Children and Their Development

Children and Their Development

Seventh Edition

Global Edition

Robert V. Kail
Purdue University

Boston   Columbus   Indianapolis   New York   San Francisco   Amsterdam
Cape Town   Dubai   London   Madrid   Milan   Munich   Paris   Montréal   Toronto   Delhi
Mexico City   São Paulo   Sydney   Hong Kong   Seoul   Singapore   Taipei   Tokyo

VP, Product Development: Dickson Musslewhite
Head of Learning Asset Acquisition, Global Edition:
     Laura Dent
Senior Acquisitions Editor: Amber Chow
Editorial Assistant: Luke Robbins
Acquisitions Editor, Global Edition: Sandhya Ghoshal
Associate Project Editor, Global Edition: Binita Roy
VP, Director of Marketing: Brandy Dawson
Director, Project Management Services: Lisa Iarkowski
Project Team Lead: Linda Behrens
Project Manager: Shelly Kupperman
Program Team Lead: Amber Mackey
Program Manager: Diane Szulecki
Director of Field Marketing: Jonathan Cottrell
Senior Product Marketer: Lindsey
     Prudhomme Gill

Executive Field Marketer: Kate Stewart
Marketing Assistant, Field Marketing:
     Paige Patunas
Marketing Assistant, Product Marketing:
     Jessica Warren
Procurement Manager: Mary Fischer
Procurement Specialist: Diane Peirano
Senior Manufacturing Controller,
     Production, Global Edition: Trudy Kimber
Associate Director of Design: Blair Brown
Cover Designer: Lumina Datamatics
Interior Designer: Kathryn Foot
Digital Media Project Manager: Pamela Weldin
Full-Service Project Management and Composition:
     Integra Software Services Pvt. Ltd.
Cover Image: © RuthChoi/Shutterstock

Credits and acknowledgments borrowed from other sources and reproduced, with permission, in this textbook appear on the appropriate page of appearance or in the Credits on pages 561–564.

Pearson Education Limited
Edinburgh Gate
Harlow
Essex CM20 2JE
England

and Associated Companies throughout the world

Visit us on the World Wide Web at:
www.pearsonglobaleditions.com

ISBN 10: 1-292-07376-4
ISBN 13: 978-1-292-07376-7

British Library Cataloguing-in-Publication Data
A catalogue record for this book is available from the British Library

ARP impression 98

Typeset in 10/13 Palatino LT Std Roman by Integra Software Services Pvt. Ltd.

Printed and bound in Great Britain by Ashford Colour Press Ltd.

To Laura, Matt, and Ben

Brief Contents

1 Child Development: Theories, Themes, and Research   20

2 Heredity, Environment, and Child Development   56

3 Prenatal Development, Birth, and the Newborn   78

4 Growth and Health   118

5 Perceptual Processes and Motor Development   148

6 Theories of Cognitive Development   178

7 Memory, Problem Solving, and Academic Skills   214

8 Intelligence and Individual Differences in Cognition   250

9 Language and Communication   278

10 Emotional Development   312

11 Understanding Self and Others   340

12 Moral Understanding and Behavior   368

13 Gender: Stereotypes, Differences, Identity, and Roles   400

14 Family Relationships   428

15 Influences Beyond the Family   462

Contents

Welcome   12
About the Author   18

1 Child Development: Theories, Themes, and Research   20

1.1 Setting the Stage   21
   Historical Views of Children and Childhood   22
   Origins of a New Science   23
   Applying Results of Research   24
1.2 Foundational Theories of Child Development   25
   The Biological Perspective   26
   The Psychodynamic Perspective   27
   The Learning Perspective   28
   The Cognitive-Developmental Perspective   29
   The Contextual Perspective   31
1.3 Themes in Child-Development Research   33
   Continuity of Development   33
   Impact of Nature and Nurture   34
   The Active Child   34
   Links Between Different Domains of Development   35
1.4 Doing Child-Development Research   36
   Measurement in Child-Development Research   37
   General Designs for Research   41
   Designs for Studying Age-Related Change   46
   Ethical Responsibilities   50
   Communicating Research Results   51
   See for Yourself • Summary • Test Yourself • Key Terms

2 Heredity, Environment, and Child Development   56

2.1 Mechanisms of Heredity   57
   The Biology of Heredity   57
   Single Gene Inheritance   59
Cultural Influences: Why Do African Americans Inherit Sickle-Cell Disease?   61
   Genetic Disorders   62
Improving Children's Lives: Genetic Counseling   63
2.2 Heredity, Environment, and Development   65
   Behavioral Genetics   66
Focus on Research: Hereditary Bases of Children's Peer Relationships   68
   Paths from Genes to Behavior   71
Unifying Themes: Nature and Nurture   75
   See for Yourself • Summary • Test Yourself • Key Terms

3 Prenatal Development, Birth, and the Newborn   78

3.1 From Conception to Birth   79
   Period of the Zygote (Weeks 1–2)   79
   Period of the Embryo (Weeks 3–8)   80
   Period of the Fetus (Weeks 9–38)   81
Improving Children's Lives: Five Steps Toward a Healthy Baby   84
3.2 Influences on Prenatal Development   86
   General Risk Factors   86
Spotlight on Theories: A Theory of the Risks Associated with Teenage Motherhood   88
   Teratogens   90
   How Teratogens Influence Prenatal Development   93
   Prenatal Diagnosis and Treatment   96
3.3 Happy Birthday!   99
   Labor and Delivery   99
   Approaches to Childbirth   100
   Adjusting to Parenthood   101
Focus on Research: Links Between Maternal Depression and Children's Behavior Problems   102
   Birth Complications   104
Cultural Influences: Infant Mortality   106
3.4 The Newborn   108
   Assessing the Newborn   108
   The Newborn's Reflexes   109
   Newborn States   110
Child Development and Family Policy: Safe Sleeping   113
   Perception and Learning in the Newborn   114
Unifying Themes: Continuity   114
   See for Yourself • Summary • Test Yourself • Key Terms

4 Growth and Health   118

4.1 Physical Growth   119
   Features of Human Growth   119
   Mechanisms of Physical Growth   122
Improving Children's Lives: What's the Best Food for Babies?   123
   The Adolescent Growth Spurt and Puberty   125
Cultural Influences: Adolescent Rites of Passage   126
Spotlight on Theories: A Paternal Investment Theory of Girls' Pubertal Timing   128

4.2 Challenges to Healthy Growth 131
Malnutrition 131
Eating Disorders: Anorexia and Bulimia 133
Focus on Research: Evaluating a Program for Preventing Eating Disorders 134
Obesity 135
Disease 136
Accidents 137
4.3 The Developing Nervous System 138
Organization of the Mature Brain 139
The Developing Brain 140
Child Development and Family Policy: Teenagers and the Law 142
Unifying Themes: Connections 145
See for Yourself • Summary • Test Yourself • Key Terms

5 Perceptual Processes and Motor Development 148
5.1 Basic Sensory and Perceptual Processes 149
Smell, Taste, and Touch 150
Hearing 151
Improving Children's Lives: Hearing Impairment in Infancy 152
Seeing 152
Integrating Sensory Information 154
Spotlight on Theories: The Theory of Intersensory Redundancy 154
5.2 Complex Perceptual and Attentional Processes 156
Perceiving Objects 156
Attention 161
Attention Deficit Hyperactivity Disorder 163
Child Development and Family Policy: What's the Best Treatment for ADHD? 164
5.3 Motor Development 165
Locomotion 166
Cultural Influences: Cultural Practices That Influence Motor Development 168
Fine-Motor Skills 169
Focus on Research: Adjusting Grasps to Objects 170
Physical Fitness 172
Unifying Themes: Active Children 174
See for Yourself • Summary • Test Yourself • Key Terms

6 Theories of Cognitive Development 178
6.1 Setting the Stage: Piaget's Theory 179
Basic Principles of Piaget's Theory 180
Stages of Cognitive Development 181
Piaget's Contributions to Child Development 187

6.2 Modern Theories of Cognitive Development 189
The Sociocultural Perspective: Vygotsky's Theory 190
Cultural Influences: How Do Parents in Different Cultures Scaffold Their Children's Learning? 192
Information Processing 193
Core-Knowledge Theories 197
6.3 Understanding in Core Domains 200
Understanding Objects and Their Properties 201
Focus on Research: Distinguishing Liquids from Solids 202
Understanding Living Things 204
Understanding People 206
Improving Children's Lives: Theory of Mind in Autism 208
Unifying Themes: Active Children 210
See for Yourself • Summary • Test Yourself • Key Terms

7 Memory, Problem Solving, and Academic Skills 214
7.1 Memory 215
Origins of Memory 215
Strategies for Remembering 216
Knowledge and Memory 218
Spotlight on Theories: Fuzzy Trace Theory 220
Child Development and Family Policy: Interviewing Children Effectively 224
7.2 Problem Solving 225
Developmental Trends in Solving Problems 225
Features of Children's and Adolescents' Problem Solving 226
Scientific Thinking 230
Focus on Research: Learning to Design Experiments 231
7.3 Academic Skills 232
Reading 233
Improving Children's Lives: Rhyme Is Sublime Because Sounds Abound 234
Writing 237
Knowing and Using Numbers 240
Cultural Influences: Fifth Grade in Taiwan 245
Unifying Themes: Active Children 246
See for Yourself • Summary • Test Yourself • Key Terms

8 Intelligence and Individual Differences in Cognition 250
8.1 What Is Intelligence? 251
Psychometric Theories 252
Gardner's Theory of Multiple Intelligences 253
Sternberg's Theory of Successful Intelligence 255

Cultural Influences: How Culture Defines What is Intelligent 256

8.2 Measuring Intelligence 257
Binet and the Development of Intelligence Testing 258
Features of IQ Scores 261
Hereditary and Environmental Factors 262

Child Development and Family Policy: Providing Children with a Head Start for School 263
Impact of Ethnicity and Socioeconomic Status 265

Focus on Research: Making Tests Less Threatening 267

8.3 Special Children, Special Needs 268
Gifted Children 269

Improving Children's Lives: Fostering Creativity 270
Children with Disability 270

Spotlight on Theories: Impaired Reading Comprehension Is Impaired Language Comprehension 272

Unifying Themes: Nature and Nurture **274**
See for Yourself • Summary • Test Yourself • Key Terms

9 Language and Communication 278

9.1 The Road to Speech 279
Elements of Language 279
Perceiving Speech 280

Child Development and Family Policy: Are Cochlear Implants Effective for Young Children? 283
First Steps to Speech 284

9.2 Learning the Meanings of Words 285
Understanding Words as Symbols 285
Fast Mapping Meanings to Words 286

Spotlight on Theories: A Shape-Bias Theory of Word Learning 288
Individual Differences in Word Learning 290

Focus on Research: Why Does Exposure to Parents' Speech Increase Children's Vocabulary? 291
Encouraging Word Learning 292

Cultural Influences: Growing Up Bilingual 293
Beyond Words: Other Symbols 295

9.3 Speaking in Sentences 296
From Two-Word Speech to Complex Sentences 297
Mastering Grammar 298

Improving Children's Lives: Promoting Language Development 302

9.4 Using Language to Communicate 303
Taking Turns 304
Speaking Effectively 305
Listening Well 306

Unifying Themes: Connections **308**
See for Yourself • Summary • Test Yourself • Key Terms

10 Emotional Development 312

10.1 Emerging Emotions 313
The Function of Emotions 313
Experiencing and Expressing Emotions 314

Improving Children's Lives: "But I Don't Want to Go to School!" 317
Recognizing and Using Others' Emotions 318
Regulating Emotions 320

10.2 Temperament 322
What Is Temperament? 322

Spotlight on Theories: A Theory of the Structure of Temperament in Infancy 323
Hereditary and Environmental Contributions to Temperament 324

Cultural Influences: Why Is Yoshimi's Son So Tough? 325
Stability of Temperament 326
Temperament and Other Aspects of Development 326

Focus on Research: Temperament Influences Outcomes in Adolescence and Adulthood 327

10.3 Attachment 329
The Growth of Attachment 329
The Quality of Attachment 331

Child Development and Family Policy: Determining Guidelines for Child Care for Infants and Toddlers 336

Unifying Themes: Active Children **336**
See for Yourself • Summary • Test Yourself • Key Terms

11 Understanding Self and Others 340

11.1 Who Am I? Self-Concept 341
Origins of Self-Recognition 341
The Evolving Self-Concept 342
The Search for Identity 344

Cultural Influences: Dea's Ethnic Identity 346

11.2 Self-Esteem 350
Developmental Change in Self-Esteem 350
Variations in Self-Esteem Associated with Ethnicity and Culture 352
Sources of Self-Esteem 353
Low Self-Esteem: Cause or Consequence? 354

11.3 Understanding Others 355
Describing Others 356
Understanding What Others Think 357
Prejudice 359

Spotlight on Theories: Developmental Intergroup Theory 360

Focus on Research: Who Is Resilient in the Face of Discrimination? 362

**Child Development and Family Policy:
Ending Segregated Schools**   363

Unifying Themes: Nature and Nurture   **365**
See for Yourself • Summary • Test Yourself • Key Terms

12 Moral Understanding and Behavior   368

12.1 Self-Control   369
Beginnings of Self-Control   370
Influences on Self-Control   371
Improving Children's Self-Control   371

**Focus on Research: Engaging Preschool Children
to Help Them Delay Gratification**   372

12.2 Reasoning About Moral Issues   374
Piaget's Views   374
Kohlberg's Theory   375
Beyond Kohlberg's Theory   378

Cultural Influences: Lies, White Lies, and Blue Lies   379

12.3 Helping Others   381
Development of Prosocial Behavior   382
Skills Underlying Prosocial Behavior   383
Situational Influences   384
The Contribution of Heredity   384
Socializing Prosocial Behavior   385

12.4 Aggression   387
Change and Stability   388
Roots of Aggressive Behavior   389

**Spotlight on Theories: Social-Information-Processing
Theory and Children's Aggressive Behavior**   392
Victims of Aggression   394

**Child Development and Family Policy:
The KiVa Antibullying Program**   395

Unifying Themes: Continuity   **396**
See for Yourself • Summary • Test Yourself • Key Terms

13 Gender: Stereotypes, Differences, Identity, and Roles   400

13.1 Gender Stereotypes   401
How Do We View Men and Women?   401
Learning Gender Stereotypes   403

**Focus on Research: Reasoning About
Gender-Related Properties**   404

13.2 Differences Related to Gender   405
Differences in Physical Development and
Behavior   406
Differences in Intellectual Abilities and
Achievement   408

**Cultural Influences: A Cross-Cultural Look
at Gender Differences in Math**   410
Differences in Personality and Social Behavior   410
Frank Talk About Gender Differences   413

13.3 Gender Identity   415
The Socializing Influences of People and the Media   415
Cognitive Theories of Gender Identity   418

Spotlight on Theories: Gender-Schema Theory   418
Biological Influences   420

13.4 Gender Roles in Transition   421
Emerging Gender Roles   422
Beyond Traditional Gender Roles   422

**Improving Children's Lives: Encouraging
Valuable Traits, Not Gender Traits**   423

Unifying Themes: Connections   **424**
See for Yourself • Summary • Test Yourself • Key Terms

14 Family Relationships   428

14.1 Parenting   429
The Family as a System   429
Styles of Parenting   431
Parental Behavior   434
Influences of the Marital System   436
Children's Contributions   438

14.2 The Changing Family   439
Impact of Divorce on Children   440

**Improving Children's Lives: Helping Children
Adjust After Divorce**   442

**Focus on Research: Evaluation of a Program
to Help Parents and Children Adjust to Life
After Divorce**   443
Blended Families   444
The Role of Grandparents   445

**Cultural Influences: Grandmothers
in African American Families**   446
Children of Gay and Lesbian Parents   447

14.3 Brothers and Sisters   448
Firstborn, Laterborn, and Only Children   448

**Child Development and Family Policy: Assessing
the Consequences of China's One-Child Policy**   449
Qualities of Sibling Relationships   450

**14.4 Maltreatment: Parent–Child Relationships
Gone Awry**   453
Consequences of Maltreatment   453
Causes of Maltreatment   454
Preventing Maltreatment   457

Unifying Themes: Active Children   **458**
See for Yourself • Summary • Test Yourself • Key Terms

15 Influences Beyond the Family   462

15.1 Peers   463
Development of Peer Interactions   464
Friendship   468

Focus on Research: Influence of Best Friends on Sexual Activity 471

Romantic Relationships 472

Groups 474

Popularity and Rejection 476

Cultural Influences: Keys to Popularity 476

15.2 Electronic Media 478

Television 478

Improving Children's Lives: Get the Kids Off the Couch! 481

New Media 482

15.3 Institutional Influences 483

Child Care and After-School Activities 484

Part-Time Employment 486

Neighborhoods 488

Spotlight on Theories: The Family Economic Stress Model 489

School 491

Unifying Themes: Continuity **494**

See for Yourself • Summary • Test Yourself • Key Terms

Glossary 498

Answers 507

References 509

Credits 561

Name Index 565

Subject Index 580

Welcome

Like many professors-turned-textbook-authors, I wrote this book because none of the texts available met the aims of the child-development classes that I teach. In the next few paragraphs, I want to describe those aims and how this book is designed to achieve them.

Goal 1: Use effective pedagogy to promote students' learning. The focus on a student-friendly book begins with the structure of the chapters. Each chapter consists of three or four modules that provide a clear and well-defined organization to the chapter. Each module begins with a set of learning objectives and a vignette that introduces the topic to be covered. Special topics that are set off in other textbooks as feature boxes are fully integrated with the main text. Each module ends with several questions intended to help students check their understanding of the major ideas in the module.

The end of each chapter includes several additional study aids. "Unifying Themes" links the ideas in the chapter to a major developmental theme. "See for Yourself" suggests activities that allow students to observe topics in child development firsthand. "Test Yourself" questions further confirm and cement students' understanding of the chapter material. The "Summary" is a concise review of the chapter.

These different pedagogical elements *do* work; students using previous editions frequently comment that the book is easy to read and presents complex topics in an understandable way.

Goal 2: Use fundamental developmental issues as a foundation for students' learning of research and theory in child development. The child-development course sometimes overwhelms students because of the sheer number of topics and studies. In fact, today's child-development science is really propelled by a concern with a handful of fundamental developmental issues, such as the continuity of development and the roles of nature and nurture in development. In *Children and Their Development*, four of these foundational issues are introduced in Chapter 1 and then reappear in subsequent chapters to scaffold students' understanding. As I mentioned already, the end of the chapter includes the "Unifying Themes" feature, in which the ideas from the chapter are used to illustrate one of the foundational themes. By occurring repeatedly throughout the text, the themes remind students of the core issues that drive child-development science.

Goal 3: Teach students that child-development science draws on many complementary research methods, each of which contributes uniquely to scientific progress. In Module 1.4, I portray child-development research as a dynamic process in which scientists make a series of decisions as they plan their work. In the process, they create a study that has both strengths and weaknesses. Each of the remaining chapters of the book contains a "Focus on Research" feature that illustrates this process by showing—in an easy-to-read, question-and-answer format—the different decisions that investigators made in designing a particular study. The results are shown, usually with an annotated figure, so that students can learn how to interpret graphs. The investigators' conclusions are described, and I end each "Focus on Research" feature by mentioning the kind of converging evidence that would strengthen the authors' conclusions. Thus, the research methods introduced in Chapter 1 reappear in every chapter, depicting research as a collaborative enterprise that depends on the contributions of many scientists using different methods.

Goal 4: Show students how the findings from child-development research can improve children's lives. Child-development scientists and students alike want to know how the findings of research can be used to promote children's development. In Chapter 1, I describe the different means by which researchers can use their work to improve children's lives. In the chapters that follow, these ideas come alive in two special features: "Improving Children's Lives" provides research-based solutions to common problems in children's lives; "Child Development and Family Policy" demonstrates how research has inspired change in social policies that affect children and families. From these features, students realize that child-development research really matters—parents, teachers, and policymakers can use research to foster children's development.

New to the Seventh Edition

In updating the coverage of research, I have added hundreds of new citations to research published since 2010. I have also added significant new content to every chapter. Of particular note:

Chapter 1 includes updated examples of different research methods.

Chapter 2 has a new Focus on Research feature on hereditary bases of peer relationships, extensively revised material on molecular genetics, and new material about methylation as an epigenetic mechanism.

Chapter 3 has new material on environmental pollutants, an updated section on the impact of cocaine, revised material on the impact of epidural analgesia, a new Focus on Research feature on links between maternal depression and children's behavior problems, and a revised Child Development and Family Policy feature.

Chapter 4 includes much-revised material on sleep, an updated section on ways to encourage young children to eat healthfully, much-revised material on the impact of timing of maturation on boys' development, a new list of factors that lead to obesity, a new Focus on Research feature on evaluating a program for preventing eating disorders, and a new Child Development and Family Policy feature on teenagers and the law.

Chapter 5 has much-revised coverage of face perception, new coverage of attention, and a new Focus on Research feature on infants' grasping.

Chapter 6 contains much-revised coverage of executive function and of naïve psychology (now called folk psychology).

Chapter 7 includes new material on the impact of children's misconceptions on their scientific thinking, a new Focus on Research feature on ways to teach children to design experiments, and much-revised coverage of reading and of quantitative reasoning.

Chapter 8 has completely revised coverage of dynamic assessment (formerly, dynamic testing), a new Focus on Research feature on making tests less threatening, a new Spotlight on Theory feature on the nature of impaired reading comprehension, and much-reorganized material on gifted children.

Chapter 9 contains revised coverage of the role of sentence cues in word learning, a new Focus on Research feature on why exposure to parents' speech increases children's vocabulary, and much-revised coverage on language acquisition in bilingual children.

Chapter 10 includes new material on perception of frightening stimuli, a much-revised Spotlight on Theories feature, a much-revised description of the stability of temperament and its links to personality, and a new Focus on Research feature on the long-term consequences of temperament.

Chapter 11 has reorganized coverage of self-awareness, new material on narcissism, a much-revised section on prejudice that includes new material on the impact of discriminatory behavior, and a new Focus on Research feature on factors that buffer youth from the impact of discriminatory behavior.

Chapter 12 contains new material on moral thinking as a core domain, a much-revised Cultural Influences feature, new material on the role of oxytocin in promoting social behavior, an updated Spotlight on Theories feature, and much-revised coverage of victims of aggression, including a new Child Development and Family Policy feature on an antibullying program.

Chapter 13 has extensively revised coverage of gender-related differences including new information on differences in memory and in effortful control, as well as new material on the "pink frilly dress" phenomenon and on tomboys.

Chapter 14 contains new material on genetic influence on parental style, on intervention programs that teach parenting skills, and on grandmothers as co-parents with incarcerated mothers, plus much-revised coverage of adopted children, including new material on open adoption.

Chapter 15 includes new material on children's play with pets, a revised feature on cultural differences in popularity, much-revised coverage of "new media" (e.g., smartphones, video games) and of day care, along with new material on links between poverty, stress, and children's health; on the impact of political violence and homelessness on children's development; and on contributions to school success of programs for mentoring and teacher training.

Ancillaries

Children and Their Development, Seventh Edition, is accompanied by a superb set of ancillary materials for instructors.

Download Instructor Resources at the Instructor's Resource Center

Register or log in to the Instructor Resource Center to download supplements from our online catalog. Go to www.pearsonglobaleditions.com/Kail.

For technical support for any of your Pearson products, you and your students can contact http://247.pearsoned.com.

MyVirtualChild

MyVirtualChild is an interactive simulation that allows students to raise a child from birth to age 18 and monitor the effects of their parenting decisions over time. By incorporating physical, social, emotional, and cognitive development at several age levels, MyVirtualChild helps students think critically as they apply their course work to the practical experiences of raising a virtual child. You can access MyVirtualChild within MyPsychLab.

Instructor's Resource Manual (ISBN 1292073810)

Each chapter in the manual includes the following resources: Chapter Learning Objectives; Key Terms; Lecture Suggestions and Discussion Topics; Classroom Activities, Demonstrations, and Exercises; Out-of-Class Assignments and Projects; Lecture Notes, and Handouts. Designed to make your lectures more effective and save you preparation time, this extensive resource gathers together the most effective activities and strategies for teaching your developmental psychology course. Available for download on the Instructor's Resource Center at **www.pearsonglobaleditions.com/Kail.**

Test Item File (ISBN 1292073861)

The test bank contains multiple-choice, true/false, short-answer, and essay questions. An additional feature for the test bank is the identification of each question as factual, conceptual, or applied. All questions have been tagged to learning objectives for this edition. This allows professors to customize their tests and to ensure a balance of question types and content coverage. Each chapter of the test item file begins with the Total Assessment Guide, and easy-to-reference grid that makes creating tests easier by organizing the test questions by text section and question type. Available for download on the Instructor's Resource Center at **www.pearsonglobaleditions.com/Kail.**

PowerPoint Slides (ISBN 1292073845)

The PowerPoints provide an active format for presenting concepts from each chapter and feature prominent figures and tables from the text. The PowerPoint Lecture Slides are available for download on the Instructor's Resource Center at **www.pearsonglobaleditions.com/Kail.**

MyPsychLab™ (ISBN 1292073829)

Available at www.mypsychlab.com, **MyPsychLab**™ is an online homework, tutorial, and assessment program that truly engages students in learning. It helps students better prepare for class, quizzes, and exams—resulting in better performance in the course. It provides educators a dynamic set of tools for gauging individual and class performance:

- *Customizable* MyPsychLab is customizable. Instructors choose what a students' course looks like. Homework, applications, and more can easily be turned on and off.
- *Blackboard Single Sign-On* MyPsychLab can be used by itself or linked to any course management system.

Blackboard single sign-on provides deep linking to all new MyPsychLab resources.

- *Pearson eText* Like the printed text, students can highlight relevant passages and add notes. The Pearson eText can be accessed through laptops, iPads, and tablets. Download the free Pearson eText app to use on tablets.
- *Assignment Calendar & Gradebook* A drag and drop assignment calendar makes assigning and completing work easy. The automatically graded assessment provides instant feedback and flows into the gradebook, which can be used in the MyPsychLab or exported.
- *Personalized Study Plan* Students' personalized plans promote better critical thinking skills. The study plan organizes students' study needs into sections, such as Remembering, Understanding, Applying, and Analyzing.

Acknowledgments

Textbook authors do not produce books on their own. I want to thank the many reviewers who generously gave their time and effort to help sharpen my thinking about child development and shape the development of this text. I am especially grateful to the following people who reviewed various aspects of the manuscript:

Johnny Castro, Brookhaven College
Judith Danovitch, Michigan State University
Cheree Anthony-Encapera, Butler Community College
Vivian Hsu, Rutgers University
Jennifer Lee, Cabrillo College
Kristy vanMarle, University of Missouri

Thanks, as well, to those who reviewed the previous editions of this book: Mark B. Alcorn, University of Northern Colorado; John Bates, Indiana University; R. M. J. Bennett, University of Dundee; Rebecca Bigler, University of Texas; Matiko Bivins, University of Houston–Downtown; James Black, University of Illinois; Tanya Boone, California State University–Bakersfield; Ty W. Boyer, University of Maryland; Renate Brenneke, Kellogg Community College; K. Robert Bridges, Pennsylvania State University; Maureen Callanan, University of California–Santa Cruz; Li Cao, University of West Georgia; Jessica Carpenter, Elgin Community College; Barbara Carr, Wayland Baptist University; Andrew L. Carrano, Southern Connecticut State University; Sharon Carter, Davidson County Community College; Grace E. Cho, University of Illinois at Urbana–Champaign; Jane E. Clark, University of Maryland; Wanda Clark, South Plains College; Malinda Colwell, Texas Tech University; Joan Cook, County College of Morris; Sandra Crosser, Ohio Northern University; E. Mark Cummings, University of Notre Dame;

Jim Dannemiller, University of Wisconsin–Madison; Tara Dekkers, Northwestern College; Lisabeth DiLalla, Southern University School of Medicine; Janet DiPietro, Johns Hopkins University; Linda Dunlap, Marist College; Kathleen Fox, Salisbury State University; Janet Gebelt, Westfield State University; Sara Goldstein, Montclair State University; Vernon C. Hall, Syracuse University; Susan Harris, Southern Methodist University; Myra Harville, Holmes Community College; Beth Hentges, University of Houston–Clear Lake; Laura Hess, Purdue University; Erika Hoff, Florida Atlantic University; George Hollich, Purdue University; William Holt, UMASS–Dartmouth; Carol S. Huntsinger, College of Lake County; Alisha Janowsky, University of Central Florida; Jyotsna Kalavar, Penn State University–New Kensington Campus; Jennifer Kampmann, South Dakota State University; William Kimberlin, Lorain County Community College; Anastasia Kitsantas, George Mason University; Suzanne Koprowski, Waukesha County Technical College; Gary E. Krolikowski, SUNY–Geneseo; Gary Ladd, University of Illinois; Marta Laupa, University of Nevada; Elizabeth Lemerise, Western Kentucky University; Dennis A. Lichty, Wayne State College; Brenda Lohman, Iowa State University; Frank Manis, University of Southern California; Kirsten Matthews, Harper College; Susan McClure, Westmoreland County Community College; Monica L. McCoy, Converse College; Michael S. McGee, Radford University; Jack Meacham, University of Buffalo; Michael Meehan, Maryville University–St. Louis; Rick Medlin, Stetson University; Jacquelyn Mize, Auburn University; Terri Mortensen, Nova Southeastern University; Lois Muir, University of Montana; Lonna M. Murphy, Iowa State University; Lisa Oakes, University of Iowa; Robert Pasnak, George Mason University; Linda Petroff, Central Community College; Brady Phelps, South Dakota State University; Brad Pillow, Northern Illinois University; Laura Pirazzi, San Jose State University; Christopher Radi, University of New Mexico; Arlene Rider, Marist College; Glenn I. Roisman, University of Illinois at Urbana–Champaign; Lori Rosenthal, Lasell College; Karen Rudolph, University of Illinois; Alice C. Schermerhorn, University of Notre Dame; Ariane Schratter, Maryville College; Russell Searight, Lake Superior State University; Tony Simon, Furman University; Cynthia Stifter, Pennsylvania State University; Dawn Strongin, California State University–Stanislaus; Marianne Taylor, University of Puget Sound; Lee Ann Thompson, Case Western Reserve University; Lesa Rae Vartanian, Indiana University–Purdue University Fort Wayne; Jennifer Vu, University of Delaware; May X. Wang, Metropolitan State College of Denver; Jared Warren, Brigham Young University; Everett Waters, SUNY–Stony Brook; Amy Weiss, University of Iowa; Gaston Weisz, Adelphi University/University of Phoenix Online; Adam Winsler, George Mason University; Ric Wynn, County College of Morris; Barbara Zimmerman, Dana College; Joan Zook, SUNY–Geneseo.

Without their thoughtful comments, this book would be less complete, less accurate, and less interesting.

I also owe a debt of thanks to many people who helped bring this project to fruition. Amber Chow helped to guide the revision. Kristin Jobe and Diane Szulecki skillfully orchestrated the many activities that were involved in actually producing the book.

I am particularly grateful to Harriett Prentiss and Susan Moss for their special contributions to *Children and Their Development*. Over the years and many editions of this book, they labored long to make my writing clear and inviting. To all these individuals, many, many thanks.

— *Robert V. Kail*

To the Student

In this book, we'll trace children's development from conception through adolescence. Given this goal, you may expect to find chapters devoted to early childhood, middle childhood, and the like. But this book is organized differently—around topics. Chapters 2 through 5 are devoted to the genetic and biological bases of human development, and the growth of perceptual and motor skills. Chapters 6 through 9 cover intellectual development—how children learn, think, reason, and solve problems. Chapters 10 through 15 concern social and emotional development— how children acquire the customs of their society and learn to play the social roles expected of them.

This organization reflects the fact that when scientists conduct research on children's development, they usually study how some specific aspect of how a child develops. For example, a researcher might study how memory changes as children grow or how friendship in childhood differs from that in adolescence. Thus, the organization of this book reflects the way researchers actually study child development.

Organization of Chapters and Learning Aids

Each of the 15 chapters in the book includes two to four modules that are listed at the beginning of each chapter. Each module begins with a set of learning objectives phrased as questions, a mini-outline listing the major subheadings of the module, and a brief vignette that introduces the topic to be covered in the module. The learning objectives, mini-outline, and vignette tell you what to expect in the module.

Each module in Chapters 2 through 15 includes at least one special feature that expands on or highlights a topic. There are five different kinds of features:

Focus on Research provides details on the design and methods used in a particular research study. Closely examining specific studies demystifies research and shows that scientific work is a series of logical steps conducted by real people.

Cultural Influences shows how culture influences children and illustrates that developmental journeys are diverse. All children share the biological aspects of development, but their cultural contexts differ. This feature celebrates the developmental experiences of children from different backgrounds.

Improving Children's Lives shows how research and theory can be applied to improve children's development. These practical solutions to everyday problems show the relevance of research and theory to real life.

Child Development and Family Policy shows how results from research are used to create social policy that is designed to improve the lives of children and their families.

Spotlight on Theories examines an influential theory of development and shows how it has been tested in research.

Two other elements of the book are designed to help you focus on the main points of the text. First, whenever a key term is introduced in the text, it appears in *italic* like this and the definition appears in **black boldface type**. This format should make key terms easier for you to find and learn. Second, Summary Tables throughout the book review key ideas and provide a capsule account of each.

Each module concludes with "Check Your Learning" questions to help you review the major ideas in that module. There are three kinds of questions: recall, interpret, and apply. If you can answer the questions in "Check Your Learning" correctly, you are on your way to mastering the material in the module. However, do not rely exclusively on "Check Your Learning" as you study for exams. The questions are designed to give you a quick check of your understanding, not a comprehensive assessment of your knowledge of the entire module.

At the end of each chapter are several additional study aids. "Unifying Themes" links the contents of the chapter to the developmental themes introduced in Module 1.3. "See for Yourself" suggests some simple activities for exploring issues in child development on your own. "Test Yourself" questions further confirm and cement your understanding of the chapter material. Finally, the "Summary" provides a concise review of the entire chapter, organized by module and the primary headings within the module.

Terminology

Every field has its own terminology, and child development is no exception. I use several terms to refer to different periods of infancy, childhood, and adolescence. Although these terms are familiar, I use each to refer to a specific range of ages:

Newborn	Birth to 1 month
Infant	1 month to 1 year
Toddler	1 to 2 years
Preschooler	2 to 6 years
School-age child	6 to 12 years
Adolescent	12 to 18 years
Adult	18 years and older

Sometimes, for the sake of variety, I use other terms that are less tied to specific ages, such as *babies, youngsters*, and *elementary-school children*. When I do, you will be able to tell from the context what groups are being described.

I also use specific terminology in describing research findings from different cultural and ethnic groups. The appropriate terms to describe different cultural, racial, and ethnic groups change over time. For example, the terms *colored people, Negroes, Black Americans*, and *African Americans* have all been used to describe Americans who trace their ancestry to individuals who emigrated from Africa. In this book, I use the term *African American* because it emphasizes the unique cultural heritage of this group of people. Following this same line of reasoning, I use the terms *European American* (instead of *Caucasian* or *White*), *Native American* (instead of *Indian* or *American Indian*), *Asian American*, and *Hispanic American*.

These labels are not perfect. Sometimes they blur distinctions within ethnic groups. For example, the term *Hispanic American* ignores differences between individuals who came to the United States from Puerto Rico, Mexico, and Guatemala; the term *Asian American* blurs variations among people whose heritage is Japanese, Chinese, or Korean. Whenever researchers identified the subgroups in their research sample, I use the more specific terms in describing results. When you see the more general terms, remember that conclusions may not apply to all subgroups within the ethnic group.

A Final Word

I wrote this book to make child development come alive for my students at Purdue. Although I can't teach you directly, I hope this book sparks your interest in children and their development. Please let me know what you like and dislike about the book so that I can improve it in later editions. You can send email to me at **rkail@purdue.edu**—I'd love to hear from you.

Pearson wishes to thank and acknowledge the following people for their work on the Global Edition:

Contributor

Paromita Mitra Bhaumik, Consultant Psychologist, Belle Vue Clinic, Kolkata

Reviewers

Jyotsna Agrawal, Indian Institute of Technology Patna

Rachana Chattopadhyay, IMI Kolkata

Bhavani Ravi, Consultant

About the Author

Robert V. Kail is Distinguished Professor of Psychological Sciences at Purdue University. His undergraduate degree is from Ohio Wesleyan University, and his Ph.D. is from the University of Michigan. Kail is editor of *Child Development Perspectives* and the editor emeritus *of Psychological Science*. He received the McCandless Young Scientist Award from the American Psychological Association, was named the Distinguished Sesquicentennial Alumnus in Psychology by Ohio Wesleyan University, and is a fellow of the Association for Psychological Science. He has also written *Scientific Writing for Psychology: Lessons in Clarity and Style*. His research focuses on cognitive development during childhood and adolescence. Away from the office, he enjoys photography and working out. His Web site is: **http://www2.psych.purdue.edu/~rk/home.html**

Children and Their Development

Chapter 1
Child Development: Theories, Themes, and Research

Modules

1.1 Setting the Stage

1.2 Foundational Theories of Child Development

1.3 Themes in Child-Development Research

1.4 Doing Child-Development Research

Beginning as a microscopic cell, every person takes a fascinating journey designed to lead to adulthood. This trip is filled with remarkably interesting and challenging events. In this book, we'll trace this journey as we learn about the science of child development, a multidisciplinary study of all aspects of growth from conception to young adulthood. As an adult, you've already lived the years that are the heart of this book. I hope you enjoy reviewing your own developmental path from the perspective of child-development research, and that this perspective leads you to new insights into the forces that have made you the person you are today.

Chapter 1 sets the stage for our study of child development. We begin, in **Module 1.1**, by looking at the philosophical foundations for child development and the events that led to the creation of child development as a new science. In **Module 1.2**, we examine theories that are central to the science of child development. In **Module 1.3**, we explore themes that guide much research in child development. Finally, in **Module 1.4**, we learn about the methods scientists use to study children and their development.

 # Setting the Stage

LEARNING OBJECTIVES

LO1   What ideas did philosophers have about children and childhood?

LO2   How did the modern science of child development emerge?

LO3   How do child-development scientists use research findings to improve children's lives?

OUTLINE

Historical Views of Children and Childhood

Origins of a New Science

Applying Results of Research

Kendra loves her 12-month-old son Joshua, but she's eager to return to her job as a loan officer at a local bank. Kendra knows a woman in her neighborhood who has cared for some of her friends' children, and they all think she is wonderful. But down deep Kendra wishes she knew more about whether this type of care is really best for Joshua. She also wishes that her neighbor's day-care center had a "stamp of approval" from someone who knows how to evaluate this kind of facility.

Kendra's concern about the best way to care for her infant son is the most recent in a long line of questions that she's had about Joshua since he was born. When Joshua was a newborn, Kendra wondered if he could recognize her face and her voice. As her son grows, she'll continue to have questions: Why is he so shy at preschool? Should he take classes for gifted children, or would he be better off in regular classes? What can she do to be sure that he doesn't use drugs?

These questions—and hundreds more like them—touch issues and concerns that parents such as Kendra confront regularly as they rear their children. And parents aren't the only ones asking these questions. Many professionals who deal with children—teachers, health care providers, and social workers, for example—often wonder what's best for children's development. Does children's self-esteem affect their success in school? Should we believe young children when they claim they've been abused? And government officials must decide what programs and laws provide the greatest benefit for children and their families. How does welfare reform affect families? Are teenagers less likely to have sex when they participate in abstinence-only programs?

So many questions, and all of them important! Fortunately, the field of child development, which traces physical, mental, social, and emotional development from conception to maturity, provides answers to many of them. To begin, let's look at the origins of child development as a science.

Historical Views of Children and Childhood

LO1 **What ideas did philosophers have about children and childhood?**

For thousands of years, philosophers have speculated on the fundamental nature of childhood and the conditions that foster children's well-being. Plato (428–347 BC) and Aristotle (384–322 BC), the famous Greek philosophers, believed that schools and parents were responsible for teaching children the self-control that would make them effective citizens. But both philosophers, particularly Aristotle, worried that too much discipline would stifle children's initiative and individuality, making them unfit to be leaders.

Plato and Aristotle also had ideas about knowledge and how it was acquired. Plato argued that children are born with knowledge of many concrete objects, such as animals and people, as well as with knowledge of abstractions such as courage, love, and goodness. In Plato's view, children's experiences simply trigger knowledge they've had since birth. The first time a child sees a dog, her innate knowledge allows her to recognize it as such; no learning is necessary. In contrast, Aristotle denied the existence of innate knowledge; instead, he theorized that knowledge is rooted in perceptual experience. Children acquire knowledge piece by piece, based on the information provided by their senses.

These contrasting views resurfaced during the Age of Enlightenment. The English philosopher John Locke (1632–1704), portrayed the human infant as a *tabula rasa* or "blank slate" and claimed that experience molds the infant, child, and adolescent into a unique individual. According to Locke, parents should instruct, reward, and discipline young children, gradually relaxing their authority as children grow. In our opening vignette, Locke would advise Kendra that Joshua's experiences in child care will surely affect his development (though Locke would not specify how).

During the following century, Locke's view was challenged by the French philosopher Jean Jacques Rousseau (1712–1778), who believed that newborns are endowed with a sense of justice and morality that unfolds naturally as children grow. During this unfolding, children move through the developmental stages that we recognize today—infancy, childhood, and adolescence. Instead of emphasizing parental discipline, Rousseau argued that parents should be responsive and receptive to their children's needs. Rousseau would emphasize the value of caregivers who are responsive to Joshua's needs.

Rousseau shared Plato's view that children begin their developmental journeys well prepared with a stockpile of knowledge. Locke, like Aristotle 2,000 years before him, believed that children begin these journeys packed lightly, but pick up necessary knowledge along the way, through experience. These philosophical debates might have continued for millennia except for a landmark event: the emergence of child development as a science.

 QUESTION 1.1

Anne lets her 2-year-old explore and socialize on his own. She guides her son to discover his potential by encouraging him to make his own decisions and by letting him participate in activities. She prefers to let her son experience new things rather than give him strict instructions on how to behave. In which philosophy of child development is Anne's parenting rooted?

Origins of a New Science

LO2 **How did the modern science of child development emerge?**

The push toward child development as a science came from two unexpected events in England in the 19th century. One was the Industrial Revolution. Beginning in the mid-1700s, England was transformed from a largely rural nation relying on agriculture to an urban-oriented society organized around factories, including textile mills that produced cotton cloth. Children moved with their families to cities and worked long hours in factories, under horrendous conditions, for little pay. Accidents were common and many children were maimed or killed. In the textile mills, for example, the youngest children often were tasked with picking up loose cotton from beneath huge power looms as the machines were running.

Reformers were appalled at these conditions and worked to enact laws that would limit child labor and put more children in schools. These initiatives were the subject of prominent political debates throughout much of the 1800s; after all, the factory owners were among the most powerful people in Britain, and they opposed efforts to limit their access to plentiful, cheap labor. But the reformers carried the day and in the process made the well-being of children a national concern.

Also setting the stage for a new science of child development was Charles Darwin's groundbreaking work on evolution. He argued that individuals within a species differ: some individuals are better adapted to a particular environment, making them more likely to survive and to pass along their characteristics to future generations. Some scientists of the day noted similarities between Darwin's description of evolutionary change in species and age-related changes in human behavior. **This prompted many scientists—including Darwin himself—to write** *baby biographies*, **detailed, systematic observations of individual children.** The observations in the biographies were often subjective and conclusions were sometimes reached based on minimal evidence. Nevertheless, the systematic and extensive records in baby biographies paved the way for objective, analytic research.

Taking the lead in the new science at the dawn of the 20th century was G. Stanley Hall (1844–1924), who generated theories of child development based on evolutionary theory and conducted studies to determine age trends in children's beliefs about a range of topics. More importantly, Hall founded the first scientific journal in English that published findings from child-development research. Hall also founded a child-study institute at Clark University and was the first president of the American Psychological Association.

Meanwhile, in France Alfred Binet (1857–1911) had begun to devise the first mental tests, which we'll examine in Module 8.2. In Austria, Sigmund Freud (1856–1939) had startled the world by suggesting that the experiences of early childhood accounted for behavior in adulthood; and in the United States, John B. Watson (1878–1958), the founder of behaviorism, had begun to write and lecture on the importance of reward and punishment for child-rearing practices. (You'll learn more about Freud's and Watson's contributions in Module 1.2.)

In 1933, these emerging scientific forces came together in a new interdisciplinary organization, the Society for Research in Child Development (SRCD). Among its members were psychologists, physicians, educators, anthropologists, and biologists, all linked by a common interest in discovering the conditions that would promote children's welfare and foster their development (Parke, 2004). In the ensuing years, SRCD has grown to a membership of more than 5,000 scientists and is now the main professional organization for child-development researchers. SRCD, along with similar organizations devoted to child-development science (e.g., International Society for the Study of Behavioural Development, International Society on Infant Studies, Society for Research on Adolescence) promotes multidisciplinary research and encourages application of research findings to improve children's lives.

Applying Results of Research

LO3 How do child-development scientists use research findings to improve children's lives?

Child-development researchers have learned about ways to enhance children's development. Because of this success, a new branch of child-development research has emerged. *Applied developmental science* **uses developmental research to promote healthy development, particularly for vulnerable children and families** (Lerner, Fisher, & Giannino, 2006). Scientists with this research interest contribute to sound family policy through a number of distinct pathways (Shonkoff & Bales, 2011). Some ensure that consideration of policy issues and options is based on factual knowledge derived from child-development research: When government officials need to address problems affecting children, child-development experts can provide useful information about children and their development (Shonkoff & Bales, 2011). Others contribute by serving as advocates for children. Working with a child-advocacy group, child-development researchers can alert policymakers to children's needs and can argue for family policy that addresses those needs. Still other child-development experts evaluate the impact of government policies (e.g., the No Child Left Behind Act) on children and families (Yarrow, 2011). Finally, a particularly good way to sway policymakers is to create a working program. When researchers create a program that effectively combats problems affecting children or adolescents (e.g., sudden infant death syndrome or teenage pregnancy), this can become powerful ammunition for influencing policy (Huston, 2008).

Thus, from its origins more than 100 years ago, modern child-development science has become a mature discipline, generating a vast catalog of knowledge of children. Scientists actively use this knowledge to improve children's lives, as we'll see in the "Child Development and Family Policy" features that appear in many chapters throughout the book. The research that you'll encounter throughout this book is rooted in a set of developmental theories that provide the foundation of modern child-development research; they are the focus of the next module.

 Check Your Learning

RECALL What two events set the stage for the creation of child-development science?

Who were the leaders of the new field of child development before the formation of the SRCD?

INTERPRET Explain the similarities between Rousseau and Plato's views of child development; how did their views differ from those shared by Locke and Aristotle?

APPLY Suppose a child-development researcher was an expert on the impact of nutrition on children's physical and emotional development. Describe several different ways in which the researcher might help to inform public policy concerning children's nutrition.

Foundational Theories of Child Development

LEARNING OBJECTIVES

LO4   What are the major tenets of the biological perspective?

LO5   How do psychodynamic theories account for development?

LO6   What is the focus of learning theories?

LO7   How do cognitive-developmental theories explain changes in children's thinking?

LO8   What are the main elements of the contextual approach?

OUTLINE

The Biological Perspective

The Psychodynamic Perspective

The Learning Perspective

The Cognitive-Developmental Perspective

The Contextual Perspective

Will has just graduated from high school, first in his class. For his proud mother, Betty, this is a time to reflect on Will's past and ponder his future. Will has always been a happy, easygoing child and he's always been interested in learning. Betty wonders why he is so perpetually good natured and so curious. If she knew the secret, she laughed, she could write a best-selling book and be a guest on The Colbert Report!

Before you read on, stop for a moment and think about Betty's question. How would you explain Will's good nature, his interest in learning, and his curiosity? Perhaps Betty has been a fantastic mother, doing all the right things at just the right time? Perhaps year after year his teachers quickly recognized Will's curiosity and encouraged it? Or was it simply Will's destiny to be this way?

Each of these explanations is a simple theory: Each tries to explain Will's curiosity and good nature. In child-development research, theories are much more complicated, but the purpose is the same: to explain behavior and development. **In child-development science, a** *theory* **is an organized set of ideas that is designed to explain and make predictions about development.**

A theory leads to hypotheses that we can test in research; in the process, each hypothesis is confirmed or rejected. Think about the different explanations for Will's behavior. Each one leads to unique hypotheses. If, for example, teachers' encouragement has caused Will to be curious, we hypothesize that he should no longer be curious if teachers stop encouraging that curiosity. When the outcomes of research are as hypothesized, the theory gains support. When results run counter to the hypothesis, the theory is incorrect and is revised. These revised theories then provide the basis for new hypotheses, which lead to new research, and the cycle continues. With each step along the way, the theory comes closer to becoming a complete account. Throughout the book, in Spotlight on Theories features, we'll look at specific theories, the hypotheses derived from them, and the outcome of research testing those hypotheses.

Over the history of child development as a science, many theories have guided research and thinking about children's development. The earliest developmental theories paved the way for newer, improved theories. In this module, I describe the theories that provide the scientific foundation for modern ones because the newer theories that I describe later in the book are best understood in terms of their historical roots.

Many early theories shared assumptions and ideas about children and development. Grouped together, they form five major theoretical perspectives in child-development research: the biological, psychodynamic, learning, cognitive-developmental, and contextual perspectives.

The Biological Perspective

LO4 What are the major tenets of the biological perspective?

According to the biological perspective, intellectual and personality development, as well as physical and motor development, are rooted in biology. One of the first biological theories, maturational theory, was proposed by Arnold Gesell (1880–1961). **According to *maturational theory*, child development reflects a specific and prearranged scheme or plan within the body.** In Gesell's view, development is simply a natural unfolding of a biological plan; experience matters little. Like Jean Jacques Rousseau 200 years before him, Gesell encouraged parents to let their children develop naturally. Without interference from adults, Gesell claimed, such behaviors as speech, play, and reasoning would emerge spontaneously according to a predetermined developmental timetable.

Maturational theory was discarded because it had little to say about the impact of the environment on children's development. However, other biological theories give greater weight to experience. *Ethological theory* **views development from an evolutionary perspective.** In this theory, many behaviors are adaptive; that is, they have survival value. For example, clinging, grasping, and crying are adaptive for infants because they elicit caregiving from adults. Ethological theorists assume that people inherit many of these adaptive behaviors.

So far, ethological theory seems like maturational theory, with a dash of evolution for taste. How does experience fit in? Ethologists believe that all animals are biologically programmed so that some kinds of learning occur only at certain ages. **A *critical period* is the time in development when a specific type of learning can take place; before or after the critical period, the same learning is difficult or even impossible.**

One well-known example of a critical period comes from the work of Konrad Lorenz (1903–1989), a zoologist who noticed that newly hatched chicks follow their mother. He theorized that chicks are biologically programmed to follow the first moving object that they see. **Usually this was the mother, so following her was the first step in *imprinting*, creating an emotional bond with the mother.** Lorenz tested his theory by showing that if some other object moved by newborn chicks, they would follow that object and treat it as "Mother." As the photo shows, this included Lorenz himself! But the chick had to see the moving object within about a day of hatching. Otherwise, the chick would not imprint on the moving object. In other words, the critical period for imprinting lasts about a day; when chicks experience the moving object outside of the critical period, imprinting does not take place. Even though the underlying mechanism is biological, experience is essential for triggering programmed, adaptive behaviors.

Newly hatched chicks follow the first moving object they see, treating it as "Mother" even when it's a human.

Ethological theory and maturational theory both highlight the biological bases of child development.

Biological theorists remind us that children's behavior is the product of a long evolutionary history. Consequently, a biological theorist would tell Betty that Will's good nature and his outstanding academic record are both largely products of his biological endowment—his heredity.

The Psychodynamic Perspective

LO5   How do psychodynamic theories account for development?

The psychodynamic perspective is the oldest scientific perspective on child development, originating in the work of Sigmund Freud (1856–1939) in the late 19th and early 20th centuries. Freud was a physician whose patients were adults with disorders that seemed to have no obvious biological causes. As Freud listened to his patients describe their problems and their lives, he became convinced that early experiences establish patterns that endure throughout a person's life. **Using his patients' case histories, Freud created the first** *psychodynamic theory,* **which holds that development is largely determined by how well people resolve conflicts they face at different ages.**

The role of conflict is evident in Freud's description of the three primary components of personality. **The** *id* **is a reservoir of primitive instincts and drives.** From birth, the id presses for immediate gratification of bodily needs and wants. A hungry baby crying illustrates the id in action. **The** *ego* **is the practical, rational component of personality.** The ego begins to emerge during the first year of life, as infants learn that they cannot always have what they want. The ego tries to resolve conflicts that occur when the instinctive desires of the id encounter the obstacles of the real world. The ego often tries to channel the id's impulsive demands into socially more acceptable channels. For example, in the photo, the child without the toy is obviously envious of the child who has the toy. According to Freud, the id would urge the child to grab the toy, but the ego would encourage the child to play with the peer and, in the process, the attractive toy.

The third component of personality, the *superego,* **is the "moral agent" in the child's personality.** It emerges during the preschool years as children begin to internalize adult standards of right and wrong. If the peer in the previous example left the attractive toy unattended, the id might tell the child to grab the toy and run; the superego would remind the child that taking another's toy would be wrong.

Today, scientists recognize many shortcomings that undermine Freud's theory as a whole (e.g., some key ideas are too vague to be tested in research). Nevertheless, two of Freud's insights have had lasting impact on child-development research and theory. First, he noted that early experiences can have enduring effects on children's development. Second, he suggested that children often experience conflict between what they want to do and what they know they should do.

Erikson's Psychosocial Theory Erik Erikson (1902–1994), Freud's student, embraced Freud's idea of conflict, but he emphasized the psychological and social aspects of conflict rather than the biological

 QUESTION 1.2
Keunho and Young-shin are sisters who moved to Toronto from Korea when they were 15 and 10 years old, respectively. Although both of them have spoken English almost exclusively since their arrival in Canada, Keunho still speaks with a bit of an accent and occasionally makes grammatical errors; Young-shin's English is flawless—she speaks like a native. How could you explain Young-shin's greater skill in terms of a critical period?

According to Freud's theory, the id would encourage the child on the right to grab the toy away from the other child, but the superego would remind her that this would be wrong.

TABLE 1-1

ERIKSON'S EIGHT STAGES OF PSYCHOSOCIAL DEVELOPMENT

Psychosocial Stage	Age	Challenge
Basic trust versus mistrust	Birth to 1 year	To develop a sense that the world is safe, a "good place"
Autonomy versus shame and doubt	1 to 3 years	To realize that one is an independent person who can make decisions
Initiative versus guilt	3 to 6 years	To develop a willingness to try new things and to handle failure
Industry versus inferiority	6 years to adolescence	To learn basic skills and to work with others
Identity versus identity confusion	Adolescence	To develop a lasting, integrated sense of self
Intimacy versus isolation	Young adulthood	To commit to another in a loving relationship
Generativity versus stagnation	Middle adulthood	To contribute to younger people, through child rearing, child care, or other productive work
Integrity versus despair	Late life	To view one's life as satisfactory and worth living

and physical aspects. **In Erikson's** *psychosocial theory,* **development consists of a sequence of stages, each defined by a unique crisis or challenge.** The complete theory includes the eight stages shown in Table 1-1. The name of each stage reflects the challenge that individuals face at a particular age. For example, the challenge for adolescents is to develop an identity. Adolescents who do not meet this challenge will not establish truly intimate relationships but will become overly dependent on their partners as a source of identity.

Whether we call them conflicts, challenges, or crises, the psychodynamic perspective emphasizes that the trek to adulthood is difficult because the path is strewn with obstacles. Outcomes of development reflect the manner and ease with which children surmount life's barriers. When children overcome early obstacles easily, they are better able to handle the later ones. Returning to this module's opening vignette, a psychodynamic theorist would tell Betty that Will's cheerful disposition and his academic record suggest that he handled life's early obstacles well, which is a good sign for his future development.

The Learning Perspective

LO6 What is the focus of learning theories?

Early Learning Theories Learning theorists endorse John Locke's view that the infant's mind is a blank slate on which experience writes. John Watson was the first theorist to apply this approach to child development, arguing that learning from experience determines what children will be.

Watson did little research to support his claims, but B. F. Skinner (1904–1990) filled this gap. **Skinner studied** *operant conditioning,* **in which the consequences of a behavior determine whether a behavior is repeated.** Skinner showed that two kinds of consequences were especially influential. **A** *reinforcement* **is a consequence that increases the future likelihood of the behavior that it follows.** Positive reinforcement consists of giving a reward—such as chocolate, gold stars, or paychecks—to increase the likelihood of repeating a previous behavior. When parents want to encourage their daughter to clean her room, they could use positive reinforcement by rewarding her with praise, food, or money whenever she completed the chore. Negative reinforcement consists of rewarding people by taking away unpleasant things. The same parents could use negative reinforcement by saying that whenever their daughter cleaned her room, she wouldn't have to wash the dishes or fold laundry.

A *punishment* is a consequence that decreases the future likelihood of the behavior that it follows. Punishment suppresses a behavior by either adding something aversive or by withholding a pleasant event. When the child failed to clean her room, the parents could punish her by making her do extra chores (adding something aversive) or by not allowing her to watch television (withholding a pleasant event).

Applied properly, reinforcement and punishment are powerful influences on children. However, children often learn without reinforcement or punishment. **Children learn much simply by watching those around them, which is known as** *imitation* or *observational learning.* For example, imitation occurs when one toddler throws a toy after seeing a peer do so, or when a school-age child offers to help an older adult carry groceries because she's seen her parents do the same, or, as in the photo, when a son tries to shave like his father.

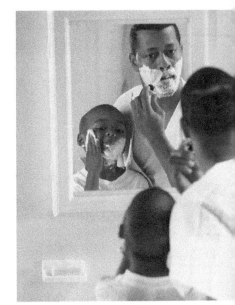

Throughout development, children learn much from imitating the actions of others.

Social Cognitive Theory Perhaps imitation makes you think of "monkey-see, monkey-do," or simple mimicking. Early investigators had this view, too, but research quickly showed that this was wrong. Children do not always imitate what they see around them. Instead, children are more likely to imitate when the person they see is popular, smart, or talented. They're also more likely to imitate when the behavior they see is rewarded than when it is punished. Findings like these imply that imitation is more complex than sheer mimicry. Children do not mechanically copy what they see and hear; instead, they look to others for information about appropriate behavior. When popular, smart peers are reinforced for behaving in a particular way, it makes sense to imitate them.

Albert Bandura (1925–) based his *social cognitive theory* **on this more complex view of reward, punishment, and imitation.** Bandura calls his theory "cognitive" because he believes that children are actively trying to understand what goes on in their world; the theory is "social" because, along with reinforcement and punishment, what other people do is an important source of information about the world (Bandura, 2006, 2012).

Bandura also argues that experience gives children a sense of *self-efficacy,* **beliefs about their own abilities and talents.** Self-efficacy beliefs help determine when children imitate others. A child who sees himself as athletically untalented, for example, will not try to imitate LeBron James dunking a basketball, despite the fact that LeBron is obviously talented and popular. But the youngster in the photo is likely to imitate LeBron because he believes he's talented and thus it makes sense to try to imitate LeBron. Thus, whether children imitate others depends on who the other person is, whether that person's behavior is rewarded, and children's beliefs about their own talents.

Bandura's social cognitive theory is a far cry from Skinner's operant conditioning. The social cognitive child, who actively interprets events, has replaced the operant conditioning child, who responds mechanically to reinforcement and punishment. Nevertheless, Skinner, Bandura, and all learning theorists share the view that experience propels children along their developmental journeys. Returning to this module's opening scenario, they would tell Betty that she can thank experience for making Will both happy and successful academically.

When someone is as talented as LeBron James, it makes sense for others to try to imitate him—and young children often do just that, they mimic LeBron and other talented people.

The Cognitive-Developmental Perspective

LO7 How do cognitive-developmental theories explain changes in children's thinking?

The *cognitive-developmental perspective* **focuses on how children think and on how their thinking changes as they grow.** Jean Piaget (1896–1980) proposed

In Piaget's theory, even infants have rudimentary theories about objects and their properties.

the best known of these theories. He believed that youngsters naturally try to make sense of their world. Infants, children, and adolescents want to understand the workings of both the physical and the social world. For example, infants want to know about objects: "What happens when I push this toy off the table?" And they want to know about people: "Who is this person who feeds and cares for me?"

Piaget argued that as children try to comprehend their world, they act like scientists in creating theories that organize what they know about objects and people. These theories are tested daily by experience because they lead children to expect certain things to happen. As with real scientific theories, when the predicted events occur, a child's belief in her theory grows stronger. When the predicted events do not occur, the child revises her theory. For example, think about the baby in the photo. Her theory of objects like the rattle she's holding might include the idea that "If I let go of a rattle, it will fall to the floor." If the infant drops some other object—a plate or an article of clothing—she will find that it, too, falls to the floor and she can make the theory more general: Objects that are dropped fall to the floor.

Piaget also believed that at a few critical points in development, children realize their theories have basic flaws. When this happens, children revise their theories radically. These changes are so fundamental that the revised theory is, in many respects, a brand-new theory. Piaget claimed that radical revisions occur three times in development: once at about age 2, a second time at about age 7, and a third time just before adolescence. These radical changes mean that children go through four distinct stages in cognitive development. Each stage represents a fundamental change in how children understand and organize their environment, and each stage is characterized by more sophisticated types of reasoning. For example, the sensorimotor stage begins at birth and lasts until about age 2. As the name implies, sensorimotor thinking is closely linked to the infant's sensory and motor skills. This stage and the three later stages are shown in Table 1-2.

According to Piaget, children's thinking becomes more sophisticated as they develop, reflecting the more sophisticated theories that children create. Returning to our opening scenario, Piaget would have little to say about Will's good nature. As for his academic success, Piaget would explain that all children naturally want to understand their worlds; Will is simply unusually skilled in this regard. In Module 6.1, we will further explore Piaget's contribution to our understanding of cognitive development, as well as more modern theories.

TABLE 1-2

PIAGET'S FOUR STAGES OF COGNITIVE DEVELOPMENT

Stage	Approximate Age	Characteristics
Sensorimotor	Birth to 2 years	Infant's knowledge of the world is based on senses and motor skills. By the end of the period, infant uses mental representations.
Preoperational	2 to 6 years	Child learns how to use symbols such as words and numbers to represent aspects of the world but relates to the world only through his or her perspective.
Concrete operational	7 to 11 years	Child understands and applies logical operations to experiences, provided the experiences are focused on the here and now.
Formal operational	Adolescence and beyond	Adolescent or adult thinks abstractly, speculates on hypothetical situations, and reasons deductively about what may be possible.

The Contextual Perspective

LO8 **What are the main elements of the contextual approach?**

Most developmentalists agree that the environment is an important force in children's lives. Traditionally, most theories of child development have emphasized environmental forces that affect children directly. Examples of direct environmental influences would be a parent praising a child, an older sibling teasing a younger one, and a nursery-school teacher discouraging girls from playing with trucks. These direct influences are important in children's lives, but in the contextual perspective they are simply one part of a much larger system, in which each element of the system influences all other elements. This larger system includes one's parents and siblings as well as important individuals outside of the family, such as extended family, friends, and teachers. The system also includes institutions that influence development, such as schools, television, the workplace, and a church, temple, or mosque.

All these people and institutions fit together to form a person's *culture—* **the knowledge, attitudes, and behavior associated with a group of people.** *Culture* can refer to a particular country or people (e.g., French culture); to a specific point in time (e.g., popular culture of the 1990s); or to groups of individuals who maintain specific, identifiable cultural traditions, such as African American families that celebrate Kwanzaa. A culture provides the context in which a child develops and thus is a source of many important influences on development throughout childhood and adolescence.

One of the first theorists to emphasize cultural context in children's development was Lev Vygotsky (1896–1934). A Russian psychologist, Vygotsky focused on ways that adults convey to children the beliefs, customs, and skills of their culture. Vygotsky believed that because a fundamental aim of all societies is to enable children to acquire essential cultural values and skills, every aspect of a child's development must be considered against this backdrop. For example, many parents in the United States want their children to work hard in school and to go to college. In the same way, Efe parents living in Africa want their children to learn to gather food, build houses, and, as you can see in the photo, to hunt; these skills are fundamental to the Efe because they are critical for survival in their environment. Vygotsky viewed development as an apprenticeship in which children develop when they work with skilled adults, including teachers and parents. In Module 6.2, we'll learn more about Vygotsky's distinctive contributions to our understanding of cognitive development.

Returning to our opening vignette, Vygotsky would agree with learning theorists in telling Betty that the environment has been pivotal in her son's amiable disposition and his academic achievements. However, the contextual theorist would insist that "environment" means much more than the reinforcements, punishments, and observations that are central to learning theory. The contextual theorist would emphasize the manner in which Betty had conveyed the value of curiosity and academic success to her son; also contributing to Will's development was Betty's membership in a cultural group that values doing well in school.

According to the contextual view, parents help children master the essential values and skills of their culture, such as learning how to hunt.

The Big Picture   Comparing the basics of five major perspectives in six pages is like trying to see all the major sights of a large city in a day: It can be done, but it's demanding and, after a while, everything blurs together. Relax. Summary Table 1-1 gives a capsule account of all five perspectives and their important theories.

These perspectives are the basis for contemporary theories that I introduce throughout this book. For example, Piaget's theory is the forerunner of modern explanations of infants' understanding of objects and of preschoolers' theory of mind (both described in Module 6.3). Similarly, Erikson's theory has contributed to work on mother–infant attachment (see Module 10.3) and formation of identity during adolescence (see Module 11.1).

The modern theories described throughout the book are derived from all five perspectives listed in Summary Table 1-1. Why? Because no single perspective provides a truly complete explanation of all aspects of children's development. Theories from the cognitive-developmental perspective are useful for understanding how children's thinking changes as they grow older. By contrast, theories from the contextual and learning perspectives are particularly valuable in explaining how environmental forces such as parents, peers, schools, and culture influence children's development. By drawing on all the perspectives, we'll be better able to understand the different forces that contribute to children's development. Just as you can better appreciate a beautiful painting by examining it from different vantage points, child-development researchers often rely on multiple perspectives to understand why children develop as they do.

Another way to understand the forces that shape development is to consider several themes of development—themes that cut across different theoretical perspectives and specific research topics. We'll look at these themes in Module 1.3.

SUMMARY TABLE 1-1

CHARACTERISTICS OF DEVELOPMENTAL PERSPECTIVES

Perspective	Key Assumptions	Illustrative Theories
Biological	Development is determined primarily by biological forces.	*Maturational theory:* emphasizes development as a natural unfolding of a biological plan
		Ethological theory: emphasizes that children's and parents' behavior has adapted to meet specific environmental challenges
Psychodynamic	Development is determined primarily by how a child resolves conflicts at different ages.	*Freud's theory:* emphasizes the conflict between primitive biological forces and societal standards for right and wrong
		Erikson's theory: emphasizes the challenges posed by the formation of trust, autonomy, initiative, industry, and identity
Learning	Development is determined primarily by a child's environment.	*Skinner's operant conditioning:* emphasizes the role of reinforcement and punishment
		Bandura's social cognitive theory: emphasizes children's efforts to understand their world, using reinforcement, punishment, and others' behavior
Cognitive-Developmental	Development reflects children's efforts to understand the world.	*Piaget's theory:* emphasizes the different stages of thinking that result from children's changing theories of the world
Contextual	Development is influenced by immediate and more distant environments, which typically influence each other.	*Vygotsky's theory:* emphasizes the role of parents (and other adults) in conveying culture to the next generation

Check Your Learning

RECALL Describe different theories that typify the biological perspective on child development.

What are the main features of the contextual perspective on child development?

INTERPRET Explain the similarities and the differences in Erikson and Piaget's stages of children's development.

APPLY A friend complains that his 1-year-old seems to cry a lot compared to other 1-year-olds. How would theorists from each of the five perspectives listed in Summary Table 1-1 explain his son's excessive crying?

 # Themes in Child-Development Research

LEARNING OBJECTIVES

LO9 How well can developmental outcomes be predicted from early life?

LO10 How do heredity and environment influence development?

LO11 What role do children have in their own development?

LO12 Is development in different domains connected?

OUTLINE

Continuity of Development

Impact of Nature and Nurture

The Active Child

Links Between Different Domains of Development

Javier Suarez smiled broadly as he held his newborn grandson for the first time. So many thoughts rushed into his mind: What would Ricardo experience growing up? Would the poor neighborhood they live in prevent him from reaching his potential? Would the family genes for good health be passed on? How would Ricardo's life growing up as a Chicano in the United States differ from Javier's own experiences growing up in Mexico?

Like many grandparents, Javier wonders what the future holds for his grandson. His questions actually reflect four basic themes in development that are the focus of this module. These themes will provide you with a foundation for understanding and organizing the many specific facts about child development that fill the rest of this book. To help you do this, at the end of Chapters 2 through 15, the "Unifying Themes" feature links the contents of the chapter to one of the themes.

Continuity of Development

LO9 How well can developmental outcomes be predicted from early life?

This theme concerns the predictability of development. Do you believe that happy, cheerful 5-year-olds remain outgoing and friendly throughout their lives? If you do, this shows that you believe development is a continuous process: According to this view, once a child begins down a particular developmental path, he or she stays on that path throughout life. In other words, if Ricardo is friendly and smart as a 5-year-old, he should be friendly and smart as a 15- and 25-year-old. The other view is that development is not continuous; according to this view, Ricardo might be friendly and smart as a 5-year-old but obnoxious and foolish at 15 and quiet but wise at 25! **Thus, the *continuity–discontinuity issue***

QUESTION 1.3

As a child, Heather was painfully shy and withdrawn, but as an adult she was outgoing, the life of many a party. What does Heather's life tell us about the continuity or discontinuity of shyness?

is really about the "relatedness" of development: Are early aspects of development consistently related to later aspects?

In reality, neither of these views is accurate. Development is not perfectly predictable. A friendly, smart 5-year-old does not guarantee a friendly, smart 15- or 25-year-old, but the chances of a friendly, smart adult are greater than if the child were obnoxious and foolish. There are many ways to become a friendly and smart 15-year-old; being a friendly and smart 5-year-old is not a required step, but it is probably the most direct route!

Impact of Nature and Nurture

LO10 How do heredity and environment influence development?

I want to introduce this theme with a story about my sons. Ben, my first son, was a delightful baby and toddler. He awoke each morning with a smile on his face, eager to start another fun-filled day. Ben was rarely upset; when he was, he was quickly consoled by being held or rocked. I presumed that his cheerful disposition must reflect fabulous parenting. Consequently, I was stunned when my second son, Matt, spent much of the first year of his life being fussy and cranky. He was easily irritated and hard to soothe. Why wasn't the all-star parenting that had been so effective with Ben working with Matt? The answer, of course, is that Ben's parenting wasn't the sole cause of his happiness. I thought environmental influences accounted for his amiable disposition, but in fact, biological influences also played an important role.

This anecdote illustrates the *nature–nurture issue*: **How do biology (nature) and environment (nurture) shape a child's development?** If Ricardo is outgoing and friendly, is it due to his heredity or his experiences? Scientists once hoped to answer questions like this by identifying either heredity or environment as *the* cause. Their goal was to be able to say, for example, that intelligence was due to heredity or that personality was due to experience. Today, we know that virtually no aspects of child development are exclusively the result of either heredity or environment. Instead, development is always shaped by both—nature and nurture interact (Sameroff, 2010). In fact, a major goal of child-development research is to understand how heredity and environment jointly determine children's development.

The Active Child

LO11 What role do children have in their own development?

I often ask students in my child-development classes about their plans for when they have children. How will they rear them? What do they want their children to grow up to be? It's interesting to hear students' responses. Many have big plans for their future children. It's just as interesting, though, to watch students who already have children roll their eyes in a "You-don't-have-a-clue" way at what the others say. The parent-students in class admit that they, too, once had grand designs about child rearing. However, they quickly learned that their children shaped the way in which they parented.

These two points of view illustrate the *active–passive child issue*: **Are children simply at the mercy of the environment (passive child), or do children actively influence their own development through their own unique individual characteristics (active child)?** The passive view corresponds to Locke's description of the child as a blank slate on which experience writes; the active view corresponds to Rousseau's view of development as a natural unfolding that takes place within the child. Today, we know that experiences are indeed crucial, but not always in the way Locke envisioned. Often, it's a child's interpretation of experiences that shapes his or her development. From birth, children like Ricardo are trying to make sense of their world, and in the process they help shape their own destinies.

Also, a child's unique characteristics may cause him or her to have some experiences but not others. Think about the child in the photo, who loves having parents read picture books. Her excitement is contagious and makes her parents eager to read to her night after night. In contrast, if a child squirms or seems bored during reading, parents may not take the time to read to the child. In both cases, children's behavior during reading influences whether parents read to them in the future.

Links Between Different Domains of Development

LO12 Is development in different domains connected?

Child-development researchers usually examine different domains or areas of development, such as physical growth, cognition, language, personality, and social relationships. One researcher might study how children learn to speak grammatically; another might explore children's reasoning about moral issues. Of course, you should *not* think of each aspect of development as an independent entity, completely separate from the others. To the contrary, development in different domains is always intertwined. Cognitive and social development, for example, are not independent; advances in one area affect advances in the other. Ricardo's cognitive growth (e.g., he becomes an excellent student) will influence his social development (e.g., he becomes friends with peers who share his enthusiasm for school).

This youngster's obvious enjoyment makes it more likely that her parents will read to her more in the future, showing that children can influence their own development.

Having introduced the themes, let's see them together once before we move on.

- *Continuity:* Early development is related to later development but not perfectly.
- *Nature and nurture:* Development is always jointly influenced by heredity and environment.
- *Active children:* Children influence their own development.
- *Connections:* Development in different domains is connected.

Most child-development scientists would agree that these are important general themes in children's development. However, just as lumber, bricks, pipe, and wiring can be used to assemble a variety of houses, these themes show up in different ways in the major theories of child development. Think, for example, about the nature–nurture issue. Of the five perspectives, the biological perspective is at one extreme in emphasizing the impact of nature; at the other extreme are the learning and contextual perspectives, which emphasize nurture.

The perspectives also see different degrees of connectedness across different domains of development. Piaget's cognitive-developmental theory emphasizes connections: Because children strive to have an integrated theory to explain the world, cognitive and social growth are linked closely. In contrast, the learning perspective holds that the degree of connectedness depends entirely on the nature of environmental influences. Similar environmental influences in different domains of children's lives produce many connections; dissimilar environmental influences would produce few connections.

Check Your Learning

RECALL Describe the difference between continuous development and discontinuous development.

Cite examples showing that development in different domains is connected.

INTERPRET Explain the difference between nature and nurture and how these forces are thought to affect children's development.

APPLY How might parents respond differently to an active child compared to a quiet child?

 # 1.4 Doing Child-Development Research

OUTLINE

Measurement in Child-Development Research

General Designs for Research

Designs for Studying Age-Related Change

Ethical Responsibilities

Communicating Research Results

LEARNING OBJECTIVES

LO13 How do scientists measure topics of interest in children's development?

LO14 What general research designs are used in child-development research?

LO15 What designs are unique to the study of age-related change?

LO16 What ethical procedures must researchers follow?

LO17 How do researchers communicate results to other scientists?

Leah and Joan are both mothers of 10-year-old boys. Their sons have many friends, but the basis for the friendships is not obvious to the mothers. Leah believes that opposites attract: children form friendships with peers who have complementary interests and abilities. Joan doubts this; her son seems to seek out other boys who are near-clones of himself in their interests and abilities.

Suppose Leah and Joan know you're taking a course in child development, so they ask you to settle their argument. You know, from Module 1.2, that Leah and Joan each have simple theories about children's friendships. Leah's theory is that complementary children are more often friends, whereas Joan's theory is that similar children are more often friends. You know that these theories should be tested with research. But how? In fact, like all scientists, child-development researchers follow the scientific method, which involves several steps:

- Identify a question to be answered or a phenomenon to be understood.
- Form a hypothesis that is a tentative answer to the question or a tentative explanation of the phenomenon.
- Select a method for collecting data that can be used to evaluate the hypothesis.

In our vignette, Leah and Joan have already taken the first two steps: They want to know why children become friends and each has a simple theory of this phenomenon, a theory that can be used to generate hypotheses. What remains is to find a method for collecting data, which is our focus for the rest of this module.

How do child-development scientists select methods for gathering evidence that's useful for testing hypotheses about child development?

In fact, in devising methods, child-development scientists must make several important decisions. They need to decide how to measure the phenomenon of interest; they must design their study; they must be sure their proposed research respects the rights of the individuals participating; and, after the study is complete, they must communicate their results to other researchers.

Child-development researchers do not always stick to this sequence of steps. For example, researchers usually consider the rights of research participants as they make each of the other decisions, perhaps rejecting a procedure because it violates those rights. Nevertheless, for simplicity, I will use this sequence to describe the steps in doing developmental research.

Measurement in Child-Development Research

LO13 How do scientists measure topics of interest in children's development?

Research usually begins by deciding how to measure the topic or behavior of interest. For example, the first step toward answering Leah and Joan's question about friendships would be to decide how to measure friendships. Child-development researchers typically use one of four approaches: observing children, using tasks to sample behavior, asking children for self-reports, and measuring physiological responses.

Systematic Observation   As the name implies, *systematic observation* involves watching children and carefully recording what they do or say. Two forms of systematic observation are common. In *naturalistic observation*, children are observed as they behave spontaneously in a real-life situation. Of course, researchers can't keep track of everything that a child does. Beforehand they must decide which *variables*—factors that can take on different values—to record. Researchers studying friendship, for example, might decide to observe children in a school lunchroom like the one in the photo. They would record where each child sits and who talks to whom. They might also decide to observe children at the start of the first year in middle school, because many children make new friends at this time.

Naturalistic observation is illustrated in research by Gunderson et al. (2013), who studied interactions between mothers and their children at 14, 26, and 38 months of age. They used video cameras to record 90 minutes of routine daily activities (e.g., getting dressed, meals, play). From these videotapes, the researchers measured the number of times that mothers praised their children, with praise defined as a remark that provided positive feedback to the child, either explicitly ("Great job!") or implicitly ("You did it yourself!").

In *structured observation*, the researcher creates a setting likely to elicit the behavior of interest. Structured observations are particularly useful for studying behaviors that are difficult to observe naturally because they are uncommon or occur in private settings. For example, an investigator using naturalistic observation to study children's responses to emergencies wouldn't make much progress because emergencies don't occur at

In naturalistic observation, researchers record children's spontaneous behavior in natural environments, such as this school cafeteria.

Structured observation involves creating a situation—asking children to play a game—that is likely to lead to behaviors of interest, such as competition.

predetermined times and locations. However, using structured observation, an investigator might stage an emergency, perhaps by having a nearby adult cry for help and then observing children's responses. Similarly, naturalistic observation of interactions with friends is difficult because they often take place at home. In structured observation, friends could be asked to come to the researcher's laboratory, which might be furnished with chairs and tables. Children would be asked to perform some activity typical of friends—such as playing a game—and researchers observe their behavior, sometimes through a one-way mirror.

A good example of structured observation comes from a study by Sturge-Apple, Davies, and Cummings (2010) of parenting strategies. These researchers asked a mother to join her 6-year-old child in a room that included many attractive toys. Mother and child were encouraged to play with the toys for five minutes, then mothers were told to encourage the child to help clean up the toys. The play and cleanup sessions were videotaped and later the researchers used the tapes to measure parental behavior, including, for example, the extent to which mothers used praise and approval to encourage their children to clean up. By creating a situation that would be moderately challenging for mothers—most 6-year-olds would rather continue playing, not clean up!—Sturge-Apple et al. hoped to gain insights into parental behavior.

Structured observations allow researchers to observe behaviors that would otherwise be difficult to study, but investigators must be careful that the settings they create do not disturb the behavior of interest. For instance, observing friends as they play a game in a researcher's lab has many artificial aspects to it: The friends are not in their own homes, they were told (in general terms) what to do, and they know they're being observed. Similarly, the moms in the study by Sturge-Apple et al. knew that they were being videotaped and may have wanted to show their best parenting behavior. Any or all of these factors may cause children and parents to behave differently than they would in the real world. Researchers must be careful that their method does not distort the behavior they are observing.

Sampling Behavior with Tasks When investigators can't observe a behavior directly, an alternative is to create tasks that sample the behavior of interest. For example, to measure memory, investigators sometimes use a digit span task: Children listen as a sequence of numbers is presented aloud. After the last digit is presented, children try to repeat the digits in the exact order in which they heard them. To measure children's ability to recognize different emotions, investigators sometimes use the task shown in Figure 1-1 on page 39. The child has been asked to look at the facial expressions and point to the person who looks happy.

Sampling behavior with tasks is popular with child-development researchers because it is so convenient. However, a potential problem is that the task may not accurately measure the behavior of interest. For example, asking children to judge emotions from photographs may not be valid because it underestimates what children do in real life. Can you think of reasons why this might be the case? I mention several reasons on page 52, just before Check Your Learning.

Figure 1-1

Self-Reports   The third approach to measurement, using self-reports, is actually a special case of using tasks to measure children's behavior. *Self-reports* **are simply children's answers to questions about the topic of interest.** When questions are posed in written form, the report is a questionnaire; when questions are posed aloud, the report is an interview. In either format, questions are created that probe different aspects of the topic of interest. For example, to examine the impact of similarity on friendship, you might tell research participants the following:

> Jacob and Dave just met each other at school. Jacob likes to read and plays the clarinet in the school orchestra; Dave likes to play games on his Xbox 360 and is a star on the basketball team. Do you think Jacob and Dave will become friends?

Children participating in the study would rate the odds that Jacob and Dave will become friends.

A typical questionnaire comes from a study by Yip, Douglass, and Shelton (2013), who were interested in measuring the extent to which Asian American adolescents' ethnic identity was affected by the diversity within their school. To measure adolescents' ethnic identity, they used a questionnaire that included statements such as "I feel good about people from my racial or ethnic group," and "In general, my race or ethnicity is an important part of my self-image." Adolescents indicated how much each statement was true of them, using a 7-point scale that ranged from "strongly disagree" to "strongly agree."

Self-reports are useful because they can lead directly to information on the topic of interest. They are also relatively convenient, particularly when they can be administered to groups of children or adolescents. However, self-reports are not always valid measures of children's behavior because children's answers are sometimes inaccurate. Why? When asked about past events, children may not remember them accurately. For example, an adolescent asked about childhood friends may not remember those friendships well. **Also, children sometimes answer incorrectly because of** *response bias*—**some responses may be more socially acceptable than others, and children are more likely to select those than socially unacceptable answers.** For example, some adolescents in the Yip et al. (2013) study may have been reluctant to admit that they had little sense of an ethnic identity. But, as long as investigators keep these weaknesses in mind, self-reports are a valuable tool for child-development research.

Physiological Measures   A final approach is less common but can be powerful: measuring children's physiological responses. Heart rate, for example,

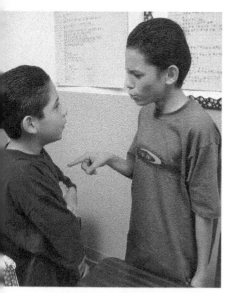

If arguments like this one are more common among boys than girls, then that difference should be evident in observations of children's behavior as well as in other measures, such as self-reports.

often slows down when children are paying close attention to something interesting. Consequently, researchers often measure heart rate to determine a child's degree of attention. As another example, the hormone cortisol is often secreted in response to stress. By measuring cortisol levels in children's saliva, scientists can determine when children are experiencing stress (Koss et al., 2013).

As both of these examples suggest, physiological measures are usually specialized, focusing on a particular aspect of a child's behavior (attention and stress in the two examples). What's more, they're often used with other behaviorally oriented methods. A researcher studying stress might observe children, looking for overt signs of stress; ask parents to rate their children's stress; and also measure cortisol in children's saliva. If all three measures lead to the same conclusions about stress, then the researcher can be much more confident about the conclusions.

Another important group of physiological measures includes those used to study brain activity. Techniques developed during the past 25 years allow modern scientists to record many facets of brain functioning as children are performing specific tasks. I describe these methods in Module 4.3. For now, the important point is that child-development scientists are making great strides in identifying the brain regions associated with reasoning, memory, emotions, and other psychological functions.

The four approaches to measurement are presented in Summary Table 1-2.

Evaluating Measures After researchers choose a method of measurement, they must show that it is reliable and valid. **A measure is *reliable* if the results are consistent over time.** A measure of friendship, for example, would be reliable if it yields the same results about friendship each time it is administered. **A measure is *valid* if it really measures what researchers think it measures.** For example, a measure of friendship is valid only if it can be shown to actually measure friendship (and not, for example, popularity). Validity is often established by showing that the measure is closely related to another measure known to be valid. We could confirm that a questionnaire measuring friendship is valid by showing that scores on the questionnaire are related to peers' and parents' ratings of friendship.

SUMMARY TABLE 1-2

WAYS OF MEASURING BEHAVIOR IN CHILD-DEVELOPMENT RESEARCH

Method	Strength	Weakness
Systematic observation		
Naturalistic observation	Captures children's behavior in its natural setting	Difficult to use with behaviors that are rare or that typically occur in private settings
Structured observation	Can be used to study behaviors that are rare or that typically occur in private settings	May be invalid if the structured setting distorts the behavior
Sampling behavior with tasks	Convenient; can be used to study most behaviors	May be invalid if the task does not sample behavior as it occurs naturally
Self-reports (questionnaires and interviews)	Convenient; can be used to study most behaviors	May be invalid because children answer incorrectly because of forgetting or response bias
Physiological measures	Can provide independent, converging evidence that can confirm behavioral measures	Are often specific to particular types of behaviors and, consequently, may not be available for all topics

Throughout this book, you'll come across many studies using these different methods. You'll also see that studies of the same topic or behavior often use different methods. This is desirable: Because the approaches to measurement have different strengths and weaknesses, finding the same results regardless of the approach leads to particularly strong conclusions. Suppose, for example, that a researcher using self-reports claims that arguments, like the one shown in the photo, are more common in boys' friendships than in girls' friendships. It would be reassuring that other investigators have found the same result from systematic observation and from sampling behavior with tasks.

Much research is based on samples of children living in developed countries in North America and other parts of the world; those results may not generalize to children living in developing nations.

Representative Sampling Valid measures depend not only on the method of measurement but also on the children who are tested. **Researchers are usually interested in broad groups of children called *populations*.** Examples of populations would be all American 7-year-olds or all African American adolescents. However, it would be extremely difficult for researchers to study every member of such large groups. **Virtually all studies include only a *sample* of children, a subset of the population.** Researchers must take care that their sample really represents the population of interest. An unrepresentative sample can lead to invalid research. For example, what would you think of a study of children's friendship if you learned that the sample consisted entirely of 8-year-olds whose friends were primarily preschool children? This sample of 8-year-olds would seem to be unusual, and you would hesitate to generalize the results from this sample back to the population at large.

As you read on, you'll discover that much of the research I describe was conducted with samples of middle-class European American youngsters. Are these samples representative of all children in the United States? Of children like those in the photo who grow up in developing countries? Sometimes, but not always. Be careful not to assume that findings from this group necessarily apply to people in other groups (Jensen, 2012).

General Designs for Research

LO14 What general research designs are used in child-development research?

Having formulated a hypothesis, identified variables, and selected a method to collect data on the topic or behavior of interest, researchers must then choose an overall conceptual approach called a *research design*. Child-development researchers usually use one of two designs: correlational or experimental studies.

Correlational Studies In a *correlational study*, **investigators look at relations between variables as they exist naturally in the world.** In the simplest possible correlational study, a researcher measures two variables then sees how they are related. Imagine a researcher who wants to test the idea that smarter children have more friends. To test this claim, the researcher would measure two variables for each child: the number of friends the child has and the child's intelligence.

The results of a correlational study are usually expressed as a *correlation coefficient*, abbreviated *r*, which stands for the direction and strength of a relation between two variables. Correlations can range from −1.0 to +1.0:

- *When **r** equals 0, two variables are completely unrelated:* Children's intelligence is unrelated to the number of friends they have.
- *When **r** is greater than 0, scores are related positively:* Children who are smart tend to have more friends than children who are not as smart. That is, greater intelligence is associated with having more friends.
- *When **r** is less than 0, scores are related, but inversely:* Children who are smart tend to have fewer friends than children who are not as smart. That is, greater intelligence is associated with having fewer friends.

In interpreting a correlation coefficient, you need to consider the sign *and* the size of the correlation. The sign indicates the *direction* of the relation between variables. For example, Belsky, Houts, and Pasco Fearon (2010) wondered whether the age at which girls entered puberty was related to the security of their emotional attachment to their mother during infancy (a topic that we'll examine in detail in Module 10.3). The investigators assessed security of mother–infant attachment when girls were 15 months old and used data from physical exams to determine when girls entered puberty. The correlation was .47, indicating that, in general, daughters with more secure attachment as infants tended to enter puberty at an older age.

The *strength* of a relation is measured by how much the correlation differs from 0, either positively or negatively. If the correlation between intelligence and number of friends were .75, the relation between these variables would be strong: Knowing a child's intelligence, you could accurately predict how many friends the child has. If, instead, the correlation were .25, the link between intelligence and number of friends would be relatively weak: Although more intelligent children would have more friends on the average, there would be many exceptions to this rule. Similarly, a correlation of −.75 would indicate a strong negative relation between intelligence and number of friends, but a correlation of −.25 would indicate a weak negative relation. Thus, in the study by Belsky et al. (2010) on links between attachment and onset of puberty, the correlation of .47 indicates a medium-sized relation between attachment security and age of onset of puberty. Many girls with secure attachment to their mother as infants entered puberty at a relatively older age, but not all of them; some girls with secure attachment started puberty at a relatively younger age.

The results of a correlational study tell whether variables are related, but this design doesn't address the question of cause and effect between the variables. In other words, finding a correlation between variables does not necessarily imply a causal relation between them. Suppose a researcher finds that the correlation between intelligence and number of friends is .7. This means that children who are smarter have more friends than children who are not as smart. How would you interpret this correlation? Figure 1-2 on page 43 shows that three interpretations are possible. Maybe being smart causes children to have more friends. Another interpretation is that having more friends causes children to be smarter. A third interpretation is that neither variable causes the other; instead, intelligence and number of friends are caused by a third variable that was not measured in the study. Perhaps parents who are warm and supportive tend to have children who are smart and who also have many friends. Any of these interpretations could be true. Cause and effect cannot be distinguished in a correlational study.

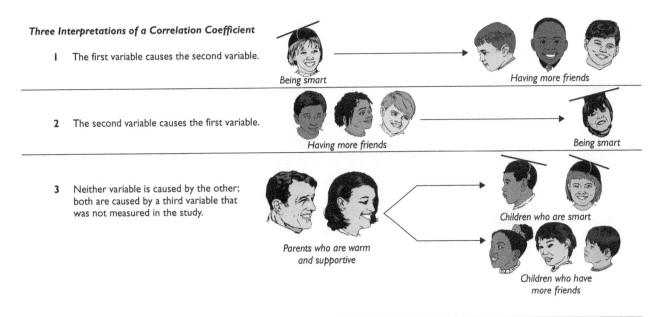

Three Interpretations of a Correlation Coefficient

1 The first variable causes the second variable.

Being smart → *Having more friends*

2 The second variable causes the first variable.

Having more friends → *Being smart*

3 Neither variable is caused by the other; both are caused by a third variable that was not measured in the study.

Parents who are warm and supportive → *Children who are smart* / *Children who have more friends*

Figure 1-2

Consequently, when investigators want to track down causes, they use a different design, an experimental study.

Experimental Studies In an *experiment,* an investigator systematically varies the factors thought to cause a particular behavior. The factor that is varied is called the *independent variable*; the behavior that is measured is called the *dependent variable.* In an experiment, the investigator randomly assigns children to different groups or conditions that are treated alike except for the single factor that varies across groups (i.e., the independent variable). The dependent variable is then measured in all groups. Because children have been assigned to groups randomly, differences between the groups reflect the different treatment the children received in the experiment.

Suppose that an investigator hypothesizes that children share more with friends than with children they do not know. Figure 1-3 on page 44 shows how the investigator might test this hypothesis. Based on random assignment, some fifth-grade children come to the investigator's laboratory with a good friend. Other fifth-graders come to the laboratory site without a friend and are paired with a child they don't know. The laboratory itself is decorated to look like a comfortable room in a house. The investigator creates a task in which one child is given an interesting object to play with—perhaps a Wii video game console—but the other child receives nothing. The experimenter explains the task to the children and then claims that she needs to leave the room briefly. Actually, the experimenter goes to a room with a one-way mirror and observes whether the child with the Wii offers to let the other child play with it.

This same scenario is used with all pairs of children: The room and Wii are the same and the experimenter is always away for the same amount of time. The circumstances are held as constant as possible for all children, except that some children participate with friends but others do not. If children who participated with friends shared the Wii more often, the investigator could conclude that children are more likely to share with their friends than with children they don't know. Conclusions about cause and effect are possible because there was a direct

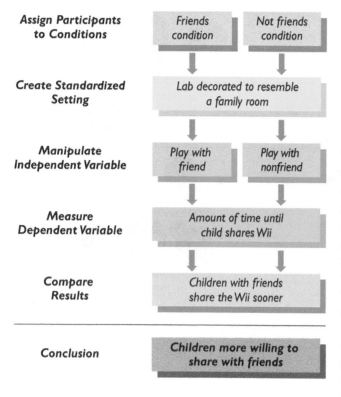

Assign Participants to Conditions

Friends condition | Not friends condition

Create Standardized Setting

Lab decorated to resemble a family room

Manipulate Independent Variable

Play with friend | Play with nonfriend

Measure Dependent Variable

Amount of time until child shares Wii

Compare Results

Children with friends share the Wii sooner

Conclusion

Children more willing to share with friends

Figure 1-3

manipulation of an independent variable (participating with a friend or with an unknown child) under controlled conditions.

You can see the use of an experiment in a study by Buttelmann and colleagues (2013). Infants readily imitate other's actions. However, are infants selective in their imitation? For example, are they more likely to imitate an adult who seems to be a member of their cultural group? To answer this question, Buttelmann and colleagues randomly assigned 14-month-olds to observe either an adult speaking in the infant's native language or an adult speaking in a foreign language. The adult told a few simple stories—either in the native or foreign language—then silently demonstrated some novel actions with an unfamiliar object (e.g., turning on an unfamiliar lamp-in-a-box by touching the side of the box with his head). Finally, infants were shown the unfamiliar objects (e.g., the lamp-in-a-box) and encouraged to play with it.

In this experiment, the independent variable was whether the infant observed an adult telling stories in a native or foreign language; the dependent variable was the extent to which infants imitated the adult by performing the novel action. In fact, infants were more likely to imitate the adult who spoke in a native language: 44% of the infants imitated the adult when he spoke in a native language but only 31% did so when he spoke in a foreign language. Because infants were randomly assigned to conditions, Buttelmann et al. (2013) could conclude that the adult's language *caused* infants to be more likely to imitate.

Child-development researchers usually conduct experiments such as this one in laboratory-like settings to control all the variables that might influence the outcome of the research. A shortcoming of laboratory work is that behavior is sometimes not studied in its natural setting. Consequently, the results may be invalid because they are artificial—specific to the laboratory setting and not representative of the behavior in the natural environment.

To avoid this limit, researchers sometimes rely on a special type of experiment. **In a *field experiment*, the researcher manipulates independent variables in a natural setting so that the results are more likely to be representative of behavior in real-world settings.** To illustrate a field experiment, let's return to the hypothesis that children share more with friends. We might conduct the research in a classroom where students must complete a group assignment. In collaboration with teachers, we place the children in groups of three: in some groups, all three children are good friends; in others, the three children are acquaintances but not friends. When the assignment is complete, the teacher gives each group leader many stickers and tells the leader to distribute them to group members based on how much each child contributed. We predict that leaders will share more (i.e., distribute the stickers more evenly) when group members are friends than when they are not.

A good example of a field experiment is a study by DeLoache and colleagues (2010), who wondered whether videos designed to promote vocabulary learning actually help babies learn words. They assigned 1-year-olds randomly to one of three conditions: in one, several times each week the infant and parent watched a commercial DVD designed to increase the infant's vocabulary; in a second condition, parents were simply told the 25 words featured in the DVD and encouraged to help their infants master them; in a third, control condition, infants saw no videos and parents weren't told the words. After four weeks, experimenters tested infants' knowledge of the 25 words in the DVD. Infants were shown two objects, one depicting a word shown in the video. The experiment said the word and asked infants to point to the corresponding object.

In this experiment, the independent variable was the type of exposure to the words (via DVD, from parents, none) and the dependent variable was the number of times that infants pointed to the correct object upon hearing the word. Was the video useful? No. Infants who had watched the video knew the same number of words as infants in the control condition. And infants in both of these groups knew *fewer* words than infants whose parents had been encouraged to teach words. Because infants were randomly assigned to conditions, DeLoache and colleagues (2010) could conclude that the type of exposure to words *caused* differences in the number of words that infants learned.

Field experiments allow investigators to draw strong conclusions about cause and effect because they embed manipulation of an independent variable in a natural setting. However, field experiments are often impractical because of logistical problems. In most natural settings, children are supervised by adults (e.g., parents and teachers) who must be willing to become allies in the proposed research. Adults may not want to change their routines to fit a researcher's needs. In addition, researchers usually sacrifice some control in field experiments. In the study by DeLoache of baby videos, for example, the investigators relied upon parents to show the videos as instructed and to provide honest reports of how often they watched the videos with their children. No doubt some parents complied with instructions better than others and some parents were more truthful in their reports of how often they watched videos.

Another important variation is the *quasi-experiment*, which typically involves examining the impact of an independent variable by using groups that were not created with random assignment. Think, for example, about how child-development researchers could study the consequences for children's development of (a) a mother's smoking, (b) exposure to natural disasters such as Hurricane Katrina, or (c) growing up in a rural area instead of a city. In these instances, conducting a true experiment is either impossible or unethical—children can't be randomly assigned to a mother who smokes or to grow up on a farm. However, children living in these conditions can be compared with children living in contrasting situations (e.g., with children whose mothers don't smoke or with children living in cities). The tricky part is that, because children weren't assigned to groups randomly, the groups may differ along other dimensions as well. For example, people with less education are more likely to smoke; consequently, a difference favoring children of women who don't smoke might reflect the tendency for these women to be better educated. This problem can be addressed, somewhat, by using statistical analyses that hold these other variables constant (i.e., that can control for the fact that groups differ along other variables, such as education).

Like most designs, quasi-experiments have strengths and weaknesses. Consequently, no single investigation can definitely answer a question, and researchers rarely rely on one study or even one method to reach conclusions. Instead, they prefer to find converging evidence from studies using as many different kinds of methods as possible. Suppose, for example, that our hypothetical laboratory and field experiments show that children do indeed share more readily with their friends. One way to be more confident of this conclusion would be to do correlational research, perhaps by observing children during lunch and measuring how often they share food with different people.

Designs for Studying Age-Related Change

LO15 What designs are unique to the study of age-related change?

Sometimes child-development research is directed at a single age group, such as fifth-grade children (as in the experiment on sharing between friends and nonfriends), memory in preschool-age children, or mother–infant relationships in 1-year-olds. When this is the case, after deciding how to measure the behavior of interest and whether the study will be correlational or experimental, the investigator could skip directly to the last step and determine whether the study is ethical.

However, much research in child development concerns changes that occur as children develop. Consequently, in conjunction with the chosen general research design, investigators must also select a strategy for assessing age-related change. Three strategies are used to incorporate different age groups into experimental and correlational research: the longitudinal approach, the cross-sectional approach, and the longitudinal-sequential approach.

Longitudinal Design In a *longitudinal design*, **the same individuals are observed or tested repeatedly at different points in their lives.** As the name implies, the longitudinal approach takes a lengthwise view of development and is the most direct way to watch growth occur. As Figure 1-4 shows, in a longitudinal study, children might be tested first at age 6 and then again at ages 9 and 12. The longitudinal approach is well suited to studying almost any aspect of development. More important, it is the only way to answer questions about the continuity or discontinuity of behavior: Will characteristics such as aggression, dependency, or mistrust observed in infancy or early childhood persist into adulthood? Will a traumatic event, such as being abandoned by one's parents, influence later social and intellectual development? Such questions can be explored only by testing children early in development and then retesting them later. For example, the study of parenting by Belsky et al. (2010) (described on page 42) was part of an ongoing longitudinal study of more than 1,000 children born in the United States in 1991, in which children were tested repeatedly

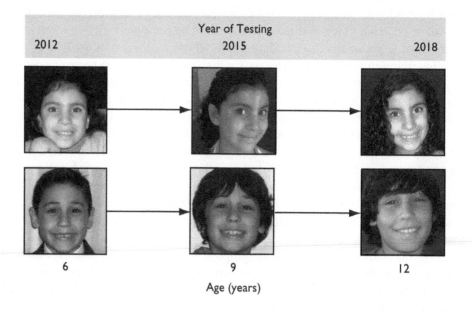

Figure 1-4

during childhood, adolescence, and young adulthood. Consequently, investigators can see how children's experiences during the preschool years affect them as adolescents and young adults.

Usually the repeated testing of longitudinal studies extends over years, but not always. **In a special type of longitudinal design known as a *microgenetic study*, children are tested repeatedly over a span of days or weeks, typically with the aim of observing change directly as it occurs.** For example, researchers might test children every week, starting when they are 12 months old and continuing until 18 months. Microgenetic studies are particularly useful when investigators have hypotheses about a specific period when developmental change should occur. In this case, researchers arrange to test children frequently before, during, and after this period, hoping to see change as it happens (e.g., Opfer & Siegler, 2007).

The longitudinal approach, however, has disadvantages that frequently offset its strengths. An obvious one is cost: The expense of keeping up with a large sample of people over several years can be staggering. Other problems are not so obvious:

- *Practice effects:* When children are given the same test many times, they may become "test-wise." Improvement over time that is attributed to development may actually stem from practice with a particular test. Changing the test from one session to the next solves the practice problem but can make it difficult to compare responses to different tests.

- *Selective attrition:* Another problem is the constancy of the sample over the course of research. Some children may drop out because they move away. Others may simply lose interest and choose not to continue. These dropouts often differ significantly from their peers, which can distort the outcome. For example, a study might find that memory improves between 8 and 11 years. What has actually happened, however, is that 8-year-olds who found the testing too difficult quit the study, thereby raising the group average when children were tested as 11-year-olds.

- *Cohort effects:* **When children in a longitudinal study are observed over a period of several years, the developmental change may be specific to a specific generation of people known as a *cohort*.** For example, the longitudinal study that I described previously includes babies born in 1991 in the United States. The results of this study may be general (i.e., apply to infants born in 1950 as well as infants born in 2000), but they may reflect experiences that were unique to infants born in the early 1990s.

Because of these problems with longitudinal studies, child-development researchers also use cross-sectional studies.

Cross-Sectional Design In a *cross-sectional design* **developmental changes are identified by testing children of different ages at one point in their development.** In other words, as shown in Figure 1-5 on page 48, a researcher might chart differences in some attribute between, say, 6-, 9-, and 12-year-olds. For example, when Verkuyten and De Wolf (2007) studied age-related change in children's preference for their own group, they tested 6-, 8-, and 10-year-olds. This was much faster than waiting the four years for the 6-year-olds to become 10-year-olds, and avoided many of the problems associated with longitudinal studies, including practice effects and selective attrition. But cohort effects are still a problem: The results may apply to children who are 6, 9, and 12 years old at the time of testing (in the example in the figure, 2015) and not generalize to

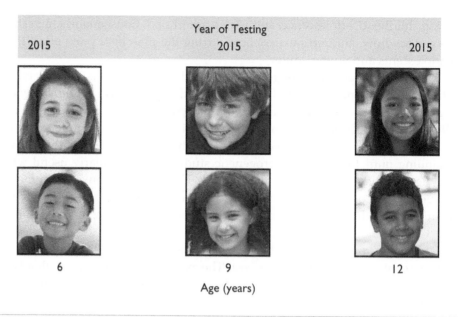

Figure 1-5

previous or future generations. Cross-sectional studies also have a unique short-coming: Because children are tested at only one point in their development, we learn nothing about the continuity of development. Consequently, we cannot tell whether an aggressive 6-year-old remains aggressive at ages 9 and 12 because an individual child would be tested at age 6, 9, or 12, but not at all three ages.

Longitudinal-Sequential Studies Because longitudinal and cross-sectional have weaknesses, investigators sometimes use a hybrid design: A longitudinal-sequential study includes sequences of samples, each studied longitudinally. For example, researchers might start with 6- and 9-year-olds. As shown in Figure 1-6, each group is tested twice—at the beginning of the study and again three years

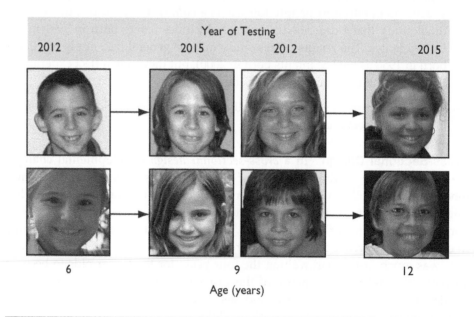

Figure 1-6

later. As in a pure longitudinal study, the longitudinal-sequential design provides some information about continuity of development: Researchers can determine whether aggressive 6-year-olds become aggressive 9-year-olds and whether aggressive 9-year-olds become aggressive 12-year-olds. Of course, to determine whether aggressive 6-year-olds become aggressive 12-year-olds would require a full-fledged longitudinal study.

Longitudinal-sequential studies allow researchers to determine whether their study is plagued by practice effects or cohort effects: The key is to compare the results for the age common to both sequences (in the example in the figure, 9-year-olds). Practice and cohort effects tend to make scores different for the two groups of 9-year-olds; if scores are the same, practice and cohort effects are probably not a problem in the study.

Each of these designs for studying development (longitudinal, cross-sectional, longitudinal-sequential) shown in Summary Table 1-3 can be combined with the two general research designs (observational, experimental), resulting in six prototypic designs. To illustrate the different possibilities, think back to our hypothetical laboratory experiment on children's sharing with friends and non-friends (described on page 43). If we tested 7- and 11-year-olds with either friends or nonfriends, this would be a cross-sectional experimental study. If instead we observed 7-year olds' spontaneous sharing at lunch, then observed the same children four years later, this would be a longitudinal correlational study.

In this book, you'll read about studies using all of the designs but the two cross-sectional designs will show up more frequently than the others. Why? For most developmentalists, the ease of cross-sectional studies compared to longitudinal studies more than compensates for the limitations of cross-sectional studies.

Integrating Findings from Different Studies   Several times in this module, I've emphasized the value of conducting multiple studies on a topic using different methods. The advantage of this approach, of course, is in showing that multiple methods all point to the same conclusion.

SUMMARY TABLE 1-3

DESIGNS USED IN CHILD-DEVELOPMENT RESEARCH

Type of Design	Definition	Strengths	Weaknesses
GENERAL DESIGNS			
Correlational	Observe variables as they exist in the world and determine their relations	Behavior is measured as it occurs naturally	Cannot determine cause and effect
Experimental	Manipulate independent and dependent variables	Control of variables allows conclusions about cause and effect	Work is often laboratory based, which can be artificial
DEVELOPMENTAL DESIGNS			
Longitudinal	One group of children is tested repeatedly as they develop	Only way to chart an individual's development and look at the continuity of behavior over time	Expensive; participants drop out; repeated testing can distort performance
Cross-sectional	Children of different ages are tested at the same time	Convenient; solves most problems associated with longitudinal studies	Cannot study continuity of behavior; cohort effects complicate interpretation of differences between groups
Longitudinal-sequential	Different sequences of children are tested longitudinally	Provides information about continuity; researchers can determine the presence of practice and cohort effects	Provides less information about continuity than a full longitudinal study and is more time consuming than a cross-sectional study

In reality, though, findings are often inconsistent. Suppose, for example, that many researchers find that children often share with friends, some researchers find that children share occasionally with friends, and a few researchers find that children never share with friends. What results should we believe? What should we conclude? *Meta-analysis* **is a tool that allows researchers to synthesize the results of many studies to estimate relations between variables** (Cooper, Hedges, & Valentine, 2009). In conducting a meta-analysis, investigators find all studies published on a topic over a substantial period of time (e.g., 10 to 20 years), then record and analyze the results and important methodological variables.

The usefulness of meta-analysis is illustrated in a study by Juffer and van IJzendoorn (2007), who asked whether adopted children differ from non-adopted children in terms of self-esteem. They found 88 studies, published between 1970 and 2007, that included nearly 11,000 adopted persons. In each of the 88 studies, self-esteem was measured, often by asking participants to rate themselves on scales containing items such as "I am a worthwhile person." Analyzing across the results of all 88 studies, Juffer and van IJzendoorn found that self-esteem did not differ in adopted and nonadopted individuals. This was true regardless of the age of the child when adopted and was true for international versus domestic adoptions as well as for children adopted by parents of their own race versus parents of another race. Evidently, adoption has no impact on self-esteem.

Thus, meta-analysis is a particularly powerful tool because it allows scientists to determine whether a finding generalizes across many studies that used different methods. In addition, meta-analysis can reveal the impact of those different methods on results (e.g., whether self-reports suggests more sharing between friends than observational studies).

Ethical Responsibilities

LO16 What ethical procedures must researchers follow?

Having selected a way of measuring the behavior of interest and having chosen a research design, scientists must confront an important remaining step: Determining whether their research is ethical, that is, that it does not violate the rights of the children who participate. Of course, scientists must always consider the ethics of research with humans, but especially for children, who are vulnerable and sensitive. Professional organizations and government agencies have codes of conduct that specify the rights of research participants and procedures to protect those participants. The following guidelines are included in all those codes:

- *Minimize risks to research participants:* Use methods that have the least potential for harm to or stress on research participants. During the research, monitor the procedures to avoid any unforeseen stress or harm.
- *Describe research to potential participants so they can determine whether they wish to participate:* **Prospective research participants should understand the research so they can make an educated decision about participating, which is known as obtaining** *informed consent.* Children are minors and are not legally capable of giving consent; consequently, as shown in the photograph, researchers must describe the study to parents and ask them for permission for their children to participate.
- *Avoid deception; if participants must be deceived, provide a thorough explanation of the true nature of the research as soon as possible:* Providing

complete information about a study in advance sometimes distorts participants' responses. Consequently, investigators may provide only partial information or even mislead participants about the true purpose of the study. As soon as it is feasible—typically just after the experiment—any false information must be corrected and the reasons for the deception must be provided.

- *Keep results anonymous or confidential:* Research results should be anonymous, which means that participants' data cannot be linked to their names. When anonymity is not possible, research results should be confidential, which means that only the investigator conducting the study knows the identities of the individuals.

Before children can participate in research, a parent or legal guardian must provide written consent.

Before researchers can conduct a study, they must convince review boards that they have carefully addressed each of these ethical points. If the review board objects to some aspects of the proposed study, the researcher must revise them and present the study anew for the review board's approval.

Much child-development research does not raise ethical red flags because the methods are harmless and avoid deception. However, some methods involve risk or deception; in these cases, review boards must balance the rights of children against the value of the research for contributing to knowledge and thereby improving children's lives. For example, in Module 10.3 we'll see that one tool for studying mother–infant relationships involves separating mothers and infants briefly, then watching infants' responses. Many infants are upset when the mother leaves and some are difficult to console when she returns. Obviously, this method is not pleasant for infants. But scientists have determined that it produces no lasting harm and therefore is suitable as long as parents receive a thorough description of the study beforehand and they consent to participate.

 QUESTION 1.4

Ethan, a 10-year-old, was at school when a researcher asked if he wanted to earn $10 doing an experiment. The money sounded good to Ethan, so he participated. Despite the pay, Ethan left the experiment upset because he overheard the experimenter telling his teacher how poorly Ethan had done. What are three ethical problems with this research?

Communicating Research Results

LO17 How do researchers communicate results to other scientists?

When the study is complete and the data have been analyzed, researchers write a report of their work. This report uses a standard format that usually includes four main sections: an introduction that describes the topic or question that was studied and the authors' hypotheses; a method section that describes the research design and the procedures; a results section that presents the findings; and a discussion section in which the authors explain the links between their results and their hypotheses.

Researchers submit the report to a scientific journal that specializes in child-development research, such as *Child Development*, *Developmental Psychology*, and *Developmental Science*. The editor of the journal asks other scientists to evaluate the report to decide whether the work was well done and the findings represent a substantial advance in understanding of a topic. If the reviewing scientists recommend that the report be published, it will appear in the journal, where other child-development researchers can learn of the results.

These reports of research are the basis for most of the information I present in this book. As you read, you'll see names in parentheses, followed by a date, like this: (Levine, Waite, & Bowman, 2007). This indicates the person(s) who did the research and the year the report describing the research was published. By looking in the References section, which begins on page 509 and is organized alphabetically, you can find the title of the article and the journal in which it was published.

Maybe all these different steps in research seem tedious and involved to you. However, for a child-development researcher, one of the most creative and stimulating parts of research is planning a novel study that will further our understanding of children's development and provide useful information to other specialists.

The Focus on Research features that appear in the remaining chapters of this book are designed to convey the creativity and the challenge of doing child-development research. Each feature focuses on a specific study. Some are studies published recently; others are classics that defined a new area of investigation or provided definitive results in some area. In each Focus feature, I trace the decisions that researchers made as they planned their study. In the process, you'll see the ingenuity of researchers as they pursue questions of child development. You'll also see that any individual study has limitations. Only when converging evidence from many studies—each using a unique combination of measurement methods and designs—points to the same conclusion can we feel confident about research results.

Responses to question on page 38 about using photographs to measure children's understanding of emotions: Children's understanding of emotions depicted in photographs may be less accurate than in real life because in real life (1) facial features are usually moving—not still, as in the photographs—and movement may be one of the clues that children naturally use to judge emotions; (2) facial expressions are often accompanied by sounds, and children may use both sight and sound to understand emotion; and (3) children often judge facial expressions of people they know (e.g., parents, siblings, peers), and knowing the "usual" appearance of a face may help children determine emotions accurately.

 ## Check Your Learning

RECALL List the ethical responsibilities of scientists who do research with children.

What steps are involved in reporting the results of research to the scientific community?

INTERPRET Compare the strengths and weaknesses of different approaches to measurement in child-development research.

APPLY Suppose you wanted to determine the impact of divorce on children's academic achievement. What would be the merits of correlational versus experimental research on this topic? How would a longitudinal study differ from a cross-sectional study?

See for Yourself

One good way to see how children influence their own development is to interview parents who have more than one child. Ask them if they used the same child-rearing methods with each child or if they used different techniques with each. If they used different techniques, find out why. You should see that, although parents try to be consistent in a general philosophy for rearing their children, many of the specific parenting techniques will vary from one child to the next, reflecting the children's influence on the parents. See for yourself!

Summary

Setting the Stage

Historical Views of Children and Childhood
Plato and Aristotle provided the first philosophical views of childhood. Their ideas were picked up in the 17th century. Locke emphasized the role of experience in children's lives, but Rousseau viewed development as a natural unfolding.

Origins of a New Science
Child development emerged as a science in the 19th century, reflecting reformers' concern for children's well-being and enthusiasm for Darwin's theory of evolution. Leaders in the new field were G. Stanley Hall (theories of child development), Binet (mental tests), Freud (early experience), and Watson (behaviorism).

Applying Results of Research
Child-development researchers help shape family policy by providing knowledge about children so that policies can be based on accurate information. They also contribute by serving as advocates for children, by evaluating the impact of social programs and by developing effective programs that can be implemented elsewhere.

Foundational Theories of Child Development

Theories provide explanations for development and hypotheses for research. Traditionally, five broad perspectives have guided researchers.

The Biological Perspective
According to this perspective, biological factors are critical for development. In maturational theory, child development reflects a natural unfolding of a prearranged biological plan. Ethological theory states that children's and parents' behavior is often adaptive.

The Psychodynamic Perspective
Freud emphasized the roles of early experience and conflict in children's development. Erikson proposed that psychosocial development consists of eight stages, each characterized by a particular struggle.

The Learning Perspective
Operant conditioning is based on reinforcement, punishment, and environmental control of behavior. Social learning theory proposes that people learn by observing others. Social cognitive theory emphasizes that children actively interpret what they see.

The Cognitive-Developmental Perspective
The cognitive-developmental perspective focuses on thought processes. Piaget proposed that children's thinking progresses through four stages.

The Contextual Perspective
Vygotsky emphasized the role of culture in children's development. He argued that skilled adults help children acquire the beliefs, customs, and skills of their culture.

Themes in Child-Development Research

Four themes help unify the findings from child-development research that are presented throughout this book.

Continuity of Development
Early development is related to later development but not perfectly. In other words, development is not perfectly predictable; early development sets the stage for later development but does not fix it.

Impact of Nature and Nurture
Development is always jointly influenced by heredity and environment. That is, heredity and environment are interactive forces that work together to chart the course of development.

The Active Child
Children constantly interpret their experiences and, by their individual characteristics, often influence the experiences they have.

Links Between Different Domains of Development

Development in different domains of children's lives is always connected. Cognitive development affects social development and vice versa.

 ## Doing Child-Development Research

Measurement in Child-Development Research

Research typically begins by determining how to measure the phenomenon. Systematic observation involves recording children's behavior as it takes place, in either a natural environment or a structured setting. Researchers sometimes create tasks to obtain samples of children's behavior. In self-reports, children answer questions posed by the experimenter. Sometimes researchers also measure physiological responses (e.g., heart rate). Researchers must also obtain a sample that is representative of a larger population.

General Designs for Research

In correlational studies, investigators examine relations between variables as they occur naturally. In experimental studies, they manipulate an independent variable to determine the impact on a dependent variable. Field studies involve manipulation of independent variables in a natural setting. Quasi-experiments take advantage of natural assignments of children to groups or conditions. The best approach is to use both experimental and correlational studies to provide converging evidence.

Designs for Studying Age-Related Change

To study developmental change, some researchers use a longitudinal design in which the same children are observed repeatedly as they grow. A cross-sectional design involves testing children in different age groups. Meta-analysis synthesizes the results of different studies on the same topic.

Ethical Responsibilities

Experimenters must minimize the risks to potential research participants, describe the research so that potential participants can decide whether they want to participate, avoid deception, and keep results anonymous or confidential.

Communicating Research Results

Investigators write reports describing their findings and publish them in scientific journals. These publications form the foundation of scientific knowledge about child development.

Test Yourself

1. The view of a child's mind as a *tabula rasa* emphasizes the role of _____ in shaping a child's development.
   a. experience
   b. active children
   c. genetics

2. The first mental test for children was developed by _____.
   a. Alfred Binet
   b. G. Stanley Hall
   c. Gesell

3. The _____ theory of child development states that development reflects a specific and prearranged scheme or plan within the body.
   a. maturational
   b. ethnological
   c. social cognitive

4. Hatched chicks typically follow the mother. This illustrates _____.
   a. positive reinforcement
   b. imitation
   c. imprinting

5. According to psychodynamic theories, development is determined by _____.
   a. how supportive the environment is
   b. how well conflicts are resolved at different stages
   c. how well children comprehend their physical and social worlds

6. In Erikson's psychosocial theory, adolescents need to resolve conflict between _____.
   a. identity and identity confusion
   b. the concrete operational stage and the formal operational stage
   c. positive and negative reinforcement

7. Operant conditioning + _____ = social cognitive theory.
   a. maturation
   b. cultural context
   c. observational learning

8. _____ was the first to apply the approach of learning theories to child development.
   a. Skinner
   b. Gesell
   c. Watson

9. A reinforcement is a _____.
   a. consequence that increases the future likelihood of the behavior that it follows
   b. consequence that is a punishment
   c. consequence that decreases the future likelihood of the behavior that follows it

10. According to the _____ of children, they are masters of their own destinies.
   a. continuous view
   b. nature–nurture
   c. active view

11. The social cognitive child _____.
   a. mechanically responds to reinforcement and punishment
   b. actively interprets events
   c. depends on his genes to interpret events

12. Piaget's last stage of cognitive development, in which adolescents can think abstractly, is _____.
   a. concrete operational
   b. formal operational
   c. transitional

13. A measure is _____ when it actually measures what it's supposed to measure.
   a. reliable
   b. biased
   c. valid

14. In a(n) _____, a researcher manipulates an independent variable and measures its effect on a dependent variable.
   a. longitudinal study
   b. experiment
   c. structured observation

15. One of the ethical responsibilities of a researcher in child development is to _____.
   a. ensure that the research is cost-effective
   b. minimize the risk to the participants and keep results confidential or anonymous
   c. ensure that parents know about the results of the study

Key Terms

active–passive child issue   34
applied developmental science   24
baby biographies   23
cognitive-developmental perspective   29
cohort   47
continuity–discontinuity issue   33
correlation coefficient   42
correlational study   41
critical period   26
cross-sectional design   47
culture   31
dependent variable   43
ego   27
ethological theory   26
experiment   43
field experiment   44

id   27
imitation   29
imprinting   26
independent variable   43
informed consent   50
longitudinal design   46
maturational theory   26
meta-analysis   50
microgenetic study   47
naturalistic observation   37
nature–nurture issue   34
observational learning   29
operant conditioning   28
populations   41
psychodynamic theory   27
psychosocial theory   27
punishment   29

quasi-experiment   45
reinforcement   28
reliability   40
research design   41
response bias   39
sample   41
self-efficacy   29
self-reports   39
social cognitive theory   29
structured observation   37
superego   27
systematic observation   37
theory   25
validity   40
variables   37

Chapter 2
Heredity, Environment, and Child Development

Modules

2.1 Mechanisms of Heredity

2.2 Heredity, Environment, and Development

I wish I had a dollar for every time my parents or in-laws said about one of my children, "He (or she) comes by that naturally." The usual prompt for their comment is that the child has just done something exactly as I or my wife did at that same age. By their remarks, grandparents remind us that many behavioral characteristics are inherited from parents just as physical characteristics like height and hair color are inherited.

In this chapter, we'll see how heredity influences children and their development. We'll start, in **Module 2.1**, by examining the basic mechanisms of heredity. Then, in **Module 2.2**, we'll see how heredity and environment work together to shape children's development.

 # 2.1 Mechanisms of Heredity

LEARNING OBJECTIVES

LO1 What are chromosomes and genes?

LO2 What are dominant and recessive traits? How are they inherited?

LO3 What disorders are inherited? Which are caused by too many or too few chromosomes?

OUTLINE

The Biology of Heredity

Single Gene Inheritance

Genetic Disorders

Leslie and Glenn have decided to try to have a baby. They are thrilled at the thought of starting their own family but also worried because Leslie's grandfather had sickle-cell disease and died when he was just 20 years old. Leslie is terrified that their baby could inherit the disease that killed her grandfather. Leslie and Glenn wish someone could reassure them that their baby will be okay.

How could we reassure Leslie and Glenn? For starters, we need to know more about sickle-cell disease. Red blood cells, like the ones in the photo, carry oxygen and carbon dioxide to and from body tissues. When a person has sickle-cell disease, the red blood cells look like those in the photo on page 58: long and curved like a sickle. These stiff, misshapen cells can't pass through small capillaries, so oxygen can't reach all parts of the body. Consequently, people with sickle-cell disease are often tired, may experience acute pain for hours or days, and are prone to infections. About 10% of people with the disease die by age 20 and 50% die by age 50 (Kumar et al., 2010).

Sickle-cell disease is inherited and is relatively common in African Americans like Leslie's grandfather. Will Leslie's baby necessarily inherit the disease from her grandfather? To answer this question, we need to examine the mechanisms of heredity.

The Biology of Heredity

LO1 What are chromosomes and genes?

The teaspoon of semen released into the vagina during an ejaculation contains 200 to 500 million sperm. Only a few hundred actually complete the 6- or 7-inch journey to the fallopian tubes. If an egg is present, many sperm simultaneously begin to burrow their way through the cluster of nurturing cells that surround the egg. When a sperm, like the

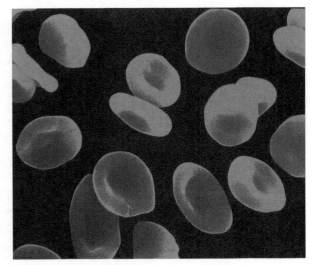

Red blood cells carry oxygen throughout the body.

one in the photo, penetrates the cellular wall of the egg, chemical changes occur immediately that block all other sperm. **Each egg and sperm cell contains 23** *chromosomes*, **tiny structures in the nucleus that contain genetic material.** When a sperm penetrates an egg, their chromosomes combine to produce 23 pairs of chromosomes. The development of a new human being is under way.

For most of history, the merging of sperm and egg took place only after sexual intercourse. No longer. In 1978, Louise Brown captured the world's attention as the first test-tube baby conceived in a laboratory dish instead of in her mother's body. Today, assisted reproductive technology is no longer experimental; it is used more than 160,000 times annually with U.S. women, producing more than 60,000 babies (Centers for Disease Control and Prevention, 2013). Many new techniques are available to couples who cannot conceive a child through sexual intercourse. **The best known,** *in vitro fertilization*, **involves mixing sperm and egg together in a laboratory dish and then placing several fertilized eggs in a woman's uterus.** The photo shows this laboratory version of conception, with the sperm in the dropper being placed in the dish containing the eggs. If the eggs are fertilized, in about 24 hours they are placed in a woman's uterus, with the hope that they will become implanted in the wall of her uterus.

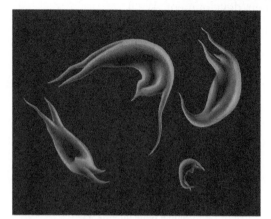

Sickle-shaped blood cells associated with sickle-cell disease cannot pass through the body's smallest blood vessels.

The sperm and egg usually come from the prospective parents, but sometimes they are provided by donors. Occasionally the fertilized egg is placed in the uterus of a surrogate mother who carries the baby throughout pregnancy. Thus, a baby could have as many as five "parents": the man and woman who provide the sperm and egg, the surrogate mother who carries the baby, and the couple who rears the child.

New reproductive techniques offer hope for couples who have long wanted a child but have been unable to conceive, and studies of the first generation of children conceived via these techniques indicates that their social and emotional development is perfectly normal (Golombok, 2013). But there are difficulties as well. Only about one-third of the attempts at in vitro fertilization succeed. What's more, when a woman becomes pregnant, she is more likely to have twins or triplets because multiple eggs are transferred to increase the odds that at least one fertilized egg will implant in her uterus. She is also at greater risk for giving birth to a baby with low birth weight or birth de-

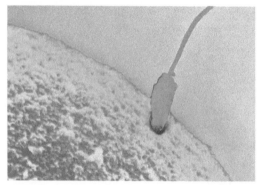

Fertilization takes place when a sperm penetrates an egg cell.

fects. Finally, the procedure is expensive—the typical cost in the United States of a single cycle of treatment is between $10,000 and $15,000—and often is not covered by health insurance. These problems emphasize that, although technology has increased the alternatives for infertile couples, pregnancy-on-demand is still in the realm of science fiction.

Whatever the source of the egg and sperm, and wherever they meet, their merger is a momentous event: The resulting 23 pairs of chromosomes define a child's heredity—what he or she "will do naturally." For Leslie and Glenn, this moment also determines whether their child inherits sickle-cell disease.

To understand how heredity influences child development, let's begin by taking a closer look at chromosomes. The photo shows all 46 chromosomes,

Sperm being placed in a dish that contains egg cells.

organized in pairs ranging from the largest to the smallest. **The first 22 pairs of chromosomes are called** *autosomes*; **and the chromosomes in each pair are about the same size.** In the 23rd pair, however, the chromosome labeled *X* is much larger than the chromosome labeled *Y*. **The 23rd pair determines the sex of the child; hence, these two are known as the** *sex chromosomes*. An egg always contains an X 23rd chromosome, but a sperm contains either an X or a Y. When an X-carrying sperm fertilizes the egg, the 23rd pair is XX and the result is a girl. When a Y-carrying sperm fertilizes the egg, the 23rd pair is XY and the result is a boy.

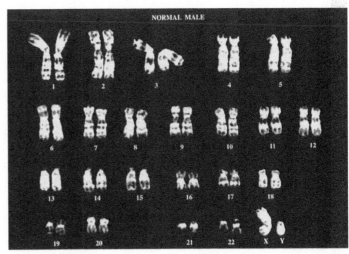

Humans have 23 pairs of chromosomes: 22 pairs of autosomes, and one pair of sex chromosomes.

Each chromosome actually consists of one molecule of *deoxyribonucleic acid*; **DNA for short.** The DNA molecule resembles a spiral staircase. As you can see in Figure 2-1, the rungs of the staircase carry the genetic code, which consists of pairs of nucleotide bases: Adenine is paired with thymine, and guanine is paired with cytosine. The order of the nucleotide pairs is the code that causes the cell to create specific amino acids, proteins, and enzymes—important biological building blocks. **Each group of nucleotide bases that provides a specific set of biochemical instructions is a** *gene*. For example, three consecutive thymine nucleotides is the instruction to create the amino acid phenylalanine.

Figure 2-2 on page 60 summarizes these links between chromosomes, genes, and DNA. The figure shows that each cell contains chromosomes that carry genes made up of DNA.

A child's 46 chromosomes include about 20,500 genes. Chromosome 1 has the most genes (nearly 3,000) and the Y chromosome has the fewest (slightly more than 200). Most of these genes are the same in all people—fewer than 1% of genes cause differences between people (Human Genome Project, 2003). **The complete set of genes makes up a person's heredity and is known as the person's** *genotype*. Through biochemical instructions that are coded in DNA, genes regulate the development of all human characteristics and abilities. **Genetic instructions, in conjunction with environmental influences, produce a** *phenotype*, **an individual's physical, behavioral, and psychological features.**

In the rest of this module, we'll see the different ways that instructions contained in genes produce different phenotypes.

Single Gene Inheritance

LO2 What are dominant and recessive traits? How are they inherited?

How do genetic instructions produce the misshapen red blood cells of sickle-cell disease? **Genes come in different forms that are known as** *alleles*. In the case of red blood cells, for example, one of two alleles can be present on chromosome 11. One allele has instructions for normal red blood cells; the other allele has instructions for sickle-shaped red blood cells. **Sometimes the alleles in a pair of chromosomes are the same, which makes them** *homozygous*. **Sometimes the alleles differ, which makes them** *heterozygous*. In Leslie's case, her baby could be homozygous, in which case it would have two alleles for normal cells or two alleles for sickle-shaped cells. Leslie's baby might also be heterozygous, which means that it would have one allele for normal cells and one for sickle-shaped cells.

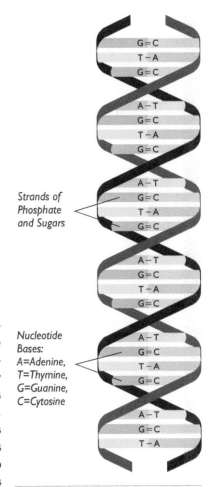

Strands of Phosphate and Sugars

Nucleotide Bases:
A=Adenine,
T=Thymine,
G=Guanine,
C=Cytosine

Figure 2-1

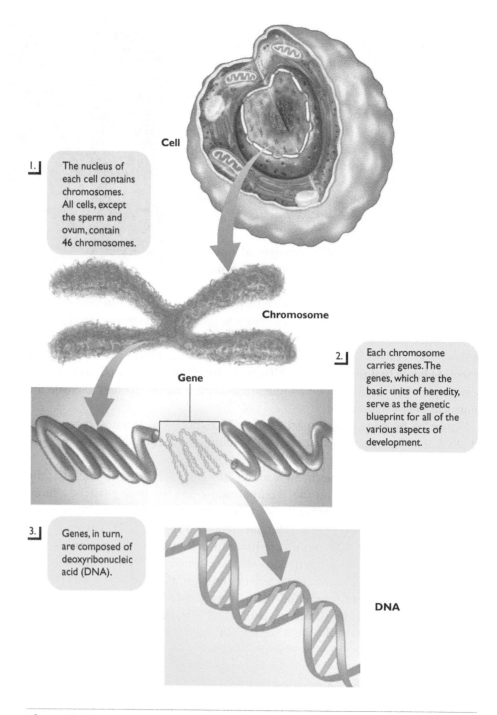

Cell

1. The nucleus of each cell contains chromosomes. All cells, except the sperm and ovum, contain 46 chromosomes.

Chromosome

2. Each chromosome carries genes. The genes, which are the basic units of heredity, serve as the genetic blueprint for all of the various aspects of development.

Gene

3. Genes, in turn, are composed of deoxyribonucleic acid (DNA).

DNA

Figure 2-2

How does a genotype produce a phenotype? The answer is simple when a person is homozygous. When both alleles are the same and therefore have chemical instructions for the same phenotype, that phenotype usually results. (We'll see some exceptions in Module 2.2.) If Leslie's baby had alleles for normal red blood cells on both of the chromosomes in its 11th pair, the baby would be almost guaranteed to have normal cells. If, instead, the baby had two alleles for sickle-shaped cells, her baby would almost certainly suffer from the disease.

When a person is heterozygous, the process is more complex. **Often one allele is _dominant_, which means that its chemical instructions are followed whereas** instructions of the other, the *recessive* allele, are ignored. In the case of sickle-cell disease, the allele for normal cells is dominant and the allele for sickle-shaped cells is recessive. This is good news for Leslie: As long as either she or Glenn contributes the allele for normal red blood cells, her baby will not develop sickle-cell disease.

Figure 2-3 summarizes what we've learned about sickle-cell disease. *A* denotes the allele for normal blood cells, and *a* denotes the allele for sickle-shaped cells. In the diagram, Glenn's genotype is homozygous dominant because he's positive that no one in his family has had sickle-cell disease. From Leslie's family history, she could be homozygous dominant or heterozygous; the diagram assumes the latter. You can see that Leslie and Glenn cannot have a baby with sickle-cell disease. However, their baby might be affected in another way. **Sometimes one allele does not dominate another completely, a situation known as** *incomplete dominance*. In incomplete dominance, the phenotype that results often falls between the phenotype associated with either allele. This is the case for the genes that control red blood cells. **Individuals with one dominant and one recessive allele have** *sickle-cell trait*: **In most situations they have no problems, but when they are seriously short of oxygen they suffer a temporary, relatively mild form of the disease.** Thus, sickle-cell trait is likely to appear when the person exercises vigorously, becomes dehydrated, or is at high altitudes (Fidler, 2012). Leslie and Glenn's baby would have sickle-cell trait if it inherited a recessive gene from Leslie and a dominant gene from Glenn, as shown in Figure 2-3.

One aspect of sickle-cell disease that we haven't considered so far is why this disorder primarily affects African American children. The "Cultural Influences" feature addresses this point and, in the process, tells more about how heredity operates.

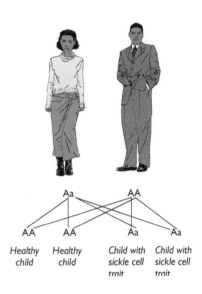

Figure 2-3

 QUESTION 2.1

If Glenn learned that he was heterozygous for sickle-cell disease instead of homozygous dominant, how would this affect the odds that he and Leslie would have a child with sickle-cell disease?

Cultural Influences

Why Do African Americans Inherit Sickle-Cell Disease?

Sickle-cell disease affects about 1 in 400 African American children. In contrast, virtually no European American children have the disorder. Why? Because the sickle-cell allele has a benefit: Individuals with this allele are more resistant to malaria, an infectious disease that is one of the leading causes of childhood death worldwide. Malaria is transmitted by mosquitoes, so it is most common in warm climates, including many parts of Africa. Compared to Africans who have alleles for normal blood cells, Africans with the sickle-cell allele are less likely to die from malaria, which means that the sickle-cell allele is passed along to the next generation.

This explanation of sickle-cell disease has two implications. First, sickle-cell disease should be found in any group of people living where malaria is common. In fact, sickle-cell disease affects Hispanic Americans who trace their roots to malaria-prone regions of the Caribbean, Central America, and South America. Second, malaria is rare in the United States, which means that the sickle-cell allele has no survival value to African Americans. Accordingly, the sickle-cell allele should become less common in successive generations of African Americans, and indeed this is happening.

There is an important lesson here. An allele may have survival value in one environment but not in others. In more general terms, the impact of heredity depends on the environment. We'll explore this lesson in more detail in Module 2.2.

TABLE 2-1

SOME COMMON PHENOTYPES ASSOCIATED WITH SINGLE PAIRS OF GENES

Dominant Phenotype	Recessive Phenotype
Curly hair	Straight hair
Normal hair	Pattern baldness (men)
Dark hair	Blond hair
Thick lips	Thin lips
Cheek dimples	No dimples
Normal hearing	Some types of deafness
Normal vision	Nearsightedness
Farsightedness	Normal vision
Normal color vision	Red-green color blindness
Type A blood	Type O blood
Type B blood	Type O blood
Rh-positive blood	Rh-negative blood

Source: Data from the Online Mendelian Inheritance in Man (OMIM). National Center for Biotechnology Information, U.S. National Library of Medicine. http://www.ncbi.nlm.nih.gov/omim.

The genetic mechanism responsible for sickle-cell disease, involving a single gene pair with one dominant allele and one recessive allele, is also responsible for many other common traits, as shown in Table 2-1. In each case, individuals with the recessive phenotype have two recessive alleles, one from each parent. Individuals with the dominant phenotype have at least one dominant allele.

Most of the traits listed in Table 2-1 are biological and medical phenotypes. These same patterns of inheritance can cause serious disorders, as we'll see in the next section.

Genetic Disorders

LO3 **What disorders are inherited? Which are caused by too many or too few chromosomes?**

Genetics can harm development in two ways. First, some disorders are inherited. Sickle-cell disease is an example of an inherited disorder. Second, sometimes eggs or sperm have more or fewer than the usual 23 chromosomes. In the next few pages, we'll see how inherited disorders and abnormal numbers of chromosomes can alter a child's development.

Inherited Disorders Sickle-cell disease is one of many disorders that are homozygous recessive—triggered when a child inherits recessive alleles from both parents. Table 2-2 lists four more disorders that are commonly inherited in this manner.

Relatively few serious disorders are caused by dominant alleles. Why? If the allele for the disorder is dominant, every person with at least one of these alleles will have the disorder. But individuals affected with these disorders typically do not live long enough to reproduce, so dominant alleles that produce fatal disorders soon vanish from the species. **An exception is *Huntington's disease*, a fatal disease characterized by progressive degeneration of the nervous system.** Individuals who inherit this disorder develop normally through childhood, adolescence, and young adulthood. However, during middle age, nerve cells in the

TABLE 2-2

COMMON DISORDERS ASSOCIATED WITH RECESSIVE ALLELES

Disorder	Frequency	Characteristics
Albinism	1 in 15,000 births	Skin lacks melanin, which causes visual problems and extreme sensitivity to light.
Cystic fibrosis	1 in 3,000 births among European Americans; less common in African and Asian Americans	Excess mucus clogs respiratory and digestive tracts. Lung infections are common.
Phenylketonuria (PKU)	1 in 10,000 births	Phenylalanine, an amino acid, accumulates in the body and damages the nervous system, causing mental retardation.
Tay–Sachs disease	1 in 2,500 births among Jews of European descent	The nervous system degenerates in infancy, causing deafness, blindness, mental retardation, and, during the preschool years, death.

Source: Based on American Lung Association, 2007; Committee on Genetics, 1996; Hellekson, 2001; Online Mendelian Inheritance in Man, 2013; Thompson, 2007.

brain begin to deteriorate; by this time many adults with Huntington's have already had children, many of whom will develop the disease themselves.

Fortunately, most inherited disorders are rare. Phenylketonuria (PKU), for example, occurs once in every 10,000 births, and Huntington's disease occurs even less frequently. Nevertheless, adults who believe that these disorders run in their family often want to know whether their children will be affected. The "Improving Children's Lives" feature shows how these couples can get help.

Improving Children's Lives

Genetic Counseling

Family planning is not easy for couples who fear that their children may inherit serious or even fatal diseases. The best advice is to seek the help of a genetic counselor before a woman becomes pregnant. With the couple's help, a genetic counselor constructs a detailed family history that can be used to decide whether it's likely that either the man or the woman has the allele for the disorder that concerns them.

A family tree for Leslie and Glenn, the couple from the opening vignette, would confirm that Leslie is likely to carry the recessive allele for sickle-cell disease. The genetic counselor would then take the next step, obtaining a sample of Leslie's DNA (typically from her blood or saliva). The sample would be analyzed to determine whether the 11th chromosome carries the recessive allele for sickle-cell disease. If Leslie learns that she is homozygous—has two dominant alleles for healthy blood cells—then she and Glenn can be assured their children will not have sickle-cell disease. If Leslie learns that she has one recessive allele, then she and Glenn will know they have a 50% risk of having a baby with sickle-cell trait. Tests can also be administered after a woman is pregnant to determine whether the child she is carrying has an inherited disorder. We'll learn about these tests in Chapter 3.

Children with Down syndrome typically have upward-slanting eyes, with a fold over the eyelid; a flattened facial profile; and a smaller-than-average nose and mouth.

More common than inherited diseases are disorders caused by the wrong number of chromosomes, as we'll see next.

Abnormal Number of Chromosomes   When children are born with extra, missing, or damaged chromosomes, development is always disturbed. **The best example is *Down syndrome*, a genetic disorder that is caused by an extra 21st chromosome and that results in intellectual disability.**[1] Like the child in the photo, persons with Down syndrome have almond-shaped eyes and a fold over the eyelid. The head, neck, and nose of a child with this disorder are usually smaller than normal. During the first several months, babies with Down syndrome seem to develop normally. Thereafter, though, their mental and behavioral development begins to lag behind the average child's. For example, a child with Down syndrome might not sit up without help until about 1 year, not walk until 2, or not talk until 3—months or even years behind children without Down syndrome. By childhood, motor and mental development is substantially delayed.

Rearing a child with Down syndrome presents special challenges. During the preschool years, children with Down syndrome need special programs to prepare them for school. Educational achievements of children with Down syndrome are likely to be limited and their average life expectancy is about 50 years (Coppus, 2013). Nevertheless, as we'll see in Chapter 8, many persons with Down syndrome lead fulfilling lives.

What causes Down syndrome? Individuals with Down syndrome typically have an extra 21st chromosome that is usually provided by the egg (Vraneković et al., 2012). Why the mother provides two 21st chromosomes is unknown. However, the odds that a woman will bear a child with Down syndrome increase markedly as she gets older. For a woman in her late 20s, the risk of giving birth to a baby with Down syndrome is about 1 in 1,000; for a woman in her early 40s, the risk is about 1 in 50. The increased risk may be because a woman's eggs have been in her ovaries since her own prenatal development. Eggs may deteriorate over time as part of aging, or eggs may become damaged because an older woman has a longer history of exposure to hazards in the environment, such as X-rays.

An extra autosome (as in Down syndrome), a missing autosome, or a damaged autosome always has far-reaching consequences for development because the autosomes contain huge amounts of genetic material. In fact, nearly half of all fertilized eggs abort spontaneously within two weeks, primarily because of abnormal autosomes. Thus, most eggs that could not develop normally are removed naturally (Moore, Persaud, & Torchia, 2012).

Abnormal sex chromosomes can also disrupt development. Table 2-3 lists four of the more frequent disorders associated with atypical numbers of X and Y chromosomes. Keep in mind that *frequent* is a relative term; although these disorders occur more frequently than PKU or Huntington's disease, the table shows that most are rare. Notice that no disorders consist solely of Y chromosomes. The presence of an X chromosome appears to be necessary for life.

---

[1] The scientific name is trisomy 21 because a person with the disorder has three 21st chromosomes instead of two. But the common name is Down syndrome, reflecting the name of the English physician, John Langdon Down, who identified the disorder in the 1860s.

TABLE 2-3			
COMMON DISORDERS ASSOCIATED WITH THE SEX CHROMOSOMES			
Disorder	**Sex Chromosomes**	**Frequency**	**Characteristics**
Klinefelter's syndrome	XXY	1 in 500 to 1,000 male births	Tall, small testicles, sterile, below-normal intelligence, passive
XYY complement	XYY	1 in 1,000 male births	Tall, some cases apparently have below-normal intelligence
Turner's syndrome	X	1 in 2,500 to 5,000 female births	Short, limited development of secondary sex characteristics, problems perceiving spatial relations
XXX syndrome	XXX	1 in 500 to 1,200 female births	Normal stature but delayed motor and language development

Source: Based on Milunsky, A. (2002). *Your genetic destiny: Know your genes, secure your health, and save your life.* Cambridge, MA: Perseus Publishing.

These genetic disorders demonstrate the remarkable power of heredity. Nevertheless, to fully understand how heredity influences development, we need to consider the environment, which we'll do in Module 2.2.

Check Your Learning

RECALL Describe the difference between dominant and recessive alleles.

Distinguish genetic disorders that are inherited from those that involve abnormal numbers of chromosomes.

INTERPRET Why do relatively few genetic disorders involve dominant alleles?

APPLY Suppose that a friend of yours discovers that she may have the recessive allele for the disease cystic fibrosis. What advice would you give her?

Heredity, Environment, and Development

LEARNING OBJECTIVES

LO4 What methods do scientists use to study the impact of heredity and environment on children's development?

LO5 How do heredity and environment work together to influence child development?

OUTLINE

Behavioral Genetics

Paths from Genes to Behavior

Sadie and Molly are fraternal twins. As babies, Sadie was calm and easily comforted, but Molly was fussy and hard to soothe. When they entered school, Sadie relished contact with other people and preferred play that involved others. Meanwhile, Molly was more withdrawn and was quite happy to play alone. Their grandparents wonder why these twins seem so different.

Why are Sadie and Molly so different despite having similar genes? To answer this question, we'll first look at the methods that child-development scientists use to study hereditary and environmental influences on children's development. Then we'll examine some basic principles that govern hereditary and environmental influences.

Behavioral Genetics

LO4   **What methods do scientists use to study the impact of heredity and environment on children's development?**

Most of the traits we examined in Module 2.1 (e.g., those shown in Table 2.1) are either–or phenotypes that are controlled by a single gene. For example, whether a person has Rh-positive or Rh-negative blood is determined by the RHD gene on chromosome 1. In contrast, most behavioral and psychological characteristics are not either–or cases but represent an entire range of different outcomes. Take extroversion as an example. You probably know a few extremely outgoing individuals and a few intensely shy persons, but most of your friends and acquaintances are somewhere in between; extroversion forms a continuum ranging from extreme extroversion at one end to extreme introversion at the other.

Many behavioral and psychological characteristics, including intelligence and aspects of personality, are distributed in this fashion, with a few individuals at the ends of the continuum and most near the middle. **Phenotypes distributed like this often reflect the combined activity of many separate genes, a pattern known as *polygenic inheritance*.** To see how many genes work together to produce a behavioral phenotype that spans a continuum, let's consider a hypothetical example. Suppose that four pairs of genes contribute to extroversion, that the allele for extroversion is dominant, and that the total amount of extroversion is simply the total of the dominant alleles. If uppercase letters represent dominant alleles and lowercase letters represent the recessive allele, the four gene pairs would be *Aa, Bb, Cc,* and *Dd.*

These four pairs of genes produce 81 different genotypes and 9 distinct phenotypes. For example, a person with the genotype *AABBCCDD* has 8 alleles for extroversion (a party animal). A person with the genotype *aabbccdd* has no alleles for extroversion (a wallflower). All other genotypes involve some combinations of dominant and recessive alleles, so these are associated with phenotypes representing intermediate levels of extroversion. In fact, Figure 2-4 on page 67 shows that the most common outcome is for people to inherit exactly 4 dominant and 4 recessive alleles: 19 of the 81 genotypes produce this pattern (e.g., *AABbccDd, AaBbcCDd*). A few extreme cases (very outgoing or very shy), when coupled with many intermediate cases, produce the familiar bell-shaped distribution that characterizes many behavioral and psychological traits.

Remember, this example is completely hypothetical. Extroversion is *not* based on the combined influence of four pairs of genes. But this example shows how several genes working together could produce a continuum of phenotypes. Something like our example is probably involved in the inheritance of numerous human behavioral traits, except that many more pairs of genes are involved and the environment also influences the phenotype (Plomin, 2013).

Determining the impact of heredity on behavioral and psychological traits is the aim of *behavioral genetics*. In the rest of Module 2.2, we'll see what behavioral genetics has revealed about the influence of heredity on children's psychological development.

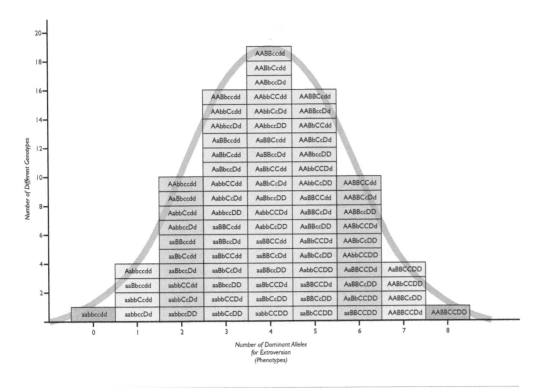

Figure 2-4

Methods of Behavioral Genetics   If many behavioral phenotypes involve count-less genes, how can we hope to unravel the influence of heredity? Traditionally, behavior geneticists have relied on statistical methods in which they compare groups of people known to differ in their genetic similarity. Twins, for example, provide important clues about the influence of heredity. **Identical twins are called** *monozygotic twins* **because they come from a single fertilized egg that splits in two.** Because identical twins come from the same fertilized egg, they have the same genes that control body structure, height, and facial features, which explains why identical twins like those in the photo look alike. **In contrast, fraternal or** *dizygotic twins* **come from two separate eggs fertilized by two separate sperm.**

Genetically, fraternal twins are just like any other siblings; on average, about half their genes are the same. In twin studies, scientists compare identical and fraternal twins; heredity is implicated when identical twins are more alike than fraternal twins.

An example will help illustrate the logic underlying comparisons of identical and fraternal twins. Suppose we want to determine whether extroversion is inherited. We would first mea-sure extroversion in a large number of identical and fraternal twins. We might use a questionnaire with scores ranging from 0 to 100 (100 indicating extreme extroversion). Some of the hypothetical results are shown in Table 2-4 on page 68.

Look first at the results for the fraternal twins. Most have similar scores: The Burress twins both have high scores but the Manning twins have low

Identical twins are called *monozygotic* twins because they came from a single fertilized egg that split in two; consequently, they have identical genes.

TABLE 2-4

TWINS' HYPOTHETICAL SCORES ON A MEASURE OF EXTROVERSION

	Fraternal Twins				Identical Twins		
Family	One Twin	Other Twin	Difference Between Twins	Family	One Twin	Other Twin	Difference Between Twins
Burress	80	95	15	Brady	100	95	5
Jacobs	70	50	20	Moss	32	30	2
Manning	10	35	25	Seau	18	15	3
Strahan	25	5	20	Vrabel	55	60	5
Toomer	40	65	25	Welker	70	62	8

scores. Looking at the identical twins, their scores are even more alike, typically differing by no more than five points. This greater similarity among identical twins than among fraternal twins would be evidence that extroversion is inherited, just as the fact that identical twins look more alike than fraternal twins is evidence that facial appearance is inherited.

You can see the distinctive features of this approach in the "Focus on Research" feature, which describes a twin study that examined the influence of heredity on children's relationships with peers.

Focus on Research

Hereditary Bases of Children's Peer Relationships

Who were the investigators, and what was the aim of the study? Children differ in the ease with which they get along with classmates and make friends. For some, interactions with peers are easy and rewarding; for others, peer interactions are troubled and painful. Michele Boivin and his colleagues (2013)—Mara Brendgen, Frank Vitaro, Ginette Dionne, Alain Girard, Daniel Pérusse and Richard Tremblay—wondered whether heredity contributed to children's success in peer relations; to find out, they conducted a twin study.

How did the investigators measure the topic of interest? Children were shown photos of their classmates and asked to select the three classmates they enjoyed playing with the most and the three they liked playing with the least. A measure of children's success in peer relations was created by counting the number of times that each child was selected as a preferred playmate and subtracting the number of times that the child was selected as an unpreferred playmate. Larger scores on this measure reflect many choices as a preferred playmate and few as an unpreferred playmate.

Who were the children in the study? Initially, the sample included 198 pairs of identical twins and 276 pairs of fraternal twins, all in first grade. Three years later, peer relationships were measured again; this

time 182 pairs of identical twins and 257 pairs of fraternal twins participated.

What was the design of the study? This study was correlational because Boivin and his colleagues examined similarity of children's peer relationships in identical and fraternal twins. The study was also longitudinal because peer relationships were assessed twice, once in first grade and again in fourth grade.

Were there ethical concerns with the study? No. Parents provided consent for their children to participate and peer selections were kept confidential.

What were the results? The primary results are correlations for children's peer relationships, shown in Figure 2-5, separately for identical and fraternal twins. All the correlations are positive, a result indicating that when one twin had successful peer relations, the other often did as well. However, at both grades the correlation for identical twins is greater than the correlation for fraternal twins, indicating a much closer match in quality of peer relations for identical twins.

What did the investigators conclude? Because success in peer relations was more similar among identical twins than among fraternal twins, this suggests an important role for heredity in the ease with which children interact with their peers. Of course "success in interacting with peers" is not inherited directly. What's more likely is that children inherit certain tendencies—they're hyperactive or too aggressive—that are obstacles for successful peer interactions.

What converging evidence would strengthen these conclusions? First, although the peer selection task is a widely used and valid measure of the quality of children's peer interactions, it would be useful to determine whether these results would hold when peer interactions were observed directly. Second, the sample was not large enough to analyze the data separately for boys and girls. Such analyses, from larger samples, would be informative because boys and girls interact differently with their peers (as we'll see in Chapters 13 and 15).

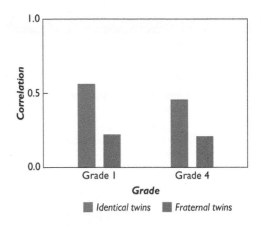

Figure 2-5

Adopted children are another important source of information about heredity. They are compared with their biological parents, who provide the child's genes, and their adoptive parents, who provide the child's environment. If an adopted child's behavior resembles that of his or her biological parents, this shows the impact of heredity; if the adopted child's behavior resembles his or her adoptive parents, this shows the influence of the environment.

To use an adoption study to determine whether extroversion is inherited, we would measure extroversion in a sample of adopted children, their biological mothers, and their adoptive mothers. (Why just mothers? Obtaining data from biological fathers of adopted children is often difficult.) The results of this hypothetical study are shown in Table 2-5.

Overall, children's scores are similar to their biological mothers' scores: Extroverted children, like Michael, tend to have extroverted biological mothers. Introverted children, like Troy, tend to have introverted biological mothers. In contrast, children's scores aren't related consistently to their adoptive mothers' scores. For example, although Michael has the highest score and Troy has the lowest, their adoptive mothers have similar scores. Children's greater similarity to biological than to adoptive parents is evidence indicating genetic influence on extroversion.

The key features of an adoption study are evident in work reported by Plomin and colleagues (Plomin et al., 1997). They wanted to determine hereditary and environmental contributions to intelligence. Consequently, they administered

TABLE 2-5

HYPOTHETICAL SCORES FROM AN ADOPTION STUDY ON A MEASURE OF EXTROVERSION

Child's Name	Child's Score	Biological Mother's Score	Adoptive Mother's Score
Anila	60	70	35
Jerome	45	50	25
Kerri	40	30	80
Michael	90	80	50
Troy	25	5	55

SUMMARY TABLE 2-1

PRIMARY RESEARCH METHODS FOR BEHAVIORAL GENETICS

Method	Defined	Evidence for Heredity	Main Weakness
Twin study	Compares monozygotic and dizygotic twins	Monozygotic twins more alike than dizygotic twins	Others may treat monozygotic twins more similarly than they treat dizygotic twins
Adoption study	Compares children with their biological and adoptive parents	Children more like biological parents than adoptive parents	Selective placement: Children's adoptive parents may resemble their biological parents

intelligence tests to biological mothers in the last few months of pregnancy and to adoptive mothers in the year following adoption. Every few years, the children took an intelligence test. At every age, children's intelligence was correlated more strongly with the biological mother's intelligence than with the adoptive mother's intelligence, which suggests that heredity plays an important role in determining intelligence.

Twin studies and adoption studies, which are described in Summary Table 2-1, are powerful tools. They are not foolproof, however. A potential flaw in twin studies is that parents and others may treat identical twins more similarly than they treat fraternal twins. This would make identical twins more similar than fraternal twins in their experiences as well as in their genes. Adoption studies have their own Achilles' heel. Adoption agencies sometimes try to place youngsters in homes like those of their biological parents. For example, if an agency believes that the biological parents are bright, the agency may try harder to have the child adopted by parents that the agency believes are bright. This can bias adoption studies because biological and adoptive parents end up being similar.

The problems associated with twin and adoption studies are not insurmountable. Because twin and adoption studies have different faults, if the two kinds of studies produce similar results on the influence of heredity, we can be confident of those results. In addition, behavioral geneticists are moving beyond traditional methods such as twin and adoption studies to connect behavior to molecular genetics (Plomin, 2013). Today, researchers can obtain DNA by gathering cheek cells from inside a child's mouth. A solution containing the DNA is placed on a microarray—a "chip" about the size of a postage stamp—that contains thousands of known sequences of DNA. Every match between the child's DNA and the known sequences is recorded, creating a profile of the child's genotype. Researchers then look to see if the genotype is associated with behavior phenotypes. For example, in one study 10 alleles were linked with children's skill in mathematics (Docherty et al., 2010).

This kind of molecular genetics research is challenging, in part because detecting the tiny effects of individual genes requires samples of thousands of children. But this research has the promise of linking individual genes to behavior. And when used with traditional methods of behavioral genetics (e.g., adoption studies), the new methods promise much greater understanding of how genes influence behavior and development (Plomin, 2013).

Which Psychological Characteristics Are Affected by Heredity?   Research reveals consistent genetic influence in many psychological areas, including personality, mental ability, psychological disorders, and attitudes and interests. One expert summarized this work by saying, "Nearly every … psychological phenotype (normal and abnormal) is significantly influenced by genetic factors" (Bouchard, 2004, p. 151). In the examples of twin and adoption studies, we've already seen the impact of heredity on peer relations and intelligence. You can see the range of genetic influence from a trio of twin studies, each involving young children:

- The number of letter sounds that children knew (e.g., "kuh" for k, which is an important prerequisite for learning to read) was correlated .68 for identical twins but .53 for fraternal twins (Taylor & Schatschneider, 2010).
- Scores on a measure of the ability to resist temptation—that is, obeying an instruction to not eat a tempting snack or touch an attractive gift—were correlated .38 for identical twins but .16 for fraternal twins (Gagne & Saudino, 2010).
- Scores on a measure of aggressive play with peers were correlated .55 for identical twins but .16 for fraternal twins (Brendgen et al., 2011).

Each of these studies shows the familiar signature of genetic influence: Be it knowing letter sounds, resisting temptation, or aggressing against peers, identical twins were more alike than were fraternal twins (i.e., larger correlations for identical twins than for fraternal twins).

We will look at the contributions of heredity (and environment) to children's development throughout this book. For now, keep in mind two conclusions from twin studies and adoption studies like those I've described so far. On the one hand, the impact of heredity on behavioral development is substantial and widespread. Heredity has a sizable influence on such different aspects of development as intelligence and personality. In understanding children and their development, we must always think about how heredity may contribute. On the other hand, heredity is never the sole determinant of behavioral development. If genes alone were responsible, then identical twins should have identical behavioral and psychological phenotypes. But we've seen that the correlations for identical twins fall short of 1, which would indicate identical scores of identical twins. Correlations of .5 and .6 mean that identical twins' scores are not perfectly consistent. One twin may, for example, play aggressively with peers but the other does not. These differences reflect the influence of the environment. In fact, as we saw in Chapter 1, scientists agree that virtually all psychological and behavioral phenotypes involve nature and nurture working together to shape development (LaFreniere & MacDonald, 2013).

Paths from Genes to Behavior

LO5 How do heredity and environment work together to influence child development?

How do genes work together to make, for example, some children brighter than others and some children more outgoing than others? That is, how does the information in strands of DNA influence a child's behavioral and psychological development? The specific paths from genes to behavior are largely uncharted (Meaney, 2010), but in the next few pages we'll discover some of their general properties.

Heredity and Environment Interact Dynamically Throughout Development
A traditional view is that heredity provides the clay of life and experience does the sculpting. In fact, genes and environments constantly interact to produce phenotypes throughout a child's development (LaFreniere & MacDonald, 2013). To illustrate, the link between genotype and phenotype is often described as direct—given a certain genotype, a specific phenotype occurs, necessarily and automatically. In fact, the path from genotype to phenotype is massively more complicated and less direct than this. A more accurate description would be that a genotype leads to a phenotype but only if the environment "cooperates" in the usual manner.

A good example of this is the disease PKU, which can be expressed only when children inherit a recessive gene on chromosome 12 from both parents (i.e., the child is homozygous recessive). Children with this genotype lack an enzyme that breaks down phenylalanine, an amino acid. Consequently, phenylalanine accumulates in the child's body, damaging the nervous system and leading to retarded mental development. Phenylalanine abounds in foods that most children eat regularly—meat, chicken, eggs, cheese—so the environment usually provides the input (phenylalanine) necessary for the phenotype (PKU) to emerge. However, in the middle of the 20th century, the biochemical basis for PKU was discovered and now newborns are tested for the disorder. Infants who have the genotype for the disease are immediately placed on a diet that limits phenylalanine and the disease does not appear; the nervous system of such a child develops normally. In more general terms, a genotype is expressed differently (no disease) when it is exposed to a different environment (one lacking phenylalanine).

The effect can work in the other direction, too, with the environment triggering genetic expression. That is, children's experiences can help to determine how and when genes are activated. For instance, teenage girls begin to menstruate at a younger age if they've had a stressful childhood (Belsky, Houts, & Fearon, 2010). The exact pathway of influence is unknown (though it probably involves the hormones that are triggered by stress and those that initiate ovulation), but this is a clear case in which the environment advances the genes that regulate the developmental clock (Ellis, 2004).

I've used a rare disease (PKU) and a once-in-a-lifetime event (onset of menstruation) to show intimate connections between nature and nurture in children's development. These examples may make it seem as if such connections are relatively rare, but nothing could be further from the truth. At a biological level, genes always operate in a cellular environment. There is constant interaction between genetic instructions and the nature of the immediate cellular environment, which can be influenced by a host of much broader environmental factors (e.g., hormones triggered by a child's experiences). **This continuous interplay between genes and multiple levels of the environment (from cells to culture) that drives development is known as** *epigenesis*. Returning to the analogy of sculpting clay, an epigenetic view of molding would be that new and different forms of genetic clay are constantly being added to the sculpture, leading to resculpting by the environment, which causes more clay to be added, and the cycle continues. Hereditary clay and environmental sculpting are continuously interweaving and influencing each other.

Research in molecular genetics has begun to reveal ways in which experiences get "under the skin." Sometimes experiences change the expression of DNA— the genetic code is preserved but some genes are "turned off." **This process is known as** *methylation* **because the chemical silencer is a methyl molecule** (van IJzendoorn, Bakermans-Kranenburg, & Ebstein, 2011). To illustrate, in one study bullying by peers was associated with increased methylation of a gene that has been linked to mood (Oullet-Morin et al., 2013). In other words, an experience (bullying) led to changes in heredity (a gene linked to mood was "turned off").

Because of the epigenetic principle, you need to be wary when you read statements like "X percent of a trait is due to heredity." **In fact, behavioral geneticists often use correlations from twin and adoption studies to calculate a** *heritability coefficient,* **which estimates the extent to which differences between people reflect heredity.** For example, intelligence has a heritability coefficient of about .5, which means that about 50% of the differences in intelligence between people is a result of heredity (Bouchard, 2004).

Why be cautious? One reason is that many people mistakenly interpret heritability coefficients to mean that 50% of *an individual's* intelligence is due to heredity; this is incorrect because heritability coefficients apply to groups of people, not to a single person.

A second reason for caution is that heritability coefficients apply only to a specific group of people living in a specific environment. They cannot be applied to other groups of people living in the same environment or to the same people living elsewhere. For example, a child's height is certainly influenced by heredity, but the value of a heritability coefficient depends on the environment. When children grow in an environment that has ample nutrition—allowing all children to grow to their full genetic potential—heritability coefficients are large. But when some children receive inadequate nutrition, this aspect of their environment will limit their height and, in the process, reduce the heritability coefficient.

Similarly, the heritability coefficient for children's cognitive skill is larger among parents who are well educated than among parents who aren't (Tucker-Drob, Briley, & Harden, 2013). Why? Well-educated parents more often provide the academically stimulating environment that fosters a child's cognitive development; consequently, cognitive skill in this group usually reflects heredity. In contrast, less-educated parents less often provide the needed stimulation, and thus cognitive skill reflects a mixture of genetic and environmental influences.

This brings us back to the principle that began this section: "Heredity and environment interact dynamically throughout development." Both genes and environments are powerful influences on development, but we can only understand one by considering the other, too. This is another reason why it is essential to expand research beyond the middle-class, European American youngster that has been the favorite of child-development scientists. Only by studying diverse groups of children can we really understand the many ways in which genes and environments propel children along their developmental journeys (Tucker-Drob et al., 2013).

Genes Can Influence the Kind of Environment to Which a Child Is Exposed

In other words, "nature" can help determine the kind of "nurturing" that a child receives (Scarr, 1992; Scarr & McCartney, 1983). A child's genotype can lead people to respond to the child in a specific way. For example, imagine a child who is bright and outgoing (both due, in part, to the child's genes). That child may receive plenty of attention and encouragement from teachers. In contrast, a child who is not as bright and more withdrawn (again, due in part to heredity) may easily be overlooked by teachers. In addition, as children grow and become more independent, they actively seek environments related to their genetic makeup. Children who are bright (due in part to heredity) may actively seek peers, adults, and activities that strengthen their intellectual development. Similarly, children like the one in the photo, who are outgoing (due in part to heredity), seek the company of other people, particularly extroverts like themselves. **This process of deliberately seeking environments that fit one's heredity is called *niche-picking*.** Niche-picking is first seen in childhood and becomes more common as children get older and can control their environments. Through niche-picking, the environment amplifies genetic differences as, for example, bright children seek intellectually stimulating environments that make them even smarter

Children who are outgoing often like to be with other people and deliberately seek them out, a phenomenon known as *niche-picking*.

and extroverted children seek socially stimulating environments that make them even more outgoing (Tucker-Drob et al., 2013).

Niche-picking is a prime example of the interaction between nature, nurture, and development. Experiences determine which phenotypes emerge, and genotypes influence the nature of children's experiences. The story of Sadie and Molly also makes it clear that, to understand how genes influence development, we need to look carefully at how environments work, our next topic.

Environmental Influences Typically Make Children Within a Family Different

One of the fruits of behavioral genetic research is greater understanding of the manner in which environments influence children (Harden, 2014). Traditionally, scientists considered some environments beneficial for children and others detrimental. This view has been especially strong with regard to family environments. Some parenting practices are thought to be more effective than others, and parents who use these effective practices are believed to have children who are, on average, better off than children of parents who don't use these practices. This view leads to a simple prediction: Children within a family should be similar because they all receive the same type of effective (or ineffective) parenting. However, dozens of behavioral genetic studies show that, in reality, siblings are not very much alike in their cognitive and social development (Plomin & Spinath, 2004).

Does this mean that family environment is not important? No. **These findings point to the importance of** *nonshared environmental influences*, **the environmental forces that make siblings different from one another.** Although environmental forces are important, they usually affect each child in a unique way, which makes siblings differ. For example, parents may be more affectionate with one child than another, they may use more physical punishment with one child than another, or they may have higher expectations for school achievement for one child than another. One teenager may have friends who like to drink while a sibling has friends who discourage drinking (e.g., Tarantino et al., 2014). All of these contrasting environmental influences tend to make siblings different, not alike. Environments are important, but, as I describe their influence throughout this book, you should remember that each child in a family experiences a unique environment.

Much of what I have said about genes, environment, and development is summarized in Figure 2-6. Parents are the source of children's genes and, at least for young children, the primary source of children's experiences. Children's genes also influence the experiences they have and the impact of those experiences on them. However, to capture the idea of nonshared environmental influences, we would need a separate diagram for each child, reflecting the fact that parents provide unique genes and a unique family environment for each of their offspring. And to capture the idea that genes are expressed across a child's lifetime, we would need to repeat the diagram for each child many times, emphasizing that heredity–environment influences at any given point are affected by prior heredity–environment exchanges.

Using this framework, we can speculate about why Sadie and Molly, the fraternal twins from this module's opening vignette, are so different. Perhaps their parents passed along more genes for sociability

Q&A **QUESTION 2.2**
Erik, 19, and Jason, 16, are brothers. Erik excels in school: he gets straight A's, is president of the math club, and enjoys tutoring younger children. Jason hates school and his grades show it. How can nonshared environmental influences explain these differences?

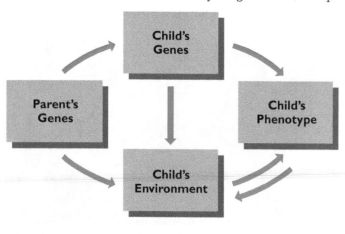

Figure 2-6

to Sadie than to Molly. During infancy, their parents included both girls in play groups with other babies. Sadie found this exciting, but Molly found it annoying and a bit stressful. Over time, their parents unwittingly worked hard to foster Sadie's relationships with her peers. They worried less about Molly's peer relationships because she seemed to be perfectly content to look at books, to color, or to play alone with puzzles. Apparently heredity gave Sadie a slighter larger dose of sociability, but experience ended up accentuating the difference between the sisters.

In a similar manner, throughout the rest of this book we'll examine links between nature, nurture, and development. An excellent place to see the interaction of nature and nurture is during prenatal development, which is the topic of Chapter 3.

 ## Check Your Learning

RECALL What is polygenic inheritance and how does it explain behavioral phenotypes?

Describe the basic features, logic, and weaknesses of twin and adoption studies.

INTERPRET Explain how niche-picking shows the interaction between heredity and environment.

APPLY Leslie and Glenn, the couple from Module 2.1 who were concerned that their baby could have sickle-cell disease, are already charting their baby's life course. Leslie, who has always loved to sing, is confident that her baby will be a fantastic musician and easily imagines a regular routine of music lessons, rehearsals, and concerts. Glenn, a pilot, is just as confident that his child will share his love of flying; he is already planning trips the two of them can take together. Are Leslie's and Glenn's ideas more consistent with the active or passive views of children? What advice might you give to Leslie and Glenn about factors they are ignoring?

 ## Unifying Themes   Nature and Nurture

This entire chapter is devoted to a single theme: *Development is always jointly influenced by heredity and environment.* We have seen, again and again, how heredity and environment are essential ingredients in all developmental recipes, though not always in equal parts. In sickle-cell disease, an allele has survival value in malaria-prone environments but not in environments in which malaria has been eradicated. Children with genes for above-average intelligence seek out intellectually stimulating environments that make them even more intelligent. Nature and nurture...development always depends on both.

See for Yourself

The Human Genome Project, completed in 2003, was designed to identify the exact location of all 20,500 human genes in human DNA and to determine the sequence of roughly 3 billion pairs of nucleotides like those shown in the diagram on page 59. At www.genome.gov you can learn about the history of the project, about the health implications of the project, and about some of the ethical issues that are raised by mapping of the human genome. See for yourself!

Summary

Mechanisms of Heredity

The Biology of Heredity

At conception, the 23 chromosomes in the sperm merge with the 23 chromosomes in the egg. The 46 chromosomes that result include 22 pairs of autosomes plus 2 sex chromosomes. Each chromosome is one molecule of DNA, which consists of nucleotides organized in a structure that resembles a spiral staircase. A section of DNA that provides specific biochemical instructions is called a gene. All of a person's genes make up a genotype; phenotype refers to the physical, behavioral, and psychological characteristics that develop when the genotype is exposed to a specific environment.

Single Gene Inheritance

Different forms of the same gene are called alleles. A person who inherits the same allele on a pair of chromosomes is homozygous; in this case, the biochemical instructions on the allele are followed. A person who inherits different alleles is heterozygous; in this case, the instructions of the dominant allele are followed, whereas those of the recessive allele are ignored. In incomplete dominance, the person is heterozygous but the phenotype is midway between the dominant and recessive phenotypes.

Genetic Disorders

Most inherited disorders are carried by recessive alleles. Examples include sickle-cell disease, albinism, cystic fibrosis, phenylketonuria, and Tay–Sachs disease. Inherited disorders are rarely carried by dominant alleles because individuals with such a disorder usually don't live long enough to have children. An exception is Huntington's disease, which doesn't become symptomatic until middle age.

Most fertilized eggs that do not have 46 chromosomes are aborted spontaneously soon after conception. One exception is Down syndrome, caused by an extra 21st chromosome. Down-syndrome individuals have a distinctive appearance and are intellectually disabled. Disorders of the sex chromosomes, such as Klinefelter's syndrome, are more common because these chromosomes contain less genetic material.

Heredity, Environment, and Development

Behavioral Genetics

Behavioral and psychological phenotypes that reflect an underlying continuum (such as intelligence) often involve polygenic inheritance. In polygenic inheritance, the phenotype reflects the combined activity of many distinct genes. Polygenic inheritance has been examined traditionally by studying twins and adopted children, and more recently, through molecular genetics. These studies indicate substantial influence of heredity in many areas, including intelligence, psychological disorders, and personality.

Paths from Genes to Behavior

The impact of heredity on a child's development depends on the environment in which the genetic instructions are carried out; these heredity–environment interactions occur throughout a child's life. A child's genotype can affect the kinds of experiences he or she has; children and adolescents often actively seek environments related to their genetic makeup. Environments affect siblings differently (nonshared environmental influence): Each child in a family experiences a unique environment.

Test Yourself

1. Each sperm and egg carries _____.
   a. 23 chromosomes
   b. 23 pairs of chromosomes
   c. 22 chromosomes

2. The genetic code, which determines heredity, is carried by _____.
   a. autosomes
   b. DNA
   c. phenotype

3. Phenotypes, the physical, behavioral, and psychological features of a person, are produced by _____.
   a. the environment

   b. physical features
   c. genetic instructions in interaction with the environment

4. The sickle-cell trait is caused by _____.
   a. a dominant allele
   b. one dominant and one recessive allele
   c. being homozygous dominant

5. Extra, missing, or damaged chromosomes _____.
   a. always disrupt development
   b. always lead to spontaneous abortion
   c. rarely affect development

6. Down syndrome _____.
   a. is most likely in teenage mothers
   b. is typified by development that is slower than normal
   c. is usually caused by a missing 21st chromosome

7. _____ is the branch of genetics concerned with the inheritance of behavioral and psychological traits.
   a. Molecular genetics
   b. Behavioral genetics
   c. Applied developmental science

8. Polygenic inheritance _____.
   a. reflects the combined influence of many pairs of genes
   b. is responsible for most either–or traits
   c. is the genetic mechanism responsible for diseases but not behaviors

9. Fraternal twins come from _____.
   a. a single fertilized egg split into two
   b. two separate eggs fertilized by two separate sperms
   c. an extra chromosome

10. Twin studies _____.
    a. are based on the assumption that heredity is implicated when identical twins resemble each other more than fraternal twins resemble each other
    b. are not useful for studying polygenic traits
    c. are far more useful than adoption studies

11. One of the most common disorders associated with abnormal sex chromosomes is _____.
    a. mental retardation
    b. PKU
    c. Klinefelter's syndrome

12. If the heritability coefficient of intelligence is 0.5, it means that _____.
    a. 50% of the differences in intelligence between people is a result of heredity
    b. 50% of an individual's intelligence is due to heredity
    c. chances of inherited intelligence in an individual is 50%

13. A bright child deliberately seeks an environment that is intellectually stimulating. This illustrates _____.
    a. nature and nurture
    b. niche-picking
    c. epigenesis

14. Which of the following is *incorrect* about nonshared environmental influences?
    a. Environmental forces make siblings different.
    b. Parents show the same behavior toward all their children.
    c. Environmental forces affect each child in a unique way.

15. In a twin study, an inherited trait will cause _____.
    a. fraternal twins to be more alike than identical twins
    b. identical twins to be more alike than fraternal twins
    c. fraternal twins to be more alike than other siblings

Key Terms

alleles 59
autosomes 59
behavioral genetics 66
chromosomes 58
deoxyribonucleic acid—DNA 59
dizygotic twins 67
dominant 60
Down syndrome 64
epigenesis 72

gene 59
genotype 59
heritability coefficient 72
heterozygous 59
homozygous 59
Huntington's disease 62
incomplete dominance 61
in vitro fertilization 58
methylation 72

monozygotic twins 67
niche-picking 73
nonshared environmental influences 74
phenotype 59
polygenic inheritance 66
recessive 61
sex chromosomes 59
sickle-cell trait 61

Chapter 3
Prenatal Development, Birth, and the Newborn

Modules

3.1 From Conception to Birth

3.2 Influences on Prenatal Development

3.3 Happy Birthday!

3.4 The Newborn

If you ask parents to name the most memorable experiences of their lives, many mention events associated with pregnancy and childbirth. From the exciting news that a woman is pregnant through birth nine months later, the entire experience evokes awe and wonder. The events of pregnancy and birth provide the foundation on which all child development is built. In **Module 3.1**, we'll trace the events of prenatal development that transform sperm and egg into a living, breathing human being. In **Module 3.2**, we'll learn about some developmental problems that can occur before birth. In **Module 3.3**, we'll turn to birth. We'll see what happens during labor and delivery, and we'll consider some problems that can arise. In **Module 3.4**, we'll discover what newborn babies are like.

3.1 From Conception to Birth

LEARNING OBJECTIVES

LO1   What happens to a fertilized egg in the first 2 weeks after conception?

LO2   When do body structures and internal organs emerge in prenatal development?

LO3   When do body systems begin to function well enough to support life?

OUTLINE

Period of the Zygote (Weeks 1–2)

Period of the Embryo (Weeks 3–8)

Period of the Fetus (Weeks 9–38)

Eun Jung has just learned that she is pregnant with her first child. Like many other parents-to-be, she and her husband, Kinam, are ecstatic. But they also realize how little they know about "what happens when" during pregnancy. Eun Jung is eager to visit her obstetrician to learn more about the normal timetable of events during pregnancy.

The changes that transform a fertilized egg into a newborn human make up *prenatal development*. Prenatal development takes an average of 38 weeks, which are divided into three stages: the period of the zygote, the period of the embryo, and the period of the fetus. Each period gets its name from the term used to describe the baby-to-be at that point in prenatal development.

In this module, we'll trace the major developments during each period. As we go, you'll learn the answer to the what-happens-when question that intrigues Eun Jung.

Period of the Zygote (Weeks 1–2)

LO1   What happens to a fertilized egg in the first 2 weeks after conception?

The diagram in Figure 3-1 on page 80 traces the major events of the first period of prenatal development, which begins with fertilization and lasts about 2 weeks. **It ends when the fertilized egg, called a** *zygote*, **implants itself in the wall of the uterus.** During these 2 weeks, the zygote grows rapidly through cell division and travels down the fallopian tube toward the uterus. Within hours, the zygote divides for the first time; then division occurs every 12 hours. Occasionally, the zygote separates into two clusters that develop into identical twins. Fraternal twins, which are more common, are created when two eggs are released and each is fertilized by a different sperm cell. **After about 4 days, the zygote consists of about 100 cells, resembles a hollow ball, and is called a** *blastocyst*.

By the end of the first week, the zygote reaches the uterus. **The next step is** *implantation*: **The blastocyst burrows into the uterine wall and establishes**

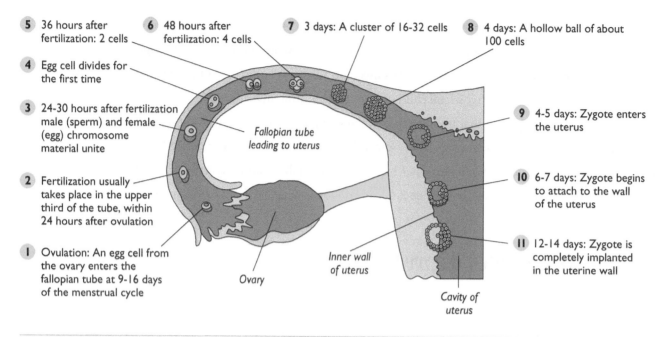

5 36 hours after fertilization: 2 cells

6 48 hours after fertilization: 4 cells

7 3 days: A cluster of 16-32 cells

8 4 days: A hollow ball of about 100 cells

4 Egg cell divides for the first time

3 24-30 hours after fertilization male (sperm) and female (egg) chromosome material unite

9 4-5 days: Zygote enters the uterus

2 Fertilization usually takes place in the upper third of the tube, within 24 hours after ovulation

10 6-7 days: Zygote begins to attach to the wall of the uterus

1 Ovulation: An egg cell from the ovary enters the fallopian tube at 9-16 days of the menstrual cycle

11 12-14 days: Zygote is completely implanted in the uterine wall

Fallopian tube leading to uterus

Ovary

Inner wall of uterus

Cavity of uterus

Figure 3-1

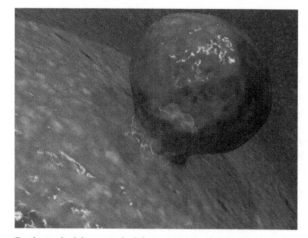

By the end of the period of the zygote, the fertilized egg has been implanted in the wall of the uterus and has begun to make connections with the mother's blood vessels.

connections with the mother's blood vessels. Implantation takes about a week to complete and triggers hormonal changes that prevent menstruation, letting the woman know she is pregnant.

As shown in the photograph, the implanted blastocyst is less than a millimeter in diameter, yet its cells have already begun to differentiate. In Figure 3-2 on page 81, which shows a cross-section of the blastocyst and the wall of the uterus, you can see different layers of cells. **A small cluster of cells near the center of the blastocyst, the *germ disc*, eventually develops into the baby.** The other cells are destined to become structures that support, nourish, and protect the developing organism. **The layer of cells closest to the uterus becomes the *placenta*, a structure for exchanging nutrients and wastes between the mother and the developing organism.**

Implantation and differentiation of cells mark the end of the period of the zygote. Comfortably sheltered in the uterus, the blastocyst is well prepared for the remaining 36 weeks of the journey to birth.

Period of the Embryo (Weeks 3–8)

LO2 When do body structures and internal organs emerge in prenatal development?

After the blastocyst is completely embedded in the uterine wall, it is called an *embryo*. This new period typically begins the third week after conception and lasts until the end of the eighth week. During the period of the embryo, body structures and internal organs develop. At the beginning of the period, three layers form in the embryo. **The outer layer or *ectoderm* will become hair, the outer layer of skin, and the nervous system; the middle layer or *mesoderm* will form muscles, bones, and the circulatory system; the inner layer or *endoderm* will form the digestive system and the lungs.**

One dramatic way to see the changes that occur during the embryonic period is to compare a 3-week-old embryo with an 8-week-old embryo. The 3-week-old

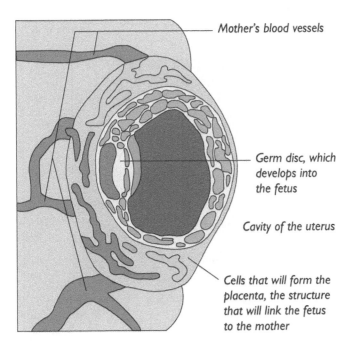

Mother's blood vessels

Germ disc, which develops into the fetus

Cavity of the uterus

Cells that will form the placenta, the structure that will link the fetus to the mother

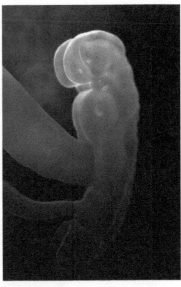

At 3 weeks after conception, the fertilized egg is about 2 millimeters long and resembles a salamander.

Figure 3-2

embryo shown in the top photo is about 2 millimeters long. Cell specialization is under way, but the organism looks more like a salamander than a human being. But growth and specialization proceed so rapidly that the 8-week-old embryo shown in the bottom photo looks distinctively human with eyes, arms, and legs. The brain and the nervous system are also developing rapidly, and the heart has been beating for nearly a month. Most of the organs found in a mature human are in place, in some form. (The sex organs are a notable exception.) Yet, being only an inch long and weighing a fraction of an ounce, the embryo is too small for the mother to feel its presence.

The embryo's environment is shown in Figure 3-3. **The embryo rests in an** *amniotic sac*, **which is filled with** *amniotic fluid* **that cushions the embryo and maintains a constant temperature.** The embryo is linked to the mother by two structures. **The** *umbilical cord* **houses blood vessels that join the embryo to the placenta.** In the placenta, the blood vessels from the umbilical cord run close to the mother's blood vessels but aren't actually connected to them. **Instead, the blood flows through** *villi*, **finger-like projections from the umbilical blood vessels that are shown in** Figure 3-3. Villi lie close to the mother's blood vessels and allow nutrients, oxygen, vitamins, and waste products to be exchanged between mother and embryo.

With body structures and internal organs in place, another major milestone passes in prenatal development. What's left is for these structures and organs to begin working properly. This is accomplished in the final period of prenatal development, as we'll see next.

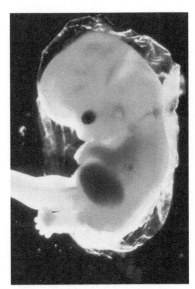

At 8 weeks after conception, near the end of the period of the embryo, the fertilized egg is obviously recognizable as a baby-to-be.

Period of the Fetus (Weeks 9–38)

LO3 When do body systems begin to function well enough to support life?

The final and longest phase of prenatal development, the *period of the fetus*, **extends from the ninth week after conception until birth.** During this period, the baby-to-be becomes much larger and its bodily systems begin to work. The increase in size is remarkable. At the beginning of this period, the fetus weighs

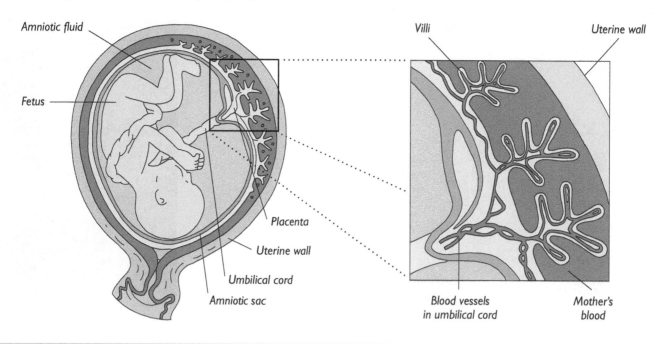

Figure 3-3

less than an ounce. At about 4 months, the fetus weighs roughly 4 to 8 ounces, enough for the mother to feel it move: Pregnant women often describe these fluttering movements as feeling like popcorn popping or a goldfish swimming inside them! During the last 5 months of pregnancy, the fetus gains an average of an additional 7 or 8 pounds before birth. Figure 3-4, which depicts the fetus at one-eighth of its actual size, shows this incredible increase in size.

During the fetal period, the finishing touches are put on the body systems that are essential to human life, such as the nervous, respiratory, and digestive systems. Some highlights of this period include the following:

- At 4 weeks after conception, a flat set of cells curls to form a tube. One end of the tube swells to form the brain; the rest forms the spinal cord. By the start of the fetal period, the brain has distinct structures and has begun to regulate body functions. **During the period of the fetus, all regions of the brain grow, particularly the** *cerebral cortex,* **the wrinkled surface of the brain that regulates many important human behaviors.**

- Near the end of the embryonic period, male embryos develop testes and female embryos develop ovaries. In the third month, the testes in a male fetus secrete a hormone that causes a set of cells to become a penis and scrotum; in a female fetus, this hormone is absent, so the same cells become a vagina and labia.

- During the fifth and sixth months after conception, eyebrows, eyelashes, and scalp hair emerge. **The skin thickens and becomes covered with a thick greasy substance,** *vernix,* **that protects the fetus during its long bath in amniotic fluid.**

- By about 6 months after conception, fetuses differ in their usual heart rates and in how much their heart rate changes in response to physiological stress. In one study (DiPietro et al., 2007), fetuses with greater heart rate variability were, as 2-month-olds, more advanced in their motor, mental, and language development. Greater heart rate variability may be a sign that the nervous system is responding efficiently to environmental change (as long as the variability is not extreme).

With these and other rapid changes, by 22 to 28 weeks most systems function well enough that a fetus born at this time has a chance to survive, which is

 QUESTION 3.1
Rachel is 8 months pregnant and spends hours each day talking to her baby-to-be. Rachel's husband considers this a waste of time, but Rachel's convinced that her baby-to-be must benefit. What do you think?

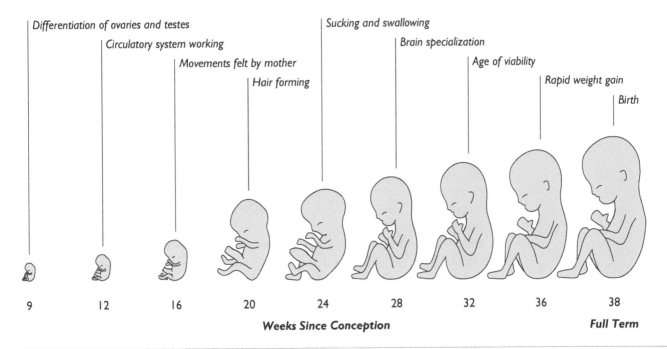

Differentiation of ovaries and testes

Circulatory system working

Movements felt by mother

Hair forming

Sucking and swallowing

Brain specialization

Age of viability

Rapid weight gain

Birth

| 9 | 12 | 16 | 20 | 24 | 28 | 32 | 36 | 38 |

Weeks Since Conception

Full Term

Figure 3-4

SOURCE: Based on Moore and Persaud: *Before We Are Born* (1993).

why this age range is called the *age of viability*. By this age, the fetus has a distinctly baby-like look, as you can see in the photo. However, babies born this early have trouble breathing because their lungs are not yet mature. Also, they cannot regulate their body temperature very well because they lack the insulating layer of fat that appears in the eighth month after conception. With modern neonatal intensive care, infants born this early can survive, but they face other challenges, as I'll describe in Module 3.3.

Fetal Behavior   During the fetal period, the fetus actually starts to behave (Joseph, 2000). The delicate movements that were barely noticeable at 4 months are now obvious. In fact, the fetus is a budding gymnast and kick-boxer rolled into one, punching, kicking, and turning somersaults. When active, the fetus moves about once a minute (DiPietro et al, 2004). However, these bursts of activity are followed by times when the fetus is still, as regular activity cycles emerge. Although movement is common in a healthy pregnancy, some fetuses are more active than others, and these differences predict infants' behavior: An active fetus is more likely than an inactive fetus to be an unhappy, difficult baby (DiPietro et al., 1996).

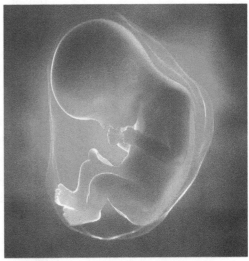

At 22 to 28 weeks after conception, the fetus has achieved the age of viability, meaning that it has a chance of surviving if born prematurely.

Another sign of growing behavioral maturity is that the senses work. The fetus can hear the mother's heart beating and hear her speaking (Lecanuet, Granier-Deferre, & Busnel, 1995). And as the fetus swallows amniotic fluid, it responds to different flavors in the fluid. Late in pregnancy enough light passes through the abdominal wall for a fetus to see (Del Giudice, 2011).

The fetus can remember these sensory experiences. For example, the fetus responds distinctively (its heart rate changes) to a recording of its mother voice compared with recordings of an unfamiliar female's voice (Kisilevsky et al., 2009). And after birth babies can remember events experienced in the uterus. Infants and children prefer foods that they tasted during prenatal development. In one study (Mennella, Jagnow, & Beauchamp, 2001), women drank carrot juice several days a week during the last month of pregnancy. When their infants were 5 and

6 months old, they preferred cereal flavored with carrot juice. In another study (Hepper et al., 2013), 8- and 9-year-olds were more likely to prefer garlic-flavored potatoes if their mothers ate garlic while pregnant.

In addition, infants recognize speech that they heard during prenatal development. In one study (DeCasper & Spence, 1986), newborns recognized *The Cat in the Hat* when their mother had read it daily for the last several weeks of pregnancy. In another study (Partanen et al., 2013), newborns recognized novel words presented during the fetal period of prenatal development. These longlasting effects of prenatal experiences with foods and sounds illustrate that prenatal development leaves babies well prepared for life outside the uterus.

After reading about findings like these, you may be tempted to buy products that claim to "teach" the fetus, by providing auditory stimulation (e.g., rhythmic sounds, speech, music). Makers of these products claim that a fetus exposed to this stimulation will reach developmental milestones earlier and be better prepared for school. However, I suggest that you save your money. The learning shown in the studies described in the previous paragraph—such as recognizing voices—occurs quite rapidly after birth without prenatal "education." Also, some of the more sophisticated forms of learning that are claimed to occur are probably impossible in utero, either because they require simultaneous visual stimulation (e.g., to pair voices with faces) or because they depend on brain development that takes place after birth.

The prenatal changes described in this module are summarized in Summary Table 3-1. The milestones listed in the table make it clear that prenatal development does a remarkable job of preparing the fetus for independent living as a newborn baby. But these astonishing prenatal changes can take place only when a woman provides a healthy environment for her baby-to-be. The "Improving Children's Lives" feature describes what pregnant women should do to provide the best foundation for prenatal development.

Improving Children's Lives

Five Steps Toward a Healthy Baby

1. Visit a health care provider for regular prenatal checkups. You should have monthly visits until you get close to your due date, when you will have a checkup every other week or maybe even weekly.

2. Eat healthy foods. Your diet should include foods from each of the five major food groups (cereals, fruits, vegetables, dairy products, and meats and beans). Your health care provider may recommend that you supplement your diet with vitamins, minerals, and iron to be sure you are providing your baby with all the nutrients it needs.

3. Stop drinking alcohol and caffeinated beverages. Stop smoking. Consult your health care provider before taking any over-the-counter medications or prescription drugs.

4. Exercise throughout pregnancy. If you are physically fit, your body is better equipped to handle the needs of the baby as well as the demands of labor and delivery.

5. Get enough rest, especially during the last 2 months of pregnancy. Also, attend childbirth education classes so that you'll be prepared for labor, delivery, and your new baby.

SUMMARY TABLE 3-1

CHANGES DURING PRENATAL DEVELOPMENT

Trimester	Period	Weeks	Size	Highlights
First	Zygote	1–2		Fertilized egg becomes a blastocyst that is implanted in the uterine wall
	Embryo	3–4	1/4 inch	Period of rapid growth; most body parts, including nervous system (brain and spinal cord), heart, and limbs are formed
	Embryo	5–8	1 inch, fraction of an ounce	
	Fetus	9–12	3 inches, about an ounce	Rapid growth continues, most body systems begin to function
Second	Fetus	13–24	12–15 inches, about 2 pounds	Continued growth; fetus is now large enough for the mother to feel its movements, fetus is covered with vernix
Third	Fetus	25–38	20 inches, 7–8 pounds	Continued growth; body systems become mature in preparation for birth, layer of fat is acquired, reaches the age of viability

As critically important as these steps are, they unfortunately do not guarantee a healthy baby. In Module 3.2, we'll see how prenatal development can sometimes go awry.

Check Your Learning

RECALL Describe the three stages of prenatal development. What are the highlights of each?

What findings show that the fetus behaves?

INTERPRET Compare the events of prenatal development that precede the age of viability with those that follow it.

APPLY In the last few months before birth, the fetus has some basic perceptual and motor skills; a fetus can hear, see, taste, and move. What are the advantages of having these skills in place months before they're really needed?

Influences on Prenatal Development

3.2

OUTLINE

General Risk Factors

Teratogens

How Teratogens Influence Prenatal Development

Prenatal Diagnosis and Treatment

LEARNING OBJECTIVES

LO4 How is prenatal development influenced by a pregnant woman's nutrition, the stress she experiences while pregnant, and her age?

LO5 What is a teratogen, and what specific diseases, drugs, and environmental hazards can be teratogens?

LO6 How do teratogens affect prenatal development?

LO7 How can prenatal development be monitored? Can abnormal prenatal development be corrected?

Chloe was barely 2 months pregnant at her first prenatal checkup. As she waited for her appointment, she looked at the list of questions that she wanted to ask her obstetrician. "I spend much of my workday talking on my cell phone. Is radiation from the phone harmful to my baby?" "When my husband and I get home from work, we'll have a glass of wine to help unwind from the stress of the day. Is moderate drinking like this okay?" "I'm 38. I know older women more often give birth to babies with disabilities. Is there any way I can know if my baby will have disabilities?"

All of Chloe's questions concern potential harm to her baby-to-be. She worries about the safety of her cell phone, about her nightly glass of wine, and about her age. Chloe's concerns are well founded. Beginning with conception, environmental factors influence the course of prenatal development, and they are the focus of this module. If you're sure you can answer all of Chloe's questions, skip this module and go directly to Module 3.3 on page 98. Otherwise, read on to learn about problems that sometimes arise in pregnancy.

General Risk Factors

LO4 How is prenatal development influenced by a pregnant woman's nutrition, the stress she experiences while pregnant, and her age?

As the name implies, general risk factors can have widespread effects on prenatal development. Scientists have identified three general risk factors: nutrition, stress, and a mother's age.

Nutrition The mother is the developing child's sole source of nutrition, so a balanced diet that includes foods from each of the five major food groups is vital. Most pregnant women need to increase their intake of calories by about 10% to 20% to meet the needs of prenatal development. A woman should expect to gain between 25 and 35 pounds during pregnancy, assuming that her weight was normal before pregnancy. A woman who was underweight before becoming pregnant may gain as much as 40 pounds; a woman who was overweight should gain at least 15 pounds (Institute of Medicine, 1990).

Sheer amount of food is only part of the equation for a healthy pregnancy. *What* a pregnant woman eats is also important. Proteins, vitamins, and minerals are essential for normal prenatal development. For example, folic acid, one of the B vitamins, is important for the nervous system to develop properly (Goh & Koren,

2008). **When mothers do not consume adequate amounts of folic acid, their babies are at risk for** *spina bifida*, **a disorder in which the embryo's neural tube does not close properly during the first month of pregnancy.** When the neural tube does not close properly, the result is permanent damage to the spinal cord and the nervous system; consequently, many children with spina bifida use crutches, braces, or wheelchairs (National Institute of Neurological Disorders and Stroke, 2013). In addition, inadequate macronutrients (e.g., protein) and micronutrients (e.g., zinc, iron) during prenatal development lead to problems in attention, memory, and intelligence (Monk, Georgieff, & Osterholm, 2013). Consequently, health care providers typically recommend that pregnant women supplement their diet with additional proteins, vitamins, and minerals.

When pregnant women experience chronic stress, they're more likely to give birth early or have smaller babies, but this may be because women who are stressed are more likely to smoke or drink and less likely to rest, exercise, and eat properly.

Stress   Does a pregnant woman's mood affect the zygote, embryo, or fetus in her uterus? Is a woman who is happy during pregnancy more likely to give birth to a happy baby? Is a pregnant woman like the harried office worker in the photo more likely to give birth to an irritable baby?

These questions address the impact on prenatal development of chronic *stress*, **which refers to a person's physical and psychological responses to threatening or challenging situations.** Women who report greater anxiety during pregnancy more often give birth early or have babies who weigh less than average (Copper et al., 1996; Tegethoff et al., 2010). What's more, when pregnant women are anxious, their children are less able to pay attention and more prone to behavioral problems as preschoolers (Loomans et al., 2012; O'Connor et al., 2002). Similar results emerged from studies of pregnant women exposed to disasters, such as the September 11 attacks on the World Trade Center: their children's physical, cognitive, and language development was affected (Engel et al., 2005; King et al., 2012). Finally, the harmful effects of stress are not linked to anxiety in general but are specific to worries about pregnancy, particularly in the first few months (Davis & Sandman, 2010; DiPietro et al., 2006).

Increased stress can harm prenatal development in several ways. First, when a pregnant woman experiences stress, her body secretes hormones that reduce the flow of oxygen to the fetus while increasing its heart rate and activity level (Monk et al., 2000). Second, stress can weaken a pregnant woman's immune system, making her more susceptible to illness (Cohen & Williamson, 1991), which can, in turn, damage fetal development. Third, pregnant women under stress are more likely to smoke or drink alcohol and less likely to rest, exercise, and eat properly (DiPietro, 2004; Monk et al., 2013). Fourth, stress may produce epigenetic changes (described on page 72) in which genes that help children to regulate their behavior are made less effective (Monk, Spicer, & Champagne, 2012). All these can endanger prenatal development.

I want to emphasize that the results described here apply to women who experience *chronic* stress. Virtually all women are sometimes anxious or upset while pregnant. But occasional, relatively mild anxiety is not thought to have harmful consequences for prenatal development.

Mother's Age   Traditionally, the 20s were thought to be the prime childbearing years. Teenage women as well as women who were 30 or older were considered less fit for the rigors of pregnancy. Is being a 20-something really important for a successful pregnancy? Let's answer this question separately for teenage and older women. Compared to women in their 20s, teenage girls are at greater risk to give birth early and to give birth to babies low in birth weight (Khashan, Baker, & Kenny, 2010). This is largely because pregnant teenagers are more likely to be living in poverty and do not receive good prenatal care. Nevertheless, even when a teenager receives adequate prenatal care and gives birth to a healthy baby, all is not rosy. Children of teenage mothers generally do less well in school and more often have behavioral problems (D'Onofrio et al., 2009; Fergusson & Woodward, 2000). For example, as adolescents they're much more likely to be convicted of crimes (Coyne et al., 2013). In the "Spotlight on Theories" feature, we'll see one explanation that child-development researchers have proposed for why these problems occur.

Spotlight on Theories
A Theory of the Risks Associated with Teenage Motherhood

BACKGROUND   Children born to teenage mothers typically don't fare very well. During childhood and adolescence, these children usually have lower scores on mental-ability tests, they get lower grades in school, and they more often have behavioral problems (e.g., they're too aggressive). However, why teen motherhood leads to these outcomes remains poorly understood.

THE THEORY   Sara Jaffee (2003) believes that teenage motherhood leads to harmful consequences through two distinct mechanisms. **One mechanism, called** *social influence*, **refers to events set in motion when a teenage girl gives birth—events that make it harder for her to provide a positive environment for her child's development.** For example, she may drop out of school, limiting her employment opportunities. Or she may try to finish school but become a neglectful parent because she spends so much time studying.

According to the second mechanism, called *social selection*, **some teenage girls are more likely than others to become pregnant, and those same factors that cause girls to become pregnant may put their children at risk.** For example, teenage girls with conduct disorder—who often lie, break rules, and are aggressive physically and verbally—are more likely to get pregnant than girls who don't have conduct disorder. The behaviors that define conduct disorder don't bode well for effective parenting. In addition, conduct disorder has a genetic component, which teenage mothers could pass along to their children.

According to social selection, the mother's age at birth is not really critical; these girls would have difficulty parenting effectively even if they delayed motherhood into their 20s or 30s. Instead, the factors that put girls at risk for becoming pregnant as teenagers also put children from those pregnancies at risk.

Hypothesis: According to the social influence mechanism, measures of the child-rearing environment should predict outcomes for children born to teenage moms. For example, if teenage motherhood results in less education and less income, then these variables should predict children's outcomes. According to the social selection mechanism, the same characteristics that are associated with a teenage girl's becoming pregnant should predict outcomes for her children. For example, if teenage girls are more likely to get pregnant when they're not as smart and have conduct disorder, then these same variables should predict outcomes for the children of these teenage moms.

Test: Jaffee (2003) evaluated both hypotheses in a 20-year longitudinal study conducted in New Zealand in which about 20% of the mothers had given birth while teenagers. She measured mothers' antisocial behavior as well as their education and income. She also assessed children's outcomes. For simplicity, we'll consider just one outcome: whether the children had, as adolescents or young adults, committed any criminal offenses.

Jaffee found that, compared to children born to older mothers, children born to teenage mothers were nearly three times more likely to have committed a criminal offense. This was as a result of both social influence and social selection mechanisms. Consistent with the social influence mechanism, teenage moms were less educated and had lower incomes, and these variables predicted their children's criminal activity. Consistent with the social selection mechanism, teenage moms were more likely to have a history of antisocial behavior, and this history predicted their children's criminal activity.

Conclusion: The adverse outcomes associated with teenage motherhood don't have a single explanation. Some of the adversity can be traced to cascading events brought on by giving birth as a teenager: Early motherhood limits education and income, hindering a mother's efforts to provide an environment that's conducive to a child's development. But some of the adversity does not reflect early motherhood per se; instead, girls who become pregnant teenagers often have characteristics that lead to adverse outcomes regardless of the age at which they gave birth.

Application: Policymakers have created many social programs designed to encourage teenagers to delay childbearing. Jaffee's work suggests two additional needs. First, policies are needed to limit the cascading harmful effects of childbearing for those teens who do get pregnant (e.g., programs to allow them to complete their education without neglecting their children). Second, many of the problems associated with teenage pregnancy are only coincidentally related to the fact that the mother is a teenager; programs are needed to help these girls learn effective parenting methods.

Of course, not all teenage mothers and their infants follow this dismal life course. Some teenage mothers finish school, find good jobs, and have happy marriages; their children do well in school, academically and socially. These successes are more likely when teenage moms live with a relative—typically the child's grandmother (Gordon, Chase-Lansdale, & Brooks-Gunn, 2004). And they're more likely when teenage moms participate in home-visiting programs in which registered nurses visit teenage moms to provide assistance, advice, and encouragement (Kitzman et al., 2010). However, teenage pregnancies with "happy endings" are definitely the exception; for many teenage mothers and their children, life is a struggle. Educating teenagers about the true consequences of teen pregnancy is crucial. Fortunately, the pregnancy rate among U.S. teenagers has declined steadily from its peak in the early 1990s (Martin et al., 2012).

Are older women better suited for pregnancy? This is an important question because present-day U.S. women typically are waiting longer than ever to become pregnant. Completing an education and beginning a career often delay childbearing. In fact, the birthrate in the 2000s among 40- to 44-year-olds is at its highest since the 1960s (Hamilton et al., 2010).

Older women have more difficulty getting pregnant and are more likely to have miscarriages, but they are quite effective mothers.

Older women like the one in the photo have more difficulty getting pregnant and are less likely to have successful pregnancies. Women in their 20s are twice as fertile as women in their 30s (Dunson, Colombo, & Baird, 2002), and past 35 years of age, the risks of miscarriage and stillbirth increase rapidly. For example, among 40- to 45-year-olds, pregnancies are much more likely to result in miscarriage or in babies with low birth weight (Khalil et al., 2013). What's more, women in their 40s are more liable to give birth to babies with Down syndrome. However, as mothers, older women are quite effective. For example, they are just as able to provide the sort of sensitive, responsive caregiving that promotes a child's development (Bornstein et al., 2006).

In general, then, prenatal development is most likely to proceed normally when women are between the ages of 20 and 35, are healthy and eat right, get good health care, and lead lives that are free of chronic stress. But even in these optimal cases, prenatal development can be disrupted, as we'll see in the next section.

Teratogens

LO5 What is a teratogen, and what specific diseases, drugs, and environmental hazards can be teratogens?

In the late 1950s, many pregnant women in Germany took thalidomide, a drug to help them sleep. Soon, however, came reports that many of these women were giving birth to babies with deformed arms, legs, hands, or fingers. **Thalidomide was a powerful** *teratogen*, **an agent that causes abnormal prenatal development.** Ultimately, more than 10,000 babies worldwide were harmed before thalidomide was withdrawn from the market (Kolberg, 1999).

Prompted by the thalidomide disaster, scientists began to study teratogens extensively. Today, we know a great deal about the three primary types of teratogens: diseases, drugs, and environmental hazards. Let's look at each.

Diseases Sometimes women become ill while pregnant. Most diseases, such as colds and many strains of flu, do not affect the developing organism. However, several bacterial and viral infections can be harmful and, in some cases, fatal to the embryo or fetus; five of the most common of these are listed in Table 3-1.

Some of these diseases pass from the mother through the placenta to attack the embryo or fetus directly. They include cytomegalovirus (a type of herpes), rubella, and syphilis. Other diseases attack at birth: The virus is present in the lining of the birth canal, and the baby is infected during the birth process. Genital herpes is transmitted this way. AIDS is transmitted both ways—through the placenta and during passage through the birth canal.

TABLE 3-1

TERATOGENIC DISEASES AND THEIR CONSEQUENCES

Disease	Potential Consequences
AIDS	Frequent infections, neurological disorders, death
Cytomegalovirus	Deafness, blindness, abnormally small head, developmental disabilities
Genital herpes	Encephalitis, enlarged spleen, improper blood clotting
Rubella (German measles)	Developmental disabilities; damage to eyes, ears, and heart
Syphilis	Damage to the central nervous system, teeth, and bones

TABLE 3-2	
TERATOGENIC DRUGS AND THEIR CONSEQUENCES	
Drug	**Potential Consequences**
Accutane	Abnormalities of the central nervous system, eyes, and ears
Alcohol	Fetal alcohol spectrum disorder, cognitive deficits, retarded growth
Aspirin	Deficits in intelligence, attention, and motor skills
Caffeine	Lower birth weight, decreased muscle tone
Cocaine and heroin	Retarded growth, irritability in newborns
Marijuana	Lower birth weight, less motor control
Nicotine	Retarded growth, possible cognitive impairments

The only way to guarantee that these diseases do not harm prenatal development is for a woman to not contract the disease before or during her pregnancy. Medication may help the woman but does not prevent the disease from damaging the developing baby.

Drugs Thalidomide illustrates the harm that drugs can cause during prenatal development. Table 3-2 lists other drugs that are known teratogens.

Notice that most of the drugs in the list are substances that you may use routinely: Accutane (used to treat acne), alcohol, aspirin, caffeine, and nicotine. Nevertheless, when consumed by pregnant women, they present special dangers (Behnke & Eyler, 1993).

Cigarette smoking is typical of the potential harm from teratogenic drugs (Cornelius et al., 1995; Espy et al., 2011). The nicotine in cigarette smoke constricts blood vessels and thus reduces the oxygen and nutrients that can reach the fetus through the placenta. Therefore, pregnant women who smoke are more likely to miscarry (abort the fetus spontaneously) and to bear children who are smaller than average at birth (Cnattingius, 2004). Furthermore, as children develop, they are more likely to show signs of impaired cognitive skills, reduced academic achievement, and behavioral problems (Clifford et al., 2012; Wakschlag et al., 2006). Finally, even secondhand smoke is harmful: When pregnant women don't smoke but their environment is filled with tobacco smoke, their babies tend to be smaller at birth and to be born early (Meeker & Benedict, 2013). Most of these harmful effects depend on degree of exposure—heavy smoking is more harmful than moderate smoking—and on the fetal genotype: Some children inherit genes that are more effective in defending, in utero, against the toxins in cigarette smoke (Price et al., 2010).

Alcohol also carries serious risk. **Pregnant women who regularly consume quantities of alcoholic beverages may give birth to babies with** *fetal alcohol spectrum disorder (FASD).* The most extreme form, fetal alcohol syndrome (FAS), is most likely among pregnant women who are heavy drinkers—for example, they drink 15 or more cans of beer over a weekend (May et al., 2013). Children with FAS usually grow more slowly than normal and have misshapen faces. Like the child in the photo, youngsters with FAS often have a small head, a thin upper lip, a short nose, and widely spaced eyes. FAS is the leading cause of developmental disabilities in the United States, and children with FAS have serious attentional, cognitive, and behavioral problems (Davis et al., 2013).

Does this mean that moderate drinking is safe? No. When women drink moderately throughout pregnancy, their children are often afflicted with partial fetal alcohol syndrome (p-FAS), which refers to children whose physical growth is normal but who have some facial abnormalities and impaired cognitive

When pregnant women drink large amounts of alcohol, their children often have fetal alcohol syndrome. Children with fetal alcohol syndrome tend to have a small head and a thin upper lip as well as developmental disabilities.

QUESTION 3.2

Nita, 22, is three-months pregnant and this is her first pregnancy. She enjoys drinking beer when she relaxes at home during weekends. Nita's best friend warned her that alcohol could be very harmful for the baby she was carrying. Should Nita listen to her friend?

skills. Another less-severe variant is alcohol-related neurodevelopmental disorder (ARND). Children with ARND are normal in appearance but have deficits in attention, memory, and intelligence (Pettoni, 2011).

Is there any amount of drinking that's safe during pregnancy? Maybe, but that amount has yet to be determined. Gathering definitive data is complicated by two factors: First, researchers usually determine the amount a woman drinks by her responses to interviews or questionnaires. If for some reason she does not accurately report her consumption, it is impossible to accurately estimate the amount of harm associated with drinking. Second, any safe level of consumption is probably not the same for all women. Based on their health and heredity, some women may be able to consume more alcohol more safely than others.

These factors make it impossible to guarantee safe levels of alcohol or any of the other drugs listed in Table 3-2. The best policy, therefore, is for a pregnant woman to avoid drugs if at all possible (including over-the-counter, prescription, and illegal drugs) and to consult a health care professional before using essential drugs.

Environmental Hazards As a by-product of life in an industrialized world, people are often exposed to toxins in food they eat, fluids they drink, and air they breathe. Chemicals associated with industrial waste are the most common environmental teratogens, and the quantities involved are usually minute. However, as is true for drugs, amounts that go unnoticed by an adult can cause serious damage to a developing fetus (Moore, 2003). Table 3-3 lists five well-documented environmental teratogens.

Polychlorinated biphenyls (PCBs) illustrate the danger of environmental teratogens. These chemicals were used in electrical transformers and paints, until the U.S. government banned them in the 1970s. However, like many industrial by-products, they seeped into the waterways, where they contaminated fish and wildlife. The amount of PCBs in a typical contaminated fish does not affect adults, but when pregnant women ate large numbers of PCB-contaminated fish, their children's cognitive skills and reading achievement were impaired (Jacobson & Jacobson, 1996; Winneke, 2011).

In developed nations, the most common teratogen is polluted air. Exposure to highly polluted air is associated with greater risk for premature births and lower birth weight (Currie, 2013). For example, in a clever natural experiment (Currie & Walker, 2011), researchers studied pregnant women living near highway toll plazas. When devices are installed that allow drivers to pay tolls electronically, without stopping, air pollution drops substantially (because cars neither wait to pay nor accelerate back to highway speed). Collecting tolls electronically produced a 10% drop in prematurity and low birth weight among pregnant women living near the

TABLE 3-3

ENVIRONMENTAL TERATOGENS AND THEIR CONSEQUENCES

Hazard	Potential Consequences
Air pollutants	Low birth weight, premature birth, lower test scores
Lead	Developmental disabilities
Mercury	Retarded growth, developmental disabilities, cerebral palsy
PCBs	Impaired memory and verbal skills
X-rays	Retarded growth, leukemia, developmental disabilities

Note: Air pollutants include carbon monoxide, ozone, lead, sulfur dioxide, and nitrous oxides.

toll plazas. Similar results are found when researchers examine the impact on prenatal development of closing industrial plants that emit toxic chemicals (Currie, 2013).

You may be wondering about one ubiquitous feature of modern environments that doesn't appear in Table 3-3: cell phones. Is a pregnant woman's cell-phone usage hazardous to the health of her fetus? At this point, there's no definitive answer to that question. The radiofrequency radiation that cell phones generate has sometimes been linked to health risks in adults (e.g., cancer), but the findings are inconsistent (Verschaeve, 2009; Vijayalaxmi & Prihoda, 2012). There are few scientific studies of the impact of cell phones on prenatal development. In a study conducted in Denmark, cell-phone use during *and after* pregnancy was associated with increased risk for behavior problems in childhood (Divan et al., 2012), but in a study conducted in the Netherlands, cell-phone use during pregnancy was unrelated to children's behavioral problems (Guxens et al., 2013). At this point, more research is needed to know if radiofrequency radiation from a pregnant woman's cell phone is a health risk. Of course, we know one way in which cell phones represent a huge health risk for pregnant women: Talking while driving is incredibly distracting and increases the odds of being in an accident by more than 50% (Asbridge, Brubacher, & Chan, 2013). So, while we wait for research to provide more information, the best advice for a pregnant woman would be to keep a cell phone at a distance when it's not being used and *never* use it while driving.

Environmental teratogens like those shown in Table 3-3 are treacherous because people are often unaware of their presence in the environment. The women in the Jacobson and Jacobson (1996) study, for example, did not realize they were eating PCB-laden fish. This invisibility makes it more difficult for a pregnant woman to protect herself from environmental teratogens. Pregnant women need to be particularly careful of the foods they eat and the air they breathe. They should be sure all foods are cleaned thoroughly to rid them of insecticides and should avoid convenience foods, which often contain many chemical additives. And they should stay away from air that's been contaminated by household products such as cleansers, paint strippers, and fertilizers. Women in jobs that require contact with potential teratogens (e.g., housecleaners, hairdressers) should switch to less potent chemicals. For example, they should use baking soda instead of more chemically laden cleansers. They should also wear protective gloves, aprons, and masks to reduce their contact with potential teratogens. Finally, because environmental teratogens continue to increase, check with a health care provider to learn if other materials should be avoided.

How Teratogens Influence Prenatal Development

LO6 **How do teratogens affect prenatal development?**

By assembling all the evidence of harm caused by diseases, drugs, and environmental hazards, scientists have identified five important general principles about how teratogens usually work (Hogge, 1990; Jacobson & Jacobson, 2000; Vorhees & Mollnow, 1987):

1. **The impact of a teratogen depends on the genotype of the organism.** A substance may be harmful to one species but not to another. To determine the safety of thalidomide, researchers had tested thalidomide in pregnant rats and rabbits, whose offspring developed normal limbs. Yet, when pregnant women took the same drug in comparable doses, many produced children with deformed limbs. Thalidomide was harmless to rats and rabbits but not to people. What's more, some women who took thalidomide gave birth to

babies with normal limbs, yet others who took comparable doses at the same time in their pregnancies gave birth to babies with deformities. Apparently, heredity makes some individuals more susceptible than others to a teratogen.

2. **The impact of teratogens changes over the course of prenatal development.** The timing of exposure to a teratogen is critical. Figure 3-5 shows how the consequences of teratogens differ for the periods of the zygote, embryo, and fetus. During the period of the zygote, exposure to teratogens usually causes the fertilized egg to be aborted spontaneously. During the embryonic period, exposure produces major defects in body structure. For example, women who took thalidomide during the embryonic period had babies with ill-formed or missing limbs. Women who contract rubella during the embryonic period have babies with heart defects. During the fetal period, exposure to teratogens either produces minor defects in body structure or causes body systems to function improperly. For example, when women drink large quantities of alcohol during the fetal period, the fetus develops fewer brain cells.

Even within the different periods of prenatal development, developing body parts and systems are more vulnerable at certain times. The blue shading in Figure 3-5 indicates a time of maximum vulnerability; orange shading indicates a time when the developing organism is less vulnerable. The heart, for example, is most sensitive to teratogens during the first two-thirds of the embryonic period. Exposure to teratogens before this time rarely produces heart damage; exposure after this time results in milder damage.

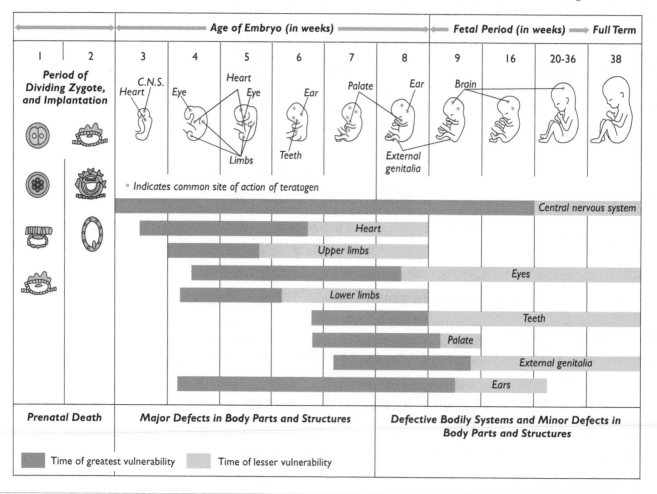

Figure 3-5

SOURCE: Based on Moore and Persaud: *Before We Are Born* (1993).

3. **Each teratogen affects a specific aspect (or aspects) of prenatal development.** Said another way, teratogens do not harm all body systems; instead, damage is selective. If a pregnant woman contracts rubella, her baby may have problems with eyes, ears, and heart, but normal limbs. If she consumes PCB-contaminated fish, her baby may have below-average cognitive skills but normal body parts and normal motor skills.

4. **The impact of teratogens depends on the dose.** Just as a single drop of oil won't pollute a lake, small doses of teratogens may not harm the fetus. In research on PCBs, for example, cognitive skills were affected only among children who had the greatest prenatal exposure to these by-products. In general, the greater the exposure, the greater the risk for damage (Adams, 1999).

   An implication of this principle is that researchers should be able to determine safe levels for a teratogen. In reality, this is difficult because sensitivity to teratogens is not the same for all people (and it's not practical to establish separate safe amounts for each person). Hence, the safest rule is zero exposure to teratogens.

5. **Damage from teratogens is not always evident at birth, but may appear later in life.** In the case of malformed infant limbs or babies born addicted to cocaine, the effects of a teratogen are obvious immediately. A cocaine baby goes through withdrawal—shaking, crying, and inability to sleep. Sometimes, however, the damage from a teratogen becomes evident only as the child develops. For example, between 1947 and 1971 many pregnant women in North America and Europe took the drug diethylstilbestrol (DES) to prevent miscarriages. Their babies were apparently normal at birth. As adults, however, daughters of women who took DES are more likely to have breast cancer or a rare cancer of the vagina. And they sometimes have abnormalities in their reproductive tract that make it difficult to become pregnant. Sons of women who took DES are at risk for testicular abnormalities and for testicular cancer (National Cancer Institute, 2006). In this case, the impact of the teratogen is not evident until decades after birth.

The Real World of Prenatal Risk   I have discussed risk factors individually, as if each were the only potential threat to prenatal development. In reality, many infants are exposed to multiple general risks and multiple teratogens. Pregnant women who drink alcohol often smoke (Baron et al., 2013). Pregnant women who are under stress often drink alcohol and may self-medicate with aspirin or other over-the-counter drugs. Many of these same women live in poverty, which means they may have inadequate nutrition and receive minimal medical care during pregnancy. When all the risks are combined, prenatal development is rarely optimal (Yumoto, Jacobson, & Jacobson, 2008).

This pattern explains why it's often challenging for child-development researchers to determine the harm associated with individual teratogens. Cocaine is a perfect example. You may remember stories in newspapers and magazines about "crack babies" and their developmental problems. Children exposed to cocaine during prenatal development suffer from a range of problems in physical growth, cognitive development, behavioral regulation, and psychopathology (e.g., Buckingham-Howes et al., 2013; Schuetze, Molnar, & Eiden, 2012). However, many of the problems associated with cocaine reflect, in part, the impact of concurrent smoking and drinking during pregnancy and the inadequate parenting that these children receive (Lambert & Bauer, 2012). Similarly, harmful effects attributed to smoking during pregnancy may also stem from the fact that pregnant women who smoke are more likely to be less educated and to have a history of psychological problems, including antisocial behavior (D'Onofrio et al., 2010).

Of course, findings like these don't mean that pregnant women should feel free to light up (or to shoot up). Instead, they highlight the difficulties involved in determining the harm associated with a single risk factor (e.g., smoking) when it usually occurs alongside many other risk factors (e.g., inadequate parenting, continued exposure to smoke after birth).

From what you've read in the past few pages, you might think that the developing fetus has little chance of escaping harm. But most babies are born in good health. Of course, a good policy for pregnant women is to avoid diseases, drugs, and environmental hazards that are known teratogens. This, coupled with thorough prenatal medical care and adequate nutrition, is the best recipe for normal prenatal development.

Prenatal Diagnosis and Treatment

LO7   How can prenatal development be monitored? Can abnormal prenatal development be corrected?

"I really don't care whether I have a boy or girl, just as long as my baby's healthy." Legions of parents worldwide have felt this way, but until recently all they could do was hope for the best. However, advances in technology give parents a much better idea of whether their baby is developing normally.

Even before a woman becomes pregnant, a couple may go for genetic counseling, which I described in Module 2.1. A counselor constructs a family tree for each prospective parent to check for heritable disorders. If one (or both) carries a disorder, further tests can determine the person's genotype. With this more detailed information, a genetic counselor can discuss choices with the prospective parents. They may choose to go ahead and conceive "naturally," taking their chances that the child will be healthy. Or they could decide to use sperm or eggs from other people. Yet another choice would be to adopt a child.

After a woman is pregnant, how can we know if prenatal development is progressing normally? Traditionally, obstetricians gauged development by feeling the size and position of the fetus through a woman's abdomen. This technique was not precise and, of course, couldn't be done at all until the fetus was large enough to feel. However, new techniques have revolutionized our ability to monitor prenatal growth and development. **A standard part of prenatal care in North America is *ultrasound*, a procedure that uses sound waves to generate a picture of the fetus.** As the photo shows, an instrument about the size of a hair dryer is rubbed over the woman's abdomen; the image is shown on a nearby TV monitor.

Ultrasound can be used as early as 4 or 5 weeks after conception; before this time the fetus is not large enough to generate an interpretable image. Ultrasound pictures are useful for determining the date of conception, which enables the physician to predict the due date more accurately. Ultrasound pictures are also valuable in showing the position of the fetus and placenta in the uterus, and they can be used to identify gross physical deformities, such as abnormal growth of the head. Ultrasound can also help in detecting twins or other multiple pregnancies. Finally, beginning at about 20 weeks after conception, ultrasound images can reveal the child's sex.

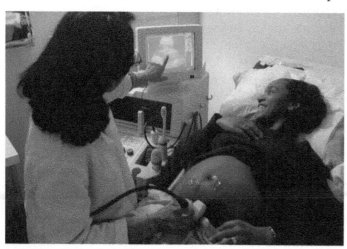

A standard part of prenatal care is ultrasound, in which sound waves are used to generate an image of the fetus.

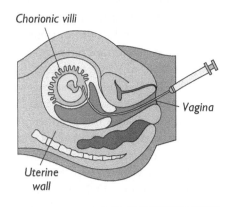

Figure 3-6   Figure 3-7

When a genetic disorder is suspected, two other techniques are particularly valuable because they provide a sample of fetal cells that can be analyzed. **In** *amniocentesis*, **a needle is inserted through the mother's abdomen to obtain a sample of the amniotic fluid that surrounds the fetus.** Amniocentesis is typically performed at approximately 16 weeks after conception. As you can see in Figure 3-6, ultrasound is used to guide the needle into the uterus. The fluid contains skin cells that can be grown in a laboratory dish and then analyzed to determine the genotype of the fetus.

In *chorionic villus sampling (CVS)*, **a sample of tissue is obtained from the chorion (a part of the placenta) and analyzed.** Figure 3-7 shows that a small tube, inserted through the vagina and into the uterus, is used to collect a small plug of cells from the placenta. CVS is often preferred over amniocentesis because it can be done about 9 to 12 weeks after conception, nearly 4 to 6 weeks earlier than amniocentesis. (Amniocentesis can't be performed until the amniotic sac is large enough to provide easy access to amniotic fluid.)

Results are returned from the lab in about 2 weeks following amniocentesis and in 7 to 10 days following CVS. (The wait is longer for amniocentesis because genetic material can't be evaluated until enough cells have reproduced for analysis.) With samples obtained from either amniocentesis or CVS, about 200 different genetic disorders can be detected. For example, for pregnant women in their late 30s or 40s, either amniocentesis or CVS is often used to determine whether the fetus has Down syndrome. These procedures are virtually error free, but they have a price: Miscarriages are slightly more likely after amniocentesis or CVS (Wilson, 2000). These procedures are described in Summary Table 3-2.

SUMMARY TABLE 3-2

METHODS OF PRENATAL DIAGNOSIS

Procedure	Description	Primary Uses
Ultrasound	Sound waves used to generate an image of the fetus	Determine due date and position of fetus in uterus; check for physical deformities, multiple births, and child's sex
Amniocentesis	Sample of fetal cells is obtained from amniotic fluid	Screen for genetic disorders
Chorionic villus sampling (CVS)	Sample of tissue is obtained from the chorion (part of the placenta)	Screen for genetic disorders

Ultrasound, amniocentesis, and CVS have made it much easier to determine if prenatal development is progressing normally. But what happens when it is not? Until recently a woman's options were limited: She could continue the pregnancy or end it. But options are expanding. **A whole new field called *fetal medicine* is concerned with treating prenatal problems before birth.** Many tools are available to solve problems that are detected during pregnancy (Rodeck & Whittle, 2009). One approach is to treat disorders medically, by administering drugs or hormones to the fetus. For example, in fetal hypothyroidism, the fetal thyroid gland does not produce enough hormones, leading to retarded physical and mental development. This disorder can be treated by injecting the necessary hormones directly into the amniotic cavity, resulting in normal growth.

Another way to correct prenatal problems is fetal surgery (Warner, Altimier, & Crombleholme, 2007). For example, spina bifida has been corrected with fetal surgery in the seventh or eighth month of pregnancy. Surgeons cut through the mother's abdominal wall to expose the fetus, then cut through the fetal abdominal wall; the spinal cord is repaired and the fetus is returned to the uterus. When treated with prenatal surgery, infants with spina bifida are less likely to need a shunt to drain fluid from the brain and, as preschoolers, are more likely to be able to walk without support (Adzick, et al. 2011).

Another potential approach to treating prenatal problems is *genetic engineering*—replacing defective genes with synthetic normal genes. Take sickle-cell disease as an example. Remember, from Module 2.1, that if a baby inherits the recessive allele for sickle-cell disease from both parents, the child will produce misshapen red blood cells that can't pass through capillaries. In theory, it should be possible to take a sample of cells from the fetus, remove the recessive genes from the 11th pair of chromosomes, and replace them with the dominant genes. These "repaired" cells could then be injected into the fetus, where they would multiply and cause normal red blood cells to be produced (David & Rodeck, 2009). As with fetal surgery, however, translating idea into practice is challenging (O'Brien, 2013). Researchers are still studying these techniques with nonhuman animals and there have been some successful applications with older children (Coutelle et al., 2005; Maguire et al., 2009). However, routine use of this method in fetal medicine is still years away.

Answers to Chloe's questions: Return to Chloe's questions in the module-opening vignette (page 86) and answer them for her. If you're not certain, I'll help by giving you the pages in this module where the answers appear:

- **Question about her cell phone—page 93**
- **Question about her nightly glass of wine—page 92**
- **Question about giving birth to a baby with developmental disabilities—page 90**

 ## Check Your Learning

RECALL What are the important general factors that pose risks for prenatal development?

Describe the main techniques for prenatal diagnosis that are available today.

INTERPRET Explain how the impact of a teratogen changes over the course of prenatal development.

APPLY What would you say to a 45-year-old woman who is eager to become pregnant but unsure about the possible risks associated with pregnancy at this age?

3.3 Happy Birthday!

LEARNING OBJECTIVES

LO8 What are the stages in labor and delivery?

LO9 What are "natural" ways of coping with the pain of childbirth? Is childbirth at home safe?

LO10 What is postpartum depression and what are its effects?

LO11 What are some complications that can occur during birth?

OUTLINE

Labor and Delivery

Approaches to Childbirth

Adjusting to Parenthood

Birth Complications

Dominique is 6 months pregnant; soon she and her partner will begin childbirth classes at the local hospital. She is relieved that the classes are finally starting because this means that pregnancy is nearly over. But all the talk she has heard about "breathing exercises" and "coaching" sounds mysterious to her. Dominique wonders what's involved and how the classes will help her during labor and delivery.

As women near the end of pregnancy, they find that sleeping and breathing become more difficult, they tire more rapidly, and their legs and feet swell. Women look forward to birth, both to relieve their discomfort and, of course, to see their baby. In this module, we'll see the different stages involved in birth, review various approaches to childbirth, and look at problems that can arise. We'll also look at childbirth classes like the one Dominique will be taking.

Labor and Delivery

LO8 What are the stages in labor and delivery?

In a typical pregnancy, a woman goes into labor about 38 weeks after conception, an event that's triggered by the flow of hormonal signals between the fetus, the mother, and the placenta (Smith et al., 2012). *Labor* is named appropriately because it involves intense, prolonged physical effort; it is usually divided into the three stages shown in Figure 3-8 and described in Summary Table 3-3. The first stage begins when the muscles of the uterus start to contract. These contractions force amniotic fluid up against the cervix, the opening at the bottom of the uterus that is the entryway to the birth canal. The wavelike motion of the amniotic fluid with each contraction causes the cervix to enlarge gradually.

The Three Stages of Labor

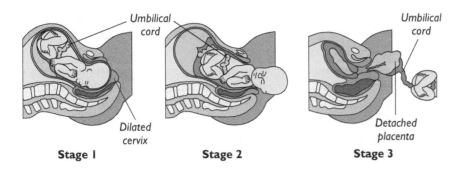

Umbilical cord

Umbilical cord

Dilated cervix

Detached placenta

Stage 1　　　　**Stage 2**　　　　**Stage 3**

Figure 3-8

SUMMARY TABLE 3-3

STAGES OF LABOR

Stage	Duration	Primary Milestone
1	12–24 hours	Cervix enlarges to 10 cm
2	1 hour	Baby moves down the birth canal
3	10–15 minutes	Placenta is expelled

At the beginning of this stage, contractions are weak and spaced irregularly. They gradually become stronger and more frequent. At the end of Stage 1, in the transition phase, contractions are intense and sometimes occur without interruption. Women report that the transition phase is the most painful part of labor. By the end of transition, the cervix is about 10 centimeters (4 inches) in diameter.

Stage 1 lasts from 12 to 24 hours for the birth of a first child, and most of the time is spent in the relative tranquility of the early phase. Stage 1 is usually shorter for subsequent births, with 3 to 8 hours being common. However, as the wide ranges suggest, these times are only rough approximations; the actual times vary greatly among women and are virtually impossible to predict.

When the cervix is fully enlarged, the second stage of labor begins. Most women feel a strong urge to push the baby out, using their abdominal muscles. This pushing, along with uterine contractions, propels the baby down the birth canal. **Soon the top of the baby's head appears, an event known as** *crowning*. In about an hour for first births and less for later births, the baby passes through the birth canal and emerges from the mother's body. **Most babies arrive head first, but a small percentage come out feet or bottom first, which is known as a** *breech presentation*. (I was one of these rare bottom-first babies and have been the butt of bad jokes ever since.) The baby's birth marks the end of the second stage of labor.

With the baby born, you might think that labor is over, but there is a third stage, in which the placenta is expelled from the uterus. This stage is quite brief, typically lasting 10 to 15 minutes.

Approaches to Childbirth

LO9 **What are "natural" ways of coping with the pain of childbirth? Is childbirth at home safe?**

When my mother went into labor (with me), she was admitted to a nearby hospital, where she soon was administered a general anesthetic. My father went to a waiting room, where he and other fathers-to-be awaited news of their babies. After my mother recovered from anesthesia, she learned that she had given birth to a healthy baby boy. My father had grown tired of waiting and gone back to work, where he got the good news in a phone call.

These were standard hospital procedures in 1950, and virtually all U.S. babies were born this way. No longer. In the middle of the 20th century, two European physicians—Grantly Dick-Read (1959) and Ferdinand Lamaze (1958)—criticized the traditional view in which labor and delivery had come to involve elaborate medical procedures that were often unnecessary and that often left women afraid of giving birth. A pregnant woman's fear led her to be tense, thereby increasing the pain she experienced during labor. These physicians argued for a more "natural" or prepared approach to childbirth, viewing labor and delivery as life events to be celebrated rather than medical procedures to be endured.

Today many varieties of prepared childbirth are available to pregnant women. However, most share some fundamental beliefs. One is that birth is more likely to be problem free and rewarding when mothers and fathers understand what's happening during pregnancy, labor, and delivery. Consequently, *prepared childbirth* means going to classes to learn basic facts about pregnancy and childbirth (like the material presented in this chapter).

A second common element is that natural methods of dealing with pain are emphasized over medical procedures, which involve possible side effects or complications. For example, the most common procedure in the United States is epidural analgesia, in which drugs are injected into the space below the spinal cord. These reduce the pain of childbirth but sometimes cause women to experience headaches or decreased blood pressure (American College of Obstetricians and Gynecologists, 2011b). One key to reducing birth pain without drugs is relaxation. Because pain often feels greater when a person is tense, pregnant women learn to relax during labor, through deep breathing or by visualizing a reassuring, pleasant scene or experience. Whenever they begin to experience pain during labor, they use these methods to relax.

A third common element of prepared childbirth is the involvement of a supportive adult, who may be the father-to-be, a relative, a close friend, or a trained birth assistant (known as a doula). These people provide emotional support, act as advocates (communicating a woman's wishes to health care personnel), and help a woman use techniques for managing pain. When pregnant women are supported in this manner, their labor tends to be shorter, they use less medication, and they report greater satisfaction with childbirth (Hodnett et al., 2012).

Another premise of the trend toward natural childbirth is that birth need not always take place in a hospital. Nearly all babies in the United States are born in hospitals; only 1% are born at home (Martin et al., 2013). For Americans accustomed to hospital delivery, home delivery can seem like a risky proposition and some medical professionals remain skeptical (Declercq, 2012). However, many women are more relaxed during labor in their homes, and they enjoy the greater control they have over labor and birth in a home delivery. That said, women should consider birth at home only if they are healthy, their pregnancy has been problem free, labor and delivery are expected to be problem free, a trained health care professional is present to assist, and comprehensive medical care is readily available should the need arise (Wax, Pinette, & Cartin, 2010).

Adjusting to Parenthood

L10 **What is postpartum depression and what are its effects?**

For parents, the time immediately after a trouble-free birth is full of excitement, pride, and joy—the much-anticipated baby is finally here! But it is also a time of adjustments for parents (and for siblings, as we'll see in Module 14.3). A woman experiences many physical changes after birth. Her breasts begin to produce milk and her uterus gradually becomes smaller, returning to its normal size in 5 or 6 weeks. Meanwhile, levels of female hormones (e.g., estrogen) drop.

Parents must also adjust psychologically. They reorganize old routines, particularly for first-born children, to fit the young baby's sleep–wake cycle (which is described in Module 3.4). In the process, fathers sometimes feel left out as mothers devote most of their attention to the baby.

Researchers once believed that an important part of parents' adjustment involved forming an emotional bond with the infant. That is, the first few days of life were thought to be a critical period for close physical contact between parents and babies; without such contact, parents and babies would find it difficult to bond emotionally (Klaus & Kennell, 1976). Today, however, we know that such contact in the first few days after birth—although beneficial for babies and pleasurable for babies and parents alike—is not essential for normal development (Eyer, 1992). In Module 10.3, we'll learn what steps are essential to forge these emotional bonds and when they typically take place.

Becoming a parent can be a huge adjustment, so it's not surprising that roughly half of all new mothers find that their initial excitement gives way to irritation, resentment, and crying spells—the so-called "baby blues." These feelings usually last a week or two and probably reflect both the stress of caring for a new baby and the physiological changes that take place as a woman's body returns to a nonpregnant state (Brockington, 1996).

For 10% to 15% of new mothers, however, irritability continues for months and is often accompanied by feelings of low self-worth, disturbed sleep, poor appetite, and apathy—a condition known as *postpartum depression*. Postpartum depression does not strike randomly. Biology contributes: Change in hormonal levels following birth place some women at risk for postpartum depression (O'Hara & McCabe, 2013). Experience also contributes: Women are more likely to experience postpartum depression when they are single, were depressed before pregnancy, are coping with other life stresses (e.g., death of a loved one or moving to a new residence), did not plan to become pregnant, or lack other adults (e.g., the father) to support their adjustment to motherhood (Edwards et al., 2012; O'Hara, 2009).

Women who are lethargic and emotionless do not mother warmly and enthusiastically. They don't touch and cuddle their new babies much or talk to them. And depressed moms are less effective in the common but essential tasks of feeding and sleep routines (Field, 2010). When postpartum depression persists over years, children's development is affected (Goodman et al., 2011). In the "Focus on Research" feature, for example, you'll see how maternal depression can lead children to have behavioral problems.

 QUESTION 3.3

Rosa gave birth a week ago. Once or twice a day she has crying spells and usually gets angry at her husband, even though he's been quite helpful to her and the baby. Do you think Rosa has postpartum depression?

Focus on Research

Links Between Maternal Depression and Children's Behavior Problems

Who were the investigators, and what was the aim of the study? When mothers are depressed, they don't parent effectively. However, this might not be due to depression per se because the same factors that put women at risk for experiencing postpartum depression—for example, being single, lacking social support, and experiencing stress—may contribute to their ineffective parenting. Edward Barker and his colleagues (Barker et al., 2012) hoped to better understand how maternal depression affects children's development.

How did the investigators measure the topic of interest? Barker and colleagues were interested in three variables: maternal depression, maternal risk factors associated with depression that might impair children's development, and children's behavioral problems. They measured the first two with questionnaires: When children were 1½ years old, moms completed a depression questionnaire; at various points between birth and their child's second birthday, moms completed questionnaires measuring exposure to risk factors such as being single, being exposed to stressful events such as cruelty from a partner, and having an inadequate support network. When children were 7 or 8 years old, their behavioral problems were diagnosed by experienced clinicians from teachers' and parents' reports of children's behavior.

Who were the children in the study? The sample was drawn from the Avon Longitudinal Study of Parents and Children, a project conducted in England that investigates children's health and development. Data on all three variables were available for 7,429 mothers and children.

What was the design of the study? The study was correlational because the investigators were interested in the relation that existed naturally among depression, risk factors, and children's problem behaviors. The study was longitudinal because children and parents were tested multiple times (and are still being tested because the study is ongoing).

Were there ethical concerns with the study? No. The measures were ones commonly used with parents and children; they posed no known risks. The investigators obtained permission from the parents and their children to participate.

What were the results? Using the mothers' replies to a depression questionnaire, Barker and his colleagues distinguished moms who had been depressed when their child was 1½ years old from moms who were not depressed. Then they compared rates of behavioral problems in children of the two groups of moms; those results are shown in Figure 3-9. For each of the five disorders, 7- and 8-year-olds were much more likely to have behavioral problems if their mom had been depressed, and overall, they were 2.56 times more likely to have problems. Next, Barker and his colleagues confirmed that, as expected, risk rates were greater for depressed moms. For example, depressed moms were five times more likely to have experienced cruelty from a partner and four times more likely to have inadequate support. Nevertheless, when these differences in exposure to risk were equated statistically, children

with depressed moms were still 1.92 times more likely to have behavioral problems.

What did the investigators conclude? The depression that some women experience following childbirth influences children in two ways. One is that depression symptoms per se are harmful for children: Depressed moms are less able to parent effectively and this may lead to behavioral problems. A second path is that the same factors that put moms at risk for depression (e.g., inadequate support) can impair a child's development, perhaps because they lead moms to parent less effectively.

What converging evidence would strengthen these conclusions? These findings are based largely on mothers' reports of their depression, risk factors, and their children's behavior. It would be valuable to have independent estimates of these variables (e.g., observation of children's antisocial behavior that contributes to the diagnosis of conduct disorder). In addition, nearly one third of the mothers dropped out of the study and those dropping out were more likely to have been exposed to risk. The present findings would be strengthened if they were replicated in a sample that was more stable over time.

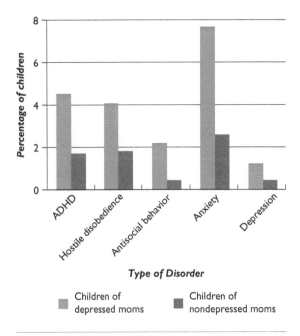

Figure 3-9

Findings like those in the Focus on Research feature show that postpartum depression should not be taken lightly: If a mother's depression doesn't lift after a few weeks, she should seek help. Home visits by trained health care professionals can be valuable (O'Hara & McCabe, 2013). During these visits, health-care professionals show moms better ways to cope with the many changes that accompany the new baby; they also provide emotional support by being a caring, sensitive listener; and, if necessary, they can refer the mother to other needed resources in the community. Finally, it's worth mentioning one simple way to reduce the risk of postpartum depression: breast-feeding. Moms who breast-feed are less likely to become depressed, perhaps because breast-feeding releases hormones that are antidepressants (Gagliardi, 2005).

Birth Complications

LO11 **What are some complications that can occur during birth?**

Women who are healthy when they become pregnant usually have a normal pregnancy, labor, and delivery. When women are not healthy or don't receive adequate prenatal care, problems can surface during labor and delivery. (Of course, even healthy women can have problems, but not as often.) The more common birth complications are listed in Table 3-4.

Some of these complications, such as a prolapsed umbilical cord, are dangerous because they can disrupt the flow of blood through the umbilical cord. **If this flow of blood is disrupted, infants do not receive adequate oxygen, a condition known as** *hypoxia*. Hypoxia sometimes occurs during labor and delivery because the umbilical cord is pinched or squeezed shut, cutting off the flow of blood. Hypoxia is serious because it can lead to developmental disabilities or death (Hogan et al., 2006).

To guard against hypoxia, fetal heart rate is monitored during labor, either by ultrasound or with a tiny electrode that is passed through the vagina and attached to the scalp of the fetus. An abrupt change in heart rate can be a sign that the fetus is not receiving enough oxygen. If the heart rate does change suddenly, a health care professional will try to determine whether the fetus is in distress, perhaps by measuring fetal heart rate with a stethoscope on the mother's abdomen.

When a fetus is in distress or when the fetus is in an irregular position or is too large to pass through the birth canal, a physician may decide to remove it from the mother's uterus surgically (American College of Obstetricians and Gynecologists, 2011a). **In a** *cesarean section (C-section),* **an incision is**

TABLE 3-4	
COMMON BIRTH COMPLICATIONS	
Complication	**Features**
Cephalopelvic disproportion	The infant's head is larger than the pelvis, making it impossible for the baby to pass through the birth canal.
Irregular position	In shoulder presentation, the baby is lying crosswise in the uterus and the shoulder appears first; in breech presentation, the buttocks or feet appear first.
Preeclampsia	A pregnant woman has high blood pressure, protein in her urine, and swelling in her extremities (as a result of fluid retention).
Prolapsed umbilical cord	The umbilical cord precedes the baby through the birth canal and is squeezed shut, cutting off oxygen to the baby.

made in the abdomen to remove the baby from the uterus. A C-section is riskier for mothers than a vaginal delivery because of increased bleeding and greater danger of infection. A C-section poses little risk for babies, although they are often briefly lethargic from the anesthesia that the mother receives before the operation. Mother–infant interactions are much the same for babies delivered vaginally or by planned or unplanned C-sections (Durik, Hyde, & Clark, 2000).

Birth complications not only are hazardous for a newborn's health, but also have long-term effects. When babies experience many birth complications, they are at risk for becoming aggressive or violent and for being at risk for psychiatric disorders (e.g., de Haan et al., 2006; Fazel et al., 2012). This is particularly true for newborns with birth complications who later experience family adversity, such as living in poverty. In one study (Arseneault et al., 2002), boys who had life-threatening birth complications such as umbilical cord prolapse or pre-eclampsia were more aggressive as 6-year-olds and more violent as 17-year-olds (e.g., they participated in gang fights or carried weapons). But this was only true when boys had also experienced family adversity, such as limited income or the absence of a parent. This outcome underscores the importance of receiving excellent health care throughout pregnancy and labor and a supportive environment throughout childhood.

Prematurity and Low Birth Weight   Normally, gestation takes 38 weeks from conception to birth. *Premature infants* **are born at 35 weeks after conception (or earlier).** *Small-for-date infants* **are substantially smaller than would be expected based on the length of time since conception.** Sometimes these two complications coincide, but not necessarily. Some, but not all, small-for-date infants are premature; conversely, some, but not all, premature infants are small-for-date. In other words, an infant can go the full 9-month term and be under the average 7- to 8-pound birth weight of newborns; the child is therefore small-for-date but not premature. Similarly, an infant born at 7 months that weighs 3 pounds (the average weight of a 7-month fetus) is only premature. But if the baby born after 7 months weighs less than the average, it is both premature and small-for-date.

Of the two complications, prematurity is the less serious. In the first year or so, premature infants often lag behind full-term infants in many facets of development, but by age 2 or 3 years, differences vanish and most premature infants develop normally thereafter (Greenberg & Crnic, 1988).

Prospects are usually not so optimistic for small-for-date babies such as the one shown in the photo. These infants are most often born to women who smoke or drink alcohol frequently during pregnancy or who do not eat enough nutritious food (Chomitz, Cheung, & Lieberman, 1995). Babies who weigh less than 1,500 grams (3.3 pounds) at birth often do not survive; when they do, their cognitive and motor development are usually delayed (Kavsek & Bornstein, 2010).

Small-for-date babies who weigh more than 1,500 grams have better prospects if they receive appropriate care. Like the infant in the photo, small-for-date babies are placed in special, sealed beds where temperature and air quality are regulated carefully. These beds effectively isolate infants, depriving them of environmental stimulation. Consequently, they often receive auditory stimulation, such as a tape recording of soothing music or their mother's voice, or visual stimulation provided from a mobile placed over the bed. Infants also receive

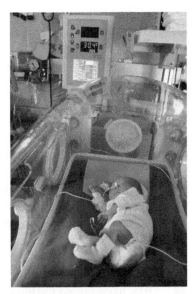

Small-for-date babies often survive, but their cognitive and motor development typically is delayed.

tactile stimulation—they are "massaged" several times daily. These forms of stimulation foster physical and cognitive development in small-for-date babies (Field, Diego, & Hernandez-Reif, 2010).

This special care should continue when infants leave the hospital for home. Consequently, interventions for small-for-date babies typically include training programs designed for parents of infants and young children. In these programs, parents learn how to respond appropriately to their child's behaviors. For example, they are taught the signs that a baby is in distress, overstimulated, or ready to interact. Parents also learn games and activities to use to foster their child's development. In addition, children are enrolled in high-quality child-care centers where the curriculum is coordinated with the parent training. This sensitive care promotes development in low-birth-weight babies; for example, sometimes they catch up to full-term infants in terms of cognitive development (Hill, Brooks-Gunn, & Waldfogel, 2003).

Long-term positive outcomes for these infants depend critically on providing a supportive and stimulating home environment. Unfortunately, not all at-risk babies have these optimal experiences. Many experience stress or disorder in their family lives. In these cases, development is usually affected (Poehlmann et al., 2011). The importance of a supportive environment for at-risk babies was dramatically demonstrated in a longitudinal study of all children born in 1955 on the Hawaiian island of Kauai (Werner & Smith, 2001). At-risk newborns who grew up in stable homes were indistinguishable from children born without birth complications. ("Stable family environment" was defined as two supportive, mentally healthy parents present throughout childhood.) When at-risk newborns had an unstable family environment because of divorce, parental alcoholism, or mental illness, for example, they lagged behind their peers in intellectual and social development.

The Hawaiian study underscores a point I have made several times in this chapter: Development is best when pregnant women receive good prenatal care and children live in a supportive environment. The "Cultural Influences" feature makes the same point in a different way, by looking at infant mortality around the world.

Cultural Influences

Infant Mortality

If you were the proud parent of a newborn and a citizen of Afghanistan, the odds would be 1 in 6 that your baby would die before his or her first birthday; worldwide, Afghanistan has the highest infant mortality rate, defined as the percentage of infants who die before their first birthday. In contrast, if you were a parent and a citizen of the Czech Republic, Iceland, Finland, or Japan, the odds are less than 1 in 300 that your baby would die in his or her first year because these countries have among the lowest infant mortality rates.

The graph in Figure 3-10 on page 107 puts these numbers in a broader, global context, depicting infant mortality rates for 15 developed nations as well as for 15 least-developed countries. Not surprisingly, risks to infants are far greater—about 20 times, on average—in the least-developed nations compared to developed nations (Central Intelligence Agency, 2013). In fact, the differences are so great that the graphs for the two groups of nations must be drawn on different scales.

If you're an American, you may be surprised to see that the United States ranks near the bottom of the list of developed nations. The difference is small, but if the United States were to reduce its infant mortality rate to the 4% that's common in European countries, this would mean that every year 8,000 American babies who now die before their first birthday would live.

What explains these differences in infant mortality rates? For U.S. infants, low birth weight is critical. The United States has more babies with low birth weight than virtually all other developed countries, and we've already seen that low birth weight places an infant at risk. Low birth weight can usually be prevented when a pregnant woman gets regular prenatal care, but many pregnant women in the United States receive inadequate or no prenatal care because they have no health insurance (Cohen, Martinez, & Ward, 2010). Virtually all the countries that rank ahead of the United States provide complete prenatal care at little or no cost. Many of these countries also provide paid leaves of absence for pregnant women (OECD, 2006).

In the least-developed countries, inadequate prenatal care is common and mothers often have inadequate nutrition. After birth, infants in these countries face the twin challenges of receiving adequate nutrition and avoiding disease. However, with improved prenatal care and improved health care and nutrition for infants, the global infant mortality rate has been cut in half since 1990 (UNICEF, 2007). With continued improvements in such care, the main challenges for infants worldwide will be walking, talking, and bonding with parents, not sheer survival.

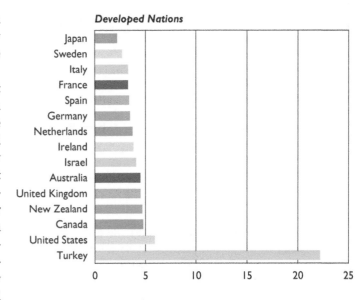

Figure 3-10

 Check Your Learning

RECALL What are the three stages of labor? What are the highlights of each?

Describe the main features of prepared approaches to childbirth.

INTERPRET Explain why some at-risk newborns develop normally but others do not.

APPLY Lynn is pregnant with her first child and would like to give birth at home. Her husband is totally against the idea and claims that it's much too risky. What advice would you give them?

The Newborn

OUTLINE

Assessing the Newborn

The Newborn's Reflexes

Newborn States

Perception and Learning in the Newborn

LEARNING OBJECTIVES

LO12 How do we determine if a baby is healthy and adjusting to life outside the uterus?

LO13 How do reflexes help newborns interact with the world?

LO14 What behavioral states are observable in newborns?

LO15 How well do newborns experience the world? Can they learn from experience?

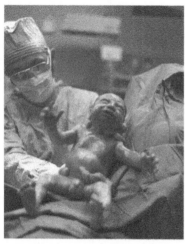

This newborn baby—my son, Ben—is covered with vernix and is bow-legged; his head is distorted from the journey down the birth canal.

Lisa and Matt, the proud but exhausted parents, were astonished at how their lives revolved around 10-day-old Hannah's eating and sleeping. Lisa felt as if she were feeding Hannah around the clock. When Hannah napped, Lisa would think of many things she should do but usually napped herself because she was so tired. Matt wondered when Hannah would start sleeping through the night so that he and Lisa could get a good night's sleep themselves.

The newborn baby that thrills parents like Lisa and Matt is actually rather homely, as this photo of my son Ben shows. I took it when he was 20 seconds old. Like other newborns, Ben is covered with blood and vernix, the white-colored "grease" that protects the fetus's skin during the many months of prenatal development. His head is temporarily distorted from coming through the birth canal, he has a potbelly, and he is bow-legged. But we thought he was beautiful and were glad he'd arrived.

What can newborns like Hannah and Ben do? We'll answer that question in this module and, as we do, learn when Lisa and Matt can expect to resume a full night's sleep.

Assessing the Newborn

LO12 How do we determine if a baby is healthy and adjusting to life outside the uterus?

Imagine that a mother has just asked you if her newborn baby is healthy. How would you decide? **The *Apgar score*, a measure devised by Virginia Apgar, is used to evaluate the newborn baby's condition.** Health professionals look for five vital signs, including breathing, heartbeat, muscle tone, presence of reflexes (e.g., coughing), and skin tone. As you can see in Table 3-5, each of the five vital signs receives a score of 0, 1, or 2, with 2 being optimal.

TABLE 3-5

FIVE SIGNS EVALUATED IN THE APGAR SCORE

Points	Activity	Pulse	Grimace (response to irritating stimulus)	Appearance (skin color)	Respiration
2	Baby moves limbs actively	100 beats per minute or more	Baby cries intensely	Normal color all over	Strong breathing and crying
1	Baby moves limbs slightly	Fewer than 100 beats per minute	Baby grimaces or cries	Normal color except for extremities	Slow, irregular breathing
0	No movement; muscles flaccid	Not detectable	Baby does not respond	Baby is blue-gray, pale all over	No breathing

The five scores are added together, with a score of 7 or more indicating a baby in good physical condition. A score of 4 to 6 means that the newborn will need special attention and care. A score of 3 or less signals a life-threatening situation that requires emergency medical care (Apgar, 1953).

The Apgar score provides a quick, approximate assessment of the newborn's status by focusing on the body systems needed to sustain life. For a comprehensive evaluation of the newborn's well-being, pediatricians and child-development specialists use the Neonatal Behavioral Assessment Scale, or NBAS (Brazelton & Nugent, 1995). The NBAS is used with newborns to 2-month-olds to provide a detailed portrait of the baby's behavioral repertoire. The scale includes 28 behavioral items along with 18 items that test reflexes. The baby's performance is used to evaluate functioning of four systems:

- *Autonomic.* The newborn's ability to control body functions such as breathing and temperature regulation
- *Motor.* The newborn's ability to control body movements and activity level
- *State.* The newborn's ability to maintain a state (e.g., staying alert or staying asleep)
- *Social.* The newborn's ability to interact with people

The NBAS is based on the view that newborns are remarkably competent individuals who are well prepared to interact with the environment. Reflecting this view, examiners go to great lengths to bring out a baby's best performance. They do everything possible to make a baby feel comfortable and secure during testing. Also, if the infant does not first succeed on an item, the examiner provides some assistance (Alberts, 2005).

Not only is the NBAS useful to clinicians in evaluating the well-being of individual babies, researchers have found it a valuable tool as well. Sometimes performance on the NBAS is used as a dependent variable. For example, harm associated with teratogens has been shown by lower scores on the NBAS (e.g., Engel et al., 2009). Researchers also use scores on the NBAS to predict later development (e.g., Stjernqvist, 2009).

The Newborn's Reflexes

LO13 **How do reflexes help newborns interact with the world?**

As we've just seen, the NBAS was based on a view—shared widely by child-development researchers—that newborns are well prepared to begin interacting with their world. **An important part of this preparation is a rich set of** *reflexes*, **unlearned responses that are triggered by a specific form of stimulation.** Table 3-6 on page 110 lists the many reflexes commonly found in newborns.

Some reflexes pave the way for newborns to get the nutrients they need to grow: Rooting and sucking ensure that the newborn is ready to begin a new diet of life-sustaining milk. Other reflexes protect the newborn from danger in the environment. The blink and withdrawal reflexes, for example, help newborns avoid unpleasant stimulation. Yet other reflexes serve as the foundation for larger, voluntary patterns of motor activity. For example, the stepping reflex looks like a precursor to walking.

Reflexes indicate whether the newborn's nervous system is working properly. For example, infants with damage to their sciatic nerve, which is found in the spinal cord, do not show the withdrawal reflex; infants who have problems with the lower part of the spine do not show the Babinski reflex. If these or other reflexes are weak or missing altogether, a thorough physical and behavioral assessment is called for (Falk & Bornstein, 2005).

TABLE 3-6

SOME MAJOR REFLEXES FOUND IN NEWBORNS

Name	Response	Significance
Babinski	A baby's toes fan out when the sole of the foot is stroked from heel to toe.	Unknown
Blink	A baby's eyes close in response to bright light or loud noise.	Protects the eyes
Moro	A baby throws its arms out and then inward (as if embracing) in response to a loud noise or when its head falls.	May help a baby cling to its mother
Palmar	A baby grasps an object placed in the palm of its hand.	Precursor to voluntary grasping
Rooting	When a baby's cheek is stroked, it turns its head toward the stroking and opens its mouth.	Helps a baby find the nipple
Stepping	A baby who is held upright by an adult and is then moved forward begins to step rhythmically.	Precursor to voluntary walking
Sucking	A baby sucks when an object is placed in its mouth.	Permits feeding
Withdrawal	A baby withdraws its foot when the sole is pricked with a pin.	Protects a baby from unpleasant stimulation

Newborn States

LO14 **What behavioral states are observable in newborns?**

Newborns spend most of their day alternating among four states (St. James-Roberts & Plewis, 1996; Wolff, 1987):

- *Alert inactivity.* The baby is calm, with eyes open and attentive; the baby looks as if he is deliberately inspecting his environment.
- *Waking activity.* The baby's eyes are open, but they seem unfocused; the baby moves her arms or legs in bursts of uncoordinated motion.
- *Crying.* The baby cries vigorously, usually accompanying this with agitated but uncoordinated motion.
- *Sleeping.* The baby's eyes are closed and the baby drifts back and forth from periods of regular breathing and stillness to periods of irregular breathing and gentle arm and leg motion.

Researchers have been particularly interested in crying, because parents want to know why babies cry and how to calm them, and sleeping, because babies spend so much time asleep!

Crying Newborns spend 2 to 3 hours each day crying or on the verge of crying. If you haven't spent much time around newborns, you might think that all crying is pretty much alike. In fact, babies cry for different reasons and cry differently for each one. In fact, scientists and parents can identify three distinctive types of cries (Snow, 1998). A *basic cry* starts softly, then gradually becomes more intense and usually occurs when a baby is hungry or tired; a *mad cry* is a more intense version of a basic cry; and a *pain cry* begins with a sudden, long burst of crying, followed by a long pause and gasping.

Parents are naturally concerned when their baby cries, and if they can't quiet a crying baby, their concern mounts and can easily give way to frustration and annoyance. It's no surprise, then, that parents develop little tricks for soothing their babies. Many Western parents will lift a baby to the shoulder and walk or gently rock the baby. Sometimes they will also sing lullabies, pat the baby's back, or give the baby a pacifier. Yet another method is to put a newborn into a car seat and go for a drive; I remember doing this, as a last resort, at 2:00 AM with my son Ben when he was 10 days old. After about the 12th time around the block, he finally stopped crying and fell asleep!

Another useful technique is *swaddling*, **in which an infant is wrapped tightly in a blanket.** Swaddling, shown in the photo, is used in many cultures around the world, including Turkey and Peru as well as countries in Asia. Swaddling provides warmth and tactile stimulation that usually works well to soothe a baby (Delaney, 2000).

Parents are sometimes reluctant to respond to their crying infant for fear of producing a baby who cries constantly. Yet they hear their baby's cry as a call for help that they shouldn't ignore. Should parents respond? "Yes" until their baby is about 3 months old. However, with older babies parents should consider why their infant is crying and the intensity of the crying (St James-Roberts, 2007). When an older baby wakes during the night and cries quietly, a parent should wait before responding, giving the baby a chance to calm herself. Of course, if parents hear a loud noise from an infant's bedroom followed by a mad cry, they should respond immediately. Parents need to remember that crying is actually the newborn's first attempt to communicate with others. They need to decide what the infant is trying to tell them and whether that warrants a quick response or whether they should let the baby soothe herself.

 QUESTION 3.4
When Mary's 4-month-old son cries, she rushes to him immediately and does everything possible to console him. Is this a good idea?

Sleeping   Crying may get parents' attention, but sleep is what newborns do more than anything else. They sleep 16 to 18 hours daily. The problem for tired parents like Lisa and Matt from the vignette is that newborns sleep in naps taken round the clock. Newborns typically go through a cycle of wakefulness and sleep about every 4 hours. That is, they will be awake for about an hour, sleep for 3 hours, then start the cycle anew. During the hour when newborns are awake, they regularly move between the different waking states several times. Cycles of alert inactivity, waking activity, and crying are common.

As babies grow older, the sleep–wake cycle gradually begins to correspond to the day–night cycle (St. James-Roberts & Plewis, 1996). Most babies begin sleeping through the night when they are about 3 or 4 months old, a major milestone for bleary-eyed parents like Lisa and Matt.

By 6 months, most North American infants are sleeping in a crib in their own rooms. Although this practice seems "natural" to North American parents, in much of the rest of the world, children sleep with their parents throughout infancy and the preschool years. Such parent–child "co-sleeping" is commonly found in cultures where people define themselves less as independent individuals and more as part of a group. For parents in cultures that value such interdependence—including Egypt, Italy, Japan, Korea, and Malaysia as well as the Maya in Guatemala and the Inuit in Canada—co-sleeping is an important step in forging parent–child bonds, just as sleeping alone is an important step toward independence in cultures that value self-reliance (Nelson, Schiefenhoevel, & Haimerl, 2000; Tan, 2009; Worthman & Brown, 2007).

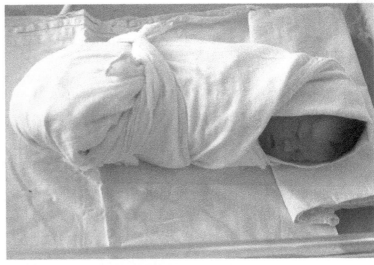
Swaddling is an effective way to soothe a baby who's upset.

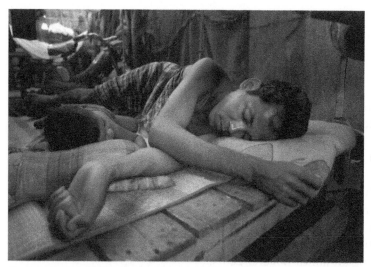

Co-sleeping, in which infants and young children sleep with their parents, is common in many countries around the world.

How does co-sleeping work? Infants may sleep in a cradle placed next to their parents' bed or in a basket that's in their parents' bed. When they outgrow this arrangement, they sleep in the bed with their mother; depending on the culture, the father may sleep in the same bed (as shown in the photo), in another bed in the same room, in another room, or in another house altogether!

You might think that co-sleeping would make children more dependent on their parents or lead to other behavioral problems, but research provides no evidence of this (Barajas et al., 2011; Okami, Weisner, & Olmstead, 2002). Plus, co-sleeping has the benefit of avoiding the lengthy, elaborate rituals that are often involved in getting youngsters to sleep in their own rooms, alone. With co-sleeping, children and parents simply go to bed together, with few struggles.

While asleep, babies alternate between two types of sleep. **In *rapid-eye-movement (REM) sleep*, babies move their arms and legs, they may grimace, and their eyes may dart beneath their eyelids.** Brain waves register fast activity, the heart beats more rapidly, and breathing is more rapid. **In regular or *non-REM sleep*, breathing, heart rate, and brain activity are steady and babies lie quietly without the twitching associated with REM sleep.** Newborns spend about equal amounts of time in REM and non-REM sleep. REM sleep becomes less frequent as infants grow: By the first birthday, REM sleep drops to about 33%, not far from the adult average of 20% (Lushington et al., 2013).

The function of REM sleep is still debated. Older children and adults dream during REM sleep, and brain waves during REM sleep resemble those of an alert, awake person. Consequently, many scientists believe that REM sleep stimulates the brain in some way that helps foster growth in the young baby's brain (Halpern et al., 1995; Roffwarg, Muzio, & Dement, 1966).

Sudden Infant Death Syndrome For many parents of young babies, sleep is sometimes a cause of concern. **In *sudden infant death syndrome (SIDS)*, a healthy baby dies suddenly, for no apparent reason.** Approximately 1 to 3 of every 1,000 U.S. babies dies from SIDS. Most of them are between 2 and 4 months old.

Scientists don't know the exact causes of SIDS, but one idea is that 2- to 4-month-old infants are particularly vulnerable to SIDS because many newborn reflexes are waning during these months and thus infants may not respond effectively when breathing becomes difficult. They may not reflexively move the head away from a blanket or pillow that is smothering them (Lipsitt, 2003).

Researchers have also identified several risk factors associated with SIDS (Carpenter et al., 2013; Sahni, Fifer, & Myers, 2007). Babies are more vulnerable if they were born prematurely or with low birth weight. They are also more vulnerable when their parents smoke. SIDS is more likely when a baby sleeps on its stomach (face down) than when it sleeps on its back (face up). Finally, SIDS is more likely during winter, when babies sometimes become overheated from too many blankets and too-heavy sleepwear (Carroll & Loughlin, 1994). Evidently, SIDS infants, many of whom were born prematurely or with low birth weight, are less able to withstand physiological stresses and imbalances that are brought on by cigarette smoke, breathing that is temporarily inter-rupted, or overheating (Simpson, 2001).

As evidence about causes of SIDS accumulated, child advocates called for action. The result is described in the "Child Development and Family Policy" feature.

Child Development and Family Policy

Safe Sleeping

Based on mounting evidence that SIDS more often occurred when infants slept on their stomachs, in 1992 the American Academy of Pediatrics (AAP) began advising parents to put babies to sleep on their backs or sides. In 1994, the AAP joined forces with the U.S. Public Health Service to launch a national program to educate parents about the dangers of SIDS and the importance of putting babies to sleep on their backs. The "Back to Sleep" campaign was widely publicized through brochures, posters like the one shown in Figure 3-11, and videos. Since the "Back to Sleep" campaign began, the incidence of SIDS has been cut in half but it still remains the leading cause of death in 1- to 12-month-olds (Trachtenberg et al., 2012). Consequently, in the 21st century the National Institutes of Health (NIH) focused on groups in which SIDS is more common, including African Americans and Native Americans. The NIH developed ways to convey the "Back to Sleep" message in a culturally appropriate manner to African American communi-ties (NICHD, 2004). In addition, the NIH developed educational programs for nurses and pharmacists. In 2012, the campaign was named Safe to Sleep and included additional recommendations to keep infants safe while asleep. Through these policies, the NIH hopes to spread the word to parents and others who care for infants: the keys to safe sleeping include keeping babies away from smoke, putting them on a firm mattress on their backs to sleep, and not overdressing them or wrapping them too tightly in blankets.

Figure 3-11

SOURCE: Courtesy of the National Institute of Health.

Perception and Learning in the Newborn

LO15 How well do newborns experience the world? Can they learn from experience?

Do you believe it is important to talk to newborns and give them fuzzy little toys? Should their rooms be bright and colorful? If you do, you really believe two things about newborns. First, you believe that newborns can have perceptual experiences—they can see, smell, hear, taste, and feel. Second, you believe that sensory experiences are somehow registered in the newborn through learning and memory, because unless experiences are registered, they can't influence later behavior. You'll be happy to know that research confirms your beliefs. All the basic perceptual systems are operating at some level at birth. The world outside the uterus can be seen, smelled, heard, tasted, and felt (Cohen & Cashon, 2003; Slater et al., 2010). Moreover, newborns show the capacity to learn and remember. They change their behavior based on their experiences (Rovee-Collier & Barr, 2010).

We'll discuss these perceptual changes in more detail in Chapter 5, and we'll discuss learning and memory in Chapter 7. For now, the important point is that newborns are remarkably prepared to interact with the world. Adaptive reflexes coupled with perceptual and learning skills provide a solid foundation for the rest of child development.

 ## Check Your Learning

RECALL What are the different functions of reflexes?

Describe the four primary states of infant behavior.

INTERPRET Compare the Apgar and the NBAS as measures of a newborn baby's well-being.

APPLY What would you recommend to parents of a 2-month-old who worry about SIDS?

 # Unifying Themes   Continuity

This chapter is a good opportunity to highlight the theme that *early development is related to later development but not perfectly*. Remember the Hawaiian study? This study showed that outcomes for at-risk infants are not uniform. When at-risk infants grow up in a stable, supportive environment, they become quite normal children. But when they grow up in stressful environments, they lag intellectually and socially. Similarly, SIDS is more likely to affect babies born prematurely and with low birth weight, yet not all of these babies die of SIDS. When premature and low-birth-weight babies sleep on their backs, are not overheated, and do not inhale smoke, they're unlikely to die from SIDS. Traumatic events early in development, such as being born early or underweight, do not predetermine the rest of a child's life, but they do make some developmental paths easier to follow than others.

See for Yourself

Words can hardly capture the miracle of a newborn baby. If you have never seen a newborn, you need to see one, or even better, a roomful. Arrange to visit the maternity ward of a local hospital, which will include a nursery for newborns. These babies will no longer be covered with blood or vernix, but you will be able to see how the newborn's head is often distorted by its journey through the birth canal. As you watch the babies, look for reflexive behavior and changes in states. Watch while a baby sucks its fingers. Find a baby who seems to be awake and alert, then note how long the baby stays this way. When alertness wanes, watch for the behaviors that replace it.

Finally, observe how different the newborns look and act from each other. The wonderful variety and diversity found among human beings is already evident in those who are hours or days old. See for yourself!

Summary

From Conception to Birth

Period of the Zygote (Weeks 1–2)
The first period of prenatal development lasts 2 weeks. This period begins when the egg is fertilized.

Period of the Embryo (Weeks 3–8)
The second period of prenatal development is when most major body structures are formed.

Period of the Fetus (Weeks 9–38)
In the third period of prenatal development, the fetus becomes much larger and body systems begin to function.

Influences on Prenatal Development

General Risk Factors
Prenatal development can be harmed if a pregnant woman does not provide adequate nutrition for the developing organism or experiences considerable stress. Teenagers often have problem pregnancies because they rarely receive adequate prenatal care. After age 35, women are less fertile and more likely to have problem pregnancies, but they are effective mothers.

Teratogens
Teratogens are agents that can cause abnormal prenatal development. Several diseases and drugs are teratogens. Environmental teratogens are particularly dangerous because a pregnant woman may not know when these substances are present.

How Teratogens Influence Prenatal Development
The effect of teratogens depends on the genotype of the organism as well as the timing and amount of exposure. The impact of a teratogen may not be evident until later in life.

Prenatal Diagnosis and Treatment
Ultrasound uses sound waves to generate a picture of the fetus that reveals the position of the fetus, its sex, and any gross physical deformities. When genetic disorders are suspected, amniocentesis or chorionic villus sampling is used to determine the genotype of the fetus. Fetal medicine corrects problems of prenatal development medically, surgically, or through genetic engineering.

Happy Birthday!

Labor and Delivery
Labor consists of three stages. In Stage 1, the muscles of the uterus contract, causing the cervix to enlarge. In Stage 2, the baby moves through the birth canal. In Stage 3, the placenta is delivered.

Approaches to Childbirth
In prepared childbirth, mothers-to-be come to understand what takes place during birth and learn to cope with pain through relaxation and the help of a supportive adult.

Although most U.S. babies are born in hospitals, home birth can be considered when the mother is healthy, the delivery is expected to be trouble free, and a health care professional is present.

Adjusting to Parenthood
Following the birth of a child, a woman's body changes physically. Both parents also adjust psychologically and sometimes fathers feel left out. After giving birth, some women experience postpartum depression: They are irritable, have poor appetite and disturbed sleep, and are apathetic. Women with postpartum depression should seek treatment because it interferes with effective parenting.

Birth Complications
During labor and delivery, the flow of blood to the fetus can be disrupted, causing hypoxia, a lack of oxygen to the fetus. If the fetus is endangered, the doctor may do a cesarean section, removing it from the uterus surgically. Babies with many birth complications are at risk for becoming aggressive and developing psychiatric disorders.

Premature babies develop more slowly at first but catch up in a few years. Small-for-date babies who weigh less than 1,500 grams often do not develop normally; larger small-for-date babies fare well when their environment is stimulating and stress-free.

Infant mortality is relatively high in many countries around the world, primarily because of inadequate care before birth and inadequate nutrition and disease after birth.

The Newborn

Assessing the Newborn
The Apgar score measures five vital signs to determine a newborn's physical well-being. The Neonatal Behavioral Assessment Scale evaluates a baby's behavioral and physical status.

The Newborn's Reflexes
Some reflexes help infants to adjust to life outside the uterus, some protect them, and some are the basis for later motor behavior.

Newborn States
Newborns spend their day in one of four states: alert inactivity, waking activity, crying, and sleeping. A newborn's crying includes a basic cry, a mad cry, and a pain cry.

Newborns spend approximately two-thirds of every day asleep and go through a complete sleep–wake cycle once every 4 hours or so. Newborns spend about half their time in REM sleep, which may stimulate nervous system growth.

Some healthy babies die from sudden infant death syndrome (SIDS). Babies are vulnerable to SIDS when they are premature, have low birth weight, sleep on their stomachs, are overheated, or are exposed to cigarette smoke. Encouraging parents to place babies on their backs for sleeping has reduced the number of SIDS cases.

Perception and Learning in the Newborn
Newborns' perceptual and learning skills function reasonably well, which allows them to experience the world.

Test Yourself

1. The fertilized egg implants in the wall of the uterus during the period of the _____.
   a. zygote
   b. fetus
   c. embryo

2. Internal organs develop during the period of the _____.
   a. embryo
   b. fetus
   c. zygote

3. The developing organism becomes much larger and its bodily systems begin to work during the period of the _____.
   a. embryo
   b. fetus
   c. zygote

4. The age of viability (22–28 weeks) signifies that _____.
   a. the internal organs have just started to function
   b. the heart has started functioning
   c. a fetus born at this time has a chance of survival

5. Consuming insufficient amounts of folic acid by the mother puts her baby at risk for _____.
   a. inattention
   b. spina bifida
   c. low birth weight

6. Which of the following is not a general risk factor?
   a. stress
   b. drugs
   c. a mother's age

7. _____ is a procedure that generates an image of the fetus, which can be used to determine its sex and the existence of multiple pregnancies.
   a. Ultrasound
   b. Chorionic villus sampling
   c. Amniocentesis

8. Which of the following is the least helpful when checking to see if a fetus has genetic disorders?
   a. amniocentesis
   b. ultrasound
   c. chorionic villus sampling

9. The first stage of labor is usually the longest; the baby is born in the _____ stage.
   a. first
   b. second
   c. fourth

10. The presence of a genetic disorder in a fetus can be confirmed by _____.
   a. X-ray
   b. amniocentesis and chorionic villus sampling
   c. ultrasound

11. A potential approach to treating sickle-cell disease at the prenatal level is _____.
   a. genetic engineering
   b. use of medicines
   c. amniocentesis

12. In breech presentation, the baby comes out
    _____.
    a. head first
    b. feet first
    c. sideways

13. Which of the following statements about postpartum depression is *incorrect*?
    a. Change in hormonal levels puts some mothers at risk for postpartum depression.
    b. Experience plays no role in the development of postpartum depression.
    c. Women with postpartum depression are not effective mothers.

14. The sleeping baby moves its arms and legs very often during _____.
    a. a state of alert inactivity
    b. REM sleep
    c. non-REM sleep

15. The national program to eliminate sudden infant death syndrome (SIDS) encouraged parents to have their babies _____.
    a. sleep on their back
    b. be kept very warm while sleeping
    c. sleep on a soft mattress

Key Terms

age of viability   83
amniocentesis   97
amniotic fluid   81
amniotic sac   81
Apgar score   108
basic cry   110
blastocyst   79
breech presentation   100
cerebral cortex   82
cesarean section (C-section)   104
chorionic villus sampling (CVS)   97
crowning   100
ectoderm   80
embryo   80
endoderm   80

fetal alcohol spectrum disorder (FASD)   91
fetal medicine   98
genetic engineering   98
germ disc   80
hypoxia   104
implantation   79
mad cry   110
mesoderm   80
non-REM sleep   112
pain cry   110
period of the fetus   81
placenta   80
postpartum depression   102
premature infants   105
prenatal development   79

rapid-eye-movement (REM) sleep   112
reflexes   109
small-for-date infants   105
social influence   88
social selection   88
spina bifida   87
stress   87
sudden infant death syndrome (SIDS)   112
swaddling   111
teratogen   90
ultrasound   96
umbilical cord   81
vernix   82
villi   81
zygote   79

Chapter 4
Growth and Health

Modules

4.1 Physical Growth

4.2 Challenges to Healthy Growth

4.3 The Developing Nervous System

Humans take longer to mature physically than any other animal. We spend about 20% of our lives—all of childhood and adolescence—growing physically. This slow journey to physical maturity is an interesting story in itself. But physical growth is just as important for its impact on other aspects of children's development, including cognition, social behavior, and personality. As children grow physically, they depend less on others for care, they're treated differently by adults, and they view themselves as older and more mature. By knowing more about children's physical growth, you'll be better prepared to understand other aspects of development that we'll study in the rest of this book.

In this chapter, we'll learn how children grow physically. In **Module 4.1**, we'll look at different facets of physical growth and some of the reasons why people differ in their physical growth and stature. Then, in **Module 4.2**, we'll explore problems that can disrupt physical growth. In **Module 4.3**, we'll look at physical growth that's not so obvious—the development of the brain.

 # Physical Growth

LEARNING OBJECTIVES

| | | OUTLINE |

LO1   What are the important features of physical growth during childhood? How do they vary from child to child?

Features of Human Growth

LO2   How do sleep and nutrition contribute to healthy growth?

Mechanisms of Physical Growth

LO3   What are the physical changes associated with puberty, and what are their consequences?

The Adolescent Growth Spurt and Puberty

Pete has just had his 15th birthday, but, as far as he is concerned, there is no reason to celebrate. Although most of his friends have grown about 6 inches in the past year or so, have a much larger penis and larger testicles, and have mounds of pubic hair, Pete looks just as he did when he was 10 years old. He is embarrassed by his appearance, particularly in the locker room, where he looks like a little boy among men. "Won't I ever change?" he wonders.

For parents and children alike, physical growth is a topic of great interest. Parents marvel at how quickly babies add pounds and inches; 2-year-olds proudly proclaim, "I bigger now!" Many adolescents take great satisfaction in finally becoming taller than a parent; others, like Pete, suffer through their teenage years as they wait for the physical signs of maturity.

In this module, we'll examine some of the basic features of physical growth and variations in growth patterns. We'll also consider the mechanisms responsible for growth. Finally, we'll end the module by studying puberty, a phase of physical growth so special that it should be considered separately.

Features of Human Growth

LO1   What are the important features of physical growth during childhood? How do they vary from child to child?

Describing Growth Probably the most obvious way to measure physical growth is in terms of sheer size—height and weight. The growth charts in Figure 4-1 on page 120 show the average changes in height and weight that take

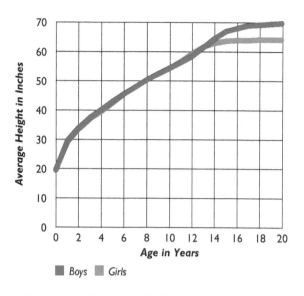

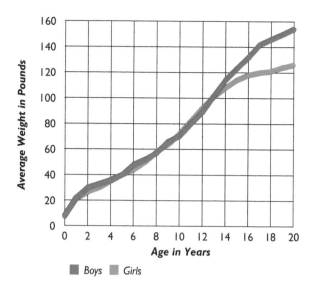

Figure 4-1

place from birth to age 20. Between birth and 2 years, for example, average height increases from 19 to 32 inches; average weight increases from 7 to 22 pounds. (An interesting rule of thumb is that boys achieve half their adult height by 2 years, and girls by 18 months.)

What is not so obvious from growth charts is that increases in height and weight are not steady. Looking at the average increase in weight and height annually—as opposed to the average total weight and height for each year—gives quite a different picture of the pattern of physical growth. Figure 4-2 shows that growth is extraordinarily rapid during the first year, when the average baby gains about 10 inches and 15 pounds. Growth is fairly steady through the preschool and elementary-school years: about 3 inches and 7 to 8 pounds each year. In early adolescence, growth is rapid again. During this growth spurt, which corresponds to the peaks in the middle of the charts in Figure 4-2, teenagers typically

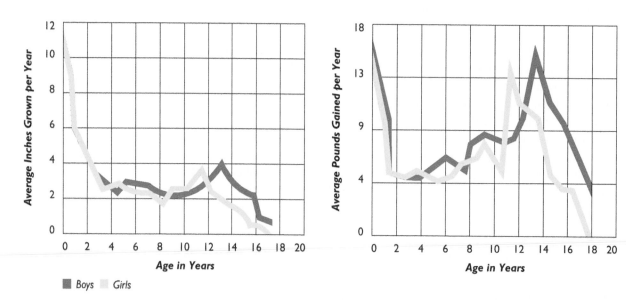

Figure 4-2

grow 4 inches and gain 16 to 17 pounds each year. After this spurt, which begins 1 to 2 years earlier in girls, growth again slows as children reach adulthood.

As children grow, their body parts develop at different rates: The head and trunk grow faster than the legs. Consequently, infants and young children are not simply scaled-down versions of adults. As you can see in Figure 4-3, infants and toddlers have disproportionately large heads and trunks, making them look top-heavy compared to older children and adolescents. As growth of the hips, legs, and feet catches up later in childhood, bodies take on proportions that are more adultlike.

Muscle, Fat, and Bones Other important features of physical growth take place inside the body, with the development of muscle, fat, and bones. Most of the body's muscle fibers are present at birth. During childhood, muscles become longer and thicker as individual fibers fuse together. This process accelerates during adolescence, particularly for boys.

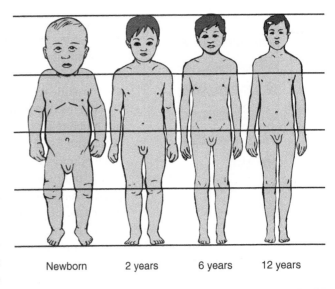

Newborn   2 years   6 years   12 years

Figure 4-3

A layer of fat appears under the skin near the end of the fetal period of prenatal development. Just as insulation in walls stabilizes the temperature inside a house, fat helps the fetus and infant regulate body temperature. Fat continues to accumulate rapidly during the first year after birth, producing the familiar look we call *baby fat*. During the preschool years, children actually become leaner, but in the early elementary-school years they begin to acquire more fat again. This happens gradually at first, then more rapidly during adolescence. The increase in fat in adolescence is more pronounced in girls than in boys.

Bone begins to form during prenatal development, starting as *cartilage*, a soft, flexible tissue. During the embryonic period, the center of the tissue turns to bone. **Then, shortly before birth, the ends of the cartilage structures, known as *epiphyses*, turn to bone.** Now the structure is hard at each end and in the center. Working from the center, cartilage turns to bone until finally the enlarging center section reaches the epiphyses, ending skeletal growth.

If you combine the changes in muscle, fat, and bone with changes in body size and shape, you have a fairly complete picture of physical growth during childhood. What's missing? The central nervous system, which we cover separately in Module 4.3.

Variations on the Average Profile The picture of children's physical growth that I have described so far is a typical profile; there are important variations on this prototype. For example, when the University of Oregon Ducks won the first NCAA men's basketball tournament in 1939, the average height of their starting lineup was 6 feet, 2 inches. When the University of Kentucky Wildcats won the tournament in 2012, the average height of the starting lineup was 6 feet, 6 inches, a difference of 4 inches that reflects changes in the U.S. population at large. Today, adults and children are taller and heavier than previous generations, largely as a result of improved health and nutrition. **Changes in physical development from one generation to the next are known as *secular growth trends*.** Secular trends have been huge. A medieval knight's armor would fit today's 10- to 12-year-old boy; the average height of U.S. sailors in the War of 1812 was 5 feet 2 inches!

"Average" physical growth varies not only from one generation to the next, but also from one country to another. Figure 4-4 on page 122 shows the

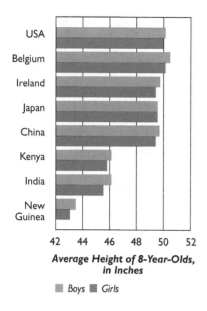

Figure 4-4

average height of 8-year-old boys and girls in several countries around the world. Youngsters from the United States, Western European countries, Japan, and China are about the same height, approximately 49 inches. Children in Africa and India are shorter, averaging just under 46 inches; and 8-year-olds in Polynesia are shorter still, averaging 43 inches.

We need to remember that *average* and *normal* are not the same. Many children are much taller or shorter than average and perfectly normal. For example, among American 8-year-old boys, normal weights range from approximately 44 pounds to 76 pounds. In other words, an extremely light but normal 8-year-old boy would weigh only slightly more than half as much as his extremely heavy but normal peer. What is normal can vary greatly, and this applies not only to height and other aspects of physical growth, but to all aspects of development. Whenever a "typical" or average age is given for a developmental milestone, you should remember that the normal range for passing the milestone is much wider. Some children pass the milestone sooner than the stated age and some later, but all are normal.

We've seen that children's heights vary within a culture, across time, and between cultures. What accounts for these differences? To answer this question, we need to look at the mechanisms responsible for human growth.

Mechanisms of Physical Growth

LO2 **How do sleep and nutrition contribute to healthy growth?**

Physical growth is easily taken for granted. Compared to other milestones of child development, such as learning to read, physical growth seems to come so easily. Like weeds, children seem to sprout without any effort at all. In reality, physical growth is complicated. Of course, heredity is involved: As a general rule, two tall parents will have tall children; two short parents will have short children; and one tall parent and one short parent will have average-height offspring.

How are genetic instructions translated into actual growth? Sleep and nutrition are both involved.

Sleep In Module 3.4, we saw that infants spend more time asleep than awake. The amount of time that children spend asleep drops gradually, from roughly 11 hours at age 3 to 10 hours at age 7 and 9 hours at age 12 (Snell, Adam, & Duncan, 2007). **Sleep is essential for normal growth because about 80% of the hormone that stimulates growth—named, appropriately, *growth hormone*—is secreted while children and adolescents sleep** (Smock, 1998). Growth hormone is secreted during sleep by the pituitary gland in the brain; from the brain, growth hormone travels to the liver, where it triggers the release of another hormone, somatomedin, which causes muscles and bones to grow (Tanner, 1990).

Sleep also affects children's psychological development. When children are chronically sleepy—because they wake often during the night or don't sleep a consistent amount nightly—they are prone to behavioral problems such as depression and anxiety (El-Sheikh et al., 2013). What's more, when children do not get enough sleep, they do less well in school (Astill et al., 2012). When deprived of sleep, children are less able to control their own behavior and thus it's more difficult for them to complete school tasks. In addition, sleep is a time when new learning is consolidated with existing knowledge (Henderson et al., 2012). Disrupted sleep may interfere with this consolidation; in other words, new information and skills presented during the school day may not "gel" as readily in a sleep-deprived child.

Findings like these show that children benefit from a "good night's sleep." One way for parents to help children sleep better and longer is to have a regular bedtime routine that includes the same sequence of activities beginning at about the same time every night. In addition, children sleep better when they share a bedroom with few other people (Buckhalt, El-Sheikh, & Keller, 2007).

Sleep loss can be a particular problem for adolescents. On the one hand, adolescents often stay up later at night, finishing ever-larger amounts of homework, spending time with friends, or working at a part-time job. On the other hand, adolescents often start school earlier than younger elementary-school students. The result is often a sleepy adolescent who struggles to stay awake during the school day (Carskadon, 2002). Many adolescents compound the problem by sacrificing sleep to study longer. This strategy often backfires: at school during the day after their late-night studying, teenagers often have trouble understanding material presented in class and do poorly on tests (Gillen-O'Neel, Huynh, & Fuligni, 2013). Thus, for adolescents and children, a good night's sleep is important for healthy physical and psychological development.

Nutrition The fuel for growth comes from the foods children eat and the liquids they drink. Nutrition is particularly important during infancy, when physical growth is so rapid. In a 2-month-old, roughly 40% of the body's energy is devoted to growth. Because growth requires so much high energy, young babies must consume about 50 calories per pound of weight (compared with 15–20 calories per pound for an adult). What's the best way for babies to receive the calories they need? The "Improving Children's Lives" feature has some answers.

Improving Children's Lives
What's the Best Food for Babies?

Breast-feeding is the best way to ensure that babies get nourishment. Human milk contains the proper amounts of carbohydrates, fats, protein, vitamins, and minerals for babies. Breast-feeding also has several other advantages compared to bottle-feeding (Dewey, 2001). First, when babies like the one in the photo are breast-fed, they are ill less often because a mother's breast milk contains antibodies that kill bacteria and viruses. Second, breast-fed babies are less prone to diarrhea and constipation. Third, breast-fed babies typically make the transition to solid foods more easily, apparently because they are accustomed to changes in the taste of breast milk that reflect a mother's diet. Fourth, breast milk cannot be contaminated (as long as a nursing mother avoids certain drugs, such as cocaine); in contrast, contamination is often a significant problem when formula is used in developing countries to bottlefeed babies.

The many benefits of breast-feeding do not mean that bottle-feeding is harmful. When prepared in sanitary conditions, formula provides generally the same nutrients as human milk. But formula does not protect infants from disease and is more likely to lead to allergies. However, bottle-feeding does have advantages. A mother who cannot readily breast-

Breast-feeding provides babies with all the nutrients they need, protects babies from disease, and eases the transition to solid foods.

feed can still enjoy the intimacy of feeding her baby, and other family members can participate in feeding. In fact, breast- and bottle-fed babies forge comparable emotional bonds with their mothers (Jansen, de Weerth, & Riksen-Walraven, 2008), so women in industrialized countries can choose either method and know that their babies' dietary and psychological needs will be met.

Experts recommend that children be breast-fed until they are 2 years old and that they be introduced to solid food at 6 months (UNICEF, 2010). In fact, in many developing countries mothers approximate these guidelines, breast-feeding their children up to 2 years of age (Arabi et al., 2012). But in the United States and other developed nations, roughly half of mothers stop breast-feeding by 6 months, in part because it is inconvenient when they return to full-time work (U.S. Centers for Disease Control, 2012).

QUESTION 4.1

Tameka is pregnant with her first child and wonders whether breast-feeding is really worthwhile. What advantages of breast-feeding would you mention to her?

Preschoolers grow more slowly than infants and toddlers, so they need to eat less per pound than before. One rule of thumb is that preschoolers should consume about 40 calories per pound of body weight, which works out to be roughly 1,500 to 1,700 calories daily for many children in this age group.

More important than the sheer number of calories, however, is a balanced diet that includes all five major food groups (grains, vegetables, fruits, milk, and meat and beans). A healthy diet also avoids too much sugar and, especially, too much fat. For preschool children, no more than approximately 30% of the daily caloric intake should come from fat, which works out to roughly 500 calories from fat. Unfortunately, too many preschool children like the ones in the photo become hooked on fast-food meals, which are notoriously high in fat. Excessive fat intake is the first step toward obesity (which I'll discuss later in this chapter), so parents need to watch what their preschool children eat (Whitaker et al., 1997).

Encouraging preschool children to eat healthy foods is tough for parents because some preschoolers become notoriously picky eaters. Like the little girl in the photo, toddlers and preschool children find foods that they once ate willingly "yucky." My daughter loved green beans as a toddler but as a 2-year-old she decided that green beans were awful and refused to eat them. Though such finickiness can be annoying, it may actually be adaptive for increasingly independent preschoolers. Because preschoolers don't know what is safe to eat and what isn't, eating only familiar foods protects them from potential harm (Aldridge, Dovey, & Halford, 2009).

Many U.S. children eat far too many fast-food meals, which are notoriously high in calories.

Parents should not be overly concerned about this finicky period. Although some children eat less than before (in terms of calories per pound), virtually all picky eaters get adequate food for growth. Nevertheless, several methods can be used to encourage youngsters to eat more healthfully:

- Reward children when they eat healthy foods; in one study (Cooke et al., 2011), when 4- to 6-year-olds received a sticker if they tasted a vegetable, consumption increased sixfold and persisted for three months after rewards were dropped.
- Show young children photos of same-age, same-sex peers who look happy when eating the target food; children are more likely to imitate such models (Frazier et al., 2012).
- Teach children about nutrition, emphasizing that different body functions require a diverse diet that includes a variety of nutrients; in one study

(Gripshover & Markman, 2013), preschoolers taught these concepts from story books ate twice as many vegetables.

- At meals, offer children new foods one at a time and in small amounts; encourage but don't force children to eat new foods; and when children reject a new food, continue to offer it over several meals so that it will become familiar (American Academy of Pediatrics, 2008).

Collectively, these guidelines can help children receive the nutrition they need to grow.

The Adolescent Growth Spurt and Puberty

LO3 What are the physical changes associated with puberty, and what are their consequences?

The biological start of adolescence is *puberty,* **which refers to the adolescent growth spurt and sexual maturation.** The adolescent growth spurt is easy to see in the graphs in Figure 4-1 on page 120. Physical growth is slow during the elementary-school years: In an average year, a 6- to 10-year-old girl or boy gains about 5 to 7 pounds and grows 2 to 3 inches. In contrast, during the peak of the adolescent growth spurt, a girl may gain as many as 20 pounds in a year and a boy, 25 (Tanner, 1970). This growth spurt lasts a few years.

The figure also shows that girls typically begin their growth spurt about 2 years before boys do. That is, girls typically start the growth spurt at about age 11, reach their peak rate of growth at about 12, and achieve their mature stature at about age 15. In contrast, boys start the growth spurt at 13, hit peak growth at 14, and reach mature stature at 17. This 2-year difference in the growth spurt can lead to awkward social interactions between 11- and 12-year-old boys and girls because, as the photo shows, at those ages girls are often taller and more mature looking than boys.

During the growth spurt, bones become longer (which, of course, is why adolescents grow taller) and become more dense. Bone growth is accompanied by several other changes that differ for boys and girls. Muscle fibers become thicker and denser during adolescence, producing substantial increases in strength. However, muscle growth is more pronounced in boys than in girls (Smoll & Schutz,

Beginning at about 2 years of age, many youngsters become picky eaters; they reject foods that they once ate willingly.

During the growth spurt, girls are often much taller than boys of the same age.

1990). Body fat also increases during adolescence, but more rapidly in girls than in boys. Finally, heart and lung capacities increase more in adolescent boys than in adolescent girls. Together, these changes help to explain why the typical adolescent boy is stronger and quicker and has greater endurance than the typical adolescent girl.

Adolescents not only become taller and heavier, but also become mature sexually. **Sexual maturation includes change in** *primary sex characteristics*, **which refer to organs that are directly involved in reproduction.** These include the ovaries, uterus, and vagina in girls and the scrotum, testes, and penis in boys. **Sexual maturation also includes change in** *secondary sex characteristics*, **which are physical signs of maturity that are not linked directly to the reproductive organs.** These include the growth of breasts and the widening of the pelvis in girls, the appearance of facial hair and the broadening of shoulders in boys, and the appearance of body hair and changes in voice and skin in both boys and girls.

Changes in primary and secondary sexual characteristics occur in a predictable sequence for boys and for girls. For girls, puberty begins with growth of the breasts and the growth spurt, followed by the appearance of pubic hair. *Menarche*, **the onset of menstruation, typically occurs at about age 13.** Early menstrual cycles are usually irregular and without ovulation.

For boys, puberty usually commences with the growth of the testes and scrotum, followed by the appearance of pubic hair, the start of the growth spurt, and growth of the penis. **At about age 13, most boys reach** *spermarche*, **the first spontaneous ejaculation of sperm-laden fluid.** Initial ejaculations often contain relatively few sperm; only months or sometimes years later are there enough sperm to fertilize an egg (Dorn et al., 2006).

The onset of sexual maturity is one of the first signs that an adolescent is on the threshold of adulthood. As we'll see in the "Cultural Influences" feature, many cultures celebrate this transition.

Cultural Influences
Adolescent Rites of Passage

Throughout history, many cultures have had special rituals or rites of passage that recognize adolescence as a unique phase in an individual's life. In ancient Japan, for example, a ceremony was performed for 12- and 14-year-old boys and girls in which they received adult clothing and adult hairstyles. Traditionally, as adolescents, indigenous Australian males walked alone in the wilderness, retracing their ancestors' paths.

Modern variants of these ceremonies include bar and bat mitzvah, which recognize that young Jewish adolescents are now responsible for their own actions, and Quinceañera (shown in the photo), which celebrates coming of age in 15-year-old girls in many Spanish-speaking regions in North, Central, and South America.

The Western Apache, Native Americans who live in the southwest portion of the United States, have a traditional ceremony—often called the Sunrise Dance—to celebrate a girl's menarche (Basso, 1970). After a girl's first menstrual period, a group of older

Quinceañera is a ritual practiced among Spanish-speaking cultures in the Americas; it honors a girl's 15th birthday.

adults select a sponsor—a woman of good character and wealth (she helps to pay for the ceremony) who is unrelated to the initiate. On the day before the ceremony, the sponsor serves a large feast for the girl and her family; at the end of the ceremony, the family reciprocates, symbolizing that the sponsor is now a member of their family.

The ceremony itself begins at sunrise and lasts a few hours. As shown in the photo, the initiate dresses in ceremonial attire. The ceremony includes eight phases in which the initiate dances or chants, sometimes accompanied by her sponsor or a medicine man. The intent of these actions is to transform the girl into "Changing Woman," a heroic figure in Apache myth. With this transformation comes longevity and perpetual strength.

Ceremonies like the Sunrise Dance, bar and bat mitzvah, and Quinceañera serve many of the same

The Apache celebrate menarche with a special ceremony in which a girl is said to become a legendary hero.

functions. They tell the community that the initiate is now an adult and remind initiates that their community now has adult-like expectations for them.

Mechanisms of Maturation What causes the many physical changes that occur during puberty? The pituitary gland in the brain is the key player. As I mentioned on page 122, the pituitary helps to regulate physical development by releasing growth hormone. In addition, the pituitary regulates pubertal changes by signaling other glands to secrete hormones. During the early elementary-school years—long before there are any outward signs of puberty—the pituitary signals the adrenal glands to release androgens, initiating the biochemical changes that will produce body hair. A few years later, in girls the pituitary signals the ovaries to release estrogen, which causes the breasts to enlarge, the female genitals to mature, and fat to accumulate. In boys the pituitary signals the testes to release the androgen testosterone, which causes the male genitals to mature and muscle mass to increase.

The timing of pubertal events is regulated, in part, by genetics (Cousminer et al., 2013). This is shown by the closer synchrony of pubertal events in identical twins than in fraternal twins: If one identical twin has body hair, the odds are that the other twin will, too (Mustanski et al., 2004). Genetic influence is also shown by the fact that a mother's age at menarche is related to her daughter's age at menarche (Belsky, Bakermans-Kranenburg, & van IJzendoorn, 2007). However, these genetic forces are strongly influenced by the environment, particularly an adolescent's nutrition and health. In general, puberty occurs earlier in adolescents who are well nourished and healthy than in adolescents who are not (St. George, Williams, & Silva, 1994).

Other findings underscore the importance of nutrition and health for the onset of puberty. Menarche occurs earlier in regions of the world where nutrition and health care are adequate. Also, within regions, socioeconomic status matters: Girls from affluent homes are more likely to receive adequate nutrition and health care and, consequently, they reach menarche earlier (Steinberg, 1999). Finally, in many industrialized countries around the world, the average age of menarche has declined steadily over the past 150 years, reflecting improvements in general health and better health care over this period (Ellis, 2004).

You may remember, from Chapter 1, that the social environment also influences the onset of puberty, at least for girls. Menarche occurs at younger ages in girls who experience chronic stress or who are depressed (James et al., 2012). For example, Belsky et al. (2010) discovered that girls have their first menstrual period at a younger age when their mothers used harsh punishment with them as preschoolers and young children.

The exact nature of these links is not known, but many explanations focus on the circumstances that would trigger the release of hormones that regulate menarche. One proposal is that when young girls experience chronic socio-emotional stress—their family life is harsh and they lack warm, supportive parents—the hormones elicited by this stress may help to activate the hormones that trigger menarche. This mechanism would even have an evolutionary advantage: If events of a girl's life suggest that her future reproductive success is uncertain—as indicated by chronic socio-emotional stress—then it may be adaptive to reproduce as soon as possible instead of waiting until later when she would be more mature and better able to care for her offspring. That is, the evolutionary gamble in this case might favor "lower-quality" offspring early over "higher-quality" offspring later (Ellis, 2004).

A related account, one that emphasizes the role of fathers, is described in the "Spotlight on Theories" feature.

Spotlight on Theories
A Paternal Investment Theory of Girls' Pubertal Timing

BACKGROUND Environmental factors can cause adolescent girls to enter puberty earlier. Some scientists believe that stress is the main factor in an adolescent girl's life that may cause her to mature early, but other scientists have continued to look for other factors that influence the onset of puberty in girls.

THE THEORY Bruce J. Ellis (Ellis & Essex, 2007; Ellis et al., 2003) has proposed a paternal investment theory that emphasizes the role of fathers in determining the timing of puberty. This theory is rooted in an evolutionary perspective that links timing of puberty—and, in the process, timing of reproduction—to the resources (defined broadly) in the child's environment. When an environment is predictable and rich in resources, it is adaptive to delay reproduction, because this allows an adolescent girl to complete her own physical, cognitive, and socio-emotional development, with the end result that she is a better parent. In contrast, when an environment is unstable and has few resources, it may be adaptive to mature and reproduce early rather than risk the possibility that reproduction may be impossible later.

According to Ellis, a father's presence and his behavior may provide important cues to girls about the quality of prospective mates. A father present and invested in his daughters signals an environment filled with high-quality males, which may delay onset of maturation. An absent father or one who is present but uninvolved with his daughter signals an environment in which high-quality males are rare, triggering early maturation. Delaying puberty is adaptive when high-quality fathers are plentiful, because it allows girls to develop the skills needed to develop a long-term relationship with a high-quality male; but accelerating puberty is adaptive when high-quality fathers are rare, because giving birth at a younger age means that the girl's mother is more likely to be able to help with child care.[1]

Hypothesis: If a girl's childhood experiences with paternal investment influence the timing of maturation, then the quantity and quality of a girl's experiences with her own father should predict the age when she enters puberty. Girls who have infrequent or negative interactions with their fathers should enter puberty earlier than girls who have frequent or positive interactions with their fathers, because infrequent or negative experiences would indicate that the environment has few high-quality fathers.

Test: Tither and Ellis (2008) studied two groups of biological sisters. In one group the father was absent as a result of divorce or separation; in the other, families were intact. Tither and Ellis measured the quality of the father's parenting and the age when daughters experienced menarche.

Two main findings support the theory. First, younger sisters had experienced a longer absence of the father—greater disruption—than older sisters and thus they should have experienced menarche earlier. They did, beginning to menstruate at an earlier age than both their older sisters and younger sisters from intact families. Second, this effect was most pronounced in daughters whose fathers were psychologically distant or had mental health problems. These girls experienced a double dose of ineffective fathering: He was usually absent and did more harm than good when he was present.

Conclusion: As predicted, pubertal timing was influenced by the quantity and quality of father–daughter interactions. Puberty was earlier when father–daughter interactions were uncommon or negative, which, according to Ellis, indicates that the environment contains relatively few high-quality fathers.

Application: We saw in Module 3.2 that teenage moms and their children usually travel a rocky road; it's always best if adolescent girls delay childbearing until they're older. Paternal investment theory suggests that one way to reduce teen pregnancy is to encourage fathers to have more and more positive interactions with their daughters. This will help delay the onset of puberty, reducing the odds that she'll become pregnant as a teenager and helping in other ways as well, as we'll see on pages 330–331. Of course, a father's investment in his daughters (as well as his sons) has benefits that extend far beyond physical maturation, as we'll see throughout the book.

---

[1] These are not conscious mechanisms: young girls are not saying to themselves, "The men around here are losers, so I might as well get on with it." Instead, neural pathways that are sensitive to the presence of caring men may act to suppress the paths that trigger puberty.

As teenagers enter puberty, they become concerned with their appearance.

Because children enter puberty at different ages, early-maturing children often tower over their late-maturing agemates.

These and other theories are being actively studied today. Where scientists agree, however, is that onset of menarche is *not* just under genetic and biological control; social and emotional factors also contribute.

Psychological Impact of Puberty Of course, teenagers are well aware of the changes taking place in their bodies. Not surprisingly, some of these changes affect adolescents' psychological development. For example, compared to children and adults, adolescents are much more concerned about their overall appearance. Like the girl in the photo, many teenagers look in the mirror regularly, checking for signs of additional physical change. Generally, girls worry more than boys about appearance and are more likely to be dissatisfied with their appearance (Vander Wal & Thelen, 2000). Girls are particularly likely to be unhappy with their appearance when appearance is a frequent topic of conversation with friends, leading girls to spend more time comparing their own appearance with that of their peers. Peers have relatively little influence on boys' satisfaction with their appearance; instead, boys are unhappy with their appearance when they expect to have an idealized strong, muscular body but don't (Jones, 2004).

In addition, adolescents are affected by the timing of maturation: Many children begin puberty years before or after these norms. An early-maturing boy might begin puberty at age 11, whereas a late-maturing boy might start at age 15 or 16. An early-maturing girl might start puberty at 9; a late-maturing girl may start at 14 or 15. For example, the girls shown in the photo on bottom of this page are the same age, but only one has reached puberty.

Maturing early can be harmful for girls. Girls who mature early often lack self-confidence, are less popular, are more likely to be depressed and have behavior problems, and are more likely to smoke and drink (Mendle, Turkheimer, & Emery, 2007; Schelleman-Offermans, Knibbe, & Kuntsche, 2013). Part of the problem is that early maturation may lead girls to relationships with older boys and these girls are ill prepared to cope with the demands of these relationships (Stattin, Kerr, & Skoog, 2011). In turn, this can result in life-changing effects on early-maturing girls who are pressured into sex and become mothers while still teenagers: as adults they typically have less prestigious, lower-paying jobs (Mendle et al., 2007). These harmful outcomes are more likely when early-maturing girls live in poverty or fight with parents (Lynne-Landsman, Graber, & Andrews, 2010; Rudolph & Troop-Gordon, 2010). Fortunately, when early-maturing girls have warm, supportive parents, they are less likely to suffer the harmful consequences of early maturation (Ge et al., 2002).

Maturing early can be harmful for boys, too. Early-maturing boys are at risk for psychological disorders such as depression; they are also more prone to substance abuse and to sexual activity (Mendle & Ferrero, 2012). Being physically advanced for their age may cause early-maturing boys to have problems with their peers who have not yet matured (leading to depression) and cause them to spend more time with older boys (exposing them to risky behavior). However, the effects of early maturation are weaker for boys than they are for girls (Graber, 2013).

For boys and girls, maturing late poses few risks. Late-maturing girls fare well; late-maturing boys are at somewhat greater risk for depression (Mendle & Ferrero, 2012). But otherwise Pete, the late-maturing boy in the opening vignette, has nothing to worry about. When he finally matures, others will treat him like an adult and the few extra years of being treated like a child will not be harmful (Weichold & Silbereisen, 2005).

Check Your Learning

RECALL Summarize the mechanisms of physical growth.

What is puberty and how does it differ for boys and girls?

INTERPRET Why is sleep important for healthy growth and development?

APPLY At first blush, the onset of puberty would seem to result entirely from biology. In fact, the child's environment influences the onset of puberty. Summarize the ways in which biology and experience interact to trigger the onset of puberty.

Challenges to Healthy Growth

LEARNING OBJECTIVES		OUTLINE
LO4	What is malnutrition? What are its consequences? What is the solution to malnutrition?	**Malnutrition**
LO5	How do nature and nurture lead some adolescent girls to diet excessively?	**Eating Disorders: Anorexia and Bulimia**
LO6	Why do some children become obese? How can they lose weight permanently?	**Obesity**
LO7	What diseases are life-threatening to children around the world?	**Disease**
LO8	What accidents are particularly risky for children and adolescents?	**Accidents**

Ricardo, 12, has been overweight for most of his life. He dislikes the playground games that entertain most of his classmates during recess, preferring to stay indoors. He has relatively few friends and is not particularly happy with his lot in life. Many times Ricardo has lost weight from dieting, but he's always regained it quickly. His parents know that being overweight is a health hazard, and they wonder what they could do to help their son.

Compared to many childhood tasks, physical growth seems easy. To paraphrase a famous line from the movie *Field of Dreams*, "If you feed them, they will grow." In reality, many children face obstacles on the path of healthy physical growth. Some obstacles concern nutrition. Growth requires enormous reserves of energy, and many children do not eat enough food to provide this energy. Other children and adolescents eat too much. Other problems are diseases and accidents, which affect millions of children worldwide. We'll look at these problems in this module, and as we do, we'll understand some of the reasons why Ricardo is overweight and what he can do about it.

Malnutrition

LO4 What is malnutrition? What are its consequences? What is the solution to malnutrition?

An adequate diet is only a dream to many of the world's children. **Worldwide, about one in four children younger than age 5 suffers from** *malnutrition,* **as indicated by being small for their age** (UNICEF-WHO-The World Bank, 2012).

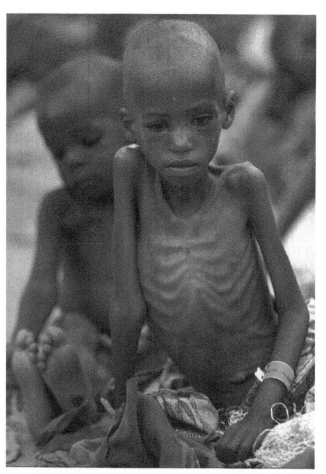

Malnutrition is acute in third-world countries, where one child in three is malnourished.

Many, like the children in the photo, are from third-world countries. In fact, nearly half of the world's undernourished children live in India, Bangladesh, and Pakistan (UNICEF, 2006). But malnutrition is regrettably common in industrialized countries, too. Many U.S. children growing up homeless and in poverty are malnourished. Approximately 15% of U.S. households have difficulty at some point in providing adequate food for all family members (Coleman-Jensen, Nord, & Singh, 2013).

Malnourishment is especially damaging during infancy because growth is so rapid during these years. By the school-age years, children with a history of infant malnutrition often have difficulty maintaining attention in school; they are easily distracted. Malnutrition during rapid periods of growth apparently damages the brain, affecting a child's abilities to pay attention and learn (Morgane et al., 1993; Nyaradi et al., 2013).

Malnutrition would seem to have a simple cure: an adequate diet. But the solution is more complex than that. Malnourished children are frequently listless and inactive, behaviors that are useful because they conserve energy. At the same time, when children are routinely unresponsive and lethargic, parents may provide fewer and fewer experiences that foster their children's development. For example, parents who start out reading to their children may stop because their malnourished children seem uninterested and inattentive. The result is a self-perpetuating cycle in which malnourished children are forsaken by parents, who feel that nothing they do gets a response, so they quit trying. A biological influence—lethargy stemming from insufficient nourishment—causes a profound change in the experiences—parental teaching—that shape a child's development (Worobey, 2005).

To break the vicious cycle, children need more than an improved diet. Their parents must also be taught how to foster their children's development. Programs that combine dietary supplements with parent training offer promise in treating malnutrition (Nahar et al., 2012). Children in these programs often catch up with their peers in physical and intellectual growth, showing that the best way to treat malnutrition is by addressing both biological and sociocultural factors (Super, Herrera, & Mora, 1990).

Short-Term Hunger Breakfast should provide about one-fourth of a child's daily calories. Yet, many children—in developed and developing countries—do not eat breakfast (Grantham-McGregor, Ani, & Gernald, 2001). When children eat a nutritious breakfast regularly, they're often more successful in school (Adolphus, Lawton, & Dye, 2013).

One strategy to attack this problem is to provide free and reduced-price meals for children at school. Lunch programs are the most common, but breakfast and dinner are sometimes available, too. These programs have a tremendous positive impact on children. Because they are better fed, children are absent from school less often and their achievement scores improve (Grantham-McGregor et al., 2001).

Eating Disorders: Anorexia and Bulimia

LO5   How do nature and nurture lead some adolescent girls to diet excessively?

In 2010, French model and actress Isabelle Caro died of respiratory disease, just months after turning 26. Near her death she weighed less than 75 pounds; Caro suffered from an eating disorder: *Anorexia nervosa* **is a disorder marked by a persistent refusal to eat and an irrational fear of being overweight.** Individuals with anorexia nervosa have a grossly distorted image of their own body. Like the girl in the photo, they claim to be overweight despite being painfully thin (Wilson, Heffernan, & Black, 1996). Anorexia is a serious disorder that can damage the heart, brain, or kidneys, sometimes causing death. A related eating disorder is bulimia nervosa. **Individuals with** *bulimia nervosa* **alternate between binge eating periods when they eat uncontrollably and purging through self-induced vomiting or with laxatives.** The frequency of binge eating varies remarkably among people with bulimia nervosa, from a few times a week to more than 30 times.

Adolescent girls with anorexia nervosa believe that they are overweight and refuse to eat.

Anorexia and bulimia are alike in many respects. Both disorders primarily affect females and emerge in adolescence (Wang & Brownell, 2005). What's more, many of the same factors put teenage girls at risk for both eating disorders. A meta-analysis (Jacobi et al., 2004) of studies of individuals with eating disorders indicated that heredity puts some girls at risk, and molecular genetic studies have implicated genes that regulate both anxiety and food intake (Klump & Culbert, 2007). Several psychosocial factors also put people at risk for eating disorders. When children have a history of eating problems, such as being a picky eater or being diagnosed with pica (i.e., eating nonfood objects such as chalk, paper, or dirt), they're at greater risk for anorexia and bulimia during adolescence. Teenagers who experience negative self-esteem or mood or anxiety disorders are at risk (Hutchinson, Rapee, & Taylor, 2010) as are girls who are harassed sexually by their peers (Petersen & Hyde, 2013). However, the most important risk factors for adolescents are being overly concerned about one's body and weight and having a history of dieting (George & Franko, 2010). Teenage girls are at risk when they frequently watch TV shows that emphasize attractive, thin characters and when their friends frequently talk about weight and diet constantly to stay thin (Grabe, Hyde, & Ward, 2008; Rancourt et al., 2013).

The meta-analysis also identified some risk factors that are unique to anorexia and bulimia. For example, overprotective parenting is associated with anorexia but not bulimia. In contrast, obesity in childhood is associated with bulimia but not anorexia.

Although eating disorders are more common in girls, boys make up about 10% of diagnosed cases of eating disorders. Because boys with eating disorders are far less common, researchers have conducted much less research with males. However, some of the known risk factors are childhood obesity, low self-esteem, pressure from parents and peers to lose weight, and participating in sports that emphasize being lean (Ricciardelli & McCabe, 2004; Shoemaker & Furman, 2009).

Fortunately, there are programs to help protect teens from eating disorders (Stice & Shaw, 2004). The most effective programs are designed for at-risk youth (e.g., teens who are unhappy with their body). These programs work to change attitudes toward being thin and ways to resist social pressure to be thin. One such program is described in the "Focus on Research" feature.

Focus on Research

Evaluating a Program for Preventing Eating Disorders

Who were the investigators, and what was the aim of the study? One way to prevent teenage girls from developing eating disorders is help them see faults in the thin female body that is often idealized in the media. Teens who participate in activities critiquing this ideal are less prone to eating disorders; for example, they no longer find the thin ideal as attractive, they're less likely to diet, and they report fewer symptoms of eating disorders. However, the research demonstrating the effectiveness of this prevention has been conducted under highly controlled conditions (e.g., in a research center, with facilitators who are highly trained and closely monitored); Eric Stice and his colleagues (2009) wanted to confirm that the prevention would work when administered in a more realistic setting, in this case by school personnel (e.g., nurses, counselors) in a high school.

How did the investigators measure the topic of interest? Stice and his colleagues recruited high-school girls who had concerns about their body image. Half the girls were assigned to a control condition in which they were given a brochure describing eating disorders and suggesting ways to improve one's body image. The other half were assigned to an intervention condition in which they attended four 1-hour sessions that included a variety of exercises designed to show girls the costs of the thin ideal. For example, they engaged in role play in which they tried to convince group leaders why girls shouldn't pursue the thin ideal and they completed homework in which they listed pressures they experienced to be thin and ways to resist those pressures. Before the intervention started and at 1, 6, and 12 months after it ended, girls in both groups completed questionnaires measuring their adherence to the thin ideal, their body dissatisfaction, their dieting behavior, and their symptoms of eating disorders.

Who were the participants in the study? The researchers tested 306 adolescent girls; 139 in the intervention condition and 167 in the control condition.

What was the design of the study? This study was experimental because Stice and his colleagues were interested in comparing the impact of the prevention program, relative to the control condition, on adolescent girls' attitudes and behaviors related to eating disorders. The researchers did not investigate age differences, so the study was neither cross-sectional nor longitudinal.

Were there ethical concerns with the study? No. The researchers obtained informed consent from the adolescents and from their parents. The measures and the prevention program posed no obvious risks to participants. Any girls in either condition who showed symptoms of eating disorders were referred for treatment.

What were the results? The results were similar for the different outcome measures. For simplicity, I focus on dieting behavior, which was measured with a questionnaire that included items such as "Do you try to eat less at meal times than you would like to eat?" and "Do you deliberately eat foods that are slimming?" Scores on the scale ranged from 1 (never) to 5 (always). The results, shown in Figure 4-5, indicate that at the pretest girls in both groups occasionally endorsed dieting-related behaviors. What's noteworthy is that these responses were reasonably stable for girls in the control condition but declined for girls in the prevention group. In other words, the prevention condition caused girls to be less likely to report dieting-related behaviors.

What did the investigators conclude? These findings, like the prior work, illustrate that girls change their body- and eating-related attitudes and behaviors after participating in a prevention emphasizing the costs and shortcomings of an ideal thin body. As Stice and his colleagues put it, "the findings from the present trial suggest that positive intervention effects still emerge when real-world providers deliver

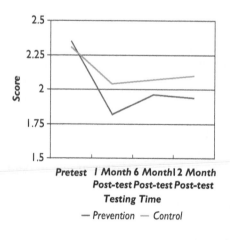

Figure 4-5

the prevention program in ecologically valid settings with a heterogeneous population" (p. 831).

What converging evidence would strengthen these conclusions? All four outcome measures were obtained from questionnaires completed by the adolescents themselves. An obvious way to provide converging evidence would be to measure some of these outcomes differently, such as by asking parents to describe their daughter's dieting-related behaviors, by using experimental tasks to estimate body dissatisfaction, or by obtaining physiological measures that reflect eating disorders.

Programs like the one described in the "Focus on Research" feature are effective: At-risk adolescents who participate in these programs are more satisfied with their appearance and less likely to diet or overeat (Stice, South, & Shaw, 2012). For those teens affected by eating disorders, treatment is available: Like prevention programs, treatment typically focuses on modifying key attitudes and behaviors (Puhl & Brownell, 2005).

Obesity

LO6   Why do some children become obese? How can they lose weight permanently?

Ricardo, the boy in this module's opening vignette, is overweight; he is heavy for his height. **The technical definition for obesity is based on the body mass index (BMI), which is an adjusted ratio of weight to height.** Children and adolescents who are in the upper 5% (very heavy for their height) are defined as being obese. Childhood obesity in the United States has reached epidemic proportions. In the past 25 to 30 years, the number of overweight children has doubled and the number of overweight adolescents has tripled, so that today roughly one child or adolescent out of six is overweight (U.S. Department of Health and Human Services, 2010). This trend is not unique to the United States: it's evident in many developed nations and in developing nations as they adopt diets and lifestyles like those in Western countries (World Health Organization, 2010).

Like the boy in the photo, overweight youngsters are often unpopular, have low self-esteem, and do poorly in school (Gable, Krull, & Chang, 2012; Puhl & Latner, 2007). Furthermore, throughout life they are at risk for many medical problems, including high blood pressure and diabetes, because the vast majority of overweight children and adolescents become overweight adults (U.S. Department of Health and Human Services, 2010).

No single factor causes children to become obese. Instead, several factors contribute, including:

Childhood obesity has reached epidemic proportions in the United States and in other parts of the world.

- Heredity—Obesity runs in families, showing that genes contribute, perhaps by causing some people to overeat, to be sedentary, or to be less able to convert fat to fuel (Cheung & Mao, 2012).
- Parents—Many parents urge children to "clean their plates" even when the children are no longer hungry and other parents routinely use food to comfort children who are upset; these practices cause children to rely on external cues to eat instead of eating only when they're hungry (Coelho et al., 2009; Wansink & Sobal, 2007).
- Sedentary lifestyle—Children are more prone to obesity when they are physically inactive, such as watching television instead of playing outdoors (Tremblay et al., 2011).

Q&A QUESTION 4.2

Joshua is a 10-year-old who is 25 pounds overweight. What can he and his parents do to help him lose weight?

• Too little sleep—Children and adolescents who do not sleep enough tend to gain weight, perhaps because being awake longer affords them more opportunities to eat, by increasing their feelings of hunger, or by making them too tired to exercise (Magee & Hale, 2012).

Individually these factors may not lead to obesity. But collectively they may put children on the path to obesity: A child is at greater risk if he or she is genetically prone to overeat, is sedentary, and chronically sleepy. To understand childhood obesity, we need to consider all of these risk factors, as well as the amount and quality of food that's available in the child's environment (Harrison et al., 2011).

Obese youth can lose weight. The most effective weight-loss programs focus on changing children's eating habits and encouraging them to become more active. Children set goals for eating and exercise; parents help them set realistic goals, reward them for progress, and monitor their own eating and exercising. When programs incorporate these features, obese children do lose weight (Oude Luttikhuis et al., 2009; West et al., 2010). However, even after losing weight, many children participating in these programs remain overweight. Consequently, it is best to avoid overweight and obesity in the first place by encouraging children to eat healthfully and to be active physically.

Disease

LO7 **What diseases are life-threatening to children around the world?**

Around the world, nearly 8 million children die before their fifth birthday; countries in Africa account for more than half of these childhood deaths (World Health Organization, 2013). These are staggering numbers—roughly the equivalent of *all* U.S. 1-, 2-, and 3-year-olds dying in a single year. The leading killers of young children worldwide are pneumonia, diarrhea, malaria, and malnutrition (World Health Organization, 2012). The majority of these deaths can be prevented with proven, cost-effective treatments. For example, diarrhea kills by dehydrating youngsters, yet children can avert death by promptly drinking water that contains salt and potassium.

As part of a vigorous effort to prevent childhood illness, for the past two decades the World Health Organization (WHO) has worked to vaccinate children worldwide. Because of these efforts, vaccination rates have skyrocketed in many developing countries. WHO has also joined with the United Nations Children's Fund (UNICEF) to create Integrated Management of Childhood Illness (IMCI), a program to combat pneumonia, diarrhea, measles, malaria, and malnutrition (World Health Organization, 2004). Because many children who are ill have symptoms related to two or more of these five conditions, IMCI uses an integrated strategy that focuses on the overall health of the child. One component of IMCI is training health care professionals to become more skilled in dealing with childhood illnesses. A second component is improving health care systems so that they respond more effectively to childhood illness (e.g., ensuring that required medicines are available). A third component involves changing family and community practices to make them more conducive to healthy growth. For example, to protect children from mosquitoes that

One way to protect young children from disease is to adopt practices that foster healthy growth, such as having them sleep in netting that protects them from mosquitoes that carry malaria.

carry malaria, children are encouraged to sleep in netting, as the baby in the photo is doing. IMCI has been adopted in more than 60 countries and is playing a pivotal role in improving children's health worldwide (Bhutta et al., 2010; Victora et al., 2006).

Accidents

LO8 **What accidents are particularly risky for children and adolescents?**

In the United States, most infant deaths are due to medical conditions associated with birth defects or low birth weight. From age 1 on, however, children are far more likely to die from accidents than from any other single cause (Federal Interagency Forum on Child and Family Statistics, 2013). Motor vehicle accidents are the most common cause of accidental death in children. Regrettably, many of these deaths could have been prevented had children and adolescents been wearing seat belts or had infants and children been restrained properly in an approved infant car seat like the one shown in the photo. Without such restraint, children and adolescents typically suffer massive head injuries when thrown through the windshield or onto the road.

A simple way to protect infants, toddlers, and young children is to insist that they be restrained in an approved seat when riding in a car.

Many infants and toddlers also drown, die from burns, or suffocate. Often these deaths result because young children are supervised inadequately (Morrongiello & Schell, 2010; Petrass & Blitvich, 2013). All too common, for example, are reports of young children who wander away, jump, or fall into an unfenced swimming pool, then drown. Parents need to remember that children are often eager to explore their environs, but are unable to recognize many hazards. Parents must constantly keep a protective eye on their young children. With older children, parents must be careful that they don't overestimate their children's skills. Some accidents happen because parents have too much confidence in their children's cognitive and motor skills. They may allow a child like the girl in the photo to ride to school in a bike lane adjacent to a street filled with commuters, even though many children may not consistently pay attention while biking or sometimes attempt to cross busy streets when there's not enough time to do so safely (Morrongiello, Klemencic, & Corbett, 2008; Stevens et al., 2013).[2]

Children sometimes have accidents because parents overestimate their children's abilities and thus allow them to engage in dangerous activities, such as riding bikes on unsafe streets.

For adolescents, motor vehicle accidents remain the leading cause of death. The difference, of course, is that adolescents are no longer passengers but are driving. Sadly, far too many adolescents are killed because they drive too fast, drive while drunk or texting, or drive without wearing a seat belt (Centers for Disease Control and Prevention, 2012). Among teenage boys, firearms represent a leading cause of death. In fact, firearms kill more 15- to 19-year-old African American youth than any other single cause (Federal Interagency Forum on Child and Family Statistics, 2013).

---

[2] As a 10-year-old, my son Matt crashed his new bike right into the back of a parked car because he was too busy watching the gears shift. Fortunately, he escaped with just a few scrapes, but this illustrates how easily a childhood lapse in concentration can lead to a cycling accident.

Although the term *accident* implies that the event happened by chance and no one was to blame, most accidents involving children and adolescents can be foreseen and either prevented or steps taken to reduce injury. In the case of automobile accidents, for example, the simple step of wearing a seat belt enhances safety immensely. Accidents involving firearms can be reduced by making guns less accessible to children and adolescents (e.g., locking away guns and ammunition separately). School- and community-based safety programs represent a cost-effective way to reduce childhood accidents (Nilsen, 2007; Schwebel, Davis, & O'Neal, 2012). Children can learn safe ways of walking or riding their bikes to school, then be allowed to practice these skills while supervised by an adult. With programs like these, children readily learn behaviors that foster safety.

 ## Check Your Learning

RECALL Summarize the factors that put adolescent girls at risk for anorexia nervosa and for bulimia nervosa.

What are the leading causes of death for toddlers and preschool children? For adolescents?

INTERPRET Distinguish the biological factors that contribute to obesity from the environmental factors.

APPLY How does malnutrition show the impact that children can have on their own development?

 # 4.3 The Developing Nervous System

OUTLINE	LEARNING OBJECTIVES
Organization of the Mature Brain	**LO9** What are the parts of a nerve cell? How is the brain organized?
The Developing Brain	**LO10** When is the brain formed in prenatal development? When do different regions of the brain begin to function?

While crossing the street, 10-year-old Martin was struck by a passing car. He was in a coma for a week, but then gradually became more alert, and now he is aware of his surroundings. Needless to say, Martin's mother is grateful that he survived the accident, but she wonders what the future holds for her son.

The physical changes that we see as children grow are impressive, but even more awe-inspiring are the changes we cannot see, those involving the brain and the nervous system. An infant's feelings of hunger, a child's laugh, and an adolescent's efforts to learn algebra all reflect the functioning of the brain and the rest of the nervous system. All the information that children learn, including language and other cognitive skills, is stored in the brain.

How does the brain accomplish these many tasks? How is the brain affected by an injury like the one that Martin suffered? To begin to answer these questions, let's look at how the brain is organized in adults.

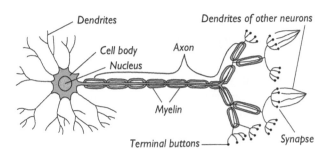

Figure 4-6

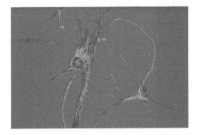

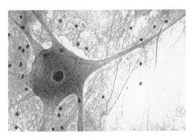

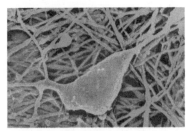

Neurons come in many shapes, but they all have the same function of transmitting information.

Organization of the Mature Brain

LO9 What are the parts of a nerve cell? How is the brain organized?

The basic unit of the brain and the rest of the nervous system is the *neuron,* **a cell that specializes in receiving and transmitting information.** Neurons come in many different shapes, as you can see in the three photos. Figure 4-6 makes it easier to understand the basic parts found in all neurons. **The** *cell body* **at the center of the neuron contains the basic biological machinery that keeps the neuron alive. The receiving end of the neuron, the** *dendrite,* **looks like a tree with many branches.** The highly branched dendrite allows one neuron to receive input from many thousands of other neurons (Morgan & Gibson, 1991). **The tubelike structure at the other end of the cell body is the** *axon,* **which sends information to other neurons. The axon is wrapped in** *myelin,* **a fatty sheath that allows it to transmit information more rapidly.** The boost in neural speed from myelin is like the difference between driving and flying: from about 6 feet per second to 50 feet per second. **At the end of the axon are small knobs called** *terminal buttons,* **which release** *neurotransmitters,* **chemicals that carry information to nearby neurons.** Finally, you'll see that the terminal buttons of one axon don't actually touch the dendrites of other neurons. **The gap between one neuron and the next is a** *synapse.* Neurotransmitters cross synapses to carry information between neurons.

Take 50 to 100 billion neurons like these and you have the beginnings of a human brain. An adult's brain weighs a little less than 3 pounds, and it easily fits into your hands. **The wrinkled surface of the brain is the** *cerebral cortex;* **made up of about 10 billion neurons, the cortex regulates many of the functions that we think of as distinctly human. The cortex consists of left and right halves, called** *hemispheres,* **that are linked by millions of axons in a thick bundle called the** *corpus callosum.* The characteristics that you value most—your engaging personality, your "way with words," your uncanny knack for reading others—are all controlled by specific regions of the cortex, many of which are shown in Figure 4-7.

Personality and your ability to make and carry out plans are largely functions of an area at the front of the cortex that is called, appropriately, the *frontal cortex.* For most people, the ability to produce and understand language, to reason, and to compute is largely because of neurons in the cortex of the left hemisphere. Also for most people, artistic and musical abilities, perception of spatial relations, and the ability to recognize faces and emotions come from neurons in the right hemisphere.

Now that we know a bit of the organization of the mature brain, let's look at how the brain develops and begins to function.

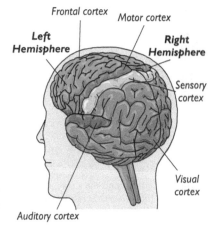

Figure 4-7

The Developing Brain

LO10 When is the brain formed in prenatal development? When do different regions of the brain begin to function?

Scientists who study brain development are guided by several key questions: How and when do brain structures develop? When do different brain regions begin to function? Why do brain regions take on different functions? In this section, we'll see how research has answered each question.

Emerging Brain Structures   We know from Module 3.1 that the beginnings of the brain can be traced to the period of the zygote. **At roughly 3 weeks after conception, a group of cells forms a flat structure known as the** *neural plate*. At 4 weeks, the neural plate folds to form a tube that ultimately becomes the brain and spinal cord. When the ends of the tube fuse shut, neurons are produced in one small region of the neural tube. Production of neurons begins about 10 weeks after conception, and by 28 weeks the developing brain has virtually all the neurons it will ever have. During these weeks, neurons form at the incredible rate of more than 3,000 per second. Surprisingly, many of these newly formed neurons are short lived: they are programmed to die, creating space for nearby neurons to form connections (Stiles, 2008).

From the neuron-manufacturing site in the neural tube, neurons migrate to their final positions in the brain. The brain is built in stages, beginning with the innermost layers. Neurons in the deepest layer are positioned first, followed by neurons in the second layer, and so on. This layering process continues until all six layers of the mature brain are in place, which occurs about 7 months after conception (Rakic, 1995). As you can see in Figure 4-8, the nerve cells move to the top by wrapping themselves around supporting cells, just as a snake might climb a pole.

In the fourth month of prenatal development, axons begin to acquire myelin—the fatty wrap that speeds neural transmission. This process continues through infancy and into childhood and adolescence (Paus, 2010). Neurons that carry sensory information are the first to acquire myelin; neurons in the cortex are among the last. You can see the effect of more myelin in improved coordination and reaction times. The older the infant and, later, the child, the more rapid and coordinated are his or her reactions. (We'll talk more about this phenomenon when we discuss fine-motor skills in Module 5.3.)

In the months after birth, the brain grows rapidly. Axons and dendrites grow longer, and, like a maturing tree, dendrites quickly sprout new limbs. As the number of dendrites increases, so does the number of synapses, reaching a peak at about the first birthday. **Soon after, synapses begin to disappear gradually, a phenomenon known as** *synaptic pruning*. Thus, beginning in infancy and continuing into early adolescence, the brain goes through its own version of "downsizing,"

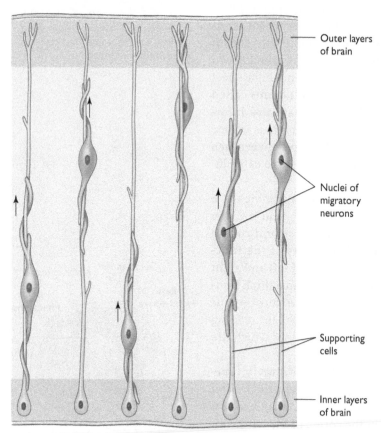

Outer layers of brain

Nuclei of migratory neurons

Supporting cells

Inner layers of brain

Just as a snake might climb a pole, neurons migrate to their final location in the brain by wrapping themselves around supporting cells.

Figure 4-8

weeding out unnecessary connections between neurons. This pruning depends on the activity of the neural circuits: synapses that are active are preserved but those that aren't active are eliminated (Webb, Monk, & Nelson, 2001). Pruning is completed first for brain regions associated with sensory and motor functions. Regions associated with basic language and spatial skills are completed next, followed by regions associated with attention and planning (Casey et al., 2005).

Growth of a Specialized Brain   Because the mature brain is specialized, with different psychological functions localized in particular regions, developmental researchers have had a keen interest in determining the origins and time course of the brain's specialization. For many years, the only clues to specialization came from children who had suffered brain injury. The logic here was to link the location of the injury to the impairment that results: If a region of the brain regulates a particular function (e.g., understanding speech), then damage to that region should impair the function.

Fortunately, relatively few children suffer brain injury. But this meant that scientists needed other methods to study brain development. **One of them,** *electroencephalography*, **involves measuring the brain's electrical activity from electrodes placed on the scalp, as shown in the top photo.** If a region of the brain regulates a function, then the region should show distinctive patterns of electrical activity while a child is using that function. **A newer technique,** *functional magnetic resonance imaging (fMRI)*, **uses magnetic fields to track the flow of blood in the brain.** With this method, shown in the bottom photo, the research participant's brain is literally wrapped in a powerful magnet that can track blood flow in the brain as participants perform different tasks (Casey et al., 2005). The logic here is that active brain regions need more oxygen, which increases blood flow to those regions.

Neither of these methods is perfect; each has drawbacks. For example, fMRI is used sparingly because it's expensive and participants must lie still for several minutes at a time. Despite these limitations, the combined outcome of research using these different approaches has identified some general principles that describe the brain's specialization as children develop.

One way to study brain functioning is to record the brain's electrical activity using electrodes placed on a child's scalp.

1. **Specialization occurs early in development.** Maybe you expect the newborn's brain to be completely unspecialized? In fact, many regions are already specialized early in infancy. For example, early specialization of the frontal cortex is shown by the finding that damage to this region in infancy results in impaired decision making and abnormal emotional responses (Anderson et al., 2001). Similarly, studies using electroencephalography show that a newborn infant's left hemisphere generates more electrical activity in response to speech than the right hemisphere (Molfese & Burger-Judisch, 1991). Thus, by the time a child is born, the cortex of the left hemisphere is already specialized for language processing. As we'll see in Chapter 9, this specialization allows language to develop rapidly during infancy. Finally, studies of children with prenatal brain damage indicate that by infancy the right hemisphere is specialized for understanding certain kinds of spatial relations (Stiles et al., 2005).

2. **Specialization takes two specific forms.** First, with development the brain regions active during processing become more focused, like a thunderstorm that covers a huge region but then concentrates that same power in a much smaller region

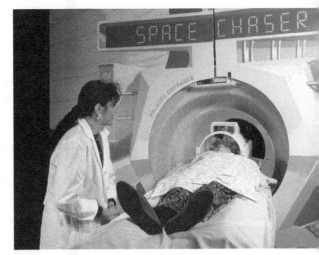

In functional magnetic resonance imaging (fMRI), a powerful magnet tracks the flow of blood to different brain regions, which shows parts of the brain that are active as children perform different tasks.

(Durston et al., 2006). Second, the kinds of stimuli that trigger brain activity shift from being general to being specific (Johnson, Grossman, & Cohen Kadosh, 2009). Processing of face-like stimuli by the brain shows both trends: it becomes focused in a particular area (the fusiform gyrus) and becomes tuned narrowly to faces (Cohen Kadosh et al., 2013; Scherf et al., 2007).

3. **Different brain systems specialize at different rates.** Think of a new housing development involving construction of many multistory homes. In each house, the first floor is completed before higher floors, but some houses are finished before others are even started. In this same way, brain regions involving basic sensory and perceptual processes specialize well before those regions necessary for higher-order processes (Fox, Levitt, & Nelson, 2010). Similarly, some brain systems that are sensitive to reward (especially to rewards from peers) may reach maturity in adolescence, but the systems responsible for self-control aren't fully specialized until adulthood (Casey & Caudle, 2013; Galván, 2013).

This differential rate of brain development may be one reason why adolescents engage in such risky behavior (e.g., drinking while driving, unprotected sex): The brain centers associated with self-control are immature relative to those associated with reward (Somerville & Casey, 2010). And these findings are leading to changes in laws that apply to adolescents, as we'll see in the Child Development and Family Policy feature.

Child Development and Family Policy
Teenagers and the Law

Child development experts recognize different stages in development (e.g., Piaget's four stages of cognitive development) but U.S. laws typically distinguish just two stages—minors who do not have adult privileges or responsibilities and adults, who do. Minors gain adult privileges and responsibilities at different ages, depending on the privilege. For example, in most U.S. states, adolescents can drive an automobile at 16 years of age and can purchase alcohol at age 21.

Traditionally, decisions about the best age for adolescents to acquire adult privileges were not based on child-development research. However, that's changed recently (Bonnie & Scott, 2013). Driving is a good example. In Module 4.2 I mentioned that automobile accidents are the leading cause of death of U.S. teenagers. Most of those deaths occur when teenagers have peers as passengers, perhaps because peers may distract teenage drivers or encourage them to drive dangerously (Laird, 2011). However, based on research showing adolescents' risk-taking and their sensitivity to peer reward, all U.S. states have implemented graduated driver licensing. The programs vary from state to state but extend the learning phase and include an intermediate phase that limits driving with peers and driving after dark. These new policies have been effective: Teen-age drivers are having fewer accidents overall and fewer that result in death (McCartt & Teoh, 2011; Zhu et al., 2013).

Another instance in which research on adolescents' brain development has influenced policy involves capital punishment—executing a convicted offender. In the late 1980s, the U.S. Supreme Court banned the use of capital punishment with juveniles who were not yet 16 when they committed the capital offense (Thompson v. Oklahoma, 1988) but upheld its use with juveniles who were at least 16 years old at the time of the crime (Stanford v. Kentucky, 1989).

This changed with a case heard before court in 2004. A 17-year-old boy had murdered a woman by tying her up and throwing her into a river to drown. The boy confessed to the crime; a jury found him guilty and recommended the death sentence, which the judge imposed. The boy appealed the death sentence and the case eventually ended up with the U.S. Supreme Court.

The American Psychological Association filed a "friend of the court" brief arguing that the death sentence for crimes committed as an adolescent constituted cruel and unusual punishment (American Psychological Association, 2004, July 19). The brief argued that because of their immature brain development adolescents are more impulsive, risk-prone, and less able than adults to anticipate the consequences of their actions. It also argued that adolescents were more vulnerable than adults to peer pressure and less capable than adults of contributing to their own defense. The Court cited these arguments in striking down capital punishment of adolescents because it was cruel and unusual punishment (Roper v. Simmons, 2005). Subsequently the Court used the same logic to rule that a sentence of mandatory life imprisonment without parole could not be imposed on adolescents (Miller v. Alabama, 2012).

Thus, behavioral and neuroscience research on adolescent risk-taking has informed public policy concerning driver licensing and capital punishment. Perhaps this same research will be used to determine the soundness of other laws affecting adolescents, such as those concerning the ages at which teenagers can (a) purchase alcohol, (b) agree to have sexual intercourse, and (c) obtain birth control pills without a parent's consent.

4. **Successful specialization requires stimulation from the environment.** To return to the analogy of the brain as a house, the newborn's brain is perhaps best conceived as a partially finished, partially furnished house: A general organizational framework is present, with preliminary neural pathways designed to perform certain functions. The left hemisphere has some language pathways and the frontal cortex has some emotion-related pathways. However, completing the typical organization of the mature brain requires input from the environment (Greenough & Black, 1992). **In this case, environmental input influences** *experience-expectant growth*: **Over the course of evolution, human infants have typically been exposed to some forms of stimulation that are used to adjust brain wiring, strengthening some circuits and eliminating others.** For example, under normal conditions, healthy human infants experience moving visual patterns (e.g., faces) and varied sounds (e.g., voices). Just as a newly planted seed depends on a water-filled environment for growth, a developing brain depends on environmental stimulation to fine-tune circuits for vision, hearing, and other systems (Black, 2003).

Of course, experiences later in life also sculpt the brain (and we'll see this in several chapters later in this book). *Experience-dependent growth* **denotes changes in the brain that are not linked to specific points in development and that vary across individuals and across cultures.** Experience-dependent growth is illustrated by a preschool child's learning of a classmate's name, an elementary-school child's discovery of a shortcut home from school, and an adolescent's mastery of the functions of a new cell phone. In each case, brain circuits are modified in response to an individual's experiences. With today's technology, we can't see these daily changes in the brain. But when they accumulate over many years—as when individuals acquire expertise in

The region of the brain that controls the fingers of the left hand is probably well developed in this skilled cellist.

 QUESTION 4.3

Ashley was distraught when her 2-year-old daughter fell down a full flight of steps and hit her head against a concrete wall, which led to a trip to the hospital. What could you say to reassure Ashley about her daughter's prognosis?

a skill—brain changes can be detected. For example, skilled cellists like the one in the photo have extensive brain regions devoted to controlling the fingers of the left hand as they are positioned on the strings (Elbert et al., 1995). Similarly, years of driving a taxicab produces changes in the hippocampus, a region of the brain implicated in navigation and way-finding (Maguire, Woollett, & Spiers, 2006).

5. **The immature brain's lack of specialization confers a benefit: greater plasticity.** Just as the structures in a housing development follow a plan that specifies the location of each house and its design, brain development usually follows a predictable course that reflects epigenetic interactions (page 72) between the genetic code and required environmental input. Sometimes, however, the normal course is disrupted. A person may experience events harmful to the brain (e.g., injured in an accident) or may be deprived of some essential ingredients of successful "brain building" (e.g., necessary experiences).

Research that examines the consequences of these atypical experiences shows that the brain has some flexibility: it is plastic. Remember Martin, the child in the vignette whose brain was damaged when he was struck by a car? His language skills were impaired after the accident. This was not surprising, because the left hemisphere of Martin's brain had absorbed most of the force of the collision. But within several months, Martin had completely recovered his language skills. Apparently other neurons took over language-related processing from the damaged neurons. This recovery of function is not uncommon, particularly for young children, and shows that the brain is plastic. In other words, young children often recover more skills after brain injury than older children and adults, apparently because functions are more easily reassigned in the young brain (Kolb & Teskey, 2012; Demir, Levine, & Goldin-Meadow, 2010).

There are, however, limits to plasticity. These are shown by studies of Romanian children who were abandoned soon after birth and lived for months—sometimes years—in orphanages where care was appalling: infants and toddlers were provided food and shelter but few toys, had minimal speech with caregivers, and did not form personal relationships with caregivers. Following adoption by families in the United Kingdom, these children progressed rapidly in their cognitive development but did not catch up to the normal course of development; what's more, cognitive deficits were greater for children who had stayed longer in the orphanages (Rutter et al., 2010). Experiences later in these children's development could not compensate for the extreme deprivation in infancy, showing that the brain is not completely plastic.

Brain-Based Education? Greater understanding of brain development and the impact of experience has led many scientists, educators, and parents to hope that this knowledge could lead to improved education. After all, if the brain is the organ of learning and the goal of school is to promote students' learning, then knowledge of brain development should yield better ways to teach. Many have jumped on the "brain-based education" bandwagon, and it is true that research on brain development is providing valuable insights into some specific academic skills, such as the nature of children's reading problems (Szücks & Goswami, 2007). However, there is reason to be cautious about redesigning an entire curriculum based on our current understanding of brain development. Many critics point out that although our current understanding of brain development may lead to a handful of general statements about the conditions that foster children's learning, we know too little to devise full-fledged curricula that are "brain-friendly" (Sylvan & Christodoulou,

2010). As Kurt Fischer, Director of Harvard's Mind, Brain, and Education Program, and his colleague Mary Helen Immordino-Yang (2008, p. xviii) put it,

> Unfortunately, most of what is called "brain-based education" has no grounding at all in brain or cognitive science.... In typical claims for brain-based education, beliefs about learning and schooling are restated in the language of brain science, but there is no brain research on which those restatements are based.

Still, there is reason to be optimistic that coming decades will provide the foundation needed for a curriculum based on solid understanding of the emerging brain (Fischer & Immordino-Yang, 2008).

 ## Check Your Learning

RECALL List the major parts of a nerve cell and the major regions of the cerebral cortex.

Describe evidence that shows the brain's plasticity.

INTERPRET Compare growth of the brain before birth with growth of the brain after birth.

APPLY How does the development of the brain, as described in this module, compare to the general pattern of physical growth described in Module 4.1?

 # Unifying Themes Connections

This chapter is an excellent opportunity to highlight the theme that *development in different domains is connected.* Consider the impact of the timing of puberty. Whether a child matures early or late affects social development (early-maturing girls are often less popular). Or consider the impact of malnutrition. Malnourished youngsters are often listless, which affects how their parents interact with them (they're less likely to provide stimulating experiences). Less stimulation, in turn, slows the children's intellectual development. Physical, cognitive, social, and personality development are linked: Change in one area generally leads to change of some kind in the others.

See for Yourself

Children love playgrounds. Unfortunately, hundreds of thousands of U.S. children are injured on playgrounds annually. Some of these accidents could have been prevented had parents (or other adults) been present, or if parents who were physically present had been paying closer attention to the children at play. Go to a local playground and watch children as they play. Notice how many children unknowingly put themselves at risk as they play. Also notice how well the children's play is monitored by adults. See for yourself!

Summary

 ## Physical Growth

Features of Human Growth

Physical growth is particularly rapid during infancy, slows during the elementary-school years, and then accelerates again during adolescence. Physical growth refers not only to increases in height and weight, but also to development of muscle, fat, and bones.

Children are taller today than in previous generations. Average heights vary around the world, and within any culture there is considerable variation in the normal range of height.

Mechanisms of Physical Growth

Physical growth depends on sleep, in part because most growth hormone is secreted while children sleep. Nutrition is also important, particularly during periods of rapid growth, such as infancy and adolescence. Breast-feeding provides babies with all the nutrients they need and has other advantages. Many children and adolescents do not get adequate nutrients because of poor diets.

The Adolescent Growth Spurt and Puberty

Puberty includes the adolescent growth spurt as well as sexual maturation. Girls typically begin the growth spurt earlier than boys, who acquire more muscle, less fat, and greater heart and lung capacities. Sexual maturation, which includes primary and secondary sex characteristics, occurs in predictable sequences for boys and girls.

Pubertal changes occur when the pituitary gland signals the adrenal gland, ovaries, and testes to secrete hormones that initiate physical changes. The timing of puberty is influenced by health, nutrition, and social environment.

Pubertal change affects adolescents' psychological functioning. Teens become concerned about their appearance. Early maturation tends to be harmful for girls and, to a lesser extent, for boys.

Challenges to Healthy Growth

Malnutrition

Malnutrition is a global problem—including in the United States—that is particularly harmful during infancy, when growth is so rapid. Malnutrition can cause brain damage, affecting children's intelligence and ability to pay attention. Treating malnutrition requires improving children's diet and training their parents to provide stimulating environments.

Eating Disorders: Anorexia and Bulimia

Anorexia and bulimia are eating disorders that typically affect adolescent girls. They are characterized by an irrational fear of being overweight. Several factors contribute to these disorders, including heredity, a childhood history of eating problems, and, during adolescence, a preoccupation with one's body and weight. Eating disorders are far less common in boys; risk factors include childhood obesity, low self-esteem, social pressure to lose weight, and participation in certain sports. Treatment and prevention programs emphasize changing adolescents' views of thinness and their eating-related behaviors.

Obesity

Many obese children and adolescents are unpopular, have low self-esteem, and are at risk for medical disorders.

Obesity reflects heredity, influences of parents, and a sedentary lifestyle. In effective programs for treating obesity in youth, children are encouraged to change their eating habits and to become more active; their parents help them set realistic goals and monitor their progress.

Disease

Millions of children around the world die annually from pneumonia, diarrhea, malaria, and malnutrition. Integrated Management of Childhood Illness is a new, integrated approach designed to promote children's health.

Accidents

In the United States, children and adolescents are more likely to die from accidents than any other single cause. Many of these fatalities involve motor vehicles and could be prevented if passengers were restrained properly. Older children and adolescents are sometimes involved in accidents because parents overestimate their abilities.

The Developing Nervous System

Organization of the Mature Brain

Nerve cells, called neurons, are composed of a cell body, a dendrite, and an axon. The mature brain consists of billions of neurons organized into nearly identical left and right hemispheres connected by the corpus callosum. The frontal cortex is associated with personality and goal-directed behavior; the cortex in the left hemisphere, with language; and the cortex in the right hemisphere, with nonverbal processes.

The Developing Brain

Brain structure begins in prenatal development, when neurons form at an incredible rate. After birth, neurons in the central nervous system become wrapped in myelin, allowing them to transmit information more rapidly. Throughout childhood, unused synapses disappear gradually through a process of pruning.

Brain specialization is evident in infancy; further specialization involves more focused brain areas and narrowing of stimuli that trigger brain activity. Different systems specialize at different rates. Specialization depends on stimulation from the environment. The relative lack of specialization in the immature brain makes it better able to recover from injury.

Test Yourself

1. Which of the following is incorrect about average physical growth?
   a. It is particularly rapid during the elementary school years.
   b. It is uniform in all countries.
   c. It varies from one generation to the next.

2. Nutritional needs during infancy are great because _____ requires a large amount of energy.
   a. respiration
   b. an infant's high activity level
   c. growth

3. Compared to bottle-fed babies, breastfed babies
   a. are ill more often.
   b. are less prone to diarrhea and constipation.
   c. have more difficulty transitioning to solid foods.

4. The onset of puberty
   a. is earlier in boys than in girls.
   b. is earlier in girls who experience stress than in girls who have less stress.
   c. is not influenced by genetics.

5. According to paternal investment theory, when the environment is unstable with few resources, it is adaptive for girls to _____.
   a. mature and reproduce early
   b. mature and reproduce late
   c. not to reproduce

6. Anorexia nervosa is an eating disorder characterized by _____.
   a. binge eating periods
   b. a very large ratio of weight to height
   c. refusal to eat due to persistent fear of weight gain

7. In _____ adolescents alternate between binge eating and purging through self-induced vomiting or with laxatives.
   a. anorexia nervosa
   b. obesity
   c. bulimia

8. The basic unit of the brain and the nervous system is the _____.
   a. neuron
   b. synapse
   c. cell

9. The leading cause of death in young children worldwide is/are _____.
   a. infectious diseases
   b. accidents
   c. birth defects

10. Synaptic pruning _____.
    a. refers to a neuron's acquisition of a fatty wrap
    b. eliminates unnecessary connections between neurons
    c. begins in early adolescence

11. Which of the following is *correct* about brain specialization?
    a. Brain specialization occurs late in development.
    b. Different brain systems specialize at different rates.
    c. Successful specialization does not require stimulation from the environment.

12. Early maturation in adolescence often leads to _____.
    a. low confidence and psychological problems
    b. better relationships
    c. high confidence and self esteem

13. Synaptic pruning is completed first for brain regions associated with _____.
    a. sensory and motor functions
    b. decision making
    c. language

14. Which of the following is *incorrect* regarding brain specialization?
    a. Different brain systems specialize at different rates.
    b. The immature brain's lack of specialization confers a benefit: greater plasticity.
    c. Specialization occurs late in development.

15. Personality, planning ability, and decision making are the major functions of the _____.
    a. right hemisphere
    b. left hemisphere
    c. frontal cortex

Key Terms

anorexia nervosa   133
axon   139
body mass index (BMI)   135
bulimia nervosa   133
cell body   139
cerebral cortex   139
corpus callosum   139
dendrite   139
electroencephalography   141
epiphyses   121
experience-dependent growth   143

experience-expectant growth   143
frontal cortex   139
functional magnetic resonance imaging (fMRI)   141
growth hormone   122
hemispheres   139
malnutrition   131
menarche   126
myelin   139
neural plate   140
neuron   139

neurotransmitters   139
primary sex characteristics   126
puberty   125
secondary sex characteristics   126
secular growth trends   121
spermarche   126
synapse   139
synaptic pruning   140
terminal buttons   139

Chapter 5
Perceptual Processes and Motor Development

Modules

5.1 Basic Sensory and Perceptual Processes

5.2 Complex Perceptual and Attentional Processes

5.3 Motor Development

When my daughter was a toddler, she often napped when her older brother needed to practice his drums. We closed her bedroom door, of course, but the thumping of the drums was still plenty loud! The first few times this happened, she would startle when the drumming began, then soon fall back to sleep. After a few days, though, she hardly stirred when the drumming began. My daughter's behavior illustrates perception in action: Our senses are assaulted with stimulation but much of it is ignored. *Sensory and perceptual processes* **are the means by which people receive, select, modify, and organize stimulation from the world.** Sensory and perceptual processes are the first step in the complex process that eventually results in "knowing." We'll begin studying perceptual development in **Module 5.1** by looking at the origins of sensory processes in infancy. In **Module 5.2** we'll see how more complex perceptual and attentional processes develop in childhood.

Perceptual processes are closely linked to *motor skills*—**coordinated movements of the muscles and limbs.** Perception often guides a child's movement: A child uses vision to avoid obstacles. In turn, a child's movement in the environment provides enormous variety in perceptual stimulation. In **Module 5.3**, we'll see how improvements in motor skill enhance children's ability to explore, understand, and enjoy the world.

 # Basic Sensory and Perceptual Processes

LEARNING OBJECTIVES	OUTLINE
LO1 Are newborn babies able to smell and taste? Do they respond to touch and experience pain?	**Smell, Taste, and Touch**
LO2 How well do infants hear? How do they use sounds to understand their world?	**Hearing**
LO3 How accurate is infants' vision? Do infants perceive color?	**Seeing**
LO4 How do infants integrate information from different senses?	**Integrating Sensory Information**

Darla adores her 3-day-old daughter, Olivia. She loves holding her, talking to her, and simply watching her. Darla is certain that Olivia is already getting to know her, coming to recognize her face and the sound of her voice. Darla's husband, Steve, thinks Darla is crazy. He tells her, "Everyone knows that babies are born blind. And they probably can't hear much either." Darla doubts that Steve is right, but she wishes someone would tell her about babies' vision and hearing.

Darla's questions are really about her newborn daughter's sensory and perceptual skills. To help her understand, we need to remember that humans have different kinds of sense organs, each receptive to a unique kind of physical energy. For example, the retina at the back of the eye is sensitive to some types of electromagnetic energy, and sight is the result. The eardrum detects changes in air pressure, and hearing is the result. Cells at the top of the nasal passage detect airborne molecules, and smell is the result. In each case, the sense organ translates the physical stimulation into nerve impulses that are sent to the brain.

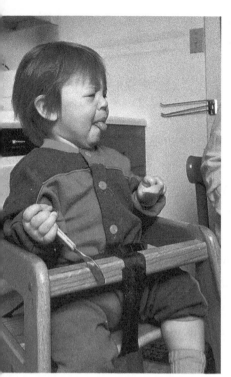

Infants and toddlers do *not* like bitter tastes!

The senses begin to function early in life, which is why this module is devoted entirely to infancy. How can we know what an infant senses? Because infants can't tell us what they smell, hear, or see, researchers have devised other ways to find out. In many studies, an investigator presents two stimuli to a baby, such as a high-pitched tone and a low-pitched tone or a sweet-tasting substance and a sour-tasting substance. Then the investigator records the baby's responses, such as heart rate, facial expression, or eye movements. If the baby consistently responds differently to the two stimuli (e.g., she looks in the direction of one tone, but not the other), the baby must be distinguishing between them.

Another approach is based on the fact that infants usually prefer novel stimuli over familiar stimuli. **When a novel stimulus is presented, babies pay much attention, but they pay less attention as it becomes more familiar, a phenomenon known as** *habituation*. Researchers use habituation to study perception by repeatedly presenting a stimulus such as a low-pitched tone until an infant barely responds. Then they present a second stimulus, such as a high-pitched tone. If the infant responds strongly, then researchers conclude that the baby distinguished the two stimuli.

In this module, you'll learn what these techniques have revealed about infants' sensory and perceptual processes. These processes are interesting in their own right—you'll see that an infant's senses are astonishingly powerful. But they are also important to study as a basis for understanding a child's complicated thoughts and feelings; before we can delve into these issues, we first need to know how skillfully infants take in information from the world around them.

Smell, Taste, and Touch

LO1   **Are newborn babies able to smell and taste? Do they respond to touch and experience pain?**

Newborns have a keen sense of smell; they respond positively to pleasant smells and negatively to unpleasant smells (Mennella & Beauchamp, 1997). They have a relaxed, contented-looking facial expression when they smell honey or chocolate, but they frown, grimace, or turn away when they smell rotten eggs or ammonia. Young babies can also recognize familiar odors. Newborns look in the direction of a pad that is saturated with their own amniotic fluid. They also turn toward a pad saturated with the odor of their mother's breast milk or her perfume (Porter & Winburg, 1999; Schaal, Soussignan, & Marlier, 2002).

Newborns also have a highly developed sense of taste. They readily differentiate salty, sour, bitter, and sweet tastes (Schwartz, Issanchou, & Nicklaus, 2009). Most infants prefer sweet and salty substances—they react to them by smiling, sucking, and licking their lips (Beauchamp & Mennella, 2011). In contrast, you can probably guess what the infant in the top photo has tasted! This grimace is typical when infants are fed bitter- or sour-tasting substances (Kaijura, Cowart, & Beauchamp, 1992). Infants are also sensitive to changes in the taste of breast milk that reflect a mother's diet. Infants nurse more after their mother has consumed a sweet-tasting substance such as vanilla (Mennella & Beauchamp, 1997).

Newborns are sensitive to touch. As I described in Module 3.4, many areas of the newborn's body respond reflexively when touched. Touching an infant's cheek, mouth, hand, or foot produces reflexive movements, documenting that infants perceive touch. What's more, babies' behavior in response to apparent pain-provoking stimuli suggests that they experience pain (Warnock & Sandrin, 2004). For example, look at the baby in the bottom photo who is receiving an inoculation. He's opened his

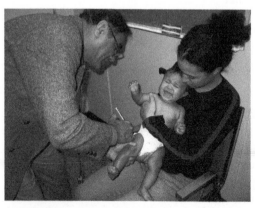

An infant's response to an inoculation—a distinctive facial expression coupled with a distinctive cry—suggests that the baby feels pain.

mouth to cry and, although we can't hear him, the sound of his cry is probably the unique pattern associated with pain. The pain cry begins suddenly, is high-pitched, and is not easily soothed. This baby is agitated, his heart rate has jumped, and he's trying to move his hands, arms, and legs (Craig et al., 1993; Goubet, Clifton, & Shah, 2001). Collectively, these signs suggest that babies experience pain.

Perceptual skills are extraordinarily useful to newborns and young babies. Smell and touch help them recognize their mothers and make it much easier for them to learn to eat. Early development of smell, taste, and touch prepares newborns and young babies to learn about the world.

Hearing

LO2   How well do infants hear? How do they use sounds to understand their world?

We know, from Module 3.1, that a fetus can hear at 7 or 8 months after conception. As you would expect from these results, newborns typically respond to sounds in their surroundings. If a parent is quiet but then coughs, an infant may startle, blink his eyes, and move his arms or legs. These responses may seem natural, but they do indeed indicate that infants are sensitive to sound.

Not surprisingly, infants do not hear as well as adults. *Auditory threshold* **refers to the quietest sound that a person can hear.** An adult's auditory threshold is fairly easy to measure: A tone is presented, and the adult simply tells when he or she hears it. Because infants can't tell us what they hear, researchers have devised a number of clever techniques to measure infants' auditory thresholds (Saffran, Werker, & Werner, 2006). For example, in one method, the infant is seated on a parent's lap. Both parent and baby wear headphones, as does an observer seated in another room who watches the baby through an observation window. An experimenter periodically presents tones over the baby's headphones; neither the observer nor the parent knows when tones are to be presented (and they can't hear them through their headphones). On each trial, the observer simply judges if the baby responds in any fashion, such as by turning her head or changing her facial expression or activity level. Afterward, the experimenter determines how well the observer's judgments match the trials: If a baby can hear the tone, the observer should have noted a response only when a tone was presented.

This type of testing reveals that, overall, adults can hear better than infants; adults can hear some quiet sounds that infants can't (Saffran et al., 2006). More important, this testing shows that infants hear sounds best that have pitches in the range of human speech—neither very high- nor very low-pitched. Infants can differentiate vowels from consonant sounds, and by $4^1/_2$ months they can recognize their own names (Jusczyk, 1995; Mandel, Jusczyk, & Pisoni, 1995). In Module 9.1, we'll learn more about infants' remarkable skill at hearing language sounds.

Infants also can distinguish different musical sounds. They can distinguish different melodies and prefer melodies that are pleasant sounding over those that are unpleasant sounding or dissonant (Trainor & Heinmiller, 1998). And infants are sensitive to the rhythmic structure of music. After infants have heard a simple sequence of notes, they can tell the difference between a new sequence that fits the original versus one that doesn't (Hannon & Trehub, 2005). This early sensitivity to music is remarkable but perhaps not so surprising when you consider that music is (and has been) central in all cultures.

Thus, by the middle of the first year, most infants respond to much of the information provided by sound. However, not all infants are able to do so, which is the topic of the "Improving Children's Lives" feature.

 QUESTION 5.1

Tiffany is worried that her 12-month-old daughter may be hearing impaired. What symptoms would suggest that she has cause for concern? If these symptoms are present, what should she do?

Improving Children's Lives

Hearing Impairment in Infancy

Some infants are born with limited hearing. Others are born deaf. (Exact figures are hard to determine because young infants' hearing is rarely tested precisely.) African, Asian, European, and Hispanic American babies are equally susceptible. Heredity is the leading cause of hearing impairment in newborns. After birth, the leading cause is meningitis, an inflammation of the membranes surrounding the brain and spinal cord.

What are signs of hearing impairment that a parent should watch for? Obviously, parents should be concerned if a young baby never responds to sudden, loud sounds. They should also be concerned if their baby has repeated ear infections, does not turn in the direction of sounds by the age of 4 or 5 months, does not respond to his own name by 8 or 9 months, and does not begin to imitate speech sounds and simple words by 12 months.

If parents notice these problems, their baby should be examined by a physician, who will check for ear problems, and an audiologist, who will measure the infant's hearing. Parents should never delay checking for possible hearing impairment. The earlier the problem is detected, the more the baby can be helped.

If testing reveals that a baby has impaired hearing, several treatments are possible, depending on the degree of hearing loss. Some children with partial hearing benefit from mechanical devices. Hearing aids help some children, but others—like the child in the photo—benefit from a cochlear implant, an electronic device placed in the ear that converts speech into electric signals that stimulate nerve cells in the inner ear. Training in lip reading helps others. Children with profound hearing loss can learn to communicate with sign language. By mastering language (either oral language or sign language) and communicating effectively, a child's cognitive and social development will be normal. The key is to recognize impairment promptly.

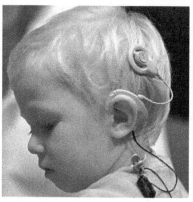

Many children with impaired hearing benefit from a cochlear implant—a device that converts speech signals into electrical impulses that stimulate the neural circuits that support hearing.

Seeing

LO3   How accurate is infants' vision? Do infants perceive color?

Babies spend much of their waking time looking around, sometimes scanning their environment broadly and sometimes seemingly focusing on nearby objects. But what do infants actually see? Is their visual world a sea of gray blobs? Or do they see the world essentially as adults do? Actually, neither is the case, but, as you'll see, the second is closer to the truth.

From birth, babies respond to light and can track moving objects with their eyes. But what is the clarity of their vision, and how can we measure it? *Visual acuity* **is defined as the smallest pattern that can be distinguished dependably.** No doubt, you've had your visual acuity measured by trying to read rows of progressively smaller letters on a chart. The same basic logic is used in tests of infants' acuity, which are based on two premises. First, most infants will look at patterned stimuli instead of plain, nonpatterned stimuli. For example, if we were to show the two stimuli in Figure 5-1 to infants, most would look longer at the striped pattern than at the gray pattern. Second, as we

Figure 5-1

make the lines narrower (along with the spaces between them), there comes a point at which the black and white stripes become so fine that they simply blend together and appear gray, just like the all-gray pattern.

To estimate an infant's acuity, we pair the gray square with squares that have different widths of stripes, like those in Figure 5-2: When infants look at the two stimuli equally, it indicates that they are no longer able to distinguish the stripes of the patterned stimulus. By measuring the width of the stripes and their distance from an infant's eye, we can estimate acuity (detecting thinner stripes indicates better acuity). Measurements of this sort indicate that newborns and 1-month-olds see at 20 feet what normal adults see at 200 to 400 feet. Infants' acuity improves rapidly, and by the first birthday, is essentially the same as that of a normal adult (Kellman & Arterberry, 2006).

Figure 5-2

Infants begin to see the world not only with greater acuity during the first year, but also in color! How do we perceive color? The wavelength of light is the source of color perception. Figure 5-3 shows that lights we see as red have a relatively long wavelength, whereas violet, at the other end of the color spectrum, has a much shorter wavelength. **We detect wavelength—and therefore color—with specialized neurons called** *cones* **that are in the retina of the eye.** Some cones are particularly sensitive to short-wavelength light (blues and violets), others are sensitive to medium-wavelength light (greens and yellows), and still others are sensitive to long-wavelength light (reds and oranges). These different kinds of cones are linked in complex circuits of neurons in the eye and in the brain, and this neural circuitry allows us to see the world in color.

These circuits gradually begin to function in the first few months after birth. Newborns and young babies can perceive few colors, but by 3 months, the three kinds of cones and their associated circuits are working and infants are able to see the full range of colors (Kellman & Arterberry, 2006). In fact, by 3 to 4 months, infants' color perception seems similar to that of adults (Adams & Courage, 1995; Franklin, Pilling, & Davies, 2005). In particular, infants, like adults, tend to see categories of color. For example, if a yellow light's wavelength is gradually increased, the infant will suddenly perceive it as a shade of red rather than a shade of yellow (Dannemiller, 1998; Ozturk et al., 2013).

The ability to perceive color, along with rapidly improving visual acuity, gives infants great skill in making sense out of their visual experiences. What makes this growing visual skill even more powerful is that, as we'll see in the next section, infants also connect information obtained from different senses.

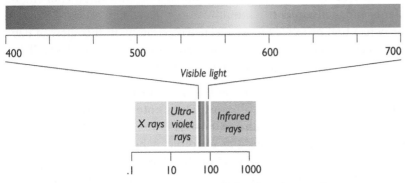

Figure 5-3

A mother who breast-feeds provides her baby with a multimedia event: the baby sees, smells, hears, feels, and tastes her!

Integrating Sensory Information

LO4 **How do infants integrate information from different senses?**

We have discussed infants' sensory systems separately, but most infant experiences are better described as "multimedia events." A nursing mother like the one in the photo provides visual and taste cues to her baby. A rattle stimulates vision, hearing, and touch. These examples show that much information spans multiple senses. Temporal information, such as duration or tempo, can be conveyed by sight or sound. For example, you can detect the rhythm of a person clapping by seeing the hands meet or by hearing the sound of hands striking. Similarly, the texture of a surface—whether it's rough or smooth, for example—can be detected by sight or by feel.

Infants readily perceive many of these relations. For example, infants can recognize visually an object that they have only touched previously (Sann & Streri, 2007). Similarly, babies can detect relations between information presented visually and auditorily; they look longer when an object's motion matches its sound (it makes higher-pitched sounds while rising but lower-pitched sounds while falling) than when it doesn't (Walker et al., 2010). They can also link the temporal properties of visual and auditory stimulation, such as duration and rhythm (Lewkowicz, 2000). Finally, they link their own body movement to their perceptions of musical rhythm, giving new meaning to the phrase "feel the beat, baby!" (Gerry, Faux, & Trainor, 2010).

Traditionally, coordinating information from different senses (e.g., vision with hearing, vision with touch) was thought to be demanding for infants. However, recent thinking challenges this view. One idea is that cross-modal perception is actually easier for infants, because in infancy regions in the brain devoted to sensory processing are not yet specialized. For example, some regions in an adult's brain respond only to visual stimuli; those same regions in an infant's brain respond to visual *and* auditory input (Spector & Maurer, 2009; Wagner & Dobkins, 2011).

Another explanation of infants' ability to integrate information from different senses is described in the "Spotlight on Theories" feature.

Spotlight on Theories
The Theory of Intersensory Redundancy

BACKGROUND Traditionally, linking information from different senses (e.g., vision with hearing, vision with touch) was said to be challenging for infants and, consequently, should emerge later, only after infants first master perceptual processes in each sense separately. In this view, a baby might perceive a favorite teddy bear's appearance, feel, and smell but would only gradually integrate these perceptions.

THE THEORY However, Lorraine Bahrick and Robert Lickliter (2002, 2012) have proposed a different view. **They note that certain information, such as duration, rate, and intensity, is** *amodal,* **in that it can be presented in different senses.** For example, when a mother claps her hands in time to music, the sounds of the claps as well as the appearance of the hands coming together and moving apart provide clues to the tempo of the music.

In Bahrick and Lickliter's *intersensory redundancy theory,* **the infant's perceptual system is particularly attuned to amodal information that**

is presented to multiple sensory modes. That is, perception is best—particularly for young infants—when information is presented redundantly to multiple senses. When an infant sees and hears the mother clapping (visual, auditory information), he focuses on the information conveyed to both senses and pays less attention to information that's only available in one sense, such as the color of the mother's nail polish or the sounds of her humming along with the tune. Or the infant can learn that the mom's lips are chapped from seeing the flaking skin and by feeling the roughness as the mother kisses him. According to intersensory redundancy theory, it's as if infants follow the rule: "Any information that's presented in multiple senses must be important, so pay attention to it!"

Hypothesis: If infants are particularly attentive to information presented redundantly to multiple senses, then they should notice changes in amodal information *at a younger age* when the information is presented to multiple senses than when it's presented to a single sense. In other words, if the mom claps slowly at first but then quickly, infants should detect this change at a younger age when they see and hear the clapping than when they only see her or only hear her.

Test: Flom and Bahrick (2007) studied infants' ability to detect differences in an adult's emotional expression—whether she was happy, angry, or sad. In the multimodal condition, infants saw a video depicting a woman who appeared to be talking directly to them. Her facial expression and tone of voice conveyed one of the three emotions. After several trials, infants saw a new video depicting the same woman expressing a different emotion. At 4 months of age, infants looked longer at the new video, showing that they detected the change in the woman's emotional expression. However, when the experiment was repeated but with the soundtrack turned off—so that emotional information was conveyed by vision alone—infants did not detect the difference in emotional expression until they were 7 months old.

Conclusion: This result supports the hypothesis. Infants detected a change in emotional expression at a younger age (4 months) when it was presented in multiple sensory modes than when it was presented in a single mode (7 months).

Application: The theory of intersensory redundancy says that infants learn best when information is simultaneously presented to multiple senses. Parents can use this principle to help babies learn. Language learning is a good example. Of course, talking to babies is beneficial (a topic we explore in depth in Chapter 9). But talking face-to-face with babies is best because then they see the visual cues that distinguish language sounds. When Mom says "oooh," her lips form a tight circle; when she says "ahhhh," her mouth is open wide. By talking face-to-face, Mom is presenting information about sounds redundantly—auditorily and visually—making it easier for her infants to distinguish these sounds (Burnham & Dodd, 2004).

Integrating information from different senses underscores the theme that has dominated this module: Infants' sensory and perceptual skills are impressive. Olivia, Darla's newborn daughter from the opening vignette, can definitely smell, taste, and feel pain. She can distinguish sounds; her vision is a little blurry but will improve rapidly, and she'll soon see the full range of colors; and she makes connections between sights and sounds and between other senses. Of course, over the coming year Olivia's perceptual skills will become more finely tuned: she'll become particularly adept at identifying stimuli that are common in her environment (Scott, Pascalis, & Nelson, 2007). But for now, Olivia, like most infants, is well prepared to make sense out of her environment.

Check Your Learning

RECALL Summarize what is known about infants' ability to smell, taste, and touch.

Describe the important developmental milestones in vision during infancy.

INTERPRET Compare the impact of nature and nurture on the development of infants' sensory and perceptual skills.

APPLY Perceptual skills are quite refined at birth and become mature rapidly. What evolutionary purposes are served by this rapid development?

5.2 Complex Perceptual and Attentional Processes

OUTLINE

Perceiving Objects

Attention

Attention Deficit Hyperactivity Disorder

LEARNING OBJECTIVES

LO5   How do infants perceive objects?

LO6   What are the components of attention? How do they develop?

LO7   What is attention deficit hyperactivity disorder? How does it affect children's development?

Soon after Stephen entered first grade, his teacher remarked that he sometimes seemed out of control. He was easily distracted, often moving aimlessly from one activity to another. He also seemed to be impulsive and had difficulty waiting his turn. This behavior continued in second grade and he began to fall behind in reading and arithmetic. His classmates were annoyed by his behavior and began to avoid him. His parents wonder whether Stephen just has lots of boyish energy or whether he has a problem.

Where we draw the dividing line between "basic" and "complex" perceptual processes is arbitrary. As you'll see, Module 5.2 is a logical extension of the information presented in Module 5.1. We'll begin by looking at how we perceive objects. We'll also look at the processes of attention and some children who have attentional problems. By the end of the module, you'll understand why Stephen behaves as he does.

Perceiving Objects

LO5   How do infants perceive objects?

Environments are filled with objects. For example, the photo shows a desk in a home office, as it might look to an infant seated on a mother's lap. You see distinct objects—a laptop computer, desk lamp, mouse—not one big object in which the

Infants use color and aligned edges to determine that the laptop computer is one object and that the lamp, mouse, and holders are different objects.

pen holder and lamp shade are part of the computer. Adults use many perceptual cues to distinguish individual objects like those on the desktop; young babies use many cues, too. Motion is one: Elements that move together are usually part of the same object. For example, on the left of Figure 5-4, a pencil appears to be moving back and forth behind a colored square. If the square were removed, you would be surprised to see a pair of pencil stubs, as shown on the right side of the diagram. The common movement of the pencil's eraser and point lead us to believe that they're part of the same pencil.

Young infants, too, are surprised by demonstrations like this. If they see a display like the moving pencils, they will then look briefly at a whole pencil, apparently because they expected it. In contrast, if after seeing the moving pencil they're shown the two pencil stubs, they look much longer, as if trying to figure out what happened (Amso & Johnson, 2006; Kellman & Spelke, 1983). Babies use common motion to identify objects and, given the right conditions, newborns do, too (Valenza & Bulf, 2011).

Motion is one clue to object unity, but infants use others, too, including color, texture, and aligned edges. As you can see in Figure 5-5 on page 158, infants more often group features together (i.e., believe they're part of the same object) when they're the same color, have the same texture, and when their edges are aligned (Johnson, 2001).

Perceptual Constancies A challenge for infants is recognizing that an object is the same even though it looks different. For example, when a mother moves away from her baby, the image that she casts on the retinas of her baby's eyes gets smaller. Do babies have a nightmare that their mother's head is shrinking as she moves away? No. **Early on, infants master** *size constancy*, **the realization that an object's actual size remains the same despite changes in the size of its retinal image.**

How do we know that infants have a rudimentary sense of size constancy? Suppose we let an infant look at an unfamiliar teddy bear. Then we show the infant the same bear, at a different distance, paired with a larger replica of the bear. If infants lack size constancy, the two bears will be equally novel and babies should respond to each similarly.

 QUESTION 5.2
When 6-month-old Sebastian watches his mother type on a keyboard, how does he know that her fingers and the keyboard are not simply one big unusual object?

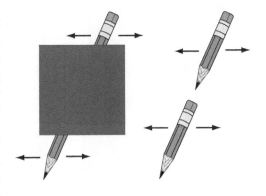

Figure 5-4

Infants believe that this display has one pencil.

Infants believe that this display has two pencils.

Cue

Color

Texture

Aligned edges

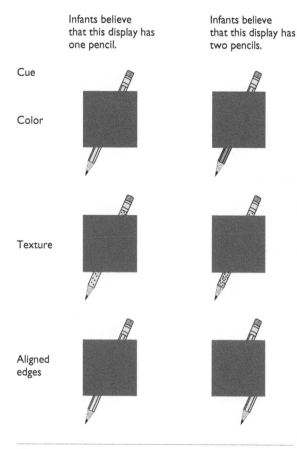

Figure 5-5

If, instead, babies have size constancy, they will recognize the first bear as familiar, the larger bear as novel, and be more likely to respond to the novel bear. In fact, by 4 or 5 months, babies treat the bear that they've seen twice at different distances—and, therefore, with different retinal images—as familiar (Granrud, 1986). This outcome is possible only if infants have size constancy. Thus, infants do not believe that mothers (and other people or objects) constantly change size as they move closer or farther away (Kellman & Arterberry, 2006).

Size is just one of several perceptual constancies. Others are brightness and color constancy as well as shape constancy, shown in Figure 5-6. All these constancies are achieved, at least in rudimentary form, by 4 months (Aslin, 1987; Dannemiller, 1998). Consequently, even young infants are not confused, thinking that the world is filled with many similar-looking but different objects. Instead, they can tell that an object is the same, even though it may look different. Mom is still Mom, whether she's nearby or far away and whether she's clearly visible outdoors or barely visible in a dimly lit room.

Depth In addition to knowing *what* an object is, babies need to know *where* it is. Determining left and right as well as high and low is relatively easy because these dimensions—horizontal, vertical—can be represented directly on the retina's flat surface. Distance or depth is more complicated because this dimension is not represented directly on the retina. Instead, many different cues are used to estimate distance or depth.

At what age can infants perceive depth? Eleanor Gibson and Richard Walk (1960) addressed this question in a classic experiment that used a specially designed apparatus. **The *visual cliff* is a glass-covered platform; on one side a pattern appears directly under the glass, but on the other it appears several feet below the glass.** Consequently, one side looks shallow but the other appears to have a steep drop-off, like a cliff. As you can see in the photo, in the experiment the baby is placed on the platform and the mother coaxes her infant to come to her. Most babies willingly crawl to their mothers when she stands on the shallow side. But virtually all babies refuse to cross the deep side, even when the mother calls the infant by name and tries to lure him or her with an attractive toy. Clearly, infants can perceive depth by the time they are old enough to crawl.

What about babies who cannot yet crawl? When babies as young as $1^1/_2$ months are simply placed on the deep side of the platform, their heartbeat slows down. Heart rate often decelerates when people notice something interesting, so this would suggest that $1^1/_2$-month-olds notice that the deep side is different. At 7 months, infants' heart rate accelerates, a sign of fear. Thus, although young babies can detect a difference between the shallow and deep sides of the visual cliff, only older, crawling babies are actually afraid of the deep side (Campos et al., 1978).

How do infants infer depth on the visual cliff and elsewhere? They use several kinds of cues. **Among the first are *kinetic cues*, in which motion is used to estimate depth.** *Visual expansion* refers to the fact that as an object moves closer, it fills an ever-greater proportion of the retina. Visual expansion is why we flinch when someone unexpectedly tosses a soda can toward us, and it's what allows a batter

Shape Constancy: Even though the door appears to change shape as it opens, we know that it really remains a rectangle.

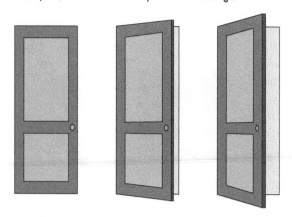

Figure 5-6

to estimate when a baseball will arrive over the plate. **Another cue, *motion parallax*, refers to the fact that nearby moving objects move across our visual field faster than those at a distance.** Motion parallax is in action when you look out the side window in a moving car: Trees next to the road move rapidly across the visual field but mountains in the distance move much more slowly. Babies use these cues in the first weeks after birth; for example, 1-month-olds blink if a moving object looks as if it's going to hit them in the face (Nánez & Yonas, 1994).

Another cue becomes important at about 4 months. ***Retinal disparity* is based on the fact that the left and right eyes often see slightly different versions of the same scene.** When objects are distant, the images appear in similar positions on the retina; when objects are near, the images appear in much different positions. Thus, greater disparity in positions of the image on the retina signals that an object is close. At about 4 months, infants use retinal disparity as a depth cue, correctly inferring that objects are nearby when disparity is great (Kellman & Arterberry, 2006).

Infants avoid the "deep side" of the visual cliff, indicating that they perceive depth.

By 7 months, infants use several cues for depth that depend on the arrangement of objects in the environment (e.g., Hemker et al., 2010). **These are sometimes called *pictorial cues* because they're the same cues that artists use to convey depth in drawings and paintings**.

Texture gradient*: The texture of objects changes from coarse but distinct for nearby objects to finer and less distinct for distant objects.* In the photo, we judge the distinct flowers to be close and the blurred ones, distant.

Interposition*: Nearby objects partially obscure more distant objects.* The glasses obscure the bottle, so we decide that the glasses are closer (and use this same cue to decide that the right glass is closer than the left glass).

Linear perspective*: Parallel lines come together at a single point in the distance.* Thus, we use the space between the lines as a cue to distance and, consequently, decide that the train in the photo is far away because the parallel tracks are close together.

Relative size*: Nearby objects look substantially larger than objects in the distance.* Knowing that the runners are really about the same size, we judge the ones that look smaller to be farther away.

The impact of motor-skill development A common theme in the past few pages is that infants develop powerful perceptual skills over their first year. This change reflects an epigenetic plan in which genetic instructions unfold in the context of a stimulating environment—and essential to this plan are the infant's own emerging motor skills. That is, as I mentioned at the beginning of this chapter, as infants' motor skills improve, they experience their environment differently and literally see their world in new and more sophisticated ways.

One example of the impact of motor skills comes from infants' growing ability to hold and manipulate objects. As we'll see in Module 5.3, 4-month-olds can hold a toy with their fingers but not until a few months later do infants become skilled at holding a toy, turning it to see its appearance on different sides, and stroking it with a finger to discover its texture. These improved motor skills allow children to learn more about the properties of objects and literally change how they perceive objects: Infants who can explore objects are more likely to understand the three-dimensional nature of objects and to notice the details of an object's appearance, such as its color (Baumgartner & Oakes, 2013; Schwarzer et al., 2013).

Another example makes use of a familiar phenomenon: When you drive down a tree-lined road, the trees rapidly move from ahead of you to behind you. Having spent many hours in a car, you interpret the changing appearance of the trees as a cue that you are moving. For this same reason, if you're sitting in an airliner parked at the gate and an airliner at an adjacent gate backs out, you feel as if you're moving forward. This experience can be simulated by placing people in rooms like the one shown in Figure 5-7, where the side walls and ceiling can move forward or backward (as shown by the arrows). If the walls move from front to back, adults seated in the middle of the room feel as if they're moving forward and they often lean back to compensate. Infants who

Figure 5-7

can move themselves by creeping or crawling do, too, but infants who can't move themselves do not (Uchiyama et al., 2008). Only after gaining the experience of propelling themselves through the environment do infants interpret front-to-back movement to mean that they are moving. Thus, just as an art-appreciation course allows you to see the *Mona Lisa* from a different perspective, infants' emerging abilities to move themselves and to manipulate objects create bold new perceptual experiences.

This same theme—perceptual skills change rapidly during infancy—is apparent in the next section, which focuses on how infants perceive faces.

Perceiving Faces   Babies depend on other people to care for them, so it's not surprising that young babies are attuned to human faces. For example, newborns prefer (a) faces with normal features over faces in which features are scrambled (Easterbrook et al., 1999); (b) upright faces over inverted faces (Mondloch et al., 1999), and (c) attractive faces over unattractive faces (Slater et al., 2000). Findings like these lead some scientists to claim that babies are innately attracted to moving stimuli that are face-like (e.g., consist of three high-contrast blobs close together). In other words, newborns' face perception may be reflexive, based on primitive circuits in the brain. At about 2 or 3 months of age, different circuits in the brain's cortex begin to control infants' looking at faces, allowing infants to learn about faces and to distinguish different faces (Morton & Johnson, 1991).

Through the first few months after birth, infants have a general prototype for a face—one that includes human and nonhuman faces (Pascalis, de Haan, & Nelson, 2002). However, over the first year infants fine-tune their prototype of a face so that it reflects faces that are familiar in their environments (Pascalis et al., 2014). For example, 3-month-olds prefer to look at faces from their own race but they can recognize faces from other races (and other species). In contrast, 6-month-olds often fail to recognize faces of individuals from other, unfamiliar races (Anzures et al., 2013).

Apparently, older infants' greater familiarity with faces of their own race leads to a more precise configuration of faces, one that includes faces of familiar racial and ethnic groups. This interpretation is supported by the finding that individuals born in Asia but adopted as infants by European parents recognize European faces better than Asian faces (Sangrigoli et al., 2005). What's more, if older infants receive extensive experience with other-race faces, they can learn to recognize them (Anzures et al., 2012).

These changes in face-recognition skill show the role of experience in fine-tuning infants' perception, a theme that will emerge again in the early phases of language learning (Module 9.1). And these improved face-recognition skills are adaptive because they provide the basis for social relationships that infants form during the rest of the first year, which we'll examine in Module 10.3.

Attention

LO6   What are the components of attention? How do they develop?

Have you ever been in a class where you knew you should be listening and taking notes, but the lecture was just so boring that you started noticing other things—the construction going on outside or an attractive person seated nearby? After a while, maybe you reminded yourself to "pay attention!" We get distracted because our perceptual systems are marvelously powerful. They provide us with far more information at any one time than we could possible interpret.

Attention **refers to processes that allow people to control input from the environment and regulate behavior.** Scientists distinguish three networks of attentional processes, each with unique functions and neural circuitry (Posner et al., 2012). The orienting network is associated with selection—it determines which stimuli will be processed further and which will be ignored. This network is well developed in infancy and is what drives, for example, an infant to turn his or her head toward a flashing light. The alerting network keeps a child's attentional processes prepared, ready to detect and respond to incoming stimuli. This network is also well developed in infancy and is illustrated by a baby who, hearing a parent's footsteps in a nearby room, looks at a doorway in anticipation of parent's arrival.

The executive network is responsible for monitoring thoughts, feelings, and responses as well as resolving conflicts that may occur. This is the most complex element of attention and the slowest to develop. For example, when 1-year-olds play with a new toy, they may be easily distracted by a program on a nearby TV: the toy and the TV program compete for attention and because the executive network is immature, the infant cannot ignore the TV to focus on the toy (Ruff & Capozzoli, 2003).

Experimental research shows the extended development of the executive network. For example, in one task there are left and right buttons and a left- or right-facing arrow is shown to indicate which button to press. When a conflict is introduced—by adding a smaller arrow pointing in the opposite direction of the large arrow—preschool children respond more slowly and less accurately; the executive network is less able to help them resolve the conflicting directions indicated by the large and small arrows (Posner & Rothbart, 2007). Similarly, when children learn to sort pictures according to one rule (e.g., sort by color) and then are asked to sort them again using a different rule (e.g., now sort by shape), preschool children often return to sorting by the old rule, even though they can describe the new rule perfectly! They are less able to ignore the conflict generated by the old rule, which causes them to sort some cards by color even when they know the new rule says to sort by shape (Zelazo et al., 2013).

Because the executive network has such a broad reach and develops so slowly, it is a crucial force in children's development, influencing their physical health, mental health, and success in school (Diamond, 2013). We'll learn more about the structure of the executive network and its link to school success in Module 6.2. And in Module 10.2 we'll see that differences in this network represent a key component of children's temperament.

In the meantime, teachers and parents *can* help young children pay attention better. For example, *Tools of the Mind* is a curriculum for preschool and kindergarten children that uses pretend play to improve the attentional processes of the executive network (Diamond & Lee, 2011). Pretend play may seem like a surprising way to improve attention but staying "in character" while pretending teaches children to inhibit inappropriate "out of character" behavior. And it encourages thinking flexibly as children respond to their playmates' improvisation. Teachers also contribute by providing visual reminders of the need to pay attention, such as showing a drawing of an ear to remind children to listen.

Parents can also help promote their children's attentional skills. In one study (Neville et al., 2013), parents and their preschool children attended an after-school program that included activities designed to improve children's attention. For example, in one task children were taught how to color carefully while being distracted by a nearby peer who was playing with a balloon. Parents were taught ways to support their children's attention. After children participated in this program, their attention improved (e.g., attending to a specified event while ignoring a distracting event).

Techniques like these improve children's attention and can be particularly useful with children who have the attentional problems—described in the next section.

Attention Deficit Hyperactivity Disorder

LO7   What is attention deficit hyperactivity disorder? How does it affect children's development?

Children with attention deficit hyperactivity disorder—ADHD for short—have special problems when it comes to paying attention. Roughly 3% to 7% of all school-age children are diagnosed with ADHD; boys outnumber girls by a 4-to-1 ratio (Goldstein, 2011). Stephen, the child in the module-opening vignette, exhibits three symptoms at the heart of ADHD (American Psychiatric Association, 2004):

- *Hyperactivity:* Like the boy in the photo, children with ADHD are unusually energetic, fidgety, and unable to keep still, especially in situations such as school classrooms where they need to limit their activity.
- *Inattention:* Youngsters with ADHD skip from one task to another. They do not pay attention in class and seem unable to concentrate on schoolwork.
- *Impulsivity:* Children with ADHD often act before thinking; they may run into a street before looking for traffic or interrupt others who are speaking.

Not all children with ADHD show all these symptoms to the same degree. Some children with ADHD are hyperactive and impulsive; others are primarily inattentive (Frick & Nigg, 2012). Children with ADHD often have problems with academic performance, conduct, and getting along with their peers (Murray-Close et al., 2010; Stevens & Ward-Estes, 2006). Many children who are diagnosed with ADHD will have problems related to overactivity, inattention, and impulsivity as adolescents and young adults (Barbaresi et al., 2013; Biederman et al., 2010). Few of these young adults complete college, and some will have work- and family-related problems (Biederman et al., 2006; Murphy, Barkley, & Bush, 2002).

Over the years, ADHD has been linked to TV, food allergies, and sugar, but research does not consistently implicate any of these as causes (e.g., Wolraich et al., 1994). Instead, scientists believe that genes put some children at risk for ADHD by affecting the alerting and executive networks of attention and the brain structures that support those networks (Gizer & Waldman, 2012; Johnson et al., 2008). But environmental factors also contribute. For example, prenatal exposure to alcohol and other drugs can place children at risk for ADHD (Milberger et al., 1997).

Because ADHD affects academic and social success throughout childhood and adolescence, researchers have worked hard to find effective treatments. The "Child Development and Family Policy" feature describes these efforts.

Tragically, many children who need these treatments do not receive them. African American and

Hyperactivity is one of three main symptoms of ADHD; the others are inattention and impulsivity.

Child Development and Family Policy

What's the Best Treatment for ADHD?

By the mid-1980s, it was clear that ADHD could be treated. For example, children with ADHD often respond well to stimulant drugs such as Ritalin. It may seem odd that stimulants are given to children who are already overactive, but these drugs stimulate the parts of the brain that normally inhibit hyperactive and impulsive behavior. Thus, stimulants actually have a calming influence for many youngsters with ADHD, allowing them to focus their attention (Barkley, 2004).

Drug therapy was not the only approach. Also effective were intervention programs like those described on page 162 that were designed to improve children's cognitive and social skills and often included home-based intervention and intensive summer programs. For example, children can be taught to remind themselves to read instructions before starting assignments. And they can be reinforced by others for inhibiting impulsive and hyperactive behavior (Lee et al., 2012; Webster-Stratton, Reid, & Beauchaine, 2011).

These treatments were well known by the late 1980s, yet many researchers were troubled by large gaps in our understanding. One gap concerned the long-term success of treatment. Most studies had measured the impact of weeks or months of treatment; virtually nothing was known about the effectiveness of treatment over longer periods. Another gap concerned the most effective combination of treatments and whether this was the same for all children. That is, is medication plus psychosocial treatment the best for all children and for all facets of children's development (i.e., academic and social)?

Prompted by these concerns, scientific advisory groups met in the late 1980s and early 1990s to identify the gaps in understanding and the research needed to fill the gaps. In 1992, the National Institute of Mental Health used reports of these groups to request proposals for research. After intensive review, the top six applications were selected and synthesized to create the Multimodal Treatment Study of Children with ADHD—the MTA for short (Richters et al., 1995). The MTA involves 18 scientists who are experts on ADHD and nearly 600 elementary-school children with ADHD. The children were assigned to different treatment modes and received treatment for 14 months. The impact of treatment has been measured every few years for several different domains of children's development.

The initial results—obtained at the end of the 14 months of treatment—showed that medication alone was the best way to treat hyperactivity per se. However, for a variety of other measures, including academic and social skills as well as parent–child relations, medication plus psychosocial treatment was somewhat more effective than medication alone (The MTA Cooperative Group, 1999). In contrast, in follow-up studies conducted 6 and 8 years after the 14-month treatment period ended, the treatment groups no longer differed and all groups fared worse than children without ADHD: Children with ADHD were more likely to be inattentive, hyperactive, and impulsive; they were more aggressive; and they were less likely to succeed in school (Molina et al., 2009).

For researchers, parents, and children with ADHD, these are disappointing results. Yet they point to an important conclusion, one with implications for policy: Several months of intensive treatment will not "cure" ADHD; instead, ADHD is perhaps better considered a chronic condition, like diabetes or asthma, one that requires ongoing monitoring and treatment (Hazell, 2009).

Hispanic American children are far less likely than European American youngsters to be diagnosed with and treated for ADHD, even when they have the same symptoms (Miller, Nigg, & Miller, 2009; Morgan et al., 2013). Why? Income plays a role. African American and Hispanic American families are more often economically disadvantaged and consequently they are less able to pay for diagnosis and treatment. Racial bias also contributes. Parents and professionals often attribute the symptoms of ADHD in European American children to a biological problem that can be treated medically; in African American or Hispanic American children, they more often attribute these symptoms to poor parenting, life stresses, or other sources that can't be treated (Bailey & Owens, 2005; Kendall & Hatton, 2002).

Obviously, all children with ADHD deserve appropriate treatment. Teachers and other professionals dealing with children must be sure that poverty and racial bias do not prevent children from receiving the care they need.

 ## Check Your Learning

RECALL Describe the cues that babies use to infer depth.

What are the main symptoms of ADHD?

INTERPRET Describe evidence showing that early experience with faces fine-tunes the infant's perception of faces.

APPLY What happens to children with ADHD when they become adolescents and young adults? How does this address the issue of continuity of development?

 # Motor Development

LEARNING OBJECTIVES

		OUTLINE
LO8	What are the component skills involved in learning to walk, and at what age do infants typically master them?	**Locomotion**
LO9	How do infants learn to coordinate the use of their hands? When and why do most children begin to prefer to use one hand?	**Fine-Motor Skills**
LO10	Are children physically fit? Do they benefit from participating in sports?	**Physical Fitness**

Nancy is 14 months old and a world-class crawler. Using hands and knees, she gets nearly anywhere she wants to go. Nancy does not walk and seems to have no interest in learning how. Her dad wonders whether he should be doing something to help Nancy progress beyond crawling. And down deep, he worries that perhaps he should have provided more exercise or training for Nancy when she was younger.

The photos on this page have a common theme. Each depicts an activity involving *motor skills*—coordinated movements of the muscles and limbs. Infants face two challenges involving motor skills. **They must learn *locomotion*, that is, to move**

Motor skills involve coordinating movements of muscles and limbs.

about in the world. Newborns are relatively immobile, but infants soon learn to crawl, stand, and walk. Learning to move through the environment upright leaves the arms and hands free, which allows infants to grasp and manipulate objects. **Infants must learn the** *fine-motor skills* **associated with grasping, holding, and manipulating objects.** In the case of feeding, for example, infants progress from being fed by others to holding a bottle, to feeding themselves with their fingers, to eating with a spoon.

Although demanding, locomotion and fine-motor skills are worth mastering because of their benefits. Being able to locomote and to grasp gives children access to an enormous amount of information about their environment. They can explore objects that look interesting, and they can keep themselves close to parents. Improved motor skills promote children's cognitive and social development, not to mention make a child's life more interesting!

In this module, we'll see how children acquire locomotor and fine-motor skills. As we do, we'll find out if Nancy's dad should be worrying about her lack of interest in walking.

Locomotion

LO8 **What are the component skills involved in learning to walk, and at what age do infants typically master them?**

In little more than a year, advances in posture and locomotion change the newborn from an almost motionless being into an upright, standing individual who walks through the environment. Figure 5-8 shows some of the important milestones in motor development and the age by which most infants achieve them. By about 4 months, most babies can sit upright with support. By 6 or 7 months, they can sit without support, and by 7 or 8 months, they can stand if they hold on to an object for support. A typical 11-month-old can stand alone briefly and walk with assistance. **Youngsters at this age are called** *toddlers*, **after the toddling manner**

Figure 5-8

of early walking. Of course, not all children walk at exactly the same age. Some walk before their first birthday; others, like Nancy, the world-class crawler in the module-opening vignette, take their first steps as late as 17 or 18 months of age. By 24 months, most children can climb steps, walk backward, and kick a ball.

Researchers once thought that these developmental milestones reflected maturation (e.g., McGraw, 1935). Walking, for example, was thought to emerge naturally when the necessary muscles and neural circuits matured. Today, however, locomotion—and, in fact, all motor development—is viewed from a new perspective. **According to** *dynamic systems theory,* **development involves many distinct skills that are organized and reorganized over time to meet the demands of specific tasks.** For example, walking includes maintaining balance, moving limbs, perceiving the environment, and having a reason to move. Only by understanding each of these skills and how they are combined to allow movement in a specific situation can we understand how walking and other skills develop (Spencer, Perone, & Buss, 2011).

In the remainder of this section, we'll see how learning to walk reflects the mastery and coalescence of many component skills.

Posture and Balance   The ability to maintain an upright posture is fundamental to walking. But upright posture is difficult for young infants because the shape of their body makes them top-heavy. Consequently, as soon as a young infant starts to lose her balance, she tumbles over. Only with growth of the legs and muscles can infants maintain an upright posture (Thelen, Ulrich, & Jensen, 1989).

After infants can stand upright, they must continuously adjust their posture to avoid falling down (Metcalfe et al., 2005). By a few months after birth, infants begin to use visual cues and an inner-ear mechanism to adjust their posture. To show the use of visual cues for balance, researchers had babies sit in a room with striped walls that moved. When adults sit in such a room, they perceive themselves as moving (not the walls) and adjust their posture accordingly; so do infants, which shows that they use vision to maintain upright posture (Bertenthal & Clifton, 1998).

Balance is not, however, something that infants master just once. Instead, infants must relearn balancing for sitting, crawling, walking, and other postures. Why? The body rotates around different points in each posture (e.g., the wrists for crawling versus the ankles for walking), and different muscle groups are used to generate compensating motions when infants begin to lose their balance. Consequently, it's hardly surprising that infants who easily maintain their balance while sitting topple over time after time when crawling. Once they walk, infants must adjust their posture further when they carry objects because these affect balance (Garciaguirre, Adolph, & Shrout, 2007). Infants must recalibrate the balance system as they take on each new posture, just as basketball players recalibrate their muscle movements when they move from dunking to shooting a three-pointer (Adolph, 2000, 2002).

Stepping   Another essential element of walking is moving the legs alternately, repeatedly transferring the weight of the body from one foot to the other. Children don't step spontaneously until approximately 10 months because they must be able to stand upright to step.

Can younger children step if they are held upright? Thelen and Ulrich (1991) devised a clever procedure to answer this question. Infants were placed on a treadmill and held upright by an adult. When the belt on the treadmill started to move, infants could respond in one of several ways. They might simply let both legs be dragged rearward by the belt. Or they might let their legs be dragged briefly, then move them forward together in a hopping motion. Many 6- and 7-month-olds

Young babies step reflexively when they are held upright and moved forward.

demonstrated the mature pattern of alternating steps on each leg that is shown in the photo. Even more amazing is that when the treadmill was equipped with separate belts for each leg that moved at different speeds, babies adjusted, stepping more rapidly on the faster belt. Apparently, the alternate stepping motion that is essential for walking is evident long before infants walk independently. Walking unassisted is not possible, though, until other component skills are mastered.

Environmental Cues Many infants learn to walk in the relative safety of flat, uncluttered floors at home. But they soon discover that the environment offers a variety of surfaces, some more conducive to walking than others. Infants use cues in the environment to judge whether a surface is suitable for walking. For example, they are more likely to cross a bridge when it's wide and has a rigid handrail than when it is narrow and has a wobbly handrail (Berger, Adolph, & Lobo, 2005; Kretch & Adolph, 2013b). And when walking down stairs, if a step is too large to descend safely, novice walkers often continue (and fall) but older, experienced walkers either stop or slide down on their backs; only experienced walkers recognize the cues that signal steps that are safe for walking (Kretch & Adolph, 2013a). If they can't decide whether a surface is safe, they depend on an adult's advice (Tamis-LeMonda et al., 2008). Results like these show that infants use perceptual cues to decide whether a surface is safe for walking.

Coordinating Skills Dynamic systems theory emphasizes that learning to walk demands orchestration of many individual skills. Each component skill must first be mastered alone and then integrated with the other skills (Werner, 1948). **That is, mastery of intricate motions requires both *differentiation*—mastery of component skills—and their *integration*—combining them in proper sequence into a coherent, working whole.** In the case of walking, not until 9 to 15 months of age has the child mastered the component skills so that they can be coordinated to allow independent, unsupported walking.

Mastering individual skills and coordinating them well does not happen overnight. Novice walkers take nearly 1500 steps per hour, covering about 1/5 of a mile, and falling more than 30 times; infants obviously get lots of natural practice (along with feedback from falls) as they master walking (Adolph et al., 2012). Similarly, we'll see in the "Cultural Influences" feature that some cultures include customs that help children learn to walk.

Cultural Influences
Cultural Practices That Influence Motor Development

In Europe and North America, most infants typically walk alone near their first birthday. But infants in other cultures often begin to walk (and reach other milestones listed on page 166) at an earlier age because child-care customs allow children to practice their emerging motor skills. For example, in some traditional African cultures, infants sit and walk at younger ages. Why? Infants are commonly carried by their parents in the "piggyback" style shown in the photo, which helps develop muscles in the infants' trunk and legs.

Some cultures even take a further step. They believe that practice is essential for motor skills

to develop normally and so parents (or siblings) provide daily training sessions. For example, the Kipsigis of Kenya help children learn to sit by having them sit while propped up (Super, 1981). Among the West Indians of Jamaica, mothers have an exercise routine that allows babies to practice walking (Hopkins & Westra, 1988). Not surprisingly, infants with these opportunities learn to sit and walk earlier, findings that are confirmed by experimental work in which some parents participate in activities that let babies practice controlling their bodies (Lobo & Galloway, 2012).

You may be surprised that some cultures do just the opposite: They have practices that discourage motor development. The Ache, an indigenous group in Paraguay, protect infants and toddlers from harm by carrying them constantly (Kaplan & Dove, 1987). In Chinese cities, parents often allow their children to crawl only on a bed surrounded by pillows, in part because they don't want their children crawling on a dirty floor (Campos et al., 2000). In both cases, infants reach motor milestones a few months later than the ages listed on page 166.

Similarly, today infants in developed nations are crawling at older ages than they did in previous generations (Dewey et al., 1998; Lung & Shu, 2011). This generational difference reflects the effectiveness of programs that encourage parents to have their babies sleep on their back (see page 113). Because today's babies spend less time on their tummies, they have fewer opportunities to discover that they can propel themselves by creeping, which would otherwise prepare them for crawling.

Thus, cultural practices can accelerate or delay the early stages of motor development, depending on the nature of practice that infants and toddlers receive (Adolph & Robinson, 2013). In the long run, however, the age of mastering various motor milestones is not critical for children's development. All healthy children learn to walk, and whether this

In many African cultures, infants are routinely carried piggyback style, which strengthens the infants' legs, allowing them to walk at a younger age.

happens a few months before or after the "typical" ages shown on page 166 has no bearing on children's later development (Lung & Shu, 2011).

Beyond Walking If you can recall the feeling of freedom that accompanied your first driver's license, you can imagine how the world expands for infants and toddlers as they learn to move independently. The first tentative steps soon are followed by others that are more skilled. With more experience, infants take longer, straighter steps. Like adults, they begin to swing their arms, rotating the left arm forward as the right leg moves, then repeating with the right arm and left leg (Ledebt, 2000; Ledebt, van Wieringen, & Saveslsbergh, 2004). Children's growing skill is evident in their running and hopping. Most 2-year-olds have a hurried walk instead of a true run; they move their legs stiffly (rather than bending them at the knees) and are not airborne as is the case when running. By 5 or 6 years, children run easily, quickly changing directions or speed.

Infants use their new walking skills to get distant objects—a favorite toy that's in a different room of the house—and carry them to share with other people (Karasik, Tamis-Lemonda, & Adolph, 2011). In the next section, we'll see how infants' fine-motor skills allow them to grasp objects.

Fine-Motor Skills

LO9 How do infants learn to coordinate the use of their hands? When and why do most children begin to prefer to use one hand?

A major accomplishment in infancy is skilled use of the hands (Bertenthal & Clifton, 1998). Newborns have little apparent control of their hands, but 1-year-olds are extraordinarily talented.

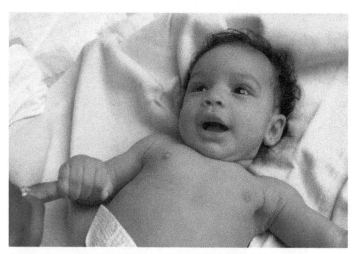

A typical 4-month-old grasps an object with fingers alone.

Reaching and Grasping   At about 4 months, infants can successfully reach for objects (Bertenthal & Clifton, 1998). These early reaches often look clumsy, and for a good reason. When infants reach, their arms and hands don't move directly and smoothly to the desired object (as is true for older children and adults). Instead, the infant's hand moves like a ship under the direction of an unskilled navigator. It moves a short distance, slows, then moves again in a slightly different direction, a process that's repeated until the hand finally contacts the object (McCarty & Ashmead, 1999). As infants grow, their reaches have fewer movements, though they are still not as continuous and smooth as older children's and adults' reaches (Berthier, 1996).

Reaching requires that an infant move the hand to the location of a desired object. Grasping poses a different challenge: Now the infant must coordinate movements of individual fingers to grab an object. Grasping, too, becomes more efficient during infancy. Most 4-month-olds just use their fingers to hold objects. Like the baby in the photo, they wrap an object tightly with their fingers alone. Not until 7 or 8 months do most infants use their thumbs to hold objects (Siddiqui, 1995). At about this age, infants begin to position their hands to make it easier to grasp an object. In trying to grasp a long, thin rod, for example, infants place their fingers perpendicular to the rod, which is the best position for grasping (Wentworth, Benson, & Haith, 2000). And they reach more slowly for smaller objects that require a more precise grip (Berthier & Carrico, 2010). However, as we'll see in the "Focus on Research" feature, not until their first birthday do babies make multiple adjustments when reaching for objects.

Focus on Research

Adjusting Grasps to Objects

Who were the investigators, and what was the aim of the study? Grasping an object effectively often requires that infants adjust their hands in several ways. For example, the best way to grasp a small object that's oriented horizontally is to use two or three fingers with the back of the hand oriented horizontally. In contrast, the best way to grasp a large object that's oriented vertically is to use the entire hand, with the back of the hand oriented vertically. Nina Schum and her colleagues—Bianca Jovanic and Gudrun Schwarzer (2011)—wanted to know whether babies would make both adjustments while grasping (i.e., changing their grip *and* the orientation of their hand).

How did the investigators measure the topic of interest? Schum and colleagues presented colorful pencils to infants, who were seated on the mother's lap, about eight inches from the pencil (a distance well within the baby's reach). The pencils were either large or small and were presented either vertically or horizontally. The baby's reaches were recorded on video.

Who were the participants in the study? The study included 38 10-month-olds and 32 12-month-olds.

What was the design of the study? This study was experimental. The independent variables included the size of the pencil (large, small) and its orientation (vertical, horizontal). The dependent variable was the kind of grip, which could be classified as (a) using the entire hand or just two to three fingers, and (b) with the back of the hand oriented vertically or horizontally. The study was cross-sectional because 10- and 12-month-olds were each tested.

Were there ethical concerns with the study? No. There was no obvious harm associated with reaching for the pencils.

What were the results? The researchers examined the videos and classified the baby's hand position just before the fingers touched the pencil. Each reach could be appropriate on either or both dimensions. For example, using two to three fingers is appropriate for small objects but the whole hand is appropriate for a larger pencil; the back of the hand should be oriented vertically for vertically oriented pencils but horizontally for horizontally oriented pencils.

Figure 5-9 shows the percentage of infants that used appropriate grips. Most 12-month-olds grasped objects appropriately—adjusting their hand's orientation and the number of fingers; in contrast, fewer than half of the 10-month-olds did so. The next two panels show that 10-month-olds typically adjusted their hand's orientation, but not the number of fingers that they used.

What did the investigators conclude? In a follow-up control study, Schum et al. showed that 10-month-olds adjust the number of fingers correctly when pencils varied only in size, not in orientation. Thus, the problem for 10-month-olds is not adjusting the number of fingers per se but one of adjusting their hands on multiple dimensions simultaneously as they grasp objects.

What converging evidence would strengthen these conclusions? One useful extension of this work would be to see how infants make other kinds of adjustments

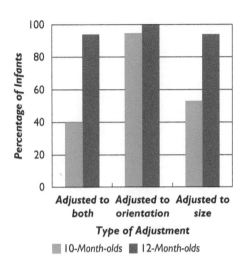

Figure 5-9

simultaneously (e.g., reaching for heavier versus lighter objects that differ in orientation). Another extension would be to observe infants as they reach for objects naturally, at home.

Infants' growing control of each hand is accompanied by greater coordination of the two hands. Although 4-month-olds use both hands, each hand seems to have a mind of its own. Infants may hold a toy motionless in one hand while shaking a rattle in the other. At roughly 5 to 6 months of age, infants coordinate the motions of their hands so that each hand performs different actions that serve a common goal. For example, a child might hold a toy animal in one hand and pet it with the other (Karniol, 1989). These skills continue to improve after children's first birthday: 1-year-olds reach for most objects with one hand; by 2 years, they reach with one or two hands, as appropriate, depending on the size of the object (van Hof, van der Kamp, & Savelsbergh, 2002).

These changes in reaching and grasping are well illustrated as infants learn to feed themselves. At about 6 months, they are often given "finger foods" (e.g., sliced bananas). Infants easily pick up such foods, but getting them into the mouth is another story. The hand grasping the food may be raised to the cheek, then moved to the edge of the lips, and finally shoved into the mouth. Mission accomplished—but only with many detours along the way! Eye–hand coordination improves rapidly, so before long foods that vary in size, shape, and texture reach the mouth directly.

At about the first birthday, youngsters usually try to eat with a spoon. At first, they simply play with the spoon, dipping it in and out of a dish filled with food or sucking on an empty spoon. With a little help, they learn to fill the spoon with food and place it in the mouth, though the motion is awkward because they don't rotate the wrist. Instead, most 1-year-olds fill a spoon by placing it directly over a dish and lowering it until the bowl of the spoon is full. Then, they raise the spoon to the mouth, all the while keeping the wrist rigid. In contrast, 2-year-olds rotate

By age 5, fine-motor skills are developed to the point that most youngsters can dress themselves.

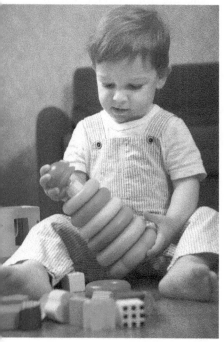

Most toddlers use the left hand to hold an object steady and the right hand to explore the object.

QUESTION 5.3

Jenny and Ian are both left-handed and they fully expected their son, Tyler, to prefer his left hand, too. But he's 8 months old already and seems to use both hands to grasp toys and other objects. Should Jenny and Ian give up their dream of being the three left-handed musketeers?

the hand at the wrist while scooping food from a dish and placing the spoon in the mouth—the same motion that adults use.

After infancy, fine-motor skills progress rapidly. Preschool children become more dexterous, making many precise and delicate movements with their hands and fingers. Greater fine-motor skill means that preschool children can begin to care for themselves, eating and dressing without a parent's help. For example, a 2- or 3-year-old can put on some simple clothing and use zippers but not buttons; by 3 or 4 years, children can fasten buttons and take off their clothes when going to the bathroom; like the child in the top photo, most 5-year-olds can dress and undress themselves, except for tying shoes, which children typically master at about age 6.

In each of these actions, the principles of dynamic systems theory apply as seen in our previous discussion about locomotion. Complex acts involve many component movements. Each must be performed correctly and in the proper sequence. Development involves first mastering the separate elements and then assembling them to form a smoothly functioning whole. Eating finger food, for example, requires grasping food, moving the hand to the mouth, then releasing the food. As the demands of tasks change and as children develop, the same skills are often reassembled to form a different sequence of movements.

Handedness   When young babies reach for objects, they don't seem to prefer one hand over the other; they use their left and right hands interchangeably. They may shake a rattle with their left hand and moments later pick up blocks with their right. By the first birthday, most youngsters are emergent right-handers. Like the toddler in the bottom photo, they use the left hand to steady the toy while the right hand manipulates the object. This early preference for one hand becomes stronger and more consistent during the preschool years and is well established by kindergarten (Marschik et al., 2008; Nelson, Campbell, & Michel, 2013).

What determines whether children become left- or right-handed? Some scientists believe that a gene biases children toward right-handedness (Corballis, Badzakova-Trajkova, & Häberling, 2012). Consistent with this idea, identical twins are more likely than fraternal twins to have the same handedness— both are right-handed or both are left-handed (Meland et al., 2009). But experience also contributes to handedness. Many cultures have traditionally viewed left handedness as evil and have punished children for using their left hand to eat or write. Not surprisingly, left-handed children are rare in these cultures. Similarly, in many developed nations, elementary-school teachers used to urge left-handed children to write with their right hands. As this practice was abandoned, the percentage of left-handed children has increased (Provins, 1997). Thus, handedness is influenced by both heredity and environment.

Physical Fitness

LO10 Are children physically fit? Do they benefit from participating in sports?

Using one's motor skills—that is, being active physically—has many benefits for children. It promotes growth of muscles and bone, cardiovascular health, and cognitive processes (Best, 2010; Biddle & Asare, 2011; Hillman et al., 2009) and can help to establish a lifelong pattern of exercise (Perkins et al., 2004). Individuals who exercise regularly—30 minutes, at least 3 times a week—reduce their risk for obesity, cancer, heart disease, diabetes, and psychological disorders, including depression and anxiety (Tomson et al., 2003). Running, vigorous walking, swimming, aerobic dancing, biking, and cross-country skiing are all examples of activities that can provide this level of intensity.

Unfortunately, when children's and adolescents' fitness is tested objectively, with items such as the mile run and pull-ups, fewer than half usually meet standards for fitness on all tasks (Morrow et al., 2010). Many factors contribute to low levels of fitness. In most schools, physical education classes meet only once or twice a week and are usually not required of high-school students (Johnston, Delva, & O'Malley, 2007). Even when students are in these classes, they spend nearly half the time standing around instead of exercising (Lowry et al., 2001; Parcel et al., 1989). Television and other sedentary leisure-time activities may contribute, too. Youth who spend much time online or watching TV often tend to be less fit physically (Lobelo et al., 2009), but the nature of this relation remains poorly understood: Children glued to a TV or computer screen likely have fewer opportunities to exercise, but perhaps children in poor physical condition chose sedentary activities over exercise.

Participating in sports can enhance children's physical, motor, cognitive, and social development.

Many experts believe that U.S. schools should offer physical education more frequently each week. And many suggest that physical education classes should offer a range of activities in which all children can participate and that can be the foundation for a lifelong program of fitness (National Association for Sport and Physical Fitness, 2004). Thus, instead of emphasizing team sports such as touch football, physical education classes should emphasize activities such as running, walking, racquet sports, and swimming; these can be done throughout childhood, adolescence and adulthood, either alone or with another person. Families can encourage fitness, too. Instead of spending an afternoon watching TV and eating popcorn, they can, go biking together. Or families can play exergames, which are digital games like *Dance Dance Revolution* that combine video gaming with exercise; playing these regularly enhances physical fitness (Staiano & Calvert, 2011).

Participating in Sports Many children and adolescents get exercise by participating in team sports, including baseball, softball, basketball, and soccer. Obviously, when children such as the girls in the photo play sports, they get exercise and improve their motor skills. But there are other benefits, too. Sports can enhance participants' self-esteem and can help them to learn initiative (Bowker, 2006; Eime et al., 2013). Sports can also give children a chance to learn important social skills, such as how to work effectively as part of a group, often in complementary roles. Finally, playing sports allows children to use their emerging cognitive skills as they devise new playing strategies or modify the rules of a game.

These benefits of participating in sports are balanced by potential hazards. Several studies have linked youth participation in sports to delinquent and antisocial behavior (e.g., Gardner, Roth, & Brooks-Gunn, 2009). However, outcomes are usually positive when sports participation is combined with

When adult coaches emphasize winning or frequently criticize players, many children lose interest and quit.

participation in activities that involve adults, such as school, religious, or youth groups (Linver, Roth, & Brooks-Gunn, 2009; Zarrett et al., 2009). Still, these potential benefits hinge on the adults who are involved. When adult coaches encourage their players and emphasize skill development, children usually enjoy playing, often improve their skills, and increase their self-esteem (Coatsworth & Conroy, 2009). In contrast, when coaches—like the man in the photo—emphasize winning over skill development and criticize or punish players for bad plays, children lose interest and stop playing. When adolescents find sports too stressful, they often get "burned out": they lose interest and quit (Raedeke & Smith, 2004).

To encourage youth to participate, adults (and parents) need to have realistic expectations for children and coach positively, praising children instead of criticizing them. They need to remember that children play games for recreation, which means they should have fun!

Check Your Learning

RECALL Describe the skills that infants must master to be able to walk.

How do fine-motor skills improve with age?

INTERPRET What are the pros and cons of children and adolescents participating in organized sports?

APPLY Describe how participation in sports illustrates connections between motor, cognitive, and social development.

 # Unifying Themes   Active Children

Each module in this chapter touched on the theme that *children influence their own development*. That is, repeatedly we saw that infants are extremely well equipped to interpret and explore their environments. In Module 5.1, we saw that most sensory systems function quite well in the first year, providing infants with accurate raw data to interpret. In Module 5.2, we learned that attentional skills originate in infancy; through habituation, infants ignore some stimuli and attend to others. Finally, in Module 5.3, we discovered that locomotor and fine-motor skills improve rapidly in infancy; by the first birthday, infants can move independently and handle objects skillfully. Collectively, these accomplishments make the infants extraordinarily well prepared to explore their world and make sense of it.

See for Yourself

To see the origins of attention, you need a baby and a small bell. A 1- to 5-month-old is probably best because babies at this age can't locomote, so they won't wander away. While the infant is awake, place it on its back. Then move behind the baby's head (out of sight) and ring the bell a few times. You don't need to ring the bell loudly—an "average" volume will do. The baby will open its eyes wide and perhaps try to turn in the direction of the sound. Every two or three minutes, ring the bell again. You should see the baby respond less intensely each time until, finally, it ignores the bell completely. Attention in action! See for yourself!

Summary

 ### Basic Sensory and Perceptual Processes

Smell, Taste, and Touch
Newborns are able to smell and can recognize their mother's odor; they also taste, preferring sweet substances and responding negatively to bitter and sour tastes. Infants respond to touch. Judging from their responses to painful stimuli, which are similar to older children's, we can say they experience pain.

Hearing
Babies can hear, although they are less sensitive to high- and low-pitched sounds than are adults. Babies can distinguish different sounds (both from language and music).

Seeing
A newborn's visual acuity is relatively poor, but 1-year-olds can see as well as adults with normal vision. Color vision develops as different sets of cones begin to function; by 3 or 4 months, children can see color as well as adults can.

Integrating Sensory Information
Infants begin to integrate information from different senses (e.g., sight and sound, sight and touch). Infants are often particularly attentive to information presented redundantly to multiple senses.

 ### Complex Perceptual and Attentional Processes

Perceiving Objects
Infants use motion, color, texture, and edges to distinguish objects. By about 4 months, infants have begun to master size, brightness, shape, and color constancy. Infants first perceive depth by means of kinetic cues, including visual expansion and motion parallax. Later, they use retinal disparity and pictorial cues (linear perspective, texture gradient, relative size, interposition) to judge depth. Infants perceive faces early in the first year. Experience leads infants to fine-tune their facial template so that it resembles the faces they see most often.

Attention
Attention includes the orienting and alerting networks, which function well in infancy, and the executive network, which develops more slowly. Teachers and parents can teach young children strategies for paying attention more effectively.

Attention Deficit Hyperactivity Disorder
Children with ADHD are typically inattentive, hyperactive, and impulsive. They sometimes have conduct problems and do poorly in school. According to the Multimodal Treatment Study of Children with ADHD, in the short term the most effective approach to ADHD combines medication with psychosocial treatment.

 ### Motor Development

Locomotion
Infants progress through a sequence of motor milestones during the first year, culminating in walking a few months after the first birthday. Like most motor skills, learning to walk involves differentiation of individual skills, such as maintaining balance and stepping on alternate legs, and then integrating these skills into a coherent whole. This differentiation and integration of skills is central to the dynamic systems theory of motor development. Experience can accelerate specific motor skills.

Fine-Motor Skills
Infants first use only one hand at a time, then both hands independently, then both hands in common actions, and finally, both hands in different actions with a common purpose.

Most people are right-handed, a preference that emerges after the first birthday and that becomes well established during the preschool years. Handedness is influenced by heredity and environment.

Physical Fitness
Although children report spending much time being physically active, in fact, fewer than half of U.S. school children meet all standards for physical fitness. Part of the explanation for the lack of fitness is inadequate physical education in school. Television may also contribute. Experts recommend that physical education in the schools be more frequent and more oriented toward developing patterns of lifetime exercise. Families can become more active, thereby encouraging children's fitness.

Participating in sports can promote motor, cognitive, and social development. But participation in sports sometimes leads to antisocial behavior, and children sometimes quit playing when coaches emphasize winning over skill development.

Test Yourself

1. Smell, touch, and taste _____.
   a. develop early, which help children to recognize their mothers and learn to eat
   b. develop later than hearing and sight
   c. have little value to infants

2. Infants _____.
   a. are particularly sensitive to high-pitched sounds
   b. hear as well as adults do
   c. cannot distinguish different musical sounds

3. Which child is at greatest risk for a possible hearing impairment?
   a. A 1-year-old who has had repeated ear infections
   b. A 2-month-old who does not respond to his name
   c. A 6-month-old who overreacts to loud sounds

4. An infant's color vision is similar to an adult's color vision _____.
   a. at birth.
   b. by 7 to 8 months of age.
   c. by 3 to 4 months of age.

5. According to the theory of intersensory redundancy, infants learn best when information is _____.
   a. presented one by one to the sense organs
   b. presented simultaneously to multiple senses
   c. presented through sight and sound only

6. Size, shape, and color constancy are achieved in a rudimentary form by _____ of age.
   a. 4 months
   b. 6 months
   c. 12 months

7. Which of these statements is not true about the way newborns perceive faces?
   a. Infants prefer faces with normal features.
   b. Infants prefer upright faces over inverted ones.
   c. Infants cannot distinguish attractive from unattractive faces.

8. The phenomenon in which the left and the right eye often see slightly different versions of the same scene is called _____.
   a. retinal disparity
   b. pictorial cues
   c. depth perception

9. Which of the following is *true* concerning the development of attention?
   a. The orienting and alerting networks are mature at birth but the executive network develops slowly.
   b. All attention networks are mature at birth.
   c. All attention networks develop gradually over infancy, the preschool years, and the early elementary school years.

10. Children with attention deficit hyperactivity disorder (ADHD) _____.
    a. often act before thinking
    b. are well liked by their peers
    c. have below average levels of intelligence

11. The ability to write is an example of _____.
    a. fine motor skills
    b. gross motor skills
    c. intelligence

12. According to dynamic systems theory, development involves _____.
    a. maturation, which remains fixed for all at specific ages
    b. the organization and reorganization of many distinct skills over time
    c. only specific skills, like learning to walk

13. Which of the following statements concerning reaching and grasping is *true*?
    a. When 4-month-olds reach for an object, they repeatedly move their hand a short distance, slow down, and adjust direction.
    b. Most 3-month-olds use their fingers and thumb to hold objects.
    c. By 6 months of age, most infants can adjust their grip to match the size and orientation of an object.

14. Which of the following is incorrect about "handedness"?
    a. It emerges by the first birthday.
    b. There is genetic bias in handedness.
    c. Right handedness and left handedness are both accepted in all cultures.

15. To encourage children in sports a coach should _____.
    a. have realistic expectations
    b. constantly be vigilant and criticize to improve performance
    c. make it clear that playing a sport is a discipline and not recreation

Key Terms

amodal 154
attention 162
auditory threshold 151
cones 153
differentiation 168
dynamic systems theory 167
fine-motor skills 166
habituation 150
integration 168
interposition 159

intersensory redundancy
   theory 154
kinetic cues 158
linear perspective 159
locomotion 165
motion parallax 159
motor skills 149
pictorial cues 160
relative size 159
retinal disparity 159

sensory and perceptual
   processes 149
size constancy 157
texture gradient 159
toddlers 166
visual acuity 152
visual cliff 158
visual expansion 158

Chapter 6
Theories of Cognitive Development

Modules

6.1 Setting the Stage: Piaget's Theory

6.2 Modern Theories of Cognitive Development

6.3 Understanding in Core Domains

On the TV show *Family Guy*, Stewie is a 1-year-old who can't stand his mother (Stewie: "Hey, mother, I come bearing a gift. I'll give you a hint: It's in my diaper and it's not a toaster.") and hopes to dominate the world. Much of the humor turns on the idea that babies are capable of sophisticated thinking—they just can't express it. Of course, few adults would really attribute such advanced thinking skills to a baby. But what thoughts *do* lurk in the mind of an infant who does not yet speak? And how do an infant's fledgling thoughts blossom into the powerful reasoning skills that older children, adolescents, and adults use daily? In other words, how does thinking change as children develop; and why do these changes take place?

For many years, the best answers to these questions came from the theory proposed by Jean Piaget that was mentioned in Module 1.2. We'll look at this theory in more detail in **Module 6.1**. In **Module 6.2**, we'll examine some of the modern theories that guide today's research on children's thinking. Finally, in **Module 6.3**, we'll see how children acquire knowledge of objects, living things, and people.

6.1 Setting the Stage: Piaget's Theory

LEARNING OBJECTIVES

LO1 What are the key ideas in Piaget's theory of cognitive development?

LO2 How does thinking change as children move through Piaget's four stages of development?

LO3 What are the lasting contributions of Piaget's theory? What are some of its shortcomings?

OUTLINE

Basic Principles of Piaget's Theory

Stages of Cognitive Development

Piaget's Contributions to Child Development

When 2½-year-old Ethan saw a monarch butterfly for the first time, his mother, Kat, told him, "Butterfly, butterfly; that's a butterfly, Ethan." A few minutes later, a zebra swallowtail landed on a nearby bush and Ethan shouted in excitement, "Butterfly, Mama, butterfly!" A bit later, a moth flew out of another bush; with even greater excitement in his voice, Ethan shouted, "Butterfly, Mama, more butterfly!" Even as Kat was telling Ethan, "No, honey, that's a moth, not a butterfly," she marveled at how rapidly Ethan seemed to grasp new concepts with so little direction from her. How was this possible?

For much of the 20th century, scientists would have answered Kat's question by referring to Jean Piaget's theory. Piaget was trained as a biologist, but he developed a keen interest in epistemology, the branch of philosophy dealing with the nature and origins of knowledge. He decided to investigate the origins of knowledge not as philosophers had—through discussion and debate—but by doing experiments with children.

Because Piaget's theory led the way to all modern theories of cognitive development, it's a good introduction to the study of children's thinking. We'll first consider some basic principles of the theory, where we will discover why

Ethan understands as quickly as he does. Then we'll look at Piaget's stages of development and end the module by examining the enduring contributions of Piaget's work to child-development science.

Basic Principles of Piaget's Theory

LO1 **What are the key ideas in Piaget's theory of cognitive development?**

Piaget believed that children are naturally curious. They want to make sense out of their experience and, in the process, construct their understanding of the world. For Piaget, children at all ages are like scientists in that they create theories about how the world works. Of course, children's theories are often incomplete, and sometimes incorrect. Nevertheless, theories are valuable to the child because they make the world seem more predictable.

In using their theories to make sense of what's going on around them, children often have new experiences that are readily understood within the context of these theories. **According to Piaget, *assimilation* occurs when new experiences are readily incorporated into a child's existing theories.** Imagine an infant like the one in the photo who knows that the family dog barks and often licks her in the face. When she has the same experience at a relative's house, this makes sense because it fits her simple theory of dogs. Thus, understanding the novel dog's behavior represents assimilation. But sometimes theories are incomplete or incorrect, causing children to have unexpected experiences. **For Piaget, *accommodation* occurs when a child's theories are modified based on experience.** The baby with a theory of dogs is surprised the first time she encounters a cat—it resembles a dog but meows instead of barks and rubs up against her instead of licking. Revising her theory to include this new kind of animal illustrates accommodation.

Assimilation and accommodation are illustrated in the vignette at the beginning of the module. When Kat named the monarch butterfly for Ethan, he formed a simple theory, something like "butterflies are bugs with big wings." The second butterfly differed in color but was still a bug with big wings, so it was readily assimilated into Ethan's new theory of butterflies. However, when Ethan referred to the moth as a butterfly, Kat corrected him. Ethan had to accommodate to this new experience. The result was that he changed his theory of butterflies to make it more precise; the new theory might be something like "butterflies are bugs with thin bodies and big, colorful wings." He also created a new theory, something like "a moth is a bug with a bigger body and plain wings."

In this example, assimilation and accommodation involve ideas, but they begin much earlier, in a young baby's actions. For example, a baby who can grasp a ball soon discovers that she can grasp blocks, rattles, and other small objects; extending grasping to new objects illustrates assimilation. When she discovers that some objects can't be grasped unless she uses two hands, this illustrates accommodation: Her revised "theory of grasping" now distinguishes objects that can be grasped with one hand from those that require two hands.

Assimilation and accommodation are usually in balance, or equilibrium. That is, children find

This infant's "theory of dogs" includes the facts that dogs are friendly and like licking people's faces.

they can readily assimilate most experiences into their existing theories, but occasionally they need to accommodate their theories to adjust to new experiences. This balance between assimilation and accommodation is illustrated both by the baby's theories of dogs and cats as well as by Ethan's understanding of butterflies.

However, periodically the balance is upset, causing a state of disequilibrium. Children discover that their current theories are not adequate because they are spending much more time accommodating than assimilating. **When disequilibrium occurs, children reorganize their theories to return to a state of equilibrium, a process that Piaget called** *equilibration*. To restore the balance, current but now-outmoded ways of thinking are replaced by a qualitatively different, more advanced theory.

Returning to the metaphor of the child as a scientist, sometimes scientists find that a theory contains critical flaws. When this occurs, they can't simply revise; they must create a new theory that draws on the older theory but is fundamentally different. For example, when the astronomer Copernicus realized that the Earth-centered theory of the solar system was wrong, he retained the concept of a central object but proposed that it was the Sun, a fundamental change in the theory. In much the same way, children periodically reach a point when their current theories seem to be wrong much of the time, so they abandon these theories in favor of more advanced ways of thinking about their physical and social worlds.

According to Piaget, these revolutionary changes in thought occur three times, at approximately 2, 7, and 11 years of age. This divides cognitive development into four stages: the *sensorimotor stage* (birth to age 2, encompassing infancy); the *preoperational stage* (ages 2 to 6, encompassing preschool and early elementary school); the *concrete operational stage* (ages 7 to 11, encompassing middle and late elementary school); and the *formal operational stage* (ages 11 and up, encompassing adolescence and adulthood).

Piaget held that all children go through these four stages in exactly this sequence. For example, sensorimotor thinking should always lead to preoperational thinking; a child cannot "skip" preoperational thinking and move directly from sensorimotor to concrete operational thought. However, the ages listed are only approximate: Some youngsters move through the stages more rapidly than others, depending on their ability and their experience. In the next section, we'll look more closely at each stage.

Stages of Cognitive Development

LO2 **How does thinking change as children move through Piaget's four stages of development?**

Just as you can recognize a McDonald's restaurant by the golden arches and Nike products by the swoosh, each of Piaget's stages is marked by a distinctive way of thinking about and understanding the world. In the next few pages, we'll learn about these unique trademarks of Piaget's stages.

The Sensorimotor Stage We know from Chapter 5 that infants' perceptual and motor skills improve quickly. Piaget proposed that these rapidly changing perceptual and motor skills in the first two years of life form a distinct phase in human development: **The *sensorimotor stage* spans birth to 2 years, a period during which the infant progresses from simple reflex actions to symbolic processing.** In the 24 months of this stage, infants' thinking progresses remarkably along three important fronts.

Between 4 and 8 months, infants eagerly explore new objects.

Adapting to and Exploring the Environment Newborns respond reflexively to many stimuli, but between 1 and 4 months, reflexes are first modified by experience. An infant may accidentally touch his lips with his thumb, which leads to sucking and the pleasing sensations associated with sucking. Later, the infant tries to recreate these sensations by guiding his thumb to his mouth. Sucking no longer occurs only reflexively when a mother places a nipple at the infant's mouth; instead, the infant can initiate sucking by himself.

Between 4 and 8 months, the infant shows greater interest in the world, paying far more attention to objects. For example, the infant shown in the photo accidentally shook a new rattle. Hearing the interesting noise, the infant grasped the rattle again, tried to shake it, and expressed great pleasure at the sound that resulted. This sequence was repeated several times.

At about 8 months of age, infants reach a watershed: the onset of deliberate, intentional behavior. For the first time, the "means" and "end" of activities are distinct. For example, if a father places his hand in front of a toy, an infant will move his hand to be able to play with the toy. "Moving the hand" is the means to achieve the goal of "grasping the toy." Using one action as a means to achieve another end is the first indication of purposeful, goal-directed behavior during infancy.

Beginning at about 12 months, infants become active experimenters. An infant may deliberately shake different objects trying to discover which ones produce sounds. Or an infant may decide to drop different objects to see what happens. An infant will discover that stuffed animals land quietly but bigger toys often make a more satisfying "clunk" when they hit the ground. These actions represent a significant extension of intentional behavior: Now babies repeat actions with different objects solely for the purpose of seeing what will happen.

Understanding Objects The world is filled with animate objects such as dogs, spiders, and college students, as well as inanimate objects such as cheeseburgers, socks, and this book. But they all share a fundamental property: They exist independently of our actions and thoughts concerning them. Much as we may dislike spiders, they still exist when we close our eyes or wish they would go away. **Understanding that objects exist independently is called** *object permanence*. Piaget made the astonishing claim that infants lack this understanding for much of the first year. That is, he proposed that an infant's understanding of objects could be summarized as "out of sight, out of mind." For infants, objects are fleeting, existing when in sight and no longer existing when out of sight.

If a tempting object such as an attractive toy is placed in front of a 4- to 8-month-old, the infant will probably reach for and grasp the object. However if the object is then hidden by a barrier or covered with a cloth, the infant will neither reach nor search. Instead, the infant seems to lose all interest in the object, as if the now-hidden object no longer exists. Paraphrasing the familiar phrase, "out of sight, out of existence!"

At about 8 months, infants search for an object that an experimenter has covered with a cloth. In fact, many 8- to 12-month-olds love to play this game—an adult covers the object and the infant sweeps away the cover, laughing and smiling all the while! But, despite this accomplishment, Piaget believed that infants' understanding of object permanence is incomplete. At this age, when infants see an object hidden under one container several times, then see it hidden under a second container, they usually look for the toy under the first container. This fascinating phenomenon is known as the "A not B error" (because babies reach for an object at the first location, A, not the second location, B), and Piaget claimed that it shows infants' limited understanding of objects: Infants do not distinguish the object from the actions they use to locate it, such as reaching for a particular container. In fact, according to Piaget, infants do not have full understanding of object permanence until about 18 months of age.

Using Symbols By 18 months, most infants have begun to talk and gesture, evidence of the emerging capacity to use symbols. Words and gestures are symbols that stand for something else. When the baby in the photo waves, this is just as effective and symbolic as saying "goodbye" to bid farewell. Children also begin to engage in pretend play, another use of symbols. A 20-month-old may move her hand back and forth in front of her mouth, pretending to brush her teeth.

By 18 months of age, most toddlers will use simple gestures, which is evidence of their emerging ability to use symbols.

Once infants can use symbols, they begin to anticipate the consequences of actions mentally instead of having to perform them. Imagine that an infant and parent construct a tower of blocks next to an open door. Leaving the room, a 12- to 18-month-old might close the door, knocking over the tower, because he cannot foresee the outcome of closing the door. But an 18- to 24-month-old can anticipate the consequence of closing the door and move the tower beforehand.

In just 2 years, the infant progresses from reflexive responding to actively exploring the world, understanding objects, and using symbols. These achievements are remarkable and set the stage for preoperational thinking, which we'll examine next.

The Preoperational Stage With the magic power of symbols, the child crosses the hurdle into preoperational thinking. **The *preoperational stage*, which spans ages 2 to 7, is marked by the child's use of symbols to represent objects and events.** Throughout this period, preschool children gradually become proficient at using common symbols, such as words, gestures, graphs, maps, and models. Although preschool children's ability to use symbols represents a huge advance over sensorimotor thinking, their thinking remains limited compared to that of school-age children. Why? To answer this question, we need to look at some important characteristics of thought during the preoperational stage.

Preoperational children typically believe that others see the world—literally and figuratively—exactly as they do. *Egocentrism* **refers to young children's difficulty in seeing the world from another's viewpoint.** When youngsters stubbornly cling to their own way, they are not being contrary. Instead, preoperational children do not comprehend that other people have different ideas and feelings.

Suppose, for example, you ask the preschooler in Figure 6-1 to select the image that shows how the objects on the table look to you. Most select the drawing on the far left, which shows how the objects look to the child, rather than the drawing on the far right—the correct choice. Preoperational youngsters evidently suppose that the mountains are seen the same way by all; they presume that theirs is the only view, rather than one of many conceivable views (Piaget & Inhelder, 1956).

Egocentrism sometimes leads preoperational youngsters to attribute their own thoughts and feelings to others. **Preoperational children sometimes credit inanimate objects with life and lifelike properties, a phenomenon known as**

Figure 6-1

animism (Piaget, 1929). A rainy-day conversation that I had with Christine, a 3½-year-old, illustrates preoperational animism.

CHRISTINE: The sun is sad today.

RK: Why?

CHRISTINE: Because it's cloudy. He can't shine. And he can't see me!

RK: What about your trike? Is it happy?

CHRISTINE: No. He's sad, too.

RK: Why is that?

CHRISTINE: 'Cause I can't ride him. And because he's all alone in the garage.

Caught up in her egocentrism, Christine believes that objects like the sun and her tricycle think and feel as she does.

Children in the preoperational stage also have the psychological equivalent of tunnel vision: They often concentrate on one aspect of a problem but ignore other, equally relevant aspects. **Centration is Piaget's term for this narrowly focused thought that characterizes preoperational youngsters.** Piaget demonstrated centration in his experiments involving conservation, which tested when children realize that important properties of objects (or sets of objects) stay the same despite changes in their physical appearance.

A typical conservation problem, involving conservation of liquid quantity, is shown in the photos. A child is shown identical glasses filled with the same amount of juice. After the child agrees that the two glasses have the same amount, juice is poured from one glass into a taller, thinner glass. The juice looks different in the tall, thin glass—it rises higher—but of course the amount is unchanged. Nevertheless, a preoperational child typically claims that the tall, thin glass has more juice than the original glass. (And, if the juice is poured into a wider glass, a preoperational child believes it has less.)

What is happening here? According to Piaget, preoperational children center on the level of the juice in the glass. If the juice is higher after it is poured, preoperational children believe that there must be more juice now than before. Because

In the conservation task, preoperational children believe that the tall, thin glass has more liquid, an error reflecting the centered thought that is common in children at this stage.

preoperational thinking is centered, these youngsters ignore the fact that the change in the level of the juice is always accompanied by a change in the diameter of the glass.

Centration and egocentrism are major limits to preoperational children's thinking, but these are overcome in the next stage, the concrete operational stage.

The Concrete Operational Stage   During the early elementary-school years, children enter a new stage of cognitive development that is distinctly more adult-like and much less childlike. **In the** *concrete operational stage,* **which spans ages 7 to 11, children first use mental operations to solve problems and to reason.** What are the mental operations that are essential to concrete operational thinking? *Mental operations* **are strategies and rules that make thinking more systematic and more powerful.** Some mental operations apply to numbers. For example, addition, subtraction, multiplication, and division are familiar arithmetic operations that concrete operational children use. Other mental operations apply to categories of objects. For example, classes can be added (mothers + fathers = parents) and subtracted (parents – mothers = fathers). Still other mental operations apply to spatial relations among objects. For example, if point A is near points B and C, then points B and C must be close to each other.

Another important property of mental operations is that they can be reversed. Each operation has an inverse that can "undo" or reverse the effect of an operation. If you start with 5 and add 3, you get 8; by subtracting 3 from 8, you reverse your steps and return to 5. For Piaget, reversibility of this sort applied to all mental operations. Concrete operational children are able to reverse their thinking in a way that preoperational youngsters cannot. In fact, reversible mental operations explain why concrete operational children pass the conservation task shown on page 184: Concrete operational thinkers understand that if the transformation were reversed (for example, the juice was poured back into the original container), the quantities would be identical.

Concrete operational thinking is much more powerful than preoperational thinking. Remember that preoperational children are egocentric (believing that others see the world as they do) and centered in their thinking; neither of these limits applies to children in the concrete operational stage. But concrete operational thinking has its own shortcomings. As the name implies, concrete operational thinking is limited to the tangible and real, to the here and now. The concrete operational youngster takes "an earthbound, concrete, practical-minded sort of problem-solving approach, one that persistently fixates on the perceptible and inferable reality right there in front of him" (Flavell, 1985, p. 98). That is, thinking abstractly and hypothetically is beyond the ability of concrete operational thinkers.

The Formal Operational Stage   In the *formal operational stage,* **which extends from roughly age 11 into adulthood, children and adolescents apply mental operations to abstract entities; they think hypothetically and reason deductively.** Freed from the concrete and the real, adolescents explore the possible; formal operational thinkers understand that reality is not the only possibility. They can envision alternative realities and examine the consequences of those propositions. For example, ask a concrete operational child, "What would happen if gravity meant that objects floated up?" or "What would happen if men gave birth?" and you're likely to get a confused or irritated look and comments like "It doesn't—they fall" or "They don't—women have babies." Reality is the foundation of concrete operational thinking. In contrast, formal operational adolescents use hypothetical

QUESTION 6.1

Richa is a 3-year-old girl who takes care of all her toys as if they are living things. She offers them food to eat and puts them to bed at night. She often talks to them and insists on bringing them along with her on trips so that they don't feel "lonely." How would Piaget's theory explain Richa's behavior?

Children in the concrete operational stage often solve problems by "plunging right in" instead of thinking hypothetically to come up with a well-defined set of solutions to a problem.

reasoning to probe the implications of fundamental change in physical or biological laws.

Formal operations also allow adolescents to take a more sophisticated approach to problem solving. Formal operational thinkers solve problems by creating hypotheses (sets of possibilities) and testing them. Piaget (Inhelder & Piaget, 1958) showed this aspect of adolescent thinking by presenting children and adolescents with several flasks, each containing what appeared to be the same clear liquid. They were told that one combination of the clear liquids would produce a blue liquid and were asked to determine the necessary combination.

A typical concrete operational youngster, like the ones in the photo, plunges right in, mixing liquids from different flasks haphazardly. In contrast, formal operational adolescents understand that the key is setting up the problem in abstract, hypothetical terms. The problem is not really about pouring liquids but about systematically forming hypotheses about different combinations of liquids and testing them systematically. A teenager might mix liquid from the first flask with liquids from each of the other flasks. If none of these combinations produces a blue liquid, he or she would mix the liquid in the second flask with each of the remaining liquids. A formal operational thinker would continue in this manner until he or she found the critical pair that produced the blue liquid.

Because adolescents' thinking is not concerned solely with reality, they are also better able to reason logically from premises and draw appropriate conclusions. **The ability to draw appropriate conclusions from facts is known as** *deductive reasoning*. Suppose we tell a person the following two facts:

1. If you hit a glass with a hammer, the glass will break.

2. Don hit a glass with a hammer.

The correct conclusion is that "the glass broke," a conclusion that formal operational adolescents will reach. Concrete operational youngsters, too, will sometimes reach this conclusion, but based on their experience and not because the conclusion is logically necessary. To see the difference, imagine that the two facts are now:

1. If you hit a glass with a feather, the glass will break.

2. Don hit a glass with a feather.

The conclusion "the glass broke" follows from these two statements just as logically as it did from the first pair. In this instance, however, the conclusion is counterfactual—it goes against what experience tells us is really true. Concrete operational 10-year-olds resist reaching conclusions that are counter to known facts; they reach conclusions based on their knowledge of the world. In contrast, formal operational 15-year-olds often reach counterfactual conclusions. They understand that these problems are about abstract entities that need not correspond to real-world relations.

Hypothetical reasoning and deductive reasoning are powerful tools for formal operational thinkers. In fact, we can characterize this power by paraphrasing the quotation about concrete operational thinking that appears on page 185: "Formal operational youth take an abstract, hypothetical approach to problem solving; they are not constrained by the reality that is staring them in the face but

TABLE 6-1

PIAGET'S FOUR STAGES OF COGNITIVE DEVELOPMENT

Stage	Approximate Age	Characteristics
Sensorimotor	Birth to 2 years	Infant's knowledge of the world is based on senses and motor skills. By the end of the period, infant uses mental representations and understands object permanence.
Preoperational	2 to 6 years	Child learns how to use symbols such as words and numbers to represent aspects of the world, but relates to the world only through his or her own perspective. Thinking is centered.
Concrete operational	7 to 11 years	Child understands and applies logical operations to experiences, provided they are focused on the here and now.
Formal operational	Adolescence and beyond	Adolescent or adult thinks abstractly, speculates on hypothetical situations, and reasons deductively about what may be possible.

are open to different possibilities and alternatives." The ability to ponder different alternatives makes possible the experimentation with lifestyles and values that occurs in adolescence, topics we'll encounter on several occasions later in this book.

With the achievement of formal operations, cognitive development is over in Piaget's theory. Adolescents and adults acquire more knowledge as they grow older, but in Piaget's view their fundamental way of thinking remains unchanged. Table 6-1 summarizes Piaget's description of cognitive changes between birth and adulthood.

Piaget's Contributions to Child Development

LO3   What are the lasting contributions of Piaget's theory? What are some of its shortcomings?

Piaget's theory dominated child-development research and theory for much of the 20th century. As one expert phrased it, "many of Piaget's contributions have become so much a part of the way we view cognitive development nowadays that they are virtually invisible" (Flavell, 1996, p. 202). Three of these contributions are worth emphasizing (Brainerd, 1996; Siegler & Ellis, 1996):

- *The study of cognitive development itself.* Before Piaget, child-development scientists paid little attention to cognitive development. Piaget showed why cognitive processes are central to development and offered some methods that could be used to study them.
- *A new view of children.* Piaget emphasized *constructivism*, **the view that children are active participants in their own development who systematically construct ever-more sophisticated understandings of their worlds.** This view now pervades thinking about children (so much so that it's one of the themes in this book), but it began with Piaget.
- *Fascinating, often counterintuitive discoveries.* One reason why Piaget's work attracted so much attention is that many of the findings were completely unexpected and became puzzles that child-development researchers couldn't resist trying to solve. For example, researchers have tested thousands of youngsters trying to understand the "A not B" error (page 183) and to understand why children fail the conservation task (page 185). In the words of one expert, "Piaget had the greenest thumb ever for unearthing fascinating and significant developmental progressions" (Flavell, 1996, p. 202).

Teaching Practices That Foster Cognitive Growth: Educational Applications of Piaget's Theory Piaget's contributions extend beyond research. In fact, his view of cognitive development helps to identify teaching practices that promote cognitive growth:

- *Facilitate rather than direct children's learning.* Cognitive growth occurs as children construct their own understanding of the world, so the teacher's role is to create environments where children can discover for themselves how the world works. A teacher shouldn't simply tell children that addition and subtraction are complementary, but instead should provide children with materials that allow them to discover the complementarity themselves.

- *Recognize individual differences when teaching.* Cognitive skills develop at different rates in different children. Consequently, instruction geared to an entire class is often boring for some students and much too challenging for others. *Instruction is most effective when it is tailored to individual students.* For some students in a classroom, the goal of addition instruction may be to master basic facts; for others, it may be to learn about properties such as commutativity and associativity.

- *Be sensitive to children's readiness to learn.* Children profit from experience only when they can interpret this experience with their current cognitive structures. It follows, then, that *the best teaching experiences are slightly ahead of children's current level of thinking.* As a youngster begins to master basic addition, don't jump right to subtraction, but first go to slightly more difficult addition problems.

- *Emphasize exploration and interaction.* Cognitive growth can be particularly rapid when children discover inconsistencies and errors in their own thinking (Legare, Gelman, & Wellman, 2010). *Teachers should therefore encourage children to look at the consistency of their thinking but then let children take the lead in sorting out the inconsistencies.* If a child is making mistakes in borrowing on subtraction problems, a teacher shouldn't correct the error directly; rather, the teacher should encourage the child to look at a large number of these errors to discover what he or she is doing wrong.

Weaknesses of Piaget's Theory Although Piaget's contributions to child development are legendary, some elements of his theory have held up better than others (Miller, 2011; Newcombe, 2013; Siegler & Alibali, 2005).

- *Piaget's theory underestimates cognitive competence in infants and young children and overestimates cognitive competence in adolescents.* In Piaget's theory, cognitive development is steady in early childhood but not particularly rapid. In contrast, a main theme of modern child-development science is that of the extraordinarily competent infant and toddler. By using more sensitive tasks than Piaget's, modern investigators have shown that infants and toddlers are vastly more capable than expected based on Piaget's theory. For example, we'll see in Module 6.3 that infants have much greater understanding of objects than Piaget believed. Paradoxically, however, Piaget *overestimated* cognitive skill in adolescents, who often fail to reason according to formal operational principles and revert to less sophisticated reasoning. For example, we'll see in Module 7.2 that adolescents often let their beliefs bias their reasoning.

- *Piaget's theory is vague concerning mechanisms of change.* Many of the key components of the theory, such as accommodation and assimilation, turned out to be too vague to test scientifically. Consequently, scientists abandoned them in favor of other cognitive processes that could be evaluated more readily and provide more convincing accounts of children's thinking.

- *Piaget's stage model does not account for variability in children's performance.* In Piaget's view, each stage of intellectual development has unique characteristics that leave their mark on everything a child does. Preoperational thinking is defined by egocentrism and centration; formal operational thinking is defined by abstract and hypothetical reasoning. Consequently, children's performance on different tasks should be consistent. In fact, children's thinking falls far short of this consistency. A child's thinking may be sophisticated in some domains but naïve in others (Siegler, 1981). This inconsistency does not support Piaget's view that children's thinking should always reflect the distinctive imprint of their current stage of cognitive development. In other words, cognitive development is not as stage-like as Piaget believed.

- *Piaget's theory undervalues the influence of the sociocultural environment on cognitive development.* Returning to the metaphor of the child as scientist, Piaget describes the child as a lone scientist, constantly trying to figure out by herself how her theory coordinates with data and experience. In reality, a child's effort to understand her world is a far more social enterprise than Piaget described. Her growing understanding of the world is profoundly influenced by interactions with family members, peers, and teachers and takes place against the backdrop of cultural values. Piaget's theory did not neglect these social and cultural forces entirely, but they are not prominent in the theory.

Because of the criticisms of Piaget's theory, many researchers have taken several different paths in studying cognitive development. In the next module, we'll look at three different approaches that are linked to Piaget's work.

Check Your Learning

RECALL What are the stages of cognitive development in Piaget's theory? What are the defining characteristics of each?

Summarize the main shortcomings of Piaget's account of cognitive development.

INTERPRET Piaget championed the view that children participate actively in their own development. How do the sensorimotor child's contributions differ from the formal operational child's contributions?

APPLY Based on what you know about Piaget's theory, what would his position have been on the continuity–discontinuity issue discussed in Module 1.3?

 # Modern Theories of Cognitive Development

6.2

LEARNING OBJECTIVES

LO4 In Vygotsky's sociocultural theory, how do adults and other people contribute to children's cognitive development?

LO5 According to information-processing psychologists, how does thinking change with development?

LO6 What naïve theories do children hold about physics, psychology, and biology?

OUTLINE

The Sociocultural Perspective: Vygotsky's Theory

Information Processing

Core-Knowledge Theories

Four-year-old Victoria loves solving jigsaw puzzles with her dad. She does the easy ones by herself. But she often has trouble with the harder ones, so her dad helps—he orients pieces correctly and reminds Victoria to look for edge pieces. Victoria may do 10 to 12 puzzles before she loses interest, then delights in telling her mom, in great detail, about all the puzzles she solved. After these marathon puzzle sessions, Victoria's dad is often surprised that a child who is sophisticated in her language skills struggles with the harder puzzles.

Many theories have built on the foundation of Piaget's pioneering work. In this module, we'll look at three different theoretical approaches, each designed to take research in cognitive development beyond Piaget's theory. As we do, you'll learn more about Victoria's cognitive and language skills.

The Sociocultural Perspective: Vygotsky's Theory

LO4 In Vygotsky's sociocultural theory, how do adults and other people contribute to children's cognitive development?

Child-development scientists often refer to child development as a journey that can proceed along many different paths. As we've seen, in Piaget's theory, children make the journey alone as they interact with the physical world. Other people (and culture in general) certainly influence the direction that children take, but the child is seen as a solitary adventurer–explorer boldly forging ahead.

In contrast, according to the *sociocultural perspective,* children are products of their culture: Children's cognitive development is not only brought about by social interaction, it is inseparable from the cultural contexts in which children live. Cultural contexts organize cognitive development in several ways. First, culture often defines which cognitive activities are valued: U.S. youngsters are expected to learn to read but not to navigate using the stars (Gauvain & Munroe, 2012). Second, culture provides tools that shape the way children think (Gauvain & Munroe, 2009). The cognitive skills that children use to solve arithmetic problems, for example, depend on whether their culture provides an abacus like the one in the photograph, or paper and pencil, or a handheld calculator. Third, higher-level cultural practices help children to organize their knowledge and communicate it to others. For instance, in most U.S. schools, students are expected to think and work alone rather than to collaborate (Matusov, Bell, & Rogoff, 2002). Thus, "culture penetrates human intellectual functioning and its development at many levels, and it does so through many organized individual and social practices" (Gauvain, 1998, p.189).

One of the original—and still quite influential—sociocultural theories was proposed by Lev Vygotsky (1896–1934), the Russian psychologist described in Chapter 1. Vygotsky saw development as an apprenticeship in which children advance when they collaborate with others who are more skilled. That is, according to Vygotsky (1978), child development is never a solitary journey. Instead, children always travel with others and usually progress most rapidly when they walk hand-in-hand with an expert partner. **For Vygotsky and other sociocultural theorists, the social nature of cognitive development is captured in the concept of *intersubjectivity,* which refers to mutual, shared understanding among participants in an activity.** When Victoria and her father solve puzzles together, they share an understanding of the goals of their activity and of their roles in solving the puzzles. Such shared understanding allows Victoria and her dad to work together in complementary fashion on the puzzles. **Such interactions typify *guided participation,* in which cognitive growth results from children's involvement in structured activities with others who are more skilled than they.** Through guided participation, children learn from others how to connect new experiences and new skills with what they already know (Rogoff, 2003). Guided participation is shown when a child learns a new video game from a peer or an adolescent learns a new karate move from a partner.

Sociocultural theories emphasize that cultures influence cognitive development by the tools that are available to support children's thinking, such as an abacus.

Vygotsky died of tuberculosis when he was only 37 years old, so he never had the opportunity to formulate a complete theory of cognitive development like that of Piaget. Nevertheless, his ideas are influential because they fill some gaps in Piaget's account of cognitive development. Three of Vygotsky's most important contributions are the concepts of zone of proximal development, scaffolding, and private speech.

The Zone of Proximal Development   Angela likes helping her 11-year-old son with his math homework, particularly when it includes word problems. Her son does most of the work but Angela often gives him hints. For example, she might help him decide what arithmetic operations are required. When Angela's son tries to solve these problems by himself, he rarely succeeds. **The difference between what Angela's son can do with assistance and what he can do alone defines the** *zone of proximal development*. That is, the zone refers to the difference between the level of performance a child can achieve when working independently and the higher level of performance that is possible when working under the guidance of more skilled adults or peers (Daniels, 2011; Wertsch & Tulviste, 1992).

Think, for example, about a preschooler who is asked to clean her bedroom. She doesn't know where to begin. By structuring the task for the child—"start by putting away your books, then your toys, then your dirty clothes"—an adult can help the child accomplish what she cannot do by herself. Similarly, the zone of proximal development explains why Victoria, in the module-opening vignette, solves difficult jigsaw puzzles with a bit of help from her dad. Just as training wheels help children learn to ride a bike by allowing them to concentrate on other aspects of bicycling, collaborators help children perform effectively by providing structure, hints, and reminders.

The idea of a zone of proximal development follows naturally from Vygotsky's basic premise that cognition develops first in a social setting and only gradually comes under the child's independent control. Understanding how the shift from social to individual learning occurs brings us to the second of Vygotsky's key contributions.

Scaffolding   Have you ever had the good fortune to work with a master teacher, one who seemed to know exactly when to say the right thing to help you over an obstacle but otherwise let you work uninterrupted? *Scaffolding* **refers to a teaching style that matches the amount of assistance to the learner's needs.** Early in learning a new task, when a child knows little, teachers such as the one in the photo provide a lot of direct instruction. But, as the child begins to catch on to the task, the teacher provides less instruction and only occasional reminders (Gauvain, 2001).

We saw previously how a parent helping a preschooler clean her room must provide detailed structure. As the child does the task more often, the parent needs to provide less structure. Similarly, when high-school students first try to do proofs in geometry, the teacher must lead them through each step; as the students begin to understand how proofs are done and can do more on their own, the teacher gradually provides less help.

Do parents worldwide scaffold their children's learning? If so, do they use similar methods? The "Cultural Influences" feature answers these questions.

Experienced teachers often provide much direct instruction as children first encounter a task, then provide less instruction as children "catch on."

Cultural Influences
How Do Parents in Different Cultures Scaffold Their Children's Learning?

Cross-cultural research by Barbara Rogoff and her colleagues (1993) suggests that parents and other adults in many cultures scaffold learning, but they do it in different ways. These researchers studied parents and 1- to 2-year-olds in four different settings: a medium-sized U.S. city, a small tribal village in India, a large city in Turkey, and a town in the highlands of Guatemala. In one part of the study, parents tried to get their toddlers to operate a novel toy (for example, a wooden doll that danced when a string was pulled). No ground rules or guidelines concerning teaching were given; parents were free to be as direct or uninvolved as they cared.

What did parents do? In all four cultural settings, the vast majority attempted to scaffold their children's learning, either by dividing a difficult task into easier subtasks or by doing parts of the task themselves,

particularly the more complicated parts. However, as the graphs in Figure 6-2 show, parents in different cultures scaffold in different ways. Turkish parents give the most verbal instruction and use some gestures (pointing, nodding, and shrugging). U.S. parents also use these methods, but to slightly lesser degrees. Turkish and U.S. parents almost never touch (such as nudging a child's elbow) or gaze (use eye contact, such as winking or staring). Indian parents seem to use roughly equal amounts of speech, gesture, and touch or gaze to scaffold. Guatemalan parents also use all three techniques, and, overall, Guatemalan parents give the most scaffolding of the four cultures. Evidently, parents worldwide try to simplify learning tasks for their children, but the methods they use to scaffold learning vary across cultures.

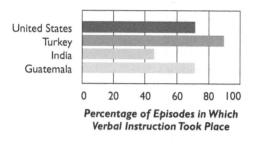

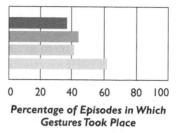

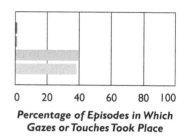

Percentage of Episodes in Which Verbal Instruction Took Place

Percentage of Episodes in Which Gestures Took Place

Percentage of Episodes in Which Gazes or Touches Took Place

Figure 6-2

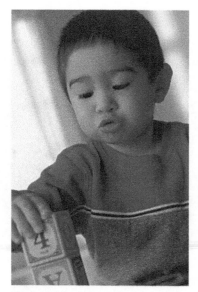

Young children often talk to themselves as they're performing difficult tasks; this helps them control their own behavior.

The defining characteristic of scaffolding—giving help but not more than is needed—clearly promotes learning (Cole, 2006). Youngsters do not learn readily when they are constantly told what to do or when they are simply left to struggle through a problem unaided. However, when teachers collaborate with them—allowing children to take on more and more of a task as they master its different elements—they learn more effectively (Murphy & Messer, 2000). Scaffolding is an important technique for transferring skills from others to the child, both in formal settings like schools and in informal settings like the home or playground (Bernier, Carlson, & Whipple, 2010).

Private Speech The little boy in the photo is talking to himself as he plays. **This behavior demonstrates** *private speech,* **comments not directed to others but intended to help children regulate their own behavior.** Vygotsky viewed private speech as an intermediate step toward self-regulation of cognitive skills (Fernyhough, 2010). At first, children's behavior is regulated by speech from other people that is directed toward them. When youngsters first try to control their own behavior and thoughts without others present, they instruct themselves by speaking aloud. **Finally, as children gain ever-greater skill, private speech becomes** *inner speech,* **Vygotsky's term for thought.**

If children use private speech to help control their behavior, then we should see children using it more often on difficult tasks than on easy tasks, and more often after a mistake than after a correct response. These predictions are generally supported in research (Berk, 2003), which documents the power of language in helping children learn to control their own behavior and thinking.

Vygotsky's view of cognitive development as an apprenticeship, a collaboration between expert and novice, complements the Piagetian view of cognitive development described in Module 6.1. Also like Piaget's theory, Vygotsky's perspective has several implications for helping children to learn. We've already seen that a teacher's main mission is to scaffold student's learning, not direct it. In other words, teachers should provide an environment that will allow students to learn on their own. This involves finding a middle ground: Students learn little when teachers provide too much instruction (e.g., "Here's how you do it and here's the right answer") or too little instruction ("Try to figure it out yourself"). Instead, a teacher needs to determine a child's current knowledge and provide the experience—in the form of a suggestion, question, or activity—that propels the child to more sophisticated understanding (Polman, 2004; Scrimsher & Tudge, 2003).

Perhaps even more important is Vygotsky's emphasis on learning as a cooperative activity in which students work together. Sometimes this collaboration takes the form of peer tutoring, in which students teach each other. Tutors often acquire a richer and deeper understanding of the topic they teach; tutees benefit, too, in part because teaching is one-on-one but also because tutees are more willing to tell a peer when an explanation is not clear.

Another form of cooperative learning involves groups of students working together on projects (e.g., a group presentation) or to achieve common goals (e.g., deciding rules for a classroom). These activities help students to take responsibility for a project and to become good "team players." Students also learn how to consider different viewpoints and how to resolve conflicts.

Cooperative learning does pay off for students. They do learn—achievement scores increase (Rohrbeck et al., 2003). What's more, cooperative learning improves students' self-concepts—students feel more competent—and they learn social skills, such as how to negotiate, build consensus, and resolve conflicts (Ginsburg-Block, Rohrbeck, & Fantuzzo, 2006).

Information Processing

LO5 According to information-processing psychologists, how does thinking change with development?

In Module 6.1, we saw that the mechanisms of change proposed by Piaget—accommodation, assimilation, and equilibration—were vague and difficult to study scientifically. Consequently, identifying mechanisms of growth has been a priority of child-development scientists, and in the 1960s researchers first began to use computer systems to explain how thinking develops. **Just as computers consist of both hardware and software that the computer runs,** *information-processing theory* **proposes that human cognition consists of mental hardware and mental software.** Figure 6-3 on page 194 shows how information-processing psychologists use the computer analogy to examine human cognition. The mental hardware has three components: sensory memory, working memory, and long-term memory.

Sensory memory is where information is held briefly in raw, unanalyzed form (no longer than a few seconds). For example, look at your hand as you

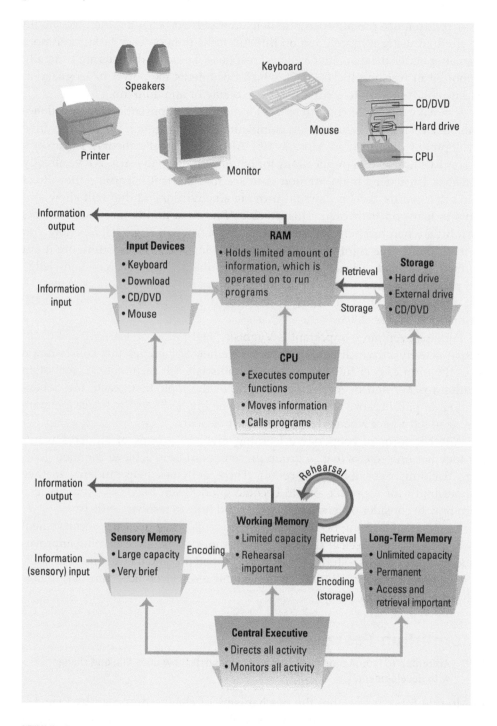

Figure 6-3

clench your fist, rapidly open your hand (to extend your fingers), and then rapidly reclench your fist. If you watch carefully, you'll see an image of your fingers that lasts momentarily after you reclench your hand. What you're seeing is an image stored in sensory memory.

Working memory **is the site of ongoing cognitive activity.** In a personal computer, RAM (random-access memory) holds the software that we're using and stores data used by the software. In much the same way, working memory includes both ongoing cognitive processes and the information that they require

(Baddeley, 2012). For example, as you read these sentences, part of working memory is allocated to the cognitive processes responsible for determining the meanings of individual words; working memory also briefly stores the results of these analyses while they are used by other cognitive processes to give meaning to sentences.

***Long-term memory* is a limitless, permanent storehouse of knowledge of the world.** Long-term memory is like a computer's hard drive, a fairly permanent storehouse of programs and data. It includes facts (e.g., Charles Lindbergh flew the Atlantic in the *Spirit of St. Louis*), personal events (e.g., "I moved to Maryland in July 1999"), and skills (e.g., how to play the cello).

Information in long-term memory is rarely forgotten, though it is sometimes hard to access. For example, do you remember the name of the African American agricultural chemist who pioneered crop rotation methods and invented peanut butter? If his name doesn't come to mind, look at this list:

Marconi   Carver   Fulton   Luther

Now do you know the answer? (If not, it appears before "Check Your Learning," on page 199.) Just as books are sometimes misplaced in a library, you sometimes cannot find a fact in long-term memory. Given a list of names, though, you can go directly to the location in long-term memory associated with each name and determine which is the famed chemist.

Coordinating all these activities is the *central executive* (also called *executive functioning*), which refers to the executive network of attention described in **Module 5.2 and resembles a computer's operating system** (e.g., Windows 8 or Linux). Executive function includes three related components: inhibiting inappropriate thoughts and actions; shifting from one action, thought, or task to another; and updating the contents of working memory (Bull & Lee, 2014).

When children are thinking—whether reading, finding their way to a friend's house, or deciding what to eat for dessert—the system in Figure 6-3 is involved, usually in conjunction with specialized strategies that are designed for particular tasks. Reading, for example, calls on strategies for identifying sounds associated with specific letters; way-finding calls on strategies for recognizing familiar landmarks as a way to verify that one is "on course." Thus, in the information-processing view, thinking involves the general system shown in Figure 6-3 implementing specialized strategies, just as a computer is a general-purpose system that runs specialized software (e.g., word-processing software, graphing software) to accomplish different tasks.

How Information Processing Changes with Development For Piaget, accommodation, assimilation, and equilibration are behind the steady age-related march to ever-more sophisticated thinking. In contrast, information-processing psychologists describe several mechanisms that drive cognitive development (Halford & Andrews, 2011; Siegler & Alibali, 2005). Let's look at some of them.

Better Strategies Older children usually use better strategies to solve problems (Bjorklund, 2012). That is, as children develop, they use strategies that are faster, more accurate, and easier. For example, trying to find a parent in a crowded auditorium, a younger child might search each row, looking carefully at every person; an older child might remember that the parent is wearing a purple sweater and only look at people in purple. Both children will probably find the parent, but the older child's approach is more efficient. Thus, as children get older and more knowledgeable, their mental software becomes more sophisticated and more powerful, just as the current version of PowerPoint is vastly more capable than PowerPoint 1.0 (which ran only in black and white when it was released in 1987!).

How do children learn more effective strategies? Of course, parents and teachers often help youngsters learn new strategies. By structuring children's actions and providing hints, adults demonstrate new strategies and how best to use them. However, youngsters also learn new strategies by watching and working with more-skilled children (Tudge, Winterhoff, & Hogan, 1996). For example, children and adolescents watch others play video games to learn good game strategies. Children also discover new strategies on their own (Tsubota & Chen, 2012). For example, when my daughter was 5, I watched her match words with their antonyms in a language workbook. The pages always had an equal number of words and antonyms, so she quickly learned to connect the last word with the one remaining antonym, without thinking about the meaning of either.

More Effective Executive Functioning The components of executive functioning improve steadily during childhood. As children develop, they are better able to inhibit inappropriate thoughts or actions. For example, an older child would be better able to ignore classmates whispering nearby and listen to her teacher's directions. Similarly, with development, children become more flexible at shifting from one task to another. To illustrate, older children are better able to move smoothly from practicing arithmetic facts to writing a short story. Finally, updating also improves with age: An older girl who is playing basketball is better able to update the game's score after each team makes a basket (Diamond, 2013). These age-related improvements in executive functioning fuel many cognitive-development changes, including improved reasoning and mastery of academic skills (Bull & Lee, 2014; Richland & Burchinal, 2013).

Increased Automatic Processing Think back to when you were learning a new skill, such as how to type. At first, you had to think about every step in the process, remembering the location of each letter and deciding which finger to use. But as your skill grew, each step became easier until you could type without thinking about the individuals letters; your fingers seemed to move automatically to the right keys, in the right sequence. **Cognitive activities that require virtually no effort are known as** *automatic processes.*

To understand how automatic processes affect developmental change, we need to return to working memory. In the early phases of learning a skill, each individual step must be stored in working memory. Because there are so many steps, an unmastered skill often occupies much of working memory. In contrast, when a skill has been mastered, individual steps are no longer stored in working memory, leaving capacity available for other activities.

Compared to adolescents and adults, children have limited experience in most tasks, so they perform few processes automatically. Instead, their processing requires substantial working memory capacity. As children gain experience, however, some processes become automatic, freeing working memory capacity for other processes (Rubinstein et al., 2002). Thus, when faced with complex tasks involving many processes, older children are more likely to succeed because they can perform some of the processes automatically. In contrast, younger children must think about all or most of the processes, taxing or even exceeding the capacity of their working memory.

Increased Speed of Processing As children develop, they complete most mental processes at an ever-faster rate (Cerella & Hale, 1994). Improved speed is obvious

As children and adolescents acquire greater skill at new tasks such as typing, some aspects of the task are performed automatically, which means they require no effort.

when we measure how fast children of different ages respond on tasks. Across a wide range of cognitive tasks, such as deciding which of two numbers is greater, naming a pictured object, and searching memory, 4- and 5-year-olds are generally one-third as fast as adults, whereas 8- and 9-year-olds are one-half as fast as adults (Kail et al., 2013).

Age differences in processing speed are critical when a specified number of actions must be completed in a fixed period of time. For example, perhaps you've had the unfortunate experience of trying to understand a professor who lectures at warp speed. The instructor's speech was so rapid that your cognitive processes couldn't keep up, which meant that you didn't get much out of the lecture. The problem is even more serious for children, who process information much more slowly than adults.

The four types of developmental change shown in Summary Table 6-1 represent powerful mechanisms for driving cognitive development during childhood and adolescence. These mechanisms produce steady age-related increases in cognitive skill. In contrast to Piaget's theory, there are no abrupt or qualitative changes that create distinct cognitive stages.

Finally, what would information-processing researchers say about Victoria, from the module-opening vignette? They would probably want to explain why she finds some puzzles harder than others. Using the list of developmental mechanisms that we've examined in the past few pages, they would note that complex puzzles may require more sophisticated strategies that are too demanding for her limited working-memory capacity. However, as she does more and more puzzles with her dad, some parts of these complex strategies may become automated, making it easier for Victoria to use the strategy.

Q&A QUESTION 6.2

Fifteen-year-old Quinn has just completed driver training, and he loves to get behind the wheel. For the most part, his parents are okay with his performance, but they absolutely refuse to let him listen to the radio while he's driving. Quinn thinks this is a stupid rule. Do you?

Core-Knowledge Theories

LO6 What naïve theories do children hold about physics, psychology, and biology?

Imagine a 12-year-old (a) trying to download apps for her new iPad, (b) wondering why her dad is grouchy today, and (c) taking her pet dog for a walk. According to Piaget and most information-processing theories, in each case the same basic mechanisms of thinking are at work, even though the contents of the child's thinking range from objects to people to pets. In this view, different types of knowledge

---

SUMMARY TABLE 6-1

TYPES OF DEVELOPMENTAL CHANGE IN INFORMATION PROCESSING

Type of Developmental Change	Defined	Example
Better strategies	Older children use faster, more accurate, and easier strategies.	Younger children may "sound out" a word's spelling, but older children simply retrieve it from memory.
More effective executive functioning	Older children are more skilled at inhibiting, shifting, and updating.	Asked by a teacher to format assignments in a new way (e.g., write their name in a different location on the page), older children are more successful in adapting to the new format.
Increased automatic processing	Older children execute more processes automatically (without using working memory).	Asked to get ready for bed, an older child goes through all the tasks (e.g., brush teeth, put on pajamas) while thinking about other things, but a younger child focuses on each task as well as what to do next.
Increased speed of processing	Older children can execute mental processes more rapidly than younger children.	Shown a picture of a dog, older children can retrieve the name "dog" from memory more rapidly.

are like different kinds of cars—they come in countless numbers of makes, models, and colors, but down deep they are alike in consisting of an engine, four wheels, doors, windows, and so on.

In contrast to this view, *core-knowledge theories* **propose distinctive domains of knowledge, some of which are acquired very early in life** (Newcombe, 2013; Spelke & Kinzler, 2007). In this view, knowledge is more like the broader class of vehicles: Much knowledge is general, represented by the large number of cars. But there are also distinct, specialized forms of knowledge, represented by buses, trucks, and motorcycles. Returning to our hypothetical 12-year-old, core-knowledge theorists would claim that her thinking about objects, people, and pets may reflect fundamentally different ways of thinking.

Core-knowledge theories were created, in part, to account for the fact that most children acquire some kinds of knowledge relatively easily and early in life. For example, think about learning language (a native language, not a second language) versus learning calculus. Most children learn to talk—in fact, the *inability* to talk is a sign of atypical development—and they do so with little apparent effort. (When was the last time you heard a 3-year-old complaining that learning to talk was just *too* hard?) Calculus, in comparison, is mastered by relatively few, usually only after hours of hard work solving problem after problem.

According to core-knowledge theorists, some forms of knowledge are so important for human survival that specialized systems have evolved to simplify learning of those forms of knowledge. In the case of language, for example, spoken communication has been so essential throughout human history that mental structures evolved to simplify language learning. Other evolutionarily important domains of knowledge include knowledge of objects and simple understanding of people.

The nature of these mental structures, or *modules*, is very much a matter of debate. Some core-knowledge theorists believe they're like the math or graphics coprocessor on a computer: They're prewired to analyze one kind of data efficiently (numbers and images, respectively, for the computer) but nothing else. The language module, for example, would be sensitive to speech sounds and would be prewired to derive grammatical rules from sequences of words. Another view of these specialized mental structures borrows from Piaget's metaphor of the child as a scientist who creates informal theories of the world. However, core-knowledge theorists believe that children's theories are focused on core domains, rather than being all-encompassing as Piaget proposed. Also, in creating their theories, children don't start from scratch; instead, a few innate principles provide the starting point. For example, infants' early theories of objects seem to be rooted in a few key principles, such as the principle of cohesion, the idea that objects move as connected wholes (Spelke & Kinzler, 2007). Both of these ideas of mental structures may be right: that is, some forms of knowledge may be better described as modular, but others may be more consistent with the child-as-scientist view.

What are the domains of knowledge that have these specialized mental structures? Language was the first core domain identified by scientists; there is so much to learn about children's mastery of language that I've devoted an entire chapter to it (Chapter 9). In addition, many child-development researchers agree that young children rapidly acquire knowledge of objects, people, and living things. That is, they create informal or naïve theories of physics, psychology, and biology. Like language, acquiring knowledge in each of these domains has been central to human existence: Naïve physics allows children to predict where and how objects will move in the environment; naïve psychology makes for more

SUMMARY TABLE 6-2

CHARACTERISTICS OF MODERN THEORIES OF COGNITIVE DEVELOPMENT

Approach	Characteristics
Vygotsky's sociocultural theory	Views cognitive development as a sociocultural enterprise; experts use scaffolding to help a novice acquire knowledge; children use private speech to regulate their own thinking.
Information processing	Based on the computer metaphor, views cognitive change in terms of better strategies, increased capacity of working memory, more effective inhibitory and executive processing, more automatic processing, and faster processing speed.
Core knowledge	Views cognitive development as an innate capability to easily acquire knowledge in such specialized domains of evolutionary importance as language, knowledge of objects, and understanding of people.

successful interactions with others; and naïve biology is important in avoiding predators and maintaining health.

Finally, if core-knowledge theorists were asked to comment on Victoria (from the module-opening vignette), they would emphasize the contrast between her sophisticated language skill and her relatively undeveloped puzzle-solving skill. Language represents an evolutionarily important domain, so Victoria's precocity here is not surprising; doing jigsaw puzzles is not a specialized domain with evolutionary significance, which explains her relative lack of skill in that task.

We'll see how knowledge in core domains changes with development in Module 6.3. For now, Summary Table 6-2 reviews the defining features of the three theories that we've explored in Module 6.2.

As you think about the three theoretical perspectives listed in Summary Table 6-2, keep in mind that each goes beyond Piaget's theory in a unique direction. The sociocultural approach expands the focus of cognitive development research from a solitary child to one who is surrounded by people and the culture they represent; the information-processing perspective expands the focus of developmental mechanisms from accommodation and assimilation to executive functioning, processing speed, and other mechanisms derived from mental hardware and mental software; core-knowledge theories expand the focus to recognize distinct domains of evolutionarily significant knowledge. Thus, these three perspectives provide complementary, not competing, accounts of cognitive development.

> *Response to question on page 195.* The agricultural chemist who pioneered crop rotation while on the faculty of Tuskegee Institute of Technology is George Washington Carver.

 # Check Your Learning

RECALL What three concepts are fundamental to Vygotsky's sociocultural theory?

What specialized domains of knowledge have been identified by core-knowledge theorists?

INTERPRET Do the developmental mechanisms in the information-processing perspective emphasize nature, nurture, or both? How?

APPLY How might an information-processing theorist explain sociocultural influences on cognitive development (e.g., scaffolding)?

6.3 Understanding in Core Domains

OUTLINE

Understanding Objects and Their Properties

Understanding Living Things

Understanding People

LEARNING OBJECTIVES

LO7 What do infants understand about the nature of objects?

LO8 When and how do young children distinguish between living and nonliving things?

LO9 How do young children acquire a theory of mind?

Amy, a reporter for a magazine that reviews products, was assigned to do a story on different kinds of "sippy cups"—plastic cups with a lid and spout that are spill-proof that are perfect for babies who are learning to use a cup. Amy brought home 12 different sippy cups and used each one for a day with her 14-month-old son. She discovered that some definitely worked better than others, but what amazed her was that after the first day her son always knew what to do with the cup. Despite differences in color, size, and the shape of the spout, he apparently recognized each one as a sippy cup because he immediately lifted each new style to his mouth and started drinking. Amy wondered how he could do this.

The world is filled with endless varieties of "stuff," including sippy cups, cats, and basketball players. Recognizing different instances of the same kind of thing—that is, being able to categorize—is essential for young children. By knowing that an object belongs to a category, we learn some of its properties, including what it can do, and where we're likely to find it. Amy's son, for example, quickly learned the essentials of a sippy cup; later he recognized each different cup as being a member of the general category of sippy cups and knew exactly what to do with them. If he couldn't categorize, every experience would be novel—on seeing yet another slightly different sippy cup, he'd need to figure out what to do with it as if it were a uniquely new object.

How do infants form categories? Important clues come from perceptual features and their organization. A sippy cup, for example, consists of a cylinder with a spout at one end. After infants have learned these features and how they're related, they can recognize sippy cups regardless of their color or size (Quinn, 2004, 2011). Similarly, they can learn the features that distinguish, for example, dogs from cats, or flowers from chairs. One popular view is that infants' first categories denote groups of objects with many similar perceptual features—the "dog" category includes four-legged animals with a distinctive snout, the "tree" category includes large bark-covered objects with limbs (Rakison & Yermolayeva, 2010).

Perceptual features aren't the only basis for children's categories. Functions are also important. When two objects look different but perform the same function (e.g., make the same sound when shaken), children judge them to be in the same category. Similarly, when adults label objects that look different with the same word, young children believe that the objects are in the same category (Gelman & Meyer, 2011).

Children's earliest categories are often formed at a basic level, where category members look similar or have similar functions. Examples would be trees, flowers, dogs, birds, cars, and chairs. But children also learn that trees and flowers are part of the more general category of plants and they learn that dogs and birds are part of the more general category of animals (Mareschal & Tan, 2007). At the same time, children learn that their first categories can also be subdivided; for example, they recognize that flowers include the subcategories of rose, tulip, and daisy.

In the remainder of this module, we'll see how infants and older children use these categorization skills to carve the world into domains and create theories within those domains. We'll consider infants' knowledge of objects, living things, and people.

Understanding Objects and Their Properties

LO7 **What do infants understand about the nature of objects?**

As adults, we know much about objects and their properties. For example, we know that if we place a coffee cup on a table, it will remain there unless moved by another person; it will not move by itself or simply disappear. And we don't release a coffee cup in midair because we know that an unsupported object will fall. Young children's understanding of these properties has long interested child-development researchers, in part because Piaget claimed that understanding of objects develops slowly, taking many months to become complete. However, other investigators have used clever procedures to show that babies understand objects much earlier than Piaget claimed. Renée Baillargeon (1987, 1994), for example, assessed object permanence using a procedure in which infants first saw a silver screen that appeared to be rotating back and forth. When they were familiar with this display, one of two new displays was shown. In the realistic event, a red box appeared in a position behind the screen, making it impossible for the screen to rotate as far back as it had previously. Instead, the screen rotated until it made contact with the box, then rotated forward. In the unrealistic event, shown in Figure 6-4, the red box

1. The silver screen is lying flat on the table and the red box is fully visible.

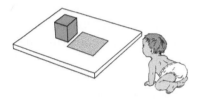

2. The silver screen has begun to rotate, but the red box is largely visible.

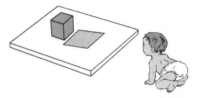

3. The silver screen is now vertical, blocking the red box.

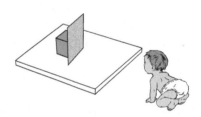

4. The silver screen continues to rotate, blocking the red box, which has started to drop through the trap door.

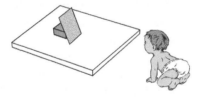

5. The silver screen is completely flat, apparently having "rotated through" the red box, which is actually now under the table.

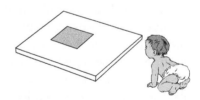

6. The silver screen is rotating back toward the infant but still blocks the red box.

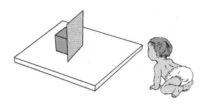

7. The silver screen is again flat and the box fully visible to the infant.

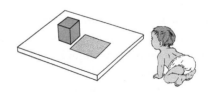

Figure 6-4

appeared but the screen continued to rotate as before. The screen rotated back until it was flat, then rotated forward, again revealing the red box. The illusion was possible because the box was mounted on a movable platform that allowed it to drop out of the way of the moving screen. However, from the infant's perspective, the box seemed to vanish behind the screen, only to reappear.

The disappearance and reappearance of the box violates the idea that objects exist permanently. Consequently, an infant who understands that objects are permanent should find the unrealistic event a truly novel stimulus and look at it longer than the realistic event. In fact, 4½-month-olds looked longer at the unrealistic event than the realistic event. Apparently they thought that the unrealistic event was novel, just as we are surprised when an object vanishes from a magician's scarf. Evidently, then, infants have some understanding of object permanence early in the first year of life.

Infants know more about objects than permanence. They know that objects move continuously on a path, not magically moving from one spot to another; they know that objects are solid and that objects cannot "pass through" each other; and they know that one object must contact another to cause movement— objects do not move spontaneously (Hespos & vanMarle, 2012). And, as we'll see in the "Focus on Research" feature, infants distinguish properties of solid objects from properties of liquids.

Focus on Research
Distinguishing Liquids from Solids

Who were the investigators, and what was the aim of the study? A property of solid objects is that they have a shape that is maintained as the object moves; in contrast, substances like liquids and sand change their "shape" depending on the kind of vessel that contains them. Susan Hespos, Alissa Ferry, and Lance Rips (2009) wanted to determine whether 5-month-olds understand these unique properties of solids and liquids.

How did the investigators measure the topic of interest? Infants were assigned to one of two conditions, shown in Figure 6-5: In a liquid condition, they saw a clear plastic drinking cup filled with a blue liquid. For several familiarization trials, the experimenter rotated the cup back and forth; as she did, movement was apparent as the surface of the liquid remained horizontal. In the solid condition, the clear plastic drinking cup was filled with a blue resin that looked just like the blue liquid. However, when the experimenter rotated the cup back and forth, the resin did not move and the top of the resin remained perpendicular to the sides of the glass.

On test trials, infants in both conditions saw two events, shown at the bottom of Figure 6-5. In one, a drinking cup containing blue liquid was lifted and tilted so that the liquid poured into the second cup; in the other event, a drinking cup containing the blue resin was lifted and tilted so that the resin slid into the second cup. Research assistants recorded how long infants looked at each event. If infants distinguish liquids and solids, those familiarized with the liquid should be surprised (and look longer) at the event showing the resin slide from one cup to the other (because they believe that the blue entity is a liquid). By the same logic, infants familiarized with the solid should be surprised at the event showing the liquid pour from one cup to the other (because they believe that the entity is a solid).

Who were the children in the study? Hespos and her colleagues tested 32 5-month-olds: 16 in the liquid condition and 16 in the solid condition.

What was the design of the study? The study was experimental. The independent variables were the type of entity shown on the familiarization trials (solid vs. liquid) and the kind of event shown on the test trials (pouring vs. sliding). The dependent variable was the time spent looking at each event. The study was not developmental because only 5-month-olds were tested.

Were there ethical concerns with the study? No. Most babies typically enjoyed watching these events. Occasionally babies would get fussy during the course of the experiment—perhaps because they were bored or tired—and when this happened the experiment was stopped.

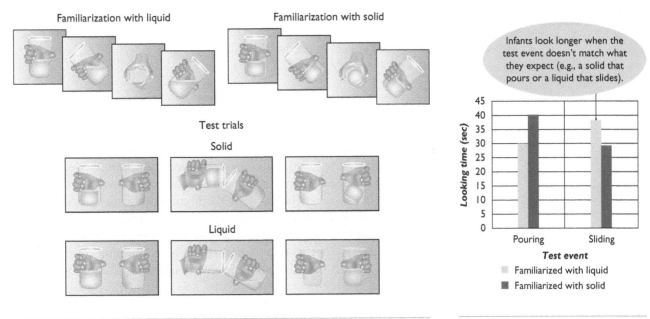

Figure 6-5

Figure 6-6

What were the results? Figure 6-6 shows the amount of time that infants spent looking at sliding and pouring, separately for the infants who were familiarized with liquids and those familiarized with solids. In each case, infants looked longer at the unexpected events: When familiarization trials led infants to believe that the cup contained a solid, they were surprised when the "solid" poured from one cup into the other. When familiarization trials led infants to believe that the cup contained a liquid, they were surprised when the "liquid" slid from one cup into the other.

What did the investigators conclude? By 5 months, infants know some of the differences between liquids and solids. They understand that solids keep their shape when moved but that liquids do not. In other words, "[i]nfants are capable of noticing the characteristic difference between the movement of liquids and solids, and they can use this difference to predict later properties of these entities" (p. 609).

What converging evidence would strengthen these conclusions? Rigid versus changing shape is just one property that distinguishes solids and liquids. One way to strengthen conclusions about infants' understanding of objects would be to test their expectations about other properties that distinguish solids and liquids. For example, objects can pass through a liquid but not through a solid; solids can be carried in containers that have holes (e.g., a sieve or colander) but liquids cannot. Showing that infants recognize these differences would provide additional evidence that they understand the unique properties of solids and liquids.

These amazing demonstrations attest to the fact that the infant is indeed an accomplished naïve physicist (Baillargeon, 2004). Of course, the infant's theories are far from complete; physical properties can be understood at many different levels (Hood, Carey, & Prasada, 2000). Using gravity as an example, infants expect unsupported objects to fall, elementary-school children know that such objects fall because of gravity, and physics students know that the force of gravity equals the mass of an object times the acceleration caused by gravity. Obviously, infants do not understand objects at the level of physics students. And some properties of objects aren't learned until after infancy. For example, not until the preschool years do children understand ownership—that people can acquire objects by receiving them as gifts, by buying them, or by creating them (Nancekivell, Van de Vondervoort, & Friedman, 2013). However, the important point is that infants rapidly create a reasonably accurate theory of some basic properties of objects, a theory that helps them to expect that objects such as toys will act in predictable ways.

Understanding Living Things

LO8 **When and how do young children distinguish between living and nonliving things?**

Fundamental to adults' naïve theories is the distinction between living and nonliving things. For example, adults know that living things are made of cells, inherit properties from parents, and move spontaneously. Knowledge of living things begins in infancy, when babies first distinguish animate objects (e.g., people, insects, other animals) from inanimate objects (e.g., rocks, plants, furniture, tools). Motion is critical in early understanding of the difference between animate and inanimate objects: That is, infants and toddlers use motion to identify animate objects; by 12 to 15 months children have determined that animate objects are self-propelled, can move in irregular paths, and act to achieve goals (Biro & Leslie, 2007; Opfer & Gelman, 2011; Rakison & Hahn, 2004).

By the preschool years, children's naïve theories of biology have come to include many of the specific properties associated with living things (Wellman & Gelman, 1998). Many 4-year-olds' theories of biology include the following elements:

- *Movement:* Children understand that animals can move themselves but inanimate objects can only be moved by other objects or by people. Shown the events in Figure 6-7—an animal and a toy car hopping across a table in exactly the same manner—preschoolers claim that only the animal can really move itself (Gelman & Gottfried, 1996).

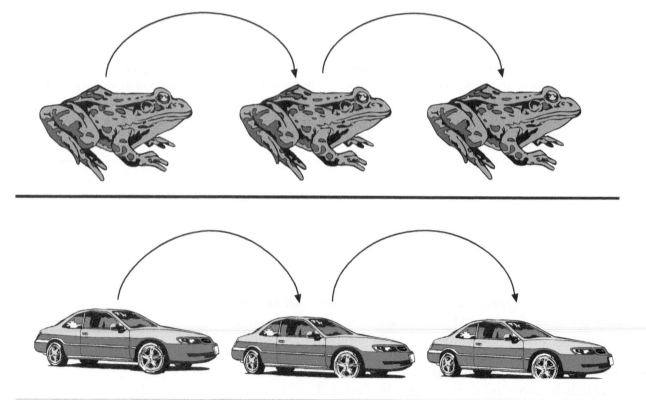

Figure 6-7

- *Growth:* Children understand that, from their first appearance, animals get bigger and physically more complex but that inanimate objects do not. They believe, for example, that sea otters and termites become larger as time goes by but that tea kettles and teddy bears do not (Margett & Witherington, 2011; Rosengren et al., 1991).

- *Internal parts:* Children know that the insides of animate objects contain different materials than the insides of inanimate objects. Preschool children judge that blood and bones are more likely to be inside an animate object but that cotton and metal are more likely to be inside an inanimate object (Simons & Keil, 1995).

- *Inheritance:* Children realize that only living things have offspring that resemble their parents. Asked to explain why a dog is pink, preschoolers believe that some biological characteristic of the parents probably made the dog pink; asked to explain why a phone is pink, preschoolers rely on mechanical causes (e.g., a worker used a machine), not biological ones (Diesendruck et al., 2013; Weissman & Kalish, 1999).

- *Illness:* Preschoolers believe that permanent illnesses such as color blindness or food allergies are more likely to be inherited from parents, but that temporary illnesses such as a sore throat or a runny nose are more likely to be transmitted through contact with other people (Raman & Gelman, 2005). They also understand that people can become ill when they eat contaminated food (Legare, Wellman, & Gelman, 2009).

- *Healing:* Children understand that, when injured, animate things heal by regrowth whereas inanimate things must be fixed by humans. Preschoolers know that hair will grow back when cut from a child's head but must be repaired by a person when cut from a doll's head (Backscheider, Shatz, & Gelman, 1993).

QUESTION 6.3

One afternoon, 15-month-old Brandon and 6-month-old Justin saw a dragonfly for the first time as it flew around in the backyard, hunting mosquitoes. Would either Brandon or Justin be likely to conclude that a dragonfly is a living thing?

By 4 years, children's understanding of living things is so sophisticated that children aren't fooled by lifelike robots: 4-year-olds know that robots are machines that (a) do not eat or grow and (b) are made by people and can break (Jipson & Gelman, 2007). Nevertheless, preschoolers believe that robots represent a special kind of machine because youngsters attribute human-like traits (e.g., being friendly) to robots (Kahn, Gary, & Shen, 2013).

A fundamental part of young children's theory of living things is a commitment to *teleological explanations*—children believe that living things and parts of living things exist for a purpose. A child like the one in the photo may say that fish have smooth skin so that they won't cut other fish that swim alongside them (Kelemen, 2003). Similarly, a child may explain that lions exist so that people can see them in a zoo. One view is that teleological explanations are based on children's knowledge that objects such as tools and machines are usually made with a purpose in mind. Children may follow a similar logic in thinking that living things (and their parts) were designed with a specific purpose in mind (Kelemen & DiYanni, 2005). This teleological thinking echoes the animistic thinking described on page 184: children attribute their own intentions and goals to other living objects.

Young children's theories of living things are also rooted in *essentialism*: children believe that all living things have an essence that can't be seen but gives a living thing its identity. All birds share an underlying "bird-ness" that distinguishes them from dogs, which, of course, share an underlying "dog-ness." And bird-ness is what allows birds to fly and sing (Gelman, 2003). Young children's essentialism explains why 4-year-olds believe that a baby kangaroo adopted by goats will still hop and have a pouch and why they believe that a

Young children's thinking about living things is often teleological: Children believe that objects and parts of objects were created with a purpose in mind. For example, a fish has smooth skin so that it won't cut other fish swimming next to it.

watermelon seed planted in a cornfield will produce watermelons (Solomon & Zaitchik, 2012). The baby kangaroo and the watermelon seed have kangaroo-ness and watermelon-ness that cause properties of kangaroos and watermelons to emerge in maturity.

Most children in Western cultures do not have well-defined ideas about what essences are. They believe that essences are inside an animal because they think that removing an animal's inside parts changes the animal's identity: for example, a dog that has blood and bones removed is no longer a dog (Gelman & Wellman, 1991). But their ideas about essences are limited to a vague notion of "inside parts" located near the center of the body (Newman & Keil, 2008). However, preschool children living in a Native American community in Wisconsin—the Menominee—have more refined ideas. Blood relations matter a great deal in this community because, for example, regulations regarding school funding and hunting are based in part on the number of "full-blooded" Menominee living in the community. Preschool Menominee children believe that a baby cow raised by pigs would grow up to look and act like a cow, which is the usual essentialist response. But, when told that a baby cow received a complete blood transfusion from its adoptive pig parent, now preschool children believed that the cow would grow up to be a pig. For Menominee preschoolers, blood is the essence of cow-ness or pig-ness (Waxman, Medin, & Ross, 2007).

Where do children get this knowledge of living things? Some of it comes just by watching animals, which children love to do. But parents also contribute: When reading books about animals to preschoolers, they frequently mention the properties that distinguish animals, including self-initiated motion (e.g., "the seal is jumping in the water") and psychological properties (e.g., "the bear is really mad!"). Such talk helps to highlight important characteristics of animals for youngsters (Gelman et al., 1998).

Of course, although preschoolers' naïve theories of biology are complex, their theories aren't complete. Preschoolers don't know, for instance, that genes are the biological basis for inheritance (Springer & Keil, 1991). And, although preschoolers know that plants grow and heal, they nevertheless don't consider plants to be living things. It's not until 7 or 8 years that children routinely decide that plants are alive. Preschoolers' reluctance to call plants living things may stem from their belief in goal-directed motion as a key property of living things: This is not easy to see in plants, but when 5-year-olds are told that plants move in goal-directed ways—for example, tree roots turn toward a source of water or a Venus flytrap closes its leaves to trap an insect—they decide that plants are alive after all (Opfer & Siegler, 2004).

Despite these limits, children's naïve theories of biology, when joined with their naïve theory of physics, provide powerful tools for making sense of their world and for understanding new experiences.

Understanding People

LO9 **How do young children acquire a theory of mind?**

The last of the three fundamental theories concerns *folk psychology*, **which refers to our informal beliefs about other people and their behavior.** Think back to the last time you wanted to figure out why someone—a friend, lover, coworker, sibling, or parent—acted as he or she did. Why did your friend go to a movie with someone else instead of going to a concert with you? Why did your brother say nothing about your brand-new coat? In common situations like this, adults are often amateur psychologists, explaining people's actions in terms of their desires or goals (Carlson, Koenig, & Harms, 2013). Your friend went to the movie because she was mad at you for not loaning her your car; your brother didn't comment on your coat because he was preoccupied with something else. Just as naïve physics allows us to predict how objects act and naïve biology allows us to understand living things, naïve psychology allows us to predict how people act.

A cornerstone of folk psychology is the idea that people's behavior is often intentional—designed to achieve a goal (Woodward, 2009). Imagine a father who says, "Where are the crackers?" in front of his 1-year-old daughter, then begins opening kitchen cabinets, moving some objects to look behind them. Finding the box of crackers, he says, "There they are!" An infant who understands intentionality would realize how her father's actions—searching, moving objects—were related to the goal of finding the crackers.

Many clever experiments have revealed that 1-year-olds understand intentionality. For example, in one study infants watched an adult reaching over a barrier for a ball, but failing because the ball was just out of reach. Then the barrier was removed and infants saw an adult either use the same "over the barrier" reaching motion or reach directly for the ball; in both cases, the adult grasped the ball. By 10 months, infants were surprised to see the adult relying on the "over the barrier" reach when it was no longer needed. In other words, with the barrier removed, infants expected to see the adult reach directly because that was the best way to achieve the goal of getting the ball; they were surprised when the actor relied on the familiar but no longer necessary method of reaching (Brandone & Wellman, 2009).

Other evidence for infants' understanding of intentionality comes from studies in which adults demonstrate novel toys to babies. During the demonstration, adults occasionally say things suggesting that some actions are mistakes (e.g., "Oops!). Later, when allowed to play with the toys, babies less often imitate the mistaken actions; apparently they understand that these were not related to achieving the goal (Sakkalou et al., 2013). Similarly, in other research, infants see two adults working together—one opening the lid to a box and the other retrieving an object in the box. Infants apparently understand that both adults have the same goal—to get the object—because they are surprised if the box-opening adult seems more interested in the box than in the object (Henderson et al., 2013). Findings like these document that infants readily interpret human acts as being purposeful, to achieve goals (Woodward, 2013).

From this early understanding of intentionality, young children's naïve psychology expands rapidly. **Between ages 2 and 5, children develop a *theory of mind*, a naïve understanding of the relations between mind and behavior.** One of the leading researchers on theory of mind, Henry Wellman (2002, 2011, 2012), believes that children's theory of mind moves through several phases during the preschool years. In the earliest phase, preschoolers understand that people can have different desires: One child might want raisins for a snack whereas another child wants crackers. In the next phase, children know that people can have different beliefs: In trying to find a missing shoe, one child might believe that the shoe is in the kitchen and another child believes that it's in the car. In the third phase, children understand that different experiences can lead to different states of knowledge: A child who has seen a toy hidden in a drawer knows what's in the now-closed drawer but a child who did not see the toy hidden does not.

The next phase represents a fundamental shift in children's theory of mind: Children understand that behavior is based on a person's beliefs about events and situations, *even when those beliefs are wrong*. Children's understanding of the influence of such false beliefs is revealed in tasks like the one shown in Figure 6-8 on page 208. Anne knows that the marble has been moved to the box, but Sally

This is Sally. Sally has a basket.

This is Anne. Anne has a box.

Sally has a marble.

She puts the marble into her basket.

Sally goes out for a walk.

Anne takes the marble out of the basket and puts it into the box.

Now Sally comes back. She wants to play with her marble. Where will she look for her marble?

Figure 6-8

believes that the marble is still in the basket. Not until 4 years of age do most children correctly say that Sally will look for the marble in the basket (acting on her false belief); 4-year-olds understand that Sally's behavior is based on her beliefs, even though her belief is wrong.

In the final phase, children understand that people may feel one emotion but show another. For example, a child who is disappointed by a birthday present smiles anyway because she doesn't want her parents to know how she really feels.

Thus, children's theory of mind becomes more sophisticated over the preschool years. This general pattern is found for children around the world, with one twist: The five-phase sequence I've described here is common in many Western nations, but in China and Iran, preschoolers typically understand differences in knowledge (phase 3) before differences in beliefs (Shahaeian et al., 2011; Wellman, Fang, & Peterson, 2011). One explanation for this difference is that compared to Western parents, parents in China and Iran emphasize knowledge to their young children ("knowing the right things") and are less tolerant of different beliefs (Wellman, 2012).

The early phases of children's theory of mind seem clear. How these emerge is very much a matter of debate, however. One of the first explanations for the development of a theory of mind suggested that it is based on an innate, specialized module coming online in the preschool years that automatically recognizes behaviors associated with different mental states such as wanting, pretending, and believing. This view was prompted, in part, by the finding that children with autism, a disorder in which individuals are uninterested in other people and have limited social skills, lag behind typically developing children in understanding false belief (Peterson, Wellman, & Slaughter, 2012). As we'll see in the "Improving Children's Lives" feature, although autistic children definitely find false-belief tasks to be challenging, the proper interpretation of that result is very much debated.

Improving Children's Lives

Theory of Mind in Autism

Autism is the most serious of a family of disorders known as Autism Spectrum Disorders (ASD). Individuals with ASD acquire language later than usual and their speech often echoes what others say to them. They sometimes become intensely interested in objects (e.g., making the same actions with a toy over and over), sometimes to the exclusion of everything else. They often seem uninterested in other people, and when they do interact, those exchanges are often awkward, as if the individuals with ASD aren't following the rules that govern social interactions. Symptoms usually emerge early in life, typically by 18 to 24 months of age. Roughly one out of every 200–300 U.S. children is diagnosed with ASD; about 80% of them are boys (Landa et al., 2013; Mash & Wolfe, 2010). ASD is heritable and many studies point to atypical brain functioning, perhaps due to abnormal levels of neurotransmitters (NINDS, 2009).

As I mentioned, children with ASD grasp false belief slowly, and this performance leads some researchers to conclude that the absence of a theory of mind—sometimes called "mindblindness" (Baron-Cohen, 2005)—is the defining characteristic of ASD (Tager-Flusberg, 2007). Other scientists aren't convinced. Although no one doubts that autistic children find false-belief tasks puzzling, some scientists say that mindblindness is a by-product of other deficits and not the cause of the symptoms associated with ASD. One idea is that ASD reflects problems in executive function (described on page 196): According to this view, autistic children's social interactions are impaired because they are relatively unable to plan, to inhibit irrelevant actions, and to shift smoothly between actions (Pellicano, 2013). Another idea emphasizes a focused processing style that is common in ASD. For example, children with ASD find hidden objects faster than typically developing children do (Chen et al., 2012), but this emphasis on perceptual details usually comes at the expense of maintaining a coherent overall picture. Consequently, in social interactions, children with ASD may focus on one facet of another person's behavior (e.g., gestures) but ignore other verbal and nonverbal cues (e.g., speech, facial expressions, body language) that collectively promote fluid interactions. Research to evaluate these claims is still ongoing; it's likely that the answers will indicate that multiple factors contribute to ASD.

ASD can't be cured. However, therapy can be used to improve language and social skills in children with autism. In addition, medications can be used to treat some of the symptoms, such as reducing repetitive behavior (Leekam, Prior, & Uljarevic, 2011). When ASD is diagnosed early and autistic children grow up in supportive, responsive environments and receive appropriate treatments, they can lead satisfying and productive lives.

The theory-of-mind module that some suspect is missing in autistic children is thought to emerge during the preschool years in typical development. But, just as the role for this module has been challenged in autism, not everyone is convinced that it drives theory of mind in typical development. Some evidence points to a role for executive function in the onset of theory of mind: Children's scores on tasks designed to measure executive function predict their scores on false-belief tasks (e.g., Lackner et al., 2012). Other evidence emphasizes the contribution of language, which develops rapidly during the same years that theory of mind emerges (as we'll see in Chapter 9). Some scientists believe that children's language skills contribute to growth of theory of mind, perhaps reflecting the benefit of an expanding vocabulary that includes verbs describing mental states, such as *think, know, believe* (Pascual et al., 2008). Or the benefits may reflect children's mastery of grammatical forms that can be used to describe a setting where a person knows that another person has a false belief (Farrant, Maybery, & Fletcher, 2012).

A different view is that a child's theory of mind emerges from interactions with other people, interactions that provide children with insights into different mental states (Dunn & Brophy, 2005; McAlister & Peterson, 2013). Through conversations with parents and siblings that focus on other people's mental states, children learn facts of mental life, and this helps children to see that others often have different perspectives than they do. In other words, when children frequently participate in conversations that focus on other people's moods, their feelings, and their intentions, they learn that people's behavior is based on their beliefs, regardless of the accuracy of those beliefs.

Probably through some combination of these forces, preschool children attain a theory of mind. After these years, their folk psychology moves beyond theory of mind and embraces an ever-expanding range of psychological phenomena. For example, at about age 10, children know that such psychological states as being nervous or frustrated can produce physical states such as vomiting or having a headache (Notaro, Gelman, & Zimmerman, 2001). For now, the important point is that children's folk psychology flourishes in the preschool years, allowing them to see that other people's behavior is not unpredictable, but follows regular patterns. When joined with their theories of naïve biology and naïve physics, young children have extensive knowledge of the physical and social world, knowledge that they can use to function successfully in those worlds.

 Check Your Learning

RECALL Summarize the evidence indicating that Piaget underestimated infants' understanding of object permanence.

What properties of living things are featured in young children's theories of biology?

INTERPRET A typical 1-year-old's understanding of objects exceeds his or her understanding of people. Why might this be the case?

APPLY What do you think would happen if you conducted a meta-analysis on studies of infants' understanding of objects? Would the pattern of age-related change in understanding objects be much the same around the world?

 # Unifying Themes   Active Children

This chapter emphasizes that *children influence their own development*. This idea is the cornerstone of Piaget's theory and of the core-knowledge account of development. Beginning in infancy and continuing through childhood and adolescence, children are constantly trying to make sense out of what goes on around them. Experiences provide intellectual food for children to digest. Parents, teachers, and peers are important in cognitive development, not so much for what they teach directly as for the guidance and challenges they provide. Thus, throughout the developmental journey, the child is a busy navigator, trying to understand the routes available and trying to decide among them.

See for Yourself

The best way to see some of the developmental changes that Piaget described is to test some children with the same tasks that Piaget used. The conservation task shown on page 184 is good because it's simple to set up and children usually enjoy it. Get yourself some glasses and colored liquids, then ask a 3- or 4-year-old and a 7- or 8-year-old to confirm that the two quantities are the same. Next, pour one liquid as shown on page 184 and ask children if the quantities are still the same. Ask them to explain their answers. The differences between 3- and 7-year-olds' answers are truly remarkable. See for yourself!

Summary

 ### Setting the Stage: Piaget's Theory

Basic Principles of Piaget's Theory

In Piaget's view, children construct theories that reflect their understanding of the world. Children's theories are constantly changing, based on their experiences. In assimilation, experiences are readily incorporated into existing theories. In accommodation, experiences cause theories to be modified to encompass new information.

When accommodation becomes much more frequent than assimilation, it is a sign that children's theories are inadequate, so children reorganize them. This reorganization produces four different stages of mental development from infancy through adulthood. All individuals go through all four phases, but not necessarily at the same rate.

Stages of Cognitive Development

The first 2 years of life constitute Piaget's sensorimotor stage. Over these 2 years, infants adapt to and explore their environment, understand objects, and begin to use symbols.

From ages 2 to 7 years, children are in Piaget's preoperational stage. Although now capable of using symbols, their thinking is limited by egocentrism, the inability to see the world from another's point of view. Preoperational children also are centered in their thinking, focusing narrowly on particular parts of a problem.

Between ages 7 and 11, children begin to use and can reverse mental operations to solve perspective-taking and conservation problems. The main limit to thinking at this stage is that it is focused on the concrete and real.

With the onset of formal operational thinking, adolescents can think hypothetically and reason abstractly. In deductive reasoning, they understand that conclusions are based on logic, not experience.

Piaget's Contributions to Child Development

Among Piaget's enduring contributions are emphasizing the importance of cognitive processes in development, viewing children as active participants in their own development, and discovering many counterintuitive developmental phenomena. The theory's weaknesses include poorly defined mechanisms of change and an inability to account for variability in children's performance.

 ## Modern Theories of Cognitive Development

The Sociocultural Perspective: Vygotsky's Theory

Vygotsky believed that cognition develops first in a social setting but gradually comes under the child's independent control. The difference between what children can do with assistance and what they can do alone defines the zone of proximal development.

Control of cognitive skills is most readily transferred from others to the child through scaffolding, a teaching style that allows children to take on more and more of a task as they master its different components.

Information Processing

According to the information-processing approach, cognition involves a general-purpose information-processing system that includes a central executive along with sensory, working, and long-term memories. Any specific cognitive activity involves this system plus specialized "software" that is specific to the task at hand.

Information-processing psychologists believe that cognitive development reflects more effective strategies, more effective executive processing (inhibiting, shifting, updating), more frequent automatic processing, and increased speed of processing.

Core-Knowledge Theories

According to core-knowledge theories, there are distinctive domains of knowledge (e.g., language, understanding of objects), some of which are acquired by infants, toddlers, and preschoolers. These domains have typically evolved because they were essential for human survival. Some theorists believe these domains of knowledge are rooted in prewired systems; others use Piaget's metaphor of child-as-scientist and describe them as specialized theories.

 ## Understanding in Core Domains

Understanding Objects and Their Properties

Infants understand that objects exist independently. They also know that objects move along continuous paths and do not move through other objects.

Understanding Living Things

Infants and toddlers use motion to distinguish animate from inanimate objects. By the preschool years, children know that living things move themselves, grow bigger and physically more complex, have different internal parts than objects, resemble their parents, inherit some diseases from parents but contract other diseases from contact with people, and heal when injured. Preschoolers' thinking about living things is often marked by teleological explanations and essentialism.

Understanding People

By age 1, infants recognize that people perform many acts intentionally, with a goal in mind. During the preschool years, children's theory of mind becomes progressively more sophisticated. One landmark is the understanding that people's behavior is based on beliefs about events and situations, even when those beliefs are wrong. Contributing to children's acquisition of a theory of mind are a specialized cognitive module, basic psychological processes such as language, and social interactions that allow children to experience different mental states.

Test Yourself

1. According to Piaget's theory, _____ is when children modify their views about the world based on their experiences.
   a. assimilation
   b. accommodation
   c. knowledge

2. Object permanence is a process by which a child realizes that _____.
   a. a rattle is an object
   b. only those objects exist that he thinks about
   c. certain objects exist, even when he has no thoughts or actions about them

3. A child uses symbols to represent objects and events in the _____.
   a. preoperational stage
   b. concrete operational stage
   c. formal operational stage

4. When a preschooler clings to his own views of the world and his own ways, without accepting others' views, this is called _____.
   a. animism
   b. selfishness
   c. egocentrism

5. During the _____ stage, thinking is rule-oriented and logical but limited to the tangible and real.
   a. preoperational stage
   b. concrete operational stage
   c. formal operational stage

6. Which of the following is not an educational application of Piaget's theory?
   a. to recognize individual differences when teaching
   b. to encourage exploration and interaction while teaching
   c. to guide children by giving direct instructions while teaching

7. The zone of proximal development refers to _____.
   a. the highest level of achievement a child can reach by himself
   b. the difference between what a child can do with and without help
   c. a teaching style that matches the amount of assistance to the learner's need

8. _____ is a teaching style in which teachers provide just enough instruction so that students can take on more and more of a task.
   a. The zone of proximal development

b. Scaffolding
   c. Equilibration

9. Information-processing theorists refer to sensory memory, working memory, and long-term memory as mental _____.
   a. software
   b. strategies
   c. hardware

10. _____ is the site of ongoing cognitive processes and the data they require.
    a. Working memory
    b. Sensory memory
    c. Long-term memory

11. Which of the following is *not* a function of the central executive?
    a. inhibiting inappropriate thoughts and actions
    b. shifting from one action, thought, or task to another
    c. talking softly to oneself to regulate behavior

12. Which of the following is *not* a type of developmental change associated with the information-processing view?
    a. reorganizing mental structures to achieve equilibration
    b. faster information processing
    c. use of more effective strategies

13. Which modern theory views cognitive development as an apprenticeship?
    a. information processing
    b. Vygotsky's theory
    c. core-knowledge theory

14. Which of the following statements concerning the development of folk psychology is *incorrect*?
    a. One-year-olds understand that people's behavior is often intentional, designed to achieve a goal.
    b. In one of the earliest phases of the development of a theory of mind, preschool children understand that people can have different desires.
    c. A fundamental shift occurs when children understand that behavior is based on a person's beliefs about events and situations, as long as those beliefs are correct.

15. Infants' naïve theory of living things includes the idea that _____.
    a. animate objects grow but inanimate objects do not
    b. animate objects are self-propelled but inanimate objects are not
    c. when damaged, animate objects heal by regrowth but inanimate objects must be repaired

Key Terms

accommodation   180

animism   184

assimilation   180

automatic processes   196

central executive   195

centration   184

concrete operational stage   185

constructivism   187

core-knowledge theories   198

deductive reasoning   186

egocentrism   183

equilibration   181

essentialism   205

executive functioning   195

folk psychology   206

formal operational stage   185

guided participation   190

information-processing theory   193

inner speech   192

intersubjectivity   190

long-term memory   195

mental operations   185

object permanence   182

preoperational stage   183

private speech   192

scaffolding   191

sensorimotor stage   181

sensory memory   193

sociocultural perspective   190

teleological explanations   205

theory of mind   207

working memory   194

zone of proximal development   191

Chapter 7
Memory, Problem Solving, and Academic Skills

⌄ Modules

7.1 Memory

7.2 Problem Solving

7.3 Academic Skills

A few weeks ago I spent a morning in a first-grade classroom watching 6- and 7-year-olds learn to read, to spell simple words, and to do simple addition problems. I then spent the afternoon in a fifth-grade classroom. Like the younger students, these 10- and 11-year-olds devoted much of their time to the traditional three Rs, but with much more complicated material. They were reading books with hundreds of pages, writing two-page essays, and solving story problems that involved multiplication and division.

This remarkable transformation over the course of just a few years became possible, in part, because of profound changes in children's thinking. We'll examine these changes in **Module 7.1**, where we'll see how memory expands as children grow, and also in **Module 7.2**, where we'll consider children's and adolescents' problem-solving skills. Finally, in **Module 7.3** we'll take a closer look at academic skills, tracing children's evolving mastery of reading, writing, and mathematics.

7.1 Memory

LEARNING OBJECTIVES

LO1 How well do infants remember?

LO2 How do strategies help children to remember?

LO3 How does children's knowledge influence what they remember?

OUTLINE

Origins of Memory

Strategies for Remembering

Knowledge and Memory

One afternoon 4-year-old Cheryl came home sobbing and reported that Mr. Johnson, a neighbor and longtime family friend, had taken down her pants and touched her "private parts." Her mother was shocked. Mr. Johnson had always seemed an honest, decent man, which made her wonder if Cheryl's imagination had simply run wild. Yet, at times, he did seem a bit peculiar, so her daughter's claim had a ring of truth.

Sadly, episodes like this are all too common in the United States today. When child abuse is suspected and the child is the sole eyewitness, the child often testifies during prosecution of the alleged abuser. But can preschool children like Cheryl be trusted to recall events accurately on the witness stand? To answer this question, we need to understand more about how memory develops. We'll start by examining the origins of memory in infancy, then see what factors contribute to its development in childhood and adolescence.

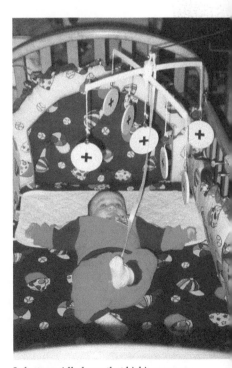

Infants rapidly learn that kicking moves the mobile; days later, babies will kick immediately, showing that they remember the connection between their action and the mobile's movement.

Origins of Memory

LO1 How well do infants remember?

The roots of memory are laid down soon after birth (Bauer, Larkina, & Deocampo, 2011). Young babies remember events for days or even weeks at a time. Among the studies that opened our eyes to the infant's ability to remember were those conducted by Carolyn Rovee-Collier (1997, 1999). The method used in her studies is shown in the photo. A ribbon from a mobile is attached to a 2- or 3-month-old's leg; within a few minutes, babies learn to kick to make the mobile move. When Rovee-Collier brought the mobile to the infants' homes several days or a few weeks later, babies would still kick to make the mobile move. If Rovee-Collier waited several weeks to return, most babies forgot that kicking moved the mobile. When that happened, she gave them a reminder—she moved the mobile herself without attaching the ribbon to the infant's foot. Then she would return the next day, hook up the apparatus, and the babies would kick to move the mobile.

Rovee-Collier's experiments show that three important features of memory exist as early as 2 and 3 months of age: (1) an event from the past is remembered; (2) over time, the event can no longer be recalled; and (3) a cue can serve to dredge up a forgotten memory.

From these humble origins, memory improves rapidly in older infants and toddlers. Youngsters can recall more of what they experience and remember it longer (Bauer & Leventon, 2013; Bauer & Lukowski, 2010). When shown novel actions with toys and later asked to imitate what they saw, toddlers can remember more than infants and can remember the actions for longer periods (Bauer, San Souci, & Pathman, 2010). For example, if shown how to make a rattle by first placing a wooden block inside a container, then putting a lid on the container, toddlers are more likely than infants to remember the necessary sequence of steps.

In addition, memory is more flexible in older infants and toddlers: They are able to remember past events even when the context associated with those events has changed (Bauer et al., 2010). For example, when asked to imitate sequences of novel actions, younger infants' memory is typically disrupted by any change between presentation of the actions and the memory test (e.g., testing by a different experimenter or in a different room); such changes are less disruptive for memory in older infants and toddlers (Patel, Gaylord, & Fagen, 2013).

Brain Development and Memory These improvements in memory can be traced, in part, to growth in the brain regions that support memory (Bauer et al., 2010). The brain structures primarily responsible for the initial storage of information, such as the hippocampus, develop during the first year. However, structures responsible for retrieving these stored memories—the frontal cortex, for example—develop much later, into the second year. In addition, part of the hippocampus is not mature until about 20 to 24 months. Thus, development of memory during the first 2 years reflects growth in these two different brain regions.

Once youngsters begin to talk, we can study their memory skills using most of the same methods we use with older children and adults. Research using these methods has linked age-related improvement in memory to two factors (Pressley & Hilden, 2006). First, as children grow, they use more effective strategies for remembering. Second, children's growing factual knowledge of the world allows them to organize information more completely and, therefore, to remember better. We'll look at each of these factors in the next few pages.

Strategies for Remembering

LO2 How do strategies help children to remember?

When you've studied for exams, you may have outlined chapters in a text or highlighted important passages; when you've had several errands to complete, you have created a list; and when you've misplaced your iPad, you may have thought back to where you know you had it last. **Each of these actions is a *memory strategy*, an action to promote remembering.** Children begin to use memory strategies early. Preschool children look at or touch objects that they've been told to remember (DeLoache, 1984). Looking and touching aren't effective strategies, but they tell us that preschoolers understand that they should be doing *something* to try to remember; remembering doesn't happen automatically! During the elementary-school years, children begin to use more powerful strategies (Schwenck, Bjorklund, & Schneider, 2009). **For example, 7- and 8-year-olds use** *rehearsal*, **a strategy of repetitively naming information that is to be remembered.** A child wanting to call a new friend will rehearse the phone number from the time she hears it until she places the call.

As children get older, they learn other memory strategies. **One is** *organization*: **structuring material to be remembered so that related information is placed together.** For example, a seventh-grader trying to remember major battles of the U.S Civil War could organize them geographically (e.g., Shiloh and Fort Donelson in Tennessee, Antietam and Monocacy in Maryland). **Another strategy is** *elaboration*, **embellishing information to be remembered to make it more memorable.** To see elaboration in action, imagine a child who can never remember if the second syllable of *rehearsal* is spelled *her* (as it sounds) or *hear*. The child could remember the correct spelling by reminding herself that *rehearsal* is like *re-hear-ing*. Thus, imagining herself "re-hearing" a sound would make it easier to remember the spelling of *rehearsal*. Finally, as children grow they're also more likely to use external aids to memory: They are more likely to make notes and to write down information on calendars so that, like the girl in the photo, they won't forget future events (Eskritt & Lee, 2002; Eskritt & McLeod, 2008).

School-age children often use external aids to help them remember, such as writing down events on a calendar.

Metacognition   Just as there's not much value to a filled toolbox if you don't know how to use the tools, memory strategies aren't much good unless children know when to use them. For example, rehearsal is great for remembering phone numbers, but lousy for remembering amendments to the U.S. Constitution or the plot of *Hamlet*. During the elementary-school years and adolescence, children gradually learn to identify different kinds of memory problems and the memory strategies most appropriate to each. For example, when reading a textbook or watching a television newscast, outlining or writing a summary are good strategies because they identify the main points and organize them. Children gradually become more skilled at selecting appropriate strategies, but even high-school students do not always use effective learning strategies when they should (Grammer et al., 2011; Pressley & Hilden, 2006).

After children choose a memory strategy, they need to monitor its effectiveness. For example, by self-testing—asking themselves questions about the material—children can determine whether the strategy is helping them learn. If it's not, they need to begin anew, reanalyzing the memory task to select a better approach. If the strategy is working, they should determine the portion of the material they have not yet mastered and concentrate their efforts there. Monitoring improves gradually with age. Even preschool children can distinguish what they know from what they don't (Ghetti, Hembacher, & Coughlin, 2013), but older children and adolescents do so more accurately (Bjorklund, 2005).

Diagnosing memory problems accurately and monitoring the effectiveness of memory strategies are two important elements of *metamemory*, **which refers to a child's informal understanding of memory.** As children develop, they learn more about how memory operates and devise intuitive theories of memory that represent an outgrowth of the theory of mind described in Module 6.3 (Lockl & Schneider, 2007). For example, children learn that memory is fallible (i.e., they sometimes forget!) and that some types of memory tasks are easier than others (e.g., remembering the main idea of the Gettysburg Address is simpler than remembering it word for word). This growing knowledge of memory helps

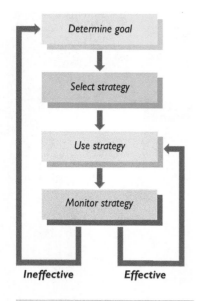

Figure 7-1

children to use memory strategies more effectively, just as an experienced carpenter's accumulated knowledge of wood tells her when to use nails, screws, or glue to join two boards (Ghetti & Lee, 2011).

Children's growing understanding of memory is paralleled by growing understanding of all cognitive processes. **Such knowledge and awareness of cognitive processes is called** *metacognitive knowledge*. Metacognitive knowledge increases rapidly during the elementary-school years: Children come to know much about perception, attention, intentions, knowledge, and thinking (Flavell, 2000; McCormick, 2003). For example, school-age children know that sometimes they deliberately direct their attention—as when searching for a parent's face in a crowd. But they also know that sometimes events capture attention—as with an unexpected clap of thunder (Parault & Schwanenflugel, 2000).

One of the most important features of children's metacognitive knowledge is their understanding of the connections among goals, strategies, monitoring, and outcomes. That is, as shown in Figure 7-1, children come to realize that on a broad spectrum of tasks—ranging from learning words in a spelling list to learning how to spike a volleyball to learning to get along with an overly talkative classmate seated nearby—they need to regulate their learning by understanding the goal and selecting a means to achieve that goal. Then they determine whether the chosen method is working. **Effective** *cognitive self-regulation*—**that is, skill at identifying goals, selecting effective strategies, and monitoring accurately—is a characteristic of successful students** (Usher & Pajares, 2009; Zimmerman, 2001). A student may decide that writing each spelling word twice before the test is a good way to get all the words right. When the student gets only 70% correct on the first test, he switches to a new strategy (e.g., writing each word four times, plus writing its definition), showing the adaptive nature of cognitive processes in self-regulated learners.

Some students do not master these learning strategies spontaneously, but they may acquire them when teachers emphasize them in class (Grammer, Coffman, & Ornstein, 2013; Ornstein et al., 2010). In addition, several programs teach students strategies for studying more effectively (Pressley, 2002). For example, teachers demonstrate several strategies that promote greater reading comprehension, including: first selecting a goal for reading, making a mental picture of what's going on in the text, periodically predicting what will happen next, and summarizing aloud what's happened so far. Children practice these strategies separately and as part of a reading "tool kit." Empowered with reading strategies like these, students' understanding of text is deeper and they typically obtain greater scores on standardized tests of reading comprehension (Pressley & Hilden, 2006).

Strategies, metamemory, and metacognition are essential for effective learning and remembering, but as you'll see in the next few pages, knowledge is also an aid to memory (Schneider, 2011).

Knowledge and Memory

LO3 **How does children's knowledge influence what they remember?**

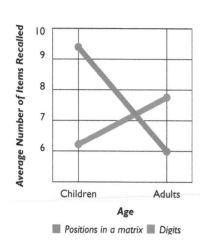

Figure 7-2

To see how knowledge influences memory, let's look at a study in which 10-year-olds and adults tried to remember sequences of numbers (Chi, 1978). As shown in Figure 7-2, adults remembered more numbers than children. Next participants tried to remember the positions of objects in a matrix. This time, 10-year-olds' recall was much better than that of adults.

What was responsible for this surprising outcome? Actually, the objects were chess pieces on a chessboard, positioned as they would be in actual games. The adults were novice players but the children were experts. For the adults, who lacked knowledge of chess, the patterns seemed arbitrary. In contrast, the children had prior knowledge that helped them organize and give meaning to the patterns, and thus could recognize and then recall the whole configuration instead of many isolated pieces. It was as if the adults were seeing this meaningless pattern:

nnccbasbccbn

but children were seeing this:

nbc cbs abc cnn

Usually the knowledge that allows a child to organize information and give it meaning increases gradually with age (Schneider & Bjorklund, 1998). Researchers often depict knowledge as a network like the one in Figure 7-3, which shows part of a 13-year-old's knowledge of animals. The entries in the network are linked by different types of associations. Some of the links denote membership in categories (a Dalmatian is a dog), and others denote properties (an elephant has a trunk). **Still others denote a** *script*, **a memory structure used to describe the sequence in which events occur.** The list of events in walking the dog is a script.

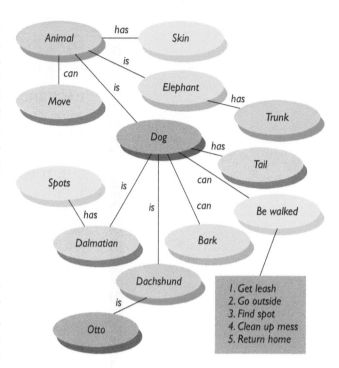

Figure 7-3

A network diagram like this for a younger child would have fewer entries and fewer and weaker connecting links. Consequently, the youngster cannot organize information as extensively, which makes remembering more difficult than for an older child.

Nevertheless, the knowledge that young children have is organized; and this turns out to be a powerful aid to memory. In the case of events that fit scripts, for example, they needn't try to remember each individual activity; instead, they simply remember the script. When the preschoolers in the photo want to tell their dad about baking cookies, they can simply retrieve the "baking cookies" script and use it to organize their recall. Knowledge can also distort memory. If a specific experience does not match a child's knowledge (e.g., it differs from a script), the experience is sometimes forgotten or distorted so that it conforms to the existing knowledge (Farrar & Boyer-Pennington, 1999; Williams & Davidson, 2009). For example, told a story about a female helicopter pilot, many youngsters will remember the pilot as a man because their knowledge network specifies that pilots are men.

Because older children often have more knowledge than younger children, they are sometimes more prone to memory distortions than younger children (Brainerd, Reyna, & Ceci, 2008). In the "Spotlight on Theories" feature, we'll see one theory that accounts for this surprising finding.

Highly familiar activities, such as baking cookies, are often stored in memory as scripts, which denote the events in the activity and the sequence in which they occur.

Spotlight on Theories
Fuzzy Trace Theory

BACKGROUND Children's knowledge of the world usually helps them remember, but sometimes it leads to inaccurate or distorted memory. Such memory errors, although common for children and adolescents, are still poorly understood.

THE THEORY According to *fuzzy trace theory*, developed by Charles J. Brainerd and Valerie Reyna (2005, 2013), most experiences can be stored in memory exactly (verbatim) or in terms of their basic meaning (gist). A 10-year-old who reads an invitation to a birthday party may store the information in memory as "the party starts at 7:30 PM" (verbatim) or as "the party is after dinner" (gist). A 14-year-old who gets a grade on a science test may store it as "I got 75% correct" (verbatim) or "I got an average grade" (gist).

Throughout development, children store information in memory in both verbatim and gist formats, but young children are biased toward verbatim memory traces; during childhood and adolescence, a bias toward gist traces emerges. That is, older children and adolescents typically represent experiences and information in terms of gist, instead of verbatim. (The theory gets its name from its emphasis on gist memory traces that are vague or fuzzy.)

Hypothesis: Some memory errors depend on gist processing. If older children and adolescents are biased to gist processing, they should be more prone to those errors than are younger children. For example, a common error occurs when people are asked to remember related words such as *rest, awake, bed, snooze, blanket, snore,* and *dream.* Typically, about three-fourths of adults will claim to have seen *sleep* even though it was not presented. Because older children and adolescents extract the gist of the meanings of these words ("they're about sleep"), they should be more susceptible to the illusion than younger children, who more often store the words verbatim.

Test: Brainerd et al. (2010) presented words to 7- and 11-year-olds and adults. As in the previous example, many words in the list were highly associated with a critical word that was not presented. Later, another list of words was presented, including some that were part of the first list and some that were not. Participants were asked to recognize the words that were part of the first list. Not surprisingly, word recognition increased substantially with age: adults recognized 88% of the words, compared with 76% for 11-year-olds and 71% for 7-year-olds. More interesting is how frequently children and adults "recognized" the critical word that had not actually been presented: adults did so 60% of the time, compared with 40% for 11-year-olds and 22% for 7-year-olds.

Conclusion: False memories—in this case "recognizing" a word that was never presented—were less common in young children than in older children and adults. This result is consistent with fuzzy trace theory, in which these memory errors are a consequence of the greater tendency for older children and adults to remember the gist of what they've experienced. Fuzzy trace theory is also supported by the finding that when children are encouraged to abstract the gist of the words in the list—to look for similar meanings—they respond like adults in "recognizing" the critical word (Brainerd, 2013).

Application: Siblings sometimes argue about past events—who did (or said) something in the past. For example:

OLDER CHILD: "I took the trash out last night just like I always do."

YOUNGER CHILD: "Nuh-uh. You were too busy. So I did it."

Listening to these arguments, it's tempting for parents to side with the older child, assuming that older children usually remember past events more accurately. That's not a bad assumption, but the paradox is that the same processes that enhance older children's remembering also make them more prone to certain kinds of memory errors. Consequently, parents need to be cautious and be certain that the situation is not one in which an older child's memory is likely to be inaccurate, an illusion caused by the older child's greater reliance on gist processing. In the example here, the older child's memory of what happened may actually be based on his well-established script of what he *usually* does in the evening.

Thus, although children's growing knowledge usually helps them to remember, sometimes it can interfere with accurate memory. In the next section, we'll look at another link between knowledge and memory: children's memory of their own lives.

Autobiographical Memory Do you remember the name of your teacher in fourth grade or where your high-school graduation was held? In answering these questions, you searched memory, just as you would search memory to answer questions such as "What is the capital of Canada?" and "Who invented the sewing machine?" However, answers to questions about Canada and sewing machines are based on general knowledge that you have not experienced personally; in contrast, answers to questions about your fourth-grade teacher and your high-school graduation are based on knowledge unique to your own life. *Autobiographical memory refers to people's memory of the significant events and experiences of their own lives.* Autobiographical memory is important because it helps people construct a personal life history. In addition, autobiographical memory allows people to relate their experiences to others, creating socially shared memories (Bauer, 2006).

Autobiographical memory originates in the preschool years. According to one influential theory (Nelson & Fivush, 2004), autobiographic memory emerges gradually, as children acquire different skills. Infants and toddlers have the basic memory skills that allow them to remember past events. Layered on top of these memory skills during the preschool years are language skills and a child's sense of self. Language allows children to become conversational partners. After infants begin to talk, parents often converse with them about past and future events—particularly about personal experiences in the child's past and future. Parents may talk about what the child did today at day care or remind the child about what she will be doing this weekend. In conversations like these, parents teach their children the important features of events and how events are organized (Fivush, Reese, & Haden, 2006). Children's autobiographical memories are richer when parents talk about past events in detail and, specifically, when they encourage children to expand their description of past events by, for example, using open-ended questions (e.g., "Where did Mommy go last night?"). When parents use this conversational style with their preschool children, as young adolescents they have earlier memories of childhood (Jack et al., 2009).

The richness of parent–child conversations also helps to explain a cultural difference in autobiographical memory. Compared with adults living in East Asia, Europeans and North Americans typically remember more events from their early years and remember those events in more detail (Ross & Wang, 2010). This difference in early memories can be traced to cultural differences in parent–child conversational styles: The elaborative style is less common among Asian parents, which means that Asian youngsters have fewer opportunities for the conversations about past events that foster autobiographical memory (Kulkofsky, Wang, & Koh, 2009; Schröder et al., 2013). Similarly, parent–child conversations explain why women's autobiographical memories tend to be richer—more vivid, more emotion-laden, and more elaborate than men's emotional memories: Parents more often use the elaborative conversational style with daughters than with sons (Grysman & Hudson, 2013).

An emergent sense of self also contributes to autobiographical memory. I describe sense of self in detail in Module 11.1, but the key idea is that 1- and 2-year-olds rapidly acquire a sense that they exist independently, in space and time. An emerging sense of self thus provides coherence and continuity to children's experience. Children realize that the self who went to the park a few days ago is the same self who is now at a birthday party and is the same self who will read a book with Dad before bedtime. The self provides a personal timeline that anchors a child's recall of the past (and anticipation of the future). Thus, a sense of self, language skills that allow children to converse with parents about past and future, and basic memory skills all contribute to the emergence of autobiographical memory in preschool children.

Older children, adolescents, and adults remember few events from their lives that took place before autobiographical memory is in place. *Infantile amnesia* **refers to the inability to remember events from one's early life.** Adults and school-age children recall nothing from the first two years of life and relatively little from the preschool years (Hayne & Jack, 2011). For example, when the 2-year-old in the photo is older, he won't remember his brother's birth (Peterson & Rideout, 1998; Quas et al., 1999).* But there's a good chance that the older boy will remember his brother's second—and certainly his third—birthday.

Many of the same factors that forge an autobiographical memory contribute to infantile amnesia (Hayne & Jack, 2011). For example, once children learn to talk (beginning at about 12 to 15 months), they tend to rely on language to represent their past. Consequently, their earlier, prelingual experiences may be difficult to retrieve from memory, just as after you reorganize your bedroom you may have trouble finding things (Simcock & Hayne, 2002). Some theorists also argue that because infants and toddlers have no sense of self, they lack the autobiographical timeline that's used to organize experiences later in life (Howe & Courage, 1997).

Thus, personal experiences from our earliest years usually can't be recalled, because of inadequate language or inadequate sense of self (Hayne & Jack, 2011). Beginning in the preschool years, however, autobiographical memory provides

Infantile amnesia is the inability to remember events from early in one's life, such as the birth of a younger sibling.

---

* Perhaps you're not convinced because you vividly recall significant events that occurred when you were 2, such as the birth of a sibling, a move to a different home, or the death of a close friend or relative. In reality, you are probably not remembering the actual event. Instead, I can almost guarantee that you're remembering others' retelling of these events and your role in them, not the events themselves. Events like these are often socially shared memories, and that's the basis for your memory.

a cohesive framework for remembering significant life events. Unfortunately, some children's autobiographical memories include memories of abuse. Can these memories be trusted? We'll see in the next section.

Eyewitness Testimony Remember Cheryl, the 4-year-old in the module-opening vignette who claimed that a neighbor had touched her "private parts"? If Cheryl's comments lead to a police investigation, Cheryl's testimony will be critical. But can her recall of events be trusted? This question is difficult to answer. In legal proceedings, children are often interviewed repeatedly—perhaps as many as 10 to 15 times—with interviewers sometimes asking leading questions or making suggestive remarks. Over the course of repeated questioning, the child may confuse what actually happened with what others suggest may have happened. For example, in one famous case in which a preschool teacher named Kelly was accused of sexually abusing children in her class, the children were asked the following leading questions (among many, many others):

> Do you think that Kelly was not good when she was hurting you all?
> When did Kelly say these words? Piss, shit, sugar?
> When Kelly kissed you, did she ever put her tongue in your mouth? (Bruck & Ceci, 1995)

Each of the questions is misleading by implying that something happened when actually it might not have. When, as in the situation in the photo, the questioner is an adult in a position of authority, children often believe that what is suggested by the adult actually happened (Candel et al., 2009; Ceci & Bruck, 1998).

Children's memories can also be tainted simply by overhearing others—adults or peers—describe events. For example, when some children in a class experience an event (e.g., a special class visitor, such as a magician), they often talk about the event with classmates who weren't there; later, these absent classmates readily describe what happened and often insist that they were actually there (Principe & Ceci, 2002; Principe & Schindewolf, 2012).

Preschool children are particularly suggestible. Why? One idea is that they are less able than older children and adults to know the source of information that they remember (Poole & Lindsay, 1995). For example, a father recalling his daughter's piano recitals knows the source of many of his memories: Some are from personal experience (he attended the recital), some he saw on video, and some are based on his daughter's descriptions. Preschool children are not particularly skilled at such source monitoring. When recalling past events, they become confused about who did or said what and, when confused in this manner, they frequently assume that they must have experienced something personally. Consequently, when preschool children are asked leading questions (e.g., "When the man touched you, did it hurt?'), this information is also stored in memory, but without the source. Because preschool children are not skilled at monitoring sources, they have trouble distinguishing what they actually experienced from what interviewers imply that they experienced (Ghetti, 2008).

Perhaps you're skeptical of findings like these. Surely it must be possible to tell when a young child is describing events that never happened. In fact, although law enforcement officials and child-protection workers believe they can usually tell whether children are telling the truth, research shows that they often cannot (Klemfuss & Ceci, 2012).

Findings like these emphasize the need to find effective ways to interview children that increase the chances of obtaining accurate descriptions of past events. The "Child Development and Family Policy" feature tells how this has been done.

When trying to remember past events, young children sometimes "remember" what others suggest might have happened in the past, particularly when the suggestion comes from a person in authority.

 QUESTION 7.1
Ravi is 6 and loves to talk about the good time he had at his uncle's wedding four years ago. He describes events vividly and remembers many incidents in great detail. Ravi's parents wonder if he can really remember so much from the time he was only 2. What do you think is more likely?

Child Development and Family Policy

Interviewing Children Effectively

By the end of the 20th century, the number of child-abuse cases had skyrocketed, followed soon by reports that some adults had been wrongly convicted based on children's false memories. Consequently, many state and federal agencies created task forces to determine the best way to respond to the challenges of evaluating allegations of child abuse. In Michigan, for example, the Governor's Task Force on Children's Justice, created in 1992, quickly identified the need for a standard protocol for interviewing children in child-abuse cases, one that would avoid contaminating children's testimony by using, for example, misleading questions like those listed on page 223. Debra Poole, a psychologist at Central Michigan University and a leading expert on children's eyewitness testimony, was hired to develop the protocol. Poole was an obvious choice because she had recently written a book with Michael E. Lamb, *Investigative Interviews of Children: A Guide for Helping Professionals*, which was published by the American Psychological Association in 1998. Working with agencies in nine Michigan counties, Poole devised a preliminary interview protocol that was tested in those counties. The revised protocol was then published by the Governor's Task Force (1998) and the procedures were implemented statewide. These procedures, derived largely from the research described here, are designed to "reduce trauma to children, make the information gained more credible in the court process, and protect the rights of the accused" (Governor's Task Force, 1998, p. v).

Revised versions of the Michigan protocol were released in 2004 and 2011. Similar protocols have been created in other U.S. states, and the National Institutes of Child Health and Human Development have also developed a structured-interview protocol. These protocols make similar recommendations regarding "best practices" for interviewing children. Specifically, interviewers should:

- Interview children as soon as possible after the event in question.
- Encourage children to tell the truth, to feel free to say "I don't know" to questions and to correct interviewers when they say something that's incorrect.
- Start by asking children to describe the event in their own words ("Tell me what happened after school…") and follow up with open-ended questions ("Can you tell me more about what happened while you were walking home?") and minimize the use of specific questions (because they may suggest to children events that did not happen).
- Allow children to understand and feel comfortable in the interview format by beginning with a neutral event (e.g., a birthday party or holiday celebration) before moving to the event of interest.
- Avoid use of props (e.g., anatomical dolls) with young children.
- Ask questions that consider alternate explanations of the event (i.e., explanations that don't involve abuse).

Following guidelines like these foster the conditions under which children recall past events accurately and therefore are better witnesses (Hershkowitz et al., 2012; Poole & Bruck, 2012).

 Check Your Learning

RECALL Describe how children use strategies to help them remember.

Summarize the processes that give rise to autobiographical memory in toddlers.

INTERPRET Distinguish the situations in which gist processing of experience is advantageous (i.e., it leads to better memory) from those in which it is not.

APPLY Describe how research on children's eyewitness testimony illustrates connections among emotional, cognitive, and social development.

7.2 Problem Solving

OUTLINE

Developmental Trends in Solving Problems

Features of Children's and Adolescents' Problem Solving

Scientific Thinking

LEARNING OBJECTIVES

LO4   Do older children and adolescents typically solve problems better than younger children?

LO5   What factors contribute to children's and adolescents' success in solving problems?

LO6   Can children and adolescents reason scientifically?

Brad, age 12, wanted to go to a hobby shop on New Year's Day. His mother, Terri, doubted that the store would be open on a holiday, so she asked Brad to call first. Moments later Brad returned and said, "Let's go!" When they arrived at the hobby shop, it was closed. Annoyed, Terri snapped, "I thought you called!" Brad answered, "I did. They didn't answer, so I figured they were too busy to come to the phone." Later that day, Brad's 3-year-old sister grabbed an opened can of soda from the kitchen counter, looked at Terri, and said, "This is yours 'cause there's lipstick." Terri thought her daughter's inference was sophisticated, particularly when compared with her son's illogical reasoning earlier in the day.

According to Piaget's theory, reasoning and problem solving become progressively more sophisticated as children develop. Piaget believed that young children's reasoning (reflected in the name "preoperational thought") was particularly limited and that adolescents' reasoning (reflected in the name "formal operational thought") was quite powerful. But research has since shown that this account was wrong in two ways. First, it underestimated young children, who, like Brad's sister, often astonish us with the inferences they draw. Second, it overestimated adolescents who, like Brad, frequently frustrate us with their flawed logic.

In this module, we'll trace the growth of problem-solving skills in childhood and adolescence. We'll see that young children do indeed solve problems with far greater skill than predicted by Piaget but that, throughout development, many factors limit the success with which children, adolescents, and adults solve problems.

Developmental Trends in Solving Problems

LO4   Do older children and adolescents typically solve problems better than younger children?

Solving problems is as much a part of children's daily lives as eating and sleeping. Think about some common examples:

- After dinner, a child tries to figure out how to finish homework and watch his favorite TV program.
- A child wants to get her bike out of the garage, where it's trapped behind the car and the lawn mower.
- A teenager wants to come up with a way to avoid raking the leaves.

In each case, there's a well-defined goal (e.g., riding the bike, avoiding a chore) and the child is deciding how to achieve it.

As a general rule, as children get older they solve problems like these more often and solve them more effectively. Of course, this doesn't mean that

Even infants can solve some problems effectively, for example, by pulling on the string to bring the toy within reach.

younger children are always inept at solving problems. In fact, research has produced many instances in which young children solve problems successfully. For example, when asked what they could do if they went to the beach but forgot to bring lunch, most 4- and 5-year-olds suggest plausible, effective solutions, such as buying lunch at the concession stand (Hudson, Shapiro, & Sosa, 1995). What's more, even infants can solve simple problems (Barrett, Davis, & Needham, 2007). If an attractive toy is placed out of reach, like the baby in the photo, infants will use other means to bring the toy to them, such as pulling on a string, or, if the toy is on a cloth, pulling the cloth. Both are simple but wonderfully effective methods of achieving the goal of playing with an interesting toy (Willatts, 1999).

Also, as Brad's behavior in the vignette reveals, adolescents are not always skilled problem solvers. Their problem solving is often inefficient, haphazard, or just plain wrong. Think about the following problem:

> Imagine that you want to enter one of two raffles. The first one advertises, "50 tickets, 5 winners, so you have a 10% chance of winning!" The second advertises, "500 tickets, 40 winners, so you have an 8% chance of winning!" Which raffle would you enter?

Many adolescents choose to enter the second raffle—even though they've just read that the odds of winning are less (8% versus 10%)—apparently because they see that there are 40 winning tickets, not just 5 (Kokis et al., 2002). Of course, in the process, they ignore the fact that the second raffle has 460 losing tickets compared to only 45 in the first raffle!

Thus, research confirms what we saw in the vignette with Brad and his sister: Although children tend to become more effective problem solvers as they get older, even young children sometimes show remarkable problem-solving skill and adolescents can be error prone. In the next section, we'll look at some of the elements that govern children's success in solving problems.

Features of Children's and Adolescents' Problem Solving

LO5 What factors contribute to children's and adolescents' success in solving problems?

Because problem solving is such an important skill, child-development scientists have been eager to reveal the circumstances that promote children's problem solving. The results of this work are described in the next few pages, organized around important themes that characterize children's problem solving.

Young Children Sometimes Fail to Solve Problems Because They Don't Encode All the Important Information in a Problem When solving a problem, people construct a mental representation that includes the important features of a problem. *Encoding processes* **transform the information in a problem into a mental representation.** For example, when the problem is to get a bike that's trapped in the back of the garage, encoding creates a representation that includes the goal (get the bike) as well as other critical elements of the problem (e.g., the location of obstacles).

Often children's representations of problems are incorrect or incomplete. They fail to encode problem features (or encode them incorrectly), making it unlikely that they will solve problems. On conservation of liquid problems like the one shown on page 184, young children's representations often include the heights of the containers but not their diameters. Or when shown mathematical equivalence problems such as "6 + 2 = 5 + ___" they often mistakenly encode the problem as "6 + 2 + 5 = ____" (McNeil, 2014).

When young children's representations lack these key features, it's not surprising that they fail to solve problems. As children grow, their encodings are more likely to be complete, perhaps due to increases in the capacity of working memory and because of greater knowledge of the world.

Young Children Sometimes Fail to Solve Problems Because They Don't Plan Ahead Solving problems, particularly complex ones, often requires planning ahead. For example, the goal "get ready for school" requires planning because it involves coordinating a number of goals—get dressed, eat breakfast, brush teeth, find backpack—which must be completed under time pressure. Faced with problems like this one, young children rarely come up with effective plans. Why? Several factors contribute (Ellis & Siegler, 1997; McCormack, 2011):

- Young children often believe—unrealistically—that they can solve a problem by boldly forging ahead without an explicit plan. Like many people who hate to read directions that come with new toys, games, or software, young children often find it difficult to inhibit the urge to "let's get moving" in favor of "let's figure this out."
- Planning is hard work, and if young children find that their plans often fail, they may see little point in investing the effort.
- Young children may expect parents and other adults to solve complex problems for them.

These factors don't mean that young children never plan or can't plan. For example, when 4-year-olds are asked to solve mazes and are urged to avoid "dead ends" in the maze, they typically pause before drawing and look ahead to find a solution (Gardner & Rogoff, 1990). Thus, young children can plan, if they're asked to and the problem is not too complex. But many problems make it difficult or even pointless for young children to plan.

Successful Problem Solving Typically Depends on Knowledge Specific to the Problem as Well as General Processes Solving a problem often requires that children know some critical facts. For example, during the elementary-school years, children become much more adept at solving arithmetic word problems such as this one: "Joe has two candy bars, then Jessica gives him four more. How many candy bars does Joe have in all?" This improvement comes about as children master basic arithmetic facts and as they learn how to map different types of word problems onto arithmetic problems (Kail & Hall, 1999). Because older children usually have more of the knowledge relevant to solving a problem, they are more successful.

Effective problem solving depends on more than problem-specific knowledge. Children often use generic strategies—ones not specific to particular tasks or problems—to find a solution. **An example is** *means-ends analysis,* **in which a person determines the difference between the current and desired situations, then does something to reduce the difference**. If no single action leads directly to the goal, then a person establishes a subgoal, one that moves her closer to the goal. To illustrate, think of a 9-year-old who has pangs of hunger while reading in her bedroom. Her goal is getting something to eat. There's no food in her bedroom, so "go to the kitchen" becomes a subgoal and, once there, she can achieve her goal. Likewise, the baby on page 226 used means-ends analysis in pulling the string toward himself to achieve the main goal of grabbing the toy.

QUESTION 7.2

Ten-year-old Kayla wakes to see the season's first snowfall. She can hardly wait to get outside, but then remembers that her sled is hanging on a hook in the garage, beyond her reach. Use means-ends analysis to show how she could achieve her goal of sledding.

Even preschool children use means-ends analyses to solve problems. For example, a 2½-year-old who wants a favorite book that is out of reach on a shelf will find a chair to stand on. The chair is the means to achieve the subgoal of "getting within reach of the book." However, means-end analyses work for young children mainly when used on simple problems in which the difference between the current and desired situations can be achieved in a few moves. Younger children struggle with more complex problems that require generating many subgoals and keeping track of them while en route to the overall goal (DeLoache, Miller, & Pierroutsakos, 1998; McCormack, 2011).

Children and Adolescents Use a Variety of Strategies to Solve Problems In Piaget's view, children and adolescents solve problems in fundamentally different ways: 8-year-olds, for example, consistently do so using concrete operational logic, but 13-year-olds do so using formal operational logic. The modern view, introduced in Module 6.2, differs: Children and adolescents call on several different strategies to solve problems. For example, while playing board games in which a roll of the dice determines how many spaces to move, young children use many strategies to determine the number of moves from the dice (Bjorklund & Rosenblum, 2002). If the dice show 5 and 2, sometimes a child counts aloud "1, 2, 3, 4, 5, 6, 7" and then moves seven spaces; sometimes the child simply counts "5...6, 7" and moves; and other times the child glances briefly at the dice, then moves, as if she recalled the sum from memory.

Much the same thing happens, of course, when older children or adolescents learn a new game or a new skill. Initially, they try many different ways to solve a problem. As they gain experience solving a particular type of problem, they learn the easiest, most effective strategy and use it as often as possible (Siegler, 2000).

This general approach is captured in Siegler's (1996, 2007) overlapping waves model, in which children use multiple strategies to solve problems and, over time, they tend to use strategies that are faster, more accurate, and take less effort. The model is illustrated in Figure 7-4, which shows how often different hypothetical strategies are used, based on a person's age. Strategy A, for example, is common among young children but becomes less common with age; Strategy E shows the opposite profile, becoming more common with age. The vertical lines make it easy to see how often various strategies are used at different ages. Among 7-year-olds, Strategy A is most common, followed by B and D; in contrast, among 14-year-olds, Strategy D is most common, followed by C and E. Thus, children and adolescents are alike in choosing from a well-stocked tool kit to solve problems; they differ in that adolescents typically have a more sophisticated set of tools.

Some theorists go further and imagine that the problem-solving toolbox includes two general kinds of tools (Klaczynski, 2004; Stanovich, West, & Toplak, 2011). **Sometimes children and adolescents solve problems using *heuristics*—rules of thumb that do not guarantee a solution but are useful in solving a range of problems.** Heuristics tend to be fast and require little effort. But sometimes children and adolescents solve problems analytically; depending on the problem, they may compute an answer mathematically or use logical rules.

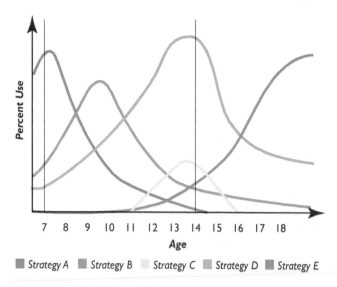

Figure 7-4

SOURCE: *Emerging Minds: The Process of Change in Children's Thinking* by Sigler (1996) Fig.4.4 p.89 © 1996 by Oxford University Press, Inc. By permission of Oxford University Press, USA.

To see the difference between heuristic and analytic solutions, think about the following problem:

> Erica wants to go to a baseball game to try to catch a fly ball. She calls the main office and learns that almost all fly balls have been caught in section 43. Just before she chooses her seats, she learns that her friend Jimmy caught 2 fly balls last week while sitting in section 10. Which section is most likely to give Erica the best chance to catch a fly ball? (Kokis et al., 2002, p. 34)

The heuristic solution relies on personal experience: When in doubt, imitate other people who have been successful. In this case, that means sitting where the friend sat. The analytic solution, in contrast, involves relying on the statistical information that, historically, the odds of catching a fly ball are greatest in section 43. Adolescents are more likely than children to solve problems like this one analytically, but some children solve them analytically and some adolescents rely on the heuristic approach (Kokis et al., 2002). In fact, this is a general pattern: heuristic and analytic solutions are both used throughout childhood and adolescence, but use of analytic solutions becomes more frequent as children develop (Furlan, Agnoli, & Reyna, 2013; Kail, 2013).

Collaboration Often Enhances Children's Problem Solving In research, children typically solve problems by themselves, but in life beyond the laboratory they often collaborate with parents, siblings, and peers. This collaboration is usually beneficial when the partner is a parent, older child, or more knowledgeable peer. As we saw in Module 6.2, parents and older children often scaffold children's efforts to solve problems, providing structure and direction that allow younger children to accomplish more than they could alone. In laboratory studies, for example, parents often tailor help to the child's needs, watching quietly when children are making headway but giving words of encouragement and hints when their children are stumped (Rogoff, 1998).

Collaboration with peers is sometimes but not always productive, and the settings that are conducive to effective peer collaboration remain a mystery (Siegler & Alibali, 2005). On the one hand, collaboration involving young children like the ones shown in the photo often fails, simply because preschool children lack many of the social and linguistic skills needed to work as part of a team. Peer collaboration is also often unproductive when problems are so difficult that neither child has a clue about how to proceed. On the other hand, peer collaboration works when both children are invested in solving the problem and when they share responsibility for doing so.

Despite its virtues, collaboration doesn't come easily to children attending schools in the United States, Canada, and Europe, where they are exposed to instruction that emphasizes an individual student's participation and achievement. In contrast, in some schools in the rest of the world—for example, in Mexico and Japan—students are taught to support their classmates, to learn from and build on their ideas and suggestions, and to view classmates as resources. In this setting, collaboration comes naturally to children (Chavajay, 2008; Silva, Correa-Chávez, & Rogoff, 2010).

Collaborative problem solving is often ineffective with young children because they lack the cognitive and social skills needed to work together.

Scientific Thinking

LO6 Can children and adolescents reason scientifically?

In Chapter 6, we saw that many child-development researchers rely on the child-as-scientist metaphor, in which experiences provide the "data" from which children construct theories that capture their understanding of the material and social world. These theories are usually described as informal because they lack the rigor of real scientific theories and because children and adolescents rarely conduct true experiments designed to test their theories. However, when it comes to the skills associated with real scientific reasoning, children and even adolescents typically have some conspicuous faults (Kuhn, 2012):

- *Children and adolescents often have misconceptions of scientific phenomena that interfere with their scientific thinking.* In other words, through experience with the physical and social worlds, children and adolescents construct mental models that help them to understand those worlds, even though the models are often wrong. For example, 6-year-olds often believe that the earth is stationary but that the sun and moon move up and down (Klahr, Zimmerman, & Jirout, 2011). Similarly, young children often believe that energy is a property of people or living things, not all physical systems or objects (Nordine, Krajcik, & Fortus, 2011). Unlearning these flawed conceptions is often a necessary first step in children's and adolescents' scientific thinking (Klahr et al., 2011).

- *Children and adolescents often devise experiments in which variables are confounded—they are combined instead of evaluated independently—so that the results are ambiguous.* For example, if asked to determine how the size of a car's engine, wheels, and tail fins affect its speed, children often manipulate more than one variable at a time. They compare a car with a large engine, large wheels, and large tail fins against a car with a small engine, small wheels, and small tail fins. Not until adulthood do individuals routinely devise experiments in which only one variable is manipulated (e.g., size of the wheels) and the rest are held constant, which allows clear conclusions regarding cause and effect (Schauble, 1996).

- *Children and adolescents often reach conclusions prematurely, basing them on too little evidence.* Instead of conducting all of the experiments necessary to isolate the impact of variables, children and adolescents typically conduct a subset of the experiments, and then reach conclusions prematurely (Zimmerman, 2007). In the previous example about determining a car's speed, children rarely do enough experimentation to provide conclusive evidence about each variable. They might perform experiments showing that a car runs fast with a large engine and slower with large tail fins, but also assume that wheel size has no effect without actually doing the critical experiments (Kuhn et al., 1995).

- *Children and adolescents often have difficulty using data to evaluate theories.* If the results of an experiment don't support children's and adolescents' own beliefs, they tend to discount the value of the study (Croker & Buchanan, 2011; Klaczynski, 2004). To illustrate, if Baptist adolescents read about a flawed experiment, they tend to overlook the flaws if the results show that Baptists make better parents but not when the results show that Baptists make worse parents. (The same is true of adolescents of other faiths.) In these cases, adolescents use less rigorous standards to evaluate experiments when the evidence supports what they believe (Jacobs & Klaczynski, 2002; Klaczynski, 2000).

These findings suggest that children and adolescents have limited scientific skills. Other findings, however, indicate that young children have some rudimentary scientific skill. For example, children can sometimes identify the kind of evidence that would support a hypothesis. If trying to determine whether an animal has a good sense of smell, 6- to 8-year-olds know that it's better to conduct an experiment that uses a weak-smelling food than a strong-smelling food. If trying to decide whether a mouse that's loose in a house is large or small, they know that it's better to place a piece of food in a box that has a small opening instead of one with a large opening (Sodian, Zaitchik, & Carey, 1991). In these studies, young children are not designing complete experiments on their own; instead, they are simply evaluating part of an experiment that someone else has planned, which may explain their improved skill (DeLoache et al., 1998).

And it's clear that even young children can be trained to think more scientifically. The "Focus on Research" feature highlights work on teaching elementary-school children how to avoid confounded experiments by manipulating one variable at a time.

Focus on Research

Learning to Design Experiments

Who were the investigators, and what was the aim of the study? Laboratory studies show that children can be taught to conduct experiments properly by manipulating variables of interest and holding others constant. However, researchers have disagreed on the best way to teach experimental design. Some argue for discovery learning—allowing students to identify properties of good experiments by evaluating the results of studies they conduct themselves. Other experts argue that providing explicit instruction about principles of sound experimentation is also necessary. Robert Lorch and his colleagues (2010) wanted to identify the most effective method for teaching experimental design to elementary-school children.

How did the investigators measure the topic of interest? To begin, students completed a questionnaire that described experiments in which some variables were confounded as well as experiments in which one variable was manipulated and the others were controlled. Students judged which experiments were "good" and which were "bad." Next, students were assigned to one of three conditions. In one condition, students were asked to identify the variables that influence how far a ball travels after rolling down a ramp. They were told to do experiments to study the impact of the steepness of the ramp, its surface (smooth or rough), the length of the ball's run on the ramp (i.e., the ball's starting position), and the color of the ball. Other students had brief instruction from

their teacher about the need to manipulate one variable (e.g., the ramp's steepness) while holding the others constant. Students in a third group received the instruction and had the opportunity to conduct their own experiments. Finally, students completed another questionnaire measuring their understanding of good experiments.

Who were the children in the study? The children included 797 fourth-grade students.

What was the design of the study? This study was experimental. The independent variable was the teaching condition: (a) discovery, (b) explicit instruction, or (c) discovery plus instruction. The dependent variable was the number of correct answers on the questionnaire completed after teaching. Because the study included only fourth graders, it was not developmental.

Were there ethical concerns with the study? The hypothetical problems were straightforward and posed no special risks to children.

What were the results? Lorch et al. defined children as "experts" in experimental design if they correctly identified 87% of the "good" and "bad" experiments on the questionnaire. The percentage of experts in each of the teaching conditions is shown in Figure 7-5. The results are clear in showing that discovery alone was the least effective and that discovery plus explicit instruction was the most effective.

What did the investigators conclude? According to Lorch et al. (2010), their findings show that

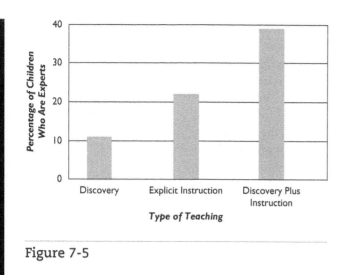

Figure 7-5

"combining explicit instruction with experimentation is much more effective than experimentation alone" (p. 98). That said, only a minority of students mastered the basic principles of experimental design with any method; most students need additional instruction to become skilled experimenters.

What converging evidence would strengthen these conclusions? In the questionnaire assessing knowledge of experimental principles, students were not designing experiments; they were evaluating experiments that others had designed. A true demonstration of the effectiveness of discovery plus instruction would be showing that it improves the experiments that students design themselves, from scratch.

Thus, the general developmental trend for scientific reasoning resembles the one we saw previously for general problem solving: Overall, children's skill improves steadily as they grow, but young children are sometimes amazingly skilled whereas older children and adolescents are sometimes surprisingly inept (Kuhn, 2011). In the next module, we'll see whether children's academic skills (reading, writing, arithmetic) develop in a similar manner.

 Check Your Learning

RECALL Describe findings that counter the general trend in which children are more successful at solving problems as they get older.

Summarize the reasons why young children often fail to solve problems.

INTERPRET Compare the widely held metaphor of "children as scientists" with the outcomes from research on actual scientific reasoning by children and adolescents.

APPLY Based on what you know about children's success at solving problems collaboratively, would you recommend that children and adolescents work together on homework?

 Academic Skills

OUTLINE	LEARNING OBJECTIVES	
Reading	LO7	What are the components of skilled reading?
Writing	LO8	As children develop, how does their writing improve?
Knowing and Using Numbers	LO9	When do children understand and use quantitative skills?

When Jasmine, a bubbly 3-year-old, is asked how old she'll be on her next birthday, she proudly says, "Four!" while holding up five fingers. Asked to count four objects, whether they're candies, toys, or socks, Jasmine almost always says, "1, 2, 6, 7 . . . SEVEN!" Jasmine's older brothers find all this funny, but her mother thinks that, notwithstanding the obvious mistakes, Jasmine's behavior shows that she knows a lot about numbers and counting. But what, exactly, does Jasmine understand? That question has her mother stumped!

Children and adolescents use their cognitive skills to accomplish many tasks in a variety of settings. Among the most important of these, however, are the school-related tasks of learning to read, write, and do math. Skill in these domains is an entry point for a developmental path that leads to higher education and to occupations with more income and prestige (Ritchie & Bates, 2013). Consequently, they've been studied extensively by child-development researchers. In this module, we'll examine the traditional three Rs. We'll start with reading, then examine writing, and end with numbers, where you'll learn why Jasmine counts as she does.

Reading

LO7 What are the components of skilled reading?

Try reading the following sentence:

Андрей достал билеты на концерт.

Unless you know Russian, you probably didn't make much headway, did you? Now try this one:

Snore secretary green plastic sleep trucks.

You probably read these words easily, but did you get anything more out of this sentence than the one in Russian? These examples show two important processes involved in skilled reading. *Word decoding* **is the process of identifying a unique pattern of letters.** Without knowing Russian, your word recognition was not successful in the first sentence. You did not know that билеты means "tickets" or that концерт means "concert." What's more, because you could not recognize individual words, you had no idea of the meaning of this sentence. *Comprehension* **is the process of extracting meaning from a sequence of words.** In the second sentence, your word recognition was perfect, but comprehension was still impossible because the words were ordered randomly. These examples remind us just how difficult learning to read can be.

In the next few pages, we'll look at how children read. We'll start with the skills that children must have if they are to learn to read, then move to word recognition and comprehension.

Foundations of Reading Skill Reading involves extracting meaning from print, and children have much to learn to do this successfully. Children need to know that reading is done with words made of letters, not with pictures or scribbles; that words on a page are separated by spaces; and that in English words are read from left to right. And, of course, they need to know the names of individual letters. These skills improve gradually over the preschool years, particularly when children are frequently involved in literacy-related activities such as reading with an adult, playing with magnetic letters, or trying to print simple words. Not surprisingly, children who know more about letters and word forms learn to read more easily than their peers who know less (Levy et al., 2006; Treiman & Kessler, 2003).

A second essential skill is sensitivity to language sounds. **The ability to distinguish the sounds in spoken words is known as** *phonological awareness*. English words consist of syllables and a syllable is made up of a vowel that's usually but not always accompanied by consonants. For example, *dust* is a one-syllable word that includes the initial consonant *d*, the vowel *u*, and the final consonant cluster *st*. Phonological awareness is shown when children can decompose words in this manner by, for example, correctly answering "What's the first sound in *dust*?" or "*Dust* without the *d* sounds like what?" Phonological awareness is strongly related to success in learning to read: Children who can readily identify different sounds in spoken words learn to read more readily than children who do not (Melby-Lervåg, Lyster, & Hulme, 2012). In fact, as we'll see in Module 8.3, an insensitivity to language sounds is one of the core features of reading disability.

Learning to read in English is particularly challenging because English is often inconsistent in the way that letters are pronounced (e.g., compare the sound of "a" in *bat, far, rake,* and *was*) and the way that sounds are spelled (e.g., the long "e" sound is the same in each of these spellings: team, feet, piece, lady, receive, magazine).* In contrast, many other languages—Greek, Finnish, German, Italian, Spanish, Dutch—are far more consistent, which simplifies the mapping of sounds to letters. In Italian, for example, most letters are pronounced in the same way; reading a word like *domani* (tomorrow) is simple because beginning readers just move from left to right, converting each letter to sound using simple rules: *d, m,* and *n* are pronounced as in English, *o* as in *cold, a* as in *car,* and *i* as in *see* (Barca, Ellis, & Burani, 2007). In fact, even though children learn to read more rapidly in languages where letter-sound rules are more consistent, phonological awareness remains the single best predictor of reading success in many languages (Caravolas et al., 2012; Ziegler et al., 2010).

If cracking the letter-sound code is essential for learning to read in so many languages, how can we help children master language sounds? The "Improving Children's Lives" feature describes one easy way.

Improving Children's Lives
Rhyme Is Sublime Because Sounds Abounds

The Cat in the Hat and *Green Eggs and Ham* are two books in the famous Dr. Seuss series. You probably know these stories for their zany plots and extensive use of rhyme. When parents frequently read rhymes—not just Dr. Seuss, but also Mother Goose and other nursery rhymes—their children become more aware of word sounds. Rhyming passages ("Is Spot hot? No, he's not!") draw children's attention to the different sounds that make up words.

The more parents read rhymes to their children, the greater their children's phonological awareness, which makes learning to read much easier (Bradley & Bryant, 1983; Ehri et al., 2001).

So, the message is clear: Read to children—the more, the better. As the photo shows, children love it when adults read to them, and learning more about word sounds is icing on the cake!

Picture-book reading is mutually enjoyable for parent and child and often fosters a child's prereading skills.

---

* The famous British playwright George Bernard Shaw ridiculed English spelling by writing *fish* as *ghoti,* with *gh* as in *laugh, o* as in *women,* and *ti* as in *motion*!

Storybook reading like that described in the feature is an informal way that parents can foster prereading skills. The benefits are not limited to the first steps in learning to read; rather, they persist into the middle elementary-school years and are just as useful for children learning to read other languages, such as Chinese (Chow et al., 2008; Sénéchal & LeFevre, 2002).

This sort of reading is also an important feature of preschool programs—for good reason: When preschool teachers use storybook reading to talk about reading-related skills, their students typically read better in elementary school. For example, in one study (Piasta et al., 2012), preschool teachers in one condition read a different book to their students every week. In another condition, teachers read a book but added comments about print (e.g., "Here are the cat's words. She says, 'I'm thirsty!'"), about letters (e.g., "This is a C."), and about words (e.g., "This word is cat."). When their teachers pointed to reading-related features of the storybooks, children read more skillfully in first grade (Piasta et al., 2012).

Recognizing Words At the beginning of reading, children sometimes learn to read a few words "by sight," but they have no understanding of the links between printed letters and the word's sound. However, the first step in true reading is learning to decode printed words by sounding out the letters in them: Beginning readers like the boy in the photo often say the sounds associated with each letter and then blend the sounds to produce a recognizable word. After a word has been sounded out a few times, it becomes a known word that can be read by retrieving it directly from long-term memory. That is, children decode words by recognizing familiar patterns of letters and syllables (Nunes, Bryant & Barros, 2012).

Thus, from their first efforts to read, most children use retrieval for some words. From that point on, the general strategy is to try retrieval first and then, if that fails, to sound out the word or ask a more skilled reader for help (Siegler, 1986). For example, when my daughter Laura was just beginning to read, she knew *the, Laura,* and several one-syllable words that ended in *at*, such as *bat, cat,* and *fat*. Shown a sentence like

Laura saw the fat cat run.

she would say, "Laura s-s-s…ah-h…wuh…saw the fat cat er-r-r…uh-h-h…n-n-n…run." Familiar words were retrieved rapidly, but the unfamiliar ones were slowly sounded out. With more reading experience, children sound out fewer words and retrieve more (Siegler, 1986). That is, by sounding out novel words, children store information about words in long-term memory that is required for direct retrieval (Cunningham et al., 2002; Share, 2008).

Educational Implications for Teaching Reading
Teaching young children to read is probably the most important instructional goal for most U.S. elementary schools. Historically, teachers have used one of three methods to teach reading (Rayner et al., 2001, 2002). The oldest is teaching phonics: for hundreds of years, U.S. children have learned to read by first focusing on letter names, then their typical sounds, and then moving on to syllables and words. Young children might be taught that *b* sounds like "buh" and that *e* sounds like "eeee," so that putting them together makes "buh-eee…be."

Beginning readers rely heavily on "sounding out" to recognize words, but even beginning readers retrieve some words from memory.

Learning all the letters and their associated sounds can be tedious, perhaps discouraging children from their efforts to learn to read. Consequently, teachers have looked to other methods. In the whole-word method, children are taught to recognize whole words by sight. This usually begins with a small number (50 to 100) of familiar words, which are repeated over and over to help children learn their appearance (e.g., "Run, Spot, run!"). In the whole-language method, which has been quite popular in the United States for 25 years, learning to read is thought to occur naturally as a by-product of immersing the child in language-related activities, such as following print as a teacher reads aloud or writing their own stories, inventing spellings as necessary (e.g., "Hr nak wz sor."). Teaching phonics is discouraged.

Although each of these three methods has some strengths, research clearly shows that phonics instruction is *essential* (Rayner et al., 2001, 2002). Children are far more likely to become successful readers when they're taught letter–sound correspondences, and this is particularly true for children at risk for reading failure. That is, the mapping of sounds onto letters, which is the basis of all alphabet-based languages such as English and German, is not something that most children master naturally and incidentally; most children need to be taught letter–sound relations explicitly.

Of course, mindless drilling of letter–sound combinations can be deathly boring. But flash cards and drills aren't the only way to master this knowledge; children can acquire it in the context of language games and activities that they enjoy. And, teaching children to read some words visually is a good practice, as is embedding reading instruction in other activities that encourage language literacy. However, these practices should be designed to complement phonics instruction, not replace it (Rayner et al., 2001, 2002).

Comprehension As we saw at the beginning of this module (page 233), decoding words accurately does not guarantee that children will understand what they've read. This phenomenon is captured in the Simple View of Reading model in which reading comprehension is viewed as the product of two general processes: word decoding and language comprehension (Gough & Tunmer, 1986). Children can't comprehend what they read when either a word can't be decoded or it's decoded but not recognized as a familiar word. Thus, skilled reading depends on accurate decoding coupled with understanding the meaning of the decoded word.

As children gain more reading experience, they better comprehend what they read. Several factors contribute to this improved comprehension (Siegler & Alibali, 2005):

- *Children's language skills improve, which allows them to understand words that they've decoded*: As children's vocabulary expands, they are more likely to recognize words that they've decoded. For example, a first grader with good decoding skills might be able to decode "prosper" but not understand it; by fifth or sixth grade, children's larger vocabulary means that they could decode and understand "prosper." In addition, older children know more about grammatical structure of sentences, knowledge that helps them comprehend the meaning of an entire sentence (Muter et al., 2004; Oakhill & Cain, 2012).

- *Children become more skilled at recognizing words, allowing more working memory capacity to be devoted to comprehension* (Zinar, 2000): When children struggle to recognize individual words, they often cannot link them to derive the meaning of a passage. In contrast, when children recognize words effortlessly, they can focus their efforts on deriving meaning from the whole sentence.

- *Working memory capacity increases, which means that older and better readers can store more of a sentence in memory as they try to identify the ideas it contains* (De Beni & Palladino, 2000; Nation et al., 1999): This extra capacity is handy when readers move from sentences like "Kevin hit the ball" to "In the bottom of the ninth, with the bases loaded and the Cardinals down 7 to 4, Kevin put a line drive into the left-field bleachers, his fourth home run of the series."

- *Children acquire more general knowledge of their physical, social, and psychological worlds, which allows them to understand more of what they read* (Ferreol-Barbey, Piolat, & Roussey, 2000; Graesser, Singer, & Trabasso, 1994): For example, even if a 6-year-old could recognize all of the words in the longer sentence about Kevin's home run, the child would not fully comprehend the meaning of the passage because he or she lacks the necessary knowledge of baseball.

- *With experience, children better monitor their comprehension:* When skilled readers don't grasp the meaning of a passage because it is difficult or confusing, they read it again (Baker & Brown, 1984). Try this sentence (adapted from Carpenter & Daneman, 1981): "The Midwest State Fishing Contest would draw fishermen from all around the region, including some of the best bass guitarists in Michigan." When you first encountered "bass guitarists," you probably interpreted *bass* as a fish. This didn't make much sense, so you reread the phrase to determine that *bass* refers to a type of guitar. Older readers are better able to realize that their understanding is not complete and take corrective action.

- *With experience, children use more appropriate reading strategies:* The goal of reading and the nature of the text dictate how you read. When reading a popular or romance novel, for example, do you often skip sentences (or perhaps paragraphs or entire pages) to get to the "good parts"? This approach makes sense for casual reading, but not for reading textbooks, recipes, or how-to manuals. Reading a textbook requires attention to both the overall organization and the relationship of details to that organization. Older, more experienced readers are better able to select a reading strategy that suits the material being read; in contrast, younger, less-skilled readers less often adjust their reading strategies to fit the material (Brown et al., 1996; Cain, 1999).

Collectively, greater language and word recognition skills, greater working memory capacity, greater world knowledge, greater monitoring skill, and use of more appropriate reading strategies allow older and more experienced readers to get more meaning from what they read.

Writing

LO8 As children develop, how does their writing improve?

Though few of us end up being a Maya Angelou, a Sandra Cisneros, or a John Grisham, most adults do write, both at home and at work. Learning to write begins early but takes years. Before children enter school, they know some of the essentials of writing. For example, 4- and 5-year-olds often know that writing involves placing letters on a page to communicate an idea (McGee & Richgels,

2004). But skilled writing develops gradually because it requires coordinating cognitive and language skills to produce coherent text.

Developmental improvements in children's writing can be traced to a number of factors (Adams, Treiman, & Pressley, 1998; Siegler & Alibali, 2005).

Greater Knowledge of and Access to Knowledge About Topics   Writing is about telling "something" to others. With age, children have more to tell as they gain more knowledge about the world and incorporate this knowledge into their writing (Benton et al., 1995). For example, asked to write about a mayoral election, children are apt to describe it as like a popularity contest; in contrast, adolescents often describe it in terms of political issues that are both subtle and complex. Of course, students are sometimes asked to write about topics quite unfamiliar to them. In this case, older children and adolescents' writing is usually better because they are more adept at finding reference material and including it in their writing.

Greater Understanding of How to Organize Writing   One difficult aspect of writing is organizing the necessary information in a manner that readers find clear and interesting. In fact, children and young adolescents organize their writing differently than older adolescents and adults (Bereiter & Scardamalia, 1987). **Young writers often use a *knowledge-telling strategy*, writing down information on the topic as they retrieve it from memory.** For example, asked to write about the day's events at school, a second-grader wrote:

> It is a rainy day. We hope the sun will shine. We got new spelling books. We had our pictures taken. We sang "Happy Birthday" to Barbara (Waters, 1980, p. 155).

The story has no obvious structure. The first two sentences are about the weather, but the last three deal with completely independent topics. Apparently, the writer simply described each event as it came to mind.

During adolescence, writers begin to use a *knowledge-transforming strategy*, deciding what information to include and how best to organize it for the point they wish to convey to their readers. This approach involves considering the purpose of writing (e.g., to inform, to persuade, to entertain) and the information needed to achieve this purpose. It also involves considering the needs, interests, and knowledge of the anticipated audience.

Asked to describe the day's events, older adolescents can select from among genres in creating a piece of writing, depending on their purpose for writing and the intended audience. An essay written to entertain peers about humorous events at school, for example, would differ from a persuasive one written to convince parents about problems with the required course load (Midgette, Haria, & MacArthur, 2008). And both of these essays would differ from one written to inform an exchange student about a typical day in a U.S. high school. In other words, although children's knowledge-telling strategy gets words on paper, the more mature knowledge-transforming strategy produces a more cohesive text for the reader.

Greater Ease in Dealing with the Mechanical Requirements of Writing   Soon after I earned my pilot's license, I took my son Matt for a flight. A few days later, he wrote the following story for his second-grade weekly writing assignment:

> This weekend I got to ride in a one propellered plane. But this time my dad was alone. He has his license now. It was a long ride. But I fell asleep after five minutes. But when we landed I woke up. My dad said, "You missed a good ride." My dad said, "You even missed the jets!" But I had fun.

Matt spent more than an hour writing this story, and the original (hanging in my office) is filled with erasures where he corrected misspelled words, ill-formed letters, and incorrect punctuation. Had Matt simply described our flight aloud (instead of writing it), his task would have been much easier. In oral language, he could ignore capitalization, punctuation, spelling, and printing of individual letters. These many mechanical aspects of writing can be a burden for all writers, but particularly for young writers.

In fact, research shows that when youngsters such as the one in the photo are absorbed by the task of printing letters correctly, the quality of their writing usually suffers; as children master printed and cursive letters, they can pay more attention to other aspects of writing (Medwell & Wray, 2014; Olinghouse, 2008). Similarly, correct spelling and good sentence structure are particularly hard for younger writers; as they learn to spell and to generate clear sentences, they write more easily and more effectively (Graham et al., 1997; McCutchen et al., 1994).

Young children often find writing difficult because of the problems they experience in printing letters properly, spelling words accurately, and using correct punctuation.

Greater Skill in Revising   Few authors get it down right the first time. Instead, they revise and revise, then revise some more. Unfortunately, young writers often don't revise at all—the first draft is usually the final draft. To make matters worse, when young writers revise, the changes do not necessarily improve their writing (Fitzgerald, 1987). Effective revision requires being able to detect problems and knowing how to correct them (Baker & Brown, 1984; Beal, 1996). As children develop, they're better able to find problems with their writing and to know how to correct them (Limpo, Alves, & Fidalgo, 2014), particularly when the topic is familiar to them and when more time passes between initial writing and revising (Chanquoy, 2001; McCutchen, Francis, & Kerr, 1997).

These past few paragraphs make it clear why good writing is so gradual in developing. Many different skills are involved and each is complicated in its own right. Word-processing software makes writing easier by handling some of these skills (e.g., checking spelling, simplifying revision), and research indicates that writing improves when people use word processors (Clements, 1995; Rogers & Graham, 2008).

Fortunately, students *can* be taught to write better. When instruction focuses on the building blocks of effective writing—strategies for planning, drafting, and revising text—students' writing improves substantially (Graham & Perin, 2007; Tracy, Reid, & Graham, 2009). For example, one successful program for teaching writing—the Self-Regulated Strategy Development in Writing program—tells students that POW + TREE is a trick that good writers use. As you can see in Figure 7-6 on page 240, POW provides young writers with a general plan for writing, and TREE tells them how to organize their writing in a nicely structured paragraph (Harris et al., 2008).

This kind of instruction is most effective when students write frequently—like any other skill, skilled writing requires lots of practice. In addition, the most productive writing instruction takes place in supportive classrooms: Writing is challenging and students have the best chance to succeed when teachers scaffold and praise students' writing (Graham, Gillespie, & McKeown, 2013).

Of course, mastering the full set of writing skills is a huge challenge, one that spans all of childhood, adolescence, and adulthood. Much the same can be said for mastering quantitative skills, as we'll see in the next section.

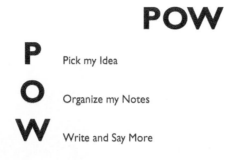

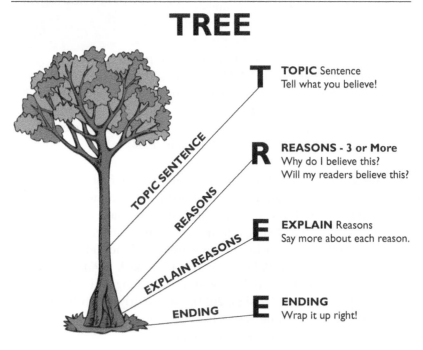

Figure 7-6

SOURCE: Harris, K. R., Graham, S., Mason, L., & Friedlander, B. (2008). *Powerful writing strategies for all students.* Baltimore, MD: Brookes.

Knowing and Using Numbers

LO9 **When do children understand and use quantitative skills?**

Basic number skills originate in infancy, long before babies learn names of numbers. Many babies experience daily variation in quantity. They play with two blocks and see that another baby has three; they watch as a father sorts laundry and finds two black socks but only one blue sock, and they eat one hot dog for lunch while an older brother eats three.

Do babies appreciate that quantity or amount is one of the ways in which objects in the world can differ? Yes. This conclusion is based on research in which babies are tested with sequences of pictures like those shown in Figure 7-7. The actual objects in the pictures differ, as do their size, color, and position; however, the first three pictures each show two things: two flowers, two cats, two butterflies. When the first of these pictures is shown, infants look at it for several seconds. But, as more pictures of two things are presented, infants habituate (become familiar with them; see Module 5.1): They glance at the picture briefly, then look away. But if a picture of a single object or, like the last drawing in the figure, a picture of three objects is then shown, infants again look for several seconds, their interest apparently renewed. Because the only systematic change

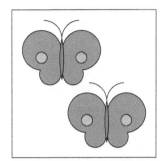
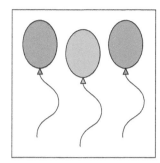

Figure 7-7

is the number of objects depicted in the picture, we conclude that babies can distinguish stimuli on the basis of number.

Research using this method shows that by six months, infants can distinguish one object from two and two objects from three. However, when sets include four or more objects, infants distinguish them only when one set is at least twice as large as the other. In other words, infants can't distinguish four objects from six objects but they can distinguish six from twelve (Cantrell & Smith, 2013; Opfer & Siegler, 2012). One idea is that infants use different systems to represent numbers. One is used for sets of one to three objects and is precise; the other is used for larger sets and estimates numbers approximately. Supporting this distinction, different regions in the infant's brain are activated when small and large sets of objects are shown (Hyde & Spelke, 2011).

What's more, young babies can do simple addition and subtraction—as long as it's *very* simple. In experiments using the method shown in Figure 7-8, infants

Sequence of events I + I = I or 2

1. Object placed in case

2. Screen comes up

3. Second object added

4. Hand leaves empty

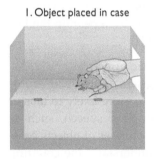
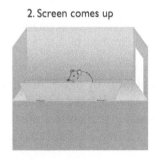
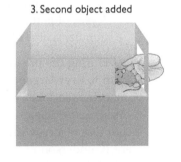

Then either: possible outcome   **or: impossible outcome**

5. Screen drops ...   revealing 2 objects   5. Screen drops ...   revealing I object

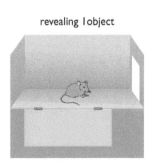

Figure 7-8

view a stage with one mouse. A screen hides the mouse and then a hand appears with a second mouse, which is placed behind the screen. When the screen is removed and reveals one mouse, 5-month-olds look longer than when two mice appear. Apparently, 5-month-olds expect that one mouse plus another mouse should equal two mice and they look longer when this expectancy is violated (Wynn, 1992). And when the stage first has two mice, one of which is removed, infants are surprised when the screen is removed and two mice are still on the stage. These experiments only work with small numbers, indicating that the means by which infants add and subtract are simple and probably unlike the processes that older children use (Mix, Huttenlocher, & Levine, 2002).

Learning to Count Names of numbers are not among most babies' first words, but by 2 years, youngsters know some number words and have begun to count. Usually, their counting is full of mistakes. In Jasmine's counting sequence that was described in the vignette—"1, 2, 6, 7"—she skips 3, 4, and 5. But research has shown that if we ignore her mistakes momentarily, the counting sequence reveals that she does understand a great deal. Gelman and Meck (1986) simply placed several objects in front of a child and asked, "How many?" By analyzing children's answers to many of these questions, they discovered that by age 3 most children have mastered three basic principles of counting, at least when it comes to counting up to five objects.

- *One-to-one principle:* **There must be one and only one number name for each object that is counted.** A child who counts three objects as "1, 2, a" understands this principle because the number of number words matches the number of objects to be counted.
- *Stable-order principle:* **Number names must be counted in the same order.** A child who counts in the same sequence—for example, consistently counting four objects as "1, 2, 4, 5"—shows understanding of this principle.
- *Cardinality principle:* **The last number name differs from the previous ones in a counting sequence by denoting the number of objects.** Typically, 3-year-olds reveal their understanding of this principle by repeating the last number name, often with emphasis: "1, 2, 4, 8…EIGHT!"

During the preschool years, children master these basic principles and apply them to ever-larger sets of objects. By age 5, most youngsters apply these counting principles to as many as nine objects. And children are more likely to master counting principles when parents mention numbers in their speech, such as counting objects with their children or simply saying the number of objects present (Gunderson & Levine, 2011). (To see whether you understand the counting principles, go back to Jasmine's counting in the vignette and decide which principles she has mastered; my answer is given before "Check Your Learning" on page 246.)

Of course, children's understanding of these principles does not mean that they always count accurately. To the contrary, children can apply all these principles consistently while counting incorrectly. They must master the conventional sequence of the number names and the counting principles to learn to count accurately. Learning the number names beyond 9 is easier because the counting words can be generated based on rules for combining decade number names (20, 30, 40) with unit names (1, 2, 3, 4). Later, similar rules are used for hundreds, thousands, and so on. By age 4, most youngsters know the numbers to 20, and some can count to 99 (Siegler & Robinson, 1982).

Learning to count beyond 10 is more complicated in English than in other languages. For example, *eleven* and *twelve* are completely irregular names, following no rules. Also, the remaining "teen" number names differ from the 20s, 30s, and the rest in that the decade number name comes after the unit (thir-*teen*, four-*teen*) rather than before (*twenty*-three, *thirty*-four). Also, some decade names only loosely correspond to the unit names on which they are based: *twenty*, *thirty*, and *fifty* resemble *two*, *three*, and *five* but are not the same.

In contrast, the Chinese and Korean number systems are almost perfectly regular. *Eleven* and *twelve* are expressed as *ten-one* and *ten-two*. There are no special names for the decades: *Two-ten* and *two-ten-one* are names for 20 and 21. These simplified number names help explain why youngsters growing up in Asian countries count more accurately than U.S. preschool children of the same age (Miller et al., 1995). What's more, the direct correspondence between the number names and the base-10 system makes it easier for Asian youngsters to learn some mathematical concepts. For example, if a child has 10 blocks, then gets 6 more, an American 5-year-old will carefully count the additional blocks to determine that he now has 16. In contrast, a Chinese 5-year-old will not count but quickly say "16" because she understands that in the base-10 system, 10 + 6 = 16 (Ho & Fuson, 1998).

Adding and Subtracting By 4 or 5 years of age, most children have encountered arithmetic problems that involve simple addition or subtraction. A 4-year-old might put one green bean on her plate, then watch in dismay as her dad gives her three more. Now she wonders, "Now how many do I have to eat?" Like the child in the photo, many youngsters solve this sort of problem by counting. They first count out four fingers on one hand, then count out two more on the other. Finally, they count all six fingers on both hands. To subtract, they do the same procedure in reverse (Siegler & Jenkins, 1989; Siegler & Shrager, 1984).

Youngsters soon abandon this approach for a slightly more efficient method. Instead of counting the fingers on the first hand, they simultaneously extend the number of fingers on the first hand corresponding to the larger of the two numbers to be added. Next, they count out the smaller number with fingers on the second hand. Finally, they count all of the fingers to determine the sum (Groen & Resnick, 1977).

After children begin to receive formal arithmetic instruction in first grade, addition problems are solved less frequently by counting aloud or by counting fingers (Jordan et al., 2008). Instead, children add and subtract by counting mentally. That is, children act as if they are counting silently, beginning with the larger number, and adding on. By age 8 or 9, children have learned the addition tables so well that sums of the single-digit integers (from 0 to 9) are facts that are simply retrieved from memory (Ashcraft, 1982).

These counting strategies do *not* occur in a rigid developmental sequence. Instead, as I mentioned in describing the overlapping waves model (on page 228), individual children use many different strategies for addition, depending on the problem. Children usually begin by trying to retrieve an

Young children use many strategies to solve simple arithmetic problems, including counting on their fingers.

Q&A QUESTION 7.3

Barb enjoys asking her 6-year-old, Erin, to solve simple arithmetic problems, such as 4 + 2 and 3 + 1. Erin likes solving these problems, but Barb finds it puzzling that Erin may solve a problem by counting on her fingers one day and simply saying the answer aloud on the next day. Is Erin's behavior unusual?

answer from memory. If they are not reasonably confident that the retrieved answer is correct, then they resort to counting aloud or on fingers (Siegler, 1996). Retrieval is most likely for problems with small addends (e.g., 1 + 2, 2 + 4) because these problems are presented frequently in textbooks and by teachers. Consequently, the sum is highly associated with the problem, which makes the child confident that the retrieved answer is correct. In contrast, problems with larger addends, such as 9 + 8, are presented less often. The result is a weaker link between the addends and the sum and, consequently, a greater chance that children need to determine an answer by resorting to a backup strategy such as counting.

Arithmetic skills continue to improve as children move through elementary school. They become more proficient in addition and subtraction, learn multiplication and division, and in high school and college move on to the more sophisticated mathematical concepts involved in algebra, geometry, trigonometry, and calculus (De Brauwer & Fias, 2009). Of course, these math skills and concepts come more easily to some children than others. By the time they enter kindergarten, children differ substantially in their math skill. One factor that's associated with early math skill is the approximate number system described on page 241: preschoolers with better math skills have a more finely tuned approximate number system. In other words, they approximate quantities more precisely (Bonny & Lourenco, 2013; Fuhs & McNeil, 2013). However, other findings suggest that knowing numbers (e.g., pointing to "6" when an experimenter says, "six") may be the most important prerequisite for success in mastering arithmetic (Göbel et al., 2014), just as knowing letters and their sounds is a prerequisite for success in learning to read.

Similarly, research has identified several factors that predict those elementary-school children who will succeed in math during middle school and high school. Some are specific to math, such as mastery of arithmetic and understanding of fundamental math concepts (e.g., fractions, the number line) but others are more general such as working memory and processing speed (Geary, 2011; Siegler et al., 2012). In short, children are successful in math when they can draw on a solid base of math skills and knowledge as well as powerful cognitive skills.

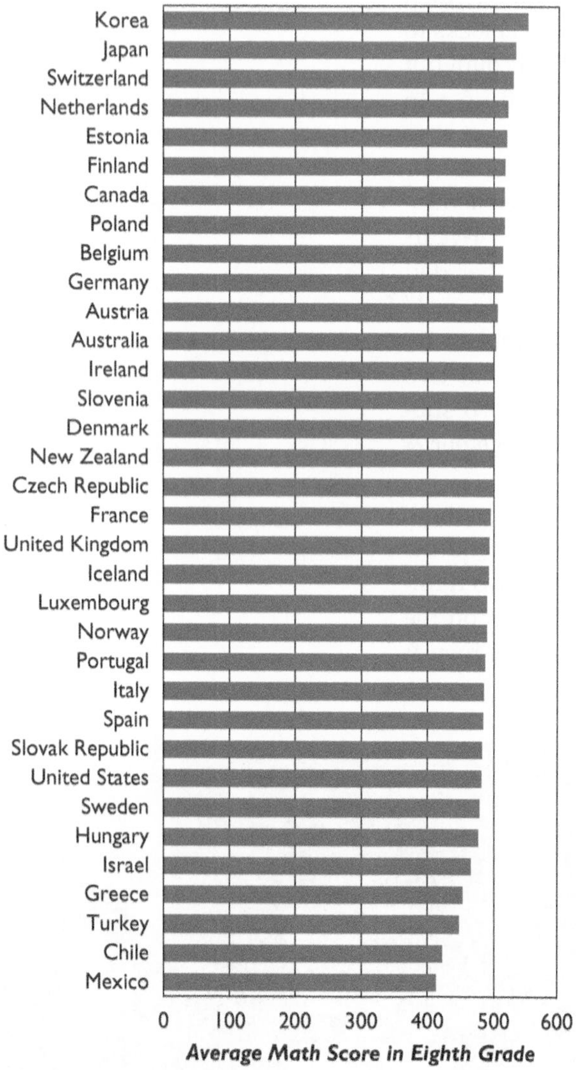

Comparing U.S. Students with Students in Other Countries

Let's return to the issue of cultural differences in mathematical competence. When compared to students worldwide in terms of math skills, U.S. students don't fare well. For example, Figure 7-9 shows the math results from a major international comparison (Kelly et al., 2013). U.S. high-school students have substantially lower scores than high-school students in several nations. Phrased another way, the best U.S. students only perform at the level of average students in many Asian countries. What's more, these differences in math achievement have been found for at least 25 years and for achievement in elementary school, middle school and high school (Stevenson & Lee, 1990).

Why do U.S. students rate so poorly? The "Cultural Influences" feature gives some answers.

Chart: Average Math Score in Eighth Grade

Korea, Japan, Switzerland, Netherlands, Estonia, Finland, Canada, Poland, Belgium, Germany, Austria, Australia, Ireland, Slovenia, Denmark, New Zealand, Czech Republic, France, United Kingdom, Iceland, Luxembourg, Norway, Portugal, Italy, Spain, Slovak Republic, United States, Sweden, Hungary, Israel, Greece, Turkey, Chile, Mexico

(x-axis: 0, 100, 200, 300, 400, 500, 600)

Average Math Score in Eighth Grade

Figure 7-9

SOURCE: Gonzales, P., Williams, T., Jocelyn, L., Roey, S., Kastberg, D., & Brenwald, S. (2008). Highlights from TIMSS 2007: Mathematics and science achievement of U.S. fourth-and eighth-grade students in an international context. Washington, DC: U.S. Department of Education.

Cultural Influences

Fifth Grade in Taiwan

Shin-ying is an 11-year-old attending school in Taipei, the largest city in Taiwan. Like most fifth-graders, Shin-ying is in school from 8:00 AM until 4:00 PM daily. Most evenings, she spends 2 to 3 hours doing homework. This academic routine is grueling by U.S. standards, where fifth-graders typically spend 6 to 7 hours in school each day and less than an hour doing homework. I asked Shin-ying what she thought of school and schoolwork. Her answers surprised me.

RK: Why do you go to school?

SHIN-YING: I like what we study.

RK: Any other reasons?

SHIN-YING: The things that I learn in school are useful.

RK: What about homework? Why do you do it?

SHIN-YING: My teacher and my parents think it's important. And I like doing it.

RK: Do you think that you would do nearly as well in school if you didn't work so hard?

SHIN-YING: Oh no. The best students are always the ones who work the hardest.

Schoolwork is the focal point of Shin-ying's life. Although many U.S. schoolchildren are unhappy when schoolwork intrudes on time for play and television, Shin-ying is enthusiastic about school and school-related activities.

Shin-ying is not unusual among Chinese elementary-school students. Many of her comments illustrate findings that emerge from detailed analyses of classrooms, teachers, students, and parents in studies comparing students in Japan, Taiwan, and the United States (Ni, Chiu, & Cheng, 2010; Stevenson & Lee, 1990; Pomerantz et al., 2014; Stigler, Gallimore, & Hiebert, 2000):

- *Time in school and how it is used.* By fifth grade, students in Japan and Taiwan spend 50% more time than U.S. students in school, more of this time is devoted to academic activities than in the United States, and instruction in Asian schools is often better organized and more challenging.

- *Time spent on homework and attitudes toward it.* Students in Taiwan and Japan spend more time on homework and value homework more than U.S. students do.
- *Parents' attitudes.* U.S. parents are more often satisfied with their children's performance in school; in contrast, Japanese and Taiwanese parents set much higher standards for their children.
- *Parents' beliefs about effort and ability.* Japanese and Taiwanese parents believe more strongly than U.S. parents that effort, not native ability, is the key factor in school success.

Thus, students in Japan and Taiwan excel because they spend more time both in and out of school on academic tasks. Furthermore, their parents (and teachers) set loftier scholastic goals and believe that students can attain these goals with hard work. Japanese classrooms even post a motto describing ideal students: *gambaru kodomo*—those who strive the hardest.

Parents underscore the importance of schoolwork in many ways to their children. For example, even though homes and apartments in Japan and China are small by U.S. standards, Asian youngsters, like the child in the photo, typically have a desk in a quiet area where they can study undisturbed (Stevenson & Lee, 1990). For Japanese and Taiwanese teachers and parents, academic excellence is paramount, and it shows in their children's success.

Many Asian schoolchildren have a quiet area at home where they can study undisturbed.

Educational Implications of Cross-Cultural Findings on Academic Achievement What can Americans learn from Japanese and Taiwanese educational systems? Experts (Stevenson & Stigler, 1992; Tucker, 2011) suggest several ways U.S. schools could be improved:

- Improve teachers' training by allowing them to work closely with older, more experienced teachers and give them more free time to prepare lessons and correct students' work.
- Organize instruction around sound principles of learning, such as providing multiple examples of concepts and giving students adequate opportunities to practice newly acquired skills.
- Create curricula that emphasize problem solving and critical thinking.
- Set higher standards for children, who need to spend more time and effort in school-related activities to achieve those standards.

Changing teaching practices and attitudes toward achievement would begin to reduce the gap between U.S. students and students in other industrialized countries. Ignoring the problem will mean an increasingly undereducated workforce and citizenry in a more complex world.

> *Response to question about Jasmine's counting on page 242:* Because Jasmine uses four number names to count four objects ("1, 2, 6, 7 ... SEVEN!"), she understands the one-to-one principle. The four number names arealways used in the same order, so she grasps the stable-order principle. Finally, she repeats the last number name with emphasis, so she understands the cardinality principle.

 ## Check Your Learning

RECALL What are some of the prerequisite skills that children must master to learn to read?

Summarize the differences between education in China and education in the United States.

INTERPRET Compare the mathematical skills that are mastered before children enter school with those that they master after beginning school.

APPLY Review the research on pages 236–237 regarding factors associated with skilled reading comprehension. Which of these factors—if any—might also contribute to skilled writing?

 # Unifying Themes   Active Children

This chapter highlights the theme that *children influence their own development:* Japanese and Chinese elementary-school children typically enjoy studying (an attitude fostered by their parents), and this makes them quite willing to do homework for 2 or 3 hours nightly. This, in turn, contributes to their high levels of scholastic achievement. U.S. schoolchildren usually detest homework and do as little of it as possible, which contributes to their relatively lower level of scholastic achievement. Thus, children's attitudes help to determine how they behave, which determines how much they will achieve over the course of childhood and adolescence.

See for Yourself

Create several small sets of objects that vary in number. You might have two pennies, three candies, four buttons, five pencils, six erasers, seven paper clips, and so on. Place each set of objects on a paper plate. Then find some preschool children; 4- and 5-year-olds would be ideal. Put a plate in front of each child and ask, "How many?" Then watch to see what the child does. If possible, record the children's counting so that you can analyze it later. If this is impossible, try to write down exactly what each child says as he or she counts. Later, go back through your notes and determine whether the children follow the counting principles described on page 242. You should see that children, particularly younger ones, more often follow the principles while counting small sets of objects than larger sets. See for yourself!

Summary

Memory

Origins of Memory
Rovee-Collier's studies of kicking show that infants can remember, forget, and be reminded of events that occurred in the past.

Strategies for Remembering
Beginning in the preschool years, children use strategies to help them remember. With age, children use more powerful strategies, such as rehearsal and outlining. Using memory strategies successfully depends, first, on analyzing the goal of a memory task and, second, on monitoring the effectiveness of the chosen strategy. Analyzing goals and monitoring are two important elements of metamemory, which is a child's informal understanding of how memory operates.

Knowledge and Memory
A child's knowledge of the world can be used to organize information that is to be remembered. When several events occur in a specific order, they are remembered as a single script. Knowledge improves memory for children and adolescents, although older individuals often reap more benefit because they have more knowledge. Knowledge can also distort memory by causing children and adolescents to forget information that does not conform to their knowledge or to remember events that are part of their knowledge but that did not actually take place.

Autobiographical memory refers to a person's memory about his or her own life. Autobiographical memory emerges in the early preschool years, often prompted by parents' asking children about past events. Infantile amnesia—children's and adults' inability to remember events from early in life—may reflect the absence of language or a sense of self.

Young children's memory in court cases is often inaccurate because children are questioned repeatedly, which makes it hard for them to distinguish what actually occurred from what adults suggest may have occurred. Children's testimony is more reliable if children are interviewed promptly, they're encouraged to tell the truth, they're first asked to explain what happened in their own words, and interviewers ask questions that test alternate accounts of what happened.

Problem Solving

Developmental Trends in Solving Problems
As children develop they typically solve problems more often and solve them more effectively. However, exceptions to the rule are not uncommon: Young children sometimes solve problems successfully whereas adolescents sometimes fail.

Features of Children's and Adolescents' Problem Solving
Young children sometimes fail to solve problems because they don't plan ahead and because they don't encode all of the necessary information in a problem. Successful problem solving typically depends on knowledge specific to the problem, along with general processes; involves the use of a variety of strategies; and is enhanced by collaborating with an adult or older child.

Scientific Problem Solving
Although the "child-as-scientist" metaphor is popular, in fact, children's and adolescents' scientific reasoning often has many shortcomings: Children and adolescents often have misconceptions that interfere with real scientific understanding; they tend to design confounded experiments; they reach conclusions prematurely, based on inadequate evidence; and they have difficulty using data to evaluate theories.

Academic Skills

Reading
Reading encompasses a number of component skills. Prereading skills include knowing letters and the sounds

associated with them. Word recognition is the process of identifying a word. Beginning readers more often accomplish this by sounding out words; advanced readers more often retrieve a word from long-term memory. Comprehension (the act of extracting meaning from text) improves with age because of several factors: working memory capacity increases, readers gain more world knowledge, and readers are better able to monitor what they read and to match their reading strategies to the goals of the reading task.

Writing

As children develop, their writing improves, reflecting several factors: They know more about the world and so they have more to say; they use more effective ways of organizing their writing; they master the mechanics (e.g., handwriting, spelling) of writing; and they become more skilled at revising their writing.

Knowing and Using Numbers

Infants can distinguish quantities. Children begin to count by about age 2, and by 3 years most children have mastered the one-to-one, stable-order, and cardinality principles, at least when counting small sets of objects. Counting is how children first add, but it is replaced by more effective strategies such as retrieving sums directly from memory.

In mathematics, U.S. students lag behind students in most other industrialized nations, chiefly because of cultural differences in the time spent on schoolwork and homework and in parents' attitudes toward school, effort, and ability.

Test Yourself

1. Compared with memory in younger infants, memory in older infants and toddlers is _____.
   a. unchanged
   b. improved due to growth in the brain regions that support memory
   c. less flexible because memories are strongly tied to specific contexts

2. Which of the following is not a memory strategy?
   a. rehearsal
   b. elaboration
   c. metamemory

3. Research shows that as children grow older, along with effective memory strategies they also have _____.
   a. better experiences
   b. better organization of factual knowledge
   c. lesser hold on information

4. Knowledge about cognitive processes like attention, perception, and intention is called _____ knowledge.
   a. academic
   b. metacognitive
   c. cognitive

5. Autobiographical memory develops as children acquire basic memory skills, language, and _____.
   a. a sense of self
   b. metacognition
   c. scripts

6. To obtain reliable testimony from preschoolers _____.
   a. interviewers should pursue only one explanation for what happened
   b. children should first be asked to describe the event in their own words
   c. adults should suggest possible events to cue the child's memory

7. According to fuzzy trace theory, younger children remember more in _____.
   a. a gist form
   b. a verbatim form
   c. neither gist nor verbatim form

8. Which of the following is an *inaccurate* statement concerning autobiographical memory?
   a. Autobiographical memory originates in infancy.
   b. According to one influential theory, autobiographical memory reflects growth in basic memory skills, language skills, and a child's sense of self.
   c. Children's autobiographical memories are richer when parents encourage children to talk about past events in detail.

9. Which of the following is *not* one of the best practices when interviewing children about a traumatic event?
   a. The interview should take place long after the event occurred.
   b. Children should be asked to describe the event in their own words.
   c. Children should be made comfortable first by discussing a "neutral" event.

10. Which of the following is a *correct* statement concerning young children's reading?
    a. Beginning readers sound words out, but advanced readers always retrieve words from memory.
    b. Advanced readers sound words out and only beginning readers use memory retrieval.
    c. As readers become more skilled, they sound out fewer words and retrieve more words from memory.

11. Older children typically understand more of what they read because they _____.
    a. know more about the world
    b. have less working memory capacity
    c. don't reread confusing passages

12. As children get older, their writing improves because _____.
    a. they begin to write down information directly as they retrieve it from memory
    b. they don't need to spend as much time on the mechanical aspects of writing
    c. their first drafts are good and they need not waste time revising

13. Infants _____.
    a. use the one-to-one principle
    b. can distinguish two objects from three objects
    c. are not sensitive to quantity as a characteristic of stimuli

14. The basic principles of counting are achieved by the age of _____.
    a. 7 years
    b. 5 years
    c. 3 years

15. Compared with U.S. students, students in Asia spend _____.
    a. less time on homework, but value it more
    b. about the same amount of time on homework
    c. more time on homework and they value it more than do American students

Key Terms

autobiographical memory   221
cardinality principle   242
cognitive self-regulation   218
comprehension   233
confounded   230
elaboration   217
encoding processes   226
fuzzy trace theory   220

heuristics   228
infantile amnesia   222
knowledge-telling strategy   238
knowledge-transforming strategy   238
means-ends analysis   227
memory strategy   216
metacognitive knowledge   218

metamemory   217
one-to-one principle   242
organization   217
phonological awareness   233
rehearsal   217
script   219
stable-order principle   242
word decoding   233

Chapter 8
Intelligence and Individual Differences in Cognition

Modules

8.1 What Is Intelligence?

8.2 Measuring Intelligence

8.3 Special Children, Special Needs

Have you ever stopped to think how many standardized tests you've taken in your student career? You probably took either the SAT or the ACT to enter college. Before that, you took countless achievement and aptitude tests during elementary school and high school. Psychological testing began in schools early in the 20th century and continues to be an integral part of U.S. education in the 21st century.

Of all standardized tests, none attracts more attention and generates more controversy than tests designed to measure intelligence. Intelligence tests have been hailed by some as one of psychology's greatest contributions to society but cursed by others. Intelligence tests and what they measure are the focus of Chapter 8. We'll start, in **Module 8.1**, by looking at different definitions of intelligence. In **Module 8.2**, we'll see how intelligence tests work and examine factors that influence test scores. Finally, in **Module 8.3**, we'll look at special children—youngsters whose intelligence sets them apart from their peers.

 # 8.1 What Is Intelligence?

LEARNING OBJECTIVES	OUTLINE
LO1 What is the psychometric view of the nature of intelligence?	**Psychometric Theories**
LO2 How does Gardner's theory of multiple intelligences differ from the psychometric approach?	**Gardner's Theory of Multiple Intelligences**
LO3 What are the components of Sternberg's theory of successful intelligence?	**Sternberg's Theory of Successful Intelligence**

Diana is an eager fourth-grade teacher who loves history. Consequently, every year she's frustrated when she teaches a unit on the U.S. Civil War. Although she's passionate about the subject, her enthusiasm is not *contagious. Instead, her students' eyes glaze over and she can see young minds drifting off—and, of course, they never seem to grasp the historical significance of this war. Diana wishes there was a different way to teach this unit, one that would engage her students more effectively.*

Before you read further, how would you define *intelligence*? If you're typical of most Americans, your definition probably includes the ability to reason logically, connect ideas, and solve real problems. You might mention *verbal ability*, meaning the ability to speak clearly and articulately. You might also mention *social competence*, referring to an interest in the world at large and an ability to admit when you make a mistake (Sternberg & Kaufman, 1998).

As you'll see in this module, many of these ideas about intelligence are included in psychological theories of intelligence. We'll begin by considering the oldest theories of intelligence, those associated with the psychometric tradition. Then we'll look at two newer approaches and, along the way, get some insights into ways that Diana could make the Civil War come alive for her class.

Psychometric Theories

LO1 What is the psychometric view of the nature of intelligence?

Psychometricians **are psychologists who specialize in measuring psychological characteristics such as intelligence and personality.** When psychometricians want to research a particular question, they usually begin by administering a large number of tests to many individuals. They then look for patterns in performance across the different tests. The basic logic is similar to a jungle hunter trying to decide whether some dark blobs in a river are three separate rotting logs or a single alligator (Cattell, 1965). If the blobs move together, the hunter decides that they are part of the same structure, an alligator. If they do not move together, they are three different structures—three logs. Similarly, if changes in performance on one psychological test are accompanied by changes in performance on a second test—that is, if the scores move together—then the tests appear to measure the same attribute or factor.

For example, suppose you believe intelligence is broad and general. In other words, you believe that some people are smart regardless of the situation, task, or problem, whereas others are not so smart. According to this view, children's performance should be consistent across tasks. Smart children should always receive high scores and less smart youngsters should always get lower scores. In fact, more than 100 years ago, Charles Spearman (1904) reported findings supporting the idea that a general factor for intelligence, or *g*, is responsible for performance on all mental tests.

However, other researchers have found that intelligence consists of distinct abilities. For example, Thurstone and Thurstone (1941) analyzed performance on a wide range of tasks and identified seven distinct patterns, each reflecting a unique ability: perceptual speed, word comprehension, word fluency, space, number, memory, and induction. Thurstone and Thurstone also acknowledged a general factor that operated in all tasks, but they emphasized that the specific factors were more useful in assessing and understanding intellectual ability.

These conflicting findings led many psychometric theorists to propose hierarchical theories of intelligence that include both general and specific components (Deary, 2012). John Carroll (1993, 1996), for example, proposed a hierarchical theory with three levels, shown in Figure 8-1. At the top of the hierarchy is *g*, general intelligence. In the middle level are eight broad categories of intellectual skill. **For example,** *fluid intelligence* **refers to the ability to perceive relations among**

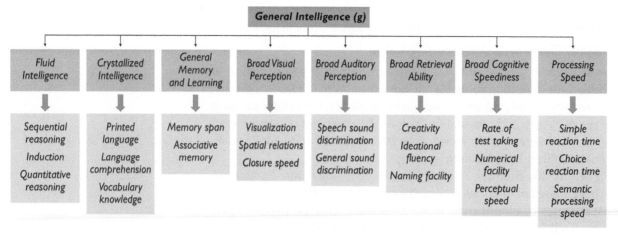

Source: Carroll, 1993.

Figure 8-1

SOURCE: Carroll, J. B. (1993). Human cognitive abilities: A survey of factor-analytic studies. New York, NY: Cambridge University Press.

stimuli. Each of the abilities in the second level is further divided into the skills listed in the bottom and most specific level. *Crystallized intelligence*, **for example, comprises a person's culturally influenced accumulated knowledge and skills, including understanding printed language, comprehending language, and knowing vocabulary.**

Carroll's hierarchical theory is a compromise between the two views of intelligence—general versus distinct abilities. But some critics still find it unsatisfactory because it ignores the research and theory on cognitive development described in Chapters 6 and 7. They believe we need to look beyond the psychometric approach to understand intelligence. In the remainder of this module, then, we'll look at two newer theories that have done just this.

Gardner's Theory of Multiple Intelligences

LO2 How does Gardner's theory of multiple intelligences differ from the psychometric approach?

Only recently have child-development researchers viewed intelligence from the perspective of modern theories of cognition and cognitive development. These new theories present a much broader perspective on intelligence and how it develops. Among the most ambitious is Howard Gardner's (1983, 1999, 2002, 2006) theory of multiple intelligences. Rather than using test scores as the basis for his theory, Gardner drew on research in child development, studies of brain-damaged persons, and studies of exceptionally talented people. Using these resources, Gardner identified seven distinct intelligences when he first proposed the theory in 1983. In subsequent work, Gardner (1999, 2002) identified two additional intelligences; the complete list is shown in Table 8-1.

The first three intelligences in this list—linguistic intelligence, logical-mathematical intelligence, and spatial intelligence—are included in psychometric

TABLE 8-1

NINE INTELLIGENCES IN GARDNER'S THEORY OF MULTIPLE INTELLIGENCES

Type of Intelligence	Definition
Linguistic	Knowing the meanings of words, using words to understand new ideas, and using language to convey ideas to others
Logical-mathematical	Understanding relations that exist among objects, actions, and ideas, as well as the logical or mathematical operations that can be performed on them
Spatial	Perceiving objects accurately and imagining in the "mind's eye" the appearance of an object before and after it has been transformed
Musical	Comprehending and producing sounds varying in pitch, rhythm, and emotional tone
Bodily-kinesthetic	Using one's body in highly differentiated ways, as dancers, craftspeople, and athletes do
Interpersonal	Identifying different feelings, moods, motivations, and intentions in others
Intrapersonal	Understanding one's emotions and knowing one's strengths and weaknesses
Naturalistic	Understanding the natural world, distinguishing natural objects from artifacts, grouping and labeling natural phenomena
Existential	Considering "ultimate" issues, such as the purpose of life and the nature of death

Source: Based on Gardner, H. (1983). *Frames of mind: The theory of multiple intelligences.* New York, NY: Basic Books; Gardner, H. (1999). *Intelligence reframed: Multiple intelligences for the 21st century.* New York, NY: Basic Books; Gardner, H. (2002). MI millennium: Multiple intelligences for the new millennium [video recording]. Los Angeles, CA: Into the Classroom Media.

theories of intelligence. The last six intelligences are not: Musical, bodily-kinesthetic, interpersonal, intrapersonal, naturalistic, and existential intelligences are unique to Gardner's theory. According to Gardner, Carlos Santana's wizardry on the guitar, the Williams sisters' remarkable shots on the tennis court, and Oprah Winfrey's grace and charm in dealing with people are all features of intelligence that are totally ignored in traditional theories.

How did Gardner arrive at these nine distinct intelligences? First, each has a unique developmental history. Linguistic intelligence, for example, develops much earlier than the other eight. Second, each intelligence is regulated by distinct regions of the brain, as shown by studies of brain-damaged persons. Spatial intelligence, for example, is regulated by particular regions in the brain's right hemisphere. Third, each has special cases of talented individuals. The field of music, for example, is well known for individuals with incredible talent at an early age. Claudio Arrau, one of the 20th century's greatest pianists, could read musical notes before he could read words; Yo-Yo Ma, the famed cellist, performed in concert at seven years of age for President John F. Kennedy.

Prompted by Gardner's theory, researchers have begun to look at other nontraditional aspects of intelligence. **Probably the best known is *emotional intelligence*, which is the ability to use one's own and others' emotions effectively for solving problems and living happily.** Emotional intelligence made headlines in 1995 because of a best-selling book, *Emotional Intelligence*, in which the author, Daniel Goleman, argued that "emotions [are] at the center of aptitudes for living" (1995, p. xiii). One major model of emotional intelligence (Salovey & Grewal, 2005; Mayer, Salovey, & Caruso, 2008) includes several distinct facets, including perceiving emotions accurately (e.g., recognizing a happy face), understanding emotions (e.g., distinguishing happiness from ecstasy), and regulating emotions (e.g., hiding one's disappointment). People who are emotionally intelligent tend to have more satisfying interpersonal relationships, have greater self-esteem, and be more effective in the workplace (Joseph & Newman, 2010; Farh, Seo, & Tesluk, 2012).

Most of the research on emotional intelligence has been done with adults, in large part because Goleman (1998; Goleman, Boyatzis, & McKee, 2002) argued that emotional intelligence can be the key to a successful career. Child-development researchers have studied emotion, but usually from a developmental angle—they've wanted to know how emotions change with age. We'll look at their research in Module 10.1.

Implications for Education The theory of multiple intelligence has important implications for education. Gardner (1993, 1995) believes that schools should foster all intelligences, rather than just the traditional linguistic and logical-mathematical intelligences. Teachers should capitalize on the strongest intelligences of individual children. That is, teachers need to know a child's profile of intelligence—the child's strengths and weaknesses—and gear instruction to the strengths (Chen & Gardner, 2005). For example, Diana, the fourth-grade teacher in the opening vignette, could help some of her students understand the Civil War by studying music of that period (musical intelligence). Other students might benefit by emphasis on maps that show armies moving in battle (spatial intelligence). Still others might profit from focusing on the experiences of African Americans living in the North and the South (interpersonal intelligence).

These guidelines do not mean that teachers should gear instruction solely to a child's strongest intelligence, pigeonholing youngsters as numerical learners or spatial learners. Instead, whether the topic is the signing of the Declaration of Independence or Shakespeare's *Hamlet*, instruction should try to engage as many different intelligences as possible (Gardner, 1999, 2002). The typical result is a much richer understanding of the topic by all students.

Some U.S. schools have enthusiastically embraced Gardner's ideas (Gardner, 1993). Are these schools better than those that have not? Educators in schools using the theory think so; they cite evidence that their students benefit in many ways (Kornhaber, Fierros, & Veenema, 2004), although some critics are not yet convinced (Waterhouse, 2006). In fact, a general criticism is that the theory has relatively little empirical support (Kaufman, Kaufman, & Plucker, 2013). Nevertheless, there is no doubt that Gardner's work has helped liberate researchers from narrow, psychometric-based views of intelligence.

A comparably broad but different view of intelligence comes from another new theory that we'll look at in the next section.

Sternberg's Theory of Successful Intelligence

LO3 **What are the components of Sternberg's theory of successful intelligence?**

Robert Sternberg has studied intelligence for more than 35 years. He began by asking how adults solve problems on intelligence tests. Over the years, this work led to a comprehensive theory of intelligence, called the theory of successful intelligence. Sternberg (1999) defines *successful intelligence* as using one's abilities skillfully to achieve one's personal goals. Goals can be short term: getting an A on a test, making a snack in the microwave, or winning the 100-meter hurdles. Or they can be longer term: having a successful career and a happy family life. Achieving these goals by using one's skills defines successful intelligence.

In achieving personal goals, people use three different kinds of abilities. *Analytic ability* **involves analyzing problems and generating different solutions.** Suppose a teenager wants to download songs to her iPod but something isn't working. Analytic intelligence is shown when she considers different causes of the problem—maybe the iPod is broken or maybe the software to download songs wasn't installed correctly.

Creative ability **involves dealing flexibly with novel situations and problems.** Returning to our teenager, suppose that she discovers her iPod is broken just as she's ready to leave on a day-long car trip. Lacking the time (and money) to buy a new player, she might show creative intelligence in dealing successfully with a novel goal: finding something enjoyable to do to pass the time on a long drive.

Finally, *practical ability* **involves knowing what solution or plan will actually work.** That is, although problems can often be solved in different ways in principle, in reality only one solution is practical. Our teenager may realize that surfing the Net for a way to fix the player is the only real choice because her parents wouldn't approve of many of the songs and she doesn't want a sibling to know that she's downloading them anyway.

Like the theory of multiple intelligence, the theory of successful intelligence suggests that students learn best when instruction is geared to their strength. A child with strong analytic ability, for example, may find algebra simpler when the course emphasizes analyses and evaluation; a child with strong practical ability may be at his best when the material is organized around practical applications. Thus, the theory of successful intelligence shows how instruction can be matched to students' strongest abilities, enhancing students' prospects for mastering the material (Grigorenko, Jarvin, & Sternberg, 2002).

QUESTION 8.1

Kathryn is convinced that her daughter is really smart because she has a huge vocabulary for her age. Would a psychometrician, Howard Gardner, and Robert Sternberg agree with Kathryn's opinion?

A key element of Sternberg's theory is that successful intelligence is revealed in people's pursuit of goals. Of course, these goals vary from one person to the next and, just as importantly, often vary even more in different cultural, ethnic, or racial groups. This makes it tricky—at best—to compare intelligence and intelligence-test scores for individuals from different groups, as we'll see in the "Cultural Influences" feature.

Cultural Influences

How Culture Defines What Is Intelligent

In Brazil, many elementary-school-age boys like the two in the photo on the left sell candy and fruit to bus passengers and pedestrians. These children often cannot identify the numbers on paper money, yet they know how to purchase their goods from wholesale stores, make change for customers, and keep track of their sales (Saxe, 1988).

Adolescents who live on Pacific Ocean islands near New Guinea learn to sail boats, like the one in the other photo, hundreds of miles across open seas to get from one small island to the next. Despite no formal training in mathematics, they use a complex navigational system based on the positions of stars and estimates of the boat's speed (Hutchins, 1983).

If either the Brazilian vendors or the island navigators were given the tests that measure intelligence in U.S. students, they would fare poorly. And they probably couldn't download music to an iPod. Does this mean they are less intelligent than U.S. children? Of course not. The specific skills and goals that are important to U.S. conceptions of successful intelligence and that are assessed on many intelligence tests are less valued in these other cultures and so are not cultivated in the young. By the same token, most bright U.S. children would be lost trying to navigate a boat in the open sea. Each culture defines what it means to be intelligent, and the specialized computing skills of vendors and navigators are just as intelligent in their cultural settings as verbal skills are in U.S. culture (Sternberg & Kaufman, 1998).

In Brazil, many school-aged boys sell candy and fruit on the streets, yet they often cannot identify the numbers on money.

Adolescents living on islands in the Pacific Ocean near New Guinea navigate small boats across hundreds of miles of open water, yet they have no formal training in mathematics.

SUMMARY TABLE 8-1

FEATURES OF MAJOR APPROACHES TO INTELLIGENCE

Approach	Distinguishing Features
Psychometric	Intelligence is a hierarchy of general and specific skills.
Gardner's theory of multiple intelligences	Nine distinct intelligences exist: linguistic, logical-mathematical, spatial, musical, bodily-kinesthetic, interpersonal, intrapersonal, naturalistic, and existential.
Sternberg's theory of successful intelligence	Successful intelligence is defined as the use of analytic, creative, and practical abilities to pursue personal goals.

As with Gardner's theory, researchers are still evaluating Sternberg's theory. As you can see in Summary Table 8-1, theorists are still debating the question of what intelligence *is*. But, however it is defined, the fact remains that individuals differ substantially in intellectual ability, and numerous tests have been devised to measure these differences. The construction, properties, and limits of these tests are the focus of the next module.

 ## Check Your Learning

RECALL Describe the psychometric perspective on intelligence.

Summarize the main features of Sternberg's theory of successful intelligence.

INTERPRET Compare and contrast the major approaches to intelligence in terms of the extent to which they make connections among different aspects of development. That is, to what extent does each perspective emphasize cognitive processes versus integrating physical, cognitive, social, and emotional processes?

APPLY On page 254, I mentioned activities that would allow Diana, the fourth-grade teacher, to take advantage of musical, spatial, and interpersonal intelligences to help engage more of her students in a unit on the U.S. Civil War. Think of activities that would allow her to engage Gardner's remaining intelligences in her teaching.

 # Measuring Intelligence

LEARNING OBJECTIVES	OUTLINE
LO4 Why were intelligence tests devised? What are modern tests like?	**Binet and the Development of Intelligence Testing**
LO5 What do they predict? How does dynamic testing differ from traditional testing?	**Features of IQ Scores**
LO6 What are the roles of heredity and environment in determining intelligence?	**Hereditary and Environmental Factors**
LO7 How do ethnicity and socioeconomic status influence intelligence test scores?	**Impact of Ethnicity and Socioeconomic Status**

Charlene, an African American third-grader, received a score of 75 on an intelligence test administered by a school psychologist. Based on the test score, the psychologist believes that Charlene is mildly mentally retarded and should receive special education. Charlene's parents are indignant; they believe that the tests are biased against African Americans and that the score is meaningless.

Between 1890 and 1915, enrollment in U.S. schools nearly doubled nationally as great numbers of immigrants arrived and as reforms restricted child labor and emphasized education. Increased enrollment meant that teachers now had more students who did not learn as readily as the "select few" who had populated their classes previously. How to deal with these less-capable children was one of the pressing issues of the day (Giordano, 2005). In this module, you'll see how intelligence tests were devised initially to address a changed school population. Then we'll look at a simple question: "How well do modern tests work?" Finally, we'll examine how race, ethnicity, social class, environment, and heredity influence intelligence, and we'll learn how to interpret Charlene's test score.

Binet and the Development of Intelligence Testing

LO4   Why were intelligence tests devised? What are modern tests like?

The problems facing educators at the beginning of the 20th century were not unique to the United States. In 1904, the minister of public instruction in France asked two noted psychologists, Alfred Binet and Theophile Simon, to devise a way to identify children who were likely to succeed in school. Binet and Simon's approach was to select simple tasks that French children of different ages should be able to do, such as naming colors, counting backward, and remembering numbers. Based on preliminary testing, Binet and Simon determined problems that typical 3-year-olds could solve, that typical 4-year-olds could solve, and so on. **Children's** *mental age or MA* **referred to the difficulty of the problems that they could solve correctly.** A child who solved problems that the typical 7-year-old could pass would have an MA of 7.

Binet and Simon used MA to distinguish "bright" from "dull" children. A bright child would have the MA of an older child; for example, a 6-year-old with an MA of 9 was considered bright. A dull child would have the MA of a younger child, for example, a 6-year-old with an MA of 4. Binet and Simon confirmed that bright children did better in school than dull children. Voilá—the first standardized test of intelligence!

The Stanford-Binet Lewis Terman, of Stanford University, revised Binet and Simon's test and published a version known as the *Stanford-Binet* in 1916. **Terman described performance as an** *intelligence quotient, or IQ,* **which was simply the ratio of mental age to chronological age, multiplied by 100:**

$$IQ = MA/CA \times 100$$

At any age, children who are perfectly average have an IQ of 100 because their mental age equals their chronological age. Figure 8-2 shows the typical distribution of test scores.

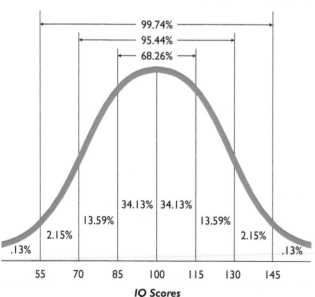

Figure 8-2

Roughly two-thirds of children taking a test have IQ scores between 85 and 115 and 95% have scores between 70 and 130.

The IQ score can also be used to compare intelligence in children of different ages. A 4-year-old with an MA of 5 has an IQ of 125 ($5/4 \times 100$), the same as an 8-year-old with an MA of 10 ($10/8 \times 100$).

IQ scores are no longer computed in this manner. Instead, children's IQ scores are determined by comparing their test performance with others their age. When children perform at the average for their age, their IQ is 100. Children who perform above the average have IQs greater than 100; children who perform below the average have IQs less than 100. Nevertheless, the concept of IQ as the ratio of MA to CA helped popularize the Stanford-Binet test.

By the 1920s, the Stanford-Binet had been joined by many other intelligence tests. Educators enthusiastically embraced the tests as an efficient and objective way to assess a student's chances of succeeding in school (Chapman, 1988). Nearly 100 years later, the Stanford-Binet remains a popular test; the latest version was revised in 2003. Like the previous versions, the modern Stanford-Binet consists of various cognitive and motor tasks, ranging from the extremely easy to the extremely difficult. The test may be administered to individuals ranging in age from approximately 2 years to adulthood, but the test items used depend on the child's age. For example, preschool children may be asked to name pictures of familiar objects, string beads, answer questions about everyday life, or fold paper into shapes. Older individuals may be asked to define vocabulary words, solve an abstract problem, or decipher an unfamiliar code. Based on a person's performance, a total IQ score is calculated, along with scores measuring five specific cognitive factors: fluid reasoning, knowledge, quantitative reasoning, visual-spatial processing, and working memory.

Another test used frequently with 6- to 16-year-olds is the Wechsler Intelligence Scale for Children-IV, or WISC-IV for short. The WISC-IV includes subtests for verbal and performance skills, some of which are shown in Figure 8-3 on page 260. Based on their performance, children receive an overall IQ score as well as scores for verbal comprehension, perceptual reasoning, working memory, and processing speed.

The Stanford-Binet and the WISC-IV are alike in that they are administered to one person at a time. Other tests can be administered to groups of individuals, with the advantage of providing information about many individuals quickly and inexpensively, typically without the need of trained psychologists. But individual testing like that shown in the photo optimizes a child's motivation and attention; it also provides an opportunity for a sensitive examiner to assess factors that may influence test performance. The examiner may notice that the child is relaxed and that test performance is a reasonable sample of the individual's talents. Or the examiner may observe that the child is so anxious that she cannot do her best. Such determinations are not possible with group tests. Consequently, most psychologists prefer individualized tests of intelligence over group tests.

Infant Tests The Stanford-Binet and the WISC-IV cannot be used to test intelligence in infants. For this purpose, many psychologists use the Bayley Scales of Infant Development (Bayley, 1970, 1993, 2006). Designed for use with 1- to 42-month-olds, the Bayley Scales consist of five scales: cognitive, language, motor, social-emotional, and adaptive behavior. To illustrate, the motor scale assesses an infant's control of its body, its coordination, and its ability to manipulate objects. For example, 6-month-olds should turn the head toward an object that the examiner drops on the floor, 12-month-olds should imitate the examiner's actions, and 16-month-olds should build a tower from three blocks.

An advantage of an individual intelligence test is that the examiner can be sure that the child is attentive and not anxious during testing.

Items Like Those Appearing on Different Subtests of the WISC-IV

Verbal Scale	Information: The child is asked questions that tap his or her factual knowledge of the world. 1. How many wings does a bird have? 2. What is steam made of?
	Comprehension: The child is asked questions that measure his or her judgment and common sense. 1. What should you do if you see someone forgot his book when he leaves a restaurant? 2. What is the advantage of keeping money in a bank?
	Similarities: The child is asked to describe how words are related. 1. In what way are a lion and a tiger alike? 2. In what way are a saw and a hammer alike?
Performance Scale	Picture arrangement: Pictures are shown and the child is asked to place them in order to tell a story. 
	Picture completion: The child is asked to identify the part that is missing from the picture. 

Figure 8-3

Stability of IQ Scores   If intelligence is a stable property of a child, then scores obtained at younger ages should predict IQ scores at older ages. In other words, smart babies should become smart elementary-school students, who should become smart adults. In fact, scores from infant intelligence tests are *not* related to IQ scores obtained later in childhood, adolescence, or adulthood (McCall, 1993). Not until 18 or 24 months of age do infant IQ scores predict later IQ scores (Kopp & McCall, 1982). Why? Infant tests measure different abilities than tests administered to children and adolescents: Infant tests emphasize sensorimotor skills more than cognitive processes such as language, thinking, and problem solving.

According to this reasoning, a measure of infant cognitive processing might yield more accurate predictions of later IQ. In fact, estimates of infants' information-processing do predict later IQ more effectively than do scores from the Bayley. For example, measures of infants' memory are related to IQ scores during middle childhood and adolescence (Bornstein, Hahn, & Wolke, 2013; Rose et al., 2012). In other words, babies who process information more efficiently and more accurately grow up to be smarter children and adolescents.

If scores on the Bayley Scales do not predict later IQs, why are these tests used at all? The answer is that they are important diagnostic tools: Researchers and health care professionals use scores from the Bayley Scales to determine whether develop-ment is progressing normally. That is, low scores on these tests are often a signal that a child may be at risk for problems later (Luttikhuizen dos Santos et al., 2013).

Although infant test scores don't reliably predict IQ later in life, scores obtained in childhood do. For example, the correlation between IQ scores at 6 years of age and adult IQ scores is about .7 (Brody, 1992; Kaufman & Lichtenberger, 2002). This is a relatively large correlation and shows that IQ scores are reasonably stable dur-ing childhood and adolescence. Nevertheless, during these years many children's IQ scores will fluctuate between 10 and 20 points (McCall, 1993; Weinert & Haney, 2003).

Features of IQ scores

LO5 **What do they predict? How does dynamic testing differ from traditional testing?**

IQ scores are remarkably powerful predictors of developmental outcomes. In fact, one expert argued that "IQ is the most important predictor of an individu-al's ultimate position within American society" (Brody, 1992). Of course, because IQ tests were devised to predict school success, it's not surprising that they do this quite well. IQ scores predict school grades, scores on achievement tests, and number of years of education; the correlations are usually between .5 and .7 (Brody, 1992; Geary, 2005).

These correlations are far from perfect, which reminds us that some young-sters with high test scores do not excel in school and others with low test scores manage to get good grades. In fact, some researchers find that self-discipline predicts grades in school even better than IQ scores do (Duckworth & Carlson, 2013). In general, however, tests do a reasonable job of predicting school success.

Not only do intelligence scores predict success in school, they also predict occupational success (Deary, 2012). Individuals with higher IQ scores are more likely to hold high-paying, high-prestige positions within medicine, law, and engineering (Oswald & Hough, 2012; Schmidt & Hunter, 2004); among scien-tists with equal education, those with higher IQ scores hold more patents and have more articles published in scientific journals (Park, Lubinski, & Benbow, 2008). Some of the linkage between IQ and occupational success occurs because these professions require more education, and we've already seen that IQ scores predict educational success. However, even within a profession—where all individuals have the same amount of education—IQ scores predict job per-formance and earnings, particularly for more complex jobs (Henderson, 2010; Schmidt & Hunter, 2004). If, for example, two teenagers have summer jobs running tests in a biology lab, the smarter of the two will probably learn the procedures more rapidly and, once learned, conduct them more accurately and efficiently.

Finally, intelligence scores even predict longevity: Individuals with greater IQ scores tend to live longer, in part because they are less likely to smoke, they drink less alcohol, they stay active physically, and they eat more healthfully (Deary, 2012).

Improving Predictions with Dynamic Testing   Traditional tests of intelligence, such as the Stanford-Binet and the WISC-IV, measure knowledge and skills that a child has accumulated up to the time of testing. These tests do not directly mea-sure a child's potential for future learning; instead, the usual assumption is that children who have learned more in the past will learn more in the future. Critics argue that tests would be more valid if they directly assessed a child's potential for future learning.

Q&A **QUESTION 8.2**

Amanda's 12-month-old son completed an intelligence test and received a slightly below-average score. Amanda is distraught because she's afraid her son's score means that he'll struggle in school. What advice would you give Amanda?

Dynamic assessment measures a child's learning potential by having the child learn something new in the presence of the examiner and with the examiner's help. Dynamic assessment differs from traditional testing in several ways (Tzuriel, 2013). First, the goal of traditional testing is to predict children's performance relative to their peers; the goal of dynamic assessment is diagnosis, revealing a child's strengths and weaknesses as a learner. Second, traditional testing follows a standardized format that focuses on a child's unaided performance; dynamic assessment is interactive and, drawing on Vygotsky's ideas of the zone of proximal development and scaffolding, focuses on the kind of guidance and feedback that children need to succeed (Sternberg & Grigorenko, 2002). Third, traditional testing focuses on the child's average performance across a variety of items; dynamic assessment focuses on a child's peak performance—identifying the circumstances where children learn best.

Dynamic assessment is most valuable for children who have difficulties learning in school, such as children with intellectual disabilities (described on pages 270–271). These children often receive low scores on traditional intelligence tests, scores that provide few insights into the child's abilities. In other words, IQ scores document that these children are less skilled than typically developing children but they don't pinpoint the skills that children do have or the conditions that promote children's use of their skills. This information is provided by dynamic assessment and estimates a child's learning potential more accurately than traditional tests do (Tzuriel, 2013).

Hereditary and Environmental Factors

LO6 What are the roles of heredity and environment in determining intelligence?

In a typical U.S. elementary school, several first-graders will have IQ scores greater than 120 and others will have IQ scores in the low 80s. What accounts for the 40-point difference in these youngsters' scores? Heredity plays an important role (Bouchard, 2009), as does experience (Bronfenbrenner & Morris, 2006).

Some of the evidence for hereditary factors is shown in Figure 8-4. If genes influence intelligence, then siblings' test scores should become more alike as siblings become more similar genetically (Plomin & Petrill, 1997). In other words, because identical twins are identical genetically, they should have virtually identical test scores (a correlation of 1). Fraternal twins have about 50% of their genes in common, just like non-twin siblings of the same biological parents. Consequently, their test scores should be (a) less similar than scores for identical

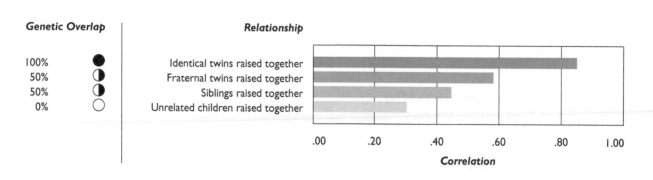

Figure 8-4

twins, (b) similar to scores of other siblings who have the same biological parents, and (c) more similar than scores of children and their adopted siblings. You can see in the graph of Figure 8-4 that each of these predictions is supported.

Studies of adopted children also suggest the impact of heredity on IQ: If heredity helps determine IQ, then children's IQs should be more like those of their biological parents than of their adoptive parents. In fact, throughout childhood and adolescence, the correlation between children's IQ and their biological parents' IQ is greater than the correlation between children's IQ and their adoptive parents' IQ. What's more, as adopted children get older, their test scores increasingly resemble those of their biological parents (Plomin & Petrill, 1997). These results are evidence for the greater impact of heredity on IQ as a child grows.

Do these results mean that heredity is the sole determinant of intelligence? No. Three areas of research show the importance of environment on intelligence. The first is research on characteristics of families and homes. If intelligence were solely the result of heredity, environment should have little or no impact on children's intelligence. In fact, children tend to have greater IQ scores when the family environment is intellectually stimulating—when parents talk frequently to the children, when they provide their children with cognitive challenging materials such as puzzles and books, and when they expose children to stimulating experiences outside the home, such as visits to museums (Nisbett et al., 2012).

The impact of the environment on intelligence is also implicated by a dramatic rise in IQ test scores during the 20th century (Flynn & Weiss, 2007). For example, scores on the WISC increased by nearly 10 points over a 25-year period (Flynn, 1999). The change may reflect industrialization, which requires a more intelligent workforce and brings about better schools, smaller families, and more stimulating leisure-time activities (Nisbett et al., 2012). Regardless of the exact causes of increased IQ scores, the increase per se shows the impact of changing environmental conditions on intelligence.

The importance of a stimulating environment for intelligence is also demonstrated by intervention programs that prepare economically disadvantaged children for school. Without preschool, children from low-income families often enter kindergarten or first grade lacking key readiness skills for academic success, which means they rapidly fall behind their peers who have these skills. Consequently, providing preschool experiences for children from poor families has long been a part of U.S. policy to eliminate poverty. The "Child Development and Family Policy" feature traces the beginnings of these programs.

Child Development and Family Policy
Providing Children with a Head Start for School

For more than 40 years, Head Start has been help.from low-income families. This program's origins can be traced to two forces. First, in the early 1960s, child-development researchers argued that environmental influences on children's development were much stronger than had been thought previously. An influential review (Hunt, 1961) of the impact of experience on intelligence concluded that children's intellectual development could reach unprecedented heights when scientists identified optimal environmental influences. In addition, a novel program in Tennessee (Gray & Klaus, 1965) gave credibility to the argument by showing that a summer program coupled with weekly home visits throughout the school year could raise intelligence and language skills in preschool children living in poverty. These findings suggested that claims of boosting children's intelligence were not simply pipe dreams.

The second force was a political twist of fate. When President Lyndon Johnson launched the War on Poverty in 1964, the Office of Economic Opportunity (OEO) was the command center. Sargent Shriver, the OEO's first director, found himself with a huge budget surplus. Most of the War on Poverty programs targeted adults; and because many of these programs were politically unpopular, Shriver was reluctant to spend more money on them. Shriver realized that no programs were aimed specifically at children and that such programs would be much less controversial politically. (After all, critics may contend that poor adults are lazy or irresponsible, but such arguments are not convincing when applied to young children.) What's more, he was personally familiar with the potential impact of programs targeted at young children through his experience as the president of the Chicago School Board and his wife's work on the President's Panel on Mental Retardation (Zigler & Muenchow, 1992).

Shriver envisioned a program that would better prepare poor children for first grade. In December 1964, he convened a 14-member planning committee that included professionals from medicine, social work, education, and psychology. Over a six-week period, the planning committee devised a comprehensive program that would, by involving professionals and parents, meet the health and educational needs of young children. In May 1965, President Johnson announced the opening of Head Start; by that summer, half a million U.S. youngsters were enrolled. The program now enrolls nearly a million U.S. children living in poverty and has, since its inception in 1965, met the needs of more than 30 million children (Administration for Children and Families, 2013).

How effectively do intervention programs like these meet the needs of preschool youngsters? Head Start takes different forms in different communities, which makes it difficult to make blanket statements about the overall effectiveness of the program. However, high-quality Head Start programs *are* effective overall. When children such as those in the photo attend good Head Start programs, they are healthier and do better in school (Ludwig & Phillips, 2007; Protzko, Aronson, & Blair, 2013). For example, Head Start graduates are less likely to repeat a grade level or to be placed in special education classes, and they are more likely to graduate from high school.

One of the most successful interventions is the Carolina Abecedarian Project (Campbell et al., 2001; Ramey & Campbell, 1991; Ramey & Ramey, 2006). This project included 111 children; most were born to African American mothers who had less than a high-school education, an average IQ score of 85, and typically no income. About half the children were assigned to a control group in which they received no special attention. The others attended a special day-care facility daily from age 4 months until 5 years. The curriculum emphasized mental, linguistic, and social development for infants, and prereading skills for preschoolers.

During elementary school and high school, children in the intervention program consistently had higher scores on a battery of cognitive tests (Campbell et al.,

2001). What's more, as adults, those who experienced the intervention were more likely to have graduated from college and more likely to be working full time (Campbell et al., 2012).

Thus, intervention works. Of course, massive intervention over many years is expensive. But so are the economic consequences of poverty, unemployment, and their by-products. In fact, economic analyses show that, in the long term, these programs more than pay for themselves in the form of increased earnings (and tax revenues) for participating children and lowered costs associated with the criminal justice system (Bartik, Gormley, & Adelstein, 2012; Reynolds et al., 2011). Programs like the Abecedarian Project show that the repetitive cycle of school failure and education can be broken. In the process, they show that intelligence is fostered by a stimulating and responsive environment.

High-quality Head Start programs are effective: Graduates of such programs are less likely to repeat a grade in school and are more likely to graduate from high school.

Impact of Ethnicity and Socioeconomic Status

LO7 How do ethnicity and socioeconomic status influence intelligence test scores?

Ethnic groups differ in their average scores on many intelligence tests: Asian Americans tend to have the highest scores, followed by European Americans, Hispanic Americans, and African Americans (Hunt & Carlson, 2007). The gaps have become smaller since the 1960s and reflect, in part, group differences in socioeconomic status (Nisbett et al., 2012; Rindermann & Thompson, 2013). Children from economically advantaged homes tend to have greater test scores than children from economically disadvantaged homes; and European American and Asian American families are more likely to be economically advantaged, whereas Hispanic American and African American families are more likely to be economically disadvantaged. Nevertheless, when children of comparable socioeconomic status are compared, group differences in IQ test scores are reduced but not eliminated (Magnuson & Duncan, 2006). Let's look at four explanations for this difference.

A Role for Genetics?   On page 262, you learned that heredity helps determine a child's intelligence: Smart parents tend to beget smart children. Does this also mean that group differences in IQ scores reflect genetic differences? No. Most researchers agree that there is no evidence that some ethnic groups have more "smart genes" than others. Instead, they believe that the environment is largely responsible for these differences (Nisbett et al., 2012).

A popular analogy (Lewontin, 1976) demonstrates the thinking here. Imagine two kinds of corn: Each kind produces both short and tall plants; and height is known to be due to heredity. If one kind of corn grows in a good soil—with plenty of water and nutrients—the mature plants will reach their genetically determined heights; some short, some tall. If the other kind of corn grows in poor soil, few of the plants will reach their full height and overall the plants of this kind will be much shorter. Even though height is quite heritable for each type of corn, the difference in height between the two groups is solely the result of the quality of the environment. Similarly, though IQ scores may be quite heritable for different groups, limited exposure to stimulating environments may mean that one group ends up with lower IQ scores overall, just like the group of plants growing up in poor soil.

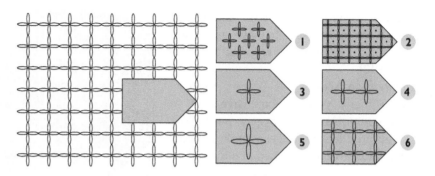

Figure 8-5

Experience with Test Contents   Some critics contend that differences in test scores reflect bias in the tests themselves. They argue that test items reflect the cultural heritage of the test creators, most of whom are economically advantaged European Americans, and so tests are biased against economically disadvantaged children from other groups (Champion, 2003). They point to test items like this one:

> A conductor is to an orchestra as a teacher is to what?
> book   school   class   eraser

Children whose background includes exposure to orchestras are more likely to answer this question correctly than children who lack this exposure.

The problem of bias led to the development of *culture-fair intelligence tests*, which include test items based on experiences common to many cultures. An example is Raven's Progressive Matrices, which consist of items like the one shown in Figure 8-5. Examinees are asked to select the piece that would complete the design correctly (6, in this case). Although items like this are thought to reduce the impact of specific experience, ethnic group differences still remain in performance on so-called culture-fair intelligence tests (Anastasi, 1988; Herrnstein & Murray, 1994). Apparently, familiarity with test-related items per se is not the key factor responsible for group differences in performance.

Stereotype Threat   When people know they belong to a group that is said to lack skill in a domain, this makes them anxious when performing in that domain for fear of confirming the stereotype, and they often do poorly as a result. **This self-fulfilling prophecy, in which knowledge of stereotypes leads to anxiety and reduced performance consistent with the original stereotype, is called *stereotype threat*.** Applied to intelligence, the argument is that African American children experience stereotype threat when they take intelligence tests, and this contributes to their lower scores (Steele, 1997; Walton & Spencer, 2009). For example, imagine two 10-year-olds taking an intelligence test for admission to a special program for gifted children. The European American child worries that if he fails the test, he won't be admitted to the program. The African American child has this same fear, but also worries that if he does poorly, it will confirm the stereotype that African American children don't do well on IQ tests (Suzuki & Aronson, 2005). Consistent with this idea, stereotype threat is reduced (and performance improves) when African American students experience self-affirmation—they remind themselves of values that are important to them and why (Sherman et al., 2013). And the "Focus on Research" feature shows that stereotype threat is also reduced when children are told that a test is an opportunity to learn new things, not a measure of ability.

Focus on Research

Making Tests Less Threatening

Who were the investigators, and what was the aim of the study? Stereotype threat works when people fear that their performance will confirm a stereotype. Consequently, one way to reduce threat should be to convince people that the task they're performing is unrelated to the stereotype. This was the approach used by Adam Alter and his colleagues (2010) to reduce stereotype threat.

How did the investigators measure the topic of interest? All participants completed 10 problems from a standardized math test. Half the participants were told that the problems measured their math ability; half were told that solving challenging math problems would help them do well in school. In addition, half the participants were asked to report their race before solving the problems, a manipulation designed to put the students at greater risk for stereotype threat; half provided this information after solving the problems, when it could not affect their performance.

Who were the participants in the study? The study included 49 African American students in grades 4-6.

What was the design of the study? This study was experimental. The independent variables included the framing of the math problems (as a measure of math ability or as a challenge that would help them do well in school) and when students reported their race (before or after solving the math problems). The dependent variable was the number of math problems solved correctly. Although the study included students in grades 4-6, the investigators did not examine age-related differences; consequently, the study was neither cross-sectional nor longitudinal.

Were there ethical concerns with the study? No. Parents provided consent for their children to participate. The math problems were common ones, taken from a test used by the school to assess students' progress. Finally, to counter any lingering effects of stereotype threat, all students were told that they'd done well on the test.

What were the results? Figure 8-6 shows the average number of problems that students solved in the four conditions. You can see that students solved the fewest problems when they provided their race before solving the problems and when the problems were portrayed as a measure of ability, an outcome that shows the impact of stereotype threat. In contrast, when stereotype threat could not operate—because the problems were portrayed as a challenging way for students to improve their learning or because race was not salient (it had not been mentioned prior to solving the problems)—students solved more problems.

What did the investigators conclude? Alter and his colleagues concluded that "reframing a threatening task as a challenge eradicated the negative effects of stereotype threat....participants who were reminded that they belonged to a marginalized group performed more poorly than their peers on an academic test, except when the test was framed as a challenge. This manipulation was subtle and inexpensive, which suggests that it might be a useful stereotype threat-management intervention" (Alter et al., 2010, p. 170).

What converging evidence would strengthen these conclusions? The results show that reframing math problems helps African American students avoid stereotype threat. It would be valuable to determine other kinds of reframing that may reduce or eliminate stereotype threat and see how well reframing works with other groups who experience stereotype threat (e.g., females and math problems).

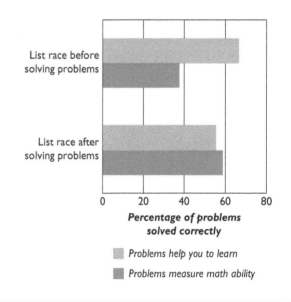

Figure 8-6

Test-Taking Styles   The impact of experience and cultural values can extend beyond particular items to a child's familiarity with the entire testing situation. Tests underestimate a child's intelligence when, for example, the child's culture encourages children to solve problems in collaboration with others and discourages them from excelling as individuals. What's more, because they are wary of questions posed by unfamiliar adults, many economically disadvantaged children often answer test questions by saying, "I don't know." Obviously, this strategy guarantees an artificially low test score. When these children are given extra time to feel at ease with the examiner, they respond less often with "I don't know" and their test scores improve considerably (Zigler & Finn-Stevenson, 1992).

Conclusion: Interpreting Test Scores   If all tests reflect cultural influences, at least to some degree, how should we interpret test scores? Remember that tests assess successful adaptation to a particular cultural context: They predict success in a school environment, which usually espouses middle-class values. Regardless of ethnic group—African American, Hispanic American, or European American—a child with a high test score is more likely to have the intellectual skills needed for academic work based on middle-class values (Hunt & Carlson, 2007). A child with a low test score, like Charlene in the module-opening vignette, apparently lacks those skills. Does a low score mean that Charlene is destined to fail in school? No. It simply means that, based on her current skills, she's unlikely to do well. Improving Charlene's skills will improve her school performance.

I want to end this module by emphasizing a crucial point: By focusing on groups of people, it's easy to overlook the fact that the average difference in IQ scores between various ethnic groups is relatively small compared to the entire range of scores for these groups (Sternberg, Grigorenko, & Kidd, 2005). You can easily find youngsters with high IQ scores from all ethnic groups, just as you can find youngsters with low IQ scores from all groups. In the next module we'll look at children at these extremes of ability.

 ## Check Your Learning

RECALL   What are modern intelligence tests like? How well do they work?

Describe the reasons why ethnic groups differ in their average scores on intelligence tests.

INTERPRET   Explain the evidence that shows the roles of heredity and environment on intelligence.

APPLY   Suppose that a local government official proposes to end all funding for preschool programs for disadvantaged children. Write a letter to this official in which you describe the value of these programs.

 # 8.3   Special Children, Special Needs

OUTLINE	LEARNING OBJECTIVES	
Gifted Children	**LO8**	What are the characteristics of gifted children?
Children with Disability	**LO9**	What are the different forms of disability?

Sanjit, a second-grader, has taken two separate intelligence tests, and both times he had above-average scores. Nevertheless, Sanjit absolutely cannot read. Letters and words are as mysterious to him as Metallica's music would be to Mozart. His parents took him to an ophthalmologist, who determined that Sanjit's vision was 20/20; nothing is wrong with his eyes. What is wrong?

Throughout history, societies have recognized children with disabilities as well as those with extraordinary talents. Today, we know much about the extremes of human talents. We'll begin this module with a look at gifted children. Then we'll look at children with disabilities and discover why Sanjit can't read.

Gifted Children

LO8 What are the characteristics of gifted children?

In many respects the boy in the photo, Bernie, is an ordinary middle-class 12-year-old: He is the goalie on his soccer team, takes piano lessons on Saturday mornings, sings in his church youth choir, and likes to go roller blading. However, when it comes to intelligence and academic prowess, Bernie leaves the ranks of the ordinary. He received a score of 175 on an intelligence test and is taking a college calculus course. **Bernie is *gifted*, which traditionally has referred to individuals with scores of 130 or greater on intelligence tests** (Horowitz & O'Brien, 1986).

Traditional definitions of giftedness emphasized test scores; modern definitions emphasize exceptional talent in a variety of areas, beginning with academic areas but also including the arts and sports.

Because giftedness was traditionally defined in terms of IQ scores, exceptional ability is often associated primarily with academic skill. But modern definitions of giftedness are broader and include exceptional talent in an assortment of areas, including art, music, creative writing, dance, and sports (Subotnik, Olszewski-Kubilius, & Worrell, 2011; Winner, 2000).

Whether the field is music or math, though, exceptionally talented children have several characteristics in common (Subotnik et al., 2011). First, their ability is substantially above average; being smart is necessary but not sufficient for being gifted. Second, gifted children are passionate about their subject and have a powerful desire to master it.

Third, gifted children are creative in their thinking, coming up with novel thoughts and actions. **Creativity is associated with *divergent thinking*, where the aim is not a single correct answer (often there isn't one) but fresh and unusual lines of thought** (Callahan, 2000). For example creativity is shown when children respond in different innovative ways to a common stimulus, as shown in Figure 8-7.

Fourth, exceptional talent must be nurtured. Without encouragement and support from parents and stimulating and challenging mentors, a youngster's talents will wither. Talented children need a curriculum that is challenging and complex; they need teachers who know how to foster talent; and they need like-minded peers who stimulate their interests (Subotnik et al., 2011). With this support, gifted children's achievement can be remarkable. In a 25-year-longitudinal study, gifted teens were, as adults, extraordinarily successful in school and in their careers (Kell, Lubinski, & Benbow, 2013). For example, more than 15% had been awarded patents before they turned 40.

Figure 8-7

The "Improving Children's Lives" feature show how parents and teachers can foster children's creativity.

Improving Children's Lives

Fostering Creativity

Here are some guidelines for helping children to be more creative.

1. Encourage children to take risks. Not all novel ideas bear fruit; some won't work and some are silly. But only by repeatedly thinking in novel and unusual ways are children likely to produce something truly original.

2. Encourage children to think of alternatives to conventional wisdom. Have them think what would happen if accepted practices were changed. For example, "What would life be like without cars?" or "Why not eat breakfast in the evening and dinner in the morning?"

3. Praise children for working hard. As the saying goes, creativity is one part inspiration and nine parts perspiration. The raw creative insight must be developed and polished to achieve the luster of a finished product.

4. Help children get over the "I'm not creative" hurdle. Too often they believe that only others are creative. Assure children that following these guidelines will make anyone more creative.

Finally, the stereotype is that gifted children are often emotionally troubled and unable to get along with their peers. In reality, gifted children and adults tend to be more mature than their peers and have fewer emotional problems (Simonton & Song, 2009; Subotnik et al., 2011), and as adults, they report being highly satisfied with their careers, relationships with others, and life in general (Lubinski et al., 2006).

Gifted children represent one extreme of human ability. At the other extreme are youngsters with disability, the topic of the next section.

Children with Disability

LO9 What are the different forms of disability?

"Little David," so named because his father was also named David, was the oldest of four children. He learned to sit only days before his first birthday, he began to walk at 2, and he said his first words as a 3-year-old. By age 5, David was far behind his age-mates developmentally. David had Down syndrome, a disorder (described in Module 2.2) that is caused by an extra 21st chromosome.

Children with Intellectual Disability Down syndrome is an example of a condition that leads to *intellectual disability*, **which refers to substantial limitations in intellectual ability as well as problems in adapting to an environment, with both emerging before 18 years of age.** Limited intellectual skill is often defined as a score of 70 or less on an intelligence test such as the Stanford-Binet. Adaptive behavior includes conceptual skills important for successful adaptation (e.g., literacy, understanding money and time), social skills (e.g., interpersonal skill), and practical skills (e.g., personal grooming, occupational skills). It is usually evaluated from interviews with a parent or other caregiver. Only individuals who are younger than the age of 18, have problems adapting in these areas, and IQ scores of 70 or less are considered to have an intellectual disability (AAIDD Ad Hoc Committee on Terminology and Classification, 2010).*

Modern explanations pinpoint four factors that place individuals at risk for intellectual disability:

- Biomedical factors, including chromosomal disorders, malnutrition, and traumatic brain injury
- Social factors, such as poverty and impaired parent–child interactions
- Behavioral factors, such as child neglect or domestic violence
- Educational factors, including impaired parenting and inadequate special education services

No individual factor in this list *necessarily* leads to intellectual disability. Instead, the risk for intellectual disability grows as more of these are present (AAIDD Ad Hoc Committee on Terminology and Classification, 2010). For example, the risk is great for a child with Down syndrome whose parents live in poverty and cannot take advantage of special education services.

As you can imagine, the many factors that can lead to intellectual disability mean that the term encompasses an enormous variety of individuals. One way to describe this variation is in terms of the kind and amount of support that they need. At one extreme, some people have so few skills that they must be supervised constantly. Consequently, they usually live in institutions for persons with intellectual disability, where they can sometimes be taught self-help skills such as dressing, feeding, and toileting (Reid, Wilson, & Faw, 1991). At the other extreme are individuals who go to school and master many academic skills, but not as quickly as a typical child does. They often work and many marry. With comprehensive training programs that focus on vocational and social skills, they're often productive citizens and satisfied human beings (Ellis & Rusch, 1991).

Children with Learning Disability   A key element of the definition of intellectual disability is substantially below-average intelligence. In contrast, by definition children with learning disability have normal intelligence. That is, **children with *learning disability*: (a) have difficulty mastering an academic subject, (b) have normal intelligence, and (c) are not suffering from other conditions that could explain poor performance, such as sensory impairment or inadequate instruction.**

In the United States, about 5% of school-age children are classified as learning disabled, which translates into nearly 3 million youngsters. The number of distinct disabilities and the degree of overlap among them are still debated (Torgesen, 2004). However, most scientists agree that three are particularly common (Hulme & Snowling, 2009): difficulties in reading individual words,

---

* What we now call intellectual disability was long known as mental retardation, and much federal and state law in the United States still uses the latter term. However, *intellectual disability* is the preferred term because it better reflects the condition not as a deficit in the person but as a poor "fit between the person's capacities and the context in which the person is to function" (AAIDD Ad Hoc Committee on Terminology and Classification, 2010, p. 13).

Youngsters with reading disability often struggle to distinguish different letter sounds.

 QUESTION 8.3

Ryan's 8-year-old daughter has been diagnosed with developmental dyslexia. Ryan is concerned that this is just a politically correct way of saying that his daughter is stupid. Is he right?

sometimes known as *developmental dyslexia*; difficulties in understanding words that have been read successfully, which is called *impaired reading comprehension*; and, finally, difficulties in mathematics, which is termed *mathematical learning disability* or *developmental dyscalculia*.

Understanding learning disabilities is complicated because each type has its own causes (Landerl et al., 2009) and thus requires its own treatment. For example, developmental dyslexia is the most common type of learning disability. (It's so common that sometimes it's just referred to as *reading disability*.) Many children with this disorder have problems in phonological awareness (described in Module 7.3), which refers to distinguishing sounds in written and oral language. For children with developmental dyslexia—like Sanjit (in the opening vignette) or the boy in the photograph—distinguishing *bis* from *bep* or *bis* from *dis* is difficult; apparently the words all sound alike (Ziegler et al., 2010).

Children with developmental dyslexia typically benefit from two kinds of instruction: training in phonological awareness—experiences that help them to identify subtle but important differences in language sounds—along with explicit instruction on the connections between letters and their sounds. With intensive instruction of this sort, youngsters with developmental dyslexia can read much more effectively (Hulme & Snowling, 2009).

Children with impaired reading comprehension have no trouble reading individual words, but they understand far less of what they read. Asked to read sentences such as *The man rode the bus to go to work* or *The dog chased the cat through the woods*, they do so easily but find it difficult to answer questions about the sentences (e.g., *What did the man ride? Where did the man go?*). In the "Spotlight on Theories" feature, we'll see why these children often struggle with meaning.

Spotlight on Theories

Impaired Reading Comprehension Is Impaired Language Comprehension

BACKGROUND In Module 7.3 we saw that reading involves decoding individual words as well as comprehending sentences or larger passages. In developmental dyslexia, children read individual words inaccurately and slowly; in impaired reading comprehension, they recognize individual words normally but have trouble making sense of what they've read.

THE THEORY Margaret Snowling, Charles Hulme, and their colleagues (2011; 2012; Clarke et al., 2014) use the Simple Model of Reading (page 236) to explain impaired reading comprehension. In this model, decoding processes convert printed words into speech; then language comprehension skills are used to understand decoded words. Specifically, reading comprehension is supported by children's knowledge of word meanings (vocabulary) and their knowledge of grammar. In Snowling and Hulme's theory, both kinds of knowledge are limited in children with impaired reading comprehension. For example, in reading *The girl could not predict the winner*, children with impaired reading comprehension may read *predict* accurately but not understand the sentence because they don't know the meaning of *predict*. Similarly, with *The teacher was hit by the ball* these children may misunderstand the sentence—thinking it's about a teacher hitting a ball—because they lack knowledge of passive voice.

Hypothesis: Snowling and Hulme's theory leads to two predictions. On the one hand, because children with impaired reading comprehension decode words skillfully, they should succeed on tasks measuring the phonological skills essential for decoding words. On the other hand, they should be less successful on tasks that measure their knowledge of word meanings and grammar.

Test: Nation et al. (2010) conducted a longitudinal study in which children's reading, language, and phonological skills were tested several times between 5 and 8 years of age. At age 8, Nation and her colleagues identified 15 children with impaired reading comprehension—children whose word reading skills were age appropriate but whose reading comprehension skills were limited. They matched these children with 15 average readers who had comparable word reading skills along with age-appropriate reading comprehension.

Next, Nation et al. compared the two groups in terms of their phonological and language skills, beginning at age 5 (before children had been taught how to read). On the one hand, the groups were similar in their phonological skills (e.g., both groups were able to say what *dish* would sound like without the *d*). On the other hand, children with impaired reading comprehension knew the meaning of fewer words and understood less grammar (e.g., they were likely to say that a drawing of a teacher hitting a ball matched *The teacher was hit by the ball*).

Conclusion: As predicted by Snowling and Hulme's account, children with impaired reading comprehension have intact phonological skills but limited knowledge of word meanings and grammar. In other words, impaired reading comprehension is really less about problems with reading per se and more about impaired language. When children have limited vocabulary and gaps in their knowledge of grammar, they comprehend less of what they hear and read.

Application: Snowling and Hulme's theory has a straightforward implication: If we improve language skills in children with impaired reading comprehension, their reading comprehension should improve. In fact such training (e.g., increasing children's vocabulary) produces substantial gains in children's reading comprehension, sometimes to the point that children who were once impaired read at an age-appropriate level (Clarke et al., 2010). This research shows an effective way to treat impaired reading comprehension and also shows the practical value of a good theory.

A third common form of learning disability is mathematical disability. Roughly 5% to 10% of young children struggle with arithmetic instruction from the beginning. These youngsters progress slowly in their efforts to learn to count, to add, and to subtract; many are also diagnosed with reading disability. As they move into second and third grade (and beyond), these children often use inefficient methods for computing solutions, such as continuing (as third-graders) to use their fingers to solve problems such as 9 + 7 (Geary, 2010; Jordan, 2007).

We know far less about mathematical learning disability, largely because mathematics engages a broader set of skills than reading (which really involves just two broad classes: decoding and comprehension). Some scientists propose that the heart of the problem is that the approximate number system (described on page 241) provides less precise estimates of quantities for children with mathematical learning disability (Geary, 2013). Another possibility is that youngsters with mathematical disability are impaired in counting and retrieving arithmetic facts from memory (Hulme & Snowling, 2009). Still others suggest that mathematical disability reflects problems in the basic cognitive processes that are used in doing arithmetic, such as working memory and processing speed (Geary et al., 2007).

Because mathematical disability is not well understood, effective interventions have just begun. For example, children at risk for mathematical learning disability benefit from intensive practice designed to increase their knowledge and understanding of numbers (Fuchs et al., 2013). As we learn more about the core problems that define mathematical disability, researchers and educators should be able to fine-tune instruction for these children. When that happens, children with mathematical disability, like children with developmental dyslexia and impaired reading comprehension, will be able to develop their full intellectual potential.

 ## Check Your Learning

RECALL Summarize the different factors that put children at risk for intellectual disability.

How is learning disability defined? What are the different types of learning disability?

INTERPRET Compare and contrast traditional and modern definitions of giftedness.

APPLY How might Jean Piaget, Howard Gardner, and Robert Sternberg define intellectual disability?

 # Unifying Themes   Nature and Nurture

In this chapter, I want to underscore the theme that *development is always jointly influenced by heredity and environment*. In no other area of child development is this theme as important, because the implications for social policy are so profound. If intelligence were completely determined by heredity, for example, intervention programs would be a waste of time and tax dollars because no amount of experience would change nature's prescription for intelligence. But we've seen several times in this chapter that neither heredity nor environment is all-powerful when it comes to intelligence. Studies of twins, for example, remind us that heredity clearly has substantial impact on IQ scores. Identical twins' IQs are consistently more alike than are fraternal twins' IQs, a result that documents heredity's influence on intelligence. Yet, at the same time, intervention studies such as Head Start and the Carolina Abecedarian Project show that intelligence is malleable. Children's intelligence can be enhanced by intensely stimulating environments.

Thus, heredity imposes some limits on how a child's intelligence will develop, but the limits are fairly modest. We can nurture all children's intelligence considerably if we are willing to invest the time and effort.

See for Yourself

We've seen that the definition of intelligence differs across cultural settings. See how parents define intelligence by asking them to rate the importance of four common aspects of intelligence:

- Problem-solving skill (thinking before acting, seeing different sides to a problem)
- Verbal skill (speaking clearly, having a large vocabulary)
- Creative skill (asking many questions, trying new things)

- Social skill (playing and working well with other people, respecting and caring for others)

Ask parents to rate the importance of each element on a 6-point scale, where 1 means extremely unimportant to intelligence and 6 means extremely important. Try to ask parents from different ethnic groups; then compare your results with other students' results to see if parents' views of intelligence are similar or different and if cultural background affects parents' definitions. See for yourself!

Summary

What Is Intelligence?

Psychometric Theories

Psychometric approaches to intelligence include theories that describe intelligence as a general factor as well as theories that include specific factors. Hierarchical theories include general intelligence as well as various specific skills, such as verbal and spatial ability.

Gardner's Theory of Multiple Intelligences

Gardner's theory of multiple intelligences proposes nine distinct intelligences. Three are found in psychometric theories (linguistic, logical-mathematical, and spatial intelligence), but six are new (musical, bodily-kinesthetic, interpersonal, intrapersonal, naturalistic, and existential intelligence). Gardner's theory has stimulated research on nontraditional forms of intelligence, such as emotional intelligence. The theory also has implications for education, suggesting, for example, that schools should adjust teaching to each child's unique intellectual strengths.

Sternberg's Theory of Successful Intelligence

According to Robert Sternberg, intelligence is defined as using skills to achieve short- and long-term goals and depends on three abilities: analytic ability to analyze problems and generate solutions, creative ability to deal adaptively with novel situations, and practical ability to know what solutions will work.

Measuring Intelligence

Binet and the Development of Intelligence Testing

Binet created the first intelligence test to identify students who would have difficulty in school. Using this work, Terman created the Stanford-Binet, which introduced the concept of the intelligence quotient (IQ). Another widely used test, the WISC-IV, yields IQ scores based on verbal

and performance subtests. Infant tests, such as the Bayley Scales, typically assess mental and motor development.

Scores on infant intelligence tests do not predict adult IQ scores, but infant information-processing predicts childhood IQs, and preschool IQ scores predict adult IQs.

Features of IQ Scores

Intelligence tests are reasonably valid measures of achievement in school. They also predict people's performance in the workplace and longevity.

Dynamic assessments measure children's potential for future learning and complement traditional tests, which emphasize knowledge acquired prior to testing.

Hereditary and Environmental Factors

Evidence for the impact of heredity on IQ comes from the findings that (a) siblings' IQ scores are more alike when siblings are more similar genetically, and (b) adopted children's IQ scores are more like their biological parents' test scores than their adoptive parents' scores. Evidence for the impact of the environment comes from the impact of home environments, historical change, and intervention programs on IQ scores.

Impact of Ethnicity and Socioeconomic Status

Ethnic groups differ in their average scores on IQ tests. This difference is not due to genetics or to familiarity with specific test items, but rather to children's familiarity and comfort with the testing situation. Nevertheless, IQ scores remain valid predictors of school success because middle-class experience is often a prerequisite for school success.

Special Children, Special Needs

Gifted Children

Traditionally, gifted children have been those with high scores on IQ tests. Modern definitions of giftedness are broader and include exceptional talent in, for example, the arts. Gifted children are substantially above average in ability, passionate about their subject, and creative. Their talent needs to be nurtured by challenging and supportive environments. Gifted children are usually socially mature and emotionally stable.

Children with Disability

Individuals with intellectual disability have IQ scores of 70 or lower and problems in adaptive behavior. Biomedical, social, behavioral, and educational factors place individuals at risk for intellectual disability.

Children with a learning disability have normal intelligence but have difficulty mastering specific academic subjects. Common variants include developmental dyslexia (difficulty decoding individual words), impaired reading comprehension (problems understanding what one has read), and mathematical learning disability. The most common is reading disability, which often can be traced to inadequate understanding and use of language sounds. When such language-related skills are taught, children's reading improves.

Test Yourself

1. The psychometric approach _____.
   a. measures intelligence using standardized intelligence tests
   b. equates intelligence with the existence of exceptional talent
   c. says that intelligent behavior always involves skillful adaptation to an environment

2. Hierarchical theories of intelligence _____.
   a. identify domains of intelligence using research in child development, studies of brain injury, and findings with talented people
   b. include both general and specific factors of intelligence
   c. emphasize the role of intelligence in achieving short- and long-term goals

3. The theory of multiple intelligences _____.
   a. suggests that one general factor of intelligence exists
   b. suggests that different intelligences are regulated by different regions of the brain
   c. is based on an extensive body of empirical work

4. Gardner's theory of multiple intelligences includes several intelligences included in psychometric theories of intelligence. Which of the following is *not* one of them?
   a. logical-mathematical
   b. musical
   c. linguistic

5. Sternberg's theory of successful intelligence includes _____, creative, and practical abilities.
   a. hierarchical
   b. general
   c. analytic

6. Compared with group intelligence tests, individual intelligence tests _____.
   a. are less expensive to administer
   b. are less likely to require a trained examiner

   c. optimize the motivation and attention of the person being tested

7. Scores from infant intelligence tests predict intelligence in childhood and adulthood _____.
   a. accurately, because sensorimotor activities are the beginning of intelligence
   b. accurately, because individual differences can be determined easily in infants
   c. inaccurately, because infant intelligence tests measure different abilities than are measured in tests used with older children

8. Dynamic assessments of intelligence _____.
   a. have been used for many years and have produced well-established results
   b. measure a child's learning potential
   c. measure what a child already knows

9. Which of these statements about heredity and intelligence is *correct*?
   a. IQ scores are usually more alike for identical twins than for fraternal twins.
   b. Adopted children's IQ scores resemble their adoptive parents' IQ scores more than their biological parents' IQ scores.
   c. Because heredity has such a strong influence on intelligence, the environment has little impact.

10. When intelligence is assessed with culture-fair intelligence tests, ethnic group differences _____.
    a. are reduced, but not eliminated
    b. remain the same
    c. are eliminated

11. Which of the following is *not* an explanation for ethnic group differences in performance on intelligence tests?
    a. heredity
    b. stereotype threat
    c. test-taking styles

12. Compared with traditional definitions of giftedness, modern definitions _____.
    a. are based solely on IQ scores
    b. rely largely on Piaget's theory of cognitive development
    c. include exceptional talent in areas such as art, music, creative writing, dance, and sports

13. Intellectual disability is defined by limited intellectual ability and _____, both emerging before 18 years of age
    a. divergent thinking
    b. emotional health
    c. problems adapting to the environment

14. Children diagnosed with a learning disability _____.
    a. typically have sensory impairments
    b. have normal intelligence but difficulty in an academic subject
    c. have below average intelligence

15. Which of the following statements concerning learning disabilities is *incorrect*?
    a. Children with developmental dyslexia have problems with phonological awareness.
    b. Children with impaired reading comprehension have problems decoding words and making sense of what they've read.
    c. Scientists know less about mathematical learning disability because math engages a broader set of skills than reading.

Key Terms

analytic ability 255
creative ability 255
crystallized intelligence 253
culture-fair intelligence tests 266
divergent thinking 269
dynamic assessment 262

emotional intelligence 254
fluid intelligence 252
gifted 269
intellectual disability 270
intelligence quotient (IQ) 258
learning disability 271

mental age (MA) 258
practical ability 255
psychometricians 252
stereotype threat 266

Chapter 9
Language and Communication

Modules

9.1 The Road to Speech

9.2 Learning the Meanings of Words

9.3 Speaking in Sentences

9.4 Using Language to Communicate

Toni Morrison, a contemporary African American writer who won the Nobel Prize in literature in 1993 and the Presidential Medal of Freedom in 2012, said, "We die. That may be the meaning of life. But we do language. That may be the measure of our lives." Language is indeed a remarkable human tool. Language allows us to express thoughts and feelings to others and to preserve our ideas and learn from the past.

Given the complexities of language, it's truly amazing that most children master it rapidly and easily. That mastery is the focus of this chapter, which examines four facets of language. We begin in **Module 9.1** by looking at the first steps in acquiring language: learning about speech sounds. **Module 9.2** concerns how children learn to speak and how they learn new words thereafter. In **Module 9.3**, we'll examine children's early sentences and the rules that children follow in creating them. Finally, in **Module 9.4**, we'll learn how children use language to communicate with others.

 # 9.1 The Road to Speech

LEARNING OBJECTIVES		OUTLINE
LO1	What are the different components of language?	Elements of Language
LO2	What are the basic sounds of speech and how well can infants distinguish them?	Perceiving Speech
LO3	What is babbling and how does it become more complex in older infants?	First Steps to Speech

As a 7-month-old, Chelsea began to make her first word-like sounds, saying "dah" and "nuh." Several weeks later, she began to repeat these syllables, saying "dah-dah" and "nuh-nuh." By 11 months her speech resembled sentences with stressed words: "dah-NUH-bah-BAH!" Chelsea's parents were astonished that her sentences could sound so much like real speech yet still be absolutely meaningless!

From birth, infants make sounds—they laugh, cry, and like Chelsea, produce sounds that resemble speech. Yet, for most of their first year, infants do not talk. This contrast raises two important questions about infants as nonspeaking creatures. First, can babies who are unable to speak understand any of the speech that is directed to them? Second, how do infants like Chelsea progress from crying to more effective methods of oral communication, such as speech? We'll answer both questions in this module, but let's begin by considering exactly what we mean by *language*.

Elements of Language

LO1   What are the different components of language?

When you think of language, what comes to mind? English, perhaps? Or maybe German, Spanish, Korean, or Zulu? What about American Sign Language? **Defined broadly,** *language* **is a system that relates sounds (or gestures) to meaning.** Languages are expressed in many forms—through speech, writing, and gestures. Furthermore, languages consist of different subsystems. Spoken languages usually involve four distinct but related elements:

- *Phonology* **refers to the sounds of a language.** About 200 different sounds are used in all known spoken languages; all the different words in English are constructed from about 45 of them.
- *Semantics* **denotes the study of words and their meaning.** *Webster's Third New International Dictionary* includes roughly half a million words; a typical college-educated English speaker has a vocabulary of about 150,000 words.
- *Syntax* **refers to rules that specify how words are combined to form sentences.** For example, one simple rule specifies that a noun followed by a verb (e.g., *dog barks, ball rolls*) is a sentence.
- *Pragmatics* **refers to the communicative functions of language and the rules that lead to effective communication.** For example, rules for effective communication specify that speakers should be clear and their comments relevant to the topic of conversation.

Learning language involves mastering each of these elements. Children must learn to hear the differences in speech sounds and how to produce them; they must learn the meaning of words and rules for combining words in sentences; and they must learn appropriate and effective ways to talk with others. In the remainder of this module (and the other three in this chapter), we'll see how children come to understand language and speak it themselves.

Perceiving Speech

LO2 **What are the basic sounds of speech and how well can infants distinguish them?**

We learned in Module 5.1 that even newborn infants hear remarkably well. Newborns also prefer to listen to speech over comparably complex nonspeech sounds (Vouloumanos et al., 2010). But can babies distinguish speech sounds? To answer this question, we first need to know more about the elements of speech. **The basic building blocks of language are** *phonemes*, **unique sounds that can be joined to create words.** Phonemes include consonant sounds, such as the sound of *t* in *toe* and *tap*, along with vowel sounds, such as the sound of *e* in *get* and *bed*. Infants can distinguish most of these sounds, many of them by as early as 1 month after birth (Aslin, Jusczyk, & Pisoni, 1998).

How do we know that infants can distinguish different vowels and consonants? Researchers have devised a number of clever techniques to determine if babies respond differently to distinct sounds. One approach is illustrated in Figure 9-1. A rubber nipple is connected to a computer so that sucking causes the computer to play a sound out of a loudspeaker. In just a few minutes, 1-month-olds learn the relation between their sucking and the sound: They suck rapidly to hear nothing more than repeated presentation of the sound of *p* as in *pin, pet*, and *pat* (pronounced "puh").

After a few more minutes, infants seemingly tire of this repetitive sound and suck less often, which represents the habituation phenomenon described in Module 5.1. But, if the computer presents a new sound, such as the sound of *b* in *bed, bat*, or *bird* (pronounced "buh"), babies begin sucking rapidly again. Evidently, they recognize that the sound of *b* is different from *p* because they suck more often to hear the new sound (Jusczyk, 1995).

Of course, the same sound is not pronounced exactly the same way by all people. For example, two native speakers of English may say *baby* differently and a nonnative speaker's pronunciation could differ even more. Only older infants consistently recognize the same words across variations in pronunciation (Schmale & Seidl, 2009).

Figure 9-1

The Impact of Language Exposure　Not all languages use the same set of pho-nemes; a distinction important in one language may be ignored in another. For example, unlike English, French and Polish differentiate between nasal and non-nasal vowels. To hear the difference, say the word *rod*. Now repeat it, but holding your nose. The subtle difference between the two sounds illustrates a nonnasal vowel (the first version of *rod*) and a nasal one (the second).

Because an infant might be exposed to any of the world's languages, it would be adaptive for young infants to be able to perceive a wide range of phonemes. In fact, research shows that infants can distinguish phonemes that are not used in their native language. For example, Japanese does not distinguish the consonant sound of *r* in *rip* from the sound of *l* in *lip*, and Japanese adults trying to learn English have great difficulty distinguishing these sounds. At about 6 to 8 months, Japanese and U.S. infants can distinguish these sounds equally well. However, by 10 to 12 months, perception of *r* and *l* improves for U.S. infants—presumably because they hear these sounds frequently—but declines for Japanese babies (Kuhl et al., 2006).

Newborns apparently are biologically capable of hearing the entire range of phonemes in all languages worldwide. But as babies grow and are more exposed to a particular language, they only notice the linguistic distinctions that are mean-ingful in their own language (Werker, Yeung, & Yoshida, 2012). This is even true for sign language: Young hearing infants notice differences in signs that older hearing infants do not (Palmer et al., 2012). Thus, specializing in one language apparently comes at the cost of making it more difficult to hear sounds in other languages. And this pattern of greater specialization in speech perception is remi-niscent of the profile for face perception described in Module 5.1. With greater exposure to human faces, babies develop a more refined notion of a human face, just as they develop a more refined notion of the sounds (and signs) that are important in their native language (Pascalis et al., 2014).

Identifying Words　Of course, hearing individual phonemes is only the first step in perceiving speech. One of the biggest challenges for infants is identify-ing recurring patterns of sounds—words, that is. Imagine, for example, an infant overhearing this conversation between a parent and an older sibling:

SIBLING:　Jerry got a new *bike*.

PARENT:　Was his old *bike* broken?

SIBLING:　No. He'd saved his allowance to buy a new mountain *bike*.

An infant listening to this conversation hears *bike* three times. Can the infant learn from this experience? Yes. When 7- to 8-month-olds hear a word repeatedly in different sentences, later they pay more attention to this word than to words they haven't heard previously. Evidently, 7- and 8-month-olds can listen to sen-tences and recognize the sound patterns that they hear repeatedly (Houston & Jusczyk, 2003; Saffran, Aslin, & Newport, 1996). Also, by 6 months of age, infants pay more attention to content words (e.g., nouns, verbs) than to function words (e.g., articles, prepositions), and they look at the correct parent when they hear "mommy" or "daddy" (Shi & Werker, 2001; Tincoff & Jusczyk, 1999).

In normal conversation, there are no silent gaps between words, so how do infants pick out words? Stress is one important clue. English contains many one-syllable words that are stressed and many two-syllable words that have a stressed syllable followed by an unstressed syllable (e.g., dough´ -nut, tooth´ -paste, bas´ -ket). Infants pay more attention to stressed syllables than unstressed syllables, which is a good strategy for identifying the beginnings of words (Bortfeld & Morgan, 2010; Thiessen & Saffran, 2003). And infants learn words more readily when the words appear at the beginning and ends of sentences, probably because the brief pause between sentences makes it easier to identify first and last words (Seidl & Johnson, 2006).

Another useful method is statistical. Infants notice syllables that go together frequently (Jusczyk, 2002). For example, in many studies, 8-month-olds heard the following sounds, which consisted of 4 three-syllable artificial words, said over and over in a random order.

<u>pa bi ku</u> <u>go la tu</u> <u>da ro pi</u> <u>ti bu do</u> <u>da ro pi</u> <u>go la tu</u> <u>pa bi ku</u> <u>da ro pi</u>

I've underlined the words and inserted gaps between them so that you can see them more easily, but in the actual studies there were no breaks at all, just a steady flow of syllables for 3 minutes. Later, infants listened to these words less than to new words that were novel combinations of the same syllables. They had detected *pa bi ku, go la tu, da ro pi,* and *ti bu do* as familiar patterns and listened to them less than to words like *tu da ro,* a new word made up from syllables they'd already heard (Aslin & Newport, 2012; Ngon et al., 2013).

Yet another way in which infants identify words is through their emerging knowledge of how sounds are used in their native language. For example, think about these two pairs of sounds: *s* followed by *t* and *s* followed by *d*. Both pairs are quite common at the end of one word and the beginning of the next: bu*s t*akes, ki*s*s *t*ook; thi*s d*og, pas*s d*irectly. However, *s* and *t* occur frequently within a word (*s*top, li*s*t, pe*s*t, *s*tink) but *s* and *d* do not. Consequently, when *d* follows an *s*, it probably starts a new word. In fact, 9-month-olds follow rules like this one because when they hear novel words embedded in continuous speech, they're more likely to identify the novel word when the final sound in the preceding word occurs infrequently with the first sound of the novel word (Mattys & Jusczyk, 2001).

Another strategy that infants use is to rely on familiar function words, such as the articles *a* and *the*, to break up the speech stream. These words are common in adults' speech; by six months most infants recognize them and use them to determine the onset of a new word (Shi, 2014). For example, for infants familiar with *a*, the sequence like *aballabataglove* becomes *a ball a bat a glove*. The new words are isolated by the familiar ones.

Thus, infants use many powerful tools to identify words in speech. Of course, they don't yet understand the meanings of these words; at this point, they simply recognize a word as a distinct configuration of sounds. Nevertheless, these early perceptual skills are important because infants who are more skilled at detecting speech sounds know more words as toddlers (Singh, Reznick, & Xuehua, 2012), and overall their language is more advanced at 4 to 6 years of age (Newman et al., 2006).

Parents (and other adults) often help infants to master language sounds by talking in a distinctive style. **In *infant-directed speech*, adults speak slowly and with exaggerated changes in pitch and loudness.** If you could hear the mother in the photo talking to her baby, you would notice that she alternates between speaking softly and loudly and between high and low pitches and that her speech seems expressive emotionally (Liu, Tsao, & Kuhl, 2007; Trainor, Austin, & Desjardins, 2000). (Infant-directed speech is also known as *motherese*, because this form of speaking was first noted in mothers, although it's now known that most caregivers talk this way to infants.)

When parents talk to babies, they often use *infant-directed speech*, which is slower and more varied in pitch and volume than adult-directed speech.

Infant-directed speech attracts infants' attention, perhaps because its slower pace and accentuated changes provide infants with salient language clues (Cristia, 2010). For example, infants can segment words more effectively when they hear them in infant-direct speech (Thiessen, Hill, & Saffran, 2005). In addition, infant-directed speech includes especially good examples of vowels (Kuhl et al., 1997), which may help infants learn to distinguish these sounds. And when talking to infants, speaking clearly is a good idea. In one study (Liu, Kuhl, & Tsao, 2003), infants who could best distinguish speech sounds had the mothers who spoke the most clearly.

Infant-directed speech, then, helps infants perceive the sounds that are fundamental to their language. Unfortunately, some babies cannot hear speech sounds because they are deaf. How can these infants best learn language? The "Child Development and Family Policy" feature addresses this question.

 QUESTION 9.1

Kristin spends hours talking to her infant son. Her husband enjoys spending time with his wife and son, but wishes that Kristin would stop using "baby talk" with their son and just talk in her regular voice. The sing-song pattern drives him crazy and he can't believe that it's any good for their son. Is he right?

Child Development and Family Policy

Are Cochlear Implants Effective for Young Children?

About 1 child out of 1,000 is born deaf or has profound hearing loss before mastering language. Of these youngsters, about 10% are born to deaf parents. In these cases, the child's deafness is usually detected early and parents communicate with their children using sign language. Deaf infants and toddlers seem to master sign language in much the same way and at about the same pace that hearing children master spoken language. For example, deaf 10-month-olds often babble in signs: They produce sequences of signs that are meaningless but resemble the tempo and duration of real signs.

The remaining 90% of deaf infants and toddlers have parents with normal hearing. For these children, communicating with signs is not an option because their parents don't know sign language. Consequently, the usual recommendation for deaf children of hearing parents is to master spoken language, sometimes through methods that emphasize lip reading and speech therapy and sometimes with these methods along with signs and gestures. Unfortunately, with any of these methods, deaf children and parents rarely master spoken language. Their ability to produce and comprehend spoken language falls years behind their peers with normal language (Hoff, 2014).

However, since the mid-1990s, deaf children have had a new option. As I described on page 152, the *cochlear implant* is a device that picks up speech sounds and converts them to electrical impulses that stimulate nerve cells in the ear. Cochlear implants are a tremendous benefit for people who lose their hearing after they master language. Adults with cochlear implants can converse readily with hearing speakers and some can converse on the phone (which is difficult otherwise because they can't lip read and because telephone lines sometimes distort speech sounds).

Cochlear implants also promote language acquisition in deaf children. When children deaf from birth receive cochlear implants, their spoken language skills end up substantially better than those of children who do not have cochlear implants. In fact, after receiving cochlear implants, some deaf children acquire language at roughly the same rate as children with normal hearing (Svirsky et al., 2000; Wie et al., 2007).

But other children benefit less from cochlear implants, an outcome that has led researchers to identify the keys to success for this procedure. Age of implantation matters as does the extent to the child's hearing loss. Cochlear implants are more successful with children who are younger and who have some residual hearing. The quality of the child's language environment also contributes: Children with cochlear implants learn language more rapidly when their parents provide a stimulating language environment, particularly when they frequently talk about what the child is looking at or doing (Cruz et al., 2013).

Thus, a cochlear implant is an effective tool that can enhance language in children who are deaf, particularly when children receive implants when they are young. However, it is not a cure: following implantation, parents need to provide a particularly rich language experience for their children to master language.

First Steps to Speech

LO3 What is babbling and how does it become more complex in older infants?

As any new parent can testify, newborns and young babies make many sounds: they cry, burp, and sneeze. However, language-based sounds don't appear immediately. **At 2 months, infants begin to produce vowel-like sounds, such as "oooooo" or "ahhhhhh," a phenomenon known as** *cooing*. Sometimes infants become quite excited as they coo, perhaps reflecting the joy of playing with sounds.

After cooing comes *babbling*, **speech-like sound that has no meaning.** A typical 6-month-old might say "dah" or "bah," utterances that sound like a single syllable consisting of a consonant and a vowel. Over the next few months, babbling becomes more elaborate as babies apparently experiment with more complex speech sounds. Older infants sometimes repeat a sound, as in "bahbah-bah," and begin to combine different sounds, "dahmahbah" (Hoff, 2014).

Babbling is not just mindless playing with sounds; instead, it's a precursor to real speech. We know this, in part, from video records of people's mouths while speaking. When adults speak, the mouth opens somewhat wider on the right side than on the left side, reflecting the left hemisphere's control of language and muscle movements on the body's right side (Graves & Landis, 1990). Infants do the same when they babble, but not when making other nonbabbling sounds, which suggests that babbling is fundamentally linguistic (Holowka & Petitto, 2002).

Other evidence for the linguistic nature of babbling comes from studies of developmental change in babbling: At roughly 8 to 11 months, babbling sounds more like real speech because infants (like Chelsea in the vignette) stress some syllables and vary the pitch of their speech (Snow, 2006). For example, in English declarative sentences, pitch rises and then falls toward the end of the sentence. However, in questions the pitch is level but then rises toward the end of the question. **This pattern of rising or falling pitch is known as** *intonation*. Older babies' babbling reflects these patterns: Babies who are brought up by English-speaking parents have both the declarative and question patterns of intonation in their babbling. Babies exposed to a language with different patterns of intonation, such as Japanese or French, reflect their language's intonation in their babbling (Levitt & Utman, 1992).

The appearance of intonation in babbling indicates a strong link between perception and production of speech: Infants' babbling is influenced by the characteristics of the speech that they hear (Goldstein & Schwade, 2008). Beginning in the middle of the first year, infants try to reproduce the sounds of language that others use in trying to communicate with them (or, in the case of deaf infants with deaf parents, the signs that others use). Hearing *dog*, an infant may first say "dod," then "gog" before finally saying "dog" correctly. In the same way that beginning typists gradually link movements of their fingers with particular keys, through babbling infants learn to use the lips, tongue, and teeth to produce specific sounds, gradually making sounds that approximate real words (Poulson et al., 1991).

The ability to produce sound, coupled with the 1-year-old's advanced ability to perceive speech sounds, sets the stage for the infant's first true words. In Module 9.2, we'll see how this happens.

 ## Check Your Learning

RECALL How do infants distinguish words in the speech they hear?

What evidence indicates that babbling is a precursor to speech?

INTERPRET Compare the developmental milestones during infancy for perceiving speech and those for producing speech.

APPLY Suppose that a 3-month-old baby born in Romania was adopted by a Swedish couple. How would the change in language environment affect the baby's language learning?

 ## Learning the Meanings of Words

LEARNING OBJECTIVES

LO4 How do children make the transition from babbling to talking?

LO5 What rules do children follow to learn new words?

LO6 What different styles of language learning do young children use?

LO7 What conditions foster children's learning of new words?

LO8 How does children's understanding of symbols progress beyond language?

OUTLINE

Understanding Words as Symbols

Fast Mapping Meanings to Words

Individual Differences in Word Learning

Encouraging Word Learning

Beyond Words: Other Symbols

Sebastien is 20 months old and loves to talk. His parents are amazed by how quickly he learns new words. For example, the day his parents brought home a computer, Sebastien watched as they set it up. The next day, he spontaneously pointed to the computer and said, "'puter." This happens all the time—Sebastien hears a word once or twice, then uses it correctly himself. Sebastien's parents wonder how he does this, particularly because learning vocabulary in a foreign language is so difficult for them!

At about their first birthday, most youngsters say their first words. In many languages, those words are similar (Nelson, 1973; Tardif et al., 2008) and include terms for mother and father, and greetings (*Hi, bye-bye*), as well as foods and toys (*juice, ball*). By age 2, most youngsters have a vocabulary of a few hundred words, and by age 6, a typical child's vocabulary includes more than 10,000 words (Bloom, 2000). Worldwide, nouns are common in children's early vocabularies, perhaps because they refer to objects that infants can perceive easily; verbs are less common than nouns but this difference is smaller (and sometimes disappears) in languages such as Korean or Chinese perhaps because verbs are more prominent in these languages or because East Asian cultures emphasize actions more than objects (Waxman et al., 2013).

Like Sebastien, most children learn new words with extraordinary ease and speed. How do they do it? We'll answer that question in this module.

Understanding Words as Symbols

LO4 How do children make the transition from babbling to talking?

When my daughter, Laura, was 9 months old, she sometimes babbled "bay-bay." A few months later, she still said "bay-bay," but with an important difference. As a 9-month-old, "bay-bay" was simply an interesting set of sounds that had no special meaning to her. As a 13-month-old, "bay-bay" was her way of saying "baby." What had happened between 9 and 13 months? Laura had begun to understand that speech is more than just entertaining sound. She realized that sounds form

Babies begin to gesture at about the same time that they say their first words; both accomplishments show that infants are mastering symbols.

words that refer to objects, actions, and properties. Put another way, Laura recognized that words are symbols, entities that stand for other entities. She already had formed concepts such as "round, bouncy things" and "furry things that bark" and "little humans that adults carry" based on her own experiences. With the insight that speech sounds can denote these concepts, she began to match sound patterns (words) and concepts (Reich, 1986).

If this argument is correct, we should find that children use symbols in other areas, not just in language. They do. Gestures are symbols, and like the baby in the photo, infants begin to gesture shortly before their first birthday (Goodwyn & Acredolo, 1993). Young children may open and close their hands to request an object or wave "bye-bye" when leaving. Infants' vocabularies of gestures and spoken words expand at about the same rate, consistent with the idea that words and gestures reflect the infant's emerging understanding of symbols (Caselli et al., 2012). In these cases, gestures and words convey a message equally well.

What's more, gestures sometimes pave the way for language. Before knowing an object's name, infants often point to it or pick it up for a listener, as if saying, "I want this!" or "What's this?" In one study, 50% of all objects were first referred to by gesture and, about 3 months later, by word (Iverson & Goldin-Meadow, 2005). Given this connection between early gestures and first spoken words, it's not surprising that toddlers who are more advanced in their use of gesture tend to have, as preschoolers, more complex spoken language (Rowe, Raudenbush, & Goldin-Meadow, 2012).

Fast Mapping Meanings to Words

LO5 What rules do children follow to learn new words?

Once children have the insight that a word can symbolize an object or action, their vocabularies grow slowly at first. A typical 15-month-old, for example, may learn two to three new words each week. **However, at about 18 months, many children experience a *naming explosion* during which they learn new words—particularly names of objects—much more rapidly than before.** Children now learn 10 or more new words each week (Fenson et al., 1994; McMurray, 2007).

This rapid rate of word learning is astonishing when we realize that most words have many plausible but incorrect referents. To illustrate, imagine what's going through the mind of the child in the photo. The mother is holding the flower and saying, "Flower. This is a flower. See the flower." To the mother (and you), this all seems crystal clear and straightforward. But what might a child learn from this episode? Perhaps the correct referent for "flower." But a youngster could, just as reasonably, conclude that "flower" refers to the petals, to the color of the flower, or to the mother's action in holding the flower."

When a parent points to an object and says a word, babies conceivably could link the name to the object, to a property of the object (e.g., color), or to the act of pointing. In fact, babies consistently interpret the word as the object's name, an assumption that allows them to learn words rapidly.

Surprisingly, most youngsters learn the proper meanings of simple words in just a few presentations. **Children's ability to connect new words to their meanings so rapidly that they cannot be considering all possible meanings for the new word is termed *fast mapping*.** How can young children learn new words so rapidly? Researchers believe that many distinct factors contribute to young children's rapid word learning (Hollich, Hirsh-Pasek, & Golinkoff, 2000).

Joint Attention Parents encourage word learning by carefully watching what interests their children. When toddlers touch or look at an object, parents often label it for them. Seeing their toddler pointing to a banana, a parent says, "Banana, that's a banana." Such labeling in the context of joint attention promotes word learning, particularly when infants and toddlers participate actively, directing their parents' attention (Beuker et al., 2013).

Of course, to take advantage of this help, infants must be able to tell when parents are labeling instead of just conversing. In fact, when adults label an unfamiliar object, young children are much more likely to assume that the label is the object's name when adults indicate that they are referring to the object, either by looking or pointing at it while labeling (Liebal et al., 2009; Nurmsoo & Bloom, 2008). Young children also consider an adult's credibility as a source: Youngsters are less likely to learn words from adults who seem uncertain, have given incorrect names for words in the past, or speak with a foreign accent (Birch, Akmal, & Frampton, 2010; Corriveau, Kinzler, & Harris, 2013). Thus, beginning in the toddler years, parents and children work together to create conditions that foster word learning: Parents label objects and youngsters rely on adults' behavior to interpret the words they hear. Finally, although joint attention helps children to learn words, it is not required: Children learn new words when those words are used in ongoing conversation and when they overhear others use novel words (Shneidman & Goldin-Meadow, 2012).

Constraints on Word Names Joint attention simplifies word learning for children, but the problem still remains: How does a toddler know that *banana* refers to the object that she's touching, as opposed to her activity (touching) or to the object's color? Young children follow several simple rules that constrain their inferences about a word's meaning. These rules have been revealed with methods illustrated in a study by Au and Glusman (1990). Preschoolers were shown a monkey-like stuffed animal with pink horns and the researcher called it a *mido. Mido* was then repeated several times, always referring to the stuffed animal with pink horns. Later, these youngsters were asked to find a *theri* in a set of stuffed animals that included several *mido.* Never having heard of a *theri,* what did the children do? They never picked a *mido;* instead, they selected other stuffed animals. Knowing that *mido* referred to monkey-like animals with pink horns, they decided that *theri* had to refer to another stuffed animal.

Apparently children were following this simple but effective rule for learning new words:

- If an unfamiliar word is heard in the presence of objects that already have names and objects that don't, the word refers to one of the objects that doesn't have a name.

    Researchers have discovered several other simple rules that help children match words with the correct referent (Hoff, 2009; Woodward & Markman, 1998):

- A name refers to a whole object, not its parts or its relation to other objects, and refers not just to this particular object but to all objects of the same type (Hollich, Golinkoff, & Hirsh-Pasek, 2007). For example, when a grandparent points to a stuffed animal on a shelf and says "dinosaur," children conclude that *dinosaur* refers to the entire dinosaur, not just its ears or nose, not to the fact that the dinosaur is on a shelf, and not to this specific dinosaur but to all dinosaur-like objects.

- If an object already has a name and another name is presented, the new name denotes a subcategory of the original name. If a child who knows the meaning of *dinosaur* sees a brother point to another dinosaur and say "T-rex," the child will conclude that *T-rex* is a special type of dinosaur.
- Given many similar category members, a word applied consistently to only one of them is a proper noun. If a child who knows *dinosaur* sees that one dinosaur is always called "Dino," the child will conclude that *Dino* is the name of that particular dinosaur.

Rules like these make it possible for children such as Sebastien, the child in the vignette, to learn words rapidly because they reduce the number of possible referents. The child in the photo on page 286 follows these rules to decide that *flower* refers to the entire object, not its parts or the action of holding it.

Sentence Cues Children hear many unfamiliar words embedded in sentences containing words they already know. The other words and the overall sentence structure can be helpful clues to a word's meaning (Yuan & Fisher, 2009). For example, when a parent describes an event using familiar words but an unfamiliar verb, children often infer that the verb refers to the action performed by the subject of the sentence (Arunachalam et al., 2013). When the youngsters in the photo hear, "The man is juggling the bats," they will infer that *juggling* refers to the man's actions because they already know the actor (*man*) and the object of the action (*bats*). Similarly, toddlers know that *a* and *the* often precede nouns and that *he, she,* and *they* precede verbs. Thus, they will conclude that "a boz" refers to an object but "she boz" refers to an action (Cauvet et al., 2014).

Cognitive Factors The naming explosion coincides with a time of rapid cognitive growth, and children's increased cognitive skills help them to learn new words. As children's thinking becomes more sophisticated and, in particular, as they start to have goals and intentions, language becomes a means to express those goals and to achieve them (Bloom & Tinker, 2001). In addition, young children's improving attentional and perceptual skills also promote word learning. In the "Spotlight on Theories" feature, we'll see how children's attention to shape (e.g., balls are round, pencils are slender rods) helps them learn new words.

Preschool children use the words they know to infer the meaning of unfamiliar words. Children in the photo already know "man" and "bats"; consequently, when they hear "The man is juggling the bats" they decide that *juggling* refers to the man's actions with the bats.

Spotlight on Theories
A Shape-Bias Theory of Word Learning

BACKGROUND Many developmental scientists believe that young children could master a complex task like word learning only by using built-in, language-specific mechanisms (e.g., fast-mapping rules such as "unfamiliar words refer to objects that don't have names"). However, not all scientists agree that specialized processes are required. Instead, they argue that word learning can be accomplished by applying basic processes of attention and learning.

THE THEORY Linda B. Smith (2000, 2009) argues that shape plays a central role in learning words. Infants and young children spontaneously pay attention to an object's shape and they use this bias to learn new words. In

Smith's theory, children first associate names with a single object: "ball" is associated with a specific tennis ball and "cup" is associated with a favorite sippy cup. However, as children encounter new balls and new cups, they hear the same words applied to similarly shaped objects and reach the conclusion that balls are round and cups are cylinders with handles. With further experience, children derive an even more general rule: Objects that have the same shape have the same name. From this, children realize that paying attention to shape is an easy way to learn names.

Hypothesis: If bias to attend to shape helps children learn names of words, then the age at which children first show the shape bias should coincide with a jump in the number of names that children learn. In other words, as soon as children realize that similarly shaped objects have the same name, they should start learning names much more rapidly.

Test: Gershkoff-Stowe and Smith (2004) conducted a longitudinal study in which parents kept detailed records of their toddlers' word learning for several months. In addition, toddlers were tested every three weeks. They were shown a multicolored U-shaped wooden object and told it was a "dax." Then they were shown several objects, some of which were also U-shaped but differed in color and material (e.g., a blue U-shaped sponge). Other objects were the same color (i.e., multicolored) or the same material (i.e., wood) but not U-shaped. Children were asked to give all the dax to the experimenter.

The crucial findings concern the age at which shape bias emerges and the age at which the naming explosion begins. Gershkoff-Stowe and Smith defined the onset of shape bias as the first session in which toddlers gave both U-shaped objects—but no others—to the experimenter. The onset of the naming explosion was defined as the first week in which toddlers learned 10 or more new words. These two ages were highly correlated— $r = .85$ —indicating a tight link between onset of shape bias and the naming explosion.

Conclusion: As predicted, once toddlers showed a shape bias—that is, they realized that a name applies to objects that have the same shape but not to objects of the same color or made of the same material—they used this knowledge to learn new words faster. This result supports Smith's theory and the general idea that word learning may not require specialized mechanisms.

Application: If shape bias helps children learn words, can we teach this bias and foster word learning? Yes. Smith and colleagues (2002) had toddlers and an experimenter play with four pairs of novel objects; each pair of objects had the same name and the same shape but differed in color and material. A dax was still a U-shaped object; a "zup" referred to an elliptical-shaped object with a slot in one end. During play, the experimenter named each object 10 times. When children played with objects in this way, they learned the names of real words rapidly. From playing with dax and zup, toddlers apparently learned that paying attention to shape is a good way to learn object names. Likewise, by systematically showing toddlers that the same name applies to many similarly shaped objects (e.g., book, crayon, comb, spoon), parents can teach youngsters the value of paying attention to shape to learn word names.

Developmental Change in Word Learning   Some of the word-learning tools described in the past few pages are particularly important at different ages (Hirsh-Pasek & Golinkoff, 2008). Before 18 months, infants learn words relatively slowly—often just one new word each day. At this age, children rely heavily on simple attentional processes (e.g., the shape bias) to learn new words. But by 24 months, most children are learning many new words daily. This faster learning reflects children's greater use of language cues (e.g., constraints on names) and a speaker's social cues. At any age, infants and toddlers rely on a mixture of word-learning tools, but with age they gradually move away from attentional cues and toward language and social cues.

Naming Errors   These many ways of learning new words are not perfect; initial mappings of words onto meanings are often only partially correct (Hoff & Naigles, 2002). **A common mistake is** *underextension*, **defining a word too narrowly.** Using *car* to refer only to the family car and *ball* to a favorite toy ball represent underextension. **Between 1 and 3 years, children sometimes make the opposite error,** *overextension*, **defining a word too broadly.** Children may use *car* to also refer to buses and trucks or use *doggie* to refer to all four-legged animals.

The overextension error occurs more frequently when children are producing words than when they are comprehending words. Two-year-old Jason may say "doggie" to refer to a goat but nevertheless correctly point to a picture of a goat when asked. Because overextension is more common in word production, it may reflect another fast-mapping rule that children follow: "If you can't remember the name for an object, say the name of a related object" (Naigles & Gelman, 1995).

Both underextension and overextension disappear gradually as youngsters refine meanings for words with more exposure to language.

Individual Differences in Word Learning

LO6   What different styles of language learning do children use?

The naming explosion typically occurs at about 18 months, but like many developmental milestones, the timing of this event varies widely for individual children. Some youngsters have a naming explosion as early as 14 months but for others it may be as late as 22 months (Goldfield & Reznick, 1990). Another way to make this point is to look at variation in the size of children's vocabulary at a specific age. At 18 months, for example, an average child's vocabulary would have about 75 words, but a child in the 90th percentile would know nearly 250 words and a child in the 10th percentile fewer than 25 words (Fenson et al., 1994).

The range in vocabulary size for normal 18-month-olds is huge—from 25 to 250 words! What can account for this difference? Heredity contributes: Twin studies find that vocabulary size is more similar in identical twins than in fraternal twins (Dionne et al., 2003). But the difference is fairly small, indicating a relatively minor role for genetics.

More important are two other factors. **One is** *phonological memory*, **the ability to remember speech sounds briefly.** This is often measured by saying a nonsense word to children—*ballop* or *glistering*—and asking them to repeat it immediately. Children's skill in recalling such words is strongly related to the size of their vocabulary (Gathercole et al., 1992; Leclercq & Majerus, 2010). Children who have difficulty remembering speech sounds accurately find word learning particularly challenging, which is not surprising because word learning involves associating meaning with an unfamiliar sequence of speech sounds.

However, the single most important factor in growth of vocabulary is the child's language environment. Children have larger vocabularies when they are exposed to a lot of high-quality language. The more words children hear, the better (Hurtado, Marchman, & Fernald, 2008). Specifically, children learn more words when their parents' speech is rich in different words and is grammatically sophisticated (Huttenlocher et al., 2010; Rowe, 2012), and when parents respond promptly and appropriately to their children's talk (Tamis-Lemonda & Bornstein, 2002).

Why does an environment filled with speech help children learn new words? One obvious mechanism is that such an environment provides children with many examples of words to learn. But, as we'll see in the "Focus on Research" feature, exposure to ample speech promotes vocabulary in another, less direct manner.

 QUESTION 9.2

Gavin and Mitch are both 16-month-olds. Gavin's vocabulary includes about 14 words but Mitch's has about 150 words, more than 10 times as many as Gavin. What factors contribute to this difference?

Focus on Research

Why Does Exposure to Parents' Speech Increase Children's Vocabulary?

Who were the investigators, and what was the aim of the study? Many studies have shown that toddlers learn more when their home environment is rich in language. But we know little about the specific ways in which such language-rich environments foster word learning. Adriana Weisleder and Anne Fernald (2013) conducted a study to test the hypothesis that abundant exposure to language hones a child's language-processing skills, making it easier for the child to learn new words.

How did the investigators measure the topic of interest? Weisleder and Fernald measured the child's language environment by having the child wear a small audio recorder that recorded all the speech that a child heard in a day. Weisleder and Fernald measured language-processing by showing children pairs of pictures of familiar objects (e.g., dog, shoe), followed by the name of one of the pictures. They measured the percentage of time that children looked at the picture that matched the name. Finally, parents completed a standard vocabulary checklist, indicating the words that their child used and understood.

Who were the children in the study? Weisleder and Fernald tested 29 toddlers.

What was the design of the study? This study was correlational: Weisleder and Fernald were interested in links between children's language environment, their language-processing efficiency, and the size of their vocabulary. The study was longitudinal: the child's language environment and language-processing efficiency was assessed when children were 19 months old; vocabulary was assessed when children were 24 months old.

Were there ethical concerns with the study? No. The tasks posed no danger to the infants or to their parents. Parents provided consent for their participation and for their child's participation.

What were the results? One striking finding was the variation in children's language environments. At one extreme were parents who directed more than 12,000 words to their child in a 10-hour day; at the other extreme were parents who directed only 670 words to their child. Overall, the amount of child-directed speech was correlated .44 with children's language-processing efficiency at 19 months and .57 with their vocabulary at 24 months. In other words, greater exposure to language was associated with more efficient language processing and a larger vocabulary. In addition, processing efficiency at 19 months was correlated .53 with vocabulary at 24 months. Using advanced statistics, Weisleder and Fernald showed that exposure to more child-directed speech led to more efficient language processing, which, in turn, yielded larger vocabularies.

What did the investigators conclude? The findings support the hypothesis that language-processing efficiency links a language-rich environment with larger vocabularies. In the words of Weisleder and Fernald, "a critical step in the path from early language experience to later vocabulary knowledge is the influence of language exposure on infants' speech-processing skill.... Infants who hear more talk have more opportunities to interpret language and to exercise skills that are vital to word learning, such as segmenting speech and accessing lexical representations" (p. 2149).

What converging evidence would strengthen these conclusions? Weisleder and Fernald used only a single measure of language-processing efficiency; it would be useful to extend the work with other measures of this construct. In addition, to determine the long-lasting effects of language-processing efficiency on children's word learning, it would be valuable to test the children again when they're older.

Word Learning Styles   Size of vocabulary is not the only way in which young children differ in their word learning. As youngsters expand their vocabulary, they often adopt a distinctive style of learning language (Bates, Bretherton, & Snyder, 1988; Nelson, 1973). **Some children have a *referential style*: their vocabularies consist mainly of words that name objects, persons, or actions.** For example, Caitlin, a referential child, had 42 name words in her 50-word vocabulary but only 2 words for social interaction or questions. **Other children have an *expressive style*: their vocabularies include some names but also many social phrases that are used like a single word, such as "go away," "what'd you want?" and "I want it."** A typical expressive child, Candace, had a more balanced vocabulary, with 22 name words and 13 for social interactions and questions.

Referential and expressive styles represent end points on a continuum; most children are somewhere in between. For children with referential emphasis, language is primarily an intellectual tool—a means of learning and talking about objects (Masur, 1995). In contrast, for children with expressive emphasis, language is more of a social tool—a way of enhancing interactions with others. Of course, both of these functions—intellectual and social—are important functions of language, which explains why most children blend the referential and expressive styles of learning language.

Encouraging Word Learning

LO7   What conditions foster children's learning of new words?

How can parents and other adults help children learn words? If children are to expand their vocabularies, they need to hear others speak. Not surprisingly, then, children learn words more rapidly if their parents speak to them frequently (Huttenlocher et al., 1991; Roberts, Burchinal, & Durham, 1999). Of course, sheer quantity of parental speech is not all that matters. Parents can foster word learning by naming objects that are the focus of a child's attention (Dunham, Dunham, & Curwin, 1993). Parents can name different products on store shelves as they point to them. During a walk, parents can label the objects—birds, plants, vehicles—that the child sees.

Parents can also help children learn words by reading books with them. Reading together is fun for parents and children alike, and it provides opportunities for children to learn new words (Song et al., 2012). However, the way that parents read makes a difference. When parents carefully describe pictures as they read, preschoolers' vocabularies increase (Reese & Cox, 1999). Asking children questions also helps (Sénéchal, Thomas, & Monker, 1995). When an adult reads a sentence (e.g., "Arthur is *angling*"), then asks a question (e.g., "What is Arthur doing?"), a child must match the new word (*angling*) with the pictured activity (fishing) and say the word aloud. When parents read without questioning, children can ignore words they don't understand. Questioning forces children to identify meanings of new words and practice saying them.

For school-age children, parents remain an important influence on vocabulary development: Children learn words when exposed to a parent's advanced vocabulary, particularly in the context of instructive and helpful interactions (Weizman & Snow, 2001). Reading is another great way to learn new words. Written material—books, magazines, newspapers, textbooks—almost always contains more unfamiliar words than conversational language, so reading is rich in opportunities to expand vocabulary (Hayes, 1988). Not surprisingly, children who read frequently tend to have larger vocabularies than children who read less often (Allen, Cipielewski, & Stanovich, 1992).

Impact of Video Television has been a regular part of U.S. children's lives since the 1950s, but video has assumed an even larger role with the ready availability of inexpensive DVD players and child-oriented DVDs. A typical preschool child in the United States spends more than two hours watching video, and infants like the one in the photo spend more than an hour watching (Linebarger & Vaala, 2010). We'll learn more about the impact of video in general in Module 15.2; for now, the issue is the influence of video in helping children to learn new words.

Although U.S. babies typically spend more than an hour every day watching video, they learn little language from such exposure.

For preschool children, viewing video can help word learning, under some circumstances. For example, preschool children who regularly watch *Sesame Street* usually have larger vocabularies than preschoolers who watch *Sesame Street* only occasionally (Wright et al., 2001). Other programs that promote word learning are those that tell a story (e.g., *Thomas the Tank Engine*), as well as programs like *Blue's Clues* and *Dora the Explorer*, which directly ask questions of the viewer. The benefits of these programs are greatest when preschoolers watch them with adults, in part because the video contents become the focus of joint attention, as described on page 287. In contrast, most cartoons have no benefit for language learning (Linebarger & Vaala, 2010).

What about videos claiming that they promote word learning in infants? Most of the evidence suggests that before 18 months of age, infant-oriented videos (e.g., *Baby Einstein, Brainy Baby*) are not effective in promoting infants' word learning (DeLoache et al., 2010; Linebarger & Vaala, 2010). One reason is that these videos are "poorly designed, insufficient to support language processing, and developmentally inappropriate" (Linebarger & Vaala, 2010, p. 184). Another reason stems from a phenomenon that we'll consider in detail at the end of this module: 12- to 18-month olds have limited understanding of relationships between real objects and their depictions in photographs and video. In other words, they have difficulty relating what they see in the video to those objects and actions as experienced in their own lives.

Research on video and on parents' influence points to a simple but powerful conclusion: Children are most likely to learn new words when they participate in activities that force them to understand the meanings of new words and use those new words (O'Doherty et al., 2011). Is learning new words (and other aspects of language) more difficult for children learning two languages? The "Cultural Influences" feature has the answer.

Cultural Influences

Growing Up Bilingual

More than 10 million U.S. children and adolescents come from homes where English is not the primary language. In many states, 25% or more of the children are bilingual, and the percentages are even greater in some urban areas (Shin & Kominski, 2010). These youngsters usually speak English and another language, such as Spanish or, like the children in the photo on page 294, Chinese.

Is learning two languages easier or harder than learning just one language? For much of the 20th century, the general view was that bilingualism harmed children's development. One child psychology text published roughly 60 years ago summarized the research by writing, "There can be no doubt that the child reared in a bilingual environment is handicapped in his language growth" (Thompson, 1952, p. 367). Today, we know this conclusion is wrong because it was based on studies of poor, immigrant children's scores on intelligence tests. In retrospect, immigrant children's test scores had more to do with their poverty and unfamiliarity with a new culture than with their bilingualism.

In fact, modern studies lead to a different picture. When children are exposed simultaneously to two (or more) languages from birth, they pass through the same milestones in each language as monolingual children but somewhat more slowly. For example, in each language their vocabulary is often slightly smaller and their grammar somewhat less complex, but their total vocabulary (i.e., words known in both languages plus words known in either language but not both) is greater than that of monolingual children (Hoff et al., 2012).

These patterns depend critically on the circumstances in which children experience multiple languages. Children's language skills progress more rapidly in the language they hear the most (Hoff et al., 2012). If a child hears English from mom and at day care, but hears Croatian only from dad, the child's skills in English will probably surpass her skills in Croatian. And children's language develops more rapidly when their language exposure comes from a native speaker (Place & Hoff, 2011). Language acquisition in bilingual children can also be affected by the relative prestige of the two languages as well as the cultures associated with the two languages (Hoff, 2014).

For some other language skills, bilingual children surpass monolingual children. Bilingual preschoolers are more likely to understand that the printed form of a word is unrelated to the meaning of the word (Bialystok, 1997; Bialystok, Shenfield, & Codd, 2000). For example, bilingual preschoolers are less likely to believe that words denoting large objects (e.g., *bus*) are longer than words denoting small objects (e.g., *bug*). Bilingual children also better understand that words are simply arbitrary symbols. Bilingual youngsters, for instance, are more likely than monolingual children to understand that, as long as all English speakers agreed, *dog* could refer to cats and *cat* could refer to dogs (Bialystok, 1988; Campbell & Sais, 1995).

Finally, bilingual children are more skilled at switching back and forth between tasks and often are better able to inhibit inappropriate responses (Barac & Bialystok, 2012; Carlson & Meltzoff, 2008). If asked to sort cards first by color, then by shape, children often continue to sort by the first rule: Instead of sorting by shape, they revert to sorting by color (the first rule). Bilingual children are less prone to this sort of mistake, perhaps because they must routinely inhibit relevant words while speaking, listening, or reading. For example, when shown a photo of a dog and asked, "What's this?" preschoolers bilingual in French and English must respond "dog" while suppressing "chien." Apparently, this experience makes bilingual children generally better at inhibiting competing responses.

Of course, many children in the U.S. can't speak English at the time when they should begin school. How to teach these children has prompted much national debate. One view is that all Americans should speak English and so all teaching should be in English. Another view is that children learn more effectively in their native tongue and so all teaching should be done in that language.

Much of the debate over the proper language of instruction is political, reflecting people's desire for a society with a universal cultural heritage and language rather than a society with pluralistic heritages and languages. Ignoring the political aspects, research shows that the best method uses both the child's native language *and* English (Castro et al., 2011). Initially, children receive basic English-language teaching while they are taught other subjects in their native language. Gradually, more instruction is done in English, in step with children's growing proficiency in the second language. When instruction is in children's native language and English, they are most likely to master academic content and literacy skills in both languages (Farver, Lonigan, & Eppe, 2009).

Bilingual children learn language nearly as rapidly as monolingual children and often have more sophisticated understanding of the underlying symbolic nature of language.

Beyond Words: Other Symbols

LO8 How does children's understanding of symbols progress beyond language?

To end this module, let's return to the topic that began the module—symbols. Words are indeed powerful and immensely useful symbols. However, as children grow they learn other symbol systems. Pictures, for example, are symbols that represent something else. The link between a picture and what it represents is often clear. Wallet photos, for example, are easily recognized as representations of familiar people (at least to the wallet's owner!). But the seemingly transparent connection between photographs and the object photographed actually poses a problem for young children—photos are not the actual object but simply a representation of it. Young children must learn that shaking a picture of a rattle will not make a noise and inverting a picture of a glass of juice will not cause it to spill. In fact, if shown realistic photos of familiar toys, 9-month-olds often try to grasp the toy in the photo, much as they would grasp the real object. By 18 months, toddlers rarely do this, indicating that toddlers understand that photos are representations of objects, not the objects themselves (Troseth, Pierroutsakos, & DeLoache, 2004).

A scale model is another kind of symbolic representation. A scale model of the solar system helps students to understand the relative distances of planets from the sun; a scale model of a college campus shows the location of campus landmarks to new students; and a scale model of an airplane allows aeronautical engineers to measure how air flows over a wing. Scale models are useful because they are realistic-looking—simply smaller versions of the real thing. Nevertheless, young children do not understand the relation between scale models and the objects the models represent: The ability to use scale models develops early in the preschool years. To illustrate, if young children watch an adult hide a toy in a full-size room, then try to find the toy in a scale model of the room that contains all the principal features of the full-scale room (e.g., carpet, window, furniture), 3-year-olds find the hidden toy readily but 2½-year-olds do not (DeLoache, 1995).

Why is this task so easy for 3-year-olds and so difficult for 2½-year-olds? Do the younger children simply forget the location of the toy by the time they look at the scale model of the room? No. If returned to the full-size room, they easily find the hidden toy. Judy DeLoache and her colleagues believe that 2½-year-olds' "attention to a scale model as an interesting and attractive object makes it difficult for them to simultaneously think about its relation to something else" (DeLoache, Miller, & Rosengren, 1997, p. 308). In other words, young children are drawn to the model as a real object and therefore find it hard to think about the model as a symbol of the full-size room.

If this argument is correct, 2½-year-olds should be more successful using the model if they don't have to think of it as a symbol for the full-size room. DeLoache and her colleagues tested this hypothesis in what is my favorite study of all time, for reasons that should soon be obvious. To test this argument, they created a condition designed to eliminate the need for children to think of the model as both an object and a symbol. Children saw the oscilloscope shown in the photograph, which was described as a shrinking machine. They saw a toy doll—"Terry the Troll"—placed in front of the oscilloscope; then the experimenter and child left the room briefly while a tape recorder played sounds that were described as sounds "the machine makes when it's shrinking something." When experimenter and child returned, Terry had shrunk from 8 inches to 2 inches. Next, Terry was hidden in the full-size room, the experimenter aimed the "shrinking machine" at the full-size room, then experimenter and child left the room. While the tape

In a study that examined children's understanding of scale models as symbols, Judy DeLoache and her colleagues convinced 2½-year-olds that this oscilloscope could shrink the doll and other objects.

recorder played shrinking sounds, research assistants quickly removed everything from the full-size room and substituted the model. Then the experimenter and child returned and the child was asked to find Terry.

Children rarely found the toy when tested with the usual instructions, but they usually did in the shrinking-machine condition. Apparently, 2½-year-olds find it difficult to think of the model as an object and as a symbol, and consequently, cannot find the hidden toy, even though the model is an exact replica of the full-size room. In contrast, when children can think of the model as the room, but much smaller, they readily find the toy.

A map is more demanding for children because it is only a two-dimensional (flat) representation of objects in the world. Nevertheless, 4- and 5-year-olds can use simple maps to find objects (Shusterman, Lee, & Spelke, 2008; Spelke, Gilmore, & McCarthy, 2011). What's more, this skill emerges when children have no exposure to maps: In a study conducted in isolated villages in South America where there were no maps, rulers, or schools, children used simple maps as capably as U.S. children did (Dehaene et al., 2006).

Of course, after children have mastered scale models and maps, a host of other symbolic forms awaits them, including graphs and musical notation. But children take their first steps toward lifelong access to symbols as infants, when they master words and gestures.

 ## Check Your Learning

RECALL What factors help children learn new words so rapidly?

Summarize some of the ways in which children's vocabularies differ quantitatively and qualitatively.

INTERPRET Explain why a child's first words are best viewed as a breakthrough in children's understanding of symbols.

APPLY Suppose you've been asked to write a brochure for first-time parents about ways they can foster word learning in their toddlers. What would you say?

 # 9.3 Speaking in Sentences

OUTLINE

From Two-Word Speech to Complex
Sentences

Mastering Grammar

LEARNING OBJECTIVES

LO9 How do children progress from speaking single words to creating complicated sentences?

LO10 How do children acquire the grammar of their native language?

Jaime's daughter, Luisa, is a curious 2½-year-old who bombards her father with questions. Jaime enjoys Luisa's questioning, but he is bothered by the way she phrases her questions. Luisa will say, "What you are doing?" and "Why she sleep?" Obviously, Jaime doesn't talk this way, so he wonders where Luisa learned to ask questions like this. Is it normal, or is it a symptom of some type of language disorder?

Not long after children begin to talk, they start combining words to form simple sentences. These simple sentences are the first step in a new area of language learning, mastering *syntax*—a language's rules for combining words to create sentences. We'll begin this module by tracing the stages in children's acquisition of syntax and, along the way, see that Luisa's way of asking questions is quite normal for youngsters learning English. Then we'll examine different factors that influence children's mastery of syntax.

From Two-Word Speech to Complex Sentences

LO9   How do children progress from speaking single words to creating complicated sentences?

At about 1½ years, children begin to combine individual words to create two-word sentences, like *more juice, gimme cookie, truck go, my truck, Mommy go, Daddy bike*. **Researchers call this kind of talk** *telegraphic speech* **because, like telegrams of days gone by, it consists of only words directly relevant to meaning.** Before text messages and e-mail, people sent urgent messages by telegraph, and the cost was based on the number of words. Consequently, telegrams were brief and to the point, containing only the important nouns, verbs, adjectives, and adverbs, much like children's two-word speech.

In their two-word speech, children follow rules to express different meanings. For example, the sentences *truck go* and *Daddy eat* are both about agents—people or objects that do something and the actions they perform. Here the rule is "agent + action." In contrast, *my truck* is about a possessor and a possession; the rule for creating these sentences is "possessor + possession."

When children are in the two-word stage, they use several basic rules to express meaning (Brown, 1973). For example, *Daddy eat* and *Mommy fall* illustrate the rule agent + action; *gimme juice* and *push truck* illustrate the rule action + object. Regardless of the language they learn, children's two-word sentences follow a common set of rules that are useful to describe people and objects, their actions, and their properties (Tager-Flusberg, 1993).

Beyond Telegraphic Speech   Beginning at about the second birthday, children move to three-word and even longer sentences. For example, at 1½ years, my daughter Laura would say, "gimme juice" or "bye-bye, Mom." As a 2½-year-old, she had progressed to "When I finish my ice cream, I'll take a shower, okay?" and "Don't turn the light out—I can't see better!" **Children's longer sentences are filled with** *grammatical morphemes*, **words or endings of words (such as -*ing*, -*ed*, or -*s*) that make a sentence grammatical.** To illustrate, a 1½-year-old might say, "kick ball," but a 3-year-old would be more likely to say, "I am kicking the ball." Compared to the 1½-year-old's telegraphic speech, the 3-year-old has added several elements, including a pronoun, *I*, to serve as the subject of the sentence; the auxiliary verb *am*; -*ing* to the verb *kick*; and an article, *the*, before *ball*. Each of these grammatical morphemes makes the older child's sentence slightly more meaningful and much more grammatical.

How do children learn all of these subtle nuances of grammar? Conceivably, a child might learn that *kicking* describes kicking that is ongoing and that *kicked* describes kicking that occurred in the past. Later, the child might learn that *raining* describes current weather and *rained* describes past weather. But learning different tenses for individual verbs—one by one—would be remarkably slow. More effective would be to learn the general rules that verb + -*ing* denotes an ongoing activity and verb + -*ed* denotes a past activity. In fact, this is what children do: They learn general rules about grammatical morphemes. For example, suppose you show preschoolers pictures of nonsense objects like the one in Figure 9-2 and label it: "This is a wug." Then you show pictures of two of the objects while saying, "Now there

This is a wug.

Now there is another one.
There are two of them.
There are two_____ .

Figure 9-2

is another one. There are two of them. There are two…" Preschoolers usually say, "Wugs" (Berko, 1958). Because *wug* is a novel word, children can answer correctly only by applying the rule of adding -*s* to indicate plural.

Sometimes, of course, applying the general rule can lead to creative communication. As a 3-year-old, my daughter would say, "unvelcro it," meaning detach the Velcro. She had never heard *unvelcro*, but she created this word from the rule that *un-* + verb means to reverse or stop the action of a verb. Creating such novel words is evidence that children learn grammar by applying rules, not by learning individual words.

Additional evidence that children master grammar by learning rules comes from preschoolers' *overregularization,* **applying rules to words that are exceptions to the rule.** Youngsters learning English may incorrectly add an -*s* instead of using an irregular plural—*two mans* instead of *two men* or *two foots* instead of *two feet*. With the past tense, children may add -*ed* instead of using an irregular past tense—*I goed* instead of *I went* or *she runned* instead of *she ran* (Maratsos, 2000; Marcus et al., 1992). Children apparently know the general rule but not all the words that are exceptions.

The rules governing grammatical morphemes range from fairly simple to complex. The rule for plurals—add -*s*—is simple to apply, and, as you might expect, it's one of the first grammatical morphemes that children master. Adding -*ing* to denote ongoing action is also simple, and it too is mastered early. More complex forms, such as the various forms of the verb *to be*, are mastered later; but, remarkably, by the end of the preschool years, children typically have mastered most of the rules that govern grammatical morphemes.

At the same time that preschoolers are mastering grammatical morphemes, they extend their speech beyond the subject-verb-object construction that is basic in English. You can see these changes in the way children ask questions. Children's questions during two-word speech are marked by intonation alone. Soon after a child can declare, "My ball," he can also ask, "My ball?" Children quickly discover *wh* words (*who, what, when, where, why*), but they don't use them correctly. Like Luisa, the 2½-year-old in the module-opening vignette, many youngsters merely attach the *wh* word to the beginning of a sentence without changing the rest of the sentence: *What he eating? What we see?* But by 3 or 3½ years, youngsters insert the required auxiliary verb before the subject, creating *What is he eating?* or *What will we see?* (deVilliers & deVilliers, 1985; Rowland et al., 2005).

Between ages 3 and 6, children also learn to use negation ("That isn't a butterfly") and embedded sentences ("Jennifer thinks that Bill took the book"). They begin to comprehend passive voice ("The ball was kicked by the girl") as opposed to the active voice ("The girl kicked the ball"), although full understanding of this form continues to develop into the elementary-school years (Hoff, 2014). In short, by the time most children enter kindergarten, they are skilled in using most of the grammatical forms of their native language.

Mastering Grammar

LO10 **How do children acquire the grammar of their native language?**

How do children master the fundamentals of grammar at such a young age? Scientists have proposed several different answers to this question.

The Behaviorist Answer   B. F. Skinner (1957) and other learning theorists once claimed that all aspects of language—sounds, words, grammar, and communication—are learned through imitation and reinforcement (Moerk,

Q&A **QUESTION 9.3**
Describing her vacation, 3-year-old Kelly said, "I sleeped in a tent!" What feature of grammatical development does her comment illustrate?

2000; Whitehurst & Vasta, 1975). But critics were quick to point to some flaws in this explanation. One problem is that most of children's sentences are novel, which is difficult to explain in terms of simple imitation of adults' speech. For example, when young children create questions by inserting a *wh* word at the beginning of a sentence ("What she doing?"), who are they imitating?

Also troublesome for the learning view is that even when children imitate adult sentences, they do not imitate adult grammar. In trying to repeat "I am drawing a picture," young children will say "I draw picture." And parents rarely reinforce their young children's speech based on its grammatical correctness; instead they respond based on its meaning, even when it is grammatically incorrect.

The Linguistic Answer   Beginning with Chomsky (1957), linguists proposed that children are born with mechanisms that simplify the task of learning grammar (Slobin, 1985). According to this view, children are born with neural circuits in the brain that allow them to infer the grammar of the language that they hear. That is, grammar itself is not built into the child's nervous system, but processes that guide the learning of grammar are. **For example, according to *semantic bootstrapping theory*, children are born knowing that nouns usually refer to people or objects and that verbs are actions; they use this knowledge to infer grammatical rules.*** Hearing sentences such as "Billy drinks," "Susan sleeps," and "Jen reads," children infer that noun + verb makes a grammatical sentence in English. Consistent with this idea, by 2 years of age, English-speaking children know that a typical transitive sentence (e.g., "the bunny ate the carrot") includes an agent (the subject), an action (the transitive verb), and a patient (the object of the action). Told that "the pig is dorping the cow," 2-year-olds match this with a video of a pig performing an action on a cow (Gertner, Fisher, & Eisengart, 2006).

The proposal that inborn mechanisms help children learn grammar might not be as intuitively appealing as imitation, but many findings indirectly support this view:

1. **Specific regions of the brain are known to be involved in language processing.** If children are born with a "grammar-learning processor," it should be possible to locate a specific region or regions of the brain that are involved in learning grammar. In fact, you may remember from Module 4.3 that for most people the left hemisphere of the brain plays a critical role in understanding language. Some functions of language have been located even more precisely. For example, the area in blue in Figure 9-3 is Broca's area—a region in the left frontal cortex that is necessary for combining words into meaningful sentences. By 2 years, specific regions of the left hemisphere are activated when sentences break simple grammatical rules, such as a noun appearing when a verb would be expected (Bernal et al., 2010). The fact that specific areas in the brain have well-defined functions for language makes it plausible that children have specialized neural circuits that help them learn grammar.

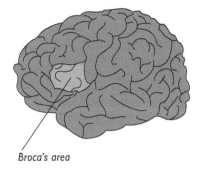

Broca's area

Figure 9-3

---

* The name for this theory comes from the phrase "pull yourself up by your bootstraps," which means improving your situation by your own efforts. The phrase is from an 18th-century fantasy tale about a baron who falls into a deep hole and escapes by pulling up on his bootstraps.

Chimpanzees can be taught very simple grammatical rules, but only after massive training that is unlike what toddlers and preschoolers experience.

2. **Only humans learn grammar readily.** If grammar is learned solely through imitation and reinforcement, then it should be possible to teach rudimentary grammar to nonhumans. If, instead, learning grammar depends on specialized neural mechanisms that are unique to humans, then efforts to teach grammar to nonhumans should fail. This prediction has been tested many times by trying to teach grammar to chimpanzees, the species closest to humans on the evolutionary ladder. For example, chimps like the one in the photo have been taught to communicate using gestures taken from sign language. The result? Chimps master a handful of grammatical rules governing two-word speech, but only with massive effort that is completely unlike the preschool child's learning of grammar. And the resulting language is unlike children's grammar in many ways (Hoff, 2014). For example, one chimp, Nim, gradually used longer sentences, but they were longer only because he repeated himself (e.g., "eat Nim eat Nim"), not because he expressed more complicated ideas. Because numerous efforts to teach grammar to chimps have failed, this suggests that children master grammar by relying on some type of mechanism specific to humans.

3. **There is a critical period for learning language.** The period from birth to about 12 years is a critical period for acquiring language generally and mastering grammar particularly. If children do not acquire language in this period, they will never truly master language later. Evidence of a critical period for language comes from studies of isolated children. In one tragic instance, a baby named Genie was restrained by a harness during the day and a straight-jacket-like device at night. No one was permitted to talk to Genie, and she was beaten when she made any noise. When Genie was discovered, at age 13, she did not speak at all. After several years of language training, her mastery of grammar remained limited, resembling the telegraphic speech of a 2-year-old (Curtiss, 1989; Rymer, 1993).

    Further evidence for a critical period for language comes from studies of individuals learning second languages. Individuals master the grammar of a foreign language at the level of a native speaker only if they are exposed to the language prior to adolescence (Newport, 1991). Why can one period of time be so much more influential for language than others? Why can't missed language experiences be made up after age 12? A critical period for language answers these questions. That is, just as females ovulate for only a limited portion of the life span, the neural mechanisms involved in learning grammar may function only during infancy and childhood.

4. **The development of grammar is tied to the development of vocabulary.** The mastery of grammar is closely related to vocabulary growth, in a way that suggests both are part of a common, emerging language system (Dixon & Marchman, 2007). One idea, for example, is that as children learn words, they learn not only a word's meaning, but also about the kinds of sentences in which a word appears and its position in those sentences. They learn the meaning of "teacher" and that "teacher" can appear as the actor and object in transitive sentences. Grammar then emerges naturally as children learn more and more words.

Two fascinating findings link growth of vocabulary and emergence of grammar. First, in bilingual children, growth of vocabulary and grammar are related within each language, but not across languages (Conboy & Thal, 2006). In other words, children's English vocabulary predicts the complexity of their English sentences (but not their Spanish sentences), and their Spanish vocabulary predicts the complexity of their Spanish sentences (but not their English sentences). In each language, children need a "critical mass" of words before grammar can emerge.

Second, children who are adopted by adults who speak another language (typically, through an international adoption) represent a valuable natural experiment. Most children are adopted as infants, toddlers, or preschoolers, which means they differ considerably in the cognitive skills they can use to learn grammar. Nevertheless, the size of children's vocabulary, not their age, predicts the complexity of their grammar (Snedeker, Geren, & Shafto, 2007). That is, if a 3-year-old and a 7-year-old each know 400 words, their grammar will be comparable, despite the age difference. This tight coupling of vocabulary and grammar in adopted and bilingual children goes well with the idea that development of vocabulary and grammar is regulated by a common, language-specific system.

Although these findings are consistent with the idea that children have innate grammar-learning mechanisms, they do *not* prove the existence of such mechanisms. Consequently, scientists have continued to look for other explanations.

The Cognitive Answer Not all researchers believe that children must have specialized mechanisms to learn grammar. Some theorists believe that children learn grammar through powerful cognitive skills that help them rapidly detect regularities in their environments, including patterns in the speech they hear. According to this approach, it's as if children establish a huge Excel spreadsheet that has the speech they've heard in one column and the context in which they heard it in a second column; periodically infants scan the columns looking for recurring patterns (Maratsos, 1998). For example, children might be confused the first time they hear -s added to the end of a familiar noun. However, as the database expands to include many instances of familiar nouns with an added -s, children discover that -s is always added to a noun when there are multiple instances of the object. Thus, they create the rule: noun + -s = plural. With this view, children learn language by searching for regularities across many examples that are stored in memory, not through an inborn grammar-learning device (Bannard & Matthews, 2008). Scientists who subscribe to this view argue that infants' impressive ability to extract regularities in the speech sounds that they hear (described on page 282) would work just as effectively to extract regularities in sentence structure (Kidd, 2012).

The Social-Interaction Answer This approach is eclectic, drawing on each of the views we've considered so far. From the behaviorist approach, it takes an emphasis on the environment; from the linguistic approach, that language learning is distinct; and, from the cognitive view, that children have powerful cognitive skills they can use to master language. The unique contribution of this perspective is emphasizing that children master language generally and grammar specifically in the context of social interactions (Bloom & Tinker, 2001). That is, much language learning takes place in the context of

According to the social-interaction account of language learning, children are eager to master grammar because it allows them to communicate their wishes and needs more effectively.

SUMMARY TABLE 9-1

DIFFERENT APPROACHES TO EXPLAINING CHILDREN'S ACQUISITION OF GRAMMAR

Approach	Children Are Thought to Master Grammar...
Behaviorist	by imitating speech they hear.
Linguistic	with inborn mechanisms that allow children to infer the grammatical rules of their native language.
Cognitive	using powerful cognitive mechanisms that allow children to find recurring patterns in the speech they hear.
Social Interaction	in the context of social interactions with adults in which both parties want improved communication.

interactions between children and adults, with both parties eager for better communication. Children have an ever-expanding repertoire of ideas and intentions that they wish to convey to others, and caring adults want to understand their children, so both parties work to improve language skills as a means toward better communication. Thus, improved communication provides an incentive for children to master language and for adults to help them.

You can see the nature of these interactions in the following example, in which a child wants a cookie (after Hulit & Howard, 2002, pp. 37–38). A 9-month-old who wants a cookie might point to it while looking at the mother. In turn, the mother gives the cookie, saying, "Here's the cookie." By age 2, a child might say, "Gimme cookie, please?" with the mother responding, "Yes, I'll give you the cookie." At 9 months and 2 years, the child's desire to have the cookie motivates communication (pointing at 9 months, spoken language at 2 years) and gives the mother opportunities to demonstrate more advanced forms of language.

None of these accounts, described briefly in Summary Table 9-1, provides a comprehensive account of how grammar is mastered. But many scientists believe the final explanation will include contributions from the linguistic, cognitive, and social-interaction accounts. That is, children's learning of grammar will be explained in terms of some mechanisms specific to learning grammar, children actively seeking to identify regularities in their environment, and linguistically rich interactions between children and adults (MacWhinney, 1998).

Of course, many parents don't care much about theories of language, but they do want to know how they can help their children master grammar and other aspects of language. The "Improving Children's Lives" feature provides some guidelines.

Improving Children's Lives
Promoting Language Development

Adults eager to promote children's language development can follow a few guidelines:

1. Talk with children frequently and treat them as partners in conversation. That is, try talking with children interactively, not directively.
2. Use a child's speech to show new language forms. Expand a child's remark to introduce new vocabulary or new grammatical forms. Rephrase a child's ungrammatical remark to show the correct grammar.

3. Encourage children to go beyond minimal use of language. Have them answer questions in phrases and sentences, not single words. Have them replace vague words such as *stuff* or *somebody* with more descriptive ones.

4. Listen. This guideline has two parts. First, because children often talk slowly, it's tempting for adults to complete their sentences for them. Don't. Let children express themselves. Second, pay attention to what children are saying and respond appropriately. Let children learn that language works.

5. Make language fun. Use books, rhymes, songs, jokes, and foreign words to increase a child's interest in learning language.

   Of course, as children's language improves during the preschool years, others can understand it more readily, which means that children become better at communicating. These emerging communication skills are described in the next module.

 Check Your Learning

RECALL Describe the major milestones that mark children's progress from two-word speech to complex sentences.

What are the main accounts of how children master grammar?

INTERPRET How do the various explanations of grammatical development differ in their view of the child's role in mastering grammar?

APPLY How might the cognitive processes described in Chapter 7 help children learn grammar?

9.4 Using Language to Communicate

LEARNING OBJECTIVES

LO11 When and how do children learn to take turns in conversation?

LO12 When do children master the skills needed to speak effectively?

LO13 When do children learn to listen well?

OUTLINE

Taking Turns

Speaking Effectively

Listening Well

Marla and Kitty, both 9-year-olds, usually are good friends, but right now they're boiling mad at each other. Marla was going to the store with her dad to buy some new markers. Kitty found out and gave Marla money to buy some markers for her, too. Marla returned with the markers, but they weren't the kind that Kitty liked, so she was angry. Marla was angry because she didn't think Kitty should be mad; after all, it was Kitty's fault for not telling her what kind to buy. Meanwhile, Marla's dad hopes they come to some understanding soon and stop all the shouting.

Imagining these girls arguing is an excellent way to learn what is needed for effective communication. Both talk at the same time, their remarks are rambling and incoherent, and neither bothers to listen to the other. For effective oral communication these girls need to follow a few simple guidelines:

- People should take turns, alternating as speaker and listener.
- A speaker's remarks should relate to the topic and be understandable to the listener.
- A listener should pay attention and let the speaker know if his or her remarks don't make sense.

Complete mastery of these guidelines is a lifelong pursuit; after all, even adults often miscommunicate with one another because they don't observe one or more of these rules. However, in this module, we'll trace the development of effective communication skills and, along the way, discover why young children like Marla and Kitty sometimes fail to communicate.

Taking Turns

LO11 **When and how do children learn to take turns in conversation?**

Many parents begin to encourage turn-taking long before infants say their first words. Parents such as the mother in the photo often structure a "conversation" around a baby's early sounds, even when those sounds lack any obvious communicative intent (Field & Widmayer, 1982):

PARENT:	Can you see the bird?
INFANT:	(COOING) ooooh
PARENT:	It *is* a pretty bird.
INFANT:	ooooh
PARENT:	You're right, it's a cardinal.

Soon after 1-year-olds begin to speak, parents encourage their youngsters to participate in conversational turn-taking. To help children along, parents often carry both sides of a conversation to demonstrate how the roles of speaker and listener alternate (Shatz, 1983):

PARENT (TO INFANT):	What's Amy eating?
PARENT (ILLUSTRATING REPLY):	She's eating a cookie.

Parents and other caregivers often work hard to allow infants and toddlers to "fit in" to a conversation. That is, caregivers scaffold youngsters' attempts to converse, making it more likely that children will succeed. However, such early conversations between caregivers and infants are not universal. In some non-Western cultures, preverbal infants are not considered appropriate conversational partners, so adults don't talk to them. Only after infants are older do others begin to converse with them (Hoff, 2009).

By age 2, spontaneous turn-taking is common in conversations between youngsters and adults (Barton & Tomasello, 1991). By age 3, children have progressed to the point that if a listener fails to reply promptly, the child repeats his or her remark to elicit a response (Garvey &

When parents speak with young babies, they often alternate roles of speaker and listener, showing conversational turn-taking.

Beringer, 1981). A 3-year-old might say, "Hi, Paul" to an older sibling who's busy reading. If Paul doesn't answer in a few seconds, the 3-year-old might say, "Hi, Paul" again. When Paul remains unresponsive, the 3-year-old is likely to shout, "PAUL!"—showing that by this age children understand the rule that a comment deserves a response. Preschool children seem to interpret the lack of a response as, "I guess you didn't hear me, so I'll say it again, louder!"

Speaking Effectively

LO12 When do children master the skills needed to speak effectively?

When do children first try to initiate communication with others? In fact, what appear to be the first deliberate attempts to communicate typically emerge at about 10 months (Golinkoff, 1993). Infants at this age may touch or point to an object while simultaneously looking at another person. They continue this behavior until the person acknowledges them. It's as if the child is saying, "This is a neat toy! I want you to see it, too."

Even before children can speak, they make gestures to communicate with others.

Beginning at 10 months, an infant may point, touch, or make noises to get an adult to do something. An infant in a highchair like the one in the photo who wants a toy that is out of reach may make noises while pointing to the toy. The noises capture an adult's attention, and the pointing indicates what the baby wants (Tomasello, Carpenter, & Liszkowski, 2007). The communication may be a bit primitive by adult standards, but it works for babies! And mothers typically translate their baby's pointing into words, so that gesturing paves the way for learning words (Goldin-Meadow, Mylander, & Franklin, 2007).

After their first birthday, children begin to use speech to communicate and often initiate conversations with adults (Bloom et al., 1996). Toddlers' first conversations are about themselves, but their conversational scope expands rapidly to include objects in the environment (e.g., toys, food). Later, conversations begin to include more abstract notions, such as hypothetical objects and past or future events (Foster, 1986).

Of course, young children are not always skilled conversational partners. At times their communications are confusing, leaving a listener to wonder, "What was that all about?" Saying something clearly is often difficult because clarity can be judged only by considering the listener's age, experience, and knowledge of the topic, along with the context of the conversation. For example, think about the simple request, "Please hand me the Phillips-head screwdriver." This message may be clear to older listeners familiar with different types of screwdrivers, but it won't mean much to younger listeners who think all screwdrivers are alike. And, if the toolbox is filled with Phillips-head screwdrivers of assorted sizes, the message won't be clear even to a knowledgeable listener.

Constructing clear messages is a fine art, but, amazingly, by the preschool years, youngsters begin to adjust their messages to match the listener and the context. In a classic study (Shatz & Gelman, 1973), 4-year-olds explained how a toy worked, once to a 2-year-old and once to an adult. The 4-year-olds talked more overall to adults than to 2-year-olds and used longer sentences with adult listeners than with 2-year-old listeners. Also, when speaking with 2-year-olds, children used simpler grammar and more attention-getting words, such as *see, look, watch,* and *hey.* Here, for example, is how one 4-year-old child explained the toy to her

 QUESTION 9.4

Shauna's older brother asked, "Where's your locker this year?" Shauna replied, "Next to Mrs. Rathert's room." When Shauna's grandmother, who lived in another city, asked the same question, Shauna's reply was much longer: "After you go in the front door, you turn left and go down a long hall until you get to some stairs. Then...." What feature of effective communication is shown in Shauna's two answers to the same question?

two different listeners (the toy was a garage with drivers and trucks that carry marbles to a dumping station):

ADULT LISTENER: You're supposed to put one of these persons in, see? Then one goes with the other little girl. And then the little boy. He's the little boy and he drives. And then they back up.... And then the little girl falls out and then it goes backwards.

2-YEAR-OLD LISTENER: Watch, Perry. Watch this. He's back in here. Now he drives up. Look, Perry. Look here, Perry. Those are marbles, Perry. Put the men in here. Now I'll do it (Shatz & Gelman, 1973, p. 13).

These findings show that preschoolers are already sensitive to characteristics of the listener in formulating a clear message. Subsequent findings also show that children consider the listener and setting in devising clear messages:

- Preschool children tailor their messages to a listener's knowledge and intentions. They give more elaborate messages to listeners who lack critical information than to listeners who have the information (Nadig & Sedivy, 2002; O'Neill, 1996). For example, a child describing where to find a toy will give more detailed directions to a listener whose eyes were covered when the toy was hidden. And if a listener wants to complete a task without help, 5-year-olds sometimes provide helpful information but conceal their intent to help, so that the listener thinks she has completed the task without assistance (Grosse, Scott-Phillips, & Tomasello, 2013).
- School-age children speak differently to adults and peers. They are more likely to speak politely with adults and be more demanding with peers (Anderson, 2000; Warren-Leubecker & Bohannon, 1989). A child might ask a parent, "May I have one of your cookies?" but say to a peer, "Gimme one of your cookies."
- Some African Americans speak *African American English*, **a variant of standard English that has slightly different grammatical rules.** For example, "He be tired" in African American English is synonymous with "He usually is tired" in standard English. Many African American children learn both African American English and standard English, and they switch back and forth, using standard English more often in school and when talking with European Americans but using African American English more often at home and when talking with African American peers (Warren & McCloskey, 1993).

All these findings show that school-age children (and sometimes preschoolers) are well on their way to understanding the factors to consider in creating clear messages. From a surprisingly young age, children express themselves to others and adjust their conversations to fit listeners. Are young children equally adept at listening? We'll find out in the next section.

Listening Well

LO13 When do children learn to listen well?

To listen well, a person must continuously decide whether a speaker's remarks make sense. If they do, then a listener needs to reply appropriately, typically by extending the conversation with another remark that's on the topic. Otherwise, the listener needs to provide feedback that the speaker was confusing (e.g., "I don't get what you mean").

Few toddlers master these fundamental conversation skills. Their replies are more likely to be unrelated to the topic than related to it (Bloom, Rocissano, & Hood, 1976). Asked "Where's the sock?" a 1½-year-old may say something like "I'm hungry!" By 3 years, children are more adept at continuing conversations by making remarks that relate to the topic being discussed.

By 4 years of age, children sometimes realize that a message is vague or confusing (Nilsen & Graham, 2012), but they often don't ask speakers to clarify their intent. Instead, young listeners often assume that they know what the speaker had in mind (Beal & Belgrad, 1990). Because young children's remarks are often ambiguous and because, as listeners, they often do not detect ambiguities, young children often miscommunicate, just like Marla and Kitty in the opening vignette. Kitty probably didn't communicate exactly what kind of markers she wanted, and Marla didn't realize that the directions were unclear. Throughout the elementary-school years, youngsters gradually master the many skills involved in determining whether a message is consistent and clear (Ackerman, 1993).

Sometimes messages are confusing because they conflict with what a listener thinks is true. For example, suppose a child is told that the family cat, which always stays indoors, has run away. Even preschoolers are more likely to believe such a message when told by a parent than by a classmate, because they know the parent is better informed about this particular topic (Robinson, Champion, & Mitchell, 1999). By the age of 7 or 8 years, children can be skeptical listeners—taking what a speaker says with a grain of salt—when, for example, a speaker has a vested interest in a topic. When a child announces to an entire class that her birthday party is going to be the "best one all year," school-age children believe her less than if they heard the information from an independent, third party (Mills & Keil, 2005).

Sometimes listeners must go beyond the words to understand the real meaning of a message. Metaphor is one example. When parents tell their teenagers, "Your bedroom is a junk yard," the remark is not to be taken literally but highlights the fact that the bedroom is a mess and filled with things that could be thrown away. Understanding of nonliteral meanings of messages develops slowly (e.g., Dews et al., 1996). In the case of metaphor, young children easily understand simple metaphors in which the nonliteral meaning is based on references to concrete objects and their properties. For example, a parent might say to a 5-year-old, "You're a fish," referring to how well the child swims and enjoys the water, and the child will likely understand.

More complex metaphors require that children make connections based on abstract relations. For example, in Shakespeare's *Romeo and Juliet*, Romeo proclaims that "Juliet is the Sun." You might interpret this line to mean that Juliet is the center of Romeo's universe or that without Juliet, Romeo will die. The first interpretation depends on your knowledge of astronomy; the second, on your knowledge of biology. Younger children lack this sort of knowledge to comprehend metaphors, so they try to interpret them literally. Only when children gain the necessary content knowledge do they understand metaphors based on abstract relations (Franquart-Declercq & Gineste, 2001).

Sarcasm is another form of communication that is not to be interpreted literally. When a soccer player misses the ball entirely and a teammate says, "Nice kick," the literal meaning of the remark is the opposite of the intended meaning. Like understanding of metaphor, understanding of sarcasm develops gradually (Creusere, 1999). When people emphasize their sarcasm by speaking in mocking or overly enthusiastic tones, school-age children can detect their meaning. However, if sarcasm must be detected solely from the context—by realizing that the comment is the opposite of what would be expected—only adolescents and adults are likely to understand the real meaning of the remark (Capelli, Nakagawa, & Madden, 1990).

This discussion of listening skills completes our catalog of the important accomplishments in communication that take place during childhood. By the time most children enter kindergarten, they have mastered many of the fundamental rules of communication, and as they grow older, they acquire even greater proficiency.

 ## Check Your Learning

RECALL What findings illustrate that preschool children are sometimes effective speakers?

Summarize children's understanding of messages that are not meant to be taken literally.

INTERPRET What are the strengths and weaknesses of infants as communicators?

APPLY In Chapter 6, we saw that Piaget characterized preschool children as egocentric. Are the findings described in this module consistent with Piaget's view?

> Unifying Themes Connections

This chapter is an appropriate occasion to stress the theme that *development in different domains is connected*: Language has important connections to biological, cognitive, and social development. A link to biological development would be children's mastery of grammar: In ways that we don't yet fully understand, children seem to be endowed with a mechanism that smoothes the path to mastering grammar. A link to cognitive development would be children's first words: Speaking words reflects the cognitive insight that speech sounds are symbols. A link to social development would be the communication skills that enable children to interact with peers and adults.

See for Yourself

Berko's (1958) "wugs" task is fun to try with preschool children. Photocopy the drawing on page 297 and show it to a preschooler, repeating the instructions that appear on that page. You should find that the child quite predictably says, "two wugs." Create some pictures of your own to examine other grammatical morphemes, such as adding *-ing* to denote ongoing activity or adding *-ed* to indicate past tense. See for yourself!

Summary

The Road to Speech

Elements of Language
Language includes four distinct elements: phonology (sounds), semantics (word meaning), syntax (rules for language structure), and pragmatics (rules for communication).

Perceiving Speech
Phonemes are the basic units of sound that make up words. Infants can hear phonemes soon after birth. They can even hear phonemes that are not used in their native language, but this ability is lost by the first birthday.

Before they speak, infants can recognize words, apparently by noticing stress and syllables that go together. Infants prefer infant-directed speech—adults' speech to infants that is slower and has greater variation in pitch—because it provides them with additional language clues.

First Steps to Speech
Newborns are limited to crying, but at about 3 months, babies coo. Babbling soon follows, consisting of a single syllable; over several months, infants' babbling includes more syllables and intonation.

Learning the Meanings of Words

Understanding Words as Symbols
Children's first words represent a cognitive accomplishment that is not specific to language. Instead, the onset of speech is a result of a child's ability to interpret and use symbols. Consistent with this view, there are parallel developments in the use of gestures.

Fast Mapping Meanings to Words
Most children learn the meanings of words too rapidly for them to consider all plausible meanings systematically. Instead, children use a number of fast-mapping rules to determine probable meanings of new words. Joint attention, constraints, sentence cues, and cognitive skills all help children learn words. The rules do not always lead to the correct meaning. An underextension denotes a child's meaning that is narrower than an adult's meaning; an overextension denotes a child's meaning that is broader.

Individual Differences in Word Learning
Individual children differ in vocabulary size; these differences are attributable to phonological memory and the quality of the child's language environment. Some youngsters use a referential word-learning style that emphasizes words as names and that views language as an intellectual tool. Other children use an expressive style that emphasizes phrases and views language as a social tool.

Encouraging Word Learning
Children's word learning is fostered by experience, including being read to, watching television, and, for school-age children, reading to themselves. The key ingredient is making children think about the meanings of new words.

Beyond Words: Other Symbols
As children learn language, they also learn about other symbol systems. By 18 months, toddlers understand that photos are representations of other objects; by 3 years, children understand that a scale model is a representation of an identical but larger object. Preschoolers can use simple maps.

Speaking in Sentences

From Two-Word Speech to Complex Sentences
Not long after their first birthday, children produce two-word sentences that are based on simple rules for expressing ideas or needs. These sentences are sometimes called *telegraphic* because they use the fewest possible words to convey meaning. Moving from two-word to more complex sentences involves adding grammatical morphemes. Children first master grammatical morphemes that express simple relations, then those that denote complex relations.

As children acquire grammatical morphemes, they also extend their speech to other sentence forms, such as questions, and later to more complex constructions, such as passive sentences.

Mastering Grammar
Behaviorists proposed that children acquire grammar through imitation, but that explanation is incorrect. Today's explanations come from three perspectives: The linguistic emphasizes inborn mechanisms that allow children to infer the grammatical rules of their native language, the cognitive perspective emphasizes cognitive processes that allow children to find recurring patterns in the speech they hear, and the social-interaction perspective emphasizes social interactions with adults in which both parties want improved communication.

Using Language to Communicate

Taking Turns
Parents encourage turn-taking even before infants talk and later demonstrate both the speaker and listener roles for their children. By age 3, children spontaneously take turns and prompt one another to speak.

Speaking Effectively
Before they can speak, infants use gestures and noises to communicate. During the preschool years, children gradually become more skilled at constructing clear messages, in part by adjusting their speech to fit their listeners' needs. They also begin to monitor their listeners' comprehension, repeating messages if necessary.

Listening Well
Toddlers are not good conversationalists because their remarks don't relate to the topic. Preschoolers are unlikely to identify ambiguities in another's speech. Also, they sometimes have difficulty understanding messages that are not to be taken literally, such as metaphor and sarcasm.

Test Yourself

1. Infants who are younger than five months of age _____.
   a. must experience speech sounds in their environment to be able to discriminate them
   b. can discriminate sounds found in their native language as well as sounds not present in their native language
   c. cannot discriminate any speech sounds, which explains why they cannot talk

2. To pick out individual words from a steady stream of speech, infants _____.
   a. pay more attention to unstressed syllables than stressed syllables
   b. notice syllables that go together frequently
   c. ignore function words and concentrate on words that have meaning

3. Which of the following statements about infant-directed speech is correct?
   a. It is useful because infants ignore it.
   b. Infant-directed speech contains few changes in pitch or volume and is unexpressive emotionally.
   c. Infant-directed speech is used frequently by adults who care for children.

4. As infants develop, _____.
   a. babbling shifts from single syllable utterances to combinations of different sounds
   b. babbling is replaced by cooing
   c. babbling no longer resembles the sound patterns of their native language

5. A child's first word probably reflects the child's mastery of _____.
   a. symbols
   b. vowels
   c. intonation

6. As young children learn new words, they _____.
   a. learn the referents of words with surprisingly few presentations
   b. systematically consider all possible hypotheses about the connection between the word and the correct referent
   c. learn equally well from credible and uncredible sources

7. Which of the following accurately describes the rules children use to learn new words?
   a. A name refers to the whole object, not to its parts.
   b. A name refers to one particular object not to all objects of the same type.

   c. If an object already has a name and another name is presented, children replace the old name with the new one.

8. Individual differences in the size of children's vocabulary _____.
   a. are unrelated to heredity
   b. reflect differences in children's ability to remember speech sounds
   c. have been linked to parents' speech: children learn fewer words when their parents' speech is grammatically sophisticated

9. If parents want to help their children learn more words, then parents should _____.
   a. encourage their children to read
   b. avoid asking their children too many questions
   c. urge their children to watch a variety of TV programs, particularly cartoons

10. Compared with monolingual children, bilingual children _____.
    a. are more skilled at switching between tasks
    b. pass most language milestones sooner
    c. are more confused about the symbolic nature of language

11. Which of the following statements about children's early sentences is correct?
    a. The sentences are based on rules that differ from language to language.
    b. Early sentences are called telegraphic because they include only words essential to meaning.
    c. As children speak in longer sentences, they no longer need grammatical morphemes.

12. The idea that children are born with a mechanism that helps them master grammar is supported by the finding that _____.
    a. most regions of the brain are involved in processing language
    b. there is a critical period for language learning
    c. chimpanzees easily learn rudimentary grammar

13. Which approach argues that children master grammar by using powerful skills to detect regularities in the speech they hear?
    a. cognitive
    b. behaviorist
    c. social-interaction

14. Parents encourage turn taking _____.
    a. soon after babies say their first words
    b. but not until their children have entered school
    c. by taking the speaker and listener roles before infants say their first words

15. Which statement accurately describes young children's communicative skills?
    a. Based on their listener's age and knowledge, preschoolers change what they say.
    b. When preschool children hear an ambiguous message, they typically ask the speaker to clarify what he or she meant.
    c. Preschool children readily interpret messages that include complex metaphors and sarcasm.

Key Terms

African American English 306
babbling 284
cooing 284
expressive style 292
fast mapping 286
grammatical morphemes 297
infant-directed speech 282
intonation 284

language 279
naming explosion 286
overextension 290
overregularization 298
phonemes 280
phonological memory 290
phonology 280
pragmatics 280

referential style 292
semantic bootstrapping theory 299
semantics 280
syntax 280
telegraphic speech 297
underextension 290

Chapter 10
Emotional Development

Modules

10.1 Emerging Emotions

10.2 Temperament

10.3 Attachment

If you're a fan of *Star Trek*, you know that Mr. Spock feels little emotion because he's half Vulcan and people from the planet Vulcan don't have emotions. Few of us would like to live an emotionless life like Mr. Spock, because feelings enrich our lives. As partial testimony to their importance, the English language has more than 500 words that refer to emotions (Averill, 1980). Joy, happiness, satisfaction, and yes, anger, guilt, and humiliation are just a few of the feelings that give life meaning.

In this chapter, we'll see how emotions emerge and how they affect development. In **Module 10.1**, we'll discuss when children first express different emotions and recognize emotions in others. Next, in **Module 10.2**, we'll see that children have different behavioral styles and that these styles are rooted, in part, in emotions. Finally, in **Module 10.3**, we'll examine the infant's first emotional relationship, the one that develops with the primary caregiver.

 # Emerging Emotions

<table>
<tr><td>

LEARNING OBJECTIVES

LO1 Why do people "feel"? Why do they have emotions?

LO2 At what ages do children begin to experience and express different emotions?

LO3 When do children begin to understand other people's emotions? How do they use this information to guide their own behavior?

LO4 When do children show evidence of regulating emotion, and why is this an important skill?

</td><td>

OUTLINE

The Function of Emotions

Experiencing and Expressing Emotions

Recognizing and Using Others' Emotions

Regulating Emotions

</td></tr>
</table>

Nicole was ecstatic that she was finally going to see her 7-month-old nephew, Claude. She rushed into the house and, seeing Claude playing on the floor with blocks, swept him up in a big hug. After a brief, puzzled look, Claude burst into angry tears and began thrashing around, as if saying to Nicole, "Who are you? What do you want? Put me down! Now!" Nicole quickly handed Claude to his mother, who was surprised by her baby's outburst and even more surprised that he continued to sob while she rocked him.

This vignette illustrates three common emotions. Nicole's initial joy, Claude's anger, and his mother's surprise are familiar to all of us. In this module, we begin by discussing *why* people have feelings at all. Then we look at when children first express emotions, how children come to understand emotions in others, and finally, how children regulate their emotions. As we do, we'll learn why Claude reacted to Nicole as he did and how Nicole could have prevented Claude's outburst.

The Function of Emotions

LO1 Why do people "feel"? Why do they have emotions?

Why do people feel emotions? Wouldn't life be simpler if people were emotionless like computers or residents of Mr. Spock's Vulcan? Probably not. Think, for example, about activities that most adults find pleasurable: a good meal, sex, holding one's children, and accomplishing a difficult but important task. These activities were and remain essential to the continuity of humans as a species, so it's not surprising that they elicit emotions (Gaulin & McBurney, 2001).

Modern theories emphasize the functional value of emotion. That is, according to the functional approach, emotions are useful because they help people adapt to their environment (Boiger & Mesquita, 2012; Shariff & Tracy, 2011). Take fear as an example. Most of us would rather not be afraid, but sometimes feeling fearful is adaptive. Imagine you are walking alone, late at night, in a poorly lighted section of campus. You become frightened and, as a consequence, are particularly attentive to sounds that might signal the presence of threat, and you probably walk quickly to a safer location. Thus, fear is adaptive because it organizes your behavior around an important goal: avoiding danger (Tooby & Cosmides, 2008).

Similarly, other emotions are adaptive. For example, happiness is adaptive in contributing to stronger interpersonal relationships: When people are happy with another person, they smile, and this often causes the other person to feel happy too, strengthening their relationship (Izard & Ackerman, 2000). Disgust is adaptive in keeping people away from substances that might make them ill: When we discover that the milk in a glass is sour, we experience disgust and push the glass away (Oaten, Stevenson, & Case, 2009). Thus, in the functional approach, most emotions developed over the course of human history to meet unique life challenges and help humans to survive.

Experiencing and Expressing Emotions

LO2 At what ages do children begin to experience and express different emotions?

Development of Basic Emotions The three emotions from the vignette—happiness, anger, and surprise—are considered "basic emotions," as are interest, disgust, sadness, and fear (Draghi-Lorenz, Reddy, & Costall, 2001). **Basic emotions are experienced by people worldwide, and each consists of three elements: a subjective feeling, a physiological change, and an overt behavior** (Izard, 2007). For example, suppose you wake to the sound of a thunderstorm and then discover that your roommate has left for class with your umbrella. Subjectively, you might feel ready to explode with anger; physiologically, your heart would beat faster; and behaviorally, you would probably be scowling.

Using facial expressions and other overt behaviors, scientists have traced the growth of basic emotions in infants. Many scientists believe that young babies simply experience broad positive and broad negative emotional states (Camras & Fatani, 2008). These broad emotional categories differentiate rapidly and by approximately 6 months of age, infants are thought to experience all basic emotions (Lewis, 2008). For example, the onset of happiness is evident in a baby's smiles. In the first month, infants smile while asleep or when touched softly. The meaning of these smiles isn't clear; they may just represent a reflexive response to bodily states. However, an important change occurs at about 2–3 months of age. *Social smiles* first appear: **Infants smile when they see another person.** As with the baby in the photo, the social smile seems to reflect the infant's pleasure in simple interactions with others. When smiling, they sometimes coo (the early form of vocalization described in Module 9.1), and they may move their arms and legs to express excitement.

Social smiles emerge at 2 to 3 months of age and seem to express an infant's happiness at interacting with others.

Anger is one of the first negative emotions to emerge from generalized distress, and typically does so between 4 and 6 months. Infants become angry, for example, if a favorite food or toy is taken away (Sullivan & Lewis, 2003). Reflecting their growing understanding of goal-directed behavior (see Module 6.1), older infants become increasingly angry when their attempts to achieve a goal are frustrated (Braungart-Rieker, Hill-Soderlund, & Karrass, 2010). For example, if a parent restrains an infant who is trying to pick up a toy, the guaranteed result is a very angry baby.

Like anger, fear emerges later in the first year. **At about 6 months, infants become wary in the presence of an unfamiliar adult, a reaction known as** *stranger wariness*. When a stranger approaches, a 6-month-old typically looks away and begins to fuss (Mangelsdorf, Shapiro, & Marzolf, 1995). The baby in the photo is showing the signs of stranger wariness. The grandmother has picked him up without giving him a chance to warm up to her, and the outcome is as predictable as it was with Claude, the baby in the vignette who was frightened by his aunt: He cries, looks frightened, and reaches with arms outstretched in the direction of someone familiar.

By 6 months, infants are wary of strangers and often become upset when they encounter people they don't know, particularly when strangers rush to greet or hold them.

Fear of strangers increases over the first two years but how wary an infant feels around strangers depends on a number of factors (Brooker et al., 2013; Thompson & Limber, 1991). First, infants tend to be less fearful of strangers when the environment is familiar and more fearful when it is not. Infants are less afraid of strangers that they see at home than strangers that they see when visiting someone for the first time. Second, the amount of anxiety depends on the stranger's behavior. Instead of rushing to greet or pick up the baby, as Nicole did in the vignette, a stranger should talk with other adults and, in a while, perhaps offer the baby a toy (Mangelsdorf, 1992). Handled this way, many infants will soon become curious about the stranger instead of afraid.

Wariness of strangers is adaptive because it emerges at the same time that children begin to master creeping and crawling (described in Module 5.3). Like Curious George, the monkey in a famous series of children's books, babies are inquisitive and want to use their new locomotor skills to explore their worlds. Being wary of strangers provides a natural restraint against the tendency to wander away from familiar caregivers. However, as youngsters learn to interpret facial expressions and recognize when a person is friendly, their wariness of strangers declines.

Of the negative emotions, we know the least about disgust. Preschool children may respond with disgust at the odor of feces or at being asked to touch a maggot or being asked to eat a piece of candy that's resting on the bottom of a brand-new potty seat (Widen & Russell, 2013). Parents likely play an important role in helping children to identify disgusting stimuli: Mothers respond quite vigorously to disgust-eliciting stimuli when in the presence of their children. They might say "That's revolting!" while moving away from the stimulus (Stevenson et al., 2010). This early sensitivity to disgust is useful because many of the cues that elicit disgust are also signals of potential harm: disgusting stimuli such as feces, vomit, and maggots can all transmit disease.

Emergence of Complex Emotions In addition to basic emotions such as happiness and anger, people feel complex emotions such as pride, shame, guilt, and embarrassment. **Sometimes known as the** *self-conscious emotions,* **they involve feelings of success when one's standards or expectations are met and feelings of failure when they aren't.** These emotions don't surface until 18 to 24 months of age, because they depend on the child having some understanding of the self, which typically occurs between 15 and 18 months. Children feel guilty, for

By 18 to 24 months, children start to experience complex emotions, including pride in accomplishing a difficult task.

QUESTION 10.1

Courtney often expresses her joy, anger, and fear, but has yet to show pride, guilt, or embarrassment. Based on this profile, how old do you think Courtney is?

example, when they've done something they know they shouldn't have done (Kochanska et al., 2002). A child who breaks a toy is thinking, "You told me to be careful. But I wasn't!" Children may show embarrassment at being asked to "perform" for grandparents by burying their face in their hands. However, children feel pride when they accomplish a challenging task for the first time. The toddler in the photo is probably thinking something like, "I've never done this before, but this time I did it—all by myself!" Thus, children's growing understanding of themselves (which I discuss in detail in Module 11.1) allows them to experience complex emotions such as pride and guilt (Lewis, 2000).

The features of basic and self-conscious emotions are listed in Summary Table 10-1.

Later Developments As children grow, their catalog of emotions continues to expand. For example, think about regret and relief, emotions that adults experience when they compare their actions with alternatives. Imagine that you're cramming for a test and decide that you have time to review your lecture notes but not reread the text. If the test questions turned out to be based largely on the lectures, you'll feel a sense of relief because your decision led to a positive outcome compared to "what might have been." If, instead, test questions cover only the text, you'll feel regret because your decision led to a terrible outcome; "If only I had reread the text!" In fact, some 5- and 6-year-olds experience regret and relief, and by 9 years of age, most children experience both emotions appropriately (Van Duijvenvoorde, Huizenga, & Jansen, 2014).

In addition to adding emotions to their repertoire, older children experience basic and complex emotions in response to different situations or events. In the case of complex emotions, cognitive growth means that elementary-school children experience shame and guilt in situations where they would not have when they were younger (Reimer, 1996). For example, unlike preschool children, many school-age children would be ashamed if they neglected to defend a classmate who had been wrongly accused of a theft.

Fear is another emotion that can be elicited in different ways, depending on a child's age. Many preschool children are afraid of the dark and of imaginary creatures. These fears typically diminish during the elementary-school years as children grow cognitively and better understand the difference between appearance and reality. Replacing these fears are concerns about school, health, and personal harm (Silverman, La Greca, & Wasserstein, 1995). Such worries are common and not cause for concern in most children. In some youngsters, however, they become so extreme that they overwhelm the child (Chorpita & Barlow, 1998). For example, a 7-year-old's worries about school would not be unusual unless her concern grew to the point that she refused to go to school. In the "Improving Children's Lives" feature, we'll look at this form of excessive fear and how it can be treated.

SUMMARY TABLE 10-1			
INFANTS' EXPRESSION OF EMOTIONS			
Type	**Defined**	**Emerge**	**Examples**
Basic	Experienced by people worldwide; include a subjective feeling, a physiological response, and an overt behavior	Birth to 9 months	Happiness, anger, fear
Self-conscious	Responses to meeting or failing to meet expectations or standards	18 to 24 months	Pride, guilt, embarrassment

Improving Children's Lives

"But I Don't Want to Go to School!"

Many youngsters plead, argue, and fight with their parents daily over going to school. For example, every school day, 9-year-old Keegan would cling to his mother and start to sob as soon as he finished his breakfast. When it was time to leave the house to catch the bus, he would drop to the floor and start kicking.

Understanding the reasons for such school refusal behavior is essential because, not surprisingly, refusing to go to school puts children on a path that leads to academic failure and leaves them with few options in the workplace. School refusal behavior sometimes reflects a child's desire to avoid school-related situations that are frightening (e.g., taking a test, speaking in front of a class, meeting new people). School refusal is sometimes an effort to get attention from parents, and sometimes reflects a child's desire to pursue enjoyable activities, such as playing video games, instead of aversive ones, such as doing schoolwork (Kearney, 2007).

Fortunately, school refusal behavior can be treated effectively, typically with a combination of behavioral and cognitive strategies. The former include gradual exposure to fear-provoking school situations, techniques for relaxing when confronting these situations, and reinforcement for attending school. The latter include providing children with strategies for coping with their anxiety and helping them reinterpret school situations (e.g., realize that teachers are *not* picking on them). In addition, parents can be trained to establish effective morning routines and reward school attendance (Kearney et al., 2011). Using these techniques, school refusal becomes much less common. In one meta-analysis (Pina et al., 2009), school attendance increased from 30% before treatment to 75% after. What's more, children's school-related fears were much reduced.

Cultural Differences in Emotional Expression Children worldwide express many of the same basic and complex emotions. However, cultures differ in the extent to which emotional expression is encouraged (Hess & Kirouac, 2000). In many Asian countries, for example, outward displays of emotion are discouraged in favor of emotional restraint. Consistent with these differences, in one study (Camras et al., 1998), European American 11-month-olds cried and smiled more often than Chinese 11-month-olds. In another study (Camras et al., 2006), U.S. preschoolers were more likely than Chinese preschoolers to smile at funny pictures and to express disgust after smelling a cotton swab dipped in vinegar.

Cultures also differ in the events that trigger emotions, particularly complex emotions. Situations that evoke pride in one culture may evoke embarrassment or shame in another. For example, U.S. elementary-school children often show pride at personal achievement, such as getting the highest grade on a test or, as shown in the photo on page 318, winning a spelling bee. In contrast, Asian elementary-school children are embarrassed by a public display of individual achievement but show great pride when their entire class is honored for an achievement (Furukawa, Tangney, & Higashibara, 2012; Lewis et al., 2010).

Children living in the United States, Canada, and Europe often express great pride at personal achievement.

Expression of anger also varies around the world. Imagine that one child has just completed a detailed drawing when a classmate spills a drink, ruining the drawing. Most U.S. children would respond with anger. In contrast, children growing up in east Asian countries that practice Buddhism (e.g., Mongolia, Thailand, Nepal) rarely respond with anger because this goes against the Buddhist tenet to extend loving kindness to all people, even those whose actions hurt others. Instead, they would probably remain quiet and experience shame that they had left the drawing in a vulnerable position (Cole, Tamang, & Shrestha, 2006).

Thus, culture can influence when and how much children express emotion. Of course, expressing emotion is only part of the developmental story. Children must also learn to recognize others' emotions, which is our next topic.

Recognizing and Using Others' Emotions

LO3 When do children begin to understand other people's emotions? How do they use this information to guide their own behavior?

Imagine that you are broke and plan to borrow $20 from your roommate when she returns from class. Shortly, she storms into your apartment, slams the door, and throws her backpack on the floor. You change your plans immediately, realizing that now is a bad time to ask for a loan. This example reminds us that, just as it is adaptive to be able to express emotions, it is adaptive to be able to recognize others' emotions and sometimes change our behavior as a consequence.

When can infants first identify emotions in others? Perhaps as early as 4 months, and definitely by 6 months, infants begin to distinguish facial expressions associated with different emotions. They can, for example, distinguish a happy, smiling face from a sad, frowning face (Bornstein & Arterberry, 2003; Montague & Walker-Andrews, 2001) and when they hear happy-sounding voices, they tend to look at happy faces, not ones that appear frustrated or angry (Vaillant-Molina, Bahrick, & Flom, 2013). What's more, like adults, infants are biased toward negative emotions (Vaish, Woodward, & Grossmann, 2008). They attend more rapidly to faces depicting negative emotions (e.g., anger) and pay attention to them longer than emotionless or happy faces (LoBue & DeLoache, 2010; Peltola et al., 2008).

Infants and young children are particularly attentive to potentially frightening stimuli (e.g., snakes, spiders), even when they've never been exposed to them previously and thus have no reason to fear them. But they quickly learn to fear such stimuli, perhaps because these skills evolve to help early humans detect and avoid threats in their environments (Leppänen & Nelson, 2012; LoBue, 2013).

Also like adults, infants use others' emotions to direct their behavior. **Infants in an unfamiliar or ambiguous environment often look at their mother or father, as if searching for cues to help them interpret the situation, a phenomenon known as** *social referencing*. If a parent looks afraid when shown a novel object, 12-month-olds are less likely to play with the new toy than if a parent looks happy (Repacholi, 1998). Infants' use of their parents' cues is precise. If two unfamiliar toys are shown to a parent, who expresses disgust at one toy but not the other, 12-month-olds will avoid the toy that elicited the disgust but not the other toy (Moses et al., 2001). And if 12-month-olds encounter an unfamiliar toy in a laboratory setting where one adult seems familiar with the toy but another adult does not, infants will look at the knowledgeable adult's expression to decide whether to play with the toy (Stenberg, 2012).

By 18 months, they're even more sophisticated: When one adult demonstrates an unfamiliar toy and a second adult comments, in an angry tone, "That's really annoying! That's so irritating!" 18-month-olds play less with the toy, compared to when the second adult makes neutral remarks in a mild manner. These youngsters apparently decided that it wasn't such a good idea to play with the toy if it might upset the second adult again (Repacholi & Meltzoff, 2007; Repacholi, Meltzoff, & Olsen, 2008). Thus, social referencing shows that infants are remarkably skilled in using other people's emotions to help them direct their own behavior.

Although infants and toddlers are adept at recognizing others' emotions, their skills are far from mature. Adults are much more skilled than infants—and school-aged children, for that matter—in recognizing the subtle signals of an emotion (Thomas et al., 2007), and adults are better able to tell when others are "faking" emotions; they can distinguish the face of a person who's really happy from the face of a person who's faking happiness (Del Giudice & Colle, 2007). Thus, facial expressions of emotion are recognized with steadily greater skill throughout childhood and into adolescence.

Understanding Emotions As their cognitive skills grow, children begin to understand why people feel as they do. By kindergarten, for example, children know that thinking about past unpleasant events can make a person feel sad (Lagattuta, 2014). Children even know that they more often feel sad when they think about the undesirable event itself (e.g., a broken toy or a friend who moves away) but feel angry when they think about the person who caused the undesirable event (e.g., the person who broke the toy or the friend's parents who wanted to live in another city). Kindergarten children also understand that a child who is feeling sad or angry may do less well on school tasks like spelling or math (Amsterlaw, Lagattuta, & Meltzoff, 2009) and that people worry when faced with the possibility that an unpleasant event may recur (Lagattuta, 2014).

During the elementary-school years, children begin to comprehend that people sometimes experience "mixed feelings." They understand that some situations may lead people to feel happy and sad at the same time (Larsen, To, & Fireman, 2007). The increased ability to see multiple, differing emotions coincides with the freedom from centered thinking that characterizes the concrete operational stage (Module 6.1).

As children develop, they also begin to learn *display rules*, **culturally specific standards for appropriate expressions of emotion in a particular setting or with a particular person or persons.** For example, adults know that expressing sadness is appropriate at funerals but expressing joy is not. Preschool children's understanding of display rules is shown by the fact that they control their anger more when provoked by peers they like than when provoked by peers they don't like (Fabes et al., 1996). Also, school-age children and adolescents are more willing to express anger than sadness and, like the child in the photo, more willing to express both anger and sadness to parents

As children develop, they learn their culture's rules for expressing emotions. For example, many children living in North America might cry in private or with parents, but would avoid crying in public, particularly when with their peers.

than to peers (Zeman & Garber, 1996; Zeman & Shipman, 1997). These display rules vary across culture: Compared with children growing up in Asian cultures, children living in Western cultures are encouraged to express their emotions more (Novin et al., 2011).

What experiences contribute to children's understanding of emotions? Parents and children frequently talk about past emotions and why people felt as they did; this is particularly true for negative emotions such as fear and anger (Lagattuta & Wellman, 2002). Not surprisingly, children learn about emotions by hearing parents talk about feelings, explaining how they differ and the situations that elicit them (Brown & Dunn, 1992; Kucirkova & Tompkins, 2014). Also, a positive, rewarding relationship with parents and siblings is related to children's understanding of emotions (Brown & Dunn, 1992; Thompson, Laible, & Ontai, 2003). The nature of this connection is still a mystery. One possibility is that within positive parent–child and sibling relationships, people express a fuller range of emotions (and do so more often) and are more willing to talk about why they feel as they do, providing children with more opportunities to learn about emotions.

Children's growing understanding of emotions in others contributes in turn to a growing ability to help others. They are more likely to recognize the emotions that signal a person's need. Better understanding of emotions in others also contributes to children's growing ability to play easily with peers because they can see the impact of their behavior on others. We'll cover empathy and social interaction in detail later in the book; for now, the important point is that recognizing emotions in others is an important prerequisite for successful, satisfying interactions. Another element of successful interactions is regulation of emotions, our next topic.

Regulating Emotions

LO4 When do children show evidence of regulating emotion, and why is this an important skill?

Think of a time when you were *really* angry at a good friend. Did you shout at the friend? Did you try to discuss matters calmly? Or did you ignore the situation altogether? Shouting is a direct expression of anger, but calm conversation and overlooking a situation are deliberate attempts to regulate emotion. People often regulate emotions; for example, we routinely try to suppress fear (because we know there's no real need to be afraid of the dark), anger (because we don't want to let a friend know just how upset we are), and joy (because we don't want to seem like we're gloating over our good fortune).

As these examples illustrate, regulating emotions skillfully depends on cognitive processes like those described in Chapters 6 through 9 (Zelazo & Cunningham, 2007). Attention is an important part of emotion regulation: We control emotions such as fear by diverting attention to other less emotional stimuli, thoughts, or feelings (Rothbart & Sheese, 2007). We also use strategies to reappraise the meaning of an event (or of feelings or thoughts), so that it provokes less emotion (John & Gross, 2007). For example, a soccer player nervous about taking a penalty kick can reinterpret her state of physiological arousal as being "pumped up" instead of being "scared to death."

Because cognitive processes are essential for emotional regulation, the research described in Chapters 6 through 9 leads us to expect that successful regulation develops gradually through childhood and adolescence and that at any age some children will be more skilled than others at regulating emotions

(Thompson, Lewis, & Calkins, 2008). In fact, both patterns are evident in research. Emotion regulation clearly begins in infancy. By 4 to 6 months, infants use simple strategies to regulate their emotions (Buss & Goldsmith, 1998; Rothbart & Rueda, 2005). When something frightens or confuses an infant—for example, a stranger or a mother who suddenly stops responding—he or she often looks away (just as older children and even adults often turn away or close their eyes to block out disturbing stimuli). Frightened infants also move closer to a parent, another effective way of helping to control their fear (Parritz, 1996). Of course, because infants and toddlers have limited ability to regulate their emotions, parents and other caregivers often help: as we saw in Module 3.4, holding, rocking, and talking softly are effective in soothing an infant who's upset (Jahromi, Putnam, & Stifter, 2004).

As children develop, they regulate their own emotions and rely less on others. For example, if preschool children are asked to wait to open a present until their mother finishes a task, they may entertain themselves (e.g., making faces in a mirror) to control their frustration at having to wait (Roben, Cole, & Armstrong, 2013). School-age children and adolescents are even more skilled at regulating emotions, in part because they can rely on cognitive strategies. For example, a child might reduce his disappointment at not receiving a much-anticipated and hoped-for gift by telling himself that he didn't really want the gift in the first place. And older children and adolescents become skilled at matching the strategies for regulating emotion to the particular setting (Zimmer-Gembeck & Skinner, 2011). For example, when faced with emotional situations that are unavoidable, such as going to the dentist to have a cavity filled, children adjust to the situation (e.g., by thinking of the positive consequences of treating the tooth) instead of trying to avoid it.

Some children regulate their emotions better than others, and those who don't tend to have problems interacting with peers and have adjustment problems (Olson et al., 2011; Zalewski et al., 2011). When children can't control their anger, worry, or sadness, they often have difficulty resolving the conflicts that inevitably surface in peer relationships (Fabes et al., 1999). For example, when children argue over which game to play or which movie to watch, their unregulated anger can interfere with finding a mutually satisfying solution. Thus, ineffective regulation of emotions leads to more frequent conflicts with peers, and, consequently, less satisfying peer relationships and less adaptive adjustment to school (Eisenberg et al., 2001; Olson et al., 2005).

In this module, we've seen how children express, recognize, and regulate emotions; in the next module, we'll discover that emotion is an important feature of children's temperament.

 ## Check Your Learning

RECALL Describe biological and cultural contributions to children's expression of emotion.

How do infants and children regulate their emotions? What are the consequences when children can't regulate their emotions well?

INTERPRET Distinguish basic emotions from self-conscious emotions.

APPLY Cite similarities between developmental change in infants' expression and regulation of emotion and developmental change in infants' comprehension and expression of speech (described in Module 9.1).

10.2 Temperament

OUTLINE

What Is Temperament?

Hereditary and Environmental Contributions to Temperament

Stability of Temperament

Temperament and Other Aspects of Development

LEARNING OBJECTIVES

LO5   What are the different features of temperament?

LO6   How do heredity and environment influence temperament?

LO7   How stable is a child's temperament across development?

LO8   What are the consequences of different temperaments?

Soon after Yoshimi arrived in the United States from Japan to begin graduate studies, she enrolled her 5-month-old son in day care. She was struck by the fact that, compared to her son, the European American babies in the day-care center were "wimps" (slang she had learned from U.S. television). The other babies cried often and with minimal provocation. Yoshimi wondered whether her son was unusually "tough" or whether he was just a typical Japanese baby.

When you've observed young babies—perhaps as part of "See for Yourself" in Chapter 3—were some babies like Yoshimi's, quiet most of the time, while others cried often and impatiently? Maybe you saw some infants who responded warmly to strangers and others who seemed shy. **Such behavioral styles, which are fairly stable across situations and are biologically based, make up an infant's** *temperament.* For example, all babies become upset occasionally and cry. However, some, like Yoshimi's son, recover quickly, but others are hard to console. These differences in emotion and style of behavior are evident in the first few weeks after birth and are important throughout life.

We'll begin this module by looking at different ways that scientists define temperament.

What Is Temperament?

LO5   What are the different features of temperament?

Alexander Thomas and Stella Chess (Thomas, Chess, & Birch, 1968; Thomas & Chess, 1977) pioneered the study of temperament with the New York Longitudinal Study, which traced the lives of 141 individuals from infancy through adulthood. Thomas and Chess interviewed parents about their babies and had individuals unfamiliar with the children observe them at home. From these interviews and observations, Thomas and Chess suggested that infants' behavior varies along nine temperamental dimensions. One dimension was *activity*, which referred to an infant's typical level of motor activity. A second was *persistence*, which referred to the amount of time that an infant devoted to an activity, particularly when obstacles were present.

Using all nine dimensions, Thomas and Chess identified three patterns of temperament. Most common were "easy" babies, who were usually happy and cheerful, tended to adjust well to new situations, and had regular routines for eating, sleeping, and toileting. A second, less common group included "difficult" babies, who tended to be unhappy, were irregular in their eating and sleeping, and often responded intensely to unfamiliar situations. Another less common

QUESTION 10.2

Ten-month-old Nina is usually cheerful, enjoys going on outings with her dad, and sleeps soundly every night. How would Thomas and Chess describe Nina's temperament?

group was made up of "slow-to-warm-up" babies. Like difficult babies, slow-to-warm-up babies were often unhappy; but unlike difficult babies, slow-to-warm-up babies were not upset by unfamiliar situations.

The New York Longitudinal Study launched research on infant temperament, but today's researchers no longer emphasize creating different categories of infants, such as easy or slow to warm up. Instead, researchers want to determine the different dimensions that underlie temperament. One modern approach to temperament is described in the "Spotlight on Theories" feature.

Spotlight on Theories
A Theory of the Structure of Temperament in Infancy

BACKGROUND Most scientists agree that *temperament* refers to biologically based differences in infants' and children's emotional reactivity and emotional self-regulation. However, scientists disagree on the number and nature of the dimensions that make up temperament.

THE THEORY Mary K. Rothbart (2011) has devised a theory of temperament that includes three different dimensions:

- *Surgency/extraversion* **refers to the extent to which a child is generally happy, active, vocal, and regularly seeks interesting stimulation.**

- *Negative affect* **refers to the extent to which a child is angry, fearful, frustrated, shy, and not easily soothed.**

- *Effortful control* **refers to the extent to which a child can focus attention, is not readily distracted, and can inhibit responses.**

These dimensions of temperament are evident in infancy, continue into childhood, and are related to dimensions of personality that are found in adolescence and adulthood. However, the dimensions are not independent: Infants who are high on effortful control tend to be high on surgency/extraversion and low on negative affect. In other words, babies who can control their attention and inhibit responses tend to be happy and active but not angry or fearful.

Hypothesis: If temperament is biologically based and includes the three dimensions of Rothbart's theory, then those dimensions of temperament should be observed in children around the world. That is, cross-cultural studies of temperament should consistently reveal the dimensions of surgency/extraversion, negative affect, and effortful control.

Test: Many scientists have examined the structure of temperament in young children growing up in different countries around the world. In most of the studies, parents of young children completed questionnaires measuring their children's temperament. For example, the Infant Behavior Questionnaire (IBQ-R) assesses different dimensions of Rothbart's theory of temperament. The items "When given a new toy, how often did the baby get very excited about getting it?" and "When put into the bath water, how often did the baby splash or kick?" both measure the surgency/extraversion dimension; "When frustrated with something, how often did the baby calm down within 5 minutes?" measures the negative-affect dimension. For each item, parents rated how often the behavior had been observed in the past 7 days, using a scale that ranged from "never" to "always."

Parents' responses are evaluated with factor analysis (described on page 252 in Module 8.1), a method that looks for patterns in parents' responses. To illustrate, the surgency/extraversion dimension would be supported if parents who judged that their infants were always excited about a new toy also said that their babies always splashed or kicked during a bath (because both items are thought to measure surgency/extraversion). In fact, factor analyses revealed that three temperamental dimensions—surgency/extraversion, negative affect, and effortful control—are evident in responses of parents from Belgium, China, Japan, the Netherlands, and the United States (Casalin et al., 2012; Sleddens et al., 2011). That is, the three basic dimensions of temperament emerge when parents worldwide describe their children.

Conclusion: As predicted, the structure of temperament was the same in many cultures. This supports Rothbart's claim that the dimensions of her theory of temperament are biologically rooted and, consequently, should be evident regardless of the specific environment or culture in which a child develops.

Application: An important theme of temperament research is that children's development proceeds best when their temperament fits well with the environment in which they grow up. That is, because temperament is rooted in biological factors, parents should accept their baby's unique temperamental characteristics and adjust their parenting accordingly. For example, babies who are quiet and shy clearly benefit when parents actively stimulate them (e.g., by describing and explaining). But these same activities are actually counterproductive with active, outgoing babies who would rather explore the world on their own (Miceli et al., 1998). Thus, Rothbart's theory, and other research on temperament, reminds us that parent–child interactions represent a two-way street in which interactions are most successful when both parties—child and parent—adjust to the needs of the other.

The hereditary contribution to temperament is shown by the fact that twins are typically similar in their level of activity.

Hereditary and Environmental Contributions to Temperament

LO6 How do heredity and environment influence temperament?

Temperament is rooted in biology, so it's not surprising that children's temperament reflects their heredity (Saudino & Wang, 2012). For example, in twin studies, identical twins are more alike in most aspects of temperament than fraternal twins. In other words, like the youngsters in the photo, if one identical twin is temperamentally active, the other usually is, too (Saudino, 2012). The impact of heredity increases with age: temperament in childhood is more influenced by heredity than is temperament in infancy (Wachs & Bates, 2001). Temperament has been linked to specific genes associated with neurotransmitters, although the findings are inconsistent (Davies et al., 2013; Saudino & Wang, 2012).

The environment also contributes to children's temperament, in at least three different ways. First, temperament can be affected directly by parents' behavior. For example, infants are less emotional when parents are responsive

(Hane & Fox, 2006; Leerkes, Blankson, & O'Brien, 2009). Second, the environment can amplify the genetic effects of temperament through the mechanisms described in Module 2.2: For example, infants with high levels of negative affect are more likely to elicit harsh parenting (Saudino & Wang, 2012).

Finally, temperament may make some children particularly susceptible to environmental influences—either beneficial or harmful (van IJzendoorn & Bakermans-Kranenburg, 2012). Several studies have focused on the DRD4 gene, which is linked to brain systems that regulate attention, motivation and reward, and novelty-seeking in adults. Children with a specific variant of the DRD4 gene are particularly susceptible to the quality of the environment: they are more likely to benefit from positive environments such as high-quality day care and more likely to be harmed by negative environments such as prenatal stress (Bakermans-Kranenburg & van IJzendoorn, 2011; Belsky & Pluess, 2013; Zohsel et al., 2014).

DRD4 is *not* a temperament gene, but it is linked to behaviors that make up temperament (e.g., novelty-seeking, fearlessness). Consequently, these findings suggest that temperament may make some children particularly sensitive to environmental influences. It's as if some children are sailboats with small rudders so that wind—representing environmental influence—can easily change their developmental course; other children have temperamentally larger rudders and are less affected by these environmental winds.

Heredity and experience may also explain why Yoshimi, the Japanese mother in the vignette, has such a hardy son. The "Cultural Influences" feature tells the story.

Cultural Influences

Why Is Yoshimi's Son So Tough?

If you've ever watched an infant getting an injection, you know the inevitable response. After the syringe is removed, the infant's eyes open wide and then the baby begins to cry, as if saying, "Wow, that hurt!" Infants differ in how intensely they cry and in how readily they are soothed, reflecting differences in the emotionality dimension of temperament, but virtually all European American babies cry.

It's easy to suppose that crying is a universal response to the pain from the inoculation, but it's not. In such stressful situations, compared with European American infants, Japanese and Chinese infants resemble Yoshimi's son: They are less likely to become upset and they are soothed more readily (Kagan et al., 1994; Lewis, Ramsay, & Kawakami, 1993). What's more, Japanese and Chinese babies smile and laugh less often and are more inhibited (Chen, Wang, & DeSouza, 2006; Gartstein et al., 2010).

Why are Asian infants less emotional than their European American counterparts? Heredity may be involved, but we can't overlook experience. Compared to European American mothers, Japanese mothers spend more time in close physical contact with their babies, constantly and gently soothing them; this may reduce the tendency to respond emotionally.

Temperament is moderately stable throughout infancy. For example, babies who as newborns cry when they experience stress tend, as 5-month-olds, to cry when they experience stress from being restrained.

Stability of Temperament

LO7   How stable is a child's temperament across development?

Do calm, easygoing babies grow up to be calm, easygoing children, adolescents, and adults? Are difficult, irritable infants destined to grow up to be cranky, whiny children? In fact, temperament is somewhat stable throughout infancy but becomes more stable in the preschool years (Shiner & Caspi, 2012). For example, when inhibited toddlers are adults, they respond more strongly to unfamiliar stimuli (Schwartz et al., 2003). Thus Sam, an inhibited 3-year-old, is more likely to be shy as a 12-year-old than Dave, an outgoing 3-year-old. However, it's not necessarily Sam's destiny to be shy as a 12-year-old. Instead, some youngsters are naturally predisposed to be sociable, emotional, or active; others *can* act in these ways, too, but only if the behaviors are nurtured by parents and others.

In many respects, temperament resembles personality, so it's not surprising that many child-development researchers have speculated about potential connections between the two. One view suggests both direct and indirect links between temperament and personality (Shiner & Caspi, 2012). The direct link is that temperamental dimensions provide a well-defined path to personality traits. For example, extroversion is a personality trait that refers to a person's warmth, gregariousness, and activity level. Extroverted individuals tend to be affectionate, prefer the company of others, and like being active; introverted people tend to be more reserved, enjoy solitude, and prefer a more sedate pace (Costa & McRae, 2001). Extroversion looks like a blend of the temperamental dimensions of positive affect and activity level, and inhibited children are more likely as adults to be introverted than extroverted (Caspi et al., 2005).

The indirect link is that a child's temperament helps to shape environmental influences and these experiences can determine the course of personality development (Shiner & Caspi, 2012). Outgoing Dave may befriend children who are outgoing like himself; experiences with these children will encourage his dispositional tendency to be gregarious and lead him to be extroverted as an adolescent and adult.

In the next section, we'll see that temperament is linked to other aspects of development, not just personality.

Temperament and Other Aspects of Development

LO8   What are the consequences of different temperaments?

In their New York Longitudinal Study, Thomas and Chess discovered that about two-thirds of the preschoolers with difficult temperaments had developed behavioral problems by the time they entered school. In contrast, fewer than one-fifth of the children with easy temperaments had behavioral problems (Thomas et al., 1968). Later studies have documented this link between a difficult temperament—youngsters who anger easily and have relatively little control—and later behavior problems, both in the United States and China (Gartstein, Putnam, & Rothbart, 2012; Zhou, Lengua, & Wang, 2009). However, difficult temperament does not necessarily lead to adjustment problems: Children with difficult temperaments can fare well when parents are warm, supportive, and respect their children's autonomy (Stright, Gallagher, & Kelley, 2008).

Other scientists have followed the lead of the New York Longitudinal Study in looking for links between temperament and outcomes of development, and they've found that temperament is an important influence on development. Consider these examples:

- Persistent children are likely to succeed in school, whereas active and distractible children are less likely to succeed (Eisenberg et al., 2014; Martin, Olejnik, & Gaddis, 1994).
- Shy, inhibited children often have difficulty interacting with their peers, often do not cope effectively with problems, and are less likely to help a stranger in distress (Eisenberg et al., 1998; Young et al., 1999).
- Anxious, fearful children are more likely to comply with a parent's rules and requests, even when the parent is not present (Kochanska et al., 2007).
- Children who are frequently angry or fearful are more prone to depression (Lengua, 2006).
- Children who are uninhibited and lack self-regulation are prone to alcohol-, drug-, and gambling-related problems as adults (Slutske et al., 2012; Zucker, Heitzeg, & Nigg, 2011).

The "Focus on Research" feature shows that temperament in childhood is also related to an array of outcomes in adolescence and adulthood.

Focus on Research

Temperament Influences Outcomes in Adolescence and Adulthood

Who were the investigators, and what was the aim of the study? Many studies show that when children regulate their emotions and behavior ineffectively, they often encounter developmental problems. However, much of the research consists of cross-sectional studies or longitudinal studies that cover just a few years. And much of the work focuses on a single problem area. Terrie Moffitt and her colleagues (2011) hoped to determine whether self-regulation in childhood was related to a range of important developmental outcomes in adolescence and adulthood.

How did the investigators measure the topic of interest? The research was based on data obtained as part of the Dunedin Multidisciplinary Health and Development Study, which has traced the lives of more than 1,000 children born in New Zealand. Between 3 and 11 years of age, self-regulation was assessed from ratings provided by parents, teachers, trained observers, and the children themselves. For example, everyone rated whether the child had difficulty completing tasks. The researchers also measured children's IQ and their family's socioeconomic status.

As adolescents, participants were asked if they smoked, had dropped out of school, or had become parents. As adults, participants had a physical exam and were interviewed about their mental health and substance use. Also, their criminal activity was determined from a computer search of court records.

Who were the children in the study? The Dunedin study began with 1,037 infants and most have been tested repeatedly through their adult years. (The study is ongoing and the participants are now in their early 40s.)

What was the design of the study? This study was correlational because Moffitt and her colleagues were interested in the relation that existed naturally between self-regulation during childhood and outcomes in adolescence and adulthood. The study was longitudinal because participants have been tested throughout childhood, adolescence, and adulthood.

Were there ethical concerns with the study? No. The measures are straightforward and without obvious risk. When participants were children, their parents provided consent; as adults, they provided their own consent.

What were the results? The graph in Figure 10-1 shows links between self-regulation in childhood and outcomes in adolescence and adulthood. The findings are expressed as the relative likelihood of an outcome for children who are skilled and less skilled in their self-regulation (defined as being at the 70th and 30th percentile of self-regulation, respectively). If children skilled and less skilled in self-regulation were equally likely to have risky outcomes, the ratio would be 1.0. However, in each

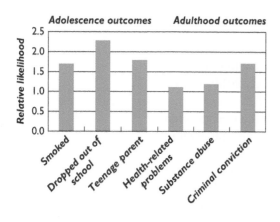

Figure 10-1

case the ratio is greater than 1, indicating that the outcomes were more likely for children who were less skilled in self-regulation. To take an extreme example, children less skilled in self-regulation were more than twice as likely to drop out of school. Similarly, they were more likely to smoke and more likely to be parents; as adults, they were more likely to have health-related problems, to have problems with substance abuse, and to be convicted of a crime.

What did the investigators conclude? When children are temperamentally unable to regulate their emotions and behavior skillfully, they are at risk for developmental paths that lead to an array of undesirable outcomes. Moffitt et al. (2011) write, "our findings imply that innovative policies that put self-control center stage might reduce...costs that now heavily burden citizens and governments" (p. 2697).

What converging evidence would strengthen these conclusions? In many ways the Dunedin study is a model of best practices in developmental science. Of course, one problem that plagues any longitudinal study is the possibility of cohort effects—the results may be specific to this particular cohort of people born in New Zealand in the early 1970s and not apply more generally. For example, as the participants entered young adulthood, New Zealand experienced a severe recession, an event that meant few jobs were available at a time when participants were eager to join the workforce. Might that unique experience affect the study's findings? The only way to know for sure is to conduct other longitudinal work in which young adults don't experience an economic recession.

Although these findings underscore that temperament is an important force in children's development, temperament rarely is the sole determining factor. Instead, the influence of temperament often depends on the environment in which children develop. To illustrate, let's consider the link between temperament and behavior problems. Infants and toddlers who temperamentally resist control—those who are difficult to manage, who are often unresponsive, and who are sometimes impulsive—tend to be prone to behavior problems, particularly aggression, when they are older. However, more careful analysis shows that resistant temperament leads to behavior problems primarily when mothers do not exert much control over their children. Among mothers who do exert control—those who prohibit, warn, and scold their children when necessary—resistant temperament is not linked to behavior problems (Bates et al., 1998).

Similarly, young adolescents are more likely to drink, smoke, and use drugs when they experience many life stressors (e.g., when someone in the family has a serious accident or illness, when a parent loses a job, or when parents and the child are frequently in conflict), and their parents themselves smoke and drink. But this is less true for young adolescents with temperaments marked by positive affect (Wills et al., 2001). That is, young adolescents who are temperamentally cheerful are less affected by life stressors, apparently because they see the world through rose-colored glasses and thus don't see the stressors as that threatening. Consequently, are less likely to turn to drink, tobacco products, or drugs.

This research reminds us that emotion is a fundamental element of temperament. In the next module, we'll look at emotion from yet another perspective, that of the emotional relationship formed between an infant and its primary caregiver.

Check Your Learning

RECALL How is temperament influenced by heredity and environment?

Summarize the influence of temperament on other aspects of development.

INTERPRET Compare and contrast the Thomas and Chess approach to temperament with Rothbart's theory of temperament.

APPLY Based on what you know about the stability of temperament, what would you say to a parent who's worried that her 15-month-old seems shy and inhibited?

 # Attachment

LEARNING OBJECTIVES

LO9 How does an attachment relationship develop between an infant and the primary caregiver?

LO10 What different types of attachment relationships are there? What are the consequences of different types of relationships?

OUTLINE

The Growth of Attachment

The Quality of Attachment

Ever since Samantha was a newborn, Karen and Dick looked forward to going to their favorite restaurant on Friday night. Karen enjoyed the break from child-care responsibilities and Dick liked being able to talk to Karen without interruptions. But recently they've had a problem. When they leave 8-month-old Samantha with a sitter, she gets a frightened look on her face and usually begins to cry hysterically. Karen and Dick wonder if Samantha's behavior is normal and if their Friday-night dinners are coming to an end.

The social-emotional relationship that develops between an infant and a parent (usually, but not necessarily, the mother) is special. This is a baby's first social-emotional relationship, so scientists and parents alike believe that it should be satisfying and trouble-free to set the stage for later relationships. In this module, we'll look at the steps involved in creating the baby's first emotional relationship. Along the way, we'll see why 8-month-old Samantha has begun to cry when Karen and Dick leave her with a sitter.

The Growth of Attachment

LO9 How does an attachment relationship development between an infant and the primary caregiver?

Today's parents are encouraged to shower their babies with hugs and kisses; the more affection young children receive, the better! This advice may seem obvious, but actually it's a relatively recent recommendation, dating from the middle of the 20th century. It emerged, in part, from observations of European children whose parents were killed during World War II. Despite being well fed and receiving necessary health care, the children's development was far from normal: their mental development was slow and they often seemed withdrawn and listless (Bowlby, 1953; Spitz, 1965). Some scientists claimed that these problems came about because the children lived in institutions (e.g., orphanages and refugee camps) where they could not form a close social-emotional bond with adults.

Soon after, studies of monkeys that were reared in isolation confirmed this idea. Although the monkeys received excellent physical care, they stayed huddled in a corner of their cages, clutching themselves, and rocking constantly; when placed with other monkeys, they avoided the others as much as they could (Harlow & Harlow, 1965). Clearly, without regular social interactions with caring adults, normal development is thrown way off course.

In explaining the essential ingredients of these early social relationships, most modern accounts take an evolutionary perspective. **According to *evolutionary psychology*, many human behaviors represent successful adaptation to the environment.** That is, over human history, some behaviors have made it more likely that people will reproduce and pass on their genes to following generations. For example, we take it for granted that most people enjoy being with other people. But evolutionary psychologists argue that our "social nature" is a product of evolution: For early humans, being in a group offered protection from predators and made it easier to locate food. Thus, early humans who were social were more likely than their asocial peers to live long enough to reproduce, passing on their social orientation to their offspring (Gaulin & McBurney, 2001). Over many, many generations, "being social" had such a survival advantage that nearly all people are socially oriented (though in varying amounts, as we know from research on temperament in Module 10.2).

Applied to child development, evolutionary psychology highlights the adaptive value of children's behavior at different points in development (Bjorklund & Jordan, 2013). For example, think about the time and energy that parents invest in child rearing. Without such effort, infants and young children would die before they were sexually mature, which means that a parent's genes could not be passed along to grandchildren (Geary, 2002). Here, too, although parenting just seems "natural," it really represents an adaptation to the problem of guaranteeing that one's helpless offspring can survive until they're sexually mature.

An evolutionary perspective of early human relationships comes from John Bowlby (1969, 1991). **According to Bowlby, children who form an *attachment*—that is, an enduring social-emotional relationship to an adult—are more likely to survive.** This person is usually the mother but need not be; the key is a strong emotional relationship with a responsive, caring person. Attachments can form with fathers, grandparents, or someone else. Bowlby described four phases in the growth of attachment:

- *Preattachment* (birth to 6–8 weeks). During prenatal development and soon after birth, infants rapidly learn to recognize their mothers by smell and sound, which sets the stage for forging an attachment relationship (Hofer, 2006). What's more, evolution has endowed infants with many behaviors that elicit caregiving from an adult. When babies cry, smile, or gaze intently at a parent's face, parents usually smile back or hold the baby. The infant's behaviors and the responses they evoke in adults create an interactive system that is the first step in the formation of attachment relationships.
- *Attachment in the making* (6–8 weeks to 6–8 months). During these months, babies begin to behave differently in the presence of familiar caregivers and unfamiliar adults. Babies now smile and laugh more often with the primary caregiver; when babies are upset, they're more easily consoled by the primary caregiver. Babies are gradually identifying the primary caregiver as the person they can depend on when they're anxious or distressed.
- *True attachment* (6–8 months to 18 months). By approximately 7 or 8 months, most infants have singled out the attachment figure—usually the mother—as a special individual. The attachment figure is now the

infant's stable social emotional base. For example, a 7-month-old like the one in the photo will explore a novel environment but periodically look toward his mother, as if seeking reassurance that all is well. The behavior suggests that the infant trusts his mother and indicates that the attachment relationship has been established. In addition, this behavior reflects important cognitive growth: It means that the infant has a mental representation of the mother, an understanding that she will be there to meet the infant's needs (Lewis, 1997). This is why infants like 8-month-old Samantha from the vignette are distressed when they're separated from the attachment figure: they've lost their secure base.

When an infant has formed an attachment with a caregiver, that person becomes a secure, stable emotional base for the infant.

- *Reciprocal relationships* (18 months on). Infants' growing cognitive and language skills and their accumulated experience with their primary caregiver make infants better able to act as true partners in the attachment relationship. They often take the initiative in interactions and negotiate with parents ("Please read me another story!"). They begin to understand parents' feelings and goals and sometimes use this knowledge to guide their own behavior (e.g., social referencing, described on page 318). And they cope with separation more effectively because they can anticipate that parents will return.

The Role of Fathers Attachment typically first develops between infants and their mothers because mothers are usually the primary caregivers of U.S. infants. Babies soon become attached to fathers, too, even though fathers in developed nations spend less time in caregiving tasks (e.g., feeding or bathing a child) than mothers do (Lamb & Lewis, 2010). Instead, fathers spend more time playing with their babies than taking care of them—and even their style of play differs. Physical play like that shown in the photo is the norm for fathers, whereas mothers spend more time reading and talking to babies, showing them toys, and playing games like patty-cake. Infants often prefer to play with fathers but rely on mothers when they are distressed (Field, 1990). However, these differences between mothers' and fathers' behaviors have become smaller as men and women have come to share responsibilities for child care and breadwinning (Lamb & Lewis, 2010).

The Quality of Attachment

LO10 What different types of attachment relationships are there? What are the consequences of different types of relationships?

Attachment between infant and mother usually occurs by 8 or 9 months of age, but the attachment can take on different forms. Mary Ainsworth (1978, 1993) pioneered the study of attachment relationships using a procedure that has come to be known as the Strange Situation. You can see in Figure 10-2 on page 332 that the Strange Situation involves a series of episodes, each about 3 minutes long. The mother and infant enter an unfamiliar room filled with interesting toys. The mother leaves briefly, then mother and baby are reunited. Meanwhile, the experimenter observes the baby, recording its response to separation and reunion.

Fathers spend much of their time with babies playing with them (instead of taking care of them) and tend to play with them more vigorously and physically than mothers do.

Steps in the Strange Situation

experimenter

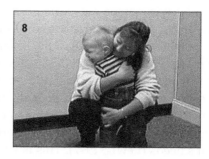

mother

1. Observer shows the experimental room to mother and infant, then leaves the room.

2. Infant is allowed to explore the playroom for 3 minutes; mother watches but does not participate.

3. A stranger enters the room and remains silent for 1 minute, then talks to the baby for a minute, and then approaches the baby. Mother leaves unobtrusively.

4. The stranger does not play with the baby but attempts to comfort it if necessary.

5. After 3 minutes, the mother returns, greets, and consoles the baby.

6. When the baby has returned to play, the mother leaves again, this time saying "bye-bye" as she leaves.

7. Stranger attempts to calm and play with the baby.

8. After 3 minutes, the mother returns and the stranger leaves.

Figure 10-2

Based on how the infant reacts, researchers identify four different types of attachment relationships (Ainsworth, 1993; Thompson, 2006). One is a secure attachment and three are insecure attachments (avoidant, resistant, disorganized):

- *Secure attachment*: **The baby may or may not cry when the mother leaves, but when she returns, the baby wants to be with her and if the baby is crying, it stops.** Babies in this group seem to be saying, "I missed you terribly, but now that you're back, I'm okay." Approximately 60 to 65% of U.S. babies have secure attachment relationships.

- *Avoidant attachment*: **The baby is not visibly upset when the mother leaves and, when she returns, may ignore her by looking or turning away.** Infants with an avoidant attachment look as if they're saying, "You left me again. I always have to take care of myself!" About 20% of U.S. infants have avoidant attachment relationships, which is one of the three forms of insecure attachment.

- *Resistant attachment*: **The baby is upset when the mother leaves and remains upset or even angry when she returns and is difficult to console.** Like the baby in the photo, these babies seem to be telling the mother, "Why do you do this? I need you desperately and yet you leave me without warning. I get so angry when you're like this." About 10 to 15% of U.S. babies have this resistant attachment relationship, which is another form of insecure attachment.

- *Disorganized (disoriented) attachment*: **The baby seems confused when the mother leaves and, when she returns, seems not to understand what's happening.** The baby often has a dazed look on its face, as if wondering, "What's going on here? I want you to be here, but you left and now you're back. I don't know whether to laugh or cry!" About 5 to 10% of U.S. babies have this disorganized attachment relationship, the last of the three kinds of insecure attachment.

The Strange Situation has long been the gold standard for studying attachment, but investigators use other methods to complement the Strange Situation. One of them, the Attachment Q-Set, can be used with young children as well as infants and toddlers. In this method, trained observers watch mothers and children interact at home; then the observer rates the interaction on many attachment-related behaviors (e.g., "Child greets mother with a big smile when she enters the room"). The ratings are totaled to measure the security of the child's attachment. Scores obtained with the Q-Set converge with assessments derived from the Strange Situation (van IJzendoorn et al., 2004).

An infant with a resistant attachment is upset or angry with the mother when reunited following a separation from her.

Patterns of Attachment Worldwide Worldwide, secure attachment is the most common form: In most countries, roughly 55 to 70% of infants are classified as being securely attached. However, the percentage of infants in the different categories of insecure attachment differs substantially across cultures (van IJzendoorn, & Sagi-Schwartz, 2008; van IJzendoorn, Schuengel, & Bakermans-Kranenburg, 1999). For example, in Japan, resistant attachment (in which the infant wants to be picked up at reunion but squirms as if to avoid the mother's hugs) is much more common than avoidant attachment (in which the infant does not wish to be picked up at all following reunion). The reverse pattern has been found in Germany (Sagi et al., 1995).

These differences may reflect cultural variations in the impact of parents' expectations about infant behavior on infants' responses in the Strange Situation. German parents, for example, are more likely to encourage independence, which may explain why avoidant attachment is more common in German infants. In contrast, Japanese parents see the mother–child relationship as particularly interdependent, and Japanese mothers spend much time holding their infants closely (Rothbaum et al., 2000). This may explain why Japanese infants rarely avoid their mothers during reunion after separation.

These cultural variations in frequency of different types of insecure attachment should not overshadow the substantial cultural consistency in the prevalence of secure attachment. Evolutionary psychologists would argue that this prevalence must mean that secure attachment is adaptive relative to the other forms. In the next section, we'll see that this is true.

Consequences of Quality of Attachment Erikson, Bowlby, and other theorists (Waters & Cummings, 2000) believe that attachment, as the first social relationship, is the basis for all of an infant's later social relationships. In this view, infants who experience the trust and compassion of a secure attachment should develop into preschool children who interact confidently and successfully with their peers. In contrast, infants who do not experience a successful, satisfying first relationship should be more prone to problems in their social interactions as preschoolers.

In fact, children with secure attachment relationships have higher-quality friendships and fewer conflicts in their friendships than children with insecure attachment relationships (McElwain, Booth-LaForce, & Wu, 2011). What's more, secure attachment in infancy is associated with higher-quality romantic relationships in adolescence and young adulthood (Collins, Welsh, & Furman, 2009; Englund et al., 2011). Finally, research consistently links insecure attachment to behavior problems involving anxiety, anger, and aggressive behavior (Kerns & Brumariu, 2014; Madigan et al., 2013).

The conclusion seems inescapable: As they grow, infants who have secure attachment relationships tend to have satisfying social interactions, but infants with disorganized attachment do not. Why? One explanation focuses on the lasting impact of this first social relationship. Secure attachment evidently leads infants to see the world positively and to trust other humans, characteristics that lead to more skilled social interactions later in childhood, adolescence, and adulthood (Dykas & Cassidy, 2011). Another view does not discount the impact of this early relationship, but adds another wrinkle: Theorists who emphasize continuity of caregiving argue that parents who establish secure attachments with infants tend to provide warm, supportive, and skilled parenting throughout their child's development (McElwain et al., 2011; Thompson, 2006). Thus, it is continuous exposure to high-quality parenting that promotes secure attachment in infancy and positive social relationships in childhood and adolescence. These accounts are *not* mutually exclusive: A successful first relationship and continued warm parenting likely work together to foster children's development.

Factors Determining Quality of Attachment   Because secure attachment is so important to a child's later development, researchers have tried to identify the factors involved. Undoubtedly the most important is the interaction between parents and their babies. A secure attachment is most likely when parents respond to infants predictably and appropriately (De Wolff & van IJzendoorn, 1997; Tomlinson, Cooper, & Murray, 2005). For example, the mother in the photo recognized that her baby was upset, responded promptly, and is soothing her baby. The mother's behavior evidently conveys that social interactions are predictable and satisfying, and apparently this behavior instills in infants the trust and confidence that are the hallmark of secure attachment.

Why does predictable and responsive parenting promote secure attachment relationships? To answer this question, think about your own friendships and romantic relationships. These relationships are usually most satisfying when we can trust the other people and depend on them in times of need. The same formula seems to hold for infants. **Infants develop an *internal working model*, a set of expectations about parents' availability and responsiveness, both generally and in times of stress.** When parents are dependable and caring, babies come to trust them, knowing they can be relied on for comfort. That is, babies develop an internal working model in which they believe their parents are concerned about their needs and will try to meet those needs (Huth-Bocks et al., 2004; Thompson, 2000).

In a particularly clever demonstration of infants' working models of attachment (Johnson et al., 2010), infants were shown animated videos depicting a large ellipse (mother) paired with a small ellipse (child). The video began with the mother and child ellipses together, then the mother moved away from the child, who began to cry. On some trials, the mother ellipse returned to the child ellipse; on other trials, she continued to move away. Securely attached infants looked longer at the trials depicting an unresponsive mother but insecurely attached infants looked longer at the trials when the mother returned. Evidently, each group has a

A key ingredient in creating a secure mother–infant attachment is for the mother to respond appropriately and predictably to her infant's needs.

working model of how parents respond—securely attached infants expect parents to respond but insecurely attached infants do not—and they look longer at the trials that violate their expectations of maternal behavior.

Not all caregivers react to babies in the reliable and reassuring manner that fosters secure attachment. Some parents respond intermittently or only after the infant has cried long and hard. And when these caregivers finally respond, they are sometimes annoyed by the infant's demands and may misinterpret the infant's intent. Over time, these babies tend to see social relationships as inconsistent and often frustrating, conditions that do little to foster trust and confidence.

Why are some parents more responsive—and thus more likely to foster secure attachment—than others? According to modern attachment theory (e.g., Cassidy, 1994), parents have internal working models of the attachment relationship with their own parents, and these working models guide interactions with their own infants. When questioned about attachment relationships with the Adult Attachment Interview (George, Kaplan, & Main, 1985; Bakermans-Kranenburg & van IJzendoorn, 2009), adults can be classified into one of three main groups, one corresponding to the secure attachment of childhood and the other two corresponding to insecure attachments:

- *Secure adults* **describe childhood experiences objectively and value the impact of the parent–child relationship on their development.**
- *Dismissive adults* **sometimes deny the value of childhood experiences and sometimes cannot recall those experiences precisely, yet they often idealize their parents.**
- *Preoccupied adults* **describe childhood experiences emotionally and often express anger or confusion regarding relationships with their parents.**

According to attachment theory, only parents with secure attachment representations are likely to provide the sensitive caregiving that promotes secure attachment relationships. In fact, many studies show that parents' secure attachment representations are associated with sensitive caregiving, and, in turn, with secure attachment in their infants (Mills-Koonce et al., 2011; Pederson et al., 1998; Tarabulsy et al., 2005). Furthermore, as I mentioned previously, infants with secure attachment relations often become young adults with secure attachment representations, completing the circle.

Fortunately, training can help mothers respond more effectively to their baby's needs (Bakermans-Kranenburg, van IJzendoorn, & Juffer, 2003; Dozier, Zeanah, & Bernard, 2013). Mothers can be taught how to interact more sensitively, affectionately, and responsively, paving the way for secure attachment and the lifelong benefits associated with a positive internal working model of interpersonal relationships.

Work, Attachment, and Child Care   Since the 1970s, more women in the workforce and more single-parent households have made child care a fact of life for U.S. families. I describe child care in detail in Module 15.3, but here I want to focus on one specific aspect: What happens to mother–infant attachment when other people care for the infant much of the time? Parents and policymakers alike have been concerned about the impact of such care. Is there, for example, a maximum amount of time per week that infants should spend in care outside the home? Is there a minimum age below which infants should not be placed in care outside the home? The "Child Development and Family Policy" feature describes work that has attempted to answer these and other questions about the impact of early child care on children's development.

Child Development and Family Policy
Determining Guidelines for Child Care for Infants and Toddlers

Because so many U.S. families need child care for their infants and toddlers, a comprehensive study of early child care was required to provide parents and policymakers with appropriate guidelines. The task fell to the U.S. National Institute of Child Health and Human Development, which began the Early Child Care study in 1991. Researchers recruited 1,364 mothers and their newborns from 12 U.S. cities. Both mothers and children have been tested repeatedly (and the testing continues because the study is ongoing).

From the outset, one of the concerns was the impact of early child care on mother–infant attachment, but the results so far show no overall effects of child-care experience on mother–infant attachment, for either 15- or 36-month-olds (NICHD Early Child Care Research Network, 1997, 2001). In other words, a secure mother–infant attachment was just as likely, regardless of the quality of child care, the time the child spent in care, the age when the child began care, how frequently the parents changed child-care arrangements, and the type of child care (e.g., at a child-care center or in the home with a nonrelative).

However, when the effects of child care were considered with characteristics of mothers, an important pattern was detected: At 15 and 36 months, insecure attachments were more common when less-sensitive mothering was combined with low-quality or large amounts of child care (NICHD Early Child Care Research Network, 1997, 2001). As the investigators put it, "poor quality, unstable, or more than minimal amounts of child care apparently added to the risks already inherent in poor mothering, so that the combined effects were worse than those of low maternal sensitivity and responsiveness alone" (1997, p. 877). These conclusions are particularly convincing because the same pattern of results was found in Israel in a large-scale study of child care and attachment that was modeled after the NICHD Early Child Care study (Sagi et al., 2002).

These results provide clear guidelines for parents. The essential ingredient for secure attachment is high-quality parenting. With such parenting, a secure attachment is likely regardless of a child's experience in child care. In Module 15.3 we'll learn more about the features that define high-quality child care and look at effects of child care on other aspects of children's development.

 QUESTION 10.3
Chantal is the mother of a 3-month-old. She's eager to return to her job as a civil engineer, but she worries that she may harm her baby by going back to work so soon. What could you say to reassure her?

 ## Check Your Learning

RECALL Describe the evolutionary perspective on mother–infant attachment.

What are the different forms of mother–infant attachment? What are the consequences of these different forms?

INTERPRET Compare the infant's contributions to the formation of mother–infant attachment with the mother's contributions.

APPLY Based on what you know about the normal developmental timetable for the formation of mother–infant attachment, what would seem to be the optimal age range for children to be adopted?

 # Unifying Themes   Active Children

Temperament is one of the best examples in this book of the theme that *children influence their own development.* Temperament helps determine how parents, peers, and other adults respond to children. Parents and peers, for example, usually respond positively to temperamentally easy children. Parents find it more straightforward to establish a secure attachment with an easy child than with a difficult child. Peers get along better with easy children than with shy, inhibited children. Children's temperament does not alone dictate the direction of their development, but it makes some directions much easier to follow than others.

See for Yourself

Arrange to visit a local day-care center where you can unobtrusively observe preschoolers for several days. As you watch the children, see if you can detect the temperamental differences that are described in Module 10.2. Can you identify an emotional child, an active child, and a social child? Also, notice how adults respond to the children. Notice if the same behaviors lead to different responses from adults, depending on the child's temperament. See for yourself!

Summary

Emerging Emotions

The Function of Emotions
Modern theories emphasize the functional value of emotion. Emotions such as fear, happiness, and disgust are valuable because they help people adapt, that is, by keeping them away from danger and strengthening social relationships.

Experiencing and Expressing Emotions
Basic emotions, which include joy, anger, and fear, emerge in the first year. Fear first appears in infancy as stranger wariness. Self-conscious emotions have an evaluative component and include guilt, embarrassment, and pride. They appear between 18 and 24 months and require more sophisticated cognitive skills than basic emotions such as happiness and fear. Cultures differ in the rules for expressing emotions and the situations that elicit particular emotions.

Recognizing and Using Others' Emotions
By 6 months, infants have begun to recognize the emotions associated with different facial expressions. They use this information to help them evaluate unfamiliar situations. Beyond infancy, children understand the causes and consequences of different emotions, that people can feel multiple emotions simultaneously, and the rules for displaying emotions appropriately.

Regulating Emotions
Infants use simple strategies to regulate emotions such as fear. As children grow, they become better skilled at regulating their emotions. Children who do not regulate emotions well tend to have problems interacting with others.

Temperament

What Is Temperament?
Temperament refers to biologically based, stable patterns of behavior that are evident soon after birth. The New York Longitudinal Study suggested three main categories of temperament, but most modern theories focus on dimensions of temperament. According to Rothbart's theory, temperament includes three main dimensions: surgency/extraversion, negative affect, and effortful control.

Hereditary and Environmental Contributions to Temperament
Twin studies show that heredity affects temperament, more in childhood than in infancy. The environment influences temperament through parents' behavior and by amplifying effects of genes. And temperament makes some children more susceptible to environmental influences.

Stability of Temperament
Temperament is somewhat stable in infancy and becomes more stable beginning in the preschool years. Temperament in childhood is somewhat related to personality in adulthood.

Temperament and Other Aspects of Development
Many investigators have shown that temperament is related to other aspects of development. Difficult babies are more likely to have behavioral problems by the time they are old enough to attend school. Persistent children are more successful in school, shy children sometimes have problems with peers, anxious children are more compliant with parents, and angry or fearful children are prone to depression. However, the impact of temperament always depends on the environment in which children develop.

Attachment

The Growth of Attachment
Attachment is an enduring social-emotional relationship between infant and parent. Bowlby's theory of attachment is rooted in evolutionary psychology and describes four stages in the development of attachment: preattachment, attachment in the making, true attachment, and reciprocal relationships.

The Quality of Attachment
Research with the Strange Situation, in which infant and mother are separated briefly, reveals four primary forms of attachment. Most common is a secure attachment, in which infants have complete trust in the mother. Less common are three types of insecure attachment relationships that lack this trust. In avoidant relationships, infants deal with the lack of trust by ignoring the mother; in resistant relationships, infants often seem angry with

her; in disorganized (disoriented) relationships, infants seem not to understand the mother's absence.

Children who have had secure attachment relationships during infancy often interact with their peers more readily and more skillfully. Secure attachment is most likely to occur when mothers respond sensitively and consistently to their infants' needs. Adults who value their relationship with their own parents are most likely to use the sensitive caregiving that promotes secure attachments with their own infants.

Test Yourself

1. Which of the following is a basic emotion?
   a. anger
   b. pride
   c. embarrassment

2. The first kind of fear to emerge in infancy is _____.
   a. fear of snakes and spiders
   b. wariness of strangers
   c. fear of imaginary creatures

3. Compared with U.S. children, Asian children are _____.
   a. more likely to express emotions outwardly
   b. more likely to be embarrassed when recognized publicly for individual accomplishments
   c. particularly likely to express anger

4. Most 12-month-olds _____.
   a. cannot distinguish happy faces from sad faces
   b. can distinguish real smiles from "fake" smiles
   c. use their parents' facial expressions to interpret unfamiliar situations

5. Which of the following statements about emotion regulation is *correct*?
   a. When children are less skilled in regulating their emotions, they tend to be less popular with peers.
   b. Infants are unable to regulate their emotions.
   c. School-age children and adolescents are relatively more skilled at regulating emotions, mainly because they no longer resort to cognitive strategies.

6. Hannah is happy, usually adjusts well to new situations, and has regular routines for eating and sleeping. Hannah fits in which of the temperamental categories described by Thomas and Chess?
   a. easy
   b. slow-to-warm-up
   c. difficult

7. Which of the following is *not* one of the temperamental dimensions proposed by Rothbart?
   a. effortful control
   b. activity
   c. negative affect

8. Research on the impact of heredity and environment on temperament shows that _____.
   a. the impact of heredity is greater in infancy than in childhood
   b. temperament may make some children particularly susceptible to environmental influence
   c. temperament is due to a few specific genes

9. Temperament _____.
   a. is moderately stable in infancy but becomes less stable in the preschool years
   b. is linked to personality directly and indirectly
   c. is stable from infancy through adulthood

10. Which of the following statements accurately describes links between temperament and other aspects of development?
    a. Children with a difficult temperament always have behavioral problems.
    b. Anxious children are more likely to comply with a parent's rules and requests.
    c. Children who are less skilled in regulating emotions and behavior are prone to problems in adolescence but not in adulthood.

11. According to the evolutionary perspective, attachment _____.
    a. evolved to increase the infant's odds of survival
    b. is learned through reinforcement and punishment
    c. has no adaptive value

12. When Emma is upset, her mom can soothe her more quickly than other people can, even though Emma savors attention from lots of people. She's still comfortable with strangers. Which of Bowlby's stages of attachment best describe Emma?
    a. preattachment
    b. attachment in the making
    c. true attachment

13. In the Strange Situation, a baby with _____ attachment is upset when the mother leaves and remains upset when she returns, sometimes to the point of being inconsolable.
    a. avoidant
    b. resistant
    c. secure

14. Compared with children who have secure attachment relationships, children with insecure attachment relationships _____.
    a. have higher quality friendships
    b. are more prone to anxiety and aggressive behavior
    c. do not differ
15. Select the statement that correctly describes influences on the quality of attachment.

   a. Secure attachment is most likely when parents are sensitive and responsive.
   b. When children are in day care, they are less likely to develop a secure attachment relationship.
   c. Secure and preoccupied adults are most likely to development secure attachment relationships with their children.

Key Terms

attachment   330
avoidant attachment   332
basic emotions   314
dismissive adults   335
disorganized (disoriented) attachment   332
display rules   319

effortful control   323
evolutionary psychology   330
internal working model   334
negative affect   323
preoccupied adults   335
resistant attachment   332
secure adults   335

secure attachment   332
self-conscious emotions   315
social referencing   318
social smiles   314
stranger wariness   315
surgency/extraversion   323
temperament   322

Chapter 11
Understanding Self and Others

Modules

11.1 Who Am I? Self-Concept

11.2 Self-Esteem

11.3 Understanding Others

A century ago, G. Stanley Hall, an influential U.S. developmental psychologist, wrote that adolescence was "strewn with wreckage of mind, body and morals" (1904, p. xiv). Judging by today's movies and media, Hall's portrayal persists: When teens aren't presented as runaways, drug addicts, and shoplifters, they're moody and withdrawn or manic. But how accurate is this picture? What does current research show about adolescence and the process of developing independence and identity?

In **Module 11.1**, we'll look at the mechanisms that give rise to a person's identity, and we'll see if adolescent "storm and stress" is a necessary step in achieving an identity. Of course, people are often happier with some aspects of themselves than with others. These evaluative aspects of identity are the focus of **Module 11.2**. Finally, in **Module 11.3**, we'll look at how we develop an understanding of others, because as we learn more about ourselves, we learn more about other people, too.

 11.1 Who Am I? Self-Concept

LEARNING OBJECTIVES	OUTLINE
LO1 When do infants first acquire a sense of self?	**Origins of Self-Recognition**
LO2 How does self-concept become more elaborate as children grow?	**The Evolving Self-Concept**
LO3 How do adolescents achieve an identity?	**The Search for Identity**

Dea was born in Seoul of Korean parents but was adopted by a Dutch couple in Michigan when she was 3 months old. Growing up, she considered herself a red-blooded American. However, in high school Dea realized that others saw her as an Asian American, an identity to which she had never given much thought. She wondered: Who am I, really? American? Dutch American? Asian American?

Like Dea, do you sometimes wonder who you are? **Answers to "Who am I?" reflect a person's** *self-concept,* **which refers to the attitudes, behaviors, and values that a person believes make him or her a unique individual.** One answer to "Who am I?"—from a 15-year-old—shows just how complex a person's self-concept can be:

> I'm smart, shy, quiet, and self-conscious, except when I'm around my friends. Then I can be loud and sometimes obnoxious! I'd like to be more outgoing all the time but that's not me. And I wish that I was more responsible, like at school. But then I'd be a real nerd and who wants that?

As an adult, your answer is probably even more complex. But how did you acquire this complex self-concept? We'll answer that question in this module, beginning with the origins of an infant's sense of self. Later, we'll see how identity becomes elaborated after infancy and see how individuals like Dea develop an ethnic identity.

Origins of Self-Recognition

LO1 When do infants first acquire a sense of self?

What is the starting point for self-concept? Following the lead of the 19th-century philosopher and psychologist William James, modern researchers believe that the foundation of self-concept is the child's awareness that he or she exists. At some

Although even very young babies enjoy looking at that "thing" in the mirror, not until about 15 months of age do babies realize that *they* are the thing in the mirror; this is one of the first signs of an emerging sense of self.

point early in life, children must realize that they exist independently of other people and objects in the environment and that their existence continues over time.

A rudimentary form of this awareness emerges in infancy. From watching their arms and legs as they move, infants become aware of their bodies. They realize that a moving hand is their hand; it belongs to them. For example, shown one monitor that displays their legs kicking (in real time) and another monitor that displays a mirror image of their legs kicking, infants look longer at the mirror images, apparently aware that "my legs don't look like that!" And infants pay more attention to videos of other people than to videos of themselves, suggesting that they distinguish themselves from other people (Rochat, 2013).

Youngsters usually reach the next landmark in self-awareness at about 18 to 24 months; this development is revealed in studies in which a mother places a red mark on her infant's nose; she does this surreptitiously, while wiping the baby's face. Then the infant is placed in front of a mirror. Many 1-year-olds touch the red mark on the mirror, showing that they notice the mark on the face in the mirror. However, between 15 and 18 months, many babies see the red mark in the mirror, then reach up and touch *their own* noses. By age 2, most children do this (Bullock & Lütkenhaus, 1990; Lewis, 1997).

This pattern of age-related change is found among infants living in communities that have no mirrors (or other reflective surfaces), which shows that toddlers' behavior is not due to their growing understanding of mirrors (Kärtner et al., 2012; Priel & deSchonen, 1986). However, self-awareness on the mirror task emerges at a younger age in Western cultures that view people as autonomous. In other words, young children become aware that they are independent beings when their cultures emphasize that independent nature (Kärtner et al., 2012).

We don't need to rely solely on the mirror task to know that self-awareness emerges between 18 and 24 months. During this same period, toddlers look more at photographs of themselves than at photos of other children. They also refer to themselves by name or with a personal pronoun, such as *I* or *me*, and sometimes they know their age and their gender. These changes, which often occur together, suggest that self-awareness is well established in most children by age 2 (Lewis & Ramsay, 2004; Kärtner et al., 2012).

During the preschool years, children begin to recognize continuity in the self over time; the "I" in the present is linked to the "I" in the past (Lazardis, 2013). Awareness of a self that is extended in time is fostered by conversations with parents about the past and the future. Through such conversations, a 3-year-old celebrating a birthday understands that she's an older version of the same person who had a birthday a year previously (Koh & Wang, 2012). And during the elementary-school years, children can project themselves into the future, anticipating what the present "I" may be like in years to come (Bohn & Berntsen, 2013).

After self-awareness is established, children begin to acquire a self-concept. That is, once children fully understand that they exist and that they have a unique mental life, they begin to wonder who they are. They want to define themselves. In the next section, we'll see how this self-concept becomes more complex as children develop.

The Evolving Self-Concept

LO2   How does self-concept become more elaborate as children grow?

Before you go any further, return to the teenager's description on page 341. It relies heavily on psychological traits and includes eight adjectives referring to these traits: *smart, shy, quiet, self-conscious, loud, obnoxious, outgoing,* and *responsible*. How do children develop such a complex view of themselves? For toddlers and preschoolers, self-concept is much simpler. If asked to describe themselves, preschoolers are likely to mention physical characteristics ("I have blue eyes"), their preferences ("I like cookies"), their possessions ("I have trucks"), and their competencies ("I can count to 50").

These features all share a focus on attributes of children that are observable and concrete (Harter, 2006). They also emphasize personal characteristics that are (relatively) unchanging across time and setting. All preschool children mention such characteristics, but they dominate European American preschoolers' descriptions of themselves. In contrast, in many Asian cultures, the self is defined, to a much greater extent, by children's social relationships. For example, in describing themselves, Chinese preschoolers are more likely than European American preschoolers to say, "I love my mommy" or "I play with Qi at school," showing that the self is embedded in relationships with others (Wang, 2006).

At about 5 to 7 years of age, children's self-descriptions begin to change (Harter, 2005). Children are more likely to mention emotions ("Sometimes I get angry"). They are also more likely to mention the social groups to which they belong ("I'm on a soccer team"). Finally, in contrast to preschool children, who simply mention their competencies, elementary school children describe their level of skill in relation to their peers ("I'm the best speller in my whole class").

Self-concepts change again as children enter adolescence (Harter, 2006). They now include attitudes ("I love algebra") and personality traits ("I'm usually a very happy person"). Adolescents also begin to make religious and political beliefs part of their self-concept ("I'm a Catholic" or "I'm a conservative Republican"). Another change is that adolescents' self-concepts often vary with the setting. A teenager might say, "I'm really shy around people I don't know, but I let loose when I'm with my friends and family."

Yet another change is that adolescents' self-concepts are often future oriented: Adolescents often describe themselves in terms of what they will be when they reach adulthood (Harter, 2005; Steinberg et al., 2009). These descriptions may include occupational goals ("I'm going to be an English teacher"), educational plans ("I plan to go to a community college to learn about computers"), or social roles ("I want to get married as soon as I finish high school").

The gradual elaboration of self-concept from the preschool years to adolescence is described in Summary Table 11-1. Two general changes are evident: First, self-concept becomes richer as children grow; adolescents simply know much more about themselves than preschoolers. Second, the type of knowledge that children have of themselves changes. Preschoolers' understanding is linked to the concrete, the real, and the here and now. Adolescents' understanding, in contrast, is more abstract and more psychological, and sees the self as evolving over time. The change in children's knowledge of themselves should not surprise you because it's exactly the type of change that Piaget described. Concrete

SUMMARY TABLE 11-1

DEVELOPMENTAL CHANGE IN SELF-CONCEPT

Preschoolers	School-Age Children	Adolescents
Possessions	Emotions	Attitudes
Physical characteristics	Social groups	Personality traits
Preferences	Comparisons with peers	Beliefs vary with the setting
Competencies		Future oriented

operational children's focus on the real and tangible extends to their thoughts about themselves, just as formal operational adolescents' focus on the abstract and hypothetical applies to their thoughts about themselves.

Adolescence is also a time of increasing self-reflection. Adolescents look for an identity that integrates the many different and sometimes conflicting elements of the self (Marcia, 1991). We'll look at this search for identity in detail in the next section.

The Search for Identity

LO3 How do adolescents acquire an identity?

Erik Erikson (1968) believed that adolescents struggle to achieve an identity that will allow them to participate in the adult world. How do they accomplish this? To learn more about possible identities, adolescents use the hypothetical reasoning skills of the formal operational stage to experiment with different selves. Adolescents' advanced cognitive skills allow them to imagine themselves in different roles.

Much of the testing and experimentation is career oriented. Some adolescents, like the ones shown in the photo, may envision themselves as rock stars; others may imagine being a professional athlete, a Peace Corps worker, or a best-selling novelist. Other testing is romantically oriented. Teens may fall in love and imagine living with the loved one. Still other exploration involves religious and political beliefs (Harre, 2007; Lopez, Huynh, & Fuligni, 2011). Teens give different identities a trial run, just as you might test-drive different cars before selecting one. By fantasizing about their future, adolescents begin to discover who they will be.

The self-absorption that marks the teenage search for identity is referred to as *adolescent egocentrism* (Elkind, 1978; Schwartz, Maynard, & Uzelac, 2008). Unlike preschoolers, adolescents know that others have different perspectives on the world. At the same time, many adolescents believe, wrongly, that they are the focus of others' thinking and attention. A teen like the one in the photo on page 345 who spills food on herself may imagine that all her friends are thinking only about the stain on her blouse and how sloppy she is. **Many adolescents feel that they are, in effect, actors whose performance is being watched constantly by their peers, a phenomenon known as the** *imaginary audience.*

Adolescent self-absorption is also demonstrated by the *personal fable*, **teenagers' tendency to believe that their experiences and feelings are unique, that no one has ever felt or thought as they do.** Whether feeling the excitement of first love, the despair of a broken relationship, or the confusion of planning for the future, adolescents often believe that they are the first to experience these feelings and that no one else could possibly understand the power of their emotions (Elkind & Bowen, 1979). **Adolescents' belief in their uniqueness also contributes to an** *illusion of invulnerability*—**the belief that misfortune only happens to others.** They think they can have sex without becoming pregnant or drive recklessly without being in an auto accident. Those misfortunes, according to them, only happen to others.

Adolescent egocentrism, imaginary audiences, personal fables, and the illusion of invulnerability become less common as adolescents make progress toward achieving an identity. What exactly is involved in achieving an identity? Most adolescents progress through different phases or *statuses*, though not necessarily in this order (Marcia, 1980, 1991):

As part of their search for an identity, adolescents often try on different roles, such as trying to imagine what life might be like as a rock star.

- *Diffusion:* Individuals in this status are confused or overwhelmed by the task of achieving an identity and are doing little to achieve one.
- *Foreclosure:* Individuals in this status have an identity determined largely by adults, rather than from personal exploration of alternatives.
- *Moratorium:* Individuals in this status are still examining different alternatives and have yet to find a satisfactory identity.
- *Achievement:* Individuals in this status have explored alternatives and have deliberately chosen a specific identity.

Adolescents often believe that others are constantly watching them, a phenomenon known as *imaginary audience*; consequently, they're often upset or embarrassed when they make obvious mistakes or blunders, such as spilling food or drink.

Unlike Piaget's stages, these four phases do not necessarily occur in sequence. Most young adolescents are in a state of diffusion or foreclosure. The common element in these phases is that teens are not exploring alternative identities. They are avoiding the crisis altogether or have resolved it by taking on an identity suggested by parents or other adults. As individuals move beyond adolescence and into young adulthood and have more opportunity to explore alternative identities, diffusion and foreclosure become less common, and achievement and moratorium become more common (Meeus et al., 2010). However, during late adolescence and young adulthood, people may alternate between moratorium and achievement statuses: For example, having explored a range of occupations and selected one provisionally, older adolescents explore the chosen occupation in depth and if it doesn't feel right—a good fit to them worthy of a deep commitment—they reconsider their choice and re-enter the moratorium status (Luyckx et al., 2013).

Typically, young people do not reach the achievement status for all aspects of identity at the same time (Goossens, 2001; Kroger & Greene, 1996). Some adolescents may reach the achievement status for occupation before achieving it for religion and politics. Others reach the achievement status for religion before other domains. Evidently, few youth achieve a complete sense of identity all at once; instead, the crisis of identity is resolved first in some areas and then in others.

What circumstances help adolescents to achieve identity? Parents are influential (Marcia, 1980). When parents encourage discussion and recognize their children's autonomy, their children are more likely to reach the achievement status. Apparently, these youth feel encouraged to undertake the personal experimentation that leads to identity. In contrast, when parents set rules with little justification and enforce them without explanation, children are more likely to remain in the foreclosure status. These teens are discouraged from experimenting personally; instead, their parents simply tell them what identity to adopt. Overall, adolescents are most likely to establish a well-defined identity in a family atmosphere in which parents encourage children to explore alternatives on their own but do not pressure them or provide explicit direction (Koepke & Denissen, 2012; Smits et al., 2010).

Beyond parents, peers are also influential. When adolescents have close friends whom they trust, they feel more secure exploring alternatives (Doumen et al., 2012). The broader social context also contributes (Bosma & Kunnen, 2001). Exploration takes time and access to resources; neither may be readily available to adolescents living in poverty (e.g., they can't explore because they drop out of school to support themselves and their family). Finally, through their personality, adolescents themselves may affect the ease with which they achieve an identity. Individuals who are more open to experience and are more agreeable (friendly, generous, helpful) are more likely to achieve an identity (Crocetti et al., 2008; Klimstra et al., 2013).

 QUESTION 11.1

Jenny thinks she might like to be an engineer, but she also enjoys dance. To help decide what path would be best for her, Jenny has taken a battery of interest inventories and her guidance counselor has suggested colleges where she could pursue both engineering and dance. Which of the four statuses best describes Jenny, at least as far as a possible occupation is concerned?

Ethnic Identity For many adolescents growing up in Europe and North America, achieving an identity is even more challenging because they are members of ethnic minority groups. The "Cultural Influences" feature describes one example.

Cultural Influences

Dea's Ethnic Identity

Dea, the adolescent in the opening vignette, belongs to the one-third of adolescents and young adults living in the United States who are members of ethnic minority groups. They include African Americans, Asian Americans, Hispanic Americans, and Native Americans. **These individuals typically develop an** *ethnic identity:* **They feel they are a part of their ethnic group and learn the special customs and traditions of their group's culture and heritage** (Phinney, 2005).

An ethnic identity seems to be achieved in three phases. Initially, adolescents have not examined their ethnic roots. A teenage Vietnamese American girl in this phase remarked, "Why should I learn about the Boat People? I'm not interested in what happened in Vietnam before I was born. Besides, I'm an American." For this girl, ethnic identity is not yet an important personal issue.

In the second phase, adolescents begin to explore the personal impact of their ethnic heritage. The curiosity and questioning that are characteristic of this stage are captured in the comments of a teenage African American girl who said, "I want to learn more about our history—back in Africa, in slavery, and during the Civil Rights movement. Going to the Black Cultural Center is one way I can find out about myself." Part of this phase involves learning cultural traditions; for example, like the girl in the photo, many adolescents learn to prepare ethnic foods.

Part of the search for an ethnic identity involves learning cultural traditions, such as learning how to prepare foods associated with one's ethnic group.

In the third phase, individuals achieve a distinct ethnic self-concept. One Mexican American adolescent explained his ethnic identification like this: "I was born in LA but my parents grew up in Mexico and came here when they were teenagers like me. I love hearing them talk about their lives there and I'm proud that I can speak Spanish with my cousins who live in Mexico. But I'm also proud to be an American and like to learn about my country's heritage."

To see if you understand the differences between these stages of ethnic identity, reread the vignette on page 341 about Dea and decide which stage applies to her. The answer appears on page 349, just before "Check Your Learning."

Older adolescents are more likely than younger ones to have achieved an ethnic identity because they are more likely to have had opportunities to explore their cultural heritage (French et al., 2006). As adolescents explore their ethnic identity, they often change the way they refer to themselves. For example, a U.S. teen whose parents were born in Vietnam might refer to herself at different times as Vietnamese, Vietnamese American, or Asian American, in no particular order (Fuligni et al., 2008).

As is true for identity formation in general, adolescents are most likely to achieve an ethnic self-concept when their parents encourage them to learn about their cultural heritage and prepare them for possible discrimination. For example, African American adolescents have a more advanced ethnic identity when their mothers tell them about Black history and encourage them to be proud of their heritage (McHale et al., 2006; Seaton et al., 2012). Similarly, Latino teens have a more advanced ethnic identity when their parents emphasize the importance of knowing their cultural heritage and routinely highlight that heritage by, for example, displaying cultural artifacts in the home (Umaña-Taylor & Guimond, 2010).

Do adolescents benefit from a strong ethnic identity? Yes. Adolescents who have achieved an ethnic identity tend to have greater self-esteem and find their interactions with family and friends more satisfying (Mandara et al., 2009; Rivas-Drake et al., 2014). They're also happier and worry less (Kiang et al., 2006). In addition, adolescents with a strong ethnic identity are less affected by discrimination—they maintain their self-worth after experiencing racial or ethnic discrimination (Neblett, Rivas-Drake, & Umaña-Taylor, 2012; Tynes et al., 2012).

However, we need to remember that racial and ethnic groups living in the United States are diverse. African American, Asian American, Hispanic American, and Native American cultures and heritages differ; thus, we should expect that the nature and consequences of a strong ethnic self-concept may differ across these and other ethnic groups (Phinney, 2005).

Even within any particular group, the nature and consequences of ethnic identity may change over successive generations (Cuellar et al., 1997). As successive generations become more assimilated into mainstream culture, they may identify less strongly with ethnic culture (Marks, Patton, & García Coll, 2011). When parents maintain strong feelings of ethnic identity that their children don't share, problems sometimes develop, as immigrant parents cling to the "old ways" but their children embrace the new culture. For example, in one study of Chinese immigrants to the United States (Kim et al., 2013), when children identified with the United States but their parents did not, parents were less supportive of their children, which caused them to do less well in school. In another study (Schofield et al., 2008), Mexican American children had more conflicts with parents and more behavioral problems when they identified themselves as Anglo but their parents identified themselves as Mexican.

Finally, let's think about adolescents for whom an ethnic identity is a particular challenge: those whose parents come from different racial or ethnic groups. Identity in biracial adolescents can be quite fluid. Some biracial adolescents first identify themselves as monoracial, then embrace a biracial identity; others shift in the opposite direction, converging on a single racial identity; still others shift from one racial identity to another (Doyle & Kao, 2007). Collectively, youth with shifting racial identities tend to have lower self-esteem than those with a consistent biracial identity (Csizmadia, Brunsma, & Cooney, 2012; Hitlin, Brown, & Elder, 2006). And U.S. biracial adolescents who identify themselves as White have less self-esteem and are less successful in school (Burke & Kao, 2013; Csizmadia & Ispa, 2014).

Storm And Stress According to novelists and filmmakers, the search for identity that I've described in the past few pages is inherently a struggle, a time of storm and stress for adolescents. Although this view may make for best-selling novels and hit movies, in reality teen rebelliousness is vastly overstated. Adolescents generally enjoy happy and satisfying relationships with their parents (Steinberg, 2001). Most teens love their parents and feel loved by them. And they embrace many of their parents' values and look to parents for advice.

Cross-cultural research provides further evidence that for most teens, adolescence is not a time of turmoil and conflict. Offer and his colleagues (1988) interviewed adolescents from 10 different countries and found that most adolescents were moving confidently and happily toward adulthood. As the graphs in Figure 11-1 on page 348 show, most adolescents around the world reported that they were usually happy, and few avoided their homes.

The Offer et al. (1988) work is more than a quarter-century old, but newer studies paint much the same picture. In one study of Arab adolescents living in Israel (Azaiza, 2005), 82% of adolescents said they felt wanted by their family and

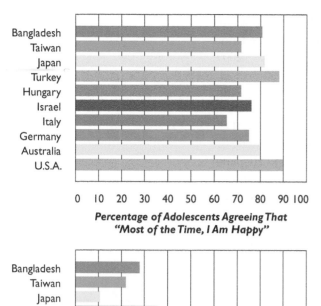

Percentage of Adolescents Agreeing That
"Most of the Time, I Am Happy"

Percentage of Adolescents Agreeing That "I Try
to Stay Away from Home Most of the Time"

Source: Offer et al., 1988.

Figure 11-1

SOURCE: Offer, D., Ostrov, E., Howard, K. I., & Atkinson, R. (1988). The teenage world: Adolescents' self-image in ten countries. New York, NY: Plenum.

89% reported that they appreciated their family. In another study (Güngör & Bornstein, 2010), adolescents in Turkey and Belgium rated their mothers as being very supportive, endorsing items such as "My mother supports me in dealing with problems" and "My mother talks to me in a comforting way." These findings are consistent with the older studies and undercut the myth of adolescence as a time when adolescent storms necessarily rain on parent–child relationships.

Of course, parent–child relations *do* change during adolescence. As teens become more independent, their relationships with their parents become more egalitarian. Parents must adjust to their children's growing sense of autonomy by treating them more like equals (Laursen & Collins, 1994). This growing independence means that teens spend less time with their parents, are less affectionate toward them, and argue more often with them about matters of style, taste, and freedom (Shanahan et al., 2007; Stanik, Riina, & McHale, 2013). Although adolescents do have more disagreements with parents, these disputes are usually relatively mild—bickering, not all-out shouting matches—and usually concern an adolescent's personal choices (e.g., hairstyle, clothing), autonomy, and responsibilities (Chen-Gaddini, 2012; Erhlich, Dykas, & Cassidy, 2012). These changes are natural by-products of an evolving parent–child relationship in which the "child" is nearly a fully independent young adult (Steinberg & Silk, 2002).

Before you think that this portrait of parent–child relationships in adolescence is too good to be true, I want to add two cautionary notes. First, conflicts between parents and their adolescent children are often distressing for *parents*, who may read far more into these conflicts than their teenagers do (Steinberg, 2001). Parents sometimes fear that arguments over attire or household chores may reflect much more fundamental disagreements about values: A mother may interpret her son's refusal to clean his room as a rejection of values concerning the need for order and cleanliness, when the son simply doesn't want to waste time cleaning a room that he knows will become a mess again in a matter of days. Second, for a minority of families—roughly 25%—parent–child conflicts in adolescence are more serious and are associated with behavior problems in adolescents (Ehrlich et al., 2012). These more harmful conflicts are more common among adolescents who don't regulate their emotions well (Eisenberg et al., 2008), and they often predate adolescence; even as children, these adolescents were prone to conflict with their parents (Steeger & Gondoli, 2013; Steinberg, 2001).

Depression The challenges of adolescence can lead some youth to become depressed (Fried, 2005). As we saw in Chapter 3, depressed individuals have pervasive feelings of sadness, are irritable, have low self-esteem, sleep poorly, and are unable to concentrate. About 5% to 15% of adolescents are depressed; adolescent girls are more often affected than boys, probably because social challenges in adolescence are often greater for girls than boys (Center for Behavioral Health Statistics and Quality, 2012; Hammen & Rudolph, 2003).

Depression is often triggered when adolescents experience a serious loss, disappointment, or failure, such as the death of a loved one or when a much-anticipated date turns out to be a fiasco (Schneiders et al., 2006). Of course, many adolescents and adults experience negative events like these, but most don't become depressed. Why? One contributing factor is temperament: Children who are less able to regulate their emotions are, as adolescents, more prone to depression (Karevold et al., 2009). Another factor is a belief system in which adolescents see themselves in an extremely negative light. Depression-prone adolescents are, for example, more likely to blame themselves for failure (Gregory et al., 2007). Thus, after the disappointing date, a depression-prone teen is likely to think, "I acted like a fool" instead of placing blame elsewhere by thinking, "Gee. He was a real jerk!"

Parents and families can also put an adolescent at risk for depression. Not surprisingly, adolescents more often become depressed when their parents are emotionally distant and uninvolved, when their parents are contemptuous and cruel, or when family life is stressful because of economic disadvantage or marital conflict (Karevold et al., 2009; Schwartz et al., 2012; Yap et al., 2014). Because African American and Hispanic adolescents more often live in poverty, they're more often depressed (Brown, Meadows, & Elder, 2007). Finally, when parents rely on punitive discipline—hitting and shouting—adolescents often resort to the negative attributions (e.g., blaming themselves) that can lead to depression (Lau et al., 2007).

Heredity also plays a role, putting some adolescents at greater risk for depression (Haeffel et al., 2008; Lau et al., 2012). Neurotransmitters may be the underlying mechanism: Some adolescents may feel depressed because lower levels of neurotransmitters make it difficult for them to experience happiness, joy, and other pleasurable emotions (Kaufman & Charney, 2003).

To treat depression, some adolescents take antidepressant drugs designed to correct the imbalance in neurotransmitters. However, drug treatment has no lasting effects—it only works while a person is taking the drugs—and it has been linked to increased risk of suicide (Vitiello & Swedo, 2004). Consequently, psychotherapy is a better choice for treating depressed adolescents. One common approach emphasizes cognitive and social skills; that is, adolescents learn how to have rewarding social interactions and to interpret them appropriately. These treatments *are* effective (Weisz, McCarty, & Valeri, 2006)—and depressed adolescents do need help. Left untreated, depression can interfere with performance in school and social relationships and may also lead to recurring depression in adulthood (Nevid, Rathus, & Greene, 2003; Rudolph, Ladd, & Dinella, 2007). Also effective are prevention programs, which can substantially reduce the number of depressive episodes in high-risk youth (Stice et al., 2009).

> *Response to question on page 346 about Dea's ethnic identity:* Dea, the Dutch Asian American high-school student, doesn't know how to integrate the Korean heritage of her biological parents with the Dutch American culture in which she was reared. This would put her in the second phase of acquiring an ethnic identity. On the one hand, she is examining her ethnic roots, which means she's progressed beyond the initial stage. On the other hand, she has not yet integrated her Asian and European roots, and so has not reached the third and final phase.

 ## Check Your Learning

RECALL What evidence indicates that sense of self emerges during the second year of life? What contributes to the emergence of a sense of self?

Describe research that undermines the view of adolescence as a period of "storm and stress."

INTERPRET Compare and contrast the three stages in the achievement of an ethnic identity with Piaget's description of the concrete and formal operational stages of cognitive development.

APPLY The Tran family has just immigrated to the United States from Vietnam. The mother and father want their two children to grow up appreciating their Vietnamese heritage, but worry that a strong ethnic identity may not be good for their kids. What advice would you give Mr. and Mrs. Tran about the impact of ethnic identity on children's development?

 # Self-Esteem

OUTLINE

Developmental Change in Self-Esteem

Variations in Self-Esteem Associated with Ethnicity and Culture

Sources of Self-Esteem

Low Self-Esteem: Cause or Consequence?

LEARNING OBJECTIVES

LO4   How does self-esteem change as children develop?

LO5   How does self-esteem vary depending on ethnicity and culture?

LO6   What factors influence the development of self-esteem?

LO7   Is children's development affected by low self-esteem?

Throughout elementary school, Amber was happy with herself—she knew she was smart, reasonably popular, and reasonably attractive. But since she entered middle school, she's worried that she's no longer so smart, popular, and attractive. Her growing self-doubt is obvious to her mom, who wonders whether Amber should see a mental-health professional.

Amber's mom is concerned about her daughter's *self-esteem,* **which refers to a person's judgment and feelings about his or her own worth.** Children with high self-esteem judge themselves favorably and feel positive about themselves. In contrast, children with low self-esteem judge themselves negatively, are unhappy with themselves, and often would rather be someone else. In this module, we'll see how self-esteem changes as children develop, what forces shape it, and whether Amber's mom should be concerned.

Developmental Change in Self-Esteem

LO4   How does self-esteem change as children develop?

Think about your own self-esteem. Do you think you have high self-esteem or low self-esteem? To help you answer this question, read each of these sentences and decide how well each applies to you:

> I'm good at schoolwork.
> I find it easy to make friends.
> I do well at all kinds of different sports.
> I'm happy with the way I look.

If you agreed strongly with each of these statements, you definitely have high self-esteem.

When children and adolescents respond to these sentences, their responses reveal two important developmental changes in self-esteem: change in the structure of self-esteem and change in overall levels of self-esteem.

Structure Of Self-Esteem   By 4 or 5 years of age, which is the earliest we can measure self-esteem, children have a differentiated view of themselves. They can distinguish overall self-esteem as well as self-esteem in specific domains (Marsh,

Ellis, & Craven, 2002). This structure should seem familiar because it's like intelligence: In Module 8.1, we saw that hierarchical theories of intelligence begin with a general intelligence that is divided into more specific abilities, such as verbal ability and spatial ability. In the case of self-esteem, overall self-esteem is at the top of the hierarchy, with self-esteem in more specialized areas underneath (Harter, 2006). In the elementary-school years, four specialized areas stand out:

- *Scholastic competence:* How competent or smart the child feels in doing schoolwork
- *Athletic competence:* How competent the child feels at sports and games requiring physical skill or athletic ability
- *Social competence:* How competent the child feels in relationships with parents and peers
- *Physical appearance:* How good-looking the child feels and how much the child likes his or her physical characteristics, such as height, weight, face, and hair

During the elementary-school years, children's academic self-concepts become even more specialized (Marsh & Craven, 2006; Marsh & Yeung, 1997). As children accumulate successes and failures in school, they form beliefs about their ability in different content areas (e.g., English, math, science), and these beliefs contribute to their overall academic self-concept. A child who believes that she is skilled at English and math but not so skilled in science will probably have a positive academic self-concept overall. But a child who believes he is untalented in most academic areas will have a negative academic self-concept.

During adolescence, other domains of self-esteem are added, including job competence, close friendships, and romantic appeal. What's more, the social component of self-esteem becomes particularly well differentiated. Adolescents distinguish self-worth in many different social relationships. A teenager may, for example, feel positive about her relationships with her parents but believe that she's a loser in romantic relationships. Another teen may feel loved and valued by his parents but think that coworkers at his part-time job can't stand him (Harter, Waters, & Whitesell, 1998).

Children's overall self-worth is *not* simply the average of their self-worth in specialized areas. Instead, self-esteem in some domains contributes more than others. For many children and adolescents, self-esteem concerning appearance has the biggest influence on overall self-esteem (Shapka & Keating, 2005). Thus, Allison, whose self-worth in the academic, athletic, and social domains is just average, has high self-esteem overall because she believes that she's very good looking. In contrast, although Colleen has high self-esteem in academics and athletics, her overall self-esteem is only average because she considers herself relatively unattractive.

Thus, between the late preschool years and adolescence, self-esteem becomes more complex because older children and adolescents identify distinct domains of self-worth. This growing complexity is not surprising—it reflects the older child's and adolescent's greater cognitive skill and the more extensive social world of older children and adolescents.

Changes in Level of Self-Esteem At what age is self-esteem greatest? The answer may surprise you: it's during the preschool years. Most preschool children have extremely positive views of themselves across many different domains (Marsh, Ellis, & Craven, 2002). This outcome isn't surprising if you think back to Piaget's description of the preoperational period (Module 6.1). Preschool children are egocentric; they have difficulty taking another person's viewpoint. Unable to see themselves as others do, preschoolers blissfully believe that they are extraordinarily competent in all domains.

Children's self-esteem is often influenced by comparisons with peers; a child who discovers that she's not a fast runner may lose athletic self-esteem.

 QUESTION 11.2

Sanjay is a well-mannered 7-year-old who excels in academics. However, he refuses to participate in any sports as he is self-conscious about being slightly overweight. He thinks he will not be able to perform well and so sees no point in trying. Which are the compromised specialized areas of self-concept in Sanjay's case?

As children progress through the elementary-school years, self-esteem usually drops somewhat. Why? In reality, of course, all children are *not* above average. During the elementary-school years, children begin to compare themselves with peers (Ruble et al., 1980). When they do, they discover that they are not necessarily the best readers or the fastest runners. They may realize that they are only average readers. Or, like the girl in the background of the photo, they come to understand that they are among the slowest runners in the class. This realization means that children's self-esteem usually drops somewhat during the elementary-school years.

By the end of the elementary-school years, children's self-esteem has usually stabilized (Harter, Whitesell, & Kowalski, 1992) as children learn their place in the "pecking order" of different domains and adjust their self-esteem accordingly. However, self-esteem sometimes drops when children move from elementary school to middle school or junior high (Twenge & Campbell, 2001). Apparently, when students from different elementary schools enter the same middle school or junior high, they know where they stand compared with their old elementary-school classmates but not compared with students from other elementary schools. Consequently, peer comparisons begin anew, and self-esteem often suffers temporarily. But, as a new school becomes familiar and students gradually adjust to the new pecking order, self-esteem again increases. Thus, Amber, the girl in the module-opening vignette, is showing the classic profile and there's no reason for her mom to worry: Amber will soon find herself again and self-doubt will wane.

Variations in Self-Esteem Associated with Ethnicity and Culture

LO5   How does self-esteem vary depending on ethnicity and culture?

The developmental changes in structure and average levels of self-esteem that I've just described are not universals. Instead, ethnicity and culture each influence important variations on these developmental trends. For example, growth of self-worth among U.S. children and adolescents varies depending on their ethnicity. Compared with European American children, African Americans and Hispanic Americans have lower self-esteem during most of the elementary-school years. However, in adolescence the gap narrows for Hispanic Americans and actually reverses for African American adolescents, who have greater self-esteem than their European American peers (Gray-Little & Hafdahl, 2000; Herman, 2004; Twenge & Crocker, 2002). In contrast, Asian American children have greater self-esteem than European American children during the elementary-school years, but less self-esteem during middle school and high school (Twenge & Crocker, 2002; Witherspoon et al., 2009).

Scientists don't fully understand why these changes take place. The differences involving Hispanic American and African American children may involve ethnic identity. Beginning in early adolescence, many African American and Hispanic American teens take pride in belonging to a distinct social and cultural group, and this raises their sense of self-worth (Gray-Little & Hafdahl, 2000; Umaña-Taylor, Diversi, & Fine, 2002).

The differences for Asian Americans may reflect their cultural heritage. Children from countries in East Asia (e.g., China, Japan, Korea) tend to have lower self-esteem than children from North America and Europe, and the difference increases in adolescence (Harter, 2012). Part of this difference is that Asian cultures emphasize modesty to a greater extent than Western cultures; as Asian youngsters internalize this cultural standard, they are reluctant to proclaim extremely positive feelings of self-worth (Cai et al., 2007).

But there is more to the story. Asian adolescents are also more willing to admit their weaknesses (Hamamura, Heine, & Paulhus, 2008). Consequently, although Western adolescents often emphasize areas of strength but ignore weaknesses when estimating overall self-esteem (e.g., the example with Allison), Asian adolescents' global self-esteem is lower because it reflects strengths *and* weaknesses. Finally, the social-comparison process that fuels self-worth in Western countries is far less common in Asian cultures. Children in Western cultures compare themselves with others in their group and feel good about themselves when they come out on top. In contrast, Asian children and adolescents see themselves as integral parts of their social groups and eschew social comparisons that could undermine group harmony (Falbo et al., 1997).

Sadly, at any age, in any domain, and in any group, it's easy to find children who do not view themselves positively. Some children are ambivalent about their self-worth; others actually feel negative about themselves. In one study (Cole, 1991), roughly 25% of 9- and 10-year-olds had negative self-esteem in at least three domains. Why do these children have so little self-worth compared to their peers? We'll answer this question in the next section.

Sources of Self-Esteem

LO6 **What factors influence the development of self-esteem?**

Why do some children feel so positive about themselves while others feel so negative? Heredity contributes, indirectly. Genes help to make some children smarter, more sociable, more attractive, and more skilled athletically. Consequently, such children are more likely to have greater self-worth because they are competent in so many domains. In other words, genes lead to greater competence, which fosters greater self-worth (Harter, 2012; Neiss, Sedikides, & Stevenson, 2006).

Children's and adolescents' self-worth is also affected by how others view them, particularly other people who are important to them. Parents matter, of course—even to adolescents. Children are more likely to view themselves positively when their parents are affectionate toward them and involved with them (Behnke et al., 2011; Ojanen & Perry, 2007). Around the world, children have greater self-esteem when families live in harmony and parents nurture their children (Scott, Scott, & McCabe, 1991). A father who routinely hugs his daughter and gladly takes her to piano lessons is saying to her, "You are important to me." When children hear this regularly from parents, they evidently internalize the message and come to see themselves positively. That said, when adults use inflated praise—saying "You played that song amazingly well!" when their playing was mediocre—this causes children with low self-esteem to shy away from challenges because they're afraid they won't succeed (Brummelman et al., 2014).

Parents' discipline also is related to self-esteem. Children with greater self-esteem generally have parents who have reasonable expectations for their children and are willing to discuss rules and discipline with their children (Awong, Grusec, & Sorenson, 2008; Laible & Carlo, 2004). Parents who fail to set rules are, in effect, telling their children that they don't care; they don't value them enough to go to the trouble of creating rules and enforcing them. In much the same way, parents who refuse to discuss discipline with their children are saying, "Your opinions don't matter to me." Not surprisingly, when children internalize these messages, the result is lower overall self-worth.

Peers' views are important, too. Children's and particularly adolescents' self-worth is greater when they believe that their peers think highly of them (Harter, 2012). Lauren's self-worth increases, for example, when she hears that Pedro, Matt, and Michael think she's the smartest girl in the eighth grade. Conversely, self-esteem drops when peers provide negative feedback, especially when those peers are popular themselves (Thomas et al., 2010).

Low Self-Esteem: Cause or Consequence?

LO7 Is children's development affected by low self-esteem?

Having low self-esteem is associated with many developmental problems (Baumeister et al., 2003). Children with low self-esteem are:

- More likely to have problems with peers (Parker et al., 2005; Rubin, Copland, & Bowker, 2009)
- More prone to psychological disorders such as depression (Boden, Fergusson, & Horwood, 2008; Orth et al., 2014)
- More likely to be involved in bullying, aggressive behavior, and criminal activity (Donnellan et al., 2005; Trzesniewski et al., 2006)
- More likely to do poorly in school (Marsh & Yeung, 1997)

These outcomes provide an excellent opportunity to remember the difficulty in identifying causal forces from correlational studies. Does low self-esteem cause children to have few friends, because peers want to avoid them? Or do poor peer relations cause children to have low self-esteem? Either claim is plausible, and longitudinal studies can help to distinguish them. For example, in research looking at the link between self-esteem and depression, the typical outcome is that low self-esteem measured early in development predicts depression later in development. However, depression detected early in development predicts low self-esteem later in development weakly or not at all (Sowislo & Orth, 2013; van Tuijl et al., 2014). In other words, a 13-year-old with low self-esteem is at risk to become a depressed 16-year-old but a depressed 13-year-old is at little risk to become a 16-year-old with low self-esteem.

What sometimes happens is that low self-esteem contributes to the outcome but is itself also caused by the outcome. For example, the claim that "low self-esteem leads to poor peer relations" is supported by findings that over the course of a school year, children with low social self-esteem often withdraw from peer interactions, and by year's end are more likely to be left out of social activities and to have few or no friends. But the claim that "poor peer relations reduce social self-worth" is also supported, this time by findings that children who have few friends at the beginning of a school year (but adequate social self-worth) tend to withdraw socially, and by year's end, their self-worth has dropped (Caldwell et al., 2004). Thus, poor peer relations reduce self-esteem in the peer context and disrupt future peer interactions, causing social self-worth to drop even more, making children even less likely to have good peer relations—the cycle goes on and on (Rubin, Coplan, & Bowker, 2009). Of course, the same kind of cycle can increase children's self-worth: success in social relationships can breed positive self-worth, which breeds more success.

Understanding this complex cause-effect-cause pattern is important in deciding how to help children with low self-esteem. Some children benefit directly from therapy that increases their low self-esteem. Others, however, who need to change their own behavior, also benefit from learning how to improve their social skills (a topic that I discuss again in Modules 12.4 and 15.1). And, we need to remember that all children have some talents that can be nurtured. Taking the time to recognize each child creates the feeling of "being special" that promotes self-esteem.

But I want to end this module on a cautionary note: Too much self-esteem is potentially as big a problem as too little self-esteem. *Narcissistic* **children and adolescents have a grandiose view of themselves, believe themselves to be better than others, and yet relish attention and compliments from others.*** Narcissistic children are prone to aggression—their overly positive view of themselves leads them to feel entitled to be aggressive when they don't get their way or believe that others are making them of them. And they're prone to depression when they notice that their inflated self-worth is at odds with reality (Pauletti et al., 2012). Given these findings, it's unfortunate that we know little about the factors that lead children and adolescents to become narcissistic. One idea is that children are at risk when they crave parents' attention and their parents are warm but manipulative (Thomaes et al., 2013).

Thus far in this chapter, we've focused on children's growing understanding of themselves. In the next module, we'll look at parallel changes that occur in children's understanding of other people.

 ## Check Your Learning

RECALL What are the salient features of self-esteem during the elementary-school years?

Summarize the ways in which self-esteem changes during childhood and adolescence.

INTERPRET Explain the forces that lead some children to have high self-esteem but others to have low self-esteem.

APPLY Suppose you attended a presentation for parents of middle-school students in which a counselor emphasized the importance of children having high self-esteem. The counselor asserts that when children have low self-esteem, they do poorly in school and don't get along well with their peers. Would you agree or disagree with the counselor's claims? Why?

 # 11.3 Understanding Others

LEARNING OBJECTIVES	OUTLINE
LO8 As children develop, how do they describe others differently?	**Describing Others**
LO9 How does understanding of others' thinking change as children develop?	**Understanding What Others Think**
LO10 When do children develop prejudice toward others?	**Prejudice**

When 12-year-old Ian agreed to baby-sit for his 5-year-old brother, Kyle, his mother reminded him to keep Kyle out of the basement because Kyle's birthday presents were there, unwrapped. But as soon as their mother left, Kyle wanted to go to the basement to ride his tricycle. When Ian told him no, Kyle burst into angry tears and shouted, "I'm gonna tell Mom you were mean to me!" Ian wished he could explain to Kyle, but he knew that would just cause more trouble!

---

*Narcissism gets its name from Narcissus, a mythological figure who fell in love with his reflection in a pool.

We know from Modules 11.1 and 11.2 that Ian, as a young adolescent, has a growing understanding of himself. This vignette suggests that his understanding of other people is also growing. He understands why Kyle is angry, and he also knows that if he gives in to Kyle, his mother will be angry when she returns. Children's growing understanding of others is the focus of this module. We'll begin by looking at how children describe others, then examine their understanding of how others think. We'll also see how children's recognition of different social groups can lead to prejudices.

Describing Others

LO8 **As children develop, how do they describe others differently?**

As children develop, their self-descriptions become richer, more abstract, and more psychological. These same changes occur in children's descriptions of others. Children begin by describing other people in terms of concrete features, such as behavior and appearance, and progress to describing them in terms of abstract traits (Livesley & Bromley, 1973). For instance, when asked to describe a girl that she liked a lot, 5-year-old Tamsen said,

> Vanessa is short. She has black hair and brown eyes. She uses a wheelchair because she can't walk. She's in my class. She has dolls just like mine. She likes to sing and read.

Tamsen's description of Vanessa is probably not too different from the way she would have described herself: The emphasis is on concrete characteristics, such as Vanessa's appearance, possessions, and preferences. Contrast this with the following description, which Tamsen gave as a 10-year-old:

> Kate lives in my apartment building. She is a very good reader and is also good at math and science. She's nice to everyone in our class. And she's very funny. Sometimes her jokes make me laugh so-o-o hard! She takes piano lessons and likes to play soccer.

Tamsen's account still includes concrete features, such as where Kate lives and what she likes to do. However, psychological traits are also evident: Tamsen describes Kate as nice and funny. By age 10, children move beyond the purely concrete and observable in describing others. During adolescence, descriptions become even more complex, as you can see in the following, from Tamsen as a 16-year-old:

> Jeannie is very understanding. Whenever someone is upset, she's there to give a helping hand. But in private Jeannie can be so sarcastic. She can say some really nasty things about people. But I know she'd never say that stuff if she thought people would hear it because she wouldn't want to hurt their feelings.

This description is more abstract: Tamsen now focuses on psychological traits such as understanding and concern for others' feelings. It's also more integrated: Tamsen tries to explain how Jeannie can be both understanding and sarcastic. Although she began, as a 7-year-old, by emphasizing concrete characteristics, as a 16-year-old she tries to integrate traits to form a cohesive picture.

More recent work also supports the trend to more abstract and richer psychological descriptions of others, but indicates that young children's understanding of other people is more sophisticated than is suggested by their verbal descriptions of people they know (Heyman, 2009). Indeed, modern work indicates that 4- and 5-year-olds have begun to think about other people in terms of psychological traits such as being smart, friendly, helpful, and shy. They can use behavioral examples to infer an underlying trait: Told about a child who won't share cookies or won't allow another child to play with a toy, 4- and 5-year-olds accurately describe the child as selfish. In addition, given information about a trait, they correctly predict future behavior: Told about a child who is shy, they believe that the child will not volunteer to help a puppeteer and will be quiet at a meal with many relatives (Liu, Gelman, & Wellman, 2007).

One idiosyncrasy of young children's descriptions of others is they see others "through rose-colored glasses"—that is, until about 10 years of age, children have a bias to look for positive traits, not negative traits, in others. Young children are willing to believe that someone is smart (or friendly or helpful) based on relatively little evidence (and based on inconsistent evidence), but require much more evidence (and more consistent evidence) to decide that someone is mean or stupid. This bias may simply be an extension of children's positive evaluations of themselves—recall from page 351 that self-esteem is greatest in preschoolers and declines gradually during the elementary-school years (Boseovski, 2010).

Understanding What Others Think

LO9 **How does understanding of others' thinking change as children develop?**

One trademark of the preschool child's thinking is difficulty in seeing the world from another's point of view. Piaget's term for this was *egocentrism*, and it was a defining characteristic of his preoperational stage of development (see Module 6.1). In much the same way, preschool children's communication is often ineffective because they don't consider the listener's perspective when they talk (see Module 9.4). As children move beyond the preschool years, though, they realize that others see the world differently, both literally and figuratively. For example, in the module-opening vignette, 12-year-old Ian knows why his little brother, Kyle, is angry: Kyle thinks that Ian is being bossy and mean. Ian understands that Kyle doesn't know there is a good reason why he can't go to the basement.

Sophisticated understanding of how others think is achieved gradually throughout childhood and adolescence. Robert Selman (1980, 1981) proposed a theory of how understanding others' thinking—or *perspective taking*—develops. Selman's theory is based on two of Piaget's key assumptions: namely, that understanding of others occurs in stages and that movement from one stage to the next is based on cognitive development. Table 11-1 shows Selman's five stages of perspective taking.

To see the progression from stage to stage, imagine two boys arguing about what to do after school. One wants to go to a playground and the other wants to watch TV. If the boys were 5-year-olds (undifferentiated stage), neither would really understand why the other wants to do something different. Their reasoning is stone simple: "If I want to go to the playground, you should too!"

During the early elementary-school years (social-informational stage), each child understands that the other wants to do something different, and they explain their differing views in terms of the other person lacking essential information. Their thinking is along the lines, "I know that you want to watch TV, but if you knew what I knew, you'd want to go to the playground." By the late

---

TABLE 11-1

SELMAN'S STAGES OF PERSPECTIVE TAKING

Stage	Approximate Ages	Description
Undifferentiated	3–6 years	Children know that self and others can have different thoughts and feelings but often confuse the two.
Social-informational	4–9 years	Children know that perspectives differ because people have access to different information.
Self-reflective	7–12 years	Children can step into another's shoes and view themselves as others do; they know that others can do the same.
Third-person	10–15 years	Children and adolescents can step outside the immediate situation to see how they and another person are viewed by a third person.
Societal	14 years to adult	Adolescents realize that a third person's perspective is influenced by broader personal, social, and cultural contexts.

---

elementary-school years (self-reflective stage), the boys would understand that each wants to do something different and they could "step into the other's shoes" to understand why: "I know you want to go to the playground because you haven't been there all week."

In early adolescence (third-person stage), the boys could step even farther apart and imagine how another person (e.g., a parent or teacher) could view the disagreement. Finally, in late adolescence (societal stage), the boys (now young men) can remove themselves even further and appreciate, for example, that many people would think it's silly to watch TV on a beautiful sunny day.

As predicted by Selman's theory, as children get older, their reasoning moves through each stage, in sequence. In addition, children at more advanced cognitive levels tend to be at more advanced stages in perspective taking (Gurucharri & Selman, 1982; Krebs & Gillmore, 1982). However, many scientists are not convinced that more sophisticated perspective taking occurs in such a stage-like fashion; they believe that it improves steadily throughout childhood and adolescence (just as cognitive development is now seen to be more continuous than Piaget's theory predicted).

Some investigators have linked improved perspective taking to the developing theory of mind, described in Module 7.3 (Chandler & Carpendale, 1998). The traditional false-belief task, for example, reveals children's understanding that another person's actions are often based on their beliefs, even when those beliefs are wrong. As an illustration, suppose children hear the following story:

> Lindsay and Angela are in the park and see some kids playing softball. Lindsay wants to play, so she runs home for her glove. Angela waits at the park for her, but while Lindsay's away, the kids decide it's too hot for softball and leave to get some ice cream.

Children understand false belief if they say that Lindsay will return to the ball field (acting on her false belief that the kids are still playing ball). But we can add a new wrinkle to the story.

> As the kids are leaving the park, one of them thinks that Lindsay might like to join them for ice cream, so she calls Lindsay and tells her the plan.

Now children are asked: "Where does Angela think Lindsay thinks the kids are?" Children understand second-order belief if they say that Angela thinks

Q&A QUESTION 11.3

Gracie is eager it for her cousin Andrew to arrive for a week-long visit. Gracie knows that Andrew will want to go swimming right away because Gracie loves to swim. Based on this example, what stage of perspective taking is Gracie in? About how old is she?

that Lindsay will go to the ball field. **This sort of "he thinks that she thinks…" reasoning is known as** *recursive thinking*. It emerges at about 5 or 6 years of age and improves steadily during the elementary-school years as a result of the combined effects of increased language skill and greater executive functioning (Miller, 2009).

One of the benefits of a developing appreciation of others' thoughts and viewpoints is that it allows children to get along better with their peers. That is, children who readily take another's perspective are typically well liked by their peers (Banerjee, Wattling, & Caputi, 2011; FitzGerald & White, 2003). Of course, mere understanding does not guarantee good social behavior; sometimes children who understand what another child is thinking take advantage of that child. In general, though, greater understanding of others seems to promote positive interactions, a topic that we'll discuss further in Chapter 12 on moral understanding and behavior.

Prejudice

LO10 When do children develop prejudice toward others?

Around the world, many adults are prejudiced against individuals solely based on their membership in a social group (e.g., a racial, ethnic, or religious group). Preferring one's group over others is first observed in 2- to 4-year-olds, becomes stronger in 5- to 7-year-olds, and remains strong thereafter (Raabe & Beelmann, 2011). But there's more to the story. By the preschool years, most children can distinguish males from females and can identify people from different racial groups (Nesdale, 2001). After children learn their membership in a specific group, they typically have an enhanced view of their own group. That is, preschool and kindergarten children attribute many positive traits, such as being friendly and smart, and few negative traits, such as being mean, to their own group (Bigler, Jones, & Lobliner, 1997; Patterson & Bigler, 2006).

Negative views of other groups form more slowly, beginning in the elementary-school years (Buttelmann & Böhm, 2014). In young children, negative views typically don't involve overt hostility; it's simply that other groups "come up short" when compared to one's own group (Aboud, 2003). During the elementary-school years, many children come to see race as a "natural kind"—determined by birth, stable, and referring to people who are similar to each other physically and behaviorally (Rhodes, 2013). At the same time, overt prejudice declines some, in part because children learn norms that discourage openly favoring their own group over others (Apfelbaum et al., 2008). But implicit bias remains—many children automatically associate their group with positive features and associate other groups with bad features (Baron & Banaji, 2006).

In the remainder of this section, we'll see why prejudice develops, look at the harm that results when prejudice leads to discriminatory behavior, and consider ways to reduce prejudice.

How Prejudice Develops   It's tempting to see prejudice as emerging from long-standing conflicts between groups of people, such as those between African and European Americans in the United States, between Protestants and Catholics in Northern Ireland, and between Muslims and Christians in some Arab nations. In this view, if the historical slate could be wiped clean, different groups would live in harmony, without prejudice.

An alternative view—in which bias and prejudice is a common by-product of children's efforts to understand their social worlds—is described in the "Spotlight on Theories" feature.

Spotlight on Theories
Developmental Intergroup Theory

BACKGROUND Bias and prejudice emerge early in development and are found in children worldwide. And, although I've emphasized racial bias in this module, children rapidly develop other biases as well, such as gender bias (the topic of Chapter 13). Why are bias and prejudice so prevalent, and why do they develop so early?

THE THEORY Rebecca Bigler and Lynn Liben (2007) believe that bias and prejudice emerge naturally out of children's efforts to understand their social world. You'll recall, from Module 6.3, that young children actively categorize animate and inanimate objects as part of their effort to understand the world around them. As children's social horizons expand beyond their parents to include peers, they continue to categorize, trying to decide how different groups of people "go together." That is, they look for obvious clues that could be used to distinguish people. They use perceptually salient features (e.g., race, gender, age) as well as verbal labels that adults may apply to different groups (e.g., "Girls go to lunch first, then the boys").

After children have identified the salient features that define peers in their environment, they begin to classify people whom they encounter along these dimensions. Jacob is now seen as a White boy; Kalika is now seen as a Black girl. Finally, children seek to learn more about each of the groups that they have defined. As they do this, their thinking is guided by essentialism, the belief that individuals who belong to the same group share internal, unseen similarities (i.e., essences). In addition, they are biased toward their own group and generate more favorable characterizations of its members.

Hypothesis: The first step in forming bias is detecting features in a setting that distinguish groups of people. Consequently, making a person-related feature more salient in an environment should make it more likely that this feature will contribute to bias. In other words, if teachers insisted that all left-handed children wear gloves on the left hand and right-handed children wear gloves on the right hand, this would make handedness a salient feature of people in the environment and should lead children to favor same-handed peers.

Test: Patterson and Bigler (2006) tested 3- to 5-year-olds attending day care. They were assigned to a "red group" or a "blue group" and wore red or blue T-shirts every day. In classrooms in the experimental group, teachers used the color names to refer to children (e.g., "Good morning, Blues!") and to organize the classroom (e.g., they created lines of Reds and Blues to leave the classroom). In classrooms in the control group, the children wore colored T-shirts but teachers never referred to them or used color names in any way.

After 3 weeks, children's perceptions and preferences were measured. As predicted, when teachers made color an important feature of the social world, children developed bias toward their own group. For example, children in these classrooms (a) believed that a new student would want to join their group, (b) said that they were happier than students in the other group, and (c) expressed greater liking for children in their own group and played with those children more often. In the control classrooms—where teachers did not mention color—children developed none of these biases.

Conclusion: As predicted, children developed bias in favor of their own color group when teachers made color salient in the day-care environment. This finding supports the general view that bias and prejudice are a natural by-product of children's efforts to determine the features in an environment that distinguish different groups.

Application: Because children are eager to know more about their social worlds and they categorize so skillfully, they easily notice features that signal group differences. This means that parents in particular and society in general face a huge challenge in reducing or eliminating bias. Parents can encourage their children to interact in multiracial groups of boys and girls, so that neither race nor gender is as salient for children. Institutions can have comparable policies. For example, teachers can be careful to avoid use of gender labels in their classrooms (just as they avoid racial labels).

The research described in the "Spotlight on Theories" feature shows that children develop biases when social groups are salient in their environment. Other work shows that the mere presence of different groups is often sufficient to generate bias. For example, if researchers ask children to join a group that's marked by the color of a shirt or a distinctive badge, young children prefer their group, attribute more positive features to their group, and ascribe negative behaviors (e.g., being stingy) to children of other groups (Dunham, Baron, & Carey, 2011; Schug et al., 2013). Even toddlers prefer their own group: They more often imitate adults who speak their native language and prefer puppets who are kind to others who like the same foods that the children like (Buttelmann et al., 2013; Hamlin et al., 2013).

Of course, children differ in the extent of their prejudice. Children and adolescents are more prejudiced when they are exposed to prejudices in their parents and other influential individuals (Castelli, Zogmaister, & Tomelleri, 2009; Degner & Dalege, 2013). Contact with other groups also matters: Even modest amounts of interactions with other groups can reduce or eliminate bias (Raabe & Beelmann, 2011).

Consequences of Discrimination   When children, adolescents, or adults act on their biases, the result is discrimination—they favor their own group over others, ignoring individuals from other groups, harassing them, or denying resources or privileges to them. Such discriminatory treatment is all too common for children and adolescents from minority groups and, as you might expect, the experience is stressful and associated with a range of harmful outcomes. African American and Latino youth who experience discrimination tend to suffer lower self-esteem and depression, are less successful in school, and have more problem behaviors (Benner & Graham, 2011; Zeiders, Umaña-Taylor, & Derlan, 2013).

Just as striking, though, is that some youth resist the harmful effects of discrimination. What factors make some children and adolescents resilient in the face of discrimination? The "Focus on Research" feature has one answer.

Focus on Research

Who Is Resilient in the Face of Discrimination?

Who were the investigators, and what was the aim of the study? When exposed to discrimination by teachers and peers, many children and adolescents end up struggling in school. Yet others resist the harm of discrimination and succeed in school. Identifying the factors that lead to such resilient behavior was the goal of a study conducted by Ming-Te Wang and James Huguley (2012).

How did the investigators measure the topic of interest? Wang and Huguley measured four constructs: (1) discrimination by teachers, with a questionnaire that included items that asked students whether they believed that, because of their race, teachers called on them less often or punished them more severely; (2) discrimination by peers, with a questionnaire that included items that asked students whether they believed that, because of their race, peers picked on them or ignored them when selecting classmates for activities or teams; (3) racial socialization, with a questionnaire that asked parents how often they emphasized racial pride with their children (e.g., talked to child about history of their racial group, celebrated holidays associated with their race); and (4) grades, obtained from school records.

Who were the children in the study? This work was part of a larger project known as the Adolescent Development in Context Study, a longitudinal study that tracked nearly 1,500 students from the time they were about 12 years old (entering middle school) until they were 21 years old. For this project Wang and Huguley used the data for 630 African American adolescents obtained when they were 14- and 17-year-olds.

What was the design of the study? This study was correlational because it involved examining relations between discrimination, racial socialization, and school grades. Although the project was longitudinal (testing participants on six occasions, beginning at age 12), the current project was neither longitudinal nor cross-sectional because it used measures of discrimination and socialization from one wave and averaged grades across two waves.

Were there ethical concerns with the study? No. The measures posed no risks and consent was obtained.

What were the results? The two graphs in Figure 11-2 show school grades (GPA) as a function of different levels of teacher discrimination (top panel) and peer discrimination (bottom panel). Within each panel, there are separate lines for children whose parents emphasized their racial heritage ("high cultural socialization") and those who did not ("low cultural socialization").

In both panels, for students whose parents had not emphasized their racial heritage, grades drop as discrimination increases. In contrast, for students whose parents had emphasized their racial heritage, discrimination has no impact on students' grades.

What did the investigators conclude? When parents emphasized racial heritage to their children, they were protected from the harmful effects of discrimination by teachers and peers. As Wang and Huguley put it, "parents' messages to their children regarding positive aspects of group membership (pride, history, and tradition) attenuate the negative effects of . . . discrimination . . ." (2012, pp. 1727–1728).

What converging evidence would strengthen these conclusions? One weakness of the study is that the researchers measured students' perceptions of discrimination, not discrimination per se. It would be valuable to have independent estimates of the amount of discrimination that students experienced from teachers and peers. A second weakness is the sample, which involved relatively older adolescents. It would be valuable to determine whether racial socialization has similar beneficial effects for children and younger adolescents.

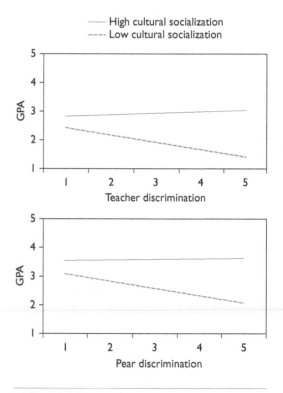

Figure 11-2

Other studies confirm that children and adolescents from minority groups are (relatively) protected from the harm of discrimination when they are well connected to their culture and have a well-established ethnic identity (Brown & Chu, 2012; Galliher, Jones, & Dahl, 2011). Of course, these children would fare best if they never experienced discrimination; in the next section we'll look at ways to rid children of the biased thinking that leads to discrimination.

Eliminating Prejudice What can parents, teachers, and other adults do to reduce or eliminate children's biases? One way is to encourage contacts between children from different groups (Aboud et al., 2012; White, Abu-Rayya, & Weitzel, 2014). Intergroup contact is most effective in reducing prejudice when:

One way to reduce children's prejudice is to have children from different groups work together toward a common goal, such as completing a school assignment.

- the participating groups of children are equal in status
- the contact between groups involves pursuing common goals (instead of competing) and encourages children to think of groups as part of a larger, common group, and
- parents and teachers support the goal of reducing prejudice (Cameron et al., 2006; Killen & McGlothlin, 2005)

To illustrate, adults might have children from different groups work together on a class project, as shown in the photo. In sports, the common task might be mastering a new skill. By working together, Gary starts to realize that Vic acts, thinks, and feels as he does simply because he's Vic, not because he's an Italian American.

Increasing interaction between children of different racial groups was one of the consequences of the U.S. Supreme Court's decision in *Brown v. Board of Education*, a case that shows how child-development research influenced social policy.

Child Development and Family Policy
Ending Segregated Schools

In 1950, African American and White children in much of the United States attended separate schools. Segregated schooling had been the law of the land for more than 100 years, bolstered by several famous Supreme Court decisions. In the fall of 1950, the chapter of the National Association for the Advancement of Colored People (NAACP) in Topeka, Kansas, decided to test the constitutionality of the law. Thirteen African American parents, including Oliver Brown, attempted to enroll their children in White-only schools; when they were turned away, the NAACP sued the Topeka Board of Education.

A key element in the NAACP's case was that separate schools were inherently harmful to African American children because such schools apparently legitimized their second-class status. To support this claim, the NAACP legal team relied on testimony from Dr. Kenneth B. Clark. In previous work, Clark (1945; Clark & Clark, 1940) had shown that African American children typically thought that White dolls were "nice" but that brown dolls were "bad." He found the same results in African American children attending segregated Topeka schools, leading him to testify that:

> these children...like other human beings who are subjected to an obviously inferior status in the society in which they live, have been definitely harmed in the development of their personalities....

In May 1954, the Supreme Court rendered the landmark decision that segregated schools were unconstitutional. The impact of Clark's research and testimony was evident in the decision in *Brown v. Board of Education*, delivered by Chief Justice Earl Warren:

> Segregation of white and colored children in public schools has a detrimental effect upon the colored children. The impact is greater when it has the sanction of the law, for the policy of separating the races is usually interpreted as denoting the inferiority of the negro group. A sense of inferiority affects the motivation of a child to learn. Segregation with the sanction of law, therefore, has a tendency to [retard] the educational and mental development of negro children and to deprive them of . . . benefits they would receive in a racial[ly] integrated school system.

After the *Brown* decision, Clark continued his work on civil rights and worked on behalf of African American youth. For his lifelong effort to inform public policy on African American children and their families, in 1987

Dr. Kenneth B. Clark's research on prejudice was influential in the Supreme Court's ruling that segregated schools are unconstitutional.

he received the Gold Medal for Life Achievement in Psychology in the Public Interest from the American Psychological Foundation; he died in 2005.

Clark's work is a compelling demonstration of the manner in which child-development research can have far-reaching implications for policy—in this case, helping to eliminate racially segregated schools in the United States. The integrated schools that resulted have helped to reduce prejudice by providing children with opportunities to learn about peers from other ethnic and racial groups.

Another useful strategy involves education—teaching children about the history and culture of other groups (Aboud et al., 2012). In one study (Hughes, Bigler, & Levy, 2007), European American elementary-school children learned about the racism that famous African Americans experienced. For example, they learned that Jackie Robinson played for a team in the old Negro Leagues because the White people in charge of Major League Baseball wouldn't allow any African Americans to play. There was also a control group in which the biographies omitted the experiences of racism. When children learned about racism directed at African Americans, they had much more positive attitudes toward African Americans.

From programs like this one, children and adolescents discover that a person's membership in a social group reveals little about that person. They also attribute differences between groups in terms of greater opportunities for some groups, not to inborn features of some groups. Finally, students in such programs are better able to detect and reject discrimination (Bigler & Wright, 2014).

Check Your Learning

RECALL Describe the different stages in Selman's theory of perspective taking.

Summarize developmental change in prejudice.

INTERPRET Compare developmental change in children's descriptions of others with developmental change in children's self-concept (described in Modules 11.1 and 11.2).

APPLY Based on what you've learned in this module, what can parents and teachers do to discourage prejudice in children?

Unifying Themes   Nature and Nurture

This chapter is a good occasion to feature the theme that *development is always jointly influenced by heredity and environment.* The emergence of self-awareness between 15 and 24 months is primarily due to biological forces. Regardless of circumstances, children become self-aware between the ages of 1 and 2. However, elaborating self-awareness into a specific self-concept depends largely on a child's experiences at home and in school. The specific direction that children take in establishing an identity is strongly influenced by those around them, particularly their parents and teachers.

See for Yourself

The mirror recognition task, described on page 342, is great fun to do, and you'll be astonished by the rapid change in children's responses between 1 and 2 years. For this task, you simply need a mirror, some tissue, blush, and a few cooperative parents of 12- to 18-month-olds. Have the parents play with their toddler near the mirror and, in the process, wipe the toddler's nose with a tissue that has blush on it. Then see how the toddler responds to the now-red nose. Some 12-month-olds will do nothing; others will touch the red nose in the mirror. When the 15- or 18-month-olds see themselves, though, they should stop, get a curious expression on their faces, and then reach up to touch their own noses. See for yourself!

Summary

Who Am I? Self-Concept

Origins of Self-Recognition

At about 15 months, infants begin to recognize themselves in the mirror, one of the first signs of self-recognition. They also begin to prefer to look at pictures of themselves, to refer to themselves by name and with personal pronouns, and sometimes to know their age and gender. Evidently, by 2 years, most children have the rudiments of self-awareness.

The Evolving Self-Concept

Preschoolers often define themselves in terms of observable characteristics, such as possessions, physical characteristics, preferences, and competencies. During the elementary-school years, self-concept begins to include emotions, a child's membership in social groups, and comparisons with peers. During adolescence, self-concept includes attitudes, personality traits, beliefs, and future plans. In general, adolescents' self-concepts are more abstract, more psychological, and more future oriented than self-concepts in younger children.

The Search for Identity

The search for identity typically involves four statuses. Diffusion and foreclosure are more common in early adolescence; moratorium and achievement are more common in late adolescence and young adulthood. Adolescents are most likely to achieve an identity when parents encourage discussion and recognize their autonomy; they are least likely to achieve an identity when parents set rules and enforce them without explanation.

Adolescents from ethnic groups often progress through three phases in acquiring an ethnic identity: initial disinterest, exploration, and identity achievement. Achieving an ethnic identity usually results in greater self-esteem.

Contrary to myth, adolescence is not usually a period of storm and stress. Most adolescents love their parents, feel loved by them, rely on them for advice, and adopt their values. The parent–child relationship becomes more egalitarian during the adolescent years, reflecting adolescents' growing independence. A small number of adolescents become depressed, often because their explanations of their own behavior are flawed.

Self-Esteem

Developmental Change in Self-Esteem

Self-esteem becomes more differentiated in older children and adolescents as they evaluate themselves on more aspects of self-esteem, including different types of academic skills. Global self-esteem is high during the preschool years but declines in the elementary-school years as children start to compare themselves to peers. Self-esteem also declines, temporarily, when children make school transitions.

Variations in Self-Esteem Associated with Ethnicity and Culture

Ethnicity and culture each influence important variations on the developmental changes in structure and average levels of self-esteem. African American and Hispanic American children have lower self-esteem in childhood but self-esteem increases in adolescence. Children from Asian countries tend to have lower self-esteem than children from North America and Europe, reflecting internalization of a cultural standard of modesty, ready admission of weaknesses, and less frequent comparison with peers.

Sources of Self-Esteem

Children's self-esteem is greater when parents are affectionate and involved with them and when parents set rules and discuss disciplinary action. Self-esteem also depends on peer comparisons. Self-esteem is usually greater when children know that others view them positively.

Low Self-Esteem: Cause or Consequence?

When children have low self-esteem, they are more likely to have poor peer relations, suffer psychological disorders such as depression, be involved in antisocial activities, and do poorly in school. Therapy and improved social skills can enhance children's self-esteem. Narcissistic children have an inflated view of their self-worth and are often too aggressive.

 Understanding Others

Describing Others

Children's descriptions of others change in much the same way that their descriptions of themselves change.

During the early elementary-school years, descriptions emphasize concrete characteristics. In the late elementary-school years, they emphasize personality traits. In adolescence, they emphasize an integrated picture of a person. Children use their descriptions to predict others' behaviors.

Understanding What Others Think

According to Selman's perspective-taking theory, children's understanding of how others think progresses through five stages. In the first, the undifferentiated stage, children often confuse their own and another's view. In the last, the societal stage, adolescents take a third person's perspective and understand that this perspective is influenced by context.

Prejudice

Prejudice, which emerges in the preschool years and becomes stronger in the elementary-school years, is a common byproduct of children's efforts to categorize social groups. Prejudiced thinking can lead to discriminatory behavior, which leads many children and adolescents to become depressed and not do well in school. Ways to reduce prejudice include exposure to individuals from other social groups and by educating children about the ills of prejudice.

Test Yourself

1. When a 12-month-old with a mark on her face looks into a mirror, she'll probably _____.
   a. ignore the image in the mirror
   b. touch the mark in the mirror
   c. touch the mark on her nose

2. Growing self-awareness between the ages of 18 and 24 months is demonstrated by the fact that at this age children _____.
   a. do not recognize themselves in a mirror
   b. prefer to look at photos of other children
   c. refer to themselves by name

3. _____ define themselves in terms of their physical characteristics, possessions, and preferences.
   a. Preschool children
   b. School-age children
   c. Adolescents

4. In the _____ status, individuals have not explored alternatives but have an identity determined largely by adults.
   a. diffusion
   b. foreclosure
   c. moratorium

5. Which statement about ethnic identity is accurate?
   a. Children who have an ethnic identity tend to have greater self-worth and get along better with peers.
   b. When parents encourage children to develop an ethnic identity, children often resist and are less likely to identify with their ethnic group.
   c. Biracial adolescents consistently identify with each of their parents' ethnic groups.

6. During adolescence, parent-child relationships _____.
   a. are filled with storm and stress
   b. become more egalitarian
   c. are marked by less time spent together but more affection

7. Which of the following is not a domain of self-esteem during the elementary-school years?
   a. scholastic competence
   b. close friendships
   c. physical appearance

8. Self-esteem is greatest during _____.
   a. the preschool years
   b. the elementary school years
   c. adolescence

9. Children with high self-esteem often have parents who _____.
   a. are affectionate and involved with them
   b. lavishly praise everything they do
   c. don't set standards for their children's behavior—their kids can do anything they want

10. Children with low self-esteem _____.
    a. generally get along well with their peers
    b. are more likely to be involved in antisocial behavior
    c. are more likely to do well in school

11. Young children's descriptions of others are unusual in emphasizing _____.
    a. positive traits over negative traits
    b. integration of traits
    c. psychological traits

12. What is typically true of children who are more skilled in taking the perspective of others?
    a. They tend to be older.
    b. They are less advanced cognitively.
    c. They do not get along well with their peers.

13. Children's prejudice _____.
    a. typically emerges in the elementary-school years
    b. is greater when their parents are biased in their thinking
    c. increases when they spend time with other social groups

14. When children and adolescents from minority groups experience discriminatory behavior, they are _____.
    a. at risk for depression but their performance in school is unaffected
    b. less at risk if they have a well-developed ethnic identity
    c. unaffected

15. Contact between diverse groups of children can reduce prejudice when _____.
    a. the minority group is given greater status
    b. the contact involves the groups pursuing mutual goals
    c. parents and teachers are not involved

Key Terms

achievement 345
adolescent egocentrism 344
diffusion 345
ethnic identity 346
foreclosure 345
illusion of invulnerability 344
imaginary audience 344
moratorium 345
narcissism 355
personal fable 344
recursive thinking 359
self-concept 341
self-esteem 350

Chapter 12
Moral Understanding and Behavior

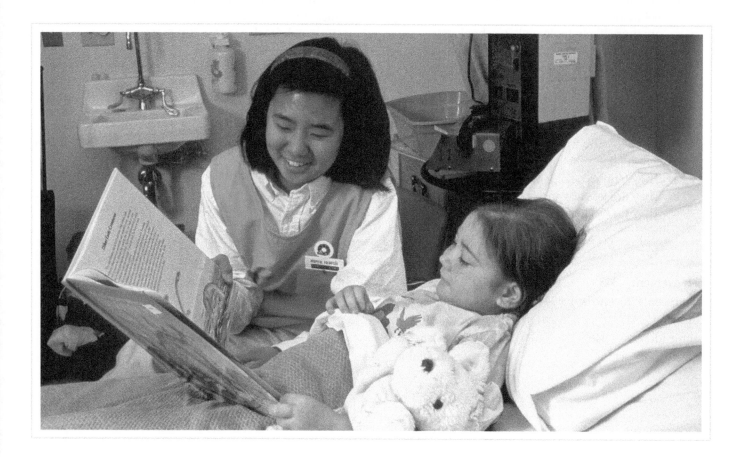

Modules

12.1 Self-Control

12.2 Reasoning About Moral Issues

12.3 Helping Others

12.4 Aggression

Imagine entering a nursery filled with 2-day-olds. Some are asleep, some are crying, others are simply lying quietly. However, the nurse tells you that the newborns include Nelson Mandela, Mother Teresa, Adolf Hitler, Mohandas Gandhi, and Martin Luther King, Jr. Although seemingly identical now, four of the newborns will rank among the 20th century's greatest figures and one will be guilty of unspeakable horrors. Why? What determines whether children act morally or immorally? Whether they care about others or take from others? Whether they become samaritans or follow a path of evil? The four modules in this chapter provide some answers to these questions. In **Module 12.1**, we'll see how children learn to control their behavior. In **Module 12.2**, we'll look at how children and adolescents reason about moral issues, and in **Module 12.3**, we'll look at factors that encourage children to be kind to others. Finally, in **Module 12.4**, we'll see why children act aggressively toward others.

 # Self-Control

LEARNING OBJECTIVES

OUTLINE

LO1 When does self-control begin, and how does it change as children develop?

Beginnings of Self-Control

LO2 What factors influence children's ability to maintain self-control?

Influences on Self-Control

LO3 What strategies can children use to improve their self-control?

Improving Children's Self-Control

Shirley came home from a long day at work tired but eager to celebrate her son Ryan's fourth birthday. Her excitement quickly turned to dismay when she discovered that Ryan had taken a huge bite of icing from the birthday cake while the babysitter fixed lunch. Before she had left for work that morning, Shirley had explicitly told Ryan not to touch the cake. Why couldn't Ryan wait? Why did he give in to temptation? What could she do to help Ryan control himself better in the future?

In this vignette, Shirley wishes that Ryan had greater *self-control*, **the ability to control one's behavior and to inhibit impulsive responding to temptations.** A child who obeys a parent's request that she not touch a nicely wrapped present is showing self-control, as is an adolescent who studies for an exam instead of going to the mall with his friends, knowing that tomorrow he can enjoy the mall and a good grade on his exam.

Self-control is one of the first steps toward moral behavior because children must learn that they cannot constantly do whatever tempts them at the moment. Instead, society has rules for behavior in certain situations, and children must learn to restrain themselves.

In this module, we'll first see how self-control emerges, then learn some of the factors that determine how well children control themselves. Finally, we'll look at strategies that children use to improve their self-control.

Beginnings of Self-Control

LO1 When does self-control begin, and how does it change as children develop?

Self-control emerges in infancy and gradually improves during the preschool years (Kopp, 1997; Li-Grining, 2007). A rough chronology looks like this:

- At about their first birthday, infants become aware that people impose demands on them and they must react accordingly. Infants learn that they are not free to behave as they wish; instead, others set limits on what they can do. These limits reflect both concern for their safety ("Don't touch! It's hot") as well as early socialization efforts ("Don't grab Ravisha's toy").
- At about 2 years, toddlers have internalized some of the controls imposed by others and are capable of some self-control in parents' absence. For example, although the boy on the right in the photo certainly looks as if he wants to play with the toy that the other toddler has, so far he has inhibited his desire to grab the toy, perhaps because he remembers that his parents have told him not to take things from others.
- At about 3 years, children become capable of self-regulation; they can devise ways to control their own behavior. To return to the example of a playmate's interesting toy, children might tell themselves that they really don't want to play with it, or they might turn to another activity that removes the temptation to grab the toy.

QUESTION 12.1

Two-year-old Amanda spilled a cup filled with juice just after she'd been asked to leave it on the counter. Amanda's dad thinks she should be disciplined for disobeying a direct instruction; her mom thinks Amanda is too young to control herself. How would you advise Amanda's parents?

Of course, although preschoolers are able to regulate impulsive behavior somewhat, effective control is achieved only gradually throughout the elementary-school years (Vazsonyi & Huang, 2010). One way to chart this long developmental trek is with studies of delay of gratification, in which children are offered the choice of a relatively small reward immediately or a much larger reward if they wait. In one study (Steelandt et al., 2012), nearly all 4-year-olds waited four minutes for a larger cookie but relatively few 2-year-olds did. In another study (Rotenberg & Mayer, 1990), children and adolescents were offered the choice of a small piece of candy immediately or an entire bag of chips if they waited 1 day. About one-third of the 6- to 8-year-olds opted to wait for the chips. In contrast, half of the 9- to 11-year-olds and nearly all the 12- to 15-year-olds waited a day for the chips. Thus, although self-control may be evident in preschoolers, mastery occurs gradually throughout childhood, probably reflecting maturation of circuitry in the brain's frontal cortex that is critical for inhibiting behavior (Berkman, Graham, & Fisher, 2012).

Even more remarkable are the results from longitudinal studies on the long-term consistency of self-control. These studies find that preschoolers' self-control predicts outcomes in adolescence and young adulthood. In Module 10.2, we saw that children who were less able to control themselves were, as teenagers, more likely to drop out of school, to smoke, and to become parents (Moffitt, Poulton, & Caspi, 2013). In addition, preschoolers who show the greatest self-control are, as adolescents, more attentive, have higher SAT scores, and are less likely to experiment with drugs and alcohol; as young adults, they are better educated, have higher self-esteem, have better cognitive control, and are less likely to be overweight (Mischel et al., 2011; Schlam et al., 2013).

By 2 years of age, many children have enough self-control that they can resist the temptation to take an interesting toy away from another child.

Obviously, individuals differ in their ability to resist temptation, and this characteristic is remarkably stable over time. But why are some children and adults better able than others to exert self-control? As you'll see in the next section of this module, parents' and children's temperament both contribute to children's self-control.

Influences on Self-Control

LO2 **What factors influence children's ability to maintain self-control?**

Parents like Shirley are disappointed and upset when their children lack self-control. What can parents do? Research consistently links greater self-control with a disciplinary style in which parents are warm and loving but establish well-defined limits on what behavior is acceptable (Feldman & Klein, 2003; Vazsonyi & Huang, 2010). Self-control is enhanced when parents discuss disciplinary issues with their children instead of simply asserting their power as parents (e.g., "You'll do it because I say so"). When Shirley disciplines Ryan, she should remind him of the clear behavioral standard (not touching the cake), explain her disappointment ("Now nobody else will see how pretty your cake was!"), and suggest ways that he could resist similar temptations in the future.

Research also shows that children's self-control is usually *less skilled* when parents are overly strict with them (Donovan, Leavitt, & Walsh, 2000; Feldman & Wentzel, 1990). By constantly directing their children to do one thing but not another, parents do not give them either the opportunity or the incentive to internalize control (Kochanska, Coy, & Murray, 2001).

But parents aren't the only important influence on children's self-control; remember, from Module 10.2, that temperament also matters. One dimension of temperament is effortful control, which describes a child's ability to focus attention, to ignore distraction, and to inhibit inappropriate responses. Thus, some children are temperamentally better suited to maintain self-control and regulate their behavior (Stifter et al., 2009).

Of course, regardless of their temperament, children are not perfectly consistent in their self-control. Children who are able to resist temptation on one occasion may give in the next time. Why do children show self-control on some tasks but not on others? As we'll see in the next section, the answer lies in children's plans for resisting temptation.

Improving Children's Self-Control

LO3 **What strategies can children use to improve their self-control?**

Imagine it's one of the first nice days of spring. You have two major exams that you should study for, but it's so-o-o-o tempting to spend the entire day with your friends, sitting in the sun. What do you do to resist this temptation and stick to studying? You might remind yourself that these exams are crucial. You might also move to a windowless room to keep your mind off the tempting weather. Stated more generally, effective ways to resist temptation include reminding yourself of the importance of long-term goals over short-term temptations and reducing the attraction of the tempting event or circumstance.

During the preschool years, some youngsters begin to use both of these methods spontaneously. In an experiment by Mischel and Ebbesen (1970), 3- to 5-year-olds were asked to sit alone in a room for 15 minutes. If they waited the entire time, they would receive a desirable reward. Children could call the experimenter back to the room at any time by a prearranged signal; in this case, they would receive a much less desirable reward.

Some children, of course, were better able than others to wait the full 15 minutes. How did they do it? Some children talked to themselves: "I've gotta wait to get the best prize!" As Vygotsky described (Module 6.2), these youngsters were using private speech to control their own behavior. Others, like the child in the photograph on page 373, looked away from the tempting prize. Still others imagined that the tempting prize was really an undesirable object. All were effective techniques for enduring 15 boring minutes to receive a desired prize.

Later studies show that children are far better able to delay gratification when they have a strategy for handling tempting situations (Mischel & Ayduk, 2004). The benefits of such a strategy are shown in the Focus on Research feature.

Focus on Research

Engaging Preschool Children to Help Them Delay Gratification

Who were the investigators, and what was the aim of the study? Philip Peake and his colleagues Michelle Hebl and Walter Mischel (2002) wanted to determine the conditions that help children delay gratification. That is, they hoped to learn ways to help children resist the temptation to take a lesser reward immediately and instead wait for a better reward later.

How did the investigators measure the topic of interest? Peake and his colleagues tested children on a classic task. Children were shown two rewards and asked which they preferred. Children in a control condition were told that the experimenter had to leave the room for a while but that if they waited patiently until the experimenter returned, they would get their chosen reward. They were also told that at any time they could ring a bell for the experimenter to return, but if they did so they would receive the less-preferred reward. Children in another condition were given these same instructions but were also shown a large bucket of colored marbles and told that they could pass the time by sorting the marbles into color-coded cups. In a third condition, a jar with a tube was decorated to look like a baby bird; children were told that they could pass the time by putting marbles down the tube to "feed the bird." (Prior work had shown that children considered this much more fun than sorting marbles.) The experimenter recorded the length of time that children waited and where they looked while waiting. For all children, both rewards remained on display, thus serving as tempting objects while they waited.

Who were the children in the study? Peake and his colleagues tested thirty 3- to 5-year-olds.

What was the design of the study? This study was experimental. The independent variable was the condition under which children waited: alone with nothing to do, with marbles to sort, or feeding the bird. The study had two dependent variables: the length of time that children waited and the amount of time they spent looking at the rewards. The study was neither longitudinal nor cross-sectional because all children were approximately the same age and each was only tested once.

Were there ethical concerns with the study? No. The tasks involved minimal risk and weren't much different from experiences that children would encounter in daily life.

What were the results? Let's begin by looking at how long children waited. The left panel of Figure 12-1 shows that children waited longest when they performed an engaging task (feeding the bird). They waited next longest when performing the boring task (sorting marbles), and waited the least when they had nothing to do. The right panel of Figure 12-1 helps to explain why: With nothing to do, children spent nearly half the time just looking at the rewards. It's no wonder that they gave into temptation early. In contrast, when children were engaged in tasks, they rarely looked at the rewards.

What did the investigators conclude? Left to their own devices—"just wait here"—preschool children weren't successful in controlling their behavior in the face of temptation. But when their attention was engaged elsewhere—particularly with the interesting task—they were much more successful in delaying gratification. Thus, a critical part of resisting temptation is "the ability to control the direction of attention, to strategically self-distract, and to move the focus of attention flexibly across a situation" (p. 325).

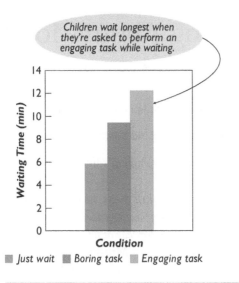

Children wait longest when they're asked to perform an engaging task while waiting.

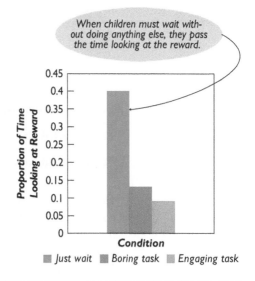

When children must wait without doing anything else, they pass the time looking at the reward.

Figure 12-1

What converging evidence would strengthen these conclusions? Peake and his colleagues measured children's self-control with a specially designed task. Consequently, a useful next step would be to complement the results from that task with observations of self-control as it occurs naturally in children's homes. Also, because 3- to 5-year-olds have hardly mastered self-control, another logical extension would be to test older children.

Overall, then, how children think about tempting objects or outcomes makes all the difference. Even preschoolers can achieve self-control by making plans that include appropriate self-instruction. For example, in the vignette, Shirley could have helped Ryan make a plan to resist temptation. She might have told him, "When you feel like you want to eat some cake, tell yourself, 'No cake until Mom gets home' and go play in your bedroom." And children can improve their self-control with the programs described in Module 5.2 for training executive function (Berkman et al., 2012).

As children learn to regulate their own behavior, they also begin to learn about moral rules—cultural rights and wrongs—which are described in the next module.

One way to resist the temptation of desirable objects is to think about something else or do something else, such as singing.

 Check Your Learning

RECALL Describe the three phases in the emergence of self-control during infancy and the preschool years.

How does temperament influence a child's self-control?

INTERPRET What does longitudinal research on preschool children's ability to delay gratification tell us about the continuity of development?

APPLY Shirley described the birthday cake episode to her own mother, who replied, "It's simple, my dear. You're the parent. He's the kid. You're the boss. Tell him what to do." What would you say to Shirley's mom?

Reasoning About Moral Issues

OUTLINE

Piaget's Views

Kohlberg's Theory

Beyond Kohlberg's Theory

LEARNING OBJECTIVES

LO4 How did Piaget describe growth in moral reasoning?

LO5 What stages of moral reasoning did Kohlberg propose?

LO6 What are some alternatives to Kohlberg's theory?

Howard, the least popular boy in the eighth grade, had been wrongly accused of stealing a sixth-grader's iPad. Min-shen, another sixth-grader, knew that Howard was innocent but said nothing to the school principal for fear of what his friends would say about siding with Howard. A few days later, when Min-shen's father heard about the incident, he was upset that his son apparently had so little "moral fiber." Why hadn't Min-shen acted in the face of an injustice?

On one of the days when I was writing this module, my local paper had two articles about youth from the area. One article was about a 14-year-girl who was badly burned while saving her younger brothers from a fire in their apartment. Her mother said she wasn't surprised by her daughter's actions because the daughter had always been an extraordinarily caring person. The other article was about two 17-year-old boys who had beaten an elderly man to death. They had only planned to steal his wallet, but when he insulted them and tried to punch them, they became enraged.

Reading articles like these makes you wonder why some people act in ways that earn our deepest respect and admiration, whereas others earn our utter contempt as well as our pity. At a more mundane level, we wonder why Min-shen didn't tell the truth about the theft to the school principal. In this module, we'll begin our exploration of moral understanding and behavior by looking at children's thinking about moral issues: How do children judge what is "good" and what is "bad"? Let's start by looking at Jean Piaget's ideas about the development of moral reasoning.

Piaget's Views

LO4 How did Piaget describe growth in moral reasoning?

When my son Matt was about 6, he and I often played Chutes and Ladders®, a board game in which you can advance rapidly when you land on a space that has a ladder but must go backward if you land on a chute. To speed up the game, I suggested to Matt that we be allowed to advance if we landed on a chute as well as a ladder. I reminded him that he liked to climb up slides at playgrounds, so my suggestion had some logic to it. Matt would have none of this. He told me, "It's a rule that you have to go backward when you land on a chute. You can't go forward. The people who made Chutes and Ladders® say so. Just read the instructions, Daddy." I tried again to persuade him (because, in my humble opinion, Chutes and Ladders® gives new meaning to "bored" games), but he was adamant.

Matt's inflexibility, which is typical of 6-year-olds, can be explained by Piaget's theory of moral development, which includes three stages. In the first stage, which lasts from age 2 years to about 4, children have no well-defined ideas about morality. **But, beginning at about 5 years and continuing through age 7, children are in a stage of** *moral realism;* **they believe that rules are** created by wise adults and therefore must be followed and cannot be changed. Another characteristic of the stage of moral realism is that children believe in *immanent justice*, the idea that breaking a rule always leads to punishment. Suppose I had forced Matt to use my new rules for Chutes and Ladders® and that, the next day, he had tripped on his way to school, scraping his knee. Believing in immanent justice, he would have seen the scraped knee as the inevitable consequence of breaking the rule the previous day.

By 8 years of age, children understand that people create rules to get along; for example, these boys may follow the rule that they'll vote to decide where to ride their skateboards.

At about age 8, children progress to the stage of *moral relativism*, the understanding that rules are created by people to help them get along. Children progress to this more advanced level of moral reasoning in part because advances in cognitive development allow them to understand the reasons for rules. Furthermore, from interactions with their peers, children come to understand the need for rules and how they are created. For example, as the boys in the photo decide where to ride their skateboards, they might follow a rule that everybody can suggest some place and then they'll vote. The boys understand that this rule isn't absolute; they follow it because it's reasonably fair and, by using this rule, they spend more time skating and less time arguing.

Children in the stage of moral relativism also understand that because people agree to set rules in the first place, they can also change them if they see the need. If the skateboarding boys decided another rule would be fairer and would help them get along better, they could adopt the new rule.

Some of Piaget's ideas about moral reasoning have stood the test of time better than others. For example, later research has showed that children's early moral reasoning does not consider adult authority final and absolute. Instead, preschool children believe adults' authority is limited. Preschoolers believe that pushing a child or damaging another child's possession is wrong even when an adult says that it's okay (Tisak, 1993). However, Piaget's idea that moral reasoning progresses through a sequence of stages set the stage for a prominent theory of moral development proposed by Lawrence Kohlberg; it's the focus of the next section.

Kohlberg's Theory

LO5 What stages of moral reasoning did Kohlberg propose?

To begin, I'd like to tell you a story about Heidi, a star player on a soccer team that I coached several years ago. Heidi was terribly upset because our team was undefeated and scheduled to play in a weekend tournament to determine the league champion. But on Sunday of this same weekend, a Habitat-for-Humanity house was to be dedicated to her grandfather, who had died a few months previously. If Heidi skipped the tournament game, her friends on the team would be upset; if she skipped the dedication, her family would be disappointed. Heidi couldn't do both and didn't know what to do.

Dilemmas like Heidi's were the starting point for Kohlberg's theory. That is, he created moral dilemmas in which any action involved some undesirable consequences and asked children, adolescents, and adults what they would do in the situation. Kohlberg was not interested in the decision per se; instead he focused on the reasoning used to justify a decision—Why should Heidi go to the tournament? Why should she go to the dedication?*

Kohlberg's best-known moral dilemma is about Heinz, whose wife is dying:

> In Europe, a woman was near death from cancer. One drug might save her, a form of radium that a druggist in the same town had recently discovered. The druggist was charging $2,000, ten times what the drug cost him to make. The sick woman's husband, Heinz, went to everyone he knew to borrow the money, but he could only get together about half of what it cost. He told the druggist that his wife was dying and asked him to sell it cheaper or let him pay later. But the druggist said, "No." The husband got desperate and broke into the man's store to steal the drug for his wife (Kohlberg, 1969, p. 379).

Although more hangs in the balance for Heinz than for Heidi, both are moral dilemmas in that the alternative courses of action have desirable and undesirable features.

Kohlberg analyzed children's, adolescents', and adults' responses to a large number of dilemmas and identified three levels of moral reasoning, each divided into two stages. Across the six stages, the basis for moral reasoning shifts. In the earliest stages, moral reasoning is based on external forces, such as the promise of reward or the threat of punishment. At the most advanced levels, moral reasoning is based on a personal, internal moral code and is unaffected by others' views or society's expectations. You can clearly see this gradual shift in the three levels:

- *Preconventional level*: **For most children, many adolescents, and some adults, moral reasoning is controlled primarily by obedience to authority and by rewards and punishments.**

  Stage 1: Obedience orientation. People believe that adults know what is right and wrong. Consequently, a person should do what adults say is right to avoid being punished. A person at this stage might argue that Heinz should not steal the drug because it is against the law (which was set by adults).

  Stage 2: Instrumental orientation. People look out for their own needs. They often are nice to others because they expect the favor to be returned in the future. A person at this stage might say it was all right for Heinz to steal the drug because his wife might do something nice for him in return (that is, she might reward him).

- *Conventional level*: **For most adolescents and most adults, moral decision making is based on social norms—what is expected by others.**

  Stage 3: Interpersonal norms. Adolescents and adults believe they should act according to others' expectations. The aim is to win the approval of others by behaving as a "good person" would behave. An adolescent or adult at this stage might argue that Heinz should not steal the drug because then others would see him as an honest citizen who obeys the law.

  Stage 4: Social system morality. Adolescents and adults believe that social roles, expectations, and laws exist to maintain order within society and to promote the good of all people. An adolescent or adult in this stage might reason that Heinz should steal the drug because a husband is obligated to do all that he possibly can to save his wife's life. Or a person in this stage might reason that Heinz should not steal the drug because stealing is against the law and society must prohibit theft.

---

* As it turned out, Heidi didn't have to resolve the dilemma. We lost our tournament game on Saturday, so she went to the dedication on Sunday.

- *Postconventional level:* **For some adults, typically those older than 25, moral decisions are based on personal, moral principles.**

Stage 5: Social contract orientation. Adults agree that members of cultural groups adhere to a "social contract" because a common set of expectations and laws benefits all group members. However, if these expectations and laws no longer promote the welfare of individuals, they become invalid. Consequently, an adult in this stage might reason that Heinz should steal the drug because social rules about property rights are no longer benefiting individuals' welfare.

Stage 6: Universal ethical principles. Abstract principles such as justice, compassion, and equality form the basis of a personal moral code that may sometimes conflict with society's expectations and laws. An adult at this stage might argue that Heinz should steal the drug because life is paramount and preserving life takes precedence over all other rights.

Summary Table 12-1 lists all the stages, providing a quick review of Kohlberg's theory.

Support for Kohlberg's Theory

Kohlberg proposed that individuals move through the six stages only in the order listed. Consequently, older and more sophisticated thinkers should be more advanced in their moral development, and they usually are (Stewart & Pascual-Leone, 1992). In addition, longitudinal studies show that individuals progress through each stage in sequence, rarely skipping stages (Colby et al., 1983).

Further support for Kohlberg's theory comes from links between moral reasoning and moral behavior. Less advanced moral reasoning reflects the influence of external forces such as rewards but more advanced reasoning is based on a personal moral code. Therefore, individuals at the preconventional and conventional levels would act morally when external forces so demand, but not otherwise. In contrast, individuals at the postconventional level, where reasoning is based on personal principles, should be compelled to moral action even when external forces may not favor it.

Consistent with this claim, adolescents who defend their principles in difficult situations tend to be more advanced in Kohlberg's stages (Gibbs et al., 1986). For example, students like those in the photograph on page 378 who protest social conditions tend to have higher moral reasoning scores. This explains why Min-shen, the boy in the vignette, said nothing. Speaking out on behalf of the unpopular student is unlikely to lead to reward and violates social norms against "squealing" on friends. Consequently, a sixth-grader—who is probably in the preconventional or

 QUESTION 12.2

When Paige was told the Heinz dilemma, she replied, "He should steal the drug. Everyone would understand why he did it. And if he just let his wife die, his family and friends would think he's a terrible husband. They would never speak to him again." Which of Kohlberg's stages best describes Paige's thinking? About how old is she?

SUMMARY TABLE 12-1

STAGES IN KOHLBERG'S THEORY OF MORAL DEVELOPMENT

Preconventional Level: Punishment and Reward

Stage 1: Obedience to authority
Stage 2: Nice behavior in exchange for future favors

Conventional Level: Social Norms

Stage 3: Live up to others' expectations
Stage 4: Follow rules to maintain social order

Postconventional Level: Moral Codes

Stage 5: Adhere to a social contract when it is valid
Stage 6: Personal morality based on abstract principles

Students who show moral courage by participating in protest movements typically have more advanced moral reasoning.

conventional level of moral reasoning—would probably let the unpopular student be punished unfairly.

On some other features, Kohlberg's theory does fare well. One is that moral reasoning is not as consistent as would be expected from the theory. Teenagers reasoning at the conventional level should always base their moral decisions on others' expectations but such consistency is not the norm. Moral reasoning may be advanced for some problems but less sophisticated for others (Krebs & Denton, 2005).

Another concern is Kohlberg's claim that the sequence of stages is universal: All people in all cultures should progress through the six-stage sequence. Children and adolescents in many cultures worldwide reason about moral dilemmas at stages 2 or 3, just like North American and European youth (Gibbs et al., 2007). However, beyond the earliest stages, moral reasoning in other cultures is often not described well by Kohlberg's theory, mainly because not all cultures and religions share the theory's emphasis on individual rights and justice. For example, the Hindu religion emphasizes duty and responsibility to others (Simpson, 1974). Consistent with this emphasis, when Hindu children and adults respond to moral dilemmas, they favor solutions that provide care for others, even when individual rights or justice may suffer (Miller & Bersoff, 1992). They sometimes condone theft if it's the best way to meet one's responsibilities to care for others. Thus, the bases of moral reasoning are not universal as Kohlberg claimed; instead, they reflect cultural values.

Beyond Kohlberg's Theory

LO6 **What are some alternatives to Kohlberg's theory?**

Kohlberg's theory triggered modern research on moral development but no longer dominates the field. Now many complementary perspectives help complete our picture of the development of moral thinking.

Gilligan's Ethic of Caring Carol Gilligan (1982; Gilligan & Attanucci, 1988) argued that Kohlberg's emphasis on justice applies more to males than to females, whose reasoning about moral issues is often rooted in concern for others. According to Gilligan, this "ethic of care" leads females like the girls in the photo to put a priority on fulfilling obligations to other people, and those obligations guide their moral decision making.

Research yields little evidence supporting Gilligan's claim that females and males differ in the bases of their moral reasoning. In a comprehensive meta-analysis (Jaffee & Hyde, 2000), males tended to get slightly greater scores on problems that emphasized justice, whereas females tended to get slightly greater scores on problems that emphasized caring. But the differences were small and do not indicate that females' moral reasoning is predominated by a concern with care or that males' moral reasoning is predominated by a concern with justice. Even though males and females do not differ as expected, Gilligan's theory is important in emphasizing that moral reasoning is broader than Kohlberg claimed: Most people think about moral issues in terms of *both* justice and caring, depending on the nature of the moral dilemma and the context (Turiel, 2006).

Development of Domains of Social Judgment Another approach notes that moral judgments (whether based on justice or care) represent just one of several important domains in which children and adults make social judgments (Smetana, 2006; Turiel, 1998). To illustrate the domains, think about the following preschool children:

- Brian often kicks or pushes his younger brother when their mom isn't looking.
- Kathryn never puts her toys away when she's done playing with them.
- Brad likes to wear his underpants inside out.

Although each child's behavior is in some sense "wrong," only the first child's behavior—kicking and pushing—represents a moral transgression because Brian's actions can harm another person. **In contrast, *social conventions* are arbitrary standards of behavior agreed to by a cultural group to facilitate interactions within the group.** Thus, social convention says that we can eat French fries but not green beans with our fingers and that children like Kathryn should clean up after themselves. **Finally, the *personal domain* pertains to choices concerning one's body (e.g., what to eat and wear) and choices of friends or activities.** Decisions here are not right or wrong, but instead are seen as personal preferences left to the individual (Smetana, 2002). Thus, Brad's decision to wear his underpants inside out is unusual but not wrong.

During the preschool years, children begin to differentiate these domains (Lagattuta, Nucci, & Bosacki, 2010; Turiel, 1998; Yau, Smetana, & Metzger, 2009). For example, they believe that breaking a moral rule is more serious and should be punished more severely than breaking a social convention. And preschool children believe that moral rules apply regardless of the situation (e.g., it's *never* okay to hit other children) and can't be overruled by adults. In contrast, preschoolers claim that social conventions are established by adults, which means they can be changed (e.g., it's okay for a school to say that students should address teachers by their first names). Finally, even preschoolers believe that the personal domain is just that: one where the individual should choose and not have the choices dictated by others.

Moral rules are common across cultures, but by definition, social conventions are not. The "Cultural Influences" feature shows how a social convention governing the same behavior—polite lying—takes different forms in Western and Asian cultures.

In Gilligan's theory, the most advanced level of moral reasoning is based on the understanding that caring is the cornerstone of all human relationships, ranging from parent–child relationships to the one that exists between a homeless person and a volunteer at a shelter.

Cultural Influences
Lies, White Lies, and Blue Lies

Preschool children claim that lying is wrong—telling a lie to hide one's transgressions is violating a moral rule. But older children have a more nuanced view and claim that "polite lying" is justified if it helps the welfare of others or would prevent an injustice. In other words, school-age children have mastered their culture's view that polite lies are social conventions designed to protect others (Lee, 2013).

Nevertheless, the circumstances that justify polite lying vary with culture. White lies are common in Western culture: Children often lie to protect another person. When asked by an experimenter if they like an undesirable gift (e.g., a bar of soap), most school-age children say "yes." Such white lies are more common as children develop and the usual justification is that it would be rude to tell the truth;

the white lie makes a person happy, which is more important than telling the truth (Popliger, Talwar, & Crossman, 2011).

In contrast, in China polite lying is more likely to take the form of a "blue lie," one that helps the group and, in the process, hurts an individual. If a classmate who sings poorly wants to join the choir, Chinese children believe that lying to the child ("Sorry, but there are no spaces left in the choir") is acceptable because it protects the quality of the choir. Western children are more likely to believe that lying to the choir ("My friend sings really well") is acceptable because it makes the friend happy (Fu et al., 2007). These cultural standards for polite lying reflect more general differences between Asian and Western cultures in their emphasis on the group and the individual (e.g., recall, from Module 10.1, that Asian children take pride in group achievement but North American children take pride in individual achievement). And they show that social conventions vary in predictable ways across cultures.

The "Cultural Influences" feature shows that children's understanding of these different domains is shaped, in part, by their experiences. Parents' responses to different kinds of transgressions also play a role (Turiel, 1998). When a child breaks a moral rule, adults talk about the impact of the act on the victim and how that person could be hurt. In contrast, when a child violates a social convention, adults more often talk about the need to follow rules and to obey parents, teachers, and other people in authority. Finally, conversations about the personal domain are different: Here adults typically do not specify a "right" or "wrong" choice, but instead encourage children to make their own choices (Nucci & Weber, 1995).

Origins of Moral Reasoning in Infancy Research on domains of social judgment shows that by 3 years, children understand moral rules are special—they can't be changed and they apply broadly (Smetana et al., 2012). Other research suggests that moral reasoning may begin at even younger ages: 19-month-olds expect resources to be divided evenly (Sloane, Baillargeon, & Premack, 2012) and 6- to 10-month-olds prefer helpful actors over those who hinder others (Hamlin, Wynn, & Bloom, 2007).

Findings like these have led some scientists to propose an evolutionary basis to moral judgments (Hamlin, 2014; Tomasello & Vaish, 2013). The gist of the argument is that a sense of morality evolved to allow early humans to live together in groups: Because people are often selfish, a moral sense evolved to allow them to cooperate with others, sometimes sacrificing their own interests for those of the group.

According to this account, an innate moral sense would include three essential components: (1) moral goodness—feeling concern for other people and helping them in time of need; (2) moral evaluation—identifying and disliking group members who do not cooperate; and (3) moral retribution—punishing group members whose behavior undermines the group. Consistent with the theory, each of these components has been observed in infants: they are concerned when others are upset, they favor people who help and dislike those who don't, and they punish uncooperative individuals by denying them rewards (Davidov et al., 2013; Hamlin, 2013). Although this work on infants' moral reasoning is just beginning, many scientists believe that moral reasoning may represent another core domain like those described in Module 6.2, one that evolved because it was a form of knowledge essential for humans to survive in groups.

The Role of Emotions So far we've considered moral development primarily in cognitive terms: as a rational decision-making process in which children deliberately evaluate the virtues of different actions. Yet moral decision making is often quite emotional (e.g., in the module-opening vignette,

Min-shen actually became quite upset as he debated whether to tell authorities who had stolen the iPad) and activates emotional centers in the brain (Greene, 2007). Consequently, scientists have begun to study the interplay of cognition and emotion in shaping the development of moral judgments (Nucci & Gingo, 2011).

One idea is that emotional responses to events provide the raw data that allow children to create categories of morally relevant concepts (Arsenio, Gold, & Adams, 2006). For example, even preschool children know that a boy would feel sad if someone stole his dessert or took his turn on a swing. And they know that a girl would feel happy if she helped a peer who dropped a stack of papers or shared her lunch with a friend who forgot hers. Repeated experience with these kinds of events leads children to form scripts (see page 219) about the emotional consequences of different actions, and children then create categories of events that lead to similar emotional outcomes. For example, one script in which a child becomes sad after a theft or another script in which a child becomes sad following unprovoked aggression may lead children to create a concept of unfair victimization.

Thus, children's emotional response to social-moral events is an important step in creating different categories of moral concepts. In Modules 12.3 and 12.4, we'll see that the nature of children's emotional responses to social interactions predicts whether they act prosocially or act aggressively.

 ## Check Your Learning

RECALL Summarize research that supports and refutes Kohlberg's theory of moral reasoning.

What are the different domains of social judgment? What do young children understand about each of them?

INTERPRET How do Piaget's stages of moral realism and moral relativism fit with Kohlberg's six stages?

APPLY Imagine that you were the father of Min-shen, the boy in the vignette who did not stand up for the other boy who was wrongly accused of stealing the iPod. Based on the research described in this module, what might you do to try to advance Min-shen's level of moral reasoning?

 # 12.3 Helping Others

LEARNING OBJECTIVES	OUTLINE
LO7 At what age do children begin to act prosocially? How does prosocial behavior change with age?	**Development of Prosocial Behavior**
LO8 What skills do children need to behave prosocially?	**Skills Underlying Prosocial Behavior**
LO9 What features of situations influence children's prosocial behavior?	**Situational Influences**
LO10 How does heredity contribute to children's prosocial behavior?	**The Contribution of Heredity**
LO11 How can parents encourage their children to act prosocially?	**Socializing Prosocial Behavior**

Six-year-old Juan got his finger trapped in the DVD player when he tried to remove a disc. While he cried and cried, his 3-year-old brother, Antonio, and his 2-year-old sister, Carla, watched but did not help. Later, when their mother had soothed Juan and saw that his finger was not injured, she worried about her younger children's reactions. In the face of their brother's obvious distress, why had Antonio and Carla done nothing?

Most parents, most teachers, and most religions try to teach children to act in cooperative, helping, giving ways—at least most of the time and in most situations. **Actions that benefit others are known as** *prosocial behavior*. Of course, cooperation often "works" because individuals gain more than they would by not cooperating. *Altruism* **is prosocial behavior that helps another with no direct benefit to the individual.** Altruism is driven by feelings of responsibility for other people. Two youngsters pooling their funds to buy a candy bar to share demonstrates cooperative behavior. One youngster giving half her lunch to a friend who forgot his own lunch demonstrates altruism.

Many scientists believe that humans are biologically predisposed to be helpful, to share, to cooperate, and to be concerned for others (Hastings, Zahn-Waxler, & McShane, 2006). Why has prosocial behavior evolved over time? The best explanation has nothing to do with lofty moral principles; instead, it's much more pragmatic: People who frequently help others are more likely to receive help themselves, and this increases the chance that they'll pass along their genes to future generations.

But, as the story of Juan and his siblings shows, children (and adults, for that matter) are not always helpful or cooperative. In this module, you'll learn how prosocial behavior changes with age and discover some factors that promote prosocial behavior.

Development of Prosocial Behavior

LO7 At what age do children begin to act prosocially? How does prosocial behavior change with age?

Simple acts of altruism can be seen by 18 months of age. When toddlers and preschoolers see other people who are obviously hurt or upset, they appear concerned. And their sympathetic nervous system is activated, which is a common by-product of experiencing distressing or threatening events (Hepach, Vaish, & Tomasello, 2012). Like the child in the photo, they try to comfort the person by hugging him or patting him (Zahn-Waxler et al., 1992). Apparently, at this early age, children recognize signs of distress. And if an adult is in obvious need of help—a teacher accidentally drops markers on a floor—most 18-month-olds spontaneously help get the markers (Warneken & Tomasello, 2006).

During the toddler and preschool years, children gradually begin to understand others' needs and learn more appropriate altruistic responses (van der Mark, van IJzendoorn, & Bakermans-Kranenburg, 2002). When 3-year-old Alexis sees her father trying, unsuccessfully, to get her mother's attention, she may poke her mom to get her attention and then point to her father (Beier, Over, & Carpenter, 2014). These early attempts at altruistic behavior often are limited because young children's knowledge of what they can do to help is modest. As youngsters acquire more strategies to help others, their preferred strategies become more adultlike (Eisenberg, Fabes, & Spinrad, 2006).

Even toddlers recognize when others are upset, and try to comfort them.

Thus, as a general rule, intentions to act prosocially increase with age, as do children's strategies for helping. Of course, not all children respond to the needs of others, either in toddlerhood or at later ages. Some children tend to look out for their own interests. What makes some children more likely than others to help? We'll answer this question in the next section.

Skills Underlying Prosocial Behavior

LO8 **What skills do children need to behave prosocially?**

Think back to an occasion when you helped someone. How did you know that the person needed help? Why did you decide to help? Although you didn't realize it at the time, your decision to help was probably based on several skills:

- *Perspective taking.* In Module 6.1, you learned about Piaget's concept of egocentrism, the preoperational youngster's inability to see things from another's point of view. Egocentrism limits children's ability to share or help because they simply do not realize the need for prosocial behavior. They have only one perspective—their own. For example, young children might not help someone carrying many packages because they cannot envision that carrying lots of bulky things is a burden. However, older children can take the perspective of others, so they recognize the burden and are more inclined to help. In general, the better children understand the thoughts and feelings of other people, the more willing they are to share and help others (Strayer & Roberts, 2004; Vaish, Carpenter, & Tomasello, 2009).
- *Empathy*. **The ability to experience another person's emotions is** *empathy*. Children who deeply feel another person's fear, disappointment, sorrow, or loneliness are more inclined to help that person than are children who do not feel these emotions (Eisenberg et al., 2006; Malti & Krettenauer, 2013). In other words, youngsters like the one in the photo, who is obviously distressed by what she is seeing, are most likely to help others.
- *Moral reasoning.* In Module 12.2, you learned that reward and punishment influence young children's moral reasoning, whereas a concern for moral principles characterizes adolescents' and adults' moral decision making. Therefore, as you would expect, prosocial behavior in young children is usually determined by the chance of reward or punishment. It also follows that, as children mature and begin to make moral decisions on the basis of fairness and justice, they become more prosocial. Consistent with this idea, Eisenberg, Zhou, and Koller (2001) found that Brazilian 13- to 16-year-olds were more likely to act prosocially when their moral reasoning was more advanced (e.g., based on internalized moral standards).

In sum, children and adolescents who help others tend to be better able to take another's view, to feel another's emotions, and to act on the basis of principles, rather than rewards, punishments, or social norms. For example, a 15-year-old who spontaneously loans his favorite video game to a friend does so because he sees that the friend would like to play the game, he feels the friend's disappointment at not owning the game, and he believes that friends should share with each other.

Of course, perspective taking, empathy, and moral reasoning skills do not guarantee that children always act altruistically. Even when children have the skills needed to act altruistically, they may not because of the particular situation, as we'll see in the next section.

Children who are empathic—they understand how others feel—are more likely to help others in need.

Situational Influences

LO9 What features of situations influence children's prosocial behavior?

Kind children occasionally disappoint us by being cruel, and children who are usually stingy sometimes surprise us with their generosity. Why? The setting helps determine whether children act altruistically or not.

- *Feelings of responsibility.* Children act altruistically when they feel responsible to the person in need. They are more likely to help siblings and friends than strangers, simply because they feel responsible for people they know well (Costin & Jones, 1992). And they're more likely to help when prompted with photos showing two people who look to be friends (Over & Carpenter, 2009). In other words, a simple reminder of the importance of friendship (or affiliation with others) can be enough to elicit helping.
- *Feelings of competence.* Children act altruistically when they feel that they have the skills necessary to help the person in need. Suppose, for example, that a child is growing more and more upset because she can't figure out how to work a computer game. A classmate who knows little about computer games is not likely to help because he doesn't know what to do to help. By helping, he could end up looking foolish (Peterson, 1983).
- *Mood.* Children act altruistically when they are happy or feeling successful but not when they are sad or feeling as if they have failed (Wentzel, Filisetti, & Looney, 2007). In other words, a preschooler who has just spent an exciting morning as the "leader" in nursery school is more inclined to share treats with siblings than is a preschooler who was punished by the teacher (Eisenberg, 2000).
- *Cost of altruism.* Children act altruistically when it entails few or modest sacrifices. A preschooler who has received a snack that she doesn't particularly like is more inclined to share it than is a child who has received her favorite snack (Eisenberg & Shell, 1986).

When, then, are children most likely to help? When they feel responsible to the person in need, have the skills that are needed, are happy, and do not think they have to give up a lot by helping. When are children least likely to help? When they feel neither responsible for nor capable of helping, are in a bad mood, and believe that helping will entail a large personal sacrifice.

Using these guidelines, how do you explain why Antonio and Carla, the children in the vignette, watched idly as their older brother cried? Here's a hint: The last two factors—mood and cost—are not likely to be involved but the first two may explain Antonio and Carla's failure to help their older brother. My explanation appears on page 386, just before "Check Your Learning."

So far, we've seen that altruistic behavior is determined by children's skills (such as perspective taking) and by characteristics of situations (such as whether children feel competent to help in a particular situation). Whether children are altruistic is also determined by genetics and by socialization, as we'll see in the remaining two sections in this module.

The Contribution of Heredity

LO10 How does heredity contribute to children's prosocial behavior?

As I mentioned on page 382, many scientists believe that prosocial behavior represents an evolutionary adaptation: People who help others are more likely to be helped themselves and thus are more likely to survive and have offspring.

According to this argument, we should expect to find evidence for heritability of prosocial behavior, and in fact that's the case: Twin studies consistently find that identical twins are more alike in their prosocial behavior than are fraternal twins (Gregory et al., 2009).

One likely path of genetic influence involves oxytocin, a hormone that influences many social behaviors (e.g., nurturance, empathy, affiliation, and cooperation) and that's been linked to a few specific genes. In this account, some children may inherit oxytocin-promoting genes that facilitate their prosocial behavior (Carter, 2014; Keltner et al., 2014).

Genes may also affect prosocial behavior indirectly, by their influence on temperament. For example, children who are temperamentally less able to regulate their emotions (in part because of heredity) may help less often because they're so upset by another's distress that taking action is impossible (Eisenberg et al., 2007). Another temperamental influence may be via inhibition (shyness). Children who are temperamentally shy are often reluctant to help others, particularly people they don't know well (Young, Fox, & Zahn-Waxler, 1999). Even though these children realize that others need help and are upset by another person's apparent distress, shy children's reticence means that these feelings don't translate into action. Thus, in both cases, children are aware that others need help. But in the first instance, they're too upset themselves to figure out how to help, and in the second instance they know how to help but are too inhibited to follow through.

Socializing Prosocial Behavior

LO11 How can parents encourage their children to act prosocially?

Dr. Martin Luther King, Jr. said that his pursuit of civil rights for African Americans was particularly influenced by three people: Henry David Thoreau (a 19th-century American philosopher), Mohandas Gandhi (the leader of the Indian movement for independence from England), and his father, Dr. Martin Luther King, Sr. As is true of many humanitarians, Dr. King's prosocial behavior started in childhood, at home. But how do parents foster altruism in their children? Several factors contribute:

- *Modeling.* When children see adults helping and caring for others, they often imitate such prosocial behavior (Eisenberg et al., 2006). Parents who report frequent feelings of warmth and concern for others tend to have children who experience stronger feelings of empathy. When a mother is helpful and responsive, her children often imitate her by being cooperative, helpful, sharing, and less critical of others. In a particularly powerful demonstration of the impact of parental modeling, people who had risked their lives during World War II to protect Jews from the Nazis often reported their parents' emphasis on caring for all people (Oliner & Oliner, 1988).
- *Disciplinary practices.* Children behave prosocially more often when their parents are warm and supportive, set guidelines, and provide feedback; in contrast, prosocial behavior is less common when parenting is harsh, threatening, and includes frequent physical punishment (Eisenberg & Fabes, 1998; Knight & Carlo, 2012; Moreno, Klute, & Robinson, 2008). Particularly important is parents' use of reasoning as a disciplinary tactic, with the goal of helping children see how their actions affect others. For example, after 4-year-old Annie grabbed some crayons from a playmate, her father told Annie, "You shouldn't just grab things away from people. It makes them angry and unhappy. Ask first, and if they say 'no,' then you mustn't take them."

 QUESTION 12.3
Rebecca was astonished when her son Ron wanted to spend a few hours distributing sweets at a nearby old-age home on his 13th birthday. She was sure that none of Ron's friends did something like that. What do you think made Ron take this decision?

After children and adolescents have had the opportunity to help others, they often continue to be helpful because they better understand the needs of others.

- *Opportunities to behave prosocially.* You need to practice to improve motor skills, and the same is true of prosocial behaviors: Children and adolescents are more likely to act prosocially when they're routinely given the opportunity to help and cooperate with others. At home, children can help with household tasks, such as cleaning and setting the table. Adolescents can be encouraged to participate in community service, such as working at a food pantry or, like the teenager in the photo, helping older adults. Experiences like these help to sensitize children and adolescents to the needs of others and allow them to enjoy the satisfaction of helping (Grusec, Goodnow, & Cohen, 1996; McLellan & Youniss, 2003). Such experiences help to explain why Mexican American youth are often more prosocial than their European American peers: Many Mexican American mothers emphasize the importance of families and expect their children to help with household chores such as caring for siblings, experiences that lead children to be attentive to others' needs (Knight & Carlo, 2012).

Thus, many factors, listed in Summary Table 12-2, contribute to children's prosocial behavior. Combining all these ingredients, we can describe the development of children's altruistic behavior this way: As children get older, their perspective-taking and empathic skills develop, which enables them to see and feel another's needs. Nonetheless, children are never invariably altruistic (or, fortunately, invariably nonaltruistic) because properties of situations dictate altruistic behavior, too.

As parents and other adults try to encourage children's prosocial behavior, one of the biggest obstacles is aggressive behavior, which is common throughout childhood and adolescence. In the next module, we'll look at some of the forces that contribute to children's aggression.

Answer to question on page 384 about why Antonio and Carla didn't help: Here are two explanations: First, neither Antonio nor Carla may have felt sufficiently responsible to help because (a) with two children who could help, each child's feeling of individual responsibility is reduced, and (b) younger children are less likely to feel responsible for an older brother. Second, both children likely

SUMMARY TABLE 12-2

FACTORS CONTRIBUTING TO CHILDREN'S PROSOCIAL BEHAVIOR

General Category	Types of Influence	Children Are More Likely to Help When...
Skills	Perspective taking	they can take another person's point of view.
	Empathy	they feel another person's emotions.
	Moral reasoning	they base moral decisions on fairness.
Situational influences	Feelings of responsibility	they feel responsible to the person in need.
	Feelings of competence	they feel competent to help.
	Mood	they're in a good mood.
	Cost of altruism	the cost of prosocial behavior is small.
Heredity	Temperament	they're not shy and can control their emotions.
Parents' influence	Modeling	parents behave prosocially themselves.
	Discipline	parents reason with them.
	Opportunities	they practice at home and elsewhere.

have been told not to use the DVD player by themselves. Consequently, they don't feel competent to help: they don't know what to do to help Juan remove his finger.

 ## Check Your Learning

RECALL Describe developmental change in prosocial behavior.

What are the situations in which children are most likely to help others?

INTERPRET Why must a full account of children's prosocial behavior include an emphasis on skills (e.g., empathy) as well as situations (e.g., whether a child feels responsible)?

APPLY Helping with household chores and voluntary community service often increase children's prosocial behavior. Of the skills underlying prosocial behavior (page 383), which do you think are most affected by children's experiences helping at home and elsewhere?

 # Aggression

LEARNING OBJECTIVES	OUTLINE
LO12 When does aggressive behavior first emerge? How stable is aggression across childhood, adolescence, and adulthood?	**Change and Stability**
LO13 How do families, television, and the child's own thoughts contribute to aggression?	**Roots of Aggressive Behavior**
LO14 Why are some children victims of aggression?	**Victims of Aggression**

Every day, 7-year-old Reza follows the same routine when he gets home from school: He watches one action-adventure cartoon after another on TV until it's time for dinner. Reza's mother is disturbed by her son's constant TV viewing, particularly because of the amount of violence in the shows that he likes. Her husband tells her to stop worrying: "Let him watch what he wants to. It won't hurt him and, besides, it keeps him out of your hair."

If you think back to your years in elementary school, you can probably remember a class "bully"—a child who was always teasing classmates and picking fights. **Such acts typify** *aggression*, **behavior meant to harm others.** Aggressiveness is not the same as assertiveness, even though laypeople often use these words interchangeably. You've probably heard praise for an "aggressive businessperson" or a ballplayer who was "aggressive at running the bases." However, psychologists and other behavioral scientists would call these behaviors *assertive*. Assertive behaviors are goal-directed actions to further the legitimate interests of individuals or the groups they represent, while respecting the rights of other persons. In contrast, aggressive behavior, which may be physical or verbal, is intended to harm, damage, or injure and is carried out without regard for the rights of others.

In this module, we will examine aggressive behavior in children and see how it changes with age. Then we'll examine some causes of children's aggression and, in the process, learn more about the impact of Reza's TV watching on his behavior.

Change and Stability

LO12 **When does aggressive behavior first emerge? How stable is aggression across childhood, adolescence, and adulthood?**

By the time infants have their first birthday, most have mastered the motor skills needed for simple aggression—grabbing and pushing—and many youngsters uses these skills to get what they want (e.g., taking a toy from a peer, Hay et al., 2011). **In such *instrumental aggression*, a child uses aggression to achieve an explicit goal.** In elementary school, instrumental aggression might take the form of one child shoving another to get to the head of a lunch line. In the elementary-school years, another form of aggression emerges (Coie et al., 1991). *Hostile aggression* **is unprovoked; apparently, its sole goal is to intimidate, harass, or humiliate another child.** Hostile aggression is illustrated by a child who spontaneously says, "You're stupid!" and then kicks the other child. **Yet another common type of aggression is *reactive aggression*, in which one child's behavior leads to another child's aggression.** Reactive aggression would include a child who loses a game and then punches the child who won, or a child not chosen for the starring role in a play kicking the child who was selected.

Instrumental, hostile, and reactive aggression are most likely to be expressed physically by younger children. As children get older, they more often use language to express their aggression (Dodge, Coie, & Tremblay, 2006). **A particularly common form of verbal aggression is *relational aggression*, in which children try to hurt others by undermining their social relationships.** In relational aggression, which is more typical of girls than boys, children try to hurt others by telling friends to avoid a particular classmate, by spreading malicious gossip, or by making remarks meant to hurt others (Côté et al., 2007; Crick et al., 2004). Two true stories from my child-development students portray relational aggression. After a heated argument in second grade, one student's former friend wrote "Erin is a big jerk" in block letters on the sidewalk where everyone walking to school would see the message. Another student, Beth, told me that after she'd beaten a classmate in the fifth-grade spelling bee, the classmate's friends formed the "I Hate Beth" club.

Stability of Aggression Over Time Forms of aggression change with development, but individual children's tendencies to behave aggressively are stable, particularly for children who are highly aggressive at a young age (Kjeldsen et al., 2014). Each of the following longitudinal studies shows that many aggressive young children grow up to be adolescents and adults who are aggressive, sometimes violent, and often commit crimes:

- In a study of more than 250 infants and toddlers growing up in Wales (Hay et al., 2014), 6-month-olds who tried to bite or strike other people were as 3-year-olds more likely to kick or hit peers to obtain toys.
- In a study of more than 900 Canadian girls (Côté et al., 2001), 6-year-olds who had been rated by their teachers as frequently disrupting class (e.g., they were disobedient or they bullied classmates) were four to five times more likely to be diagnosed, as teenagers, with conduct disorder, a disorder in which individuals are chronically aggressive, destroy property, and lie or steal.
- In a study involving more than 200 German preschool children (Asendorpf, Denissen, & van Aken, 2008), those children who were judged by teachers to be most aggressive were, as young adults, 12 times more likely than the least aggressive children to have been charged for criminal activity.

Violent behavior in adulthood is not the only long-term outcome of childhood aggression; poor adjustment to high school (e.g., dropping out, failing a grade) and unemployment are others (Asendorpf et al., 2008; Ladd, 2003). In one study, aggressive 8-year-olds tended to do poorly in high school, leaving them few options for work as young adults and putting them at risk for problem drinking. By their early 30s, many highly aggressive children have limited education and low-status jobs; others are chronically unemployed (Alatupa et al., 2013; Kokko & Pulkkinen, 2000).

Findings from these and similar studies show that aggression is *not* simply a case of playful pushing and shoving that children always outgrow. To the contrary, a small minority of children who are highly aggressive develop into young adults who create havoc in society. What causes children to behave aggressively? Let's look at some of the roots of aggressive behavior.

Roots of Aggressive Behavior

LO13 **How do families, television, and the child's own thoughts contribute to aggression?**

Psychologists once believed that aggression was caused by frustration. The idea was that when children or adults were blocked from achieving a goal, they became frustrated and acted aggressively, often against the interfering person or object. However, scientists now look to many other causes, including biological factors, the family, the child's community and culture, and the child's own thoughts.

Biological Contributions *Born to Be Bad* is the title of at least two movies, two CDs (one by George Thorogood and one by Joan Jett), and three books. Implicit in this popular title is the idea that, from birth, some individuals follow a developmental track that leads to destructive, violent, or criminal behavior. In other words, the claim is that biology sets the stage for people to be aggressive long before experience can affect development.

Is there any truth to this idea? In fact, biology and heredity *do* contribute to aggressive and violent behavior. For example, in twin studies, identical twins are usually more alike in their levels of physical aggression than are fraternal twins (Brendgen et al., 2006; Lacourse et al., 2014). But these studies do not tell us that aggression per se is inherited; instead, they indicate that some children inherit factors that place them at risk for aggressive or violent behavior. Temperament seems to be one such factor: Youngsters who are temperamentally difficult, overly emotional, or inattentive are, for example, more likely to be aggressive (Joussemet et al., 2008; Xu, Farver, & Zhang, 2009). Hormones represent another factor: Higher levels of the hormone testosterone are often associated, weakly, with greater aggression and stronger responses to provocation (Carré, McCormick, & Hariri, 2011). Finally, some children may have a deficit in the neurotransmitters that inhibit aggressive behavior (van Goozen et al., 2007).

None of these factors—temperament, testosterone, or neurotransmitters—*causes* a child to be aggressive, but they do make aggressive behavior more likely. For instance, children who are emotional and easily irritated may be disliked by their peers and be in frequent conflict with them, opening the door for aggressive responses. Thus, biological factors place children at risk for aggression. To understand which children actually become aggressive, we need to look at interactions between inherited factors and children's experiences (Moffitt, 2005).

Impact of the Family Although few parents deliberately teach their children to harm others, family experiences are a prime training ground for learning patterns of aggression. Parents' approach to discipline is crucial. When parents use physical punishment or threats to discipline their children, the hidden message

When parents often use physical punishment, their children are more likely to become aggressive.

to children is that physical force "works" as a means of controlling others. A parent like the one in the photo is saying, in effect, "The best way to get people to do what you want is to hurt them" (Lee, Altschul, & Gershoff, 2013; Gershoff, 2013).

But strong or aggressive parental responses are not the only path to making a child aggressive. Some parents frequently threaten to withhold their love, express disappointment, and are overly possessive with their children, behaviors that represent the sort of social and emotional manipulation that defines relational aggression. Consequently, it's not surprising that children who experience heavy doses of such parenting are more likely to be relationally aggressive (Kuppens et al., 2013).

In many families with aggressive children, a vicious circle seems to develop (Keijsers et al., 2011). Compared with families with nonaggressive children, both aggressive children and their parents are more likely to respond to neutral behavior with aggression. What's more, after an aggressive exchange has begun, both parents and children are likely to escalate the exchange, rather than break it off. And once a child has been labeled aggressive by parents and others, that child is more likely to be accused of aggression and to be singled out for punishment, even when the child has been behaving entirely appropriately on the occasion in question (Patterson, 2008). The "aggressive child" will be accused of all things that go wrong—from missing cookies to broken appliances—and other children's misbehaviors will be ignored.

Another aspect of parental behavior that's been linked to aggression is *monitoring*, **which refers to parents' knowledge of where their children are, what they're doing, and who they're with.** When parents don't monitor their children's behavior, the children are more frequently aggressive (Patterson, 2008; Vieno et al., 2009). Of course, monitoring requires children's cooperation to a certain extent, and children who are chronically aggressive are often reluctant to tell parents what they're doing (e.g., teenagers not answering their cell phones when they see that a parent is calling), in part because they see monitoring as intrusive (Racz & McMahon, 2011).

So far we've seen that children's aggression is linked to parents' use of physical punishment and to their lack of monitoring. To this list we need to add another critical aspect of family life: the presence of conflict. When parents constantly argue and fight, their children are much more likely to be aggressive (Cummings et al., 2006; Narayan, Englund, & Englund, 2013). Of course, children have ringside seats for many of these confrontations, and thus they can see firsthand how parents use verbal and physical aggression against each other. Sadly, children often come to believe that these patterns of interacting represent "natural" ways of solving problems within a family (Graham-Bermann & Brescoll, 2000).

Influence of Community and Culture Parents are hardly alone in giving important lessons about aggression. Other influential voices within children's lives deliver powerful messages about aggressive behavior:

- *Television and media games.* Most TV programs targeted at children contain acts of physical aggression (Wilson et al., 2002). The average American youngster will see several *thousand* murders on TV before reaching adolescence (Waters, 1993). (If you find these numbers hard to believe, try the activities described in "See for Yourself" at the end of this chapter.) What does research tell us about this steady diet of televised mayhem and violence? Will Reza, the avid cartoon watcher in the vignette at the beginning of the module, become more aggressive? Or, as his father believes, is his TV watching simply fun?

In fact, longitudinal studies have consistently found that children exposed to much media violence often grow up to be aggressive and violent adults. This is true even when controlling for parents' education and family income (Fuld et al., 2009). What's more, playing violent video games seems to lead to aggressive and violent behavior in much the same way that watching violent TV does (Willoughby, Adachi, & Good, 2012), particularly when children play habitually and identify with aggressive game characters (Konijn, Nije Bijvank, & Bushman, 2007). Playing violent video games also leads players to see targets of aggression as less human, making aggression against them more acceptable (Greitemeyer & McLatchie, 2011). In short, Reza's father is wrong: Frequent exposure to media violence makes children more aggressive.

- *Peers.* Aggressive children often befriend other aggressive children. The outcome is hardly surprising: Aggressive friends support and encourage each other's aggressive behavior (Banny et al., 2011; Powers, Bierman, & The Conduct Problems Prevention Research Group, 2013). Just as friends drawn together by a mutual interest in music enjoy listening to CDs together, friends whose bond is their aggressive behavior enjoy teaming up to attack their peers; they often "share" targets of aggression (Card & Hodges, 2006). Aggressive adolescents often join gangs, which has a catalytic effect on aggressive and violent behavior. That is, even though adolescents who join gangs are already aggressive, their membership in a gang leads to more frequent and more violent antisocial behavior (Thornberry et al., 2003).

- *Failure in school.* Aggressive children are often uninterested in school and their grades reflect this disinterest. One interpretation of this finding is that aggressive children's behavior interferes with their learning. Instead of spending time on school tasks such as learning to add, aggressive youngsters are busy creating mayhem or being disciplined; in the process, they create conflicted relationships with their teachers—another impediment to school success (Stipek & Miles, 2008). Another interpretation is that children who have difficultly learning in school become frustrated and unhappy, and they express their frustration by aggressing against their peers.

  Both views may be right (Masten et al., 2005; Miles & Stipek, 2006). School failure may breed aggressive behavior and aggressive behavior, in turn, leads to school failure. In other words, this may be a vicious circle in which the starting point can be either aggressive behavior or school failure. Once started, the other soon follows and the cycle grows. A 5-year-old boy who kicks and pushes classmates struggles to learn to read. His failure breeds even greater anger and aggression toward his classmates, which causes him to fall further behind academically. Over time, he becomes more aggressive and more of a failure in school (Masten et al., 2005).

- *Poverty.* Aggressive and antisocial behavior is more common among children living in poverty than among children who are economically advantaged (Williams, Conger, & Blozis, 2007). Some of the impact of poverty can be explained by factors that we've already considered. For example, living in poverty is extremely stressful for parents and often leads to the parental behaviors that promote aggression—harsh discipline and lax monitoring (Shaw & Shelleby, 2014). But poverty also contributes to violent behavior in another manner, by helping to create a culture of violence.

- *Culture of violence.* Violent crime is far more common in poverty-stricken neighborhoods, and exposure to such violence fosters aggressive behavior in adolescents. For example, in a group of Chicago adolescents, those living in poverty were more likely to be exposed to firearms violence (e.g., seeing someone shot) and, as they got older, were more likely to be aggressive and violent themselves (Bingenheimer, Brennan, & Earls, 2005). Similarly, individuals living in the South and West regions of the United States often endorse a "culture of honor" that endorses aggressive and violent behavior to defend one's honor, family, and property (Hayes & Lee, 2005). In such states, adolescents are more likely to report carrying firearms to school, and school shootings like those at Columbine High School are more common (Brown, Osterman, & Barnes, 2009). Finally, on a much smaller scale, elementary-school classrooms that contain many aggressive children often create a climate that sanctions aggression and aggressive behavior is contagious, spreading from one child to the next (Powers et al., 2013). In other words, just as frequent exposure within a family to physical punishment and marital conflict leads children to believe that aggression is a natural way to solve problems, exposure in the classroom or at the community level to violence and pro-aggression attitudes leads adolescents to condone aggressive and violent behavior.

Cognitive Processes   The perceptual and cognitive skills described in Chapters 6 through 8 also play a role in aggression. One general factor is executive functioning, described on page 195. Children who are less skilled in inhibiting, shifting, and updating behaviors and thoughts are prone to aggressive behavior (Ellis, Weiss, & Lochman, 2009; McQuade et al., 2013; Schoemaker et al., 2013).

Cognitive processes contribute to aggression in another way, too: Aggressive youth often respond aggressively because they are not skilled at interpreting other people's intentions and, without a clear interpretation in mind, they respond aggressively by default (Dodge, Bates, & Pettit, 1990). Far too often, they think, "I don't know what you're up to, and, when in doubt, attack." In the "Spotlight on Theories" feature, we'll learn more about a theory of cognitive processing that helps to reveal how aggressive children think about other people.

Spotlight on Theories
Social-Information-Processing Theory and Children's Aggressive Behavior

BACKGROUND   Genetics, parents, TV, peers, and poverty all contribute to make some children prone to aggression. What these influences have in common is that they lead some children to see the world as a hostile place in which they must be wary of other people. Nonetheless, precisely characterizing the aggressive child's hostile view has been a challenge.

THE THEORY   To explain how children perceive, interpret, and respond to people, Nicki R. Crick and Kenneth Dodge (1994; Dodge & Crick, 1990; Fontaine & Dodge, 2006) formulated an information-processing model of children's thinking, which is shown in Figure 12-2. According to the model, responding to a social stimulus involves several steps. First, children selectively attend to certain features of the social stimulus but do not attend to others. Second, children try to interpret the features that

they have processed; that is, they try to give meaning to the social stimulus. Third, children evaluate their goals for the situation. Fourth, children retrieve from memory a behavioral response that is associated with the interpretation and goals of the situation. Fifth, children evaluate this response to determine if it is appropriate. Finally, the child proceeds with the behavior.

Applied to aggressive children, the theory says that aggressive children's processing is biased and restricted in many of the steps in the diagram, and that this flawed information processing is part of what leads these children to be more aggressive: They systematically misperceive people's actions (Crick & Werner, 1998; Egan, Monson, & Perry, 1998).

Hypothesis: According to social-information-processing theory, aggressive children's processing of social information (e.g., people) is biased in each of the stages depicted in Figure 12-2. In the fourth and fifth stages of processing—accessing response options and evaluating them—this bias leads to the hypothesis that aggressive children should respond hostilely when this interpretation is not warranted. For example, when an aggressive child picks up a book from a desk and another child says, "That's my book" in a nonprovocative manner, aggressive children are expected to be more likely to respond in a hostile way ("I was just looking at it. I didn't know it was yours. No need to jump all over me.") than in a neutral way ("Okay, I was wondering whose it was.").

Test: Fontaine et al. (2009) evaluated this hypothesis by asking adolescents to watch videos in which one person's action (e.g., picking up a book) leads to another person's neutral response ("That's my book."). Then the videos showed hostile and non-hostile responses; adolescents in the study were asked how easily they would act in these ways and how they would feel in doing so. Aggressive adolescents more often endorsed the hostile response but

less aggressive adolescents tended to endorse the nonhostile response.

Conclusion: When confronted with situations in which a person's actions aren't clear, aggressive children and adolescents often respond in a hostile manner by default. In other words, aggressive children view the world through suspicious eyes—as if the others are always "out to get them," and consequently they respond to many neutral interactions with unwarranted hostility and anger.

Application: If aggressive children are unskilled at interpreting and responding to others' actions, would training in these skills reduce their aggressive behavior? The answer seems to be yes. When children are taught more sophisticated social-cognitive skills—including better strategies for resolving conflicts—they become better able to recognize other people's emotions, to interpret others' intentions, and to deal with peer-related problems without aggressing. Collectively, these improved social skills mean that children are less prone to antisocial behaviors such as aggression (Dodge, Godwin, & The Conduct Problems Prevention Research Group, 2013).

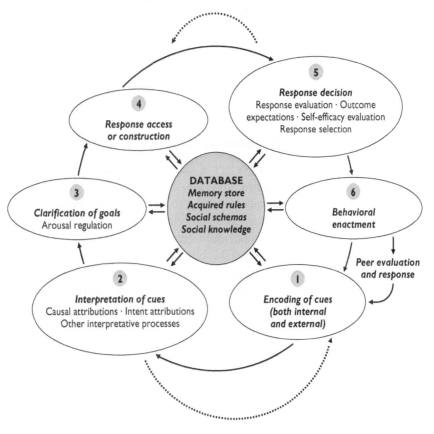

Figure 12-2

Multiple, Cascading Risks Many factors contribute to make some children and adolescents more prone to aggressive, sometimes violent behavior. When these factors mount up in children's lives, they are at ever-greater risk for aggressive behavior (Greenberg et al., 1999). What's more, many of the factors operate in a cascading fashion, such that later risk factors build on prior factors (Vaillancourt et al., 2013): Poverty or maternal depression can lead to harsh, ineffective parenting. In turn, this leads children to be unprepared for school (both academically and socially), which leads to school failure and conduct problems. These difficulties cause some parents to become less active and less invested in parenting, which means that they monitor their children less often, allowing them to associate with deviant, aggressive peers (Dodge, Greenberg, & Malone, 2008).

Thus, the developmental journey that leads to a violent, aggressive, antisocial adolescent starts in early childhood but gains momentum along the way. Consequently, efforts to prevent children from taking this path must begin early, be maintained over childhood, and target both children and their parents. An example of a successful intervention program is Fast Track (Bierman et al., 2013; Conduct Problems Prevention Research Group, 2011), which is designed to teach academic and social skills to elementary-school children as well as life and vocational skills to adolescents. In addition, parents are taught skills for effective child rearing and, later, how to stay involved with their children and to monitor their behavior. At 12th grade—two years after the program had ended—aggressive and destructive behavior among children who were at highest risk in kindergarten was cut in half compared to similar high-risk children assigned to a control condition.

Of course, this sort of successful program comes with a high price tag. But its cost is a fraction of that associated with the by-products of aggressive behavior: One analysis suggests that each violent and aggressive American adolescent costs $2–$5 million in payments to victims, court costs, and costs of incarceration (Cohen & Piquero, 2009). Thus, programs like Fast Track not only improve children's lives (and the lives of people around them) but are also cost-effective.

Victims of Aggression

LO14 Why are some children victims of aggression?

Every aggressive act is directed at someone. Most children are the targets of an occasional aggressive act—a shove or kick to gain a desired toy, or a stinging insult by someone trying to save face. However, a small percentage of children are chronic targets of bullying. In both Europe and the United States, 10–25% of elementary-school children and adolescents are chronic victims of physical attacks, name calling, backstabbing, and similar aggressive acts (Juvonen & Graham, 2014). In recent years, some youth have become victims of electronic bullying, in which they are harassed via cell phones or the Internet (Raskauskas & Stoltz, 2007).

As you can imagine, being tormented daily by their peers is hard on children. Research consistently shows that children who are chronic victims of aggression are often lonely, anxious, and depressed; they dislike school and their peers; and they have low self-esteem (Ladd & Ladd, 1998; Rudolph, Troop-Gordon, & Flynn, 2009). As adults, they're prone to poor health and unsatisfying social relationships (Wolke et al., 2013). Ironically, the impact of bullying is reduced when children see others being bullied, apparently because they feel that they're not being singled out for harassment (Nishina & Juvonen, 2005).

Why do some children suffer the sad fate of being victims? Some victims are actually aggressive themselves (van Lier et al., 2012; Veenstra et al., 2005). These youngsters often overreact, are restless, and are easily irritated. Their aggressive

 **QUESTION 12.4**
Brandon is constantly picked on by other kids at his school: The girls tease him and the boys often start fights with him. What could he and his parents do to improve his peer relations?

peers soon learn that these children are easily baited. A group of children will, for example, insult or ridicule such a child, knowing that he or she will probably start a fight even though he or she is outnumbered. Other victims tend to be withdrawn, submissive, and have low self-esteem. They are unwilling or unable to defend themselves from their peers' aggression, and so they are usually referred to as *passive victims* (Guerra, Williams, & Sadek, 2011; Ladd & Ladd, 1998; Salmivalli & Isaacs, 2005). When attacked, like the child in the photo, they show obvious signs of distress and usually give in to their attackers, thereby rewarding the aggressive behavior. Thus, both aggressive and withdrawn–submissive children end up as victims—and this pattern holds for children in China as well as for children in North America (Schwartz, Chang, & Farver, 2001).

When children give in to aggressive children, they often become chronic victims.

Other factors contribute to make children victims of bullying. Children are more likely to be bullied when they are obese, depressed, disabled, or immigrants. In essence, any feature that would make children different from their peers puts them in the sights of bullies (Juvonen & Graham, 2014; Strohmeier, Kärnä, & Salmivalli, 2011).

Victimized children can learn ways of dealing with bullying that are more effective than either overreacting or withdrawing passively, including not lashing out when insulted and not showing fear when threatened. In addition, increasing self-esteem can help. When attacked, children with low self-esteem may think, "I'm a loser and have to put up with this because I have no choice." Increasing children's self-esteem makes them less tolerant of personal attacks (Egan et al., 1998). Another useful way to help victims is to foster their friendships with peers. When children have friends, they're less likely to be victimized (Veenstra et al., 2010).

Of course, the best solution is to prevent bullying and victimization altogether; as we'll see in the "Child Development and Family Policy" feature, an effective way to do this is to create a school climate in which bullying is not condoned and victims are supported by their peers.

Child Development and Family Policy

The KiVa Antibullying Program

Beginning in the 1990s, Finland became concerned about the prevalence of bullying in Finnish schools. Consequently, the Ministry of Education asked Dr. Christina Salmivalli, an expert on bullying from the University of Turku, to create a school-based antibullying program. The result was KiVa, which comes from the Finnish words for "against bullying" *kiusaamista vastaan*. The heart of the program is creating a classroom climate in which bullying is not tolerated. Through lessons and discussions about respect for others, role playing (e.g., playing the part of the victim), and computer games, children who witness bullying are empowered to act, supporting victims and reporting bullying to

teachers. In addition, teachers learn strategies for dealing with cases of bullying. For example, they help a bully think about ways to change his or her aggressive behavior and they provide support for victims (Rubin, 2012).

The KiVa program is effective—bullying and victimization are reduced in schools where it's implemented (Kärnä et al., 2013). Because of its success, KiVa has been adopted in nearly 3,000 schools in Finland as well as in schools in Japan, Sweden, the Netherlands, the United Kingdom, and the United States (Rubin, 2012). KiVa's success shows how research on factors that drive bullying can be used create effective programs to eliminate it.

Check Your Learning

RECALL Describe the different forms of aggression and the ages when they typically appear.

Summarize the primary phases of decision making in Crick and Dodge's information-processing model and the biases that are found in aggressive children's decision making.

INTERPRET Compare the impact of nature and nurture on children's aggressive behavior.

APPLY Suppose that a group of elementary-school teachers wanted to know how to reduce the amount of aggressive behavior in their classrooms. What advice would you give them?

 # Unifying Themes   Continuity

This chapter has some nice illustrations of the theme that *early development is related to later development, but not perfectly.* For example, we learned on page 370 that preschoolers who were best able to delay gratification were, as adolescents, less likely to yield to temptation and to be distractible. Yet the relation was not perfect: Many preschoolers who quickly gave into temptation became adolescents who were not distractible. The same conclusion is evident in the results of longitudinal studies of aggressive children (pages 388–389). Many of these children commit serious crimes as adults, but not all do. Behaving aggressively in childhood definitely increases the odds of adult criminal activity, but it does not guarantee it.

See for Yourself

This assignment may seem like a dream come true—you are being required to watch TV! Pick an evening when you can watch network television programming from 8:00 until 10:00 PM (prime time). Your job is to count each instance of (a) physical force by one person against another and (b) threats of harm to compel another to act against his or her will. Select one network randomly and watch the program for 10 minutes. Then turn to another network and watch that program for 10 minutes. Continue changing the channels every 10 minutes until the 2 hours are over. Of course, it won't be easy to follow the plots of all these programs, but you will end up with a wider sample of programming this way. Repeat this procedure on a Saturday morning when you can watch 2 hours of children's cartoons (not *South Park!*).

Now simply divide the total number of aggressive acts by four to estimate the amount of aggression per hour. Then multiply this figure by 11,688 to estimate the number of aggressive acts seen by an average adolescent by age 19. (Why 11,688? Two hours of daily TV viewing—a conservative number—multiplied by 365 days and 16 years.) Then ponder the possible results of that large number. If your parents told you, nearly 12,000 times, that stealing was okay, would you be more likely to steal? Probably. Then what are the consequences of massive exposure to the televised message, "Solve conflicts with aggression"? See for yourself!

Summary

 ## Self-Control

Beginnings of Self-Control

At 1 year, infants are first aware that others impose demands on them; by 3 years, youngsters can devise plans to regulate their behavior. During the school-age years, children become better able to control their behavior.

Children differ in their self-control, but individuals are fairly consistent over time: Preschoolers who have good self-control tend to become adolescents and adults with good self-control.

Influences on Self-Control

Children who have the best self-control tend to have parents who are loving, set limits, and discuss discipline with them. When parents are overly strict, their children have less self-control, not more. Temperament also influences children's self-control: Some children are temperamentally better suited to focus attention and to inhibit responses.

Improving Children's Self-Control

Children are better able to regulate their own behavior when they have plans to help them remember the importance of the goal and something to distract them from tempting objects.

Reasoning About Moral Issues

Piaget's Views

Piaget theorized that 5- to 7-year-olds are in a stage of moral realism. They believe that rules are created by wise adults; therefore, rules must be followed and cannot be changed. At about 8 years, children enter a stage of moral relativism, believing that rules are created by people to help them get along.

Kohlberg's Theory

Kohlberg proposed that moral reasoning includes preconventional, conventional, and postconventional levels. Moral reasoning is first based on rewards and punishments, and, later, on personal moral codes. As predicted by Kohlberg's theory, people progress through the stages in sequence and do not regress, and morally advanced reasoning is associated with more frequent moral behavior. However, few people attain the most advanced levels, and cultures differ in the bases for moral reasoning.

Beyond Kohlberg's Theory

Gilligan proposed that females' moral reasoning is based on caring and responsibility for others, not justice. Research does not support consistent sex differences, but has found that males and females both consider caring as well as justice in their moral judgments, depending on the situation.

During the preschool years, children differentiate moral rules, social conventions, and personal choices. They believe, for example, that social conventions can be changed but moral rules cannot. And, they understand that breaking a moral rule produces a harsher punishment than breaking a social convention. Some scientists believe that infants have an innate moral sense because they feel concern for others and dislike group members who do not cooperate. Children's emotional responses to events may help them form categories of morally relevant concepts.

Helping Others

Development of Prosocial Behavior

Even toddlers know when others are upset, and they try to offer comfort. As children grow older, they more often see the need to act prosocially and are more likely to have the skills to do so.

Skills Underlying Prosocial Behavior

Children are more likely to behave prosocially when they are able to take others' perspectives, are empathic, and have more advanced moral reasoning.

Situational Influences

Children's prosocial behavior is often influenced by situational characteristics. Children more often behave prosocially when they feel that they should and can help, when they are in a good mood, and when they believe that they have little to lose by helping.

The Contribution of Heredity

Genes influence prosocial behavior via oxytocin, a hormone that's linked to social behaviors and through temperament: Some children are unlikely to help because they're too shy or they become too upset themselves (because they can't control their emotions).

Socializing Prosocial Behavior

Parenting approaches that promote prosocial behavior include modeling prosocial behavior, using reasoning in discipline, and giving children frequent opportunities inside and outside the home to use their prosocial skills.

Aggression

Change and Stability

Typical forms of aggression in young children include instrumental, hostile, and reactive aggression. As children grow older, physical aggression decreases and relational aggression becomes more common. Overall levels of aggression are fairly stable, which means that very aggressive young children often become involved in violent and criminal activities as adolescents and adults.

Roots of Aggressive Behavior

Children's aggressive behavior has many sources: genetics, harsh parenting, viewing violence on TV and in other media, aggressive peers, school failure, living in poverty, and biased interpretation of people's behavior.

Victims of Aggression

Children who are chronic targets of aggression are often lonely and anxious. Some victims of aggression tend to overreact when provoked; others tend to withdraw and submit. Bullying and victimization can be reduced by KiVa, a school-based program that creates a classroom climate in which bullying is not tolerated.

Test Yourself

1. By their first birthday, most children _____.
   a. are aware that others impose demands on them
   b. have internalized some controls imposed by others
   c. are capable of self-regulation

2. Preschoolers who show the greatest self-control _____.
   a. have better self-esteem as adults
   b. are more likely to drop out of school during adolescence
   c. often experiment with drugs as teenagers

3. Children have better self-control when parents _____.
   a. are strict with them
   b. are warm but establish limits
   c. don't discuss discipline with them

4. Children who are in Piaget's stage of moral realism typically believe that _____.
   a. breaking a rule leads directly to punishment
   b. rules were created by people to get along
   c. rules can be changed if necessary

5. A child who judges whether an act is good in terms of what is expected by other people is reasoning at which of Kohlberg's levels?
   a. preconventional level
   b. conventional level
   c. postconventional level

6. Which of the following statements about Kohlberg's work is *incorrect*?
   a. Older children typically reason at more advanced levels.
   b. Individuals who reason at more advanced levels are more likely to help others in need.
   c. Most children and adolescents around the world progress through the six-stage sequence.

7. At Happy Hollow Elementary School, the principal decided that children with cell phones had to leave them in their desk during the school day. This rule applies to which domain?
   a. moral reasoning
   b. social conventions
   c. the personal domain

8. Which of the following statements about moral reasoning is *correct*?
   a. Research on infants' moral reasoning has ruled out the possibility of an innate moral sense.
   b. In China and the United States, children tell lies to protect their friends, even if it hurts their group.
   c. Children's emotional responses to events help them to create categories of morally relevant concepts.

9. Which child would be *most* likely to help another child?
   a. A child who relies on rewards and punishments to help others.
   b. A child with low levels of empathy.
   c. A child skilled in perspective-taking.

10. Prosocial behavior is most likely when children _____.
    a. must sacrifice a lot help
    b. feel sad
    c. feel competent to help

11. Parents can foster their children's prosocial behavior by _____.
    a. helping others themselves
    b. not disciplining their children
    c. making sure that their children have plenty of free time by not burdening them with household chores

12. In _____ aggression, children use aggressive behavior to achieve a specific goal, such as getting to go down a playground slide before others.
    a. hostile
    b. instrumental
    c. reactive

13. When parents _____, their children are more likely to behave aggressively.
    a. use physical punishment often
    b. monitor their children's behavior
    c. get along well with each other

14. Which of the following is a *correct* statement concerning the influence of community and culture on children's aggressive behavior?
    a. Poverty is unrelated to aggressive behavior.
    b. When children watch much violent TV, they're less aggressive and have more empathy for targets of violence.
    c. School failure may breed aggressive behavior, which, in turn, leads to school failure.

15. Children who are chronic victims of bullies _____.
    a. are affected by the bullying briefly but not in the long term
    b. are withdrawn and submissive but not aggressive
    c. are better able to deal with bullying if they have friends

Key Terms

aggression 387

altruism 382

conventional level 376

empathy 383

hostile aggression 388

immanent justice 375

instrumental aggression 388

monitoring 390

moral realism 374

moral relativism 375

personal domain 379

postconventional level 377

preconventional level 376

prosocial behavior 382

reactive aggression 388

relational aggression 388

self-control 369

social conventions 379

Chapter 13
Gender: Stereotypes, Differences, Identity, and Roles

Modules

13.1 Gender Stereotypes

13.2 Differences Related to Gender

13.3 Gender Identity

13.4 Gender Roles in Transition

You barely have the phone to your ear before your brother-in-law shouts, "Camille had the baby!"

"A boy or a girl?" you ask. Why are people so interested in a baby's sex? The answer is that being a boy or a girl is not simply a biological distinction. **Instead, these terms are associated with distinct *social roles* that are cultural guidelines for people's behavior. Starting in infancy, children learn about *gender roles*—behaviors considered appropriate for males and females.** As youngsters learn these roles, they begin to identify with one of these groups. **Children forge a *gender identity*, the perception of the self as either male or female.**

In this chapter, we will see how children acquire a gender role and a gender identity. We'll begin, in **Module 13.1**, by considering cultural stereotypes of males and females. In **Module 13.2**, we will examine actual psychological differences between boys and girls. In **Module 13.3**, we'll focus on how children come to identify with one sex. Finally, in **Module 13.4**, we'll discuss recent changes in gender roles. Throughout this chapter, I'll use *sex* to refer to aspects of males and females that are clearly biological (such as differences in anatomy) and the term *gender* to refer to all other characteristics that relate to maleness and femaleness.

 # Gender Stereotypes

LEARNING OBJECTIVES

LO1   What are gender stereotypes, and how do they differ for males and females?

LO2   How do gender stereotypes influence behavior?
      When do children learn their culture's stereotypes for males and females?

OUTLINE

How Do We View Men and Women?

Learning Gender Stereotypes

When Nancy was 7 months pregnant, her 11-year-old son, Clark, announced that he really wanted a brother, not a sister. Clark explained, "A sister would drive me crazy. Girls never make up their minds about stuff, and they get all worked up over nothin'." "Where did Clark get these ideas?" Nancy wondered. "Is this typical for 11-year-olds?"

All cultures have *gender stereotypes*: beliefs about how males and females differ in personality traits, interests, and behaviors. Of course, because stereotypes are beliefs, they may or may not be true. In this module, we'll look at the features associated with gender stereotypes and discover when children like Clark learn gender stereotypes.

How Do We View Men and Women?

LO1   What are gender stereotypes, and how do they differ for males and females?

"Terry is active, independent, competitive, and aggressive." As you were reading this sentence, did you assume that Terry was a male? Why? *Terry* is a common name for both males and females, but the adjectives used here to describe

Terry are more commonly associated with men than with women. In fact, most adults associate different traits with men and women, and these views have changed little since the 1960s (***Ruble, Martin, & Berenbaum, 2006***). Men are said to be independent, competitive, aggressive, outgoing, ambitious, self-confident, and dominant. **These male-associated traits are called *instrumental* because they describe individuals who act on the world and influence it.** In contrast, women are said to be emotional, kind, creative, considerate, gentle, excitable, and aware of others' feelings. **Female-associated traits are called *expressive*, because they describe emotional functioning and individuals who value inter-personal relationships.**

Are these views shared by adults worldwide? The graphs in Figure 13-1 provide the answer for four traits from seven countries (Williams & Best, 1990). You can see that each trait varies across cultures. For example, virtually all American participants consider men aggressive, but only a slight majority of Nigerian participants do. Thus, American views of men and women are not shared world-wide. In fact, what's notable about the research results is that Americans' gender stereotypes are more extreme than those of any other country listed. Keep this in mind as you think about what men and women can and cannot do and what they should and should not do. Your ideas about gender are shaped by your culture's beliefs, beliefs that are not held universally.

Understanding our tendency to stereotype gender behavior is important because stereotypes are limiting (Smith & Mackie, 2000). If we have stereotyped views, we expect males to act in particular ways and females to act in other ways, and we respond to males and females solely on the basis of gender, not as individuals. For example,

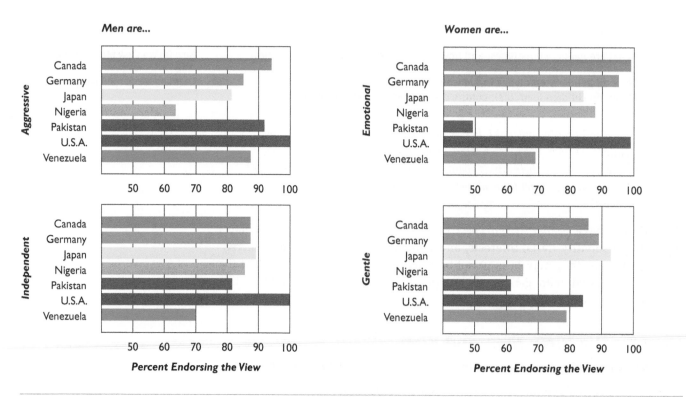

Figure 13-1

do you assume the youngster in the photo is a girl based on her taste in toys? Assuming the child is a girl may lead you to think she plays more quietly and is more easily frightened than if you assume the child is a boy (Karraker, Vogel, & Lake, 1995). Making stereotyped assumptions about gender leads to a whole host of inferences about behavior and personality that may not be true.

When do children begin to learn their culture's stereotypes for males and females? We'll answer this question in the next section.

Gender stereotypes lead us to assume that this child is a girl simply because the child is playing with a doll.

Learning Gender Stereotypes

LO2 How do gender stereotypes influence behavior?
When do children learn their culture's stereotypes for males and females?

Children don't live in a gender-neutral world for long. Although 12-month-old boys and girls look equally at gender-stereotyped toys, 18-month-olds do not: Girls look longer at pictures of dolls than pictures of trucks, but boys look longer at pictures of trucks (Serbin et al., 2001). By 4 years, children's knowledge of gender-stereotyped activities is extensive: They believe that girls play hopscotch but that boys play football; girls help bake cookies but boys take out the trash; and women feed babies but men chop wood (Gelman, Taylor, & Nguyen, 2004). And they've begun to learn about behaviors and traits that are stereotypically masculine or feminine. Preschoolers believe that boys are more often aggressive physically but girls tend to be aggressive verbally (Giles & Heyman, 2005).

During the elementary-school years, children expand their knowledge of gender-stereotyped traits and behaviors. They learn stereotypes about personality traits—boys are tough and girls are gentle—and about academic subjects—math is for boys and reading is for girls (Cvencek, Meltzoff, & Greenwald, 2011; Heyman & Legare, 2004). By the time they enter middle school, their ideas of gender stereotypes are virtually as well formed as those of adults.

During the elementary-school years, children also learn that occupations associated with males tend to earn more money and have greater power than those associated with females (Weisgram, Bigler, & Liben, 2010). Children apparently learn a simple rule—something like "Jobs for men are better than jobs for women"—because children learning unfamiliar jobs (e.g., a chandler makes candles) rate these occupations as more prestigious if they're illustrated with men than with women (Liben, Bigler, & Krogh, 2001).

As children develop, they also begin to understand that gender stereotypes do not always apply; older children are more willing than younger children to ignore stereotypes when judging other children. For example, told about a boy who likes to play with girls and pretend to iron, preschoolers think he would still want to play with masculine toys. By the middle elementary-school years, however, children realize that this boy's interests are not stereotypic and he would rather play with stereotypically feminine toys (Blakemore, 2003).

Thus, although older children are more familiar with gender stereotypes, they see these stereotypes as general guidelines for behavior that are not necessarily binding for all boys and girls (Conry-Murray & Turiel, 2012). This developmental trend toward greater flexibility is evident in the study described in the "Focus on Research" feature.

 QUESTION 13.1

Abigail believes that girls are gentler than boys, and that boys are stronger than girls, but that boys and girls are equally talkative and confident. With these stereotypic beliefs, how old is Abigail likely to be?

Focus on Research

Reasoning About Gender-Related Properties

Who were the investigators, and what was the aim of the study? Do children believe that physical and behavioral properties of boys and girls are inherent and stable? Do they believe, for example, that boys *necessarily* like to build things and grow up to have a beard? Do they believe that girls *necessarily* like to play with dolls and grow up to have breasts? Marianne Taylor, Marjorie Rhodes, and Susan Gelman (2009) conducted a study to answer these questions.

How did the investigators measure the topic of interest? Taylor and colleagues told participants about a baby girl who, immediately after birth, went to live on an island inhabited only by men, including her uncle. She had no contact with females. Participants were then shown a photo of the baby as a "big kid" and were asked several questions about her physical properties (e.g., "Will she grow up to be a mommy or a daddy?") and some about her behavioral properties (e.g., "Will she like to play with a tea set or with trucks?"). They were also told about a baby boy who lives on an island with his aunt and other women and then were asked the same questions.

Who were the participants in the study? The study included 68 5-year-olds, 64 10-year-olds, and 32 college students. At each age, half of the children were girls.

What was the design of the study? This study was experimental because Taylor and colleagues were interested in the impact of the domain—physical versus behavioral—on participants' judgments. The study was cross-sectional because it included 5-year-olds, 10-year-olds, and college students, each tested once.

Were there ethical concerns with the study? No; the children enjoyed hearing stories about babies growing up on the island.

What were the results? The investigators recorded the percentage of responses that were consistent with the baby's biological sex (e.g., predicting that the baby girl would like a tea set and want to be a nurse, and that she'll grow up to be a mom and have breasts). The results are shown in Figure 13-2, separately for physical and behavioral properties.

Let's start with the physical properties. There's little developmental change in these judgments: at all ages, participants expected the baby to acquire physical properties associated with its biological sex. However, the pattern is quite different for behavioral properties, where there is a steady downward developmental trend. Five-year-olds tend to believe that boys and girls will engage in gender-stereotypic behaviors, though they see these as slightly more flexible than physical properties. In contrast, adults believe that a boy brought up by women will behave in a feminine-stereotypic manner and that a girl brought up by men will behave in a masculine-stereotypic manner. A final result to note is that participants at all ages claimed greater flexibility in behavioral properties for girls than for boys; they thought that girls were more likely to be influenced in a masculine direction than boys were to be influenced in a feminine direction.

What did the investigators conclude? Taylor and colleagues concluded that "young children treat the concepts of 'boy' and 'girl' as equivalent to species,

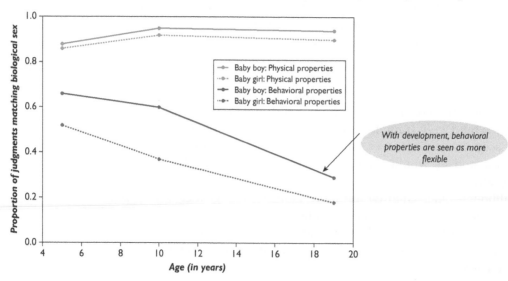

Figure 13-2

in the extent to which features are inborn, inflexible, and intrinsically linked to category membership.... [By] adulthood, participants viewed both male and female behavior as more open to the environment and flexible..." (2009, p. 475).

What converging evidence would strengthen these conclusions? The children in this sample came from university towns in the U.S. Midwest, and most were European American. It would be important to see whether children from different backgrounds responded in a similar fashion. In addition, it would be valuable to extend the list of properties to, for example, psychological properties (e.g., personality) to determine whether they're considered more like physical properties or more like behavioral properties in terms of flexibility.

Increased age is not the only factor leading to more flexible views of stereotypes. Girls tend to be more flexible about stereotypes (Ruble, Martin, & Berenbaum, 2006), perhaps because they see that male-stereotypic traits are more attractive and have more status than female-stereotypic traits. Social class also contributes. Adolescents and young adults (but not children) from middle-class homes tend to have more flexible ideas about gender than individuals from lower-class homes (e.g., Serbin, Powlishta, & Gulko, 1993). This difference may be due to education: Better-educated, middle-class parents may impart less rigid views of gender to their children.

Ethnicity is another factor associated with flexible views of gender. Some studies find that African American youngsters have more flexible ideas about gender than their European American peers (e.g., Rowley et al., 2007). Compared with European American mothers, African American mothers are more frequently employed outside the home, and this may contribute to their children's more open attitudes.

At this point, perhaps you're wondering whether there's any truth to gender stereotypes. For example, are boys really more dominant than girls? Are girls really more excitable than boys? For answers to these questions, let's go to Module 13.2.

 ## Check Your Learning

RECALL How do older children's gender stereotypes differ from those of younger children?

What groups of children tend to have more flexible views of gender stereotypes?

INTERPRET Compare and contrast instrumental traits with expressive traits.

APPLY How might Jean Piaget have explained older children's more flexible views of gender stereotypes?

 # Differences Related to Gender

LEARNING OBJECTIVES	OUTLINE
LO3 How do boys and girls differ in physical development?	**Differences in Physical Development and Behavior**
LO4 What are the gender differences in intellectual abilities?	**Differences in Intellectual Abilities and Achievement**
LO5 In personality and social behavior, how do boys and girls differ?	**Differences in Personality and Social Behavior**
LO6 What are the implications of gender differences for boys' and girls' development?	**Frank Talk About Gender Differences**

The high-school student council was discussing a proposal to hold the prom in an expensive hotel in a nearby big city. Maggie thought this was a truly terrible idea, but most of the group seemed to like the plan, so she decided not to say anything. Just as she decided to keep quiet, her friend Charles announced that he was going to vote against the proposal and, as he described his reasons, Maggie realized that they were exactly the ones that she'd thought of but hadn't voiced.

Maggie and Charles both thought the proposal was flawed, but only Charles expressed those concerns. Why? We'll answer that question in this module as we explore gender-related differences in different domains of development. This territory was first charted in *The Psychology of Sex Differences*, a book by Eleanor Maccoby and Carol Jacklin published in 1974, that summarized results from approximately 1,500 research studies. Maccoby and Jacklin concluded that gender differences had been established in only four areas: Girls have greater verbal ability, whereas boys have greater mathematical and visual–spatial ability, and boys are more aggressive than girls. Just as importantly, Maccoby and Jacklin did *not* find evidence to support popular ideas that girls are more social and suggestible than boys, have lower self-esteem, are less analytic in thinking, and lack achievement motivation.

Some critics challenged Maccoby and Jacklin on the grounds that they had included some weak studies and defined behaviors in ways that other researchers might not (Block, 1978). The debate stimulated more research; some of this research applied new statistical techniques that allowed for finer analysis, such as meta-analysis. Many developmentalists now believe that gender differences are more extensive than Maccoby and Jacklin suggested, but their book remains a classic because its comprehensiveness provided an excellent starting point for further research.

In the remainder of this module, we'll see what we've discovered about gender differences since Maccoby and Jacklin's classic analysis. We'll focus on differences in physical development, cognitive processes, and social behavior.

Differences in Physical Development and Behavior

LO3 How do boys and girls differ in physical development?

Of course, differences in the reproductive system are what differentiate boys from girls, along with differences in secondary sex characteristics such as lower voice and facial hair in boys and breast development and wider hips in girls. Boys are usually larger and stronger than girls, which means that they often physically outperform girls. You can see the difference at high-school track meets: Boys usually run faster, jump higher, and throw objects farther and more accurately. And, as Figure 13-3 shows, long before high school, boys throw and jump farther than girls. Outside of sports, on tasks that involve fine-motor coordination, such as tracing and drawing, girls do better than boys (Thomas & French, 1985).

Some of the gender differences in gross-motor skills that require strength reflect the fact that as children approach and enter puberty, girls' bodies have proportionately more fat and less muscle than boys' bodies. This difference explains why, for example, boys can hang from a bar using their arms and hands much longer than girls can. However, for other gross-motor skills, such as running, throwing, and catching, body composition is much less important (Smoll & Schutz, 1990). In these cases, children's experience is crucial.

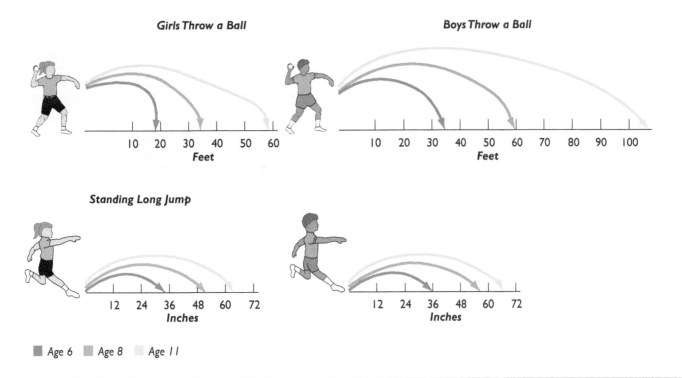

Girls Throw a Ball

Boys Throw a Ball

Standing Long Jump

■ Age 6 ■ Age 8 ■ Age 11

Figure 13-3

Many girls and their parents believe that sports and physical fitness are less valuable for girls than for boys. Consequently, girls spend less time in these sports- and fitness-related activities than boys, depriving them of opportunities to practice, which is essential for developing motor skills (Eccles & Harold, 1991). During recess, for example, elementary-school girls are more often found swinging, jumping rope, or perhaps talking quietly in a group; in contrast, boys are often playing football or shooting baskets. Consistent with this argument, gender differences in throwing are much smaller among Australian Aborigines, a group that traditionally expected girls to be able to throw while hunting (Thomas et al., 2010).

As infants, boys are more active than girls, and this difference increases during childhood (Alexander & Wilcox, 2012; Saudino, 2009). For example, in a classroom, boys are more likely than girls to have a hard time sitting still. On playgrounds like those in the photos on page 408, boys more often play vigorously and girls quietly. And, recall from Module 5.2 that boys are three times more likely than girls to be diagnosed with attention deficit hyperactivity disorder.

Girls tend to be healthier than boys. Female embryos are more likely than male embryos to survive prenatal development. This trend continues after birth. Infant boys are more prone to birth complications, and throughout life, boys are more prone to many diseases and dysfunctions (Jacklin, 1989). Finally, as the brain matures in adolescence, girls' brains tend to have more cell bodies and dendrites but boys' brains have more glial cells (which provide nutrients and oxygen and destroy pathogens) and more myelinated axons (Nisbett et al., 2012).

To summarize, boys tend to be bigger, stronger, and more active; girls tend to have better fine-motor coordination and to be healthier. In the next section, which concerns intellectual skills, you'll again see that gender differences vary from one skill to the next.

Boys are physically more active than girls, a difference that's evident when you watch children on a playground.

Differences in Intellectual Abilities and Achievement

LO4 **What are the gender differences in intellectual abilities?**

Of the four gender-based differences discovered by Maccoby and Jacklin (1974), three concern intellectual skills: Girls tend to have greater verbal skill but boys tend to have greater mathematical and visual–spatial skill. Since Maccoby and Jacklin's work was published, we've learned much about the nature of gender differences in these areas.

Verbal Ability Girls have larger vocabularies than boys and are more talkative (Feldman et al., 2000; Leaper & Smith, 2004). During elementary school and high school, girls read better than boys, and this difference is found in virtually all industrialized countries (Miller & Halpern, 2014). Finally, more boys are diagnosed with language-related problems such as reading disability (Halpern, 2012).

Why are girls more talented verbally than boys? One idea is that the brain plays a role. Some studies find that brain regions involved in reading differ for boys and girls (Burman et al., 2013), in a manner that suggests more efficient language processing in girls' brains. However, the findings are inconsistent (Eliot, 2013; Wallentin, 2009); the brain's contribution to sex differences in reading remains a puzzle. In contrast, evidence is more consistent regarding the role of experience. Parents often provide more verbal stimulation for daughters than sons. For example, during the toddler years, mothers talk more to daughters than to sons (Fivush et al., 2000). And by the elementary-school years, reading is often stereotyped as an activity for girls (Plante et al., 2013), which may make girls more willing than boys to invest time and effort in mastering verbal skills such as reading. Finally, teachers contribute; they expect girls to read better than boys, by an amount that exceeds the actual difference (Ready & Wright, 2011).

Spatial Ability In Module 8.1, you saw that spatial ability is a component of most models of intelligence. **One aspect of spatial ability is *mental rotation*, the ability to imagine how an object will look after it has been**

moved in space. For example, mental rotation is involved in determining whether Figure 13-4 shows different objects or the same object in different orientations. During childhood and adolescence, boys tend to have better mental-rotation skill than girls (Govier & Salisbury, 2000; Voyer, Voyer, & Bryden, 1995). Even as infants, boys are more likely than girls to recognize stimuli that have been rotated in space (Alexander & Wilcox, 2012). However, on other spatial tasks, such as mental rotation in two dimensions, sex differences are smaller and on other spatial tasks, they vanish (Miller & Halperin, 2014).

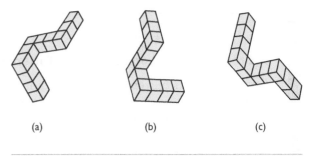

(a)   (b)   (c)

Figure 13-4

Some explanations for gender differences in mental rotation and other spatial abilities emphasize biology. Some scientists argue that spatial skill was essential for successful hunting—in navigating and in calculating trajectories for weapons—and may represent an evolutionary adaptation for males (Halpern et al., 2007). And some findings link better spatial skill to androgen, a hormone found in larger amounts in boys (Miller & Halperin, 2014).

But experience certainly contributes too. Boys are more likely than girls to participate in activities that foster spatial skill, such as estimating the trajectory of an object moving through space (e.g., a baseball), using two-dimensional plans to assemble an object such as a scale model (Baenninger & Newcombe, 1995), or, like the boy in the photo, playing video games that involve visual–perceptual skills (Okagaki & Frensch, 1994; Terlecki & Newcombe, 2005). And parents may provide richer stimulation for sons on tasks that foster spatial skill. In one study (Levine et al., 2012), parents provided more challenging puzzles to sons and used more spatial language while solving the puzzles (e.g., referring to the shape, location, and orientation of puzzle pieces). However, among children from lower-socioeconomic-status homes, boys and girls have comparable spatial skills (Levine et al., 2005), a result suggesting that some experience associated with middle-class living is critical for the sex differences to emerge.

Playing video games can enhance a child's spatial skill; because boys play video games more often than girls, this may contribute to a gender difference in spatial skill.

Of course, these explanations are not necessarily mutually exclusive. Biological and experiential forces may both contribute to gender differences in spatial ability, just as both contribute to gender differences in verbal ability. Thus, parents and others can foster verbal and spatial abilities in both boys and girls because each is influenced considerably by experience, training, and practice (Newcombe, 2002; Uttal et al., 2013).

Mathematics During the elementary-school years, girls are usually more advanced than boys in arithmetic and mastery of basic math concepts, a difference that may be a by-product of girls' greater language skill (Wei et al., 2012). During high school and college, boys used to get higher scores than girls on standardized math tests, but that difference has diminished substantially over the past 25 years; now boys have a negligible advantage (Lindberg et al., 2010). This change apparently reflects efforts to encourage girls to pursue mathematics generally and to take more math courses specifically. For example, American boys and girls are now equally likely to take calculus courses in high school (National Science Foundation, 2008). And, as we'll see in the "Cultural Influences" feature, cross-cultural comparisons also point to an important role for cultural expectations in explaining gender differences in mathematics.

Cultural Influences

A Cross-Cultural Look at Gender Differences in Math

Several math achievement tests are administered internationally, and the results provide useful insights into the forces that drive gender differences in math. For example, the Programme for International Student Assessment (PISA) is administered in more than 60 countries, with thousands of high-school students in each country taking tests measuring math, reading, and science abilities (Organisation for Economic Co-operation and Development, 2010). In many countries, there are small differences favoring boys (e.g., France, Germany). However, in some countries (e.g., Republic of Korea, the Slovak Republic), boys have substantially greater scores. And in Iceland, girls have the advantage (Else-Quest, Hyde, & Linn, 2010).

Why should the pattern vary so much? One view is that it reflects cultural differences in math-related career opportunities for men and women. When girls (and their parents and their teachers) see math as a means to achieve success, they will be interested in math and take math courses. In contrast, if girls see

math-related careers as "for boys only," they will have little reason to invest time and energy in mastering math. This line of thinking leads to a straightforward prediction: In countries where women have much the same access to education, occupations, and political power as men, gender differences in math should be negligible. In contrast, where women are limited to traditionally feminine-stereotypic occupations that do not require math skills, gender differences in math should remain. Exactly this pattern is found in international comparisons of PISA math data (Else-Quest et al., 2010). For example, educational and professional opportunities are substantial in Iceland (where girls excel in math) but not in the Republic of Korea (where test results favor boys). In other words, these cross-cultural comparisons seem to suggest that "girls will perform at the same level as their male classmates when they are encouraged to succeed, are given the necessary educational tools, and have visible female role models excelling in mathematics" (Else-Quest et al., 2010, p. 125).

Memory According to Maccoby and Jacklin, verbal, spatial, and math abilities were domains in which boys and girls differed. One other domain has been added to the list by subsequent research: memory. Compared with boys and men, girls and women often remember the identity of objects as well as their location more accurately (Miller & Halpern, 2014; Voyer et al., 2007). For example, if shown photos of faces, girls remember those faces more accurately than boys do (Herlitz & Lovén, 2013). In addition, when describing past events (e.g., a trip to a museum, a special visitor at school), girls tend to provide more elaborate and more emotion-filled descriptions (Grysman & Hudson, 2013).

Because these gender-related differences in memory have been documented only recently, they're not well understood. One suggestion is that they may be consequences of gender differences in other domains. For example, girls' advantage in language and recognizing emotions (described on pages 408 and 411) may allow them to construct more elaborate representations of stimuli and events, representations that are more resistant to forgetting. Another possibility links the differences in memory to the hippocampus, a brain structure that's critical for memory and is larger in girls than in boys (Lenroot & Giedd, 2010).

Q&A **QUESTION 13.2**

Brianna is the mother of fraternal twins, a boy and a girl, who are just starting elementary school. She's determined that both of her children will excel in reading and math. Are Brianna's goals realistic?

Differences in Personality and Social Behavior

LO5 In personality and social behavior, how do boys and girls differ?

Are there differences in personality and social behavior between boys and girls? In the 1970s, Maccoby and Jacklin (1974) found convincing evidence of only one gender difference in this realm: Boys were more aggressive than girls. In this section, we'll see what researchers have discovered in the ensuing 35 years.

Aggressive Behavior No one doubts Maccoby and Jacklin's conclusion that boys are more aggressive physically than girls. As mentioned in Module 12.4 and as you can see in the photo, the gender difference in physical aggression is readily observed, as early as 17 months of age (Hyde, 2014).

Because boys and men are more aggressive in virtually all cultures, and because males in nonhuman species are also more aggressive, scientists are convinced that biology contributes heavily to this gender difference. **Aggressive behavior has been linked to** *androgens*, **hormones secreted by the testes.** Androgens do not lead directly to aggression.

Physical aggression is far more common among boys than among girls.

Instead, androgens make it *more likely* that boys will be aggressive by making them more competitive, quicker to anger, and less able to control their emotions (Archer, 2006; Dodge, Coie, & Lynam, 2006; Hay, 2007).

Even though hormones are involved, we can't ignore experience. The media are filled with aggressive male models—from Vin Diesel to Jedi knights—who are rewarded for their behavior. What's more, parents are more likely to use physical punishment with sons than with daughters and are more tolerant of aggressive behavior in sons than in daughters (Condry & Ross, 1985; Martin & Ross, 2005). As we saw in Module 12.4, these are just the sort of experiences that precipitate a vicious cycle of increasing aggression; and this cycle is much more common for boys than for girls. Although biology may make boys more prone to aggression, experience encourages boys rather than girls to express their aggression physically.

Boys' aggression may be more obvious because of its physical nature, but girls can be aggressive, too (Ostrov & Godleski, 2010). In Module 12.4, we saw that girls often rely upon relational aggression, in which they try to hurt others by damaging their relationships with peers (Crick & Grotpeter, 1995). They may call other children names, make fun of them, spread rumors about them, or—just as bad—pointedly ignore them. Boys aggress in this manner, too, but it's less obvious because physical aggression is so common and so salient for boys (Archer, 2004).

Emotional Sensitivity According to the stereotypes listed on page 401, girls are better able to express their emotions and interpret others' emotions. In fact, this gender difference is supported by research. For example, throughout infancy, childhood, and adolescence, girls identify facial expressions (e.g., happy face versus a sad face) more accurately than boys do (Alexander & Wilcox, 2012; Thompson & Voyer, 2014). In addition, girls are more likely to express happiness and sadness, but boys are more likely to express anger (Chaplin & Aldao, 2013). Finally, for the complex (self-conscious) emotions described on pages 315–316, adolescent girls report experiencing shame and guilt more often than boys do (Else-Quest et al., 2012).

Most developmentalists believe that the gender difference in emotional sensitivity reflects both nature and nurture. One idea is that because boys are more active and less able to regulate their behavior, parents discourage sons from expressing emotions as a way of promoting self-regulation. In contrast, parents encourage daughters to express emotions because this is consistent with gender roles in which females are expected to be nurturing and supportive (Brody & Hall, 2008).

Social Influence Another gender stereotype is that females are more easily influenced by others—that is, that they are more persuadable. In fact, young girls are more likely than young boys to comply with an adult's request, and they are more likely to seek an adult's help (Jacklin & Maccoby, 1978). Girls and women are also influenced more than boys and men by persuasive messages and others' behavior, especially when they are under group pressure (Becker, 1986; Eagly, Karau, & Makhijani, 1995). However, these gender differences may stem from the fact that females value group harmony more than boys and thus seem to give in to others (Miller, Danaher, & Forbes, 1986; Strough & Berg, 2000). For instance, at a meeting like the one described in the module-opening vignette, girls are just as likely as boys to recognize the flaws in a bad idea, but like Maggie, girls are more willing to go along simply because they don't want the group to start arguing.

Effortful Control During story time in a preschool classroom, many children sit quietly, listening to the teacher read. But if there's a child fidgeting or pestering a nearby child, the odds are that it's a boy. Consistent with this example, girls are more skilled at effortful control; compared with boys, they are better able to regulate their behavior, to inhibit inappropriate responding, and to focus their attention (Else-Quest et al., 2006; Gagné, Miller, & Goldsmith, 2013). In addition, boys are far more likely to be diagnosed with attentional disorders such as ADHD (Hyde, 2014).

Earlier we saw that effortful control and ADHD have biological bases; these may contribute to gender-related differences. That is, the average girl is more likely than the average boy to be biologically programmed to have skilled self-control. But the environment can amplify these differences. For example, when parents discover that their 2-year-old son refuses to sit still in quiet settings (e.g., an older sibling's orchestra concert), they may stop taking him, depriving him of the opportunity to learn to control his behavior.

Depression During adolescence, girls are more likely than boys to report negative events such as fights with friends, and they report being more upset by these events than boys (Flook, 2011). Such episodes can lead some teens—especially girls—to be depressed; they feel chronically sad and irritable and have low self-esteem (Mezulis et al., 2014).

Several factors converge to make teenage girls more prone to depression. First, they experience more frequent stressors, such as dissatisfaction with their appearance after pubertal change or conflict with close friends (Hankin, Mermelstein, & Roesch, 2007). Second, girls like the one in the photo are more apt to interpret these negative life events in harmful terms, emphasizing social-emotional consequences to a far greater extent than boys do. For example, if a teenage girl were to fail a major exam, she would be more likely than a boy to interpret this event harshly, thinking, "I'm so stupid; my friends won't want to be with me if they know I'm this dumb." Third, much more than boys, girls are prone to ruminate about their problems: thinking about them over and over, and talking about them with friends (Cox, Mezulis, & Hyde, 2010; Rood et al., 2009). Fourth, hormonal changes at puberty may make teenage girls particularly vulnerable to interpersonal stressors (Martel, 2013).

During adolescence, girls are more likely than boys to suffer from depression.

Frank Talk About Gender Differences

LO6 What are the implications of gender differences for boys' and girls' development?

The gender differences we've discussed in this module are listed in Summary Table 13-1. As you think about the differences, it's essential to remember that the gender differences described in this module represent differences in the *average scores* for boys and girls—differences that are relatively small. For example, Figure 13-5 on page 414 shows the distribution of scores on a hypothetical reading test. As we would expect, overall girls do better than boys. However, the distributions of girls' and boys' scores overlap substantially. The area shaded in yellow shows the large percentage of boys who have higher reading scores than the average girl, and the area shaded in red shows the large percentage of girls who have lower reading scores than the average boy. The diagram makes it obvious that a difference in average scores does *not* mean that girls read well and boys read poorly. Consequently, a boy who wants to become a writer should not be deterred because of small differences in average scores for boys and girls. Of course, we could draw similar diagrams in the other domains in which boys and girls differ, with the same conclusion. The vast majority of gender differences are small—a majority corresponding to correlations of .20 or less—which means that boys' and girls' scores overlap considerably (Hyde, 2014).

Figure 13-5 also helps to explain why gender differences often seem more striking than they are. The tails of the distribution show a small number of extreme cases. In Figure 13-5 the handful of "super readers" are much more likely to be girls than boys. If Figure 13-5 showed the distribution of mental

---

SUMMARY TABLE 13-1

SEX DIFFERENCES IN PHYSICAL AND BEHAVIORAL DEVELOPMENT

General	Specific Domain	Nature of Difference
Physical Development	Motor skills	Boys excel at tasks that require strength, but girls do better on tasks that require fine-motor coordination.
	Activity	Beginning in infancy, boys are more active than girls.
	Health	From conception through adulthood, girls are healthier.
Intellectual Abilities	Verbal ability	Girls have larger vocabularies; they also read better and are less likely to have language-related impairments.
	Spatial ability	Boys are better on mental-rotation tasks and in determining relations between objects in space.
	Mathematics	Boys get higher scores on standardized tests, but primarily in countries where girls have limited educational and career opportunities.
	Memory	Girls remember the identity of objects and location of objects more accurately; also, their descriptions of past events are more elaborate.
Personality and Social Behavior	Aggression	Boys are more aggressive physically; girls rely more on relational aggression.
	Emotional sensitivity	Girls are better able to identify and express emotions.
	Social influence	Because girls value group harmony more than boys do, girls are more susceptible to others' influence.
	Effortful control	Girls are better able to regulate their behavior, to inhibit inappropriate responding, and to focus their attention; boys are more likely to be diagnosed with ADHD.
	Depression	Beginning in adolescence, girls are more prone to depression than boys.

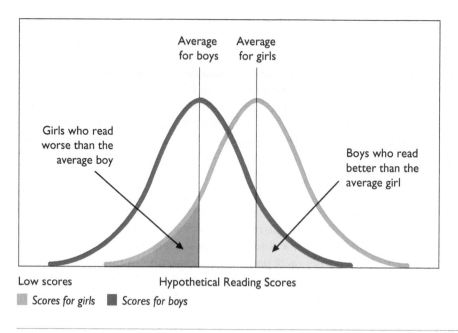

Figure 13-5

rotation skill, the distributions for boys and girls would be swapped and the small number of "super mental rotators" would probably be boys. These extreme cases stand out, are easily remembered, and bias us—incorrectly—to think that all girls are outstanding readers and all boys are exceptional mental rotators.

It's also essential to think about the large number of abilities, behaviors, and traits that have not been considered in this module. Boys and girls do not differ in many, many aspects of cognition, personality, and social behavior, a point that is easily lost when focusing on gender differences. In reality, a list of ways in which boys and girls are similar is much longer than a list of differences (Hyde, 2014). In intelligence, reasoning, and understanding of people—to name just a few areas—boys and girls are much more alike than different. If development is a journey, both boys and girls have many choices as they travel; few, if any, routes have signs that say "for girls only" or "for boys only."

In this module, we've focused on the behaviors and skills in which boys and girls differ; in the next, we'll see how children acquire a gender identity, a sense of "being a boy" or "being a girl."

Check Your Learning

RECALL What were the primary gender differences that Maccoby and Jacklin described in their 1974 book?

Summarize features of personality and social behavior in which boys and girls differ.

INTERPRET How do nature and nurture contribute to gender differences in intellectual abilities and achievement?

APPLY Based on what you know about differences between boys and girls in intellectual abilities and social behavior, how might Module 13.2 differ in the 40th edition of this book, published in 2106?

13.3 Gender Identity

LEARNING OBJECTIVES

LO7 How do parents, peers, and the media influence children's learning of gender roles?

LO8 How do cognitive theories explain children's learning of gender roles?

LO9 How does biology influence children's learning of gender roles?

OUTLINE

The Socializing Influences of People and the Media

Cognitive Theories of Gender Identity

Biological Influences

Taryn, who has just turned 4, knows that she's a girl but is convinced that she'll grow up to be a man. Taryn plays almost exclusively with boys and her favorite toys are trucks and cars. Taryn tells her parents that when she's bigger, she'll grow a beard and be a daddy. Taryn's father is confident that his daughter's ideas are a natural part of a preschooler's limited understanding of gender, but her mother wonders if they've neglected some important aspect of Taryn's upbringing.

According to the old saying, "Boys will be boys and girls will be girls"—but how, in fact, do boys become boys and girls become girls when it comes to gender roles? That is, how do children acquire and internalize their culture's roles for males and females? And how do children develop a sense of identity as a male or female? We'll answer these questions in this module and, as we do, learn whether Taryn's wish to grow up to be a man is typical for youngsters her age.

The Socializing Influences of People and the Media

LO7 How do parents, peers, and the media influence children's learning of gender roles?

Folklore holds that parents and other adults—teachers and television characters, for example—directly shape children's behavior regarding the roles associated with their sex. Boys are rewarded for boyish behavior and punished for girlish behavior.

The folklore even has a theoretical basis: According to social cognitive theorists such as Albert Bandura (1977, 1986; Bandura & Bussey, 2004) and Walter Mischel (1970), children learn gender roles in much the same way they learn other social behaviors—by watching the world around them and learning the outcomes of actions. Thus, children learn what their culture considers appropriate behavior for males and females simply by watching how adults and peers act. How well does research support social cognitive theory? Let's look first at research done with parents.

Parents An extensive meta-analysis of 172 studies involving 27,836 children (Lytton & Romney, 1991) found that parents often treat sons and daughters similarly: Parents interact equally with sons and daughters, are equally warm to both, and encourage both sons and daughters to succeed and be independent. However, in behavior related to gender roles, parents respond differently to sons and daughters (Lytton & Romney, 1991). Activities such as playing with dolls, dressing up, or helping an adult are encouraged more often in daughters than in sons; rough-and-tumble play and playing with blocks are encouraged more in sons than in daughters. Parents tolerate mild aggression more in sons than in daughters (Martin & Ross, 2005), and following the birth of a child (especially a firstborn), parents

Fathers are more likely than mothers to treat their children in a stereotyped manner.

become more traditional in their attitudes regarding gender (Katz-Wise, Priess, & Hyde, 2010).

Fathers are more likely than mothers to treat sons and daughters differently. More than mothers, fathers such as the one in the photo often encourage gender-related play. Fathers also push their sons to achieve more but accept dependence in their daughters (Snow, Jacklin, & Maccoby, 1983). A father, for example, may urge his frightened young son to jump off the diving board ("Be a man!") but not be so insistent with his daughter ("That's okay, honey."). Apparently, mothers are more likely to respond based on their knowledge of the individual child's needs, but fathers respond based on gender stereotypes. A mother responds to her son knowing that he's smart but unsure of himself; a father may respond because of what he thinks boys should be like.

Of course, adults differ in their views on the relative rights and roles of males and females. Some have traditional views, believing, for example, that men should be hired preferentially for some jobs and that it's more important for sons than daughters to attend college; others have more gender-neutral views, believing, for example, that women should have the same business and professional opportunities as men and that daughters should have the same educational opportunities as sons. It would be surprising if parents did not convey these attitudes to their children, and indeed they do (Crouter et al., 2007). A meta-analysis of 48 studies, including more than 10,000 pairs of parents and children, showed that children's gender-related interests, attitudes, and self-concepts are more traditional when their parents have traditional views and more gender-neutral when their parents have nontraditional views (Tenenbaum & Leaper, 2002).

Teachers   After parents, teachers may be the most influential adults in children's lives. Many teachers help to differentiate gender roles by making gender salient in the classroom. In elementary schools, students may be told to form separate lines for boys and girls; teachers may praise the girls as a group for being quiet during a video while criticizing the boys for laughing (Thorne, 1993). In addition, teachers spend more time interacting with boys than with girls. Teachers call on boys more frequently, praise them more for their schoolwork, and spend more time scolding them for disruptive classroom behavior (Good & Brophy, 1996). By using sex as a basis for differentiating children and by giving boys more attention, teachers foster the idea that boys differ from girls and that each has a distinct social role (Ruble, Martin, & Berenbaum, 2006).

Preschool children often tease their peers who engage in cross-gender play.

Peers   By the age of 3, most children's play shows the impact of gender stereotypes—boys prefer blocks and trucks, whereas girls prefer tea sets and dolls—and youngsters are critical of peers who engage in gender-inappropriate play (Aspenlieder et al., 2009). This is particularly true of boys who like feminine toys or who choose feminine activities. Boys who play with dolls and girls (like the one in the photo) who play with trucks will both be ignored, teased, or ridiculed by their peers, but a boy will receive harsher treatment than a girl (Levy, Taylor, & Gelman, 1995). Once children learn rules about gender-typical play, they often harshly punish peers who violate those rules.

Peers influence gender roles in another way, too. During the preschool years, children begin to prefer playing with same-sex peers (Halim et al., 2013). Little boys play together with cars, and little girls play together with dolls. Segregation of playmates by sex occurs spontaneously and children often resist playing with members of the other sex, even in gender-neutral activities such as playing tag or coloring (Maccoby, 1990, 1998).

This preference increases during childhood, reaching a peak in preadolescence. By age 10 or 11, the vast majority of peer activity is with same-sex children, and most of this involves sex-typed play. Boys are playing sports or playing with cars or action figures; girls are doing artwork or playing with pets or dolls (McHale et al., 2004). Then the tide begins to turn, but even in adulthood time spent at work and at leisure is quite commonly segregated by gender (Hartup, 1983).

Why do boys and girls seem so attracted to same-sex play partners? One reason is self-selection by sex. Boys and girls want to play with others like themselves and after they know their sex, they pick others on that basis (Martin et al., 2013). Second, boys and girls differ in their styles of play. Boys prefer rough-and-tumble play and generally are more competitive and dominating in their interactions; in contrast, girls' play is more cooperative, prosocial, and conversation-oriented (Martin et al., 2011; Rose & Rudolph, 2006). Generally, boys don't enjoy the way that girls play and girls are averse to boys' style of play (Maccoby, 1990, 1998).

Third, when girls and boys play together, girls do not readily influence boys. **Girls' interactions with one another are typically** *enabling*—**their actions and remarks tend to support others and sustain the interaction.** When drawing together, one girl might say to another, "Cool picture" or "What do you want to do now?" **In contrast, boys' interactions are often** *constricting*—**one partner tries to emerge as the victor by threatening or contradicting the other, by exaggerating, and so on.** In the same drawing task, one boy might say to another, "My picture's better" or "Drawing is stupid—let's watch TV." When these styles are brought together, girls find that their enabling style is ineffective with boys. The same subtle overtures that work with other girls have no impact on boys. Boys ignore girls' polite suggestions about what to do and ignore girls' efforts to resolve conflicts with discussion (Rose & Rudolph, 2006).

Some theorists believe that these contrasting styles may have an evolutionary basis (Geary et al., 2003). Boys' concerns about dominating others may stem from a concern with establishing one's rank among a group of males because those males at the upper ranks have better access to mates and better access to resources needed for offspring. Girls' concerns about affiliation may be a by-product of the fact that women traditionally left their own communities (and relatives) to live in a husband's community. Having no relatives nearby enhanced the value of a close friend, which placed a premium on the affiliative behaviors that lead to and maintain friendships.

Regardless of the exact cause, early segregation of playmates by style of play means that boys learn primarily from boys and girls from girls. Over time, such social segregation by sex reinforces gender differences in play. Martin and Fabes (2001), for example, conducted a longitudinal study of same-sex play in preschool and kindergarten children. When young boys spent most of their time playing with other boys at the beginning of the school year, their play was more active and more aggressive by the end of the year. In contrast, when young girls spent most of their time playing with other girls at the beginning of the school year, their play was less active and less aggressive by the end of the year. Boys and girls who spent more time playing with other-sex children didn't show these changes. Thus, young boys and girls teach each other gender-appropriate play. As they do, this helps solidify a youngster's emerging sense of membership in a particular gender group and sharpens the contrast between genders.

Television Another source of influence on gender-role learning is television. For decades, males and females have been depicted on TV in stereotypical ways.

 QUESTION 13.3

Rick has encouraged his 4-year-old son to play with the 5-year-old girl who lives next door, but his son will have none of it; he refuses every time. Rick thinks that his son is being unreasonable and stubborn. Do you agree?

Women tend to be cast in family roles; they are depicted as emotional, passive, and weak. Men are more often cast in management roles and are depicted as rational, active, and strong (Leaper et al., 2002; Smith et al., 2012). As you can imagine, children who watch a lot of TV end up with more stereotyped views of males and females. In other words, TV viewing causes children to adopt many of the distorted portraits of males and females that dominate television programming (Oppliger, 2007; Signorielli & Lears, 1992).

Let's now return to our original question: How well does research support the social learning explanation of gender roles? Studies of parents, teachers, and peers show that children learn much about gender roles simply by observing males and females, but simple observation of real-life models or television characters cannot be the entire explanation. After all, young boys traditionally have far more opportunities to observe their mother's behavior than their father's, but they are more likely to imitate their father (for example, by using hammer and saw) than their mother (for example, by cooking). Thus, an important element in learning about gender is identifying with one gender and then actively seeking out activities that are typical for that gender. This aspect of gender-role learning is the focus of cognitive theories, which we'll examine in the next section.

Cognitive Theories of Gender Identity

LO8   How do cognitive theories explain children's learning of gender roles?

One of the first descriptions of children's understanding of gender was proposed by Lawrence Kohlberg (1966; Kohlberg & Ullian, 1974), the same theorist who described moral development as a sequence of stages (pages 375–378). In Kohlberg's account, toddlers know that they are either boys or girls and label themselves accordingly. During the preschool years, children begin to understand that gender is stable; boys become men and girls become women. Yet at this age, they believe that a girl who wears her hair like a boy will become a boy and that a boy who plays with dolls will become a girl. Not until about 5 or 6 years do children come to understand that maleness and femaleness do not change over situations or according to personal wishes. They understand that a child's sex is unaffected by the clothing that a child wears or the toys that a child likes.

Taryn, the 4-year-old in the opening vignette, is in the first stage: she knows that she's a girl. However, she does not yet understand that gender is stable and consistent.

As soon as children understand that gender is stable, they begin learning about gender-typical behavior. Explaining how that learning takes place is the aim of a theory that the focus of the "Spotlight on Theories" feature.

Spotlight on Theories

Gender-Schema Theory

BACKGROUND   Preschool children learn gender roles rapidly. The environment, of course, provides many clues about typical roles for males and females. But how do children use these clues to learn about the behaviors and characteristics typically associated with their sex?

THE THEORY   A theory proposed by Carol Martin (Martin & Ruble, 2004; Martin et al., 1999), illustrated in Figure 13-6, addresses how children learn about gender. **In *gender-schema theory*, children first decide whether an object, activity, or behavior is female or male, then use this information to decide**

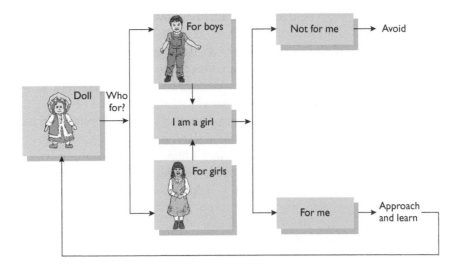

Figure 13-6

whether or not they should learn more about the object, activity, or behavior. That is, once children know their gender, they pay attention primarily to experiences and events that are gender appropriate (Martin & Halverson, 1987; Zosuls, Ruble, & Tamis-Lemonda, 2014). According to gender-schema theory, a preschool boy who is watching a group of girls playing in sand will decide that playing in sand is for girls and that, because he is a boy, playing in sand is not for him. Seeing a group of older boys playing football, he will decide that football is for boys, and because he is a boy, football is acceptable and he should learn more about it.

Hypothesis: According to gender-schema theory, children first establish gender identity, then begin actively learning about gender roles. Consequently, children who have established a gender identity should know much about gender roles, but children who have not established a gender identity should know little about gender roles.

Test: Zosuls et al. (2009) recorded children's language development from 10 to 21 months, looking for occasions when children referred to themselves as a boy or as a girl. In addition, at 17 and 21 months, children were observed as they played with several gender-stereotypic toys (truck, doll) and gender-neutral toys (telephone, miniature people). The investigators found that children who referred to themselves by gender played more often with gender-stereotypic toys. In other words, Beth, who has referred to herself as a girl, plays with dolls but not with trucks. In contrast, James, who has never referred to himself as a boy, plays with dolls and trucks equally.

Conclusion: As predicted, children's understanding that they are a boy (or girl) is the catalyst for learning about gender roles. As Martin and Ruble put it, "Children are gender detectives who search for cues about gender—who should or should not engage in a particular activity, who can play with whom, and why girls and boys are different" (2004, p. 67).

Application: After children understand gender, it's as if they see the world through special glasses that allow only gender-typical activities to be in focus (Liben & Bigler, 2002). For parents who don't want their children limited to traditional views of gender and traditional gender roles, it may be tempting to encourage children to remove the gender-tinted glasses in favor of more neutral glasses. But once a child has acquired gender identity, that's probably easier said than done. A better strategy may be to expose children to many counter-stereotypical examples: By showing girls women who fly planes, work in construction, and manage companies, and by showing boys men who are nurses, preschool teachers, or dental hygienists, children can learn a much broader definition of what it means to be male or female.

After children realize that gender is stable, they begin to learn all that they can about their gender's role. This leads some preschool girls to like frilly dresses that symbolize traditional feminine roles.

Gender-schema theory shows that "male" and "female" become much more salient in children's worlds after they understand gender. Consistent with this theory, I remember vividly taking my 4-year-old daughter Laura to watch my son Ben play football. I wondered if she would become so bored and restless that we'd have to leave. Wrong. Laura immediately discovered the cheerleaders (all girls) and insisted that we sit right in front of them. Throughout the game (and the rest of the season), Laura's eyes were riveted to the cheerleaders' every move, and when we got home, she'd imitate their routines. According to gender-schema theory, 4-year-old Laura knew that cheerleading was for girls and that because she was a girl, she needed to learn everything about it.*

This account also helps to explain why many 3- to 5-year-old girls, like the one in the photo, adore wearing exceedingly feminine clothing such as pink frilly dresses yet by the elementary-school years they become tomboys, wearing pants, playing sports, and avoiding feminine-stereotyped toys and activities (Bailey, Bechtold, & Berenbaum, 2002; Halim et al., 2014). A young girl's love of frilly dresses likely reflects the pursuit of salient symbols that match her newly acquired gender identity. However by school age, children know that gender roles are flexible (e.g., wearing pants doesn't make a girl into boy, wearing nail polish doesn't make a boy into a girl) and that masculine roles often have more status. Consequently, elementary-school girls realize that by being a tomboy they can have some of the status associated with being a boy without jeopardizing their identity as a girl (Halim, Ruble, & Amodio, 2011).

Biological Influences

LO9 How does biology influence children's learning of gender roles?

Most child-development researchers agree that biology contributes to gender roles and gender identity. Evolutionary developmental psychology, for example, reminds us that men and women performed vastly different roles for much of human history: Women were more invested in child rearing and men were more invested in providing important resources (e.g., food, protection) for their offspring (Geary, 2002). In adapting to these roles, different traits and behaviors evolved for men and women. For example, men became more aggressive because that was adaptive in helping them to hunt and to ward off predators.

If gender roles are based in part on our evolutionary heritage, then behavioral genetic research should show the impact of heredity on gender-role learning. Indeed, twin studies show a substantial hereditary contribution to gender-role learning (Iervolino et al., 2005). For identical twins, if one strongly prefers sex-typical toys and activities, the other one usually does, too. Fraternal twins are also similar in their preference for sex-typical toys and activities, but not to the same extent as identical twins.

Twin studies point to a biological basis for gender-role learning, but don't tell us what factors are responsible. Some scientists believe that the sex hormones are key players; consistent with this idea, for both boys and girls, exposure to testosterone during prenatal development leads to greater interest in masculine sex-typed activities during the elementary-school years (Constantinescu & Hines, 2012). **This link is particularly vivid in studies of children with *congenital adrenal hyperplasia (CAH)*, a genetic disorder in which, beginning in prenatal**

---

* But, during the elementary school years, she abandoned cheerleading for soccer and basketball.

development, the adrenal glands secrete large amounts of androgen. During childhood and adolescence, girls with CAH prefer masculine activities (such as playing with cars instead of dolls) and male playmates to a much greater extent than girls not exposed to these amounts of androgen, despite strong encouragement from parents to play with feminine toys (Miller & Halpern, 2014; Pasterski et al., 2005). Apparently, the androgen affects the prenatal development of brain regions critical for masculine and feminine gender-role behavior.

Perhaps the most accurate conclusion to draw is that biology, the socializing influence of people and media, and the child's own efforts to understand gender-typical behavior all contribute to gender roles and differences. Recognizing the interactive nature of these influences on gender learning also enables us to better understand how gender roles are changing today, which is the focus of the last module.

 ## Check Your Learning

RECALL Describe the forces of socialization that contribute to a child's development of gender identity.

Describe cognitive theories of gender identity.

INTERPRET How does children's acquisition of gender identity compare with growth in self-concept, described in Module 11.1?

APPLY The popular view is that children learn gender roles from adults (and society at large). But children are active participants in gender-role learning. Describe how children influence their own learning of gender roles.

 # Gender Roles in Transition

LEARNING OBJECTIVES

LO10 What is androgyny, and how is it related to traditional conceptions of masculinity and femininity?

LO11 Can parents rear gender-neutral children?

OUTLINE

Emerging Gender Roles

Beyond Traditional Gender Roles

Meda and Perry want their 6-year-old daughter, Hope, to pick activities, friends, and ultimately a career based on her interests and abilities, rather than on her gender. They have done their best to encourage gender-neutral values and behavior. Both are therefore astonished that Hope seems to be totally indistinguishable from other 6-year-olds reared by conventional parents. Hope's close friends are all girls. When Hope is with her friends, they play house or play with dolls. What seems to be going wrong with Meda and Perry's plans for a gender-neutral girl?

Gender roles are not etched in stone; they change with the times. In the United States, the range of acceptable roles for girls and boys and women and men has never been greater than today. For example, fathers such as the man in the photo stay home to be the primary caregivers for children, and some women work full-time as sole support for the family. What is the impact of these changes on children? In this module, we'll answer this question by looking at new gender roles and at efforts by parents like Meda and Perry to rear gender-neutral children.

Gender roles continue to evolve, and the range of acceptable roles for men and women continues to expand.

Emerging Gender Roles

LO10 **What is androgyny, and how is it related to traditional conceptions of masculinity and femininity?**

Traditionally, masculinity and femininity were seen as ends of a continuum: Children possessing many traits associated with males were considered highly masculine, and youngsters possessing many traits associated with females were considered highly feminine. A newer view of gender roles is based on the independent dimensions of instrumentality and expressiveness that were described in Module 13.1. In this view, traditional males are rated high on instrumentality but low on expressiveness, whereas traditional females are low on instrumentality but high on expressiveness. In other words, this approach recognizes that other combinations of traits are possible. *Androgynous* **persons are rated high on both the instrumental and expressive dimensions.** That is, androgynous individuals can be independent and emotional, self-confident and considerate, ambitious and creative.

Many theorists (e.g., Bem, 1996) argue that the ability to react with both instrumental and expressive behaviors is psychologically healthier than reacting primarily with one or the other. In fact, androgynous children often are better adjusted than children whose gender roles are highly stereotyped (DiDonato & Berenbaum, 2011; Norlander, Erixon, & Archer, 2000). However, the benefits of androgyny are greater for girls than for boys. Androgynous girls have greater self-esteem than expressive girls and are more likely to express their thoughts and feelings publicly (Harter, Waters, & Whitesell, 1998). For example, a girl like the one in the photo, who is independent and ambitious as well as considerate and creative, is more likely to feel positive about herself than a girl who embodies only the expressive traits traditionally associated with females.

Evidently, a balance of expressiveness and instrumentality may be especially adaptive across life's many tasks. Being independent and confident has benefits at home and work, but so does being kind and considerate. However, as we'll see in the next section, teaching children to adopt nontraditional views of gender is challenging.

Beyond Traditional Gender Roles

LO11 **Can parents rear gender-neutral children?**

Girls benefit from an androgynous gender role that combines the independence and self-confidence of the instrumental dimension with the emotional and considerate aspects of the expressive dimension.

Many researchers (e.g., Hyde, 2014) believe that gender is overemphasized to children. They argue that adults often unnecessarily group children by gender. Consider, for example, a minister who rewards perfect church attendance with blue pencils for boys and pink pencils for girls. Children's gender is irrelevant to the reason for the reward, yet distinguishing boys and girls makes gender seem important and increases children's gender stereotypes (Bigler, 1995).

Many developmentalists believe that gender should be linked strictly to reproductive function instead of, as it is now, to traits, behaviors, and abilities. Is this possible? Can children learn less stereotyped views of gender? Yes. School-age children can be taught that whether a person is well suited for a job depends on the person's skills and interests, not the person's sex (Bigler & Liben, 1990). In addition, children can be taught how to identify gender prejudice and how to respond to sexist remarks (Brinkman et al., 2011; Lamb et al., 2009; Pahlke, Bigler, & Martin, 2014).

Accomplishing long-term change in a natural setting may be more complicated, based on results of the Family Lifestyles Project (Weisner & Wilson-Mitchell, 1990; Weisner, Garnier, & Loucky, 1994). This research examined families in which the parents were members of the 1960s' and 1970s' counterculture and deeply committed to rearing their children without traditional gender stereotypes. In these families, men and women shared the household, financial, and child-care tasks.

The Family Lifestyle Project indicates that parents like Meda and Perry in this module's opening vignette can influence some aspects of gender stereotyping more readily than others. The children studied in the Family Lifestyles Project had few stereotypes about occupations; they agreed that girls could be president of the United States and drive trucks and that boys could be nurses and secretaries. They also had fewer stereotyped attitudes about the use of objects. Boys and girls were equally likely to use an iron, a shovel, hammer and nails, and needle and thread. Nevertheless, children in these families tended to have same-sex friends, and they liked gender-stereotypic activities; the boys enjoyed physical play and the girls enjoyed drawing and reading.

It should not surprise you that some features of gender roles and identities are influenced more readily by experience than others. For 250,000 years, *Homo sapiens* have existed in small groups of families, hunting animals and gathering vegetation. Because women have borne the children and cared for them, it has been adaptive for women to be caring and nurturing. As we saw in Module 10.3, a nurturing caregiver increases the odds of a secure attachment and, ultimately, the survival of the infant. Men's responsibilities included hunting and protecting the family unit from predators, roles for which physical strength and aggressiveness were crucial.

Circumstances of life in the 21st century differ substantially: Often men and women are employed outside the home and share child care (Eagly & Wood, 2013). Nevertheless, the cultural changes of the past few decades cannot erase hundreds of thousands of years of evolutionary history. We should not be surprised that boys and girls play differently, that girls tend to be more supportive in their interactions with others, and that boys are usually more aggressive physically.

The "Improving Children's Lives" feature suggests ways children can be helped to go beyond traditional gender roles and learn the best from both roles.

 QUESTION 13.4

Ms. Bower has her second-grade class form two lines—one for boys and one for girls—before they walk to the cafeteria for lunch. What do you think of this practice?

Improving Children's Lives

Encouraging Valuable Traits, Not Gender Traits

Parents and other adults can encourage children to learn the best from both of the traditional gender roles. Being independent, confident, caring, and considerate is valuable for all people, not just for boys or girls. Here are some guidelines to help achieve these aims:

- Because children learn gender roles from those around them, parents should be sure that they themselves are not gender bound. Mothers and fathers can mow lawns, make repairs, and work outside the home. Mothers and fathers can prepare meals, do laundry, and care for the young. This *does* make a difference: I've always done most of the laundry in our house, and my daughter, at age 5, was astonished when I told her that in most homes mothers do the wash.

- Parents should not base decisions about children's toys, activities, and chores on the child's sex. They should decide whether a toy, activity, or chore is appropriate for the child as an individual (based on age, abilities, and interests), rather than because the child is a boy or a girl.

- Forces outside the home, such as media and teachers, often work against parents who want their children to go beyond traditional gender roles. It's neither feasible nor wise to shelter children from these influences, but parents can encourage children to think critically about others' gender-based decisions. When band teachers insist that boys play trumpets and trombones while girls play clarinets and flutes, parents should ask children whether this makes sense. When a TV program shows a man coming to aid the stereotypic damsel in distress, parents should ask the child why the woman simply didn't get herself out of her predicament.

By following these guidelines, adults can help children to develop all of their talents, not just those that fit traditional views associated with males and females.

 ## Check Your Learning

RECALL What characteristics make up androgyny?

What elements of gender stereotyping seem fairly easy to change? What elements seem more resistant to change?

INTERPRET Why might girls benefit more than boys from an androgynous gender role?

APPLY What advice would you give to a mother who wants her daughter to grow to be gender-free in her attitudes, beliefs, and aspirations?

 # Unifying Themes   Connections

Research on gender illustrates the theme that development in different domains is connected. Think about how children learn gender roles. According to conventional wisdom, children acquire masculine or feminine traits and behaviors through socialization by parents and other knowledgeable or authoritative persons in the child's culture. This process is important, but we have seen that learning gender roles is not simply a social phenomenon:

Cognitive processes are essential. Children don't really begin to learn about gender roles until they understand that gender is stable; when they do, gender-schema theory shows how children use this information to decide which experiences are relevant to them. Biology apparently contributes, too, although we still don't really understand how. Biology, cognition, and social forces all shape the unique gender role that individual boys or girls play.

See for Yourself

To see that older children know more about gender stereotypes and understand that stereotypes are not binding, you'll need to create some simple stories that illustrate stereotypical traits. I suggest that you use *independent, confident, appreciative,* and *gentle*. Each story should include two to three sentences that describe a child. Be sure that your stories contain no other clues that would hint that the child in the story is a boy or a girl. For example, this story illustrates independent:

> I know a child who likes to do things without help from adults. This child likes to do homework without help and enjoys traveling alone to visit cousins who live in another city.

Read your stories to some 11- and 12-year-olds. After you've read each story, ask, "Is this child a boy, a girl,

or could it be either?" Record the reply, and then ask, "Would most people think that the child is a boy, or would most think that the child is a girl?"

With the first question, you're measuring children's understanding that gender stereotypes are flexible. You should find that children answer with "either one" about half of the time, indicating that they believe in some, but not total, flexibility in gender stereotypes. With the second question, you're measuring children's awareness of gender stereotypes. You should find that most children always answer the second question stereotypically: that people would identify the independent and confident children as boys and the appreciative and gentle children as girls. See for yourself!

Summary

 Gender Stereotypes

How Do We View Men and Women?

Instrumental traits describe individuals who act on the world and are usually associated with males. Expressive traits describe individuals who value interpersonal relationships and are usually associated with females.

Learning Gender Stereotypes

By age 4, children have substantial knowledge of gender-stereotypic activities; during the elementary-school years, they come to know gender-stereotypical traits and behaviors. Older children also understand that traits and occupations associated with males have higher social status and that stereotypes are not necessarily binding.

 Differences Related To Gender

In *The Psychology of Sex Differences*, published in 1974, Eleanor Maccoby and Carol Jacklin concluded that males and females differed in only four areas: verbal ability, spatial ability, math achievement, and aggression. Subsequent investigators have used their work as the starting point for analyzing gender differences.

Differences in Physical Development and Behavior

Boys tend to be bigger, stronger, and more active than girls, who tend to have better fine-motor coordination and to be healthier.

Differences in Intellectual Abilities and Achievement

Girls excel in verbal skills whereas boys excel in spatial ability. Boys once had an advantage in math achievement, but the gap is now negligible because girls have more exposure to women who pursue math-relevant careers. Girls remember objects and their locations more accurately than boys do. Differences in intellectual abilities reflect both hereditary and environmental factors.

Differences in Personality and Social Behavior

Boys are more aggressive physically than girls, and biology probably contributes heavily to this difference. Girls usually express their aggression by trying to damage other children's relations with peers. Girls are more sensitive to others' feelings and are more influenced by others; both differences are probably due to experience. Girls are more skilled in effortful control but in adolescence are more prone to depression than are adolescent boys.

Frank Talk About Gender Differences

Most gender differences are fairly small, which means that abilities for boys and girls overlap considerably. Also, despite the emphasis on gender differences, boys and girls are quite similar in many aspects of cognition, personality, and social behavior.

 Gender Identity

The Socializing Influences of People and the Media

Parents treat sons and daughters similarly, except in gender-related behavior. Fathers may be particularly important in teaching about gender because they are more likely to treat sons and daughters differently. Teachers foster gender-role learning by making gender salient.

By the preschool years, peers discourage cross-gender play by ridiculing peers who engage in it. Peers also influence gender roles because children play almost exclusively with same-sex peers.

Television depicts men and women in a stereotypical fashion, and children who watch a lot of television are likely to have stereotyped views of men and women.

Cognitive Theories of Gender Identity

Children gradually learn that gender is constant over time and cannot be changed according to personal wishes. After children understand that gender is constant, they begin to learn gender-typical behavior. According to gender-schema theory, children learn about gender by paying attention to behaviors of members of their own sex and ignoring behaviors of members of the other sex.

Biological Influences

The idea that biology influences some aspects of gender roles is supported by research on females exposed to male hormones during prenatal development.

 Gender Roles in Transition

Emerging Gender Roles

Androgynous persons embody both instrumental and expressive traits. Androgynous girls have greater self-esteem than traditional girls and are more likely to express themselves publicly; androgynous boys have about the same level of self-esteem as traditional boys.

Beyond Traditional Gender Roles

Training studies show that children can learn less stereotyped views of gender, but studies of parents trying to rear gender-neutral children suggest that many stereotyped behaviors are resistant to change.

Test Yourself

1. Instrumental traits _____.
   a. are associated with females
   b. describe people who act on the world
   c. describe people who value interpersonal relationships

2. During the _____ years, children's knowledge of gender stereotypes expands to include personality traits.
   a. toddler
   b. elementary-school
   c. high-school

3. By the middle elementary-school years, children know more gender stereotypes, but they also see stereotypes as _____.
   a. more flexible and not binding
   b. rigid, just like physical properties associated with a child's biological sex
   c. holding more strongly for girls than for boys

4. Compared with girls, boys tend to _____.
   a. be stronger and more active
   b. have better fine-motor coordination
   c. be healthier

5. In the intellectual domain, _____.
   a. boys outperform girls on all spatial tasks
   b. girls read better than boys but girls also have more language-related problems
   c. girls remember objects and their locations more accurately than boys do

6. In mathematics, _____.
   a. girls do as well as boys in math in cultures where males and females have comparable access to education
   b. boys have greater understanding of math concepts but girls get higher scores on achievement tests administered in high school
   c. girls used to be more advanced than boys in arithmetic but this gap has vanished in the last 25 years

7. Which of the following is an *accurate* description of sex differences in aggression?
   a. Parents are more likely to punish sons than daughters for being physically aggressive.
   b. Boys rely exclusively on physical aggression, not relational aggression.
   c. Androgen probably contributes to boys' aggressive behavior by making them more competitive and quicker to anger.

8. In the domains of personality and social behavior, girls are _____.
   a. more sensitive emotionally
   b. less able to control their behavior
   c. less prone to depression

9. Boys and girls differ in their average scores in several domains, _____.
   a. but the distributions of scores for boys and girls overlap considerably
   b. and most of the differences are quite large
   c. but boys and girls are equally likely to get very high or very low scores

10. Research on the impact of parents on children's learning of gender shows that _____.
    a. fathers are more likely than mothers to treat sons and daughters the same
    b. parents with traditional views of gender tend to have children with traditional gender-related interests, attitudes, and self-concepts
    c. parents interact more with daughters than with sons but more strongly encourage their sons to achieve

11. Children's play is usually segregated by sex because _____.
    a. children like to play with children who are like themselves
    b. boys prefer conversation-oriented play
    c. when boys and girls play together, boys cannot readily influence girls

12. According to cognitive theories of gender identity, _____.
    a. toddlers understand that gender is stable, that boys become men and girls become women
    b. playing with sex-typed toys is crucial for children to learn a gender identity
    c. typically girls become tomboys only after they realize that gender roles are flexible

13. Which of the following is an *accurate* description of biological influences on gender roles?
    a. Girls exposed to large amounts of testosterone during prenatal development prefer feminine activities.
    b. According to evolutionary developmental psychology, different traits and behaviors evolved for males and females.
    c. Twin studies show that fraternal and identical twins are similar in their preference for sex-typical toys and activities.

14. Which child is likely to have the lowest self-esteem?
    a. An androgynous girl
    b. A masculine-stereotyped boy
    c. A feminine-stereotyped girl

15. Interventions designed to influence children's thinking about gender stereotypes show that _____

    a. school-age children cannot be taught to recognize sexism and prejudice.

    b. it is fairly easy to change children's stereotyped views of occupations.

    c. after training, most children have as many same-sex as other-sex friends.

Key Terms

androgens 411

androgynous 422

congenital adrenal hyperplasia (CAH) 420

constricting 417

enabling 417

expressive 402

gender identity 401

gender roles 401

gender-schema theory 418

gender stereotypes 401

instrumental 402

mental rotation 408

social roles 401

Chapter 14
Family Relationships

Modules

14.1 Parenting

14.2 The Changing Family

14.3 Brothers and Sisters

14.4 Maltreatment: Parent–Child Relationships Gone Awry

Family. The term is as sacred to most Americans as baseball, apple pie, and Chevrolet. But what comes to mind when you think of family? Television gives us one answer: from *Leave It to Beaver* to *Family Ties* to *The Middle*, the American family is portrayed as a mother, a father, and their children. In reality, of course, American families are as diverse as the people in them. Some families consist of a single parent and an only child. Others include two parents, many children, and grandparents or other relatives.

All these family configurations, however, have a common goal: nurturing children and helping them become full-fledged adult members of their culture. To learn how families achieve these goals, we'll begin, in **Module 14.1**, by looking at relationships between parents and children. Next, in **Module 14.2**, we'll see how families are changing in the 21st century. Then, in **Module 14.3**, we'll look at relationships between siblings. Finally, in **Module 14.4**, we'll examine the forces that can cause parents to abuse their children.

14.1 Parenting

LEARNING OBJECTIVES

		OUTLINE
LO1	What is a systems view of family dynamics?	**The Family as a System**
LO2	What are the different styles of parenting?	**Styles of Parenting**
LO3	What parental behaviors affect children's development?	**Parental Behavior**
LO4	How are children influenced by the quality of their parents' marital relationship?	**Influences of the Marital System**
LO5	How do children help determine how parents rear them?	**Children's Contributions**

Tanya and Sheila, both sixth graders, wanted to go to a Miley Cyrus concert with two boys from their school. When Tanya asked if she could go, her mom said, "No way!" Tanya responded defiantly, "Why not?" In return, her mother exploded, "Because I say so. That's why. Stop pestering me." Sheila wasn't allowed to go either. When she asked why, her mom said, "I just think you're still too young to be dating. I don't mind your going to the concert. If you want to go just with Tanya, that would be fine. What do you think of that?"

The vignette illustrates what we all know well from personal experience: Parents go about child rearing in many different ways. In this module, you'll learn about different approaches that parents take to raising children. But let's begin by thinking about parents as an important element in the family system.

The Family as a System

LO1 What is a systems view of family dynamics?

Families are rare in the animal kingdom. Only human beings and a handful of other species form family-like units. Why? Compared to the young in other species, children develop slowly. Because children are unable to care for themselves for many years, the family structure evolved as a way to protect and nurture young children as they develop into full-fledged members of their culture (Bjorklund, Yunger, & Pellegrini, 2002). Of course, modern families serve many other functions

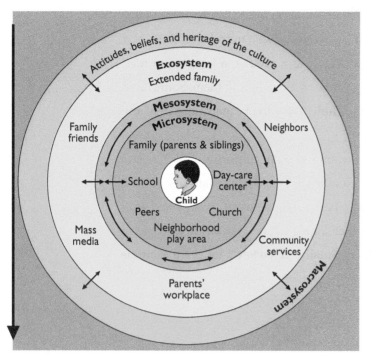

Figure 14-1

According to a systems approach to parenting, a parent who has a frustrating day at work may be a less effective parent when she gets home.

as well—they're economic units and they provide emotional support—but child rearing remains the most salient and probably the most important family function.

As we think about original and modern families, it's tempting to believe that parents' actions are all that really matter. That is, through their behavior, parents directly and indirectly determine their children's development. This view of parents as "all powerful" was part of early psychological theories (e.g., Watson, 1925) and is held even today by some first-time parents. But most theorists now view families from a contextual perspective (described in Module 1.2). That is, families form a system of interacting elements, in which parents and children influence one another (Cox & Paley, 2003; Schermerhorn & Cummings, 2008), and families are part of a much larger system that includes extended family, friends, and teachers as well as institutions that influence development (e.g., schools).

This systems view of children and families is exemplified in a theory proposed by Bronfenbrenner (1995; Bronfenbrenner & Morris, 2006), which holds that the developing child is embedded in a series of complex and interactive systems. As Figure 14-1 shows, the environment is divided into five components: the microsystem, the mesosystem, the exosystem, the macrosystem, and the chronosystem. **At any point in life, the *microsystem* consists of the people and objects in an individual's immediate environment.** These are the people closest to a child, such as parents or siblings. Some children have more than one microsystem; for example, a young child might have the microsystems of the family and of the day-care setting. As you can imagine, microsystems strongly influence development.

Microsystems themselves are connected to create the *mesosystem*. The mesosystem represents the fact that what happens in one microsystem is likely to influence what happens in others. Perhaps you've found that if you have a stressful day at work or school, you're grouchy at home. This indicates that your mesosystem is alive and well; your microsystems of home and work are connected emotionally for you.

The *exosystem* **refers to social settings that a person may not experience firsthand but that still influence development.** For example, a mother's work environment is part of her child's exosystem, because she may pay more attention to her child when her work is going well and less attention when she's under a great deal of work-related stress. Although the influence of the exosystem is at least secondhand, its effects on the developing child can be quite strong. Think about the woman in the photo, who doesn't look as if she's having a good day at work; do you think she'll do her best mothering when she gets home? Probably not, which means that the workplace has affected her child's development.

The broadest environmental context is the *macrosystem*, the subcultures and cultures in which the microsystem, mesosystem, and exosystem are embedded. A mother, her workplace, her child, and the child's school are part of a larger cultural setting, such as Asian Americans living in southern California or Muslim Americans living in large cities on the East Coast. Members of these cultural groups share a common identity, a common heritage, and common values.

Finally, these systems all change over time, a dimension known as the *chronosystem*. This dimension reminds us that microsystem, mesosystem, exosystem, and macrosystem are not static but are constantly in flux. For example, the child's microsystem changes when an older sister leaves home to attend college and the child's exosystem changes when a mother leaves an easy but low-paying job for a more challenging but higher-paying job. And, of course, children themselves are changing over time, which often influences the way in which they are affected by the other elements in the system. For example, a family's move to a distant city may affect a school-age child more than a toddler because the older child must change schools and replace long-term friends (Adams, 2004).

When viewed as part of an interactive system like the one shown in Figure 14-1, parents still influence their children, both directly—for example, by encouraging them to study hard—and indirectly—for example, by being generous and kind to others. However, the influence is no longer exclusively from parent to children; it is mutual. Children influence their parents, too. By their behaviors, attitudes, and interests, children affect how their parents behave toward them. When children resist discipline, for example, parents may become less willing to reason with them and more inclined to use force.

Even more subtle influences become apparent when families are viewed as systems of interacting elements. For example, fathers' behaviors can affect mother–child relationships. A demanding husband may leave his wife with little time, energy, or interest in helping her daughter with homework. Or when siblings argue constantly, parents may become preoccupied with avoiding problems rather than encouraging their children's development.

These examples show that narrowly focusing on parents' impact on children misses the complexities of family life. But there is even more to the systems view. The family itself is embedded in other social systems, such as neighborhoods and religious institutions (Parke & Buriel, 1998). These other institutions can affect family dynamics. Sometimes they simplify child rearing, as when neighbors are trusted friends and can help care for each other's children. Other times, however, they complicate child rearing. Grandparents who live nearby can create friction within the family. At times, the impact of the larger systems is indirect, as when work schedules cause a parent to be away from home or when schools must eliminate programs that benefit children.

In the remainder of this module, we'll describe parents' influences on children and then see how children affect their parents' behavior.

Styles of Parenting

LO2 What are the different styles of parenting?

Parenting can be described in terms of general dimensions that are like personality traits in that they represent stable aspects of parental behavior—aspects that remain across different situations, creating a characteristic manner or style in which parents interact with their children (Holden & Miller, 1999). When parenting is viewed this way, two general dimensions of parental behavior emerge. One is the degree of warmth and responsiveness that parents show their children. At one end of the spectrum are parents who are openly warm and affectionate with their children. They are involved with them, respond to their emotional needs, and spend much time with them. At the other end of the spectrum are parents who are relatively uninvolved with their children and sometimes even hostile toward them. These parents often seem more focused on their own needs and interests than those of their children.

Warm parents enjoy hearing their children describe the day's activities; uninvolved or hostile parents aren't interested, considering it a waste of their time. Warm parents see when their children are upset and try to comfort them; uninvolved or hostile parents pay little attention to their children's emotional states and invest little effort in comforting them when they're upset. As you might expect, children benefit from warm and responsive parenting (Pettit, Bates, & Dodge, 1997; Zhou et al., 2002).

A second general dimension of parental behavior involves control, which comes in two forms (Grusec, 2011). Psychological control refers to parents' efforts to manipulate their children's emotional states by, for example, withdrawing their love or making children feel guilty. Behavioral control refers to parents' efforts to set rules for their children and to impose limits on what children can and cannot do. Some parents are dictatorial: They try to regulate every facet of their children's lives, like a puppeteer controlling a marionette. At the other extreme are parents who exert little or no control over their children: These children do whatever they want without asking parents first or worrying about their parents' response.

What's best for children is minimal psychological control combined with an intermediate amount of behavioral control in which parents set reasonable standards for their children's behavior, expect their children to meet those standards, and monitor their children's behavior (i.e., they also usually know where their children are, what they're doing, and with whom). When parents have reasonable expectations for their children and keep tabs on their activity—for example, a mother knows that her 12-year-old is staying after school for choir practice, then going to the library—their children tend to be better adjusted (Kilgore, Snyder, & Lentz, 2000).

When the dimensions of warmth and control are combined, the result is four prototypic styles of parenting, as shown in Figure 14-2 (Baumrind, 1975, 1991).

- *Authoritarian parenting* **combines high control with little warmth.** These parents lay down the rules and expect them to be followed without discussion. Hard work, respect, and obedience are what authoritarian parents wish to cultivate in their children. There is little give-and-take between parent and child because authoritarian parents do not consider children's needs or wishes. This style is illustrated by Tanya's mother in the opening vignette, who feels no obligation whatsoever to explain her decisions.
- *Authoritative parenting* **combines a fair degree of parental control with warmth and responsivity to children.** Authoritative parents explain rules and encourage discussion. This style is exemplified by Sheila's mother in the opening vignette. She explained why she did not want Sheila going to the concert and encouraged her daughter to discuss the issue with her.
- *Permissive parenting* **offers warmth and caring but little parental control.** These parents generally accept their children's behavior and punish them infrequently. A permissive parent would readily agree to Tanya's or Sheila's request to go to the concert, simply because it is something the child wants to do.
- *Uninvolved parenting* **provides neither warmth nor control.** Uninvolved parents provide for their children's basic physical and emotional needs but little else. These parents try to minimize the amount of time spent with their children and avoid becoming emotionally involved with them. Returning to the vignette, if Tanya had uninvolved parents, she might simply have gone to the concert without asking, knowing that her parents wouldn't care and would rather not be bothered.

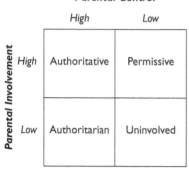

Parental Control

	High	Low
High	Authoritative	Permissive
Low	Authoritarian	Uninvolved

(Parental Involvement)

Figure 14-2

SOURCE: Data from Baumrind, D. (1975). *Early socialization and the discipline controversy.* Morristown, NJ: General Learning Press; Baumrind, D. (1991). Parenting styles and adolescent development. In R. M. Lerner, A. C. Petersen, & J. Brooks-Gunn (Eds.), *Encyclopedia of adolescence.* New York, NY: Garland.

Research consistently shows that authoritative parenting is best for most children, most of the time. Children with authoritative parents tend to be responsible, self-reliant, and friendly, and have higher grades (Amato & Fowler, 2002; Simons & Conger, 2007). In contrast, children with authoritarian parents are often unhappy, have low self-esteem, and are often aggressive (e.g., Braza et al., 2014; Silk et al., 2003; Zhou et al., 2008). Finally, children with permissive parents are often impulsive and have little self-control, whereas children with uninvolved parents often do poorly in school and are aggressive (Aunola, Stattin, & Nurmi, 2000; Driscoll, Russell, & Crockett, 2008). Thus, children typically thrive on a parental style that combines control, warmth, and affection.

Variations Associated with Culture and Socioeconomic Status The general aim of child rearing—helping children become contributing members of their cultures—is much the same worldwide (Whiting & Child, 1953), and warmth and control are universal aspects of parents' behavior. But views about the "proper" amount of warmth and the "proper" amount of control vary by culture. European Americans want their children to be happy and self-reliant individuals; they believe that these goals are best achieved when parents are warm and exert moderate control (Goodnow, 1992). However, in many countries around the world, individualism is less important than cooperation and collaboration (Wang, Pomerantz, & Chen, 2007). In China, for example, emotional restraint and obedience are seen as the keys to family harmony (Chao, 2001). Consequently, parents in China often rely on an authoritarian style in which they are infrequently affectionate and expect their children to obey them without question (Lin & Fu, 1990; Zhou et al., 2008).

Another common pattern worldwide is for parents to be warm and controlling (Deater-Deckard et al., 2011). For example, Latino culture typically places greater emphasis on strong family ties and respecting the roles of all family members, particularly adults; these values lead parents to be more protective of their children and to set more rules for them (Halgunseth, Ispa, & Rudy, 2006). Thus, cultural values help specify culturally appropriate ways for parents to interact with their offspring.

Not only do parental styles vary *across* cultures, but they also vary *within* cultures, depending on parents' socioeconomic status. Within the United States, parents with lower socioeconomic status tend to be more controlling and more punitive—characteristics associated with the authoritarian parenting style—than are parents with higher socioeconomic status (Hoff-Ginsberg & Tardif, 1995). This difference may reflect educational differences that help to define socioeconomic status. Parents with higher socioeconomic status are, by definition, more educated, and consequently often see development as a more complex process that requires the more nuanced and child-friendly approach that marks authoritative parenting (Skinner, 1985). Another contributing factor derives from another variable that defines socioeconomic status: income (Melby et al., 2008). Because of their limited financial resources, parents with lower socioeconomic status often lead more stressful lives (e.g., they wonder whether they'll have enough money at the end of the month for groceries) and are far more likely to live in neighborhoods where violence, drug abuse, and crime are commonplace. Thus, parents with lower socioeconomic status may be too stressed to invest the energy needed for authoritative parenting, and the authoritarian approach—with its emphasis on the child's immediate compliance—may actually protect children who are growing up in dangerous neighborhoods (Parke & Buriel, 1998; Smetana, 2011).

Genetic Influences on Parenting Families and parenting are adaptations that evolved to provide for children until they mature. In other words, genes linked to behaviors that make for effective parenting (e.g., being nurturing) were more likely to be passed on because they helped children to reach maturity. Consistent with this view, research on twins as parents shows the impact of genetics on parental style. For example, parental warmth is influenced by heredity, as is parental negativity (Klahr & Burt, 2014). That is, heredity makes it easier for some people to be warm, caring, supporting, and responsive parents and makes it easier for other people to be hostile, angry, and abusive parents. Behavior genetic studies also reveal several environmental influences on parental style, including the quality of the parents' marital relationship and the children themselves (Klahr & Burt, 2014); we'll examine these later in this module.

Parental Behavior

LO3   What parental behaviors affect children's development?

A *style* is a broad characterization of how parents typically behave. For example, if I describe a parent as using an authoritarian style, you immediately have a sense of that parent's typical ways of interacting with his or her children. Nevertheless, the price for such a general description is that it tells us little about how parents behave in specific situations and how these parental behaviors influence children's development. Put another way, what specific behaviors can parents use to influence their children? Researchers who study parents name three: direct instruction and coaching, modeling, and feedback.

Direct Instruction and Coaching   Parents often tell their children what to do. But simply playing the role of drill sergeant in ordering children around—"Clean your room!" "Turn off the TV!"—is not very effective. **A better approach is *direct instruction*, telling a child what to do, when, and why.** Instead of just shouting "Share your candy with your brother!" a parent should explain when and why it's important to share with a sibling.

In addition, just as coaches help athletes master sports skills, parents can help their youngsters master social and emotional skills. Parents can explain links between emotions and behavior—"Catlin is sad because you broke her crayon" (Gottman, Katz, & Hooven, 1996). They can also teach how to deal with difficult social situations—"When you ask Lindsey if she can sleep over, do it privately so you won't hurt Kaycee's or Hannah's feelings" (Mize & Pettit, 1997). In general, children who get this sort of parental "coaching" tend to be more socially skilled and, not surprisingly, get along better with their peers. (I'll say more about this in Module 15.1.)

Learning by Observing   Children learn much from parents simply by watching them. For example, in Module 12.4 we saw that youngsters often learn how to interact with others by watching how their parents interact. *Observational learning* can also produce *counterimitation*, learning what should not be done. If an older sister like the one in the photo has been mean to a classmate and the mother punishes her, the younger sister may learn to be friendly instead of mean.

Observational learning likely contributes to intergenerational continuity of parenting behavior. Parental behavior is often consistent from one generation to the next. When, for example, parents often use harsh physical punishment to discipline their children, these children will, when they are parents, follow suit (Bailey et al., 2009).

By watching others (observational learning), children can learn behaviors that are expected (and may be rewarded) as well as behaviors that are considered inappropriate (and may lead to punishment).

Feedback By giving feedback to their children, parents indicate whether a behavior is appropriate and should continue or is inappropriate and should stop. Feedback comes in two general forms. *Reinforcement* **is any action that increases the likelihood of the response that it follows.** Parents may use praise to reinforce a child's studying or give a reward for completing household chores. *Punishment* **is any action that discourages the reoccurrence of the response that it follows.** Parents may forbid children to watch television when they get poor grades in school or make children go to bed early for neglecting household chores.

Of course, parents have been rewarding and punishing their children for centuries, so what do psychologists know that parents don't know already? **The most surprising discovery is that parents often unwittingly reinforce the very behaviors they want to discourage, a situation called the** *negative reinforcement trap* (Patterson, 1980). This trap occurs in three steps, most often between a mother and her son. In the first step, the mother tells her son to do something he doesn't want to do. She might tell him to clean up his room, to come inside while he's outdoors playing with friends, or to study instead of watching television. In the next step, the son responds with some behavior that most parents find intolerable: He argues, complains, or whines—not just briefly, but for an extended period. In the last step, the mother gives in—saying that the son needn't do as she told him initially—simply to get the son to stop the behavior that is so intolerable.

The feedback to the son is that arguing (or complaining or whining) works; the mother rewards that behavior by withdrawing the request or command that the son did not like. That is, although we usually think a behavior is strengthened when it is followed by the presentation of something that is valued, behavior is also strengthened when it is followed by removing something that is disliked.

As for punishment, research shows that it works best when:

- It is administered directly after the undesired behavior occurs, rather than hours later.
- An undesired behavior always leads to punishment, rather than usually or occasionally.
- It is accompanied by an explanation of why the child was punished and how punishment can be avoided in the future.
- The child has a warm, affectionate relationship with the person administering the punishment.

At the same time, research reveals some serious drawbacks to punishment. One is that the impact of punishment is temporary if children do not learn new behaviors to replace those that were punished. For example, denying TV to brothers who are fighting stops the undesirable behavior, but fighting is likely to recur unless the boys learn new ways of solving their disputes.

A second drawback is that punishment can have undesirable side effects. Children become upset as they are being punished, which means they often miss the feedback that punishment is meant to convey. A child denied TV for misbehaving may become angry over the punishment itself and ignore why he's being punished.

Spanking illustrates the problems with punishment. Although used by many parents in the United States and around the world, it is ineffective in getting children to comply with parents and often leads them to be aggressive (Gershoff, 2013). And harsher forms of physical punishment are associated with a range of negative outcomes including mental health problems, impaired parent–child relationships, and delayed cognitive development (Berlin et al., 2009; Gershoff & Bitensky, 2007). Because physical punishment is so harmful to children, many

 QUESTION 14.1

When 10-year-old Dylan's family got a puppy, he agreed to walk it every day after school. But when his mom asks him to do this, he gets angry because he'd rather watch TV. They argue for about 15 minutes, then Dylan's mom gives up and walks the dog herself, while Dylan goes back to watching TV. Analyze this situation. What could Dylan's mom do to prevent these regular arguments?

Time-out, in which children are isolated socially, is an effective form of punishment.

countries around the world (e.g., Costa Rica, the Netherlands, New Zealand, and Spain) have banned it altogether (Global Initiative to End All Corporal Punishment of Children, 2011).

One method retains the best features of punishment but avoids its shortcomings. **In *time-out*, a child who misbehaves must briefly sit alone in a quiet, unstimulating location.** Some parents have children sit alone in a bathroom; others have children sit alone in a room, as shown in the photo. Time-out is punishing because it interrupts the child's ongoing activity and isolates the child from other family members, toys, books, and, generally, all forms of rewarding stimulation.

The period is sufficiently brief—usually just a few minutes—for a parent to use the method consistently. During time-out, both parent and child typically calm down. Then, when time-out is over, a parent can talk with the child and explain why the punished behavior is objectionable and what the child should do instead. "Reasoning" like this—even with preschool children—is effective because it emphasizes why a parent punished initially and how punishment can be avoided in the future.

These techniques can be taught to parents. Many meta-analyses document the effectiveness of programs that teach parenting skills (e.g., using positive reinforcement and using nonphysical punishment consistently), that promote good communication within families, and that make parents feel confident in their ability to be good parents. These kinds of intervention programs make parents feel more satisfied with their parenting, lead them to parent more effectively, and reduce children's behavior problems (Brotman et al., 2011; Sanders, 2014). Thus, although research on genetics shows that the path to good parenting may be easier for some people than others, most adults can master the skills that foster children's development.

Influences of the Marital System

LO4   How are children influenced by the quality of their parents' marital relationship?

When Derek returned from 7-Eleven with a six-pack of beer and a bag of chips instead of diapers and baby food, Anita exploded in anger. "How could you! I used the last diaper an hour ago!" Huddled in the corner of the kitchen, their son Randy watched yet another episode in the daily soap opera that featured Derek and Anita.

Although Derek and Anita aren't arguing about Randy—in fact, they're so wrapped up in their conflict that they forget he's in the room—it's hard to conceive that a child would emerge unscathed from such constant parental conflict. Indeed, research shows that chronic parental conflict is harmful for children: When parents are constantly in conflict, children and adolescents often become anxious, withdrawn, aggressive, and are more prone to chronic diseases and to be abusive in their own romantic relationships (Miller & Chen, 2010; Narayan, Englund, & Egeland, 2013; Rhoades, 2008). Parental conflict affects children's development through three distinct mechanisms. First, seeing parents fight jeopardizes a child's feeling that the family is stable and secure, making a child feel anxious, frightened, and sad (Cummings et al., 2012; Davies, Cicchetti, & Martin, 2012). Second, chronic conflict between parents often spills over into the parent–child relationship. A wife who finds herself frequently arguing with and confronting her husband may adopt a similarly ineffective style in interacting with her children (Cox, Paley, & Harter, 2001). Third, when parents invest time and energy fighting with each other, they're often too tired or too preoccupied to invest themselves in high-quality parenting (Katz & Woodin, 2002).

Of course, all marriages experience conflict at some point. Does this mean that all children bear at least some scars? Not necessarily. Many parents resolve conflicts in a manner that's constructive instead of destructive. To see this, suppose that one parent believes their child should attend a summer camp, but the other parent believes it's too expensive and not worth it because the child attended the previous summer. Instead of shouting and name-calling (e.g., "You're always so cheap!"), some parents seek mutually acceptable solutions: The child could attend the camp if she earns money to cover part of the cost or the child could attend a different, less expensive camp. When families like the one

When parents resolve conflicts constructively, their children respond positively to conflict.

in the photo routinely resolve disagreements this way, children actually respond *positively* to conflict, apparently because it shows that their family is cohesive and able to withstand and overcome life's problems (Goeke-Morey et al., 2003). And youth exposed to this sort of constructive approach rely on it when solving conflicts in their peer and romantic relationships (Miga, Gdula, & Allen, 2012).

The extent and resolution of conflict is an obvious way in which the parental system affects children, but it's not the only way. Many mothers and fathers form an effective parental team, working together in a coordinated and complementary fashion toward goals that they share for their child's development. For example, Mom and Dad may agree that their daughter is smart and athletically skilled and that she should excel in both domains. Consequently, they're quite happy to help her achieve these goals. Mom gives her basketball tips and Dad edits her school essays.

But not all parents work together well. Sometimes they don't agree on goals: One parent values sports over schoolwork while the other reverses these priorities. Sometimes parents actively compete for their child's attention: Mom may want to take the child shopping but Dad wants to take her to a ball game. Finally, parents sometimes act as gatekeepers, limiting one another's participation in parenting. Mom may feel that infant care is solely her turf and not allow Dad to participate. Or Dad may claim all school-related tasks and discourage Mom from getting involved.

These many examples show that, just as a doubles tennis team won't win many matches when each player ignores his or her partner, parenting is far less effective when parents try to "go it alone" instead of working together, collaborating as co-parents to achieve goals that they share and using methods that they both accept. Lack of teamwork, competition, and gatekeeping can lead to problems, causing children, for example, to become withdrawn and less likely to behave prosocially (McHale et al., 2002; Scrimgeour et al., 2013).

Thus far, we've seen that to understand parents' impact on children's development, we need to consider the nature of the marital relationship as well as parenting style and specific parenting behaviors (e.g., use of feedback). In addition, Figure 14-1 reminds us that forces outside the family can influence parenting and children's development. To illustrate, let's consider work-related influences. One such influence is a parent's job security: Children and adolescents lose self-esteem and find it difficult to concentrate in school when their parents become unemployed, or for that matter, when they simply worry that their parents may become unemployed (Barling, Zacharatos, & Hepburn, 1999; Kalil & Ziol-Guest, 2005).

Another well-known factor is work-related stress. Not surprisingly, when men and women lead stressful lives at work, they parent less effectively. Sometimes frazzled parents withdraw from family interactions. Over time, this gives the appearance that the parent is detached and disinterested, which makes children anxious and upset. And sometimes work-stressed parents are less accepting and less tolerant, leading to conflicts with their children (Crouter & Bumpus, 2001; Lim & Kim, 2014; Maggi et al., 2008).

Thus, a person's work life can profoundly affect children and adolescents by changing the parenting they experience. In Module 15.3, we'll look at another system-level influence on children: the neighborhood where children live. For now, another way to view family systems in action is by switching perspectives and seeing how children affect parenting behavior.

Children's Contributions

LO5 How do children help determine how parents rear them?

I emphasized previously that the family is a dynamic, interactive system in which parents and children influence each other. In fact, children begin at birth to influence the way their parents treat them. Let's look at two characteristics of children that influence how parents treat them.

Age Parenting changes as children grow. The same parenting that is marvelously effective with infants and toddlers is inappropriate for adolescents. These age-related changes in parenting are evident in the two basic dimensions of parental behavior: warmth and control. Warmth is beneficial throughout development; toddlers and teens alike enjoy knowing that others care about them. But the manifestation of parental affection changes, becoming more reserved as children develop. The enthusiastic hugging and kissing that delights toddlers embarrasses adolescents (Shanahan et al., 2007).

Parental control also changes as children develop (Maccoby, 1984; Vazsonyi, Hibbert, & Snider, 2003). As children enter adolescence, they believe that parents have less authority to make decisions for them, especially in the personal domain (Darling, Cumsille, & Martínez, 2008). In fact, parents gradually relinquish control—though sometimes not as rapidly as adolescents want them to—and increases in decision-making autonomy are associated with greater adolescent well-being (Qin, Pomerantz, & Wang, 2009; Wray-Lake, Crouter, & McHale, 2010).

An example of the impact of children's behavior on parents is that, when children respond to parents defiantly, their parents often resort to harsher forms of punishment.

Temperament and Behavior A child's temperament can have a powerful effect on parental behavior (Brody & Ge, 2001). To illustrate the reciprocal influence of parents and children, imagine two preschoolers with different temperaments as they respond to a parent's authoritative style. The first child has an "easy" temperament, complying readily with parental requests and responding well to family discussions about parental expectations. These parent–child relations are a textbook example of successful authoritative parenting. But suppose that, like the child in the photo, the second child has a "difficult" temperament and complies reluctantly and sometimes not at all. Over time, the parent becomes more controlling and less affectionate. The child in turn complies even less in the future, leading the parent to adopt an authoritarian parenting style (Bates et al., 1998; Paulussen-Hoogeboom et al., 2007).

As this example illustrates, parenting behaviors and styles often evolve as a consequence of the child's behavior. With a moderately active young child who is eager to please adults, a parent may discover that a modest amount of control is adequate. But for a very active child who is not as eager to please, a parent may need to be more controlling and directive (Brody & Ge, 2001; Hastings & Rubin, 1999). Influence is reciprocal: Children's behavior helps determine how parents treat them and the resulting parental behavior influences children's behavior, which in turn causes parents to again change their behavior (Choe, Olson, & Sameroff, 2013; Schermerhorn, Chow, & Cummings, 2010).

As time goes by, these reciprocal influences lead many families to adopt routine ways of interacting with each other. Some families end up functioning smoothly: Parents and children cooperate, anticipate each other's needs, and are generally happy. Unfortunately, other families end up troubled: Disagreements are common, parents spend much time trying unsuccessfully to control their defiant children, and everyone is often angry and upset. Still others are characterized by disengagement: Parents withdraw from each other and are not available to their children (Sturge-Apple, Davies, & Cummings, 2010). Over the long term, such troubled families do not fare well, so it's important that these negative reciprocal influences get nipped in the bud (Carrere & Gottman, 1999; Christensen & Heavey, 1999).

 ## Check Your Learning

RECALL Describe ways in which the marital system contributes to children's development.

What are some of the ways in which children influence their own development?

INTERPRET Compare the styles approach to parenting with the approach that focuses on parental behavior per se. What are the strengths of each?

APPLY Imagine a family in which Mom and Dad both work full-time outside the home. Mom's employer wants her to take a new position in a distant small town. Mom is tempted because the position represents a promotion with much more responsibility and much higher pay. However, because the town is so small, Dad couldn't get a job comparable to the one he has now, which he loves. Based on what you know about Bronfenbrenner's family systems theory (pages 430–431), how might the move affect the couple's 10-year-old daughter and 4-year-old son?

 # 14.2 The Changing Family

LEARNING OBJECTIVES	OUTLINE
LO6 What are some of the effects of divorce on children?	Impact of Divorce on Children
LO7 How do children adjust to a parent's remarriage?	Blended Families
LO8 How do grandparents contribute to childrearing?	The Role of Grandparents
LO9 How effective are gay parents?	Children of Gay and Lesbian Parents

Jack has lived with his dad for the four years since his parents' divorce; he visits his mother every other weekend. Although Jack was confused and depressed when his parents divorced, he has come to terms with the new situation. He's excelling in school, where he is well liked by peers and teachers. One of Jack's friends is Troy. Troy's parents are married but bicker constantly since Troy's dad lost his job. His parents are unable to agree on anything; the pettiest event or remark triggers an argument. Troy's grades have fallen, and whereas he was once a leader among the boys in his class, now he prefers to be alone.

The American family has been changing steadily since the middle of the 20th century. First, people are older when they marry. The age of first marriage is up from the early 20s in the 1950s and 1960s to the late 20s today, and consequently, the age at which women first bear children has increased. Second, families are smaller, having decreased from an average of more than three children in 1960 to fewer than two children today (U.S. Census Bureau, 2011). Third, in the 1950s and 1960s few mothers of young children worked outside of the home; today, most do (Bureau of Labor Statistics, 2013). Finally, more children are growing up in single-parent families as a result of a doubling of the divorce rate since the 1960s and a doubling of the percentage of babies born to unwed mothers (Children's Defense Fund, 2010).

Because of these and other societal changes, today the family takes on many different forms in the United States and in other industrialized nations. In this module, we'll look at several of these forms and see how children develop within them. As we do, we'll look at the impact of divorce on Jack and the impact of marital conflict on Troy.

Impact of Divorce on Children

LO6 **What are some of the effects of divorce on children?**

Like Jack, many American youngsters' parents divorce. According to all theories of child development, divorce is distressing for children because it involves conflict between parents and usually separation from one of them. Do the disruptions, conflict, and stress associated with divorce affect children? Of course they do. Having answered this easy question, many more difficult questions remain: Are *all* aspects of children's lives affected equally by divorce? *How* does divorce influence development? *Why* is divorce more stressful for some children than others?

What Aspects of Children's Lives Are Affected by Divorce? Hundreds of studies of divorce have been conducted, involving tens of thousands of preschool- through college-age children. Comprehensive meta-analyses of this research reveal that in school achievement, conduct, adjustment, self-concept, and parent–child relations, children whose parents had divorced fared poorly compared to children from intact families (Amato, 2001; Amato & Keith, 1991; Lansford, 2009). However, the effects of divorce dropped from the 1970s to 1980s, perhaps because as divorce became more frequent in the 1980s, it became more familiar and less frightening. The effects of divorce increased again in the 1990s, perhaps reflecting a widening gap in income between single- and two-parent families (Amato, 2001).

When children of divorced parents become adults, the effects of divorce persist. As adults, children of divorce are more likely to experience conflict in their own marriages, to have negative attitudes toward marriage, and to become divorced themselves. Also, they report less satisfaction with life and are more likely to become depressed (Hetherington & Kelly, 2002; Segrin, Taylor, & Altman, 2005). And women sometimes experience low self-esteem and are less successful in intimate relationships (Mustonen et al., 2011). These findings don't mean that children of divorce are destined to have unhappy, conflict-ridden marriages that inevitably lead to divorce, but children of divorce are at greater risk for such an outcome.

The first year following a divorce is often rocky for parents and children alike. But beginning in the second year, most children begin to adjust to their new circumstances (Hetherington & Kelly, 2002). Children adjust to divorce more readily if their divorced parents cooperate with each other, especially on disciplinary matters (Buchanan & Heiges, 2001). **In *joint custody*, both parents retain legal custody of the children.** Children benefit from joint custody *if* their parents get along well (Bauserman, 2002). Unfortunately, relatively few divorced couples get along well enough for joint custody to succeed; most divorced couples fight or simply ignore each other (Amato, Kane, & James, 2011).

When joint custody is not an option, mothers have traditionally been awarded custody; when this happens, children benefit when fathers remain involved in parenting (Fabricius & Luecken, 2007). In recent years fathers have increasingly often been given custody, especially of sons. This practice coincides with findings that children such as Jack, the other boy in the opening vignette, often adjust better when they live with the same-sex parent: Boys often fare better with fathers and girls fare better with mothers (McLanahan, 1999). One reason boys are often better off with their fathers is that boys are likely to become involved in negative reinforcement traps (described in Module 14.1) with their mothers. Another explanation is that both boys and girls may forge stronger emotional relationships with same-sex parents than with other-sex parents (Zimiles & Lee, 1991).

How Does Divorce Influence Development?   Divorce usually results in several changes in family life that affect children (Amato & Keith, 1991). First, the absence of one parent means that children lose a role model, a source of parental help and emotional support, and a supervisor. For instance, a single parent may have to choose between helping one child complete an important paper or watching another child perform in a school play. Because the parent can't do both, one child will miss out.

Second, single-parent families often experience economic hardship, which creates stress and often means that activities once taken for granted are no longer available (Lansford, 2009). A single parent may no longer be able to afford books for pleasure reading, music lessons, or other activities that promote child development. Moreover, when a single parent worries about having enough money for food and rent, he or she has less energy and effort to devote to parenting.

Third, as we saw in Module 14.1, conflict between parents is extremely distressing to children and adolescents (Leon, 2003), particularly for children who are emotionally insecure (Davies & Cummings, 1998). In fact, many of the problems ascribed to divorce are really caused by marital conflict occurring before the divorce (Amato, 2010; Shaw, Winslow, & Flanagan, 1999). Children like Troy, the boy in the opening vignette whose parents are married but fight constantly, often show many of the same effects associated with divorce (Katz & Woodin, 2002).

Which Children Are Most Affected by Divorce? Why?   Some children are more affected by divorce than others. For example, children who are temperamentally more emotional tend to be more affected by divorce (Lengua et al., 1999). What's more, divorce is more harmful when it occurs during childhood and adolescence than during the preschool or college years (Amato & Keith, 1991), and the consequences differ for children and adolescents. Following divorce, children more often become anxious or develop behavioral problems, but adolescents more often do worse in school (Lansford et al., 2006).

Some children suffer more from divorce because of their tendency to interpret events negatively. We know, from Module 12.4, that two children often have differing interpretations of exactly the same social event. Suppose, for example, that a father forgets to take a child on a promised outing. One child might believe that an emergency prevented the father from taking the child. A second child might believe that the father hadn't really wanted to spend time with the child in the first place and will never make similar plans again. Children who—like the second child—tend to interpret life events negatively are more likely to have behavioral problems following divorce (Mazur et al., 1999).

Finally, children's efforts to cope with divorce-related stress can influence the impact of divorce. When children actively cope with their parents' divorce—either by trying to solve a problem or by trying to make it feel less threatening—they gain confidence in their ability to control future events in their lives. This protects children from behavioral disorders such as anxiety or depression (Sandler et al., 2000).

Just as children can reduce the harm of divorce by being active problem solvers, parents can make divorce easier on their children. The "Improving Children's Lives" feature has some tips on ways parents can make divorce less stressful for their children.

Improving Children's Lives

Helping Children Adjust after Divorce

Divorce causes major changes in children's lives that are very stressful. Here are some ways parents can reduce stress and help children adjust to their new life circumstances. Parents should:

- Explain together to children why they are divorcing and what their children can expect to happen to them.
- Reassure children that they will always love them and always be their parents; parents must back up these words with actions by remaining involved in their children's lives, despite the increased difficulty of doing so.
- Expect that their children will sometimes be angry or sad about the divorce, and they should encourage children to discuss these feelings with them.

Parents should not:

- Compete with each other for their children's love and attention; children adjust to divorce best when they maintain good relationships with both parents.
- Take out their anger with each other on their children.
- Criticize the ex-spouse in front of the children.
- Ask children to mediate disputes; parents should work out problems without putting the children in the middle.

Following all these rules all the time is not easy. After all, divorce is stressful and painful for adults, too. Fortunately, there are effective programs that can help parents and children adjust to life following divorce. The "Focus on Research" feature describes one of them.

Focus on Research

Evaluation of a Program to Help Parents and Children Adjust to Life After Divorce

Who were the investigators, and what was the aim of the study? Throughout this module, we've seen that divorce puts children at risk for reduced school achievement, behavioral problems, and other undesirable outcomes. Clorinda Vélez, Sharlene Wolchik, Jenn-Yun Tein, and Irwin Sandler (2011) wanted to determine the benefits for children of an intervention program for mothers that focused primarily on the quality of the mother–child relationship and effective disciplinary methods.

How did the investigators measure the topic of interest? Vélez and her colleagues assigned mothers to one of two conditions: in the intervention condition, mothers participated in five group sessions that discussed ways that a mother can foster quality relationships with her children and three sessions that were devoted to discipline. In the control condition, mothers were simply provided books that described how to adjust to divorce and a reading guide. Before mothers were assigned to conditions and at four points later, mothers and children completed several questionnaires designed to measure parenting quality (defined as being warm and communicating effectively). In addition, children completed questionnaires designed to measure whether they were coping effectively with divorce-related adjustment (e.g., being proactive in making changes, being optimistic).

Who were the participants in the study? The study included 240 mothers who had been divorced within the previous two years and who had at least one child between 9 and 12 years of age. The mothers had not remarried and had no plans to do so in the near future.

What was the design of the study? This study was experimental because Vélez and her colleagues assigned mothers randomly to either an intervention condition or a control condition. The study was longitudinal because mothers and children were tested five times: prior to the experimental treatment and immediately after the treatment, as well as at three months, sixth months, and six years after.

Were there ethical concerns with the study? No; the questionnaires that parents and children completed were ones commonly used to study parent–child relationships and family interactions.

What were the results? Correlations were computed between experimental conditions, relationship quality, and children's active coping. They revealed that parent–child relationships (as reported by both mothers and children) were of higher quality when mothers participated in the intervention condition and that higher-quality relationships were associated with more active coping on the part of children. In other words, the intervention condition improved mother–child relationships and this improvement, in turn, resulted in children's use of more active coping to deal with their problems.

What did the investigators conclude? Vélez and her colleagues concluded that "by increasing one of children's most important interpersonal resources, mother–child relationship quality, the [intervention program] improved youth's coping efficacy and active coping" (2011, p. 255). In other words, when children have a high-quality relationship with their mother—she is warm with them and communicates well with them—they are empowered to deal with the unique challenges they face as they adjust to life after their mother's divorce.

What converging evidence would strengthen these conclusions? There are two limits to these findings. First, the children were all in middle childhood; would intervention be equally effective with preschool children or with adolescents? Second, mothers and children were mainly middle class; would intervention work as well with divorced women living in poverty, who face additional stresses and obstacles to effective parenting? Answering these questions would provide more convincing evidence of the effectiveness of intervention programs designed to help children and mothers adjust to life following divorce.

Blended Families

LO7 How do children adjust to a parent's remarriage?

As divorce became more common in the 20th century, so did blended families, in which children live with a stepparent and sometimes with stepsiblings.

Following divorce, most children live in a single-parent household for about five years. However, like the adults in the photo, most men and women eventually remarry (Sweeney, 2010). **The resulting unit, consisting of a biological parent, stepparent, and children, is known as a *blended family*.** (Other terms for this family configuration are *remarried family* and *reconstituted family*.)

Because mothers are more often granted custody of children, the most common form of blended family is a mother, her children, and a stepfather. Most stepfathers do not participate actively in child rearing; they often seem reluctant to become involved (Clarke-Stewart & Bretano, 2005). Overall, becoming part of a blended family does not cause adjustment problems for children (Ryan & Claessens, 2013). Indeed, children typically benefit from a warm and involved stepfather (King, 2006). However, preadolescent girls sometimes do not adjust readily to their mother's remarriage, apparently because it disrupts the intimate relationship they have established with her (Visher, Visher, & Pasley, 2003).

Adjusting to life in a blended family is more difficult when a stepfather brings his own biological children to the mix. In such families, parents sometimes favor their biological children over their stepchildren, being more involved with and warmer toward their biological children. Such preferential treatment almost always leads to conflict and unhappiness (Dunn & Davies, 2001; Sweeney, 2010). Also, when the mother and stepfather argue, children usually side with their biological parents (Dunn, O'Connor, & Cheng, 2005).

The best strategy for stepfathers is to be interested in their new stepchildren but avoid encroaching on established relationships. Newly remarried mothers must be careful that their enthusiasm for their new spouse does not come at the expense of time and affection for their children. What's more, both parents and children need to have realistic expectations. The blended family can be successful and beneficial for children and adolescents, but it takes effort because of the complicated relationships, conflicting loyalties, and jealousies that usually exist (Sweeney, 2010; White & Gilbreth, 2001).

Over time, children adjust to the blended family. If the marriage is happy, most children profit from the presence of two caring adults. Nevertheless, when compared to children from intact families, children in blended families do less well in school and experience more symptoms of depression (Halpern-Meekin & Tach, 2008). Unfortunately, second marriages are somewhat more likely than first marriages to end in divorce, particularly when stepchildren are involved (Teachman, 2008). This means that many children relive the trauma of divorce. Fortunately, effective programs are available to help members of blended families adjust to their new roles (Bullard et al., 2010). These emphasize effective co-parenting (described on page 437) and, in particular, ways of dealing with the behavioral problems that children often display with stepparents. These programs result in fewer behavioral problems and greater marital satisfaction.

The Role of Grandparents

LO8 How do grandparents contribute to childrearing?

With people living longer, three-generation families—with child, parents, and grandparents—are becoming the norm in many industrialized nations. Many American children see their grandparents at least once a month, more often if they live nearby. And approximately 12% of American children live with their grandparents (Dunifon, 2013).

Grandmothers, especially maternal grandmothers, are usually more involved with grandchildren than grandfathers, and some scientists believe that this is an evolutionary adaptation (Pollett, Nettle, & Nelissen, 2007). That is, for most of human history, the onset of menopause has coincided, approximately, with the birth of grandchildren. Genetically speaking, middle-aged women may be more valuable in caring for their grandchildren—making sure that they survive to bear further children—than in bearing additional children of their own (Coall & Hertwig, 2011).

What roles do grandparents play in children's lives? One analysis suggests five specific styles of grandparenting (Mueller & Elder, 2003):

- *Influential grandparents* are very close to their grandchildren, are very involved in their lives, and frequently perform parental roles, including discipline.
- *Supportive grandparents* are similar to influential grandparents—close and involved with grandchildren—but do not take on parental roles.
- *Authority-oriented grandparents* provide discipline for their grandchildren but otherwise are not particularly active in their grandchildren's lives.
- *Passive grandparents* are caught up in their grandchildren's development but not with the intensity of influential or supportive grandparents; they do not assume parental roles.
- *Detached grandparents* are uninvolved with their grandchildren.

The first two grandparental roles—influential and supportive—are those in which grandparents are most involved with their grandchildren. Several factors determine whether grandparents assume these involved roles. Some factors are practical: Grandparents are more involved when they live near their grandchildren and when they have few rather than many grandchildren. Other factors relate to grandparents' relationships with their children and their own grandparents: Grandparents are more concerned when their children (i.e., the grandchildren's parents) encourage such involvement and when they knew their own maternal grandparent.

Sometimes grandparents take a more active role in child rearing because the child's parents are unable to perform these responsibilities because of mental illness, substance use, or domestic violence. For example, when mothers are incarcerated, children often live with grandparents, an arrangement that leads incarcerated mothers to stay in touch with their children (via phone calls and visits), but only when the mother and grandmother have a warm, accepting relationship (Loper & Clark, 2013). What's more, when incarcerated mothers and grandmothers have a satisfying co-parent relationship, children have fewer behavior problems and mothers parent more effectively when released from prison (Baker et al., 2010).

Not surprisingly, children and adolescents benefit from close ties with their grandparents. For example, children experience fewer emotional problems and are more prosocial when their grandparents are actively involved in child rearing (Attar-Schwartz et al., 2009; Barnett et al., 2010). Strong grandparent–child relationships are particularly valuable when children and adolescents experience stress, such as that associated with divorce (Henderson et al., 2009): Strong relationships with grandparents are associated with better adjustment by children.

 QUESTION 14.2

Ollie, a 4-year-old, sees his grandparents several times a week. They take him to preschool on Monday and Wednesday and try to do something special, such as getting an ice cream cone, each week. And they don't hesitate to remind him to say "please" and "thank you" and to wait his turn. What grandparental role best describes Ollie's grandparents?

Grandparents are especially active in the lives of immigrant and minority children, often taking on parental roles (Hernandez, 2004; Minkler-Fuller & Thomson, 2005). The "Cultural Influences" feature describes the important role of grandmothers in African American family life.

Cultural Influences

Grandmothers in African American Families

Approximately 1 in 10 African American children lives with a grandmother, compared to only 1 in 25 European-American children (U.S. Census Bureau, 2011). Why is this? A quarter of all African American children grow up in chronic poverty, and living with relatives is one way of sharing—and thereby reducing—the costs associated with housing and child care.

African American grandmothers often play an active role in rearing their grandchildren, which benefits the grandchildren.

African American grandmothers who live with their daughters and their children frequently become involved in rearing their grandchildren, taking on the role of influential grandparent (Oberlander, Black, & Starr, 2007). When the daughter is a teenage mother, the grandmother may be the child's primary caregiver, an arrangement that benefits both the adolescent mother and the child. Freed from the obligations of child rearing, the adolescent mother is able to improve her situation by, for example, finishing school. The child benefits because grandmothers are often more effective mothers than teenage mothers: Grandmothers are less punitive and, like the grandmother in the photo, are very responsive to their grandchildren (Chase-Lansdale, Brooks-Gunn, & Zamsky, 1994; Smith & Drew, 2002). Another benefit is that when the young mother and young father have positive relationships with grandmothers, they get along better with each other, and parent more effectively (Krishnakumar & Black, 2003).

This family arrangement works well for children. In terms of achievement and adjustment, children living with their mothers and grandmothers resemble children living in two-parent families (Dunifon, 2013). Even when grandmothers are not living in the house, children benefit when their mothers receive social and emotional support from grandmothers and other relatives: Children are more self-reliant and less likely to become involved in delinquent activities such as drug use and vandalism (Taylor & Roberts, 1995).

Thus, grandmothers and other relatives can ease the burden of child rearing in African American families living in poverty, and, not surprisingly, children benefit from the added warmth, support, and guidance of an extended family.

By acting as surrogate parents, grandparents can affect their grandchildren's lives directly. However, grandparents also affect their grandchildren indirectly, through intergenerational transmission of parental attitudes and practices. For example, if parents are affectionate with their children, when these children become parents themselves, they will tend to be affectionate with their own children. In other words, the grandparents' affectionate behavior results in their grandchildren experiencing affectionate care. Thus, it is important to think about the indirect as well as the direct influences that grandparents have on their grandchildren (Smith & Drew, 2002).

Children of Gay and Lesbian Parents

LO9 How effective are gay parents?

Many youngsters in the United States have a gay or lesbian parent. In most of these situations, children were born in a heterosexual marriage that ended in divorce when one parent revealed his or her homosexuality. Less frequent, but becoming more common, are children born to single lesbians or to lesbian couples who have children through artificial insemination or adoption.

As parents, gay and lesbian couples are more similar to heterosexual couples than they are different, although lesbian and gay couples more often share child-rearing tasks evenly (Farr & Patterson, 2013). There is no indication that gay and lesbian parents are less effective parents than heterosexual parents. In fact, some evidence suggests that lesbian and gay couples may be especially warm and responsive to children's needs (Golombok et al., 2014).

Children reared by gay and lesbian parents seem to develop much like children reared by heterosexual couples (Golombok et al., 2003; Patterson, 2006). In fact, in research that directly pits the impact on children of family structure (heterosexual parents versus lesbian or gay parents) against family process variables (e.g., parental stress, parental discipline), process variables predict children's outcomes, but family structure does not (Farr, Forssell, & Patterson., 2010; Golombok et al., 2014). For example, preschool boys and girls apparently identify with their own sex and acquire the usual accompaniment of gender-based preferences, interests, activities, and friends. As adolescents, most are heterosexual, although there is some evidence that daughters of lesbian mothers may be somewhat more likely to explore same-sex relationships (Gartrell, Bos, & Goldberg, 2011; Wainwright, Russell, & Patterson, 2004). In other respects—such as self-concept, social skill, peer relations, moral reasoning, behavior problems, and intelligence—children of lesbian mothers resemble children of heterosexual parents (Farr & Patterson, 2013; Patterson, 2006; Wainwright & Patterson, 2008). And, as is the case with heterosexual parents, children benefit from close relationships with warm, caring gay and lesbian parents (Farr et al., 2010; Wainright & Patterson, 2008). Finally, some children of lesbian mothers report being treated unfairly because their mother is lesbian; they're at some risk for anxiety and depression, particularly if they don't get along with their mother or don't fit in with peers (Van Gelderen et al., 2012).

Research on children reared by gay and lesbian couples, along with findings concerning African American grandmothers, reminds us that "good parenting" can assume many different forms. These research results also challenge the conventional wisdom that a two-parent family with mother and father both present *necessarily* provides the best circumstances for development. Multiple adults *are* important—that's evident from research on the impact of divorce on children—but *who* the adults are seems to matter less than what they do. Children benefit from good parenting skills, whether it's a mother and father or grandparents—or two women or two men—doing the parenting.

Check Your Learning

RECALL Describe the different grandparental roles and the factors that influence which roles grandparents take on.

What is known about development in children of gay and lesbian parents?

INTERPRET From a child's perspective, what are the pros and cons of a blended (remarried) family?

APPLY Suppose that a couple argues constantly. They've tried to resolve their differences in counseling, but this was unsuccessful and now they're considering a divorce. They are the parents of two school-age children. What advice would you give them?

 # 14.3 Brothers and Sisters

OUTLINE

Firstborn, Laterborn, and Only Children

Qualities of Sibling Relationships

LEARNING OBJECTIVES

LO10 How do firstborn, laterborn, and only children differ?

LO11 How do sibling relationships change as children grow? What determines how well siblings get along?

Bob and Alice adored their 2-year-old son, Robbie, who was friendly, playful, and always eager to learn new things. In fact, Bob thought Robbie was nearly perfect and saw no reason to tempt fate by having another child. However, Alice had heard stories that only children were conceited, spoiled, and unfriendly. Alice was sure that Robbie would grow up like this unless she and Bob had another child. What to do?

For most of a year, all firstborn children are only children like Robbie. Some children remain "onlies" forever, but most get brothers and sisters, particularly when firstborns are outgoing and smart (Jokela, 2010). Some firstborns are joined by many siblings in rapid succession; others are simply joined by a single brother or sister. As the family acquires these new members, parent–child relationships become more complex (McHale, Updegraff, & Whiteman, 2013). Parents can no longer focus on a single child, but must adjust to the needs of multiple children. Just as important, siblings influence each other's development, not just during childhood but throughout life. To understand sibling influence, let's first look at differences between firstborns, laterborns, and only children.

Firstborn, Laterborn, and Only Children

LO10 How do firstborn, laterborn, and only children differ?

Firstborn children are often "guinea pigs" for most parents, who have lots of enthusiasm but little practical experience in rearing children. Parents typically have high expectations for their firstborns and are more affectionate, more controlling, and more demanding with them (Furman & Lanthier, 2002). As more children arrive, parents become more adept at their roles, having learned "the tricks of the parent trade" with prior children. With laterborn children, parents have more realistic expectations and are more relaxed in their discipline (e.g., Baskett, 1985).

The different approaches that parents take with their firstborns and laterborns help explain differences that are commonly observed between these children.

Firstborn children generally have higher scores on intelligence tests and are more likely to go to college. They are also more willing to conform to parents' and adults' requests. Laterborn children, perhaps because they are less concerned about pleasing parents and adults but need to get along with older siblings, are more popular with their peers and more innovative (Beck, Burnet, & Vosper, 2006; Bjerkedal et al., 2007).

What about only children? Alice, the mother in the opening vignette, was well acquainted with the conventional wisdom, which says that parents like the ones in the photo dote on "onlies," with the result that the children are selfish and egotistical. Is the folklore correct? No. Only children are more likely to succeed in school than other children and to have higher levels of intelligence and self-esteem but don't differ in popularity, adjustment, and personality (Falbo & Polit, 1986; Falbo, 2012).

Contrary to the folklore, only children are not spoiled brats; instead, they tend to do well in school and often are leaders.

This research has important implications for China, where only children are the norm because of government efforts to limit family size. The "Child Development and Family Policy" feature tells the story.

Child Development and Family Policy
Assessing the Consequences of China's One-Child Policy

With more than a billion citizens, the People's Republic of China has the largest population in the world. In the middle of the 20th century, Chinese leaders recognized that a large, rapidly growing population was a serious obstacle to economic growth and improvements in the standard of living. Consequently, the Chinese government implemented several programs to limit family size and since 1979 has had a policy of one child per family. The policy was promoted with billboards, like the one in the photo, advertising the benefits of having only one child. Parents were encouraged to use contraceptives; more importantly, one-child families received many economic benefits, such as cash bonuses, better health and child care, and more desirable housing.

The policy has been effective in reducing the birth rate in China; and now social scientists are evaluating the impact of the one-child policy on children and their families. For example, traditionally the Chinese have valued well-behaved children who get along well with others. Would the only children in today's China be less cooperative and more self-centered than previous generations of Chinese youngsters? The answer seems to be no. Many studies have compared only and non-only children in China; most comparisons find no differences. One of the few differences is that Chinese only children, like Western only children, are more successful in school (Falbo, 2012; Liu, Lin, & Chen, 2010).

As Chinese only children enter adulthood, a new concern will be care of the elderly. Traditionally, children have been responsible for their aging parents. This task becomes more demanding—financially and psychologically—when it cannot be shared with other siblings. Consequently, the Chinese government now encourages older parents and their adult children to sign a Family Support Agreement, which is a voluntary contract specifying the kinds and amounts of support that children will provide for their aging parents (Chou, 2011).

Since 1979, the Chinese government has had a policy of encouraging parents to have only one child.

Adopted Children   The U.S. government doesn't keep official statistics on the number of adopted children, but the best estimate is that about 2% to 4% of U.S. children are adopted. The most common form of adoption is for a foster parent or relative to adopt children who are in foster care because their birth families mistreated them. About 50,000 children are adopted annually in this manner, typically at about 6 or 7 years of age. Also common is for children to be adopted through private agencies, most often because young parents believe that they cannot provide adequately for the child. Roughly 14,000 children are adopted annually in this way, usually as infants. Finally, about 10,000 children are adopted annually from other countries, such as China and Ethiopia. These adoptions involve infants and preschool children (Grotevant & McDermott, 2014).

Adopted children often experience adversity before being adopted. For example, children adopted from foster care have often experienced maltreatment that led them to be placed in foster care; many children adopted internationally were abandoned and lived in institutions prior to adoption. These circumstances aren't optimal for children's development, so it's not surprising that adopted children are at risk for many problems, including antisocial and aggressive behavior, depression and anxiety, and learning problems (Grotevant & McDermott, 2014). However, outcomes are quite varied. Most adopted children develop within the typical range. Problems are most likely when children are adopted after infancy and when their care before adoption was poor (e.g., they were institutionalized or lived in a series of foster homes). For example, the fall of the Ceauşescu regime in Romania in 1989 revealed hundreds of thousands of children living in orphanages under incredibly primitive conditions. Beginning in the 1990s, many of these children were adopted internationally. Some have shown remarkable catch-up growth, but many show multiple impairments, such as delayed cognitive development and disordered attachment (Kreppner et al., 2007).

Thus, although adoption per se is not a fundamental developmental challenge for most children, quality of life before adoption certainly places some adopted children at risk. And these children often fare well when they receive excellent care after adoption (Grotevant & McDermott, 2014).

Today, many adoptees and their parents wonder whether to have contact with the child's birth families, which is known as an *open adoption*. Traditionally this practice was discouraged because of fear that it might lead children to be confused about their "real" parents. But such confusion does not surface in research: Youth who experience open adoptions are as well adjusted as those who experience closed adoptions. Furthermore, youth in open adoptions have a deeper, more consistent identity as an adoptee, in part because open adoptions prompt conversations with parents about the nature of adoption (Grotevant et al., 2013).

In discussing firstborn, laterborn, only, and adopted children, we have not yet considered relationships that exist between siblings. These can be powerful forces on development, as we'll see in the next section.

Qualities of Sibling Relationships

LO11 How do sibling relationships change as children grow? What determines how well siblings get along?

From the very beginning, sibling relationships are complicated. Expectant parents typically are excited by the prospect of another child, and their enthusiasm is contagious: Their children, too, eagerly await the arrival of the newest family member. However, the baby's arrival prompts varied responses: Some children are distressed, sad, and less responsive to parents, responses that are more common with younger children (Volling, 2012). Parents can minimize their older children's distress by remaining attentive to their needs (Howe & Ross, 1990).

Many older siblings enjoy helping their parents take care of newborns. Older children play with the baby, console it, feed it, or change its diapers. In middle-class Western families, such caregiving often occurs in the context of play, with parents nearby. But in some cultures, children—particularly girls like the one in the photo—play an important role in providing care for their younger siblings (Zukow-Goldring, 2002).

As the infant grows, interactions between siblings become more frequent and more complicated. For example, toddlers tend to talk more to parents than to older siblings. But, by the time the younger sibling is 4 years old, the situation is reversed: Now young siblings talk more to older siblings than to their mother (Brown & Dunn, 1992). Older siblings become a source of care and comfort for younger siblings when they are distressed or upset (Kim et al., 2007; Gass, Jenkins, & Dunn, 2007), and older siblings serve as teachers for their younger siblings, teaching them to play games or how to cook simple foods (Maynard, 2002). Finally, when older children do well in school and are popular with peers, younger siblings often follow suit (Brody et al., 2003).

As time goes by, some siblings grow close, becoming best friends in ways that nonsiblings can never be. Other siblings constantly argue, compete, and simply do not get along with each other. The basic pattern of sibling interaction seems to be established early in development and remains fairly stable (Kramer, 2010). In general, siblings who get along as preschoolers continue to get along as young adolescents, but siblings who quarrel as preschoolers often quarrel as young adolescents.

Why are some sibling relationships filled with love and respect, but others are dominated by jealousy and resentment? First, children's sex and temperament matter. Sibling relations are more likely to be warm and harmonious between siblings of the same sex than between siblings of the opposite sex (Dunn & Kendrick, 1981) and when neither sibling is temperamentally emotional (Brody, Stoneman, & McCoy, 1994). Age is also important: Sibling relationships generally improve as the younger child approaches adolescence because siblings begin to perceive one another as equals (Kim et al., 2007; McHale et al., 2013).

Parents contribute to the quality of sibling relationships, both directly and indirectly (Brody, 1998). The direct influence stems from parents' treatment. Siblings more often get along when they believe that parents have no "favorites" but treat all siblings fairly (McGuire & Shanahan, 2010). When parents lavishly praise one child's accomplishments while ignoring another's, children notice the difference and their sibling relationship suffers (Updegraff, Thayer, et al., 2005).

This doesn't mean that parents must treat all their children the same. Children understand that parents should treat their kids differently—based on their age or personal needs. Only when differential treatment is not justified do sibling relationships deteriorate (Kowal & Kramer, 1997). In fact, during adolescence, siblings get along better when each has a unique, well-defined relationship with parents (Feinberg et al., 2003).

The indirect influence of parents on sibling relationships stems from the quality of the parents' relationship with each other: A warm, harmonious relationship between parents fosters positive sibling relationships. Conflict between parents is associated with conflict between siblings, although intense marital conflict sometimes leads siblings to become closer, as they support each other emotionally (McHale et al., 2013).

In many developing countries, older siblings are actively involved in caring for their younger siblings.

 QUESTION 14.3

Calvin, age 8, and his younger sister, Hope, argue over just about everything and constantly compete for their parents' attention. Teenage sisters Melissa and Caroline love doing everything together and enjoy sharing clothes and secrets about their teen romances. Why might Calvin and Hope get along so poorly but Melissa and Caroline get along so well?

Preschool children often argue because they lack the social skills to settle disagreements in a mutually beneficial manner.

Many of the features associated with high-quality sibling relationships, such as the sex of the siblings, are common across different ethnic groups. However, some unique features also emerge. For example, in a study of African American families, sibling relations were more positive when children had a stronger ethnic identity (McHale et al., 2007). And a study of Mexican American families found that siblings feel closer and spend more time together when siblings have a strong commitment to their family—that is, when they felt obligated to their family and viewed it as an important source of support (Updegraff, McHale, et al., 2005).

One practical implication of these findings is that in their pursuit of family harmony (what many parents call "peace and quiet"), parents can influence some of the factors affecting sibling relationships but not others. Parents can help reduce friction between siblings by being equally affectionate, responsive, and caring with all of their children and by caring for one another. And they can encourage the sorts of behaviors that promote positive sibling relationships, including being engaged in mutually enjoyable activities, being supportive of each other, and appreciating their shared experiences (Kramer, 2010).

At the same time, some dissension is natural in families, especially those with young boys and girls: Children's different interests lead to arguments, like the one in the photo. Faced with common simple conflicts—Who decides which TV show to watch? Who gets to eat the last cookie? Who gets to hold the new puppy?—a 3-year-old brother and a 5-year-old sister *will* argue because they lack the social and cognitive skills that allow them to find mutually satisfying compromises.

When siblings do fight—particularly young children—parents should intervene. When parents explain one sibling's behavior to another (e.g., "He covered his eyes 'cause he was scared"), siblings have more positive interactions (Kojima, 2000). Also, by helping their children to settle differences, parents show children more sophisticated ways to negotiate; later, children often try to use these techniques themselves instead of fighting (McHale et al., 2013). Parents especially need to intervene when conflicts escalate to the point that siblings are acting aggressively, yelling or swearing, or making denigrating comments. Obviously, parents need to protect their children from each other in the immediate situation. More importantly, though, if left unchecked, such conflicts can lead to behavior problems over time (Garcia et al., 2000).

Fortunately, parents can be shown how to mediate siblings' disputes. Smith and Ross (2007) administered brief training—90 minutes—in which parents were shown how to have children (1) identify points of agreement and disagreement, (2) discuss what they want to achieve (i.e., their goals for the situation), and (3) think of ways to resolve their dispute. After parents know how to mediate, siblings are better able to resolve conflicts successfully, and in doing so, they're more likely to talk calmly (instead of arguing), listen, apologize, and explain their actions. Thus, parents needn't listen to their children argue endlessly; instead, they can show them social skills that will help them solve their conflicts successfully.

Check Your Learning

RECALL Summarize what's known about the psychological development of adopted children.

How do sibling relationships change as children grow?

INTERPRET What research findings suggest continuity in the quality of sibling relationships? What findings suggest discontinuity?

APPLY Suppose your sister has a 2-year-old child. She and her husband are deciding whether to have another child. Describe to her the advantages and disadvantages of having two children versus only one.

 # Maltreatment: Parent–Child Relationships Gone Awry

LEARNING OBJECTIVES

LO12 What is the impact of maltreatment on children?

LO13 What factors cause parents to mistreat their children?

LO14 How can maltreatment be prevented?

OUTLINE

Consequences of Maltreatment

Causes of Maltreatment

Preventing Maltreatment

The first time 7-year-old Max came to school with bruises on his face, he said he'd fallen down the basement steps. When Max showed up with similar bruises a few weeks later, his teacher spoke with the school principal, who contacted local authorities. They discovered that Max's mother hit him with a paddle for even minor misconduct; for serious transgressions, she beat Max and made him sleep alone in an unheated, unlighted basement.

Unfortunately, cases like Max's occur far too often in modern America. Maltreatment comes in many forms (Cicchetti & Toth, 2006). The two that often come to mind first are physical abuse involving assault that leads to injuries and sexual abuse involving fondling, intercourse, or other sexual behaviors. Another form of maltreatment is *neglect*, not giving children adequate food, clothing, or medical care. Children can also be gravely harmed by psychological abuse— ridicule, rejection, and humiliation (Wicks-Nelson & Israel, 2006).

The frequency of these various forms of child maltreatment is difficult to estimate because so many cases go unreported. According to the U.S. Department of Health and Human Services (2013), nearly 700,000 children annually suffer maltreatment or neglect. About 80% are neglected, about 20% are abused physically, about 10% are abused sexually, and 5% are maltreated psychologically. (The percentages sum to more than 100 because some children experience more than one form of abuse.)

We'll begin this module by looking at the consequences of maltreatment, then look at some causes, and finally, examine ways to prevent maltreatment. As we do, we'll discover what led Max to suffer as he did.

Consequences of Maltreatment

LO12 **What is the impact of maltreatment on children?**

You probably aren't surprised to learn that the prognosis for youngsters like Max is not very good. Some, of course, suffer permanent physical damage. Even when there is no lasting physical damage, children's social and emotional development is often disrupted. They tend to have poor relationships with peers, often because they are too aggressive (Alink et al., 2012; Appleyard, Yang, & Runyan, 2010). Their cognitive development and academic performance are also disturbed. Abused youngsters typically get lower grades in school, score lower on standardized achievement tests, and are more frequently retained in a grade rather than promoted. Also, school-related behavior problems, such as being disruptive in class, are common, in part because maltreated children are often socially unskilled, don't regulate their emotions well, and don't recognize others' emotions accurately (Burack et al., 2006; Kim-Spoon, Cicchetti, & Rogosch, 2013; Luke & Banerjee, 2013). Abuse often leads children and adolescents to become depressed (Appleyard et al., 2010; Harkness, Lumley, & Truss, 2008). Finally, adults who were abused as children are more prone to think about or attempt suicide, and are more likely to abuse spouses and their own children (Malinosky-Rummell & Hansen, 1993). In short, when children are maltreated, the effects are usually widespread and long lasting.

Resilience Although the overall picture is bleak, some children are remarkably resilient to the impact of abuse. In other words, in a group of children and adolescents who have been abused, many will show some (or all) of the consequences that I've just described. For a handful, though, the impact of abuse is much reduced. Why are some children protected from the damaging effects of abuse when others are vulnerable?

One factor that protects children is their *ego-resilience*, **which denotes children's ability to respond adaptively and resourcefully to new situations.** The effects of abuse tend to be smaller when children are flexible in responding to novel and challenging social situations (Flores, Cicchetti, & Rogosch, 2005). Another protective factor is being engaged in school: When maltreated children are cognitively engaged in school—they pay attention, complete tasks, and are well organized—they are less prone to antisocial and aggressive behavior (Pears et al., 2013).

A final preventive factor is a positive mother–child relationship: When children have a positive representation of their mother—they describe her as "kind" and "loving," for example—they suffer relatively few symptoms of maltreatment (Valentino et al., 2008). However, the buffering value of such a positive view only holds for children who have been neglected. Children who are abused physically suffer the typical maltreatment-related symptoms even when they have a positive representation of their mother.

Q&A QUESTION 14.4

Kevin has never physically abused his 10-year-old son, Alex, but he constantly torments him emotionally. For example, when Alex got an *F* on a spelling test, Kevin screamed, "I skipped *Monday Night Football* just to help you but you still flunked. You're such a dummy." When Alex began to cry, Kevin taunted, "Look at Alex, crying like a baby." These interactions occur nearly every day. What are the likely effects of such repeated episodes of emotional abuse?

Causes of Maltreatment

LO13 **What factors cause parents to mistreat their children?**

Why would a parent abuse a child? Maybe you think parents would have to be severely disturbed to harm their own flesh and blood. Not really. The vast majority of abusing parents are not suffering from any specific mental or psychological disorder (Wolfe, 1985). Instead, a host of factors puts some children at risk for abuse and protects others; the number and combination of factors determine if the child is a likely target for abuse (Cicchetti & Toth, 2006). Let's look at three of the most important factors: cultural context and community, the parents, and the children themselves.

Culture and Community The most general category of contributing factors has to do with cultural values and the social conditions of the community in which parents rear their children. For example, a culture's view of physical punishment may contribute to child maltreatment. Many countries in Europe and Asia have strong cultural prohibitions against physical punishment. In many countries, including Austria, Croatia, Germany, Israel, and Sweden, spanking is against the law. It simply isn't done, and would be viewed in much the same way we would view American parents who punished by not feeding their child for a few days. Nevertheless, in the United States physical punishment is common. Condoning physical punishment in this manner opens the door for child maltreatment.

In addition to cultural values, the communities in which children live can put them at risk for maltreatment and abuse. Living in poverty is one important risk factor: Maltreatment is more common in families living in poverty, in part because lack of money increases the stress of daily life (Duncan & Brooks-Gunn, 2000). When parents are worrying about whether they can buy groceries or pay the rent, they are more likely to punish their children physically instead of making the extra effort to reason with them. Similarly, abuse is more common among military families when a soldier is deployed in a combat zone (Gibbs et al., 2007). In this case, maltreatment may be rooted in stress stemming from concern over the absent parent and temporary single parenthood.

A second risk factor is social isolation: Abuse is more likely when families are socially isolated from other relatives or neighbors, because isolation deprives children of adults who could protect them and deprives parents of social support that would help them cope with life stresses (Coulton et al., 2007).

Cultural values and community factors clearly contribute to child abuse, but they are only part of the puzzle. After all, although maltreatment is more common among families living in poverty, it does not occur in a majority of these families, and it does occur in middle-class families, too. Consequently, we need to look for additional factors to explain why abuse occurs in some families but not others.

Parents Faced with the same cultural values and living conditions, why do only a handful of parents abuse or mistreat their children? That is, which characteristics increase the odds that a parent will abuse his or her children? Child-development researchers have identified several important factors (Berlin, Appleyard, & Dodge, 2011; Bugental & Happaney, 2004). First, parents who maltreat their children often were maltreated themselves, which may lead them to believe that abuse is simply a normal part of childhood. This does not mean that abused children inevitably become abusing parents—only about one-third do. But a history of child abuse clearly places adults at risk for mistreating their own children (Berlin et al., 2011; Cicchetti & Toth, 2006). Second, parents who mistreat their children often use ineffective parenting techniques (e.g., inconsistent discipline), have such unrealistic expectations that their children can never meet them, and often believe that they are powerless to control their children. For example, when abusive parents do not get along with their children, they often chalk this up to factors out of their control, such as children having a difficult temperament or being tired that day; they're less likely to think that their own behavior contributed to unpleasant interactions. Third, in families where abuse occurs, the couple's interactions are often unpredictable, unsupportive, and unsatisfying for both husbands and wives. In other words, mistreatment of children is simply one symptom of family dysfunction. This marital discord makes life more stressful and makes it more difficult for parents to invest effort in child rearing.

Children's Contributions To place the last few pieces in the puzzle, we must look at the abused children themselves. Our discussion in Module 14.1

of reciprocal influence between parents and children should remind you that children may inadvertently, through their behavior, bring on their own abuse (Sidebotham et al., 2003). In fact, infants and preschoolers are abused more often than older children. Why? They are easier targets of abuse and they are less able to regulate aversive behaviors that elicit abuse. You've probably heard stories about a parent who shakes a baby to death because the baby won't stop crying. Because younger children are more likely to cry or whine excessively—behaviors that irritate all parents sooner or later—they are more likely to be the targets of abuse.

For much the same reason, children who are chronically ill or who suffer disabilities like those described in Module 8.3 are more often abused (Govindshenoy & Spencer, 2007; Sherrod et al., 1984). When children are sick, they're more likely to cry and whine, annoying their parents. Also, when children are sick or disabled, they need extra care, which means additional expense. By increasing the level of stress in a family, sick children can inadvertently become the targets of abuse.

Stepchildren form another group at risk for abuse (Archer, 2013). Just as Cinderella's stepmother doted on her biological children but abused Cinderella, stepchildren are more prone to be victims of abuse and neglect than are biological children. Adults are less invested emotionally in their stepchildren, and this lack of emotional investment leaves stepchildren more vulnerable.

Obviously, in all of these instances children are *not* at fault and do not deserve the abuse. Nevertheless, normal infant or child behavior can provoke anger and maltreatment from some parents.

Thus, many factors, listed in Summary Table 14-1, all contribute to child maltreatment. Any single factor will usually not result in abuse; maltreatment is more likely when risk factors start to add up. For example, several factors placed Max, the boy in the module-opening vignette, at risk for abuse: His family had moved to the community recently because his stepfather thought he could find work in the local plant; but the plant wasn't hiring, so his stepfather was unemployed and the family had little money saved. And Max had asthma, which meant there was regular expense for medication and occasional visits to the emergency room

---

SUMMARY TABLE 14-1

FACTORS THAT CONTRIBUTE TO CHILD ABUSE

General Category	Specific Factor
Cultural and community contributions	Abuse is more common in cultures that tolerate physical punishment.
	Abuse is more common when families live in poverty because of the stress associated with inadequate income. Abuse is more common when families are socially isolated because parents lack social support.
Parents' contributions	Parents who abuse their children were often maltreated themselves as children. Parents who abuse their children often have poor parenting skills (e.g., unrealistic expectations, inappropriate punishment).
Children's contributions	Young children are more likely to be abused because they cannot regulate their behavior. Ill children are more likely to be abused because their behavior while ill is often aversive. Stepchildren are more likely to be abused because stepparents are less invested in their stepchildren.

when he had a severe attack. All these factors combined to put Max at risk for maltreatment. (How many risk factors? My answer appears just before "Check Your Learning" on page 458.)

Preventing Maltreatment

LO14 **How can maltreatment be prevented?**

The complexity of child abuse dashes any hopes for a simple solution (Kelly, 2011). Because maltreatment is more apt to occur when several contributing factors are present, eradicating child maltreatment would entail a massive effort. American attitudes toward "acceptable" levels of punishment and poverty would have to change. American children will be abused as long as physical punishment is considered acceptable and as long as poverty-stricken families live in chronic stress from simply trying to provide food and shelter. Parents also need counseling and training in parenting skills. Abuse will continue as long as parents remain ignorant of effective methods of parenting and discipline.

It would be naïve to expect all of these changes to occur overnight. However, by focusing on some of the more manageable factors, the risk of maltreatment can be reduced. Social supports help. When parents know they can turn to other helpful adults for advice and reassurance, they better manage the stresses of child rearing that might otherwise lead to abuse. Families can also be taught more effective ways of coping with situations that might otherwise trigger abuse (Wicks-Nelson & Israel, 2006). Through role-playing sessions, parents can learn the benefits of authoritative parenting and effective ways of using feedback and modeling (described in Module 14.1) to regulate children's behavior.

Providing social supports and teaching effective parenting are typically done when maltreatment and abuse have already occurred. Of course, preventing maltreatment in the first place is more desirable and more cost-effective. For prevention, one useful tool is familiar: early childhood intervention programs. That is, maltreatment and abuse can be cut in half when families participate for two or more years in intervention programs that include preschool education along with family support activities aimed at encouraging parents to become more involved in their children's education (Reynolds & Robertson, 2003). When parents participate in these programs, they become more committed to their children's education. This leads their children to be more successful in school, reducing a source of stress and enhancing parents' confidence in their child-rearing skills, reducing the risks of maltreatment in the process.

Another successful approach focuses specifically on parenting skills in families where children are at risk for maltreatment. In one program (Bugental & Schwartz, 2009), mothers of infants at risk for abuse (because of medical problems at birth) participated in an extensive training program in which they learned to identify likely causes of problems associated with recurring problems encountered while caring for their babies (e.g., problems associated with feeding, sleeping, crying). They were then given help in devising methods to deal with those problems and in monitoring the effectiveness of the methods. When mothers participated in the program, they were less likely to use harsh punishment (a known risk factor for child maltreatment) and their children were less likely to suffer injuries at home (a common measure of parental neglect).

There are also effective programs targeting parents of older children who are at risk for maltreatment. One program, Parent-Child Interaction Therapy, focuses on (1) helping parents to build warm and positive relationships with their children, and (2) developing reasonable expectations for their children and using more effective disciplinary practices. When parents of at-risk children participate in this program, they report less stress, their behavior with their children becomes more positive (more praise and fewer commands), and critically, suspected abuse is less (Thomas & Zimmer-Gimbeck, 2011, 2012).

As we end this module, it's important to remember that most parents who have mistreated their children deserve compassion rather than censure. In most cases, parents and children are attached to each other; maltreatment is a consequence of ignorance and burden, not malice.

Answer to question on page 457 about the number of risk factors: Four factors put Max at risk: social isolation (just moved to the community), poverty (unemployed, no savings), he is a stepchild, and he has a chronic illness.

 ## Check Your Learning

RECALL Describe the different factors that lead to child abuse.

How can we prevent child abuse?

INTERPRET How does child abuse demonstrate, in an unfortunate way, that children are sometimes active contributors to their own development?

APPLY Suppose that you read a letter to the editor of your local paper in which the author claims that parents who abuse their children are mentally ill. If you were to write a reply, what would you say?

 # Unifying Themes Active Children

In this chapter, I want to emphasize the theme that *children influence their own development*. This may seem to be an unusual chapter to emphasize this theme because, after all, we usually think of how parents influence their children. But several times in this chapter we've seen that parenting is determined, in part, by children themselves. We saw that parents change their behavior as their children grow older. Parents also adjust their behavior depending on how their children respond to previous efforts to discipline. And, in discussing causes of child maltreatment, we discovered that younger and sick children often unwittingly place themselves at risk for abuse because of their behavior. Constant whining and crying is trying for all parents and prompts a small few to harm their children.

Of course, parents do influence their children's development in many important ways. Effective parenting recognizes that there is no all-purpose formula that works for all children or for that matter, for all children in one family. Instead, parents must tailor their child-rearing behavior to each child, recognizing his or her unique needs, strengths, and weaknesses.

See for Yourself

Many students find it hard to believe that parents actually use the different styles described in Module 14.1. To observe how parents differ in their warmth and control, visit a place where parents and children interact together. Shopping malls and fast-food restaurants are two good examples. Observe parents and children, then judge their warmth (responsive to the child's needs versus uninterested) and degree of control (relatively controlling versus uncontrolling). As you observe, decide whether parents are using feedback and modeling effectively. You will most likely observe an astonishing variety of parental behavior, some effective and some not. See for yourself!

Summary

 ## 14.1 Parenting

The Family as a System

According to the systems approach, the family is an evolutionary adaptation that consists of interacting elements; parents and children influence each other. The family itself is embedded in a context of interconnected systems that range from the microsystem (people and objects in the child's immediate environment) to the macrosystem (the cultures and subcultures in which all the other systems are embedded).

Styles of Parenting

One dimension of parenting is the degree of parental warmth: Children clearly benefit from warm, caring parents. Another dimension is control. Effective parental control involves setting appropriate standards and enforcing them consistently. Combining warmth and control yields four parental styles: (1) authoritarian parents who are controlling but uninvolved, (2) authoritative parents who are controlling but responsive to their children, (3) indulgent–permissive parents who are loving but exert little control, and (4) indifferent–uninvolved parents who are neither warm nor controlling. Authoritative parenting is usually best for children.

Child rearing is influenced by culture and family configuration. Compared to American parents, Chinese parents are more controlling and less affectionate. Parents living in poverty often rely more heavily on authoritarian parenting.

Parental Behavior

Parents influence development by direct instruction and coaching. In addition, parents serve as models for their children, who sometimes imitate parents' behavior directly and sometimes in ways that are the opposite of what they've seen (counterimitation).

Parents also use feedback to influence children's behavior. Sometimes parents fall into the negative reinforcement trap, inadvertently reinforcing behaviors that they want to discourage. Punishment is effective when it is prompt, consistent, accompanied by an explanation, and delivered by a person with whom the child has a warm relationship. Time-out is one useful form of punishment.

Influences of the Marital System

Chronic conflict is harmful to children, but children can actually benefit when their parents solve disagreements constructively. Not all parents work well together, because they disagree about child-rearing goals or methods.

Children's Contributions

Parenting is influenced by characteristics of children themselves, such as their age and temperament.

 ## 14.2 The Changing Family

Impact of Divorce on Children

Divorce harms children in many ways, ranging from school achievement to adjustment. The impact of divorce stems from less supervision of children, economic hardship, and parental conflict.

Blended Families

The blended family can be successful and beneficial for children and adolescents, but it takes effort because of the complicated relationships, conflicting loyalties, and jealousies that usually exist. When a mother remarries, daughters sometimes have difficulty adjusting because the new stepfather encroaches on an intimate mother–daughter relationship. Best strategies include avoiding preferential treatment of biological children, showing warmth and caring to all family members, and maintaining a harmonious marital relationship.

The Role of Grandparents

Grandparents play many different roles with their grandchildren; the influential and supportive roles are two in which grandparents are particularly active in rearing grandchildren. In African American families, grandmothers often live with their daughters, an arrangement that benefits children. Grandparents also influence their grandchildren indirectly, through the way they reared the child's parents.

Children of Gay and Lesbian Parents

Research on gay and lesbian parents suggests that they are more similar to heterosexual parents than different and that their children develop much like children reared by heterosexual couples.

 ## 14.3 Brothers and Sisters

Firstborn, Laterborn, and Only Children

Firstborn children often are more intelligent and more likely to go to college, but laterborn children are more popular and more innovative. Only children are comparable to children with siblings along most dimensions. Some adopted children have problems, primarily when they were adopted at an older age and when their quality of care before adoption was poor.

Qualities of Sibling Relationships

The birth of a sibling can be stressful for older children, particularly when parents ignore their older child's needs. Siblings get along better when they are of the same sex, believe that parents treat them fairly, enter adolescence, and have parents who get along well.

14.4 Maltreatment: Parent–Child Relationships Gone Awry

Consequences of Maltreatment
Children who are maltreated sometimes suffer permanent physical damage. Their peer relationships are often poor, and they tend to lag in cognitive development and academic performance.

Causes of Maltreatment
A culture's views on violence, poverty, and social isolation can foster child maltreatment. Parents who abuse their children are often unhappy, socially unskilled individuals. Younger, unhealthy children are more likely to be targets of maltreatment, as are stepchildren.

Preventing Maltreatment
Prevention programs often focus on providing families with new ways of coping with problems and providing parents with resources to help them cope with stress.

Test Yourself

1. The _____ refers to social settings that a person may not experience firsthand but that still influence development.
   a. microsystem
   b. mesosystem
   c. exosystem

2. _____ parenting combines a fair degree of parental control with warmth.
   a. Authoritarian
   b. Uninvolved
   c. Authoritative

3. Children of authoritarian parents _____.
   a. are often unhappy
   b. have high levels of self-esteem
   c. rarely are involved in misconduct at school

4. In _____, parents inadvertently reinforce the behaviors that they hope to discourage.
   a. permissive parenting
   b. time out
   c. a negative reinforcement trap

5. Which statement is an *accurate* description of the influences on children of the marital system?
   a. Children suffer whenever they experience conflict between their parents.
   b. Most parents are skilled at preventing work-related stress from affecting their children.
   c. Parenting is more effective when parents work together to achieve shared goals for their children.

6. As children get older, their parents _____.
   a. are more reserved when they express affection
   b. are more controlling, particularly in the personal domain
   c. are no longer influenced by their children's temperament or behavior

7. When parents divorce, _____.
   a. their children's peer relations often suffer but their school achievement does not
   b. children benefit from joint custody if parents get along
   c. children are particularly affected if they usually interpret events positively

8. In blended families, stepfathers _____.
   a. should be interested in their new stepchildren but not step on established relationships
   b. usually find that their stepdaughters adjust more readily than their stepsons
   c. are typically very eager to get involved in child rearing

9. Grandparents are more likely to be involved with their grandchildren when _____.
   a. they have few grandchildren
   b. they live far away from their grandchildren
   c. their children (their grandchildren's parents) don't care if grandparents are involved

10. Children whose parents are gay or lesbian _____.
    a. usually grow up to gay or lesbian themselves
    b. are as intelligent as children reared by heterosexual parents but are less skilled socially and have lower self-concept
    c. are sometimes treated unfairly because their mother is lesbian

11. Which of the following statements about adoption is *correct*?
    a. Youth who experience open adoptions are as well adjusted as those who experience closed adoptions.
    b. Quality of life after adoption affects an adopted child's development but quality of life before adoption does not.

c. Most adopted children experience developmental problems.

12. Siblings get along best when they're _____.
    a. both emotional
    b. of the opposite sex
    c. both adolescents

13. _____ is the most common form of child maltreatment.
    a. Physical abuse
    b. Sexual abuse
    c. Neglect

14. Parents who abuse their children _____.
    a. are often socially isolated
    b. were rarely maltreated themselves
    c. often have a supportive and satisfying marital relationship

15. Children are more likely to be targets of abuse when they are _____.
    a. healthy rather than ill
    b. biological children rather than stepchildren
    c. infants and preschoolers rather than school-age children

Key Terms

authoritarian parenting   432
authoritative parenting   432
authority-oriented grandparents   445
blended family   444
chronosystem   431
counterimitation   434
detached grandparents   445
direct instruction   434
ego-resilience   454
exosystem   430
influential grandparents   445
joint custody   441
macrosystem   430
mesosystem   430
microsystem   430
negative reinforcement trap   435
observational learning   434
open adoption   450
passive grandparents   445
permissive parenting   432
punishment   435
reinforcement   435
supportive grandparents   445
time-out   436
uninvolved parenting   432

Chapter 15
Influences Beyond the Family

Modules

 15.1 Peers

15.2 Electronic Media

15.3 Institutional Influences

If you stand outside a kindergarten classroom on the first day of school, you'll probably see some children crying, fearful of facing a novel environment on their own. What may surprise you is that many parents, too, are struggling to hold back their tears. Why? Parents realize that when children begin school, they are taking an important step toward independence. Other forces now become influential in children's lives, some challenging parents' influence. Among these forces are children's peers, the media, and school itself. In this chapter, we'll look at peer influence in **Module 15.1**. Next, in **Module 15.2**, we'll see how electronic media—particularly television and computers—affect children's development. Finally, in **Module 15.3**, we'll examine the influences on children's development of other cultural institutions, including day care, the workplace, neighborhoods, and schools.

15.1 Peers

LEARNING OBJECTIVES

LO1 When do youngsters first begin to interact with each other, and how do these interactions change during infancy, childhood, and adolescence?

LO2 Why do children become friends, and what are the benefits of friendship?

LO3 When do romantic relationships emerge in adolescence?

LO4 What are the important features of groups in childhood and adolescence? How do groups influence individuals?

LO5 Why are some children more popular than others? What are the causes and consequences of being rejected?

OUTLINE

Development of Peer Interactions

Friendship

Romantic Relationships

Groups

Popularity and Rejection

For six months, 17-year-old Gretchen has been dating Jeff, an 18-year-old. They have had sex several times, each time without contraception. Gretchen suggested to Jeff that he buy some condoms, but he didn't want to because someone might see him at the drug store and that would be too embarrassing. She has not pressed the issue because, although she never mentions it to Jeff, Gretchen sometimes thinks that getting pregnant would be cool; then she and Jeff could move into their own apartment and begin a family.

Many of the major developmental theorists—including Freud, Erikson, Piaget, and Vygotsky—believed that children's development is strongly shaped by their interactions and relationships with peers. Whether occurring with classmates, a small circle of friends, or in a romantic relationship like Gretchen's, children's and adolescents' interactions with peers are important developmental events.

In this module, we'll trace the development of peer interactions. Then we'll look at friendship and romantic relationships; here we'll come to better understand why Gretchen and Jeff are having unprotected sex. Finally, we'll consider children's membership in groups, including their social status within those groups.

Development of Peer Interactions

LO1 When do youngsters first begin to interact with each other, and how do these interactions change during infancy, childhood, and adolescence?

In parallel play, children play alone but pay close attention to what other nearby children are doing as they play.

Peer interactions begin surprisingly early in infancy. Two 6-month-olds together will look, smile, and point at one another. Over the next few months, infants laugh and babble when with other infants (Rubin, Bukowski, & Parker, 2006).

Beginning at about the first birthday and continuing through the preschool years, peer relations rapidly become more complex. In a classic early study, Parten (1932) proposed a developmental sequence in which children first play alone or watch others play, then progress to more elaborate forms of play with each child having a well-defined role. Today, researchers no longer share Parten's view that children move through each stage of play in a rigid sequence, but the different forms of play that Parten distinguished are useful nonetheless.

The first type of social play to appear—soon after the first birthday—is *parallel play:* **youngsters play alone but maintain a keen interest in what other children are doing.** For example, each girl in the photo has her own toy but is watching the other play, too. During parallel play, exchanges between youngsters begin to occur. When one talks or smiles, the other usually responds (Howes, Unger, & Seidner, 1990).

Beginning at roughly 15 to 18 months, toddlers no longer just watch one another at play. **In** *associative play,* **youngsters engage in similar activities, talk or smile at one another, and offer each other toys.** Play is now truly interactive (Howes & Matheson, 1992). An example of associative play would be two 20-month-olds pushing toy cars along the floor, making "car sounds," and periodically trading cars.

Toward the second birthday, *cooperative play* begins: **Now children organize their play around a distinct theme and take on special roles based on the theme.** For example, children may play hide-and-seek and alternate roles of hider and finder, or they may have a tea party and alternate being the host and guest. By the time children are 3½ to 4 years old, parallel play is much less common and cooperative play is the norm. Cooperative play typically involves peers of the same sex, a preference that increases until, by age 6, youngsters choose same-sex playmates about two-thirds of the time (LaFreniere, Strayer, & Gauthier, 1984).

When preschool children engage in make-believe, they often use props to support their play; these props are usually concrete with younger preschoolers but can be more abstract with older preschoolers.

Make-Believe During the preschool years, cooperative play often takes the form of make-believe. Preschoolers have telephone conversations with imaginary partners or pretend to drink imaginary juice. In early phases of make-believe, children rely on realistic props to support their play. While pretending to drink, younger preschoolers use a real cup; while pretending to drive a car, they use a toy steering wheel. In later phases of make-believe, children no longer need realistic props; instead, they can imagine that a block is the cup, or like the girl in the photo, that the pile of sand is pancake batter. Of course, this gradual movement toward more abstract make-believe is possible because of cognitive growth that occurs during the preschool years (Striano, Tomasello, & Rochat, 2001).

Although make-believe is a particularly striking feature of preschoolers' play, it emerges earlier. By 16 to 18 months, toddlers have an inkling of the difference between pretend play and reality. If toddlers see an adult who pretends to fill two glasses with water and then drinks from one of the glasses, they will pretend to drink from the other glass (Bosco, Friedman, & Leslie, 2006).

Of course, the first time that a parent pretends, the activity must be puzzling for toddlers. They probably wonder why Mom is drinking from an empty glass or eating cereal from an empty bowl. But mothers help toddlers make sense out of this behavior: When mothers pretend, they typically look directly at the child and grin, as if to say, "This is just for fun—it's not real!" And toddlers return the smile, as if responding, "I get it! We're playing!" (Nishida & Lillard, 2007). When children are older, they usually tell play partners that they want to pretend ("Let's pretend"), then describe those aspects of reality that are being changed ("I'll be the pilot and this is my plane," referring to the couch). It's as if children mutually agree to enter a parallel universe that's governed by its own set of rules (Rakoczy, 2008; Skolnick Weisberg & Bloom, 2009).

As you might suspect, culture influences the development of make-believe. In some cultures (e.g., India, Peru) parents do not routinely engage in pretend play with their children. Without such parental support, children don't begin pretend play until they're older (Callaghan et al., 2011). In addition, the contents of pretend play reflect the values important in a child's culture (Gosso, Morais, & Otta, 2007). For example, adventure and fantasy are favorite themes for European American youngsters, but family roles and everyday activities are favorites of Korean American children. Thus, cultural values influence both the emergence and the content of make-believe (Farver & Shin, 1997).

Not only is make-believe play entertaining for children, but it also promotes cognitive development. Children who spend much time in make-believe play tend to be more advanced in language, memory, and executive functioning (Bergen & Mauer, 2000; Lillard et al., 2013). They also tend to have a more sophisticated understanding of other people's thoughts, beliefs, and feelings (Lindsey & Colwell, 2003).

Yet another benefit of make-believe is that it allows children to explore topics that frighten them. Children who are afraid of the dark may reassure a doll who is also afraid of the dark. By explaining to the doll why she shouldn't be afraid, children come to understand and regulate their own fear of darkness. Or children may pretend that a doll has misbehaved and must be punished, which allows them to experience the parent's anger and the doll's guilt. Make-believe allows children to explore other emotions, too, including joy and affection (Gottman, 1986; Lillard et al., 2013).

For many preschool children, make-believe play involves imaginary companions. Imaginary companions were once thought to be fairly rare, but many preschoolers, particularly firstborn and only children, report imaginary companions (Taylor et al., 2004). Children can usually describe what their imaginary playmates look and sound like (Tahiroglu, Mannering, & Taylor, 2011). Having an imaginary companion is associated with many *positive* social characteristics (Davis, Meins, & Fernyhough, 2011; Gleason & Hohmann, 2006; Roby & Kidd, 2008); compared with preschool children who lack imaginary friends, preschoolers with imaginary friends tend to be more sociable, have more real friends, and have greater self-knowledge than other preschoolers. Among older children who are at risk for developing behavior problems, an imaginary companion promotes better adjustment during adolescence (Taylor, Hulette, & Dishion, 2010).

Many children also play with nonhuman animals, particularly family pets. Most families in the United States and Europe have pets, and children often consider them to be family members. Only children and children without younger siblings are particularly likely to play with pets. Such play sometimes resembles cooperative play, particularly when dogs are involved. For example, "fetch" has the roles of "thrower" and "retriever" that are understood by child and dog. In other common forms of child–animal play, children sometimes pretend to be an animal like the pet (e.g., barking at the pet) or they pretend that the pet is human and hold conversations in which they speak for it and themselves (Melson, 2003, 2010).

Solitary Play   At times throughout the preschool years, many children prefer to play alone. Should parents be worried? Usually, no. Solitary play comes in many forms and most are normal—even healthy. Spending free playtime alone coloring, solving puzzles, or assembling Legos® is not a sign of maladjustment. Many youngsters enjoy solitary activities and, at other times, choose very social play (Coplan & Ooi, 2014).

However, some forms of solitary play *are* signs that children are uneasy about interacting with others (Coplan et al., 2001; Harrist et al., 1997). One type of unhealthy solitary play is wandering aimlessly. Sometimes children go from one preschool activity center to the next, as if trying to decide what to do. But really they just keep wandering, never settling into play with others or into constructive solitary play. Another unhealthy type of solitary play is hovering: A child stands near peers who are playing, watching them play but not participating. Over time, these behaviors do not bode well for youngsters because they cause peers to avoid or reject them (Coplan & Armer, 2007); it's best for these youngsters to see a professional who can help them overcome their reticence in social situations.

Parental Influence   Parents get involved in their young children's play in several ways (Parke & O'Neil, 2000):

- *Playmate*. Many parents enjoy the role of playmate (and many parents deserve an Oscar for their performances). They use the opportunity to scaffold their children's play (see Module 6.2), often raising it to more sophisticated levels (Tamis-LeMonda & Bornstein, 1996). For example, if a toddler is stacking toy plates, a parent might help the child stack the plates (play at the same level) or might pretend to wash each plate (play at a more advanced level). When parents demonstrate the reciprocal, cooperative nature of play, their children's play with peers is more successful (Lindsey, Cremeens, & Caldera, 2010).

- *Social director*. It takes two to interact, and young children rely on parents to create opportunities for social interactions. Many parents of young children arrange visits with peers, enroll children in activities (e.g., preschool programs), and take children to settings that attract young children (e.g., parks, swimming pools). All this effort is worth it: Children whose parents provide them with frequent opportunities for peer interaction tend to get along better with their peers (Ladd & Pettit, 2002).

- *Coach*. Successful interactions require a host of skills, including how to initiate an interaction, make joint decisions, and resolve conflicts. When parents help their children acquire these skills, children tend to be more competent socially and more accepted by their peers (Grusec, 2011; Mounts, 2011). For example, when mothers emphasize how targets of relational aggression feel, their children are less likely to resort to relational aggression (Werner et al., 2014). But there's a catch: The coaching must be constructive for children to benefit. Parent-coaches sometimes make suggestions that are misguided. Bad coaching is worse than none at all because it harms children's peer relations (Russell & Finnie, 1990).

- *Mediator*. When young children play, they often disagree, argue, and sometimes fight. As shown in the photo, children play more cooperatively and longer when parents are present to help iron out conflicts (Mize, Pettit, & Brown, 1995). When young children can't agree on what to play, a parent can negotiate a mutually acceptable activity. When both youngsters want to play with the same toy, a parent can arrange for them to share. Here, too, parents scaffold their preschoolers' play, smoothing the interaction by providing some of the social skills that preschoolers lack.

In addition to these direct influences on children's play, parents influence children's play indirectly, via the quality of the parent–child attachment relationship. Recall from Module 10.3 that peer relationships in childhood and adolescence are most successful when the children, as infants, had a secure attachment relationship with their mother (Bascoe et al., 2009; Brown & Bakken, 2011). A child's relationship with his or her parents is the internal working model for all future social relationships. When the parent–child relationship is of high quality and emotionally satisfying, children are encouraged to

One way in which parents facilitate their children's play is by taking on the role of mediator; parents help to resolve the disputes that inevitably develop when young children play.

form relationships with other people. Another possibility is that a secure attachment relationship with the mother makes an infant feel more confident about exploring the environment, which, in turn, provides more opportunities to interact with peers. These two views are not mutually exclusive; both may contribute to the relative ease with which securely attached children interact with their peers (Hartup, 1992).

Peer Relations After Preschool When children attend elementary school, the context of peer relations changes dramatically (Rubin et al., 2006). Not only does the sheer number of peers increase, but children are also often exposed to a far more diverse set of peers than before. In addition, children find themselves interacting with peers in situations that range from reasonably structured with much adult supervision (e.g., a classroom) to largely unstructured with minimal adult supervision (e.g., a playground during recess).

An obvious change in children's peer relations during the elementary-school years is that, because of more experience with peers, as well as cognitive and language development, children get along better than when they were younger. They become more skilled at initiating and maintaining interactions. They also use more sophisticated methods to resolve conflicts, such as negotiation (Laursen, Finkelstein, & Betts, 2001).

What do school-age children do when they're together? In one study (Zarbatany, Hartmann, & Rankin, 1990), investigators asked Canadian students in grades 5 and 6 how they spent their time with peers. The students in the study indicated how often they participated with peers in each of 29 different activities. The results, shown in the graph in Figure 15-1, are not too surprising, eh? The most common activities with peers are simple—just being together and talking. This is true of high-school students as well: They spend more time talking and hanging out with friends

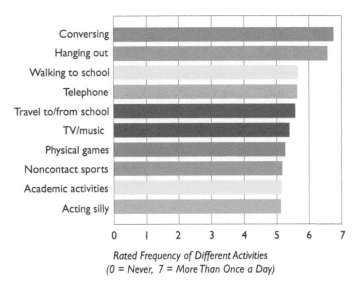

Rated Frequency of Different Activities
(0 = Never, 7 = More Than Once a Day)

Figure 15-1

than in watching videos, doing homework, or participating in school activities (Nelson & Gastic, 2009).

The graph also highlights another important feature of peer relations during the elementary-school years. Children reported that they played physical games a few times each week, which reflects, in part, the emergence of a special type of play in school-age children. **In *rough-and-tumble play*, children playfully chase, punch, kick, shove, fight, and wrestle with peers.** Notice the word *play* in this definition: Unlike aggression, where the intention is to do harm, rough-and-tumble play is for fun. When children are involved in rough-and-tumble play, they are usually smiling and sometimes laughing (Pellis & Pellis, 2007). When parents or teachers intervene, the youngsters usually explain that there's no problem; they're just playing. Rough-and-tumble play is more common among boys than girls, and girls' rough-and-tumble play tends to emphasize running and chasing over wrestling and fighting.

As children move into adolescence, three features of their peer relationships loom large: Friendships become more intimate, youth have their first romantic relationships, and groups take on greater significance. These changes are so important that we'll consider each one separately. Let's start with friendship.

Friendship

LO2 Why do children become friends, and what are the benefits of friendship?

Over time, even young children develop special relationships with certain peers. *Friendship* **is a voluntary relationship between two people involving mutual liking.** By age 4 or 5 years, most children claim to have a "best friend." If you ask them how they can tell a child is their best friend, their response will probably resemble 5-year-old Katelyn's:

> INTERVIEWER: Why is Heidi your best friend?
>
> KATELYN: Because she plays with me. And she's nice to me.
>
> INTERVIEWER: Are there any other reasons?
>
> KATELYN: Yeah, Heidi lets me play with her dolls.

Thus, the key elements of friendship for preschool and younger elementary-school children are that children like each other and enjoy playing together.

As children develop, their friendships become more complex. For older elementary-school children (8 to 11 years), mutual liking and shared activities are joined by features that are more psychological in nature, such as trust and assistance. At this age, children expect that they can depend on their friends; their friends will be nice to them, will keep their promises, and won't say mean things about them to others. And they expect friends to step forward in times of need: A friend should willingly help with homework or willingly share a snack.

Adolescence adds another layer of complexity to friendships. Mutual liking, common interests, and trust remain. In fact, trust becomes even more important in adolescent friendships. New to adolescence is intimacy: Friends now confide in one another, sharing personal thoughts and feelings. Teenagers will reveal their excitement over a new romance or disappointment at not being cast in a school musical. Intimacy is more common in friendships among girls, who are more likely than boys to have one exclusive "best friend" (Markovits, Benenson, & Dolenszky, 2001). Because intimacy is at the core of their friendships, girls are also more likely to be concerned about the faithfulness of their friends and worry about being rejected (Benenson & Christakos, 2003; MacEvoy & Asher, 2012; Poulin & Chan, 2010).

The emergence of intimacy in adolescent friendships means that friends also come to be seen as sources of social and emotional support. Elementary-school children generally rely on close family members—parents, siblings, and grandparents—as primary sources of support when they need help or are upset. But adolescents turn to close friends instead. Because adolescent friends share intimate thoughts and feelings, they can provide support during emotional or stressful periods (del Valle, Bravo, & Lopez, 2010; Levitt, Guacci-Franco, & Levitt, 1993).

Hand in hand with the emphasis on intimacy is loyalty. Having confided in friends, adolescents expect friends to stick with them through good and bad times. If a friend is disloyal, adolescents are afraid that they may be humiliated because their intimate thoughts and feelings will become known to a much broader circle of people (Berndt & Perry, 1990).

QUESTION 15.1

If Heidi is still Katelyn's best friend in high school, how will Katelyn's description of their friendship differ from the description she gave as a 5-year-old?

Who Become Friends? In childhood and adolescence, most friends are like those in the photo: alike in age, sex, and race (Hamm, 2000; Mehta & Strough, 2009). Because friends are supposed to treat each other as equals, friendships are rare between an older, more experienced child and a younger, less experienced child. Because children typically play with same-sex peers (see Module 13.3), boys and girls become close friends infrequently.

Although children's friendships are overwhelmingly with members of their own sex, a few children have friendships with other-sex children. Children with same- *and* other-sex friendships tend to be well adjusted, whereas children with only other-sex friendships tend to be unpopular and less competent academically and socially and have lower self-esteem. Apparently, children with both same- *and* other-sex friends are so socially skilled and popular that both boys and girls are eager to be their friends. In contrast, children with only other-sex friendships are socially unskilled, unpopular youngsters who are rejected by their same-sex peers and form friendships with other-sex children as a last resort (Bukowski, Sippola, & Hoza, 1999).

Other-sex friendships are more common among teenagers (Arndorfer & Stormshak, 2008). By mid-adolescence, boys make up about 33% of girls' friends, but only 20% of boys' friends are girls. Boys benefit more from these other-sex friendships: Female friends provide more help and support to boys than male friends provide to girls (Poulin & Pedersen, 2007; Sears, Graham, & Campbell, 2009).

Friendships are more common between children and adolescents from the same race or ethnic group than between those from different groups, reflecting racial segregation in US society. Friendships among children of different groups are more common in schools where classes are smaller (Hallinan & Teixeira, 1987) and when a child's school and neighborhood are ethnically diverse (Quillian & Campbell, 2003). Although such cross-group friendships are uncommon, they are valuable: Children from majority groups typically form more positive attitudes toward a minority group following a friendship with a youth from that group (Feddes, Noack, & Rutland, 2009). And children in cross-group friendships are less often targets of relational aggression (Kawabata & Crick, 2011).

Of course, friends are usually alike not only in age, sex, and race. They tend to be alike in popularity:

Friends tend to be alike in age, sex, race, and interests.

Highly popular youth befriend popular peers and avoid friendships with less popular peers (Dijkstra, Cillessen, & Borch, 2013). In addition, friends have similar attitudes toward school, recreation, drug use, and plans for the future (Hamm, 2000; Newcomb & Bagwell, 1995). Children and adolescents befriend others who are similar to themselves and, as time passes, friends become more similar in their attitudes and values (Popp et al., 2008; Van Zalk et al., 2010). Nevertheless, friends are not photocopies of each other; friends are less similar, for example, than spouses or dizygotic twins (Rushton & Bonds, 2005).

Quality and Consequences of Friendship You probably remember some childhood friendships that were long lasting and satisfying, whereas others rapidly wore thin and soon dissolved. What accounts for these differences in the quality and longevity of friendships? Sometimes friendships are brief because children have the skills to create friendships—they know funny stories, they kid around, they know good gossip—but lack the skills to sustain those friendships—they can't keep secrets, are too bossy, or are too emotional (Blair et al., 2014; Jiao, 1999; Parker & Seal, 1996). Sometimes friendships end because, when conflicts arise, children are more concerned about their own interests and are unwilling to compromise or negotiate (Glick & Rose, 2011; Rose & Asher, 1999). At other times, friendships dissolve when children discover that their needs and interests aren't as similar as they thought initially (Ellis & Zarbatany, 2007; Poulin & Boivin, 2000).

Considering that friendships disintegrate for many reasons, you're probably reminded that truly good friends are to be treasured. In fact, researchers consistently find that children benefit from having good friends. Compared to children who lack friends, children with good friends have higher self-esteem, are less likely to be lonely and depressed, and more often act prosocially—sharing and cooperating with others (Burk & Laursen, 2005; Hartup & Stevens, 1999). Children with good friends cope better with stressful experiences, such as doing poorly on an exam or being rejected by peers (Adams, Santo, & Bukowski, 2011; McDonald et al., 2010). And they're less likely to be victimized by peers (Schwartz et al., 2000). What's more, the benefits of friendship are long lasting: Children who have friends have greater self-worth as young adults (Bagwell, Newcomb, & Bukowski, 1998). Thus, for many adolescents, friends are important resources. Children learn from their friends and turn to them for support in times of stress.

Although children and adolescents benefit from their friends' support, there can be costs as well. **Sometimes friends spend much of their time together discussing each other's personal problems, which is known as** *co-rumination.* Girls do this more than boys (consistent with the fact that intimacy is more important to girls' friendships). Such co-rumination strengthens girls' friendships but also puts them at risk for greater depression and anxiety. In other words, when Avanti and Mishra spend day after day talking about problems with their parents and their schoolwork, they grow closer but also more troubled (Brendgen et al., 2010; Schwartz-Mette & Rose, 2012).

There are other ways in which friendships can be hazardous (Bagwell, 2004). For example, when aggressive children are friends, they often encourage each other's aggressive behavior (Dishion, Poulin, & Burraston, 2001; Piehler & Dishion, 2007). Similarly, when teens engage in risky behavior (e.g., they drink, smoke, or have sex), they often reinforce the other's risky behavior (Bot et al., 2005; Henry et al., 2007). The "Focus on Research" feature describes a study that shows this impact of friends.

Focus on Research

Influence of Best Friends on Sexual Activity

Who were the investigators, and what was the aim of the study? James Jaccard, Hart Blanton, and Tonya Dodge (2005) set out to determine whether close friends influence adolescents' sexual behavior. That is, they wanted to know whether adolescents were more likely to be sexually active when their closest same-sex friend was sexually active.

How did the investigators measure the topic of interest? Jaccard and his colleagues used data from the *Add Health* database, which includes information obtained from more than 20,000 US adolescents in grades 7–12. They completed questionnaires and were interviewed on a wide range of topics concerning adolescent health and development. Best friends were determined by asking adolescents to name five same-sex friends and then indicate the time spent with each in the past week. Sexual activity was determined by asking teens whether they had ever had sexual intercourse, and, if so, how recently.

Who were the children in the study? The investigators focused on a subsample of nearly 1,700 adolescents—837 boys and 851 girls—who were interviewed twice and who were not married.

What was the design of the study? This study was correlational because Jaccard and colleagues were interested in the relation that existed naturally between two variables: whether an adolescent was sexually active and whether an adolescent's best friend was sexually active. The study was longitudinal because adolescents were interviewed twice, approximately a year apart.

Were there ethical concerns with the study? You bet. This is one of the few child-development studies that's been debated on the floor of the US Congress! The initial version of the project, proposed in the late 1980s, was motivated by the growing AIDS epidemic and focused solely on adolescent sexual risk-taking. After the National Institutes of Health (NIH) decided to fund the project, many conservative groups protested, arguing that the project actually endorsed the adolescent sexual behaviors that it was designed to study. The NIH withdrew the funds but a compromise was reached in 1993: The U.S. Congress passed legislation calling for a much broader longitudinal study, one that would examine adolescent health and well-being, the factors that jeopardize adolescent health, and behaviors that promote health. The result was the National Longitudinal Study of Adolescent Health—*Add Health* for short.

Parents and adolescents both gave consent to participate. In addition, the *Add Health* project went to great lengths to ensure that no individual's name could be linked to his or her responses to any question. For example, for questions on sensitive topics, adolescents listened to questions played on a tape recorder and they entered their answers directly into a laptop computer.

What were the results? When adolescents were interviewed the first time, the correlation between an adolescent being sexually active and an adolescent's best friend being sexually active was .34 for boys and .40 for girls. This shows a tendency for best friends to be alike in their sexual experience. But are adolescents more likely to be sexually active when their best friends are? The investigators answered this question by examining adolescents' sexual activity over the year. They found that when best friends were sexually active over the year, 56% of adolescents were sexually active during the same period; in contrast, when best friends were sexually inactive, only 24% of adolescents were sexually active. Thus, over time, adolescents were more likely to be sexually active when their best friend was, too. This was true for adolescents who were sexually active at the initial interview as well as for those who had been inactive sexually.

What did the investigators conclude? Adolescent friendships are based on similarity and, once friendships are formed, like-minded friends can encourage and support each other's behavior. In this case, they can support each other's sexual activity or inactivity. However, friendships are not all-powerful in this regard. When adolescents' best friends were sexually active over the year, 56% of the adolescents followed their friends in becoming sexually active but 44% did not. As Jaccard and colleagues put it, "adolescent peer and social networks exert considerable impact on a wide range of behaviors, such as musical interests, clothing preference, and extracurricular activities.... [However]...peer influence is just one of a number of factors that contribute to adolescent risk behavior" (2005, p. 144).

What converging evidence would strengthen these conclusions? One useful step would be to continue the longitudinal study to examine the influence of friends over a longer term. Another important addition would be to examine the impact of an extended peer network, not simply an adolescent's best friend.

Finally, it's important to note that many youth are involved in relationships that are just the opposite of friendships. Mutual antipathies are characterized by shared dislike for each other, including some in which the feelings are quite intense (e.g., "I hate your guts!") as well as those in which the feelings are milder (e.g., children simply avoid each other). About one-third of US children and adolescents have mutual antipathic relationships; those who do are more likely to be aggressive and be withdrawn (Card, 2010). These relationships sometimes reflect dissimilarities between children (Nangle et al., 2004). Tom, who enjoys school, likes to read, and plans to go to Harvard, loathes Barry, who thinks that school is stupid, listens to his iPod constantly, and plans to quit high school to become a rock star; Barry feels the same way about Tom. Sometimes antipathies emerge from the wreckage of a broken friendship (Casper & Card, 2010). For example, when Kerri shares Regan's intimate secrets with the rest of their group, Regan retaliates by doing the same with Kerri's secrets; their friendship dissolves and they quickly develop an antipathic relationship. Finally, sometimes antipathies emerge as a way for highly popular children and adolescents to distance themselves from less popular peers (Berger & Dijkstra, 2013).

Romantic Relationships

LO3 **When do romantic relationships emerge in adolescence?**

The social landscape adds a distinctive landmark in adolescence: romantic relationships. These are uncommon during elementary school, but by high school roughly two-thirds of US adolescents have had a romantic relationship within the previous 1½ years and most have been involved in a romance lasting nearly a year (Carver, Joyner, & Udry, 2003).

But cultural factors influence the timing of romantic relationships. Traditional Hispanic American and Asian American parents emphasize family ties and loyalty to parents. Because romantic relationships are a sign of independence and usually result in less time spent with family, it's not surprising that Hispanic American and Asian American adolescents often begin to date at an older age and date less frequently (Collins, Welsh, & Furman, 2009).

Romantic relationships build on friendships. Like friends, romantic partners tend to be similar in popularity and physical attractiveness. And a best friendship serves both as a prototype for and a source of support during ups-and-downs of close relationships (Collins et al., 2009). What's more, romantic relationships change over time in ways that resemble changes in friendship: For younger adolescents, romantic relationships offer companionship (like that provided by a best friend) and an outlet for sexual exploration. For older adolescents like those in the photo, intimacy, trust, and support become important features of romantic relationships (Shulman & Kipnis, 2001). Finally, like friendships, when children have high-quality parenting, they more readily invest in romantic relationships as adults (Oriña et al., 2011).

It's tempting to dismiss teen romances as nothing more than "puppy love," but they are often developmentally significant (Collins et al., 2009). On the one hand, adolescents involved in a romantic relationship are often more self-confident and have higher self-esteem, and high-quality adolescent romances are associated with positive relationships during adulthood. On the other hand, adolescents in romantic relationships report more emotional upheaval and conflict (Joyner & Udry, 2000). In addition, early dating with many different partners is associated with a host of problems in adolescence (e.g., drug use, lower grades) and is associated with less satisfying romantic relationships in adulthood (Collins, 2003).

When older adolescents are romantically involved, they believe that trust and support are an important part of their relationship.

Sexual Behavior   Sexual exploration is an important feature of romantic relationships for younger adolescents. In fact, by the end of high school, roughly two-thirds of US adolescents will have had intercourse at least once (Eaton et al., 2008). No single factor predicts adolescent sexual behavior. Instead, adolescents are more likely to be sexually active when they acquire (from parents, peers, and media) permissive attitudes toward sex, when their parents don't monitor their behavior, when they are more physically mature, and when they drink alcohol regularly (Belsky et al., 2010; Collins et al., 2011; Hipwell et al., 2010; Zimmer-Gembeck & Helfand, 2008). What's more, adolescents exposed to harsh environments (e.g., living in poverty) start sex at younger ages, but adolescents with better executive functioning start at older ages (Carlson, Mendle, & Harden, 2014; Khurana et al., 2012).

Adolescents' sexual behavior is a cause for concern because, among US adolescent girls who have ever had intercourse, approximately 1 in 6 becomes pregnant. The result is that nearly a half million babies are born to US teenagers annually. African American and Hispanic American adolescents are the most likely to become pregnant (Ventura et al., 2008).

Teen pregnancy is common because sexually active teens often do not use birth control consistently or correctly (Guttmacher Institute, 2013). Why? Several factors contribute (Gordon, 1996). First, many adolescents are ignorant of basic facts of conception and many believe that they are invulnerable—that only others become pregnant. Second, some teenagers do not know where to obtain contraceptives, and others, like Jeff in the module-opening vignette, are embarrassed to buy them (Ralph & Brindis, 2010). Still others don't know how to use contraceptives. Third, for some adolescent girls, like Gretchen from the vignette, becoming pregnant is appealing (Phipps et al., 2008). They think having a child is a way to break away from parents, gain status as an independent-living adult, and have "someone to love them."

The best way to reduce adolescent sexual behavior and teen pregnancy is with comprehensive sex education programs (Kirby & Laris, 2009). These programs teach the biological aspects of sex and emphasize responsible sexual behavior or abstinence from premarital sex altogether. They also include discussions of the pressures to become involved sexually and ways to respond to this pressure. A key element is that in role-playing sessions, students practice strategies for refusing to have sex. Youth who participate in programs like these are less likely to have intercourse; when they do have intercourse, they are more likely to use contraceptives. In contrast, there is little evidence that programs focusing solely on abstinence are effective in reducing sexual activity or encouraging contraceptive use.

Sexual Orientation   For most adolescents, sexual behavior involves members of the other sex. However, in early and mid-adolescence, roughly 15% of teens experience a period of sexual questioning, during which they sometimes report emotional and sexual attractions to members of their own sex (Carver, Egan, & Perry, 2004). For most adolescents, these experiences are simply a part of the larger process of role experimentation common to adolescence. However, like the teens in the photo, about 5% of teenage boys and girls identify their sexual orientation as gay (Rotherman-Borus & Langabeer, 2001).

The roots of attraction to members of the same sex are poorly understood. One idea is that genes and hormones may lead some boys to feel "different" during childhood and early adolescence, and these feelings lead to an interest in gender-atypical activities and, later, attraction to other males. For females, the path to same-sex attraction is less predictable. Attraction to other females usually does not emerge until mid- or late adolescence, and in some cases, not until middle or old age. What's more, for many lesbian women, same-sex attraction grows out of deep feelings for a particular woman that, over time, extends to other females (Diamond, 2007).

About 5% of adolescents find themselves attracted to members of their own sex and identify themselves as gay or lesbian.

Although the origins of same-sex attraction are not yet well understood, it is clear that gay and lesbian youth face many challenges. Their family and peer relationships are often disrupted (Pearson & Wilkinson, 2013) and they endure verbal and physical attacks (Duncan & Hatzenbuehler, 2014). Given these problems, it's not surprising that gay and lesbian youth often experience mental health problems, including depression and anxiety (Burton, Marshal, & Chisolm, 2014). In recent years, social changes have helped gay and lesbian youth respond more effectively to these challenges, including more (and more visible) role models and more centers for gay and lesbian youth. These resources are making it easier for gay and lesbian youth to understand their sexual orientation and to cope with the many other demands of adolescence; most end up as well adjusted as heterosexual youth (Saewyc, 2011).

In concluding this section, we need to recognize that sexual behavior and sexuality are enormously complicated and emotionally charged issues, even for adults. Adults who deal with adolescents need to recognize this complexity and help provide teenagers with skills for dealing with the issues involved in their emerging sexuality.

Groups

LO4 **What are the important features of groups in childhood and adolescence? How do groups influence individuals?**

During adolescence, groups become an important feature of social life. Two types of groups are particularly common during adolescence. **A *clique* consists of four to six individuals who are good friends and, consequently, tend to be similar in age, sex, race, and interests.** Members of a clique spend time together and often dress, talk, and act alike. Cliques are often part of a larger group, too. **A *crowd* is a larger mixed-sex group of older children or adolescents who have similar values and attitudes and are known by a common label.** Maybe you remember some of the different crowds from your own youth? *Jocks, preppies, burnouts, nerds,* and *brains*—adolescents use these or similar terms to refer to crowds of older children or adolescents (Brown & Klute, 2003). Ethnic minority youth typically belong to such crowds, but some belong to ethnically based crowds instead (Brown et al., 2008).

Some crowds have more status than others. For example, students in many junior and senior high schools claim that the jocks are the most prestigious crowd, whereas the burnouts are among the least prestigious. Self-esteem in older children and adolescents often reflects the status of their crowd. During the school years, youths from high-status crowds tend to have greater self-esteem than those from low-status crowds (Sussman et al., 2007). Finally, youth in crowds that support adult values, such as jocks and preppies, are less prone to psychological disorders such as depression than youth in crowds that don't support these values, such as burnouts (Doornward et al., 2012).

Why do some students become nerds while others join the burnouts? Adolescents' interests and abilities matter, obviously. Brighter students who enjoy school gravitate to the brain or nerd crowds and athletically talented teens become part of the jock crowd (Prinstein & LaGreca, 2004). Adolescents' crowds also reveal parents' influence. When parents practice authoritative parenting—they are warm but controlling—their children become involved with crowds that endorse adult standards of behavior (for example, normals, jocks, brains). But, when parents' style is neglectful or permissive, their children are less likely to identify with adult standards of behavior and, instead, join crowds like druggies that disavow adult standards. This seems to be true of African American, Asian American, European American, and Hispanic American children and their parents (Brown et al., 1993).

Group Structure Groups—whether in school, at a summer camp, or anyplace else—typically have a well-defined structure. **Most groups have a** *dominance hierarchy* **consisting of a leader to whom all other members of the group defer.** Other members know their position in the hierarchy. They yield to members who are above them in the hierarchy and assert themselves over members who are below them. A dominance hierarchy is useful in reducing conflict and allocating resources within groups, because every member knows his or her place.

What determines where members stand in the hierarchy? With children, especially boys, physical power is often the basis for the dominance hierarchy. The leader is usually the most physically intimidating child (Hawley, 1999). Among girls and older boys, leaders have high self-esteem, good relationships with peers, and skills useful to the group. At a summer camp, for example, the leaders most often are the children with the greatest camping experience. Among Girl Scouts, girls chosen to be patrol leaders tend to be bright and goal oriented and to have new ideas (Edwards, 1994). These characteristics are appropriate because the primary function of patrols is to help plan activities for the entire troop. Similarly, in a study of classroom discussion groups, the children who became leaders had good ideas and were outgoing (Li et al., 2007). Thus, leadership based on key skills is effective because it gives the greatest influence to those with the skills most important to group functioning.

Peer Pressure Groups establish *norms*—standards of behavior that apply to all group members—and groups may pressure members to conform to these norms. Such "peer pressure" is often characterized as an irresistible, harmful force. The stereotype is that teenagers exert enormous pressure on each other to behave antisocially. In reality, peer pressure is neither all-powerful nor always evil. For example, most adolescents resist peer pressure to behave in ways that are clearly antisocial, such as stealing (Cook, Buehler, & Henson, 2009), and such resistance increases from mid- to late adolescence (Steinberg & Monahan, 2007). Peer pressure can be positive, too. Peers often urge one another to work hard in school; to participate in school activities, such as trying out for a play or working on the yearbook; or to become involved in community action projects, such as Habitat for Humanity (Kindermann, 2007; Molloy, Gest, & Rulison, 2011).

Of course, peer influence is common throughout the life span. As we saw in Module 1.1, children and adults often imitate their peers' behavior, particularly when the peer has high status and the behavior is rewarded. But adolescents may be particularly susceptible to peer influence because they are forging an identity (Module 11.1) and matching the behavior of a valued peer group may help to foster that identity. If Jordan sees that popular kids smoke and part of her emerging identity is that she's in the popular group, she may start smoking too (Brechwald & Prinstein, 2011).

Peer pressure is *not* all-powerful. Instead, peer influence is stronger when (1) youth are younger and more socially anxious; (2) peers are high-status friends, and (3) standards for appropriate behavior are not clear-cut, as in the case of tastes in music or clothing or standards for smoking and drinking (Allen et al., 2012; Brechwald & Prinstein, 2011). Thus, when 14-year-old Doug's best friend (who's one of the most popular kids in school) gets his hair cut like Justin Beiber, Doug may go along because he's young, the peer is popular and his friend, and there are no fixed standards for hair style. But when an unpopular kid that 18-year-old Kelly barely knows suggests to her that they go to the mall and shoplift some earrings, Kelly will resist because she's older, the peer is unpopular and not a friend, and norms for shoplifting are clear.

Popularity and Rejection

LO5 Why are some children more popular than others?
What are the causes and consequences of being rejected?

Eileen is definitely the most popular child in her class. Her peers always want to play with her and sit near her at lunch or on the school bus. In contrast, Jay is the least popular child in the class. When he tries to join a game of four square, the others quit. Students in the class dislike Jay as much as they like Eileen.

Popular and rejected children like Eileen and Jay can be found in every classroom and neighborhood. In fact, studies of popularity (Hymel et al., 2004) reveal that most children can be placed in one of five categories:

- *Popular children* are liked by many classmates.
- *Rejected children* are disliked by many classmates.
- *Controversial children* are both liked and disliked by classmates.
- *Average children* are liked and disliked by some classmates but without the intensity found for popular, rejected, or controversial children.
- *Neglected children* are ignored by classmates.

Of these categories, we know most about popular and rejected children. Each of these categories actually includes two subtypes. Most popular children are skilled academically and socially. They are good students who are usually friendly, cooperative, and helpful. They are more skillful at communicating and regulating themselves as well as being better at integrating themselves into an ongoing conversation or play session; they "fit in" instead of "barging in" (Graziano, Keane, & Calkins, 2007; Kam et al., 2011; Véronneau et al., 2010). A smaller group of popular youth includes physically aggressive boys who pick fights with peers and relationally aggressive girls who, like the "Plastics" in the film *Mean Girls*, thrive on manipulating social relationships. Although these youth are not particularly friendly, their antisocial behavior nevertheless garners respect from peers (Kuryluk, Cohen, & Audley-Piotrowski, 2011; Xie et al., 2006).

Are these avenues to popularity specific to US children, or do they apply more generally? The "Cultural Influences" feature has the answer.

Cultural Influences
Keys to Popularity

In the United States, popular children seem to know how to get along with others. These results don't apply just to US children; they hold for children in many cultures around the world, including Canada, European countries, Israel, and China (e.g., Casiglia, Coco, & Zappulla, 1998; Chung-Hall & Chen, 2010). However, sometimes popular children have other characteristics that are unique to their cultural setting. In Israel, for example, popular children are more likely to be direct and assertive than in other countries (Krispin, Sternberg, & Lamb, 1992). In China, historically shy children were often popular because their restrained behavior was taken as a sign of social maturity. However, economic reforms in China in the past 25 years have resulted in greater emphasis on taking initiative and being assertive. Consequently, shy children living in urban areas that have experienced economic reform are now rejected by peers but they remain popular in more traditional rural areas (Chen, Wang, & Cao, 2011). Evidently, good social skills are at the core of popularity in most countries, but other features may also be important, reflecting culturally specific values that may change over time.

As for rejected children, many are overly aggressive, hyperactive, socially unskilled, and unable to regulate their emotions. These children are usually much more hostile than popular aggressive children and seem to view aggression as an end—which peers dislike—instead of using aggression as a means toward other ends—which peers may not actually like but grudgingly respect (Prinstein & Cillessen, 2003). Other rejected children are shy, withdrawn, timid, and, not surprisingly, lonely (Coplan et al., 2013; Rubin, Coplan, & Bowker, 2009).

Consequences of Rejection   No one enjoys being rejected. Not surprisingly, peer rejection is a major obstacle in children's development. Over time rejected youngsters become less involved in classroom activities; they end up feeling lonely and disliking school (Ladd, Herald-Brown, & Reiser, 2008; Sturaro et al., 2011). Repeated peer rejection in childhood can also have serious long-term consequences (Ladd, 2006; Rubin et al., 2009). Rejected youngsters are more likely than youngsters in the other categories to drop out of school, commit juvenile offenses, and suffer from psychopathology.

Causes of Rejection   Peer rejection can be traced, at least in part, to parental influence (Ladd, 1998). Children see how their parents respond to different social situations and often imitate these responses later. Parents who are friendly and cooperative with others demonstrate effective social skills. Parents who are belligerent and combative demonstrate much less effective social skills. In particular, when parents typically respond to interpersonal conflict like the couple in the photo—with intimidation or aggression—their children may imitate them; this hampers their development of social skills and makes them less popular in the long run (Keane, Brown, & Crenshaw, 1990).

Parents' disciplinary practices also affect their children's social skill and popularity. Inconsistent discipline—punishing a child for misbehaving one day and ignoring the same behavior the next—is associated with antisocial and aggressive behavior, paving the way to rejection (Dishion, 1990). Consistent punishment that is tied to parental love and affection is more likely to promote social skill and, in the process, popularity (Dekovic & Janssens, 1992).

In sum, parenting can lead to an aggressive interpersonal style in a child, which in turn leads to peer rejection. The implication, then, is that by teaching youngsters (and their parents) more effective ways of interacting with others, we can make rejection less likely. With improved social skills, rejected children would not need to resort to antisocial behaviors. Rejected children (and other types of unpopular children) can be taught how to initiate interaction, communicate clearly, and be friendly. They can also be discouraged from behaviors that peers dislike, such as whining and fighting. This training is similar to training for aggressive adolescents, who are typically unpopular (see Module 12.4). Training of this sort does work. Rejected children can learn skills that lead to peer acceptance and thereby avoid the long-term harm associated with being rejected (LaGreca, 1993; Mize & Ladd, 1990).

Throughout this module, we've seen that peers affect children's development in many ways—for example, through different forms of play, through friendships, and through participation in social groups. Beginning in the next module, we'll look at important *nonsocial* influences on children's development, starting with media such as television and computers.

Many rejected children are too aggressive, and some learn this style of interaction from watching their parents in conflict.

Check Your Learning

RECALL Describe the factors that seem to contribute to an adolescent's or young adult's sexual orientation.

How and when are teenagers most susceptible to peer pressure?

INTERPRET How might developmental change in peer interactions during infancy and the preschool years be explained by Piaget's stages of cognitive development, described in Module 6.1?

APPLY On page 476, you met Jay, who is the least popular child in his class. Jay's mom is worried about her son's lack of popularity and wants to know what she can do to help her son. Jay's dad thinks that Jay's mom is upset over nothing; he argues that, like fame, popularity is fleeting, and that Jay will turn out okay in the end. What advice would you give to Jay's parents?

 # Electronic Media

OUTLINE

Television

New Media

LEARNING OBJECTIVES

LO6   How does watching television affect children's attitudes and behavior?
How does TV viewing influence children's cognitive development?

LO7   How do children use computers, smartphones, and other digital media?

Whenever Bill visits his granddaughter, Harmony, he is struck by the amount of time Harmony spends watching television. Many of the programs she watches are worthwhile. Nevertheless, Bill wonders if such a steady diet of TV watching might somehow be harmful. Images pop on and off the screen so rapidly that Bill wonders how Harmony will ever learn to pay attention, particularly in other settings that aren't as rich in video stimulation.

In generations past, children learned their culture's values from parents, teachers, religious leaders, and print media. These sources of cultural knowledge are still with us, but they coexist with new technologies that do not always reflect parents' values; these include satellite TV, DVD players, video game players, iPads, smartphones, and the Internet. More forces than ever before can potentially influence children's development. Two of these technologies—television and computers— are the focus of this module. As we look at their influence, we'll see whether Bill's concern for his granddaughter is well founded.

Television

LO6   How does watching television affect children's attitudes and behavior?
How does TV viewing influence children's cognitive development?

The cartoon exaggerates TV's impact on US children, but only somewhat. If you were a typical US child and adolescent, you spent much more time watching TV than interacting with your parents or friends or in school. The numbers tell an incredible story. School-age children spend about 20 to 25 hours each week watching TV (Rideout, Foehr, & Roberts, 2010). Extrapolated through adolescence, the typical US high-school graduate has watched 15,000 hours of TV—nearly 2 full years of watching TV 24/7! No wonder scientists and laypeople alike think TV plays an important role in socializing US children.

For most youngsters, viewing time increases gradually during the preschool and elementary-school years, reaching a peak just before adolescence. Boys watch more TV than girls. Also, children with lower IQs watch more than those with higher IQs; children from lower-income families watch more TV than children from higher-income families (Rideout et al., 2010).

It is hard to imagine that all this TV viewing would not affect children's behavior. For this reason, scientists have been studying the impact of TV since the 1950s. Early research addressed the impact of the medium per se; later research examined the impact of the contents of TV programs (Huston & Wright, 1998). In this section, we'll look at the results of both types of research.

"MRS. HORTON, COULD YOU STOP BY SCHOOL TODAY?"

The Medium is the Message—Or is it? Some critics argue that the medium itself—independent of the contents of programs—harms children (Huston & Wright, 1998). Among the criticisms are these:

- Because TV programs consist of many brief segments presented rapidly, children who watch much TV develop short attention spans and have difficulty concentrating in school.
- Because TV provides ready-made, simple-to-interpret images, children who watch much TV become passive, lazy thinkers and become less creative.
- Children who watch TV often spend less time in more productive and valuable activities, such as reading, participating in sports, and playing with friends.

As stated, none of these criticisms is consistently supported by research. The first criticism—TV watching reduces attention span—is the easiest to dismiss. Research repeatedly shows that increased TV viewing does not lead to reduced attention, greater impulsivity, reduced task persistence, or increased activity levels (Foster & Watkins, 2010). The *contents* of TV programs can influence these dimensions of children's behavior—for example, children who watch impulsive models behave more impulsively themselves—but TV, per se, does not harm children's ability to pay attention. Bill, the grandfather in the opening vignette, need not worry that his granddaughter's TV viewing will limit her ability to pay attention later in life.

As for the criticism that TV viewing fosters lazy thinking and stifles creativity, the evidence is mixed. On the one hand, some educational programs depict people being creative and encourage children to pretend; when children watch these programs frequently, they're often more creative. On the other hand, when children often watch programs that are action oriented, they may be less creative. The content and pacing of these often do not provide viewers with the time to reflect that is essential for creativity (Calvert & Valkenburg, 2013).

Finally, according to the last criticism, TV viewing replaces other socially more desirable activities: The simple-minded view is that every hour of TV viewing replaces an hour of some more valuable activity, such as reading or doing homework. To illustrate the problems with this view, let's look at reading. The correlation between time spent watching TV and reading tends to be negative; heavy TV viewers read less (Ennemoser & Schneider, 2007; Schmidt & Vandewater, 2008). But we need to be cautious in interpreting this correlation (see Figure 1-2 on page 43). The easy interpretation is that watching much TV causes children to read less. However, an alternate interpretation is plausible: Children who are poor readers (and thus are unlikely to spend much time reading) end up watching a lot of TV. For youngsters who read poorly, an hour spent watching TV replaces some activity, but not necessarily an hour that would have been spent reading (Huston & Wright, 1998).

Research does reveal one way in which the medium itself is harmful. In many homes, the TV is on constantly—from morning until bedtime—even though no one is explicitly watching a specific program. In this case, TV is often a powerful distraction. Young children will make frequent, brief glances at the TV, enough to disrupt the quality of their play. Similarly, during parent–child interaction, parents will steal quick looks at the TV, which reduces the quantity and quality of parent–child interactions (Kirkorian et al., 2009; Setliff & Courage, 2011).

When we move past the medium per se and consider the contents of programs, TV does substantially affect children's development (Anderson & Hanson, 2009), as you'll see in the next three sections.

Influence on Attitudes and Social Behavior   Children are definitely influenced by what they see on TV (Browne & Hamilton-Giachritsis, 2005; Huesmann, 2007). On the one hand, children become more aggressive after viewing violence on television (Module 12.4) and adopt gender stereotypes from TV (Module 13.3). In addition, exposure to videos that portray sexual activity can lead teenagers to engage in sex at younger ages (O'Hara et al., 2012). On the other hand, TV watching can also lead to more positive outcomes, helping children become more generous and cooperative and have greater self-control. For example, when children and adolescents watch TV shows that emphasize prosocial behavior (e.g., *Arthur, Dora the Explorer*), they are more likely to behave prosocially, in part because viewing makes them more empathic (Prot et al., 2014; Wilson, 2008). However, prosocial behaviors are portrayed on TV less frequently than aggressive behaviors, so opportunities to learn the former from television are limited; we are far from harnessing the power of television for prosocial uses.

Influence on Consumer Behavior   Sugary cereals, hamburgers and French fries, snack foods, toys, jeans, and athletic shoes—a phenomenal number of TV advertisements for these products are directed toward children and adolescents. A typical US youth may see more than 40,000 commercials in a year (Calvert, 2008)! Children as young as 3 years can distinguish commercials from programs, though preschoolers believe commercials are simply a different form of entertainment—one designed to inform viewers. Not until age 8 or 9 do children begin to understand the persuasive intent of commercials; a few years later, children realize that commercials are not always truthful (Linn, 2005; Oates, Blades, & Gunter, 2002). They understand that a toy rocket will not really fly or that a doll will not really talk, contrary to how they're shown in commercials. However, even school-age children don't fully understand the purpose of advertising that is embedded in programs, such as a character drinking from a can of Coke Zero® (Owen et al., 2012).

Even though children and adolescents come to understand the real intent of commercials, commercials are still effective sales tools (Smith & Atkin, 2003). Children grow to know many of the products advertised on TV (Buijzen, Schuurman, & Bomhof, 2008) and urge parents to buy products they've seen on television. And among adolescents, exposure to TV programs that contain commercials for alcohol (e.g., beer ads) is associated with more frequent drinking of alcohol (Stacy et al., 2004). This selling power of TV has long concerned

Q&A QUESTION 15.2
Brent is a 6-year-old boy who loves to read. His parents wonder whether they should limit his TV viewing because they're afraid it will cut into the time he spends reading. Do research findings suggest that Brent's parents are on the right track?

advocates for children because so many commercials are for foods that have little nutritional value and can lead to obesity and tooth decay. The US government once regulated the amount and type of advertising on children's TV programs (Huston, Watkins, & Kunkel, 1989), but today the responsibility falls largely to parents.

Influence on Cognition The cast of *Sesame Street*, shown in the photo, has been educating preschool children for more than 40 years. Today, mothers and fathers who watched *Sesame Street* as preschoolers are watching with their own youngsters. Remarkably, the time preschool children spend watching *Sesame Street* predicts their grades in high school and the amount of time they spend reading as adolescents (Anderson et al., 2001).

For more than four decades, *Sesame Street* has had tremendous success in helping preschool children acquire many of the skills needed for success in school, such as knowing the names of letters and knowing how to count.

Sesame Street has been joined by programs designed to teach young children about language and reading skills (*Martha Speaks, Super Why!, Word Girl*) and programs that teach basic science and math concepts (*Cyberchase, Curious George, Dinosaur Train, Sid the Science Kid*). Programs like these (and older programs, such as *Electric Company, 3-2-1 Contact*, and *Square One TV*) show that the power of TV can be harnessed to help children learn important academic skills (Ennemoser & Schneider, 2007).

The "Improving Children's Lives" feature includes some guidelines for ensuring that TV's influence on children is positive.

Improving Children's Lives

Get the Kids Off the Couch!

If you know a child who sits glued to the TV screen from after school until bedtime, it's time to act. Here are some suggestions:

- Children need rules concerning the amount of TV and the types of programs that they can watch. These rules should be enforced consistently.

- Children shouldn't fall into the trap of "I'm bored, so I'll watch TV." Children should be encouraged to know what they want to watch *before* they turn on the TV.

- Adults should watch TV with children and discuss the programs. For example, parents can express their disapproval of a character's use of aggression and suggest other means of resolving conflicts. Parents can also point to the stereotypes that are depicted. The aim is for children to learn to watch TV critically.

- Parents need to be good TV viewers themselves. The first two tips listed here apply to viewers of all ages. When a child is present, parents shouldn't watch violent programs or others that are inappropriate for the young. And parents should watch TV deliberately and selectively, instead of mindlessly channel surfing.

New Media

LO7 How do children use computers, smartphones, and other digital media?

Some observers believe that computers, video games, and smartphones are creating a "digital childhood"—an era in which new media are transforming the lives of US children. In this section, we'll look at the impact of these new media on children's development.

Computers in the Classroom New technologies soon find themselves in the classroom. Personal computers are no exception; virtually all US public schools now use personal computers to aid instruction. Computers serve many functions in the classroom (Roschelle et al., 2000). One is that of instructor: As shown in the photo, children use computers to learn reading, spelling, arithmetic, science, and social studies. Computers allow instruction to be individualized and interactive. Students proceed at their own pace, receiving feedback and help when necessary (Hurts, 2008; Roschelle et al., 2010). Computers are also a valuable medium for experiential learning. Simulation programs allow students to explore the world in ways that would be impossible or dangerous otherwise. Students can change the law of gravity or see what happens to a city when no taxes are imposed. Finally, computers can help students achieve traditional academic goals (Steelman, 1994). A graphics program can allow artistically untalented students to produce beautiful illustrations. A word-processing program can relieve much of the drudgery associated with revising, thereby encouraging better writing.

Personal Use of New Media More than 90% of US youth live in homes with a computer and three-fourths have access to a tablet device such as an iPad (Rideout 2013; Rideout et al., 2010). And they begin to use these devices at a remarkably young age; more than a third of US children aged two years or younger have used a mobile device to play games (e.g., *Jake and the Neverland Pirates*) or watch videos (Rideout, 2013). Overall, boys, older children, and children from middle-class homes spend more time using these media than do girls, younger children, and children from lower-class homes (Whitty, 2014).

Most children and adolescents use media to pursue three activities: watching videos such as those posted on YouTube, playing video games, and communicating with peers through social networking sites such as Facebook (Rideout et al., 2010). Viewing videos online likely affects children in much the same way that viewing videos on TV does: content matters. For example, viewing YouTube videos that portray males and females in traditional roles reinforces gender stereotypes.

Similarly, the contents of video games determine their influence on children and adolescents. On the one hand, many games, including *Tetris* and *Star Fox*, emphasize perceptual–spatial skills, such as estimating the trajectory of a moving object, responding rapidly, and shifting efficiently from one task goal to another. When children play such games frequently, they improve their spatial skills, processing speed, and executive functioning (Best, 2014; Mackey et al., 2011; Subrahmanyam et al., 2001). On the other hand, many popular games, such as *Manhunt* and *Grand Theft Auto*, are violent, with players killing game characters in extraordinarily gruesome ways. Just as exposure to televised violence can make children behave more aggressively, playing violent video games can make children more aggressive (Gentile, 2011).

Computerized instruction can be extremely useful because it allows instruction to be individualized and interactive, which allows students to work at their own pace and receive personalized feedback.

What's more, a minority—roughly 10%—of youth get "hooked" on video games (Gentile, 2009). They show many of the same symptoms associated with pathological gambling: Playing video games comes to dominate their lives, it provides a "high," and it leads to conflict with others. Not surprisingly, extreme video-game playing is associated with less success in school, apparently because youth spend time playing games instead of studying (Weis & Cerankosky, 2010).

The third main use of new media is communicating, through social networking sites or via text messages, often through social networking sites such as Facebook, Twitter, and Instagram. Most teens are online daily, typically to connect with friends met offline (Spies Shapiro & Margolin, 2014). Online communication seems to promote self-disclosure, which produces high-quality friendships and, in turn, adolescents' well-being (Valkenburg & Jochen, 2009). And such communication allows youth who are socially unskilled to connect with peers in a more comfortable medium (Spies Shapiro & Margolin, 2014). However, a growing number of youth are subject to cyberbullying in which they are the targets of rude, nasty, or threatening comments posted online. About 10% of youth report being victims of cyberbullying—most of them girls—and they often report lower self-esteem, greater feelings of depression, and increased antisocial behavior (Jones, Mitchell, & Finkelhor, 2013; Patchin, 2013).

In many respects, new technologies have changed the *how* of childhood and adolescence but not the *what*. As with previous generations, children and adolescents still play games, connect with peers, and do homework. Technology like a home computer simply provides a different means for accomplishing these tasks.

Check Your Learning

RECALL Summarize research that has examined the impact on children of TV as a medium.

What are the primary ways in which computers are used in schools?

INTERPRET Compare and contrast the ways in which TV viewing and being online may affect children's development.

APPLY What if you had the authority to write new regulations for children's TV programs? What shows would you encourage? What shows would you want to limit?

 # Institutional Influences

LEARNING OBJECTIVES

LO8 How are children affected by nonparental child care?

LO9 What is the impact of part-time employment on children's development?

LO10 How are children influenced by their neighborhoods?

LO11 What are the hallmarks of effective schools and effective teachers?

OUTLINE

Child Care and After-School Activities

Part-Time Employment

Neighborhoods

School

When 15-year-old Aaron announced that he wanted an after-school job at the local supermarket, his mother was delighted, believing that he would learn much from the experience. Five months later, she had her doubts. Aaron had lost interest in school, and they argued constantly about how he spent his money.

So far in this chapter, we've seen the potent influences of peers and media on children's development. Yet there are other noteworthy influences on children and their development: namely, cultural institutions where children spend much of their lives. In this module, we'll look at four such institutions: day care, the workplace, neighborhoods, and school. As we do, we'll see whether part-time jobs like Aaron's help or harm youth.

Child Care and After-School Activities

LO8 **How are children affected by nonparental child care?**

Each day, millions of US children age 5 and under are cared for by someone other than their mother, a phenomenon linked to more dual-earner couples and to more single-parent households in the United States in the 21st century (US Department of Health and Human Services, Health Resources and Services Administration, Maternal and Child Health Bureau, 2013). Three forms of child care are most common: (1) children stay at home, where they receive care from a relative such as a father or grandparent, (2) children receive care in the home of a child-care provider, and (3) children attend day-care or nursery-school programs.

Many mothers and fathers have misgivings about their children spending so much time in the care of others. Should parents worry? Does nonmaternal care harm children? Before turning to research for answers to these questions, let's put them in historical and cross-cultural perspective. Although nonmaternal care of children is often portrayed as unnatural—and therefore potentially harmful—for much of history and in many cultures, most children have been cared for by someone other than the mother, at least some of the time (Lamb, 1999; Leinaweaver, 2014). When viewed from the larger perspectives of history and other cultures, there is nothing "natural" or "traditional" about mothers having sole responsibility for child care.

Nevertheless, in the United States and many other industrialized countries since World War II, the cultural ideal has been that children are better off when cared for at home by their mothers. Does research support the cultural ideal? In answering this question, most researchers worried about the impact of child care on mother–infant attachment. But, as we saw in Module 10.3, the Early Child-Care study conducted by the National Institute of Child Health and Human Development showed that attachment security was affected by child care only when less sensitive mothers had their infants in low-quality child care.

Similar patterns emerge when researchers study the influence of child care on other aspects of children's development. The most important factor in understanding the impact of child care is the quality of care that children receive: Better care is linked consistently to better outcomes. Children thrive when child care has a relatively small number of children per caregiver (e.g., three infants or toddlers per caregiver) and the caregivers are well-trained, responsive, provide age-appropriate stimulating activities, and communicate well with parents (American Academy of Pedatrics, 2011). For example, when children receive high-quality child care, their cognitive and language development is more advanced (Li et al., 2013). Similarly, children who receive high-quality care tend to be well adjusted and less prone to antisocial, aggressive behavior (Vandell et al., 2010). In contrast, children in low-quality care often fall behind in their cognitive and social development. What's more, the harmful effects of low-quality care on children's development are often multiplied when children are genetically very responsive to the environment (Belsky & Pleuss, 2013), experience less skilled parenting (Burchinal, Vandell, & Belsky, 2014; Watamura et al., 2011), or frequently change from one low-quality program to another (Morrissey, 2009).

Thus, as long as child care is high quality, parents can enroll their youngsters with no fear of harmful consequences. And a side benefit is that when children who attend high-quality care enter school, their mothers are more involved in their child's schooling (Crosnoe, Augustine, & Huston, 2012).

When children enter elementary school, child care becomes easier for working parents. However, many children still need care after school. Historically, after-school programs have focused on recreation: children played games and sports, did arts and crafts, or participated in musical or dramatic productions. Recently, however, many after-school programs have focused more on academics. Children attending such programs often show modest improvements in school achievement, particularly when they attend higher-quality programs (Vandell, Pierce, & Dadisman, 2005).

In addition, many children and adolescents participate in structured activities after school. The most common activities are sports, school clubs, and community service or religious organizations (Fredricks & Eccles, 2006; Larson, Hansen, & Moneta, 2006). As a general rule, children and adolescents benefit from participating: They often are more successful in school, are better adjusted, and are less likely to have behavioral problems (Beal & Crockett, 2010; Feldman Farb & Matjasko, 2012). The main exception is participation in sports, where the findings are mixed. Some studies (e.g., Fauth, Roth, & Brooks-Gunn, 2007) show that adolescents involved in sports are more likely to drink alcohol and to have lower grades. But not all studies report this outcome (e.g., O'Connor & Jose, 2012). The results may depend, for example, on attitudes toward sports in the school and on the specific sports in which the child is involved (Metzger et al., 2011; Wilson et al., 2010).

Of course, some students participate in many activities, and such diverse participation is beneficial. Students who participate in multiple school activities tend to be better adjusted, more successful in school, less prone to drug use, and more involved in their communities (Feldman Farb & Matjasko, 2012; Fredricks & Eccles, 2006). This may surprise you in light of media reports that US youth—particularly affluent youth—are stressed out because they're overscheduled after school. But research suggests that most teenagers are not distressed by a busy after-school schedule; most children participate in activities because they enjoy them, not because they're pressured into them by achievement-oriented parents (Luthar, Shoum, & Brown, 2006).

Finally, many school-age children and adolescents—about one-third of US middle-school students and one-half of high-school students—care for themselves after school at least once a week (Mahoney & Parente, 2009). **Children who care for themselves are sometimes called** *latchkey children,* **a term that originated more than 200 years ago to describe children who raised a door latch to enter their own homes.** Some latchkey children, like the child in the photo, stay at home alone (sometimes with parental supervision in absentia via phone calls and text messages). Others may stay at friends' homes where adults are sometimes present, or they may be unsupervised in public places such as shopping malls.

The popular perception is that latchkey children are a frightened, endangered lot. In fact, research suggests that self-care can be risky under certain circumstances. Youth who care for themselves can get into trouble—abuse alcohol and drugs, become aggressive, and begin to fail in school—when they spend their

Many US children care for themselves after school, an arrangement that can be safe, depending on the child's age and maturity, the neighborhood, and the rules established for the child.

after-school hours away from home, unsupervised, and when they live in neighborhoods plagued by high crime rates. When these circumstances don't apply, older children and adolescents can care for themselves successfully (Mahoney & Parente, 2009).

Parents need to consider several factors when deciding whether they can leave their child home alone (Child Welfare Information Gateway, 2013). At the top of the list is the child's age—many experts recommend that children are not capable of self-care until they're 12, but others say that some 8-year-olds can care for themselves briefly (1 to 1½ hours) during the day. More important than age is the child's maturity: Is the child responsible? Does the child make good decisions on his or her own? Parents should also consider the child's attitudes and feelings about being left alone: Is the child anxious about being alone in the house? Finally, it's important for parents to consider their neighborhood: Is it safe? Are there trusted neighbors that the child can turn to if necessary?

If questions like these can be answered yes, then self-care will probably work. But it's important that children be prepared for self-care. They need to know after-school routines (e.g., acceptable ways of getting home from school and how to check in with a parent), rules for their own behavior after school (e.g., acceptable and unacceptable activities), guidelines on how to handle emergencies, and emergency phone numbers (Child Welfare Information Gateway, 2013).

Part-Time Employment

LO9 **What is the impact of part-time employment on children's development?**

The teens in the photo are engaged in a U.S. adolescent ritual: the part-time job. More than half of today's high-school seniors hold part-time jobs, typically in retail (Bachman et al., 2011; U.S. Department of Labor, 2000). Many adults praise teens for working, believing that early exposure to the workplace teaches self-discipline, self-confidence, and important job skills. However, for many adolescents part-time work is harmful, for several reasons:

1. **School performance suffers.** When students work more than approximately 20 hours per week, they become less engaged in school and are less likely to be successful in college, particularly if they are relatively affluent European Americans (Bachman et al., 2013; Monahan, Lee, & Steinberg, 2011). Many high-school students apparently do not have the foresight and discipline necessary to consistently meet the combined demands of work and school.

2. **Teens experience mental health and behavioral problems.** Adolescents who work more than 20 hours a week are more likely to experience anxiety and depression, and their self-esteem often suffers. Many adolescents find themselves in jobs that are repetitive and boring but stressful, and such conditions undermine self-esteem and breed anxiety. Extensive part-time work frequently leads to substance abuse and frequent problem behavior (e.g., antisocial behavior, including theft), especially for younger teens who attend school sporadically (Monahan et al., 2011; Monahan, Steinberg, & Cauffman, 2013).

Many US adolescents hold part-time jobs; these can be beneficial, but not when adolescents work more than 15-20 hours weekly.

Why employment is associated with all of these problems is not clear. Perhaps employed adolescents turn to drugs to help them cope with the anxiety and depression brought on by work. Arguments with parents may become more common because anxious, depressed adolescents are more prone to argue or because wage-earning adolescents may believe that their freedom should match their income. Whatever the exact mechanism, extensive part-time work is clearly detrimental to the mental health of most adolescents.

3. **Teens learn bad habits for handling money.** Adults sometimes argue that work is good for teenagers because it teaches them "the value of a dollar," but the typical teenage pattern is "earn and spend." Working adolescents spend most of their earnings on themselves—to buy clothing, snack food, or cosmetics, and to pay for entertainment. Few working teens set aside much of their income for future goals, such as a college education, or use it to contribute to their family's expenses (Shanahan et al., 1996a, 1996b). Because parents customarily pay for many of the essential expenses associated with truly independent living—rent, utilities, and groceries, for example—working adolescents often have a vastly higher percentage of their income available for discretionary spending than working adults. Thus, for many teens, part-time work provides unrealistic expectations about how income can be allocated (Darling et al., 2006; Zhang, Cartmill, & Ferrence, 2008).

The message that emerges repeatedly from research on part-time employment is hardly encouraging. Like Aaron, the teenage boy in the vignette, many adolescents who work long hours at part-time jobs do not benefit from the experience. Instead, they do worse in school, are more likely to have behavioral problems, and learn how to spend money rather than how to manage it. These effects are similar for adolescents from different ethnic groups (Steinberg & Dornbusch, 1991) and are comparable for boys and girls (Bachman & Schulenberg, 1993). Ironically, though, there is a long-term benefit: Young adults who had a stressful part-time job as an adolescent are better able to cope with stressful adult jobs (Mortimer & Staff, 2004).

Does this mean that teenagers who are still in school should never work part-time? Not necessarily. Part-time employment *can* be a good experience, depending on the circumstances. One key is the number of hours of work: Most students could easily work 5 hours weekly without harm, and many could work 10 hours weekly. Another key is the type of job. When adolescents have jobs that allow them to use existing skills (e.g., computing), acquire new skills, and receive effective mentoring, self-esteem is enhanced, and they learn from their work experience (Staff & Schulenberg, 2010; Vazsonyi & Snider, 2008). Yet another factor is the link between work and school: Teens often benefit from apprenticeships or internships that are explicitly linked to school so that work experiences complement classroom experiences (Symonds, Schwartz, & Ferguson, 2011). A final factor is how teens spend their earnings. When they save their money or use it to pay for clothes and school expenses, relations with their parents often improve and teens learn to balance saving and spending (Marsh & Kleitman, 2005; Shanahan et al., 1996b).

By these criteria, who is likely to show the harmful effects of part-time work? A teen who spends 30 hours a week bagging groceries and spends most of it on CDs or videos. And who is likely to benefit from part-time work? A teen who likes to tinker with cars, who spends Saturdays working in a repair shop, and who sets aside some of his earnings for college.

 QUESTION 15.3

Nick is a 16-year-old who would love to have a career in the entertainment industry—TV, movies, or maybe in music. For now, he works two nights a week (about 8 hours total) as an usher at a local movie theater. At his parents' request, one-third of his take-home pay goes into a college fund. Is this part-time job likely to be harmful to Nick?

Finally, summer jobs typically do not involve conflict between work and school. Consequently, many of the harmful effects associated with part-time employment during the school year do not hold for summer employment. In fact, such employment sometimes enhances adolescents' self-esteem, especially when they save part of their income for future plans (Marsh, 1991).

Neighborhoods

LO10 How are children influenced by their neighborhoods?

For years, Mr. Rogers welcomed preschool children into a neighborhood that was safe and nurturing. Unfortunately, not all children are so fortunate; their neighborhoods are neither safe nor nurturing. Do these differences in neighborhoods affect children's lives? Yes; all other things being equal, children benefit from living in a neighborhood where most of the adults are well educated and economically advantaged. These benefits are seen for both school achievement and psychological adjustment. In other words, when children live in economically advantaged neighborhoods, they tend to do better in school and are somewhat less likely to have behavioral and emotional problems (Ackerman & Brown, 2006; Murray et al., 2011).

Researchers agree that neighborhoods per se do not influence children's behavior. Instead, as we would expect from the contextual model of parenting (described in Module 14.1), the impact of neighborhoods is indirect, transmitted through people (mainly parents and peers) and other social institutions. Several pathways of influence are possible (Leventhal & Brooks-Gunn, 2000). One concerns the availability of institutional resources: Economically advantaged neighborhoods more often have the kinds of resources that enhance children's development: libraries, museums, quality day care, and good schools to foster children's cognitive development; medical services to provide for children's physical and mental health; and opportunities for adolescents to find work. In economically advantaged neighborhoods that tend to have these resources, children are more likely to have experiences that lead to school success, to good health, and to the ability to find part-time jobs as teenagers. In contrast, in economically disadvantaged neighborhoods that frequently lack these resources, children are often prepared inadequately for school, receive little medical care, and are unable to find jobs as teenagers, so they turn to delinquent or criminal behavior.

A second way in which neighborhoods affect children and adolescents is based on the fact that, because economically advantaged neighborhoods are more likely to be stable, they are more cohesive and close-knit, which means residents take a greater interest in neighborhood events and activities, including those of children and adolescents (Chung & Steinberg, 2006; Odgers et al., 2009). Suppose, for example, adults see the two boys in the photo slugging it out in the park. In a cohesive neighborhood, adults are more likely to intervene (e.g., break up the fight and scold the children for fighting) because they are committed to its residents; in a less cohesive neighborhood, adults

People living in poorer neighborhoods are less likely to know their neighbors and consequently, are less likely to get involved in their neighbors' lives; for example, when children are fighting, they may be reluctant to stop the fight because they don't know the children.

might ignore the children because they don't want the hassle of getting involved. Thus, in cohesive neighborhoods, residents more often monitor the activities of neighborhood children, making it more difficult for children to get into trouble.

Yet another link between poverty and children's development reflects the fact that when children live in poverty, their home life is often described as chaotic (Chen, Cohen, & Miller, 2010). Their residence is often crowded and noisy and their lives are often relatively unstructured and unpredictable. For example, children may not have a set time for doing homework, or even a place to do it. Living in such chaos often engenders a sense of helplessness: Children feel as if they have little control over their own lives, and these feelings of helplessness are often associated with mental health problems and school failure (Bradley & Corwyn, 2002; Evans et al., 2005). In addition, when children experience chronic poverty, as adults they're often less healthy because constant exposure to poverty-related stress overwhelms the developing child's physiological systems that battle stress (Evans & Kim, 2013; Hostinar & Gunnar, 2013). This begins very early: When a mother responds physiologically to stress, her baby does too (Waters, West, & Mendes, 2014).

Finally, neighborhoods affect children through their impact on parenting behavior. One account of this link is the focus of the "Spotlight on Theories" feature.

Spotlight on Theories
The Family Economic Stress Model

BACKGROUND The harmful effects of poverty on children have been known for decades; but only recently have researchers attempted to understand the many different ways in which poverty harms children. Among the most difficult to understand is the way in which poverty causes children to receive less effective parenting.

THE THEORY Adults living in chronic poverty often experience much stress, from constantly worrying about whether they will have enough money to buy food and clothing or to pay rent. Rand Conger and Glen Elder (1994) proposed the Family Economic Stress Model (FESM) to explain how such poverty-induced stress could affect children's development. According to the FESM, economic hardship results in a series of consequences:

1. Parents find that their income is not adequate to meet their needs.

2. This economic pressure affects parents' mental health, causing some to become depressed.

3. Once depressed, the quality of the marital relationship declines.

4. This results in less effective parenting (parents are not as warm with their children, praise them

less frequently, and instead, are often angry and impatient with them).

5. Because children receive less effective parenting, behavioral problems are common (e.g., children become anxious or angry).

Thus, in the FESM, poverty harms children's development because parents struggling to make ends meet become depressed and parent less effectively.

Hypothesis: When parents' economic situation changes for the worse—for example, one or both parents lose a job and can't find a comparable new job—this should start the cascade of consequences described in the FESM: Diminished income causes economic stress, which leads to depression, which leads to marital conflict and ineffective parenting, which finally disrupts children's development.

Test: Solantaus, Leinonen, and Punamäki (2004) provided a novel evaluation of this hypothesis by looking at families in Finland in the early 1990s, when that country experienced a deep economic decline that compared to the Great Depression in the United States in the 1930s. They took advantage of the fact that a large cross-section of Finnish families had been studied in the late 1980s, before the onset of the depression. Children and their families were studied again in 1994 when the economic recession was at its peak. Solantaus and colleagues obtained measures of all the key constructs in the FESM: family economic hardship, parental mental health, quality of marital interaction, parenting quality, and children's mental health. All were measured with questionnaires, which were completed by parents, children, and the children's teachers. Each of the links in the FESM was supported: (1) families who experienced more economic pressure reported more mental health problems, (2) parents who had more mental problems reported that their marriages were less satisfying, (3) a less-satisfying marriage was associated with lower-quality parenting, and (4) lower-quality parenting was associated with more frequent mental health problems in children.

Conclusion: Solantaus and colleagues found the outcomes predicted by the FESM: Economic hardship triggered a sequence of events that ultimately harmed children's mental health. As they phrased it, "[The family] is a relationship unit, but it is also an economic unit....This means that economic and relationship issues are intertwined, making the relationships vulnerable when the economy collapses" (2004, p. 425).

Application: Based on these findings, we can add "improving children's mental health" to the long list of reasons to eliminate poverty. Until that happens, these findings and the FESM remind us of the difficulties of parenting effectively while living in poverty. Families living in poverty often need immediate help (e.g., services for parents and children who have mental health problems) as they pursue their longer-term goal of leaving poverty.

Chronic poverty is particularly hard for parents because they usually have few social supports to help them cope with stress. When adults living in economically advantaged neighborhoods find life so stressful that they need help, they can turn to neighbors or health care professionals. In contrast, adults living in poverty are less likely to turn either to a neighbor (because they don't know anyone well enough because of instability in the neighborhood) or to a health care professional (because one is not available nearby or they can't afford it). In other words, adults living in chronic poverty experience a "double whammy"—more stress and fewer resources to cope with stress—that contributes to less effective parenting.

Thus, children growing up in economically disadvantaged neighborhoods typically have access to fewer institutional resources, are monitored less often by neighbors, often lead chaotic lives, and experience less effective parenting brought on by chronic stress. At the same time, research suggests that an effective way to invest in poverty-ridden neighborhoods is by providing additional institutional resources (Huston et al., 2005). When neighborhoods have good child care and good schools, many opportunities for recreation, and effective health care, children benefit directly. They also benefit indirectly because when parents feel less stress, they parent more effectively, and because residents are less likely to move, contributing to neighborhood cohesiveness. And boosting family income—either by providing cash supplements or increasing tax credits—increases children's achievement (Duncan & Magnuson, 2012).

Neighborhoods—be they advantaged or disadvantaged—are usually relatively stable institutions where change occurs gradually, over months or years. But sometimes neighborhoods or entire communities are affected by disasters (e.g., floods, earthquakes, industrial accidents). In the United States, roughly one child in seven will experience some sort of disaster during childhood or adolescence (Becker-Blease, Turner, & Finkelhor, 2010). Not surprisingly, exposure to disasters is traumatic for

Exposure to disasters such as Hurricane Katrina is stressful for youth, particularly when they're younger, dealing with other stresses in their lives, and don't regulate their emotions well.

children; mental health problems such as depression are frequent following exposure to disasters and risks typically increase with the degree of exposure (Masten & Narayan, 2012).

Other children experience upheaval because their neighborhoods are the site of political violence. Children living in such neighborhoods are more anxious, more depressed, and more aggressive, often because political violence undermines the child's view that their neighborhood is safe and stable (Cummings et al., 2014). Still other children lack neighborhoods altogether; they're homeless or often moving from one temporary residence to another. Not surprisingly, children living in these conditions are often less successful in school and are at risk for behavioral problems (Masten et al., 2014).

However, as we've seen several times before, children and adolescents respond differently to adversity. Youth cope better with a disaster-related adversity when they're not also trying to deal with other family- or school-related stress, when they're better able to regulate their emotions and behavior, and in the case of political violence, when they identify strongly with their ethnic group (Cummings et al., 2014; Kithakye et al., 2010; Kronenberg et al., 2010; Masten et al., 2014). However, for children who do not cope well with this adversity, cognitive-behavioral treatment can help modify their disaster-related thinking and teach them ways to respond to stress-related feelings (LaGreca & Silverman, 2009). Following a disaster, all children are helped when familiar institutions are restored as soon as possible. Foremost among these are schools (Masten & Osofsky, 2010), which are the focus of the next (and last!) section.

School

LO11 What are the hallmarks of effective schools and effective teachers?

At age 5 or 6, most US children head off to kindergarten, starting an educational journey that lasts 13 years for most and more than 17 years for some. How do schools influence children's development? Answering this question is difficult because US education is a smorgasbord, reflecting local control by communities throughout the United States. Schools differ on many dimensions, including their emphasis on academic goals and parent involvement. Teachers, too, differ in many ways, such as how they run their classrooms and how they teach. These and other variables affect how much students learn, as you'll see in the next few pages. Let's begin with school-based influences.

School-Based Influences on Student Achievement   Roosevelt High School, in the center of Detroit, has an enrollment of 3,500 students in grades 9 to 12. Opened in 1936, the building shows its age. The rooms are drafty, the desks are decorated with generations of graffiti, and new technology means an overhead projector. Nevertheless, attendance at Roosevelt is good, most students graduate, and many continue their education at community colleges and state universities. Southport High School, in Boston, has about the same enrollment as Roosevelt High and the building is about the same age. Yet truancy is commonplace at Southport, where fewer than half the students graduate and almost none go to college.

These schools are hypothetical, but accurately portray US education. Some schools are much more successful than others, regardless of whether success is defined in terms of the percentage of students who are literate, graduate, or go to college. Why are some schools successful and not others? Researchers (DuBois et al., 2011; El Nokali, Bachman, & Votruba-Drzal, 2010;

Successful schools encourage parents to become involved; for example, they may encourage parents to tutor students.

Good & Brophy, 2008; Pianta, 2007) have identified a number of factors linked with successful schools:

- *Staff and students alike understand that academic excellence is the primary goal and standards are set accordingly.* The school day emphasizes instruction, and students are recognized publicly for their academic accomplishments.
- *The school climate is safe and nurturing.* Students know that they can devote their energy to learning (instead of worrying about being harmed in school), and they know the staff truly wants to see them succeed.
- *Parents are involved.* In some cases, this may be through formal arrangements, such as parent–teacher organizations. Or it may be informal. Parents may spend some time each week in school grading papers or, like the mom in the photo, tutoring a child. Such involvement signals both teachers and students that parents are committed to students' success.
- *Mentoring programs allow children and adolescents to learn from nonparental adults.* When youth come under the guidance of adults who have similar interests to theirs and who are supported in their advocacy and teaching roles, youth do better in school and improve their self-esteem as well as their peer relationships; these effects are often largest for children and adolescents at risk.
- *Progress of students, teachers, and programs is monitored.* The only way to know if schools are succeeding is by measuring performance. Students, teachers, and programs must be evaluated regularly, using objective measures that reflect academic goals. In schools that follow these guidelines, students usually succeed. In schools where the guidelines are ignored, students more often fail.

Of course, on a daily basis, individual teachers have the most potential for impact. Let's see how teachers can influence their students' achievement.

Teacher-Based Influences   Take a moment to recall your teachers in elementary school, junior high, and high school. Some you probably remember fondly, because they were enthusiastic and innovative and they made learning fun. You may remember others with bitterness. They seemed to have lost their love of teaching and children, making class a living hell. Your experience tells you that some teachers are better than others, but what exactly makes a good teacher? Personality and enthusiasm are not the key elements. Although you may enjoy warm and eager teachers, research (Good & Brophy, 2008; Gregory et al., 2014; Pianta, 2007; Walberg, 1995) shows that several other factors are critical when it comes to students' achievement. Students tend to learn the most when teachers:

- *Manage the classroom effectively so they can devote most of their time to instruction.* When teachers spend a lot of time disciplining students, or when students do not move smoothly from one class activity to the next, instructional time is wasted, and students are apt to learn less.
- *Believe they are responsible for their students' learning and that their students will learn when taught well.* When students don't understand a new topic, these teachers repeat the original instruction (in case the student missed something) or create new instruction (in case the student heard everything but just didn't "get it"). These teachers keep plugging away because they feel at fault if students don't learn.
- *Pay careful attention to pacing.* They present material slowly enough that students can understand a new concept, but not so slowly that students get bored.

- *Emphasize mastery of topics*. Teachers should introduce a topic, then give students many opportunities to understand, practice, and apply the topic. Just as you'd find it hard to go directly from driver's ed to driving a race car, students more often achieve when they grasp a new topic thoroughly, then gradually move on to other, more advanced topics.
- *Teach actively*. The best teachers don't just talk or give students an endless stream of worksheets. Instead, they demonstrate topics concretely or have hands-on demonstrations for students. They also have students participate in class activities and encourage students to interact, generating ideas and solving problems together.
- *Value tutoring*. Good teachers work with students individually or in small groups, so they can gear their instruction to each student's level and check each student's understanding. They also encourage peer tutoring, in which more capable students tutor less capable students. Children who are tutored by peers do learn, and so do the tutors, evidently because teaching helps tutors organize their knowledge.
- *Teach children techniques for monitoring and managing their own learning*. Students are more likely to achieve when they are taught how to recognize the aims of school tasks and know effective strategies for achieving those aims (like those described on pages 216–218).
- *Have access to resources that allow them to improve their teaching*. When teachers work directly with an expert teacher who provides feedback about their current teaching and offers evidence-based methods to improve it, their students fare better.

Thus, what makes for effective schools and teachers? No single element is crucial. Instead, many factors contribute to make some schools and teachers remarkably effective. Some of the essential ingredients include parents who are involved, teachers who care deeply about their students' learning and manage classrooms well, and a school that is safe, nurturing, and emphasizes achievement.

Of course, many schools are not successful. However, as parents, teachers, and concerned citizens, we need to resist the idea that any single magic potion can cure a school's ills. As we have seen throughout this book, the outcome of development—in this case, academic achievement—is determined by many factors, including environmental forces (e.g., parents, teachers) as well as the contributions of children themselves. To foster academic success, we need to consider all these factors and not focus narrowly on only one or two.

Finally, as we consider the features of effective schools and effective teachers, it's important to remember that children's skills when they enter school are powerful predictors of their achievement in school. Longitudinal studies clearly show that kindergarten children who know letters, some words, numbers, and simple quantitative concepts are on the path to success in school; this is true regardless of a child's socioeconomic status or ethnicity (Duncan et al., 2007; Marks & García Coll, 2007). Of course, as we've seen repeatedly, continuity across development is not perfect: Some 5-year-olds who don't know their numbers will get As in calculus as high-school seniors. But they're the exception, not the rule. Consequently, it's crucial for children to begin kindergarten with a solid foundation of pre-reading and pre-arithmetic skills.

On a more general note, understanding why and how children succeed in school (and in other domains of life) is indeed a challenging puzzle. Nevertheless, scientists are making remarkable progress in solving the child-development puzzle; as we end the book, I hope you've enjoyed learning about their discoveries. Thanks for reading.

Check Your Learning

RECALL What is known about the impact of part-time employment on adolescents?

Summarize the ways in which poverty can influence children's development.

INTERPRET Compare and contrast the ways in which schools (as institutions) affect children's learning with the ways in which teachers affect children's learning.

APPLY Imagine that you've taken a new job, which means that your 10-year-old daughter would need to care for herself at home from after school until about 6:00 P.M. What would you do to decide whether she's capable of such self-care? If you decided that she is capable, what would you do to prepare her?

 # Unifying Themes   Continuity

In this last chapter of the book, I want to remind you that *early development is related to later development, but not perfectly.* Children who are rejected by their peers are, over time, more likely to do poorly in school, have lower self-esteem, and have behavioral problems. Of course, not all rejected children suffer this fate. Some do well in school, have high self-esteem, and avoid behavioral problems. Positive outcomes are more likely to occur when children learn effective skills for interacting with others. As we've seen many times in previous chapters, early experiences often point children toward a particular developmental path, but later experiences can cause them to change course.

See for Yourself

The best way to understand the differences between good and bad teaching is to visit some actual school classrooms. Try to visit three or four classes in at least two different schools. (You can usually arrange this by speaking with the school's principal.) Take along the principles of good teaching that are listed on pages 492–493. Start by watching how the teachers and children interact; then decide how much the teacher relies on each of the principles. You'll probably see that most teachers use some but not all of these principles. You'll also see that, in today's classroom, consistently following all the principles is challenging. See for yourself!

Summary

 ### 15.1 Peers

Development of Peer Interactions

Children's first real social interactions, at about 12 to 15 months, take the form of parallel play, in which infants play alone while watching each other. At about 2 years, cooperative play organized around a theme becomes common.

Make-believe play is also common and, in addition to being fun, promotes cognitive development and lets children examine frightening topics. Most solitary play is harmless. Parents foster children's play by acting as skilled playmates, serving as social director for their children, coaching social skills, and mediating disputes.

Beyond preschool, peer relations improve and emphasize talking and being together, as well as rough-and-tumble play.

Friendship

Friendships among preschoolers are based on common interests and getting along well. As children grow, loyalty, trust, and intimacy become more important features in their friendships. Friends are usually similar in age, sex, race, and attitudes. Children with friends are more skilled socially and better adjusted.

Romantic Relationships

For younger adolescents, romantic relationships offer companionship and the possibility of sexual exploration;

for older adolescents, they provide trust and support. Pregnancy is common because many adolescents engage in unprotected sex. Comprehensive sex education is effective in reducing teenage sexual activity. Adolescents often wonder about their sexual orientation, but only a small percentage report having homosexual experiences.

Groups

Older children and adolescents often form cliques— small groups of like-minded individuals that become part of a crowd. Members of higher-status crowds often have higher self-esteem.

Most groups have a dominance hierarchy, a well-defined structure with a leader at the top. Physical power often determines the dominance hierarchy, particularly among younger boys. With older children and adolescents, dominance hierarchies are more often based on skills that are important to group functioning.

Peers are particularly influential when standards of behavior are unclear, such as for taste in music or clothing, or concerning drinking.

Popularity and Rejection

Many popular children are socially skilled; they generally share, cooperate, and help others. Other popular children use aggression to achieve social goals. Some children are rejected by their peers because they are too aggressive; others are rejected for being shy. Both groups of rejected children are often unsuccessful in school and have behavioral problems.

Electronic Media

Television

Many popular criticisms about TV as a medium (e.g., it shortens children's attention span) are not supported by research. However, the content of TV programs can affect children. Youngsters who frequently watch prosocial TV become more skilled socially, and preschoolers who watch programs like *Sesame Street* improve their academic skills and adjust more readily to school.

New Media

Computers are used in school as tutors, to provide experiential learning, and as a multipurpose tool to achieve traditional academic goals. At home, children use computers to play video games (and are influenced by the contents of the games they play) and to communicate with friends via the Internet.

Institutional Influences

Child Care and After-School Activities

Many US children are cared for by a father or other relative, in a day-care provider's home, or in a day-care center. When children attend high-quality child care, this fosters their cognitive and socio-emotional development. After-school programs and structured activities are often beneficial, too. Children can care for themselves after school if they are mature enough, live in a safe neighborhood, and are monitored by a parent.

Part-Time Employment

Adolescents who are employed more than 15–20 hours per week during the school year typically do poorly in school, often have lowered self-esteem and increased anxiety, and have problems interacting with others. Employed adolescents save relatively little of their income. Instead, they spend most of it on themselves, which can give misleading expectations about how to allocate income.

Part-time employment can be beneficial if adolescents work relatively few hours, if the work allows them to develop skills and is linked to school, and if teens save some of their earnings. Summer employment can also be beneficial.

Neighborhoods

Children are more likely to thrive when they grow up in a neighborhood that is economically advantaged and stable. These neighborhoods are better for children because more institutional resources (e.g., schools) are available, because residents are more likely to monitor neighborhood children's behavior, because home life is predictable, and because parents are not living in the chronic stress associated with poverty.

School

Schools influence students' achievement in many ways. Students are most likely to achieve when their school emphasizes academic excellence, has a safe and nurturing environment, monitors pupils' and teachers' progress, and encourages parents to be involved.

Students achieve at higher levels when their teachers manage classrooms effectively, take responsibility for their students' learning, teach mastery of material, pace material well, value tutoring, and show children how to monitor their own learning.

Test Yourself

1. In _____, which emerges at about two years of age, children organize their play around a distinct theme and take on special roles based on the theme.
   a. parallel
   b. cooperative
   c. associative

2. _____ play allows children to explore topics that frighten them.
   a. Make-believe
   b. Solitary
   c. Parallel

3. A new feature of friendships in adolescence is _____.
   a. mutual liking
   b. trust
   c. intimacy

4. Which of the following is an *incorrect* statement concerning romantic relationships?
   a. Romantic relationships build on friendships.
   b. Hispanic American and Asian American adolescents often date at older ages.
   c. Adolescents in romantic relationships typically have lower self-esteem and lack self confidence.

5. Peer pressure _____.
   a. is a powerful influence on adolescents, one that easily leads them to behave antisocially
   b. is especially powerful when children are forging an identity
   c. is strongest when standards for behavior are clear-cut

6. Children who are rejected _____.
   a. often feel lonely, dislike school, and commit juvenile offenses
   b. are almost always shy, withdrawn, and timid
   c. often have parents who were consistent in their discipline

7. When children watch much TV, _____.
   a. they have difficulty concentrating in school
   b. they are sometimes found to be less creative
   c. this causes them to read less well

8. Select the *correct* statement concerning the impact of TV programs on children.
   a. Children can learn aggressive behavior from TV programs but not prosocial behavior
   b. Preschool children understand that the goal of commercials is to persuade viewers
   c. Programs like *Sesame Street* can teach children important academic skills

9. When personal computers are used in schools to aid instruction, students _____.
   a. receive feedback but instruction is not individualized
   b. cannot proceed at their own pace
   c. can use simulation programs for experiential learning

10. When children play video games _____.
    a. they learn aggressive behaviors but do not improve their perceptual–spatial skills
    b. unlike TV, they are unaffected by the contents of the games they play
    c. a small percentage become addicted to game playing

11. Research on the impact of day care on children shows that _____.
    a. most children who attend day care do not become emotionally attached to their mothers
    b. the quality of care is the most important factor: Better care is associated with better outcomes
    c. children thrive in day care regardless of the quality of the caregivers

12. Participating in after-school activities is _____.
    a. beneficial, except perhaps for participating in sports
    b. beneficial but only when children participate in a single activity, not multiple activities
    c. is much more beneficial than having children care for themselves because such latchkey children almost always get into trouble

13. Part-time employment _____.
    a. is harmful regardless of the amount of time that adolescents work
    b. is less harmful than summer employment
    c. can cause adolescents to be less successful in school and become depressed

14. Poverty-stricken neighborhoods _____.
    a. are more likely to be close-knit and provide more monitoring of neighborhood children
    b. often cause adults to experience more stress, leading to less effective parenting
    c. typically have access to more resources

15. Which of the following teachers is likely to be most effective?
    a. One who spends much time disciplining students, thereby creating a quiet classroom.
    b. One who understands that some students will not learn regardless of the type of instruction.
    c. One who teaches students techniques for monitoring their own learning.

Key Terms

associative play   464

clique   474

cooperative play   464

co-rumination   470

crowd   474

dominance hierarchy   475

friendship   468

latchkey children   485

parallel play   464

rough-and-tumble play   468

Glossary

A

accommodation According to Piaget, changing existing knowledge based on new knowledge.

achievement The identity status in Marcia's theory in which adolescents have explored alternative identities and are now secure in their chosen identities.

active–passive child issue The issue of whether children are simply at the mercy of the environment (passive child) or actively influence their own development through their own unique individual characteristics (active child).

adolescent egocentrism The self-absorption that is characteristic of teenagers as they search for identity.

African American English A dialect of Standard English spoken by some African Americans; has slightly different grammatical rules than Standard English.

age of viability The age at which a fetus can survive because most of its bodily systems function adequately, typically at 7 months after conception.

aggression Behavior meant to harm others.

allele A variation of a specific gene.

altruism Prosocial behavior, such as helping and sharing, in which the individual does not benefit directly from his or her behavior.

amniocentesis A prenatal diagnostic technique that involves withdrawing a sample of amniotic fluid through the abdomen using a syringe.

amniotic fluid Fluid in the amnion that cushions the embryo and maintains a constant temperature.

amniotic sac An inner sac in which the developing child will rest.

amodal information Information that can be presented to different senses, such as duration, rate, and intensity.

analytic ability In Sternberg's theory of intelligence, the ability to analyze problems and generate different solutions.

androgens Hormones secreted by the testes that influence aggressive behavior.

androgynous Having a combination of gender-role traits that includes both instrumental and expressive behaviors.

animism A phenomenon, common in preschool children, in which they attribute life and lifelike properties to inanimate objects.

anorexia nervosa A persistent refusal to eat, accompanied by an irrational fear of being overweight.

Apgar score A measure to evaluate the newborn's condition, based on breathing, heart rate, muscle tone, presence of reflexes, and skin tone.

applied developmental science A scientific discipline that uses child-development research to promote healthy development, particularly for vulnerable children and families.

assimilation According to Piaget, taking in information that is compatible with what one already knows.

associative play A form of play in which toddlers engage in similar activities, talk or smile at one another, and offer each other toys.

attachment The affectionate, reciprocal relationship that is formed at about 6 or 7 months between an infant and his or her primary caregiver, usually the mother.

attention Processes that determine which information will be processed further by an individual.

auditory threshold The quietest sound that a person can hear.

authoritarian parenting A style of parenting that combines high levels of control with low levels of warmth toward children.

authoritative parenting A style of parenting that combines a moderate degree of behavioral control with being warm and responsive toward children.

authority-oriented grandparents Grandparents who provide discipline for their grandchildren but otherwise are not particularly active in their grandchildren's lives.

autobiographical memory A person's memory of the significant events and experiences of his or her own life.

automatic processes Cognitive activities that require virtually no effort.

autosomes The first 22 pairs of chromosomes.

avoidant attachment A relationship in which infants turn away from their mothers when they are reunited following a brief separation.

axon A tubelike structure that emerges from the cell body and transmits information to other neurons.

B

babbling Speechlike sounds that consist of vowel–consonant combinations.

baby biographies Detailed, systematic observations of individual children, often by famous scientists, that helped to pave the way for objective research on children.

basic cry A cry that starts softly and gradually becomes more intense; often heard when babies are hungry or tired.

basic emotions Emotions that are experienced by people worldwide and that consist of a subjective feeling, a physiological change, and an overt behavior; examples include happiness, anger, and fear.

behavioral genetics The branch of genetics that deals with inheritance of behavioral and psychological traits.

blastocyst The fertilized egg 4 days after conception; consists of about 100 cells and resembles a hollow ball.

blended family A family consisting of a biological parent, a stepparent, and children.

body mass index (BMI)   An adjusted ratio of weight to height used to define overweight.

breech presentation   A birth in which the feet or bottom are delivered first, before the head.

bulimia nervosa   An eating disorder in which individuals alternate between bingeing (when they eat uncontrollably) and purging through self-induced vomiting or with laxatives.

C

cardinality principle   The counting principle that the last number name denotes the number of objects being counted.

cell body   The center of the neuron that keeps the neuron alive.

central executive   The component of the information-processing system, analogous to a computer's operating system, that coordinates the activities of the system.

centration   Narrowly focused thinking characteristic of Piaget's preoperational stage.

cerebral cortex   The wrinkled surface of the brain that regulates many distinctly human functions.

cesarean section (C-section)   A surgical procedure in which an incision is made in the mother's abdomen to remove the baby from the uterus.

chorionic villus sampling (CVS)   A prenatal diagnostic technique that involves taking a sample of tissue from the chorion.

chromosomes   Threadlike structures in the nucleus of the cell that contain genetic material.

chronosystem   In Bronfenbrenner's systems view, the idea that the microsystem, mesosystem, exosystem, and macrosystem are not static but change over time.

clique   Small groups of friends who are similar in age, sex, race, and interests.

cognitive-developmental perspective   An approach to development that focuses on how children think and on how their thinking changes over time.

cognitive self-regulation   Skill at identifying goals, selecting effective strategies, and accurate monitoring; a characteristic of successful students.

cohort   A group of people born in the same year or same generation.

comprehension   The process of extracting meaning from a sequence of words.

concrete operational stage   The third of Piaget's stages, from approximately 7 to 11 years, in which children first use mental operations to solve problems and to reason.

cones   Specialized neurons in the back of the eye that detect the wavelength of light and, therefore, lead to perception of color.

confounded   As applied to the design of experiments, an error in which variables are combined instead of evaluated independently, making the results of the experiment ambiguous.

congenital adrenal hyperplasia (CAH)   A genetic disorder in which girls are masculinized because the adrenal glands secrete large amounts of androgen during prenatal development.

constricting   An interaction style, common among boys, in which one child tries to emerge as the victor by threatening or contradicting the others, or by exaggerating.

constructivism   The view, associated with Piaget, that children are active participants in their own development who systematically construct ever-more-sophisticated understandings of their worlds.

continuity–discontinuity issue   An issue concerned with whether a developmental phenomenon follows a smooth progression throughout the life span or a series of abrupt shifts.

conventional level   The second level of reasoning in Kohlberg's theory, where moral reasoning is based on society's norms.

cooing   Early vowel-like sounds that babies produce.

cooperative play   Play that is organized around a theme, with each child taking on a different role; begins at about 2 years of age.

core-knowledge theories   The view that infants are born with rudimentary knowledge of the world that is elaborated based on children's experiences.

corpus callosum   A thick bundle of neurons that connects the two cerebral hemispheres.

correlation coefficient   A statistic that reveals the strength and direction of the relation between two variables.

correlational study   A research design in which investigators look at relations between variables as they exist naturally in the world.

co-rumination   Conversations with friends that focus on each other's personal problems; sometimes contributes to depression in adolescent girls.

counterimitation   A type of observational learning in which the child observes and learns what should not be done.

creative ability   In Sternberg's theory of intelligence, the ability to deal adaptively with novel situations and problems.

critical period   A time in development when a specific type of learning can take place; before or after the critical period, the same learning is difficult or even impossible.

cross-sectional design   A research design in which people of different ages are compared at the same point in time.

crowd   A large group that includes many cliques with similar attitudes and values.

crowning   During labor, the appearance of the top of the baby's head.

crystallized intelligence   A person's culturally influenced accumulated knowledge and skills, including understanding printed language, comprehending language, and knowing vocabulary.

culture   The knowledge, attitudes, and behavior associated with a group of people.

culture-fair intelligence tests   Tests designed to reduce the impact of different experiences by including items based on experiences common to many cultures.

D

deductive reasoning   Drawing conclusions from facts; characteristic of formal operational thought.

dendrite   The end of the neuron that receives information; looks like a tree with many branches.

deoxyribonucleic acid (DNA)   A molecule composed of four nucleotide bases; the biochemical basis of heredity.

dependent variable   In an experiment, the behavior that is observed after other variables are manipulated.

detached grandparents   Grandparents who are uninvolved with their grandchildren.

differentiation   Distinguishing and mastering individual motions.

diffusion   The identity status in Marcia's theory in which adolescents do not have an identity and are doing nothing to achieve one.

direct instruction   A parental behavior in which adults try to influence their children's behavior by telling them what to do, when, and why.

dismissive adults (attachment representation)   A representation of parent–child relations in which adults describe childhood experiences in very general terms and often idealize their parents.

disorganized (disoriented) attachment   A relationship in which infants don't seem to understand what's happening when they are separated from and later reunited with their mothers.

display rules   Culturally specific standards for appropriate expressions of emotion in a particular setting or with a particular person or persons.

divergent thinking   Thinking in novel and unusual directions.

dizygotic (fraternal) twins   Twins that are the result of the fertilization of two separate eggs by two sperm.

dominance hierarchy   An ordering of individuals within a group in which group members with lower status defer to those with greater status.

dominant   The form of an allele whose chemical instructions are followed.

Down syndrome   A disorder, caused by an extra chromosome, that causes intellectual disability and a distinctive appearance.

dynamic assessment   An approach to intelligence testing that measures a child's learning potential by having the child learn something new in the presence of the examiner and with the examiner's help.

dynamic systems theory   A theory that views development as involving many distinct skills that are organized and reorganized over time to meet demands of specific tasks.

E

ectoderm   The outer layer of the embryo, which becomes the hair, outer layer of skin, and nervous system.

effortful control   A dimension of temperament that refers to the extent to which a child can focus attention, is not easily distracted, and can inhibit responses.

ego   According to Freud, the rational component of the personality; develops during the first few years of life.

egocentrism   Difficulty in seeing the world from another's point of view; typical of children in Piaget's preoperational stage.

ego-resilience   The ability to respond adaptively and resourcefully to new situations; a factor that protects children from the impact of maltreatment.

elaboration   A memory strategy in which information is embellished to make it more memorable.

electroencephalography   A method in which a pattern of brain waves is recorded from electrodes placed on the scalp.

embryo   The name given to the developing baby after the zygote is completely embedded in the uterine wall.

emotional intelligence   The ability to use one's own and others' emotions effectively for solving problems and living happily.

empathy   Experiencing another person's feelings.

enabling   An interaction style, common among girls, in which children's actions and remarks tend to support others and to sustain the interaction.

encoding processes   The cognitive processes that transform the information in a problem into a mental representation.

endoderm   The inner layer of the embryo, which becomes the lungs and the digestive system.

epigenesis   The continuous interplay between genes and multiple levels of the environment (from cells to culture).

epiphyses   Ends of bone tissue, which are formed first before the center is formed.

equilibration   According to Piaget, the process by which children reorganize their schemes and, in the process, move to the next developmental stage.

essentialism   The belief, common among young children, that all living things have an underlying essence that cannot be seen but that gives a living thing its identity.

ethnic identity   The feeling that one is part of an ethnic group and the understanding of special customs and traditions of the group's culture and heritage.

ethological theory   A theory in which development is seen from an evolutionary perspective and behaviors are examined for their survival value.

evolutionary psychology   The theoretical view that many human behaviors represent successful adaptation to the environment.

executive functioning   A mechanism of growth that includes inhibitory processes, planning, and cognitive flexibility.

exosystem   According to Bronfenbrenner, social settings that influence one's development even though one does not experience them firsthand.

experience-dependent growth   Changes in the brain due to experiences that are not linked to specific ages and that vary across individuals and across cultures.

experience-expectant growth   Changes in the brain from environmental influences that typically occur at specified points in development and for all children.

experiment   A systematic way of manipulating factors that a researcher thinks cause a particular behavior.

expressive style   A style of language learning that describes children whose vocabularies include many social phrases that are used like one word.

expressive traits   Psychological characteristics that describe a person who is focused on emotions and interpersonal relationships.

F

fast mapping   The fact that children make connections between new words and referents so quickly that they cannot be considering all possible meanings.

fetal alcohol spectrum disorder (FASD)   A disorder affecting babies whose mothers consumed large amounts of alcohol while they were pregnant.

fetal medicine   The branch of medicine that deals with treating prenatal problems.

field experiment   A type of experiment in which the researcher manipulates independent variables in a natural setting so that the results are more likely to be representative of behavior.

fine-motor skills   Motor skills associated with grasping, holding, and manipulating objects.

fluid intelligence   The ability to perceive relations among stimuli.

folk psychology   Our informal beliefs about other people and their behavior.

foreclosure   The identity status in Marcia's theory in which adolescents have an identity that was chosen based on advice from adults, rather than one that was a result of personal exploration of alternatives.

formal operational stage   The fourth of Piaget's stages, from roughly age 11 into adulthood, in which children and adolescents can apply mental operations to abstract entities, allowing them to think hypothetically and reason deductively.

friendship   A voluntary relationship between two people involving mutual liking.

frontal cortex   A brain region that regulates personality and goal-directed behavior.

functional magnetic resonance imaging (fMRI)   A technique for measuring brain activity that uses magnetic fields to track the flow of blood in the brain.

fuzzy trace theory   A theory proposed by Brainerd and Reyna in which experiences can be stored in memory verbatim or in terms of their basic meaning (gist).

G

gender identity   The perception of oneself as either male or female.

gender role   Culturally prescribed behaviors considered appropriate for males and females.

gender-schema theory   A theory that children learn gender roles by first deciding whether an object, activity, or behavior is female or male, then using this information to decide whether they should learn more about the object, activity, or behavior.

gender stereotypes   Beliefs and images about males and females that are not necessarily true.

gene   A group of nucleotide bases that provides a specific set of biochemical instructions.

genetic engineering   A branch of fetal medicine in which defective genes are replaced with synthetic normal genes.

genotype   A person's hereditary makeup.

germ disc   A small cluster of cells near the center of the zygote that develops into the baby.

gifted   Traditionally, individuals with intelligence test scores of at least 130.

grammatical morphemes   Words or endings of words that make a sentence grammatical.

growth hormone   A hormone, secreted by the pituitary gland during sleep, that regulates growth by triggering the release of other hormones that cause muscles and bones to grow.

guided participation   According to Vygotsky, structured interactions between a child and another more knowledgeable person; they are thought to promote cognitive growth.

H

habituation   Becoming unresponsive to a stimulus that is presented repeatedly.

hemispheres   The right and left halves of the cortex.

heritability coefficient   A measure of the extent to which heredity contributes to individual differences in a trait for a group of people.

heterozygous   When the alleles for a trait differ from each other.

heuristics   Rules of thumb that are handy for solving problems but that do not guarantee a solution.

homozygous   When the alleles for a trait are the same.

hostile aggression   Aggression that is unprovoked; its goal is to intimidate, harass, or humiliate others.

Huntington's disease   A type of dementia caused by a dominant allele; characterized by degeneration of the nervous system beginning in middle age.

hypoxia   Lack of oxygen during delivery, typically because the umbilical cord becomes pinched or tangled during delivery.

I

id   According to Freud, the element of personality that desires immediate gratification of bodily wants and needs; present at birth.

illusion of invulnerability   The belief, common among adolescents, that misfortune only happens to others.

imaginary audience   Adolescents' belief that their behavior is constantly being watched by their peers.

imitation (observational learning)   Learning that takes place simply by observing others.

immanent justice   A characteristic of the stage of moral realism in which children believe that breaking a rule always leads to punishment.

implantation   The process in which the zygote burrows into the uterine wall and establishes connections with the mother's blood vessels.

imprinting   Learning that occurs during a critical period soon after birth or hatching, as demonstrated by chicks creating an emotional bond with the first moving object they see.

incomplete dominance   The situation in which one allele does not dominate another completely.

independent variable   The factor that is manipulated by the researcher in an experiment.

infant-directed speech   Speech that adults use with babies that is slow and loud and has exaggerated changes in pitch; thought to foster infants' language learning.

infantile amnesia   The inability to remember events from early in one's life.

influential grandparents   Grandparents who are very close to their grandchildren, are very involved in their lives, and frequently perform parental roles, including discipline.

information-processing theory   A view that human cognition consists of mental hardware and mental software.

informed consent A person's decision to participate in research after having been told enough about the research to make an educated decision; children are not legally capable of giving informed consent.

inner speech Vygotsky's term for thought.

instrumental aggression Aggression used to achieve an explicit goal.

instrumental traits Psychological characteristics that describe a person who acts on and influences the world.

integration Linking individual motions into a coherent, coordinated whole.

intellectual disability A disorder formerly known as mental retardation in which, before 18 years of age, individuals have substantially below-average intelligence and problems adapting to an environment.

intelligence quotient (IQ) A ratio of mental age to chronological age, multiplied by 100.

internal working model An infant's understanding of how responsive and dependable the mother is; thought to influence close relationships throughout the child's life.

interposition A perceptual cue to depth based on the fact that nearby objects partially obscure more distant objects.

intersensory redundancy theory A view, proposed by Bahrick and Lickliter, that the infant's perceptual system is particularly attuned to amodal information that is presented to multiple sensory modes.

intersubjectivity According to Vygotsky, mutual, shared understanding among people who are participating in an activity together.

intonation A pattern of rising and falling pitch in speech or babbling that often indicates whether the utterance is a statement, question, or command.

in vitro fertilization The technique of fertilizing eggs with sperm in a Petri dish and then transferring several of the fertilized eggs to the mother's uterus, where they might implant in the lining of the uterine wall.

J

joint custody When both parents retain legal custody of their children following a divorce.

K

kinetic cues Depth cues based on motion, such as visual expansion and motion parallax.

knowledge-telling strategy A strategy for writing, often used by younger writers, in which information is written in sequence as it is retrieved from memory.

knowledge-transforming strategy A strategy for writing, often used by older writers, in which they decide what information to include and how best to organize it for the point they wish to convey to the reader.

L

language Any rule-based system for expressing ideas.

latchkey children Children who care for themselves after school.

learning disability When a child with normal intelligence has difficulty mastering at least one academic subject.

linear perspective A cue to depth perception based on the fact that parallel lines come together at a single point in the distance.

locomotion The ability to move around in the world.

longitudinal design A research design in which a single cohort is studied over multiple times of measurement.

long-term memory A permanent storehouse for memories that has unlimited capacity.

M

macrosystem According to Bronfenbrenner, the cultural and subcultural settings in which the microsystems, mesosystems, and exosystems are embedded.

mad cry A more intense version of a basic cry.

malnutrition Being small for one's age because of inadequate nutrition.

maturational theory The view that child development reflects a specific and prearranged scheme or plan within the body.

means-ends analysis A problem-solving heuristic in which people determine the difference between the current and desired situations, then do something to reduce the difference.

memory strategies Activities that improve remembering.

menarche The onset of menstruation.

mental age (MA) In intelligence testing, a measure of children's performance corresponding to the chronological age of those whose performance equals the child's.

mental operations Cognitive actions that can be performed on objects or ideas.

mental rotation An aspect of spatial ability involving the ability to imagine how an object will appear after it has been moved in space.

mesoderm The middle layer of the embryo, which will become the muscles, bones, and circulatory system.

mesosystem According to Bronfenbrenner, the interrelations between different microsystems.

meta-analysis A tool that allows researchers to synthesize the results of many studies to estimate relations between variables.

metacognitive knowledge A person's knowledge and awareness of cognitive processes.

metamemory A person's informal understanding of memory; includes the ability to diagnose memory problems accurately and to monitor the effectiveness of memory strategies.

methylation A process by which experience changes the expression of DNA—the genetic code is preserved but a gene is silenced by a methyl molecule

microgenetic study A special type of longitudinal study in which children are tested repeatedly over a span of days or weeks, with the aim of observing change directly as it occurs.

microsystem According to Bronfenbrenner, the people and objects that are present in one's immediate environment.

monitoring As applied to parent–child relations, parents' knowledge of where their children are, what they're doing, and with whom.

monozygotic (identical) twins Twins that result when a single fertilized egg splits to form two new individuals.

moral realism A stage described by Piaget that begins at about age 5 and continues through age 7, in which children believe that rules are created by wise adults and therefore must be followed and cannot be changed.

moral relativism A stage described by Piaget that begins at about age 8, in which children understand that rules are created by people to help them get along.

moratorium The identity status in Marcia's theory in which adolescents are still examining different alternatives and have yet to find a satisfactory identity.

motion parallax A kinetic depth cue in which nearby moving objects move across a person's visual field faster than distant objects.

motor skills Coordinated movements of the muscles and limbs.

myelin A fatty sheath that surrounds neurons in the central nervous system and allows them to transmit information more rapidly.

N

naming explosion A period, beginning at about age 18 months, in which children learn new words very rapidly.

Narcissistic personality Children and adolescents who have a grandiose view of themselves, believe themselves to be better than others, and yet relish attention and compliments from others.

naturalistic observation A method of observation in which children are observed as they behave spontaneously in a real-life situation.

nature–nurture issue An issue concerning the manner in which genetic and environmental factors influence development.

negative affect A dimension of temperament that refers to the extent to which a child is angry, fearful, frustrated, shy, and not easily soothed.

negative reinforcement trap A situation in which parents often unwittingly reinforce the very behaviors they want to discourage; particularly likely between mothers and sons.

neural plate A flat group of cells present in prenatal development that becomes the brain and spinal cord.

neuron A cell that is the basic unit of the brain and nervous system; specializes in receiving and transmitting information.

neurotransmitters Chemicals released by terminal buttons that carry information to nearby neurons.

niche-picking The process of deliberately seeking environments compatible with one's genetic makeup.

non-REM (regular) sleep Sleep in which heart rate, breathing, and brain activity are steady.

nonshared environmental influences Forces within a family that make children different from one another.

O

object permanence The understanding, acquired in infancy, that objects exist independently of oneself.

observational learning Learning based on watching others; imitation.

one-to-one principle The counting principle stating that there must be one and only one number name for each object counted.

open adoption A form of adoption in which adopted children have contact with their birth families.

operant conditioning A view of learning, proposed by Skinner, that emphasizes reward and punishment.

organization A memory strategy in which information to be remembered is structured so that related information is placed together.

overextension When children define words more broadly than adults do.

overregularization Children's application of rules to words that are exceptions to the rule; used as evidence that children master grammar by learning rules.

P

pain cry A cry that begins with a sudden, long burst, followed by a long pause and gasping.

parallel play When children play alone but are aware of and interested in what another child is doing; occurs soon after the first birthday.

passive grandparents Grandparents who are caught up in their grandchildren's development but not with the intensity of influential or supportive grandparents; they do not assume parental roles.

period of the fetus The longest period of prenatal development, extending from the ninth week after conception until birth.

permissive parenting A style of parenting that offers warmth and caring but little parental control over children.

personal domain The domain of decisions concerning one's body (e.g., what to eat and wear) and choices of friends or activities.

personal fable The feeling of many adolescents that their feelings and experiences are unique and have never been experienced by anyone else.

phenotype The physical, behavioral, and psychological features that are the result of the interaction between one's genes and the environment.

phonemes Unique speech sounds that can be used to create words.

phonological awareness The ability to hear the distinctive sounds associated with specific letters.

phonological memory The ability to remember speech sounds briefly; a key component for learning new words easily.

phonology The sounds of a language.

pictorial cues Depth cues like those used by artists to convey depth in drawings and paintings; examples include linear perspective and interposition.

placenta The structure through which nutrients and wastes are exchanged between the mother and the developing child.

polygenic inheritance When phenotypes are the result of the combined activity of many separate genes.

population A broad group of children that is the usual focus of research in child development.

postconventional level   The third level of reasoning in Kohlberg's theory, in which morality is based on a personal moral code.

postpartum depression   A condition affecting 10% to 15% of new mothers in which irritability continues for months and is often accompanied by feelings of low self-worth, disturbed sleep, poor appetite, and apathy.

practical ability   In Sternberg's theory of intelligence, the ability to know which solutions to problems are likely to work.

pragmatics   How people use language to communicate effectively.

preconventional level   The first level of reasoning in Kohlberg's theory, where moral reasoning is based on external forces.

premature infant   A baby born before the 38th week after conception.

prenatal development   The many changes that turn a fertilized egg into a newborn human.

preoccupied adults (attachment representation)   A representation of parent–child relations in which adults describe childhood experiences emotionally and often express anger or confusion regarding relationships with their parents.

preoperational stage   The second of Piaget's stages, from 2 to 7 years, in which children first use symbols to represent objects and events.

primary sex characteristics   Changes in bodily organs directly involved in reproduction (i.e., the ovaries, uterus, and vagina; the scrotum, testes, and penis) that are signs of physical maturity.

private speech   Comments that are not intended for others but that help children regulate their own behavior.

prosocial behavior   Any behavior that benefits another person.

psychodynamic theory   A view first formulated by Freud in which development is largely determined by how well people resolve conflicts they face at different ages.

psychometricians   Psychologists who specialize in the measurement of psychological characteristics such as intelligence and personality.

psychosocial theory   A theory proposed by Erikson in which personality development is the result of the interaction of maturation and societal demands.

puberty   A collection of physical changes that marks the onset of adolescence, such as the growth spurt and the growth of breasts or testes.

punishment   Applying an aversive stimulus (e.g., a spanking) or removing an attractive stimulus (e.g., TV viewing); an action that discourages the reoccurrence of the response that it follows.

Q

quasi-experiment   A variation of an experiment in which the impact of an independent variable is examined by groups that are created after the fact, not by random assignment, and are equated statistically.

R

rapid-eye-movement (REM) sleep (irregular sleep)   Irregular sleep in which an infant's eyes dart rapidly beneath the eyelids, while the body is quite active.

reactive aggression   Aggression prompted by another child's behavior.

recessive   An allele whose instructions are ignored when it is combined with a dominant allele.

recursive thinking   A child's ability to think about what others are thinking, particularly when another person's thoughts refer to the child (e.g., "He thinks that I think…").

referential style   A style of language learning that describes children whose vocabularies are dominated by names of objects, persons, or actions.

reflexes   Unlearned responses that are triggered by specific stimulation.

rehearsal   A memory strategy that involves repetitively naming information that is to be remembered.

reinforcement   A consequence that increases the likelihood that a behavior will be repeated.

relational aggression   A form of verbal aggression in which children try to hurt others by undermining their social relationships.

relative size   A perceptual cue to depth based on the fact that nearby objects look larger than objects in the distance.

reliability   As applied to tests, how consistent test scores are from one testing time to another.

research design   An overall conceptual plan for research; the most common are correlational and experimental designs.

resistant attachment   A relationship in which, after a brief separation, infants want to be held but are difficult to console.

response bias   The tendency for research participants to respond in ways that are socially acceptable.

retinal disparity   A perceptual cue to depth based on the fact that, when a person views an object, the retinal images in the left and right eyes differ.

rough-and-tumble play   A form of play common during the elementary-school years in which children playfully chase, punch, kick, shove, fight, and wrestle with peers.

S

sample   A group of children drawn from a population that participates in research.

scaffolding   A teaching style in which adults adjust the amount of assistance that they offer, based on the learner's needs.

script   The means by which people remember common events consisting of sequences of activities.

secondary sex characteristics   Physical signs of maturity in body parts not linked directly to the reproductive organs (e.g., growth of breasts, the appearance of facial hair, the appearance of body hair).

secular growth trends   Changes in physical development from one generation to the next; for example, the fact that people in industrialized societies are larger and are maturing earlier than in previous generations.

secure adults (attachment representation)   A representation of parent–child relations in which adults describe childhood experiences objectively and mention both positive and negative aspects of their parents.

secure attachment A relationship in which infants have come to trust and depend on their mothers.

self-concept Attitudes, behaviors, and values that a person believes make him or her a unique individual.

self-conscious emotions Emotions such as pride, guilt, or embarrassment that involve feelings of success when one's standards or expectations are met and feelings of failure when they aren't; emerge between 18 to 24 months of age.

self-control The ability to rise above immediate pressures and not give in to impulse.

self-efficacy The belief that one is capable of performing a certain task.

self-esteem A person's judgment and feelings about his or her own worth.

self-reports A measurement method in which children respond to questions about specific topics.

semantic bootstrapping theory A view that children rely on their knowledge of word meanings to discover grammatical rules.

semantics The study of words and their meaning.

sensorimotor stage The first of Piaget's four stages of cognitive development, which lasts from birth to approximately 2 years, in which infants progress from responding reflexively to using symbols.

sensory and perceptual processes The means by which the nervous system receives, selects, modifies, and organizes stimulation from the world.

sensory memory A type of memory in which information is held in raw, unanalyzed form very briefly (no longer than a few seconds).

sex chromosomes The 23rd pair of chromosomes; these determine the sex of the child.

sickle-cell trait A disorder in which individuals show signs of mild anemia only when they are seriously deprived of oxygen; occurs in individuals who have one dominant allele for normal blood cells and one recessive sickle-cell allele.

size constancy The realization that an object's actual size remains the same despite changes in the size of its retinal image.

small-for-date infants Newborns who are substantially smaller than would be expected based on the length of time since conception.

social cognitive theory A theory developed by Bandura in which children use reward, punishment, and imitation to try to understand their world.

social conventions Arbitrary standards of behavior agreed to by a cultural group to help coordinate interactions of individuals within the group.

social influence As applied to teen pregnancies, the view that when teenage girls give birth, this triggers a set of events that make it harder for them to provide a positive environment for their children's development.

social referencing A phenomenon in which infants in an unfamiliar or ambiguous environment look at their mother or father, as if searching for cues to help them interpret the situation.

social role A set of cultural guidelines about how one should behave, especially with other people.

social selection As applied to teen pregnancies, the view that the same factors that make some teenage girls more likely than others to become pregnant make those girls less effective as parents.

social smiles Smiles that first appear at about 2 months of age, when infants see another human face.

sociocultural perspective The view, associated with Vygotsky, that children's cognitive development can only be understood by considering the cultural contexts in which children develop.

spermarche The first spontaneous ejaculation of sperm-laden fluid; typically occurs at age 13.

spina bifida A disorder in which the embryo's neural tube does not close properly during the first month of pregnancy.

stable-order principle The counting principle which states that number names must always be counted in the same order.

stereotype threat The self-fulfilling prophecy in which knowledge of stereotypes leads to anxiety and reduced performance consistent with the original stereotype.

stranger wariness An infant's apparent concern or anxiety in the presence of an unfamiliar adult; typically observed at about 6 months of age.

stress A person's physical and psychological responses to threatening or challenging situations.

structured observation A method in which a researcher creates a setting to elicit the behavior of interest.

sudden infant death syndrome (SIDS) A disorder in which a healthy baby dies suddenly, for no apparent reason; typically occurs between 2 and 4 months of age.

superego According to Freud, the moral component of the personality that has incorporated adult standards of right and wrong.

supportive grandparents Grandparents who are very close to and involved with their grandchildren, but do not take on parental roles.

surgency/extraversion A dimension of temperament that refers to the extent to which a child is happy, active, vocal, and seeks interesting stimulation.

swaddling A technique for calming a crying baby in which the baby is wrapped tightly in a blanket.

synapse The gap between one neuron and the next.

synaptic pruning Gradual loss of unused synapses, beginning in infancy and continuing into early adolescence.

syntax Rules that specify how words are combined to form sentences.

systematic observation A method of observation in which investigators watch children and record what they do or say.

T

telegraphic speech A style of speaking, common in 1-year-olds, that includes only words directly relevant to meaning.

teleological explanation As applied to children's naïve theories of living things, the belief that living things and parts of living things exist for a purpose.

temperament   A consistent style or pattern of behavior.

teratogen   An agent that causes abnormal prenatal development.

terminal buttons   Small knobs at the end of an axon that release neurotransmitters.

texture gradient   A perceptual cue to depth based on the fact that the texture of objects is coarse but distinct for nearby objects but finer and less distinct for distant objects.

theory   An organized set of ideas that is designed to explain development.

theory of mind   An intuitive understanding of the connections among thoughts, beliefs, intentions, and behavior; develops rapidly in the preschool years.

time-out   Punishment that involves removing a child who is misbehaving to a quiet, unstimulating environment.

toddler   A young child who has just learned to walk.

U

ultrasound   A prenatal diagnostic technique that involves bouncing sound waves off the fetus to generate an image of the fetus.

umbilical cord   A structure containing veins and arteries that connects the developing child to the placenta.

underextension   When children define words more narrowly than adults do.

uninvolved parenting   A style of parenting that provides neither warmth nor control and that minimizes the amount of time parents spend with children.

V

validity   As applied to tests, the extent to which the test measures what it purports to measure.

variable   Any factor subject to change.

vernix   A thick, greasy substance that covers the fetus and protects it during prenatal development.

villi   Finger-like projections from the umbilical blood vessels that are close to the mother's blood vessels and thus allow nutrients, oxygen, vitamins, and waste products to be exchanged between mother and embryo.

visual acuity   The smallest pattern that one can distinguish reliably.

visual cliff   A glass-covered platform that appears to have a "shallow" side and "deep" side; used to study infants' depth perception.

visual expansion   A kinetic depth cue in which approaching objects fill an ever-greater proportion of the retina.

W

word decoding   The ability to identify individual words, either by retrieving them or sounding them out.

working memory   A type of memory in which a small number of items can be stored briefly.

Z

zone of proximal development   The difference between what children can do with assistance and what they can do alone.

zygote   The fertilized egg.

Answers to Test Yourself Questions

Chapter 1

1. a
2. a
3. a
4. c
5. b
6. a
7. c
8. c
9. a
10. c
11. b
12. b
13. a
14. c
15. b

Chapter 2

1. a
2. b
3. c
4. b
5. a
6. b
7. b
8. a
9. b
10. a
11. c
12. a
13. b
14. b
15. c

Chapter 3

1. a
2. a
3. b
4. c
5. b
6. a
7. a

8. b
9. b
10. b
11. a
12. b
13. a
14. b
15. a

Chapter 4

1. b
2. c
3. b
4. b
5. a
6. c
7. c
8. a
9. a
10. a
11. b
12. a
13. a
14. c
15. c

Chapter 5

1. a
2. b
3. a
4. c
5. b
6. a
7. c
8. a
9. a
10. a
11. a
12. b
13. a
14. a
15. a

Chapter 6

1. b
2. c
3. a
4. c
5. b
6. c
7. b
8. c
9. c
10. a
11. c
12. b
13. c
14. c
15. c

Chapter 7

1. a
2. c
3. b
4. b
5. a
6. b
7. b
8. a
9. a
10. c
11. a
12. b
13. b
14. c
15. c

Chapter 8

1. a
2. b
3. b
4. b
5. c
6. c
7. c

8. b
9. a
10. a
11. a
12. c
13. c
14. b
15. b

Chapter 9

1. b
2. b
3. c
4. a
5. a
6. a
7. a
8. b
9. a
10. a
11. b
12. b
13. a
14. c
15. a

Chapter 10

1. a
2. b
3. b
4. c
5. a
6. a
7. b
8. b
9. b
10. b
11. a
12. b
13. b
14. b
15. a

Chapter 11

1. b
2. c
3. a
4. b
5. a
6. b
7. b
8. a
9. a
10. b
11. a
12. a
13. b
14. b
15. b

Chapter 12

1. a
2. a
3. b
4. a
5. b
6. c
7. b
8. c
9. c
10. c
11. a
12. b
13. a
14. c
15. c

Chapter 13

1. b
2. b
3. a
4. a
5. c
6. a
7. c
8. a
9. a
10. b
11. a
12. c
13. b
14. c
15. b

Chapter 14

1. c
2. c
3. a
4. c
5. c
6. a
7. b
8. a
9. a
10. c
11. a
12. c
13. c
14. a
15. c

Chapter 15

1. b
2. a
3. c
4. c
5. b
6. a
7. b
8. c
9. c
10. c
11. b
12. a
13. c
14. b
15. c

References

AAIDD Ad Hoc Committee on Terminology and Classification. (2010). *Intellectual disability* (11th ed.). Washington, DC: American Association on Intellectual and Developmental Disabilities.

Aboud, F. E. (2003). The formation of in-group favoritism and out-group prejudice in young children: Are they distinct attitudes? *Developmental Psychology, 39*, 48–60.

Aboud, F. E., Tredoux, C., Tropp, L. R., Brown, C. S., Niens, U., Noor, N. M. et al. (2012). Interventions to reduce prejudice and enhance inclusion and respect for ethnic differences in early childhood: A systematic review. *Developmental Review, 32*, 307–336.

Ackerman, B. P. (1993). Children's understanding of the speaker's meaning in referential communication. *Journal of Experimental Child Psychology, 55*, 56–86.

Ackerman, B. P., & Brown, E. D. (2006). Income poverty, poverty co-factors, and the adjustment of children in elementary school. In R. V. Kail (Ed.), *Advances in child development and behavior* (Vol. 34, pp. 91–129). Amsterdam: Elsevier Academic Press.

Adams, J. (1999). On neurodevelopmental disorders: Perspectives from neurobehavioral teratology. In H. Tager-Flusberg (Ed.), *Neurodevelopmental disorders* (pp. 451–468). Cambridge, MA: MIT Press.

Adams, E. K. (2004). Beyond quality: Parental and residential stability and children's adjustment. *Current Directions in Psychological Science, 13*, 210–213.

Adams, R. J., & Courage, M. L. (1995). Development of chromatic discrimination in early infancy. *Behavioral Brain Research, 67*, 99–101.

Adams, R. E., Santo, J. B., & Bukowski, W. M. (2011). The presence of a best friend buffers the effects of negative experiences. *Developmental Psychology, 47*, 1786–1791.

Adams, M. J., Treiman, R., & Pressley, M. (1998). Reading, writing, and literacy. In W. Damon (Ed.), *Handbook of child psychology* (Vol. 4, pp. 275–355). New York, NY: Wiley.

Administration for Children and Families. (2013). *Head Start facts fiscal year 2012*. Washington DC: Author.

Adolph, K. E. (2000). Specificity of learning: Why infants fall over a veritable cliff. *Psychological Science, 11*, 290–295.

Adolph, K. (2002). Learning to keep balance. In R. V. Kail (Ed.), *Advances in child development and behavior* (Vol. 30, pp. 1–40). Orlando, FL: Academic Press.

Adolph, K. E., Cole, W. G., Komati, M., Garciaguirre, J. S., Badaly, D., Lingeman, J. M., et al. (2012). How do you learn to walk? Thousands of steps and dozens of falls per day. *Psychological Science, 23*, 1387–1394.

Adolph, K. E., & Robinson, S. R. (2013). The road to walking: What learning to walk tells us about development. In P. Zelazo (Ed.) *Oxford handbook of developmental psychology* (pp. 403–443). New York NY: Oxford University Press.

Adolphus, K., Lawton, C. L., & Dye, L. (2013). The effects of breakfast on behavior and academic performance in children and adolescents. *Frontiers in Human Neuroscience, 7*, Article 425.

Adzick, N. S., Thom, E. A., Spong, C Y., Brock, J. W., Burrows, P. K., Johnson, M. P., et al. (2011). A randomized trial of prenatal versus postnatal repair of myelomeningocele. *The New England Journal of Medicine, 364*, 993–1004.

Ainsworth, M. S. (1978). The development of infant–mother attachment. In B. M. Caldwell & H. N. Ricciuti (Eds.), *Review of child development research* (Vol. 3, pp. 1–94). Chicago, IL: University of Chicago Press.

Ainsworth, M. S. (1993). Attachment as related to mother–infant interaction. *Advances in Infancy Research, 8*, 1–50.

Alatupa, S., Pulkki-Råback, L., Hintsanen, M., Elovainio, M., Mullola, S., & Keltikangas-Järvinen, L. (2013). Disruptive behavior in childhood and socioeconomic position in adulthood: a prospective study over 27 years. *International Journal of Public Health, 58*, 247–256.

Alberts, A. E. (2005). Neonatal behavioral assessment scale. In C. B. Fisher & R. M. Lerner (Eds.), *Encyclopedia of applied developmental science* (Vol. 1, pp. 111–115). Thousand Oaks, CA: Sage.

Aldridge, V., Dovey, T. M., & Halford, J. C. G. (2009). The role of familiarity in dietary development. *Developmental Review, 29*, 32–44.

Alexander, G. M., & Wilcox, T. (2012). Sex differences in early infancy. *Child Development Perspectives, 6*, 400–406.

Alink, L. R. A., Cicchetti, D., Kim, J., & Rogosch, F. A. (2012). Longitudinal associations among child maltreatment, social functioning, and cortisol regulation. *Developmental Psychology, 48*, 224–236.

Allen, J. P., Chango, J., Szwedo, D., Schad, M., & Marston, E. (2012). Predictors of susceptibility to peer influence regarding substance use in adolescence. *Child Development, 83*, 337–350.

Allen, L., Cipielewski, J., & Stanovich, K. E. (1992). Multiple indicators of children's reading habits and attitudes: Construct validity and cognitive correlates. *Journal of Educational Psychology, 84*, 489–503.

Alter, A. L., Aronson, J., Darley, J. M., Rodriguez, C., & Ruble, D. N. (2010). Rising to the threat: Reducing stereotype threat by reframing the threat as a challenge. *Journal of Experimental Social Psychology, 46*, 166–171.

Amato, P. R. (2001). Children of divorce in the 1990s: An update of the Amato and Keith (1991) meta-analysis. *Journal of Family Psychology, 15*, 355–370.

Amato, P. R. (2010). Research on divorce: Continuing trends and new developments. *Journal of Marriage and Family, 72*, 650–666.

Amato, P. R., & Fowler, F. (2002). Parenting practices, child adjustment, and family diversity. *Journal of Marriage & the Family, 64*, 703–716.

Amato, P. R., Kane, J. B., & James, S. (2011). Reconsidering the "good divorce." *Family Relations, 60*, 511–524.

Amato, P. R., & Keith, B. (1991). Parental divorce and the well-being of children: A meta-analysis. *Psychological Bulletin, 110*, 26–46.

American Academy of Pediatrics. (2008). *Feeding kids right isn't always easy: Tips for preventing food hassles*. Elk Grove Village, IL: Author.

American Academy of Pediatrics. (2011). *Caring for our children: National health and safety performance standards; guidelines for early child care and education programs* (3rd ed.). Elk Grove Village, IL: Author.

American College of Obstetricians and Gynecologists. (2011a). *Frequently asked questions: Cesarean birth*. Washington DC: Author.

American College of Obstetricians and Gynecologists. (2011b). *Frequently asked questions: Pain relief during labor and delivery*. Washington DC: Author.

American Lung Association. (2007). *State of lung disease in diverse communities: 2007*. New York, NY: Author.

American Psychological Association. (2004, July 19). [Amicus curiae brief filed in U.S. Supreme Court in *Roper v. Simmons*, 543 U.S. 551 (2005)].

American Psychiatric Association. (2004). *Diagnostic and statistical manual of mental disorders* (4th ed.). Washington, DC: Author.

Amso, D., & Johnson, S. P. (2006). Learning by selection: Visual search and object perception in young infants. *Developmental Psychology, 42,* 1236–1245.

Amsterlaw, J., Lagattuta, K. H., & Meltzoff, A. N. (2009). Young children's reasoning about the effects of emotional and physiological states on academic performance. *Child Development, 80,* 115–133.

Anastasi, A. (1988). *Psychological testing* (6th ed.). New York, NY: Macmillan.

Anderson, E. (2000). Exploring register knowledge: The value of "controlled improvisation." In L. Menn & N. B. Ratner (Eds.), *Methods for studying language production* (pp. 225–248). Mahwah, NJ: Erlbaum.

Anderson, S. W., Damasio, H., Tranel, D., & Damasio, A. R. (2001). Long-term sequelae of prefrontal cortex damage acquired in early childhood. *Developmental Neuropsychology, 18,* 281–296.

Anderson, D. R., & Hanson, K. G. (2009). Children, media, and methodology. *American Behavioral Scientist, 52,* 1204–1219.

Anzures, G., Quinn, P. C., Pascalis, O., Slater, A. M., Tanaka, J. W., & Lee, K. (2013). Developmental origins of the other-race effect. *Current Directions in Psychological Science, 22,* 173–178.

Anzures, G., Wheeler, A., Quinn, P. C., Pascalis, O., Slater, A. M., Heron-Delaney, M., et al. (2012). Brief daily exposures to Asian females reverses perceptual narrowing for Asian faces in Caucasian infants. *Journal of Experimental Child Psychology, 112,* 484–495.

Apfelbaum, E. P., Pauker, K., Ambady, N., Sommers, S. R., & Norton, M. I. (2008). Learning (not) to talk about race: When older children underperform in social categorization. *Developmental Psychology, 44,* 1513–1518.

Apgar, V. (1953). A proposal for a new method of evaluation of the newborn infant. *Current Researches in Anesthesia & Analgesia, 32,* 260–267.

Appleyard, K., Yang, C. M., & Runyan, D. K. (2010). Delineating the maladaptive pathways of child maltreatment: A mediated moderation analysis of the roles of self-perception and social support. *Development & Psychopathology, 22,* 337–352.

Arabi, M., Frongillo, E. A., Avula, R., & Mangasaryan, N. (2012). Infant and young child feeding in developing countries. *Child Development, 83,* 32–45.

Archer, J. (2004). Sex differences in aggression in real-world settings: A meta-analytic review. *Review of General Psychology, 8,* 291–322.

Archer, J. (2006). Testosterone and human aggression: An evaluation of the challenge hypothesis. *Neuroscience and Biobehavioral Reviews, 30,* 319–345.

Archer, J. (2013). Can evolutionary principles explain patterns of family violence? *Psychological Bulletin, 139,* 403–440.

Arndorfer, C. L., & Stormshak, E. A. (2008). Same-sex versus other-sex best friendship in early adolescence: Longitudinal predictors of antisocial behavior throughout adolescence. *Journal of Youth & Adolescence, 37,* 1059–1070.

Arseneault, L., Tremblay, R. E., Boulerice, B., & Saucier, J. F. (2002). Obstetrical complications and violent delinquency: Testing two developmental pathways. *Child Development, 73,* 496–508.

Arsenio, W. F., Gold, J., & Adams, E. (2006). Children's conceptions and displays of moral emotions. In M. Killen & J. G. Smetana (2006), *Handbook of moral development* (pp. 581–609). Mahwah, NJ: Erlbaum.

Arunachalam, S., Escovar, E., Hansen, M. A., & Waxman, S. R. (2013). Out of sight, but not out of mind: 21-month-olds use syntactic information to learn verbs even in the absence of a corresponding event. *Language and Cognitive Processes, 28,* 417–425.

Asbridge, M., Brubacher, J. R., & Chan, H. (2013). Cell phone use and traffic crash risk: A culpability analysis. *International Journal of Epidemiology, 42,* 259–267.

Asendorpf, J. B., Denissen, J. J. A., & van Aken, M. A. G. (2008). Inhibited and aggressive preschool children at 23 years of age: Personality and social transitions into adulthood. *Developmental Psychology, 44,* 997–1011.

Ashcraft, M. H. (1982). The development of mental arithmetic: A chronometric approach. *Developmental Review, 2,* 212–236.

Aslin, R. N. (1987). Visual and auditory discrimination in infancy. In J. D. Osofsky (Ed.), *Handbook of infant development* (2nd ed.). New York, NY: Wiley.

Aslin, R. N., Jusczyk, P. W., & Pisoni, D. B. (1998). Speech and auditory processing during infancy: Constraints on and precursors to language. In W. Damon (Ed.), *Handbook of child psychology* (Vol. 2). New York, NY: Wiley.

Aslin, R. N., & Newport, E. L. (2012). Statistical learning: From acquiring specific items to forming general rules. *Current Directions in Psychological Science, 21,* 170–176.

Aspenlieder, L., Buchanan, C. M., McDougall, P., & Sippola, L. K. (2009). Gender nonconformity and peer victimization in pre- and early adolescence. *European Journal of Developmental Science, 3,* 3–16.

Astill, R. G., van der Heijden, K. B., van IJzendoorn, M. H., & van Someren, E. J. W. (2012). Sleep, cognition, and behavioral problems in school-age children: A century of research meta-analyzed. *Psychological Bulletin, 138,* 1109–1138.

Attar-Schwartz, S., Tan, J. P., Buchanan, A., Fluri, E., & Griggs, J. (2009). Grandparenting and adolescent adjustment in two-parent biological, lone-parent, and step families. *Journal of Family Psychology, 23,* 67–75.

Au, T. K., & Glusman, M. (1990). The principle of mutual exclusivity in word learning: To honor or not to honor? *Child Development, 61,* 1474–1490.

Aunola, K., Stattin, H., & Nurmi, J.-E. (2000). Parenting styles and adolescents' achievement strategies. *Journal of Adolescence, 23,* 205–222.

Averill, J. A. (1980). A constructivist view of emotion. In R. Plutchik & H. Kellerman (Eds.), *Emotion: Theory, research, and experience: Vol. 1 Theories of emotion.* New York, NY: Academic Press.

Awong, T., Grusec, J. E., & Sorenson, A. (2008). Respect-based control and anger as determinants of children's socio-emotional development. *Social Development, 17,* 941–959.

Azaiza, F. (2005). Parent-child relationships as perceived by Arab adolescents living in Israel. *International Journal of Social Welfare, 14,* 297–304.

Bachman, J. G., & Schulenberg, J. (1993). How part-time work intensity relates to drug use, problem behavior, time use, and satisfaction among high school seniors: Are these consequences or merely correlates? *Developmental Psychology, 29,* 229–230.

Bachman, J. G., Staff, J., O'Malley, P. M., & Freedman-Doan, P. (2013). Adolescent work intensity, school performance, and substance use: Links vary by race/ethnicity and socioeconomic status. *Developmental Psychology, 49,* 2125–2134.

Bachman, J. G., Staff, J. G., O'Malley, P. M., Schulenberg, J. E., & Freedman-Doan, P. (2011). Twelfth-grade student work intensity linked to later educational attainment and substance use: New longitudinal evidence. *Developmental Psychology, 47,* 344–363.

Backscheider, A. G., Shatz, M., & Gelman, S. A. (1993). Preschoolers' ability to distinguish living kinds as a function of regrowth. *Child Development, 64,* 1242–1257.

Baddeley, A. (2012). Working memory: Theories, models, and controversies. *Annual Review of Psychology, 63*, 1–29.

Baenninger, M., & Newcombe, N. (1995). Environmental input to the development of sex-related differences in spatial and mathematical ability. *Learning & Individual Differences, 7*, 363–379.

Bagwell, C. L. (2004). Friendships, peer networks and antisocial behavior. In J. B. Kupersmidt & K. A. Dodge (Eds.), *Children's peer relations* (pp. 37–57). Washington, DC: American Psychological Association.

Bagwell, C. L., Newcomb, A. F., & Bukowski, W. M. (1998). Preadolescent friendship and peer rejection as predictors of adult adjustment. *Child Development, 69*, 140–153.

Bahrick, L. E., & Lickliter, R. (2002). Intersensory redundancy guides early perceptual and cognitive development. In R. V. Kail (Ed.), *Advances in child development and behavior* (Vol. 30, pp. 153–177). Orlando, FL: Academic Press.

Bahrick, L. E., & Lickliter, R. (2012). The role of intersensory redundancy in early perceptual, cognitive, and social development. In A. Bremner, D.J. Lewkowicz, and C. Spence (Eds.), *Multisensory development* (pp. 183–205). Oxford, England: Oxford University Press.

Bailey, J. M., Bechtold, K. T., & Berenbaum, S. A. (2002). Who are tomboys and why should we study them? *Archives of Sexual Behavior, 31*, 333–341.

Bailey, J. A., Hill, K. G., Oesterle, S., & Hawkins, J. D. (2009). Parenting practices and problem behavior across three generations: Monitoring, harsh discipline, and drug use in the intergenerational transmission of externalizing behavior. *Developmental Psychology, 45*, 1214–1226.

Bailey, R. K., & Owens, D. L. (2005). Overcoming challenges in the diagnosis and treatment of attention-deficit/hyperactivity disorder in African Americans. *Journal of the National Medical Association, 97*, 5S–10S.

Baillargeon, R. (1987). Object permanence in 3½- and 4½-month-old infants. *Developmental Psychology, 23*, 655–664.

Baillargeon, R. (1994). How do infants learn about the physical world? *Current Directions in Psychological Science, 3*, 133–140.

Baillargeon, R. (2004). Infants' reasoning about hidden objects: Evidence for event-general and event-specific expectations. *Developmental Science, 7*, 391–424.

Baker, L., & Brown, A. L. (1984). Metacognitive skills and reading. In P. D. Pearson (Ed.), *Handbook of reading research: Part 2*. New York, NY: Longman.

Baker, J., McHale, J., Strozier, A., & Cecil, D. (2010). Mother-grandmother coparenting relationships in families with incarcerated mothers: A pilot investigation. *Family Process, 49*, 165–184.

Bakermans-Kranenburg, M. J., & van IJzendoorn, M. H. (2009). The first 10,000 Adult Attachment Interviews: distributions of adult attachment representations in clinical and non-clinical groups. *Attachment and Human Development, 11*, 223–263.

Bakermans-Kranenburg, M. J., & Van IJzendoorn, M. H. (2011). Differential susceptibility to rearing environment depending on dopamine-related genes: New evidence and a meta-analysis. *Development and Psychopathology, 23*, 39–52.

Bakermans-Kranenburg, M., van IJzendoorn, M. H., & Juffer, F. (2003). Less is more: Meta-analyses of sensitivity and attachment interventions in early childhood. *Psychological Bulletin, 129*, 195–215.

Bandura, A. (1977). *Social learning theory*. Englewood Cliffs, NJ: Prentice-Hall.

Bandura, A. (1986). *Social foundations of thought and action: A social-cognitive theory*. Englewood Cliffs, NJ: Prentice-Hall.

Bandura, A. (2006). Toward a psychology of human agency. *Perspectives on Psychological Science, 1*, 164–180.

Bandura, A. (2012). On the functional properties of self-efficacy revisited. *Journal of Management, 38*, 9–44.

Bandura, A., & Bussey, K. (2004). On broadening the cognitive, motivational, and sociostructural scope of theorizing about gender development and functioning: Comment on Martin, Ruble, and Szkrybalo (2002). *Psychological Bulletin, 130*, 691–701.

Banerjee, R., Watling, D., & Caputi, M. (2011). Peer relations and the understanding of faux pas: Longitudinal evidence for directional associations. *Child Development, 82*, 1887–1905.

Bannard, C., & Matthews, D. (2008). Stored word sequences in language learning: The effect of familiarity on children's repetition of four-word combinations. *Psychological Science, 19*, 241–248.

Banny, A. M., Heilbron, N., Ames, A., & Prinstein, M. (2011). Relational benefits of relational aggression: Adaptive and maladaptive associations with adolescent friendship quality. *Developmental Psychology, 47*, 1153–1166.

Barac, R., & Bialystok, E. (2012). Bilingual effects on cognitive and linguistic development: Role of language, cultural background, and education. *Child Development, 83*, 413–422.

Barajas, R. G., Martin, A. Brooks-Gunn, J., & Hale, L. (2011). Mother-child bed-sharing in toddlerhood and cognitive and behavioral outcomes. *Pediatrics, 128*, e339–e347.

Barbaresi, W. J., Colligan, R. C., Weaver, A. L., Voigt, R. G., Killian, J. M., & Katusic, S. K. (2013). Mortality, ADHD, and psychosocial adversity in adults with childhood ADHD: A prospective study. *Pediatrics, 131*, 637–644.

Barca, L., Ellis, A. W., & Burani, C. (2007). Context-sensitive rules and word naming in Italian children. *Reading & Writing, 20*, 495–509.

Barker, E. D., Copeland, W., Maughan, B., Jaffee, S. R., & Uher, R. (2012). Relative impact of maternal depression and associated risk factors on offspring psychopathology. *The British Journal of Psychiatry, 200*, 124–129.

Barkley, R. A. (2004). Adolescents with attention deficit/hyperactivity disorder: An overview of empirically based treatments. *Journal of Psychiatric Review, 10*, 39–56.

Barling, J., Zacharatos, A., & Hepburn, C. G. (1999). Parents' job insecurity affects children's academic performance through cognitive difficulties. *Journal of Applied Psychology, 84*, 437–444.

Barnett, M. A., Scaramella, L. V., Neppl, T. K., Ontai, L. L., & Conger, R. D. (2010). Grandmother involvement as a protective factor for early childhood social adjustment. *Journal of Family Psychology, 24*, 635–645.

Baron, A. S., & Banaji, M. R. (2006). The development of implicit attitudes: Evidence of race evaluations from ages 6 and 10 and adulthood. *Psychological Science, 17*, 53–58.

Baron, R., Manniën, J., de Jonge, A., Heymans, M.W., Klomp, T., Hutton, E. K., et al. (2013) Socio-demographic and lifestyle-related characteristics associated with self-reported any, daily and occasional smoking during pregnancy. *PLoS ONE 8(9)*, e74197.

Baron-Cohen, S. (2005). The Empathizing System: A revision of the 1994 model of the Mind Reading System. In B. J. Ellis & D. F. Bjorklund (Eds.), *Origins of the social mind: Evolutionary psychology and child development* (pp. 468–492). New York, NY: Guilford.

Barrett, T. M., Davis, E. F., & Needham, A. (2007). Learning about tools in infancy. *Developmental Psychology, 43*, 352–368.

Bartik, T. J., Gormley, W., & Adelstein, S. (2012). Earning benefits of Tulsa's pre-K program for different income groups. *Economics of Education Review, 31*, 1143–1161.

Barton, M. E., & Tomasello, M. (1991). Joint attention and conversation in mother-infant-sibling triads. *Child Development, 62*, 517–529.

Bascoe, S. M., Davies, P. T., Sturge-Apple, M. L., & Cummings, E. M. (2009). Children's representations of family relationships, peer information processing, and school adjustment. *Developmental Psychology, 45,* 1740–1751.

Baskett, L. M. (1985). Sibling status effects: Adult expectations. *Developmental Psychology, 21,* 441–445.

Basso, K. H. (1970). *The Cibecue Apache.* New York, NY: Holt, Rinehart, & Winston.

Bates, E., Bretherton, I., & Snyder, L. (1988). *From first words to grammar: Individual differences and dissociable mechanisms.* New York, NY: Cambridge University Press.

Bates, J. E., Pettit, G. S., Dodge, K. A., & Ridge, B. (1998). Interaction of temperamental resistance to control and restrictive parenting in the development of externalizing behavior. *Developmental Psychology, 34,* 982–995.

Bauer, P. J. (2006). Event memory. In W. Damon & R. M. Lerner (Eds.), *Handbook of child psychology* (6th ed., Vol. 2). New York, NY: Wiley.

Bauer, P. J., Larkina, M., & Deocampo, J. (2011). Early memory development. In U. Goswami (Ed.), *The Wiley-Blackwell handbook of cognitive development* (2nd ed., pp.153–179). West Sussex UK: Wiley-Blackwell.

Bauer, P. J., & Leventon, J. S. (2013). Memory for one-time experiences in the second year of life: Implications for the status of episodic memory. *Infancy, 18,* 755–781.

Bauer, P. J., & Lukowski, A. F. (2010). The memory is in the details: Relations between memory for the specific features of events and long-term recall during infancy. *Journal of Experimental Child Psychology, 107,* 1–14.

Bauer, P. J., San Souci, P., & Pathman, T. (2010). Infant memory. *WIREs Cognitive Science, 1,* 267–277.

Baumeister, R. F., Campbell, J. D., Krueger, J. I., & Vohs, K. D. (2003). Does high self-esteem cause better performance, interpersonal success, happiness, or healthier lifestyles? *Psychological Science in the Public Interest, 4,* 1–44.

Baumgartner, J. A., & Oakes, L. M. (2013). Investigating the relation between infants' manual activity with objects and their perception of dynamic events. *Infancy, 18,* 983–1006.

Baumrind, D. (1975). *Early socialization and the discipline controversy.* Morristown, NJ: General Learning Press.

Baumrind, D. (1991). Parenting styles and adolescent development. In R. M. Lerner, A. C. Petersen, & J. Brooks-Gunn (Eds.), *Encyclopedia of adolescence.* New York, NY: Garland.

Bauserman, R. (2002). Child adjustment in joint-custody versus sole-custody arrangements: A meta-analytic review. *Journal of Family Psychology, 16,* 91–102.

Bayley, N. (1970). Development of mental abilities. In P. H. Mussen (Ed.), *Carmichael's manual of child psychology.* New York, NY: Wiley.

Bayley, N. (1993). *Bayley scales of infant development: Birth to two years* (2nd ed.). San Antonio, TX: Psychological Corporation.

Bayley, N. (2006). *Bayley scales of infant and toddler development–Third edition.* San Antonio, TX: Harcourt Assessment, Inc.

Beal, C. R. (1996). The role of comprehension monitoring in children's revision. *Educational Psychology Review, 8,* 219–238.

Beal, C. R., & Belgrad, S. L. (1990). The development of message evaluation skills in young children. *Child Development, 61,* 705–712.

Beal, S. J., & Crockett, L. J. (2010). Adolescents' occupational and educational aspirations and expectations: Links to high school activities and educational attainment. *Developmental Psychology, 46,* 258–265.

Beauchamp, G. K., & Mennella, J. A. (2011). Flavor perception in human infants: Development and functional significance. *Digestion, 83,* 1–6.

Beck, E., Burnet, K. L., & Vosper, J. (2006). Birth-order effects on facets of extraversion. *Personality & Individual Differences, 40,* 953–959.

Becker, B. J. (1986). Influence again: An examination of reviews and studies of gender differences in social influence. In J. S. Hyde & M. C. Linn (Eds.), *The psychology of gender differences. Advances through meta-analysis.* Baltimore, MD: Johns Hopkins University Press.

Becker-Blease, K. A., Turner, H. A., & Finkelhor, D. (2010). Disasters, victimization, and children's mental health. *Child Development, 81,* 1040–1052.

Behnke, M., & Eyler, F. D. (1993). The consequences of prenatal substance use for the developing fetus, newborn, and young child. *International Journal of the Addictions, 28,* 1341–1391.

Behnke, A. O., Plunkett, S. W., Sands, T., & Bámaca-Colbert, M. Y. (2011). The relationship between Latino adolescents' perceptions of discrimination, neighborhood risk, and parenting on self-esteem and depressive symptoms. *Journal of Cross-Cultural Psychology, 42,* 1179–1197.

Beier, J. S., Over, H., & Carpenter, M. (2014). Young children help others to achieve their social goals. *Developmental Psychology, 50,* 934–940.

Belsky, J., Bakermans-Kranenburg, M. J., & van IJzendoorn, M. H. (2007). For better and for worse: Differential susceptibility to environmental influences. *Current Directions in Psychological Science, 16,* 300–304.

Belsky, J., Houts, R. M., & Pasco Fearon, R. M. (2010). Infant attachment security and the timing of puberty: Testing an evolutionary hypothesis. *Psychological Science, 21,* 1195–1201.

Belsky, J., & Pluess, M. (2013). Genetic moderation of early child-care effects on social functioning across childhood: A developmental analysis. *Child Development, 84,* 1209–1225.

Belsky, J., Steinberg, L., Houts, R. M., Halpern-Felsher, B. L., & the NICHD Early Child Care Research Network. (2010). The development of reproductive strategy in females: Early maternal harshness → earlier menarche → increased sexual risk taking. *Developmental Psychology, 46,* 120–128.

Bem, D. J. (1996). Exotic becomes erotic: A developmental theory of sexual orientation. *Psychological Review, 103,* 320–335.

Benenson, J. F., & Christakos, A. (2003). The greater fragility of females' versus males' closest same-sex friendships. *Child Development, 74,* 1123–1129.

Benner, A. D., & Graham, S. (2011). Latino adolescents' experiences of discrimination across the first 2 years of high school: Correlates and influences on educational outcomes. *Child Development, 82,* 508–519.

Benton, S. L., Corkill, A. J., Sharp, J. M., Downey, R. G., & Khramtsova, I. (1995). Knowledge, interest, and narrative writing. *Journal of Educational Psychology, 87,* 66–79.

Bereiter, C., & Scardamalia, M. (1987). *The psychology of written composition.* Hillsdale, NJ: Erlbaum.

Bergen, D., & Mauer, D. (2000). Symbolic play, phonological awareness, and literacy skills at three age levels. In K. A. Roskos & J. F. Christie (Eds.), *Play and literacy in early childhood: Research from multiple perspectives* (pp. 45–62). Mahwah, NJ: Erlbaum.

Berger, S. E., Adolph, K. E., & Lobo, S. A. (2005). Out of the toolbox: Toddlers differentiate wobbly and wooden handrails. *Child Development, 76,* 1294–1307.

Berger, C., & Dijkstra, J. K. (2013). Competition, envy, or snobbism? How popularity and friendships shape antipathy networks of adolescents. *Journal of Research on Adolescence, 23,* 586–595.

Berk, L. E. (2003). Vygotsky, Lev. In L. Nadel (Ed.), *Encyclopedia of cognitive science* (Vol. 6). London: Macmillan.

Berkman, E. T., Graham, A. M., & Fisher, P. A. (2012). Training self-control: A domain-general translational neuroscience approach. *Child Development Perspectives, 6,* 374–384.

Berko, J. (1958). The child's learning of English morphology. *Word, 14,* 150–177.

Berlin, L. J., Appleyard, K., & Dodge, K. A. (2011). Intergenerational continuity in child maltreatment: Mediating mechanisms and implications for prevention. *Child Development, 82*, 162–176.

Berlin, L. J., Ispa, J. M., Fine, M. A., Malone, P. S., Brooks-Gunn, J., Brady-Smith, C., et al. (2009). Correlates and consequences of spanking and verbal punishment for low-income White, African Americans and Mexican American toddlers. *Child Development, 80*, 1403–1420.

Bernal, S., Dehaene-Lambertz, G., Millotte, S., & Christophe, A. (2010). Two-year-olds compute syntactic structure on-line. *Developmental Science, 13*, 69–76.

Berndt, T. J., & Perry, T. B. (1990). Distinctive features and effects of adolescent friendships. In R. Montemayer, G. R. Adams, & T. P. Gullotta (Eds.), *From childhood to adolescence: A transition period?* London: Sage.

Bernier, A., Carlson, S. M., & Whipple, N. (2010). From external regulation to self-regulation: Early parenting precursors of young children's executive functioning. *Child Development, 81*, 326–339.

Bertenthal, B. H., & Clifton, R. K. (1998). Perception and action. In W. Damon (Ed.), *Handbook of child psychology* (Vol. 2). New York, NY: Wiley.

Berthier, N. E. (1996). Learning to reach: A mathematical model. *Developmental Psychology, 32*, 811–823.

Berthier, N., & Carrico, R. L. (2010). Visual information and object size in infant reaching. *Infant Behavior and Development, 33*, 555–566.

Best, J. R. (2010). Effects of physical activity on children's executive function: Contributions of experimental research on aerobic exercise. *Developmental Review, 30*, 331–351.

Best, J. R. (2014). Relations between video gaming and children's executive functions. In F. C. Blumberg (Ed.), *Learning by playing: Video gaming in education* (pp. 42–53). New York, NY: Oxford.

Beuker, K. T., Rommelse, N. N. J., Donders, R., & Buitelaar, J. K. (2013). Development of early communication skills in the first two years of life. *Infant Behavior and Development, 36*, 71–83.

Bhutta, Z. A., Chopra, M., Axelson, H., Berman, P., Boerma, T., Bryce, J., et al. (2010). Countdown to 2015 decade report (2000–10): Taking stock of maternal, newborn, and child survival. *Lancet, 375*, 2032–2044.

Bialystok, E. (1988). Levels of bilingualism and levels of linguistic awareness. *Developmental Psychology, 24*, 560–567.

Bialystok, E. (1997). Effects of bilingualism and biliteracy on children's emerging concepts of print. *Developmental Psychology, 33*, 429–440.

Bialystok, E., Shenfield, T., & Codd, J. (2000). Languages, scripts, and the environment: Factors in developing concepts of print. *Developmental Psychology, 36*, 66–76.

Biddle, S. J. H., & Asare, M. (2011). Physical activity and mental health in children and adolescents: a review of reviews. *British Journal of Sports Medicine, 45*, 886–895.

Biederman, J., Monuteaux, M. C., Mick, E., Spencer, T., Wilens, T. E., Silva, J. M., et al. (2006). Young adult outcome of attention deficit hyperactivity disorder: A controlled 10-year follow-up study. *Psychological Medicine, 362*, 167–179.

Biederman, J., Petty, C. R., Evans, M., Small, J., & Faraone, S. V. (2010). How persistent is ADHD? A controlled 10-year follow-up study of boys with ADHD. *Psychiatry Research, 177*, 299–304.

Bierman, K. L., Coie, J., Dodge, K., Greenberg, M., Lochman, J., McMohan, R., et al. (2013). School outcomes of aggressive-disruptive children: Prediction from kindergarten risk factors and impact of the Fast Track Prevention Program. *Aggressive Behavior, 39*, 114–130.

Bigler, R. S. (1995). The role of classification skills in moderating environmental influences on children's gender stereotyping: A study of the functional use of gender in the classroom. *Child Development, 66*, 1072–1087.

Bigler, R. S., Jones, L. C., & Lobliner, D. B. (1997). Social categorization and the formation of intergroup attitudes in children. *Child Development, 68*, 530–543.

Bigler, R. S., & Liben, L. S. (1990). The role of attitudes and interventions in gender-schematic processing. *Child Development, 61*, 1440–1452.

Bigler, R. S., & Liben, L. S. (2007). Developmental intergroup theory: Explaining and reducing children's social stereotyping and prejudice. *Current Directions in Psychological Science, 16*, 162–166.

Bigler, R. S., & Wright, Y. F. (2014). Reading, writing, arithmetic, and racism? Risks and benefits to teaching children about intergroup biases. *Child Development Perspectives, 8*, 18–23.

Bingenheimer, J. B., Brennan, R. T., & Earls, F. J. (2005). Firearm violence exposure and serious violent behavior. *Science, 308*, 1323–1326.

Birch, S. A., Akmal, N., & Frampton, K. (2010). Two-year-olds are vigilant of others' non-verbal cues to credibility. *Developmental Science, 13*, 363–369.

Biro, S., & Leslie, A. M. (2007). Infants' perception of goal-directed actions: Development through cue-based bootstrapping. *Developmental Science, 8*, 36–43.

Bjerkedal, T., Kristensen, P., Skjeret, G. A., & Brevik, J. I. (2007). Intelligence test scores and birth order among young Norwegian men (conscripts) analyzed within and between families. *Intelligence, 35*, 503–514.

Bjorklund, D. F. (2005). *Children's thinking: Cognitive development and individual differences* (4th ed.). Belmont, CA: Wadsworth.

Bjorklund, D. F. (2012). *Children's thinking* (5th ed). Belmont, CA: Wadsworth.

Bjorklund, D. F., & Jordan, A. C. (2013). Human parenting from an evolutionary perspective. In W. B. Wilcox & K. K. Kline (Eds.), *Gender and parenthood: Biological and social scientific perspectives* (pp. 61–90). New York, NY: Columbia University Press.

Bjorklund, D. F., & Rosenblum, K. E. (2002). Context effects in children's selection and use of simple arithmetic strategies. *Journal of Cognition & Development, 3*, 225–242.

Bjorklund, D. F., Yunger, J. L., & Pellegrini, A. D. (2002). The evolution of parenting and evolutionary approaches to childrearing. In M. H. Bornstein (Ed.), *Handbook of parenting. Vol. 2: Biology and ecology of parenting* (pp. 3–30). Mahwah, NJ: Erlbaum.

Black, J. E. (2003). Environment and development of the nervous system. In I. B. Weiner, M. Gallagher, & R. J. Nelson (Eds.), *Handbook of psychology, Vol. 3: Biological psychology* (pp. 655–668). Hoboken, NJ: Wiley.

Blair, B. L., Perry, N. B., O'Brien, M., Calkins, S. D., Keane, S. P., & Shanahan, L. (2014). The indirect effects of maternal emotion socialization on friendship quality in middle childhood. *Developmental Psychology, 50*, 566–576.

Blakemore, J. E. O. (2003). Children's beliefs about violating gender norms: Boys shouldn't look like girls, and girls shouldn't act like boys. *Sex Roles, 48*, 411–419.

Block, J. H. (1978). Another look at sex differentiation in the socialization behavior of mothers and fathers. In J. Sherman & F. L. Denmark (Eds.), *Psychology of women: Future directions for research* (pp. 29–87). New York, NY: Psychological Dimensions.

Bloom, P. (2000). *How children learn the meanings of words.* Cambridge MA: MIT Press.

Bloom, L., Margulis, C., Tinker, E., & Fujita, N. (1996). Early conversations and word learning: Contributions from child and adult. *Child Development, 67*, 3154–3175.

Bloom, L., Rocissano, L., & Hood, L. (1976). Adult-child discourse: Developmental interaction between information processing and linguistic knowledge. *Cognitive Psychology, 8*, 521–552.

Bloom, L., & Tinker, E. (2001). The intentionality model and language acquisition. *Monographs of the Society for Research in Child Development, 66* (Serial No. 267).

Boden, J. M., Fergusson, D. M., & Horwood, L. J. (2008). Does adolescent self-esteem predict later life outcomes? A test of the causal role of self-esteem. *Development & Psychopathology, 20,* 319–339.

Bohn, A., & Berntsen, D. (2013). The future is bright and predictable: The development of prospective life stories across childhood and adolescence. *Developmental Psychology, 49,* 1232–1241.

Boiger, M., & Mesquita, B. (2012). The construction of emotion in inter-actions, relationships, and cultures. *Emotion Review, 4,* 221–229.

Boivin, M., Brendgen, M., Vitaro, F., Dionne, G., Girard, A., Pérusse, D., & Tremblay, R. E. (2013). Strong genetic contribution to peer relationship difficulties at school entry: Findings from a longitudinal twin study. *Child Development, 84,* 1098–1114.

Bonnie, R. J., & Scott, E. S. (2013). The teenage brain: Adolescent brain research and the law. *Current Directions in Psychological Science, 22,* 158–161.

Bonny, J. W., & Lourenco, S. F. (2013). The approximate number system and its relation to early math achievement: Evidence from the pre-school years. *Journal of Experimental Child Psychology, 114,* 375–388.

Bornstein, M. H., & Arterberry, M. E. (2003). Recognition, discrimination, and categorization of smiling by 5-month-old infants. *Developmental Science, 6,* 585–599.

Bornstein, M. H., Hahn, C-S., & Wolke, D. (2013). Systems and cascades in cognitive development and academic achievement. *Child Development, 84,* 154–162.

Bornstein, M. H., Putnick, D. L., Suwalsky, J. T., & Gini, M. (2006). Maternal chronological age, prenatal and perinatal history, social support, and parenting of infants. *Child Development, 77,* 875–892.

Bortfeld, H., & Morgan, J. L. (2010). Is early word-form processing stress-full? How natural variability supports recognition. *Cognitive Psychology, 60,* 241–266.

Bosco, F. M., Friedman, O., & Leslie, A. M. (2006). Recognition of pretend and real actions in play by 1- and 2-year-olds: Early success and why they fail. *Cognitive Development, 21,* 3–10.

Boseovski, J. J. (2010). Evidence for "rose-colored glasses": An examina-tion of the positivity bias in young children's personality judgments. *Child Development Perspectives, 4,* 212–218.

Bosma, H. A., & Kunnen, E. S. (2001). Determinants and mechanisms in ego identity development: A review and synthesis. *Developmental Review, 21,* 39–66.

Bot, S. M., Engels, R. C. M. E., Knibbe, R. A., & Meeus, W. H. J. (2005). Friend's drinking behavior and adolescent alcohol consumption: The moderating role of friendship characteristics. *Addictive Behaviors, 30,* 929–947.

Bouchard, T. J. (2004). Genetic influence on human psychological traits. *Current Directions in Psychological Science, 13,* 148–151.

Bouchard, T. J. (2009). Genetic influence on human intelligence (Spearman's g): How much? *Annals of Human Biology, 36,* 527–544.

Bouchard, T. J., & McGue, M. (1981). Familial studies of intelligence: a review. *Science, 212,* 1055–1059.

Bowker, A. (2006). The relationship between sports participation and self-esteem during early adolescence. *Canadian Journal of Behavioral Science, 38,* 214–229.

Bowlby, J. (1953). *Child care and the growth of love.* London, UK: Penguin.

Bowlby, J. (1969). *Attachment and loss* (Vol. 1). New York, NY: Basic Books.

Bowlby, J. (1991). Ethological light on psychoanalytical problems. In P. Bateson (Ed.), *The development and integration of behaviour: Essays in honour of Robert Hinde* (pp. 301–313). New York, NY: Cambridge University Press.

Bradley, L., & Bryant, P. E. (1983). Categorising sounds and learning to read—a causal connection. *Nature, 301,* 419–421.

Bradley, R. H., & Corwyn, R. F. (2002). Socioeconomic status and child development. *Annual Review of Psychology, 53,* 371–399.

Brainerd, C. J. (1996). Piaget: A centennial celebration. *Psychological Science, 7,* 191–203.

Brainerd, C. J. (2013). Developmental reversals in false memory: A new look at the reliability of children's evidence. *Current Directions in Psychological Science, 22,* 335–341.

Brainerd, C. J., Holliday, R. E., Reyna, V. F., Yang, Y., & Toglia, M. P. (2010). Developmental reversals in false memory: Effects of emotional valence and arousal. *Journal of Experimental Child Psychology, 107,* 137–154.

Brainerd, C. J., & Reyna, V. F. (2005). *The science of false memory.* New York, NY: Oxford University Press.

Brainerd, C. J., & Reyna, V. F. (2013). Dual processes in memory development: Fuzzy-trace theory. In P. J. Bauer & R. Fivush (Eds.), *Wiley-Blackwell handbook on the development of children's memory.* New York, NY: Wiley-Blackwell.

Brainerd, C. J., Reyna, V. F., & Ceci, S. J. (2008). Developmental reversals in false memory: A review of data and theory. *Psychological Bulletin, 134,* 343–382.

Brandone, A. C., & Wellman, H. M. (2009). You can't always get what you want: Infants understand failed goal-directed actions. *Psychological Science, 20,* 85–91.

Braungart-Rieker, J. M., Hill-Soderlund, A. L., & Karrass, J. (2010). Fear and anger reactivity trajectories from 4 to 16 months: The roles of temperament, regulation, and maternal sensitivity. *Developmental Psychology, 46,* 791–804.

Braza, P., Carreras, R., Muñoz, J. M., Braza, F., Azurmendi, A., Pascual-Sagastizábal, E., et al. (2014). Negative maternal and paternal parenting styles as predictors of children's behavioral problems: Moderating effects of the child's sex. *Journal of Child and Family Studies,* in press.

Brazelton, T. B., & Nugent, J. K. (1995). *Neonatal behavioral assessment scale* (3rd ed). London: MacKeith.

Brechwald, W. A., & Prinstein, M. J. (2011). Beyond homophily: A decade of advances in understanding peer influence processes. *Journal of Research on Adolescence, 21,* 166–179.

Brendgen, M., Boivin, M., Dionne, G., Barker, E. D., Vitaro, F., Girard, A. et al. (2011). Gene-environment processes linking aggression, peer victimization, and the teacher-child relationship. *Child Development, 82,* 2021–2036.

Brendgen, M., Lamarche, V., Wanner, B., & Vitaro, F. (2010). Links between friendship relations and early adolescents' trajectories of depressed mood. *Developmental Psychology, 46,* 491–501.

Brendgen, M., Vitaro, F., Boivin, M., Dionea, G., & Perusse, D. (2006). Examining genetic and environmental effects on reactive versus proactive aggression. *Developmental Psychology, 42,* 1299–1312.

Brinkman, B. G., Jedinak, A., Rosen, L. A., & Zimmerman, T. S. (2011). Teaching children fairness: Decreasing gender prejudice among children. *Analyses of Social Issues and Social Policy, 11,* 61–81.

Brockington, I. (1996). *Motherhood and mental health.* Oxford, UK: Oxford University Press.

Brody, N. (1992). *Intelligence* (2nd ed.). San Diego, CA: Academic Press.

Brody, G. H. (1998). Sibling relationship quality: Its causes and consequences. *Annual Review of Psychology, 49,* 1–24.

Brody, G. H., & Ge, X. (2001). Linking parenting processes and self-regulation to psychological functioning and alcohol use during early adolescence. *Journal of Family Psychology, 15,* 82–94.

Brody, L. R., & Hall, J. A. (2008). Gender and emotion in context. In M. Lewis, J. M. Haviland-Jones, & L. F. Barrett (Eds.), *Handbook of emotions* (3rd ed., pp. 395–408). New York, NY: Guilford.

Brody, G. H., Kim, S., Murry, V. M., & Brown, A. C. (2003). Longitudinal direct and indirect pathways linking older sibling competence to the development of younger sibling competence. *Developmental Psychology, 39*, 618–628.

Brody, G. H., Stoneman, A., & McCoy, J. K. (1994). Forecasting sibling relationships in early adolescence from child temperament and family processes in middle childhood. *Child Development, 65*, 771–784.

Bronfenbrenner, U. (1995). Developmental ecology through space and time: A future perspective. In P. Moen, G. H. Elder, Jr., & K. Luscher (Eds.), *Examining lives in context: Perspectives on the ecology of human development*. Washington, DC: American Psychological Association.

Bronfenbrenner, U., & Morris, P. (2006). The ecology of developmental processes. In W. Damon & R. M. Lerner (Eds.), *Handbook of child psychology* (6th ed., Vol. 1, pp. 793–829). New York, NY: Wiley.

Brooker, R. J., Buss, K. A., Lemery-Chalfant, K., Aksan, N., Davidson, R. J., & Goldsmith, H. H. (2013). The development of stranger fear in infancy and toddlerhood: Normative development, individual differences, antecedents, and outcomes. *Developmental Science, 16*, 864–878.

Brotman, L. M., Calzada, E., Huang, K-Y., Kingston, S., Dawson-McClure, S., Kamboukos, D., et al. (2011). Promoting effective parenting practices and preventing child behavior problems in school among ethnically diverse families from underserved, urban communities. *Child Development, 82*, 258–276.

Brown, R. (1973). *A first language: The early stages*. Cambridge, MA: Harvard University Press.

Brown, B. B., & Bakken, J. P. (2011). Parenting and peer relationships: Reinvigorating research on family-peer linkages in adolescence. *Journal of Research on Adolescence, 21*, 153–165.

Brown, C. S., & Chu, H. (2012). Discrimination, ethnic identity, and academic outcomes of Mexican immigrant children: The importance of school context. *Child Development, 83*, 1477–1485.

Brown, J., & Dunn, J. (1992). Talk with your mother or your sibling? Developmental changes in early family conversations about feelings. *Child Development, 63*, 336–349.

Brown, B. B., Herman, M., Hamm, J. V., & Heck, D. J. (2008). Ethnicity and image: Correlates of crowd affiliation among ethnic minority youth. *Child Development, 79*, 529–546.

Brown, B. B., & Klute, C. (2003). Friends, cliques, and crowds. In G. R. Adams & M. D. Berzonsky (Eds.), *Blackwell handbook of adolescence* (pp. 330–348). Malden, MA: Blackwell.

Brown, J., Meadows, S. O., & Elder, G. H., Jr. (2007). Race-ethnic inequality and psychological distress: Depressive symptoms from adolescence to young adulthood. *Developmental Psychology, 43*, 1295–1311.

Brown, B. B., Mounts, N., Lamborn, S. D., & Steinberg, L. (1993). Parenting practices and peer group affiliation in adolescence. *Developmental Psychology, 64*, 467–482.

Brown, R. P., Osterman, L. L., & Barnes, C. D. (2009). School violence and the culture of honor. *Psychological Science, 20*, 1400–1405.

Brown, R., Pressley, M., Van Meter, P., & Schuder, T. (1996). A quasi-experimental validation of transactional strategies instruction with low-achieving second-grade readers. *Journal of Educational Psychology, 88*, 18–37.

Browne, K. D., & Hamilton-Giachritsis, C. (2005). The influence of violent media on children and adolescents: A public-health approach. *Lancet, 365*, 702–710.

Bruck, M., & Ceci, S. J. (1995). Amicus brief for the case of *State of New Jersey vs Michaels* presented by Committee of Concerned Social Scientists. *Psychology, Public Policy, & Law, 1*, 272–322.

Brummelman, E., Thomaes, S., Orobio de Casto, B., Overbeek, G., & Bushman, B. J. (2014). "That's not just beautiful—that's incredibly beautiful!" The adverse impact of inflated praise on children with low self-esteem. *Psychological Science, 25*, 728–735.

Buchanan, C. M., & Heiges, K. L. (2001). When conflict continues after the marriage ends: Effects of postdivorce conflict on children. In J. Grych & F. D. Fincham (Eds.), *Interparental conflict and child development* (pp. 337–362). New York, NY: Cambridge University Press.

Buckhalt, J. A., El-Sheikh, M., & Keller, P. (2007). Children's sleep and cognitive functioning: Race and socioeconomic status as moderators of effects. *Child Development, 78*, 213–231.

Buckingham-Howes, S., Berger, S. S., Scaletti, L. A., & Black, M. M. (2013). Systematic review of prenatal cocaine exposure and adolescent development. *Pediatrics, 131*, e1917–d1936.

Bugental, D. B., & Happaney, K. (2004). Predicting infant maltreatment in low-income families: The interactive effects of maternal attributions and child status at birth. *Developmental Psychology, 40*, 234–243.

Bugental, D. B., & Schwartz, A. (2009). A cognitive approach to child maltreatment prevention among medically at-risk infants. *Developmental Psychology, 45*, 284–288.

Buijzen, M., Schuurman, J., & Bomhof, E. (2008). Associations between children's television advertising exposure and their food consumption patterns: A household diary-survey study. *Appetite, 50*, 231–239.

Bukowski, W. M., Sippola, L. K., & Hoza, B. (1999). Same and other: Interdependency between participation in same- and other-sex friendships. *Journal of Youth & Adolescence, 28*, 439–459.

Bull, R., & Lee, K. (2014). Executive functioning and mathematics achievement. *Child Development Perspectives, 8*, 36–41.

Bullard, L., Wachlarowicz, M., DeLeeuw, J., Snyder, J., Low, S., Forgatch, M., et al. (2010). Effects of the Oregon model of Parent Management Training (PMTO) on marital adjustment in new stepfamilies: A randomized trial. *Journal of Family Psychology, 24*, 485–496.

Bullock, M., & Lütkenhaus, P. (1990). Who am I? The development of self-understanding in toddlers. *Merrill-Palmer Quarterly, 36*, 217–238.

Burack, J. A., Flanagan, T., Peled, T., Sutton, H. M., Zygmuntowicz, C., & Manly, J. T. (2006). Social perspective-taking skills in maltreated children and adolescents. *Developmental Psychology, 42*, 207–217.

Burchinal, M. R., Vandell, D. L., & Belsky, J. (2014). Is the prediction of adolescent outcomes from early child care moderated by later maternal sensitivity? Results from the NICHD Study of Early Child Care and Youth Development. *Developmental Psychology, 50*, 542–553.

Bureau of Labor Statistics. (2013). *Employment characteristics of families—2012*. Washington DC: U.S. Department of Labor.

Burk, W. J., & Laursen, B. (2005). Adolescent perceptions of friendship and their associations with individual adjustment. *International Journal of Behavioral Development, 29*, 156–164.

Burke, R., & Kao, G. (2013). Bearing the burden of whiteness: The implications of racial self-identification for multiracial adolescents' school belonging and academic achievement. *Ethnic and Racial Studies, 36*, 747–773.

Burman, D. D., Minas, T., Bolger, D. J., & Booth, J. R. (2013). Age, sex, and verbal abilities affect location of linguistic connectivity in ventral visual pathway. *Brain & Language, 124*, 184–193.

Burnham, D., & Dodd, B. (2004). Auditory-visual speech integration by prelinguistic infants: Perception of an emergent consonant in the McGurk effect. *Developmental Psychobiology, 45*, 204–220.

Burton, C. M., Marshal, M. P., & Chisolm, D. J. (2014). School absenteeism and mental health among sexual minority youth and heterosexual youth. *Journal of School Psychology, 52*, 37–47.

Buss, K. A., & Goldsmith, H. H. (1998). Fear and anger regulation in infancy: Effects on the temporal dynamics of affective expression. *Child Development, 69,* 359–374.

Buttelmann, D., & Böhm, R. (2014). The ontogeny of the motivation that underlies in-group bias. *Psychological Science, 25,* 921–927.

Buttelmann, D., Zmyj, N., Daum, M., & Carpenter, M. (2013). Selective imitation of in-group over out-group members in 14-month-old infants. *Child Development, 84,* 422–428.

Cai, H., Brown, J. D., Deng, C., & Oakes, M. A. (2007). Self-esteem and culture: Differences in cognitive self-evaluations or affective self-regard? *Asian Journal of Social Psychology, 10,* 162–170.

Cain, K. (1999). Ways of reading: How knowledge and use of strategies are related to reading comprehension. *British Journal of Developmental Psychology, 17,* 293–312.

Caldwell, M. S., Rudolph, K. D., Troop-Gordon, W., & Kim, D-Y. (2004). Reciprocal influences among relational self-views, social disengagement, and peer stress during early adolescence. *Child Development, 75,* 1140–1154.

Callaghan, T., Moll, H., Rakoczy, H., Warneken, F., Liszkowski, U., Behne, T., et al. (2011). Early social cognition in three cultural contexts. *Monographs of the Society for Research in Child Development, 76,* Serial No. 299.

Callahan, C. M. (2000). Intelligence and giftedness. In R. J. Sternberg (Ed.), *Handbook of intelligence* (pp. 159–175). Cambridge, UK: Cambridge University Press.

Calvert, S. L. (2008). Children as consumers: Advertising and marketing. *The Future of Children, 18,* 205–234.

Calvert, S. L., & Valkenburg, P. M. (2013). The influence of television, video games, and the internet on children's creativity. In M. Taylor (Ed.), *The Oxford handbook of the development of imagination* (pp. 438–450). New York, NY: Oxford.

Cameron, L., Rutland, A., Brown, R., & Douch, R. (2006). Changing children's intergroup attitudes toward refugees: Testing different models of extended contact. *Child Development, 77,* 1208–1219.

Campbell, F. A., Pungello, E. P., Burchinal, M., Kainz, K., Pan, Y., Wasik, B. H., et al. (2012). Adult outcomes as a function of an early childhood educational program: An Abecedarian Project follow-up. *Developmental Psychology, 48,* 1033–1043.

Campbell, F. A., Pungello, E. P., Miller-Johnson, S., Burchinal, M., & Ramey, C. T. (2001). The development of cognitive and academic abilities: Growth curves from an early childhood educational experiment. *Developmental Psychology, 37,* 231–242.

Campbell, R., & Sais, E. (1995). Accelerated metalinguistic (phonological) awareness in bilingual children. *British Journal of Developmental Psychology, 13,* 61–68.

Campos, J. J., Anderson, D. I., Barbu-Roth, M. A., Hubbard, E. M., Hertenstein, M. J., & Witherington, D. (2000). Travel broadens the mind. *Infancy, 1,* 149–219.

Campos, J. J., Hiatt, S., Ramsay, D., Henderson, C., & Svedja, M. (1978). The emergency of fear on the visual cliff. In M. Lewis & L. Rosenblum (Eds.), *The origins of affect.* New York, NY: Plenum.

Camras, L. A., Chen, Y., Bakeman, R., Norris, K., & Cain, R. T. (2006). Culture, ethnicity, and children's facial expressions: A study of European American, Mainland Chinese, Chinese American, and adopted Chinese girls. *Emotion, 6,* 103–114.

Camras, L. A., Ester, H., Campos, J., Campos, R., Ujiie, T., Miyake, K., et al. (1998). Production of emotional facial expressions in European, American, Japanese, and Chinese infants. *Developmental Psychology, 34,* 616–628.

Camras, L. A., & Fatani, S. S. (2008). The development of facial expressions: Current perspectives on infant emotions. In M. Lewis, J. M. Haviland-Jones, & L. F. Barrett (Eds.), *Handbook of emotions* (3rd ed., pp. 291–303). New York, NY: Guilford.

Candel, I., Hayne, H., Strange, D., & Prevoo, E. (2009). The effect of suggestion on children's recognition memory for seen and unseen details. *Psychology, Crime, & Law, 15,* 29–39.

Cantrell, L., & Smith, L. B. (2013). Open questions and a proposal: A critical review of the evidence on infant numerical abilities. *Cognition, 128,* 331–352.

Capelli, C. A., Nakagawa, N., & Madden, C. M. (1990). How children understand sarcasm: The role of context of information. *Child Development, 61,* 1824–1841.

Caravolas, M., Lervåg, A., Mousikou, P., Efrim, C., Litavský, M., Onochie-Quintanilla, E., et al. (2012). Common patterns of prediction of literacy development in different alphabetic orthographies. *Psychological Science, 23,* 678–686.

Card, N. A. (2010). Antipathetic relationships in child and adolescent development: A meta-analytic review and recommendations for an emerging area of study. *Developmental Psychology, 46,* 516–529.

Card, N. A., & Hodges, E. V. (2006). Shared targets for aggression by early adolescent friends. *Developmental Psychology, 42,* 1327–1338.

Carlson, S. M., Koenig, M. A., & Harms, M. B. (2013). Theory of mind. *WIREs Cognitive Science, 4,* 391–402.

Carlson, S. M., & Meltzoff, A. N. (2008). Bilingual experience and executive functioning in young children. *Developmental Science, 11,* 282–298.

Carlson, M. D., Mendle, J., & Harden, K. P. (2014). Early adverse environments and genetic influences on age at first sex: Evidence for gene × environment interaction. *Developmental Psychology, 50,* 1532–1554.

Carpenter, P. A., & Daneman, M. (1981). Lexical retrieval and error recovery in reading: A model based on eye fixations. *Journal of Verbal Learning & Verbal Behavior, 20,* 137–160.

Carpenter, R., McGarvey, C., Mitchell, E. A., Tappin, D. M., Vennemann, M. M., Smuk, M., et al. (2013). Bedsharing when parents do not smoke: Is there a risk of SIDS? An individual level analysis of five major case-control studies. *British Medical Journal Open, 3:*e002299.

Carré, J. M., McCormick, C. M., & Hariri, A. R. (2011). The social neuroendocrinology of human aggression. *Psychoneuroendocrinology, 36,* 935–944.

Carrere, S., & Gottman, J. M. (1999). Predicting the future of marriages. In E. M. Hetherington (Ed.), *Coping with divorce, single parenting, and remarriage: A risk and resiliency perspective.* Mahwah, NJ: Erlbaum.

Carroll, J. B. (1993). *Human cognitive abilities: A survey of factor-analytic studies.* New York, NY: Cambridge University Press.

Carroll, J. B. (1996). A three-stratum theory of intelligence: Spearman's contribution. In I. Dennis & P. Tapsfield (Eds.), *Human abilities: Their nature and measurement.* Mahwah, NJ: Erlbaum.

Carroll, J. L., & Loughlin, G. M. (1994). Sudden infant death syndrome. In F. A. Oski, C. D. DeAngelis, R. D. Feigin, J. A. McMillan, & J. B. Warshaw (Eds.), *Principles and practice of pediatrics.* Philadelphia, PA: Lippincott.

Carskadon, M. A. (2002). Factors influencing sleep patterns of adolescents. In M. A. Carskadon (Ed.), *Adolescent sleep patterns: Biological, social, and psychological influences* (pp. 4–26). New York, NY: Cambridge University Press.

Carter, C. S. (2014). Oxytocin pathways and the evolution of human behavior. *Annual Review of Psychology, 65,* 17–39.

Carver, P. R., Egan, S. K., & Perry, D. G. (2004). Children who question their heterosexuality. *Developmental Psychology, 40,* 43–53.

Carver, K., Joyner, K., & Udry, J. R. (2003). National estimates of adolescent romantic relationships. In P. Florsheim (Ed.), *Adolescent romantic relations and sexual behavior: Theory, research, and practical implications* (pp. 23–56). Mahwah, NJ: Erlbaum.

Casalin, S., Luyten, P., Vliegen, N., & Meurs, P. (2012). The structure and stability of temperament from infancy to toddlerhood: A one-year prospective study. *Infant Behavior and Development, 35,* 94–108.

Caselli, M. C., Rinaldi, P., Stefanini, S., & Volterra, V. (2012). Early action and gesture "vocabulary" and its relation with word comprehension and production. *Child Development, 83,* 526–542.

Casey, B. J., & Caudle, K. (2013). The teenage brain: Self control. *Current Directions in Psychological Science, 22,* 82–87.

Casey, B. J., Tottenham, N., Liston, C., & Durston, S. (2005). Imaging the developing brain: What have we learned about cognitive development? *Trends in Cognitive Neuroscience, 9,* 104–110.

Casiglia, A. C., Coco, A. L., & Zappulla, C. (1998). Aspects of social reputation and peer relationships in Italian children: A cross-cultural perspective. *Developmental Psychology, 34,* 723–730.

Casper, D. M., & Card, N. A. (2010). "We were best friends, But…": Two studies of antipathetic relationships emerging from broken friendships. *Journal of Adolescent Research, 25,* 499–526.

Caspi, A., Roberts, B. W., & Shiner, R. L. (2005). Personality development: Stability and change. *Annual Review of Psychology, 56,* 453–484.

Cassidy, J. (1994). Emotion regulation: Influences of attachment relationships. *Monographs of the Society for Research in Child Development, 59* (Serial No. 240), 228–283.

Castelli, L., Zogmaister, C., & Tomelleri, S. (2009). The transmission of racial attitudes within the family. *Developmental Psychology, 45,* 586–591.

Castro, D. C., Páez, M. M., Dickinson, D. K., & Frede, E. (2011). Promoting language and literacy in young dual language learners: Research, practice, and policy. *Child Development Perspectives, 5,* 15–21.

Cattell, R. B. (1965). *The scientific analysis of personality.* Baltimore, MD: Penguin.

Cauvet, E., Limissuri, R., Millotte, S., Skoruppa, K., Cabrol, D., & Christophe, A. (2014). Function words constrain on-line recognition of verbs and nouns in French 18-month-olds. *Language Learning and Development, 10,* 1–18.

Ceci, S. J., & Bruck, M. (1998). Children's testimony: Applied and basic issues. In W. Damon (Ed.), *Handbook of child psychology* (Vol. 4). New York, NY: Wiley.

Center for Behavioral Health Statistics and Quality. (2012). *Depression triples between the ages of 12 and 15 among adolescent girls.* Rockville MD: Substance Abuse and Mental Health Services Administration.

Centers for Disease Control and Prevention. (2012). Youth risk behavior surveillance—United States, 2011. *Morbidity and Mortality Weekly Report, 61.* Atlanta GA: Author.

Centers for Disease Control and Prevention. (2013). *2011 Assisted Reproductive Technology Fertility Clinic Success Rates Report.* Atlanta, GA: Author.

Central Intelligence Agency. (2013). *The world factbook* 2013–14. Washington, DC: Author.

Cerella, J., & Hale, S. (1994). The rise and fall in information-processing rates over the life span. *Acta Psychologica, 86,* 109–197.

Champion, T. B. (2003). A "matter of vocabulary": Performance of low-income African-American Head Start children on the Peabody Picture Vocabulary Test. *Communication Disorders Quarterly, 24,* 121–127.

Chandler, M. J., & Carpendale, J. I. M. (1998). Inching toward a mature theory of mind. In M. D. Ferrari & R. J. Sternberg (Eds.), *Self-awareness: Its nature and development* (pp. 148–190). New York, NY: Guilford Press.

Chanquoy, L. (2001). How to make it easier for children to revise their writing: A study of text revision from 3rd to 5th grades. *British Journal of Educational Psychology, 71,* 15–41.

Chao, R. K. (2001). Extending research on the consequences of parenting style for Chinese Americans and European Americans. *Child Development, 72,* 1832–1843.

Chaplin, T. M., & Aldao, A. (2013). Gender differences in emotion expression in children: A meta-analytic review. *Psychological Bulletin, 139,* 735–765.

Chapman, P. D. (1988). *Schools as sorters: Lewis M. Terman, applied psychology, and the intelligence testing movement, 1890–1930.* New York, NY: New York University Press.

Chase-Lansdale, P. L., Brooks-Gunn, J., & Zamsky, E. S. (1994). Young African-American multigenerational families in poverty: Quality of mothering and grandmothering. *Child Development, 65,* 373–393.

Chavajay, P. (2008). Organizational patterns in problem solving among Mayan fathers and children. *Developmental Psychology, 44,* 882–888.

Chen, E., Cohen, S., & Miller, G. E. (2010). How low socioeconomic status affects 2-year-hormonal trajectories in children. *Psychological Science, 21,* 31–37.

Chen, J., & Gardner, H. (2005). Assessment based on multiple intelligences theory. In D. P. Flanagan & P. L. Harrison (Eds.), *Contemporary intellectual assessment: Theories, tests, and issues* (pp. 77–102). New York, NY: Guilford Press.

Chen, Y., Norton, D. J., McBain, R., Gold, J., Frazier, J. A. & Coyle, J. T. (2012). Enhanced local processing of dynamic visual information in autism: Evidence from speed discrimination. *Neuropsychologia, 50,* 733–739.

Chen, X., Wang, L., & Cao, R. (2011). Shyness-sensitivity and unsociability in rural Chinese children: relations with social, school, and psychological adjustment. *Child Development, 82,* 1531–1543.

Chen, X., Wang, L., & DeSouza, A. (2006). Temperament, socioemotional functioning, and peer relationships in Chinese and North American children. In X. Chen, D. C. French, & B. H. Schneider (Eds.), *Peer relationships in cultural context* (pp. 123–147). New York, NY: Cambridge University Press.

Chen-Gaddini, M. (2012). Chinese mothers and adolescents' views of authority and autonomy: A study of parent-adolescent conflict in urban and rural China. *Child Development, 83,* 1846–1852.

Cheung, W. W., & Mao, P. (2012). Recent advances in obesity: Genetics and beyond. *ISRN Endocrinology,* Article ID 536905.

Chi, M. T. H. (1978). Knowledge structures and memory development. In R. Siegler (Ed.), *Children's thinking: What develops?* Hillsdale, NJ: Erlbaum.

Child Welfare Information Gateway. (2013). *Leaving your child home alone.* Washington DC: Children's Bureau.

Children's Defense Fund. (2010). *State of America's children: 2010.* Washington, DC: Author.

Choe, D. E., Olson, S. L., & Sameroff, A. J. (2013). The interplay of externalizing problems and physical and inductive discipline during childhood. *Developmental Psychology, 49,* 2029–2039.

Chomitz, V. R., Cheung, L. W. Y., & Lieberman, E. (1995). The role of lifestyle in preventing low birth weight. *The Future of Children, 5,* 121–138.

Chomsky, N. (1957). *Syntactic structure.* The Hague, The Netherlands: Mouton.

Chorpita, B. F., & Barlow, D. H. (1998). The development of anxiety: The role of control in the early environment. *Psychological Bulletin, 124,* 3–21.

Chou, R. J. A. (2011). Filial piety by contract? The emergence, implementation, and implications of the "Family Support Agreement" in China. *Gerontologist, 51,* 3–16.

Chow, B. W., McBride-Chang, C., Cheung, H., & Chow, C. S. (2008). Dialogic reading and morphology training in Chinese children: Effects on language and literacy. *Developmental Psychology, 44,* 233–244.

Christensen, A., & Heavey, C. L. (1999). Intervention for couples. *Annual Review of Psychology, 50,* 165–190.

Chung, H. L., & Steinberg, L. (2006). Relations between neighborhood factors, parenting behaviors, peer deviance, and delinquency among serious juvenile offenders. *Developmental Psychology, 42,* 319–331.

Chung-Hall, J., & Chen, X. (2010). Aggressive and prosocial peer group functioning: Effects on children's social, school, and psychological adjustment. *Social Development, 19,* 659–680.

Cicchetti, D., & Toth, S. L. (2006). Developmental psychopathology and preventive intervention. In W. Damon & R. M. Lerner (Eds.), *Handbook of child psychology* (Vol. 4.) New York, NY: Wiley.

Clark, K. B. (1945). A brown girl in a speckled world. *Journal of Social Issues, 1,* 10–15.

Clark, K. B., & Clark, M. K. (1940). Skin color as a factor in racial identification of Negro preschool children. *Journal of Social Psychology, 11,* 159–169.

Clarke, P. J., Snowling, M. J., Truelove, E., & Hulme, C. (2010). Ameliorating children's reading-comprehension difficulties: A randomized controlled trial. *Psychological Science, 21,* 1106–1116.

Clarke, P. J., Truelove, E., Hulme, C., & Snowling, M. J. (2014). *Developing reading comprehension.* Chichester, West Sussex, UK: Wiley.

Clarke-Stewart, K. A., & Bretano, C. (2005). *Till divorce do us part.* New Haven, CT: Yale University Press.

Clements, D. H. (1995). Teaching creativity with computers. *Educational Psychology Review, 7,* 141–161.

Clifford, A., Lang, L. D., & Chen, R. L. (2012). Effects of maternal cigarette smoking during pregnancy on cognitive parameters of children and young adults: A literature review. *Neurotoxicology and Teratology, 34,* 560–570.

Cnattingius, S. (2004). The epidemiology of smoking during pregnancy: Smoking prevalence, maternal characteristics, and pregnancy outcomes. *Nicotine & Tobacco Research, 6,* S125–S140.

Coall, D. A., & Hertwig, R. (2011). Grandparent investment: A relic of the past or a resource for the future? *Current Directions in Psychological Science, 20,* 93–98.

Coatsworth, J. D., & Conroy, D. E. (2009). The effects of autonomy-supporting coaching, need satisfaction, and self-perceptions on initiative and identity in youth swimmers. *Developmental Psychology, 45,* 320–328.

Coelho, J. S., Jansen, A., Roefs, A., & Nederkoom, C. (2009). Eating behavior in response to food-cue exposure: Examining the cue-reactivity and counteractive-control models. *Psychology of Addictive Behaviors, 23,* 131–139.

Cohen, L. B., & Cashon, C. H. (2003). Infant perception and cognition. In R. M. Lerner, D. K. Freedheim, I. B. Weiner, M. A. Easterbrooks, & J. Mistry (Eds.), *Handbook of psychology: Developmental psychology.* Hoboken, NJ: Wiley.

Cohen, R. W., Martinez, M. E., & Ward, B. W. (2010). *Health insurance coverage: Early release of estimates from the National Health Interview Survey, 2009.* Hyattsville MD: National Center for Health Statistics.

Cohen, M., & Piquero, A. R. (2009). New evidence on the monetary value of saving a high risk youth. *Journal of Quantitative Criminology, 25,* 25–49.

Cohen, S., & Williamson, G. M. (1991). Stress and infectious disease in humans. *Psychological Bulletin, 109,* 5–24.

Cohen Kadosh, K., Johnson, M. H., Dick, F., Cohen Kadosh, R., & Blakemore, S-J. (2013). Effects of age, task performance, and structural brain development on face processing. *Cerebral Cortex, 23,* 1630–1642.

Coie, J. D., Dodge, K. A., Terry, R., & Wright, V. (1991). The role of aggression in peer relations: An analysis of aggression episodes in boys' play groups. *Child Development, 62,* 812–826.

Colby, A., Kohlberg, L., Gibbs, J. C., & Lieberman, M. (1983). A longitudinal study of moral development. *Monographs of the Society for Research in Child Development, 48* (Serial No. 200).

Cole, C. A. (1991). Change in self-perceived competence as a function of peer and teacher evaluation. *Developmental Psychology, 27,* 682–688.

Cole, M. (2006). Culture and cognitive development in phylogenetic, historical and ontogenetic perspective. In W. Damon & R. M. Lerner (Eds.), *Handbook of child psychology* (6th ed., Vol. 2). New York, NY: Wiley.

Cole, P. M., Tamang, B. L., & Shrestha, S. (2006). Cultural variations in the socialization of young children's anger and shame. *Child Development, 77,* 1237–1251.

Coleman-Jensen, A., Nord, M., & Singh, A. (2013). Household food security in the United States in 2012. *Economic Research Report,* Number 155, U.S. Department of Agriculture.

Collins, W. A. (2003). More than myth: The developmental significance of romantic relationships during adolescence. *Journal of Research on Adolescence, 13,* 1–24.

Collins, R. L., Martino, S. C., Elliot, M. N., & Miu, A. (2011). Relationships between adolescent sexual outcomes and exposure to sex in media: Robustness to propensity-based analysis. *Developmental Psychology, 47,* 585–591.

Collins, W. A., Welsh, D. P., & Furman, W. (2009). Adolescent romantic relationships. *Annual Review of Psychology, 60,* 631–652.

Committee on Genetics. (1996). Newborn screening fact sheet. *Pediatrics, 98,* 473–501.

Conboy, B. T., & Thal, D. J. (2006). Ties between the lexicon and grammar: Cross-sectional and longitudinal studies of bilingual toddlers. *Child Development, 77,* 712–735.

Condry, J. C., & Ross, D. F. (1985). Sex and aggression: The influence of gender label on the perception of aggression in children. *Child Development, 56,* 225–233.

Conduct Problems Prevention Research Group. (2011). The effects of the Fast Track preventive intervention on the development of conduct disorder across childhood. *Child Development, 82,* 331–345.

Conger, R. D., & Elder, G. H. (1994). *Families in troubled times: Adapting to change in rural America.* New York, NY: Aldine de Gruyter.

Conry-Murray, C., & Turiel, E. (2012). Jimmy's baby doll and Jenny's truck: Young children's reasoning about gender norms. *Child Development, 83,* 146–158.

Constantinescu, M., & Hines, M. (2012). Relating prenatal testosterone exposure to postnatal behavior in typically developing children: Methods and findings. *Child Development Perspectives, 6,* 407–413.

Cook, E. C., Buehler, C., & Henson, R. (2009). Parents and peers as social influences to deter antisocial behavior. *Journal of Youth & Adolescence, 38,* 1204–1252.

Cooke, L. J., Chambers, L. C., Añez, E. V., Croker, H. A. Boniface, D.,Yeomans, M. R., et al. (2011). Eating for pleasure or profit: The effects of incentives on children's enjoyment of vegetables. *Psychological Science, 22,* 190–196.

Cooper, H., Hedges, L. V., & Valentine, J. C. (Eds.). (2009). *The handbook of research synthesis and meta-analysis* (2nd ed.). New York: Russell Sage Foundation.

Coplan, R. J., & Armer, M. (2007). A "multitude" of solitude: A closer look at social withdrawal and nonsocial play in early childhood. *Child Development Perspectives, 1,* 26–32.

Coplan, R. J., Gavinski-Molina, M. H., Lagace-Seguin, D. G., & Wichman, C. (2001). When girls versus boys play alone: Nonsocial play and adjustment in kindergarten. *Developmental Psychology, 37,* 464–474.

Coplan, R. J., & Ooi, L. (2014). The causes and consequences of "playing alone" in childhood. In R. J. Coplan & J. C. Bowker (Eds.), *The handbook of solitude: Psychological perspectives on social isolation, social withdrawal, and being alone* (pp. 111–128). Chichester, West Sussex, UK: Wiley.

Coplan, R. J., Rose-Krasnor, L., Weeks, M., Kingsbury, A., Kingsbury, M., & Bullock, A. (2013). Alone is a crowd: Social motivations, social withdrawal, and socioemotional functioning in later childhood. *Developmental Psychology, 49,* 861–875.

Copper, R. L., Goldenberg, R. L., Das, A., Elder, N., Swain, M., Norman, G. et al. (1996). The preterm prediction study: Maternal stress is associated with spontaneous preterm birth at less than thirty-five weeks' gestation. *American Journal of Obstetrics & Gynecology, 175,* 1286–1292.

Coppus, A. M. W. (2013). People with intellectual disability: What do we know about adulthood and life expectancy. *Developmental Disabilities Research Reviews, 18,* 6–16.

Corballis, M. C., Badzakova-Trajkova, G., & Häberling, I. S. (2012). Right hand, left brain: Genetic and evolutionary assymetries for language and manual action. *WIREs Cognitive Science, 3,* 1–17.

Cornelius, M., Taylor, P., Geva, D., & Day, N. (1995). Prenatal tobacco exposure and marijuana use among adolescents: Effects on offspring gestational age, growth, and morphology. *Pediatrics, 95,* 738–743.

Corriveau, K. H., Kinzler, K. D., & Harris, P. L. (2013). Accuracy trumps accent in children's endorsement of object labels. *Developmental Psychology, 49,* 470–479.

Costa, P. T., & McRae, R. R. (2001). A theoretical context for adult temperament. In T. D. Wachs & G. A. Kohnstamm (Eds.), *Temperament in context* (pp. 1–21). Mahwah, NJ: Erlbaum.

Costin, S. E., & Jones, D. C. (1992). Friendship as a facilitator of emotional responsiveness and prosocial interventions among young children. *Developmental Psychology, 28,* 941–947.

Côté, S. M., Vaillancourt, T., Barker, E. D., Nagin, D., & Tremblay, R. E. (2007). The joint development of physical and indirect aggression: Predictors of continuity and change during childhood. *Development and Psychopathology, 19,* 37–55.

Côté, S., Zoccolillo, M., Tremblay, R. E., Nagin, D., & Vitaro, F. (2001). Predicting girls' conduct disorder in adolescence from childhood trajectories of disruptive behaviors. *Journal of the American Academy of Child and Adolescent Psychiatry, 40,* 678–684.

Coulton, C. J., Crampton, D. S., Irwin, M., Spilsbury, J. C., & Korbin, J. E. (2007). How neighborhoods influence child maltreatment: A review of the literature and alternative pathways. *Child Abuse & Neglect, 31,* 1117–1142.

Cousminer, D. L., Berry, D. J., Timpson, N. J., Ang, W., Thiering, E., Byrne, E. M., et al. (2013). Genome-wide association and longitudinal analyses reveal genetic loci linking pubertal height growth, pubertal timing, and childhood adiposity. *Human Molecular Genetics, 22,* 2735–2747.

Coutelle, C. Themis, M., Waddington, S. N., Buckley, S. M., Gregory, L. G., Nivsarkar, M. S., et al. (2005). Gene therapy progress and prospects: Fetal gene therapy—first proofs of concept—some adverse effects. *Gene Therapy, 12,* 1601–1607.

Cox, S. J., Mezulis, A. H., & Hyde, J. S. (2010). The influence of child gender role and maternal feedback to child stress on the emergence of the gender difference in depressive rumination in adolescence. *Developmental Psychology, 46,* 842–852.

Cox, M. J., & Paley, B. (2003). Understanding families as systems. *Current Directions in Psychological Science, 12,* 193–196.

Cox, M. J., Paley, B., & Harter, K. (2001). Interparental conflict and parent–child relationships. In J. H. Grych & F. D. Fincham (Eds.), *Interparental conflict and child development* (pp. 249–272). New York, NY: Cambridge University Press.

Coyne, C. A., Långström, N., Rickert, M. E., Lichtenstein, P., & D'Onofrio, B. M. (2013). Maternal age at first birth and offspring criminality: Using the children of twins design to test causal hypotheses. *Development and Psychopathology, 25,* 17–35.

Craig, K. D., Whitfield, M. F., Grunau, R. V. E., Linton, J., & Hadjistavropoulos, H. D. (1993). Pain in the preterm neonate: Behavioral and physiological indices. *Pain, 52,* 238–299.

Creusere, M. A. (1999). Theories of adults' understanding and use of irony and sarcasm: Applications to and evidence from research with children. *Developmental Review, 19,* 213–262.

Crick, N. R., & Dodge, K. A. (1994). A review and reformulation of social-information processing mechanisms in children's social adjustment. *Psychological Bulletin, 115,* 74–101.

Crick, N. R., & Grotpeter, J. K. (1995). Relational aggression, gender, and social-psychological adjustment. *Child Development, 66,* 710–722.

Crick, N. R., Ostrov, J. M., Appleyard, K., Jansen, E., & Casas, J. F. (2004). Relational aggression in early childhood: You can't come to my birthday party unless…In M. Putallaz & K. Bierman (Eds.), *Aggression, antisocial behavior, and violence among girls: A developmental perspective* (pp. 71–89). New York, NY: Guilford.

Crick, N. R., & Werner, N. E. (1998). Response decision processes in relational and overt aggression. *Child Development, 69,* 1630–1639.

Cristia, A. (2010). Phonetic enhancement of sibilants in infant-directed speech. *Journal of the Acoustical Society of America, 128,* 424–434.

Crocetti, E., Rubini, M., Luyckx, K., & Meeus, W. (2008). Identity formation in early and middle adolescence from various ethnic groups: From three dimensions to five statuses. *Journal of Youth & Adolescence, 37,* 983–996.

Croker, S., & Buchanan, H. (2011). Scientific reasoning in a real-world context: The effect of prior belief and outcome on children's hypothesis-testing strategies. *British Journal of Developmental Psychology, 29,* 409–424.

Crosnoe, R., Augustine, J. M., & Huston, A. C. (2012). Children's early child care and their mothers' later involvement with schools. *Child Development, 83,* 758–772.

Crouter, A. C., & Bumpus, M. F. (2001). Linking parents' work stress to children's and adolescents' psychological adjustment. *Current Directions in Psychological Science, 10,* 156–159.

Crouter, A. C., Whiteman, S. D., McHale, S. M., & Osgood, D. (2007). Development of gender attitude traditionality across middle childhood and adolescence. *Child Development, 78,* 911–926.

Cruz, I., Quittner, A. L., Marker, C., DesJardin, J. L. and the DCaCI Investigative Team. (2013). Identification of effective strategies to promote language in deaf children with cochlear implants. *Child Development, 84,* 543–559.

Csizmadia, A., Brunsma, D. L., & Cooney, T. M. (2012). Racial identification and developmental outcomes among Black-White multiracial youth: A review from a life course perspective. *Advances in Life Course Research, 17,* 34–44.

Csizmadia, A., & Ispa, J. M. (2014). Black-White biracial children's social development from kindergarten to fifth grade: Links with racial identification, gender, and socioeconomic status. *Social Development, 23*, 157–177.

Cuellar, I., Nyberg, B., Maldonado, R. E., & Roberts, R. E. (1997). Ethnic identity and acculturation in a young adult Mexican-origin population. *Journal of Community Psychology, 25*, 535–549.

Cummings, E. M., George, M. R. W., McCoy, K., P., & Davies, P. T. (2012). Interparental conflict in kindergarten and adolescent adjustment: Prospective investigation of emotional security as an explanatory mechanism. *Child Development, 83*, 1703–1715.

Cummings, E. M., Goeke-Morey, M. C., Merrilees, C. E., Taylor, L. K., & Shirlow, P. (2014). A social-ecological, process-oriented perspective on political violence and child development. *Child Development Perspectives, 8*, 82–89.

Cummings, E., Schermerhorn, A. C., Davies, P. T., Goeke-Morey, M. C., & Cummings, J. S. (2006). Interparental discord and child adjustment: Prospective investigations of emotional security as an explanatory mechanism. *Child Development, 77*, 132–152.

Cunningham, A. E., Perry, K. E., Stanovich, K. E., & Share, D. L. (2002). Orthographic learning during reading: Examining the role of self-teaching. *Journal of Experimental Child Psychology, 82*, 185–199.

Currie, J. (2013). Pollution and infant health. *Child Development Perspectives, 7*, 237–242.

Currie, J., & Walker, R. (2011). Traffic congestion and infant health: Evidence from EZPass. *American Economic Journals: Applied Economics, 3*, 65–90.

Curtiss, S. (1989). The independence and task-specificity of language. In M. H. Bornstein & J. S. Bruner (Eds.), *Interaction in human development* (pp. 105–137). Hillsdale, NJ: Erlbaum.

Cvencek, D., Meltzoff, A. N., & Greenwald, A. G. (2011). Math-gender stereotypes in elementary school children. *Child Development, 82*, 766–779.

Daniels, H. (2011). Vygotsky and psychology. In U. Goswami (Ed.), *The Wiley-Blackwell handbook of childhood cognitive development* (2nd ed., pp. 673–696). West Sussex, UK: Wiley-Blackwell.

Dannemiller, J. L. (1998). Color constancy and color vision during infancy: Methodological and empirical issues. In V. Walsh & J. Kulikowski (Eds.), *Perceptual constancy: Why things look as they do*. New York, NY: Cambridge University Press.

Darling, N., Cumsille, P., & Martínez, M. L. (2008). Individual differences in adolescents' beliefs about the legitimacy of parental authority and their own obligation to obey: A longitudinal investigation. *Child Development, 79*, 1103–1118.

Darling, H., Reeder, A. I., McGee, T., & Williams, S. (2006). Brief report: Disposable income, and spending on fast food, alcohol, cigarettes, and gambling by New Zealand secondary school students. *Journal of Adolescence, 29*, 837–843.

David, A., & Rodeck, C. H. (2009). Fetal gene therapy. In C. H. Rodeck & M. J. Whittle (Eds.), *Fetal medicine: Basic science and clinical practice*. London: Churchill Livingstone.

Davidov, M., Zahn-Waxler, C., Roth-Hanania, R., & Knafo, A. (2013). Concern for others in the first year of life: Theory, evidence, and avenues for research. *Child Development Perspectives, 7*, 126–131.

Davies, P. T., Cicchetti, D., Hentges, R. F., & Sturge-Apple, M. L. (2013). The genetic precursors and the advantageous and disadvantageous sequelae of inhibited temperament: An evolutionary perspective. *Developmental Psychology, 49*, 2285–2300.

Davies, P. T., Cicchetti, D., & Martin, M. J. (2012). Toward greater specificity in identifying associations among interparental aggression, child emotional reactivity to conflict, and child problems. *Child Development, 83*, 1789–1804.

Davies, P. T., & Cummings, E. M. (1998). Exploring children's emotional security as a mediator of the link between marital relations and child adjustment. *Child Development, 69*, 124–139.

Davis, K. M., Gagnier, K. R., Moore, T. E., & Todorow, M. (2013). Cognitive aspects of fetal alcohol spectrum disorder. *WIREs Cognitive Science, 4*, 81–92.

Davis, P. E., Meins, E., & Fernyhough, C. (2011). Self-knowledge in childhood: Relations with children's imaginary companions and understanding of mind. *British Journal of Developmental Psychology, 29*, 680–686.

Davis, E. P., & Sandman, C. A. (2010). The timing of prenatal exposure to maternal cortisol and psychosocial stress is associated with human cognitive development. *Child Development, 81*, 131–148.

Deary, I. (2012). Intelligence. *Annual Review of Psychology, 63*, 453–482.

Deater-Deckard, K., Lansford, J. E., Malone, P. S., Alampay, L. P. Sorbring, E., Bacchini, D., et al. (2011). The association between parental warmth and control in thirteen cultural groups. *Journal of Family Psychology, 25*, 790–794.

De Beni, R., & Palladino, P. (2000). Intrusion errors in working memory tasks: Are they related to reading comprehension ability? *Learning & Individual Differences, 12*, 131–143.

De Brauwer, J., & Fias, W. (2009). A longitudinal study of children's performance on simple multiplication and division problems. *Developmental Psychology, 45*, 1480–1496.

DeCasper, A. J., & Spence, M. J. (1986). Prenatal maternal speech influences newborns' perception of speech sounds. *Infant Behavior & Development, 9*, 133–150.

Declercq, E. (2012). The politics of home birth in the United States. *Birth, 39*, 281–285.

Degner, J., & Dalege, J. (2013). The apple does not fall far from the tree or does it? A meta-analysis of parent-child similarity in intergroup attitudes. *Psychological Bulletin, 139*, 1270–1304.

de Haan, M., Wyatt, J. S., Roth, S., Vargha-Khadem, F., Gadian, D., & Mishkin, M. (2006). Brain and cognitive-behavioral development after asphyxia at term birth. *Developmental Science, 9*, 441–442.

Dehaene, S., Izard, V., Pica, P., & Spelke, E. (2006). Core knowledge of geometry in an Amazonian indigene group. *Science, 311*, 381–384.

Dekovic, M., & Janssens, J. M. (1992). Parents' child-rearing style and child's sociometric status. *Developmental Psychology, 28*, 925–932.

Delaney, C. (2000). Making babies in a Turkish village. In J. S. DeLoache & A. Gottlieb (Eds.), *A world of babies: Imagined child care guides for seven societies*. New York, NY: Cambridge University Press.

Del Giudice, M. (2011). Alone in the dark? Modeling the conditions for visual experience in human fetuses. *Developmental Psychobiology, 53*, 214–219.

Del Giudice, M., & Colle, L. (2007). Differences between children and adults in the recognition of enjoyment smiles. *Developmental Psychology, 43*, 796–803.

DeLoache, J. S. (1984). Oh where, oh where: Memory-based searching by very young children. In C. Sophian (Ed.), *Origins of cognitive skills*. Hillsdale, NJ: Erlbaum.

DeLoache, J. S. (1995). Early understanding and use of models: The modal model. *Current Directions in Psychological Science, 4*, 109–113.

DeLoache, J. S., Chiong, C., Sherman, K., Islam, N., Vanderborght, M., Troseth, G. L., Strouse, G. A., & O'Doherty, K. (2010). Do babies learn from baby media? *Psychological Science, 21*, 1570–1574.

DeLoache, J. S., Miller, K. F., & Pierroutsakos, S. L. (1998). Reasoning and problem solving. In W. Damon (Ed.), *Handbook of child psychology* (5th ed., Vol. 2, pp. 801–850). New York, NY: Wiley.

DeLoache, J. S., Miller, K. F., & Rosengren, K. S. (1997). The incredible shrinking room: Very young children's performance with symbolic and nonsymbolic relations. *Psychological Science, 8*, 308–313.

del Valle, J. F., Bravo, A., & Lopez, M. (2010). Parents and peers as providers of support in adolescents' social network: A developmental perspective. *Journal of Community Psychology, 38*, 16–27.

Demir, A., Levine, S. C., & Goldin-Meadow, S. (2010). Narrative skill in children with unilateral brain injury: A possible limit to functional plasticity. *Developmental Science, 13*, 636–647.

deVilliers, J. G., & deVilliers, P. A. (1985). The acquisition of English. In D. I. Slobin (Ed.), *The cross-linguistic study of language acquisition*. Hillsdale, NJ: Erlbaum.

Dewey, K. G. (2001). Nutrition, growth, and complementary feeding of the breastfed infant. *Pediatric Clinics of North America, 48*, 87–104.

Dewey, C., Fleming, P., Goldin, J., & the ALSPAC Study Team. (1998). Does the supine sleeping position have any adverse effects on the child? II. Development in the first 18 months. *Pediatrics, 101*, e5.

De Wolff, M. S., & van IJzendoorn, M. H. (1997). Sensitivity and attachment: A meta-analysis on parental antecedents of infant attachment. *Child Development, 68*, 571–591.

Dews, S., Winner, E., Kaplan, J., Rosenblatt, E., Hunt, M., Lim, K., et al. (1996). Children's understanding of the meaning and functions of verbal irony. *Child Development, 67*, 3071–3085.

Diamond, A. (2007). Interrelated and interdependent. *Developmental Science, 10*, 152–158.

Diamond, A. (2013). Executive functions. *Annual Review of Psychology, 64*, 135–168.

Diamond, A., & Lee, K. (2011). Interventions shown to aid executive function development in children 4 to 12 years old. *Science, 333*, 959–964.

Dick-Read, G. (1959). *Childbirth without fear*. New York, NY: Harper & Brothers.

DiDonato, M. D., & Berenbaum, S. A. (2011). The benefits and drawbacks of gender typing: How different dimensions are related to psychological adjustment. *Archives of Sexual Behavior, 40*, 457–463.

Diesendruck, G., Birnbaum, D., Deeb, I., & Segall, G. (2013). Learning what is essential: Relative and absolute changes in children's beliefs about the heritability of ethnicity. *Journal of Cognition and Development, 14*, 546–560.

Dijkstra, J. K., Cillessen, A. H. N., & Borch, C. (2013). Popularity and adolescent friendship networks: Selection and influence dynamics. *Developmental Psychology, 49*, 1242–1252.

Dionne, G., Dale, P.S., Boivin, M., & Plomin, R. (2003). Genetic evidence for bidirectional effects of early lexical and grammatical development. *Child Development, 74*, 394–412.

DiPietro, J. A. (2004). The role of maternal stress in child development. *Current Directions in Psychological Science, 13*, 71–74.

DiPietro, J. A., Bornstein, M. H., Hahn, C. S., Costigan, K., & Achy-Brou, A. (2007). Fetal heart rate and variability: Stability and prediction to developmental outcomes in early childhood. *Child Development, 78*, 1788–1798.

DiPietro, J. A., Caulfield, L., Costigan, K. A., Merialdi, M., Nguyen, R. H. N., Zavaleta, N., et al. (2004). Fetal neurobehavioral development: A tale of two cities. *Developmental Psychology, 40*, 445–456.

DiPietro, J. A., Hodgson, D. M., Costigan, K. A., & Milton, S. C. (1996). Fetal neurobehavioral development. *Child Development, 67*, 2553–2567.

DiPietro, J. A., Novak, M. F., Costigan, K. A., Atella, L. D., & Reusing, S. P. (2006). Maternal psychological distress during pregnancy in relation to child development at age two. *Child Development, 77*, 573–587.

Dishion, T. J. (1990). The family ecology of boys' peer relations in middle childhood. *Child Development, 61*, 874–892.

Dishion, T. J., Poulin, F., & Burraston, B. (2001). Peer group dynamics associated with iatrogenic effects in group interventions with high-risk young adolescents. In D. W. Nangle & C. A. Erdley (Eds.), *The role of friendship in psychological adjustment* (pp. 79–92). San Francisco, CA: Jossey-Bass.

Divan, H. A., Kheifets, L., Obel, C., & Olsen, J. (2012). Cell phone use and behavioral problems in young children. *Journal of Epidemiology and Community Health, 66*, 524–529.

Dixon, J. A., & Marchman, V. A. (2007). Grammar and the lexicon: Developmental ordering in language acquisition. *Child Development, 78*, 190–212.

Docherty, S. J., Davis, O. S. P., Kovas, Y., Meaburn, E. L., Dale P. S., Petrill, S. A., et al. (2010). A genome-wide association study identifies multiple loci associated with mathematics ability and disability. *Genes, Brain, and Behavior, 9*, 234–247.

Dodge, K. A., Bates, J. E., & Pettit, G. S. (1990). Mechanisms in the cycle of violence. *Science, 250*, 1678–1683.

Dodge, K. A., Coie, J. D., & Lynam, D. (2006). Aggression and antisocial behavior in youth. In N. Eisenberg (Ed.), *Handbook of child psychology: Vol. 3. Social, emotional, and personality development* (6th ed., pp. 719–788). New York, NY: Wiley.

Dodge, K. A., Coie, J. D., & Tremblay, R. E. (2006). Aggression. In W. Damon & R. M. Lerner (Eds.), *Handbook of child psychology, Vol. 3* (6th ed.). New York, NY: Wiley.

Dodge, K. A., & Crick, N. R. (1990). Social information-processing bases of aggressive behavior in children. *Personality & Social Psychology Bulletin, 16*, 8–22.

Dodge, K. A., Godwin, J., & The Conduct Problems Prevention Research Group. (2013). Social-information-processing patterns mediate the impact of preventive intervention on adolescent antisocial behavior. *Psychological Science, 24*, 456–465.

Dodge, K. A., Greenberg, M. T., & Malone, P. S. (2008). Testing an idealized dynamic cascade model of the development of serious violence in adolescence. *Child Development, 79*, 1907–1927.

Donnellan, M. B., Trzesniewski, K. H., Robins, R. W., Moffitt, T. E., & Caspi, A. (2005). Low self-esteem is related to aggression, antisocial behavior, and delinquency. *Psychological Science, 16*, 328–335.

D'Onofrio, B. M., Goodnight, J. A., Van Hulle, C. A., Rodgers, J. L., Rathouz, P. J., Waldman, I. D., et al. (2009). Maternal age at childbirth and offspring disruptive behaviors: Testing the causal hypothesis. *Journal of Child Psychology & Psychiatry, 50*, 1018–1028.

D'Onofrio, B. M., Singh, A. L., Iliadou, A., Lambe, M., Hultman, C. M., Neiderhiser, J. M., et al. (2010). A quasi-experimental study of maternal smoking during pregnancy and offspring academic achievement. *Child Development, 81*, 80–100.

Donovan, W. L., Leavitt, L. A., & Walsh, R. O. (2000). Maternal illusory control predicts socialization strategies and toddler compliance. *Developmental Psychology, 36*, 402–411.

Doornwaard, S. M., Branje, S., Meeus, W. H. J., & ter Bogt, T. F. M. (2012). Development of adolescents' peer crowd identification in relation to changes in problem behaviors. *Developmental Psychology, 48*, 1366–1380.

Dorn, L. D., Dahl, R. E., Woodward, H. R., & Biro, F. (2006). Defining the boundaries of early adolescence: A user's guide to assessing pubertal status and pubertal timing in research with adolescents. *Applied Developmental Science, 10*, 30–56.

Doumen, S., Smits, I., Luyckx, K., Duriez, B., Vanhalst, J., Verschueren, K., et al. (2012). Identity and perceived peer relationship quality in emerging adulthood: The mediating role of attachment-related emotions. *Journal of Adolescence, 35*, 1417–1425.

Doyle, J. M., & Kao, G. (2007). Are racial identities of multiracials stable? Change self-identification among single and multiple race individuals. *Social Psychology Quarterly, 70,* 405–423.

Dozier, M., Zeanah, C. H., & Bernard, K. (2013). Infants and toddlers in foster care. *Child Development Perspectives, 7,* 166–171.

Draghi-Lorenz, R., Reddy, V., & Costall, A. (2001). Rethinking the development of "nonbasic" emotions: A critical review of existing theories. *Developmental Review, 21,* 263–304.

Driscoll, A. K., Russell, S. T., & Crockett, L. J. (2008). Parenting styles and youth well-being across immigrant generations. *Journal of Family Issues, 29,* 185–209.

DuBois, D. L., Portillo, N., Rhodes, J. E., Silverthorn, N., & Valentine, J. C. (2011). How effective are mentoring programs for youth? A systematic assessment of the evidence. *Psychological Science in the Public Interest, 12,* 57–91.

Duckworth, A. L., & Carlson, S. M. (2013). Self-regulation and school success. In B.W. Sokol, F. M. E. Grouzet, & U. Müller (Eds.), *Self-regulation and autonomy: Social and developmental dimensions of human conduct* (pp. 208–230). New York, NY: Cambridge University Press.

Duncan, G. J., & Brooks-Gunn, J. (2000). Family poverty, welfare reform, and child development. *Child Development, 71,* 188–196.

Duncan, G. J., Dowsett, C. J., Claessens, A., Magnuson, K., Huston, A. C., Klebanov, P., et al. (2007). School readiness and later achievement. *Developmental Psychology, 43,* 1428–1446.

Duncan, D. T., & Hatzenbuehler, M. L. (2014). Lesbian, gay, bisexual, and transgender hate crimes and suicidality among a population-based sample of sexual-minority adolescents in Boston. *American Journal of Public Health, 104,* 272–278.

Duncan, G. J., & Magnuson, K. (2012). Socioeconomic status and cognitive functioning: moving from correlation to causation. *WIREs Cognitive Science, 3,* 377–386.

Dunham, Y., Baron, A. S., & Carey, S. (2011). Consequences of "minimal" group affiliations in children. *Child Development, 82,* 793–811.

Dunham, P. J., Dunham, F., & Curwin, A. (1993). Joint-attentional states and lexical acquisition at 18 months. *Developmental Psychology, 29,* 827–831.

Dunifon, R. (2013). The influence of grandparents on the lives of children and adolescents. *Child Development Perspectives, 7,* 55–60.

Dunn, J., & Brophy, M. (2005). Communication, relationships, and individual differences in children's understanding of mind. In J. W. Astington & J. A. Baird (Eds.), *Why language matters for theory of mind* (pp. 50–69). New York, NY: Oxford.

Dunn, J., & Davies, L. (2001). Sibling relationships and interpersonal conflict. In J. Grych & F. D. Fincham (Eds.), *Interparental conflict and child development* (pp. 273–290). New York, NY: Cambridge University Press.

Dunn, J., & Kendrick, C. (1981). Social behavior of young siblings in the family context: Differences between same-sex and different-sex dyads. *Child Development, 52,* 1265–1273.

Dunn, J., O'Connor, T. G., & Cheng, H. (2005). Children's responses to conflict between their different parents: Mothers, stepfathers, nonresident fathers, and nonresident stepmothers. *Journal of Clinical Child & Adolescent Psychology, 34,* 223–234.

Dunson, D. B., Colombo, B., & Baird, D. D. (2002). Changes in age in the level and duration of fertility in the menstrual cycle. *Human Reproduction, 17,* 1399–1403.

Durik, A. M., Hyde, J. S., & Clark, R. (2000). Sequelae of cesarean and vaginal deliveries: Psychosocial outcomes for mothers and infants. *Developmental Psychology, 36,* 251–260.

Durston, S., Davidson, M. C., Tottenham, N., Galvan, A., Spicer, J., Fossella, J. A., et al. (2006). A shift from diffuse to focal cortical activity with development. *Developmental Science, 9,* 1–8.

Dykas, M. J., & Cassidy, J. (2011). Attachment and the processing of social information across the life span: Theory and evidence. *Psychological Bulletin, 137,* 19–46.

Eagly, A. H., Karau, S. J., & Makhijani, M. G. (1995). Gender and the effectiveness of leaders: A meta-analysis. *Psychological Bulletin, 117,* 125–145.

Eagly, A. H., & Wood, W. (2013). The nature-nurture debates: 25 years of challenges in understanding the psychology of gender. *Perspectives on Psychological Science, 8,* 340–357.

Easterbrook, M. A., Kisilevsky, B. S., Muir, D. W., & Laplante, D. P. (1999). Newborns discriminate schematic faces from scrambled faces. *Canadian Journal of Experimental Psychology, 53,* 231–241.

Eaton, D. K., Kann, L., Kinchen, S., Shanklin, S., Ross, J., Hawkins, J., et al. (2008). Youth risk behavior surveillance—United States, 2007. *Morbidity & Mortality Weekly Report, 57,* 1–131.

Eccles, J. S., & Harold, R. D. (1991). Gender differences in sport involvement: Applying the Eccles expectancy-value model. *Journal of Applied Sports Psychology, 3,* 7–35.

Edwards, C. A. (1994). Leadership in groups of school-age girls. *Developmental Psychology, 30,* 920–927.

Edwards, R. C., Thullen, M. J., Isarowong, N., Shiu, C-S., Henson, L., & Hans, S. L. (2012). Supportive relationships and the trajectory of depressive symptoms among young, African American mothers. *Journal of Family Psychology, 26,* 585–594.

Egan, S. K., Monson, T. C., & Perry, D. G. (1998). Social-cognitive influences on change in aggression over time. *Developmental Psychology, 34,* 996–1006.

Ehri, L., Nunes, S., Willows, D., Schuster, B., Yaghoub-Zadeh, Z., & Shanahan, T. (2001). Phonemic awareness instruction helps children learn to read: Evidence from the National Reading Panel's meta-analysis. *Reading Research Quarterly, 36,* 250–287.

Ehrlich, K. B., Dykas, M. J., & Cassidy, J. (2012). Tipping points in adolescent adjustment: Predicting social functioning from adolescents' conflict with parents and friends. *Journal of Family Psychology, 26,* 776–783.

Eime, R. M., Young, J. A., Harvey, J. T., Charity, M. J., & Payne, W. R. (2013). A systematic review of the psychological and social benefits of participation in sport for children and adolescents: informing development of a conceptual model of health through sport. *International Journal of Behavioral Nutrition and Physical Activity, 10:* 98.

Eisenberg, N. (2000). Emotion, regulation, and moral development. *Annual Review of Psychology, 51,* 665–697.

Eisenberg, N., Duckwork, A. L., Spinrad, T. L., & Valiente, C. (2014). Conscientiousness: origins in childhood? *Developmental Psychology,* in press.

Eisenberg, N., & Fabes, R. A. (1998). Prosocial development. In W. Damon (Ed.), *Handbook of child psychology* (Vol. 3, pp. 701–778). New York, NY: Wiley.

Eisenberg, N., Fabes, R. A., & Spinrad, T. (2006). Prosocial development. In W. Damon & R. M. Lerner (Eds.), *Handbook of child psychology, Vol. 3* (6th ed.). New York, NY: Wiley.

Eisenberg, N., Michalik, N., Spinrad, T. L., Hofer, C., Kupfer, A., Valiente, C., et al. (2007). The relations of effortful control and impulsivity to children's symptoms: A longitudinal study. *Cognitive Development, 22,* 544–567.

Eisenberg, N., & Shell, R. (1986). Prosocial moral judgment and behavior in children: The mediating role of cost. *Personality & Social Psychology Bulletin, 12,* 426–433.

Eisenberg, N., Shepard, S. A., Fabes, R. A., Murphy, B. C., & Guthrie, I. K. (1998). Shyness and children's emotionality, regulation, and coping: Contemporaneous, longitudinal, and across-context relations. *Child Development, 69,* 767–790.

Eisenberg, N., Zhou, Q., & Koller, S. (2001). Brazilian adolescents' prosocial moral judgment and behavior: Relations to sympathy, perspective taking, gender-role orientation, and demographic characteristics. *Child Development, 72,* 518–534.

Elbert, T., Pantev, C., Weinbruch, C., Rockstroh, B., & Taub, E. (1995). Increased cortical representation of the fingers of the left hand in strings players. *Science, 270,* 305–307.

Eliot, L. (2013). Single-sex education and the brain. *Sex Roles, 69,* 363–381.

Elkind, D. (1978). *The child's reality: Three developmental themes.* Hillsdale, NJ: Erlbaum.

Elkind, D., & Bowen, R. (1979). Imaginary audience behavior in children and adolescents. *Developmental Psychology, 15,* 38–44.

Ellis, B. J. (2004). Timing of pubertal maturation in girls: An integrated life history approach. *Psychological Bulletin, 130,* 920–958.

Ellis, B. J., Bates, J. E., Dodge, K. A., Fergusson, D. M., Horwood, L. J., Pettit, G. S., et al. (2003). Does father absence place daughters at special risk for early sexual activity and teenage pregnancy? *Child Development, 74,* 801–821.

Ellis, B. J., & Essex, M. J. (2007). Family environments, adrenarche, and sexual maturation: A longitudinal test of a life history model. *Child Development, 78,* 1799–1817.

Ellis, W. K., & Rusch, F. R. (1991). Supported employment: Current practices and future directions. In J. L. Matson & J. A. Mulick (Eds.), *Handbook of mental retardation* (2nd ed.). New York, NY: Pergamon.

Ellis, S., & Siegler, R. S. (1997). Planning and strategy choice, or why don't children plan when they should? In S. L. Friedman & E. K. Scholnick (Eds.), *The developmental psychology of planning: Why, how, and when do we plan?* (pp. 183–208). Hillsdale, NJ: Erlbaum.

Ellis, M. L., Weiss, B., & Lochman, J. E. (2009). Executive functions in children: Associations with aggressive behavior and appraisal processing. *Journal of Abnormal Child Psychology, 37,* 945–956.

Ellis, W. E., & Zarbatany, L. (2007). Explaining friendship formation and friendship stability—the role of children's and friends' aggression and victimization. *Merrill-Palmer Quarterly, 53,* 79–104.

El Nokali, N. E., Bachman, H. J., & Votruba-Drzal, E. (2010). Parent involvement and children's academic and social development in elementary school. *Child Development, 81,* 988–1005.

Else-Quest, N. M., Higgins, A., Allison, C., & Morton, L. C. (2012). Gender differences in self-conscious emotional experience: A meta-analysis. *Psychological Bulletin, 138,* 947–981.

Else-Quest, N. M., Hyde, J. S., Goldsmith, H. H., & Van Hulle, C. A. (2006). Gender differences in temperament: A meta-analysis. *Psychological Bulletin, 132,* 33–72.

Else-Quest, N. M., Hyde, J. S., & Linn, M. C. (2010). Cross-national patterns of gender differences in mathematics: A meta-analysis. *Psychological Bulletin, 136,* 103–127.

El-Sheikh, M., Bub, K. L., Kelly, R. J., & Buckhalt, J. A. (2013). Children's sleep and adjustment: A residualized change analysis. *Developmental Psychology, 49,* 1591–1601.

Engel, S. M., Berkowitz, G. S., Wolff, M. S., & Yehuda, R. (2005). Psychological trauma associated with the World Trade Center attacks and its effect on pregnancy outcome. *Paediatric & Perinatal Epidemiology, 19,* 334–341.

Engel, S. M., Zhu, C., Berkowitz, G. S., Calafat, A. M., Silva, M. J., Miodovnik, A., et al. (2009). Prenatal phthalate exposure and performance on the Neonatal Behavioral Assessment Scale in a multiethnic birth cohort. *Neurotoxicology, 30,* 522–528.

Englund, M. M., Kuo, S. I., Puig, J., & Collins, W. A. (2011). Early roots of adult competence: The significance of close relationships from infancy to early adulthood. *International Journal of Behavioral Development, 35,* 490–496.

Ennemoser, M., & Schneider, W. (2007). Relations of television viewing and reading: Findings from a 4-year longitudinal study. *Journal of Educational Psychology, 99,* 349–368.

Erikson, E. H. (1968). *Identity: Youth and crisis.* New York, NY: Norton.

Eskritt, M., & Lee, K. (2002). Remember when you last saw that card?: Children's production of external symbols as a memory aid. *Developmental Psychology, 38,* 254–266.

Eskritt, M., & McLeod, K. (2008). Children's note taking as a mnemonic tool. *Journal of Experimental Child Psychology, 101,* 52–74.

Espy, K. A., Fang, H., Johnson, C., Stopp, C., Wiebe, S. A., & Respass, J. (2011). Prenatal tobacco exposure: Developmental outcomes in the neonatal period. *Developmental Psychology, 47,* 153–169.

Evans, G. W., Gonnella, C., Marcynyszyn, L. A., Gentile, L., & Salpekar, N. (2005). The role of chaos in poverty and children's socioemotional adjustment. *Psychological Science, 16,* 560–565.

Evans, G. W., & Kim, P. (2013). Childhood poverty, chronic stress, self-regulation, and coping. *Child Development Perspectives, 7,* 43–48.

Eyer, D. E. (1992). *Mother–infant bonding: A scientific fiction.* New Haven, CT: Yale University Press.

Fabes, R. A., Eisenberg, N., Jones, S., Smith, M., Guthrie, I., Poulin, R., et al. (1999). Regulation, emotionality, and preschoolers' socially competent peer interactions. *Child Development, 70,* 432–442.

Fabes, R. A., Eisenberg, N., Smith, M. C., & Murphy, B. C. (1996). Getting angry at peers: Associations with liking of the provocateur. *Child Development, 67,* 942–956.

Fabricius, W. V., & Luecken, L. J. (2007). Postdivorce living arrangements, parent conflict, and long-term physical health correlates for children of divorce. *Journal of Family Psychology, 21,* 195–205.

Falbo, T. (2012). Only children: An updated review. *Journal of Individual Psychology, 68,* 38–49.

Falbo, T., & Polit, E. F. (1986). Quantitative review of the only child literature: Research evidence and theory development. *Psychological Bulletin, 100,* 176–186.

Falbo, T., Poston, D. L., Triscari, R. S., & Zhang, X. (1997). Self-enhancing illusions among Chinese schoolchildren. *Journal of Cross-Cultural Psychology, 28,* 172–191.

Falk, D., & Bornstein, M. H. (2005). Infant reflexes. In C. B. Fisher & R. M. Lerner (Eds.), *Encyclopedia of applied developmental science* (Vol. 1, pp. 581–582). Thousand Oaks, CA: Sage.

Farh, C. I. C. C., Seo, M-G., & Tesluk, P. E. (2012). Emotional intelligence, teamwork effectiveness, and job performance: The moderating role of job context. *Journal of Applied Psychology, 97,* 890–900.

Farr, R. H., Forssell, S. L., & Patterson, C. J. (2010). Parenting and child development in adoptive families: Does parental sexual orientation matter? *Applied Developmental Science, 14,* 164–178.

Farr, R. H., & Patterson, C. J. (2013). Coparenting among lesbian, gay, and heterosexual couples: Associations with adopted children's outcomes. *Child Development, 84,* 1226–1240.

Farrant, B. M., Maybery, M. T., & Fletcher, J. (2012). Language, cognitive flexibility, and explicit false belief understanding: Longitudinal analysis in typical development and specific language impairment. *Child Development, 83,* 223–235.

Farrar, M. J., & Boyer-Pennington, M. (1999). Remembering specific episodes of a scripted event. *Journal of Experimental Child Psychology, 73,* 266–288.

Farver, J. M., Lonigan, C. J., & Eppe, S. (2009). Effective early literacy skill development for young Spanish-speaking English language learners: An experimental study of two methods. *Child Development, 80,* 703–719.

Farver, J. M., & Shin, Y. L. (1997). Social pretend play in Korean- and Anglo-American preschoolers. *Child Development, 68,* 544–556.

Fauth, R. C., Roth, J. L., & Brooks-Gunn, J. (2007). Does the neighborhood context alter the link between youth's after-school time activities and developmental outcomes? A multilevel analysis. *Developmental Psychology, 43*, 760–777.

Fazel, S., Bakiyeva, L., Cnattingius, S., Grann, M., Hultman, C. M., Litchtenstein, P., et al. (2012). Perinatal risk factors in offenders with severe personality disorder: A population-based investigation. *Journal of Personality Disorders, 26*, 737–750.

Feddes, A. R., Noack, P., & Rutland, A. (2009). Direct and extended friendship effects on minority and majority children's interethnic attitudes: A longitudinal study. *Child Development, 80*, 377–390.

Federal Interagency Forum on Child and Family Statistics. (2013). *America's Children: Key National Indicators of Well-Being, 2013.* Washington, DC: U.S. Government Printing Office.

Feinberg, M. E., McHale, S. M., Crouter, A. C., & Cumsille, P. (2003). Sibling differentiation: Sibling and parental relationships trajectories in adolescence. *Child Development, 74*, 1261–1274.

Feldman, H. M., Dollaghan, C. A., Campbell, T. F., Kurs-Lasky, M., Janosky, J. E., & Paradise, J. L. (2000). Measurement properties of the MacArthur Communicative Development Inventories at one and two years. *Child Development, 71*, 310–322.

Feldman, R., & Klein, P. S. (2003). Toddler's self-regulated compliance to mothers, caregivers, and fathers: Implications for theories of socialization. *Developmental Psychology, 39*, 680–692.

Feldman, S. S., & Wentzel, K. R. (1990). The relationships between parental styles, sons' self-restraint, and peer relations in early adolescence. *Journal of Early Adolescence, 10*, 439–454.

Feldman Farb, A., & Matjasko, J. L. (2012). Recent advances in research on school-based extracurricular activities and adolescent development. *Developmental Review, 32*, 1–48.

Fenson, L., Dale, P. S., Reznick, J. S., Bates, E., Thal, D., & Pethick, S. (1994). Variability in early communicative development. *Monographs of the Society for Research in Child Development, 59* (Whole No. 173).

Fergusson, D. M., & Woodward, L. J. (2000). Teenage pregnancy and female educational underachievement: A prospective study of a New Zealand birth cohort. *Journal of Marriage & the Family, 62*, 147–161.

Fernyhough, C. (2010). Inner speech. In H. Pashler (Ed.), *Encyclopaedia of the mind.* Thousand Oaks, CA: Sage.

Ferreol-Barbey, M., Piolat, A., & Roussey, J. (2000). Text recomposition by eleven-year-old children: Effects of text length, level of reading comprehension, and mastery of prototypical schema. *Archives de Psychologie, 68*, 213–232.

Fidler, E. (2012). Sickle cell trait: A review and recommendations for training. *Strength and Conditioning Journal, 34*, 28–32.

Field, T. (2010). Postpartum depression effects on early interactions, parenting, and safety practices: A review. *Infant Behavior & Development, 33*, 1–6.

Field, T. M. (1990). *Infancy.* Cambridge, MA: Harvard University Press.

Field, T., Diego, M., & Hernandez-Reif, M. (2010). Preterm infant message therapy research: A review. *Infant Behavior and Development, 33*, 115–124.

Field, T. M., & Widmayer, S. M. (1982). Motherhood. In B. J. Wolman (Ed.), *Handbook of developmental psychology.* Englewood Cliffs, NJ: Prentice Hall.

Fischer, K. W., & Immordino-Yang, M. H. (2008). The fundamental importance of the brain and learning for education. In *The Jossey-Bass reader on the brain and learning.* San Francisco, CA: Jossey-Bass.

Fitzgerald, J. (1987). Research on revision in writing. *Review of Educational Research, 57*, 481–506.

FitzGerald, D. P., & White, K. J. (2003). Linking children's social worlds: Perspective-taking in parent-child and peer contexts. *Social Behavior & Personality, 31*, 509–522.

Fivush, R., Brotman, M. A., Buckner, J. P., & Goodman, S. H. (2000). Gender differences in parent-child emotion narratives. *Sex Roles, 42*, 233–253.

Fivush, R., Reese, E., & Haden, C. A. (2006). Elaborating on elaborations: Role of maternal reminiscing style in cognitive and socioemotional development. *Child Development, 77*, 1568–1588.

Flavell, J. H. (1985). *Cognitive development* (2nd ed.). Englewood Cliffs, NJ: Prentice Hall.

Flavell, J. H. (1996). Piaget's legacy. *Psychological Science, 7*, 200–203.

Flavell, J. H. (2000). Development of children's knowledge about the mental world. *International Journal of Behavioral Development, 24*, 15–23.

Flom, R., & Bahrick, L. E. (2007). The development of infant discrimination of affect in multimodal and unimodal stimulation: The role of intersensory redundancy. *Developmental Psychology, 43*, 238–252.

Flook, L. (2011). Gender differences in adolescents' daily interpersonal events and well-being. *Child Development, 82*, 454–461.

Flores, E., Cicchetti, D., & Rogosch, F. A. (2005). Predictors of resilience in maltreated and nonmaltreated Latino children. *Developmental Psychology, 41*, 338–351.

Flynn, J. R. (1999). Searching for justice: The discovery of IQ gains over time. *American Psychologist, 54*, 5–20.

Flynn, J. R., & Weiss, L. G. (2007). American IQ gains from 1932 to 2002: The WISC subtests and educational progress. *International Journal of Testing, 7*, 209–224.

Fontaine, R. G., & Dodge, K. A. (2006). Real-time decision making and aggressive behavior in youth: A heuristic model of response evaluation and decision (RED). *Aggressive Behavior, 32*, 604–624.

Fontaine, R. G., Yang, C., Dodge, K. A., Pettit, G. S., & Bates, J. E. (2009). Development of response evaluation and decision (RED) and antisocial behavior in childhood and adolescence. *Developmental Psychology, 45*, 447–459.

Foster, E. M., & Watkins, S. (2010). The value of reanalysis: TV viewing and attention problems. *Child Development, 81*, 368–375.

Foster, S. H. (1986). Learning discourse topic management in the preschool years. *Journal of Child Language, 13*, 231–250.

Fox, S. E., Levitt, P., & Nelson, C. A. (2010). How the timing and quality of early experiences influence the development of brain architecture. *Child Development, 81*, 28–40.

Franklin, A., Pilling, M., & Davies, I. (2005). The nature of infant color categorization: Evidence from eye movements on a target detection task. *Journal of Experimental Child Psychology, 91*, 227–248.

Franquart-Declercq, C., & Gineste, M. (2001). Metaphor comprehension in children. *Annee Psychologique, 101*, 723–752.

Frazier, B. N., Gelman, S. A., Kaciroti, N., Russell, J. W., & Lumeng, J. C. (2012). I'll have what she's having: The impact of model characteristics on children's food choices. *Developmental Science, 15*, 87–98.

Fredricks, J. A., & Eccles, J. S. (2006). Is extracurricular participation associated with beneficial outcomes? Concurrent and longitudinal relations. *Developmental Psychology, 42*, 698–713.

French, S. E., Seidman, E., Allen, L., & Aber, J. (2006). The development of ethnic identity during adolescence. *Developmental Psychology, 42*, 1–10.

Frick, P. J., & Nigg, J. T. (2012). Current issues in the diagnosis of attention deficit hyperactivity disorder, oppositional defiant disorder, and conduct disorder. *Annual Review of Clinical Psychology, 8*, 77–107.

Fried, A. (2005). Depression in adolescence. In C. B. Fisher & R. M. Lerner (Eds.), *Encyclopedia of applied developmental science* (Vol. 1, pp. 332–334). Thousand Oaks, CA: Sage.

Fu, G., Xu, F., Cameron, C. A., Herman, G., & Lee, K. (2007). Cross-cultural differences in children's choices, categorizations, and evaluations of truths and lies. *Developmental Psychology, 43,* 278–293.

Fuchs, L. S., Geary, D. C., Compton, D. L., Fuchs, D., Schatschneider, C., Hamlett, C. L., et al. (2013). Effects of first-grade number knowledge tutoring with contrasting forms of practice. *Journal of Educational Psychology, 105,* 58–77.

Fuhs, M. W., & McNeil, N. M. (2013). ANS acuity and mathematics ability in preschoolers from low-income homes: Contributions of inhibitory control. *Developmental Science, 16,* 136–148.

Fuld, G. L., Mulligan, D. A., Altmann, T. R., Brown, A., Christakis, D. A., Clarke-Pearson, K., et al. (2009). Policy statement—media violence. *Pediatrics, 124,* 1495–1503.

Fuligni, A. J., Kiang, L., Witkow, M. R., & Baldelomar, O. (2008). Stability and change in ethnic labeling among adolescents from Asian and Latin American immigrant families. *Child Development, 79,* 944–956.

Furlan, S., Agnoli, F., & Reyna, V. F. (2013). Children's competence or adults' incompetence: Different developmental trajectories in different tasks. *Developmental Psychology, 49,* 1466–1480.

Furman, W., & Lanthier, R. (2002). Parenting siblings. In M. Bornstein (Ed.), *Handbook of parenting: Practical issues in parenting* (Vol. 5, pp. 165–188). Mahwah, NJ: Erlbaum.

Furukawa, E., Tangney, J., & Higashibara, F. (2012). Cross-cultural continuities and discontinuities in shame, guilt, and pride: A study of children residing in Japan, Korea, and the USA. *Self and Identity, 11,* 90–133.

Gable, S., Krull, J. L., & Chang, Y. (2012). Boys' and girls' weight status and math performance from kindergarten entry through fifth grade: A mediated analysis. *Child Development, 83,* 1822–1839.

Gagliardi, A. (2005). Postpartum depression. In C. B. Fisher & R. M. Lerner (Eds.), *Encyclopedia of applied developmental science* (Vol. 2, pp. 867–870). Thousand Oaks, CA: Sage.

Gagné, J. R., Miller, M. M., & Goldsmith, H. H. (2013). Early—but modest—gender differences in focal aspects of childhood temperament. *Personality and Individual Differences, 55,* 95–100.

Gagne, J. R., & Saudino, K. J. (2010). Wait for it! A twin study of inhibitory control in early childhood. *Behavior Genetics, 40,* 327–337.

Galliher, R. V., Jones, M. D., & Dahl, A. (2011). Concurrent and longitudinal effects of ethnic identity and experiences of discrimination on psychosocial adjustment of Navajo adolescents. *Developmental Psychology, 47,* 509–526.

Galván, A. (2013). The teenage brain: Sensitivity to rewards. *Current Directions in Psychological Science, 22,* 88–93.

Garcia, M. M., Shaw, D. S., Winslow, E. G., & Yaggi, K. E. (2000). Destructive sibling conflict and the development of conduct problems in young boys. *Developmental Psychology, 36,* 44–53.

Garciaguirre, J. S., Adolph, K. E., & Shrout, P. E. (2007). Baby carriage: Infants walking with loads. *Child Development, 78,* 664–680.

Gardner, H. (1983). *Frames of mind: The theory of multiple intelligences.* New York, NY: Basic Books.

Gardner, H. (1993). *Multiple intelligences: The theory in practice.* New York, NY: Basic Books.

Gardner, H. (1995). Reflections on multiple intelligences: Myths and messages. *Phi Delta Kappan, 77,* 200–203, 206–209.

Gardner, H. (1999). *Intelligence reframed: Multiple intelligences for the 21st century.* New York, NY: Basic Books.

Gardner, H. (2002). *MI millennium: Multiple intelligences for the new millennium* [video recording]. Los Angeles, CA: Into the Classroom Media.

Gardner, H. (2006). *Multiple intelligences: New horizons.* New York, NY: Basic Books.

Gardner, W., & Rogoff, B. (1990). Children's deliberateness of planning according to task circumstances. *Developmental Psychology, 26,* 480–487.

Gardner, M., Roth, J., & Brooks-Gunn, J. (2009). Sports participation and juvenile delinquency: The role of the peer context among adolescent boys and girls with varied histories of problem behavior. *Developmental Psychology, 45,* 341–353.

Gartrell, N. K., Bos, H. M. W., & Goldberg, N. G. (2011). Adolescents of the U. S. National Longitudinal Lesbian Family Study: Sexual orientation, sexual behavior, and sexual risk exposure. *Archives of Sexual Behavior, 40,* 1199–1209.

Gartstein, M. A., Putnam, S. P., & Rothbart, M. K. (2012). Etiology of preschool behavior problems: Contributions of temperament attributes in early childhood. *Infant Mental Health Journal, 33,* 197–211.

Gartstein, M. A., Slobodskaya, H. R., Zylicz, P. O., Gosztyla, D., & Nakagawa, A. (2010). A cross-cultural evaluation of temperament: Japan, USA, Poland, and Russia. *International Journal of Psychology and Psychological Therapy, 10,* 55–75.

Garvey, C., & Beringer, G. (1981). Timing and turn taking in children's conversations. *Discourse Processes, 4,* 27–59.

Gass, K., Jenkins, J., & Dunn, J. (2007). Are sibling relationships protective? A longitudinal study. *Journal of Child Psychology & Psychiatry, 48,* 167–175.

Gathercole, S. E, Willis, C. S., Emslie, H., & Baddeley, A. D. (1992). Phonological memory and vocabulary development during the early school years: A longitudinal study. *Developmental Psychology, 28,* 887–898.

Gaulin, S. J. C., & McBurney, D. H. (2001). *Psychology: An evolutionary approach.* Upper Saddle River, NJ: Prentice-Hall.

Gauvain, M. (1998). Cognitive development in social and cultural context. *Current Directions in Psychological Science, 7,* 188–192.

Gauvain, M. (2001). *The social context of cognitive development.* New York NY: Guilford.

Gauvain, M., & Munroe, R. L. (2009). Contributions of social modernity to cognitive development: A comparison of four cultures. *Child Development, 80,* 1628–1642.

Gauvain, M., & Munroe, R. L. (2012). Cultural change, human activity, and cognitive development. *Human Development, 55,* 205–228.

Ge, X., Brody, G. H., Conger, R. D., Simons, R. L., & Murphy, V. M. (2002). Contextual amplification of pubertal transition effects on deviant peer affiliation and externalizing behavior among African American children. *Developmental Psychology, 38,* 45–54.

Geary, D. C. (2002). Sexual selection and human life history. In R. V. Kail (Ed.), *Advances in child development and behavior* (Vol. 30, pp. 41–102). San Diego, CA: Academic Press.

Geary, D. C. (2005). *The origin of mind: Evolution of brain, cognition, and general intelligence.* Washington, DC: American Psychological Association.

Geary, D. C. (2010) Mathematical learning disabilities. In P. Bauer (Ed.), *Advances in child development and behavior* (Vol. 38, pp. 45–77). San Diego CA: Academic Press.

Geary, D. C. (2011). Cognitive predictors of achievement growth in mathematics: A 5-year longitudinal study. *Developmental Psychology, 47,* 1539–1552.

Geary, D. C. (2013). Early foundations for mathematics learning and their relations to learning disabilities. *Current Directions in Psychological Science, 22*, 23–27.

Geary, D. C., Byrd-Craven, J., Hoard, M. K., Vigil, J., & Numtee, C. (2003). Evolution and development of boys' social behavior. *Developmental Review, 23*, 444–470.

Geary, D. C., Hoard, M. K., Byrd-Craven, J., Nugent, L., & Numtee, C. (2007). Cognitive mechanisms underlying achievement deficits in children with mathematical learning disability. *Child Development, 78*, 1343–1359.

Gelman, S. A. (2003). *The essential child.* New York, NY: Oxford.

Gelman, S. A., Coley, J. D., Rosengren, K. S., Hartman, E., & Pappas, A. (1998). Beyond labeling: The role of maternal input in the acquisition of richly structured categories. *Monographs of the Society for Research in Child Development, 63*, Serial No. 253.

Gelman, S. A., & Gottfried, G. M. (1996). Children's causal explanations of animate and inanimate motion. *Child Development, 67*, 1970–1987.

Gelman, R., & Meck, E. (1986). The notion of principle: The case of counting. In J. Hiebert (Ed.), *Conceptual and procedural knowledge: The case of mathematics.* Hillsdale, NJ: Erlbaum.

Gelman, S. A., & Meyer, M. (2011). Child categorization. *WIREs Cognitive Science, 2*, 95–105.

Gelman, S. A., Taylor, M. G., & Nguyen, S. P. (2004). Mother-child conversations about gender. *Monographs of the Society for Research in Child Development, 69* (Serial No. 275).

Gelman, S. A., & Wellman, H. M. (1991). Insides and essences: Early understandings of the non-obvious. *Cognition, 38*, 213–244.

Gentile, D. (2009). Pathological video-game use among youth ages 8 to 18: A national study. *Psychological Science, 20*, 594–602.

Gentile, D. A. (2011). The multiple dimensions of video game effects. *Child Development Perspectives, 5*, 75–81.

George, J. B. F., & Franko, D. L. (2010). Cultural issues in eating pathology and body image among children and adolescents. *Journal of Pediatric Psychology, 35*, 231–242.

George, C., Kaplan, N., & Main, M. (1985). *The adult attachment interview.* Unpublished manuscript, Department of Psychology, University of California, Berkeley.

Gerry, D. W., Faux, A. L., & Trainor, L. J. (2010). Effects of Kindermusik training on infants' rhythmic enculturation. *Developmental Science, 13*, 545–551.

Gershoff, E. T. (2013). Spanking and child development: We know enough now to stop hitting our children. *Child Development Perspectives, 7*, 133–137.

Gershoff, E. T., & Bitensky, S. H. (2007). The case against corporal punishment of children: Converging evidence from social science research and international human rights law and implications for U.S. public policy. *Psychology, Public Policy, & the Law, 13*, 231–272.

Gershkoff-Stowe, L., & Smith, L. B. (2004). Shape and the first hundred nouns. *Child Development, 75*, 1098–1114.

Gertner, Y., Fisher, C., & Eisengart, J. (2006). Learning words and rules: Abstract knowledge of word order in early sentence comprehension. *Psychological Science, 17*, 684–691.

Ghetti, S. (2008). Rejection of false events in childhood: A metamemory account. *Current Directions in Psychological Science, 17*, 16–20.

Ghetti, S., Hembacher, E., & Coughlin, C. A. (2013). Feeling uncertain and acting on it during the preschool years: A metacognitive approach. *Child Development Perspectives, 7*, 160–165.

Ghetti, S., & Lee, J. (2011). Children's episodic memory. *WIREs Cognitive Science, 2*, 365–373.

Gibbs, J. C., Clark, P. M., Joseph, J. A., Green, J. L., Goodrick, T. S., & Makowski, D. (1986). Relations between moral judgment, moral courage, and field independence. *Child Development, 57*, 185–193.

Gibbs, D. A., Martin, S. L., Kupper, L. L., & Johnson, R. E. (2007). Child maltreatment in enlisted soldiers' families during combat-related deployments. *Journal of the American Medical Association, 298*, 528–535.

Gibson, E. J., & Walk, R. D. (1960). The "visual cliff." *Scientific American, 202*, 64–71.

Giles, J. W., & Heyman, G. D. (2005). Reconceptualizing children's suggestibility: Bidirectional and temporal properties. *Child Development, 76*, 40–53.

Gillen-O'Neel, C., Huynh, V. W., & Fuligni, A. J. (2013). To study or to sleep? The academic costs of extra studying at the expense of sleep. *Child Development, 84*, 133–142.

Gilligan, C. (1982). *In a different voice: Psychological theory and women's development.* Cambridge, MA: Harvard University Press.

Gilligan, C., & Attanucci, J. (1988). Two moral orientations: Gender differences and similarities. *Merrill-Palmer Quarterly, 34*, 223–237.

Ginsburg-Block, M. D., Rohrbeck, C. A., & Fantuzzo, J. W. (2006). A meta-analytic review of social, self-concept, and behavioral outcomes of peer-assisted learning. *Journal of Educational Psychology, 98*, 732–749.

Giordano, G. (2005). *How testing came to dominate American schools: The history of educational assessment.* New York, NY: Peter Lang.

Gizer, I. R., & Waldman, I. D. (2012). Double dissociation between lab measures of inattention and impulsivity and the dopamine transporter gene (*DAT1*) and the dopamine D4 receptor gene (*DRD4*). *Journal of Abnormal Psychology, 121*, 1011–1023.

Gleason, T. R., & Hohmann, L. M. (2006). Concepts of real and imaginary friendships in early childhood. *Social Development, 15*, 128–144.

Glick, G. C., & Rose, A. J. (2011). Prospective associations between friendship adjustment and social strategies: Friendship as a context for building social skills. *Developmental Psychology, 47*, 1117–1132.

Global Initiative to End All Corporal Punishment of Children. (2011). *States with full prohibition.* Retrieved March 26, 2011, from http://www.endcorporalpunishment.org.

Göbel, S. M., Watson, S. E., Lervåg, A. & Hulme, C. (2014). Children's arithmetic development: It is number knowledge, not the approximate number sense, that counts. *Psychological Science, 25*, 789–798.

Goeke-Morey, M. C., Cummings, E. M., Harold, G. T., & Shelton, K. H. (2003). Categories and continua of destructive and constructive conflict tactics from the perspective of U.S. and Welsh children. *Journal of Family Psychology, 17*, 327–338.

Goh, Y. I., & Koren, G. (2008). Folic acid in pregnancy and fetal outcomes. *Journal of Obstetrics and Gynecology, 28*, 3–13.

Goldfield, B. A., & Reznick, J. S. (1990). Early lexical acquisition: Rate, content, and the vocabulary spurt. *Journal of Child Language, 17*, 171–184.

Goldin-Meadow, S., Mylander, C., & Franklin, A. (2007). How children make language out of gesture: Morphological structure in gesture systems developed by American and Chinese deaf children. *Cognitive Psychology, 55*, 87–135.

Goldstein, S. (2011). Attention-deficit/hyperactivity disorder. In S. Goldstein and C. R. Reynolds (Eds.), *Handbook of neurodevelopmental and genetic disorders in children* (2nd ed., pp. 131–150). New York, NY: Guilford.

Goldstein, M. H., & Schwade, J. A. (2008). Social feedback to infants' babbling facilitates rapid phonological learning. *Psychological Science, 19*, 515–523.

Goleman, D. (1995). *Emotional intelligence: Why it can matter more than IQ*. New York, NY: Bantam.

Goleman, D. (1998). *Working with emotional intelligence*. New York, NY: Bantam.

Goleman, D., Boyatzis, R., & McKee, A. (2002). *Primal leadership: Realizing the power of emotional intelligence*. Boston, MA: Harvard University Press.

Golinkoff, R. M. (1993). When is communication a "meeting of minds"? *Journal of Child Language, 20*, 199–207.

Golombok, S. (2013). Families created by reproductive donation: Issues and research. *Child Development Perspectives, 7*, 61–65.

Golombok, S., Mellish, L., Jennings, S., Casey, P., Tasker, F., & Lamb, M. E. (2014). Adoptive gay father families: Parent-child relationships and children's psychological adjustment. *Child Development, 85*, 456–468.

Golombok, S., Perry, B., Burston, A., Murray, C., Mooney-Somers, J., Stevens, M., et al. (2003). Children with lesbian parents: A community study. *Developmental Psychology, 39*, 20–33.

Good, T. L., & Brophy, J. E. (2008). *Looking in classrooms*. Boston, MA: Pearson/Allyn & Bacon.

Goodman, S. H., Rouse, M. H., Connell, A. M., Broth, M. R., Hall, C. M., & Heyward, D. (2011). Maternal depression and child psychopathology: A meta-analytic review. *Clinical Child and Family Psychology Review, 14*, 1–27.

Goodnow, J. J. (1992). *Parental belief systems: The psychological consequences for children*. Hillsdale, NJ: Erlbaum.

Goodwyn, S. W., & Acredolo, L. P. (1993). Symbolic gesture versus word: Is there a modality advantage for onset of symbol use? *Child Development, 64*, 688–701.

Goossens, L. (2001). Global versus domain-specific statuses in identity research: A comparison of two self-report measures. *Journal of Adolescence, 24*, 681–699.

Gordon, C. P. (1996). Adolescent decision making: A broadly based theory and its application to the prevention of early pregnancy. *Adolescence, 31*, 561–584.

Gordon, R. A., Chase-Lansdale, P. L., & Brooks-Gunn, J. (2004). Extended households and the life course of young mothers: Understanding the associations using a sample of mothers with premature, low birth weight babies. *Child Development, 75*, 1013–1038.

Gosso, Y., Morais, M. L. S., & Otta, E. (2007). Pretend play of Brazilian children: A window into different cultural worlds. *Journal of Cross-Cultural Psychology, 38*, 539–558.

Gottman, J. M. (1986). The world of coordinated play: Same- and cross-sex friendships in children. In J. M. Gottman & J. G. Parker (Eds.), *Conversations of friends*. New York, NY: Cambridge University Press.

Gottman, J. M., Katz, L. F., & Hooven, C. (1996). Parental meta-emotion philosophy and the emotional life of families: Theoretical models and preliminary data. *Journal of Family Psychology, 10*, 243–268.

Goubet, N., Clifton, R. K., & Shah, B. (2001). Learning about pain in preterm newborns. *Journal of Developmental & Behavioral Pediatrics, 22*, 418–424.

Gough, P. B., & Tunmer, W. E. (1986). Decoding, reading and reading disability. *Remedial & Special Education, 7*, 6–10.

Governor's Task Force on Children's Justice. (1998). *Forensic interviewing protocol*. Lansing, MI: Author.

Govier, E., & Salisbury, G. (2000). Age-related sex differences in performance on a side-naming spatial task. *Psychology, Evolution, & Gender, 2*, 209–222.

Govindshenoy, M., & Spencer, N. (2007). Abuse of the disabled child: A systematic review of population-based studies. *Child Care, Health, & Development, 33*, 552–558.

Grabe, S., Hyde, J. S., & Ward, L. M. (2008). The role of the media in body image concerns among women: A meta-analysis of experimental and correlational studies. *Psychological Bulletin, 134*, 460–476.

Graber, J. A. (2013). Pubertal timing and the development of psychopathology in adolescence and beyond. *Hormones and Behavior, 64*, 262–269.

Graesser, A. C., Singer, M., & Trabasso, T. (1994). Constructing inferences during narrative text comprehension. *Psychological Review, 101*, 371–395.

Graham, S., Berninger, V. W., Abbott, R. D., Abbott, S. P., & Whitaker, D. (1997). Role of mechanics in composing of elementary school students: A new methodological approach. *Journal of Educational Psychology, 89*, 170–182.

Graham, S., Gillespie, A., & McKeown, D. (2013). Writing: Importance, development, and instruction. *Reading and Writing, 26*, 1–15.

Graham, S., & Perin, D. (2007). A meta-analysis of writing instruction for adolescent students. *Journal of Educational Psychology, 99*, 445–476.

Graham-Bermann, S. A., & Brescoll, V. (2000). Gender, power, and violence: Assessing the family stereotypes of the children of batterers. *Journal of Family Psychology, 14*, 600–612.

Grammer, J., Coffman, J. L., & Ornstein, P. (2013). The effect of teachers' memory-relevant language on children's strategy use and knowledge. *Child Development, 84*, 1989–2002.

Grammer, J. K., Purtell, K. M., Coffman, J. L., & Ornstein, P. A. (2011). Relations between children's metamemory and strategic performance: Time-varying covariates in early elementary school. *Journal of Experimental Child Psychology, 108*, 139–155.

Granrud, C. E. (1986). Binocular vision and spatial perception in 4- and 5-month-old infants. *Journal of Experimental Psychology: Human Perception & Performance, 12*, 36–49.

Grantham-McGregor, S., Ani, C., & Gernald, L. (2001). The role of nutrition in intellectual development. In R. J. Sternberg & E. L. Grigorenko (Eds.), *Environmental effects on cognitive abilities* (pp. 119–155). Mahwah, NJ: Erlbaum.

Graves, R., & Landis, T. (1990). Asymmetry in mouth opening during different speech tasks. *International Journal of Psychology, 25*, 179–189.

Gray, S. W., & Klaus, R. A. (1965). An experimental preschool program for culturally deprived children. *Child Development, 36*, 887–898.

Gray-Little, B., & Hafdahl, A. R. (2000). Factors influencing racial comparisons of self-esteem: A quantitative review. *Psychological Bulletin, 126*, 26–54.

Graziano, P. A., Keane, S. P., & Calkins, S. D. (2007). Cardiac vagal regulation and early peer status. *Child Development, 78*, 264–278.

Greenberg, M. T., & Crnic, K. A. (1988). Longitudinal predictors of developmental status and social interaction in premature and full-term infants at age two. *Child Development, 59*, 554–570.

Greenberg, M. T., Lengua, L. J., Coie, J. D., Pinderhughes, E. E., & the Conduct Problems Prevention Research Group. (1999). Predicting developmental outcomes at school entry using a multiple-risk model: Four American communities. *Developmental Psychology, 35*, 403–417.

Greene, J. (2007). The secret joke of Kant's soul. In W. Sinnott-Armstrong (Ed.), *Moral psychology: The neuroscience of morality, emotion, brain disorders, and development* (pp. 35–80). Cambridge, MA: MIT.

Greenough, W. T., & Black, J. E. (1992). Induction of brain structure by experience: Substrates for cognitive development. In M. Gunnar & C. Nelson (Eds.), *Minnesota symposia on child psychology: Vol. 24: Developmental behavioral neuroscience* (pp. 155–200). Hillsdale, NJ: Erlbaum.

Gregory, A., Allen, J. P., Mikami, A. Y., Hafen, C. A., & Pianta, R. C. (2014). Effects of a professional development program on behavioral engagement of students in middle and high school. *Psychology in the Schools, 51*, 143–163.

Gregory, A. M., Light-Häusermann, J. H., Rijsdijk, F., & Eley, T. C. (2009). Behavioral genetic analyses of prosocial behavior in adolescents. *Developmental Science, 12*, 165–174.

Gregory, A. M., Rijsdijk, F., Lau, J. Y. F., Napolitano, M., McGuffin, P., & Eley, T. C. (2007). Genetic and environmental influences on interpersonal cognitions and associations with depressive symptoms in 8-year-old twins. *Journal of Abnormal Psychology, 116*, 762–775.

Greitemeyer, T., & McLatchie, N. (2011). Denying humanness to others: A newly discovered mechanism by which violent video games increase aggressive behavior. *Psychological Science, 22*, 659–665.

Grigorenko, E. L., Jarvin, L., & Sternberg, R. J. (2002). School-based tests of the triarchic theory of intelligence: Three settings, three samples, three syllabi. *Contemporary Educational Psychology, 27*, 167–208.

Gripshover, S. J., & Markman, E. M. (2013). Teaching young children a theory of nutrition: Conceptual change and the potential for increased vegetable consumption. *Psychological Science, 24*, 1541–1553.

Groen, G. J., & Resnick, L. B. (1977). Can preschool children invent addition algorithms? *Journal of Educational Psychology, 69*, 645–652.

Grosse, G., Scott-Phillips, T. C., & Tomasello, M. (2013). Three-year-olds hide their communicative intentions in appropriate contexts. *Developmental Psychology, 49*, 2095–2101.

Grotevant, H. D., & McDermott, J. M. (2014). Adoption: Biological and social processes linked to adaptation. *Annual Review of Psychology, 65*, 235–265.

Grotevant, H. D., McRoy, R. G., Wrobel, G. M., & Ayers-Lopez, S. (2013). Contact between adoptive and birth families: Perspectives from the Minnesota/Texas adoption research project. *Child Development Perspectives, 7*, 193–198.

Grusec, J. E. (2011). Socialization processes in the family: Social and emotional development. *Annual Review of Psychology, 62*, 243–269.

Grusec, J. E., Goodnow, J. J., & Cohen, L. (1996). Household work and the development of concern for others. *Developmental Psychology, 32*, 999–1007.

Grysman, A., & Hudson, J. A. (2013). Gender differences in autobiographical memory: Developmental and methodological considerations. *Developmental Review, 33*, 239–272.

Guerra, N. G., Williams, K. R., & Sadek, S. (2011). Understanding bullying and victimization during childhood and adolescence: A mixed methods study. *Child Development, 82*, 295–310.

Gunderson, E. A., Gripshover, S. J., Romero, C., Dweck, C. S., Goldin-Meadow, S., & Levine, S. C. (2013). Parent praise to 1- to 3-year-olds predicts children's motivational frameworks 5 years later. *Child Development, 84*, 1526–1541.

Gunderson, E. A., & Levine, S. C. (2011). Some types of parent number talk count more than others: relations between parents' input and children's cardinal-number knowledge. *Developmental Science, 14*, 1021–1032.

Güngör, D., & Bornstein, M. H. (2010). Culture-general and -specific associations of attachment avoidance and anxiety with perceived parental warmth and psychological control among Turk and Belgian adolescents. *Journal of Adolescence, 33*, 593–602.

Gurucharri, C., & Selman, R. L. (1982). The development of interpersonal understanding during childhood, preadolescence, and adolescence: A longitudinal follow-up study. *Child Development, 53*, 924–927.

Guttmacher Institute. (2013). *Facts on American teens' sexual and reproductive health.* New York, NY: Author.

Guxens, M., van Eijsden, M., Vemeulen, R., Loomans, E., Vrijkotte, T. G. M., Komhout, H., et al. (2013). Maternal cell phone and cordless phone use during pregnancy and behaviour problems in 5-year-old children. *Journal of Epidemiology and Community Health, 67*, 432–438.

Haeffel, G. J., Getchell, M., Koposov, R. A., Yrigollen, C. M., DeYoung, C. G., af Klinteberg, B., et al. (2008). Associations between polymorphisms in the dopamine transporter gene and depression: Evidence for a gene-environment interaction in a sample of juvenile detainees. *Psychological Science, 19*, 62–69.

Halford, G. S., & Andrews, G. (2011). Information-processing models of cognitive development. In U. Goswami (Ed.), *The Wiley-Blackwell handbook of childhood cognitive development* (2nd ed., pp. 697–722). West Sussex, UK: Wiley-Blackwell.

Halgunseth, L. C., Ispa, J. M., & Rudy, D. (2006). Parental control in Latino families: An integrated review of the literature. *Child Development, 77*, 1282–1297.

Halim, M. L., Ruble, D. N., & Amodio, D. M. (2011). From pink frilly dresses to 'one of the boys': A social-cognitive analysis of gender identity development and gender bias. *Social and Personality Psychology Compass, 5*, 933–949.

Halim, M. L., Ruble, D., Tamis-Lemonda, C., & Shrout, P. E. (2013). Rigidity in gender-typed behaviors in early childhood. *Child Development, 84*, 1269–1284.

Halim, M. L., Ruble, D. N., Tamis-Lemonda, C. S., Zosuls, K. M., Lurye, L. E., & Greulich, F. K. (2014). Pink frilly dresses and the avoidance of all things "girly": Children's appearance rigidity and cognitive theories of gender development. *Developmental Psychology*, in press.

Hall, G. S. (1904). *Adolescence, 1.* New York, NY: Appleton.

Hallinan, M. T., & Teixeira, R. A. (1987). Opportunities and constraints: Black-white differences in the formation of interracial friendships. *Child Development, 58*, 1358–1371.

Halpern, D. F. (2012). *Sex differences in cognitive abilities* (4th ed.). New York, NY: Psychology Press.

Halpern, D. F., Benbow, C. P., Geary, D. C., Gur, R. C., Hyde, J. S., & Gernsbacher, M. A. (2007). The science of sex differences in science and mathematics. *Psychological Science in the Public Interest, 8*, 1–51.

Halpern, L. F., MacLean, W. E., & Baumeister, A. A. (1995). Infant sleep-wake characteristics: Relation to neurological status and the prediction of developmental outcome. *Developmental Review, 15*, 255–291.

Halpern-Meekin, S., & Tach, L. (2008). Heterogeneity in two-parent families and adolescent well-being. *Journal of Marriage & Family, 70*, 435–451.

Hamamura, T., Heine, S. J., & Paulhus, D. L. (2008). Cultural differences in response styles: The role of dialectical thinking. *Personality and Individual Differences, 44*, 932–942.

Hamilton, B. E., Martin, J. A., & Ventura, S. J. (2010). Births: Preliminary data for 2008. *National Vital Statistics Reports*, Vol. 58. Hyattsville, MD: National Center for Health Statistics.

Hamlin, J. K. (2013). Moral judgment and action in preverbal infants and toddlers: Evidence for an innate moral core. *Current Directions in Psychological Science, 22*, 186–193.

Hamlin, J. K. (2014). The origins of human morality: Complex sociomoral evaluations by preverbal infants. In J. Decety & Y. Christen (Eds.), *New frontiers in social neuroscience* (pp. 175–188). New York, NY: Springer.

Hamlin, J. K., Mahajan, N., Liberman, Z., & Wynn, K. (2013). Not like me! Bad: Infants prefer those who harm dissimilar others. *Psychological Science, 24*, 589–594.

Hamlin, J. K., Wynn, K., & Bloom, P. (2007). Social evaluation by preverbal infants. *Nature, 450*, 557–559.

Hamm, J. V. (2000). Do birds of a feather flock together? The variable bases for African American, Asian American, and European American adolescents' selection of similar friends. *Developmental Psychology, 36,* 209–219.

Hammen, C., & Rudolph, K. D. (2003). Childhood mood disorders. In E. J. Mash & R. A. Barkley (Eds.), *Child psychopathology* (2nd ed., pp. 233–278). New York, NY: Guilford.

Hane, A. A., & Fox, N. W. (2006). Ordinary variations in maternal caregiving influence human infants' stress reactivity. *Psychological Science, 17,* 550–556.

Hankin, B. L., Mermelstein, R., & Roesch, L. (2007). Sex differences in adolescent depression: Stress exposure and reactivity models. *Child Development, 78,* 279–295.

Hannon, E. E., & Trehub, S. E. (2005). Metrical categories in infancy and adulthood. *Psychological Science, 16,* 48–55.

Harden, K. P. (2014). Genetic influences on adolescent sexual behavior: Why genes matter for environmentally oriented researchers. *Psychological Bulletin, 140,* 434–465.

Harkness, K. L., Lumley, M. N., & Truss, A. E. (2008). Stress generation in adolescent depression: The moderating role of child abuse and neglect. *Journal of Abnormal Child Psychology, 36,* 421–432.

Harlow, H. F., & Harlow, M. K. (1965). The affectional systems. In A. M. Schier, H. F. Harlow, & F. Stollnitz (Eds.), *Behavior of nonhuman primates* (Vol. 2.). New York, NY: Academic Press.

Harre, N. (2007). Community service or activism as an identity project for youth. *Journal of Community Psychology, 35,* 711–724.

Harris, K. R., Graham, S., Mason, L., & Friedlander, B. (2008). *Powerful writing strategies for all students.* Baltimore, MD: Brookes.

Harrison, K., Bost, K. K., McBride, B. A., Donovan, S. M., Grigsby-Toussaint, D. S., Kim, J., et al., (2011). Toward a developmental conceptualization of contributors to overweight and obesity in childhood: The Six-Cs model. *Child Development Perspectives, 5,* 50–58.

Harrist, A. W., Zaia, A. F., Bates, J. E., Dodge, K. A., & Pettit, G. S. (1997). Subtypes of social withdrawal in early childhood: Sociometric status and social-cognitive differences across four years. *Child Development, 68,* 278–294.

Harter, S. (2005). Self-concepts and self-esteem, children and adolescents. In C. B. Fisher & R. M. Lerner (Eds.), *Encyclopedia of applied developmental science* (Vol. 2, pp. 972–977). Thousand Oaks, CA: Sage.

Harter, S. (2006). The self. In W. Damon & R. M. Lerner (Eds.), *Handbook of child psychology* (6th ed., Vol. 3). New York, NY: Wiley.

Harter, S. (2012). *The construction of the self: Developmental and sociocultural foundations* (2nd ed.). New York, NY: Guilford.

Harter, S., Waters, P., & Whitesell, N. R. (1998). Relational self-worth: Differences in perceived worth as a person across interpersonal contexts among adolescents. *Child Development, 69,* 756–766.

Harter, S., Whitesell, N. R., & Kowalski, P. S. (1992). Individual differences in the effects of educational transitions on young adolescents' perceptions of competence and motivational orientation. *American Educational Research Journal, 29,* 777–807.

Hartup, W. W. (1983). Peer relations. In P. H. Mussen (Ed.), *Handbook of child psychology* (Vol. 4). New York, NY: Wiley.

Hartup, W. W. (1992). Friendships and their developmental significance. In H. McGurk (Ed.), *Contemporary issues in childhood social development.* London: Routledge.

Hartup, W. W., & Stevens, N. (1999). Friendships and adaptation across the life span. *Current Directions in Psychological Science, 8,* 76–79.

Hastings, P. D., & Rubin, K. H. (1999). Predicting mothers' beliefs about preschool-aged children's social behavior: Evidence for maternal attitudes moderating child effects. *Child Development, 70,* 722–741.

Hastings, P. D., Zahn-Waxler, C., & McShane, K. (2006). We are, by nature, moral creatures: Biological bases of concern for others. In M. Killen & J. G. Smetana (2006), *Handbook of moral development* (pp. 483–516). Mahwah, NJ: Erlbaum.

Hawley, P. H. (1999). The ontogenesis of social dominance: A strategy-based evolutionary perspective. *Developmental Review, 19,* 7–132.

Hay, D. F. (2007). The gradual emergence of sex differences in aggression: Alternative hypotheses. *Psychological Medicine, 37,* 1527–1537.

Hay, D. F., Mundy, L., Roberts, S., Carta, R., Waters, C. S., Perra, O., et al. (2011). Known risk factors for violence predict 12-month-old infants' aggressiveness with peers. *Psychological Science, 22,* 1205–1211.

Hay, D. F., Waters, C. S., Perra, O., Swift, N., Kairis, V., Phillips, R., et al. (2014). Precursors to aggression are evident by 6 months of age. *Developmental Science, 17,* 471–480.

Hayes, D. P. (1988). Speaking and writing: Distinct patterns of word choice. *Journal of Memory & Language, 27,* 572–585.

Hayes, T. C., & Lee, M. R. (2005). The Southern culture of honor and violent attitudes. *Sociological Spectrum, 25,* 593–617.

Hayne, H., & Jack, F. (2011). Childhood amnesia. *WIREs Cognitive Science, 2,* 136–145.

Hazell, P. L. (2009). 8-year follow-up of the MTA sample. *Journal of the American Academy of Child & Adolescent Psychiatry, 48,* 461–462.

Hellekson, K. L. (2001). NIH consensus statement on phenylketonuria. *American Family Physician, 63,* 1430–1432.

Hemker, L., Granrud, C. E., Yonas, A., & Kavsek, M. (2010). Infant perception of surface texture and relative height as distance information: A preferential-reaching study. *Infancy, 15,* 6–27.

Henderson, N. D. (2010). Predicting long-term firefighter performance from cognitive and physical ability measures. *Personnel Psychology, 63,* 999–1039.

Henderson, C. E., Hayslip, B., Sanders, L. M., & Louden, L. (2009). Grandmother-grandchild relationship quality predicts psychological adjustment among youth from divorced families. *Journal of Family Issues, 30,* 1245–1264.

Henderson, A. M. E., Wang, Y., Matz, L. E., & Woodward, A. L. (2013). Active experience shapes 10-month-old infants' understanding of collaborative goals. *Infancy, 18,* 10–39.

Henderson, L. M., Weighall, A. R., Brown, H., & Gaskell, M. G. (2012). Consolidation of vocabulary is associated with sleep in children. *Developmental Science, 15,* 674–687.

Henry, D. B., Schoeny, M. E., Deptula, D. P., & Slavick, J. T. (2007). Peer selection and socialization effects on adolescent intercourse without a condom and attitudes about the costs of sex. *Child Development, 78,* 825–838.

Hepach, R., Vaish, A., & Tomasello, M. (2012). Young children are intrinsically motivated to see others helped. *Psychological Science, 23,* 967–972.

Hepper, P. G., Wells, D. L., Dornan, J. C., & Lynch, C. (2013). Long-term flavor recognition in humans with prenatal garlic experience. *Developmental Psychobiology, 55,* 568–574.

Herlitz, A., & Lovén, J. (2013). Sex differences and the own-gender bias in face recognition: A meta-analytic review. *Visual Cognition, 21,* 1306–1336.

Herman, M. (2004). Forced to choose: Some determinants of racial identification in multiracial adolescents. *Child Development, 75,* 730–748.

Hernandez, D. J. (2004). Demographic change and the life circumstances of families. *Future of Children, 14,* 17–47.

Herrnstein, R. J., & Murray, C. (1994). *The bell curve: Intelligence and class structure in American life.* New York, NY: Free Press.

Hershkowitz, I., Lamb, M. E., Orbach, Y., Katz, C., & Horowitz, D. (2012). The development of communicative and narrative skills among preschoolers: Lessons from forensic interviews about child abuse. *Child Development, 83,* 611–622.

Hespos, S. J., Ferry, A. L., & Rips, L. J. (2009). Five-month-old infants have different expectations for solids and liquids. *Psychological Science, 20,* 603–611.

Hespos, S. J., & vanMarle, K. (2012). Physics for infants: Characterizing the origins of knowledge about objects, substances, and number. *WIREs Cognitive Science, 3,* 19–27.

Hess, U., & Kirouac, G. (2000). Emotion expression in groups. In M. Lewis & J. Haviland-Jones (Eds.), *Handbook of emotions* (2nd ed., pp. 368–381). New York, NY: Guilford.

Hetherington, E. M., & Kelly, J. (2002). *For better or for worse: Divorce reconsidered.* New York, NY: W. W. Norton.

Heyman, G. D. (2009). Children's reasoning about traits. In P. Bauer (Ed.), *Advances in child development and behavior* (Vol. 37, pp. 105–143). London, UK: Elsevier.

Heyman, G. D., & Legare, C. H. (2004). Children's beliefs about gender differences in the academic and social domains. *Sex Roles, 50,* 227–239.

Hill, J. L., Brooks-Gunn, J., & Waldfogel, J. (2003). Sustained effects of high participation in an early intervention for low-birth-weight premature infants. *Developmental Psychology, 39,* 730–744.

Hillman, C. H., Buck, S. M., Themanson, J. R., Pontifex, M. B., & Castelli, D. M. (2009). Aerobic fitness and cognitive development: Event-related brain potential and task performance indices of executive control in preadolescent children. *Developmental Psychology, 45,* 114–129.

Hipwell, A. E., Keenan, K., Loeber, R., & Battista, D. (2010). Early predictors of sexually intimate behaviors in an urban sample of young girls. *Developmental Psychology, 46,* 366–378.

Hirsh-Pasek, K., & Golinkoff, R. M. (2008). King Solomon's take on word learning: An integrative account from the radical middle. In R. V. Kail (Ed.), *Advances in child development and behavior* (Vol. 36, pp. 1–29). San Diego, CA: Elsevier.

Hitlin, S., Brown, J., & Elder, G. H., Jr. (2006). Racial self-categorization in adolescence: Multiracial development and social pathways. *Child Development, 77,* 1298–1308.

Ho, C. S., & Fuson, K. C. (1998). Children's knowledge of teen quantities as tens and ones: Comparisons of Chinese, British, and American kindergartners. *Journal of Educational Psychology, 90,* 536–544.

Hodnett, E. D., Gates, S., Hofmeyr, G. J., & Sakala, C. (2012). Continuous support for women during childbirth. *Cochrane Database of Systematic Reviews,* Issue 10.

Hofer, M. A. (2006). Psychobiological roots of early attachment. *Current Directions in Psychological Science, 15,* 84–88.

Hoff, E. (2009). *Language development* (2nd ed.). Belmont, CA: Wadsworth Cengage Learning.

Hoff, E. L. (2014). *Language development* (5th ed.). Belmont, CA: Wadsworth, Cengage Learning.

Hoff, E., Core, C., Rumiche, R., Señor, M., & Parra, M. (2012). Dual language exposure and early bilingual development. *Journal of Child Language, 39,* 1–27.

Hoff, E., & Naigles, L. (2002). How children use input to acquire a lexicon. *Child Development, 73,* 418–433.

Hoff-Ginsburg, E., & Tardif, T. (1995). Socioeconomic status and parenting. In M. H. Bornstein (Ed.), *Handbook of parenting* (Vol. 2, pp. 161–188). Mahwah, NJ: Erlbaum.

Hogan, A. M., de Haan, M., Datta, A., & Kirkham, F. J. (2006). Hypoxia: An acute, intermittent and chronic challenge to cognitive development. *Developmental Science, 9,* 335–337.

Hogge, W. A. (1990). Teratology. In I. R. Merkatz & J. E. Thompson (Eds.), *New perspectives on prenatal care.* New York, NY: Elsevier.

Holden, G. W., & Miller, P. C. (1999). Enduring and different: A meta-analysis of the similarity in parents' child rearing. *Psychological Bulletin, 125,* 223–254.

Hollich, G. J., Golinkoff, R. M., & Hirsh-Pasek, K. (2007). Young children associate novel words with complex objects rather than salient parts. *Developmental Psychology, 43,* 1051–1061.

Hollich, G. J., Hirsh-Pasek, K., & Golinkoff, R. M. (2000). Breaking the language barrier: An emergentist coalition model for the origins of word learning. *Monographs of the Society for Research in Child Development, 65* (Serial No. 262).

Holowka, S., & Petitto, L. A. (2002). Left hemisphere cerebral specialization for babies while babbling. *Science, 297,* 1515.

Hood, B., Carey, S., & Prasada, S. (2000). Predicting the outcomes of physical events: Two-year-olds fail to reveal knowledge of solidarity and support. *Child Development, 71,* 1540–1554.

Hopkins, B., & Westra, T. (1988). Maternal handling and motor development: An intercultural study. *Genetic, Social, & General Psychology Monographs, 14,* 377–420.

Horowitz, F. D., & O'Brien, M. (1986). Gifted and talented children: State of knowledge and directions for research. *American Psychologist, 41,* 1147–1152.

Hostinar, C. E., & Gunnar, M. R. (2013). The developmental effects of early life stress: An overview of current theoretical frameworks. *Current Directions in Psychological Science, 22,* 400–406.

Houston, D. M., & Jusczyk, P. W. (2003). Infants' long-term memory for the sound patterns of words and voices. *Journal of Experimental Psychology: Human Perception & Performance, 29,* 1143–1154.

Howe, M. L., & Courage, M. L. (1997). The emergence and early development of autobiographical memory. *Psychological Review, 104,* 499–523.

Howe, N., & Ross, H. S. (1990). Socialization, perspective taking and the sibling relationship. *Developmental Psychology, 26,* 160–165.

Howes, C., & Matheson, C. C. (1992). Sequences in the development of competent play with peers: Social and social pretend play. *Developmental Psychology, 28,* 961–974.

Howes, C., Unger, O., & Seidner, L. B. (1990). Social pretend play in toddlers: Parallels with social play and with solitary pretend. *Child Development, 60,* 77–84.

Hudson, J. A., Shapiro, L. R., & Sosa, B. B. (1995). Planning in the real world: Preschool children's scripts and plans for familiar events. *Child Development, 66,* 984–998.

Huesmann, L. R. (2007). The impact of electronic media violence: Scientific theory and research. *Journal of Adolescent Health Care, 41,* S6–S13.

Hughes, J. M., Bigler, R. S., & Levy, S. R. (2007). Consequences of learning about historical racism among European American and African American children. *Child Development, 78,* 1689–1705.

Hulit, L. M., & Howard, M. R. (2002). *Born to talk: An introduction to speech and language development* (3rd ed.). Boston, MA: Allyn & Bacon.

Hulme, C., & Snowling, M. J. (2009). *Developmental disorders of language learning and cognition.* Chichester, West Sussex, UK: Wiley-Blackwell.

Hulme, C., & Snowling, M. J. (2011). Children's reading comprehension difficulties: Nature, causes, and treatments. *Current Directions in Psychological Science, 20,* 139–142.

Human Genome Project. (2003). *Genomics and its impact on science and society: A 2003 primer.* Washington, DC: U.S. Department of Energy.

Hunt J. M. (1961). *Intelligence and experience.* New York, NY: Ronald.

Hunt, E., & Carlson, J. (2007). Considerations relating to the study of group differences in intelligence. *Perspectives on Psychological Science, 2,* 194–213.

Hurtado, N., Marchman, V. A., & Fernald, A. (2008). Does input influence uptake? Links between maternal talk, processing speed, and vocabulary size in Spanish-learning children. *Developmental Science, 11,* F31–F39.

Hurts, K. (2008). Building cognitive support for the learning of long division skills using progressive schematization: Design and empirical validation. *Computers & Education, 50,* 1141–1156.

Huston, A. C. (2008). From research to policy and back. *Child Development, 79,* 1–12.

Huston, A. C., Duncan, G. J., McLoyd, V. C., Crosby, D. A., Ripke, M. N., Weisner, T. S., et al. (2005). Impacts on children of a policy to promote employment and reduce poverty for low-income parents: New hope after 5 years. *Developmental Psychology, 41,* 902–918.

Huston, A. C., Watkins, B. A., & Kunkel, D. (1989). Public policy and children's television. *American Psychologist, 44,* 424–433.

Huston, A. C., & Wright, J. C. (1998). Mass media and children's development. In W. Damon (Ed.), *Handbook of child psychology* (Vol. 4). New York, NY: Wiley.

Hutchins, E. (1983). Understanding Micronesian navigation. In D. A. Gentner & A. Stevens (Eds.), *Mental models.* Hillsdale, NJ: Erlbaum.

Hutchinson, D. M., Rapee, R. M., & Taylor, A. (2010). Body dissatisfaction and eating disturbances in early adolescence: A structural modeling investigation examining negative affect and peer factors. *Journal of Early Adolescence, 30,* 489–517.

Huth-Bocks, A. C., Levendosky, A. A., Bogat, G. A., & von Eye, A. (2004). The impact of maternal characteristics and contextual variables on infant–mother attachment. *Child Development, 75,* 480–496.

Huttenlocher, J., Haight, W., Bryk, A., Seltzer, M., & Lyons, T. (1991). Early vocabulary growth: Relation to language input and gender. *Developmental Psychology, 27,* 236–248.

Huttenlocher, J., Waterfall, H., Vasilyeva, M., Vevea, J., & Hedges, L. V. (2010). Sources of variability in children's language growth. *Cognitive Psychology, 61,* 343–365.

Hyde, J. S. (2014). Gender similarities and differences. *Annual Review of Psychology, 65,* 373–398.

Hyde, D. C., & Spelke, E. S. (2011). Neural signatures of number processing in human infants: Evidence for two core systems underlying numerical cognition. *Developmental Science, 14,* 360–371.

Hymel, S., Vaillancourt, T., McDougall, P., & Renshaw, P. D. (2004). Peer acceptance and rejection in childhood. In P. K. Smith & C. H. Hart (Eds.), *Blackwell handbook of childhood social development* (pp. 265–284). Malden, MA: Blackwell.

Iervolino, A. C., Hines, M., Golombok, S. E., Rust, J., & Plomin, R. (2005). Genetic and environmental influences on sex-typed behavior during the preschool years. *Child Development, 76,* 826–840.

Inhelder, B., & Piaget, J. (1958). *The growth of logical thinking from childhood to adolescence.* New York, NY: Basic Books.

Institute of Medicine. (1990). *Nutrition during pregnancy.* Washington, DC: National Academy Press.

Iverson, J. M., & Goldin-Meadow, S. (2005). Gesture paves the way for language development. *Psychological Science, 16,* 367–371.

Izard, C. E. (2007). Basic emotions, natural kinds, emotion schemas, and a new paradigm. *Perspectives on Psychological Science, 2,* 260–280.

Izard, C. E., & Ackerman, B. P. (2000). Motivational, organizational, and regulatory functions of discrete emotions. In M. Lewis & J. Haviland-Jones (Eds.), *Handbook of emotions* (2nd ed., pp. 253–264). New York, NY: Guilford.

Jaccard, J., Blanton, H., & Dodge, T. (2005). Peer influences on risk behavior: An analysis of the effects of a close friend. *Developmental Psychology, 41,* 135–147.

Jack, F., MacDonald, S., Reese, E., & Hayne, H. (2009). Maternal reminiscing style during early childhood predicts the age of adolescents' earliest memories. *Child Development, 80,* 496–505.

Jacklin, C. N. (1989). Female and male: Issues of gender. *American Psychologist, 44,* 127–133.

Jacklin, C. N., & Maccoby, E. E. (1978). Social behavior at thirty-three months in same-sex and mixed-sex dyads. *Child Development, 49,* 557–569.

Jacobi, C., Hayward, C., de Zwaan, M., Kraemer, H. C., & Agras, W. S. (2004). Coming to terms with risk factors for eating disorders: Application of risk terminology and suggestions for a general taxonomy. *Psychological Bulletin, 130,* 19–65.

Jacobs, J. E., & Klaczynski, P. A. (2002). The development of judgment and decision making during childhood and adolescence. *Current Directions in Psychological Science, 11,* 145–149.

Jacobson, J. L., & Jacobson, S. W. (1996). Intellectual impairment in children exposed to polychlorinated biphenyls in utero. *New England Journal of Medicine, 335,* 783–789.

Jacobson, S. W., & Jacobson, J. L. (2000). Teratogenic insult and neurobehavioral function in infancy and childhood. In C. A. Nelson (Ed.), *The Minnesota Symposium on Child Psychology: Vol. 31. The effects of early adversity on neurobehavioral development* (pp. 61–112). Mahwah, NJ: Erlbaum.

Jaffe, S. R. (2003). Pathways to adversity in young adulthood among early childbearers. *Journal of Family Psychology, 16,* 38–49.

Jaffee, S., & Hyde, J. S. (2000). Gender differences in moral orientation: A meta-analysis. *Psychological Bulletin, 126,* 703–726.

Jahromi, L. B., Putnam, S. P., & Stifter, C. A. (2004). Maternal regulation of infant reactivity from 2 to 6 months. *Developmental Psychology, 40,* 477–487.

James, J., Ellis, B. J., Schlomer, G. L., & Garber, J. (2012). Sex-specific pathways to early puberty, sexual debut, and sexual risk taking: Tests of an integrated evolutionary-developmental model. *Developmental Psychology, 48,* 687–702.

Jansen, J., de Weerth, C., & Riksen-Walraven, J. M. (2008). Breastfeeding and the mother-infant relationship—A review. *Developmental Review, 28,* 503–521.

Jensen, L. A. (2012). Bridging universal and cultural perspectives: A vision for developmental psychology in a global world. *Child Development Perspectives, 6,* 98–104.

Jiao, Z. (1999, April). *Which students keep old friends and which become new friends across a school transition?* Paper presented at the 1999 meeting of the Society for Research in Child Development, Albuquerque, New Mexico.

Jipson, J. L., & Gelman, S. A. (2007). Robots and rodents: Children's inferences about living and nonliving kinds. *Child Development, 78,* 1675–1688.

John, O. P., & Gross, J. J. (2007). Individual differences in emotion regulation. In J. J. Gross (Ed.), *Handbook of emotion regulation* (pp. 351–372). New York, NY: Guilford.

Johnson, S. P. (2001). Visual development in human infants: Binding features, surfaces, and objects. *Visual Cognition, 8,* 565–578.

Johnston, L. D., Delva, J., & O'Malley, P. M. (2007). Sports participation and physical education in American secondary schools: Current levels and racial/ethnic and socioeconomic disparities. *American Journal of Preventive Medicine, 33,* S195–S208.

Johnson, S. C., Dweck, C. S., Chen, F. S., Stern, H. L., Ok, S-J., & Barth, M. (2010). At the intersection of social and cognitive development:

Internal working models of attachment in infancy. *Cognitive Science, 34*, 807–825.

Johnson, M. H., Grossman, T., & Cohen Kadosh, K. (2009). Mapping functional brain development: Building a social brain through interactive specialization. *Developmental Psychology, 45*, 151–159.

Johnson, K. A., Robertson, I. H., Barry, E., Mulligan, A., Daibhis, A., Daly, M., et al. (2008). Impaired conflict resolution and alerting in children with ADHD: Evidence from the Attention Network Task (ANT). *Journal of Child Psychology and Psychiatry, 49*, 1339–1347.

Jokela, M. (2010). Characteristics of the first child predict the parents' probability of having another child. *Developmental Psychology, 46*, 915–926.

Jones, D. C. (2004). Body image among adolescent girls and boys: A longitudinal study. *Developmental Psychology, 40*, 823–835.

Jones, L. M., Mitchell, K. J., & Finkelhor, D. (2013). Online harassment in context: Trends from three youth internet safety surveys (2000, 2005, 2010). *Psychology of Violence, 3*, 53–69.

Jordan, N. C. (2007). The need for number sense. *Educational Leadership, 65*, 63–64.

Jordan, N. C., Kaplan, D., Ramineni, C., & Locuniak, M. N. (2008). Development of number combination skill in the early school years: When do fingers help? *Developmental Science, 11*, 662–668.

Joseph, R. (2000). Fetal brain behavior and cognitive development. *Developmental Review, 20*, 81–98.

Joseph, D. L., & Newman, D. A. (2010). Emotional intelligence: An integrative meta-analysis and cascading model. *Journal of Applied Psychology, 95*, 54–78.

Joussemet, M., Vitaro, F., Barker, E. D., Côté, S., Zoccolillo, M., Nagin, D. S., et al. (2008). Controlling parenting and physical aggression during elementary school. *Child Development, 79*, 411–425.

Joyner, K., & Udry, J. R. (2000). You don't bring me anything but down: Adolescent romance and depression. *Journal of Health & Social Behavior, 41*, 369–391.

Juffer, F., & van IJzendoorn, M. H. (2007). Adoptees do not lack self-esteem: A meta-analysis of studies on self-esteem of transracial, international, and domestic adoptees. *Psychological Bulletin, 133*, 1067–1083.

Jusczyk, P. W. (1995). Language acquisition: Speech sounds and phonological development. In J. L. Miller & P. D. Eimas (Eds.), *Handbook of perception and cognition: Vol. 11. Speech, language, and communication* (pp. 263–301). Orlando, FL: Academic Press.

Jusczyk, P. W. (2002). How infants adapt speech-processing capacities to native-language structure. *Current Directions in Psychological Science, 11*, 15–18.

Juvonen, J., & Graham, S. (2014). Bullying in schools: The power of bullies and the plight of victims. *Annual Review of Psychology, 65*, 159–185.

Kagan, J., Arcus, D., Snidman, N., Feng, W. Y., Hendler, J., & Greene, S. (1994). Reactivity in infants: A cross-national comparison. *Developmental Psychology, 30*, 342–345.

Kahn, P. H., Gary, H. E., & Shen, S. (2013). Children's social relationships with current and near-future robots. *Child Development Perspectives, 7*, 32–37.

Kaijura, H., Cowart, B. J., & Beauchamp, G. K. (1992). Early developmental change in bitter taste responses in human infants. *Developmental Psychobiology, 25*, 375–386.

Kail, R. V. (2013). Influences of credibility of testimony and strength of statistical evidence on children's and adolescents' reasoning. *Journal of Experimental Child Psychology, 116*, 747–754.

Kail, R., & Hall, L. K. (1999). Sources of developmental change in children's word-problem performance. *Journal of Educational Psychology, 91*, 660–668.

Kail, R. V., McBride-Chang, C., Ferrer, E., Cho, J.-R., & Shu, H. (2013). Cultural differences in the development of processing speed. *Developmental Science, 16*, 476–483.

Kalil, A., & Ziol-Guest, K. M. (2005). Single mothers' employment dynamics and adolescent well-being. *Child Development, 76*, 196–211.

Kam, C.-M., Greenberg, M. T., Bierman, K. L., Coie, J. D., Dodge, K. A., Foster, M. E., et al. (2011). Maternal depressive symptoms and child social preference during the early school years: Mediation by maternal warmth and child emotion regulation. *Journal of Abnormal Child Psychology, 39*, 365–377.

Kaplan, H., & Dove, H. (1987). Infant development among the Ache of eastern Paraguay. *Developmental Psychology, 23*, 190–198.

Karasik, L. B., Tamis-LeMonda, C. S., & Adolph, K. E. (2011). Transition from crawling to walking and infants' actions with objects and people. *Child Development, 82*, 1199–1209.

Karevold, E., Røysamb, E., Ystrom, E., & Mathiesen, K. S. (2009). Predictors and pathways from infancy to symptoms of anxiety and depression in early adolescence. *Developmental Psychology, 45*, 1051–1060.

Kärnä, A., Voeten, M., Little, T. D., Alanen, E., Poskiparta, E., & Salmivalli, C. (2013). Effectiveness of the KiVa antibullying program: Grades 1–3 and 7–9. *Journal of Educational Psychology, 105*, 535–551.

Karniol, R. (1989). The role of manual manipulative states in the infant's acquisition of perceived control over objects. *Developmental Review, 9*, 205–233.

Karraker, K. H., Vogel, D. A., & Lake, M. A. (1995). Parents' gender-stereotyped perceptions of newborns: The eye of the beholder revisited. *Sex Roles, 33*, 687–701.

Kärtner, J., Keller, H., Chaudhary, N., & Yovsi, R. D. (2012). The development of mirror self-recognition in different sociocultural contexts. *Monographs of the Society for Research in Child Development, 77*, Serial No. 307.

Katz, L. F., & Woodin, E. M. (2002). Hostility, hostile detachment, and conflict engagement in marriages: Effects on child and family functioning. *Child Development, 73*, 636–652.

Katz-Wise, S. L., Priess, H. A., & Hyde, J. S. (2010). Gender-role attitudes and behavior across the transition to parenthood. *Developmental Psychology, 46*, 18–28.

Kaufman, J., & Charney, D. (2003). The neurobiology of child and adolescent depression: Current knowledge and future directions. In D. Cicchetti & E. Walker (Eds.), *Neurodevelopmental mechanisms in psychopathology* (pp. 461–490). New York, NY: Cambridge University Press.

Kaufman, J. C., Kaufman, S. B., & Plucker, J. A. (2013). Contemporary theories of intelligence. In D. Reisberg (Ed.), *The Oxford handbook of cognitive psychology*. New York, NY: Oxford University Press.

Kaufman, J., & Lichtenberger, E. O. (2002). *Assessing adolescent and adult intelligence* (2nd ed). Boston, MA: Allyn & Bacon.

Kavsek, M., & Bornstein, M. H. (2010). Visual habituation and dishabituation in preterm infants: A review and meta-analysis. *Research in Developmental Disabilities, 31*, 951–975.

Kawabata, Y., & Crick, N. R. (2011). The significance of cross-racial/ethnic friendships: Associations with peer victimization, peer support, sociometric status, and classroom diversity. *Developmental Psychology, 47*, 1763–1775.

Keane, S. P., Brown, K. P., & Crenshaw, T. M. (1990). Children's intention-cue detection as a function of maternal social behavior: Pathways to social rejection. *Developmental Psychology, 26*, 1004–1009.

Kearney, C. A. (2007). Forms and functions of school refusal behavior in youth: Am empirical analysis of absenteeism severity. *Journal of Child Psychology & Psychiatry, 48*, 53–61.

Kearney, C. A., Haight, C., Gauger, M., & Schafer, R. (2011) School refusal behavior and absenteeism. In R. J. R. Levesque (Ed.), *Encyclopedia of adolescence* (pp. 2489–2492). New York, NY: Springer.

Keijsers, L., Loeber, R., Branje, S., & Meeus, W. (2011). Bidirectional links and concurrent development of parent-child relationships and boys' offending behavior. *Journal of Abnormal Psychology, 120,* 878–889.

Kelemen, D. (2003). British and American children's preferences for teleo-functional explanations of the natural world. *Cognition, 88,* 201–221.

Kelemen, D., & DiYanni, C. (2005). Intuitions about origins: Purpose and intelligent design in children's reasoning about nature. *Journal of Cognition & Development, 6,* 3–31.

Kell, H. J., Lubinski, D., & Benbow, C. P. (2013). Who rises to the top? Early indicators. *Psychological Science, 24,* 648–659.

Kellman, P. J., & Arterberry, M. E. (2006). Infant visual perception. In W. Damon & R. M. Lerner (Eds.), *Handbook of child psychology: Vol. 2. Cognition, perception, and language* (6th ed., pp. 109–160). Hoboken, NJ: Wiley.

Kellman, P. J., & Spelke, E. S. (1983). Perception of partly occluded objects in infancy. *Cognitive Psychology, 15,* 483–524.

Kelly, P. (2011). Corporal punishment and child maltreatment in New Zealand. *Acta Paediatrica, 100,* 14–20.

Kelly, D., Xie, H., Nord, C. W., Jenkins, F., Chan, J. Y., & Kastberg, D. (2013). *Performance of U. S. 15-year-old students in mathematics, science, and reading literacy in an international context: First look at PISA 2012.* Washington DC: National Center for Education Statistics.

Keltner, D., Kogan, A., Piff, P. K., & Saturn, S. R. (2014). The sociocultural appraisals, values, and emotions (SAVE) framework of prosociality: Core processes from gene to meme. *Annual Review of Psychology, 65,* 425–460.

Kendall, J., & Hatton, D. (2002). Racism as a source of health disparity in families with children with attention deficit hyperactivity disorder. *Advances in Nursing Science, 25,* 22–39.

Kerns, K. A., & Brumariu, L. E. (2014). Is insecure parent-child attachment a risk factor for the development of anxiety in childhood or adolescence? *Child Development Perspectives, 8,* 12–17.

Khalil, A., Syngelaki, A., Maiz, N., Zinevich, Y., & Nicolaides, K. H. (2013). Maternal age and adverse pregnancy outcomes: A cohort study. *Ultrasound in Obstetrics and Gynecology, 42,* 634–643.

Khashan, A. S., Baker, P. N., & Kenny, L. C. (2010). Preterm birth and reduced birthweight in first and second teenage pregnancies: a register-based cohort study. *BMC Pregnancy and Childbirth, 10,* 36.

Khurana, A., Romer, D., Betancourt, L. M., Brodsky, N. L., Giannetta, J. M., & Hurt, H. (2012). Early adolescent sexual debut: The mediating role of working memory ability, sensation seeking, and impulsivity. *Developmental Psychology, 48,* 1416–1428.

Kiang, L., Yip, T., Gonzales-Backen, M., Witkow, M., & Fuligni, A. J. (2006). Ethnic identity and the daily psychological well-being of adolescents from Mexican and Chinese backgrounds. *Child Development, 77,* 1338–1350.

Kidd, E. (2012). Implicit statistical learning is directly associated with the acquisition of syntax. *Developmental Psychology, 48,* 171–184.

Kilgore, K., Snyder, J., & Lentz, C. (2000). The contribution of parental discipline, parental monitoring, and school risk to early-onset conduct problems in African American boys and girls. *Developmental Psychology, 36,* 835–845.

Killen, M., & McGlothlin, H. (2005). Prejudice in children. In C. B. Fisher & R. M. Lerner (Eds.), *Encyclopedia of applied developmental science* (Vol. 2, pp. 870–872). Thousand Oaks, CA: Sage.

Kim, S.Y., Chen, Q., Wang, Y., Shen, Y. & Orozco-Lapray, D. (2013). Longitudinal linkages among parent–child acculturation discrepancy, parenting, parent-child sense of alienation, and adolescent adjustment in Chinese immigrant families. *Developmental Psychology, 49,* 900–912.

Kim, J.-Y., McHale, S. M., Crouter, A. C., & Osgood, D. (2007). Longitudinal linkages between sibling relationships and adjustment from middle childhood through adolescence. *Developmental Psychology, 43,* 960–973.

Kim-Spoon, J., Cicchetti, D., & Rogosch, F. A. (2013). A longitudinal study of emotion regulation, emotion lability-negativity, and internalizing symptomatology in maltreated and nonmaltreated children. *Child Development, 84,* 512–527.

Kindermann, T. A. (2007). Effects of naturally existing peer groups on changes in academic engagement in a cohort of sixth graders. *Child Development, 78,* 1186–1203.

King, V. (2006). The antecedents and consequences of adolescents' relationships with stepfathers and nonresident fathers. *Journal of Marriage & the Family, 68,* 910–928.

King, S., Dancause, K., Turcotte-Tremblay, A-M., Veru, F., & Laplante, D. P. (2012). Using natural disasters to study the effects of prenatal maternal stress on child health and human development. *Birth Defects Research (Part C), 96,* 273–288.

Kirby, D., & Laris, B. A. (2009). Effective curriculum-based sex and STD/HIV education programs for adolescents. *Child Development Perspectives, 3,* 21–29.

Kirkorian, H. L., Pempek, T. A., Murphy, L. A., Schmidt, M. E., & Anderson, D. R. (2009). The impact of background television on parent-child interaction. *Child Development, 80,* 1350–1359.

Kisilevsky, B. S., Hains, S. M. J., Brown, C. A., Lee, C. T., Cowperthwaite, B., Stutzman, S. S., et al. (2009). Fetal sensitivity to properties of maternal speech and language. *Infant Behavior and Development, 32,* 59–71.

Kithakye, M., Morris, A. S., Terranova, A. M., & Myers, S. (2010). The Kenyan political conflict and children's adjustment. *Child Development, 81,* 1114–1128.

Kitzman, H. J., Olds, D. L., Cole, R. E., Hanks, C. A., Anson, E. A., Arcoleo, K. J., et al. (2010). Enduring effects of prenatal and infancy home visiting by nurses on children. *Archives of Pediatrics and Adolescent Medicine, 164,* 412–418.

Kjeldsen, A., Janson, H., Stoolmiller, M., Torgersen, L., & Mathiesen, K. S. (2014). Externalising behavior from infancy to mid-adolescence: Latent profiles and early predictors. *Journal of Applied Developmental Psychology, 35,* 25–34.

Klaczynski, P. A. (2000). Motivated scientific reasoning biases, epistemological beliefs, and theory polarization. *Child Development, 71,* 1347–1366.

Klaczynski, P. A. (2004). A dual-process model of adolescent development: Implications for decision making, reasoning, and identity. In R. Kail (Ed.), *Advances in child development and behavior* (Vol. 32, pp. 73–123). San Diego, CA: Elsevier.

Klahr, A. M., & Burt, S. A. (2014). Elucidating the etiology of individual differences in parenting: A meta-analysis of behavioral genetic research. *Psychological Bulletin, 140,* 544–586.

Klahr, D., Zimmerman, C., & Jirout, J. (2011). Educational interventions to advance children's scientific thinking. *Science, 333,* 971–975.

Klaus, M., & Kennell, H. H. (1976). *Mother-infant bonding.* St. Louis: Mosby.

Klemfuss, J. Z., & Ceci, S. J. (2012). Legal and psychological perspectives on children's competence to testify in court. *Developmental Review, 32,* 268–286.

Klimstra, T. A., Luyckx, K., Branje, S., Teppers, E., Goossens, L., & Meeus, W. H. J. (2013). Personality traits, interpersonal identity, and relationship stability: Longitudinal linkages in late adolescence and young adulthood. *Journal of Youth and Adolescence, 42,* 1661–1673.

Klump, K. L., & Culbert, K. M. (2007). Molecular genetic studies of eating disorders: Current status and future directions. *Current Directions in Psychological Science, 16,* 37–41.

Knight, G. P., & Carlo, G. (2012). Prosocial development among Mexican American youth. *Child Development Perspectives, 6,* 258–263.

Kochanska, G., Aksan, N., & Joy, M. E. (2007). Children's fearfulness as a moderator of parenting in early socialization: Two longitudinal studies. *Developmental Psychology, 43,* 222–237.

Kochanska, G., Coy, K. C., & Murray, K. T. (2001). The development of self-regulation in the first four years of life. *Child Development, 72,* 1091–1111.

Kochanska, G., Gross, J. N., Lin, M., & Nichols, K. E. (2002). Guilt in young children: Development, determinants, and relations with a broader system of standards. *Child Development, 73,* 461–482.

Koepke, S., & Denissen, J. A. (2012). Dynamics of identity development and separation-individuation in parent-child relationships during adolescence and emerging adulthood. *Developmental Review, 32,* 67–88.

Koh, J. B. K., & Wang, Q. (2012). Self-development. *WIREs Cognitive Science, 3,* 513–524.

Kohlberg, L. (1966). A cognitive-developmental analysis of children's sex-role concepts and attitudes. In E. E. Maccoby (Ed.), *The development of sex differences.* Stanford, CA: Stanford University Press.

Kohlberg, L. (1969). Stage and sequence: The cognitive-developmental approach to socialization. In D. Goslin (Ed.), *Handbook of socialization theory and research* (pp. 347–480). Chicago, IL: Rand McNally.

Kohlberg, L., & Ullian, D. Z. (1974). Stages in the development of psychosexual concepts and attitudes. In R. C. Friedman, R. M. Richart, & R. L. Van Wiele (Eds.), *Sex differences in behavior.* New York, NY: Wiley.

Kojima, Y. (2000). Maternal regulation of sibling interactions in the preschool years: Observational study in Japanese families. *Child Development, 71,* 1640–1647.

Kokis, J. V., Macpherson, R., Toplak, M. E., West, R. F., & Stanovich, K. E. (2002). Heuristic and analytic processing: Age trends and associations with cognitive ability and cognitive styles. *Journal of Experimental Child Psychology, 83,* 26–52.

Kokko, K., & Pulkkinen, L. (2000). Aggression in childhood and long-term unemployment in adulthood: A cycle of maladaptation and some protective factors. *Developmental Psychology, 36,* 463–472.

Kolb, B., & Teskey, G. C. (2012). Age, experience, injury, and the changing brain. *Developmental Psychobiology, 54,* 311–325.

Kolberg, K. J. S. (1999). Environmental influences on prenatal development and health. In T. L. Whitman & T. V. Merluzzi (Eds.), *Life-span perspectives on health and illness* (pp. 87–103). Mahwah, NJ: Erlbaum.

Konijn, E. A., Nije Bijvank, M., & Bushman, B. J. (2007). I wish I were a warrior: The role of wishful identification in the effects of violent video games on aggression in adolescent boys. *Developmental Psychology, 43,* 1038–1044.

Kopp, C. B. (1997). Young children: Emotion management, instrumental control, and plans. In S. L. Friedman & E. K. Scholnick (Eds.), *The developmental psychology of planning: Why, how, and when do we plan?* (pp. 103–124). Mahwah, NJ: Erlbaum.

Kopp, C. B., & McCall, R. B. (1982). Predicting later mental performances for normal, at-risk, and handicapped infants. In P. B. Bates & O. G. Brim (Eds.), *Life-span development and behavior* (Vol. 4). New York: Academic Press.

Kornhaber, M., Fierros, E., & Veenema, S. (2004). *Multiple intelligences: Best ideas from research and practice.* Boston, MA: Allyn & Bacon.

Koss, K. J., George, M. R. W., Cummings, E. M., Davies, P. T., El-Sheikh, M., & Cicchetti, D. (2013). Asymmetry in children's salivary cortisol and alpha-amylase in the context of marital conflict: Links to children's emotional security and adjustment. *Developmental Psychobiology, 56,* 836–849.

Kowal, A., & Kramer, L. (1997). Children's understanding of parental differential treatment. *Child Development, 68,* 113–126.

Kramer, L. (2010). The essential ingredients of successful sibling relationships: An emerging framework for advancing theory and practice. *Child Development Perspectives, 4,* 80–86.

Krebs, D. L., & Denton, K. (2005). Toward a more pragmatic approach to morality: A critical evaluation of Kohlberg's model. *Psychological Review, 113,* 672–675.

Krebs, D., & Gillmore, J. (1982). The relationships among the first stages of cognitive development, role-taking abilities, and moral development. *Child Development, 53,* 877–886.

Kreppner, J. M., Rutter, M., Beckett, C., Castle, J., Colvert, E., Groothues, C., et al. (2007). Normality and impairment following profound early institutional deprivation: A longitudinal follow-up into early adolescence. *Developmental Psychology, 43,* 931–946.

Kretch, K. S., & Adolph, K. E. (2013a). Cliff or step? Posture-specific learning at the edge of a drop-off. *Child Development, 84,* 226–240.

Kretch, K. S., & Adolph, K. E. (2013b). No bridge too high: Infants decide whether to cross based on the probability of falling not the severity of the potential fall. *Developmental Science, 16,* 336–351.

Krishnakumar, A., & Black, M. M. (2003). Family processes within three-generation households and adolescents mothers' satisfaction with father involvement. *Journal of Family Psychology, 17,* 488–498.

Krispin, O., Sternberg, K. J., & Lamb, M. E. (1992). The dimensions of peer evaluation in Israel: A cross-cultural perspective. *International Journal of Behavioral Development, 15,* 299–314.

Kroger, J., & Greene, K. E. (1996). Events associated with identity status change. *Journal of Adolescence, 19,* 477–490.

Kronenberg, M. E., Hansel, T. C., Brennan, A. M., Osofsky, H. J., Osofsky, J. D., & Lawrason, B. (2010). Children of Katrina: Lessons learned about postdisaster symptoms and recovery patterns. *Child Development, 81,* 1241–1259.

Kucirkova, N., & Tompkins, V. (2014). Personalization in mother-child emotion talk across three contexts. *Infant and Child Development, 23,* 153–169.

Kuhl, P. K., Andruski, J. E., Chistovich, I. A., Chistovich, L. A., Kozhevnikova, E. V., Ryskina, V. L., et al. (1997). Cross-language analysis of phonetic units in language addressed to infants. *Science, 277,* 684–686.

Kuhl, P. K., Stevens, E., Hayashi, A., Deguchi, T., Kiritani, S., & Iverson, P. (2006). Infants show a facilitation effect for native language phonetic perception between 6 and 12 months. *Developmental Science, 9,* F13–F21.

Kuhn, D. (2011). What is scientific thinking and how does it develop? In U. Goswami (Ed.), *The Wiley-Blackwell handbook of cognitive development* (2nd ed., pp. 497–523). West Sussex UK: Wiley-Blackwell.

Kuhn, D. (2012). The development of causal reasoning. *WIREs Cognitive Science, 3,* 327–335.

Kuhn, D., Garcia-Mila, M., Zohar, A., & Andersen, C. (1995). Strategies of knowledge acquisition. *Monographs of the Society for Research in Child Development, 60* (Serial No. 245).

Kulkofsky, S., Wang, Q., & Koh, J. B. K. (2009). Functions of memory sharing and mother-child reminiscing behaviors: Individual and cultural variations. *Journal of Cognition & Development, 10,* 92–114.

Kumar, V., Abbas, A. K., Aster, J. C., & Fausto, N. (2010). *Robbins and Cotran pathologic basis of disease, professional edition* (8th ed.). Philadelphia: W. B. Saunders.

Kuppens, S., Laurent, L., Heyvaert, M., & Onghena, P. (2013). Associations between parental psychological control and relational aggression in children and adolescents: A multilevel and sequential meta-analysis. *Developmental Psychology, 49,* 1697–1712.

Kuryluk, A., Cohen, R., & Audley-Piotrowski, S. (2011). The role of respect in the relation of aggression to popularity. *Social Development, 20,* 703–717.

Lackner, C., Sabbagh, M. A., Hallinan, E., Liu, X., & Holden, J. J. A. (2012). Dopamine receptor D4 gene variation predicts preschoolers' developing theory of mind. *Developmental Science, 15,* 272–280.

Lacourse, E., Boivin, M., Brendgen, A., Petitclerc, A., Girard, A., Vitaro, F., et al. (2014). A longitudinal twin study of physical aggression during early childhood: evidence for a developmentally dynamic genome. *Psychological Medicine, 44,* 2617–2627.

Ladd, G. W. (1998). Peer relationships and social competence during early and middle childhood. *Annual Review of Psychology, 50,* 333–359.

Ladd, G. W. (2003). Probing the adaptive significance of children's behavior and relationships in the school context: A child by environment perspective. In R. V. Kail (Ed.), *Advances in child development and behavior* (Vol. 31, p. 43–104). San Diego, CA: Academic Press.

Ladd, G. W. (2006). Peer rejection, aggressive or withdrawn behavior, and psychological maladjustment from ages 5 to 12: An examination of four predictive models. *Child Development, 77,* 822–846.

Ladd, G. W., Herald-Brown, S. L., & Reiser, M. (2008). Does chronic classroom peer rejection predict the development of children's classroom participation during the grade school years? *Child Development, 79,* 1001–1015.

Ladd, G. W., & Ladd, B. K. (1998). Parenting behaviors and parent–child relationships: Correlates of peer victimization in kindergarten? *Developmental Psychology, 34,* 1450–1458.

Ladd, G. W., & Pettit, G. S. (2002). Parents and children's peer relationships. In M. Bornstein (Ed.), *Handbook of parenting: Vol. 4* (2nd ed., pp. 377–409). Hillsdale, NJ: Erlbaum.

LaFreniere, P., & MacDonald, K. (2013). A post-genomic view of behavioral development and adaptation to the environment. *Developmental Review, 33,* 89–109.

LaFreniere, P., Strayer, F. F., & Gauthier, R. (1984). The emergence of same-sex affiliative preferences among preschool peers: A developmental/ethnological perspective. *Child Development, 55,* 1958–1965.

Lagattuta, K. (2014). Link past, present, and future: Children's ability to connect mental states and emotions across time. *Child Development Perspectives, 8,* 90–95.

Lagattuta, K. N., Nucci, L., & Bosacki, S. L. (2010). Bridging theory of mind and the personal domain: Children's reasoning about resistance to parental control. *Child Development, 81,* 616–635.

Lagattuta, K. H., & Wellman, H. M. (2002). Differences in early parent–child conversations about negative versus positive emotions: Implications for the development of psychological understanding. *Developmental Psychology, 38,* 564–580.

LaGreca, A. M. (1993). Social skills training with children: Where do we go from here? *Journal of Clinical Child Psychology, 22,* 288–298.

LaGreca, A. M., & Silverman, W. K. (2009). Treatment and prevention of posttraumatic stress reactions in children and adolescents to disasters and terrorism: What is the evidence? *Child Development Perspectives, 3,* 4–10.

Laible, D. J., & Carlo, G. (2004). The differential relations of maternal and paternal support and control to adolescent social competence, self-worth, and sympathy. *Journal of Adolescent Research, 19,* 759–782.

Laird, R. D. (2011). Teenage driving offers challenges and potential rewards for developmentalists. *Child Development Perspectives, 5,* 311–316.

Lamaze, F. (1958). *Painless childbirth.* London: Burke.

Lamb, M. E. (1999). Nonparental child care. In M. E. Lamb (Ed.), *Parenting and child development in "nontraditional" families.* Mahwah, NJ: Erlbaum.

Lamb, L. M., Bigler, R. S., Liben, L. S., & Green, V. A. (2009). Teaching children to confront peers' sexist remarks: Implications for theories of gender development and educational practice. *Sex Roles, 61,* 361–382.

Lamb, M. E., & Lewis, C. (2010). The development and significance of father-child relationships in two-parent families. In M. E. Lamb (Ed.), *The role of the father in child development* (5th ed., pp. 94–153). Hoboken, NJ: Wiley.

Lambert, B. L., & Bauer, C. R. (2012). Developmental and behavioral consequences of prenatal cocaine exposure: A review. *Journal of Perinatology, 32,* 819–828.

Landa, R. J., Gross, A. L., Stuart, E. A., & Faherty, A. (2013). Developmental trajectories in children with and without autism spectrum disorders. *Child Development, 84,* 429–442.

Landerl, K., Fussenegger, B., Moll, K., & Willburger, E. (2009). Dyslexia and dyscalculia: Two learning disorders with different cognitive profiles. *Journal of Experimental Child Psychology, 103,* 309–324.

Lansford, J. E. (2009). Parental divorce and children's adjustment. *Perspectives on Psychological Science, 4,* 140–152.

Lansford, J. E., Malone, P. S., Castellino, D. R., Dodge, K. A., Pettit, G. S., & Bates, J. E. (2006). Trajectories of internalizing, externalizing, and grades for children who have and have not experienced their parents' divorce or separation. *Journal of Family Psychology, 20,* 292–301.

Larsen, J. T., To, R. M., & Fireman, G. (2007). Children's understanding and experience of mixed emotions. *Psychological Science, 18,* 186–191.

Larson, R. W., Hansen, D. M., & Moneta, G. (2006). Differing profiles of developmental experiences across types of organized youth activities. *Developmental Psychology, 42,* 849–863.

Lau, J. Y. F., Belli, S. D., Gregory, A. M., Napolitano, M., & Eley, T. C. (2012). The role of children's negative attributions on depressive symptoms: An inherited characteristic or a product of the early environment? *Developmental Science, 15,* 569–578.

Lau, J. Y., Rijsdijk, F., Gregory, A. M., McGuffin, P., & Eley, T. C. (2007). Pathways to childhood depressive symptoms: The role of social, cognitive, and genetic risk factors. *Developmental Psychology, 43,* 1402–1414.

Laursen, B., & Collins, W. A. (1994). Interpersonal conflict during adolescence. *Psychological Bulletin, 115,* 197–209.

Laursen, B., Finkelstein, B. D., & Betts, N. T. (2001). A developmental meta-analysis of peer conflict resolution. *Developmental Review, 21,* 423–449.

Lazardis, M. (2013). The emergence of a temporally extended self and factors that contribute to its development: From theoretical and empirical perspectives. *Monographs of the Society for Research in Child Development, 78,* Serial No. 305.

Leaper, C., & Smith, T. E. (2004). A meta-analytic review of gender variations in children's language use: Talkativeness, affiliative speech, and assertive speech. *Developmental Psychology, 40,* 993–1027.

Lecanuet, J. P., Granier-Deferre, C., & Busnel, M. C. (1995). Human fetal auditory perception. In J. P. Lecanuet, W. P. Fifer, N. A. Krasnegor, & W. P. Smotherman (Eds.), *Fetal development: A psychobiological perspective.* Hillsdale, NJ: Erlbaum.

Leclercq, A-L., & Majerus, S. (2010). Serial-order short-term memory predicts vocabulary development: Evidence from a longitudinal study. *Developmental Psychology, 46,* 417–427.

Ledebt, A. (2000). Changes in arm posture during the early acquisition of walking. *Infant Behavior & Development, 23,* 79–89.

Ledebt, A., van Wieringen, P. C. W., & Saveslsbergh, G. J. P. (2004). Functional significance of foot rotation in early walking. *Infant Behavior & Development, 27,* 163–172.

Lee, K. (2013). Little liars: Development of verbal deception in children. *Child Development Perspectives, 7,* 91–96.

Lee, S. J., Altschul, I., & Gershoff, E. T. (2013). Does warmth moderate longitudinal associations between spanking and child aggression in early childhood? *Developmental Psychology, 49,* 2017–2028.

Lee, P. C., Niew, W. I., Yang, H. J., Chen, V. C. H., & Lin, K. C. (2012). A meta-analysis of behavioral parent training for children with attention deficit hyperactivity disorder. *Research in Developmental Disabilities, 33,* 2040–2049.

Leekam, S. R., Prior, M. R., & Uljarevic, M. (2011). Restricted and repetitive behaviors in autism spectrum disorders: A review of research in the last decade. *Psychological Bulletin, 137,* 562–593.

Leerkes, E. M., Blankson, A. M., & O'Brien, M. (2009). Differential effects of maternal sensitivity to infant distress and nondistress on social-emotional functioning. *Child Development, 80,* 762–775.

Legare, C. H., Gelman, S. A., & Wellman, H. M. (2010). Inconsistency with prior knowledge triggers children's causal explanatory reasoning. *Child Development, 81,* 929–944.

Legare, C. H., Wellman, H. M., & Gelman, S. A. (2009). Evidence for an explanation advantage in naïve biological reasoning. *Cognitive Psychology, 58,* 177–194.

Leinaweaver, J. (2014). Informal kinship-based fostering around the world: anthropological findings. *Child Development Perspectives, 8,* 131–136.

Lengua, L. J. (2006). Growth in temperament and parenting as predictors of adjustment during children's transition to adolescence. *Developmental Psychology, 42,* 819–832.

Lengua, L. J., Sandler, I. N., West, S. G., Wolchik, S. A., & Curran, P. J. (1999). Emotionality and self-regulation, threat appraisal, and coping in children of divorce. *Development & Psychopathology, 11,* 15–37.

Lenroot, R. K., & Giedd, J. N. (2010). Sex differences in the adolescent brain. *Brain and Cognition, 72,* 46–55.

Leon, K. (2003). Risk and protective factors in young children's adjustment to parental divorce: A review of the research. *Family Relations, 52,* 258–270.

Leppänen, J. M., & Nelson, C. A. (2012). Early development of fear processing. *Current Directions in Psychological Science, 21,* 200–204.

Lerner, R. M., Fisher, C. B., & Giannino, L. (2006). Editorial: Constancy and change in the development of applied developmental science. *Applied Developmental Science, 10,* 172–173.

Leventhal, T., & Brooks-Gunn, J. (2000). The neighborhood they live in: The effects of neighborhood residence on child and adolescent outcomes. *Psychological Bulletin, 126,* 309–337.

Levine, S. C., Ratliff, K. R., Huttenlocher, J., & Cannon, J. (2012). Early puzzle play: A predictor of preschoolers' spatial transformation skill. *Developmental Psychology, 48,* 530–542.

Levine, S. C., Vasilyeva, M., Lourenco, S. F., Newcombe, N. S., & Huttenlocher, J. (2005). Socioeconomic status modifies the sex difference in spatial skill. *Psychological Science, 16,* 841–845.

Levine, L. E., Waite, B. M., & Bowman, L. L. (2007). Electronic media use, reading, and academic distractibility in college youth. *Cyberpsychology and Behavior, 10,* 560–566.

Levitt, M. J., Guacci-Franco, N., & Levitt, J. L. (1993). Convoys of social support in childhood and early adolescence: Structure and function. *Developmental Psychology, 29,* 811–818.

Levitt, A. G., & Utman, J. A. (1992). From babbling towards the sound systems of English and French: A longitudinal two-case study. *Journal of Child Language, 19,* 19–49.

Levy, B. A., Gong, Z., Hessels, S., Evans, M. A., & Jared, D. (2006). Understanding print: Early reading development and the contributions of home literacy experiences. *Journal of Experimental Child Psychology, 93,* 63–93.

Levy, G. D., Taylor, M. G., & Gelman, S. A. (1995). Traditional and evaluative aspects of flexibility in gender roles, social conventions, moral rules, and physical laws. *Child Development, 66,* 515–531.

Lewis, M. (1997). The self in self-conscious emotions. In J. G. Snodgrass & R. L. Thompson (Eds.), *The self across psychology: Self-awareness, self-recognition, and the self-concept* (pp. 119–142). New York, NY: New York Academy of Science.

Lewis, M. (2000). The emergence of human emotions. In M. Lewis & J. Haviland-Jones (Eds.), *Handbook of emotions* (2nd ed., pp. 265–280). New York, NY: Guilford.

Lewis, M. (2008). The emergence of human emotion. In M. Lewis, J. M. Haviland-Jones, & L. F. Barrett (Eds.), *Handbook of emotions* (3rd ed., pp. 304–319). New York, NY: Guilford.

Lewis, M., & Ramsay, D. (2004). Development of self-recognition, personal pronoun use, and pretend play during the second year. *Child Development, 75,* 1821–1831.

Lewis, M., Ramsay, D. S., & Kawakami, K. (1993). Differences between Japanese infants and Caucasian American infants in behavioral and cortisol response to inoculation. *Child Development, 64,* 1722–1731.

Lewis, M., Takai-Kawakami, K., Kawakami, K., & Sullivan, M. W. (2010). Cultural differences in emotional responses to success and failure. *International Journal of Behavioral Development, 34,* 53–61.

Lewkowicz, D. J. (2000). Infants' perception of the audible, visible, and bimodal attributes of multimodal syllables. *Child Development, 71,* 1241–1257.

Lewontin, R. C. (1976). Race and intelligence. In N. J. Block & G. Dworkin (Eds.), *The IQ controversy* (pp. 78–92). New York: Pantheon Books.

Li, Y., Anderson, R. C., Nguyen-Jahiel, K., Dong, T., Archodidou, A., Kim, I.-H., et al. (2007). Emergent leadership in children's discussion groups. *Cognition & Instruction, 25,* 75–111.

Li, W., Farkas, G., Duncan, G. J., Burchinal, M. R., & Vandell, D. L. (2013). Timing of high-quality child care and cognitive, language, and preacademic development. *Developmental Psychology, 49,* 1440–1451.

Liben, L. S., & Bigler, R. S. (2002). The developmental course of gender differentiation. *Monographs of the Society for Research in Child Development, 67* (Serial No. 269).

Liben, L. S., Bigler, R. S., & Krogh, H. R. (2001). Pink and blue collar jobs: Children's judgments of job status and job aspirations in relation to sex of worker. *Journal of Experimental Child Psychology, 79,* 346–363.

Liebal, K., Behne, T., Carpenter, M., & Tomasello, M. (2009). Infants use shared experience to interpret pointing gestures. *Developmental Science, 12,* 264–271.

Li-Grining, C. P. (2007). Effortful control among low-income preschoolers in three cities: Stability, change, and individual differences. *Developmental Psychology, 43,* 208–221.

Lillard, A. S., Lerner, M. D., Hopkins, E. J., Dore, R. A., Smith, E. D., & Palmquist, C. M. (2013). The impact of pretend play on children's development: A review of the evidence. *Psychological Bulletin, 139,* 1–34.

Lim, V. K. G., & Kim, T-Y. (2014). The long arm of the job: Parents' work-family conflict and youths' work centrality. *Applied Psychology, 63*, 151–167.

Limpo, T., Alves, R. A., & Fidalgo. R. (2014). Children's high-level writing skills: Development of planning and revising and their contribution to writing quality. *British Journal of Educational Psychology, 84*, 177–193.

Lin, C. C., & Fu, V. R. (1990). A comparison of childrearing practices among Chinese, immigrant Chinese, and Caucasian-American parents. *Child Development, 61*, 429–433.

Lindberg, S. M., Hyde, J. S., Petersen, J. L., & Linn, M. C. (2010). New trends in gender and mathematics performance: A meta-analysis. *Psychological Bulletin, 136*, 1123–1135.

Lindsey, E. W., & Colwell, M. J. (2003). Preschoolers' emotional competence: Links to pretend and physical play. *Child Study Journal, 33*, 39–52.

Lindsey, E. W., Cremeens, P. R., & Caldera, Y. M. (2010). Mother-child and father-child mutuality in two contexts: Consequences for young children's peer relationships. *Infant and Child Development, 19*, 142–160.

Linebarger, D. L., & Vaala, S. E. (2010). Screen media and language development in infants and toddlers: An ecological perspective. *Developmental Review, 30*, 176–202.

Linn, S. (2005). The commercialization of childhood. In S. Oldman (Ed.), *Childhood lost: How American culture is failing our kids* (pp. 107–122). Westport, CT: Praeger.

Linver, M. R., Roth, J. L., & Brooks-Gunn, J. (2009). Patterns of adolescents' participation in organized activities: Are sports best when combined with other activities? *Developmental Psychology, 45*, 354–367.

Lipsitt, L. P. (2003). Crib death: A biobehavioral phenomenon. *Psychological Science, 12*, 164–170.

Liu, D., Gelman, S. A., & Wellman, H. M. (2007). Components of young children's trait understanding: Behavior-to-trait and trait-to-behavior predictions. *Child Development, 78*, 1543–1558.

Liu, H.-M., Kuhl, P. K., & Tsao, F.-M. (2003). An association between mothers' speech clarity and infants' speech discrimination skills. *Developmental Science, 6*, F1–F10.

Liu, R. X., Lin, W., & Chen, Z. Y. (2010). School performance, peer association, psychological and behavioral adjustments: A comparison between Chinese adolescents with and without siblings. *Journal of Adolescence, 33*, 411–417.

Liu, H.-M., Tsao, F.-M., & Kuhl, P. K. (2007). Acoustic analysis of lexical tone in Mandarin infant-directed speech. *Developmental Psychology, 43*, 912–917.

Livesley, W. J., & Bromley, D. B. (1973). *Person perception in childhood and adolescence*. New York, NY: Wiley.

Lobelo, F., Dowda, M., Pfeiffer, K. A., & Pate, R. R. (2009). Electronic media exposure and its association with activity-related outcomes in female adolescents: Cross-sectional and longitudinal analyses. *Journal of Physical Activity & Health, 6*, 137–143.

Lobo, M. A., & Galloway, J. C. (2012). Enhanced handling and positioning in early infancy advances development throughout the first year. *Child Development, 83*, 1290–1302.

LoBue, V. (2013). What are we so afraid of? How early attention shapes our most common fears. *Child Development Perspectives, 7*, 38–42.

LoBue, V., & DeLoache, J. S. (2010). Superior detection of threat-relevant stimuli in infancy. *Developmental Science, 13*, 221–228.

Lockl, K., & Schneider, W. (2007). Knowledge about the mind: Links between theory of mind and later metamemory. *Child Development, 78*, 148–167.

Loomans, E. M., van der Stelt, O., van Eijsden, M., Gemke, R. J. B. J., Vrijkotte, T. G. M., & Van den Bergh, B. R. H. (2012). High levels of antenatal maternal anxiety are associated with altered cognitive control in five-year-old children. *Developmental Psychobiology, 54*, 441–450.

Loper, A. B., & Clarke, C. N. (2013). Attachment representations of imprisoned mothers as related to child contact and the caregiving alliance: The moderating effect of children's placement with maternal grandmothers. *Monographs of the Society for Research in Child Development, 78*, Serial No. 308, 41–56.

Lopez, A. B., Huynh, V. W., & Fuligni, A. J. (2011). A longitudinal study of religious identity and participation during adolescence. *Child Development, 82*, 1297–1309.

Lorch, R. F., Lorch, E. P., Calderhead, W. J., Dunlap, E. E., Hodell, E. C., & Freer, B. D. (2010). Learning the control of variables strategy in higher and lower achieving classrooms: Contributions of explicit instruction and experimentation. *Journal of Educational Psychology, 102*, 90–101.

Lowry, R., Wechsler, H., Kann, L., & Collins, J. L. (2001). Recent trends in participation in physical education among U.S. high school students. *Journal of School Health, 71*, 145–152.

Lubinski, D., Benbow, C. P., Webb, R. M., & Bleske-Rechek, A. (2006). Tracking exceptional human capital over two decades. *Psychological Science, 17*, 194–199.

Ludwig, J., & Phillips, D. (2007). The benefits and costs of Head Start. *SRCD Social Policy Report, 21*, 3–11, 16–18.

Luke, N., & Banerjee, R. (2013). Differentiated associations between childhood maltreatment experiences and social understanding: A meta-analysis and systematic review. *Developmental Review, 33*, 1–28.

Lung, F-W., & Shu, B-C. (2011). Sleeping position and health status of children at six-, eighteen-, and thirty-six-month development. *Research in Developmental Disabilities, 32*, 713–718.

Lushington, K., Pamula, Y., Martin, J., & Kennedy, J. D. (2013). Developmental changes in sleep: Infancy and preschool years. In A. R. Wolfson and H. W. Montgomery-Downs (Eds.), *The Oxford handbook of infant, child, and adolescent sleep and behavior* (pp. 34–47). Oxford, UK: Oxford University Press.

Luthar, S. S., Shoum, K. A., & Brown, P. J. (2006). Extracurricular involvement among affluent youth: A scapegoat for "ubiquitous achievement pressures"? *Developmental Psychology, 42*, 583–597.

Luttikhuizen dos Santos, E. S., de Kieviet, J. F., Königs, M., van Elburg, R. M., & Oosterlaan, J. (2013). Predictive value of the Bayley Scales of Infant Development on development of very preterm/very low birth weight children: A meta-analysis. *Early Human Development, 89*, 487–496.

Luyckx, K., Klimsta, T. A., Duriez, B., Van Petegem, S., & Beyers, W. (2013). Personal identity processes through the late 20s: Age trends, functionality, and depressive symptoms. *Social Development, 22*, 701–721.

Lynne-Landsman, S. D., Graber, J. A., & Andrews, J. A. (2010). Do trajectories of household risk in childhood moderate pubertal timing effects on substance initiation in middle school? *Developmental Psychology, 46*, 853–868.

Lytton, H., & Romney, D. M. (1991). Parents' differential socialization of boys and girls: A meta-analysis. *Psychological Bulletin, 109*, 267–296.

Maccoby, E. E. (1984). Socialization and developmental change. *Child Development, 55*, 317–328.

Maccoby, E. E. (1990). Gender and relationships: A developmental account. *American Psychologist, 45*, 513–520.

Maccoby, E. E. (1998). *The two sexes: Growing up apart, coming together*. Cambridge, MA: Belknap Press.

Maccoby, E. E., & Jacklin, C. N. (1974). *The psychology of sex differences.* Stanford, CA: Stanford University Press.

MacEvoy, J. P., & Asher, S. R. (2012). When friends disappoint: Boys' and girls' responses to transgressions of friendship expectations. *Child Development, 83,* 104–119.

Mackey, A. P., Hill, S. S., Stone, S. I., & Bunge, S. A. (2011). Differential effects of reasoning and speed training in children. *Developmental Science, 14,* 582–590.

MacWhinney, B. (1998). Models of the emergence of language. *Annual Review of Psychology, 49,* 199–227.

Madigan, S., Atkinson, L., Laurin, K., & Benoit, D. (2013). Attachment and internalizing behavior in early childhood: A meta-analysis. *Developmental Psychology, 49,* 672–689.

Magee, L., & Hale, L. (2012). Longitudinal associations between sleep duration and subsequent weight gain: A systematic review. *Sleep Medicine Reviews, 16,* 231–241.

Maggi, S., Ostry, A., Tansey, J., Dunn, J., Hershler, R., Chen, L., & Hertzman, C. (2008). Paternal psychosocial work conditions and mental health outcomes: A case-control study. *BMC Public Health, 8,* 104.

Magnuson, K., & Duncan, G. (2006). The role of family socioeconomic resources in black and white test score gaps among young children. *Developmental Review, 26,* 365–399.

Maguire, A. M., High, K. A., Auricchio, A., Wright, J. F., Pierce, E. A., Testa, F., et al. (2009). Age-dependent effects of RPE65 gene therapy for Leber's congenital amaurosis: A phase 1 dose-escalation trial. *Lancet, 374,* 1597–1605.

Maguire, E. A., Woollett, K., & Spiers, H. J. (2006). London taxi drivers and bus drivers: A structural MRI and neuropsychological analysis. *Hippocampus, 16,* 1091–1101.

Mahoney, J. L., & Parente, M. E. (2009). Should we care about adolescents who care for themselves? What we have learned and what we need to know about youth in self-care. *Child Development Perspectives, 3,* 189–195.

Malinosky-Rummell, R., & Hansen, D. J. (1993). Long-term consequences of childhood physical abuse. *Psychological Bulletin, 114,* 68–79.

Malti, T., & Krettenauer, T. (2013). The relation of moral emotion attributions to prosocial and antisocial behavior: A meta-analysis. *Child Development, 84,* 397–412.

Mandara, J., Gaylord-Harden, N. K., Richard, M. H., & Ragsdale, B. L. (2009). The effects of changes in racial identity and self-esteem on changes in African American adolescents' mental health. *Child Development, 80,* 1660–1675.

Mandel, D. R., Jusczyk, P. W., & Pisoni, D. B. (1995). Infants' recognition of the sound patterns of their own names. *Psychological Science, 6,* 314–317.

Mangelsdorf, S. C. (1992). Developmental changes in infant–stranger interaction. *Infant Behavior & Development, 15,* 191–208.

Mangelsdorf, S. C., Shapiro, J. R., & Marzolf, D. (1995). Developmental and temperamental differences in emotional regulation in infancy. *Child Development, 66,* 1817–1828.

Maratsos, M. (1998). The acquisition of grammar. In W. Damon (Ed.), *Handbook of child psychology.* New York, NY: Wiley.

Maratsos, M. (2000). More overregularizations after all: New data and discussion on Marcus, Pinker, Ullman, Hollander, Rosen, and Xu. *Journal of Child Language, 27,* 183–212.

Marcia, J. E. (1980). Identity in adolescence. In J. Adelson (Ed.), *Handbook of adolescent psychology.* New York, NY: Wiley.

Marcia, J. E. (1991). Identity and self-development. In R. M. Lerner, A. C. Petersen, & J. Brooks-Gunn (Eds.), *Encyclopedia of adolescence* (Vol. 1). New York, NY: Garland.

Marcus, G. F., Pinker, S., Ullman, M., Hollander, M., Rosen, T. J., & Xu, F. (1992). Overregularization in language acquisition. *Monographs of the Society for Research in Child Development, 58* (Serial No. 228).

Mareschal, D., & Tan, S. H. (2007). Flexible and context-dependent categorization by eighteen-month-olds. *Child Development, 78,* 19–37.

Margett, T. E., & Witherington, D. C. (2011). The nature of preschoolers' concept of living and artificial objects. *Child Development, 82,* 2067–2082.

Markovits, H., Benenson, J., & Dolenszky, E. (2001). Evidence that children and adolescents have internal models of peer interactions that are gender differentiated. *Child Development, 72,* 879–886.

Marks, A. K., & García Coll, C. (2007). Psychological and demographic correlates of early academic skill development among American Indian and Alaska Native youth: A growth modeling study. *Developmental Psychology, 43,* 663–674.

Marks, A. K., Patton, F., & García Coll, C. (2011). Being bicultural: A mixed-methods study of adolescents' implicitly and explicitly measured multiethnic identities. *Developmental Psychology, 47,* 270–288.

Marschik, P. B., Einspieler, C., Strohmeier, A., Plienegger, J., Garzarolli, B., & Prechtl, H. F. R. (2008). From the reaching behavior at 5 months of age to hand preference at preschool age. *Developmental Psychobiology, 50,* 511–518.

Marsh, H. W. (1991). Employment during high school: Character building or a subversion of academic goals? *Sociology of Education, 64,* 172–189.

Marsh, H. W., & Craven, R. G. (2006). Reciprocal effects of self-concept and performance from a multidimensional perspective: Beyond seductive pleasure and unidimensional perspectives. *Perspectives on Psychological Science, 1,* 133–163.

Marsh, H. W., Ellis, L. A., & Craven, R. G. (2002). How do preschool children feel about themselves? Unraveling measurement and multidimensional self-concept structure. *Developmental Psychology, 38,* 376–393.

Marsh, H. W., & Kleitman, S. (2005). Consequences of employment during high school: Character building, subversion of academic goals, or a threshold? *American Educational Research Journal, 42,* 331–369.

Marsh, H. W., & Yeung, A. S. (1997). Causal effects of academic self-concept on academic achievement: Structural equation models of longitudinal data. *Journal of Educational Psychology, 89,* 41–54.

Martel, M. M. (2013). Sexual selection and sex differences in the prevalence of childhood externalizing and adolescent internalizing disorders. *Psychological Bulletin, 139,* 1221–1259.

Martin, C. L., & Fabes, R. A. (2001). The stability and consequences of young children's same-sex peer interactions. *Developmental Psychology, 37,* 431–446.

Martin, C. L., Fabes, R. A., Evans, S. M., & Wyman, H. (1999). Social cognition on the playground: Children's beliefs about playing with girls versus boys and their relationships to sex-segregated play. *Journal of Social & Personal Relationships, 16,* 751–772.

Martin, C. L., Fabes, R. A., Hanish, L., Leonard, S., & Dinella, L. M. (2011). Experienced and expected similarity to same-gender peers: Moving toward a comprehensive model of gender segregation. *Sex Roles, 65,* 421–434.

Martin, C. L., & Halverson, C. F. (1987). The roles of cognition in sex role acquisition. In D. B. Carter (Ed.), *Current conceptions of sex roles and sex typing: Theory and research* (pp. 123–137). New York, NY: Praeger.

Martin, J.A., Hamilton, B.E., Ventura, S. J., Osterman, M. J. K., & Mathews, T. J. (2013). Births: Final data for 2011. *National Vital Statistics Reports, 62,* no 1. Hyattsville, MD: National Center for Health Statistics.

Martin, J. A., Hamilton, B. E., Ventura, S. J., Osterman, M. J. K., Wilson, E. C., & Mathews, T. J. (2012). Births: Final data for 2010. *National Vital Statistics Reports, 61*. Hyattsville, MD: National Center for Health Statistics.

Martin, C. L., Kornienko, O., Schaefer, D. R., Hanish, L. D., Fabes, R. A., & Goble, P. (2013). The role of sex of peers and gender-typed activities in young children's peer affiliative networks: A longitudinal analysis of selection and influence. *Child Development, 84*, 921–937.

Martin, R. P., Olejnik, S., & Gaddis, L. (1994). Is temperament an important contributor to schooling outcomes in elementary school? Modeling effects of temperament and scholastic ability on academic achievement. In W. B. Casey & S. C. McDevitt (Eds.), *Prevention and early intervention*. New York, NY: Brunner/Mazel.

Martin, J. L., & Ross, H. S. (2005). Sibling aggression: Sex differences and parents' reactions. *International Journal of Behavioral Development, 29*, 129–138.

Martin, C. L., & Ruble, D. (2004). Children's search for gender cues: Cognitive perspectives on gender development. *Current Directions in Psychological Science, 13*, 67–70.

Mash, E. J., & Wolfe, D. A. (2010). *Abnormal child psychology* (4th ed). Belmont, CA: Cengage.

Masten, A. S., & Narayan, A. J. (2012). Child development in the context of disaster, war, and terrorism: Pathways of risk and resilience. *Annual Review of Psychology, 63*, 227–257.

Masten, A. S., & Osofsky, J. D. (2010). Diasters and their impact on child development: Introduction to the special section. *Child Development, 81*, 1029–1039.

Masten, A. S., Roisman, G. I., Long, J. D., Burt, K. B., Obradovic, J., Riley, J. R., et al. (2005). Developmental cascades: Linking academic achievement and externalizing and internalizing symptoms over 20 years. *Developmental Psychology, 41*, 733–746.

Masten, A., Cutuli, J., Herbers, J., Hinz, E., Obradovic, J., & Wenzel, A. (2014). Academic risk and resilience in the context of homelessness. *Child Development Perspectives, 8*, in press.

Masur, E. F. (1995). Infants' early verbal imitation and their later lexical development. *Merrill-Palmer Quarterly, 41*, 286–306.

Mattys, S. L., & Jusczyk, P. W. (2001). Phonotactic cues for segmentation of fluent speech by infants. *Cognition, 78*, 91–121.

Matusov, E., Bell, N., & Rogoff, B. (2002). Schooling as cultural process: Working together and guidance by children from schools differing in collaborative practices. In R. V. Kail & H. W. Reese (Eds.), *Advances in child development and behavior* (Vol. 29, pp. 129–160). San Diego, CA: Academic Press.

May, P. A., Blankenship, J., Marais, A-S., Gossage, J. P., Kalberg, W. O., Joubert, B., et al. (2013). Maternal alcohol consumption producing fetal alcohol spectrum disorders (FASD): Quantity, frequency, and timing of drinking. *Drug and Alcohol Dependence, 133*, 502–512.

Mayer, J. D., Salovey, P., & Caruso, D. R. (2008). Emotional intelligence: New ability or eclectic traits? *American Psychologist, 63*, 503–517.

Maynard, A. E. (2002). Cultural teaching: The development of teaching skills in Maya sibling interactions. *Child Development, 73*, 969–982.

Mazur, E., Wolchik, S. A., Virdin, L., Sandler, I. N., & West, S. G. (1999). Cognitive moderators of children's adjustment to stressful divorce events: The role of negative cognitive errors and positive illusions. *Child Development, 70*, 231–245.

McAlister, A. R., & Peterson, C. C. (2013). Siblings, theory of mind, and executive functioning in children aged 3–6 years: New longitudinal evidence. *Child Development, 84*, 1442–1458.

McCall, R. B. (1993). Developmental functions for general mental performance. In D. K. Detterman (Ed.), *Current topics in human intelligence* (Vol. 3, pp. 3–29). Norwood, NJ: Ablex.

McCartt, A. T., & Teoh, E. R. (2011). Strengthening driver licensing systems for teenaged drivers. *JAMA, 306*, 1142–1143.

McCarty, M. E., & Ashmead, D. H. (1999). Visual control of reaching and grasping in infants. *Developmental Psychology, 35*, 620–631.

McCormick, C. B. (2003). Metacognition and learning. In I. B. Weiner (Editor-in-Chief) and W. M. Reynolds & G. E. Miller (Eds.), *Handbook of psychology: Vol. 7. Educational psychology* (pp. 79–102). New York, NY: Wiley.

McCormack, T. A. (2011). Planning in young children: A review and synthesis. *Developmental Review, 31*, 1–31.

McCutchen, D., Covill, A., Hoyne, S. H., & Mildes, K. (1994). Individual differences in writing: Implications of translating fluency. *Journal of Educational Psychology, 86*, 256–266.

McCutchen, D., Francis, M., & Kerr, S. (1997). Revising for meaning: Effects of knowledge and strategy. *Journal of Educational Psychology, 89*, 667–676.

McDonald, K. L., Bowker, J. C., Rubin, K. H., Laursen, B., & Duchene, M. S. (2010). Interactions between rejection sensitivity and supportive relationships in the prediction of adolescents' internalizing difficulties. *Journal of Youth & Adolescence, 39*, 563–574.

McElwain, N. L., Booth-LaForce, C., & Wu, X. (2011). Infant-mother attachment and children's friendship quality: Maternal mental-state talk as an intervening mechanism. *Developmental Psychology, 47*, 1295–1311.

McGee, L. M., & Richgels, D. J. (2004). *Literacy's beginnings* (4th ed.). Boston, MA: Allyn & Bacon.

McGraw, M. B. (1935). *Growth: A study of Johnny and Jimmy*. East Norwalk, CT: Appleton-Century-Crofts.

McGuire, S., & Shanahan, L. (2010). Sibling experiences in diverse family contexts. *Child Development Perspectives, 4*, 72–79.

McHale, S. M., Crouter, A. C., Kim, J.-Y., Burton, L. M., Davis, K. D., Dotterer, A. M., et al. (2006). Mothers' and fathers' racial socialization in African American families: Implications for youth. *Child Development, 77*, 1387–1402.

McHale, S. M., Kim, J. Y., Whiteman, S. D., & Crouter, A. C. (2004). Links between sex-typed activities in middle childhood and gender development in early adolescence. *Developmental Psychology, 40*, 868–881.

McHale, J. P., Laurette, A., Talbot, J., & Pourquette, C. (2002). Retrospect and prospect in the psychological study of coparenting and family group process. In J. P. McHale & W. Grolnick (Eds.), *Retrospect and prospect in the psychological study of families* (pp. 127–165). Mahwah, NJ: Erlbaum.

McHale, S. M., Updegraff, K. A., & Whiteman, S. D. (2013). Sibling relationships. In G. W. Peterson & K. R. Bush (Eds.), *Handbook of marriage and the family* (pp. 329–351). New York, NY: Springer Science+Business Media.

McHale, S. M., Whiteman, S. D., Kim, J.-Y., & Crouter, A. C. (2007). Characteristics and correlates of sibling relationships in two-parent African American families. *Journal of Family Psychology, 21*, 227–235.

McLanahan, S. (1999). Father absence and the welfare of children. In E. M. Hetheringon (Ed.), *Coping with divorce, single parenting, and remarriage: A risk and resiliency perspective* (pp. 117–145). Mahwah, NJ: Erlbaum.

McLellan, J. A., & Youniss, J. (2003). Two systems of youth service: Determinants of voluntary and required youth community service. *Journal of Youth & Adolescence, 32*, 47–58.

McMurray, B. (2007). Defusing the childhood vocabulary explosion. *Science, 317*, 631.

McNeil, N. (2014). A "change-resistance" account of children's difficulties understanding mathematical equivalence. *Child Development Perspectives, 8*, 42–47.

McQuade, J. D., Murray-Close, D., Shoulberg, E. K., & Hoza, B. (2013). Working memory and social functioning in children. *Journal of Experimental Child Psychology, 115*, 422–435.

Meaney, M. J. (2010). Epigenetics and the biological definition of gene x environment interactions. *Child Development, 81*, 41–79.

Medland, S. E., Duffy, D. L., Wright, M. J., Geffen, G. M., Hay, D. A., Levy, F., et al., (2009). Genetic influences on handedness: Data from 25,732 Australian and Dutch twin families. *Neuropsychologia, 47*, 330–337.

Medwell, J., & Wray, D. (2014). Handwriting automaticity: The search for performance thresholds. *Language and Education, 28*, 34–51.

Meeker, J. D., & Benedict, M. D. (2013). Infertility, pregnancy loss and adverse birth outcomes in relation to maternal secondhand tobacco smoke exposure. *Current Women's Health Reviews, 9*, 41–49.

Meeus, W., van de Schoot, R., Keijsers, L., Schwartz, S. J., & Branje, S. (2010). On the progression and stability of adolescent identity formation: A five-wave longitudinal study in early-to-middle and middle-to-late adolescence. *Child Development, 81*, 1565–1581.

Mehta, C. M., & Strough, J. (2009). Sex segregation in friendships and normative contexts across the life span. *Developmental Review, 29*, 201–220.

Melby, J. N., Conger, R. D., Fang, S., Wickrama, K. A. S., & Conger, K. J. (2008). Adolescent family experiences and educational attainment during early adulthood. *Developmental Psychology, 44*, 1519–1536.

Melby-Lervåg, M., Lyster, S. H., & Hulme, C. (2012). Phonological skills and their role in learning to read: A meta-analytic review. *Psychological Bulletin, 138*, 322–352.

Melson, G. F. (2003). Child development and the human-companion animal bond. *American Behavioral Scientist, 47*, 31–39.

Melson, G. F. (2010). Play between children and domestic animals. In E. Enwokah, (Ed.), *Play as engagement and communication* (pp. 23–39). Lanham, MD: University Press of America.

Mendle, J., & Ferrero, J. (2012). Detrimental psychological outcomes associated with pubertal timing in adolescent boys. *Developmental Review, 32*, 49–66.

Mendle, J., Turkheimer, E., & Emery, R. E. (2007). Detrimental psychological outcomes associated with early pubertal timing in adolescent girls. *Developmental Review, 27*, 151–171.

Mennella, J., & Beauchamp, G. K. (1997). The ontogeny of human flavor perception. In G. K. Beauchamp & L. Bartoshuk (Eds.), *Tasting and smelling: Handbook of perception and cognition*. San Diego, CA: Academic Press.

Mennella, J. A., Jagnow, C. P., & Beauchamp, G. K. (2001). Prenatal and postnatal flavor learning by human infants. *Pediatrics, 107*, e88.

Metcalfe, J. S., McDowell, K., Chang, T.-Y., Chen, L.-C., Jeka, J. J., & Clark, J. E. (2005). Development of somatosensory-motor integration: An event-related analysis of infant posture in the first year of independent walking. *Developmental Psychobiology, 46*, 19–35.

Metzger, A., Dawes, N., Mermelstein, R., & Wakschlag, L. (2011). Longitudinal modeling of adolescents' activity involvement, problem peer associations, and youth smoking. *Journal of Applied Developmental Psychology, 32*, 1–9.

Mezulis, A., Salk, R. H., Hyde, J. S., Priess-Groben, H. A., & Simonson, J. L., (2014). Affective, biological, and cognitive predictors of depressive symptom trajectories in adolescence. *Journal of Abnormal Child Psychology, 42*, 539–550.

Miceli, P. J., Whitman, T. L., Borkowsky, J. G., Braungart-Riekder, J., & Mitchell, D. W. (1998). Individual differences in infant information processing: The role of temperament and maternal factors. *Infant Behavior & Development, 21*, 119–136.

Midgette, E., Haria, P., & MacArthur, C. (2008). The effects of content and audience awareness goals for revision on the persuasive essays of fifth- and eight-grade students. *Reading & Writing, 21*, 131–151.

Miga, E. M., Gdula, J. A., & Allen, J. P. (2012). Fighting fair: Adaptive marital conflict strategies as predictors of future adolescent peer and romantic relationship quality. *Social Development, 21*, 443–460.

Milberger, S., Biederman, J., Faraone, S. V., Guite, J., & Tsuang, M. T. (1997). Pregnancy, delivery and infancy complications, and attention deficit hyperactivity disorder: Issues of gene-environment interaction. *Biological Psychiatry, 41*, 65–75.

Miles, S. B., & Stipek, D. (2006). Contemporaneous and longitudinal associations between social behavior and literacy achievement in a sample of low-income elementary school children. *Child Development, 77*, 103–117.

Miller v. Alabama, 132 S. Ct. 2455 (2012).

Miller, S. A. (2009). Children's understanding of second-order mental states. *Psychological Bulletin, 135*, 749–773.

Miller, P. H. (2011). Piaget's theory: Past, present, and future. In U. Goswami (Ed.), *The Wiley-Blackwell handbook of childhood cognitive development* (2nd ed., pp. 649–672). West Sussex, UK: Wiley-Blackwell.

Miller, J. G., & Bersoff, D. M. (1992). Culture and moral judgment: How are conflicts between justice and interpersonal responsibilities resolved? *Journal of Personality & Social Psychology, 62*, 541–554.

Miller, G. E., & Chen, E. (2010). Harsh family climate in early life presages the emergence of proinflammatory phenotype in adolescence. *Psychological Science, 21*, 848–856.

Miller, P. M., Danaher, D. L., & Forbes, D. (1986). Sex-related strategies of coping with interpersonal conflict in children aged five to seven. *Developmental Psychology, 22*, 543–548.

Miller, D. I., & Halpern, D. F. (2014). The new science of cognitive sex differences. *Trends in Cognitive Sciences, 18*, 37–45.

Miller, T. W., Nigg, J. T., & Miller, R. L. (2009). Attention deficit hyperactivity disorder in African American children: What can be learned from the past ten years? *Clinical Psychology Review, 29*, 77–86.

Miller, K. F., Smith, C. M., Zhu, J., & Zhang, H. (1995). Preschool origins of cross-national differences in mathematical competence: The role of number-naming systems. *Psychological Science, 6*, 56–60.

Mills, C. M., & Keil, F. C. (2005). The development of cynicism. *Psychological Science, 16*, 385–390.

Mills-Koonce, W. R., Appleyard, K., Barnett, M., Deng, M., Putallaz, M., & Cox, M. (2011). Adult attachment style and stress as risk factors for early maternal sensitivity and negativity. *Infant Mental Health Journal, 32*, 277–285.

Milunsky, A. (2002). *Your genetic destiny: Know your genes, secure your health, and save your life.* Cambridge, MA: Perseus Publishing.

Minkler, M., & Fuller-Thomson, E. (2005). African American grandparents raising grandchildren: A national study using the Census 2000 American Community Survey. *Journals of Gerontology: Psychological Sciences & Social Sciences, 60B*, S82–S92.

Mischel, W. (1970). Sex-typing and socialization. In P. H. Mussen (Ed.), *Carmichael's manual of child psychology* (Vol. 2). New York, NY: Wiley.

Mischel, W., & Ayduk, O. (2004). Willpower in a cognitive-affective processing system: The dynamics of delay of gratification. In R. F. Baumeister & K. D. Vohs (Eds.), *Handbook of self-regulation* (pp. 99–129). New York, NY: Guilford.

Mischel, W., Ayduk, O., Berman, M. G., Casey, B. J., Gotlib, I. H., Jonides J., et al. (2011). "Willpower" over the life span: decomposing self-regulation. *Social Cognitive and Affective Neuroscience, 6*, 252–256.

Mischel, W., & Ebbesen, E. (1970). Attention in delay of gratification. *Journal of Personality & Social Psychology, 16,* 329–337.

Mix, K. S., Huttenlocher, J., & Levine, S. C. (2002). Multiple cues for quantification in infancy: Is number one of them? *Psychological Bulletin, 128,* 278–294.

Mize, J., & Ladd, G. W. (1990). A cognitive social-learning approach to social skill training with low-status preschool children. *Developmental Psychology, 26,* 388–397.

Mize, J., & Pettit, G. S. (1997). Mothers' social coaching, mother–child relationship style, and children's peer competence: Is the medium the message? *Child Development, 68,* 312–332.

Mize, J., Pettit, G. S., & Brown, E. G. (1995). Mothers' supervision of their children's peer play: Relations with beliefs, perceptions, and knowledge. *Developmental Psychology, 31,* 311–321.

Moerk, E. L. (2000). *The guided acquisition of first language skills.* Westport, CT: Ablex.

Moffitt, T. E. (2005). The new look of behavioral genetics in developmental psychopathology: Gene-environment interplay in antisocial behaviors. *Psychological Bulletin, 131,* 533–554.

Moffitt, T. E., Arseneault, L., Belsky, D., Dickson, N., Hancox, R. J., Harrington, H., et al. (2011). A gradient of childhood self-control predicts health, wealth, and public safety. *Proceedings of the National Academy of Sciences, 108,* 2693–2698.

Moffitt, T. E., Poulton, R., & Caspi, A. (2013). Lifelong impact of early self-control: Childhood self-discipline predicts adult quality of life. *American Scientist, 101,* 352–359.

Molfese, D. L., & Burger-Judisch, L. M. (1991). Dynamic temporal-spatial allocation of resources in the human brain: An alternative to the static view of hemisphere differences. In F. L. Ketterle (Ed.), *Cerebral laterality: Theory and research. The Toledo symposium.* Hillsdale, NJ: Erlbaum.

Molina, B. S. G., Hinshaw, S. P., Swanson, J. M., Arnold, L. E., Vitiello, B., Jensen, P. S., et al. (2009). The MTA at 8 years: Prospective follow-up of children treated for combined-type ADHD in a multisite study. *Journal of the American Academy of Child & Adolescent Psychiatry, 48,* 484–500.

Molloy, L. E., Gest, S. D., & Rulison, K. L. (2011). Peer influences on academic motivation: Exploring multiple methods of assessing youths' most "influential" peer relationships. *Journal of Early Adolescence, 31,* 13–40.

Monahan, K. C., Lee, J. M., & Steinberg, L. (2011). Revisiting the impact of part-time work on adolescent adjustment: Distinguishing between selection and socialization using propensity score matching. *Child Development, 82,* 96–112.

Monahan, K. C., Steinberg, L., & Cauffman, E. (2013). Age differences in the impact of employment on antisocial behavior. *Child Development, 84,* 791–801.

Mondloch, C. J., Lewis, T. L., Budreau, D. R., Maurer, D., Dannemiller, J. L., Stephens, B. R., et al. (1999). Face perception during early infancy. *Psychological Science, 10,* 419–422.

Monk, C., Fifer, W. P., Myers, M. M., Sloan, R. P., Trien, L., & Hurtando, A. (2000). Maternal stress responses and anxiety during pregnancy: Effects on fetal heart rate. *Developmental Psychology, 36,* 67–77.

Monk, C., Georgieff, M. K., & Osterholm, E. A. (2013). Research review: Maternal prenatal distress and poor nutrition—mutually influencing risk factors affecting infant neurocognitive development. *Journal of Child Psychology and Psychiatry, 54,* 115–130.

Monk, C., Spicer, J., & Champagne, F. A. (2012). Linking prenatal adversity to developmental outcomes in infants: The role of epigenetic pathways. *Development and Psychopathology, 24,* 1361–1376.

Montague, D. P., & Walker-Andrews, A. S. (2001). Peekaboo: A new look at infants' perception of emotion expressions. *Developmental Psychology, 37,* 826–838.

Moore, C. F. (2003). *Silent scourge: Children, pollution, and why scientists disagree.* New York, NY: Oxford University Press.

Moore, K. L., Persaud, T. V. N., & Torchia, M. G. (2012). *Before we are born: Essentials of embryology and birth defects* (8th ed.). Philadelphia: W. B. Saunders.

Moreno, A. J., Klute, M. M., & Robinson, J. L. (2008). Relational and individual resources as predictors of empathy in early childhood. *Social Development, 17,* 613–637.

Morgan, B., & Gibson, K. R. (1991). Nutritional and environmental interactions in brain development. In K. R. Gibson & A. C. Peterson (Eds.), *Brain maturation and cognitive development: Comparative and cross-cultural perspectives* (pp. 91–106). New York, NY: Aldine de Gruyter.

Morgan, P. L., Staff, J., Hillemeier, M. M., Farkas, G., & Maczuga, S. (2013). Racial and ethnic disparities in ADHD diagnosis from kindergarten to eighth grade. *Pediatrics, 132,* 85–93.

Morgane, P. J., Austin-LaFrance, R., Bronzino, J. D., Tonkiss, J., Diaz-Cintra, S., et al. (1993). Prenatal malnutrition and development of the brain. *Neuroscience & Biobehavioral Reviews, 17,* 91–128.

Morrissey, T. W. (2009). Multiple child-care arrangements and young children's behavioral outcomes. *Child Development, 80,* 59–76.

Morrongiello, B. A., Klemencic, N., & Corbett, M. (2008). Interactions between child behavior patterns and parent supervision: Implications for children's risk of unintentional injury. *Child Development, 79,* 627–638.

Morrongiello, B. A., & Schell, S. L. (2010). Child injury: The role of supervision. *American Journal of Lifestyle Medicine, 4,* 65–74.

Morrow, J. R., Martin, S. B., Welk, G. J., Zhu, W., & Meredith, M. D. (2010). Overview of the Texas Youth Fitness Study. *Research Quarterly for Exercise and Sport, 81,* S1–S5.

Mortimer, J. T., & Staff, J. (2004). Early work as a source of developmental discontinuity during the transition to adulthood. *Development & Psychopathology, 16,* 1047–1070.

Morton, J., & Johnson, M. H. (1991). CONSPEC and CONLERN: A two-process theory of infant face recognition. *Psychological Review, 98,* 164–181.

Moses, L. J., Baldwin, D. A., Rosicky, J. G., & Tidball, G. (2001). Evidence for referential understanding in the emotions domain at twelve and eighteen months. *Child Development, 72,* 718–735.

Mounts, N. S. (2011). Parental management of peer relationships and early adolescents' social skills. *Journal of Youth and Adolescence, 40,* 416–427.

The MTA Cooperative Group. (1999). Moderators and mediators of treatment response for children with attention-deficit/hyperactivity disorder. *Archives of General Psychiatry, 56,* 1088–1096.

Mueller, M. M., & Elder, G. H. (2003). Family contingencies across the generations: Grandparents–grandchild relationships in holistic perspective. *Journal of Marriage & the Family, 65,* 404–417.

Murphy, K. R., Barkley, R. A., & Bush, T. (2002). Young adults with attention deficit hyperactivity disorder: Subtype differences in comorbidity, educational, and clinical history. *Journal of Nervous & Mental Disease, 190,* 147–157.

Murphy, N., & Messer, D. (2000). Differential benefits from scaffolding and children working alone. *Educational Psychology, 20,* 17–31.

Murray, V. M., Berkely, C., Gaylord-Harden, N. K., Copeland-Linder, N., & Nation, M. (2011). Neighborhood poverty and adolescent development. *Journal of Research on Adolescence, 21,* 114–128.

Murray-Close, D., Hoza, B., Hinshaw, S. P., Arnold, L. E., Swanson, J., Jensen, P. S., et al. (2010). Developmental processes in peer problems of children with attention-deficit/hyperactivity disorder in the Multimodal Treatment Study of Children with ADHD: Developmental cascades and vicious cycles. *Development & Psychopathology, 22*, 785–802.

Mustanski, B. S., Viken, R. J., Kaprio, J., Pulkkinen, L., & Rose, R. J. (2004). Genetic and environmental influences on pubertal development: Longitudinal data from Finnish twins at ages 11 and 14. *Developmental Psychology, 40*, 1188–1198.

Mustonen, U., Huurre, T., Kiviruusu, O., Haukkala, A., & Aro, H. (2011). Long-term impact of parental divorce on intimate relationship quality in adulthood and the mediating role of psychosocial resources. *Journal of Family Psychology, 25*, 615–619.

Muter, V., Hulme, C., Snowling, M. J., & Stevenson, J. (2004). Phonemes, rimes, vocabulary, and grammatical skills as foundations of early reading development: Evidence from a longitudinal study. *Developmental Psychology, 40*, 663–681.

Nadig, A. S., & Sedivy, J. C. (2002). Evidence of perspective-taking constraints in children's online reference resolution. *Psychological Science, 13*, 329–336.

Nahar, B., Hossain, M. I., Hamadani, J. D., Ahmed, T., Huda, S. N., Grantham-McGregor, S. M., et al. (2012). Effects of a community-based approach of food and psychosocial stimulation on growth and development of severely malnourished children in Bangladesh: a randomised trial. *European Journal of Clinical Nutrition, 66*, 701–709.

Naigles, L. G., & Gelman, S. A. (1995). Overextensions in comprehension and production revisited: Preferential-looking in a study of dog, cat, and cow. *Journal of Child Language, 22*, 19–46.

Nancekivell, S. E., Van de Vondervoort, J., & Friedman, O. (2013). Young children's understanding of ownership. *Child Development Perspectives, 7*, 243–247.

Nánez, J., Sr., & Yonas, A. (1994). Effects of luminance and texture motion on infants' defensive reactions to optical collision. *Infant Behavior & Development, 17*, 165–174.

Nangle, D. W., Erdley, C. A., Zeff, K. R., Staunchfield, L. L., & Gold, J. A. (2004). Opposites do not attract: Social status and behavioral-style concordances and discordances among children and peers who like or dislike them. *Journal of Abnormal Child Psychology, 32*, 425–434.

Narayan, A. J., Englund, M. M., & Egeland, B. (2013). Developmental timing and continuity of exposure to interparental violence and externalizing behavior as prospective predictors of dating violence. *Development and Psychopathology, 25*, 973–990.

Nation, K., Adams, J. W., Bowyer-Crane, C. A., & Snowling, M. J. (1999). Working memory deficits in poor comprehenders reflect underlying language impairments. *Journal of Experimental Child Psychology, 73*, 139–158.

Nation, K., Cocksey, J., Taylor, J. S. H., & Bishop, D. V. M. (2010). A longitudinal investigation of early reading and language skills in children with poor reading comprehension. *Journal of Child Psychology and Psychiatry, 51*, 1031–1039.

National Association for Sport and Physical Education. (2004). *Appropriate practices for high school physical education.* Reston, VA: Author.

National Cancer Institute. (2006). *DES: Questions and answers.* Washington DC: Author.

National Institute of Neurological Disorders and Stroke. (2013). *Spina bifida fact sheet.* NIH Publication No. 13–309. Author: Bethesda, MD.

National Science Foundation. (2008). *Science and engineering indicators 2008.* Retrieved April 10, 2013, from http://www.nsf.gov/statistics/seind08.

Neblett, E. W., Rivas-Drake, D., & Umaña-Taylor, A. J. (2012). The promise of racial and ethnic protective factors in promoting ethnic minority youth development. *Child Development Perspectives, 6*, 295–303.

Neiss, M., B., Sedikides, C., & Stevenson, J. (2006). Genetic influences on level and stability of self-esteem. *Self and Identity, 5*, 247–266.

Nelson, K. (1973). Structure and strategy in learning to talk. *Monographs of the Society for Research in Child Development, 38* (Serial No. 149).

Nelson, E. L., Campbell, J. M., & Michel, G. F. (2013). Unimanual to bimanual: Tracking the development of handedness from 6 to 24 months. *Infant Behavior and Development, 36*, 181–188.

Nelson, K., & Fivush, R. (2004). The emergence of autobiographical memory: A social cultural developmental theory. *Psychological Review, 111*, 486–511.

Nelson, I. A., & Gastic, B. (2009). Street ball, swim team and the sour cream machine: A cluster analysis of out of school time participation portfolios. *Journal of Youth & Adolescence, 38*, 1172–1186.

Nelson, E. A. S., Schiefenhoevel, W., & Haimerl, F. (2000). Child care practices in nonindustrialized societies. *Pediatrics, 105*, e75.

Nesdale, D. (2001). The development of prejudice in children. In M. A. Augoustinos & K. J. Reynolds (Eds.), *Understanding prejudice, racism, and social conflict* (pp. 57–73). London, UK: Sage.

Nevid, J. S., Rathus, S. A., & Greene, B. (2003). *Abnormal psychology in a changing world* (5th ed.). Upper Saddle River, NJ: Prentice-Hall.

Neville, H. J., Stevens, C., Pakulak, E., Bell, T. A., Fanning, J., Klein, S., et al. (2013). Family-based training program improves brain function, cognition, and behavior in lower socioeconomic status preschoolers. *PNAS, 110*, 12138–12143.

Newcomb, A. F., & Bagwell, C. L. (1995). Children's friendship relations: A meta-analytic review. *Psychological Bulletin, 117*, 306–347.

Newcombe, N. S. (2002). The nativist-empiricist controversy in the context of recent research on spatial and quantitative development. *Psychological Science, 13*, 395–401.

Newcombe, N. (2013). Cognitive development: changing views of cognitive change. *WIREs Cognitive Science, 4*, 479–491.

Newman, G. E., & Keil, F. C. (2008). Where is the essence? Developmental shifts in children's beliefs about internal features. *Child Development, 79*, 1344–1356.

Newman, R., Ratner, N. B., Jusczyk, A. M., Jusczyk, P. W., & Dow, K. A. (2006). Infants' early ability to segment the conversational speech signal predicts later language development: A retrospective analysis. *Developmental Psychology, 42*, 643–655.

Newport, E. L. (1991). Contrasting conceptions of the critical period for language. In S. Carey & R. Gelman (Eds.), *The epigenesis of mind: Essays on biology and cognition* (pp. 111–130). Hillsdale, NJ: Erlbaum.

Ngon, C., Martin, A., Dupoux, E., Cabrol, D., Dutat, M., & Peperkamp, S. (2013). (Non)words, (non)words, (non)words: Evidence for a protolexicon during the first year of life. *Developmental Science, 16*, 24–34.

Ni, Y., Chiu, M. M., & Cheng, Z-J. (2010). Chinese children learning mathematics: From home to school. In M. H. Bond (Ed.), *Oxford handbook of Chinese psychology* (pp. 143–154). New York, NY: Oxford University Press.

NICHD. (2004). *The NICHD community connection.* Washington DC: Author.

NICHD Early Child Care Research Network. (1997). The effects of infant child care on infant–mother attachment security: Results of the NICHD Study of Early Child Care. *Child Development, 68*, 860–879.

NICHD Early Child Care Research Network. (2001). Child-care and family predictors of preschool attachment and stability from infancy. *Developmental Psychology, 37*, 847–862.

Nilsen, P. (2007). The how and why of community-based injury prevention: A conceptual and evaluation model. *Safety Science, 45,* 501–521.

Nilsen, E. S., & Graham, S. A. (2012). The development of preschoolers' appreciation of communicative ambiguity. *Child Development, 83,* 1400–1415.

Nisbett, R. E., Aronson, J., Clair, C., Dickens, W., Flynn, J., Halpern, D. F., et al. (2012). Intelligence: New findings and theoretical developments. *American Psychologist, 67,* 130–159.

Nishida, T. K., & Lillard, A. S. (2007). The informative value of emotional expressions: "Social referencing" in mother–child pretense. *Developmental Science, 10,* 205–212.

Nishina, A., & Juvonen, J. (2005). Daily reports of witnessing and experiencing peer harassment in middle school. *Child Development, 76,* 435–450.

Nordine, J., Krajcik, J., & Fortus, D. (2011). Transforming energy instruction in middle school to support integrated understanding and future learning. *Science Education, 95,* 670–699.

Norlander, T., Erixon, A., & Archer, T. (2000). Psychological androgyny and creativity: Dynamics of gender-role and personality trait. *Social Behavior & Personality, 28,* 423–435.

Notaro, P. C., Gelman, S. A., & Zimmerman, M. A. (2001). Children's understanding of psychogenic bodily reactions. *Child Development, 72,* 444–459.

Novin, S., Rieffe, C., Banerjee, R., Miers, A. C., & Cheung, J. (2011). Anger response styles in Chinese and Dutch children: A sociocultural perspective on anger regulation. *British Journal of Developmental Psychology, 29,* 806–822.

Nucci, L., & Gingo, M. (2011). The development of moral reasoning. In U. Goswami (Ed.), *The Wiley-Blackwell handbook of childhood cognitive development* (2nd ed., pp. 420–445). West Sussex, UK: Wiley.

Nucci, L., & Weber, E. (1995). Social interactions in the home and the development of young children's conception of the personal. *Child Development, 66,* 1438–1452.

Nunes, T., Bryant, P., & Barros, R. (2012). The development of word recognition and its significance for comprehension and fluency. *Journal of Educational Psychology, 104,* 959–973.

Nurmsoo, E., & Bloom, P. (2008). Preschoolers' perspective taking in word learning: Do they blindly follow eye gaze? *Psychological Science, 19,* 211–215.

Nyaradi, A., Li, J., Hickling, S., Foster, J., & Oddy, W. H. (2013). The role of nutrition in children's neurocognitive development, from pregnancy through childhood. *Frontiers in Human Neuroscience, 7,* Article 97.

Oakhill, J. V., & Cain, K. (2012). The precursors of reading ability in young readers: Evidence from a four-year longitudinal study. *Scientific Studies of Reading, 16,* 91–121.

Oaten, M., Stevenson, R. J., & Case, T. I. (2009). Disgust as a disease-avoidance mechanism. *Psychological Bulletin, 135,* 303–321.

Oates, C., Blades, M., & Gunter, B. (2002). Children and television advertising: When do they understand persuasive intent? *Journal of Consumer Behavior, 1,* 238–245.

Oberlander, S. E., Black, M. M., & Starr, R. H., Jr. (2007). African American adolescent mothers and grandmothers: A multigenerational approach to parenting. *American Journal of Community Psychology, 39,* 37–46.

O'Brien, T. (2013). Gene therapy for Type 1 diabetes moves a step closer to reality. *Diabetes, 62,* 1396–1397.

O'Connor, T., Heron, J., Golding, J., Beveridge, M., & Glover, V. (2002). Maternal antenatal anxiety and children's behavioral/emotional problems at 4 years. *British Journal of Psychiatry, 180,* 502–508.

O'Connor, S., & Jose, P. E. (2012). A propensity score matching study of participation in community activities: A path to positive outcomes for youth in New Zealand? *Developmental Psychology, 48,* 1563–1569.

Odgers, C. L., Moffitt, T. E., Tach, L. M., Sampson, R. J., Taylor, A., Matthews, C. L., et al. (2009). The protective effects of neighborhood collective efficacy on British children growing up in deprivation: A developmental analysis. *Developmental Psychology, 45,* 942–957.

O'Doherty, K., Troseth, G. L., Shimpi, P. M., Goldenberg, E., Akhtar, N., & Saylor, M. M. (2011). Third-party social interaction and word learning from video. *Child Development, 82,* 902–915.

OECD. (2006). *Starting strong II: Early childhood education and care.* Paris: OECD Publishing.

Offer, D., Ostrov, E., Howard, K. I., & Atkinson, R. (1988). *The teenage world: Adolescents' self-image in ten countries.* New York, NY: Plenum.

O'Hara, M. W. (2009). Postpartum depression: What we know. *Journal of Clinical Psychology, 65,* 1258–1269.

O'Hara, R. E., Gibbons, F. X., Gerrard, M., Li, Z., & Sargent, J. D. (2012). Greater exposure to sexual content in popular movies predicts earlier sexual debut and increased sexual risk taking. *Psychological Science, 23,* 984–993.

O'Hara, M. W., & McCabe, J. E. (2013). Postpartum depression: Current status and future directions. *Annual Review of Clinical Psychology, 9,* 379–407.

Ojanen, T., & Perry, D. G. (2007). Relational schemas and the developing self: Perceptions of mother and of self as joint predictors of early adolescents' self-esteem. *Developmental Psychology, 43,* 1474–1483.

Okagaki, L., & Frensch, P. A. (1994). Effects of video game playing on measures of spatial performance: Gender effects in late adolescence. *Journal of Applied Developmental Psychology, 15,* 33–58.

Okami, P., Weisner, T., & Olmstead, R. (2002). Outcome correlates of parent–child bedsharing: An eighteen-year longitudinal study. *Developmental & Behavioral Pediatrics, 23,* 244–253.

Oliner, S. P., & Oliner, P. M. (1988). *The altruistic personality: Rescuers of Jews in Nazi Europe.* New York, NY: Free Press.

Olinghouse, N. G. (2008). Student- and instruction-level predictors of narrative writing in third-grade students. *Reading & Writing, 21,* 3–26.

Olson, S. L., Lopez-Duran, N., Lunkenheimer, E. S., Chang, H., & Sameroff, A. J. (2011). Individual differences in the development of early peer aggression: Integrating contributions of self-regulation, theory of mind, and parenting. *Development and Psychopathology, 23,* 253–266.

Olson, S. L., Sameroff, A. J., Kerr, D. C. R., Lopez, N. L., & Wellman, H. M. (2005). Developmental foundations of externalizing problems in young children: The role of effortful control. *Development & Psychopathology, 17,* 25–45.

Olweus, D., Mattson, A., Schalling, D., & Low, H. (1988). Circulating testosterone levels and aggression in adolescent males: A causal analysis. *Psychosomatic Medicine, 50,* 261–272.

O'Neill, D. K. (1996). Two-year-old children's sensitivity to a parent's knowledge state when making requests. *Child Development, 67,* 659–677.

Online Mendelian Inheritance in Man. (2013). Nathans Institute of Genetic Medicine, Johns Hopkins University (Baltimore, MD). Retrieved from http://omim.org/ on September 22, 2013.

Opfer, J. E., & Gelman, S. A. (2011). Development of the animate-inanimate distinction. In U. Goswami (Ed.), *The Wiley-Blackwell handbook of childhood cognitive development* (2nd ed., pp. 213–238). West Sussex, UK: Wiley-Blackwell.

Opfer, J. E., & Siegler, R. S. (2004). Revisiting preschoolers' living things concept: A microgenetic analysis of conceptual change in basic biology. *Cognitive Psychology, 49,* 301–332.

Opfer, J. E., & Siegler, R. S. (2007). Representational change and children's numerical estimation. *Cognitive Psychology, 55*, 169–195.

Opfer, J. E., & Siegler, R. S. (2012). Development of quantitative thinking. In K. Holyoak & R. Morrison (Eds.), *Oxford handbook of thinking and reasoning* (pp. 585–605). New York, NY: Oxford University Press.

Oppliger, P. A. (2007). Effects of gender stereotyping on socialization. In R. W. Preiss, B. M. Gayle, N. Burrell, M. Allen, & J. Bryant (Eds.), *Mass media effects research: Advances through meta-analysis* (pp. 199–214). Mahwah, NJ: Erlbaum.

Organisation for Economic Co-operation and Development. (2010). *PISA 2009 assessment framework—Key competencies in reading, mathematics and science.* Paris: Author.

Oriña, M. M., Collins, W. A., Simpson, J. A., Salvatore, J. E., Haydon, K. C., & Kim, J. S. (2011). Developmental and dyadic perspectives on commitment in adult romantic relationships. *Psychological Science, 22*, 908–915.

Ornstein, P. A., Coffman, J., Grammer, J., San Souci, P., & McCall, L. (2010). Linking the classroom context and the development of children's memory skills. In J. L. Meece & J. S. Eccles (Eds.), *Handbook of research on schools, schooling, and human development* (pp. 42–59). New York, NY: Routledge.

Orth, U., Robins, R. W., Widaman, K. F., & Conger, R. D. (2014). Is low self-esteem a risk factor for depression? Findings from a longitudinal study of Mexican-origin youth. *Developmental Psychology, 50*, 622–633.

Ostrov, J. M., & Godleski, S. A. (2010). Toward an integrated gender-linked model of aggression subtypes in early and middle childhood. *Psychological Review, 117*, 233–242.

Oswald, F. L., & Hough, L. (2012). I-O 2.0 from Intelligence 1.5: Staying (just) behind the cutting edge of intelligence theories. *Industrial and Organizational Psychology: Perspectives on Science and Practice, 5*, 172–175.

Oude Luttikhuis, H., Baur, L., Jansen, H., Shrewsbury, V. A., O'Malley, C., Stolk, R .P., et al. (2009). Interventions for treating obesity in children. *Cochrane Database of Systematic Reviews, 3*, 1–57.

Ouellet-Morin, I., Wong, C. C. Y., Danese, A., Pariante, C. M., Papdopoulous, A. S., Mill, J. et al. (2013). Increased serotonin transport gene (SERT) DNA methylation is associated with bullying victimization and blunted cortisol response to stress in childhood: A longitudinal study of discordant monozygotic twins. *Psychological Medicine, 43*, 1813–1823.

Over, H., & Carpenter, M. (2009). Eighteen-month-old infants show increased helping following priming with affiliation. *Psychological Science, 20*, 1189–1193.

Owen, L., Hang, H., Lewis, C., & Auty, S. (2012). Children's processing of embedded brand messages: Product placement and the role of conceptual fluency. In L. J. Shrum (Ed.), *The psychology of entertainment media: Blurring the lines between entertainment and persuasion* (2nd ed., pp. 65–92). New York, NY: Taylor & Francis.

Ozturk, O., Shayan, S., Liszkowski, U., & Majid, A. (2013). Language is not necessary for color categories. *Developmental Science, 16*, 111–115.

Pahlke, E., Bigler, R. S., & Martin, C. L. (2014). Can fostering children's ability to challenge sexism improve critical analysis, internalization, and enactment of inclusive, egalitarian peer relationships? *Journal of Social Issues, 70*, 115–133.

Palmer, S. B., Fais, L., Golinkoff, R. M., & Werker, J. F. (2012). Perceptual narrowing of linguistic sign occurs in the 1st year of life. *Child Development, 83*, 543–553.

Parault, S. J., & Schwanenflugel, P. J. (2000). The development of conceptual categories of attention during the elementary school years. *Journal of Experimental Child Psychology, 75*, 245–262.

Parcel, G. S., Simons-Morton, B. G., O'Hara, N. M., Baranowksi, T., Kilbe, L. J., & Bee, D. E. (1989). School promotion of healthful diet and exercise behavior: An integration of organizational change and social learning theory interventions. *Journal of School Health, 57*, 150–156.

Park, G., Lubinski, D., & Benbow, C. P. (2008). Ability differences among people who have commensurate degrees matter for scientific creativity. *Psychological Science, 19*, 957–961.

Parke, R. D. (2004). The Society for Research in Child Development at 70: Progress and promise. *Child Development, 75*, 1–24.

Parke, R. D., & Buriel, R. (1998). Socialization in the family: Ethnic and ecological perspectives. In W. Damon (Ed.), *Handbook of child psychology* (Vol. 3). New York, NY: Wiley.

Parker, J. G., Low, C. M., Walker, A. R., & Gamm, B. K. (2005). Friendship jealousy in young adolescents: Individual differences and links to sex, self-esteem, aggression, and social adjustment. *Developmental Psychology, 41*, 235–250.

Parke, R. D., & O'Neil, R. (2000). The influence of significant others on learning about relationships: From family to friends. In R. S. L. Mills & S. Duck (Eds.), *The developmental psychology of personal relationships* (pp. 15–47). New York, NY: Wiley.

Parker, J. G., & Seal, J. (1996). Forming, losing, renewing, and replacing friendships: Applying temporal parameters to the assessment of children's friendship experiences. *Child Development, 67*, 2248–2268.

Parritz, R. H. (1996). A descriptive analysis of toddler coping in challenging circumstances. *Infant Behavior & Development, 19*, 171–180.

Partanen, E., Kujala, T., Naatanen, R., Liitola, A., Sambeth, A., & Houtilainen, M. (2013). Learning-induced neural plasticity of speech processing before birth. *PNAS, 110*, 15145–15150.

Parten, M. (1932). Social participation among preschool children. *Journal of Abnormal & Social Psychology, 27*, 243–269.

Pascalis, O., de Haan, M., & Nelson, C. A. (2002). Is face processing species-specific during the first year of life? *Science, 296*, 1321–1323.

Pascalis, O., Loevenbruck, H., Quinn, P., Kandel, S., Tanaka, J., & Lee, K. (2014). On the linkage between face processing, language processing, and narrowing during development. *Child Development Perspectives, 8*, 65–70.

Pascual, B., Aguardo, G., Sotillo, M., & Masdeu, J. C. (2008). Acquisition of mental state language in Spanish children: A longitudinal study of the relationship between the production of mental verbs and linguistic development. *Developmental Science, 11*, 454–466.

Pasterski, V. L., Geffner, M. E., Brain, C., Hindmarsh, P., Brook, C., & Hines, M. (2005). Prenatal hormones and postnatal socialization by parents as determinants of male-typical toy play in girls with congenital adrenal hyperplasia. *Child Development, 76*, 264–278.

Patchin, J. W. (2013). Cyberbullying among adolescents: Implications for empirical research. *Journal of Adolescent Health, 53*, 431–432.

Patel, S., Gaylord, S., & Fagen, J. (2013). Generalization of deferred imitation in 6-, 9-, and 12-month-old infants using visual and auditory contexts. *Infant Behavior and Development, 36*, 25–31.

Patterson, G. R. (1980). Mothers: The unacknowledged victims. *Monographs of the Society for Research in Child Development, 45* (Serial No. 186).

Patterson, C. J. (2006). Children of lesbian and gay parents. *Current Directions in Psychological Science, 15*, 241–244.

Patterson, G. R. (2008). A comparison of models for interstate wars and for individual violence. *Perspectives on Psychological Science, 3*, 203–223.

Patterson, M. M., & Bigler, R. S. (2006). Preschool children's attention to environmental messages about groups: Social categorization and the origins of intergroup bias. *Child Development, 77*, 847–860.

Pauletti, R. E., Menon, M., Menon, M., Tobin, D. D., & Perry, D. G. (2012). Narcissism and adjustment in preadolescence. *Child Development, 83*, 831–837.

Paulussen-Hoogeboom, M. C., Stams, G. J. J., Hermanns, J. M., & Peetsma, T. T. (2007). Child negative emotionality and parenting from infancy to preschool: A meta-analytic review. *Developmental Psychology, 43*, 438–453.

Paus, T. (2010). Growth of white matter in the adolescent brain: Myelin or axon? *Brain & Cognition, 72*, 26–35.

Peake, P. K., Hebl, M., & Mischel, W. (2002). Strategic attention deployment for delay gratification in working and waiting situations. *Developmental Psychology, 38*, 313–326.

Pears, K. C., Kim, H. K., Fisher, P. A., & Yoerger, K. (2013). Early school engagement and late elementary outcomes for maltreated children in foster care. *Developmental Psychology, 49*, 2201–2211.

Pearson, J., & Wilkinson, L. (2013). Family relationships and adolescent well-being: Are families equally protective for same-sex attracted youth? *Journal of Youth and Adolescence, 42*, 376–393.

Pederson, D. R., Gleason, K. E., Moran, G., & Bento, S. (1998). Maternal attachment representations, maternal sensitivity, and the infant–mother attachment relationship. *Developmental Psychology, 34*, 925–933.

Pellicano, E. (2013). Testing the predictive power of cognitive atypicalities in autistic children: Evidence from a 3-year follow-up study. *Autism Research, 6*, 258–267.

Pellis, S. M., & Pellis, V. C. (2007). Rough-and-tumble play and the development of the social brain. *Current Directions in Psychological Science, 16*, 95–98.

Peltola, M. J., Leppänen, J. M., Palokangas, T., & Hietanen, J. K. (2008). Fearful faces modulate looking duration and attention disengagement in 7-month-old infants. *Developmental Science, 11*, 60–68.

Perkins, D. F., Jacobs, J. E., Barber, B. L., & Eccles, J. S. (2004). Childhood and adolescent sports participation as predictors of participation in sports and physical fitness activities during young adulthood. *Youth & Society, 35*, 495–520.

Peterson, L. (1983). Role of donor competence, donor age, and peer presence on helping in an emergency. *Developmental Psychology, 19*, 873–880.

Petersen, J. L., & Hyde, J. S. (2013). Peer sexual harassment and disordered eating in early adolescence. *Developmental Psychology, 49*, 184–195.

Peterson, C., & Rideout, R. (1998). Memory for medical emergencies experienced by 1- and 2-year-olds. *Developmental Psychology, 34*, 1059–1072.

Peterson, C. C., Wellman, H. M., & Slaughter, V. (2012). The mind behind the message: Advancing theory-of-mind scales for typically developing children, and those with deafness, autism, or Aspberger syndrome. *Child Development, 83*, 469–485.

Petrass, L. A., & Blitvich, J. D. (2013). Unobtrusive observation of caregiver-child pairs at public pools and playgrounds: Implications for child unintentional injury risk. *International Journal of Aquatic Research and Education, 7*, 204–213.

Pettit, G. S., Bates, J. E., & Dodge, K. A. (1997). Supportive parenting, ecological context, and children's adjustment: A seven-year longitudinal study. *Child Development, 68*, 908–923.

Pettoni, A. N. (2011). Fetal alcohol effects. In S. Goldstein & J. A. Naglieri (Eds.), *Encyclopedia of child behavior and development* (pp. 649–650). New York, NY: Springer Science+Business Media.

Phinney, J. S. (2005). Ethnic identity development in minority adolescents. In C. B. Fisher & R. M. Lerner (Eds.), *Encyclopedia of applied developmental science* (Vol. 1, pp. 420–423). Thousand Oaks, CA: Sage.

Phipps, M. G., Rosengard, C., Weitzen, S., Meers, A., & Billinkoff, Z. (2008). Age group differences among pregnant adolescents: Sexual behavior, health habits, and contraceptive use. *Journal of Pediatric & Adolescent Gynecology, 21*, 9–15.

Piaget, J. (1929). *The child's conception of the world.* New York, NY: Harcourt, Brace.

Piaget, J., & Inhelder, B. (1956). *The child's conception of space.* Boston, MA: Routledge & Kegan Paul.

Pianta, R. C. (2007). Developmental science and education: The NICHD Study of Early Child Care and Youth Development findings from elementary school. In R. V. Kail (Ed.), *Advances in child development and behavior, Vol. 35* (pp. 254–296). Amsterdam: Elsevier.

Piasta, S. B., Justice, L. M., McGinty, A. S., & Kaderavek, J. N. (2012). Increasing young children's contact with print during shared reading: Longitudinal effects on literacy achievement. *Child Development, 83*, 810–820.

Piehler, T. F., & Dishion, T. J. (2007). Interpersonal dynamics within adolescent friendships: Dyadic mutuality, deviant talk, and patterns of antisocial behavior. *Child Development, 78*, 1611–1624.

Pina, A. A., Zerr, A. A., Gonzales, N. A., & Ortiz, C. D. (2009). Psychosocial interventions for school refusal behavior in children and adolescents. *Child Development Perspectives, 3*, 11–20.

Place, S., & Hoff, E. (2011). Properties of dual language exposure that influence 2-year-olds' bilingual proficiency. *Child Development, 82*, 1834–1849.

Plante, I., de la Sablonnière, R., Aronson, J. M., & Théorêt, M. (2013). Gender stereotype endorsement and achievement-related outcomes: The role of competence beliefs and task values. *Contemporary Educational Psychology, 38*, 225–235.

Plomin, R. (2013). Child development and molecular genetics: 14 years later. *Child Development, 84*, 104–120.

Plomin, R., Fulker, D. W., Corley, R., & DeFries, J. C. (1997). Nature, nurture, and cognitive development from 1 to 16 years: A parent-offspring adoption study. *Psychological Science, 8*, 442–447.

Plomin, R., & Petrill, S. A. (1997). Genetics and intelligence: What's new? *Intelligence, 24*, 53–77.

Plomin, R., & Spinath, F. (2004). Intelligence: Genes, genetics, and genomics. *Journal of Personality & Social Psychology, 86*, 112–129.

Poehlmann, J., Schwichtenberg, A. J., Bolt, D. M., Hane, A., Burnson, C., & Winters, J. (2011). Infant physiological regulation and maternal risks as predictors of dyadic interaction trajectories in families with a preterm infant. *Developmental Psychology, 47*, 91–105.

Pollett, T. V., Nettle, D., & Nelissen, M. (2007). Maternal grandmothers do go the extra mile: Factoring distance and lineage into differential contact with grandchildren. *Evolutionary Psychology, 5*, 832–843.

Polman, J. L. (2004). Dialogic activity structures for project-based learning environment. *Cognition & Instruction, 22*, 431–466.

Pomerantz, E. M., Ng, F. F., Cheung, C. S., & Qu, Y. (2014). Raising happy children who succeed in school: Lessons from China and the United States. *Child Development Perpsectives, 8*, 71–76.

Poole, D. A., & Bruck, M. (2012). Divining testimony? The impact of interviewing props on children's reports of touching. *Developmental Review, 32*, 165–180.

Poole, D. A., & Lindsay, D. S. (1995). Interviewing preschoolers: Effects of nonsuggestive techniques, parental coaching, and leading questions on reports of nonexperienced events. *Journal of Experimental Child Psychology, 60*, 129–154.

Popliger, M., Talwar, V., & Crossman, A. (2011). Predictors of children's prosocial lie-telling: Motivation, socialization variables, and moral understanding. *Journal of Experimental Child Psychology, 110*, 373–392.

Popp, D., Laursen, B., Kerr, M., Stattin, H., & Burk, W. K. (2008). Modeling homophily over time with an actor-partner interdependence model. *Developmental Psychology, 44,* 1028–1039.

Porter, R. H., & Winburg, J. (1999). Unique salience of maternal breast odors for newborn infants. *Neuroscience & Biobehavioral Reviews, 23,* 439–449.

Posner, M. I., & Rothbart, M. K. (2007). Research on attention networks as a model for the integration of psychological science. *Annual Review of Psychology, 58,* 1–23.

Posner, M. I., Rothbart, M. K., Sheese, B. E., & Voelker, P. (2012). Control networks and neuromodulators of early development. *Developmental Psychology, 48,* 827–835.

Poulin, F., & Boivin, M. (2000). The role of proactive and reactive aggression in the formation and development of boys' friendships. *Developmental Psychology, 36,* 233–240.

Poulin, F., & Chan, A. (2010). Friendship stability and change in childhood and adolescence. *Developmental Review, 30,* 257–272.

Poulin, F., & Pedersen, S. (2007). Developmental changes in gender composition of friendship networks in adolescent girls and boys. *Developmental Psychology, 43,* 1484–1496.

Poulson, C. L., Kymissis, E., Reeve, K. F., Andreatos, M., & Reeve, L. (1991). Generalized vocal imitation in infants. *Journal of Experimental Child Psychology, 51,* 267–279.

Powers, C. J., Bierman, K. L., & The Conduct Problems Prevention Research Group. (2013). The multifaceted impact of peer relations on aggressive-disruptive behavior in early elementary school. *Developmental Psychology, 49,* 1174–1186.

Pressley, M. (2002). *Reading instruction that works: The case for balanced teaching* (2nd ed). New York, NY : Guilford Press.

Pressley, M., & Hilden, K. (2006). Cognitive strategies. In D. Kuhn & R. S. Siegler (Eds.), *Handbook of child psychology* (6th ed., Vol. 2., pp. 511–556). Hoboken, NJ: Wiley.

Price, T. S., Grosser, T., Plomin, R., & Jaffee, S. R. (2010). Fetal genotype for the xenobiotic metabolizing enzyme NQO1 influences intrauterine growth among infants whose mothers smoked during pregnancy. *Child Development, 81,* 101–114.

Priel, B., & deSchonen, S. (1986). Self-recognition: A study of a population without mirrors. *Journal of Experimental Child Psychology, 41,* 237–250.

Principe, G. F., & Ceci, S. J. (2002). I saw it with my own ears: The effects of peer conversations on preschoolers' reports of nonexperienced events. *Journal of Experimental Child Psychology, 83,* 1–25.

Principe, G.F., & Schindewolf, E. (2012). Natural conversations as a source of false memories in children: Implications for the testimony of young witnesses. *Developmental Review, 32,* 205–223.

Prinstein, M. J., & Cillessen, A. H. N. (2003). Forms and functions of adolescent peer aggression associated with high levels of peer status. *Merrill Palmer Quarterly, 49,* 310–342.

Prinstein, M. J., & LaGreca, A. M. (2004). Childhood peer rejection and aggression as predictors of adolescent girls' externalizing and health risk behaviors: A 6-year longitudinal study. *Journal of Consulting & Clinical Psychology, 72,* 103–112.

Prot, S., Gentile, D. A., Anderson, C. A., Suzuki, K., Swing, E., Lim, K. M., et al. (2014). Long-term relations among prosocial-media use, empathy, and prosocial behavior. *Psychological Science, 25,* 358–368.

Protzko, J., Aronson, J., & Blair, C. (2013). How to make a young child smarter: Evidence from the Database of Raising Intelligence. *Perspectives on Psychological Science, 8,* 25–40.

Provins, K. A. (1997). Handedness and speech: a critical reappraisal of the role of genetic and environmental factors in the cerebral lateralization of function. *Psychological Review, 104,* 554–571.

Puhl, R. M., & Brownell, K. D. (2005). Bulimia nervosa. In C. B. Fisher & R. M. Lerner (Eds.), *Encyclopedia of applied developmental science* (Vol. 1, pp. 192–195). Thousand Oaks, CA: Sage.

Puhl, R. M., & Latner, J. D. (2007). Stigma, obesity, and the health of the nation's children. *Psychological Bulletin, 133,* 557–580.

Qin, L., Pomerantz, E. M., & Wang, Q. (2009). Are gains in decision-making autonomy during early adolescence beneficial for emotional functioning? The case of the United States and China. *Child Development, 80,* 1705–1721.

Quas, J. A., Goodman, G. S., Bidrose, S., Pipe, M., Craw, S., & Ablin, D. S. (1999). Emotion and memory: Children's long-term remembering, forgetting, and suggestibility. *Journal of Experimental Child Psychology, 71,* 235–270.

Quillian, L., & Campbell, M. E. (2003). Beyond black and white: The present and future of multiracial friendship segregation. *American Sociological Review, 68,* 540–566.

Quinn, P. H. (2004). Development of subordinate-level categorization in 3- to 7-month-old infants. *Child Development, 75,* 886–899.

Quinn, P. H. (2011). Born to categorize. In U. Goswami (Ed.), *The Wiley-Blackwell handbook of childhood cognitive development* (2nd ed., pp. 129–152). West Sussex, UK: Wiley-Blackwell.

Raabe, T., & Beelmann, A. (2011). Development of ethnic, racial, and national prejudice in childhood and adolescence: A multinational meta-analysis of age differences. *Child Development, 82,* 1715–1737.

Racz, S. J., & McMahon, R. J. (2011). The relationship between parental knowledge and monitoring and child and adolescent conduct problems: A 10-year update. *Clinical Child and Family Psychology Review, 14,* 377–398.

Raedeke, T. D., & Smith, A. L. (2004). Coping resources and athlete burnout: An examination of stress mediated and moderation hypotheses. *Journal of Sport & Exercise Psychology, 26,* 525–541.

Rakic, P. (1995). Corticogenesis in humans and nonhuman primates. In M. S. Gazzaniga (Ed.), *The cognitive neurosciences.* Cambridge, MA: MIT Press.

Rakison, D. H., & Hahn, E. R. (2004). The mechanisms of early categorization and induction: Smart or dumb infants? *Advances in Child Development & Behavior, 32,* 281–322.

Rakison, D. H., & Yermolayeva, Y. (2010). Infant categorization. *WIREs Cognitive Science, 1,* 894–905.

Rakoczy, H. (2008). Taking fiction seriously: Young children understand the normative structure of joint pretense games. *Developmental Psychology, 44,* 1195–1201.

Ralph, L. J., & Brindis, C. D. (2010). Access to reproductive healthcare for adolescents: Establishing healthy behaviors at a critical juncture in the lifecourse. *Current Opinion in Obstetrics & Gynecology, 22,* 369–374.

Raman, L., & Gelman, S. A. (2005). Children's understanding of the transmission of genetic disorders and contagious illnesses. *Developmental Psychology, 41,* 171–182.

Ramey, C. T., & Campbell, F. A. (1991). Poverty, early childhood education, and academic competence: The Abecedarian experiment. In A. Huston (Ed.), *Children reared in poverty.* New York, NY: Cambridge University Press.

Ramey, S. L., & Ramey, C. T. (2006). Early educational interventions: Principles of effective and sustained benefits from targeted early education programs. In S. B. Neuman & D. K. Dickinson (Eds.), *Handbook of early literacy research* (Vol. 2, pp. 445–459). New York, NY: Guilford.

Rancourt, D., Conway, C. C., Burk, W. J., & Prinstein, M. J. (2013). Gender composition of preadolescents' friendship groups moderates peers socialization of body change behaviors. *Health Psychology, 32,* 283–292.

Raskauskas, J., & Stoltz, A. D. (2007). Involvement in traditional and electronic bullying among adolescents. *Developmental Psychology, 43*, 564–575.

Rayner, K., Foorman, B. R., Perfetti, C. A., Pesetsky, D., & Seidenberg, M. S. (2001). How psychological science informs the teaching of reading. *Psychological Science in the Public Interest, 2*, 31–75.

Rayner, K., Foorman, B. R., Perfetti, C. A., Pesetsky, D., & Seidenberg, M. S. (2002). How should reading be taught? *Scientific American, 286*, 85–91.

Ready, D. D., & Wright, D. L. (2011). Accuracy and inaccuracy in teachers' perceptions of young children's cognitive abilities: The role of child background and classroom context. *American Educational Research Journal, 48*, 335–360.

Reese, E., & Cox, A. (1999). Quality of adult book reading affects children's emergent literacy. *Developmental Psychology, 35*, 20–28.

Reich, P. A. (1986). *Language development*. Englewood Cliffs, NJ: Prentice-Hall.

Reid, D. H., Wilson, P. G., & Faw, G. D. (1991). Teaching self-help skills. In J. L. Matson & J. A. Mulick (Eds.), *Handbook of mental retardation* (2nd ed.). New York, NY: Pergamon.

Reimer, M. S. (1996). "Sinking into the ground": The development and consequences of shame in adolescence. *Developmental Review, 16*, 321–363.

Repacholi, B. M. (1998). Infants' use of attentional cues to identify the referent of another person's emotional expression. *Developmental Psychology, 34*, 1017–1025.

Repacholi, B. M., & Meltzoff, A. N. (2007). Emotional eavesdropping: Infants selectively respond to indirect emotional signals. *Child Development, 78*, 503–521.

Repacholi, B. M., Meltzoff, A. N., & Olsen, B. (2008). Infants' understanding of the link between visual perception and emotion: "If she can't see me doing it, she won't get angry." *Developmental Psychology, 44*, 561–574.

Reynolds, A. J., & Robertson, D. L. (2003). School-based early intervention and later child maltreatment in the Chicago Longitudinal Study. *Child Development, 74*, 3–26.

Reynolds, A. J., Temple, J. A., White, B. A. B., Ou, S., & Robertson, D. L. (2011). Age 26 cost-benefit analysis of the child-parent center early education program. *Child Development, 82*, 379–404.

Rhoades, K. A. (2008). Children's responses to interparental conflict: A meta-analysis of their associations with child adjustment. *Child Development, 79*, 1942–1956.

Rhodes, M. (2013). How two intuitive theories shape the development of social categorization. *Child Development Perspectives, 7*, 12–16.

Ricciardelli, L. A., & McCabe, M. P. (2004). A biopsychosocial model of disordered eating and the pursuit of muscularity in adolescent boys. *Psychological Bulletin, 130*, 179–205.

Richland, L. E., & Burchinal, M. R. (2013). Early executive function predicts reasoning development. *Psychological Science, 24*, 87–92.

Richters, J. E., Arnold, L. E., Jensen, P. S., Abikoff, H., Conners, C. K., Greenhill, L. L., et al. (1995). NIMH collaborative multisite multimodal treatment study of children with ADHD: I. Background and rationale. *Journal of the American Academy of Child & Adolescent Psychiatry, 34*, 987–1000.

Rideout, V. (2013). *Zero to eight: Children's media use in America 2013*. San Francisco, CA: Common Sense Media.

Rideout, V., Foehr, U. G., & Roberts, D. F. (2010). *Generation M²: Media in the lives of 8-18 year olds*. Menlo Park, CA: Henry J. Kaiser Family Foundation.

Rindermann, H., & Thompson, J. (2013). Ability rise in NAEP and narrowing ethnic gaps? *Intelligence, 41*, 821–831.

Ritchie, S. J., & Bates, T. C. (2013). Enduring links from childhood mathematics and reading achievement to adult socioeconomic status. *Psychological Science, 24*, 1301–1308.

Rivas-Drake, D., Seaton, E. K., Markstrom, C., Quintana, S., Syed, M., Lee, R. M., et al. (2014). Ethnic and racial identity in adolescence: Implications for psychosocial, academic, and health outcomes. *Child Development, 85*, 40–57.

Roben, C. K. P., Cole, P. M., & Armstrong, L. M. (2013). Longitudinal relations among language skills, anger expression, and regulatory strategies in early childhood. *Child Development, 84*, 891–905.

Roberts, J. E., Burchinal, M., & Durham, M. (1999). Parents' report of vocabulary and grammatical development of African American preschoolers: Child and environmental associations. *Child Development, 70*, 91–106.

Robinson, E. J., Champion, H., & Mitchell, P. (1999). Children's ability to infer utterance veracity from speaker informedness. *Developmental Psychology, 35*, 535–546.

Roby, A. C., & Kidd, E. (2008). The referential communication skills of children with imaginary companions. *Developmental Science, 11*, 531–540.

Rochat, P. (2013). Self-conceptualizing in development. In P. D. Zelazo (Ed.), *The Oxford handbook of developmental psychology* (Vol. 2., *Self and Other*; pp. 378–397). Oxford, UK: Oxford University Press.

Rodeck, C. H., & Whittle, M. J. (Eds.). (2009). *Fetal medicine: Basic science and clinical practice*. London: Churchill Livingstone.

Roffwarg, H. P., Muzio, J. N., & Dement, W. C. (1966). Ontogenetic development of the human sleep-dream cycle. *Science, 152*, 604–619.

Rogers, L. A., & Graham, S. (2008). A meta-analysis of single subject design writing intervention research. *Journal of Educational Psychology, 100*, 879–906.

Rogoff, B. (1998). Cognition as a collaborative process. In W. Damon (Ed.), *Handbook of child psychology* (5th ed., Vol. 2, pp. 679–744). New York, NY: Wiley.

Rogoff, B. (2003). *The cultural nature of human development*. New York, NY: Oxford University Press.

Rogoff, B., Mistry, J., Goncu, A., & Mosier, C. (1993). Guided participation in cultural activity by toddlers and caregivers. *Monographs of the Society for Research in Child Development, 58*, Serial No. 236.

Rohrbeck, C. A., Ginsburg-Block, M. D., Fantuzzo, J. W., & Miller, T. R. (2003). Peer-assisted learning interventions with elementary school students: A meta-analytic review. *Journal of Educational Psychology, 95*, 240–257.

Rood, L., Roelofs, J., Bögels, S. M., Nolen-Hoeksema, S., & Schouten, E. (2009). The influence of emotion-focused rumination and distraction in depressive symptoms in non-clinical youth: A meta-analytic review. *Clinical Psychology Review, 29*, 607–616.

Roper v. Simmons, 543 U.S. 551 (2005).

Roschelle, J. M., Pea, R. D., Hoadley, C. M., Gordin, D. M., & Means, B. M. (2000). Changing how and what children learn in school with computer-based technologies. *Future of Children, 10*, 76–101.

Roschelle, J. M., Schechtman, N., Tatar, D., Hegedus, S., Hopkins, B., Empson, S., et al. (2010). Integration of technology, curriculum, and professional development for advancing middle school mathematics: Three large-scale studies. *American Educational Research Journal, 47*, 833–878.

Rose, A. J., & Asher, S. R. (1999). Children's goals and strategies in response to conflicts within a friendship. *Developmental Psychology, 35*, 69–79.

Rose, A. J., & Rudolph, K. D. (2006). A review of sex differences in peer relationship processes: Potential trade-offs for the emotional and behavioral development of girls and boys. *Psychological Bulletin, 132*, 98–131.

Rose, S. A., Feldman, J. F., Jankowski, J. J., & Van Rossem, R. (2012). Information processing from infancy to 11 years: Continuities and prediction of IQ. *Intelligence, 40*, 445–457.

Rosengren, K. S., Gelman, S. A., Kalish, C., & McCormick, M. (1991). As time goes by: Children's early understanding of growth in animals. *Child Development, 62*, 1302–1320.

Ross, M., & Wang, Q. (2010). Why we remember and what we remember: Culture and autobiographical memory. *Perspectives on Psychological Science, 5*, 401–409.

Rotenberg, K. J., & Mayer, E. V. (1990). Delay gratification in native and white children: A cross-cultural comparison. *International Journal of Behavioral Development, 13*, 23–30.

Rothbart, M. K. (2011). *Becoming who we are: Temperament and personality in development.* New York, NY: Guilford.

Rothbart, M. K., & Rueda, M. R. (2005). The development of effortful control. In U. Mayr, E. Awh, & S. W. Keele (Eds.), *Developing individuality in the human brain: A tribute to Michael I. Posner* (pp. 167–188). Washington, DC: American Psychological Association.

Rothbart, M. K., & Sheese, B. E. (2007). Temperament and emotion regulation. In J. J. Gross (Ed.), *Handbook of emotion regulation* (pp. 331–350). New York, NY: Guilford.

Rothbaum, F., Weisz, J., Pott, M., Miyake, K., & Morelli, G. (2000). Attachment and culture: Security in the United States and Japan. *American Psychologist, 55*, 1093–1104.

Rotherman-Borus, M. J., & Langabeer, K. A. (2001). Developmental trajectories of gay, lesbian, and bisexual youth. In A. R. D'Augelli & C. Patterson (Eds.), *Lesbian, gay, and bisexual identities among youth: Psychological perspectives* (pp. 97–128). New York, NY: Oxford University Press.

Rovee-Collier, C. (1997). Dissociation in infant memory: Rethinking the development of implicit and explicit memory. *Psychological Review, 104*, 467–498.

Rovee-Collier, C. (1999). The development of infant memory. *Current Directions in Psychological Science, 8*, 80–85.

Rovee-Collier, C., & Barr, R. (2010). Infant learning and memory. In T. D. Wachs & G. Bremner (Eds.), *Blackwell handbook of infant development*, 2nd ed. Oxford, UK: Blackwell.

Rowe, M. L. (2012). A longitudinal investigation of the role of quantity and quality of child-directed speech in vocabulary development. *Child Development, 83*, 1762–1774.

Rowe, M. L., Raudenbush, S. W., & Goldin-Meadow, S. (2012). The pace of vocabulary growth helps predict later vocabulary skill. *Child Development, 83*, 508–525.

Rowland, C. F., Pine, J. M., Lieven, E. V. M., & Theakston, A. L. (2005). The incidence of error in young children's wh-questions. *Journal of Speech, Language, & Hearing Research, 48*, 384–404.

Rowley, S. J., Kurtz-Costes, B., Mistry, R., & Feagans, L. (2007). Social status as a predictor of race and gender stereotypes in late childhood and early adolescence. *Social Development, 16*, 150–168.

Rubin, C. M. (2012, September 17). The global search for education: It takes a community. *HuffPost Education.* Retrieved from www. huffingtonpost.com.

Rubin, K. H., Coplan, R. J., & Bowker, J. C. (2009). Social withdrawal in childhood. *Annual Review of Psychology, 60*, 141–171.

Rubin, K., Bukowski, W., & Parker, J. (2006). Peer interaction and social competence. In W. Damon & R. M. Lerner (Eds.), *Handbook of child psychology* (6th ed., Vol. 3). New York, NY: Wiley.

Rubinstein, O., Henrik, A., Berger, A., & Shahar-Shalev, S. (2002). The development of internal representations of magnitude and their association with Arabic numerals. *Journal of Experimental Child Psychology, 81*, 74–92.

Ruble, D. N., Boggiano, A. D., Feldman, N. S., & Loebl, N. H. (1980). Developmental analysis of the role of social comparison in self-evaluation. *Developmental Psychology, 16*, 105–115.

Ruble, D. N., Martin, C. L., & Berenbaum, S. A. (2006). Gender development. In N. Eisenberg, W. Damon, & R. M. Lerner (Eds.), *Handbook of child psychology: Vol. 3, Social, emotional, and personality development* (6th ed., pp. 858–932). Hoboken, NJ: John Wiley & Sons.

Rudolph, K. D., Ladd, G., & Dinella, L. (2007). Gender differences in the interpersonal consequences of early-onset depressive symptoms. *Merrill-Palmer Quarterly, 53*, 461–488.

Rudolph, K. D., & Troop-Gordon, W. (2010). Personal-accentuation and contextual-amplification models of pubertal timing: Predicting youth depression. *Development & Psychopathology, 22*, 433–451.

Rudolph, K. D., Troop-Gordon, W., & Flynn, M. (2009). Relational victimization predicts children's social-cognitive and self-regulatory responses in a challenging peer context. *Developmental Psychology, 45*, 1444–1454.

Ruff, H. A., & Capozzoli, M. C. (2003). Development of attention and distractibility in the first 4 years of life. *Developmental Psychology, 39*, 877–890.

Rushton, J. P., & Bonds, T. A. (2005). Mate choice and friendship in twins. *Psychological Science, 16*, 555–559.

Russell, A., & Finnie, V. (1990). Preschool children's social status and maternal instructions to assist group entry. *Developmental Psychology, 26*, 603–611.

Rutter, M., Sonuga-Barke, E. J., Beckett, C., Castle, J., Kreppner, J., Kumsta, R., et al. (2010). Deprivation-specific psychological patterns: Effects of institutional deprivation. *Monographs of the Society for Research in Child Development, Serial No. 295, 75*(1).

Ryan, R. M., & Claessens, A. (2013). Associations between family structure changes and children's behavior problems: The moderating effects of timing and marital birth. *Developmental Psychology, 49*, 1219–1231.

Rymer, R. (1993). *Genie.* New York, NY: Harper Collins.

Saewyc, E. M. (2011). Research on adolescent sexual orientation: Development, health disparities, stigma, and resilience. *Journal of Research on Adolescence, 21*, 256–272.

Saffran, J. R., Aslin, R. N., & Newport, E. L. (1996). Statistical learning by 8-month-old infants. *Science, 274*, 1926–1928.

Saffran, J. R., Werker, J. F., & Werner, L. A. (2006). The infant's auditory world: Hearing, speech, and the beginnings of language. In W. Damon & R. M. Lerner (Eds.), *Handbook of child psychology: Vol. 2. Cognition, perception, and language* (6th ed., pp. 58–108). Hoboken, NJ: Wiley.

Sagi, A., Koren-Karie, N., Gini, M., Ziv, Y., & Joels, T. (2002). Shedding further light on the effects of various types and quality of early child care on infant–mother attachment relationship: The Haifa study of early child care. *Child Development, 73*, 1166–1186.

Sagi, A., van IJzendoorn, M. H., Aviezer, O., Donnell, F., Koren-Karie, N., Joels, T., et al. (1995). Attachments in a multiple-caregiver and multiple-infant environment: The case of the Israeli kibbutzim. In E. Waters, B. E. Vaughn, G. Posada, & K. Kondo-Ikemura (Eds.), *Caregiving, cultural, and cognitive perspectives on secure-base behavior and working models: New growing points in attachment theory and research. Monographs of the Society for Research in Child Development, 60*, Serial No. 244.

Sahni, R., Fifer, W. P., & Myers, M. M. (2007). Identifying infants at risk for sudden infant death syndrome. *Current Opinion in Pediatrics, 19*, 145–149.

Sakkalou, E., Ellis-Davies, K., Fowler, N. C., Hilbrink, E. E., & Gattis, M. (2013). Infants show stability of goal-directed imitation. *Journal of Experimental Child Psychology, 114*, 1–9.

Salmivalli, C., & Isaacs, J. (2005). Prospective relations among victimization, rejection, friendlessness, and children's self- and peer-perceptions. *Child Development, 76*, 1161–1171.

Salovey, P., & Grewal, D. (2005). The science of emotional intelligence. *Current Directions in Psychological Science, 14*, 281–285.

Sameroff, A. (2010). A unified theory of development: A dialectic integration of nature and nurture. *Child Development, 81*, 6–22.

Sanders, M. (2014). A public health approach to improving parenting and promoting children's well being. *Child Development Perspectives, 8*, in press.

Sandler, I. N., Tein, J.-Y., Mehta, P., Wolchik, S., & Ayers, T. (2000). Coping efficacy and psychological problems of children of divorce. *Child Development, 71*, 1099–1118.

Sangrigoli, S., Pallier, C., Argenti, A.-M., Ventureyra, V. A. G., & de Schonen, S. (2005). Reversibility of the other-race effect in face recognition during childhood. *Psychological Science, 16*, 440–444.

Sann, C., & Streri, A. (2007). Perception of object shape and texture in human newborns: Evidence from cross-modal transfer tasks. *Developmental Science, 10*, 399–410.

Saudino, K. J. (2009). Do different measures tap the same genetic influences? A multi-method study of activity level in young twins. *Developmental Science, 12*, 626–633.

Saudino, K. J. (2012). Sources of continuity and change in activity level in early childhood. *Child Development, 83*, 266–281.

Saudino, K. J., & Wang, M. (2012). Quantitative and molecular genetic studies of temperament. In M. Zentner & R. L. Shiner (Eds.), *Handbook of temperament* (pp. 315–346). New York, NY: Guilford.

Saxe, G. B. (1988). Candy selling and math learning. *Educational Researcher, 17*, 14–21.

Scarr, S. (1992). Developmental theories for the 1990s: Development and individual differences. *Child Development, 63*, 1–19.

Scarr, S., & McCartney, K. (1983). How people make their own environments: A theory of genotype-environment effects. *Child Development, 54*, 424–435.

Schaal, B., Soussignan, R., & Marlier, L. (2002). Olfactory cognition at the start of life: The perinatal shaping of selective odor responsiveness. In C. Rouby et al. (Eds.), *Olfaction, taste, and cognition* (pp. 421–440). Cambridge, UK: Cambridge University Press.

Schauble, L. (1996). The development of scientific reasoning in knowledge-rich contexts. *Developmental Psychology, 32*, 102–119.

Schelleman-Offermans, K., Knibbe, R. A., & Kuntsche, E. (2013). Are the effects of early pubertal timing on the initiation of weekly alcohol use mediated by peers and/or parents? A longitudinal study. *Developmental Psychology, 49*, 1277–1285.

Scherf, K. S., Behrmann, M., Humphreys, K., & Luna, B. (2007). Visual category-selectivity for faces, places and objects emerges along different developmental trajectories. *Developmental Science, 10*, F15–F30.

Schermerhorn, A. C., Chow, S., & Cummings, E. M. (2010). Developmental family processes and interparental conflict: Patterns of microlevel influences. *Developmental Psychology, 46*, 869–885.

Schermerhorn, A. C., & Cummings, E. M. (2008). Transactional family dynamics: A new framework for conceptualizing family influence processes. In R. V. Kail (Ed.), *Advances in child development and behavior* (Vol. 36, pp. 187–250). Amsterdam: Academic Press.

Schlam, T. R., Wilson, N. L., Shoda, Y., Mischel, W., & Ayduk, O. (2013). Preschoolers' delay of gratification predicts their body mass 30 years later. *The Journal of Pediatrics, 162*, 90–93.

Schmale, R., & Seidl, A. (2009). Accommodating variability in voice and foreign accent: Flexibility of early word representations. *Developmental Science, 12*, 583–601.

Schmidt, F. L., & Hunter, J. (2004). General mental ability in the world of work: Occupational attainment and job performance. *Journal of Personality & Social Psychology, 86*, 162–173.

Schmidt, M. E., & Vandewater, E. A. (2008). Media and attention, cognition, and school achievement. *Future of Children, 18*, 63–85.

Schneider, W. (2011). Memory development in childhood. In U. Goswami (Ed.), *The Wiley-Blackwell handbook of cognitive development* (2nd ed., pp. 347–376). West Sussex UK: Wiley-Blackwell.

Schneider, W., & Bjorklund, D. F. (1998). Memory. In W. Damon (Ed.), *Handbook of child psychology* (Vol. 2). New York, NY: Wiley.

Schneiders, J., Nicolson, N. A., Berkhof, J., Feron, F. J., van Os., J., & deVries, M. W. (2006). Mood reactivity to daily negative events in early adolescence: Relationship to risk for psychopathology. *Developmental Psychology, 42*, 543–554.

Schoemaker, K., Mulder, H., Dekovic, M., & Matthys, W. (2013). Executive functions in preschool children with externalizing behavior problems: A meta-analysis. *Journal of Abnormal Child Psychology, 41*, 457–471.

Schofield, T. J., Parke, R. D., Kim, Y., & Coltrane, S. (2008). Bridging the acculturation gap: Parent-child relationship quality as a moderator in Mexican American families. *Developmental Psychology, 44*, 1190–1194.

Schröder, L., Keller, H., Kärtner, J., Kleis, A., Abels, M., Yovsi, R. D. et al. (2013). Early reminiscing in cultural contexts: Cultural models, maternal reminiscing styles, and children's memories. *Journal of Cognition and Development, 14*, 10–34.

Schuetze, P., Molnar, D. S., & Eiden, R. D. (2012). Profiles of reactivity in cocaine-exposed children. *Journal of Applied Developmental Psychology, 33*, 282–293.

Schug, M. G., Shusterman, A., Barth, H., & Patalano, A. L. (2013). Minimal-group membership influences children's responses to novel experience with group members. *Developmental Science, 16*, 47–55.

Schum, N., Jovanovic, B., & Schwarzer, G. (2011). Ten- and twelve-month-olds' visual anticipation of orientation and size during grasping. *Journal of Experimental Child Psychology, 109*, 218–231.

Schwartz, D., Chang, L., & Farver, J. M. (2001). Correlates of victimization in Chinese children's peer groups. *Developmental Psychology, 37*, 520–532.

Schwartz, D., Dodge, K. A., Pettit, G. S., Bates, J. E., & The Conduct Problems Prevention Research Group. (2000). Friendship as a moderating factor in the pathway between early harsh home environment and later victimization in the peer group. *Developmental Psychology, 36*, 646–662.

Schwartz, O. S., Dudgeon, P., Sheeber, L. B., Yap, M. B. H., Simmons, J. G., & Allen, N. B. (2012). Parental behaviors during family interactions predict changes in depression and anxiety symptoms during adolescence. *Journal of Abnormal Child Psychology, 40*, 59–71.

Schwartz, C., Issanchou, S., & Nicklaus, S. (2009). Developmental changes in the acceptance of the five basic tastes in the first year of life. *British Journal of Nutrition, 102*, 1375–1385.

Schwartz, P. D., Maynard, A. M., & Uzelac, S. M. (2008). Adolescent egocentrism: A contemporary view. *Adolescence, 43*, 441–448.

Schwartz, C. E., Wright, C. I., Shin, L. M., Kagan, J., & Rauch, S. L. (2003). Inhibited and uninhibited infants "grow up": Adult amygdalar response to novelty. *Science, 300*, 1952–1953.

Schwartz-Mette, R. A., & Rose, A. J. (2012). Co-rumination mediates contagion of internalizing symptoms within youths' friendships. *Developmental Psychology, 48*, 1355–1365.

Schwarzer, G., Freitag, C., Buckel, R., & Lofruthe, A. (2013). Crawling is associated with mental rotation ability by 9-month-old infants. *Infancy, 18*, 432–441.

Schwebel, D. C., Davis, A. L., & O'Neal, E. E. (2012). Child pedestrian injury: A review of behavioral risks and preventive strategies. *American Journal of Lifestyle Medicine, 6*, 292–302.

Schwenck, C., Bjorklund, D. F., & Schneider, W. (2009). Developmental and individual differences in young children's use and maintenance of a selective memory strategy. *Developmental Psychology, 45*, 1034–1050.

Scott, L. S., Pascalis, O., & Nelson, C. A. (2007). A domain-general theory of the development of perceptual discrimination. *Current Directions in Psychological Science, 16*, 197–201.

Scott, W. A., Scott, R., & McCabe, M. (1991). Family relationships and children's personality: A cross-cultural, cross-source comparison. *British Journal of Social Psychology, 30*, 1–20.

Scrimgeour, M. B., Blandon, A. Y., Stifter, C. A., & Buss, K. A. (2013). Cooperative coparenting moderates the association between parenting practices and children's prosocial behavior. *Journal of Family Psychology, 27*, 506–511.

Scrimsher, S., & Tudge, J. (2003). The teaching/learning relationship in the first years of school: School revolutionary implications of Vygotsky's theory. *Early Education & Development, 14*, 293–312.

Sears, H. A., Graham, J., & Campbell, A. (2009). Adolescent boys' intentions of seeking help from male friends and female friends. *Journal of Applied Developmental Psychology, 30*, 738–748.

Seaton, E. K., Yip, T., Morgan-Lopez, A., & Sellers, R. M. (2012). Racial discrimination and racial socialization as predictors of African Americans adolescents' racial identity development using latent transition analysis. *Developmental Psychology, 48*, 448–458.

Segrin, C., Taylor, M. E., & Altman, J. (2005). Social cognitive mediators and relational outcomes associated with parental divorce. *Journal of Social & Personal Relationships, 22*, 361–377.

Seidl, A., & Johnson, E. L. (2006). Infants' word segmentation revisited: Edge alignment facilitates target extraction. *Developmental Science, 9*, 565–573.

Selman, R. L. (1980). *The growth of interpersonal understanding: Development and clinical analyses.* New York, NY: Academic Press.

Selman, R. L. (1981). The child as a friendship philosopher: A case study in the growth of interpersonal understanding. In S. R. Asher & J. M. Gottman (Eds.), *The development of children's friendships.* Cambridge, UK: Cambridge University Press.

Sénéchal, M., & LeFevre, J. (2002). Parental involvement in the development of children's reading skill: A five-year longitudinal study. *Child Development, 73*, 445–460.

Sénéchal, M., Thomas, E., & Monker, J. (1995). Individual differences in 4-year-old children's acquisition of vocabulary during storybook reading. *Journal of Educational Psychology, 87*, 218–229.

Serbin, L. A., Poulin-Dubois, D., Colburne, K. A., Sen, M. G., & Eichstedt, J. A. (2001). Gender stereotyping in infancy: Visual preferences for and knowledge of gender-stereotyped toys in the second year. *International Journal of Behavioral Development, 25*, 7–15.

Serbin, L. A., Powlishta, K. K., & Gulko, J. (1993). The development of sex typing in middle childhood. *Monographs of the Society for Research in Child Development, 58* (Serial No. 232).

Setliff, A. E., & Courage, M. L. (2011). Background television and infants' allocation of their attention during toy play. *Infancy, 16*, 611–639.

Shahaeian, A., Peterson, C. C., Slaughter, V., & Wellman, H. M. (2011). Culture and the sequence of steps in theory of mind development. *Developmental Psychology, 47*, 1239–1247.

Shanahan, M. J., Elder, G. H., Burchinal, M., & Conger, R. D. (1996a). Adolescent earnings and relationships with parents: The work-family nexus in urban and rural ecologies. In J. T. Mortimer & M. D. Finch (Eds.), *Adolescents, work, and family: An intergenerational developmental analysis.* Thousand Oaks, CA: Sage.

Shanahan, M. J., Elder, G. H., Burchinal, M., & Conger, R. D. (1996b). Adolescent paid labor and relationships with parents: Early work-family linkages. *Child Development, 67*, 2183–2200.

Shanahan, L., McHale, S. M., Crouter, A. C., & Osgood, D. (2007). Warmth with mothers and fathers from middle childhood to late adolescence: Within- and between-families comparisons. *Developmental Psychology, 43*, 551–563.

Shapka, J. D., & Keating, D. P. (2005). Structure and change in self-concept during adolescence. *Canadian Journal of Behavioural Sciences, 37*, 83–96.

Share, D. L. (2008). Orthographic learning, phonological recoding, and self-teaching. In R. V. Kail (Ed.), *Advances in child development and behavior* (Vol. 36, pp. 31–84). San Diego, CA: Elsevier.

Shariff, A. F., & Tracy, J. L. (2011). What are emotion expressions for? *Current Directions in Psychological Science, 20*, 395–399.

Shatz, M. (1983). Communication. In P. H. Mussen (Ed.), *Handbook of child psychology* (Vol. 3). New York, NY: Wiley.

Shatz, M., & Gelman, R. (1973). The development of communication skills: Modifications in the speech of young children as a function of listener. *Monographs of the Society for Research in Child Development, 38* (5, Serial No. 152).

Shaw, D. S., & Shelleby, E. C. (2014). Early-starting conduct problems: Intersection of conduct problems and poverty. *Annual Review of Clinical Psychology, 10*, 503–528.

Shaw, D. S., Winslow, E. B., & Flanagan, C. (1999). A prospective study of the effects of marital status and family relations on young children's adjustment among African American and European American families. *Child Development, 70*, 742–755.

Sherman, D. K., Hartson, K. A., Binning, K. R., Purdie-Vaughns, V., Garcia, J., Taborsky-Barba, S., et al. (2013). Deflecting the trajectory and changing the narrative: How self-affirmation affects academic performance and motivation under identity threat. *Journal of Personality and Social Psychology, 104*, 591–618.

Sherrod, K. B., O'Connor, S., Vietze, P. M., & Altemeier, W. A., III (1984). Child health and maltreatment. *Child Development, 55*, 1174–1183.

Shi, R. (2014). Functional morphemes and early language acquisition. *Child Development Perspectives, 8*, 6–11.

Shi, R., & Werker, J. F. (2001). Six-month old infants' preference for lexical words. *Psychological Science, 12*, 70–75.

Shin, H. B., & Kominski, R. A. (2010). *Language use in the United States: 2007.* (American Community Survey Reports, ACS-12). Washington, DC: U.S. Census Bureau.

Shiner, R. L., & Caspi, A. (2012). Temperament and the development of personality traits, adaptations, and narratives. In M. Zentner & R. L. Shiner (Eds.), *Handbook of temperament* (pp. 497–516). New York, NY: Guilford.

Shneidman, L. A., & Goldin-Meadow, S. (2012). Language input and acquisition in a Mayan village: How important is directed speech? *Developmental Science, 15*, 659–673.

Shoemaker, L. B., & Furman, W. (2009). Interpersonal influences on late adolescent girls' and boys' disordered eating. *Eating Behaviors, 10*, 97–106.

Shonkoff, J. P., & Bales, S. N. (2011). Science does not speak for itself: Translating child development research for the public and its policymakers. *Child Development, 82*, 17–32.

Shulman, S., & Kipnis, O. (2001). Adolescent romantic relationships: A look from the future. *Journal of Adolescence, 24*, 337–351.

Shusterman, A., Lee, S. A., & Spelke, E. W. (2008). Young children's spontaneous use of geometry in maps. *Developmental Science, 11,* F1–F7.

Siddiqui, A. (1995). Object size as a determinant of grasping in infancy. *Journal of Genetic Psychology, 156,* 345–358.

Sidebotham, P., Heron, J., & the ALSPAC Study Team. (2003). Child maltreatment in the "children of the nineties": The role of the child. *Child Abuse & Neglect, 27,* 337–352.

Siegler, R. S. (1981). Developmental sequences within and between concepts. *Monographs of the Society for Research on Child Development, 46,* Serial No. 189.

Siegler, R. S. (1986). Unities in strategy choices across domains. In M. Perlmutter (Ed.), *Minnesota symposia on child development* (Vol. 19). Hillsdale, NJ: Erlbaum.

Siegler, R. S. (1996). *Emerging minds: The process of change in children's thinking.* New York, NY: Oxford University Press.

Siegler, R. S. (2000). The rebirth of children's learning. *Child Development, 71,* 26–35.

Siegler, R. S. (2007). Cognitive variability. *Developmental Science, 18,* 303–307.

Siegler, R. S., & Alibali, M. W. (2005). *Children's thinking* (4th ed.). Upper Saddle River, NJ: Prentice Hall.

Siegler, R. S., Duncan, G. J., Davis-Kean, P. E., Duckworth, K., Claessens, A., Engel, M. et al. (2012). Early predictors of high school mathematics achievement. *Psychological Science, 23,* 691–697.

Siegler, R. S., & Ellis, S. (1996). Piaget on childhood. *Psychological Science, 7,* 211–215.

Siegler, R. S., & Jenkins, E. (1989). *How children discover new strategies.* Hillsdale, NJ: Erlbaum.

Siegler, R. S., & Robinson, M. (1982). The development of numerical understanding. In H. W. Reese & L. P. Lipsitt (Eds.), *Advances in child development and behavior* (Vol. 16). New York, NY: Academic Press.

Siegler, R. S., & Shrager, J. (1984). Strategy choices in addition and subtraction: How do children know what to do? In C. Sophian (Ed.), *Origins of cognitive skills.* Hillsdale, NJ: Erlbaum.

Signorielli, N., & Lears, M. (1992). Children, television, and conceptions about chores: Attitudes and behaviors. *Sex Roles, 27,* 157–170.

Silk, J. S., Morris, A. S., Kanaya, T., & Steinberg, L. D. (2003). Psychological control and autonomy granting: Opposite ends of a continuum or distinct constructs? *Journal of Research on Adolescence, 13,* 113–128.

Silva, K. G., Correa-Chávez, M., & Rogoff, B. (2010). Mexican-heritage children's attention and learning from interactions directed to others. *Child Development, 81,* 898–912.

Silverman, W. K., La Greca, A. M., & Wasserstein, S. (1995). What do children worry about? Worries and their relations to anxiety. *Child Development, 66,* 671–686.

Simcock, G., & Hayne, H. (2002). Breaking the barrier? Children fail to translate their preverbal memories into language. *Psychological Science, 13,* 225–231.

Simons, L. G., & Conger, R. D. (2007). Linking mother-father differences in parenting to a typology of family parenting styles and adolescent outcomes. *Journal of Family Issues, 28,* 212–241.

Simons, D. J., & Keil, F. C. (1995). An abstract to concrete shift in the development of biological thought: The insides story. *Cognition, 56,* 129–163.

Simonton, D. K., & Song, A. V. (2009). Eminence, IQ, physical and mental health, and achievement domain: Cox's 282 geniuses revisited. *Psychological Science, 20,* 429–434.

Simpson, E. L. (1974). Moral development research: A case study of scientific cultural bias. *Human Development, 17,* 81–106.

Simpson, J. M. (2001). Infant stress and sleep deprivation as an aetiological basis for the sudden infant death syndrome. *Early Human Development, 61,* 1–43.

Singh, L., Reznick, J. S., & Xuehua, L. (2012). Infant word segmentation and childhood vocabulary development: A longitudinal analysis. *Developmental Science, 15,* 482–495.

Skinner, B. F. (1957). *Verbal behavior.* New York, NY: Appleton-Century-Crofts.

Skinner, E. A. (1985). Determinants of mother-sensitive and contingent-responsive behavior: The role of childbearing beliefs and socioeconomic status. In I. E. Sigel (Ed.), *Parental belief systems: The psychological consequences for children* (pp. 51–82). Hillsdale, NJ: Erlbaum.

Skolnick Weisberg, D., & Bloom, P. (2009). Young children separate multiple pretend worlds. *Developmental Science, 12,* 699–705.

Slater, A., Bremner, G., Johnson, S. P., Sherwood, P., Hayes, R., & Brown, E. (2000). Newborn infants' preference for attractive faces: The role of internal and external facial features. *Infancy, 1,* 265–274.

Slater, A. M., Riddell, P., Quinn, P. C., Pascalis, O., Lee, K., & Kelly, D. J. (2010). Visual perception. In T. D. Wachs & G. Bremner (Eds.), *Blackwell handbook of infant development,* 2nd ed. Oxford, UK: Blackwell.

Sleddens, E. F. C., Kremers, S. P. J., Candel, M. J. J. M., De Vries, N. N. K., & Thijs, C. (2011). Validating the Children's Behavior Questionnaire structure in Dutch children: Psychometric properties and a cross-cultural comparison of factor structures. *Psychological Assessment, 23,* 417–426.

Sloane, S., Baillargeon, R., & Premack, D. (2012). Do infants have a sense of fairness? *Psychological Science, 23,* 196–204.

Slobin, D. I. (1985). Cross-linguistic evidence for the language-making capacity. In D. I. Slobin (Ed.), *The cross-linguistic study of language acquisition: Vol. 2. Theoretical issues.* Hillsdale, NJ: Erlbaum.

Slutske, W. S., Moffitt, T. E., Poulton, R., & Caspi, A. (2012). Undercontrolled temperament at age 3 predicts disordered gambling at age 32: A longitudinal study of a complete birth cohort. *Psychological Science, 23,* 510–516.

Smetana, J. G. (2002). Culture, autonomy, and personal jurisdiction in adolescent-parent relationships. *Advances in Child Development & Behavior, 29,* 52–87.

Smetana, J. G. (2006). Social-cognitive domain theory: Consistencies and variations in children's moral and social judgments. In M. Killen & J. G. Smetana (2006). *Handbook of moral development* (pp. 119–153). Mahwah, NJ: Erlbaum.

Smetana, J. G. (2011). Parenting beliefs, parenting, and parent-adolescent communication in African American families. In N. E. Hill, T. Mann, & H. E. Fitzgerald (Eds.), *African-American children's mental health: Vol. 1. Development and context* (pp. 173–197). Santa Barbara, CA: Praeger.

Smetana, J. G., Rote, W. M., Jambon, M., Tasopoulos-Chan, M., Villalobos, M., & Comer, J. (2012). Developmental changes and individual differences in young children's moral judgments. *Child Development, 83,* 683–696.

Smith, L. B. (2000). How to learn words: An associative crane. In R. Golinkoff & K. Hirsch-Pasek (Eds.), *Breaking the word learning barrier* (pp. 51–80). Oxford, UK: Oxford University Press.

Smith, L. B. (2009). From fragments to geometric shape: Changes in visual object recognition between 18 and 24 months. *Current Directions in Psychological Science, 18,* 290–294.

Smith, S. L., & Atkin, C. (2003). Television advertising and children: Examining the intended and unintended effects. In E. L. Palmer & B. M. Young (Eds.), *The faces of televisual media: Teaching, violence, selling to children* (pp. 301–326). Mahwah, NJ: Erlbaum.

Smith, S. L., Choueiti, M., Prescott, A., & Pieper, K. (2012). *Gender roles and occupations: A look at character attributes and job-related aspirations in film and television.* Los Angeles, CA: Geena Davis Institute on Gender in Media.

Smith, P. K., & Drew, L. M. (2002). Grandparenthood. In M. H. Bornstein (Ed.), *Handbook of parenting: Vol. 3. Status and social conditions of parenting* (2nd ed., pp. 141–172). Mahwah, NJ: Erlbaum.

Smith, L. B., Jones, S. S., Landau, B., Gershkoff-Stowe, L., & Samuelson, L. (2002). Object name learning provides on-the-job training for attention. *Psychological Science, 13,* 13–19.

Smith, E. R., & Mackie, D. M. (2000). *Social psychology* (2nd ed.). Philadelphia, PA: Psychology Press.

Smith, R., Paul, J., Maiti, K., Tolosa, J., & Gemma, M. (2012). Recent advances in understanding the endocrinology of human birth. *Trends in Endocrinology and Metabolism, 23,* 516–523.

Smith, J., & Ross, H. (2007). Training parents to mediate sibling disputes affects children's negotiation and conflict understanding. *Child Development, 78,* 790–805.

Smits, I., Soenens, B., Vansteenkiste, M., Luyckx, K., & Goossens, L. (2010). Why do adolescents gather information or stick to parental norms? Examining autonomous and controlled motives behind adolescents' identity style. *Journal of Youth & Adolescence, 39,* 1343–1356.

Smock, T. K. (1998). *Physiological psychology: A neuroscience approach.* Upper Saddle River, NJ: Prentice-Hall.

Smoll, F. L., & Schutz, R. W. (1990). Quantifying gender differences in physical performance: A developmental perspective. *Developmental Psychology, 26,* 360–369.

Snedeker, J., Geren, J., & Shafto, C. L. (2007). Starting over: International adoption as a natural experiment in language development. *Psychological Science, 18,* 79–87.

Snell, E. K., Adam, E. K., & Duncan, G. J. (2007). Sleep and the body mass index and overweight status of children and adolescents. *Child Development, 78,* 309–323.

Snow, C. W. (1998). *Infant development* (2nd ed.). Upper Saddle River, NJ: Prentice Hall.

Snow, D. (2006). Regression and reorganization of intonation between 6 and 23 months. *Child Development, 77,* 281–296.

Snow, M. E., Jacklin, C. N., & Maccoby, E. E. (1983). Sex-of-child differences in father–child interaction at one year of age. *Child Development, 54,* 227–232.

Snowling, M. J., & Hulme, C. (2012). Annual Research Review: The nature and classification of reading disorders—a commentary on proposals for DSM-5. *Journal of Child Psychology and Psychiatry, 53,* 593–607.

Sodian, B., Zaitchik, D., & Carey, S. (1991). Young children's differentiation of hypothetical beliefs from evidence. *Child Development, 62,* 753–766.

Solantaus, T., Leinonen, J., & Punamäki, R.-L. (2004). Children's mental health in times of economic recession: Replication and extension of the family economic stress model in Finland. *Developmental Psychology, 40,* 412–429.

Solomon, G. E. A., & Zaitchik, D. (2012). Folkbiology. *WIREs Cognitive Science, 3,* 105–115.

Somerville, L. H., & Casey, B. J. (2010). Developmental neurobiology of cognitive control and motivational systems. *Current Opinion in Neurobiology 20,* 236–241.

Song, L., Tamis-LeMonda, C. S., Yoshikawa, H., Kahana-Kalman, R., & Wu, I. (2012). Language experiences and vocabulary development in Dominican and Mexican infants across the first 2 years. *Developmental Psychology, 48,* 1106–1123.

Sowislo, J. F., & Orth, U. (2013). Does low self-esteem predict depression and anxiety? A meta-analysis of longitudinal studies. *Psychological Bulletin, 139,* 213–240.

Spearman, C. (1904). "General intelligence" objectively determined and measured. *American Journal of Psychology, 15,* 201–293.

Spector, F., & Maurer, D. (2009). Synesthesia: A new approach to understanding the development of perception. *Developmental Psychology, 45,* 175–189.

Spelke, E. S., Gilmore, C. K., & McCarthy, S. (2011). Kindergarten children's sensitivity to geometry in maps. *Developmental Science, 14,* 809–821.

Spelke, E. S., & Kinzler, K. D. (2007). Core knowledge. *Developmental Science, 10,* 89–96.

Spencer, J. P., Perone, S., & Buss, A. T. (2011). Twenty years and going strong: A dynamic systems revolution in motor and cognitive development. *Child Development Perspectives, 5,* 260–266.

Spies Shapiro, L. A., & Margolin, G. (2014). Growing up wired: Social networking sites and adolescent psychosocial development. *Clinical Child and Family Psychology Review, 17,* 1–18.

Spitz, R. A. (1965). *The first year of life.* New York, NY: International Universities Press.

Springer, K., & Keil, F. C. (1991). Early differentiation of causal mechanisms appropriate to biological and nonbiological kinds. *Child Development, 62,* 767–781.

Stacy, A. W., Zoog, J. B., Unger, J. B., & Dent, C. W. (2004). Exposure to televised alcohol ads and subsequent alcohol use. *American Journal of Health Behavior, 28,* 498–509.

Staff, J., & Schulenberg, J. E. (2010). Millenials and the world of work: Experiences in paid work during adolescence. *Journal of Business & Psychology, 25,* 247–255.

Staiano, A. E., & Calvert, S. L. (2011). Exergames for physical education courses: Physical, social, and cognitive benefits. *Child Development Perspectives, 5,* 93–98.

Stanford v. Kentucky, 492 U.S. 361 (1989).

Stanik, C. E., Riina, E. M., & McHale, S. M. (2013). Parent-adolescent relationship qualities and adolescent adjustment in two-parent African American families. *Family Relations, 62,* 597–608.

Stanovich, K. E., West, R. F., & Toplak, M. E. (2011). The complexity of developmental predictions from dual process models. *Developmental Review, 31,* 103–118.

Stattin, H., Kerr, M., & Skoog, T. (2011). Early pubertal timing and girls' problem behavior: Integrating two hypotheses. *Journal of Youth and Adolescence, 40,* 1271–1278.

Steeger, C. M., & Gondoli, D. M. (2013). Mother-adolescent conflict as a mediator between adolescent problem behaviors and maternal psychological control. *Developmental Psychology, 49,* 804–814.

Steelandt, S., Thierry, B., Broihanne, M-H., & Dufour, V. (2012). The ability of children to delay gratification in an exchange task. *Cognition, 122,* 416–425.

Steele, C. M. (1997). A threat in the air: How stereotypes shape intellectual identity and performance. *American Psychologist, 52,* 613–629.

Steelman, J. D. (1994). Revision strategies employed by middle level students using computers. *Journal of Educational Computing Research, 11,* 141–152.

Steinberg, L. D. (1999). *Adolescence* (5th ed.). Boston, MA: McGraw-Hill.

Steinberg, L. (2001). We know some things: Parent-adolescent relationships in retrospect and prospect. *Journal of Research on Adolescence, 11,* 1–19.

Steinberg, L., & Dornbusch, S. M. (1991). Negative correlates of part-time employment during adolescence: Replication and elaboration. *Developmental Psychology, 27*, 304–313.

Steinberg, L., Graham, S., O'Brien, L., Woolard, J., Cauffman, E., & Banich, M. (2009). Age differences in future orientation and delay discounting. *Child Development, 80*, 28–44.

Steinberg, L., & Monahan, K. C. (2007). Age differences in resistance to peer influence. *Developmental Psychology, 43*, 1531–1543.

Steinberg, L., & Silk, J. (2002). Parenting adolescents. In M. Bornstein (Ed.), *Handbook of parenting: Vol. 1* (2nd ed., pp. 103–133). Hillsdale, NJ: Erlbaum.

Stenberg, G. (2012). Why do infants look at and use positive information from some informants rather than others in ambiguous situations? *Infancy, 17*, 642–671.

Sternberg, R. J. (1999). The theory of successful intelligence. *Review of General Psychology, 3*, 292–316.

Sternberg, R. J., & Grigorenko, E. L. (2002). *Dynamic testing: The nature and measurement of learning potential.* New York, NY: Cambridge University Press.

Sternberg, R. J., Grigorenko, E. L., & Kidd, K. K. (2005). Intelligence, race, and genetics. *American Psychologist, 60*, 46–59.

Sternberg, R. J., & Kaufman, J. C. (1998). Human abilities. *Annual Review of Psychology, 49*, 479–502.

Stevens, E., Plumert, J. M., Cremer, J. F., & Kearney, J. K. (2013). Preadolescent temperament and risky behavior: Bicycling across traffic-filled intersections in a virtual environment. *Journal of Pediatric Psychology, 38*, 285–295.

Stevens, J., & Ward-Estes, J. (2006). Attention-deficit/hyperactivity disorder. In M. Hersen & J. C. Thomas (Series Eds.), & R. T. Ammerman (Vol. Ed.), *Comprehensive handbook of personality and psychopathology, Vol. 3: Child psychopathology* (pp. 316–329). Hoboken, NJ: Wiley.

Stevenson, H. W., & Lee, S. (1990). Contexts of achievement. *Monographs of the Society for Research in Child Development, 55* (Serial No. 221).

Stevenson, R. J., Oaten, M. J., Case, T. I., Repacholi, B. M., & Wagland, P. (2010). Children's response to adult disgust elicitors: Development and acquisition. *Developmental Psychology, 46*, 165–177.

Stevenson, H. W., & Stigler, J. W. (1992). *The learning gap.* New York, NY: Summit Books.

Stewart, L., & Pascual-Leone, J. (1992). Mental capacity constraints and the development of moral reasoning. *Journal of Experimental Child Psychology, 54*, 251–287.

St. George, I. M., Williams, S., & Silva, P. A. (1994). Body size and menarche: The Dunedin study. *Journal of Adolescent Health, 15*, 573–576.

Stice, E., Rohde, P., Gau, J., & Shaw, H. (2009). An effectiveness trial of a dissonance-based eating disorder prevention program for high-risk adolescent girls. *Journal of Consulting and Clinical Psychology, 77*, 825–834.

Stice, E., & Shaw, H. (2004). Eating disorder prevention programs: A meta-analytic review. *Psychological Bulletin, 130*, 206–227.

Stice, E., Shaw, H., Bohon, C., Martin, C. N., & Rohde, P. (2009). A meta-analytic review of depression prevention programs for children and adolescents: Factors that predict magnitude of intervention effects. *Journal of Consulting & Clinical Psychology, 77*, 486–503.

Stice, E., South, K., & Shaw, H. (2012). Future directions in etiologic, prevention, and treatment research for eating disorders. *Journal of Clinical Child and Adolescent Psychology, 41*, 845–855.

Stifter, C. A., Cipriano, E., Conway, A., & Kelleher, R. (2009). Temperament and the development of conscience: The moderating role of effortful control. *Social Development, 18*, 353–374.

Stigler, J. W., Gallimore, R., & Hiebert, J. (2000). Using video surveys to compare classrooms and teaching across cultures: Examples and lessons from the TIMSS video studies. *Educational Psychologists, 35*, 87–100.

Stiles, J. (2008). *Fundamentals of brain development.* Cambridge, MA: Harvard University Press.

Stiles, J., Reilly, J., Paul, B., & Moses, P. (2005). Cognitive development following early brain injury: Evidence for neural adaptation. *Trends in Cognitive Sciences, 9*, 136–143.

Stipek, D., & Miles, S. (2008). Effects of aggression on achievement: Does conflict with the teacher make it worse? *Child Development, 79*, 1721–1735.

St. James-Roberts, I. (2007). Helping parents to manage infant crying and sleeping: A review of the evidence and its implications for services. *Child Abuse Review, 16*, 47–69.

St. James-Roberts, I., & Plewis, I. (1996). Individual differences, daily fluctuations, and developmental changes in amounts of infant waking, fussing, crying, feeding, and sleeping. *Child Development, 67*, 2527–2540.

Stjernqvist, K. (2009). Predicting development for extremely low birthweight infants: Sweden. In K. Nugent, B. J. Petrauskas, & T. B. Brazelton (Eds.), *The newborn as a person: Enabling healthy infant development worldwide.* Hoboken, NJ: Wiley.

Strayer, J., & Roberts, W. (2004). Children's anger, emotional expressiveness, and empathy: Relations with parents' empathy, emotional expressiveness, and parenting practices. *Social Development, 13*, 229–254.

Striano, T., Tomasello, M., & Rochat, P. (2001). Social and object support for early symbolic play. *Developmental Science, 4*, 442–455.

Stright, A. D., Gallagher, K. C., & Kelley, K. (2008). Infant temperament moderates relations between maternal parenting in early childhood and children's adjustment in first grade. *Child Development, 79*, 186–200.

Strohmeier, D., Kärnä, A., & Salmivalli, C. (2011). Intrapersonal and interpersonal risk factors for peer victimization in immigrant youth in Finland. *Developmental Psychology, 47*, 248–258.

Strough, J., & Berg, C. A. (2000). Goals as a mediator of gender differences in high-affiliation dyadic conversations. *Developmental Psychology, 36*, 117–125.

Sturaro, C, van Lier, P. A. C., Cuijpers, P., & Koot, H. M. (2011). The role of peer relationships in the development of early school-age externalizing problems. *Child Development, 82*, 758–765.

Sturge-Apple, M. L., Davies, P. T., & Cummings, E. M. (2010). Typologies of family functioning and children's adjustment during the early school years. *Child Development, 81*, 1320–1335.

Subotnik, R. F., Olszewski-Kubilius, P., & Worrell, F. C. (2011). Rethinking giftedness and gifted education: A proposed direction forward based on psychological science. *Psychological Science in the Public Interest, 12*, 3–54.

Subrahmanyam, K., Greenfield, P., Kraut, R., & Gross, E. (2001). The impact of computer use on children's and adolescents' development. *Journal of Applied Developmental Psychology, 22*, 7–30.

Sullivan, M. W., & Lewis, M. (2003). Contextual determinants of anger and other negative expressions in young infants. *Developmental Psychology, 39*, 693–705.

Super, C. M. (1981). Cross-cultural research on infancy. In H. C. Triandis & A. Heron (Eds.), *Handbook of cross-cultural psychology: Vol. 4. Developmental psychology.* Boston, MA: Allyn & Bacon.

Super, C. M., Herrera, M. G., & Mora, J. O. (1990). Long-term effects of food supplementation and psychosocial intervention on the physical growth of Colombian infants at risk of malnutrition. *Child Development, 61*, 29–49.

Sussman, S., Pokhrel, P., Ashmore, R. D., & Brown, B. B. (2007). Adolescent peer group identification and characteristics: A review of the literature. *Addictive Behaviors, 32,* 1602–1627.

Suzuki, L., & Aronson, J. (2005). The cultural malleability of intelligence and its impact on the racial/ethnic hierarchy. *Psychology, Public Policy, & Law, 11,* 320–327.

Svirsky, M. A., Robbins, A. M., Kirk, K. I., Pisoni, D. B., & Miyamoto, R. T. (2000). Language development in profoundly deaf children with cochlear implants. *Psychological Science, 11,* 153–158.

Sweeney, M. M. (2010). Remarriage and stepfamilies: Strategic sites for family scholarship in the 21st century. *Journal of Marriage & Family, 72,* 667–684.

Sylvan, L. J., & Christodoulou, J. A. (2010). Understanding the role of neuroscience in brain based products: A guide for educators and consumers. *Mind, Brain, and Education, 4,* 1–7.

Symonds, W. C., Schwartz, R. B., & Ferguson, R. (2011). *Pathways to prosperity: Meeting the challenge of preparing young Americans for the 21st century.* Cambridge, MA: Harvard Graduate School of Education.

Szücks, D., & Goswami, U. (2007). Educational neuroscience: Defining a new discipline for the study of mental representations. *Mind, Brain, & Education, 1,* 114–127.

Tager-Flusberg, H. (1993). Putting words together: Morphology and syntax in the preschool years. In J. Berko Gleason (Ed.), *The development of language* (3rd ed.). New York, NY: Macmillan.

Tager-Flusberg, H. (2007). Evaluating the theory-of-mind hypothesis of autism. *Current Directions in Psychological Science, 16,* 311–315.

Tahiroglu, D., Mannering, A. M., & Taylor, M. (2011). Visual and auditory imagery associated with children's imaginary companions. *Imagination, Cognition, and Personality, 31,* 99–112.

Tamis-Lemonda, C. S., Adolph, K. E., Lobo, S. A., Karasik, L. B., Ishak, S., & Dimitropoulou, K. A. (2008). When infants take mothers' advice: 18-month-olds integrate perceptual and social information to guide motor action. *Developmental Psychology, 44,* 734–746.

Tamis-LeMonda, C. S., & Bornstein, M. H. (1996). Variation in children's exploratory, nonsymbolic, and symbolic play: An explanatory multidimensional framework. In C. Rovee-Collier & L. P. Lipsitt (Eds.), *Advances in infancy research* (Vol. 10). Norwood, NJ: Ablex.

Tamis-LeMonda, C. S., & Bornstein, M. H. (2002). Maternal responsiveness and early language acquisition. In R. V. Kail & H. W. Reese (Eds.), *Advances in child development and behavior* (Vol. 29, pp. 90–127). San Diego, CA: Academic Press.

Tan, K. L. (2009). Bed sharing among mother-infant pairs in Kiang District, Peninsular Malaysia, and its relationship to breast-feeding. *Journal of Developmental & Behavioral Pediatrics, 30,* 420–425.

Tanner, J. M. (1970). Physical growth. In P. H. Mussen (Ed.), *Carmichael's manual of child psychology* (3rd ed., pp. 77–135.). New York, NY: Wiley.

Tanner, J. M. (1990). *Fetus into man: Physical growth from conception to maturity* (2nd ed.). Cambridge, MA: Harvard University Press.

Tarabulsy, G. M., Bernier, A., Provost, M. A., Maranda, J., Larose, S., Moss, E., et al. (2005). Another look inside the gap: Ecological contributions to the transmission of attachment in a sample of adolescent mother–infant dyads. *Developmental Psychology, 41,* 212–224.

Tarantino, N., Tully, E. C., Garcia, S. E., South, S., Iacono, W. G., & McGue, M. (2014). Genetic and environmental influences on affiliation with deviant peers during adolescence and early adulthood. *Developmental Psychology, 50,* 663–673.

Tardif, T., Fletcher, P., Liang, W., Zhang, Z., Kaciroti, N., & Marchman, V. A. (2008). Baby's first 10 words. *Developmental Psychology, 44,* 929–938.

Taylor, M., Carlson, S. M., Maring, B. L., Gerow, L., & Charley, C. M. (2004). The characteristics of fantasy in school-age children: Imaginary companions, impersonation, and social understanding. *Developmental Psychology, 40,* 1173–1187.

Taylor, M., Hulette, A. C., & Dishion, T. J. (2010). Longitudinal outcomes of young high-risk adolescents with imaginary companions. *Developmental Psychology, 46,* 1632–1636.

Taylor, M. G., Rhodes, M., & Gelman, S. A. (2009). Boys will be boys; cows will be cows: Children's essentialist reasoning about gender categories and animal species. *Child Development, 80,* 461–481.

Taylor, R. D., & Roberts, D. (1995). Kinship support and maternal and adolescent well-being in economically disadvantaged African-American families. *Child Development, 66,* 1585–1597.

Taylor, J., & Schatschneider, C. (2010). Genetic influence on literacy constructs in kindergarten and first grade: Evidence from a diverse twin sample. *Behavior Genetics, 40,* 591–602.

Teachman, J. (2008). Complex life course patterns and the risk of divorce in second marriages. *Journal of Marriage & Family, 70,* 294–305.

Tegethoff, M., Greene, N., Olsen, J., Meyer, A. H., & Meinlschmidt, G. (2010). Maternal psychosocial adversity is associated with length of gestation and offspring size at birth: Evidence from a population-based cohort study. *Psychosomatic Medicine, 72,* 419–426.

Tenenbaum, H. R., & Leaper, C. (2002). Are parents' gender schemas related to their children's gender-related cognitions? A meta-analysis. *Developmental Psychology, 38,* 615–630.

Terlecki, M. S., & Newcombe, N. S. (2005). How important is the digital divide? The relations of computer and videogame usage to gender differences in mental rotation ability. *Sex Roles, 53,* 433–441.

Thelen, E., & Ulrich, B. D. (1991). Hidden skills. *Monographs for the Society for Research in Child Development, 56,* Serial No. 223.

Thelen, E., Ulrich, B. D., & Jensen, J. L. (1989). The developmental origins of locomotion. In M. H. Woollacott & A. Chumway-Cook (Eds.), *Development of posture and gait across the life span.* Columbia: University of South Carolina Press.

Thiessen, E. D., Hill, E., & Saffran, J. R. (2005). Infant-directed speech facilitates word segmentation. *Infancy, 7,* 53–71.

Thiessen, E. D., & Saffran, J. R. (2003). When cues collide: Use of stress and statistical cues to word boundaries by 7- to 9-month-old infants. *Developmental Psychology, 39,* 706–716.

Thomaes, S., Brummelman, E., Reijntjes, A., & Bushman, B. (2013). When Narcissus was a boy: origins, nature, and consequences of childhood narcissism. *Child Development Perspectives, 7,* 22–26.

Thomas, J. R., Alderson, J. A., Thomas, K. T., Campbell, A. C., & Elliot, B. C. (2010). Developmental gender differences for overhand throwing in Aboriginal Australian children. *Research Quarterly for Exercise & Sport, 81,* 432–441.

Thomas, A., & Chess, S. (1977). *Temperament and development.* New York, NY: Brunner/Mazel.

Thomas, A., Chess, S., & Birch, H. G. (1968). *Temperament and behavior disorders in children.* New York, NY: New York University Press.

Thomas, L. A., De Bellis, M. D., Graham, R., & LaBar, K. S. (2007). Development of emotional facial recognition in late childhood and adolescence. *Developmental Science, 10,* 547–558.

Thomas, J. R., & French, K. E. (1985). Gender differences across age in motor performance: A meta-analysis. *Psychological Bulletin, 98,* 260–282.

Thomas, R., & Zimmer-Gembeck, M. J. (2011). Accumulating evidence for parent-child interaction therapy in the prevention of child maltreatment. *Child Development, 82,* 177–192.

Thomas, R., & Zimmer-Gembeck, M. J. (2012). Parent-Child Interaction Therapy: An evidence-based treatment for child maltreatment. *Child Maltreatment, 17*, 253–266.

Thompson v. Oklahoma, 487 U.S. 815 (1988).

Thompson, G. G. (1952). *Child psychology*. Boston, MA: Houghton Mifflin.

Thompson, R. A. (2000). The legacy of early attachments. *Child Development, 71*, 145–152.

Thompson, R. A. (2006). The development of the person: Social understanding, relationships, conscience, self. In N. Eisenberg (Ed.), *Handbook of child psychology: Vol. 3. Social, emotional, and personality development* (6th ed.). Hoboken, NJ: Wiley.

Thompson, R. (2007). *What is albinism?* East Hampstead, NH: National Organization for Albinism and Hypopigmentation.

Thompson, R. A., Laible, D. J., & Ontai, L. L. (2003). Early understandings of emotion, morality, and self: Developing a working model. *Advances in Child Development & Behavior, 31*, 137–172.

Thompson, R. A., Lewis, M. D., & Calkins, S. D. (2008). Reassessing emotion regulation. *Child Development Perspectives, 2*, 124–131.

Thompson, R. A., & Limber, S. (1991). "Social anxiety" in infancy: Stranger wariness and separation distress. In H. Leitenberg (Ed.), *Handbook of social and evaluation anxiety*. New York, NY: Plenum.

Thompson, A. E., & Voyer, D. (2014). Sex differences in the ability to recognise non-verbal displays of emotion: A meta-analysis. *Cognition and Emotion, 28*, 1164–1195.

Thornberry, T. P., Krohn, M. D., Lizotte, A. J., Smith, C. A., & Tobin, K. (2003). *Gangs and delinquency in developmental perspective*. New York, NY: Cambridge University Press.

Thorne, B. (1993). *Gender play: Girls and boys in school*. New Brunswick, NJ: Rutgers University Press.

Thurstone, L. L., & Thurstone, T. G. (1941). Factorial studies of intelligence. *Psychometric Monograph, No. 2*.

Tincoff, R., & Jusczyk, P. W. (1999). Some beginnings of word comprehension in 6-month-olds. *Psychological Science, 10*, 172–175.

Tisak, M. (1993). Preschool children's judgments of moral and personal events involving physical harm and property damage. *Merrill-Palmer Quarterly, 39*, 375–390.

Tither, J. M., & Ellis, B. J. (2008). Impact of fathers on daughters' age at menarche: A genetically and environmentally controlled sibling study. *Developmental Psychology, 44*, 1409–1420.

Tomasello, M., Carpenter, M., & Liszkowski, U. (2007). A new look at infant pointing. *Child Development, 78*, 705–722.

Tomasello, M., & Vaish, A. (2013). Origins of human cooperation and morality. *Annual Review of Psychology, 64*, 231–255.

Tomlinson, M., Cooper, P., & Murray, L. (2005). The mother–infant relationship and infant attachment in a South African peri-urban settlement. *Child Development, 76*, 1044–1054.

Tomson, L. M., Pangrazi, R. P., Friedman, G., & Hutchison, H. (2003). Childhood depressive symptoms, physical activity and health related fitness. *Journal of Sport Psychology, 25*, 419–439.

Tooby, J., & Cosmides, L. (2008). The evolutionary psychology of emotions and their relationship to internal regulatory variables. In M. Lewis, J. M. Haviland-Jones, & L. F. Barrett (Eds.), *Handbook of emotions* (3rd ed., pp. 114–137). New York, NY: Guilford.

Torgesen, J. K. (2004). Learning disabilities: An historical and conceptual overview. In B. Y. L. Wong (Ed.), *Learning about learning disabilities* (3rd ed., pp. 3–40). San Diego, CA: Elsevier.

Trachtenberg, F. L., Haas, E. A., Kinney, H. C., Stanley, C., & Krous, H. F. (2012). Risk factor changes for Sudden Infant Death Syndrome after initiation of Back-to-Sleep campaign. *Pediatrics, 129*, 630–638.

Tracy, B., Reid, R., & Graham, S. (2009). Teaching young students strategies for planning and drafting stories. The impact of self-regulated strategy development. *Journal of Educational Research, 102*, 323–331.

Trainor, L. J., Austin, C. M., & Desjardins, R. N. (2000). Is infant-directed speech prosody a result of vocal expression of emotion? *Psychological Science, 11*, 188–195.

Trainor, L. J., & Heinmiller, B. M. (1998). The development of evaluative responses to music: Infants prefer to listen to consonance over dissonance. *Infant Behavior & Development, 21*, 77–88.

Treiman, R., & Kessler, B. (2003). The role of letter names in acquisition of literacy. *Advances in Child Development & Behavior, 31*, 105–135.

Tremblay, M. S., LeBlanc, A. G., Kho, M. E., Saunders, T. J., Larouche, R., Colley, R. C., et al. (2011). Systematic review of sedentary behaviour and health indicators in school-aged children and youth. *International Journal of Behavioral Nutrition and Physical Activity, 8*, Article 98.

Tremblay, R. E., Schall, B., Boulerice, B., Arsonault, L., Soussignan, R. G., & Paquette, D. (1998). Testosterone, physical aggression, and dominance and physical development in adolescence. *International Journal of Behavioral Development, 22*, 753–777.

Troseth, G. L., Pierroutsakos, S. L., & DeLoache, J. S. (2004). From the innocent to the intelligent eye: The early development of pictorial competence. In R. V. Kail (Ed.), *Advances in child development and behavior* (Vol. 32, pp. 1–35). San Diego, CA: Elsevier.

Trzesniewski, K. H., Donnellan, M. B., Caspi, A., Moffitt, T. E., Robins, R. W., & Poultin, R. (2006). Adolescent low self-esteem is a risk factor for adult poor health, criminal behavior, and limited economic prospects. *Developmental Psychology, 42*, 381–390.

Tsubota, Y., & Chen, Z. (2012). How do young children's spatio-symbolic skills change over short time scales? *Journal of Experimental Child Psychology, 111*, 1–21.

Tucker, M. S. (2011). *Surpassing Shanghai: An agenda for American education built on the world's leading systems*. Cambridge, MA: Harvard Education Press.

Tucker-Drob, E. M., Briley, D. A., & Harden, K. P. (2013). Genetic and environmental influences on cognition across development and context. *Current Directions in Psychological Science, 22*, 349–355.

Tudge, J. R. H., Winterhoff, P. A., & Hogan, D. M. (1996). The cognitive consequences of collaborative problem solving with and without feedback. *Child Development, 67*, 2892–2909.

Turiel, E. (1998). The development of morality. In W. Damon (Ed.), *Handbook of child psychology, Vol. 3: Social, emotional, and personality development* (pp. 863–932). New York, NY: Wiley.

Turiel, E. (2006). The development of morality. In W. Damon & R. M. Lerner (Eds.), *Handbook of child psychology* (6th ed., Vol. 3, pp. 789–857). Hoboken, NJ: Wiley.

Twenge, J. M., & Campbell, W. K. (2001). Age and birth cohort differences in self-esteem: A cross-temporal meta-analysis. *Personality & Social Psychology Review, 5*, 321–344.

Twenge, J. M., & Crocker, J. (2002). Race and self-esteem: Meta-analysis comparing Whites, Blacks, Hispanics, and American Indians and comment on Gray-Little and Hafdahl (2000). *Psychological Bulletin, 128*, 371–408.

Tynes, B. M., Umaña-Taylor, A. J., Rose, C. A., Lin, J., & Anderson, C. J. (2012). Online racial discrimination and the protective function of ethnic identity and self-esteem for African American adolescents. *Developmental Psychology, 48*, 343–355.

Tzuriel, D. (2013). Dynamic assessment of learning potential. In M. M. C. Mok (Ed.), *Self-directed learning oriented assessments in the Asia-Pacific* (pp. 235–235). Heidelberg, Germany: Springer Dordrecht.

Uchiyama, I., Anderson, D. I., Campos, J. J., Witherington, D., Frankel, C. B., Lejeune, L., et al. (2008). Locomotor experience affects self and emotion. *Developmental Psychology, 44*, 1225–1231.

Umaña-Taylor, A., Diversi, M., & Fine, M. (2002). Ethnic identity and self-esteem among Latino adolescents: Distinctions among Latino populations. *Journal of Adolescent Research, 17,* 303–327.

Umaña-Taylor, A. J., & Guimond, A. B. (2010). A longitudinal examination of parenting behaviors and perceived discrimination predicting Latino adolescents' ethnic identity. *Developmental Psychology, 46,* 636–650.

UNICEF. (2006). *Progress for children: A report card on nutrition, 2000–2006.* New York, NY: Author.

UNICEF. (2007). *The state of the world's children, 2008.* New York, NY: Author.

UNICEF. (2010). *Facts for life* (4th ed.). New York, NY: Author.

UNICEF-WHO-The World Bank. (2012). *UNICEF-WHO-World Bank joint malnutrition estimates.* New York, NY: Author.

Updegraff, K. A., McHale, S. M., Whiteman, S. D., Thayer, S. M., & Delgado, M. Y. (2005). Adolescent sibling relationships in Mexican American families: Exploring the role of familism. *Journal of Family Psychology, 19,* 512–522.

Updegraff, K. A., Thayer, S. M., Whiteman, S. D., Denning, D. J., & McHale, S. M. (2005). Aggression in adolescents' sibling relationships: Links to sibling and parent–adolescents relationship quality. *Family Relations: Interdisciplinary Journal of Applied Family Studies, 54,* 373–385.

U.S. Census Bureau. (2011). America's Families and Living Arrangements: 2010. Retrieved March 31, 2011 from www.census.gov/population/www/socdemo/hh-fam/cps2010.html.

U.S. Centers for Disease Control. (2012). *Breastfeeding report card—United States, 2012.* Atlanta GA: Author.

U.S. Department of Health and Human Services. (2010). *The Surgeon General's vision for a healthy and fit nation.* Rockville, MD: Author.

U.S. Department of Health and Human Services. (2013). Child maltreatment 2012. Available from http://www.acf.hhs.gov/programs/cb/research-data-technology/statistics-research/child-maltreatment.

US Department of Health and Human Services, Health Resources and Services Administration, Maternal and Child Health Bureau. (2013). *Child health USA 2013.* Rockville, MD: Author.

US Department of Labor. (2000). *Report on the youth labor force.* Washington, DC: Author.

Usher, E. L., & Pajares, F. (2009). Sources of self-efficacy in mathematics: A validation study. *Contemporary Educational Psychology, 34,* 89–101.

Uttal, D. H., Meadow, N. G., Tipton, E., Hand, L. L., Alden, A. R., Warren, C., et al. (2013). The malleability of spatial skills: A meta-analysis of training studies. *Psychological Bulletin, 139,* 352–402.

Vaillancourt, T., Brittain, H. L., McDougall, P., & Duku, E. (2013). Longitudinal links between childhood peer victimization, internalizing and externalizing problems, and academic functioning: Developmental cascades. *Journal of Abnormal Child Psychology, 41,* 1203–1215.

Vaillant-Molina, M., Bahrick, L. E., & Flom, R. (2013). Young infants match facial and vocal emotional expressions of other infants. *Infancy, 18*(S1), E97–E111.

Vaish, A., Carpenter, M., & Tomasello, M. (2009). Sympathy through affective perspective taking and its relation to prosocial behavior in toddlers. *Developmental Psychology, 45,* 534–543.

Vaish, A., Woodward, A., & Grossmann, T. (2008). Not all emotions are created equal: The negativity bias in social-emotional development. *Psychological Bulletin, 134,* 383–403.

Valentino, K., Ciccetti, D., Rogosch, F. A., & Toth, S. L. (2008). Memory, maternal representations, and internalizing symptomatology among abused, neglected, and nonmaltreated children. *Child Development, 79,* 705–719.

Valenza, E., & Bulf, H. (2011). Early development of object unity: Evidence for perceptual completion in newborns. *Developmental Science, 14,* 799–808.

Valkenburg, P. M., & Jochen, P. (2009). Social consequences of the Internet for adolescents: A decade of research. *Current Directions in Psychological Science, 18,* 1–5.

Vandell, D. L., Belsky, J., Burchinal, M., Steinberg, L., Vandergrift, N., & The NICHD Early Child Care Research Network. (2010). Do effects of early child care extend to age 15 years? Results from the NICHD Study of Early Child Care and Youth Development. *Child Development, 81,* 737–756.

Vandell, D. L., Pierce, K. M., & Dadisman, K. (2005). Out-of-school settings as a developmental context for children and youth. In R. V. Kail (Ed.), *Advances in child development and behavior* (Vol. 33, pp. 43–77). Amsterdam: Elsevier Academic Press.

van der Mark, I. L., van IJzendoorn, M. H., & Bakermans-Kranenburg, M. J. (2002). Development of empathy in girls during the second year of life: Associations with parenting, attachment, and temperament. *Social Development, 11,* 451–468.

Vander Wal, J. S., & Thelen, M. H. (2000). Eating and body image concerns among obese and average-weight children. *Addictive Behaviors, 25,* 775–778.

Van Duijvenvoorde, A. C. K., Huizenga, H. M., & Jansen, B. R. J. (2014). What is and what could have been: Experiencing regret and relief across childhood. *Cognition and Emotion, 28,* 926–935.

Van Gelderen, L., Gartrell, N. N., Bos, H. M. W., & Hermanns, J. M. A. (2012). Stigmatization and promotive factors in relation to psychological health and life satisfaction of adolescents in planned lesbian families. *Journal of Family Issues, 34,* 809–827.

van Goozen, S. H., Fairchild, G., Snoek, H., & Harold, G. T. (2007). The evidence for a neurobiological model of childhood antisocial behavior. *Psychological Bulletin, 133,* 149–182.

van Hof, P., van der Kamp, J., & Savelsbergh, G. J. P. (2002). The relation of unimanual and bimanual reaching to crossing the midline. *Child Development, 73,* 1352–1362.

Van IJzendoorn, M. H., & Bakermans-Kranenburg, M. J. (2012). Integrating temperament and attachment: The different susceptibility paradigm. In M. Zentner & R. L. Shiner (Eds.), *Handbook of temperament* (pp. 403–424). New York, NY: Guilford.

Van IJzendoorn, M. H., Bakermans-Kranenburg, M. J., & Ebstein, R. P. (2011). Methylation matters in child development: Toward developmental behavioral epigenetics. *Child Development Perspectives, 5,* 305–310.

Van IJzendoorn, M. H., & Sagi-Schwartz, A. (2008). Cross-cultural patterns of attachment: Universal and contextual dimensions. In J. Cassidy & P. R. Shaver (Eds.), *Handbook of attachment: Theory, research, and clinical applications* (pp. 713–734). New York, NY: Guilford.

van IJzendoorn, M. H., Schuengel, C., & Bakermans-Kranenburg, M. J. (1999). Disorganized attachment in early childhood: Meta-analysis of precursors, concomitants, and sequelae. *Development & Psychopathology, 11,* 225–249.

van IJzendoorn, M. H., Vereijken, C. M. J. L., Bakermans-Kranenburg, M. J., & Riksen-Walraven, J. M. (2004). Assessing attachment security with the Attachment Q-Sort: Meta-analytic evidence for the validity of the observer AQS. *Child Development, 75,* 1188–1213.

van Lier, P. A. C., Vitaro, F., Barker, E. D., Brendgen, M., Tremblay, R. E., & Boivin, M. (2012). Peer victimization, poor academic achievement, and the link between childhood externalizing and internalizing problems. *Child Development, 83,* 1775–1788.

Van Tuijl, L. A., de Jong, P. J., Sportel, B. E., de Hullu, E., & Nauta, M. H. (2014). Implicit and explicit self-esteem and their reciprocal relationship with symptoms of depression and social anxiety: A longitudinal study in adolescents. *Journal of Behavior Therapy and Experimental Psychiatry, 45,* 113–121.

Van Zalk, M., Herman, W., Kerr, M., Branje, S. J. T., Stattin, H., & Meeus, W. H. J. (2010). It takes three: Selection, influence, and de-selection processes of depression in adolescent friendship networks. *Developmental Psychology, 46,* 927–938.

Vazsonyi, A. T., Hibbert, J. R., & Snider, J. B. (2003). Exotic enterprise no more? Adolescent reports of family and parenting practices from youth in four countries. *Journal of Research on Adolescence, 13,* 129–160.

Vazsonyi, A. T., & Huang, L. (2010). Where self-control comes from: On the development of self-control and its relationship to deviance over time. *Developmental Psychology, 46,* 245–257.

Vazsonyi, A. T., & Snider, J. B. (2008). Mentoring, competencies, and adjustment in adolescents: American part-time employment and European apprenticeships. *International Journal of Behavioral Development, 32,* 46–55.

Veenstra, R., Lindberg, S., Oldenhinkel, A. J., De Winter, A. F., Verhulst, F. C., & Ormel, J. (2005). Bullying and victimization in elementary schools: A comparison of bullies, victims, bully/victims, and uninvolved preadolescents. *Developmental Psychology, 41,* 672–682.

Veenstra, R., Lindenberg, S., Munniksma, A., & Dijkstra, J. K. (2010). The complex relation between bullying, victimization, acceptance, and rejection: Giving special attention to status, affection, and sex differences. *Child Development, 81,* 480–486.

Vélez, C. E., Wolchik, S. A., Tein, J., & Sandler, I. (2011). Protecting children from the consequences of divorce: A longitudinal study of the effects of parenting on children's coping processes. *Child Development, 82,* 244–257.

Ventura, S. J., Abma, J. C., Mosher, W. D., & Henshaw, S. K. (2008). Estimated pregnancy rates by outcome for the United States, 1990–2004. *National Vital Statistics Reports, 56,* 1–26.

Verkuyten, M., & De Wolf, A. (2007). The development of in-group favoritism: Between social reality and group identity. *Developmental Psychology, 43,* 901–911.

Véronneau, M.-H., Vitaro, F., Brendgen, M., Dishion, T. J., & Tremblay, R. E. (2010). Transactional analysis of the reciprocal linkages between peer relationships and academic achievement from middle childhood to early adolescence. *Developmental Psychology, 46,* 773–790.

Verschaeve, L. (2009). Genetic damage in subjects exposed to radiofrequency radiation. *Mutation Research—Reviews in Mutation Research, 681,* 259–270.

Victora, C. G., Adam, T., Bruce, J., & Evans, D. B. (2006). Integrated management of the sick child. In D. T. Jamison et al. (Eds.), *Disease control priorities in developing countries* (2nd ed., pp. 1172–1192). New York, NY: Oxford University Press.

Vieno, A., Nation, M., Pastore, M., & Santinello, M. (2009). Parenting and antisocial behavior: A model of the relationship between adolescent self-disclosure, parental closeness, parental control, and adolescent antisocial behavior. *Developmental Psychology, 45,* 1509–1519.

Vijayalaxmi & Prihoda, T. J. (2012). Genetic damage in human cells exposed to non-ionizing radiofrequency fields: A meta-analysis of the data from 88 publications (1990–2011). *Mutation Research/Genetic Toxicology and Environmental Mutagenesis, 749,* 1–16.

Visher, E. G., Visher, J. S., & Pasley, K. (2003). Remarriage families and stepparenting. In F. Walsh (Ed.), *Normal family processes* (pp. 153–175). New York, NY: Guilford.

Vitiello, B., & Swedo, S. (2004). Antidepressant medications in children. *New England Journal of Medicine, 350,* 1489–1491.

Volling, B. L. (2012). Family transitions following the birth of a sibling: An empirical review of changes in the firstborn's adjustment. *Psychological Bulletin, 138,* 497–528.

Vorhees, C. V., & Mollnow, E. (1987). Behavior teratogenesis: Long-term influences on behavior. In J. D. Osofsky (Ed.), *Handbook of infant development* (2nd ed.). New York, NY: Wiley.

Vouloumanos, A., Hauser, M. D., Werker, J. F., & Martin, A. (2010). The tuning of human neonates' preference for speech. *Child Development, 81,* 517–527.

Voyer, D., Postma, A., Brake, B., & Imperato-McGinley, J. (2007). Gender differences in object location memory: A meta-analysis. *Psychonomic Bulletin & Review, 14,* 23–38.

Voyer, D., Voyer, S., & Bryden, M. P. (1995). Magnitude of sex differences in spatial abilities: A meta-analysis and consideration of critical variables. *Psychological Bulletin, 117,* 250–270.

Vraneković, J., Božović, I. B., Grubić, Z., Wagner, J., Pavlinić, D., Dahoun, S., et al. (2012). Down syndrome: Parental origin, recombination, and maternal age. *Genetic Testing and Molecular Biomarkers, 16,* 70–73.

Vygotsky, L. S. (1978). *Mind in society: The development of higher psychological processes* (M. Cole, V. John-Steiner, S. Scribner, & E. Soubermen, Eds.). Cambridge, MA: Harvard University Press.

Wachs, T. D., & Bates, J. E. (2001). Temperament. In G. Bremner & A. Fogel (Eds.), *Blackwell handbook of infant development* (pp. 465–501). Malden, MA: Blackwell.

Wagner, K., & Dobkins, K. R. (2011). Synaesthetic associations decrease during infancy. *Psychological Science, 22,* 1067–1072.

Wainwright, J. L., & Patterson, C. J. (2008). Peer relations among adolescents with female same-sex parents. *Developmental Psychology, 44,* 117–126.

Wainwright, J. L., Russell, S. T., & Patterson, C. J. (2004). Psychosocial adjustment, school outcomes, and romantic relationships of adolescents with same-sex parents. *Child Development, 75,* 1886–1898.

Wakschlag, L. S., Leventhal, B. L., Pine, D. S., Pickett, K. E., & Carter, A. S. (2006). Elucidating early mechanisms of developmental psychopathology: The case of prenatal smoking and disruptive behavior. *Child Development, 77,* 893–906.

Walberg, H. J. (1995). General practices. In G. Cawelti (Ed.), *Handbook of research on improvising student achievement.* Arlington, VA: Educational Research Service.

Walker, P., Bremner, J. G., Mason, U., Spring, J., Mattock, K., Slater, A., et al. (2010). Preverbal infants' sensitivity to synaesthetic cross-modality correspondences. *Psychological Science, 21,* 21–25.

Wallentin, M. (2009). Putative sex differences in verbal abilities and language cortex: A critical review. *Brain & Language, 108,* 175–183.

Walton, G. M., & Spencer, S. J. (2009). Latent ability: Grades and test scores systematically underestimate the intellectual ability of negatively stereotyped students. *Psychological Science, 20,* 1132–1139.

Wang, Q. (2006). Culture and the development of self-knowledge. *Current Directions in Psychological Science, 15,* 182–187.

Wang, S. S., & Brownell, K. D. (2005). Anorexia nervosa. In C. B. Fisher & R. M. Lerner (Eds.), *Encyclopedia of applied developmental science* (Vol. 1, pp. 83–85). Thousand Oaks, CA: Sage.

Wang, M-T., & Huguley, J. P. (2012). Parental racial socialization as a moderator of the effects of racial discrimination on educational success among African American adolescents. *Child Development 83,* 1716–1731.

Wang, Q., Pomerantz, E. M., & Chen, H. (2007). The role of parents' control in early adolescents' psychological functioning:

A longitudinal investigation in the United States and China. *Child Development, 78,* 1592–1610.

Wansink, B., & Sobal, J. (2007). Mindless eating: The 200 daily food decisions we overlook. *Environment & Behavior, 39,* 106–123.

Warneken, F., & Tomasello, M. (2006). Altruistic helping in human infants and young chimpanzees. *Science, 311,* 1301–1303.

Warner, B., Altimier, L., & Crombleholme, T. M. (2007). Fetal surgery. *Newborn & Infant Nursing Reviews, 7,* 181–188.

Warnock, F., & Sandrin, D. (2004). Comprehensive description of newborn distress behavior in response to acute pain (newborn male circumcision). *Pain, 107,* 242–255.

Warren, A. R., & McCloskey, L. A. (1993). Pragmatics: Language in social contexts. In J. Berko Gleason (Ed.), *The development of language* (3rd ed., pp. 195–238). New York, NY: Macmillan.

Warren-Leubecker, A., & Bohannon, J. N. (1989). Pragmatics: Language in social contexts. In J. Berko Gleason (Ed.), *The development of language* (2nd ed., pp. 327–368). Columbus, OH: Merrill.

Watamura, S. E., Phillips, D. A., Morrissey, T. W., McCartney, K., & Bub, K. (2011). Double jeopardy: Poorer social-emotional outcomes for children in the NICHD SECCYD experiencing home and child-care environments that confer risk. *Child Development, 82,* 48–65.

Waterhouse, L. (2006). Multiple intelligences, the Mozart effect, and emotional intelligence: A critical review. *Educational Psychologist, 41,* 207–225.

Waters, H. S. (1980). "Class news": A single-subject longitudinal study of prose production and schema formation during childhood. *Journal of Verbal Learning & Verbal Behavior, 19,* 152–167.

Waters, H. F. (1993, July 12). Networks under the gun. *Newsweek,* 64–66.

Waters, E., & Cummings, E. M. (2000). A secure base from which to explore close relationships. *Child Development, 71,* 164–172.

Waters, S. F., West, T. V., & Mendes, W. B. (2014). Stress contagion: Physiological covariation between mothers and infants. *Psychological Science, 25,* 934–942.

Watson, J. B. (1925). *Behaviorism.* New York, NY: Norton.

Wax, J. R., Pinette, M. G., & Cartin, A. (2010). Home versus hospital birth: Process and outcome. *Obstetrical & Gynecological Survey, 65,* 132–140.

Waxman, S., Fu, X., Arunachalam, S., Leddon, E., Geraghty, K., & Song, H-J. (2013). Are nouns learned before verbs? Infants provide insights into a long-standing debate. *Child Development Perspectives, 7,* 155–159.

Waxman, S., Medin, D., & Ross, N. (2007). Folkbiological reasoning from a cross-cultural developmental perspective: Early essentialist notions are shaped by cultural beliefs. *Developmental Psychology, 43,* 294–308.

Webb, S. J., Monk, C. S., & Nelson, C. A. (2001). Mechanisms of postnatal neurobiological development: Implications for human development. *Developmental Neuropsychology, 19,* 147–171.

Webster-Stratton, C. H., Reid, M. J., & Beauchaine, T. (2011). Combining parent and child training for young children with ADHD. *Journal of Clinical Child and Adolescent Psychology, 40,* 191–203.

Wei, W., Lu, H., Zhao, H., Chen, C., Dong, Q., & Zhou, X. (2012). Gender differences in children's arithmetic performance are accounted for by gender differences in language abilities. *Psychological Science, 23,* 320–330.

Weichold, K., & Silbereisen, R. K. (2005). Puberty. In C. B. Fisher & R. M. Lerner (Eds.), *Encyclopedia of applied developmental science* (Vol. 2, pp. 893–898). Thousand Oaks, CA: Sage.

Weinert, F. E., & Haney, E. A. (2003). The stability of individual differences in intellectual development: Empirical evidence, theoretical problems, and new research questions. In R. J. Sternberg, J. Lautrey, &

T. I. Lubart (Eds.), *Models of intelligence: International perspectives* (pp. 169–181). Washington, DC: American Psychological Association.

Weis, R., & Cerankosky, B. C. (2010). Effects of video-game ownership on young boys' academic and behavioral functioning: A randomized, controlled study. *Psychological Science, 21,* 463–470.

Weisgram, E. S., Bigler, R. S., & Liben, L. S. (2010). Gender, values, and occupational interests among children, adolescents, and adults. *Child Development, 81,* 778–796.

Weisleder, A., & Fernald, A. (2013). Talking to children matters: Early language experience strengthens processing and builds vocabulary. *Psychological Science, 24,* 2143–2152.

Weisner, T. S., Garnier, H., & Loucky, J. (1994). Domestic tasks, gender egalitarian values and children's gender typing in conventional and nonconventional families. *Sex Roles, 30,* 23–54.

Weisner, T. S., & Wilson-Mitchell, J. E. (1990). Nonconventional family lifestyles and sex typing in six-year-olds. *Child Development, 61,* 1915–1933.

Weissman, M. D., & Kalish, C. W. (1999). The inheritance of desired characteristics: Children's view of the role of intention in parent-offspring resemblance. *Journal of Experimental Child Psychology, 73,* 245–265.

Weisz, J. R., McCarty, C. A., & Valeri, S. M. (2006). Effects of psychotherapy for depression in children and adolescents: A meta-analysis. *Psychological Bulletin, 132,* 132–149.

Weizman, Z. O., & Snow, C. E. (2001). Lexical output as related to children's vocabulary acquisition: Effects of sophisticated exposure and support for meaning. *Developmental Psychology, 37,* 265–279.

Wellman, H. M. (2002). Understanding the psychological world: Developing a theory of mind. In U. Goswami (Ed.), *Blackwell handbook of childhood cognitive development* (pp. 167–187). Malden, MA: Blackwell.

Wellman, H. M. (2011). Developing a theory of mind. In U. Goswami (Ed.), *The Wiley-Blackwell handbook of childhood cognitive development* (2nd ed., pp. 258–284). West Sussex, UK: Wiley-Blackwell.

Wellman, H. M. (2012). Theory of mind: Better methods, clearer findings, more development. *European Journal of Developmental Psychology, 9,* 313–330.

Wellman, H. M., Fang, F., & Peterson, C. C. (2011). Sequential progressions in a theory-of-mind scale. *Child Development, 82,* 780–792.

Wellman, H. M., & Gelman, S. A. (1998). Knowledge acquisition in foundational domains. In W. Damon (Ed.), *Handbook of child psychology* (Vol. 2, pp. 523–573). New York, NY: Wiley.

Wentworth, N., Benson, J. B., & Haith, M. M. (2000). The development of infants' reaches for stationary and moving targets. *Child Development, 71,* 576–601.

Wentzel, K. R., Filisetti, L., & Looney, L. (2007). Adolescent prosocial behavior: The role of self-processes and contextual cues. *Child Development, 78,* 895–910.

Werker, J. F., Yeung, H. H., & Yoshida, K. A. (2012). How do infants become experts at native-speech perception? *Current Directions in Psychological Science, 21,* 221–226.

Werner, H. (1948). *Comparative psychology of mental development.* Chicago, IL: Follet.

Werner, N. E., Eaton, A. D., Lyle, K., Tseng, H., & Holst, B. (2014). Maternal social coaching quality interrupts the development of relational aggression during early childhood. *Social Development, 23,* 470–486.

Werner, E. E., & Smith, R. S. (2001). *Journeys from childhood to midlife: Risk, resilience, and recovery.* Ithaca, NY: Cornell University Press.

Wertsch, J. V., & Tulviste, P. (1992). L. S. Vygotsky and contemporary developmental psychology. *Developmental Psychology, 28,* 548–557.

West, F., Sanders, M. R., Cleghorn, G. J., & Davies, P. S. W. (2010). Randomised clinical trial of a family-based lifestyle intervention for childhood obesity involving parents as the exclusive agents of change. *Behaviour Research and Therapy, 48,* 1170–1179.

Whitaker, R. C., Wright, J. A., Pepe, M. S., Seidel, K. D., & Dietz, W. H. (1997). Predicting obesity in young adulthood from childhood and parental obesity. *New England Journal of Medicine, 337,* 869–873.

White, F. A., Abu-Rayya, H. M., & Weitzel, C. (2014). Achieving twelve-months of intergroup bias reduction: The dual identity-electronic contact (DIEC) experiment. *International Journal of Intercultural Relations, 38,* 158–163.

White, L., & Gilbreth, J. G. (2001). When children have two fathers: Effects of relationships with stepfathers and noncustodial fathers on adolescent outcomes. *Journal of Marriage & the Family, 63,* 155–167.

Whitehurst, G. J., & Vasta, R. (1975). Is language acquired through imitation? *Journal of Psycholinguistic Research, 4,* 37–59.

Whiting, J. W. M., & Child, I. L. (1953). *Child training and personality: A cross-cultural study.* New Haven, CT: Yale University Press.

Whitty, M. T. (2014). The internet and its implications for children, parents and family relationships. In A. Abela & J. Walker (Eds.), *Contemporary issues in family studies: Global perspectives on partnerships, parenting, and support in a changing world* (pp. 262–274). Chichester, West Sussex, UK: Wiley.

Wicks-Nelson, R., & Israel, A. C. (2006). *Behavior disorders of childhood* (6th ed.). Upper Saddle River, NJ: Pearson.

Widen, S. C., & Russell, J. A. (2013). Children's recognition of disgust in others. *Psychological Bulletin, 139,* 271–299.

Wie, O. B., Falkenberg, E.-S., Tvete, O., & Tomblin, B. (2007). Children with a cochlear implant: Characteristics and determinants of speech recognition, speech-recognition growth rate, and speech production. *International Journal of Audiology, 46,* 232–243.

Willatts, P. (1999). Development of means-end behavior in young infants: Pulling a support to retrieve a distant object? *Developmental Psychology, 35,* 651–667.

Williams, J. E., & Best, D. L. (1990). *Measuring sex stereotypes: A thirty-nation study* (rev. ed.). Newbury Park, CA: Sage.

Williams, S. T., Conger, K. J., & Blozis, S. A. (2007). The development of interpersonal aggression during adolescence: The importance of parents, siblings, and family economics. *Child Development, 78,* 1526–1542.

Williams, T. L., & Davidson, D. (2009). Interracial and intra-racial stereotypes and constructive memory in 7- and 9-year-old African-American children. *Journal of Applied Developmental Psychology, 30,* 366–377.

Willoughby, T., Adachi, P. J. C., & Good, M. (2012). A longitudinal study of the association between violent video game play and aggression among adolescents. *Developmental Psychology, 48,* 1044–1057.

Wills, T. A., Sandy, J. M., Yaeger, A., & Shinar, O. (2001). Family risk factors and adolescent substance use: Moderation effects for temperament dimensions. *Developmental Psychology, 37,* 283–297.

Wilson, R. D. (2000). Amniocentesis and chorionic villus sampling. *Current Opinion in Obstetrics & Gynecology, 12,* 81–86.

Wilson, B. J. (2008). Media and children's aggression, fear, and altruism. *Future of Children, 18,* 87–118.

Wilson, D. M., Gottfredson, D. C., Cross, A. B., Rorie, M., & Connell, N. (2010). Youth development in after-school leisure activities. *Journal of Early Adolescence, 30,* 668–690.

Wilson, G. T., Heffernan, K., & Black, C. M. D. (1996). Eating disorders. In E. J. Marsh & R. A. Barkley (Eds.), *Child psychopathology.* New York, NY: Guilford.

Wilson, B. J., Smith, S. L., Potter, W. J., Kunkel, D., Linz, D., Colvin, C. M., & Donnerstein, E. (2002). Violence in children's television programming: Assessing the risks. *Journal of Communication, 52,* 5–35.

Winneke, G. (2011). Developmental aspects of environmental neurotoxicology: Lessons from lead and polychlorinated biphenyls. *Journal of the Neurological Sciences, 308,* 9–15.

Winner, E. (2000). Giftedness: Current theory and research. *Current Directions in Psychological Science, 9,* 153–156.

Witherspoon, D., Schotland, M., Way, N., & Hughes, D. (2009). Connecting the dots: How connectedness to multiple contexts influences the psychological and academic adjustment of urban youth. *Applied Developmental Science, 13,* 199–216.

Wolfe, D. A. (1985). Child-abusive parents: An empirical review and analysis. *Psychological Bulletin, 97,* 462–482.

Wolff, P. H. (1987). *The development of behavioral states and the expression of emotions in early infancy.* Chicago, IL: University of Chicago Press.

Wolke, D., Copeland, W. E., Angold, A., & Costello, E. J. (2013). Impact of bullying on adult health, wealth, crime, and social outcomes. *Psychological Science, 24,* 1958–1970.

Wolraich, M. L., Lindgren, S. D., Stumbo, P. J., Stegink, L. D., Appelbaum, M. I., & Kiritsy, M. C. (1994). Effects of diets high in sucrose or aspartame on the behavior and cognitive performance of children. *New England Journal of Medicine, 330,* 301–307.

Woodward, A. L. (2009). Infants' grasp of others' intention. *Current Directions in Psychological Science, 18,* 53–57.

Woodward, A. L. (2013). Infant foundations of intentional understanding. In M. R. Banaji & S. A. Gelman (Eds.), *Navigating the social world: What infants, children, and other species can teach us* (pp. 75–80). New York, NY: Oxford University Press.

Woodward, A. L., & Markman, E. M. (1998). Early word learning. In W. Damon (Ed.), *Handbook of child psychology* (Vol. 2). New York, NY: Wiley.

World Health Organization. (2004). *The analytic review of the integrated management of childhood illness strategy.* Geneva, Switzerland: Author.

World Health Organization. (2010). *Population-based prevention strategies for childhood obesity.* Geneva, Switzerland: Author.

World Health Organization. (2012). *Recommendations for management of common childhood conditions.* Geneva, Switzerland: Author.

World Health Organization. (2013). *World health statistics 2013.* Geneva, Switzerland: Author.

Worobey, J. (2005). Effects of malnutrition. In C. B. Fisher & R. M. Lerner (Eds.), *Encyclopedia of applied developmental science* (Vol. 2, pp. 673–676). Thousand Oaks, CA: Sage.

Worthman, C. M., & Brown, R. A. (2007). Companionable sleep: Social regulation of sleep and cosleeping in Egyptian families. *Journal of Family Psychology, 21,* 124–135.

Wray-Lake, L., Crouter, A. C., & McHale, S. M. (2010). Developmental patterns in decision-making autonomy across middle childhood and adolescence: European American parents' perspectives. *Child Development, 81,* 636–651.

Wright, J. C., Huston, A. C., Murphy, K. C., St. Peters, M., Piñon, M., Scantlin, R. et al. (2001). The relations of early television viewing to school readiness and vocabulary of children from low-income families: The Early Window Project. *Child Development, 72,* 1347–1366.

Wynn, K. (1992). Addition and subtraction by human infants. *Nature, 358,* 749–750.

Xie, H., Li, Y., Boucher, S. M., Hutchins, B. C., & Cairns, B. D. (2006). What makes a girl (or a boy) popular (or unpopular)? African American children's perceptions and developmental differences. *Developmental Psychology, 42,* 599–612.

Xu, Y., Farver, J. A., & Zhang, Z. (2009). Temperament, harsh and indulgent parenting, and Chinese children's proactive and reactive aggression. *Child Development, 80,* 244–258.

Yap, M. B. H., Pilkington, P. D., Ryan, S. M., & Jorm, A. F. (2014). Parental factors associated with depression and anxiety in young people: A systematic review and meta-analysis. *Journal of Affective Disorders, 156,* 8–23.

Yarrow, A. L. (2011). A history of federal child antipoverty and health policy in the United States since 1900. *Child Development Perspectives, 5,* 66–72.

Yau, J., Smetana, J. G., & Metzger, A. (2009). Young Chinese children's authority concepts. *Social Development, 18,* 210–229.

Yip, T., Douglass, S., & Shelton, J. C. (2013). Daily intragroup contact in diverse settings: Implications for Asian Adolescents' ethnic identity. *Child Development, 84,* 1425–1441.

Young, S. K., Fox, N. A., & Zahn-Waxler, C. (1999). The relations between temperament and empathy in 2-year-olds. *Developmental Psychology, 35,* 1189–1197.

Yuan, S., & Fisher, C. (2009). "Really? She blicked the baby?": Two-year-olds learn combinatorial facts about verbs by listening. *Psychological Science, 20,* 619–626.

Yumoto, C., Jacobson, S. W., & Jacobson, J. L. (2008). Fetal substance exposure and cumulative environmental risk in an African American cohort. *Child Development, 79,* 1761–1776.

Zahn-Waxler, C., Radke-Yarrow, M., Wagner, E., & Chapman, M. (1992). Development of concern for others. *Developmental Psychology, 28,* 126–136.

Zalewski, M., Lengua, L. J., Wilson, A. C., Trancik, A., & Bazinet, A. (2011). Emotion regulation profiles, temperament, and adjustment problems in preadolescents. *Child Development, 82,* 951–966.

Zarbatany, L., Hartmann, D. P., & Rankin, D. B. (1990). The psychological functions of preadolescent peer activities. *Child Development, 61,* 1067–1080.

Zarrett, N., Fay, K., Li, Y., Carrano, J., Phelps, E., & Lerner, R. M. (2009). More than child's play: Variable- and pattern-centered approaches for examining effects of sports participation on youth development. *Developmental Psychology, 45,* 368–382.

Zeiders, K. H., Umaña-Taylor, A. J., & Derlan, C. L. (2013). Trajectories of depressive symptoms and self-esteem in Latino youths: Examining the role of gender and perceived discrimination. *Developmental Psychology, 49,* 951–963.

Zelazo, P. D., Anderson, J. E., Richler, J., Wallner-Allen, K., Beaumont, J. L., & Weintraub, S. (2013). NIH Toolbox Cognition Battery (CB): Measuring executive function and attention. In P. D. Zelazo and P. J. Bauer (Eds.), National Institutes of Health Toolbox Cognition Battery (NIH Toolbox CB): Validation for children between 3 and 15 years. *Monographs of the Society for Research in Child Development, 78,* Serial No. 309, 16–33.

Zelazo, P. D., & Cunningham, W. A. (2007). Executive function: Mechanisms underlying emotion regulation. In J. J. Gross (Ed.), *Handbook of emotion regulation* (pp. 135–158). New York, NY: Guilford.

Zeman, J., & Garber, J. (1996). Display rules for anger, sadness, and pain: It depends on who is watching. *Child Development, 67,* 957–973.

Zeman, J., & Shipman, K. (1997). Social-contextual influences on experiences for managing anger and sadness: The transition from middle childhood to adolescence. *Developmental Psychology, 33,* 917–924.

Zhang, B., Cartmill, C., & Ferrence, R. (2008). The role of spending money and drinking alcohol in adolescent smoking. *Addiction, 103,* 310–319.

Zhou, Q., Eisenberg, N., Losoya, S. H., Fabes, R. A., Reiser, M., Guthrie, I. K., et al. (2002). The relations of parental warmth and positive expressiveness to children's empathy-related responding and social functioning: A longitudinal study. *Child Development, 73,* 893–915.

Zhou, Q., Lengua, L., & Wang, Y. (2009). The relations of temperament reactivity and effortful control to children's adjustment problems in China and the United States. *Developmental Psychology, 45,* 724–739.

Zhou, Q., Wang, Y., Eisenberg, N., Wolchik, S., Tein, J-W., & Deng, X. (2008). Relations of parenting and temperament to Chinese children's experience of negative life events, coping efficacy, and externalizing problems. *Child Development, 79,* 493–513.

Zhu, M., Cummings, P., Chu, H., Coben, J. H., & Li, G. (2013). Graduated driver licensing and motor vehicle crashes involving teenage drivers: an exploratory age-stratified meta-analysis. *Injury Prevention, 19,* 49–57.

Ziegler, J. C., Bertrand, D., Töth, D., Csépe, V., Reis, A., Faísca, L. et al. (2010). Orthographic depth and its impact on universal predictors of reading: A cross-language investigation. *Psychological Science, 21,* 551–559.

Zigler, E., & Finn-Stevenson, M. (1992). Applied developmental psychology. In M. H. Bornstein & M. E. Lamb (Eds.), *Developmental psychology: An advanced textbook.* Hillsdale, NJ: Erlbaum.

Zigler, E. F., & Muenchow, S. (1992). *Head Start: Inside story of American's most successful educational experiment.* New York, NY: Basic Books.

Zimiles, H., & Lee, V. E. (1991). Adolescent family structure and educational progress. *Developmental Psychology, 27,* 314–320.

Zimmer-Gembeck, M. J., & Helfand, M. (2008). Ten years of longitudinal research on U.S. adolescent sexual behavior: Developmental correlates of sexual intercourse, and the importance of age, gender and ethnic background. *Developmental Review, 28,* 153–224.

Zimmer-Gembeck, M. J. & Skinner, E. A. (2011). The development of coping across childhood and adolescence: An integrative review and critique of research. *International Journal of Behavioral Development, 35,* 1–17.

Zimmerman, B. J. (2001). Theories of self-regulated learning and academic adjustment: An overview and analysis. In B. J. Zimmerman & D. H. Schunk (Eds.), *Self-regulated learning and academic achievement: Theoretical perspectives* (2nd ed., pp. 1–37). Mahwah, NJ: Erlbaum.

Zimmerman, C. (2007). The development of scientific thinking skills in elementary and middle school. *Developmental Review, 27,* 172–223.

Zinar, S. (2000). The relative contributions of word identification skill and comprehension-monitoring behavior to reading comprehension ability. *Contemporary Educational Psychology, 25,* 363–377.

Zohsel, K., Buchmann, A. F., Blomeyer, D., Hohm, E., Schmidt, M. H., Esser, G., et al. (2014). Mothers' prenatal stress and their children's antisocial outcomes—a moderating role for the dopamine receptor D4 (DRD4) gene. *Journal of Child Psychology and Psychiatry, 55,* 69–76.

Zosuls, K. M., Ruble, D. N., & Tamis-Lemonda, C. S. (2014). Self-socialization of gender in African American, Dominican immigrant, and Mexican immigrant toddlers. *Child Development, 85,* in press.

Zosuls, K. M., Ruble, D. N., Tamis-LeMonda, C. S., Shrout, P. E., Bornstein, M. H., & Greulich, F. K. (2009). The acquisition of gender labels in infancy: Implications for gender-typed play. *Developmental Psychology, 45,* 688–701.

Zucker, R. A., Heitzeg, M. M., & Nigg, J. T. (2011). Parsing the undercontrol-disinhibition pathway to substance use disorders: A multilevel developmental problem. *Child Development Perspectives, 5,* 248–255.

Zukow-Goldring, P. (2002). Sibling caregiving. In M. H. Bornstein (Ed.), *Handbook of parenting: Vol. 3. Status and social conditions of parenting* (2nd ed., pp. 253–286). Mahwah, NJ: Erlbaum.

Credits

Photographs

Chapter 1 Page 20: Blend Images/SuperStock; 26: Nina Leen/Time & Life Pictures/Getty Images; 27: Sonya Etchison/Shutterstock; 29: (top) Andy Sacks/Getty Images; 29: (bottom) Koji Sasahara/AP Images; 30: Elizabeth Crews Photography; 31: Peter Arnold Inc./Alamy; 35: Image Source/Alamy; 37: Baerbel Schmidt/Getty Images; 38: Steve Gorton/DK Images; 40: Tony Freeman/PhotoEdit; 41: Pamela Johnson Meyer/Science Source; 46: (center left) Sherry Lewis; 46: (center) Sherry Lewis; 46: (center right) Sherry Lewis; 46: (bottom left) Courtesy of Sherry Lewis; 46: (bottom center) Courtesy of Sherry Lewis; 46: (bottom right) Courtesy of Sherry Lewis; 48: (top left) Jaimie Duplass/Shutterstock; 48: (top center) Joe Belanger/Alamy; 48: (top right) Ron Levine/Digital Vision/Getty Images; 48: (top left) Monkey Business Images/Shutterstock; 48: (top center) Monkey Business Images/Shutterstock; 48: (top right) Hurst Photo/Shutterstock; 48: (bottom left) Courtesy of Sherry Lewis; 48: (bottom center) Courtesy of Sherry Lewis; 48: (bottom center) Courtesy of Sherry Lewis; 48: (bottom right) Courtesy of Sherry Lewis; 48: (bottom left) Courtesy of Sherry Lewis; 48: (bottom center) Courtesy of Sherry Lewis; 48: (bottom center) Courtesy of Sherry Lewis; 48: (bottom right) Courtesy of Sherry Lewis; 51: Ryan McVay/Photodisc/Getty Images.

Chapter 2 Page 56: MBI/Alamy; 57: SPL/Custom Medical Stock Photo; 58: (top left) SPL M108/078/Science Source; 58: (center left) David Phillips/Science Source; 58: (bottom left) Alexander Tsiaras/Science Source; 59: BioPhoto Associates/Science Source; 64: SPL M140/369/Science Source; 67: Blaine Harrington III/Alamy; 73: Chris Schmidt/Getty Images.

Chapter 3 Page 78: Picture Partners/Alamy; 80: Stocktrek Images, Inc./Alamy; 81: (top right) Science Picture Co/The Science Picture Company/Alamy; 81: (center right) Petit Format/Science Source; 83: SCIEPRO/Science Photo Library/Alamy; 87: Dennis MacDonald/PhotoEdit; 90: Chassenet/BSIP SA/Alamy; 91: Gilles Mingasson/Getty Images; 96: Keith Brofsky/Photodisc/Getty Images; 106: Bernardo Gimenez/Alamy; 108: Prof. Robert V. Kail Ph D; 111: Aynur_sh/Fotolia; 112: Steve Raymer/National Geographic Stock.

Chapter 4 Page 118: Rene Jansa/Shutterstock; 123: Ian O'Leary/Getty Images; 124: Francis Dean/The Image Works; 125: (top right) Blue Jean Images/Alamy; 125: (bottom left) Andy Reynolds/Getty Images; 126: Joanna B. Pinneo/Aurora Photos; 127: Anders Ryman/Alamy; 130: (top left) Flirt/SuperStock; 130: (bottom left) Prof. Robert V. Kail Ph D; 132: David Guttenfelder/AP Images; 133: Peter Banos/Alamy; 135: Imagestate Media Partners Limited-Impact Photos/Alamy; 136: Earl & Nazima Kowall/Corbis; 137: (top right) Francisco Cruz/Purestock/Alamy; 137: (bottom right) AllrightImages/face to face Agentur GmbH/Alamy; 139: (top right) Geostock/Photodisc/Getty Images; 139: (center right) Ed Reschke; 139: (bottom right) Don W. Fawcett/Science Source; 141: (center right) Oli Scarff/Staff/Getty Images News/Getty Images; 141: (bottom right) Richard T. Nowitz/Corbis; 143: Emmanuel Faure/Stockbyte/Getty Images.

Chapter 5 Page 148: Gorilla/Shutterstock; 150: (top left) Dion Ogust/The Image Works; 150: (bottom left) John T. Fowler/Alamy; 152: Gene J. Puskar/AP Images; 154: SelectStock/Vetta/Getty Images; 157: Professor Robert V. Kail; 159: (bottom left) SAYAM TRIRATTANAPAIBOON/Shutterstock; 159: (top right) Mark Richards/PhotoEdit; 159: (center left) Jessmine/Fotolia; 159: (center) Ivanoffotography/Shutterstock; 159: (bottom center) PCN Photography/Alamy; 163: Nicholas Prior/Stone+/Getty Images; 165: (bottom) Kevin R. Morris/Corbis; 165: (bottom left) Images-USA/Alamy; 167: Voisin/Phanie/Superstock; 169: Mitch Reardon/Science Source; 170: Corbis RF/Alamy; 171: Ross Whitaker/Getty Images; 172: Petro Feketa/Shutterstock; 173: Professor Robert V. Kail; 174: Jose Carillo/PhotoEdit.

Chapter 6 Page 178: Morgan Lane Photography/Shutterstock; 180: Lynne Siler/Lynne Harty Photography/Alamy; 182: Ruth Jenkinson/DK Images; 183: Richard Mittleman/Alamy; 184: (bottom left) Tony Freeman/PhotoEdit; 184: (bottom center) Tony Freeman/PhotoEdit; 184: (bottom right) Tony Freeman/PhotoEdit; 186: Janine Wiedel/Photolibrary/Alamy; 190: Cindy Charles/PhotoEdit; 191: Elizabeth Crews; 192: JDC/Bridge/Corbis; 196: Andersen Ross/Blend Images/Alamy; 205: Elena Yakusheva/Shutterstock.

Chapter 7 Page 214: Ian Shaw/Alamy; 215: Carolyn Rovee-Collier; 217: Prof. Robert V. Kail Ph D; 219: Corbis Super RF/Alamy; 222: Prof. Robert V. Kail Ph D; 223: Ted Foxx/Alamy; 226: Steve Shott/DK Images; 229: Elizabeth Crews/The Image Works; 234: Wavebreakmedia/Shutterstock; 235: DonSmith/Alamy; 239: Jennie Woodcock/Reflections Photolibrary/Corbis; 243: Alan Oddie/PhotoEdit; 245: Gary Conner/Photolibrary/Getty Images.

Chapter 8 Page 250: Jupiterimages/BananaStock/Thinkstock; 256: (bottom center) David R. Frazier Photolibrary, Inc./Alamy; 256: (bottom right) Anna E. Zuckerman/PhotoEdit; 259: The Image Works; 265: Bob Ebbesen/Alamy; 269: Stockbyte/Getty Images; 272: Britt Erlanson/Getty Images.

Chapter 9 Page 278: Grublee/Shutterstock; 282: KIYOKO FUKUDA/a.collectionRF/Getty Images; 286: (top left) Paul Springett 02/Alamy; 286: (bottom left) 2xSamara.com/Shutterstock; 288: Topham/The Image Works; 293: Robert V. Kail; 294: A. Ramey/PhotoEdit; 295: Judy DeLoache; 300: Susan Kuklin/Science Source; 301: Chris Rout/Alamy; 304: Areipa.lt/Shutterstock; 305: Maya Barnes Johansen/The Image Works.

Chapter 10 Page 312: Mandy GodBehear/Shutterstock; 314: Science Photo Library/Alamy; 315: Professor Robert V. Kail; 316: Myrleen Fergueson Cate/PhotoEdit; 318: Tetra Images/Alamy; 319: Jeff Greenberg/PhotoEdit; 324: Big Cheese Photo/SuperStock; 326: Jan Mika/Shutterstock; 331: (top right) Brian McEntire/Shutterstock; 331: (bottom right) Design Pics Inc./

Text Credits

Chapter 1   Page 22: John Locke, (1632–1704), Essay Concerning Human Understanding, 1689; Page 39: Yip, T., and Douglass S. (2013). The application of experience sampling approaches....*Child Development Perspectives, 7*, 211–214.

Chapter 2   Page 63: Based on American Lung Association. (2007). State of lung disease in diverse communities: New York, NY: Author; Committee on Genetics. (1996). Newborn screening fact sheet. *Pediatrics, 98*, 473–501; Hellekson, K. L. (2001). NIH consensus statement on phenylketonuria. American Family Physician, 63,1430–1432; Thompson, R. (2007). What is albinism? East Hampstead, NH: National Organization for Albinism and Hypopigmentation; Pages 70–72: Bouchard, T. J. (2004). Genetic influence on human psychological traits. *Current Directions in Psychological Science, 13*, 148–151.

Chapter 3   Page 110: St. James-Roberts, I., & Plewis, I. (1996). Individual differences, daily fluctuations, and developmental changes in amounts of infant waking, fussing, crying, feeding, and sleeping. *Child Development, 67*, 2527–2540; AND Wolf, P. H. (1987). The development of behavioral states and the expression of emotions in early infancy. Chicago, IL: University of Chicago Press.

Chapter 4   Page 134: Stice, E., Shaw, H., Bohon, C., Martin, C. N., & Rohde, P. (2009). A meta-analytic review of depression prevention programs for children and adolescents: Factors that predict magnitude of intervention effects. *Journal of Consulting & Clinical Psychology, 77*, 486–503; Page 145: Fischer, K. W., & Immordino-Yang, M. H. (2008). The fundamental importance of the brain and learning for education. In The Jossey-Bass reader on the brain and learning. San Francisco, CA: Jossey-Bass.

Chapter 5   Page 163: Based on the *Diagnostic and Statistical Manual of Mental Disorders*, Fourth Edition, (Copyright 2012). American Psychiatric Association.

Chapter 6   Pages 182–183: Piaget, J. (1929). *The child's conception of space.* Boston, MA: Routledge and Kegan Paul. Page 185: Flavell, J.H. (1985). *Cognitive development.* Englewood Cliffs, NJ: Prentice Hall; Page 186: Inhelder, B. and Piaget, A. (1958). *The growth of logical thinking from childhood to adolescence.* New York, NY: Basic Books; Page 187: Flavell, J.H. (1996). Piaget's legacy. *Psychological Science, 7,* 200–203; Pages 187–188: Data from Brainard, C.J. (1996). Piaget: A centennial celebration. *Psychological Science, 7,* 191–203; Siegler, R.S. and Ellis, S. Piaget on childhood. *Psychological Science, 7,* 211–215; Pages 190–191: Gauvain, M. Cognitive development in social and cultural context. Current Directions in *Psychological Science, 7,* 188–192; Page 202: Hespos, S.J; Ferry A.L; and Rips, L.J. (2009). Five-month-old infants have different expectations for solids and liquids. *Psychological Science, 20,* 603–611; Pages 208–209: Baron-Cohen (2005). Mindblindness: An essay on autism and theory of mind. Cambridge, MA: MIT Press/Bradford Books.

Chapter 7   Page 223: State of New Jersey vs Kelly Michaels, Jan. 31, 1994. Cited in Bruck, M., & Ceci, S. J. (1995). Amicus brief for the case of State of New Jersey vs Michaels presented by Committee of Concerned Social Scientists. *Psychology, Public Policy, & Law,* 1, 272–322; Page 224: Governor's Task Force on Children's Justice. (1998). Forensic interviewing protocol. Lansing, MI: Author, p. v; Page 224: Hershkowitz et al., 2012; Poole & Bruck, 2012; Page 227: Based on Ellis, S., & Siegler, R. S. (1997). Planning and strategy choice, or why don't children plan when they should? In S. L. Friedman & E. K. Scholnick (Eds.), *The developmental psychology of planning: Why, how, and when do we plan?* (pp. 183–208). Hillsdale, NJ: Erlbaum; Page 229: Kokis, J. V., Macpherson, R., Toplak, M. E., West, R. F., & Stanovich, K. E. (2002). Heuristic and analytic processing: Age trends and associations with cognitive ability and cognitive styles. *Journal of Experimental Child Psychology, 83*, 26–52; Page 230: Kuhn, 2012; Pages 231–232: "Learning the control of variables strategy in higher and lower achieving classrooms: Contributions of explicit instruction and experimentation" by Robert F. Lorch Jr., Elizabeth P. Lorch, William J. Calderhead, Emily E. Dunlap, Emily C. Hodell and Benjamin Dunham Freer

(*Journal of Educational Psychology*, 2010[Feb], Vol 102[1], 90-101). p. 98; Pages 236–237: Siegler & Alibali, 2005; Page 238: Waters, H. S. (1980). "Class news": A single-subject longitudinal study of prose production and schema formation during childhood, p. 155. *Journal of Verbal Learning & Verbal Behavior, 19*, 152–167; Page 245: Based on Ni, Chiu, & Cheng, 2010; Stevenson, H. W., & Lee, S. (1990). Contexts of achievement. Monographs of the Society for Research in Child Development, 55 (Serial No. 221); Stigler, J. W., Gallimore, R., & Hiebert, J. (2000). Using video surveys to compare classrooms and teaching across cultures: Examples and lessons from the TIMSS video studies. Educational Psychologists, 35, 87–100.

Chapter 8   Page 254: Daniel Goleman, *Emotional Intelligence,* Bantam Books, 1995, p. xiii; Page 261: Brody, N. (1992). *Intelligence* (2nd ed.). San Diego, CA: Academic Press; Page 267: Alter, A. L., Aronson, J., Darley, J. M., Rodriguez, C., & Ruble, D. N. (2010). Rising to the threat: Reducing stereotype threat by reframing the threat as a challenge. *Journal of Experimental Social Psychology, 46*, 166–171.

Chapter 9   Page 279: Toni Morrison, "Nobel Lecture," Nobel Foundation, 7 December 1993; Page 283: Hoff, E. (2009). *Language development* (2nd ed). Belmont, CA: Wadsworth Cengage Learning; Page 290: Naigles, L. G., & Gelman, S. A. (1995). Overextensions in comprehension and production revisited: Preferential-looking in a study of dog, cat, and cow. *Journal of Child Language, 22*, 19–46; Page 291: Weisleder, A., & Fernald, A. (2013). Talking to children matters: Early language experience strengthens processing and builds vocabulary. *Psychological Science, 24*, 2143–2152; Page 293: Linebarger, D. L., & Vaala, S. E. (2010). Screen media and language development in infants and toddlers: An ecological perspective, p. 184. *Developmental Review, 30*, 176–202; Page 293: Thompson, G. G. (1952). *Child psychology,* p. 367. Boston, MA: Houghton Mifflin; Page 295: DeLoache, J. S., Miller, K. F., & Rosengren, K. S. (1997). The incredible shrinking room: Very young children's performance with symbolic and nonsymbolic relations. *Psychological Science, 8*, 308–313; Page 298: Berko, J. (1958). The child's learning of English morphology. *Word, 14*, 150–177; Page 299: Gertner, Y., Fisher, C., & Eisengart, J. (2006). Learning words and rules: Abstract knowledge of word order in early sentence comprehension. *Psychological Science, 17*, 684–691; Page 304: Field, T. M., & Widmayer, S. M. (1982). Motherhood. In B. J. Wolman (Ed.), *Handbook of developmental psychology.* Englewood Cliffs, NJ: Prentice Hall; Page 304: Shatz, M. (1983). Communication. In P. H. Mussen (Ed.), *Handbook of child psychology* (Vol. 3). New York, NY: Wiley; Page 305: Shatz, M., & Gelman, R. (1973). The development of communication skills: Modifcations in the speech of young children as a function of listener, p. 13. *Monographs of the Society for Research in Child Development, 38* (5, Serial No. 152); Page 307: William Shakespeare, *Romeo and Juliet,* 1562.

Chapter 10   Page 320: Data from Rothbart, M. K. (2007). Temperament, development, and personality. *Current Directions in Psychological Science, 16*, 207–212; Page 325: Gartstein, M. A., Knyazev, G. G., & Slobodskaya, H. R. (2005). Cross-cultural differences in the structure of infant temperament: United States of America and Russia. *Infant Behavior and Development, 28*, 54–61; Page 327: Moffitt TE, Arseneault L, Belsky D, et al. A gradient of childhood self-control predicts health, wealth, and public safety. Proc Natl Acad Sci U S A. Feb 15 2011;108(7):2693–2698;

Page 330: Based on Bowlby, J. (1969). *Attachment and loss* (Vol. 1). New York, NY: Basic Books; Page 335: Data from George, J. B. F., & Franko, D. L. (2010). Cultural issues in eating pathology and body image among children and adolescents. *Journal of Pediatric Psychology, 35*, 231–242; Page 336: NICHD Early Child Care Research Network. (1997). The effects of infant child care on infant–mother attachment security: Results of the NICHD Study of Early Child Care. *Child Development, 68*, 860–879.

Chapter 11   Page 341: Hall, G. S. (1904). *Adolescence,* 1. New York, NY: Appleton; Page 345: Marcia, J. E. (1980). Identity in adolescence. In J. Adelson (Ed.), Handbook of adolescent psychology. New York, NY: Wiley; Marcia, J. E. (1991). Identity and self-development. In R. M. Lerner, A. C. Petersen, & J. Brooks-Gunn (Eds.), *Encyclopedia of adolescence* (Vol. 1). New York, NY: Garland; Page 346: Phinney, J. (1989). Stage of ethnic identity in minority group adolescents, p. 44. *Journal of Early Adolescence, 9*, 34–49; Page 348: Güngör, D., & Bornstein, M. H. (2010). Culture-general and -specific associations of attachment avoidance and anxiety with perceived parental warmth and psychological control among Turk and Belgian adolescents. *Journal of Adolescence, 33*, 593–602; Page 351: Harter, S. (2006). The self. In W. Damon & R. M. Lerner (Eds.), *Handbook of child psychology* (6th ed., Vol. 3). New York, NY: Wiley; Page 356: Livesley, W. J., & Bromley, D. B. (1973). *Person perception in childhood and adolescence.* New York, NY: Wiley; Page 359: Baron, A. S., & Banaji, M. R. (2006). The development of implicit attitudes: Evidence of race evaluations from ages 6 and 10 and adulthood. *Psychological Science, 17*, 53–58; Page 363: Clark, K. B., & Clark, M. K. (1940). Skin color as a factor in racial identification of Negro preschool children. *Journal of Social Psychology, 11*, 159–169; Page 372: Brown v. Board of Education, 347 U.S. 483 (1954).

Chapter 12   Page 372: Peake, P. K., Hebl, M., & Mischel, W. (2002). Strategic attention deployment for delay gratification in working and waiting situations. *Developmental Psychology, 38*, 313–326; Pages 375–377: Kohlberg, L. (1969). Stage and sequence: The cognitive-developmental approach to socialization. In D. Goslin (Ed.), *Handbook of socialization theory and research* (pp. 347–480). Chicago, IL: Rand McNally.

Chapter 13   Pages 404–405: Taylor, M. G., Rhodes, M., & Gelman, S. A. (2009). Boys will be boys; cows will be cows: Children's essentialist reasoning about gender categories and animal species. *Child Development, 80*, 461–481; Page 410: Else-Quest, N. M., Hyde, J. S., & Linn, M. C. (2010). Cross-national patterns of gender differences in mathematics: A meta-analysis, p. 125. *Psychological Bulletin, 136*, 103–127; Pages 418–419: Martin, C. L., & Ruble, D. (2004). Children's search for gender cues: Cognitive perspectives on gender development. *Current Directions in Psychological Science, 13*, 67–70.

Chapter 14   Page 432: Baumrind, D. (1975). Early socialization and the discipline controversy. Morristown, NJ: General Learning Press; Page 434: Gottman, J. M., Katz, L. F., & Hooven, C. (1996). Parental meta-emotion philosophy and the emotional life of families: Theoretical models and preliminary data. *Journal of Family Psychology, 10*, 243–268; Page 434: Mize, J., & Pettit, G. S. (1997). Mothers' social coaching, mother–child relationship style, and children's peer competence: Is the medium the message? *Child Development, 68*, 312–332; Page 443: Vélez, C. E.,

Wolchik, S. A., Tein, J., & Sandler, I. (2011). Protecting children from the consequences of divorce: A longitudinal study of the efects of parenting on children's coping processes, p. 255. *Child Development, 82,* 244–257; Page 445: Mueller, M. M., & Elder, G. H. (2003). Family contingencies across the generations: Grandparents–grandchild relationships in holistic perspective. *Journal of Marriage & the Family, 65,* 404–417.

Chapter 15 Page 476: Hymel, S., Vaillancourt, T., McDougall, P., & Renshaw, P. D. (2004). Peer acceptance and rejection in childhood. In P. K. Smith & C. H. Hart (Eds.), *Blackwell handbook of childhood social development* (pp. 265–284). Malden, MA: Blackwell; Pages 489–490: Conger, R. D., & Elder, G. H. (1994). Families in troubled times: Adapting to change in rural America. New York, NY: Aldine de Gruyter.

Name Index

A

Aboud, F. E., 363
Abu-Rayya, H. M., 363
Ackerman, B.P., 307, 314, 488
Acredolo, L. P., 286
Adachi, P. J. C., 391
Adams, E., 381
Adams, E. K., 431
Adams, M. J., 238
Adams, R. E., 470
Adams, R.J., 153
Adelstein, S., 265
Adolph, K. E., 167, 168, 169
Adolphus, K., 132
Agnoli, F., 229
Ainsworth, M. S., 332
Akmal, N., 287
Alatupa, S., 389
Alberts, A. E., 109
Aldao, A., 411
Aldridge, V., 124
Alexander, G. M., 407, 409, 411
Alibali, M. W., 188, 195, 229, 238
Alink, L. R. A., 453, 475
Allen, J. P., 437
Allen, L., 292
Alter, A., 267
Altimier, L., 98
Altman, J., 441
Altschul, I., 390
Alves, R. A., 239
Amato, P. R., 432, 440–442
Amodio, D. M., 420
Amsterlaw, J., 319
Anastasi, A., 266
Anderson, D. R., 480
Anderson, E., 306
Anderson, S. W., 141, 481
Andrews, G., 195
Andrews, J. A., 130
Ani, C., 132
Anzures, G., 161
Apfelbaum, E. P., 359
Apgar, V., 108–109
Appleyard, K., 453–454, 455
Arabi, M., 124
Archer, J., 411, 456
Archer, T., 422
Armer, M., 466
Armstrong, L. M., 321
Arndorfer, C. L., 469
Aronson, J., 264, 266
Arseneault, T., 105

Arsenio, W. F., 381
Arterberry, M. E., 153, 158–159, 318
Arunachalam, S., 288
Asare, M., 172
Asbridge, M., 93
Asendorpf, J. B., 388
Asher, S. R., 468, 470
Ashcraft, M. H., 243
Ashmead, D. H., 170
Aslin, R. N., 158, 280, 281, 282
Aspenlieder, L., 416
Astill, R. G., 122
Atkin, C., 480
Attanucci, J., 378
Attar-Schwartz, S., 445
Au, T. K., 287
Audley-Piotrowski, S., 476
Augustine, J. M., 485
Aunola, K., 433
Austin, C. M., 282
Awong, T., 353
Ayduk, O., 372
Azaiza, F., 347

B

Bachman, H. J., 491
Bachman, J. G., 486–487
Backscheider, A.G., 205
Baddeley, A., 195
Badzakova-Trajkova, G., 172
Baenninger, M., 409
Bagwell, C. L., 470
Bahrick, L., 154–155
Bahrick, L. E., 155, 318
Bailey, J. A., 434
Bailey, J. M., 420
Bailey, R. K., 164
Baillargeon, R., 201, 380
Baird, D. D., 90
Baker, J., 445
Baker, L., 237, 239
Baker, P. N., 88
Bakermans-Kranenburg, M. J., 72, 127, 325, 333, 335, 382
Bakken, J. P., 467
Bales, S. N., 24
Banaji, M. R., 359
Bandura, A., 29, 32, 415
Banerjee, R., 359, 454
Bannard, C., 301
Banny, A. M., 391
Barajas, R. G., 112
Barbaresi, W. J., 163
Barca, L., 234
Barker, E. D., 102–103

Barkley, R. A., 163, 164
Barling, J., 437
Barlow, D. H., 316
Barnes, C. D., 392
Barnett, M. A., 445
Baron, A. S., 359, 361
Baron-Cohen, S., 209
Barr, R., 114
Barrett, T. M., 226
Barros, R., 235
Bartik, T. J., 265
Bascoe, S. M., 467
Baskett, L. M., 448
Basso, K H., 126
Bates, E., 292
Bates, J. E., 328, 392, 432, 439
Bates, T. C., 233
Bauer, P. J., 216, 221
Baumeister, R. F., 354
Baumgartner, J. A., 160
Baumrind, D., 432
Bayatzis, R., 254
Bayley, N., 258
Beal, C. R., 239, 307
Beal, S. J., 485
Beauchaine, T., 164
Beauchamp, G. K., 83, 150
Bechtold, K. T., 420
Beck, E., 449
Becker, B. J., 412
Becker-Blease, K. A., 490
Beelmann, A., 361
Behnke, A. O., 353
Behnke, M., 91
Beier, J. S., 382
Belgrad, S. L., 307
Bell, N., 190
Belsky, J., 42, 46, 72, 127–128, 325, 473, 485
Bem, D. J., 422
Benbow, C. P., 261, 269
Benenson, J., 468
Benenson, J. F., 468
Benner, A. D., 361
Benson, J. B., 170
Benton, S. L., 238
Bereiter, C., 238
Berenbaum, S. A., 402, 405, 416, 420, 422
Berg, C. A., 412
Bergen, D., 465
Berger, C., 472
Berger, S. E., 168
Berk, L. E., 193
Berkman, E. T., 370, 373

Berko, J., 76, 298, 308
Berlin, L. J., 435, 455
Bernard, K., 335
Berndt, T. J., 469
Bernier, A., 192
Berntsen, D., 342
Bersoff, D. M., 378
Bertenthal, B. H., 167, 169–170
Berthier, N., 170
Berthier, N. E., 170
Best, D. L., 402
Best, J. R., 172, 482
Betts, N. T., 467
Beuker, K. T., 287
Bhutta, Z. A., 137
Bialystok, E., 294
Biddle, S. J. H., 172
Biederman, J., 163
Bierman, K. L., 391, 394
Bigler, R. S., 359–360, 364, 403,
    419, 422
Binet, A., 22, 258
Bingenheimer, J. B., 392
Birch, H. G., 322
Birch, S. A., 287
Biro, S., 202
Bitensky, S. H., 435
Bjerkedal, T., 449
Bjorklund, D. F., 195, 217, 219,
    330, 429
Black, C. M. D., 133
Black, J. E., 142
Black, M. M., 446
Blades, M., 480
Blair, B. L., 470
Blair, C., 264
Blakemore, J. E. O., 403
Blankson, A. M., 325
Blanton, H., 471
Block, J. H., 406
Bloom, L., 288, 301, 305, 307
Bloom, P., 285, 287, 380, 465
Blozis, S. A., 391
Boden, J. M., 354
Bohannon, J. N., 306
Böhm, R., 359
Bohn, A., 342
Boiger, M., 314
Boivin, M., 68–69, 470
Bomhof, E., 480
Bonds, T. A., 470
Bonnie, R. J., 142
Bonny, J. W., 244
Booth-LaForce, C., 333–334
Borch, C., 470
Bornstein, M. H., 90, 105, 109, 260, 291,
    318, 348, 466
Bortfeld, H., 282
Bos, H. M., 447
Bosaki, S. L., 379
Bosco, F. M., 464

Boseovski, J. J., 357
Bosma, H. A., 345
Bot, S. M., 470
Bouchard, T. J., 72, 262
Bowen, R., 344
Bowker, A., 173
Bowker, J. C., 354, 477
Bowlby, J., 329, 330
Bowman, L. L., 52
Boyer-Pennington, M., 219
Bradley, L., 234, 489
Brainerd, C. J., 187, 219–221
Brandone, A. C., 207
Braungart-Rieker, J. M., 315
Bravo, A., 469
Braza, P., 433
Brazelton, T. B., 109
Brechwald, W. A., 475
Brendgen, M., 71, 389, 470
Brennan, R. T., 392
Bretano, C., 444
Bretherton, I., 292
Briley, D. A., 73–74
Brindis, C. D., 473
Brinkman, B. J., 422
Brockington, I., 102
Brody, G. H., 438–439, 451
Brody, L. R., 411
Brody, N., 261
Bromley, D. B., 356
Bronfenbrenner, U., 262, 430
Brooker, R. J., 315
Brooks-Gunn, J., 89, 106, 174, 446, 455,
    485, 488
Brophy, J. E., 492
Brophy, M., 209
Brotman, L. M., 436
Brown, A. L., 237, 239
Brown, B. B., 467, 474
Brown, C. S., 363
Brown, E. G., 467
Brown, E.D., 488
Brown, J., 320, 347, 349, 451
Brown, K. D., 480
Brown, K. P., 477
Brown, P. J., 485
Brown, R., 237, 297
Brown, R. A., 111
Brown, R.P., 392
Brownell, K. D., 135
Brubacher, J. R., 93
Bruck, M., 223, 224
Brumariu, L. E., 334
Brummelman, E., 353
Brunsma, D. L., 347
Bryant, P., 235
Bryant, P. E., 234
Bryden, M. P., 409
Buchanan, C. M., 441
Buchanan, H., 230
Buckhalt, J. A., 123

Buckingham-Howes, S., 95
Buehler, C., 475
Bugental, D. B., 455, 457
Buijzen, M., 480
Bukowski, W., 464
Bukowski, W. M., 470
Bulf, H., 157
Bull, R., 195–196
Bullard, L., 444
Bullock, M., 342
Bumpus, M. F., 438
Burack, J. A., 454
Burani, C., 234
Burchinal, M., 292
Burchinal, M. R., 196, 485
Burger-Judisch, L. M., 141
Buriel, R., 431, 433
Burk, W. J., 470
Burke, R., 347
Burman, D. D., 408
Burnet, K. L., 449
Burnham, D., 155
Burraston, B., 470
Burt, S. A., 434
Burton, C. M., 474
Bush, T., 163
Bushman, B. J., 391
Busnel, M. C., 83
Buss, A. T., 167
Bussey, K., 415
Buttelmann, D., 44, 359, 361

C

Cai, H., 353
Cain, K., 236, 237
Caldera, Y. M., 466
Caldwell, M. S., 354
Calkins, S. D., 321, 476
Callaghan, T., 465
Callahan, C. M., 269
Calvert, S. L., 173, 479, 480
Cameron, L., 363
Campbell, A., 469
Campbell, F. A., 264
Campbell, J. M., 172
Campbell, M. E., 469
Campbell, R., 294
Campbell, W. K., 352
Campos, J. J., 158, 169
Camras, L. A., 116, 317, 314
Candel, I., 223
Cantrell, L., 241
Cao, R., 476
Capelli, C. A., 308
Capozzoli, M. C., 162
Caputi, M., 359
Caravolas, M., 234
Card, N. A., 391, 472
Carey, S., 201, 231, 361
Carlo, G., 353, 385–386
Carlson, J., 265, 268

Carlson, M. D., 473
Carlson, S. M., 192, 207, 261
Caro, I., 133
Carpendale, J. I. M., 358
Carpenter, M., 305, 382, 383, 384
Carpenter, R., 112
Carré, J. M., 389
Carrere, S., 439
Carrico, R. L., 170
Carroll, J. B., 252–253
Carroll, J. L., 112
Carskadon, M. A., 123
Carter, C. S., 385
Cartin, A., 101
Cartmill, C., 487
Caruso, D. R., 254
Carver, K., 472
Carver, P. R., 473
Casalin, S., 324
Case, T. I., 314
Caselli, M. C., 286
Casey, B. J., 141, 142
Cashon, C. H., 114
Casiglia, A. C., 476
Casper, D. M., 472
Caspi, A., 326, 370
Cassidy, J., 334, 335, 348
Castelli, L., 361
Castro, D. C., 294
Caudle, K., 142
Cauffman, E., 486
Cauvet, E., 288
Ceci, S. J., 219, 223
Cerankosky, B. C., 483
Cerella, J., 196
Champagne, F. A., 87
Champion, H., 307
Champion, T. B., 266
Chan, A., 468
Chan, H., 93
Chandler, M. J., 358
Chang, L., 395
Chang, Y., 135
Chanquoy, L., 239
Chao, R. K., 433
Chaplin, T. M., 411
Charney, D., 349
Chase-Lansdale, P. L., 89, 446
Chavajay, P., 229
Chen, E., 436, 489
Chen, Y., 209
Chen-Gaddini, M., 348
Chen, H., 433
Chen, J., 254
Chen, X., 325, 476
Chen, Z., 196
Chen, Z. Y., 449
Cheng, H., 444
Cheng, Z-J., 245
Chess, S., 322

Cheung, L. W. Y., 105
Cheung, W. W., 135
Chi, M. T. H., 218
Child, I. L., 433
Chisolm, D. J., 474
Chiu, M. M., 245
Choe, D. E., 439
Chomitz, V. R., 105
Chomsky, N., 299
Chorpita, B. F., 316
Chou, R. J. A., 449
Chow, B. W., 235
Chow, S., 439
Christakos, A., 468
Christensen, A., 439
Christodoulou, J. A., 144–145
Chung, H. L., 488
Cicchetti, D., 436, 453–455
Cillessen, A. H. N., 470, 477
Cipielewsi, J., 292
Claessens, A., 444
Clark, K. B., 363, 364
Clark, R., 105
Clarke, C. N., 445
Clarke, P. J., 272
Clarke-Stewart, K. A., 444
Clements, D. H., 239
Clifford, A., 91
Clifton, R. K., 151, 167, 169–170
Cnattingius, S., 91
Coall, D. A., 445
Coatsworth, J. D., 174
Coco, A. L., 476
Codd, J., 294
Coelho, J. S., 135
Coffman, J. L., 218
Cohen, M., 394
Cohen, S., 87
Cohen Kadosh, K., 142
Cohen, L.., 386
Cohen, L. B., 114
Cohen, R., 476
Cohen, R. W., 107
Coie, J. D., 388, 411
Colby, A., 377
Cole, C. A., 353
Cole, M., 192
Cole, P. M., 318, 321
Coleman-Jensen, A., 132
Colle, L., 319
Collins, R. L., 473
Collins, W. A., 334, 348, 472
Columbo, B., 90
Colwell, M. J., 465
Conboy, B. T., 301
Condry, J. C., 411
Conger, K. J., 391
Conger, R. D, 432, 489–490
Conroy, D. E., 174
Constantinescu, M., 420
Cook, E. C., 475

Cooke, L. J., 124
Cooney, T. M., 347
Cooper, H., 50
Coplan, R. J., 354, 466, 477
Copper, R. L., 87
Corballis, M. C., 172
Corbett, M., 137
Cornelius, M., 91
Correa-Chávez, M., 229
Corriveau, K. H., 287
Corwyn, R. F., 489
Cosmides, L., 314
Costa, P. T., 326
Costall, A., 314
Costin, S. E., 384
Côté, S. M., 388
Coughlin, C. A., 217
Coulton, C. J., 455
Courage, M.L., 153, 222, 480
Cousminer, D. L., 127
Coutelle, C., 98
Cowart, B. J., 150
Cox, M. J., 430, 436
Cox, S. J., 412
Coy, K. C., 371
Coyne, C. A., 88
Craig, K. D., 151
Craven, R. G., 350–351
Cremeens, P. R., 466
Crenshaw, T. M., 477
Creusere, M. A., 307
Crick, N. R., 108, 388, 392, 411, 469
Cristia, A., 283
Crnic, K. A., 105
Crocetti, E., 345
Crocker, J., 352
Crockett, L. J., 433, 485
Croker, S., 230
Crombleholme, T. M., 98
Crosnoe, R., 485
Crossman, A., 380
Crouter, A. C., 416, 438
Cruz, I., 283
Csizmadia, A., 347
Cueller, I., 347
Culbert, K. M., 133
Cummings, E., 390
Cummings, E. M., 38, 333, 430, 436, 439, 441, 491
Cumsille, P., 438
Cunningham, A. E., 235
Cunningham, W. A., 320
Currie, J., 92–93
Curtiss, S., 300
Curwin, A., 292
Cvencek, D., 403

D

Dadisman, K., 485
Dahl, A., 363
Dalege, J., 361

Danaher, D. L., 412
Daniels, H., 191
Dannemiller, J. L., 153, 158
Darling, H., 487
Darling, N., 438
David, A., 98
Davidov, M., 380
Davidson, D., 219
Davies, I., 153
Davies, L., 444
Davies, M., 324
Davies, P. T., 38, 436, 439
Davis, A. L., 138
Davis, E. F., 226
Davis, E. P., 87
Davis, K. M., 91
Davis, P. E., 465
Davis, P. T., 441
De Beni, R., 237
De Brauwer, J., 244
de Haan, M., 105, 161
de Weerth, C., 123–124
De Wolf, A., 47
De Wolff, M. S., 334
Deary, I., 252, 261
Deater-Deckard, K., 433
DeCasper, A. J., 84
Declercq, E., 101
Degner, J., 361
Dehaene, S., 296
Dekovic, M., 477
Del Giudice, M., 83, 319
del Valle, J. F., 469
Delaney, C., 111
DeLoache, J. S., 44–45, 216, 228, 231,
    293, 295, 318
Delva, J., 173
Dement, W. C., 112
Demir, A., 144
Denissen, J. A., 345
Denissen, J. J. A., 388
Denton, K., 378
Derlan, C. L., 361
deSchonen, S., 342
Desjardins, R. N., 282
DeSouza, A, 325
deVilliers, P. A., 298
Dewey, C., 169
Dewey, K. G., 123
Dews, S., 307
Diamond, A., 162, 196, 473
Dick-Read, G., 100
DiDonato, M. D., 422
Diego, M., 106
Diesendruck, G., 205
Dijkstra, J. K., 472
Dinella, L., 349
Dionne, G., 68–69, 290
DiPietro, J. A., 82–83, 87
Dishion, T. J., 470, 477
Divan, H. A., 93

Diversi, M., 352
Dixon, J. A., 300
DiYanni, C., 205
Djikstra, J.K., 470
Dobkins, K. R., 154
Docherty, S. J., 70
Dodd, B., 155
Dodge, K. A., 388, 392–394, 411, 432,
    455, 471
Dolenszky, E., 468
Donnellan, M. B., 354
D'Onofrio, B. M., 88, 95
Donovan, W. L., 371
Doornwaard, S. M., 474
Dorn, L. D., 126
Dornbusch, S. M., 487
Doumen, S., 345
Dove, H., 169
Dovey, T. M., 124
Down, J., 64
Doyle, J. M., 347
Dozier, M., 335
Draghi-Lorenz, R., 314
Drew, L. M., 447
Driscoll, A. K., 433
DuBois, D. L., 491
Duckworth, A. L., 261
Duncan, D. T., 474
Duncan, G., 265
Duncan, G. J., 455, 490, 493
Dunham, F., 292
Dunham, P. J., 292
Dunham, Y., 361
Dunifon, R., 445–446
Dunn, J., 209, 444, 451
Dunson, D. B., 90
Durham, M., 292
Durik, A. M., 105
Durston, S., 142
Dye, L., 132
Dykas, M. J., 334, 348

E

Eagly, A. H., 412, 423
Earls, F. J., 392
Easterbrook, M. A., 161
Ebbesen, E., 371
Ebstein, R. P., 72
Eccles, J. S., 485
Edwards, C. A., 475
Edwards, R. C., 102
Egan, S. K., 392, 395, 473
Egeland, B., 390, 436
Ehri, L., 234
Ehrlich, K. B., 348
Eiden, R. D., 95
Eime, R. M., 173
Eisenberg, N., 321, 327,
    382–385
Eisengart, J., 299
El Nokali, N. E., 491

El-Sheikh, M., 122
Elbert, T., 144
Elder, G. H., 349, 445,
    489–490
Elder, G. H. Jr., 347
Eliot, L., 408
Elkind, D., 344
Ellis, A. W., 234
Ellis, B. J., 54, 109, 128, 129
Ellis, L. A., 350–351
Ellis, M. L., 392
Ellis, S., 227
Ellis, W. E., 470
Ellis, W. K., 271
Else-Quest, N. M., 410–412
Emery, R. E., 130
Engel, S. M., 87
Englund, M. M., 334, 390, 436
Ennemoser, M., 479, 481
Eppe, S., 294
Erikson, E., 27–28, 32, 344, 463
Erixon, A., 422
Eskritt, M., 217
Espy, K. A., 91
Essex, M. J., 128
Evans, G. W., 489
Eyer, D. E., 102
Eyler, F. D., 91

F

Fabes, R. A., 319, 321, 382,
    385, 417
Fabricius, W. V., 441
Fagen, J., 216
Fahr, C. I. C. C., 254
Falbo, T., 353, 449
Falk, D., 109
Fang, F., 208
Fantuzzo, J. W., 193
Farr, R. H., 447
Farrar, M. J., 219
Farver, J. A., 389
Farver, J. M., 294, 395, 465
Fatani, S. S., 314
Fauth, R. C., 485
Faux, A. L., 154
Faw, G. D., 271
Fazel, S., 105
Feddes, A. R., 469
Feinberg, M. E., 451
Feldman Farb, A., 485
Feldman, H. M., 408
Feldman, R., 371
Fenson, P. S., 286, 290
Ferguson, R., 487
Fergusson, D. M., 88, 354
Fernald, A., 291
Fernyhough, C., 465
Ferrence, R., 487
Ferreol-Barbey, M., 237
Ferrero, J., 130

Ferry, A. L., 203
Fias, W., 244
Fidalgo, P., 239
Fidler, E., 61
Field, T., 102, 106
Field, T. M., 304, 331
Fierros, E., 255
Fifer, W. P., 112
Filisetti, L., 384
Fine, M., 352
Finkelhor, D., 483, 490
Finkelstein, B. D., 467
Finn-Stevenson, M., 268
Finnie, V., 466
Fireman, G., 319
Fischer, K., 145
Fischer, K. W., 145
Fisher, C., 299
Fisher, C. B., 24
Fisher, P. A., 370, 373
FitzGerald, D. P., 359
Fitzgerald, J., 239
Fivush, R., 221, 408
Flanagan, C., 441
Flavell, J. H., 185, 187, 218
Flom, R., 155, 318
Flook, L., 412
Flores, E., 454
Flynn, J. R., 263
Flynn, M., 394
Foehr, U. G., 478–479, 482
Fontaine, R. G., 392–393
Forbes, D., 412
Forssell, S. L., 447
Fortus, D., 230
Foster, E. M., 479
Foster, S. H., 305
Fowler, F., 432
Fox, N. A., 385
Fox, N. W., 325
Fox, S. E., 142
Frampton, K., 287
Francis, M., 239
Franklin, A., 153, 305
Franko, D. L., 133
Franquart-Declercq, C., 307
Frazier, B. N., 124
Fredricks, J. A., 485
French, K. E., 406
French, S. E., 346
Frensch, P. A., 409
Freud, S., 22, 27, 32, 463
Fried, A., 348
Friedman, O., 202, 464
Fu, G., 380
Fu, V. R., 433
Fuchs, L. S., 274
Fuhs, M. W., 244
Fuld, G. L., 391
Fuligni, A. J., 123, 344, 346
Fuller-Thomson, E., 446

Furlan, S., 229
Furman, W., 133, 334, 448, 472
Furukawa, E., 317
Fuson, K. C., 243

G
Gable, S., 135
Gaddis, L., 327
Gagliardi, A., 104
Gagne, J. R., 71, 412
Gallagher, K. C., 326
Galliher, R. V., 363
Gallimore, R., 245
Galloway, J. C., 168
Galván, A., 142
Garber, J., 320
García Coll, C., 347, 493
Garcia, M. M., 452
Garciaguirre, J. S., 167
Gardner, H., 253–255, 257
Gardner, M., 174
Gardner, W., 227
Garnier, H., 423
Gartrell, N. K., 447
Gartstein, M. A., 325, 326
Gass, K., 451
Gastic, B., 468
Gathercole, S. E., 290
Gaulin, S. J. C., 314, 330
Gauthier, R., 464
Gauvain, M., 130, 190, 191
Gaylord, S., 216
Gdula, J. A., 437
Ge, X., 438–439
Geary, D. C., 244, 261, 274, 330, 417, 420
Gelman, R., 242, 305
Gelman, S., 404–405
Gelman, S. A., 188, 200, 202, 204–206, 209, 290, 357, 403, 416
Gentile, D., 483
Gentile, D. A., 482
George, C., 335
George, J. B. F., 133
Georgieff, M. K., 87
Geren, J., 301
Gernald, L., 132
Gerry, D. W., 154
Gershkoff-Stowe, L., 289
Gershoff, E. T., 390, 435
Gertner, Y., 299
Gesell, A., 26
Gest, S. D., 475
Ghetti, S., 217–218, 223
Giannino, L., 24
Gibbs, D. A., 378, 455
Gibbs, J. C., 377
Gibson, E., 158
Giedd, J. N., 410
Gilbreth, J. G., 444
Giles, J. W., 403

Gillen-O'Neel, C., 123
Gilligan, C., 378
Gilmore, C. K., 296
Gineste, M., 307
Gingo, M., 381
Ginsburg-Block, M. D., 193
Giordano, G., 258
Girard, A., 68–69
Gizer, I. R., 163
Gleason, T. R., 465
Glick, G. C., 470
Glusman, M., 287
Göbel, S. M., 244
Godleski, S. A., 411
Godwin, J., 393
Goeke-Morey, M. C., 437
Goh, Y. I., 86–87
Gold, J., 381
Goldberg, N. G., 447
Goldfield, B. A., 290
Goldin-Meadow, S., 144, 286, 287, 305
Goldsmith, H. H., 412
Goldstein, M. H., 284
Goldstein, S., 163
Goleman, D., 254
Golinkoff, R. M., 286, 287, 290, 305
Golombok, S., 447
Gondoli, D. M., 348
Good, M., 391
Good, T. L., 416
Goodman, S. H., 102
Goodnow, J. J., 386, 433
Goodwyn, S., 286
Goossens, L., 345
Gordon, C. P., 473
Gordon, R. A., 89
Gormley, W., 265
Gosso, Y., 465
Goswami, U., 144
Gottfried, G. M., 204
Gottman, J. M., 434, 439, 465
Goubet, N., 151
Gough, P. B., 236
Govier, E., 409
Govindshenoy, M., 456
Grabe, S., 133
Graber, J. A., 130
Graesser, A. C., 237
Graham, A. M., 370, 373
Graham-Bermann, S. A., 390
Graham, J., 469
Graham, S., 239, 361, 394, 395
Graham, S. A., 307
Grammer, J., 218
Grammer, J. K., 217
Granier-Deferre, C., 83
Grantham-McGregor, S., 132
Graves, R., 284
Gray-Little, B., 352

Gray, S. W., 263
Graziano, P. A., 476
Greenberg, M. T., 105, 394
Greene, B., 349
Greene, J., 381
Greene, K. E., 345
Greenough, W. T., 142
Greenwald, A. G., 403
Gregory, A., 492
Gregory, A. M., 349, 385
Greitemeyer, T., 391
Grewal, D., 254
Grigorenko, E. J., 255
Grigorenko, E. L., 262, 268
Gripshover, S. J., 125
Groen, G. J., 243
Gross, J. J., 320
Grosse, G., 306
Grossman, T., 318
Grotevant, H. D., 450
Grotpeter, J. K., 411
Grusec, J. E., 353, 386,
    432, 466
Grysman, A., 222, 410
Guacci-Franco, N., 469
Guerra, N. G., 395
Guimond, A. B., 346
Gulko, J., 405
Gunderson, E. A., 37, 242
Güngör, D., 348
Gunnar, M. R., 489
Gunter, B., 480
Gurucharri, C., 358
Guxens, M., 93

H
Häberling, I. S., 172
Haden, C. A., 221
Haeffel, G. J., 349
Hafdahl, A. R., 352
Hahn, C-S., 260
Hahn, E. R., 202
Haimerl, F., 111
Haith, M. M., 170
Hale, L., 136
Hale, S., 196
Halford, G. S., 195
Halford, J. C. G., 124
Halgunseth, L. C., 433
Halim, M. L., 416, 420
Hall, G. S., 22, 340
Hall, J. A., 411
Hall, L. K., 227
Hallinan, M. T., 469
Halpern. D. F., 408–410, 421
Halpern, L. F., 112
Halpern-Meekin, S., 444
Halverson, C. F., 419
Hamamura, T., 353
Hamilton, B. E., 89
Hamlin, J. K., 361, 380

Hamm, J. V., 469–470
Hammen, C, 348
Hane, A. A., 325
Haney, E. A., 261
Hankin, B. L., 412
Hannon, E. E., 151
Hansen, D. J., 454
Hansen, D. M., 485
Hanson, K. G., 480
Happaney, K., 455
Harden, K. P., 73–74, 473
Haria, P., 238
Hariri, A. R., 389
Harkness, K. L., 454
Harlow, H. F., 330
Harlow, M. K., 330
Harms, M. B., 207
Harre, N., 344
Harris, K. R., 239
Harris, P. L., 287
Harrison, K., 136
Harrist, A. W., 466
Harter, K., 436
Harter, S., 351–354, 422
Hartmann, D. P., 467
Hartup 101, 416
Hartup, W. W., 467, 470
Hastings, P. D., 382, 439
Hatton, D., 164
Hatzenbuehler, M. L., 474
Hawley, P. H., 475
Hay, D. F., 388, 411
Hayes, T. C., 292, 392
Hayne, H., 222
Hazell, P. L., 164
Heavey, C. L., 439
Hebl, M., 372–373
Hedges, L. V., 50
Heffernan, K., 133
Heiges, K. L., 441
Heine, S. J., 353
Heinmiller, B. M., 151
Heitzeg, M. M., 327
Helfand, M., 473
Hembacher, E., 217
Hemker, L., 159
Henderson, C. E., 445
Henderson, L. M., 122
Henderson, N. D., 261
Henry, D. B., 470
Henson, R., 475
Hepach, R., 382
Hepburn, C. G., 437
Herald-Brown, S. L., 477
Herlitz, A., 410
Herman, M., 352
Hernandez, D. J., 446
Hernandez-Reif, M., 106
Herrera, M. G., 132
Herrnstein, R. J., 266
Hershkowitz, I., 224

Hertwig, R., 445
Hespos, S. J., 201, 203
Hess, U., 317
Hetherington, E. M., 441
Heyman, G. D., 356, 403
Hibbert, J. R., 438
Hiebert, J., 245
Higashibara, F., 317
Hilden, K., 216–218
Hill, E., 283
Hill, J. L., 106
Hill-Soderlund, A. L., 315
Hillman, C. H., 172
Hines, M., 420
Hipwell, A. E., 473
Hirsh-Pasek, K., 286, 287, 290
Hitlin, S., 347
Ho, C. S., 243
Hodges, E. V., 391
Hodnett, E. D., 101
Hoff, E., 287, 290, 294, 304
Hoff, E. L., 283–284, 298, 300
Hoff-Ginsberg, E., 433
Hogan, A. M., 103
Hogan, D. M., 196
Hogge, W. A., 93
Hohmann, L. M., 465
Holden, G. W., 431
Hollich, G. J., 286–287
Holowka, S., 284
Hood, B., 201
Hood, L., 307
Hooven, C., 434
Hopkins, B., 168
Horowitz, F. D., 269
Horwood, L. J., 354
Hostinar, C. E., 489
Hough, L., 261
Houston, D. M., 281
Houts, R. M., 42, 46, 72,
    128, 473
Howard, M. R., 302
Howe, M. L., 222
Howes, C., 464
Huang, L., 371
Hudson, J. A., 222, 226, 410
Huesmann, L. R., 480
Hughes, J. M., 364
Huguley, J., 362
Huizenga, M., 316
Hulit, L. M., 302
Hulme, C., 234, 271–272, 274
Hunt, E., 265, 268
Hunt, J. M., 263
Hunter, J., 261
Hurtado, N., 291
Hurts, K., 482
Huston, A. C., 24, 479–481,
    485, 490
Hutchins, E., 256
Hutchinson, D. M., 133

Huth-Bocks, A. C., 334
Huttenlocher, J., 242, 291, 292
Huynh, V. W., 123, 344
Hyde, D. C., 241
Hyde, J. S., 105, 133, 378, 410, 412, 413, 416, 422
Hymel, S., 476

I

Iervolino, A. C., 420
Immordino-Yang, M. H., 145
Inhelder, B., 186
Isaacs, J., 395
Ispa, J. M., 433
Israel, A. C., 453, 457
Issanchou, S., 150
Iverson, J. M., 286
Izard, C. E., 314

J

Jaccard, J., 471
Jack, F., 222
Jacklin, C., 406
Jacklin, C. N., 408, 410–411, 412, 416
Jacobi, C., 133
Jacobs, J. E., 230
Jacobson, J. L., 92–93, 95
Jacobson, S. W., 92–93, 95
Jaffee, S., 88–89, 378
Jagnow, C. P., 83
Jahromi, L. B., 321
James, S., 441
James, W., 342
Jansen, B. R. J., 316
Jansen, J., 123–124
Janssens, J. M., 477
Järvinen, L., 255
Jenkins, E., 243
Jenkins, J., 451
Jensen, J. L., 167
Jensen, L. A., 41
Jiao, Z., 470
Jipson, J. L., 205
Jirout, J., 230
Jochen, P., 483
John, O. P., 320
Johnson, K. A., 163
Johnson, L., 264
Johnson, M. H., 161
Johnson, S. C., 335
Johnston, L. D., 173
Jokela, M., 448
Jones, D. C., 130, 384
Jones, L. C., 359
Jones, L. M., 483
Jones, M. D., 363
Jordan, A. C., 330
Jordan, N. C., 243, 274
Jose, P. E., 485
Joseph, D. L., 254
Joussemet, M., 389

Jovanic, B., 170
Jovenen, J., 394
Joyner, K., 472
Juffer, F., 50, 335
Jusczyk, P. W., 151, 280–282
Juvonen, J., 394–395

K

Kagan, J., 325
Kaijura, H., 150
Kail, R. V., 197, 227, 229
Kalil, A., 437
Kalish, C. W., 205
Kam, C.-M., 476
Kane, J. B., 441
Kao, G., 347
Kaplan, H., 169
Kaplan, N., 335
Karasik, L. B., 169
Karau, S. J., 412
Karevold, E., 349
Kärnä, A., 395
Karniol, R., 171
Karraker, K. H., 403
Karrass, J., 315
Kärtner, J., 342
Katz, L. F., 434, 437, 441
Katz-Wise, S. L., 416
Kaufman, J., 261, 349
Kaufman, J. C., 251, 255, 256
Kaufman, S. B., 255
Kavsek, B., 105
Kawabata, Y., 469
Kawakami, K., 325
Keane, S. P., 476, 477
Kearney, C. A., 317
Keating, D. P., 351
Keijsers, L., 390
Keil, F. C., 205, 206, 307
Keith, B., 440–442
Kelemen, D., 205
Kell, H. J., 269
Keller, P., 123
Kelley, K., 326
Kellman, P. J., 153, 139, 158–159
Kelly, D., 244
Kelly, J., 441
Kelly, P., 457
Keltner, D., 385
Kendall, J., 164
Kendrick, C., 451
Kennell, H. H., 102
Kenny, L. C., 88
Kerns, K. A., 334
Kerr, M., 130
Kerr, S., 239
Kessler, B., 233
Khalil, A., 90
Khashan, A. S., 88
Khurana, A., 473

Kiang, L., 347
Kidd, E., 301, 465
Kidd, K. K., 268
Kilgore, K., 432
Killen, M., 363
Kim, J.-Y., 451
Kim, P., 489
Kim-Spoon, J., 454
Kim, S.Y., 347
Kim, T.-Y., 438
Kindermann, T. A., 475
King, S., 87
King, V., 444
Kinzler, K. D., 198, 287
Kipnis, O., 472
Kirby, D., 473
Kirkorian, H. L., 480
Kirouac, G., 317
Kisilevsky, B. S., 83
Kithakye, M., 491
Kitzman, H. J., 89
Klaczynski, P. A., 228, 230
Klahr, A. M., 230, 434
Klaus, M., 102
Klaus, R. A., 263
Klein, P. S., 371
Klemencic, N., 137
Klemfuss, J. Z., 223
Klimstra, T. A., 345
Klump, K. L., 133
Klute, M. M., 385
Knibbe, R. A., 130
Knight, G. P., 385–386
Kochanska, G., 316, 327, 371
Koenig, M. A., 207
Koepke, S., 345
Koh, J. B. K., 222, 342
Kohlberg, L., 374–378, 418
Kokis, J. V., 229
Kokko, K., 389
Kolb, B., 144
Kolberg, K. J. S., 90
Koller, S., 383
Kominski, R. A., 293
Konijn, E. A., 391
Kopp, C. B., 370
Koren, G., 86–87
Kornhaber, M., 255
Koss, K. J., 40
Kowal, A., 451
Kowalski, P. S., 352
Krajcik, J., 230
Kramer, L., 451–452
Krebs, D. L., 358, 378
Kreppner, J. M., 450
Kretch, K. E., 168
Krettenauer, T., 383
Krishnakumar, A., 446
Krispin O., 476
Kroger, J., 345
Krogh, H. R., 403

Kronenberg, M. E., 491
Krull, J. L., 135
Kucirkova, N., 320
Kuhl, P. K., 281, 282, 283
Kuhn, D., 230, 232
Kulkofsky, S., 222
Kumar, V., 57
Kunkel, D., 481
Kunnen, E. S., 345
Kuntsche, E., 130
Kuppens, S., 390
Kuryluk, A., 476

L

Lackner, C., 209
Lacourse, E., 389
Ladd, B. K., 394–395
Ladd, G. W., 349, 394–395,
    466, 477
LaFreniere, P., 71, 464
Lagattuta, K., 319
Lagattuta, K. H., 319, 320
Lagattuta, K. N., 379
LaGreca, A. M., 316, 474,
    477, 491
Laible, D. J., 320, 353
Laird, R. D., 142
Lake, M. A., 403
Lamaze, F., 100
Lamb, L. M., 422, 484
Lamb, M., 224
Lamb, M. E., 331, 476
Landerl, K., 272
Landis, T., 284
Langabeer, K. A., 473
Lansford, J. E., 440–442
Lanthier, R., 448
Laris, B. A., 473
Larsen, J. T., 319
Larson, R. W., 485
Lau, J. Y., 349
Laursen, B., 348, 467, 470
Lawton, C. I., 132
Lazardis, M., 342
Leaper, C., 408, 416, 418
Lears, M., 418
Leavitt, L. A., 371
Lecanuet, J. P., 83
Leclercq, A-L., 290
Ledebt, A., 169
Lee, J., 218
Lee, J. M., 486
Lee, K., 162, 195–196, 217, 379
Lee, M. R., 392
Lee, P. C., 164
Lee, S., 245
Lee, S. A., 296
Lee, S. J., 390
Lee, V. E., 441
Leekam, S. R., 209
Leerkes, E. M., 325

LeFevre, J., 235
Legare, C. H., 188, 205, 403
Leinaweaver, J., 484
Leinonen, J., 489–490
Lengua, L. J., 326, 327, 442
Lenroot, R. K., 410
Lentz, C., 432
Leon, K., 441
Leppänen, J. M., 318
Lerner, R. M., 24
Leslie, A. M., 202, 464
Leventhal, T., 488
Leventon, S. J., 216
Levine, L. E., 52
Levine, S. C., 144, 242, 409
Levitt, A. G., 284
Levitt, J. L., 469
Levitt, M. J., 469
Levitt, P., 142
Levy, B. A., 233
Levy, G. D., 416
Levy, S. R., 364
Lewis, C., 331
Lewis, M., 314–317, 325,
    331, 342
Lewis, M. D., 321
Lewkowicz, D. J., 154
Lewontin, R. C., 265
Li-Grining, C.P., 370
Li, W., 484
Li, Y., 475
Liben, L. S., 360, 403, 419
Lichtenberger, E. O., 261
Lickliter, R., 154–155
Liebal, K., 287
Lieberman, E., 105
Lillard, A. S., 465
Lim, V. K. G., 438
Limber, S., 315
Limpo, T., 239
Lin, C. C., 433
Lin, W., 449
Lindberg, S. M., 409
Lindsay, D. S., 223
Lindsey, E. W., 465–466
Linebarger, D. L., 293
Linn, M. C., 410
Linn, S., 480
Linver, M. R., 174
Lippsitt, L. P., 112
Liu, D., 357
Liu, H.- M., 282, 283
Liu, R. X., 449
Livesley, W. J., 356
Lizkowski, U., 305
Lobelo, F., 173
Lobliner, D. B., 359
Lobo, M. A., 168
Lobo, S. A., 168
LoBue, V., 318
Lochman, J. E., 392

Locke, J., 22, 28
Lockl, K., 217
Lonigan, C. J., 294
Loomans, E. M., 87
Looney, L., 384
Loper, A. B., 445
Lopez, A. B., 344
Lopez, M., 469
Lorch, R. F., 231–232
Lorenz, C., 26
Loucky, J., 423
Loughlin, G. M., 112
Lourenco, S. F., 244
Lovén, J., 410
Lubinski, D., 261, 269–270
Ludwig, J., 264
Luecken, L. J., 441
Luke, N., 454
Lukowski, A. F., 216
Lumley, M. N., 454
Lung, F-W., 169
Lushington, K., 112
Luthar, S. S., 485
Lütkenhaus, P., 342
Luyckx, K., 345
Lynam, D., 411
Lynne-Landsman, S. D., 130
Lyster, S. H., 234
Lytton, H., 415

M

MacArthur, C., 238
Maccoby, E. E., 406, 408,
    410–412, 416, 416–417, 438
MacDonald, K., 71
MacEvoy, J. P., 468
Mackey, A. P., 482
Mackie, D. M., 402
MacWhinney, B., 302
Madden, C. M., 308
Magee, L., 136
Maggi, S., 438
Magnuson, K., 265, 490
Maguire, A. M., 98
Maguire, E. A., 144
Mahoney, J. L., 485–486
Main, M., 335
Majerus, S., 290
Makhijani, M. G., 412
Malinosky-Rummell, R., 454
Malone, P. S., 394
Malti, T., 383
Mandara, J., 347
Mandel, D. R., 151
Mangelsdorf, S. C., 315
Mannering, A. M., 465
Mao, P., 135
Maratsos, M., 298, 301
Marchman, V. A., 291, 300
Marcia, J. E., 344–345
Marcus, G. F., 298

Mareschal, D., 200
Margett, T. E., 205
Margolin, G., 483
Markman, E. M., 125, 287
Markovits, H., 468
Marks, A. K., 347, 493
Marlier, L., 150
Marschik, P. B., 172
Marsh, H. W., 350–351, 354, 488
Marshal, M. P., 474
Martel, M. M., 412
Martin, C. L., 402, 405, 416,
    417–419, 422
Martin, J. A., 89, 101, 417
Martin, J. L., 411, 415
Martin, M. J., 436
Martin, R. P., 327
Martinez, M. E., 107
Martínez, M. L., 438
Marzolf, D., 315
Masten, A. S., 391, 491
Masur, E. F., 292
Matheson. C. C., 464
Matjasko, J. L., 485
Matthews, D., 301
Mattys, S. L., 282
Matusov, E., 190
Mauer, D., 465
Maurer, D., 154
Mayer, E. V., 370
Mayer, J. D., 254
Maynard, A. E., 451
Maynard, A. M., 344
Mazur, E., 442
McAlister, A. R., 209
McBurney, D. H., 314, 330
McCabe, J. E., 103
McCabe, M., 353
McCabe, M. P., 133
McCall, R. B., 260
McCarthy, S., 296
McCartney, K., 73
McCartt, A. T., 142
McCarty, C. A., 349
McCarty, M. E., 170
McCloskey, L. A., 306
McCormack, T. A., 227–228
McCormick, C. B., 218
McCormick, C. M., 389
McCoy, J. K., 451
McCutchen, D., 239
McDermott, J. M., 450
McDonald, K. L., 470
McElwain, N. L., 333–334
McGee, L. M., 237–238
McGlothlin, H., 363
McGraw, M. B., 167
McGuire, S., 451
McHale, J. P., 437
McHale, S. M., 346, 348, 416, 438,
    451–452

McKee, A., 254
McLanahan, S., 441
McLatchie, N., 391
McLellan, J. A., 386
McLeod, K., 217
McMahon, R. J., 390
McMurray, B., 286
McNeil, N., 227
McNeil, N. M., 244
McQuade, J. D., 392
McRae, R. R., 326
McShane, K., 382
Meadows, S. O., 349
Meaney, M. J., 71
Meck, E., 242
Medin, D., 206
Medwell, J., 239
Meeus, W., 345
Mehta, C. M., 469
Meins, E., 465
Meland, 172
Melby, J. N., 433
Melby-Lervåg, M., 234
Melson, G. F., 466
Meltzoff, A. N., 319, 403
Mendes, W. B., 489
Mendle, J., 130, 473
Mennella, J. A., 83, 150
Mermelstein, R., 412
Mesquita, B., 314
Messer, D., 192
Metcalfe, J. S., 167
Metzger, A., 379, 485
Meyer, M., 200
Mezulis, A. H., 412
Michel, G. F., 172
Midgette, E., 238
Miga, E. M., 437
Miles, S., 391
Miles, S. B., 391
Miller, D. I., 408–410, 421
Miller, J. G., 378, 436
Miller, K. F., 228, 231,
    243, 295
Miller, M. M., 412
Miller, P. C., 431
Miller, P. H., 188
Miller, P.M., 412
Miller, R. L., 164
Miller, S. A., 359
Miller, T. W., 164
Mills, C. M., 307
Mills-Koonce, W. R., 335
Milunsky, A., 65
Minkler, M., 446
Minkel, W., 415, 370–373
Mitchell, K. J., 483
Mitchell, P., 307
Mix, K. S., 242
Mize, J., 434, 467, 477
Moffitt, T. E., 327–328, 370, 389

Molfese, D. L., 141
Molina, B. S. G., 164
Mollnow, E., 93
Molloy, L. E., 475
Molnar, D. S., 95
Monahan, K. C., 475, 486
Mondloch, C. J., 161
Moneta, G., 485
Monk, C., 87
Monk, C. S., 141
Monker, J., 292
Monson, T. C., 392, 395
Montague, D. P., 318
Moore, C. F., 92
Moore, K. L., 64
Mora, J. O., 132
Morais, M. L. S., 465
Moreno, A. J., 385
Morgan, J. L., 282
Morgan, P. L., 164
Morgane, P. L., 132
Morris, P., 262, 430
Morrison, T., 279
Morrissey, T. W., 485
Morrongiello, B. A., 137
Morrow, J. R., 172
Mortimer, J. T., 487
Morton, J., 161
Moses, L. J., 318
Mounts, N. S., 466
Mueller, M. M., 445
Muenchow, S., 264
Munroe, R. L., 190
Murphy, K. R., 163
Murphy, N., 192
Murray, C., 266
Murray-Close, D., 163
Murray, K. T., 371
Murray, V. M., 488
Mustonen, U., 441
Muter, V., 236
Muzio, J. N., 112
Myers, M. M., 112
Mylander, C., 305

N
Nadig, A. S., 306
Nahar, B., 132
Naigles, L., 290
Naigles, L. G., 290
Nakagawa, N., 308
Nancekivell, S. E., 202
Nánez, J. Sr., 159
Nangle, D. W., 472
Narayan, A. J., 390, 436, 491
Nation, K., 237, 273
Neblett, E. W., 347
Needham, A., 226
Neiss, M. B., 353
Nelissen, M., 445
Nelson, C. A., 141, 142, 156, 161, 318

Nelson, E. A. S., 111
Nelson, E. L., 172
Nelson, I. A., 468
Nelson, K., 221, 285, 292
Nesdale, D., 359
Nettle, D., 445
Nevid, J. S., 349
Neville, H. J., 162
Newcomb, A. F., 470
Newcombe, N., 188, 198, 409
Newcombe, N. S., 409
Newman, D. A., 254
Newman, G. E., 206
Newman, R., 282
Newport, E. L., 281, 282, 300
Ngon, C., 282
Nguyen, S. P., 403
Ni, Y., 245
Nicklaus, S., 150
Nigg, J. T., 164, 327
Nije Bijvank, M., 391
Nilsen, E. S., 307
Nilson, P., 138
Nisbett, R. E., 263, 265, 407
Nishida, T. K., 465
Nishina, A., 394
Noack, P., 469
Nord, M., 132
Nordine, J., 230
Norlander, T., 422
Notaro, P. C., 209
Novin, S., 320
Nucci, L., 379, 380, 381
Nugent, J. K., 109
Nunes, T., 235
Nurmi, J.-E., 433
Nurmsoo, E., 287
Nyaradi, A., 132

O

Oakes, L. M., 160
Oakhill, J. V., 236
Oaten, M., 314
Oates, C., 480
Oberlander, S. E., 446
O'Brien, M., 269, 325
O'Brien, T., 98
O'Connor, S., 485
O'Connor, T., 87
O'Connor, T. G., 444
Odgers, C. L., 488
O'Doherty, K., 293
Offer, E., 347
O'Hara, M. W., 102, 103
O'Hara, R. E., 480
Ojanen, T., 353
Okagaki, L., 409
Okami, P., 112
Olejnik, S., 327
Oliner, P. M., 385
Oliner, S. P., 385

Olinghouse, N. G., 239
Olmstead, R., 112
Olsen, B., 319
Olsen, S. L., 321
Olson, S. L., 439
Olszewski-Kubilius, P., 269, 270
O'Malley, P. M., 173
O'Neal, E. E., 138
O'Neil, R., 466
O'Neill, D. K., 306
Ontai, L. L., 320
Ooi, L., 466
Opfer, J. E., 202, 206, 241
Oppliger, P. A., 418
Oriña, M. M., 472
Ornstein, P., 218
Ornstein, P. A., 218
Orth, U., 354
Osofsky, J. D., 491
Osterholm, E. A., 87
Osterman, L. L., 392
Ostrov, J. M., 411
Oswald, F. L., 261
Otta, A., 465
Oude Luttikhuis, H., 136
Ouellet-Morin, I., 72
Over, H., 382, 384
Owen, L., 480
Owens, D. L., 164
Ozturk, O., 153

P

Pahlke, E., 422
Pajares, F., 218
Paley, B., 430, 436
Palladino, P., 237
Palmer, S. B., 281
Parault, S. J., 218
Parente, M. E., 485–486
Park, G., 261
Parke, R. D., 431, 433, 466
Parker, J., 464
Parker, J. G., 354, 470
Parritz, R. H., 321
Partanen, E., 84
Parten, M., 464
Pascalis, O., 156, 161, 281
Pasco Fearon, R. M., 42, 46, 72, 128, 473
Pascual, B., 209
Pascual-Leone, J., 377
Pasley, K., 444
Pasterski, V. L., 421
Patchin, J. W., 483
Patel, S., 216
Pathman, T., 216
Patterson, C. J., 447
Patterson, G. R., 390, 435
Patterson, M. M., 359–360
Patton, F., 347
Pauletti, R. E., 355

Paulhus, D. L., 353
Paulussen-Hoogeboom, M. C., 439
Paus, T., 140
Peake, P. K., 372–373
Pears, K. C., 454
Pearson, J., 474
Pedersen, S., 469
Pederson, D. R., 335
Pellegrini, A. D., 429
Pellis, S. M., 468
Pellis, V. C., 468
Peltola, M. J., 318
Perin, D., 239
Perkins, D. F., 172
Perone, S., 167
Perry, D. G., 353, 392, 395, 473
Perry, T. B., 469
Persaud, T. V. N., 64
Pérusse, D., 68–69
Petersen, J. L., 133
Peterson, C., 222
Peterson, C. C., 208, 209
Peterson, L., 384
Petitto, L. A., 284
Petrass, L. A., 137
Petrill, S. A., 262–263
Pettit, G. S., 392, 432, 434, 466–467
Pettoni, A. N., 92
Phillips, D., 264
Phinney, J. S., 346, 347
Phipps, M. G., 473
Piaget, J., 30, 32, 35, 179–191, 193, 197–198, 201, 225, 343, 345, 357–358, 374–375, 383, 463
Pianta, R. C., 492
Piasta, S. B., 235
Piehler, T. F., 470
Pierce, K. M., 485
Pierroutsakos, S. L., 228, 231, 295
Pilling, M., 153
Pina, A. A., 317
Pinette, M. G., 101
Piolat, A., 237
Pisoni, D. B., 151, 280
Place, S., 294
Plante, I., 408
Plewis, I., 111
Plomin, R., 69–70, 74, 262–263
Plucker, J. A., 255
Pluess, M., 325, 485
Poehlmann, J., 106
Polit, E. F., 449
Pollett, T. V., 445
Polman, J. L., 193
Pomerantz, E. M., 245, 433, 438
Poole, D., 224
Poole, D. A., 223, 224
Popliger, M., 380

Popp, D., 470
Porter, R. H., 150
Posner, M. I., 162
Poulin, F., 468, 469, 470
Poulson, C. I., 284
Poulton, R., 370
Powers, C. J., 391, 392
Powlishta, K. K., 405
Prasada, S., 201
Premack, D., 380
Pressley, M., 216–218, 238
Priel, B., 342
Priess, H. A., 416
Prihoda, T. J., 93
Principe, G. F., 223
Prinstein, M. J., 474–475, 477
Prior, M. R., 209
Prot, S., 480
Protzko, J., 264
Provins, K. A., 172
Puhl, R. M., 135
Pulkkinen, L., 389
Punamaki, R-L., 489–490
Putnam, S. P., 321, 326

Q
Qin, L., 438
Quas, J. A., 222
Quillian, L., 469

R
Raabe, T., 361
Racz, S. J., 390
Raedeke, T. D., 174
Rakic, P., 140
Rakison, D. H., 200, 202
Rakoczy, H., 465
Ralph, L. J., 473
Raman, L., 205
Ramey, C. T., 264
Ramey, S. L., 264
Ramsay, D., 342
Ramsay, D. S., 325
Rancourt, S., 133
Rankin, D. B., 467
Rapee, R. M., 133
Raskauskas, J., 394
Rathus, S. A., 349
Raudenbush, S. W., 286
Rayner, K., 235–236
Ready, D. D., 408
Reddy, V., 314
Reese, E., 221
Reich, P. A., 286
Reid, D. H., 271
Reid, M. J., 164
Reid, R., 239
Reimer, M. S., 316
Reiser, M., 477
Repacholi, B. M., 319
Resnick, L. B., 243
Reyna, V. F., 219–221, 229

Reynolds, A. J., 457
Reznick, J. S., 282, 290
Rhoades, K. A., 436
Rhodes, M., 359, 404–405
Ricciardelli, L. A., 133
Richgels, D. J., 237–238
Richland, L. E., 196
Richters, J. E., 164
Rideout, R., 222
Rideout, V., 478–479, 482
Riina, E. M., 348
Riksen-Walraven, J. M., 123–124
Rinderman, H., 265
Rips, L. J., 203
Ritchie, S. J., 233
Rivas-Drake, D., 347
Roben, C. K. P., 321
Roberts, D., 446
Roberts, J. E., 292, 478–479, 482
Roberts, W., 383
Robertson, D. L., 457
Robinson, E. J., 307
Robinson, J. L., 385
Robinson, M., 242
Robinson, S. R., 169
Roby, A. C., 465
Rochat, P., 342, 464
Rocissano, L., 307
Rodeck, C. H., 98
Roesch, L., 412
Roffwarg, H. P., 112
Rogers, L. A., 239
Rogoff, B., 190, 192, 227, 229
Rogosch, F. A., 454
Rohrbeck, C. A., 193
Romney, D. M., 415
Rood, L., 412
Roschelle, J. M., 482
Rose, A. J., 417, 470
Rose, S. A., 260
Rosengren, K. S., 205, 295
Ross, D. F., 411
Ross, H., 452
Ross, H. S., 411, 415
Ross, M., 222
Ross, N., 206
Rotenberg, K. J., 370
Roth, J., 174
Roth, J. L., 174, 485
Rothbart, M. K., 162, 320, 323–324, 326
Rothbaum, F., 333
Rotherman-Borus, M. J., 473
Rovee-Collier, C., 114, 215
Rowe, M. L., 286, 291
Rowland, C. F., 298
Rowley, S. J., 405
Rubenstein, O., 196
Rubin, C. M., 395
Rubin, K., 467

Rubin, K. H., 354, 439, 464, 477
Ruble, D. N., 352, 402, 405, 416, 418, 419, 420
Rudolph, K. D., 130, 348–349, 394
Rudy, D., 433
Ruff, H. A., 162
Rulison, K. L., 475
Runyan, D. K., 453–454
Rushton, J. P., 470
Russell, A., 466
Russell, J. A., 315
Russell, S. T., 433, 447
Rutland, A., 469
Rutter, M., 144
Ryan, R. M., 444
Rymer, R., 300

S
Sadek, S., 395
Saewyc, E. M., 474
Saffran, J. R., 151, 281, 282, 283
Sagi, A., 336
Sagi-Schwartz, A., 333
Sahni, R., 112
Sais, E., 294
Sakkalou, E., 207
Salisbury, G., 409
Salmivalli, C., 395
Salovey, P., 254
Sameroff, A. J., 34, 439
San Souci, P., 216
Sanders, M., 436
Sandler, I., 443
Sandler, I. N., 442
Sandman, C. A., 87
Sandrin, D., 150
Sangrigoli, S., 161
Sann, C., 154
Santo, J. B., 470
Saudino, K. J., 71, 324–325, 407
Savelsberg, G. J. P., 171
Saveslsbergh, G. J. P., 169
Saxe, G. B., 256
Scardamalia, M., 238
Scarr, S., 73
Schaal, B., 150
Schatschneider, C., 71
Schauble, L., 230
Schell, S. L., 137
Schelleman-Offermans, K., 130
Scherf, K. S., 142
Schermerhorn, A. C., 430, 439
Scheungel, C., 333
Schiefenhoevel, W., 111
Schindewolf, E., 223
Schlam, T. R., 370
Schmale, R., 280
Schmidt, F. L., 261
Schmidt, M. E., 479

Schneider, W., 217, 218, 219, 479, 481
Schneiders, J., 348
Schoemaker, K., 392
Schröder, L., 222
Schuetze, P., 95
Schug, M. G., 361
Schulenberg, J., 487
Schulenberg, J. E., 487
Schum, N., 170
Schutz, R. W., 125–126, 406
Schuurman, J., 480
Schwade, J. A., 284
Schwanenflugel, P. J., 218
Schwartz, A., 457
Schwartz, C., 150
Schwartz, C. E., 326
Schwartz, D., 395, 470
Schwartz-Mette, R. A., 470
Schwartz, O. S., 349
Schwartz, P. D., 344
Schwartz, R. B., 487
Schwarzer, G., 160, 170
Schwebel, D. C., 138
Schwenck, C., 217
Scott, E. S., 142
Scott, L. S., 156
Scott-Phillips, T. C., 306
Scott, R., 353
Scott, W. A., 353
Scrimgeour, M. B., 437
Scrimsher, S., 193
Seal, J., 470
Sears, H. A., 469
Seaton, E. K., 346
Sedikides, C., 353
Sedivy, J. C., 306
Segrin, C., 441
Seidl, A., 280
Seidner, L. B., 464
Selman, R., 357, 358
Selman, R. L., 358
Sénéchal, M., 235, 292
Seo, M-G., 254
Serbin, L. A., 403, 405
Setliff, A. E., 480
Shafto, C. L., 301
Shah, B., 151
Shahaeian, A., 208
Shanahan, L., 451
Shanahan, M. J., 348, 438, 487
Shapiro, J. R., 315
Shapiro, L. R., 226
Shapka, J. D., 351
Share, D. L., 235
Shariff, A. F., 314
Shatz, M., 205, 305
Shaw, D. S., 391, 441
Shaw, H., 133
Sheese, B. E., 320
Shell, R., 384

Shelleby, E. C., 391
Shenfield, T., 294
Sherman, D. K., 266
Sherrod, K. B., 456
Shi, R., 281, 282
Shin, H. B., 293
Shin, Y. L., 465
Shiner, R. L., 326
Shipman, K., 320
Shneidman, L. A., 287
Shoemaker, L. B., 133
Shonkoff, J. P., 24
Shoum, K. A., 485
Shrager, J., 243
Shrestha, S., 318
Shriver, S., 264
Shrout, P. E., 167
Shu, B-C., 169
Shulman, S., 472
Shusterman, A., 296
Siddiqui, A., 170
Sidebotham, P., 456
Siegler, R. S., 187–189, 195, 206, 228–229, 235, 238, 241–244
Signorielli, N., 418
Silbereisen, R. K., 130
Silk, J., 348
Silk, J. S., 433
Silva, K. G., 229
Silva, P. A., 127
Silverman, W. K., 316, 491
Simcock, G., 222
Simon, T., 258
Simons, D. J., 205
Simons, L. G., 432
Simonton, D. K., 270
Simpson, E. L., 378
Simpson, J. M., 113
Singer, M., 237
Singh, A., 132
Singh, L., 282
Skinner, B.F., 28, 32, 298–299
Skinner, E. A., 321, 433
Skolnick Weisberg, D., 465
Skoog, T., 130
Slaughter, V., 208
Sleddens, E. F. C., 324
Sloane, S., 380
Slutske, W. S., 327
Smetana, J. G., 379, 379–380, 433
Smith, A. L., 174
Smith, E. R., 402
Smith, J., 452
Smith, L., 289
Smith, L. B., 241, 288–289
Smith, P. K., 446
Smith, R. S., 106
Smith, S. L., 99, 418, 480
Smith, T. E., 408
Smits, I., 345
Smock, T. K., 122

Smoll, F. L., 125–126, 406
Snedeker, J., 301
Snider, J. B., 438, 487
Snow, C. E., 292
Snow, C. W., 110
Snow, D., 284
Snow, M. E., 416
Snowling, M., 272
Snowling, M. J., 271–272, 274
Snyder, J., 432
Snyder, L., 292
Sobal, J., 135
Sodian, B., 231
Solantaus, T., 489–490
Solomon, G. E. A., 206
Somerville, L. H., 142
Song, A. V., 270
Song, L., 292
Sorenson, A., 353
Sosa, B. B., 226
Soussignan, R., 150
Sowislo, J. F., 354
Spearman, C., 252
Spector, F., 154
Spelke, E. S., 198, 241, 296
Spelke, E. W., 296
Spence, M. J., 84
Spencer, J. P., 167
Spencer, N., 456
Spenser, S. J., 266
Spicer, J., 87
Spiers, H. J., 144
Spies Shapiro, L. A., 483
Spinath, F., 74
Spinrad, T., 382
Spitz, R. A., 329
Springer, K., 206
St. George, I. M., 127
St. James-Roberts, I., 110–111
Stacy, A. W., 480
Staff, J., 487
Staiano, A. E., 173
Stanik, C. E., 348
Stanovich, K. E., 228, 292
Starr, R. H. Jr., 446
Stattin, H., 130, 433
Steeger, C. M., 348
Steelandt, S., 370
Steele, C. M., 266
Steelman, J. D., 482
Steinberg, L., 343, 347–348, 475, 486–488
Steinberg, L. D., 127
Stenberg, G., 319
Sternberg, K. J., 476
Sternberg, R. J., 251, 255–256, 262, 268
Stevens, E., 137
Stevens, J., 163
Stevens, N., 470
Stevenson, H. W., 244–246

Stevenson, J., 353
Stevenson, R. J., 314–315
Stewart, L., 377
Stice, E., 133–134, 349
Stifter, C. A., 321, 371
Stigler, J. W., 245, 246
Stiles, J., 140–141
Stipek, D., 391
Stoltz, A. D., 394
Stoneman, A., 451
Stormshak, E. A., 469
Strayer, F. F., 464
Strayer, J., 383
Streri, A., 154
Striano, T., 464
Stright, A. D., 326
Strohmeier, D., 395
Strough, J., 412, 469
Sturaro, C., 477
Sturge-Apple, M. L., 38, 439
Subotnik, R. F., 269, 270
Subramanyam, K., 482
Sullivan, M. W., 315
Super, C. M., 132
Sussman, S., 474
Suzuki, L., 266
Svirsky, M. A., 283
Swedo, S., 349
Sweeney, M. M., 444
Sylvan, L. J., 144–145
Symonds, W. C., 487
Szücks, D., 144

T
Tach, L., 444
Tager-Flusberg, H., 209, 297
Tahiroglu, D., 465
Talwar, V., 380
Tamang, B. L., 318
Tamis-LeMonda, C. S., 168–169, 291, 419, 466
Tan, K. L., 111
Tan, S. H., 200
Tangney, J., 317
Tanner, J. M., 122, 125
Tarabulsy, G. M., 335
Tardif, T., 285, 433
Taylor, A., 133
Taylor, J., 71
Taylor, M., 404–405, 465
Taylor, M. E., 441
Taylor, M. G., 403, 416
Taylor, R. D., 446
Teachman, J., 444
Tegethoff, M., 87
Tein, J-Y, 443
Teixeira, R. A., 469
Tenenbaum, H. R., 416
Teoh, E. R., 142
Terlecki, M. S., 409
Termon, L., 258

Teskey, G. C., 144
Tesluk, P. E., 254
Thal, D. J., 301
Thayer, S. M., 451
Thelen, E., 167
Thelen, M. H., 130
Thiessen, E. D., 282, 283
Thomaes, S., 355
Thomas, A., 322, 326
Thomas, E., 292
Thomas, J. R., 354, 406–407
Thomas, R., 458
Thompson, A. E., 411
Thompson, J., 265
Thompson, R. A., 315, 320–321, 332, 334–335
Thorne, B., 416
Thurstone, L. L., 252
Thurstone, T. G., 252
Tincoff, R., 281
Tinker, E., 288, 301
Tisak, M., 375
Tither, J. M., 129
To, R. M., 319
Tomasello, M., 304–306, 380, 382, 383, 464
Tomelleri, S., 361
Tompkins, V., 320
Tomson, L. M., 172
Tooby, J., 314
Toplak, M. E., 228
Torchia, M. G., 64
Torgesen, J. K., 271
Toth, S. L., 453–455
Trabasso, T., 237
Trachtenberg, F. L., 113
Tracy, B., 239
Tracy, J. L., 314
Trainor, L. J., 151, 154, 282
Trehub, S. E., 151
Treiman, R., 233, 238
Tremblay, M. S., 135
Tremblay, R., 68–69
Tremblay, R. E., 388
Troop-Gordon, W., 130, 394
Troseth, G. L., 295
Truss, A. E., 454
Trzesniewski, K. H., 354
Tsao, F.-M., 282–483
Tsubota, Y., 196
Tucker-Drob, E. M., 73–74
Tucker, M. S., 246
Tudge, J. H. R., 193, 196
Tulviste, P., 191
Tunmer, W. E., 236
Turiel, E., 378–380
Turkheimer, E., 130
Turner, H. A., 490
Twenge, J. M., 352
Tynes, B. M., 347
Tzuriel, D., 262

U
Uchiyama, I., 161
Udry, J. R., 472
Uljarevic, M., 209
Ullian, D. Z., 418
Ulrich, B. D., 167
Umaña-Taylor, A. J., 346–347, 352, 361
Unger, O., 464
Updegraff, K. A., 451–452, 451–452
Usher, E. L., 218
Utman, J. A., 284
Uttal, D. H., 409
Uzelac, S. M., 344

V
Vaala, S. E., 293
Vaillancourt, T., 394
Vaillant-Molina, M., 318
Vaish, A., 318, 380, 382–383
Valentine, J. C., 50
Valentino, K., 454
Valenza, E., 157
Valeri, S. M., 349
Valkenburg, P. M., 479, 483
van Aken, M. A. G., 388
Van de Vondervoort, J., 202
van der Kamp, J., 171
van der Mark, I. L., 382
Van Duijvenvoorde, A. C. K., 316
Van Gelderen, L., 447
van Goozen, S. H., 389
van Hof, P., 171
Van IJzendoorn, M. H., 50, 72, 127, 325, 333–335, 382
van Lier, P. A. C., 394
van Tuijl, L. A., 354
van Wieringen, P. C. W., 169
Van Zalk, M., 470
Vandell, D. L., 485
Vander Wal, J. S., 130
Vandewater, E. A., 479
vanMarle, K., 201
Vasta, R., 299
Vazsonyi, A. T., 370, 438, 487
Veenema, S., 255
Veenstra, R., 394–395
Vélez, C., 443
Ventura, S. J., 89, 473
Verkuyten, M., 47
Véronneau, M-H., 476
Verschaeve, L., 93
Victora, C. G., 137
Vieno, A., 390
Vijayalaxmi, 93
Visher, E. G., 444
Visher, J. S., 444
Vitaro, F., 68–69
Vitiello, B., 349
Vogel, D. A., 403

Volling, B. L., 451
Vorhees, C. V., 93
Vosper, J., 449
Votruba-Drzal, E., 491
Voyer, D., 409–411
Voyer, S., 409
Vygotsky, L., 31–32, 189–193, 199, 372, 463

W
Wagner, K., 154
Wainwright, J. L., 447
Waite, B. M., 52
Wakschlag, L. S., 91
Walberg, H. J., 492
Waldfogel, J., 106
Waldman, I. D., 163
Walk, R., 158
Walker-Andrews, A. S., 318
Walker, P., 154
Walker, R., 92
Wallentin, M., 408
Walsh, R. O., 371
Walton, G. M., 266
Wang, Q., 343
Wang, L., 325, 476
Wang, M., 324–325
Wang, M-T., 362
Wang, Q., 222, 342, 433, 438
Wang, Y., 326
Wansink, B., 135
Ward, B. W., 107
Ward-Estes, J., 163
Ward, L. M., 133
Warneken, F., 382
Warner, B., 98
Warnock, F., 150
Warren, A. R., 306
Warren, E., 364
Warren-Leubecker, A., 306
Wasserstein, S., 316
Watamura, S. E., 485
Waters, E., 333
Waters, H. F., 390
Waters, H. S., 238
Waters, P., 351, 422
Waters, S. F., 489
Watkins, B. A., 481
Watkins, S., 479
Watling, D., 359
Watson, B., 22
Watson, J., 28
Watson, J. B., 430
Wax, J. R., 101
Waxman, S., 206, 285
Webb, S. J., 141
Weber, E., 380
Webster-Stratton, C. H., 164
Wei, W., 409
Weichold, K., 130
Weinert, F. E., 261

Weis, R., 483
Weisgram, E. S., 403
Weisleder, A., 291
Weisner, T., 112
Weisner, T. S., 423
Weiss, B., 392
Weiss, L. G., 263
Weissman, M. D., 205
Weisz, J. R., 349
Weitzel, C., 363
Weizman, Z. O., 292
Wellman, H. M., 188, 204–208, 320, 357
Welsh, D. P., 334, 472
Wentworth, N., 170
Wentzel, K. R., 384
Werker, J. F., 151, 281
Werner, E. E., 106
Werner, L. A., 151
Werner, N. E., 392, 466
Wertsch, J. V., 191
West, R. F., 228
West, T. V., 489
Westra, T., 168
Whipple, N., 192
Whitaker, R. C., 124
White, F. A., 363
White, K. J., 359
White, L., 444
Whitehurst, G. J., 299
Whiteman, S. D., 451–452
Whitesell, N. R., 351–352, 422
Whiting, J. W. M., 433
Whitty, M. T., 482
Wicks-Nelson, R., 453, 457
Widen, S. C., 315
Widmayer, S. M., 304
Wie, O. B., 283
Wilcox, T., 407, 409, 411
Wilkinson, L., 474
Willatts, P., 226
Williams, J. E., 402
Williams, K. R., 395
Williams, S., 127
Williams, S. T., 391
Williams, T. L., 219
Willoughby, T., 391
Wills, T. A., 328
Wilson, B. J., 390, 480
Wilson, D. M., 485
Wilson, G. T., 133
Wilson-Mitchell, J. E., 423
Wilson, P.G., 271
Wilson, R. D., 97
Winburg, J., 150
Winneke, G., 92
Winner, E., 269
Winslow, E. B., 441
Winterhoff, P. A., 196
Witherington, D. C., 205
Witherspoon, D., 352

Wolchik, S., 443
Wolfe, D. A., 454
Wolff, P. H., 110
Wolke, D., 260, 394
Wolraich, M. L., 163
Wood, W., 423
Woodin, E. M., 437, 441
Woodward, A., 318
Woodward, A. L., 207, 287
Woodward, L. J., 88
Woollett, K., 144
Worobey, J., 132
Worrell, F. C., 269–270
Worthman, C. M., 111
Wray, D., 239
Wray-Lake, L., 438
Wright, D. L., 408
Wright, J. C., 293, 479–480
Wright, Y. F., 364
Wu, X., 333–334
Wynn, K., 242, 380

X
Xie, H., 476
Xu, Y., 389
Xuehua, L., 282

Y
Yang, C. M., 453–454
Yap, M. B. H., 349
Yarrow, A. L., 24
Yau, J., 379
Yermolayeva, Y., 200
Yeung, A. S., 351, 354
Yeung, H. H., 281
Yip, T., 39
Yonas, A., 159
Yoshida, K. A., 281
Young, S. K., 327, 385
Youniss, J., 386
Yumoto, C., 95
Yunger, J. L., 429

Z
Zacharatos, A., 437
Zahn-Waxler, C., 382, 385
Zaitchik, D., 206, 231
Zalewski, M., 321
Zamsky, E. S., 446
Zappulla, C., 476
Zarbatany, L., 467
Zarrett, N., 174
Zeanah, C. H., 335
Zeiders, K. H., 361
Zelazo, P. D., 132, 320
Zeman, J., 320
Zhang, B., 487
Zhang, Z., 389
Zhou, Q., 326, 383, 432–433
Zhu, M., 142
Ziegler, J. C., 234, 272

Zigler, E., 268
Zigler, E. F., 264
Zimiles, H., 441
Zimmer-Gembeck, M. J., 321,
    458, 473

Zimmerman, B. J., 218
Zimmerman, C., 230
Zimmerman, M. A., 209
Zinar, S., 236
Ziol-Guest, K. M., 437

Zogmaister, C., 361
Zohsel, K., 325
Zosuls, K. M., 419
Zucker, R. A., 327
Zukow-Goldring, R., 451

Subject Index

A

Abecedarian Project, 264
Academic skills, 214–249, 232–246
Accommodation, 180
Accutane, 91
Achievement, 345
Active children, 210
Active-passive child, 34–35, 174–175, 458
Adding, 243–244
ADHD. *see* Attention Deficit and Hyperactivity Disorder (ADHD)
Adolescent egocentrism, 344
Adolescent growth spurt and puberty, 125–126
Adopted children, 450
Adoption studies, 69–70
African American English, 306
African Americans and sickle cell disease, 61
After-school activities, 484–486
Age of viability, 83
Aggression, 387, 387–396
  biological contributions, 389
  change and stability, 388
  cognitive processes, 392–393
  community and culture, 390
  family and, 389–390
  gender and, 411
  multiple, cascading risks, 394
  roots of aggressive behavior, 387–396
  social-information-processing theory and, 392–393
  stability of over time, 388
  TV and media games, 390–391
  victims of aggression, 387–396
AIDS, 90
Air pollutants, 92
Albinism, 63
Alcohol, 91
Alleles, 59, 60, 63
Altruism, 382
Amniocentesis, 97
Amniotic fluid, 81
Amniotic sac, 81
Amodal, 154
Analytic ability, 255
Androgenous, 422
Androgens, 411
Animism, 184
Anorexia, 133–135
Anorexia nervosa, 133
Apgar score, 108
Applied developmental science, 24
Aspirin, 91

Assimilation, 180
Associative play, 464
Attachment, 329–336
  consequences of, 333–334
  fathers and, 331
  growth of, 329–331
  patterns of worldwide, 333
  quality of, 331–336
  work and child care and, 335–336
Attention, 149, 161–165
Attention deficit hyperactivity disorder (ADHD), 163–164
Auditory threshold, 151
Authoritarian parenting, 432
Authoritative parenting, 432
Authority-oriented grandparents, 445
Autism, 208–209
Autobiographical memory, 221–223
Automatic processes, 196
Autosomes, 59
Avoidant attachment, 332
Axon, 139

B

Babbling, 284
Babies, food for, 123–124
Babinski reflex, 109, 110
Baby biographies, 23
Basic cry, 110
Basic emotions, 314
Behavioral genetics, 59, 66–71
Birth, 100–101
Birth complications, 104–105
Blastocyst, 79
Blended families, 444
Blink reflex, 110
Bodily-kinesthetic intelligence, 253
Body mass index (BMI), 135
Brain development, 139–145
Breast-feeding, 123–124
Breech presentation, 80
Brothers and sisters, 428–461, 448–449, 450–452
Bulimia nervosa, 133–135

C

C-section, 104
Caffeine, 91
CAH. *see* Congenital adrenal hyperplasia (CAH)
Cardinality principle, 242
Carolina Abecedarian Project, 264
Cell body, 139
Central executive, 195
Centration, 184
Cerebral cortex, 82, 139

Cesarean section (C-section), 104
Changing family, 428–461
Child abuse, 453–458
Child care, 335–336, 484–486
Child development research, 20–55
  applying the results of research, 24
  communicating research results, 51–52
  design (*see* research design), 41–45
  ethical responsibilities, 50–51
  hereditary and environmental factors, 71
  history of, 23–24
  measurement, 37–41
  research designs for study of age-related change, 46–50
Childbirth, 100–101
China's one-child policy, 449–450
Chorionic villus sampling (CVS), 97
Chromosomes, 57–59
Chronosystem, 430
Clique, 474
Co-rumination, 470
Cocaine, 91
Cochlear implants, 283
Cognitive development, 178–213, 215–224
  academic skills, 214–249, 232–246
  adding, 243–244
  core-knowledge theories, 197–199
  counting, 242–243
  four stages of, 30
  information processing theory, 193–197
  intelligence, 250–277. *see also* Intelligence
  mathematics, 240–246
  memory, 215–224. *see also* memory
  modern theories of cognitive development, 189–199
  numbers, 240–246
  Piaget, 179–189. *see also* Piaget, Jean
  problem solving, 225–232
  reading, 233–237
  sociocultural perspective, 190–193
  subtracting, 243–244
  understanding in core domains, 200–210
  understanding living things, 202, 204–206
  understanding objects and their properties, 201–202
  understanding people, 206–209
  Vgotsky, 190–193
  writing, 237–240

Cognitive-developmental perspective, 29
Cognitive self-regulation, 218
Cohort, 47
Cohort effects, 47
Comprehension, 233
Concrete operational stage, 30, 185
Cones, 153
Confidentiality of results, 51
Confounded, 230
Congenital adrenal hyperplasia (CAH), 420
Connections, 308
Constricting, 417
Constructivism, 187
Continuity, 396
Continuity-discontinuity issue, 33–34, 114, 494
Conventional level, 376
Cooing, 284
Cooperative play, 464
Core-knowledge theories, 197–199
Corpus callosum, 139
Correlation coefficient, 41
Correlational studies, 41
Counterimitation, 434
Counting, 242–243
Creative ability, 255
Creative children, 271
Creativity, fostering, 270
Critical period, 26
Cross-sectional design, 47
Crowd, 474
Crowning, 100
Crystallized intelligence, 253
Cultural influences
  adolescent rites of passage, 126–127
  African Americans and sickle cell disease, 61
  cross-cultural look at gender differences in math, 410
  differences in emotional expression, 317–318
  display of emotion and, 325–326
  ethnic identity, 345–347
  fifth grade in Taiwan, 245–246
  grandmothers in African American families, 446
  growing up bilingual, 293–294
  infant mortality and, 106–107
  keys to popularity, 476–477
  lies and, 379–380
  motor development, 168–169
Culture, 31
  economic status and, 428–461
Culture-fair intelligence tests, 266
CVS, 97
Cystic fibrosis, 63
Cytomegalovirus, 90

D

Deductive reasoning, 186
Delayed gratification, 372–373
Delivery, 99–100
Dendrite, 139
Deoxyribonucleic acid (DNA), 59
Dependent variable, 43
Depression, 348–349
Designing experiments, 231–232
Detached grandparents, 445
Developing nervous system, 138–145
Developmental dyscalculia. *see* Mathematical learning disability
Developmental intergroup theory, 360–361
Differentiation, 168
Diffusion, 345
Direct instruction, 434
Diseases, prenatal development and, 90, 96–97
Dismissive adults, 335
Disorganized (disoriented) attachment, 332
Display rules, 319
Divergent thinking, 269
Dizygotic twins, 67
DNA, 59
Dominance hierarchy, 475
Dominant, 60, 62
Dominant traits, 59
Down syndrome, 64
DRD4 gene, 325
Drugs, prenatal development and, 91–92
Dynamic assessment, 262
Dynamic systems theory, 167

E

Eating disorders, 134–135
Ecosystem, 430
Ectoderm, 80
Effortful control, 323
Ego, 27
Ego-resilience, 454
Egocentrism, 183
Elaboration, 217
Electric Company, 481
Electroencephalography, 141
Electronic media, 482–483
  media games, 390–391
  television, 478–481
Embryo (weeks 3-8), 80–81
Emotional development, 312–339
  attachment, 329–336
  basic emotions, 314–315
  cultural differences, 317–318
  emergence of complex emotions, 315–316
  emerging emotions, 313–320
  function of emotions, 313–314
  recognizing and using others' emotions, 318–319
  regulating emotions, 320–321
  temperament, 322–329
  understanding emotions, 319–320
Emotional intelligence, 254
Empathy, 383
Enabling, 417
Encoding processes, 226
Endoderm, 80
Environmental hazards, prenatal development and, 92–93
Epigenesis, 72
Epiphyses, 121
Equilibration, 181
Erikson's psychosocial theory, 27–28
Essentialism, 205
Ethnic identity, 345–347
Ethological theory, 26
Evaluating measures, 40
Evolutionary psychology, 330
Executive functioning, 195
Existential intelligence, 253
Experience-dependent growth, 143
Experience-expectant growth, 143
Experiment, 43
Experimental studies, 41
Exposure to parents' speech increases children's vocabulary, 291
Expressive, 402
Expressive style, 292
Eyewitness testimony, 223

F

f-MRI, 141
Face recognition, 161
Family as a system, 429–431
Family economic stress model (FESM), 489–490
Family Lifestyle Project, 423
Family relationship, 428–461
  adopted children, 450
  blended families, 444
  brothers and sisters, 428–461
  changing family, 428–461
  child abuse, 428–461, 453–458
  children's contributions, 438–439
  culture and economic status, 428–461
  family as a system, 429–431
  gay and lesbian parents, 447
  impact of divorce on children, 440–442
  influences of the marital system, 436–438
  parental behavior and, 434–436
  parenting, 429–461
  parenting styles, 431–433
  role of grandparents, 445–446
FASD, 286–288
Fast mapping, 286

FESM, 489–490
Fetal alcohol spectrum disorder (FASD), 91
Fetal medicine, 98
Fetus (weeks 9-38), 81–85
Field experiment, 43
Fine-motor skills, 166
Fluid intelligence, 252
Folk psychology, 206
Foreclosure, 345
Formal operational stage, 30, 185–187
Foundational theories, 25–32
  biological perspective, 26–27
  cognitive-developmental perspective, 29–30
  contextual perspective, 31–32
  learning perspective, 28–29
  psychodynamic perspective, 27–28
Friendship, 468
Frontal cortex, 139
Functional magnetic resonance imaging (fMRI), 141
Fuzzy trace theory, 220–221

G
Gardner's theory of multiple intelligences, 253–255
Gay/lesbian parents, 447
Gender and development, 400–427
  aggressive behavior, 411
  depression, 412
  differences in personality and social behavior, 410–412
  differences related to gender, 406–410
  effortful control, 412
  emotional sensitivity, 411
  gender identity, 400–427
  gender roles in transition, 400–427
  gender stereotypes, 400–427
  learning gender stereotypes, 403–405
  social influence, 412
  talking about gender differences, 413–414
  views of men and women, 401–403
Gender constancy, 425
Gender identity, 401, 415–421
  beyond traditional roles, 422
  biological influences, 420–421
  cognitive theories of, 418, 420
  emerging gender roles, 421–422
  encouraging valuable traits, not gender traits, 422
  gender roles in transition, 421–422
  parents, 415–416
  peers, 416–417
  socializing influences of people and the media, 415
  teachers, 416
  television, 417–418

Gender roles, 401
Gender-schema theory, 418, 418–420
Gender stereotypes, 401
Genes, 57, 59
Genetic bases, 56–77
  behavioral genetics, 66–71
  biology of heredity, 57–59
  from genes to behavior, 71–75
  genetic disorders, 62–66
  single gene inheritance, 59–62
Genetic counseling, 63
Genetic disorders, 62–66
Genetic engineering, 98
Genital herpes, 90
Genotype, 59–60
Germ disc, 80
Gifted, 269
Gifted children, 269–271
Grammar, 297–302
Grammatical morphemes, 297
Grandparents, 445–496
Grasping, 170–171
Groups, 474–475
Growth and health, 118–147
  accidents, 137–138
  adolescent growth spurt and puberty, 125–126
  brain development, 139–145
  challenges to healthy growth, 131–138
  describing growth, 119–121
  developing nervous system, 138–145
  diseases, 136–137
  eating disorders: anorexia and bulimia, 133–135, 134–135
  malnutrition, 131–132
  mechanisms of maturation, 122, 127–128
  muscle, fat, and bones, 121
  nervous system, 138–139
  nutrition and, 123–125
  obesity, 135–136
  physical growth, 119–131
  puberty, 128–130
  sleep and, 122–123
  variations on the average profile, 121–122
Growth hormone, 122
Growth spurt, 125–126
Guided participation, 190

H
Habituation, 150
Head Start, 263–264
Hearing, 151–152
Hearing impairment in infancy, 152
Helping children adjust after divorce, 442–443
Helping others, 381–396
Hemispheres, 139
Hereditary contribution, 384–385

Heritability coefficient, 72
Heroin, 91
Heterozygous, 59
Heuristics, 228
Historical overview, 22
Homozygous, 59
Hostile aggression, 388
Human Genome Project, 75
Huntington's disease, 62
Hypoxia, 104

I
IBQ-R, 323
Illusion of invulnerability, 344
Imaginary audience, 344
IMCI, 136
Imitation, 29
Immanent justice, 375
Impact of divorce on children, 440–442
Impaired reading comprehension, 272
Implantation, 79
Imprinting, 26
In vitro fertilization, 58
Incomplete dominance, 61
Independent variable, 43
Infant Behavior Questionnaire (IBQ-R), 323
Infant-directed speech, 282
Infantile amnesia, 222
Influence of best friends on sexual activity, 471–472
Influences beyond the family, 462–497
  electronic media, 482–483
  friendship, 468–472
  groups, 474–475
  institutional influences, 483–493
  peer interactions, 464–468
  peers, 463–478
  popularity and rejection, 476–477
  romantic relationships, 472–473
  sexual behavior, 473
  sexual orientation, 473
  television, 478–481
Influences of the marital system, 436–438
Influential grandparents, 445
Information-processing theory, 193–197
Informed consent, 50
Inner speech, 192
Institutional influences, 483–493
  after-school activities, 484–486
  child care, 484–486
  neighborhoods, 488–491
  part-time employment, 486–488
  school, 491–493
Instrumental, 402
Instrumental aggression, 388
Integrated Management of Childhood Illness (IMCI), 136
Integration, 168
Intellectual disability, 270

Intelligence, 250–277
culture and, 256
ethnicity and socioeconomic status, 265–266
Gardner's theory of multiple intelligences, 253–255
hereditary and environmental factors, 71, 262–265
individual differences in cognition and, 79–80
intelligence testing, 258–262
measuring, 257–268
psychometric theories, 252–253
Sternberg's theory of successful intelligence, 255–257
Intelligence quotient (IQ), 258, 261
Internal working model, 334
Interpersonal intelligence, 253
Interposition, 159
Intersensory redundancy, 154–155
Intersubjectivity, 190
Interviewing children, 224
Intonation, 284
Intrapersonal intelligence, 253
IQ, 261

J
Joint custody, 441

K
Kinetic cues, 158
KiVa Antibullying Program, 395
Klinefelter's syndrome, 65, 76
Knowledge, 218–224
Knowledge-telling strategy, 238
Knowledge-transforming strategy, 238

L
Labor and delivery, 99–100
Language, 279
Language and communication, 278–311
beyond words: other symbols, 295–296
bilingualism, 293–294
cognitive factors, 288
constraints on word names, 287–288
developmental change in word learning, 290
elements of language, 279–280
encouraging word learning, 292–293
fast mapping meanings to words, 286–288
first steps to speech, 284
individual differences in word learning, 290–292
learning the meanings of words, 285–296
listening well, 306–308
mastering grammar, 298–302
naming errors, 290
perceiving speech, 280–283

sentence cues, 288
shape-bias theory of word learning, 288–289
speaking effectively, 305–306
speaking in sentences, 296–298
taking turns, 304–305
understanding words as symbols, 285–286
using language to communicate, 303–308
Latchkey children, 485
Lead, 92
Learning disability, 271
Lesbian parents, 447
Linear perspective, 159
Linguistic intelligence, 253
Liquids from solids, distinguishing, 28, 203–204
Listening, 306–308
Locomotion, 165
Logical-mathematical intelligence, 253
Long-term memory, 195
Longitudinal design, 46–47
Longitudinal-sequential studies, 48–49

M
MA, 258
Macrosystem, 430
Mad cry, 110
Make-believe, 464
Making tests less threatening, 267
Malnutrition, 131–132
Maltreatment, 428–461, 453–458
Marijuana, 91
Maternal depression, children's behavior problems and, 102
Mathematical learning disability, 273–274
Mathematics, 240–246
Maturational theory, 26
Means-ends analysis, 227
Memory, 215–224
autobiographical, 221–223
brain development and, 216
eyewitness testimony, 223
knowledge and, 218–224
metacognition, 217–218
origins of memory, 215–216
strategies for remembering, 215–218
Memory strategies, 216
Menarche, 126
Mental age (MA), 258
Mental operations, 185
Mental retardation, 64, 271
Mental rotation, 408
Mercury, 92
Mesoderm, 80
Mesosystem, 430
Meta-analysis, 50
Metacognition, 217–218

Metacognitive knowledge, 218
Metamemory, 217
Methylation, 72
Microgenetic study, 46
Microsystem, 430
mindblindness, 209
Monitoring, 390
Monozygotic twins, 67
Moral realism, 374
Moral relativism, 375
Moral understanding and behavior, 368–399
aggression, 368–399. *see also* Aggression
beyond Kohlberg's theory, 378–379
contribution of heredity, 384–385
domains of social judgment, 379–380
Gilligan's ethic of caring, 378–379
helping others, 368–399
Kohlberg's theory, 375–377
origins of moral reasoning in infancy, 380
Piaget's views, 374–375
prosocial behavior, 382–383
reasoning about moral issues, 373
role of emotions in, 380–381
self-control, 369–373
situational influences, 384
skills underlying prosocial behavior, 383
socializing prosocial behavior, 385–387
Moratorium, 345
Moro reflex, 110
Motion parallax, 159
Motor development, 165–174
beyond walking, 169–170
coordinating skills, 174
cultural influence, 168–169
environmental cues, 168
fine-motor skills, 169–172
handedness, 172
locomotion, 166–169
participation in sports, 173–174
physical fitness, 172–173, 172–174
posture and balance, 167
reaching and grasping, 170–172
stepping, 167–168
Motor skills, 149
Musical intelligence, 253
Myelin, 139

N
Naming errors, 290
Naming explosion, 286
Narcissism, 355
Naturalistic intelligence, 253

Naturalistic observation, 37
Nature-nurture issue, 34–35, 75, 274, 365
Negative affect, 323
Negative reinforcement trap, 435
Neighborhood, 488–491
Nervous system, 138–139
Neural plate, 140
Neuron, 139
Neurotransmitters, 139
Newborn, 108
  assessing, 108–109
  behavioral states in, 110–112
  crying, 110
  perception and learning in, 114
  reflexes of, 109–110
  SIDS, 112
Niche-picking, 73–74
Nicotine, 91
Non-REM sleep, 112
Non-shared environmental influences, 74
Numbers, 240–246
Nutrition, 86–87, 123–125

O
Obesity, 135–136
Object permanence, 182
Observational learning, 29, 434
One-to-one principle, 242
Open adoption, 450
Operant conditioning, 28
Organization, 217
Overextension, 290
Overregularization, 298

P
Pain cry, 110
Palmar reflex, 110
Parallel play, 464
Parent-Child Interaction Therapy, 458
Parental behavior, 434–436
Parenting, 429–461
Parenting styles, 431–433
Parents and children adjustment to life after divorce, programs to help, 442–443
Part-time employment, 486–488
Passive grandparents, 445
Paternal Investment Theory of Girls' Puberty Timing, 128–129
PCBs, 92
Peer pressure, 475
Peer relations
  hereditary and environmental factors, 71
Peers
  peer pressure, 475
  popularity and rejection,476–477
Perceiving faces, 161
Perceiving objects, 156

Perceptual and motor development, 148–177
  basic sensory and perceptual processes, 149–156
  complex perceptual and attentional processes, 156–165
  motor development, 165–174
Perceptual processes. *see* Sensory and perceptual processes
Period of the fetus, 81
Permissive parenting, 432
Personal domain, 379
Personal fable, 344
Phenotype, 60, 62
Phenylketoniuria (PKU), 63, 72
Phonemes, 280
Phonological awareness, 233
Phonological memory, 290
Phonology, 280
Physical growth, 119–131
Physiological measures, 39–40
Piaget, Jean, 29–30, 179–189
  basic principles, 180–181
  cognitive development, 179–189
  concrete operational stage, 30, 185
  educational applications of Piaget's theory, 188
  formal operational stage, 30, 185–187
  four stages of cognitive development, 30
  Piaget's theory, 179–189
  preoperational stage, 30, 183–185
  sensorimotor stage, 30, 181–183
  stages of cognitive development, 181–187
  weaknesses in his theory, 188–189
Pictorial cues, 160
Pituitary gland, 122
PKU, 63, 72
Placenta, 80
Play, 464
Polychlorinated biphenyls (PCBs), 92
Polygenic inheritance, 66
Populations, 41
Postconventional level, 377
Postpartum depression, 101–102
Practical ability, 255
Practice effects, 47
Pragmatics, 280
Preconventional level, 376
Prejudice, 359–364
  consequences of discrimination, 361–362
  development of intelligence testing, 359–360

eliminating, 363–364
ending segregated schools, 363–364
resilience in the face of discrimination, 362–363
Premature infants, 105
Prenatal development, 78–95
  diseases, 90, 96–97
  drugs, 91–92
  embryo (weeks 3-8), 80–81
  environmental hazards, 92–93
  fetus (weeks 9-38), 81–85
  mother's age, 87–88
  mother's nutrition, 86–87
  mother's stress, 87
  older women, 90
  prenatal risk, 95
  teenage pregnancy, 88–89
  teratogens, 90–92, 93–95
  zygote (weeks 1-2), 79–80
Prenatal risk, 95
Preoccupied adults, 335
Preoperational stage, 30, 183–185
Primary sex characteristics, 126
Private speech, 192
Problem solving, 225–232
Promoting language development, 302–303
Prosocial behavior, 382
Psychodynamic theory, 27
Psychometricians, 252
Psychosocial theory, 27–28
Puberty, 125, 128–130
Punishment, 29, 435

Q
Quasi-experiment, 45

R
Rapid-eye-movement (REM) sleep, 113
Reactive aggression, 388
Reading, 233–237, 272
Reading disability, 272
Reasoning about gender-related properties, 404–405
Recessive, 62, 63
Recessive traits, 59
Recursive thinking, 359
Referential style, 292
Reflexes, 109
Rehearsal, 217
Reinforcement, 28, 435
Rejected children, 476–477
Relational aggression, 388
Relative size, 159
Reliable, 40
REM sleep, 113
Representative sampling, 41
Research. *see* Child development research

Research design
  correlational studies, 41
  cross-sectional design, 47
  experimental studies, 41
  longitudinal design, 46–47
  longitudinal-sequential studies, 48–49
  study of age-related change, 46–50
Resistant attachment, 332
Response bias, 39
Retinal disparity, 159
Role of grandparents, 445–446
Romantic relationships, 472–473
Rooting reflex, 110
Rough-and-tumble play, 464
Rubella (German measles), 90

S
Safe sleeping, 113
Sampling behavior with tasks, 38, 40
Scaffolding, 191
School refusal behavior, 317
Scientific problem solving, 230–231
Script, 219
Search for identity, 344–345
Secondary sex characteristics, 126
Secular growth trends, 121
Secure adults, 335
Secure attachment, 332
Seeing, 152–153
Segregated schools, 363–364
Selective attrition, 47
Self-concept, 340–367
  depression, 348–349
  ethnic identity, 345–347
  evolving, 342–344
  origins of self-recognition, 341–342
  search for identity, 344–345
  storm and stress, 347–348
Self-conscious emotions, 315
Self-control, 369
Self-efficacy, 29
Self-esteem, 350, 350–364
  changes in level of, 351–352
  developmental change in, 350–351
  low self-esteem: cause or consequence?, 354–355
  sources of, 353–354
  sources of low, 350–364
  structure of, 350–351
  variations in associated with ethnicity and culture, 352
Self-reports, 39
Selman's stages of perspective taking, 358–359

Semantic bootstrapping theory, 299
Semantics, 280
Sensorimotor stage, 30, 181, 181–183
Sensory and perceptual processes, 149–156, 156–165
  attention, 161–165
  defined, 149
  hearing, 151–152
  integrating sensory information, 154–156
  perceiving faces, 161
  perceiving objects, 156
  seeing, 152–153
  smell, 150–151
  taste, 150–151
  theory of intersensory redundancy, 154–155
  touch, 150–151
Sensory information, integrating, 154–156
Sensory memory, 193
Sesame Street, 481
Sex chromosomes, 59, 65
Shape-bias theory of word learning, 288–289
Sickle-cell disease, 61
Sickle-cell trait, 61
SIDS, 112
Single gene inheritance, 59–62
Size constancy, 157
Sleep, 112–113, 122–123
Small-for-date infants, 105
Smell, 150–151
Social-cognitive theory, 29
Social conventions, 379
Social influence, 88
Social-information-processing theory, 392–393
Social-interaction approach to grammar acquisition, 298–302
Social referencing, 318
Social role, 401
Social selection, 88
Social smiles, 314
Society for Research in Child Development (SRCD), 23
Sociocultural perspective, 190–193
Spatial intelligence, 253
Special needs children, 269–274
  children with disability, 270–271
  creative children, 271
  gifted children, 269–271
  learning disability, 270–272
Spermarche, 126
Spina bifida, 87
Stable-order principle, 242
Stanford-Binet intelligence test, 258

Stepping, 109
Stepping reflex, 109, 110
Stereotype threat, 266
Strange Situation, 332–333
Stranger wariness, 315
Strategies for remembering, 215–218
Stress, 87
Structured observation, 37–38
Subtracting, 243–244
Successful intelligence, 255–257
Sucking reflex, 110
Sudden infant death syndrome (SIDS), 112
Superego, 27
Supportive grandparents, 445
Surgency/extraversion, 323
Swaddling, 111
Synapse, 139
Synaptic pruning, 140
Syntax, 297
Syphilis, 90
Systematic observation, 37–38

T
Taste, 150–151
Tay-Sachs disease, 63
Teenage pregnancy, 88–89
Teenagers and the law, 142–143
Telegraphic speech, 297
Teleological explanations, 205
Temperament, 322, 322–329
  features of, 322–323
  hereditary and environmental factors, 324–325
  influence on outcomes in adolescence and adulthood, 327–328
  other aspects of development and, 326–328
  parental behavior and, 326
  stability of, 326
  theory of the structure of in infancy, 323–324
Teratogens, 90–95
Terminal buttons, 140
Texture gradient, 159
Thalidomide, 91
Themes in child-development research, 33–35
  active-passive child, 34–35
  continuity of development, 33–34
  links between different domains of development, 35
  nature-nurture, 34
Theory of mind, 207, 208–209
Three-Two-One Contact, 481
Time-out, 436
Toddlers, 166
Touch, 150–151
Trisomy 39. *see* Down syndrome

Turner's syndrome, 65
Twin studies, 68–70

U

Ultrasound, 96
Umbilical cord, 81
Underextension, 290
Understanding others, 340–367, 355–365
   describing others, 356–357
   prejudice, 359–364
   Selman's stages of perspective
     taking, 358–359
   understanding what others think,
     357–359
Uninvolved parenting, 432

V

Valid, 40
Variables, 37
Vernix, 82
Villi, 81
Visual acuity, 152
Visual cliff, 158
Visual expansion, 158
Vygotsky, Lev, cognitive development
   theories of, 31, 190–193

W

Wechsler Intelligence Scale for
   Children-IV (WISC-IV), 259
WISC-IV, 259

Withdrawal reflex, 110
Word decoding, 233
Working memory, 194
Writing, 237–240

X

X-rays, 92
XXX syndrome, 65
XYY complement, 65

Z

Zone of proximal development, 194
Zygote (weeks 1-2), 81
   prenatal development,
     79–80